More Praise for *Reagan: His Life and Legend*

"Cogent, handsome, and well-meaning, with charm to seduce millions, Max Boot's Ronald Reagan is a leader with peerless rhetorical gifts who is overmatched by the responsibilities of leadership.... Boot's biography is essential to understanding the roots of Trumpism and is a briskly written portrait of one of the twentieth century's most enigmatic and influential presidents."

—Mark Bowden, author of *Black Hawk Down*

"Max Boot's masterwork brings to readers a penetrating portrait of Ronald Reagan, one of the most consequential presidents in American history. Here is the real Reagan, not the myth: pragmatic, dreamy, lucky, and oblivious. Boot's depiction is deeply reported, unflinching, and persuasive. A must-read."

—David E. Hoffman, author of *The Billion Dollar Spy*

"I read Max Boot's landmark biography of Ronald Reagan with great admiration and pleasure. As the editor of Reagan's autobiography, I can attest that he captured perfectly both his personal charm and his remoteness, and gives him the credit he deserves, but so seldom receives, for his many achievements. A balanced, definitive, very readable life."

—Michael Korda, author of *Ike* and *Muse of Fire*

"This is the best book on Ronald Reagan I have read. It beautifully (and judiciously) conveys the values, aspirations, and shortcomings of a complex and elusive person. The amount of research here is incredible. Even more so is the mobilization of evidence in support of broader key themes—above all the pragmatism that characterized Reagan's political career from beginning to end. It is a work of scholarship of the highest level."

—James Graham Wilson, State Department historian and author of *The Triumph of Improvisation*

"A tour de force, and a page-turner, Max Boot's *Reagan* is not only the definitive biography of our fortieth president; it is a brilliant explication of twentieth-century America." —Adam Cohen, author of *Supreme Inequality*

REAGAN

REAGAN

His Life and Legend

MAX BOOT

Liveright Publishing Corporation

An Imprint of W. W. Norton & Company
Independent Publishers Since 1923

Frontispiece: *Ronald Reagan at Rancho del Cielo, August 13, 1981.*
(RONALD REAGAN PRESIDENTIAL FOUNDATION)

For information about permission to reproduce selections from this book, write to
Permissions, Liveright Publishing Corporation, a division of W. W. Norton & Company, Inc.,
500 Fifth Avenue, New York, NY 10110

For information about special discounts for bulk purchases, please contact
W. W. Norton Special Sales at specialsales@wwnorton.com or 800-233-4830

Manufacturing by Lakeside Book Company
Book design Chris Welch
Production manager: Anna Oler

ISBN 978-0-87140-944-7

Liveright Publishing Corporation, 500 Fifth Avenue, New York, N.Y. 10110
www.wwnorton.com

W. W. Norton & Company Ltd., 15 Carlisle Street, London W1D 3BS

10 9 8 7 6 5 4 3 2 1

To two of the strongest women I have ever known,
my wife, Sue Mi Terry, and my late mother, Olga E. Kagan.
They have done as much to support me as
Nelle and Nancy did for Ronald Reagan.

All men lead their lives behind a wall of
misunderstanding they have themselves built.

—SHERWOOD ANDERSON

Contents

ACT I

SMALL-TOWN BOY

ACT II

ACTOR

ACT III

"CITIZEN POLITICIAN"

ACT IV

MR. PRESIDENT

ACT V

EX-PRESIDENT

REAGAN

Ronald Reagan's flag-draped casket being escorted on a horse-drawn caisson to the U.S. Capitol, June 7, 2004. (GETTY)

Prologue

Mourning in America

There was almost no one who did not succumb to his magic.

—SELWA "LUCKY" ROOSEVELT

The end came shortly after 1:00 p.m. on Saturday, June 5, 2004, in the secluded, ranch-style house on Saint Cloud Road in Bel-Air at the end of a winding, bougainvillea-lined driveway guarded by the Secret Service. Outside, the jacaranda trees and jasmine vines were in bloom, the jasmine filling the air with sweet, heavy perfume and the jacaranda bursting in a profusion of purple. But the dying man was not aware of the seasons or the flowers or even his own family. He could no longer recognize his loving wife of fifty-two years—his indispensable, though sharp-elbowed, companion and *consigliere* during his rise from president of the Screen Actors Guild to the president of the entire nation. Nancy Reagan, who had become his devoted caregiver during his protracted, lingering senescence, was now eighty-two and frail. She stood helplessly by, grief-stricken, watching the love of her life fade away.[1]

It had been a decade since Ronald Reagan had left the public stage with a poignant, handwritten note announcing that he had become "one of the millions of Americans" who was "afflicted with Alzheimer's Disease." "I now begin the journey that will lead me into the sunset of my life," he had written, using a cowboy trope that might have been equally appropriate for one of his Western movies. That sunset had finally arrived, producing a darkness, at least as a physical manifestation, that set in just after noon.

Once Ronald Reagan had bestridden the world; now the world had closed in on him. His post-presidential office in a Century City skyscraper— once used, as if biographically scripted, as a set for the movie *Die Hard*— had already been shuttered.[2] He had long ago been forced to give up visits to his beloved ranch in Santa Barbara, located at a hundred-mile remove from Bel-Air, after he had gotten frantic and disoriented during a drive up.

Even swimming—the sport in which he had excelled his whole life, ever since his days as a teenage lifeguard on the Rock River in Illinois—was no longer possible. Because long-term memory is often the last to go for Alzheimer's patients, he was still reminiscing about working as a lifeguard after he had forgotten everything else; he couldn't understand how his old aide Michael Deaver, who had heard the stories a hundred times before, could already know all about his teenage feats.[3] In his straitened circumstances, he was reduced to the indignity of wearing inflatable water wings while being propped up in the shallow end of the pool by a nurse and a Secret Service agent. He enjoyed using a pool rake to scoop magnolia blossoms out of the swimming pool so much that his Secret Service agents would thoughtfully throw in a few more blossoms for him to take out.[4]

But his pool time had to end after he fell in his bedroom and broke his hip in the first month of 2001. On that occasion he had landed in the same medical facility—St. John's Hospital in Santa Monica—where, on another floor, his sixty-year-old daughter, Maureen, was dying of melanoma that was now lapping at her brain. He was not aware, not even dimly, that she was there. Nor did he know when she passed away eight months later, in August. He survived his fall, but the general anesthesia used during surgery evidently worsened his dementia. There would be no physical rehabilitation from this injury as there had been after he was shot in 1981. When he returned home, he could no longer go to the park—outings he had once enjoyed, even though he could not understand why so many people recognized him. "How do they know me?" he wondered. He was now confined to a hospital bed in the room that had been his home office. Once a poster boy of ruddy good health, even during his incipient dementia, his broad shoulders and strong swimmer's legs had been reduced to skin and bones. He would simply lie and silently stare into the distance as the sun streaked across the western sky.[5]

His well-worn wooden desk, a gift from the Kitchen Cabinet that he had used in Sacramento and at the White House residence, still stood by the window and remained filled with annotated articles and notecards he had been collecting for decades on matters of concern to him. This miscellany included warnings of radicalism on college campuses, the perils of "pot" smoking and of government-provided health care, the virtues of tax cuts, the threats posed by North Vietnam and the Sandinistas, the Communist infiltration of Hollywood and the peace movement, and the horrors of nuclear war. Mixed in, incongruously, among the right-wing literature was an advertisement for Dehner riding boots ("where quality is traditional")—a reminder of his nonpolitical passion. Here lay one-liners he could deploy ("Summing it all up I'd have to say the whole Iran episode gives me the same feeling as my recent operation") and collections of his favorite political jokes ("COMMUNISM—You have two cows. The government takes them both and gives you milk. . . . BUREAUCRACY: You have two cows. The government takes both of them, shoots one of them, milks the other, and pours the milk down the drain").[6] All of it had long been unread and unused, his mental life having been cruelly sapped and extinguished years before his physical existence followed suit.

The Reagans' youngest son, Ron, who lived in Seattle, had flown all night from a Hawaii vacation to bid a final goodbye. Their daughter Patti Davis, who had long ago taken her mother's maiden name in an attempt to escape the unforgiving glare of her family's spotlight, had driven from her nearby home. Notably missing was Michael Reagan, Ronald Reagan's adopted son from his first marriage. He had visited the day before, journeying from his home in the San Fernando Valley, but his estranged stepmother, Nancy, had not summoned him this morning to his father's deathbed. He would not arrive until it was too late.[7]

Now Ron and Patti, loyal and supportive as children could be at such a dire time, stood by with their mother, alongside a doctor and a nurse, watching the patient's breathing become shallow and labored. Nancy gently stroked her dying husband's hair while Patti held his left hand and Ron touched a knee. All "murmured words of love and affection," Ron recalled. Just before the end, the dying president opened his eyes. Both Patti and Ron were astonished to see that they were vividly blue and focused in a way they had not been for at least a year. He looked straight at his wife of more than a half century. Then, Ron noted, "the blue flame guttered and extinguished. His eyes dimmed. With a quiet exhalation, my father settled back onto his pillow and died."[8]

Nancy Reagan had spent a lifetime perfecting a look of rapt adoration when her husband spoke in public, but the actress's gaze could no longer hold. She was now in tears. Having seen his eyes one last time, she whispered, "That's the greatest gift you could have given me."[9]

The Reagan family did not know what to expect after the demise of the fortieth president. He had been out of the public eye for a decade. Would people still remember him? Would they care that he was dead? The minutes after his demise revealed that he was gone but far from forgotten. News helicopters buzzed the house. So many reporters thronged the streets of the Bel-Air neighborhood that the hearse from the Gates Kingsley & Gates funeral home had trouble getting through. Television networks broke into their programming to announce the news, and newspapers splashed it across their front pages the next morning.

"Reagan Dies at 93" read the banner headline in his hometown newspaper, the *Los Angeles Times*: "Popular President Changed the Political Landscape."

The passage of years had been politically if not personally kind to Ronald Reagan. Since his departure from office in January 1989, the world had gone his way. He had called for the Berlin Wall to be torn down, and, less than a year after he left office, it was. (A piece of the wall was proudly displayed at the Reagan Library much as a big-game hunter might mount an animal head on the wall.) He had excoriated the Soviet Union as an "evil empire," and, less than three years after he left office, it—as if magically—dissolved. He had said that "government is not the solution to our problem; government is the problem," and seven years after he left office that laissez-faire outlook was ratified by a Democratic president, Bill Clinton, who proclaimed, "The era of big government is over." The president at the time of Reagan's death, George W. Bush, was the son of Reagan's vice president and claimed to be carrying on Reagan's legacy more than his father's.

Ronald Reagan had decades before exceeded the low expectations among naysayers who labeled him, in Clark Clifford's words, an "amiable dunce" and feared he would trigger another world war. While historians continue to debate to what extent he deserved credit for the Cold War's end and the economy's revival—and most cite factors beyond any president's control—he was by the time of his death seen by many as the second most consequential president of the twentieth century, behind only his onetime idol, Franklin D. Roosevelt. As Jane Wyman, Reagan's first wife and the Oscar-winning actress who had starred most recently in the prime-time soap opera *Falcon Crest*, wrote to his second wife, "You can be very proud of the mark that Ronnie has left on history. He has left strong footprints in the sands of time."[10]

While Reagan's achievements—helping to end the Cold War and reviving the nation's spirits along with the economy—loomed larger than ever in 2004, many of his failures, rightly or wrongly, had already faded into history. The Iran-Contra affair, when his administration was caught trading arms for hostages with Iran and illegally funneling the proceeds from the weapons sales to Nicaraguan guerrillas, was still the most significant scandal since Watergate, as it would remain until the Trump presidency. But it no longer loomed quite as large after another president—Bill Clinton— had been impeached, a fate Reagan had avoided. The loss of 241 Marines in Beirut in 1983 as part of an ill-conceived peacekeeping mission no longer seemed as dire compared with the far greater losses being suffered by American troops in Afghanistan and Iraq. (By 2004, nearly a thousand had been killed, and more were falling every day.) The soaring budget deficits that had resulted from Reagan's tax cuts and defense budget increases paled by comparison with George W. Bush's shortfalls: The federal budget deficit in 2004 was more than twice as large as in 1988. The failure to confront apartheid in South Africa no longer seemed to matter quite as much since that system of white supremacy had collapsed, and the failure to do more to fight HIV/AIDS no longer seemed so catastrophic once antiretroviral drugs made it possible to treat the disease. Other scandals—involving former White House aides and officials from the Department of Housing and Urban Development, the Environmental Protection Agency, and the Justice Department—were all but forgotten. Forgotten, that is, by the cavalcade of mourners, yet these setbacks and failures are remembered by historians whose task it is to contextualize Reagan's historical standing.

Despite his deviations from conservative orthodoxy—he had raised taxes more often than he cut them—the Gipper by that time had become an icon on the right, the only leader who was universally revered in the Republican Party. His many admirers could point to the recent publication of speeches, letters, and radio addresses he had written in his own hand to argue that he was smarter than he had been given credit for. Many liberals still saw him as out of touch, indeed out to lunch. They thought he, reflecting the Republican Party as a whole, had supported brutal allies abroad and exacerbated racial divisions and income disparities at home while favoring the rich with his "trickle-down economics," setting back the cause of civil rights, and ignoring the plight of AIDS victims. But even they found it hard to hold a grudge against a man with such a disarming personality who had shown such grace and good humor after being shot and who had so stoically submitted to the ravages of Alzheimer's. Although Reagan had decisively won two national elections—the second by one of the largest margins in US history—he averaged only 53 percent job approval during his presidency, below average for US presidents. He had been a polarizing figure. But no longer. By 2002, propelled by gusts of sympathy, he had wafted aloft with a 73 percent approval rating—higher than any modern president other than the martyred John F. Kennedy.[11]

What most people remembered, more than any policy achievement or failure, was Reagan's good nature, his sense of humor and humility, his optimism, and, of course, his incomparable ability to communicate. As the Reagan White House protocol chief Selwa "Lucky" Roosevelt wrote to Nancy Reagan after his death, "It was a joy to watch him in action—and there was almost no one who did not succumb to his magic."[12]

That is attested to by the outpouring of condolence letters the former first lady received from politicians, world leaders, entertainers, religious leaders, socialites, fashion designers, journalists, former aides, military officers, Secret Service agents, and waiters and servants. George J. Rubisz, a former butler and chauffeur to the publishing magnate Walter Annenberg, at whose Palm Springs estate the Reagans had luxuriously celebrated every New Year's Eve, wrote, "I went on with a career to serve many world dignitaries, but I never met a man who stood as tall, walked as straight, or spoke such truths as President Reagan." "When I think of the President, the first thing that comes to mind is his sense of humor," wrote the redoubtable actor Kirk Douglas. "It was never dull when the President was around." "Not only was he a truly great man, a great President, but one of the world's finest human beings," wrote Carol Swanson Price, an heiress who was part of the Annenbergs' social circle and whose husband was Reagan's ambassador to the United Kingdom. Reagan's vice president and successor, George H. W. Bush, confided to Nancy, "I loved your man, my President, I really did."[13]

Ordinary Americans had the chance to show their affection and pay their respects to the late president as memorial ceremonies unfolded with military precision in both Southern California and Washington, DC, over the next week—and they did. The state funeral, the first held since the death of Lyndon Johnson more than thirty-one years before, had been planned for years by the Reagans' aides in coordination with the Military District of Washington. It was known as Operation Serenade.[14] The week of events made clear that the Reagan administration's flair for showmanship—for perfect television visuals—had outlived the president himself. A veteran actor always knows how to make a memorable exit, and none did it better than Ronald Reagan.

On Monday, June 7, a formidable motorcade moved the president's body from the funeral home in Santa Monica to the Ronald Reagan Presidential Library and Museum amid the ocher-colored mountains of the Simi Valley. More than a hundred thousand people streamed by the casket on its catafalque over the next two days. On Wednesday, June 9, another motorcade took the body to the Point Mugu Naval Air Station, where Air Force One had always landed when the Reagans were heading to their Santa Barbara ranch. From there, it was off to Washington on a 747-200 that carried the designation Air Force One when it was being used by the president. There was a brief moment of panic when, just before their arrival, an unknown aircraft entered Washington's airspace. With memories of the September 11, 2001, terrorist attacks still fresh, the Capitol was evacuated, and fighter jets were scrambled. It turned out to be simply an aircraft with a transponder malfunction that was bringing the governor of Kentucky to the funeral. Governor Ernie Fletcher had been lucky not to be shot down.[15]

The flag-covered casket was taken by hearse from Andrews Air Force Base to a spot just in front of the Ellipse, within sight of the White House, where it was transferred to a horse-drawn caisson for a solemn procession to the Capitol. No detail was spared in a spectacle that might have been borrowed from a Cecil B. DeMille historical epic. A riderless horse, with the late president's favorite riding boots reversed in the saddle's stirrups, followed just behind the caisson while a military honor guard marched alongside. A limousine carried Nancy Reagan, Patti Davis, Ron Reagan, and his wife, Doria, along with two Secret Service agents. The Reagans had temporarily put aside their barely camouflaged animosities and resentments to remember an amiable if remote husband and father who had preached "family values" that, owing to circumstances and personality, he had often been unable to practice. "The four of us got along quite well for those few days," Patti recalled. "Almost like a family."[16]

But that family was not quite big enough to accommodate Michael Reagan, whose relations with Nancy were so tense that, following one loud altercation, she had insisted on a Secret Service agent being present whenever he visited.[17] For this occasion he was present, but he was riding in a separate car with his wife and two children. Maureen Reagan's widower, Dennis Revell, who had been bickering with Michael all during the trip east, rode in a third car with his girlfriend.[18]

Spectators, in rows three to five deep, thronged Pennsylvania Avenue to catch a glimpse of this melancholy but historic funeral procession, replete with military honor guards and marching bands. Ron Reagan remembered seeing a sign, "Now *there* was a president."[19] It took three teams of military pallbearers, working as if in a relay race, to haul the mahogany, marble-lined casket with the embalmed president inside—weighing a total of 750 pounds—up the long steps of the West Front to the Capitol Rotunda to the bier where it was put on display. They had practiced for days on a casket stuffed with sandbags to make sure nothing would be amiss.[20] Here, as the flag-covered casket lay in state for the next thirty-six hours, more than a hundred thousand mourners filed past, some waiting many hours for their turn. In a note to Nancy Reagan, the presidential historian Richard Norton Smith wrote that those waiting in line alongside him included "a visitor from Norfolk who had made the trip to Washington for the first time, . . . a middle-aged black mother with three children, the youngest of whom she carried in her arms, . . . military people in uniform, couples pushing strollers, and countless others too young to cast a vote for President Reagan. Their grief was equaled by their gratitude for a life that had become synonymous in their eyes with the nation itself."

"Even though the President had been offstage for nearly a decade," Smith concluded, "he seemed to loom larger and larger with every passing year."[21]

On Saturday, June 11, under gray, overcast skies, the military pallbearers took the casket out of the Capitol as artillery roared and the familiar cadences of "Hail to the Chief" rent the quiet of a late spring morning. Another motorcade, led by District of Columbia police outriders on motorcycles, bore the body on the five-mile journey to Washington National Cathedral, where nearly four thousand mourners had gathered for a state funeral that was carried live by every television network.

It was evident to onlookers that no formal obsequy had been spared. Foreign heads of state mixed with Hollywood royalty and Washington power brokers in the pews for what a reporter described as "more than two extraordinary hours of thundering organ, swelling chorus, haunting silences, and eloquent prayers."[22] Readings were given by religious leaders of different faiths and by Justice Sandra Day O'Connor, now seventy-four years old, who had been appointed the first woman on the Supreme Court by the man they were now honoring. Eulogies were also delivered by the two world leaders with whom Reagan had been closest—former British prime minister Margaret Thatcher, the so-called Iron Lady, who was present in a pew wearing a funereal black hat but speaking on video because of a series of recent strokes, and, from the pulpit, former Canadian prime minister Brian Mulroney, another jovial offspring of Eire. They were followed by two Republican presidents named Bush. The soaring stone and stained-glassed heights of the cathedral resonated to "The Battle Hymn of the Republic," "Amazing Grace," and "Ode to Joy." Presiding over the service was former Missouri Republican senator John Danforth, an Episcopalian priest who did not know Reagan well but was struck by the love he elicited from ordinary Americans. "It was a very unifying time for the country," he recalled. "I think people knew this man was more than a bundle of ideas, or a bundle of policies. He brought out the best in people."[23]

For a man whose image had been meticulously crafted by imagemakers in Hollywood, Sacramento, and Washington, it was a spectacle that would not disappoint those viewers whose historical consciousness had been shaped by the cinematic extravaganzas of the 1950s. The event was of such magnitude that it transcended the ordinary divisions of partisan politics. Once the service ended, the cathedral bell tolled forty times in honor of the fortieth president. Around the world, US military bases staged twenty-one-gun salutes at noon and fifty-gun salutes at dusk. Letitia Baldrige, who had been Jacqueline Kennedy's chief of staff in the White House, wrote to Nancy Reagan, "I've never seen Washington so wrapped in emotional knots, turning from grief into awe over our U.S. military. Of course much of it was déjà vu for me—remembering JFK's funeral. . . . All of the pomp and circumstance was perfection, and made us proud."[24]

The pomp and circumstance, however, were not quite finished. Or as

Reagan liked to say—adapting a famous line from the 1927 film *The Jazz Singer,* the first "talkie," which came out when he was still in high school— "You ain't seen nothing yet."[25]

After the cathedral service, the president, back on Air Force One, made his final trip home to California, flying for the last time over a nation that he had idolized and idealized. The final funeral service would come at the hilltop Reagan Library, carefully timed for sunset with a majestic view of the Santa Susana Mountains and the Pacific Ocean in the background, as if this were the closing credits of a John Ford–directed Western. The president's three surviving children delivered the final eulogies in front of a crowd full of movie-industry titans—including California's Austrian-accented governor, Arnold Schwarzenegger, who had enjoyed the kind of movie stardom that had eluded the late president. "Taps" was played by a US Army bugler, and Navy fighter jets flew by in the traditional "missing man" formation. The commander of the nuclear-powered aircraft carrier USS *Ronald Reagan,* which Nancy Reagan had christened in 2001, presented the folded flag from the casket to her.

Stoic all week, the widow finally broke down and wept in the crepuscular light as she paid her last goodbye to her husband before he was forever lowered into the ground. The epitaph carved on his granite tomb was a typically optimistic and uplifting credo from a speech in 1991:

I know in my heart that man is good
That what is right will always eventually triumph
And there is purpose and worth to each and every life.[26]

Ron Reagan, the president's youngest child, would recall nearly two decades later that he and the rest of the family were surprised by the vast throngs that had turned out to see the funeral processions on both coasts. On the final leg of the trip, from Point Mugu to the Reagan Library, a distance of twenty-six miles, the entire motorcade route was lined with rows of well-wishers, many standing on freeway overpasses waving flags or holding signs with messages such as "We love you Nancy."[27] "I had not anticipated this," he told me in 2017, sitting in his bungalow in Seattle, shaking his head in wonder much as his father might have done. "None of us had. It was just remarkable. You figure many people like him. Of course, it's going to be kind of a big deal, but . . . wow. We didn't quite expect the enormity of it."[28]

No one did. Who, after all, could have expected that a poor boy from Tampico, Illinois, born in the twilight of the horse-and-buggy era, would come to capture the imagination of a nation and transform the geopolitics of the entire world at the dawn of the tumultuous Computer Age?

Introduction

The Pragmatist

He was a true conservative, but, boy, was he pragmatic when
it came to governing.

—JAMES A. BAKER III

Many years have passed since Ronald Reagan's historic funeral
and even more since he left office. Yet, while countless books
and articles have been produced about one of the most influential presidents of the twentieth century, there is still no definitive biography.

The task rightly should have fallen to the late Edmund Morris, chosen as the president's official biographer and granted unprecedented, real-time access to the White House from 1985 to 1989. But he appeared to be so flummoxed by the complexities of Reagan's character that he produced *Dutch: A Memoir of Ronald Reagan,* an experimental, quasi-fictional book that was widely criticized in spite of its acute insights into the president's boyhood. Not a few people I interviewed about Ronald Reagan began by asking, "You're not going to write a book like Edmund's, are you?" No, I'm not. But while this book is strictly factual—I have resisted the temptation to insert myself as a character in Reagan's long life—I harbor some sympathy for the ordeal that this gifted writer went through to understand a man who was always hiding in plain sight. Reagan was often accused of having simplistic views, but he was hardly a simple man.

Ronald Reagan was one of the most famous people in the world from the 1930s onward, but he remained an enigma even to those who knew him, which suggests that his very inscrutability may have contributed to his appeal. He was the most affable of men—always ready with a story or joke, always genial, always polite, always thoughtful on a one-to-one basis that transcended race or class. As a result of his acting experience, he could connect with an audience like few other politicians, yet his own children said they did not know him well. Behind his practiced bonhomie was a glacial reserve that forced the person closest to him—his wife, Nancy—to say that he walled off part of himself even from her. "He was just plain hard to fig-ure out," noted one White House aide.[1] He preached family values, but he was the first divorced man and the only one other than Donald J. Trump to win the presidency. He presided over an often-dysfunctional family and did not know until long afterward that one of his children (Michael) had been molested by a camp counselor or another (Maureen) had been beaten by her first husband. He never knew the names of his children's friends.

He would call aides and acquaintances to comfort them when a parent died, and his aides were slavishly dedicated to him, but he barely noticed when aides left his employ and seldom did anything to buck up their morale while they were working for him. Sometimes, long before the onset of Alz-heimer's, he could not remember their names. James A. Baker III, his White House chief of staff and later US Treasury secretary, told me that Reagan looked on him as just one of the "hired hands," and even political consultant Stuart K. Spencer—an essential strategist on all four of Reagan's successful political campaigns going back to 1966—said that he always viewed himself as a "solid acquaintance," not a real friend of Reagan's. Spencer felt much closer to former president Gerald Ford in spite of having run only one of his campaigns. Reagan was fundamentally a loner who, by the time of his presidency, had few real friends beyond his wife and two former state police officers who worked with him on his ranch. He would have made, in the words of Spencer, "a pretty good hermit," yet he was so good-natured that he utterly lacked the resentments and paranoia of presidents such as Lyn-don Johnson, Richard Nixon, and Donald Trump.[2]

Reagan had strong convictions and could be quick on his feet as a speaker, but he lacked intellectual depth or curiosity. His mind was full of finely honed stories and factual nuggets, many of them apocryphal, some of them based on movies he had seen or acted in, others invented by right-wing propagandists. No matter how many times his claims were revealed to be false, he stubbornly kept repeating them. He often bored aides and visitors by reciting the same well-worn tales over and over instead of engaging in the intricacies of policy arguments. When he was working in Hollywood, he drove many associates to distraction with his incessant talk about pol-itics; when he was in Sacramento and Washington, he drove many associ-ates to distraction with his incessant talk about show business. Yet he was seen as more successful in implementing his agenda than such presidents as Richard Nixon, Jimmy Carter, Bill Clinton, and Barack Obama, all of whom would presumably have scored higher on an IQ test. His memoirs were ghostwritten, as were most of his presidential speeches, yet he could be an extremely effective writer in his own right, producing words that were meant to be spoken rather than read.

He could be famously stubborn. Yet he was usually willing to compromise and settle for 70 percent of what he wanted to get a deal done. He had a near-photographic memory honed by memorizing movie scripts yet claimed to not recall crucial details of decisions that proved scandalous, whether a deal he made with the Music Corporation of America (MCA) as president of the Screen Actors Guild or his administration's initiative to sell arms to Iran and funnel the proceeds to the Contras. Sometimes he could make tough decisions when he felt they were necessary—firing thousands of striking air-traffic controllers in 1981, invading Grenada in 1983, bombing Libya in 1986, walking out of the Reykjavik summit later that year rather than trading away missile defense—yet often, as in the aftermath of the 1983 Marine barracks bombing in Beirut, he was paralyzed by indecision. He was a distant and disengaged chief executive who found it impossible to fire aides, and he was terrible at managing his staff, allowing disagreements and jealousies to fester out of control.

He was a sucker for a hard-luck story and would regularly send a check to ordinary Americans who wrote to tell him of their woes. Yet he propounded economic policies that inflicted real hardship on millions of ordinary people while providing a windfall for the wealthy and exacerbating income inequality. A longtime supporter of Israel and opponent of antisemitism, he upset Jewish groups with his determination to visit a German war cemetery at Bitburg in 1985 even after it was found to contain the graves of Waffen Schutzstaffel (SS) soldiers. Similarly, although he prided himself on his lack of bigotry, he angered African Americans and the LGTBQ community with his apparent indifference to racial discrimination and the ravages of AIDS, respectively. He also prided himself on being an outdoorsman, yet he aggravated green groups with callous comments about trees causing air pollution and with his appointment of the egregious James Watt to run the Department of the Interior. He professed to be deeply religious and fervently believed in biblical prophecies such as Armageddon (hence his aversion to nuclear weapons), yet as president he seldom went to church, preferring to read the Sunday comics, and never began cabinet meetings with an invocation.

He often expressed his skepticism of the government, but federal spending soared by nearly 70 percent during his presidency and state spending by 120 percent during his governorship of California.[3] Even his famous quip "I've always felt the nine most terrifying words in the English language are: 'I'm from the government, and I'm here to help'" was uttered during a press conference in which he announced an *increase* in federal subsidies to farmers.[4] He ran for president as a "pro-life" candidate who equated abortion with murder, yet as governor of California he did more to legalize abortion than any previous person in US history. He backed the death penalty, but as governor appointed a chief justice who wrote a State Supreme Court decision holding capital punishment to be unconstitutional. And although he supported gun rights, he made California's gun laws the toughest in the nation and, after his presidency, endorsed an assault-weapons ban.

With all his myriad contradictions and inconsistencies, Ronald Reagan was not an easy man to decipher. One of his closest aides, Michael K. Deaver, confessed, "At times Ronald Reagan has been very much a puzzle to me," while his longtime secretary, Helene von Damm, wrote that "he was fundamentally a very difficult man to know."[5] But his story is worth the historian's effort because his life sheds such significant light on America's perilous, if ultimately triumphant, journey though the twentieth century.

His life inevitably is more than the story of one man. It is also the story of a nation's transformation from rural to urban and suburban; the rise of mass media—first radio, then movies and television—and their role in shaping the American imagination and American politics; the transition from isolationism to interventionism in 1941 and the rise to superpower status in 1945; bitter, often violent labor-management struggles; the Red Scare in the early years of the Cold War; the white, middle-class backlash against the civil rights movement and student radicalism in the 1960s; the growth of the New Right from a marginal movement to a dominant one; the nation's revival from the nadir of Watergate, Vietnam, and stagflation; and, finally, the Cold War's perilous final decade followed by a surprisingly peaceful denouement.

Ronald Reagan was, in one form or another, at the center of it all for a half century. It is no exaggeration to say that you cannot fully comprehend what happened to America in the twentieth century without first understanding what happened to Ronald Reagan. To know how we got here—to the America and the world of the twenty-first century—you must chart his lengthy, eventful, and consequential life, whose course was often at odds with the legend that has grown around him.

I am fortunate that Ronald Reagan's story can now be told as never before because we possess far more archival sources and far more historical perspective. The passage of more than thirty years since he left office affords the kind of understanding of his presidency that historians finally achieved only in the 1980s of the Eisenhower administration. We can now see Reagan's failures and achievements in the context of the grand sweep of historical events—and in many cases they look quite different than they did to contemporaries. For example, the economic growth rates he achieved in the 1980s look less impressive in light of the stronger expansion under President Bill Clinton in the 1990s, while the deficits he piled up do not look as daunting because they were so much smaller than the deficits under the presidents who followed Clinton. Meanwhile, Reagan's ability to pass sweeping tax and immigration reforms with bipartisan majorities looks more impressive in light of the partisan gridlock and political polarization of more recent decades. But his willingness, in common with many other politicians of his day, to cater to bigots to win elections becomes a bigger blot on his record from the vantage point of the 2020s, when Americans had been more acutely sensitized to the historical harms of racial discrimination than in the past.

Among other things, we can now see what we could not know in 1989 or even 2004, namely, how the conservative movement, which he had once personified, would continue to evolve after his exit from the stage. It is startling to realize that when Reagan was president, there was no widely available internet, no widespread use of email, no smartphones, no Fox News Channel, and, until his final year in office, no Rush Limbaugh show in national syndication. Politics seemed brutal then but appears gentle by comparison with today's blood sport. Some of Reagan's passions—for cutting taxes and appointing conservative judges—continue to animate the modern Republican Party, but his support for immigration, free trade, and alliances are as much a quaint relic of the past as his gentlemanly demeanor, willingness to compromise, and reluctance to attack opponents by name. His place as a right-wing icon has been usurped, for many, by Donald Trump. In a poll conducted in 2021, 36 percent of Republicans labeled Trump the best president in US history, while only 18 percent said it was Reagan. By 2023, in another poll of Republicans, Reagan narrowly edged out Trump, 41 percent to 37 percent.[6] It's too simplistic to say that Reagan inevitably led to Trump, but it is worth asking how we got from one to the other. Did Reaganism contain the seeds of Trumpism? That is a question a modern biographer cannot avoid.

In addition to new perspectives on the fortieth president, there are new sources to examine. The US government continues declassifying documents on pivotal episodes such as the shootdown of Korean Air Lines Flight 007, the war scares of 1983, the diplomacy with Mikhail Gorbachev, the failed peacekeeping mission to Lebanon, the development of the Strategic Defense Initiative, the Iran arms deal, and much else besides. It is now possible, for example, to read verbatim transcripts of all the Reagan-Gorbachev summits rather than simply relying on the memories of participants. The publication of the full Reagan diaries provides granular insights into his day-to-day thinking that do not exist for most other presidents. So, too, the diaries of other insiders—notably, Republican Congressman Barber Conable, House Majority Leader Jim Wright, Deputy Secretary of State Kenneth W. Dam, and Canadian Ambassador Allan Gotlieb—provide a fascinating, behind-the-scenes perspective on administration deliberations.

Even more documents will be declassified in the years ahead, but future historians will not be able to interview so many of those who knew Reagan best. I spoke with nearly a hundred of his aides, colleagues, friends, and family members, many of whom have already passed away since our conversations. I also read the ever-expanding literature on Ronald Reagan: hundreds of monographs and memoirs that provide important new information about various aspects of his life and presidency. And I traveled to the most significant locations in his life—including the area in Ireland where his father's side of the family came from; his boyhood haunts in early twentieth-century, small-town Illinois; his ranch in Santa Barbara; and the windswept building in Reykjavik where he met with Mikhail Gorbachev in 1986—in order to try to see the world through his twinkling blue eyes.

Taken together, all of this new information allows me to write about Ronald Reagan in a way that was not possible before. One theme that strongly emerged from my research, much to my surprise, was his pragmatism.

We are used to thinking of Reagan as an ideologue, and he was certainly more ideological than most presidents, at least when he was campaigning for the causes he believed in. As historian Jonathan Darman, son of Reagan White House aide Richard Darman, noted, "Pragmatism is not a virtue people usually ascribe to Reagan." But Reagan would never have gotten as far as he did if he were simply an idealist or a zealot. He had strongly held principles, but they were tempered by a keen sense of realpolitik. Put another way, the Great Communicator was also the Great Compromiser. His entire life was characterized by a series of deals—first with studio bosses, then with California Assembly Speakers Jesse "Big Daddy" Unruh and Bob Moretti, and finally, during his presidency, with House Speaker Thomas "Tip" O'Neill and Soviet leader Mikhail Gorbachev. "He was a true conservative," Jim Baker told me, "but, boy, was he pragmatic when it came to governing."[7]

Reagan's pragmatism resulted in budget deals, trade deals, welfare reform, tax legislation, immigration reform, and, most significant of all, the first US-Soviet treaty to abolish, not just limit, an entire class of nuclear weapons. Because of his unexpected flexibility in the application of his principles, he got more done than most presidents or governors, even though his party was never in complete control of Congress during his presidency and controlled the California Legislature for only two out of the eight years of his governorship. He knew that he had to cut deals with the opposition party—and he did. Long after Reagan ceased to be a member of the Democratic Party, he remained a "small-d" democrat. He believed that an elected leader had to listen to the verdict of the voters—and that, if Democrats won control of the state legislature or Congress, he felt compelled to meet them halfway.

But there was also a cynical, troubling side to Reagan's pragmatism that may dumbfound many who have confused his legend with reality. He revered his small-town roots but was so ambitious, ferociously if secretly so, that he fled the Midwest as soon as he could. He spent World War II working in an Army Air Forces film unit a few miles from home but cooperated in press coverage that gave the impression he was fighting at the front. He built his political career on vastly exaggerated, even falsified, accounts of resisting a Communist takeover of the film industry. He avoided becoming tarred with the excesses of McCarthyism yet served as an FBI informant in Hollywood and an arbiter of the blacklist. He cut sweetheart deals with his talent agency, MCA, that allowed it to become the dominant force in the entertainment industry while he received a lucrative, career-saving job as host of a popular TV show and, later, a massive, inflated windfall on the sale of his Malibu ranch.

The pattern hardly abated when Reagan entered politics. He distanced himself from the John Birch Society—a group of conspiracy-mongers so extreme they considered Dwight D. Eisenhower a Communist agent—but still repeated its bogus claims and never truly disavowed it because he counted on its members' support. He employed blatantly false "facts" and quotations, often borrowed from the Birchers, to accuse the Democratic Party of advancing a supposed Communist plot to take over America by passing social-welfare legislation. When he was governor of California, he exacerbated tensions with student radicals (he vowed a "bloodbath" if necessary) and used excessive force to quell protests in Berkeley. Although he and especially his wife had numerous gay friends, he allowed a homophobic campaign to drive out his first chief of staff in Sacramento and later allowed homophobic aides to slow-roll the federal response to the AIDS pandemic.

To win office, he made common cause with segregationists while opposing civil rights legislation and pandering to white fears of Black criminals and "welfare queens." He did not use the same racist rhetoric as George Wallace, but he consciously appealed to the same constituency. Having never criticized Richard Nixon's outreach to the Soviet Union and China when Nixon was in office, he turned into a vitriolic critic of détente when running against Gerald Ford for the Republican presidential nomination in 1976. His aides were still more ruthless: Almost certainly without his knowledge, they made use of materials stolen from Jimmy Carter's campaign to prepare for a crucial debate in 1980, conspired to pay the New York Liberal Party to endorse third-party candidate John Anderson, and may have plotted to prevent Americans held hostage in Iran from being released prior to the election.

Early in Reagan's presidency, his incendiary rhetoric against the "evil empire," combined with a massive arms buildup and secret US military provocations to test Soviet defenses, exacerbated tensions and raised the risk of nuclear war. And while he talked tough on terrorism, he traded arms for hostages with Iran and never struck back at the terrorists who blew up the US Marine barracks and the US Embassy in Beirut.

Other presidents might have made such compromises cynically. Reagan made them naively, without necessarily being aware that he was compromising anything at all. His pragmatism was always sheathed in the armor of moral certitude. His superpower was the ability to reorder the world in his mind as he wished it to be—not necessarily as it was. That allowed him to avoid any second thoughts and always convinced him that he was acting in conformity with his highest ideals—even when he was not. That is part of what made the Iran-Contra affair so traumatic for him: It forced him, for one of the few times in his life, to acknowledge that he had fallen short of the heroic role in which he had cast himself ever since his days as a teenage lifeguard pulling swimmers out of the churning waters of the Rock River.

Reagan had little guile and was congenitally incapable of deception. His son Ron said at his interment ceremony, "He was the most plainly decent man you could ever hope to meet," and few who knew him would disagree. But he was no proverbial Boy Scout and certainly no saint, and he would have been less interesting and less influential if he were. No politician, not even Ronald Reagan, could have scaled the heights of power without making some unsavory compromises along the way. (Even Jimmy Carter, the most honest and idealistic of presidents, had used code words to appeal to segregationists while concealing his support for integration during his 1970 campaign for governor of Georgia.)[8] The biographer's job is to find the compromises and expose the shibboleths and then to report on them dispassionately, not to cover them up or exaggerate their importance, so that readers can make up their own minds.

I did not vote for Ronald Reagan only because I was too young to do so. But growing up in Los Angeles in a family of Russian-Jewish refugees who had arrived from the Soviet Union in 1976, I was an ardent admirer of a president who embodied moral clarity in denouncing the "evil empire." I was desperately worried when, as an elementary school student in 1981, I heard that he had been shot—and greatly relieved he had survived. As a high school student in 1984, I attended his final campaign rally at a community college in Canoga Park, California, waiting for hours in the broiling sun to hear him speak. Ronald Reagan made me, along with many others, into a Republican, and I will always retain a residue of affection for him. But I am a Republican no longer. Nor have I become a Democrat. I am an independent, and I write not as a partisan for or against Reagan but as a historian who wants to set the story straight.

In the process, I seek to strip away many of the legends—from his role in battling Communism in Hollywood to his role in ending the Cold War—that have accreted like barnacles around the Reagan legacy. The real story is far more interesting and complex than most have realized—less flattering in some respects, more flattering in other ways.

This biography, I suspect, will not fully satisfy either Reagan worshippers or Reagan haters—and, goodness knows, there are plenty of both in the world. But I am hoping that with the passage of time readers are ready for a more dispassionate look at a once-polarizing figure. This is not intended to be either a hagiography or a hit job but, rather, a fair-minded account of a pragmatic but flawed president whose soaring vision made his presidency a success but whose inability to manage the government and aversion to uncomfortable realities inflicted heavy costs on his administration and the country as a whole. My aim is to make the reader understand who Ronald Reagan was and what legacy he left—how he was shaped by America and how he in turn shaped America as few others have.

The story begins—appropriately enough considering that Ronald Reagan cultivated a lifelong image as the most typical and wholesome of Americans—near the midpoint of the United States geographically and near the midpoint of its history.

ACT I

SMALL-TOWN BOY

(previous page) *Ronald "Dutch" Reagan in Dixon, Illinois, in the 1920s. He was a quintessential product of the small-town, early twentieth-century Midwest.* (RRPL)

1

Main Street

Reagan was a man whose belief system was based on Judeo-
Christian principles conditioned by a Midwestern ethic.

—STUART K. SPENCER

P residents, like other people, are shaped not only by the idiosyncra-
sies of their own character and upbringing but also by the norms
and mores of the society in which they are raised. Many of America's
early presidents were products of the distinctive culture of colonial Virginia;
Theodore Roosevelt and Franklin Roosevelt of Gilded Age New York; John
F. Kennedy of the Irish American elite in Boston; Lyndon B. Johnson of the
dirt-poor Texas Hill Country; George H. W. Bush of the New England WASP
aristocracy; Donald J. Trump of the outer-borough culture of Queens, New
York. Ronald Reagan would come to embody the "cowboy conservatism" of
the West. But like most of the presidents from 1860 to 1960, if few since then,
he was actually a product of the Midwest—a part of the country so characteristically American that it was hard to say where regional identity ended
and American normalcy began. The small-town, early twentieth-century
Midwest was where he spent his first twenty-six years and where he forged
the sensibility that would last a lifetime, even as his political beliefs under-
went a radical, midlife transformation.

This area was known to Americans as the Northwest Territory when
white settlers were just beginning to wrest it at gunpoint from its Native
American inhabitants in the late eighteenth century. In the nineteenth century, when states from Ohio (in 1803) to South Dakota (in 1889) were joining the Union, it became known simply as the West or the Great West—and
it became the destination for countless settlers, mainly recent European
immigrants (Ronald Reagan's forebears among them), arriving in covered
wagons and later on steamboats and railroads, looking to claim a homestead
and trying but often failing to build a better life. Only in the early twentieth century did it come to be called the Middle West, or Midwest for short,

because by then the United States stretched from "sea to shining sea" and a new "Northwest" was rising on the Pacific coast. By the time Ronald Reagan was growing up, this region had become the center of the country psychologically as well as geographically.

"Midwesterners were distinguished by their lack of distinguishing characteristics," noted historian Andrew Cayton. "Anything but flamboyant, they supposedly had no discernible accent or clothing or customs." According to the popular stereotypes, they were renowned for being sober and serious, practical and hardworking folks who were almost compulsively nice but lacking in pizzazz. Even their meat-and-potatoes cuisine, Cayton noted, was "solid, practical, unimaginative."[1]

While many Westerners and Southerners felt alienated from the American mainstream, Midwesterners *were* the mainstream. When television personalities Johnny Carson, Walter Cronkite, or Tom Brokaw spoke, it was as if they had no accent at all, because they were from the Midwest. In vaudeville days there was even a phrase—"Will it play in Peoria?"—to suggest that to be a success a show had to be pitched to the tastes of the "heartland." By contrast, *New Yorker* editor Harold Ross defiantly conceived the sophisticated magazine in 1925 as "not for the little old lady in Dubuque" to distinguish it from mainstream competitors such as the *Saturday Evening Post*.[2]

In the nineteenth century, the brutal European conquest of the Midwest had been pioneered by consummate risk-takers like Ronald Reagan's great-grandparents who were willing to leave their old lives behind to start anew, but by the mid-twentieth century, when the future of America was being forged in fast-growing Sunbelt states from Florida to California, the Midwest had become known as a sleepy paragon of the status quo and stability. This region produced many progressive reformers, from William Jennings Bryan to Hubert Humphrey, but, as exemplified by Bryan's religious fundamentalism, it remained a haven of cultural conservatism. Grant Wood, a product of rural Iowa, produced in *American Gothic* one of the region's defining images by painting an unsmiling farmer in his overalls, pitchfork in hand, and his equally grim daughter—actually the artist's dentist and sister—in front of a typical wooden farmhouse. He wrote in 1935, "This region has always stood as the great conservative section of the country."[3] Little wonder, then, that Reagan, like all the other presidents raised in the Midwest, would be a conservative. (Although Barack Obama represented Illinois in the US Senate, he grew up in Hawaii and Indonesia.)

Ronald Reagan, unlike his predecessor in the White House, Jimmy Carter of Georgia, did not grow up on a farm and had no memories of milking cows, feeding pigs, or performing other farm chores. Although the Midwest is the country's foremost agricultural region—renowned for having some of the richest soil in the world—Reagan was, like Harry S. Truman, Dwight D. Eisenhower, and Gerald R. Ford, a product of the small towns that dotted the Midwestern prairies. Those towns were commended in popular culture as a repository of homespun virtue and wisdom when they were not being reviled as a hotbed of conformity, anti-intellectualism, and hidden dysfunction. Coming from the small-town Midwest was normality squared. Reagan actually grew up in the early twentieth-century world mythologized in Disneyland's "Main Street, USA"—and brutally satirized in Sinclair Lewis's *Main Street*. Of course, both Walt Disney and Sinclair Lewis were Midwesterners too.

Ronald Reagan's ancestors, like so many other impoverished immigrants from the Old World, had arrived in what would become known as the Midwest when America was still only a few generations old. His father's people, originally called O'Regan, came from the tiny village of Doolis in County Tipperary, Ireland, which has long disappeared, like Brigadoon, into the mists of time. Where it stood are now shamrock-green fields grazed by sheep and cattle. The closest surviving town is Ballyporeen (population 318), and it has become known as the Reagan family seat.

The president's great-grandfather Michael, an impoverished, twenty-two-year-old soapmaker, fled Doolis in 1851 because of the potato famine. Between 1845 and 1855, more than a million Irish people died from starvation and disease after the failure of the potato crop.[4] Michael went first to London, where he married an Irish lass named Catherine Mulcahey; then, in 1857, they sailed to New York with their first two children.[5] The Reagans, as they came to spell their name, established a farm in Fair Haven in northwestern Illinois, but, as readers of Willa Cather and Laura Ingalls Wilder know, farm life on the Great Plains was an unrelenting struggle from sunup to sundown. Their offspring sought an easier life in nearby towns, and the family lost its farm in the 1880s following Michael's death from tuberculosis—a contagious disease as little understood in those days as AIDS would be a century later.

Michael and Catherine Reagan's son John Michael left the farm to work on a grain elevator in the bustling and seedy Mississippi River port of Fulton, Illinois, "a kind of riverside Dodge City," where he married a woman of Irish ancestry, Jennie Cusick.[6] She gave birth in 1881 to William Reagan and two years later to John Edward "Jack" Reagan, the father of a future president. Both John and Jennie Reagan also died of tuberculosis, leaving Jack an orphan by age five. He was raised by his great-aunt Margaret, who had no children of her own. In her late thirties, she had married a stolid Yankee who owned a general store first in Fulton and then in Bennett, Iowa, a frontier outpost with two saloons and a pool hall but no sidewalks or paved streets.[7] Jack was more interested in playing baseball with his friends than in studying (he was part of a team called the Junior Tigers that took on all comers), and he left school at age twelve to help in the store. By the time he was eighteen, he was clerking at the larger and more successful J. W. Broadhead Dry Goods Store in Fulton—a country cousin of the sprawling department stores, such as Marshall Field's in Chicago and Macy's in New York, that had opened in major cities. He developed a specialty in women's shoes, and with his swarthy, muscular good looks and fluent salesman's patter, he did not want for customers.

But if other ladies had their eyes on Jack, he had eyes primarily for an attractive, part-time clerk of his own age with auburn hair and blue eyes. Nelle Clyde Wilson was descended from English and Scottish immigrants. Her paternal grandfather, John Wilson, had married a fellow Scottish immigrant and established a farm in Clyde, Illinois, in 1839, only four miles away from the Reagans' future spread in Fair Haven. The Wilsons had eight children. Their son John married Mary Anne Elsey, an English immigrant who had been a domestic servant, and they in turn had seven children in rapid succession. Nelle, born in 1883, was the youngest. When Nelle was but five years old, her ne'er-do-well father abandoned the family, leaving her mother to run the farm by herself with the help of her children. Like Jack Reagan—and most other Americans of the time—Nelle's education ended at sixth grade. (In 1910, only 13.5 percent of the population had graduated from high school.)[8]

Following her mother's death in 1900, Nelle and her family left the farm and moved to Fulton with her recently returned father. At Broadhead's store, she fell in love with the charming and ambitious Jack Reagan, who, like her, came from a broken family. They were married in 1904, when they were both twenty-one, at the Catholic Church in Fulton—in the parsonage, not at the altar, because Nelle was not Catholic. Nelle was eager to get Jack away from the pernicious influence of his hard-drinking brother William, who operated a cigar store in Fulton and was prone to get into brawls when inebriated.[9]

So in 1906 Jack got a job selling clothing and shoes at the H. C. Pitney Variety Store in Tampico, Illinois, and the Reagans rented a five-room apartment on the second floor of a simple, two-story, red-brick building topped by an elegant cornice at 111 South Main Street. The ground floor was occupied by a saloon, although the Tampico Historical Society claims it was a bakery, presumably to make it seem more wholesome. In reality, the bakery did not replace the tavern until 1915—by which time the Reagans had already moved on.[10]

Tampico, with a population of just 849 people, was a rail depot and commercial entrepôt for the farmers in the surrounding area in northwestern Illinois.[11] A tiny urban oasis amid a sea of green and brown fields, it had been established in the 1870s after the arrival of the railroad in the area. The town had barely survived a series of major fires and a devastating tornado in its early days, but it had rebounded with a modest building boom in the years shortly before the Reagans' arrival. The Chicago, Burlington, and Quincy Railroad hauled local grain, cattle, and hogs to Chicago and returned with various goods that the locals wanted to buy—many of them sold either by the H. C. Pitney store or by its competitor, W. H. Harrison & Company. The town had a few two-story brick buildings scattered along Main Street; the entire business district took up just a single block. The town boasted a newspaper, the *Tampico Tornado* (named for a tornado that had swept through in 1874); a post office; two banks; a poultry plant; two grain elevators; a creamery; a pharmacy; a hotel (advertising "adequate . . . accommodation"); four churches; three physicians; one dentist; and a school with four teachers. It even had, as of 1909, a street paved with brick. A lone police officer enforced the law.[12]

Photos of the time show no automobiles on Main Street—only horse-drawn carriages. That's hardly surprising since in 1910 there were fewer than five hundred thousand automobiles in the whole country—a number destined to expand over the next seventy years to more than 150 million.[13]

But it would not be long before noisy and smoky horseless carriages started appearing on these once-quiet streets; Jack Reagan would purchase his first Ford Model T in 1913 with a loan from his boss.[14] In other ways Tampico was already on the front lines of progress. It possessed its own telephone company and its own electrical plant. Residents such as the Reagans had access to telephones and electricity at a time when most American households, especially in rural areas, did not.

Tampico does not look like much to the twenty-first-century visitor, and it wasn't much more impressive in the early twentieth century, but the *Tampico Tornado* could be forgiven for boasting that it was a "handsome, progressive, busy town in the midst of a fine farming country." After all, the newspaper noted, "not so many years ago, we were face to face with the primitive life of the frontier. The ox team furnished transportation, the tallow dip or tallow candle furnished light, log cabins or rude shacks furnished shelter, stage coaches and the pony express were the only means of communication." By 1910, even the residents of this tiny town on the prairie had become accustomed "to the many conveniences of life in . . . the early twentieth century, such as railways, steamships, telegraph, telephone, electric light, paved streets . . . even the flying machine." The *Tornado*, perhaps sensitive to the snobbery of city slickers, insisted that between the telephone and the telegraph, Tampico was "in quick touch with the whole world" and that its rail and water links gave it "direct outlets to the uttermost parts of the earth."[15]

The Reagans' first child, John Neil, was born in Tampico on September 16, 1908. To distinguish him from all the other Johns in the family, including his own father, he was known as Neil and later as "Moon" after *Moon Mullins*, a popular comic strip of the 1920s.

Nelle became pregnant again in 1910. Just as she was going in labor, on Sunday, February 5, 1911, one of the worst blizzards of the winter hit Tampico, producing a ghostly landscape reminiscent of "the Alps, Rockies, and Sierras," the *Tampico Tornado* reported. "After the wind and snow had spent its fury, the snow was ten inches to a foot on the level and drifted badly making the highways nearly impassable."[16] The doctor who was supposed to deliver the child was unavailable. Jack had to race through the snow to find a midwife. Finally, the doctor showed up around 3:00 a.m. on February

6, and the child arrived soon thereafter. It had been a difficult delivery, and the newborn's face was blue from screaming.[17]

Jack was ecstatic that mother and son were safe. The *Tampico Tornado* reported four days later—alongside news that "the champion eater of Tampico" had "packed . . . away" thirty-one large bananas in one sitting—that "John Reagan has been calling thirty-seven inches a yard and giving seventeen ounces for a pound this week at Pitney's store he has been feeling so jubilant over the arrival of a ten pound boy Monday."[18]

Nelle had been planning to call the baby Donald, but one of her sisters had already used that name for her own son. So "Donald" was crossed out on the birth certificate and "Ronald" written in.[19] His middle name was Nelle's family name—thus, Ronald Wilson Reagan. But almost no one other than his mother called him Ronald. Family legend has it that Jack took one look at the squalling newborn and said, "For such a little bit of a fat Dutchman, he makes a hell of a lot of noise, doesn't he?" Whether this was the actual origin of the nickname or not, Ronald Reagan would call himself "Dutch"—a moniker usually employed by those of Dutch or German ancestry, which he was not—until he got to Hollywood in 1937. "I never thought 'Ronald' was rugged enough for a young red-blooded American boy," he later explained.[20]

Two-and-a-half-year-old Neil was not happy to discover that his new sibling was a boy. "I had been promised a sister by my father and mother," he recalled many years later. "That's all I wanted."[21] But no sister would ever arrive. Nelle was told by her doctor that she was too weak to bear another child—which meant, in those days before the availability of reliable contraceptives, that Nelle probably refrained from sexual relations with her husband after Dutch's birth. So this would be the whole Reagan family, and it would be an unusually small and insular clan at a time when large families were common and multiple generations often lived in close proximity. (Harry S. Truman grew up in a household of at least fourteen people.)[22] Dutch and Neil were even invited to call their parents by their first names, as if they were all friends of the same age.

Despite this informality—which would be highly unusual in our day, much less in theirs—the children's upbringing was strict. Neil noted that their mother "wasn't the demonstrative type, she was reserved, serious and dedicated." Nelle was later part of a church group that put out a how-to manual for its members. It advised children to be obedient, mind their table manners ("Never keep your lips apart when chewing. . . . Never eat chicken with your fingers"), be "clean and neat looking at all times," and "never talk back to older people, especially to your mother and father" because "they know best." Infractions were swiftly punished. Neil remembered that when he was eight and Dutch was five and a half, Nelle overheard them practicing some swear words they had picked up from neighborhood kids during a baseball game. She immediately turned each boy over her knee and spanked him—and "with each whack she was telling us we shouldn't be using that language. It was an impressive lesson."[23]

That was typical of how children were raised in America in the early years of the twentieth century. They were not supposed to swear or blaspheme or talk back to adults—although, of course, in practice many often did.

In 1911, the world was still much as it had been in the nineteenth century, but it was changing with bewildering and accelerating rapidity. The United States had become an industrial giant but was still a military pygmy, with fewer men under arms than the kingdom of Italy.[24] The president, Republican William Howard Taft, was the most corpulent occupant ever of that office and the last to sport facial hair. The federal government he presided over was minuscule by modern standards. The federal income tax did not yet exist—the Sixteenth Amendment would not be ratified until 1913—so federal taxes consumed only 2 percent of gross domestic product in 1910 compared to 18 percent in 1980.[25] (No wonder Reagan thought in the 1980s that taxes were too high.) The social welfare state—which, in the future, would encompass programs from Social Security to Food Stamps—did not yet exist. The War, Navy, and State Departments, that is, the entire national security bureaucracy, fit into a single office building next to the White House—a structure that by the time of Ronald Reagan's presidency was no longer sufficient to house even the whole of his personal staff. (No wonder Reagan thought in the 1980s the government was too big.)

America was still a land of isolated farms, small towns like Tampico, and only a few major cities. New York, Chicago, and Philadelphia were the only metropolises of more than a million people. The country had yet to become an endless sprawl of cities and suburbs, chain stores and strip malls. Domestic servants were the third-largest occupational category behind farmers and factory workers.[26] Electric dishwashers, vacuum cleaners, air conditioners, electric washers and dryers, even refrigerators were unknown, with the first one for home use not invented until 1913. While electricity had come to Tampico remarkably early, most of the countryside would not receive electrical power until the advent of the New Deal of the 1930s. Even indoor plumbing and central heating were luxuries unavailable to many; as late as 1930 more than a third of Americans lived in homes without running water.[27] When the Reagans in 1911 had to relieve themselves, they still had to use either a chamber pot or walk outside to a malodorous outhouse that must have been unbearable in both winter and summer. Heat for their apartment came from a coal-burning stove. Food was chilled in an icebox. Bathing was done in a tub filled with water hauled in pails from the outdoor pump. Clothes were washed by hand. This was a lifestyle that in many respects predated the Industrial Revolution.

Nelle supplemented Jack's meager wages by taking in sewing. Few women worked outside the home, and even fewer could vote—a right that would not be recognized by the Constitution until 1920. Even wearing cosmetics was frowned on, and Nelle would never be caught doing something so frivolous. Selling contraceptives, or even providing information about them, was generally illegal under the Comstock laws. Censorship of material deemed too radical or salacious was enforced across the land.

As seems inevitable in almost any era, society was riven by terrible class and racial divides. Tycoons such as the Rockefellers, Carnegies, and Morgans lived in gilded splendor, attended by armies of liveried servants, while many ordinary workers toiled twelve hours a day, six days a week in unsafe conditions, living in overcrowded, pestilential slums and barely making enough to eat. In 1911 the Triangle Shirtwaist factory fire in New York, one of the worst industrial accidents in US history, killed 146 garment workers, in part because so many of the building's exits were locked to prevent workers from taking unauthorized breaks.

Ninety percent of African Americans still lived in the segregated South, many of them consigned to backbreaking labor as sharecroppers on land they did not own; the Great Migration to seek a better life in the industrial cities of the North and West was just beginning. What would today be called "hate crimes" were a regular occurrence; sixty African Americans were lynched in 1911 alone—more than one a week.[28] But few white Americans paid much attention to these grave racial injustices. Emblematic of the era's blinkered attitudes was the 1919 hit song "Swanee," written by George Gershwin and Irving Caesar and sung by Al Jolson in blackface, which at the time was not recognized as being racist or pernicious. The song's narrator pines for an idealized life in the Old South, with its birds singing and banjos "strummin' soft and low" and "my mammy waitin' for me." "I give the world to be / Among the folks in D-I-X-I-E," Jolson sings with apparent naivete.[29]

Ronald Reagan's worldview would be shaped profoundly, if unconsciously, not only by the region he was born into but also by the epoch. It was a world still in transition from an agricultural age to an industrial one, from empires and monarchies to democracies and dictatorships, from laissez-faire capitalism to welfare states, and from European domination to the establishment of independent states in Africa and Asia. The Victorian era had just ended. The American Century was just beginning. If, by the 1980s, Ronald Reagan often seemed like a remnant from an earlier age of US history—well, that's because he was. He was born into a country that no longer existed and that even in 1911 was fast disappearing. Yet, ever the quintessential American, he always looked to the future with hope and optimism rather than dwelling on the past.

All four of Dutch Reagan's grandparents were dead by the time he entered the world, and his father seemed to have little or no contact with his great-aunt Margaret, who had raised him. Even though he was an orphan, Jack was surely familiar with his family's story of hardship and emigration from Ireland (Margaret must have related the family lore), but he chose not to share it with his sons. "I learned very little from him about his family's background," Ronald Reagan later wrote. The boys grew up knowing little more than that "our roots were Irish and English, mostly Irish," Neil recalled. Even as an adult Ronald Reagan was under the misapprehension that his father's family came from County Cork rather than County Tipperary; that his father had been born in Bennett, Iowa, rather than in Fulton, Illinois; and that the great-aunt who raised his father was named Mary rather than Margaret.[30]

That level of unawareness indicated a willful desire to escape the tethers of his family's history of struggle and hardship. Thus, Reagan would grow up to be a model American, freed of the burden of the past and ready to make a fresh start. In other countries, the historian Bernard Lewis observed, events that had happened a thousand years ago were still sparking conflict. In the land of opportunity, by contrast, the phrase "that's history" was used to dismiss something as having "no relevance to present events, concerns or purposes."[31]

Liberated from the past, Ronald Reagan was able to cast off the ancestral grievances of the Irish against the English, their colonial masters for seven hundred years. He would think of himself as a man of the Midwest, not as a transplanted Irishman. He did not have the chip on the shoulder and the ethnic solidarity that came from being part of an often-despised minority. He was very different in that respect from his future adversary, House Speaker Thomas "Tip" O'Neill of Boston, the personification of the bulky, backslapping, Irish American machine politician.

The early twentieth century was a time of rampant anti-Catholic bigotry; the American Protective Association, a leading nativist organization, was headquartered in Clinton, Iowa, only forty miles from Tampico. Dutch, unlike his older brother, was never baptized a Catholic. Because of his father's heritage, however, he still was more sensitized to discrimination than the average white American Protestant of the early twentieth century. "I had my share of fistfights, including some that started only because I was from an Irish Catholic family," he recalled, while stressing that his family was not really Catholic: "We were religiously divided."[32]

Some other kids may have thought Dutch was somehow a foreigner, but that was not how he thought of himself. He considered himself from the start a mainstream, generic, nonhyphenated American, Midwestern born. He may have been half Irish, but he was all American. He always identified more with the homogenized white majority than with embattled ethnic minorities, and he always expressed unstinting faith in America "as a promised land."[33]

Reagan would not visit Ballyporeen until 1984, when it was seen as a way to win Irish American votes for his reelection campaign. He was startled to meet a local man named Miles O'Regan who looked so much like him that he did a "double take." "It was a shock to all of us," he told his brother Moon. Reminiscing about this trip in a memoir, he admitted, "I've never been a great one for introspection or dwelling on the past."[34]

That was putting it mildly. Ronald Reagan's interest was always in what came next, not on what had come before. As president, he would quote the radical pamphleteer Thomas Paine: "We have it within our power to begin the world over again."[35] Not a very conservative sentiment but one close to his heart. Ronald Reagan would remake his own world—repeatedly.

But however much he might change his own circumstances through sheer force of his powerful will—going from a poor boy in small-town Illinois to a star in Hollywood and then a giant in politics—one constant remained: the values he learned growing up in the Midwest. Values like do your best, work hard, follow the rules, be friendly, stay humble, tell the truth, put family first, respect your elders. It was meat-and-potatoes morality for a seemingly meat-and-potatoes guy. "Reagan was a man whose belief system was based on Judeo-Christian principles conditioned by a Midwestern ethic," explained his longtime campaign operative Stuart K. Spencer.

In Spencer's telling, Reagan's pragmatism was born in the region where he was raised. "The Midwestern ethic was that when a farmer brought his bushels of corn to a market, and he wanted ten dollars a barrel," Spencer explained, "but he got there and looked around, saw that there were thousands of bushels around, so he said, 'I ain't gonna get ten dollars a barrel, I'm only gonna get eight.' To him that was simple logic: I'll get my eight, or I'll get my seven. Better than getting nothing at all."[36] Indeed, Reagan used virtually identical language in the late 1960s to describe his governing philosophy: "I'm willing to take what I can get. You have to take what you can get and go out and get some more next year."[37]

Dutch had learned as a child to be satisfied with what he had because he didn't have much.

2

"The Sunny Side's the Only Side"

My brother and I would hear some pretty fiery arguments through the walls of our house.

—RONALD REAGAN

Nelle and Jack Reagan could not have been more different. She was Protestant, he Catholic; she devout and a teetotaler, he fun-loving and hard-drinking. The gulf between them only widened as she became more devoted to Jesus Christ and he to John Barleycorn. Like a diamond formed under intense pressure and high heat, Ronald Reagan's crystalline personality would be forged in the cauldron of parental tensions.

Nelle had been willing to allow Neil to be baptized a Catholic, but her forbearance for her husband's faith did not extend to Dutch. In the interim between the birth of her two boys, she had found religion—and it wasn't Catholicism. She had been raised a Methodist, but in Tampico on Easter Sunday 1910, shortly before becoming pregnant with Dutch, she was baptized, most likely in the nearby Hennepin Canal, as a member of the Disciples of Christ. Often known simply as the Christian Church, this was a religious denomination created in western Pennsylvania and northern Kentucky in the early nineteenth century as a populist revolt of "plain folk" against mainstream Protestant sects headquartered "back East." By 1910 it had more than 1.3 million adherents. It was an austere faith that frowned on musical instruments in religious services and avoided open displays of emotion.[1]

Disciples of Christ, such as Carrie A. Nation, agitated against alcohol (she became notorious for attacking barrooms with a hatchet), and this might have been part of the faith's attraction to someone like Nelle whose husband was besotted with demon rum. The Disciples were firmly patriotic, anti-Communist, and suspicious of unions and radicals. But there was also a more liberal strain of the faith. The church became a prominent home of the social gospel movement, which called for liberal, even socialist, reforms to address the needs of the downtrodden. Dutch combined both strands in his own early outlook: He would be conservative on personal morality and liberal on public policy.[2]

Nelle became a zealous Disciple whose devotion to good deeds was described by those who knew her as saintly. When she wasn't performing household chores or taking in sewing to help pay the bills, she could be found teaching Sunday school, organizing church activities and charities, performing in religious plays and readings, and visiting prisons, mental institutions, and hospitals to help the least fortunate. A woman who knew her said, "I can't explain in words what a wonderful woman she was. She was cheerful, lovable, and wonderful to everybody. . . . She got more pleasure out of helping others—the sick and the 'bad boys' in jail—than in doing things for herself."[3]

Nelle was a "very plain looking lady," almost severe, who wore her hair in a bun—"not a fancy dresser or anything," a neighbor recalled. She looked "just like the average wife or grandmother in the 1920s." She was so modest that, a friend said, "She always dressed and undressed inside a bedroom closet with the door closed."[4] Given her religiosity, she could easily have become a stereotypical holier-than-though scold, but, while strict, she was far from dour. She was, in fact, a high-spirited woman with a passion for dramatic recitals.

Ronald Reagan described his mother as a "frustrated actress" and recalled, "She recited classic speeches in tragic tones, wept as she flung herself into the more poignant, if less talented, passages of such melodramas as *East Lynne*, and poured out poetry by the yard." Nelle was constantly acting in amateur theatricals, beginning in Tampico, where she enlisted Jack and Neil as costars in productions staged in a second-floor theater called Burden's Opera House. Neil's first stage appearance came when he was but three or four months old, playing the part of a dying baby in a production called *The Dust of the Earth*. Dutch would be pressed into service when he was a little older—"usually," he recalled, "as the thing in a sheet at the Sunday School pageant with a character name such as 'The Spirit of Christmas Never Was.'"[5]

Toward the end of his life, Ronald Reagan was asked by Robert Lindsey, the ghostwriter of his presidential memoir, about a "Rosebud" moment that had shaped his character like the protagonist of *Citizen Kane*. Reagan could not think of anything at first—"he seldom evaluated events in an analytical way," Lindsey noted—but eventually he mentioned being coaxed by his mother at age eleven to give a public reading, probably of a poem or an excerpt from a play. It went so well that he "got a burst of applause whose intensity he remembered vividly more than half a century later." "I really liked the sound of that," he told his amanuensis.[6] It was from his mother, then, that Reagan inherited his well-known passion for performing in public—and his unacknowledged need for public adulation.

Other inheritances from Nelle included Ronald's deep-rooted religious faith, his unshakable self-confidence, and his unwavering optimism. "While my father was a cynic and tended to suspect the worst of people," Ronald Reagan was to write, "my mother was the opposite. She always expected to find the best in people and often did, even among the prisoners at our local jail to whom she frequently brought hot meals."[7] Nelle's outlook was evident in a poem she wrote in 1927:

As you journey on the road of life
Observe as you push your way
Some faces moodish, sullen, sad.
Others with smile so gay.
These last ones are on the sunny side
They see the best in life
Think lovely thoughts, ennobling the soul
Keeping them from strife. . . .
The sunny side's the only side.[8]

Nelle taught her sunny younger son, he later wrote, that "everything in life happened for a purpose," that "all things were part of God's plan, even the most disheartening setbacks, and in the end, everything worked out for the best." Remarkably, Dutch's faith included belief in heaven but not hell. "I can't believe," he said in 1950, "that an all wise and loving Father would condemn any one of his children to eternal damnation. . . . I believe in a force of God behind most people, so I put my trust in them." This might be described as a Panglossian outlook—only Lou Cannon, the reporter who covered Reagan longer and more closely than any other, wrote that "Pangloss was a sourpuss compared to Reagan."[9]

Reagan's unerring optimism, rooted in his mother's teaching, proved to be one of the secrets of his political success: He was seen by millions as a source of inspiration and hope in dark days such as the recession of 1981–1982. But always looking on the bright side can often mean denying certain unpleasant realities—and that trait would nearly prove his downfall in the Iran-Contra affair. "Nelle never saw anything evil in another human being, and Ronnie is the same way," wrote Nancy Reagan. She admitted that it could "be difficult to live with somebody so relentlessly upbeat. There were times when his optimism made me angry, or when I felt Ronnie wasn't being realistic and I longed for him to show at least a *little* anxiety." But however much it might have infuriated her, Nancy concluded, "That's how he is."[10]

Nancy's husband was the way he was because he was trying, consciously or not, to blot out the memories of a difficult, impoverished, even traumatic childhood. Although Jack Reagan had some sterling qualities, he would hardly be described as a model husband or father. In his memoirs, Ronald Reagan naturally accentuated the positive, writing that his father "had a wry, mordant humor" and that "he was the best raconteur I ever heard."[11] Dutch inherited from his handsome, garrulous father his storytelling and joke-telling abilities along with his rugged good looks and his fastidiousness about clothes.

Dutch also inherited, before turning his back on it, Jack's political allegiance. The Reagans lived in a rock-ribbed Republican region: Illinois was, as the state slogan has it, the "Land of Lincoln," and there were still old-timers around when Dutch was young who had personal memories of the martyred savior of the Union. In 1907, a year after the Reagan family arrived in Tampico, many veterans of the "war of the rebellion"—the preferred term in the North for what Southerners called the "war between the states"—attended the unveiling of a granite monument in the town's Depot Park, now Reagan Park, honoring the service of Union soldiers and those in the more recent Spanish American War.[12] But the Republican Party in those days contained a significant "know-nothing," anti-Catholic, nativist element that repelled Irish Americans like Jack Reagan. The Democrats were hardly free of prejudice—their Southern branch championed segregation and nativism—but the Northern Democratic Party, based on big-city political machines, was full of Catholics, welcomed immigrants, opposed

Prohibition, and supported the rights of labor over big business. Ronald Reagan wrote that his father was a "sentimental Democrat, who believed fervently in the rights of the workingman" and who stood opposed to bigotry and prejudice. His mother was also progressive on racial issues, even if a few of her activities and attitudes would raise concerns today. In 1926, a local newspaper reported that Nelle gave a "humorous" reading to her church's Missionary Circle "in darkey dialect."[13]

Often accused of pandering to racists during his political career, Ronald Reagan in self-defense invariably cited the story of how his father refused to let the family see D. W. Griffith's *The Birth of a Nation*, the influential 1915 film that romanticized the Ku Klux Klan. "It deals with the Ku Klux Klan against the colored folks," Jack told his kids, "and I'm damned if anyone in this family will go to see it." On another occasion, while Jack was on the road as a shoe salesman, he refused to stay at a hotel that would not admit Jews. He was said to have spent the night in his car, contracting pneumonia as a result. "We were raised to be intolerant of one thing—intolerance," President Reagan wrote to a liberal critic in 1984, yet his upbringing would not prevent him making use of racial issues in his various campaigns.[14]

But however much Ronald Reagan might pay tribute to his father, even he could not entirely blot out the impact of Jack's affliction. He had, as one neighbor remembered, "a great thirst." He was, in fact, an alcoholic—a term coined by a Swedish physician in 1849 to describe those who in an earlier age would simply have been known as drunkards but were now seen as suffering from an addiction. Jack was a binge drinker who, once he started, could not stop until he passed out. One of the most traumatic (and oft-told) memories of his childhood, Ronald Reagan later wrote, was coming home at age eleven "to find my father flat on his back on the front porch and no one there to lend a hand but me. He was drunk, dead to the world. . . . I bent over him, smelling the sharp odor of whiskey from the speakeasy. I got a fistful of his overcoat. Opening the door, I managed to drag him inside and get him to bed." Reagan's daughter Patti later asked him if this was the only time he had found his father in such a condition. He never answered.[15]

Ronald Reagan recalled that his mother, despite her own aversion to liquor, told him and his brother "that alcoholism was a sickness—that we should love and help our father and never condemn him for something that was beyond his control." But even saintly, cheerful Nelle could not help but clash with Jack, who, as Ronald Reagan recalled, "could be pretty surly" when drunk. Scenes from such classic movies about alcoholism as *The Lost Weekend* and *Come Back, Little Sheba* could have been inspired by the Reagans' home life. Jack was liable to go off on a multiday bender or spend money on whiskey that the family needed for clothes or food. "Sometimes, my father suddenly disappeared and didn't come home for days," Reagan wrote, "and sometimes when he did return, my brother and I would hear some pretty fiery arguments through the walls of our house.... Sometimes out of the blue my mother bundled us up and took us to visit one of her sisters and we'd be gone for several days." Jack would sometimes go on the wagon, but as soon as he touched a drop of alcohol, the troubles began again. Dutch learned to dread holidays like Christmas because this was when Jack was most likely to start drinking again. "There were times when he didn't open the screen door," Neil recalled of their father. "He just walked through it."[16]

Growing up in a troubled home, with parents in frequent conflict, inculcated in Ronald Reagan an "almost pathological squeamishness with regard to interpersonal conflict," wrote his son Ron Reagan. "He was always acutely uncomfortable with roiling emotion and harsh words." Michael Deaver, a longtime aide, agreed: "I had never known anyone so unable to deal with close personal conflict." Ron recalled that "my father often frustrated my mother by conveniently checking out of dinnertime confrontations. Mom and I would be going back and forth with increasing acrimony about one thing or another while, at the other end of the table, Dad kept his head down, busily spearing charred bits of roast beef or hiding his uneaten vegetables under lumps of mashed potatoes." Ron's father was behaving pretty much the same way as an adult as he had as a child when he had pretended to be asleep so his parents would not realize he could hear their screaming matches.[17]

This is one of the central paradoxes of Reagan's life: He could be famously confrontational as a politician ("Mr. Gorbachev, tear down this wall") while being completely nonconfrontational as a person. He found it so difficult to discipline his children or to fire errant aides that he seldom did either. He was an inspirational leader but a poor manager and not a particularly successful father. He often chose to believe in soothing myths and invariably tried to keep personal relationships at a superficial level of conviviality rather than to confront harsh and uncomfortable realities.

The alcoholic's son had had his fill of interpersonal conflict growing up.

Jack Reagan's tragedy was that he was, as Dutch put it, "burning with ambition to succeed" (he dreamed of opening his own shoe shop), but his weakness for the bottle sabotaged his ambitions at every turn. As Neil Reagan later said, "My dad was his own worst enemy. He talked or worked himself out of nearly every job he had." It would make for a rootless childhood for Dutch and Moon. The family would be constantly on the move, from one town to another, always staying in rented quarters and seldom for long. It did not help that the rural region where the Reagans lived was battered in the 1920s by falling crop prices after a temporary spike in demand during World War I. Even while America's industrial cities were basking in the prosperity of the Roaring Twenties, many farmers were losing their spreads in foreclosure; they did not have much money to spare for an extra pair of shoes.[18]

The family's first move came just a few months after Dutch's birth, and they did not go far: In May 1911, they moved down the road in Tampico to a small, rented, white-frame bungalow at 104 West Glassburn Street. This house came with those eagerly sought luxuries—indoor plumbing and a flush toilet. The next move, in December 1914, just a few months after the outbreak of World War I, was more momentous: The family left for Chicago when Dutch was not yet four years old.

With a population of 2.4 million people, Chicago had become one of the biggest cities in the world. In 1914, the year the Reagans moved there, Carl Sandburg wrote a now-famous poem paying tribute to his adopted hometown, which he dubbed the "City of the Big Shoulders." It was, he wrote, "proud to be Hog Butcher, Tool Maker, Stacker of Wheat, Player with Railroads and Freight Handler to the Nation." Jack Reagan, like many a newcomer, sensed opportunity in this bustling metropolis. He thought he had a position lined up at Marshall Field's, the fanciest department store in town. But that fell through. Instead, he had to settle for a job selling shoes at the discount-oriented Fair Store—so named because, in the words of its founder, it was "like a fair" in offering "many different things for sale at a cheap price." Although no Marshall Field's, the Fair Store, which took up an entire block between Dearborn and State Streets, was still an impressive temple of commerce. It had 650 feet of plate glass; nearly 6 miles of counters; 800,000 feet of floor space; and "everything necessary to clothe man, woman, or child from head to foot, or to furnish the house from top to bottom."[19] Five thousand workers kept this emporium humming—Jack among them. The family lived in a cold-water flat in a slum near the University of Chicago campus. Their apartment, Dutch wrote, "was lighted by a single gas jet brought to life with the deposit of a quarter in a slot down the hall."[20]

With his genius for wishful thinking, Ronald Reagan was later to write that when he was growing up, he did not realize his family was poor. "Only later did the government decide that it had to tell people they were poor," he wrote in his 1990 memoir, as if their lack of money was a fiction concocted by some faceless bureaucrat. Neil Reagan was more realistic and less sentimental. "We were poor, and I mean poor," he recalled. Even Dutch would concede, "Our family didn't exactly come from the wrong side of the tracks, but we were certainly always within sound of the train whistles."[21] Yet no matter how poor the family was, Nelle always insisted on tithing a tenth of their income to the church.

Nelle made all the boys' clothes herself—or, more accurately, she made all of Neil's clothes and Dutch wore Neil's hand-me-downs. She had to be creative simply to feed the family: She could make a soup bone last for days, and on Saturdays she would send Neil to the butcher to get some liver, a cheap and unpopular meat. He told the butcher it was for the family cat, which existed only in his imagination. The liver became their Sunday dinner. On other occasions, the main family meal was oatmeal mixed with hamburger to make the meat go further. Ronald later rhapsodized, "It was moist and meaty, the most wonderful thing I'd ever eaten. Of course, I didn't realize oatmeal meat was born of poverty."[22] Of course.

Tampico was a "dry" town, while Chicago was gloriously and prodigiously "wet." A history of turn-of-the-century Chicago notes, "The working-class saloon was a neighborhood institution second in importance only to the family and the parish church. . . . Sleepy workers stopped there as early as five in the morning for an 'eye-opener,' and at the screaming sound of noontime factory whistles, dirt and blood-caked men rushed out of the foundries and slaughtering mills to neighboring rows of saloons for five-cent drafts, ten-cent whiskey chasers, and a free lunch of cold meats, cheeses, pickles, and rye breads."[23] Those inviting saloons proved to be Jack Reagan's downfall. At the end of 1915, he lost his job at the Fair Store, most likely because of his drinking, and the family had to pack up once again.

Dutch was only four at the time, so he remembered little about Chicago save for a bout with pneumonia, a mishap wherein he and Neil wandered the streets by themselves, and an incident where they watched "a clanging horse-drawn fire engine race past . . . with a cloud of steam rising behind it" in the waning years before motorized fire engines replaced the horses of yore.[24] He had more memories of the family's next stop—a rented house in Galesburg, Illinois, the hometown of Carl Sandburg and of his future father-in-law, Loyal Davis. Like Tampico, Galesburg, located 140 miles west of the City of the Big Shoulders, owed its prosperity to the Chicago, Burlington and Quincy Railroad. But it had grown much larger than Dutch's birthplace. Galesburg had 23,000 inhabitants compared to fewer than a thousand in Tampico. Galesburg had three colleges, a nationally known horse track, a fine hotel, an auditorium that routinely hosted performers such as the Marx Brothers and W. C. Fields, a Minor League Baseball team, and a number of factories. Jack went to work as a shoe salesman at the O. T. Johnson Big Store on East Main Street.[25]

Galesburg may have been bustling by the standards of Tampico, but compared to Chicago it was rather bucolic. "Instead of noisy streets and crowds of people, it consisted of meadows and caves, trees and streams, and the joys of small-town life," Ronald Reagan was to write. "From that time onward, I guess I've always been partial to small towns and the outdoors."[26]

Dutch entered first grade in Galesburg at the Silas Willard School in September 1917 in the months shortly after the United States entered World War I. He was so nearsighted that he could barely read the blackboard even from the front row, but because of his prodigious memory, he found that he was good at school: "I could pick up something to read and memorize it fairly quickly, a lucky trait that made schoolwork easier for me but sometimes annoyed my brother, who did not have the same ability." A surviving first-grade report card shows that Dutch scored a 95 in reading, a 100 in spelling, and 100 in arithmetic. He was such an excellent student, in fact, that he skipped much of the second grade, advancing to third grade ahead of his peers.[27]

Edwin Meese III, one of Ronald Reagan's closest aides in both Sacramento and Washington, later speculated that his boss had learned from his early school experience that "the smartest kid in the class was not the most popular," and so he "deliberately downplayed his intellectual capabilities" to make friends.[28] Although he would never be accused of being an intellectual, Dutch would long retain—until his mind was ravaged by Alzheimer's—a near-photographic memory that would enable him to readily and easily memorize movie scripts along with anecdotes, quotations, and statistics that he could pull out for speeches.

By the time he began school, Dutch already knew how to read; he had figured it out while watching his mother read to him and Neil every night. One evening, Dutch recalled, his father came home to find him looking at a newspaper on the floor. Jack asked him what he was doing. "Reading," his son replied. Jack was skeptical. "Well, read me something," he demanded. So Dutch read him a news story about the explosion the previous day, July 30, 1916, at the Black Tom pier in New York Harbor—an act of sabotage carried out by German agents. Jack was so proud of his boy that he called the neighbors in to hear him read.[29]

This was the beginning of a voracious, lifelong reading habit. "I can barely remember a time in my life when I didn't know how to read," Ronald Reagan wrote years later, adding "I can't think of greater torture than being isolated in a guest room or a hotel room without something to read."[30] Like other American boys in this pre-broadcast and pre-internet age, he was enthralled by dime novels featuring fictional heroes such as the Yale athletic star Frank Merriwell; the Rover Boys; Tarzan, Lord of the Apes; and John Carter, Warlord of Mars. Young Dutch also spent a lot of time alone in the attic of one of the Reagans' rented houses in Galesburg, studying a collection of "birds' eggs and butterflies" left by a previous occupant. He recalled being "fascinated" by these objects, which became "gateways to the mysterious" and "symbols of the out-of-doors."[31]

Dutch was a shy, introverted youngster who was not as self-confident, athletic, or popular as his older brother. "Neil was more the outgoing, roustabout, all around kid," a neighbor recalled. By contrast, Neil described Dutch as "a very serious boy and very quiet." "In grade school," Ronald Reagan later wrote, "I wasn't especially good at sports and worried about it. . . . In baseball I was forever striking out or suffering the indignity of missing an easy fly ball." This wasn't because he was unathletic; it was because he was so nearsighted that the whole world was a big blur to him. But he didn't realize it at the time. "As a result," he wrote, "I had a lot of trouble convincing myself I was good enough to play with the other kids, a deficiency of confidence that's not a small matter when you're growing up in a youthful world dominated by sports and games."[32]

Dutch's isolation as a boy was exacerbated by the family's frequent moves. He seldom stayed in one town or one school long enough to make many friends. This combined with his father's alcoholism—the source of family shame—to make Dutch wary of other children and reluctant to let anyone get too close to him. Like his reading, this too would become a life-long habit. "In some ways," he later conceded, "I think this reluctance to get close to people never left me completely."[33]

By the time he became president, he would have no close friends aside from his wife, and he would be emotionally distant even from his own children. He would employ his natural affability and a steady supply of stories and jokes filed away in his photographic memory to keep the rest of the world at a safe, comfortable remove. "He would have made a hell of a good hermit," said Stuart Spencer, the political consultant who guided Reagan's rise to the governorship and presidency. "He was content to be alone," agreed Ed Meese, "but he did like to be popular." While Reagan was "unfailingly kind" to his staff, noted White House aide James Rosebush, "he was never really personal," and "when you left his presence, you knew he wasn't thinking about you—he wasn't engaged in your life."[34]

Even Nancy Reagan, her husband's only true friend, would describe him as a "loner" who "often seems remote." "There's a wall around him," she wrote perceptively. "He lets me come closer than anyone else, but there are times when even I feel that barrier."[35] That emotional enclosure began to be erected during his difficult childhood in the rural Illinois of the early twentieth century when, because of his family's constant uprooting, he would come to believe that no friendship would last long.

There is some uncertainty about exactly when the Reagans moved from one town to another; since the family always rented, they never left any property records behind. But in early 1918, while Dutch was in first grade, Jack Reagan seems to have lost his job in Galesburg, yet again because of his drinking. The family had to move twenty miles down the road to Monmouth, Illinois, most likely the hometown of the celebrated Western lawman Wyatt Earp, who by then was living, like many Midwesterners, in Los Angeles. Jack went to work in the E. B. Colwell Department Store on South

Main Street. If measured by the size of the towns he worked in, Jack was going down in the world: Galesburg was much smaller than Chicago, and Monmouth, with ten thousand inhabitants, was half the size of Galesburg. The town was yet another stop on the Chicago, Burlington and Quincy Railroad and a center of cattle production and pottery making; it would bill itself as the "Prime Beef Center of the World."

Always being the new boy in town proved challenging. Returning to Monmouth as a presidential candidate in 1976, Ronald Reagan told reporters that he still remembered being chased home by several boys from the Central School. Nelle ran to the front porch to scold his tormentors. Reagan said that "it was the only time in his life that he'd been truly terrified—scared to death."[36]

Although the Reagans did not spend long in Monmouth, the town produced other memories that would be etched indelibly in the future president's memory. The United States had entered World War I in April 1917 after German U-boats began preying on American merchant ships and Germany tried to entice Mexico into attacking its northern neighbor. Jack told his sons that he had tried to enlist in the army but was rejected because he was too old and the sole support for his family; he said he regretted having been too young to fight in the Spanish American War and too old for the Great War.

While living in Galesburg, Ronald remembered the townspeople dropping whatever they were doing to go to the train depot to cheer railcars full of doughboys setting out, as if messianically, "on a noble mission to save our friends in Europe." He was still in Monmouth when the war ended on the eleventh hour of the eleventh day of the eleventh month of 1918. "I'll never forget Armistice Day in downtown Monmouth," he wrote. "The streets suddenly filled up with people, bonfires were lighted, and grown-ups and children paraded down the street singing and carrying torches in the air."[37]

Dutch was not quite eight at the time, but he later wrote that he was "old enough to share the hopes of everyone in Monmouth that we have fought 'the war to end all wars.' I think the realization that some of those boys to whom I'd waved on the troop train later died on European soil made me an isolationist for a long time."[38] That World War I profoundly affected his thinking, as it did for so many of his generation, was confirmed by a short story he wrote as a Eureka College student in 1931 about a young soldier in the American Expeditionary Force who had been an idealist who talked "o sacrifice and glory and heroism." An older soldier tried to set him straight: "He cursed mentally at a world so ordered that once every generation it must be bathed in the blood of youth." After being gassed and sent home, the once-idealistic veteran is cast off by society. He becomes a tramp and loses his life under the wheels of a train he is trying to hop while seeking medical care for his war injuries. The bitterly ironic title—"Killed in Action: A Short Short Story."[39]

Reagan's boyhood revulsion against war would never entirely leave him, even though in later life he would become an ardent booster of the armed forces and advocate of muscular action against Communist regimes. Long after he had abandoned the liberalism of his early manhood, he would dream of abolishing nuclear weapons to ensure that the most destructive conflict imaginable would never be fought.

One of the most tragic and unexpected consequences of World War I was the global spread of a particularly virulent strain of influenza that became known as the Spanish flu. Nelle was one of approximately five hundred million people—a third of the world's population—who contracted the disease. The whole family was terrified. Jack, not normally a churchgoer, lit candles in the local Catholic church for her. Dutch recalled that "a gruff old family-type doctor" advised keeping "her stuffed to the gills with old green cheese, the moldier the better." Whether due to this proto-penicillin or sheer serendipity or the grace of the God in whom she so fervently believed, Nelle survived.[40]

After she recovered, the family moved in 1919 temporarily back to Tampico. Jack became the manager of the H. C. Pitney General Store where he had once worked as a lowly salesman. Dutch later remembered this short interlude in Tampico as "one of those rare Huck Finn–Tom Sawyer idylls," suggesting he never read Mark Twain's novels too closely. (As Gary Wills noted, they were "chronicles of superstition, racism and crime.")[41] The eight-year-old boy enjoyed exploring the woods outside of town, and he learned to swim in the "deep and treacherous" Hennepin Canal. There were also the typical misadventures of youth: Dutch and his friend "Monkey" Winchell experimented with a shotgun owned by Monkey's father. They blew a hole in the ceiling—and might have blown themselves to bits. Jack Reagan got it in his head that he could make some money by buying and then selling a train car full of potatoes. But the tubers sat in a hot boxcar too long, and many of them rotted, turning squishy and emitting "an odor worse than that of a decaying corpse." Dutch and Neil were forced to separate out the good potatoes from the bad, leading the boys to develop "a near permanent dislike for potatoes in any form."[42]

The best part of being back in Tampico was the kindness shown to Dutch by Emma and Jim Greenman, an elderly, childless couple next door who offered him cookies and chocolates every afternoon. They had time for him when his parents did not: Jack was busy working, and Nelle was engrossed in church activities. Dutch referred to the Greenmans, who ran a jewelry shop, as Aunt Emma and Uncle Jim. Years later, he vividly remembered the joy of being allowed to read—and dream—in the neighbors' cozy living room "with its horsehair-gargoyles of furniture, its shawls and antimacassars, globes of glass over birds and flowers, books and strange odors."[43]

He was later to write, "Those were the happiest times of my life."[44] And yet his life was just beginning. It would be in the next town where the family moved that little Dutch Reagan—a shy, lonely boy lost in his thoughts and consumed by his dreams—would begin to blossom into the man the world would come to know.

3

"A Good, Clean Town"

At our one local movie theater, blacks and whites had to
sit apart—the blacks in the balcony.

—RONALD REAGAN

"All of us have a place we go back to; Dixon is that place for me," Ronald Reagan wrote in a memoir published in 1965.[1] The Reagan family moved to this town thirty miles north of Tampico and a hundred miles west of Chicago in December 1920, when Dutch was almost ten years old. Earlier that year, in January, Prohibition had gone into effect banning the sale of alcohol. In August, the Nineteenth Amendment to the Constitution, granting women the right to vote, had been ratified by the states. And in November, the Republican nominee, Warren G. Harding of Marion, Ohio, had won the presidency by promising a "return to normalcy." It was in Dixon, Illinois—as quintessentially normal an American town as one could find, for better or worse—that Dutch would spend his adolescence and put down some semblance of roots after having lived in four towns and at least seven different homes in the previous nine years.

The town traced its history back to the arrival in 1830 of a storekeeper from New York named John Dixon who operated a ferry crossing and established a settlement on the banks of the Rock River. By 1920, Dixon had a population of 8,198 people, making it many times larger than Tampico. The most memorable sight in town was the "victory arch" with the word *DIXON* on it that had been erected over Galena Avenue in 1919 to honor veterans of the Great War. Passenger trains came to and from Chicago every day, and the town was a stop on the Lincoln Highway, the first coast-to-coast road, dedicated in 1913, but the section around Dixon was not yet paved. The city streets, some brick, others dirt, were a veritable hodgepodge of horse-drawn vehicles, automobiles, and electric streetcars. Some residents had telephones and most had electricity, but people still relied on iceboxes and outhouses.[2]

Major employers included the Reynolds Wire Company, the Borden Condensed Milk Company, the Dixon Paper Box Company, and the Grand Detour Plow Works. Early in 1921, readers of the *Dixon Evening Telegraph* were alerted to a new addition to the city's retail scene at 94 Galena Avenue: the Fashion Boot Shop. "Learn the Joys of Foot Comfort," urged its advertisement. "Our Foot Expert is a man specially trained in Dr. Scholl's Method of Foot Correction and is able to relieve all your foot troubles. Come in anytime." That "foot expert" was Jack Reagan or, as he was styled in the newspaper, J. E. Reagan. He had convinced his boss in Tampico, H. C. Pitney, who was going blind, to close his general store and open a new store devoted exclusively to shoes in Dixon. Jack would be the manager with the expectation that he would eventually buy out Pitney and make the store entirely his own. "Mr. Reagan is very enthusiastic over this work," reported the *Telegraph*, "and . . . says it is his ambition to send every person out of his shoe store with comfortable feet in neat, stylish shoes."[3]

The Reagan family found much to appreciate in this blue-collar community. Like Kings Row—the fictional Midwestern town that would be the setting of Ronald Reagan's most lauded film—Dixon could be described by its boosters as "A good, clean town. A good town to live in, and a good place to raise your children."[4] Naturally Dixon, like the fictional Kings Row, also had its dark side—one that its most famous son would never acknowledge. In typical fashion, he preferred to dwell on all the town's attractions.

Dixon had a public library, which Ronald Reagan later called "my house of magic." "I was probably as regular a patron as the library ever had," he recalled. Nearby there was a YMCA where Dutch and Moon would take part in activities such as "Basket Ball Games." There was the Rock River, a tributary of the mighty Mississippi, where the boys would go swimming in the summer and skating in the winter. And there was a lavish movie theater, the Dixon Theater, built in 1922, where young Dutch would pay thirty-five cents to be enthralled by silent movies featuring, he recalled, "the marvelous flickering antics of Tom Mix and William S. Hart as they foiled robbers and villains and escorted the beautiful girls to safety."[5] In his 1924 silent-film classic *Sherlock Jr.*, Buster Keaton depicted the comical adventures of a hapless film projectionist who dreams that he can walk into the movie screen and become a suave detective. This was a perfect metaphor for how the movies were already drawing millions of people—including young

Dutch Reagan, who would choose to be an actor rather than a detective—into their phantasmagoric world.

The other major source of local entertainment was the Rock River Assembly, a vast circular auditorium that could hold five thousand people. It was part of the Chautauqua, a religious movement started in Chautauqua, New York, in the late nineteenth century, which brought noted speakers and entertainers to rural communities for purposes of edification and entertainment. Like many Dixonians, the Reagans, Nelle and Dutch in particular, became regulars in what Teddy Roosevelt called "the most American thing in America" and Sinclair Lewis derided as "nothing but wind and chaff and . . . the laughter of yokels." This experience would have heightened Dutch's interest in public speaking.[6]

Billy Sunday, a former professional baseball player turned popular evangelist, was a regular speaker. In 1922, this staunch Republican preached what the *Dixon Evening Telegram* described as a "red hot sermon" in which he denounced "socialists and bolshevists and radicals." He said that "every man in America who preached anarchy should be deported or face [a] firing squad" and also called for anti-immigration laws to stop America from being "a dumping ground for foreign filth that the devil himself wouldn't have." (He would get his wish in 1924 with the passage of a law severely restricting immigration, particularly from Latin America and Asia.) The reverend even denounced the nascent motion-picture business, saying that "a lot of movie actors are worse than Fatty Arbuckle," the famous comedian whose career had just been ruined by unfounded accusations of rape and murder. "And then, to be sure he hadn't overlooked anybody," the newspaper wrote, "he said that the lowest down scoundrel on earth is a dancing Methodist."[7]

Billy Sunday's views, especially his fervent support of Prohibition, were enthusiastically applauded in this conservative community where liquor had been outlawed in 1916. No doubt Nelle Reagan was happy and Jack Reagan distraught that the saloons were shuttered, even if illicit liquor was still easy to come by in an area of town known as Bootleggers Knob.[8] But neither of the Reagans could have been happy about the growing power of the Ku Klux Klan, a largely northern and middle-class organization in the 1920s.

There were few African Americans in Dixon (ninety-eight, to be exact, in the 1920 census), but the town was segregated just like in the South. "At our one local movie theater," Ronald Reagan later wrote, "blacks and whites had to sit apart—the blacks in the balcony. . . . My brother's best friend was black, and when they went to the movies, Neil sat with him in the balcony."[9] (Neil's friend was Winston "Wink" McReynolds, a football teammate in high school.)[10] Reagan did not mention in either of his memoirs the power and popularity of the KKK in Dixon, and it has been almost entirely overlooked by chroniclers of his life, but it was an inescapable reality of the Midwest in the 1920s. The second coming of the Klan—the first one ended along with Reconstruction in the 1870s—was actually stronger in the North than in the South. It claimed four million to six million members (including sixteen senators, eleven governors, and dozens of congressmen), and inveighed not just against African Americans but also, in one historian's description, against "Catholics, Jews, immigrants, and bootleggers."[11]

While the original KKK was a covert terrorist organization in the post–Civil War South whose members wore hoods to hide their identity, the new reincarnation was very public, and its influence was pervasive. At age twelve in 1923, Dutch Reagan even belonged to a Klean Kids Klub at the Dixon YMCA; he was the lieutenant in charge of "B" Company. This was a seemingly harmless youth organization, similar to the Boy Scouts, whose members were taught how to care for their teeth and concentrate on their studies, but it was named in either spoof or tribute to the more notorious KKK.[12]

The real Klan held regular rallies—"Klantauquas"—at the Rock River Assembly to spew its racist, nativist, antisemitic, and anti-Catholic invective. On September 15, 1924, the *Dixon Evening Telegram* ran a large advertisement announcing a "KKK Fall Round Up": "Protestant Public Invited," "Bring Your Robes." Three days later, eight thousand people assembled to hear Charles G. Palmer, the Grand Dragon of Illinois, proclaim, "We consider the white race the superior of all races in the world and it is our desire to keep it as such." Hundreds of robed Klansmen then marched through downtown Dixon, an event no townsperson could have missed.[13]

Such pervasive incitement could easily flare into violence. Reagan told Lou Cannon in 1968 that he had seen a race riot in Dixon that broke out when "a Negro bum slashed a white bum in a card game." He recalled "whites hurling Negro children onto freight-train boxcars and the screaming kids carried hundreds of miles away in fear."[14] There is no newspaper record of this riot; like many of his memories, it may have been exaggerated or apocryphal. But such an occurrence would not have been unusual at that place and time. In Chicago, only a hundred miles from Dixon, a race riot in 1919 resulted in thirty-eight deaths, more than five hundred injured, and a thousand Black families left homeless.[15]

This was the environment in which Dutch Reagan was reared. His family was part of a Democratic minority in a very conservative Republican area, and his father was a minority twice over as an Irish Catholic among Protestants. As an adult, Ronald Reagan was to rhapsodize about Dixon as a place where people "tended to care about each other" and where he "learned standards and values that would guide me for the rest of my life." It was, he wrote, a community animated by "love and common sense of purpose."[16] That was his remembered reality, filtered through the rose-tinted spectacles of nostalgia. But he was ignoring a grittier and grimier reality beneath the picture-postcard surface. The Ku Klux Klan was animated by hate, not love, and yet it drew the support of a disturbingly large number of the Reagans' neighbors.

The grown-up Reagan also ignored another reality of Dixon: the role played by the government in building it. When he returned to his hometown as president in 1984 for the opening of his restored boyhood home, he paid tribute to the "everyday people" who had developed the town. "You know, I must say," he quipped, "that if Father [John] Dixon had to fill out environmental impact statements, report to the regulatory agencies in Washington, or wait for an area redevelopment plan, Dixon would probably still be known as Dixon's Ferry."[17] That line drew a big laugh from the audience in the high school gym—it was still a staunchly Republican area, as it remains to this day—but it overlooked how important the government had been in Dixon's development.

The federal government had sent scientific and military expeditions, led by army officers such as Zebulon Pike and Stephen Harriman Long, to explore what was then known as the Great West in the early nineteenth century. They were followed by federal surveyors to map the land and divide it into parcels that could be titled and sold. The Northwest Ordinance, passed by Congress in 1787, extended American governance over this frontier region and set the procedures for admitting new states. Federal troops and state militias evicted the Native Americans from their lands, allowing Europeans

to move in. Later laws such as the 1841 Preemption Act and the 1862 Homestead Act drew settlers, including Ronald Reagans' great-grandparents,
with the promise of rich farmland that they could buy for a pittance. The
creation of courts and police forces made it possible for communities such
as Dixon to flourish under the rule of law, with contracts enforced and criminals prosecuted. Its inhabitants also benefited greatly from the publicly
subsidized development of canals, railroads, roads, dams, bridges, electricity, water, sewerage, telegraphs, telephones, and other vital infrastructure.[18]

In his tribute to the pioneers of Dixon, Reagan was highly selective in his
history by ignoring the invaluable and irreplaceable help they received from
their government.

The Reagans' first home in Dixon was a two-story, white clapboard house
at 816 South Hennepin Avenue on the south side of the Rock River. It was
a rental costing twenty-three dollars a month, and they lived there for only
three years, but it has become a tourist attraction known as the Reagan Boyhood Home.[19] The president's visit to Dixon in 1984 was part of the celebration around the opening of this shrine, full of generic period furniture
because the Reagans' actual furnishings from the 1920s have not survived.
It is a threadbare place by modern, middle-class standards, with three
small bedrooms and a cramped bathroom on the second floor. But having
an indoor toilet and running water was a luxury in those days.

Dutch and Moon shared a single room and a single bed as did Jack and
Nelle. The third bedroom was used by Nelle to supplement the family
income by employing her prized Singer sewing machine. Downstairs was a
parlor with a fireplace where Dutch used to hide pennies behind the loose
tiles. Out front was a porch that offered welcome relief on sweltering summer evenings. Out back was a ramshackle barn where the boys raised rabbits and pigeons; Neil would kill some of the squabs and rabbits and sell
them, while Neil's younger, gentler brother preferred to study his collection
of birds' eggs.[20]

While the two brothers slept in the same bed, they were hardly on the
same page. Everyone said that Moon took more after their father, Dutch
after their mother. "Moon was always the bad boy within the family," Ronald Reagan's son Ron recalled. Dutch by contrast was, in the judgment of
his peers, a bit of a "goody-goody"—a mama's boy in the parlance of the

playground. Many years later, Neil recalled, "I was the one who, then, would go down to the one pool hall in town that was downstairs under a store, where your folks couldn't see you if they happened to walk by. . . . [Dutch] would never do anything like that. He would rather be up there, just gazing at his birds' eggs."[21]

Dutch later recalled how when he was a child, the Fourth of July was "almost as long anticipated as Christmas," even though "we didn't give too much thought to the meaning of the day." Jack would bring home as many firecrackers as he "could afford," and the boys would "count and recount" them the night before, "determined to be up with the sun so as to offer the first thunderous notice of the 4th of July." "There was a thrill never to be forgotten in seeing a tin can blown 30 ft. in the air by a giant 'cracker,'" Dutch fondly recalled.

One year, at Neil's instigation, Dutch overdid it. On the eve of the Fourth of July in 1922, Moon gave his eleven-year-old brother some illegal firecrackers known as "torpedoes" and goaded him into setting them off by a Rock River bridge. They made a loud blast. A patrolling police officer happened to see this mischief and demanded to know what Dutch was doing. The boy impudently replied, "Twinkle, twinkle little star. Who the hell do you think you are?" That uncharacteristic act of sarcasm and defiance earned Dutch a trip to jail and forced Jack to pay a fine of $14.50—big money in those days. Dutch had to do a "lot of odd jobs" to repay his debt to his dad.[22]

As soon as the family had settled in Dixon, Nelle predictably threw herself into a whirl of activities at the First Christian Church—teaching Sunday school, leading prayers, directing the choir, acting in church plays, and organizing church socials. As early as March 30, 1921, just three months after arriving in town, she gave a reading at a tea sponsored by the church's Ladies' Aid Society. "Mrs. Reagan, practically a new comer in Dixon, gave much pleasure in her reading given in a truly charming manner," the *Dixon Evening Telegraph* reported.[23]

A few years later, the newspaper noted that "Mrs. Reagan is a little body but she possesses a lot of pep and when she starts to do something . . . she will get results."[24] One of the things that Nelle set her mind to was passing along her faith to Dutch.

The Disciples of Christ did not baptize babies at birth; its adherents had to make a conscious choice later in life. Dutch made his decision when he was only eleven years old. This was shortly after he came home in early 1922 to find his father passed out in the snow in an alcoholic stupor. His mother comforted him with a book that would change his life: *That Printer of Udell's* by Disciples of Christ minister and inspirational novelist Harold Bell Wright. It tells the tale of Dick Falkner, another Midwestern boy whose father was a slave to alcohol. After his parents die, Dick goes to work as a printer for a publisher named George Udell. But he really comes into his own as part of his church's Young People's Society. He proposes a scheme to "apply Christ's teaching in our town" by helping the "deserving" poor, whom he distinguishes from the "undeserving" poor. Rather than "encourage the idle in their idleness," he advocates putting those who are impoverished through no fault of their own to work in a lumberyard—a charitable scheme he promises will soon pay for itself. The plan is implemented with great success. Dick becomes the idol of the town and marries his sweetheart. The novel ends with Dick getting elected to Congress and heading off to a "wider usefulness at the national Capitol."[25]

For a biographer, *That Printer of Udell's* brims over with insights. After all, it prefigures both Reagan's welfare-for-work initiatives and his eventual journey to Washington. But its immediate impact was to convince little Dutch to "declare [his] faith and be baptized."[26] In fact, he was so overwhelmed with religious fervor that he persuaded Neil to become baptized too, temporarily abandoning the Catholic Church. Wearing their swimsuits, the two boys were immersed on June 21, 1922.[27] Neil would revert to Catholicism within five years, but Dutch would become an active member of the Disciples of Christ, helping to lead prayer meetings and even teaching Sunday school classes for younger kids.

Many years later, Ronald Reagan would inform Harold Bell Wright's daughter-in-law that his book "had an impact I shall always remember." Dick Falkner became his "role model," he wrote: "He set me on a course I've tried to follow even unto this day. I shall always be grateful."[28] Reagan would never become ostentatiously religious, and he would never put his faith in the center of his political appeal as some other politicians did. He hardly ever attended church as president, claiming he did not want to inconvenience the congregation. But he would always remain devout, even if he would eventually come to attend a more socially prestigious Presbyterian church in Bel-Air rather than the Disciples of Christ. "All the hours in the old church in Dixon (which I didn't appreciate at the time) and all of Nelle's faith have come together in a kind of inheritance without which I'd be lost and helpless," Reagan wrote in 1973.[29]

Ronald Reagan emerged from childhood with a moralistic outlook on the world, tending to view political disputes as battles between good and evil. Whatever side he was on was always, of course, the good one. His faith in the Almighty would transfer easily to faith in himself as the Lord's servant.

A couple of years after Dutch's baptism, he experienced another epiphany. In 1924, when he was thirteen, the whole family went for a drive in Jack's Model T. Dutch noticed that Neil could read the road signs, but he could not. He picked up his mother's spectacles, and suddenly the whole world came into focus. "Until then," Dutch recalled, "a tree beside the road looked like a green blob and a billboard was a fuzzy haze. Suddenly I was able to see branches on trees and leaves on the branches. There were words as well as pictures on billboards. 'Look!' I shouted, pointing to a herd of grazing dairy cows I hadn't seen before. I was astounded."

The very next day he was fitted with a pair of "thick, black-rimmed" glasses. He despised being called "Four Eyes" by his classmates, he wrote, but "I could see and that outweighed the effects of whatever ridicule I had to endure."[30] As an adult he tried to avoid being photographed in glasses, and he started wearing contact lenses as soon as a practical plastic model became available in the late 1940s.[31]

In comic books that first appeared in 1938, a mild-mannered Midwestern farm boy named Clark Kent transformed himself into Superman by taking off his glasses. Dutch Reagan was Superman in reverse: He gained his superpowers by putting his glasses on. For the first time he could truly see what was happening in class and on the athletic field. He was not leaping tall buildings in a single bound, but his confidence would soar as he entered high school.

4

The Lifeguard

You know why I had such fun with it? Because I was the only
one up there on the guard stand; it was like a stage. A lot of
people had to look at me.

—RONALD REAGAN

I t was in high school that Dutch Reagan ceased to be a quiet, dreamy child staring at his bird eggs, reading his books, and lamenting his lack of athletic ability. He blossomed not only into a so-called big man on campus—a varsity football player, a star swimmer and thespian, and student body president—but even into a town hero who was renowned for his life-saving feats on the Rock River. This was the first of many astonishing transformations that would characterize his long, lucky life—and it began a mile removed from the "boyhood home" that tourists visit today.

The Reagans' rented home on Hennepin Avenue was a nice one by the standards of Dixon, but they could not afford to stay there for long. So in 1924—the year J. Edgar Hoover was appointed to run the Justice Department's Bureau of Investigation, University of Chicago students Richard Loeb and Nathan Leopold Jr. murdered a fourteen-year-old boy for the thrill of it, and Congress passed the nativist Johnson-Reed Act severely restricting immigration—they moved into a smaller and cheaper rental home. Their new house was located at 338 West Everett Street on the north side of the Rock River.[1]

Neil Reagan was already enrolled at Dixon's South Side High School, and he elected to remain there. "We always looked on the north side, we southsiders, as sort of the sissies' part of town," he said.[2] Dutch Reagan was just starting high school, so he went to North Side High School. The two brothers, so different in so many ways, would be united, however, in playing on the same football team: The two high schools fielded a joint squad. One thing the brothers shared, in common with many other American boys of their time, was a passion for this relatively new sport.

Football had developed in Eastern colleges in the late nineteenth century as an outgrowth of British soccer and rugby. For many years football
remained a vicious, chaotic scrum played without benefit of pads or helmets. Often employing a "flying wedge" formation, masses of players would
collide with one another like battle lines of ancient hoplites. In the ensuing
pileups they would wrestle, punch, choke, gouge, and kick to get the pigskin.
In 1905 these grisly contests killed eighteen players. Football was almost
outlawed for being too violent. To save the sport, President Theodore Roosevelt convened a White House summit in 1905 with the coaches of Yale,
Princeton, and Harvard, urging them to make the game less savage. This
spurred important changes, including the introduction of the forward pass
and leather helmets.

Football remained brutal, but it became less deadly and more popular.
The forerunner of the National Football League was created in 1920, but in
the 1920s football remained primarily a collegiate sport. Major games were
closely covered not only by newspapers and magazines but also by a new
medium: radio. College football players and coaches—Harold "Red" Grange
(the "Galloping Ghost") of the University of Illinois; Bronislau "Bronko"
Nagurski of the University of Minnesota; Knute Rockne, George Gipp, and
the "Four Horsemen" of Notre Dame; Amos Alonzo Stagg of the University
of Chicago—became celebrities.[3]

Dutch Reagan was enthralled by the whole spectacle. Indeed, the very
first letter of his that survives—written at age eleven in 1922 to an older girl
who had moved to Wisconsin—is filled mainly with football news. "Dixon
High School has played 10 games won 3 tied 1," he wrote, before noting
that he was the drum major of the YMCA band and that he had twelve rabbits "and I am going to kill 3 and eat them."[4] Dutch enjoyed playing pickup
games of football a lot more than baseball because he could see the larger
ball much more clearly. He aspired to wear the purple-and-white jersey of
the Dixon High School football team. He even began to dream of going to
college—a seemingly impossible goal for a poor boy like him—so that he
could become a football star, just like the fictional Frank Merriwell at Yale.[5]

As a high school freshman in 1924, Dutch was eager to join the football
team, but he was held back by his scrawny physique. Having skipped second grade, he was still only thirteen years old, weighing but 108 pounds

and standing five feet, three inches tall. It was hard to find a uniform small enough for him. Not surprisingly, in competition against older and bigger boys, he did not make the squad. The summer between ninth and tenth grades, he decided to build up his muscles and earn a little money for college by getting a job as a construction worker for thirty-five cents an hour. His sophomore year, a new football division was created for players weighing under 135 pounds, so Dutch was finally able to play and was even elected captain. By his junior year Dutch was five feet, ten inches tall and weighed more than 160 pounds. He finally made the varsity team as a lineman and midway through the season was elevated to the starting squad.

He was not as talented a football player as Moon, a tight end who was said to be "a good man at receiving passes." Indeed, given his poor vision, Dutch could not have been a running back or wide receiver: He could not wear glasses on the gridiron, and contact lenses did not yet exist. But Dutch was determined to succeed as an unglamorous lineman—one of the unsung heroes of the gridiron who enabled flashier players like Neil to score points. "'Dutch,' the lightest but fastest guard on the team, won his letter through sheer grit," reported his 1927 high school yearbook. Dutch was a starter all during his senior year, 1927–1928. The Dixon Dukes had a terrible season— they lost to their main rival, Sterling High School, by a score of twenty-five to zero and won only two games—but the yearbook wrote that "'Dutch' proved to be one of the strong factors in the line this year. He took care of his tackle berth in a creditable manner, and certainly had the true 'Dixon Spirit.'"[6]

Football wasn't the only sport that Dutch played in high school. He also ran track and swam competitively. In fact, he was a better swimmer than a football player. In 1928, he won a 110-yard freestyle race by half the length of the pool. "I was totally wrapped up in athletics in my younger days," he recalled.[7] Whatever he did, he exhibited boundless enthusiasm at a time when the very concept of "school spirit" was starting to seem a little quaint, a little musty, a little outdated.

The 1920s, following the mass bloodshed of World War I, was a decade of disenchantment for many of the young. The "lost generation" was fashionably trying to cast off society's strictures in bohemian haunts, from New York's Greenwich Village to Paris's Left Bank, while writers such as Theodore Dreiser, Sinclair Lewis, and H. L. Mencken were puncturing, in wholly different ways, what they considered to be the self-satisfaction and hypocrisy of Middle America. Growing up in Dixon, Dutch Reagan appeared to be largely unaffected by most of the intellectual currents of the 1920s propagated by big-city sophisticates, save for his revulsion toward the slaughter in the trenches of France. While Dutch later claimed to have read Sinclair Lewis's *Babbitt* and even named it as one of his favorite books, he was closer in spirit to the self-satisfied, small-town boosters and jingoistic local businessmen whom its author brutally satirized.[8]

As a high school junior in 1927, in fact, Dutch wrote a school essay in defense of "school spirit" that earned him a grade of 94 and was later published in the *Dixon Evening Telegram*.[9] That he felt compelled to defend the "Dixon spirit" was an indication that in those jaded times not everyone shared his dedication to boosterism. "Sad as it seems," he lamented, "school spirit is buried beneath a cloak of attempted sophistication that sneers at this show of feeling. We try to be worldly, to laugh at that sentimental side of student life, but that inexpressible feeling is more precious than all the sham ever attempted or attained." Dutch wasn't having any of this "sham" sophistication. He proudly averred his dedication to the slogan "Dixon never quits" and wrote that "the fellow who knows the smell of liniment, and the salty tang of sweated jerseys, has acquired something precious, which no one can steal."[10]

If Dutch was worried about seeming too straitlaced and unfashionable—what a later generation would label as "square"—he never showed any sign of it, and his popularity did not suffer for it. "I don't remember there was anyone who didn't like him," recalled one of his classmates. "He was a very down-to-earth fellow."[11]

Although Dutch would develop a winning sense of humor—he would be one of the best joke-tellers ever to become president—he was, and would always remain, a stranger to irony or sarcasm. Hurtful humor was as alien to his nature as disillusionment and self-awareness. As his first wife, Jane Wyman, said, "He has fun without hurting feelings."[12] That was just as well from the standpoint of his future political career. Politicians, such as John McCain, Bob Dole, and Mo Udall, whose wit is too cutting—and who are too apt to puncture their own or others' pieties and pretensions—seldom get elected to the nation's highest office. Few people would buy a political platform—or any other product—from a salesman who is less than entirely, wholeheartedly, unreservedly, and unironically convinced of its superior

virtues. And Dutch always was, whether he was promoting school spirit in his teenage years or tax cuts in his senior years. His beliefs changed over the years, but his devotion to them remained steadfast. He was, from the start, a true believer—and not just in Christianity.

In the summer of 1926, as the nation was transfixed by the mysterious disappearance of the famous evangelist Aimee Semple McPherson in Los Angeles and the premature death of thirty-one-year-old silent-screen idol Rudolph Valentino in New York, Dutch Reagan received a summer job that deeply influenced his development. He was hired as a lifeguard by Edward and Ruth Graybill, fellow members of the Disciples of Christ Church who had been granted a concession to operate a bathhouse and food stand at the municipally owned Lowell Park. The park consisted of two hundred acres of woods that opened onto a manmade beach on the fast-flowing Rock River. Dutch was young for the job—he was only fifteen—but he had already finished his second year of high school and earned a lifesaving certificate from the YMCA. So, at Jack Reagan's urging, the Graybills decided to give him a shot. He did so well that he kept working for them every summer until his graduation from college in 1932.

The Graybills paid Dutch either eighteen dollars a week (their recollection) or fifteen dollars a week (his recollection) and all the ten-cent hamburgers and nickel root beers he could consume. In return for that modest stipend, he worked up to twelve hours a day, seven days a week, except when it rained. His days began in the morning with loading up the Graybills' pickup truck with hamburgers and hot dogs, buns, soda pop, and hundreds of pounds of ice and ended when darkness fell and the park closed. When the pace was slow in the morning, he would give swimming lessons to kids, some from as far away as Chicago; his former pupils reported that he was an easygoing and understanding instructor. The swimsuit itched when it got wet, but Dutch had no replacement. He had to wear it again the next day—and the day after that. The money he earned he was saving for college.

Physically, Dutch was blossoming into a handsome young man. By the time he stopped working at Lowell Park, he had reached his adult size—six feet, one inch tall and 175 pounds. "He was the perfect specimen of an athlete, tall, willowy, muscular, brown, good-looking," recalled Bill Thompson, one of Dutch's successors as the Lowell Park lifeguard. "Of course, the girls were always flocking around him."[13] Dutch was aware of, and pleased by, his effect on female beachgoers. In a high school yearbook essay called "Meditations of a Lifeguard," he wrote of assuming "a manly worried expression, designed to touch the heart of any blonde, brunette, or unclassified female."[14]

But while the girls were "mooning" over Dutch in his bib-style swimsuit with "Life Guard" emblazoned on his chest, he largely kept his eyes on the water. Usually, he was positioned on the diving pier five feet above the water or on a bench in the middle of the beach (now on display at the Loveland History Museum in Dixon). "At the first hint of trouble, Dutch would be in the water, moving like a torpedo," Bill Thompson said.[15]

Dutch had to supervise as many as five hundred swimmers at a time all by himself. Many were inexperienced and soon got into trouble in the treacherous river currents. But there was never an unclaimed clothes basket at the end of the day. Over seven summers, he saved seventy-seven people from drowning, each time adding a notch to a driftwood log to record his accomplishment.[16]

Some cynics joked that girls feigned drowning so they could be rescued by the handsome lifeguard, and some historians and biographers—products of a more cynical age—later scoffed at his lifesaving achievements. One author even compared the "somewhat fanciful 'rescue' stories" to George Washington's mythical confession to chopping down a cherry tree.[17] But contemporary news reports and the accounts of the swimmers themselves make clear that the danger was as real as his lifesaving. In 1985, Fred Moore, then sixty-seven years old, recounted how, at age ten, he was pulled under the current about fifty feet from shore. He cried in panic but only swallowed mouthfuls of water. "I sank under the water and thought, 'So this is what it's like to die.' But then I felt an arm wrap around me and the next thing I knew my head was out of the water. . . . I wouldn't be alive today if it wasn't for his quick action." Eighty-seven-year-old Fred "Fritz" Zbinden remembered seeing Dutch rescue a four-year-old girl: "He was like Superman in action. One second he was on a raft, and the next he was pulling the girl out of the water. She was O.K. and everyone on the beach applauded."[18]

Many drowning swimmers thrashed around madly in panic, making Dutch's job more difficult, and some of those he pulled out, men in particular, were not grateful for being saved: They claimed indignantly that they didn't need to be rescued. But Reagan's lifesaving was closely covered by the local newspaper. A headline in 1932 proclaimed " 'Dutch' Reagan Has Made

Fine Mark as Guard," and the article went on to recount "several narrow escapes and thrilling rescues, both of adults and children at the beach."[19]

Dutch was learning what it was like to be a local celebrity and hero—Dixon's own version of Douglas Fairbanks Sr., Charles Lindbergh, or Babe Ruth—and, although he was generally too modest to admit it, he enjoyed the feeling. Like the heroes he would later play in the movies, he shrugged off the praise and muttered, "I'm just doing my job."[20] He only allowed his ego to peek out occasionally. In 1939, for example, he admitted in an interview with a film fan magazine, "You know why I had such fun with it? Because I was the only one up there on the guard stand; it was like a stage. A lot of people had to look at me."[21]

Ron Reagan suggested that his father's work as a lifeguard taught him not only his own self-worth but also the satisfaction that could come from helping people and setting the world right. Having grown up in a deeply troubled household, Dutch was learning that he had the power to bring order out of chaos—and to bask in the resulting praise.[22] Those were lessons that would stay with him long after the log on which he had notched his rescues floated away.

By his senior year at North Side High School (1927–1928), Dutch was not only a celebrated lifeguard and varsity football player but also president of the student body, president of the Dramatic Club, art director of the yearbook, and vice president of the Boys' Hi-Y Club, which was dedicated to promoting "Clean Speech, Clean Sports, Clean Living," and, rather puzzlingly, "Clean Scholarship." The whimsical quotation he chose for his senior-class yearbook listing—"Life is just one grand sweet song, so start the music"[23]—was indicative of an optimist and a doer who felt that the world was going his way. It was as if his life had been scored by George Gershwin, who described his jaunty, jazzy 1924 composition "Rhapsody in Blue" as "a sort of musical kaleidoscope of America, . . . of our unduplicated national pep, of our metropolitan madness."[24]

One of the few hints Dutch gave in public of his troubled, impoverished, nomadic family life with an alcoholic, self-sabotaging father was an oblique reference in a poem for his high school yearbook in which he lamented, "We make our life a struggle / When life should be a song." Dutch was turning up the volume on his own life to mute the troubles of his unsettled boyhood.

He was blossoming into an all-American striver who was one of the most popular kids in school. "In high school," Ronald Reagan later wrote, "I began to lose my old feelings of insecurity. Success . . . did a lot to give me self-confidence."[25]

He was referring to extracurricular, not academic, success. Having started elementary school as an excellent student who skipped most of second grade, by high school he had become a mediocre student whose attention was focused primarily outside the classroom. One of his female classmates even claimed years later to have written book reports for him because "he was too busy with football and sports and dramatics."[26] This was the cost of Dutch's growing athletic and social success: It came at the expense of more scholarly pursuits.

Besides football coach Arthur C. Bowers, the only high school teacher who left a major imprint on him was Bernard J. Frazer, a graduate of a small liberal-arts college who taught English and, more important, advised the drama club. He was, Ronald Reagan recalled, "a small man with spectacles almost as thick as mine who taught me things about acting that stayed with me for the rest of my life." Dutch had already been performing and winning applause at Disciples of Christ events; in 1925, for example, the local newspaper reported that he "convulsed the audience by his one-act dramatic reading."[27] But under Frazer's guidance his acting became more professional.

Frazer had the students stage recent Broadway hits and always told them to probe for their characters' motivations. He would sometimes interrupt rehearsals to ask, "What do you think your character means with that line? Why do you think he would say that?" Dutch starred in two comedies directed by Frazer: Philip Barry's 1923 play *You and I* during his junior year and Walter Hackett's 1921 play *Captain Applejack* during his senior year. He also penned numerous essays and short stories under Frazer's guidance— quite literally penned as the Reagans did not seem to have a typewriter. In his school essays, Reagan showed a talent for the kind of vivid, easy-to-understand language that would later characterize his sportscasts and speeches.

B. J. Frazer recalled that Dutch was "head and shoulders" above his other students, he "never flubbed" a line, and he could "fit into almost any kind of role you put him into." "He had a good sense of what people wanted and how they reacted—all the makings of a good politician," Frazer said, with the benefit of hindsight.[28] Decades later, Frazer's star student, by then a movie star turned governor of California, wrote, "I still think that much of what has happened that is good in my life began in the old Northside high school when I first 'trod the boards' in Phillip Barry's play, 'You and I,' under the direction of B. J. Frazier [sic]."[29]

Dutch's costar in these high school productions was his girlfriend, Margaret Cleaver, whom he nicknamed "Mugs" (her family called her Peggy). If Dutch was the big man on campus, she was the leading young woman—and a better student. The 1928 *Dixonian* yearbook identified her as "our popular all-around everything" and noted her leadership positions in student government, the drama club, the glee club, the yearbook, and the Girls Hi-Y. While Dutch was student body president, she was the senior class president. She did not possess Dutch's sense of humor, but she was as enthusiastic about drama and public speaking as he was. In her commencement address to the class of 1928, she even proposed that the high school create a Department of Public Speaking and Dramatics so as to prevent graduates from becoming "timid, backward," and unable to "compete in the rapidly-moving social life" of the day.[30]

Mugs was the daughter of the Reverend Ben Hill Cleaver, a clergyman who had arrived in Dixon, age forty-one, in 1922 to take over the Disciples of Christ Church after the death of a previous pastor. Dutch spotted Margaret in church and was immediately smitten: "I used to look at her more than I listened to the sermons," he acknowledged. "Like my mother," he recalled, in a comment that would give Freudians a field day, "she was short, pretty, auburn haired, and intelligent."[31] Other boys were sweet on Margaret, too, including the captain of the high school football team, Richard "Dick" McNicol, a doctor's son who was said by his peers to be full of "skill, pep, and raw courage."[32] But Dick was a Methodist. Dutch had the inside track as a fellow member of her father's church. Reverend Cleaver, in fact, became a surrogate father to Dutch, who was often at their house. Ronald Reagan would correspond with Ben Cleaver until the minister's death in 1975, at age ninety-three, and he would sign his letters with "Love," something he never did for anyone else outside of his immediate family. Garry Wills, who wrote one of the most perceptive books about Reagan's upbringing, noted, "He was as close to being a 'minister's kid' as one can be without actually moving into the rectory."[33]

Ben Cleaver was conservative but hardly reactionary. Margaret recalled that he was "no hair splitter in matters of theology" and that he was "very curious, very widely read." He could read Hebrew and classical Greek, and he appreciated music and theater, even though he did not think that movies should be screened on Sundays. Some members of the congregation fretted that he was "too intellectual" and not a captivating speaker, but he made up for it with his organizational abilities and dedication to the church. "When the janitor fell ill, Cleaver took over the duties," a historian noted. "When the Depression made it impossible for the church to meet its budget, he insisted the debt be retired first and he be the last paid." By 1928, four years into his ministry, Cleaver was acclaimed by the Dixon newspaper as an "able and popular minister" who had expanded his congregation and "engaged in a vigorous campaign of activity and usefulness."[34]

The reverend did not achieve popularity by pandering to his congregation. He pushed back against the capitalist gospel popular in the 1920s. (One of the best-selling books of the decade, *The Man Nobody Knows*, presented Christ as a proto-Rotarian who was "the founder of modern business.") Cleaver taught his congregation that "spiritual values" and "clean hearts . . . filled with faith" were more important than "full treasuries and receipted accounts." Later, in retirement back in his home state of Missouri, Cleaver became one of the few white residents in Cape Girardeau to join the National Association for the Advancement of Colored People. (Cape Girardeau was the hometown of right-wing radio host Rush Limbaugh, whose prominent family Cleaver probably knew.) But Cleaver was no wild-eyed liberal. He was skeptical of the New Deal, arguing that Americans "could not spend our way into prosperity." An ardent New Dealer at the time, Dutch would initially disagree, but later he would come to share this view. After leaving the presidency, Ronald Reagan would call the reverend "a wonderful man" and a "great influence."[35]

Jack Reagan's drinking was always a looming shadow menacing his son's relationship with Ben Cleaver's straitlaced daughter. Mugs strongly disapproved of alcohol, but Dutch could hardly keep his father's weakness a secret in such a small town. When Margaret mentioned one of Jack's benders, Dutch was terrified that she would break up with him. He went home to rage to Nelle that, if Mugs left him, he would never speak to his father again.

But Mugs did not force the issue, and the relationship continued. Dutch was from the start a serial monogamist. Like the narrator of Fats Waller's 1929 song, "Ain't Misbehavin'," he could say to Mugs, "I'm savin' my love for you." "For almost six years of my life," Dutch later wrote, "I was sure she was going to be my wife. I was very much in love."[36]

It was his love of Margaret as much as anything else that led Dutch Reagan to go to college following his high school graduation in 1928 and another summer of lifeguarding. She was planning to attend Eureka College, a small Disciples of Christ school ninety miles south of Dixon where her two older sisters had gone before her. As if Dutch needed any further incentive to enroll, Eureka was also the alma mater of his hometown hero: John Garland Waggoner II, son of Ben Cleaver's predecessor as the Disciples of Christ minister. Waggoner had been a star football player at Dixon High School and became one at Eureka as well.[37] Dutch wanted to follow in his footsteps and stay close to Mugs. So he decided to enroll too. It was his first, but far from last, step to escape a hometown he revered but had no desire to stay in.

During his Dixon years, Ronald Reagan had grown into a handsome young man renowned for his lifesaving feats on the Rock River, his success on the high school football field and the theater stage, and his all-around popularity. He had put behind him a nomadic, unsettled early childhood and gained the confidence to excel. Now he was ready to move on to fresh challenges in new places. Unlike so many high school stars, he was not content to endlessly replay his teenage glory days, like a flickering old film, while living a mundane, monochromatic adult existence. He was quietly ambitious for far greater success than he could have found by staying in Dixon.

5

'Neath the Elms

He was the biggest mouth of the freshman class; he was a cocky
S.O.B., a loud talker.

—HOWARD SHORT

The top-grossing movie of 1928 was the Warner Brothers tearjerker *The Singing Fool*. Al Jolson, its star, had rocketed to fame the previous year in *The Jazz Singer*, the first "talkie." Now, in *The Singing Fool*, he sang about how hard it was to keep "sittin' on top of the world."[1] Ronald Reagan, who entered college in the fall of 1928, faced a similar problem, albeit on a much smaller scale. But he would not experience the kind of tribulations that would mar life at the top for Jolson's character, a singing waiter turned star songwriter whose wife leaves him and whose son dies. Dutch would go from success to success, untroubled by the taint of failure. Indeed, there was a good deal of continuity between his high school and college years. He continued working as the Lowell Park lifeguard throughout his undergraduate summers and engaged in the same extracurricular activities—football and acting—as in high school. His years at Eureka College would merely embellish his self-identification as an accomplished striver and establishment booster, even if he was willing on one memorable occasion to take part in a student revolt against the college administration.

That Dutch Reagan made it to college in the first place was a testament to his ambition and to sheer luck. Fewer than 5 percent of Americans aged eighteen to twenty-four were enrolled in institutions of higher learning in 1920. (By 1980, that figure had grown to 40 percent.)[2] "We came from a poor family," said Neil Reagan, "and for years if anybody would have said I was going to college or he was going to college, I would have laughed. 'No possibility.'"[3]

The long odds became even longer when Jack Reagan lost his job at the Fashion Boot Shop in April 1928.[4] His cherished hopes of taking over the shop from H. C. Pitney lay shattered. In later years, Ronald Reagan would paint his father as a victim of the Great Depression, but Jack actually lost his job a year and a half before the stock market crash of 1929.[5] He was a victim of his own alcoholism, not of an economic slump. Jack would find work for a while as a traveling salesman for Red Wing Shoes, and Nelle would go to work in a dress shop to help out, but the family had even less money than before—and there was definitely none left over for college.[6]

Neil Reagan, less ambitious and less talented than his younger brother, had surrendered to the grim economic reality and went straight to work at a cement factory in Dixon after his high school graduation. But Dutch remained determined to better himself no matter what. His desire to attend Eureka only grew when he drove with Margaret Cleaver to the campus for the first time in September 1928 to help her enroll. "It was even lovelier than I'd imagined it would be," he rhapsodized sixty years later about a college that, to modern eyes, looks entirely ordinary. "There were five Georgian-style brick buildings arranged around a semicircle with windows framed in white. The buildings were covered with ivy and surrounded by acres of rolling green lawn studded with trees still lush with their summer foliage."[7]

The problem was how to pay for entry into this academic Elysium. Dutch had saved $400 from his summer lifeguarding job, but tuition at Eureka had just been raised to $180 a year while room and board cost $270.[8] His savings would be exhausted before the end of his first year. He was lucky to receive a scholarship that covered half of his tuition. To underwrite the cost of room and board, he got a job washing dishes and serving tables at the three-story, red-brick Tau Kappa Epsilon fraternity house next to the campus. This was also where he would live as a newly pledged "Teke."[9] Mugs, for her part, pledged the Delta Zeta sorority.

Our images of college life in the 1920s have been formed to a considerable extent by novels such as Evelyn Waugh's *Brideshead Revisited* (1945) and F. Scott Fitzgerald's *This Side of Paradise* (1920). They paint a sybaritic picture of privileged youths at elite institutions such as Oxford and Princeton wearing evening clothes, drinking champagne and cocktails, dancing the Charleston and the foxtrot, listening to jazz, and wearing raccoon coats. This was a cosmopolitan world far removed from the small, staid Christian college that Dutch was now entering, situated in a community of just 1,800 souls in the middle of the Corn Belt. But the winds of modernity were blowing even through Eureka.

Starting in 1828, immigrants from Kentucky who were members of the Disciples of Christ had created a rough-hewn frontier settlement along the banks of Walnut Creek in Illinois. In 1848 they opened the Walnut Grove Seminary, soon to be called Walnut Creek Academy, to educate their youngsters. In 1855 the state of Illinois granted a charter to turn that school into a college. Because there was already another township in Illinois called Walnut Grove, the new institution was named Eureka, after the ancient Greek word for "I have found it." The founders were religious but relatively liberal by the standard of the day. Ben Major, one of the early settlers, was a former slaveholder who had educated and then freed his slaves. Twenty-nine of Eureka's early students and faculty left the school in April 1861 to fight for the Union. They mustered beneath a tree on campus that became known as the Recruiting Elm. Gone now, it was still there in 1928, along with so many other trees that Eureka students referred to their campus as the place "'neath the elms."

Those who knew of Ronald Reagan only later in his life might have expected that he would attend college at an insular bastion of conservative ideology. Nothing could have been further from the truth. Eureka admitted women from the start, making it one of the first co-ed colleges in the nation, and by the late nineteenth century it would also enroll Black students at a time when most universities even in the North remained segregated. At the time Dutch enrolled, the entire school had just 220 students.[10]

Eureka would come to be associated with the Social Gospel movement that opposed racism, sought to aid the poor, and supported Progressive reforms and the New Deal. Dutch would become an economics and sociology major, a popular new combined field. His most influential professor— with whom he would take seven classes—was Alexander C. Gray, an ordained minister who had received undergraduate degrees from the University of Toronto and Yale University and master's degrees from Hiram College and the University of Michigan. Considered to be a Christian socialist, A. C. Gray wrote essays espousing immigration—"immigration brings wealth to our country"—and denouncing nativism as "the expression of dense ignorance, unreasonable prejudice, and a cocksureness that those who are different from us are inferior." "It is high time for us to do our duty to the stranger within our gate," he wrote.[11] The pastor of the Disciples of

Christ Church in Eureka during Dutch's first two years at the college, the Reverend Fred W. Helfer, was also a fiery social reformer. His credo: "I will not be blind to the worth of other men because they differ from me in color, creed or country."[12] Their teaching and preaching only strengthened the liberal beliefs that Dutch had inherited from his father.

By the 1920s, even students at a relatively staid institution such as Eureka, where chapel attendance was mandatory, were dancing, drinking, playing cards, and making out. A classmate remembered that Dutch's room at the Teke house—so large it was called "Grand Central"—was where the fraternity brothers gathered to play pinochle. Reagan later recounted that in college, despite "Jack's curse," he "had learned to drink—principally because it was against the law—and it was done out of a bottle that tasted like gasoline on the fraternity back porch or in a parked car." On one occasion, he drank so much that he became "blind drunk." The next day he had a "terrible hangover," which contributed to his abstemiousness later in life. A fellow student recalled that Dutch was "never a drinker or a playboy."[13]

A cemetery located just three minutes' walk from campus was a popular date spot at night. "Everyone had his favorite grave," Dutch noted, "usually with a large enough tombstone to provide a backrest for two and a sizable pool of shadow." One imagines Dutch and Mugs canoodling in the graveyard, at least before the Illinois weather turned too chilly, enjoying what the college yearbook described as "open air, a canopy of heaven and stars, the lazy moon, romance." Most dates were, of course, more innocent: They could involve nothing more, Dutch reminisced, than "two big cherry phosphates at the drug counter . . . and a walk home" or devouring "homemade cake" and strolling "under the campus elms."[14]

Mugs and Dutch must have been doing a lot of strolling because by their sophomore year in 1929–1930 he had given her his fraternity pin—which was tantamount to being engaged.[15] A ring would follow. There is, however, little credible evidence to substantiate the lurid suggestion made in a Reagan biography by Bob Spitz that Margaret may have left Eureka during her junior year because she was pregnant with his baby and wanted to get an abortion or to give it up for adoption. Her attendance at the University of Illinois at Urbana-Champaign during that school year (1930–1931) was well documented, including in the college transcripts and yearbooks. A straight-A student, unlike her beau, Mugs left Eureka because she wanted to challenge herself in a larger, more renowned university. But she returned to finish her studies at Eureka in her senior year and even lived with her family next to the campus—the Reverend Ben Hill Cleaver having left Dixon to take over the Christian Church in Eureka.[16]

The straitlaced administrators of this Christian college were not happy about the liberties their young charges were taking. Students could not be stopped from dancing off campus, but there was absolutely no dancing allowed on the college grounds. Smoking, too, was prohibited at a time when any fashionable "college man" sported a pipe and daring women were lighting up cigarettes. Dissatisfaction with such prohibitions helped spark a student revolt during Dutch's first semester at Eureka.

The ostensible justification for the revolt—and the only one mentioned in Ronald Reagan's memoirs—was budget cutbacks. Given its low tuition and modest endowment (just $658,000 in 1928), Eureka was constantly struggling to stay solvent. A previous college president had exhausted himself and ultimately died of illness in 1923 in his effort to drum up donations. His successor, Bert Wilson, decided in 1928 to cut courses, combine faculty departments, and lay off professors to balance the budget. There were even rumors that he wanted to move the school to Springfield and rename it Abraham Lincoln College. That sparked a revolt among the faculty—an uprising that many students were happy to join because they wanted to overturn Wilson's puritanical ban on dancing and smoking. In fact, the two issues were linked: Wilson did not want to relax the prohibition on dancing in part because he hoped to get more financial support from the Disciples of Christ Church.

A hidden dynamic was the power struggle between Wilson, a fundraiser for the church who had no academic distinction, and Dean Samuel G. Harrod, a scholar of vast girth with a PhD from Princeton University who had been acting president for a year before Wilson's arrival and felt the top job should rightly be his. Harrod had been kind to Dutch, helping to arrange his partial scholarship, and the anti-Wilson agitation centered on the Tau Kappa Epsilon house where Dutch lived, so even though he was a freshman and hardly a campus leader (yet), he was drawn into the fray.[17]

The three-week campus drama began on Friday, November 16, 1928, when the college board of trustees adopted Wilson's retrenchment agenda. An underground student organization called the Committee of 21 responded by

circulating a petition opposing the cutbacks and demanding Wilson's resignation. It was signed by 143 of 220 students, Dutch included. On November
22, a group of students met with the trustees to present the petition in person. After a lengthy discussion, they left in disgust, feeling that their intelligence had been insulted and they had been "laughed out of the meeting."[18]
The next day Wilson offered his resignation, but the students suspected
this was merely a trick so the trustees could vote to keep him and reaffirm
support for his budget cuts. Dean Harrod probably kept the students well
informed. Sure enough, on Tuesday, November 27, after an all-day meeting, the trustees emerged at 11:45 p.m. to announce that they had rejected
Wilson's resignation. The students were ready; they had deliberately not
gone home even with Thanksgiving break looming. By prearrangement,
they rang an old college bell to summon students and faculty and even some
alumni to assemble in the campus chapel for a midnight meeting as if they
were Minutemen mobilizing to meet the Redcoats.

The leaders of the Committee of 21 drafted a resolution for a student
strike, and a number of students spoke in favor of it—Dutch included. Some
accounts of Reagan's life make it seem as if he were the only speaker; in fact,
he was one of many. He was put forward as a freshman representative, a
senior named Howard Short explained to author Garry Wills, "because he
was the biggest mouth of the freshman class; he was a cocky S.O.B., a loud
talker."[19] His remarks were more significant in hindsight—this was a future
president's maiden political speech—than they appeared at the time. His
speech was not mentioned in newspaper accounts, and Margaret Cleaver
said that "it did not make waves."[20] But, in his own recollection of the meeting, Ronald Reagan was the star of the show. "For the first time in my life, I
felt my words reach out and grab an audience, and it was exhilarating," he
wrote decades later. "When I'd say something, they'd roar after every sentence, sometimes every word, and after a while, it was as if the audience and
I were one."[21]

The strike motion was approved by acclamation at 1:45 a.m. on Wednesday, November 28, with the walkout beginning that day and continuing
after Thanksgiving break. All but twelve students participated in the strike,
which also had the tacit support of much of the faculty, led by Dean Harrod.
The trustees met again on December 7, and this time they accepted Bert
Wilson's resignation while also upbraiding Harrod for inciting the insurrection and denying him the presidency he sought.[22] Yet in spite of Wilson's

departure, the trustees still went through with the planned consolidation of departments—a development that Reagan glosses over in his memoirs (just as he never mentioned Harrod's role) in his attempt to paint the strike as a straightforward morality play over the future of the college. Nor does he mention that by the early 1930s, because of the Great Depression, the college had to make even greater cutbacks, losing its accreditation for years.[23] But by the spring of 1929 supervised dances were being held on the college grounds and jazz was being played in the chapel—which was what most of the students really cared about all along.[24]

The irony of Ronald Reagan's participation in this student uprising was lost on no one when he became governor of California in 1967 and cracked down on campus radicals. But the student revolt at Eureka in 1928, while significant for that placid decade, was pretty sedate compared to the uprisings of the more tumultuous 1960s; Eureka students did not occupy the administration building or clash with police. The biggest difference is that 1960s radicals saw universities as part of an oppressive establishment that they wanted to overthrow or least reform, whereas the rebels of 1928 professed their "love" for Eureka and loyalty to "her traditions" and lacked any grand aspirations of changing society.[25]

Dutch may have revolted against the college president, but he remained devoted to the college. He would be not only a varsity swimmer and football player but also a cheerleader for the basketball team during his last three years in college and president of the Booster Club for the last two. He would write saccharine paeans for the college newspaper, the *Pegasus*, about the importance of the "Eureka spirit" just as he had done for the *Dixon Evening Telegram* about "Dixon spirit." He was no forerunner of Mario Savio, the radical icon who led the Free Speech Movement at the University of California at Berkeley in 1964. He had more in common with the character he would play in *Brother Rat* (1938)—the high-spirited but straitlaced Virginia Military Institute cadet Dan Crawford, a varsity baseball player who broke minor rules but tried to keep his roommates out of trouble.

The only time Dutch's faith in Eureka wavered was between his freshman and sophomore years when he was away from the campus. While working at his old job as a lifeguard at Lowell Park, Dutch met a surveyor who offered him a job and promised to help him get an athletic scholarship to his alma mater, the University of Wisconsin. Dutch was briefly tempted. But, he wrote, after returning to campus with Margaret to help her move in, "I was seduced by Eureka all over again." He was able to reenroll with the aid of another needy student's scholarship and a new job washing dishes in the women's dormitory known as Lida's Wood—"one of the better jobs I've ever had," he quipped during a 1980 campaign stop at Eureka.[26] He was lucky to have that modest income given that the stock market crashed shortly after the start of his sophomore year, plunging the nation into an economic depression.

At his mother's urging, Dutch convinced his brother Moon to join him by arranging a scholarship and inviting him to pledge his fraternity. Moon had little interest in going because he was making $125 a month working at a cement factory—good money in those days. But when his boss heard about the offer, he told Moon that if he wasn't "smart enough to take the good thing" his brother had "fixed up" for him, he wasn't smart enough to continue working at the company.[27] So Moon became a Eureka freshman against his will, while his younger brother was already a sophomore.

The newcomer was often referred to as "Dutch Reagan's brother." At the Teke house, Dutch even had to paddle Moon as part of the hazing ritual, and he made sure to whack him extra hard so as to avoid any suspicion of favoritism. The power dynamic between the two brothers had inverted. As Moon later noted, "It's a funny thing and I guess I've never really gotten over it completely. I automatically became the younger brother." That shift would add to the sublimated strains of the rivalrous sibling relationship. "Nothing I've done is ever right as far as he's concerned," Moon complained years later.[28]

The differences between the brothers would only become more accentuated as they grew older. As an adult, Moon would display his father's gift for storytelling, but his stories, in contrast to his brother's, would tend to meander and lack a clear point. Moon simply liked to hear himself talk and would often lose his listeners. He lacked Dutch's unerring ability to read an audience as well as his relentless ambition. Moon also lacked Dutch's charisma and good nature. Ron Reagan recalled, "Moon was cynical and sarcastic. He could be belittling to people who he was telling stories about. He was not warm. In many ways, he was quite the opposite of my father."[29]

Their contrasting attitudes toward alcohol were symbolic of their differences: Moon became a heavy drinker like their dad, while Ronald was far more abstemious, normally nursing a single glass of wine or a single cocktail all evening. Ron Reagan recalled that, when he was growing up, he would see his uncle twice a year—at Christmas and Thanksgiving—and both his mother and father did not exactly look forward to these occasions. Moon himself said of Dutch, "We didn't have what you would call great companionship. . . . If you were a casual observer, you'd say, 'Well, these two brothers don't have any association at all, do they?' "[30]

If any more indication were needed of Ronald Reagan's aloofness from others, this was it. After early childhood, he was not all that close even to his only sibling. That tendency to keep others, even those closest to him, at a remove would not change no matter how many improbable twists and turns Dutch's life took.

As in high school, Dutch Reagan's primary passion in college was football, even though he was more talented as a swimmer. As a Eureka freshman he won every event during a major swim meet except the breaststroke, and he would become a student coach for the swim team during his last two years in college.[31] Years later, he even told his son Ron that a coach for the US Olympic swim team had offered him a spot in training camp, but he had turned it down because he could not afford to give up the income he earned from lifeguarding.[32] Despite the celebrated success of American swimmer— and future movie Tarzan—Johnny Weissmuller at the 1924 and 1928 Olympics, swimming was too low profile a sport to satisfy Dutch Reagan's barely concealed quest for glory.

Only a major spectator sport like the burgeoning college competition of football could bring him the recognition he craved. Reagan saw football as more than merely "the greatest sport in the world." In 1946, he described it as "the one sport today, in a civilization that is too civilized, that gets down to the fundamental things of combat, without the tragedy of war." The players "have a clean hatred of each other," and "each gives every ounce of his energy to the battle," he explained, but when it's over "the players, as friends, not enemies, shake hands in the locker room."[33] The implication of the football-as-war metaphor was plain: Dutch, who was to wear a uniform but never take part in combat, was determined to prove his manhood on the gridiron.

Eureka's football coach was a legendary former football and basketball player, Ralph "Mac" McKinzie, who was reputed to be the best athlete in the school's history. Only five feet, eight inches tall and 145 pounds (he was called "Little Mac" behind his back), the flinty Oklahoma native made up in toughness what he lacked in physical stature. "He has never tolerated a man on his team who could not play clean, while at the same time, fighting his hardest," the yearbook proclaimed.[34]

Mac thought so little of Dutch's abilities as a lineman that he kept him on the bench for most of his freshman season. It didn't help that Dutch was unable to wear his glasses on the field, making the game a blur. Dutch admitted that he spent much of his freshman year "sulking" about his failure to make the starting squad; it was one of the great disappointments of his charmed life and may help explain why he considered leaving Eureka after his freshman year. But, to his credit, he never gave up. The Eureka yearbook reported that "he was regular at all practices, a thing which is pleasing to any coach."[35]

During his sophomore season, Dutch finally showed that he had what it took to be a starter by throwing a terrific block while practicing a sweep play: The defensive player he hit, he recalled with the trademark exaggeration of a born raconteur, "ascended as if he'd been hurled by a shot-putter and seemed to dangle in midair for several moments before plummeting to the ground."[36] Dutch became a starter on the line for the rest of his time in college, playing both defense and offense as was typical in those days. Accordingly, he got to walk around campus in a varsity letterman sweater with a big "E" on the front. The college yearbook commended him for never giving up "when the odds are against him."[37]

More than a half century later, "Mac" McKinzie, who coached into his nineties, recalled that Dutch was a "plugger"—not a star. Moon was a better player; he was a tight end who, according to the yearbook, would score touchdowns with his "sensational" runs and catches.[38] Mac said that Dutch was "slow afoot, only average in size, and lacking in many techniques. But he had about him a good attitude, he believed in conditioning and hard work, he understood self-sacrifice and self-development, he was a team man, and he cooperated well."[39] *Good attitude. Hard work. Cooperating with others.* These were qualities that would carry Ronald Reagan far in life.

Dutch initially thought that McKinzie hated him—the flinty coach was tough on his players—but by the end of his collegiate days the two men had established a fast bond. McKinzie would attend his former student's inauguration in 1981 and later visit the Oval Office. A half century after graduating from Eureka, the president of the United States still handwrote on his calendar every October 1, "Mac McKinzie Birthday." [40]

Three African Americans enrolled with Dutch Reagan at Eureka as first-year students in 1928, including Willie Sue Smith, who would become the first Black woman to graduate from the college. Some of the Black students dropped out, but a few more would arrive as transfers during Dutch's school days. None, however, were able to join fraternities or sororities as most white students did because the national Greek organizations were white-only. [41]

As a result of playing on the football team, Dutch became close with the handful of Black players—his first and last African American friends. One of them, Eudell "Lump" Watts Jr. from Kewanee, Illinois, was the grandson of an enslaved person and one of the best football players in the state. His nickname came from the "lumps" he gave opposing teams. He enrolled at Eureka because the University of Illinois football team, then a national powerhouse, was not integrated until 1943. Another teammate was Franklin "Burgie" Burghardt, who came from a family of barbers in Greenfield, Illinois, and was a distant relative of the civil rights pioneer W. E. B. (B for Burghardt) Du Bois. Burgie was the starting center, playing next to Dutch on the line, and would become co-captain in his senior season after Dutch's graduation. Many of the other college teams that the Golden Tornadoes, later the Red Devils, faced (the squad name changed while Dutch was enrolled) did not have a single Black player, and some colleges refused to play against an integrated squad. A game scheduled with a college in Missouri was canceled because it refused to permit Black players on campus. [42]

Ronald Reagan remembered the racist taunts aimed at Burgie during a game, with one player on the other team even trying to injure his knee. This had the whole Eureka squad "seething," Reagan later wrote, but Burgie got his revenge "completely within the rules" with his sharp blows aimed at his tormentor. [43]

In October 1931, during Dutch's senior year, he convinced the football team to stay in Dixon on a Friday night and stage a public practice for the hometown folks while en route to a Saturday game against Elmhurst

College. But a problem occurred when the team tried to check into a hotel. The manager was willing to provide rooms to everyone except the "two colored boys"—Burghardt and reserve tackle Jim Rattan. Coach Mac was "trembling with rage" and said they would just go to another hotel. But the manager told him that no hotel in Dixon—a town with segregation nearly as rigid as in the South—would give a room to a "colored boy." Mac then said, "We'll sleep on the bus," but this would have simply made the whole team suffer and could have fostered resentment toward the Black players.

Dutch offered a better solution: He would tell Burghardt and Rattan that there wasn't room for everyone at the hotel but that they could stay at his house. Dutch knew that his parents would be hospitable because they were "absolutely color blind when it came to racial matters." Sure enough, when Dutch showed up unannounced with his two Black teammates, Jack and Nelle "didn't even blink or act as if anything had happened that was not a daily occurrence."[44]

Ronald Reagan would recount this honorable act countless times in the future to answer accusations that he was either a racist or pandering to those who were. In truth it was more a deflection than a defense while he continued to exploit white bigotry for political gain.

Decades later, Burghardt, who voted for Reagan in 1980 and kept in touch with him, told a reporter that "we seem to have a mutual respect and admiration," but Reagan was stretching the truth when, in response to criticism from African Americans, he claimed that "we remained close friends throughout the years."[45] In truth, they seldom communicated. Burgie complimented his old teammate for his lack of racial prejudice—"I just don't think he was conscious of race at all"—but chided him for his naivete: "Reagan said that when he was growing up they didn't know they had a racial problem. It was the dumbest thing a grown person could say, but he'd never seen it. I believe that hotel was his first experience of that sort." As a Black man, Burgie, sadly, knew better. "You were always on guard," he said. "You never knew when you were going to walk in the door of a restaurant and the man would say, 'We can't serve you here.' I'm telling you how difficult it was in the Midwest."[46]

Finding out about the corrosive reality of racial inequality in America was one of the most important lessons that Ronald Reagan learned in college—and it did not happen in a classroom. Like much of what one learns in college, however, the lesson would fade over time.

Aside from athletics, Dutch's other major college interest was dramatics. His first drama teacher—the drama queen of the family—had been his mother. His second had been high school teacher B. J. Frazer. His third was a newly hired English instructor at Eureka named Ellen Marie Johnson, a young graduate of a tiny Baptist college in Illinois with a recently acquired master's degree from the University of Illinois. She shared Frazer's passion for teaching acting and organized a drama society, Alpha Epsilon Sigma. Both Dutch and Margaret starred in a number of her productions. The college yearbook commended his performance in *The Call of the Banshee*, a supernatural drama, writing, "Ronald Reagan as Dr. Neville Lacey made one actually feel the hypnotic power he was supposed to have over people."[47]

Near the end of Reagan's sophomore year, in April 1930, the Eureka College "players" earned a spot in a major national drama contest at Northwestern University, competing against nine colleges from eight states. They presented *Aria de Capo*, an antiwar play written by the poet and playwright Edna St. Vincent Millay in 1919, shortly after the guns fell silent on the western front. Dutch played a shepherd, Thyrsis, who is strangled to death. "Death scenes are always pleasant for an actor," he reminisced fondly, "and I tried to play it to the hilt." Much to the surprise of everyone, tiny Eureka College scored third place, and Dutch was one of six actors who earned honorable mentions from the judges. Reagan slightly embellished this achievement in his memoir, claiming that Eureka came in second and that he won one of three acting awards. "No Oscar show will ever be as thrilling to me," he wrote.[48] (Of course, he would never be nominated for an Academy Award, much less win one, but he did appear in feature films that were nominated and a short film that won an Oscar.)

Afterward, the head of Northwestern's School of Speech urged him to consider acting as a career. "I guess that was the day that the acting bug really bit me," he wrote.[49] But acting seemed like a remote possibility for a poor boy from rural Illinois in the middle of the Great Depression.

With all of his extracurricular activities, academics was no more a focus for Dutch Reagan in college than it had been in high school. It was hard to find time or energy to study after a grueling football practice, washing dishes at the women's dorm, and then playing pinochle with his fraternity brothers or going out on a date with Mugs Cleaver. His grades suffered as a result. His report card had more Ds than As. His Ds came in American literature, English history, and even the Life of Christ, suggesting that his religious devotion exceeded his religious knowledge. One wonders if Nelle ever found out. His only A was in a senior-year class, the "Fundamentals of Sports," most likely taught by Coach McKinzie. Mostly he received Bs and Cs—just good enough to maintain his eligibility for the football team. His highest grade-point average was in his senior year, when he achieved a 1.96, equivalent to a C.[50]

But Dutch showed no sign of caring—and to his credit he never tried to exaggerate his modest scholastic achievements by claiming that he was any kind of genius. Returning to Eureka years later to receive an honorary degree, he quipped, "I thought my first Eureka degree was an honorary one."[51] This was a less academically competitive time, and his achievements outside the classroom were impressive enough. In his senior year he was elected student body president. This was his second stint as "President Reagan," and he hadn't even graduated from college yet. At Eureka he built on and easily exceeded an already impressive record of extracurricular and social accomplishments from high school. His most impressive achievement was simply scraping together enough money to stay in school in the midst of the Great Depression when so many other students were dropping out.

Like most older people recalling their youthful haunts, Reagan would remember his college days fondly, insisting that if he had to do it all over again, he would have preferred going to Eureka rather than to one of the bigger and more prestigious University of California campuses he later supervised. "You acquired a habit of accepting personal responsibility in the college undertakings because being a small college all hands were needed," he handwrote in an alumni questionnaire in 1974. Reagan would return regularly over the years, serve on Eureka's board of trustees, and donate to his alma mater. "My heart is still very much in Eureka—'Neath the Elms Upon the Campus!" the former president wrote to a classmate in 1991.[52]

His affection for his college must have been all the greater because it offered him a temporary safe haven from the gale-force economic winds lashing the country in the 1930s. But in 1932—the very worst year of the very worst economic crisis in America's history—he would be forced to leave his academic bastion to face the storm alone and unprotected.

6

The New Dealer

*I was a child of the Depression, a Democrat by upbringing,
and very emotionally committed to FDR.*

—RONALD REAGAN

Ronald Reagan graduated from Eureka College on Tuesday, June 7, 1932, the very day that a "bonus army" of seven thousand bedraggled and impoverished World War I veterans paraded in motley uniforms through Washington, DC, demanding early payment of bonuses they had been promised for their service.[1] The bonus was not paid, and the veterans were brutally dispersed the following month by troops under the command of General Douglas MacArthur.

While Jack missed the graduation ceremony either because he was working or perhaps drinking, Nelle looked on proudly as Dutch received his diploma. "The campus was so beautiful it hurt," Dutch recalled.[2] Following an academic procession from Burgess Hall to Pritchard Gymnasium, the begowned graduates took part in a traditional ceremony: They held a strand of ivy taken from one of the brick buildings, and the new college president, Claude L. Lyon, cut off each graduate's portion. Committed couples such as Dutch and Margaret Cleaver, who had gotten "pinned" during their sophomore year and were planning to get married as soon as they could afford it, stood apart and received a double length of ivy.[3]

The college ceremony may have been idyllic, but the country was by now in the midst of a hellish ordeal that would do much to shape Dutch's early liberal outlook. In these hard times, Eureka could not even afford to publish a yearbook for his senior year. The Great Depression had started with the stock market crash in October 1929 while he was beginning his sophomore year. But fewer than 3 percent of Americans owned any stocks, so it took some time before the impact of the downturn was felt on Main Street. By the beginning of 1932, more than 4,300 banks had failed; 1,456 more would close that year. The unemployment rate spiked to 23.6 percent; among

African Americans, it was 50 percent. Gross domestic product plunged by 12.9 percent in 1932—the most calamitous decline in US history. By year's end, nearly half of all home mortgages were in default.[4] Bing Crosby's 1932 song "Brother, Can You Spare a Dime?" summed up the glum national mood.

The suffering was particularly acute in rural regions, which had never experienced the prosperity of the Roaring Twenties. By 1932, farm prices were at an all-time low—a bushel of corn was selling for less than a pack of chewing gum—while farmers' costs remained unchanged. Between 1930 and 1935, more than 750,000 farms went into bankruptcy or foreclosure.[5] "A sort of nameless dread hangs over the place," journalist Lorena Hickock wrote in 1933 from the Dakotas, with milk cows going "dry for lack of food," "dull-eyed" horses wandering around with "every rib showing," and people shivering in the cold without coats or shoes and "getting just enough food to keep them from starving."[6] Reality was even worse than the grim picture in Erskine Caldwell's best-selling 1932 novel *Tobacco Road*—soon to become a long-running Broadway play and a John Ford film—about the plight of white sharecroppers in rural Georgia.

The misery was compounded by the grasshopper infestations and drought that gripped the Great Plains beginning in 1930. The parched, over-farmed soil was lifted by the winds to form giant, swirling dust storms, ten thousand feet high, choking people and livestock alike. The dust fell like snow as far away as Washington and New York, producing darkness in the daytime, but worst hit were the southern plains of Kansas, Colorado, New Mexico, Texas, and Oklahoma—what became known as the Dust Bowl. "Cattle went blind and suffocated," Timothy Egan wrote in his harrowing history *The Worst Hard Time*. "Children coughed and gagged."[7]

Millions of Americans in both urban and rural areas were lining up to receive free food at soup kitchens. Millions more were wandering the country—many "riding the rails"—in a quest for work or food. Hobos were living in makeshift encampments made of tarpaper and cardboard that were known as "Hoovervilles" in sardonic tribute to Herbert Hoover, the Republican president who had no idea of how to relieve the suffering. He was more progressive than many members of his party, but his emphasis remained on balancing the budget, not on spending public funds to help the destitute. Two of his major initiatives, the 1930 Smoot-Hawley Tariff Act and the 1932 Revenue Act, raised taxes and thereby further damaged the economy—a lesson not lost on a Eureka graduate with a major in economics and sociology who would one day push for tax cuts to address the worst recession since the 1930s.

The federal government, still of minuscule size—as demanded by conservatives in both parties—had almost no capacity to provide assistance to the newly impoverished. On the same day Dutch graduated from Eureka, the House of Representatives passed a $2.2 billion bill to create a federal public works program and provide direct relief to the poor. New York Congressman Fiorello La Guardia, a liberal Republican, called it "the first ray of hope that has been cast in a critical situation," but a month later the parsimonious president, still in thrall to the old laissez-faire shibboleths, vetoed the legislation, claiming it was full of pork-barrel spending. He did, however, sign a smaller compromise bill.[8]

The task of caring for the impoverished fell, as it traditionally had, on state and local governments and charities, but they were simply overwhelmed. The Dixon Welfare Association, which had helped 150 destitute families through the winter of 1930–1931, now had 350 families seeking assistance. The association sought $10,000 for "groceries, coal and other necessities" but by May 1932 had collected less than $6,500; families did not have enough money to support themselves, much less to give charity to others. Volunteers from the American Legion went door to door in Dixon, begging families that had money to spend to "help in a return to prosperity." In order "to ward off starvation," the *Dixon Evening Telegram* reported, an evangelist opened a giant pantry in Assembly Park to collect and can donated food for distribution to the poor.[9]

None of it was enough. "We can no longer depend on passing the hat, and rattling the tin cup," journalist William Allen White wrote. "We have gone to the bottom of the barrel."[10]

Ronald Reagan's fiancée was lucky to graduate with a job lined up: Margaret Cleaver would teach high school in the tiny township of Cropsey, Illinois. But Dutch's future remained as murky as the country's. In 1939 he would tell a Hollywood fan magazine that he had no desire to follow in the footsteps of other collegiate athletes and become a coach or physical education teacher, get married, and raise "other little football heroes." "That," he said, "was exactly what I was afraid of. It might happen to me. Not that such a job and such a life is so bad. It's wonderful for some people—but I had an idea way back in my mind that I had to be an actor, and I knew I'd never be satisfied unless I had a crack at it at least."[11]

Hopes of Hollywood stardom could explain why Dutch boasted to his fellow Tekes when he visited Eureka's campus in the fall of 1932, "If I'm not making five thousand a year when I'm five years out of college, I'll consider these four years here were wasted."[12] This was a tidy sum at a time when the average trade and retail worker was making around $1,100 a year—and, of course, many workers had no jobs at all.[13] But the preternaturally ambitious young graduate saw no more chance of landing a job as an actor than he did of going to the moon. "If I had told anyone I was setting out to be a movie star," he later wrote, "they'd have carted me to an institution."[14]

But if he was not to become a movie star, what was to become of him? He would work as a lifeguard for one more summer. But what would happen after the Lowell Park beach closed in the fall of 1932? Dutch had no idea how he would survive. His parents were in the same predicament. They now found themselves at the bottom of the barrel like so many others in Depression-era America.

Ronald Reagan was to recall bitterly his father's downward spiral. Having already lost his job at the Fashion Boot Shop in 1928, Jack next lost his traveling salesman's job for Red Wing Shoes. The end of the line for him was managing a store that sold cheap shoes and was nearly two hundred miles from Dixon, in Springfield, Illinois—where, rumor had it, he acquired a local girlfriend, thereby straining his marriage to the long-suffering Nelle.[15]

Dutch Reagan visited the store with Moon during a trip with the Eureka football team to play a game (probably in 1931) and received a searing glimpse into the economic degradation his father was enduring, his dreams of opening his own sparkling shoe emporium long ago put aside. More than three decades later, Ronald Reagan painted the dispiriting scene, which could have come straight from *Death of a Salesman*:

His store was a grim, tiny hole-in-the-wall. Although he'd cleaned it up, there wasn't much anybody could have done with the store. There were garish orange advertisements promoting cut-rate shoes plastered on the windows, and the sole piece of furniture was a small wooden bench with iron armrests where his customers were fitted.

When I saw the store I thought of the hours he'd spent when we were boys talking about the grand shoe store he dreamed of opening one day, then remembered the Fashion Boot Shop, the elegant store that, before he lost it, had fulfilled his dream.

My eyes filled and I looked away, not wanting him to see the tears welling up in my eye.[16]

Ronald Reagan was to recall an even more poignant scene at Christmas— probably in 1932.[17] By this point Jack and Nelle had so little money that they had moved into an apartment in Dixon that was one floor of a large house. When Dutch visited, he slept on the cot on the landing. On Christmas Eve, a special-delivery letter arrived for Jack Reagan. After reading it, he quietly remarked, "Well, it's a hell of a Christmas present." Jack had been fired from the Springfield store. He was now one of the more than twelve million unemployed. Aides would later trace Ronald Reagan's lifelong aversion to firing anyone he knew personally to this trauma that his father experienced.[18]

The situation looked bleak, even hopeless. A labor leader warned in 1931, "When despite every effort to get employment, men and women find no opportunity to earn their living, desperation and blind revolt follow."[19] In one small town in Iowa, a crowd of irate farmers kidnapped a judge who was signing foreclosure orders and threatened to string him up unless he stopped, leading to a countywide declaration of martial law.[20] The very survival of capitalism and democracy appeared to be imperiled.

But hope—and help—was on the way. On November 8, 1932, voters decisively repudiated the overmatched Hoover and awarded the presidency to the jaunty, patrician governor of New York, Franklin D. Roosevelt, who would exercise a powerful pull on the imagination of Dutch Reagan along with millions of his contemporaries. Most residents of Dixon had backed Hoover, but Jack Reagan was a staunch Democrat who, in Dutch's telling, never missed "a chance to speak up for the working man or sing the praises of Roosevelt."[21]

While Neil Reagan became a Republican shortly after Roosevelt's inauguration, Dutch followed his father politically. A few months after his twenty-first birthday, he cast his first vote for the entire Democratic ticket. "I grew up a Democrat and entered upon voting age as an ardent New Dealer," he later wrote. He told his daughter Maureen that, as "a child of the Depression" and a "Democrat by upbringing," he was "very emotionally committed to FDR." In his post-presidential memoir, he went even further: "I soon idealized FDR," he proclaimed.[22] Roosevelt would in many ways remain a model for him long after he became ideologically aligned with FDR's conservative foes.

There were, of course, countless differences between the privileged scion of Hyde Park—a graduate of the Groton School, Harvard College, and Columbia Law School—and the poor boy from Dixon. Not the least of these was that the wily FDR was far more secretive and manipulative in dealing with people than the guileless and transparent Ronald Reagan. Roosevelt also was much less ideological in his approach to governance. He famously said in 1932 that "the country demands bold, persistent experimentation. It is common sense to take a method and try it: If it fails admit it frankly and try another."[23] Many said of FDR, because of his shifts of policy, that he lacked "very strong convictions";[24] no one would ever accuse Reagan of such a thing.

But in other respects the two men were eerily alike in ways both good and bad. Some of the barbed descriptions of Roosevelt by his contemporaries uncannily echoed later descriptions of Reagan: "a second-class intellect but a first-class temperament"; "amiable, pleasant, anxious to be of service, very badly informed"; "a pleasant man who, without any important qualifications for the office, would very much like to be president"; "a kind of amiable boy scout." FDR was even said to have a "professional actor's" skill at shaping his image—a comment that was not intended as a compliment. But many of the resemblances were undeniably positive. Both Reagan and Roosevelt were master communicators who employed an intimate and informal speaking style and possessed an almost mystical connection with the American people. And both men were endowed with a preternatural sunniness, unflagging optimism, copious warmth, and bountiful charm and good cheer. FDR's 1932 campaign song, "Happy Days Are Here Again," exemplified his ethos—and Reagan's. Roosevelt was said to be "all light and no darkness," and precisely the same was true of Reagan.[25]

One of the most important qualities they shared was an impressive resilience. In both cases part of the reason was a mother's devotion: Sara Roosevelt instilled as much self-confidence in Franklin as Nelle Reagan did in Dutch. Born into great wealth, FDR had not suffered as a young man, but his ordeal in overcoming polio, which he had contracted in 1921 at age thirty-nine and which left him unable to walk without heavy metal braces, had suffused him with a toughness Reagan acquired by dint of his hard-scrabble upbringing. In moments of crisis both men showed flashes of steel that surprised those who saw them as genial lightweights.

Both presidents were nearly assassinated—Roosevelt shortly before assuming the presidency, Reagan shortly afterward—and both reacted with otherworldly aplomb. Reagan famously joked as the doctors were about to operate on him, "I hope you're all Republicans." In Roosevelt's case, an assassin in Miami took aim at him on February 15, 1933, and instead hit Chicago Mayor Anton J. Cermak, who was next to him. Roosevelt cradled the wounded mayor, soon to die, in his lap on the trip to the hospital. Afterward, while the president-elect was unwinding with his inner circle, Roosevelt adviser Raymond Moley noted that "there was . . . not so much as the twitching of a muscle to indicate that it wasn't any other evening in any other place. Roosevelt was simply himself—easy, confident, poised, to all appearances unmoved."[26]

That sense of imperturbability was FDR's greatest asset in coping with the Great Depression—as it would be for Reagan in dealing with the severe recession he faced early in his presidency. "We have nothing to fear but fear itself," Roosevelt declared in his first inaugural address in 1933. With those now-famous words, he began to restore a shattered nation's self-confidence. "With the possible exception of Ronald Reagan (who voted for FDR four times)," wrote Roosevelt biographer Jean Edward Smith, "no president has ever been more serene in his conviction that whatever happened, everything would turn out all right."[27]

While Reagan shared some important character traits with Roosevelt, he also studied and emulated his idol. He memorized large swaths of FDR's first inaugural address and could do a convincing impersonation of his hero. In the 1964 speech that would launch his own political career, he borrowed a memorable phrase from FDR's 1936 speech accepting his second Democratic nomination for president: "This generation of Americans has a rendezvous with destiny." He also quoted generously from Roosevelt in his 1980 Republican convention acceptance speech. Many of the 1980 Republican delegates were taken aback—hatred of FDR, the architect of the American welfare state, had long been a staple of conservative orthodoxy—but the *New York Times* was so impressed it dubbed the GOP nominee "Franklin Delano Reagan."[28]

Roosevelt's use of radio, a new communications medium, particularly impressed the recent Eureka graduate. "During his Fireside Chats, his strong, gentle, confident voice resonated across the nation with an eloquence that brought comfort and resilience to a nation caught up in a storm and reassured us that we could lick any problem," Reagan later wrote. "I will never forget him for that."[29] Indeed, Reagan would deliver regular radio addresses during his own presidency despite the advent of television—something that few other modern occupants of the Oval Office have done.

Historian David McCullough interviewed Reagan in 1981 about the approaching centenary of FDR's birth and concluded that he "sees Roosevelt as his 'kind of guy'—confident, cheerful, theatrical, larger than life."[30]

But while Reagan showed keen appreciation of FDR's communications ability and sought to emulate it, he showed less understanding of FDR's ad hoc, empirical approach to policymaking. After converting with theological fervor to conservatism in the 1950s, Reagan thereafter excoriated Roosevelt for supposedly betraying his earlier small-government rhetoric and paving the way for "a form of veiled socialism in America." "Many people forget," Reagan lectured in his memoir, "Roosevelt ran for president on a platform dedicated to reducing waste and fat in government. . . . If he had not been distracted by war, I think he would have resisted the relentless expansion of the federal government that followed him."[31] On another occasion he lamented that FDR "departed from his original course in a drastic manner."[32]

Reagan always insisted on this point because he did not want anyone to think he was inconsistent in his beliefs. Famously stubborn, he sometimes changed his mind but seldom admitted doing so. He acknowledged that "as a young man, I did nurture ideas that perhaps utilities should be publicly owned," but otherwise, he wrote in 1971, "my basic beliefs about individual freedom seem to me to be still very much what they were then."[33] In his telling, it was the Democrats who had changed—not him. "I didn't desert my party," he often said. "It deserted me."[34]

It was a memorable line but not an accurate one. It was true that large elements of the Democratic Party before the Great Depression, especially its Southern wing, were animated by a Jeffersonian philosophy that embraced state's rights and resisted federal power. There was a similar anti-Washington outlook among conservative, pro-business Republicans such as President Calvin Coolidge who stood in opposition to the progressive wing of their own party. Many years later, President Reagan would praise Coolidge, who took office when Dutch was twelve years old, "as one of our most underrated presidents" and hang his portrait in the Cabinet Room, but "Silent Cal" would have been anathema to young Dutch.[35]

What Reagan conveniently forgot was that the anti-Washington outlook in the Democratic Party was already fast fading by the time he cast his first vote for Roosevelt—and it was long gone by the time he enthusiastically voted for Roosevelt's reelection in 1936. That year, Reagan was excited to see his idol in person for the first and only time. FDR was riding in an open limousine, waving at vast throngs in Des Moines, where Dutch was then living, and he joined in the "wave of affection and enthusiasm" that "swept the crowd . . . in those hard times."[36] That affection was shared by most Americans and nearly all Democrats, save for a few conservative Democrats, such as the party's 1928 standard-bearer Al Smith, who came to loathe Roosevelt and oppose the New Deal. But Dutch Reagan was no conservative and no Roosevelt hater; he was a progressive Midwesterner who later described himself as a "very emotional New Dealer."[37]

It was misleading to suggest, as Reagan later did, that Roosevelt was a small-government conservative who went awry to win World War II or even to combat the Depression. It is more accurate to say that Roosevelt had few fixed convictions beyond a desire to help "the forgotten man," and that the 1932 Democratic Party platform on which he had been elected was an incoherent mishmash of conservative and liberal beliefs. Democrats pledged themselves to "an immediate and drastic reduction of governmental expenditures" but also to expand public works, unemployment relief, old-age insurance, farm credit, and tougher regulation of banks, brokerages, and utility companies.[38] Reagan frequently mentioned the fiscally conservative planks but never the liberal ones.

Roosevelt's speech in Chicago accepting the 1932 Democratic presidential nomination, delivered less than a month and 150 miles removed from Reagan's college graduation, likewise had some conservative elements. But it also contained a critique of what would later be called "trickle-down economics": Roosevelt denounced the theory "that a favored few" should be helped in the hope that "some of their prosperity will leak through, sift through, to labor, to the farmer, to the small business man." More important, the speech included a pledge that "when we get the chance, the Federal Government will assume bold leadership in distress relief." In proclaiming that "the Federal Government has always had and still has a continuing responsibility for the broader public welfare," Roosevelt was breaking decisively with the conservative, small-government orthodoxy of American politics—and Dutch Reagan was no doubt listening on the radio and cheering along with most Americans.[39]

Roosevelt's nomination speech famously promised "a new deal for the American people." The details of the New Deal remained to be filled in, and indeed Roosevelt never entirely gave up his fiscal conservatism. He signed a budget that slashed spending in 1937 in order to eliminate the budget deficit—an ill-fated decision that stymied the recovery and sparked another recession, a "depression within the depression."[40] But his primary impulse was to mobilize the federal government to meet the economic emergency—and the longer he stayed in office, the more ambitious he became in crafting initiatives not only to curb the Great Depression but to redress the existing economic and social inequities that it had revealed.

FDR did not get everything he wanted—he dreamed of "cradle to grave" social insurance and a national system of health care that Reagan would later denounce as "socialized medicine"—but he did create what Reagan was later to call "an alphabet soup of federal agencies."[41] These included, in the first hundred days alone, the Federal Bank Deposit Insurance Corporation, the Agricultural Adjustment Administration (AAA), the Farm Credit Administration, the Civilian Conservation Corps, the Federal Emergency Relief Administration, the Tennessee Valley Authority, the National Recovery Administration (NRA), and the Public Works Administration. Even more ambitious programs would be implemented during the so-called Second New Deal in 1935, including the Social Security Administration, the Works Progress Administration, and the National Labor Relations Board. Reagan later claimed that these programs represented a betrayal of FDR's original vision, but they were a reflection of Roosevelt's evolving agenda, and Dutch supported all of them at the time.

Not all of the New Deal programs lasted—the NRA and AAA were invalidated by a conservative Supreme Court in 1935—and not all of them worked as intended. The New Deal ameliorated the Depression but did not end it. FDR was still too conservative to spend what was necessary to lift the nation out of the economic doldrums; it took the far higher government spending of the war years for prosperity to return. But Roosevelt's programs still represented the most ambitious expansion of the federal government in US history: The federal budget went from 3.2 percent of GDP in 1929 to 10.1 percent in 1939.[42] Roosevelt created the modern welfare state and, not coincidentally, made Democrats the dominant party in Washington for sixty years to come. His actions, which helped restore a measure of confidence in the political system, prevented extremists such as Huey Long, Gerald L. K. Smith, Father Charles Coughlin, Charles Lindbergh, and Communist leaders William Z. Foster and Earl Browder from overturning the fundamental tenets of American democracy.

Although he was dubbed a "traitor to his class" by many of the wealthy, FDR resisted populist demands to nationalize industry or redistribute income. He remained, like his distant cousin Theodore Roosevelt, a conservative reformer dedicated to rescuing capitalism from both the capitalists and communists. Far from undermining the free-market economy, as Ronald Reagan later imagined, Franklin D. Roosevelt saved it during its hour of gravest peril.

Among those rescued by the New Deal was Reagan's own family. As a loyal Democrat, Jack Reagan was put to work administering local relief efforts in Dixon. By early November 1933, he was being identified in the *Dixon Evening Telegraph* as "secretary of the local relief association" and the "receiving and distributing agent for federal relief supplies." One day, for example, he received and handed out 185 barrels of flour and 3 tons of salt-cured pork from the federal government.[43] (Yes, this was literally "pork-barrel" politics.) The unemployed, dipsomaniac shoe salesman was transformed overnight into a dedicated and effective federal bureaucrat on the front lines of the fight against the Depression. His drinking was not debilitating in this period, perhaps because of his determination to rise to the occasion. Dutch later recalled visiting his father at his office and being "shocked to see the fathers of many of my schoolmates waiting in line for handouts—men I had known most of my life, who had jobs I'd thought were as permanent as the city itself."[44]

Writing from his conservative perspective later in life, Ronald Reagan excoriated the government for extending handouts when the supplicants really wanted work. He credited his father with finding them jobs almost as if he were acting in defiance of the federal authorities.[45] In reality, as Reagan well knew, Franklin Roosevelt was as opposed to welfare dependency as any Republican. "To dole out relief in this way is to administer a narcotic, a subtle destroyer of the human spirit," FDR told Congress in 1935. "It is inimical to the dictates of sound policy. It is in violation of the traditions of America. Work must be found for able-bodied but destitute workers."[46] Reagan even quoted this statement in his first memoir.

FDR was more interested in creating jobs rather than in simply handing out food or money. In November 1933, the president created by executive order a new government body—the Civil Works Administration (CWA) led by his most trusted aide, the intensely driven New York social worker Harry Hopkins—in order to provide work for the unemployed during the winter of 1933–1934. By December, Jack had become "county certifying officer" in Lee County, which included Dixon, for the CWA—not, as his son later claimed, for the Works Progress Administration.

With $263,245.33 in federal funds at his disposal—note the exactitude, which was indicative of how carefully the Roosevelt administration managed taxpayer funds—Jack was able to employ 810 men initially.[47] Although there were 275,000 women nationwide working for the CWA, in Lee County the beneficiaries appear to have been exclusively male.[48] Jack's job was to serve as liaison with the federal authorities in Chicago, convincing them to fund local projects and monitoring how the funds were spent. By the spring of 1934, Jack Reagan could proudly boast that the CWA in Lee County had allocated money for projects such as building a new municipal airport, improvements in Lowell Park, cleaning and painting school buildings, decorating the public library, brush-cutting and ditch-cleaning, road grading, and landscaping along state highways.[49]

When some workers at the airport construction project were temporarily laid off, angry local politicians hauled in Jack Reagan to explain why. Jack did not back down. The *Dixon Evening Telegraph* reported that a "verbal bomb burst" when "J. E. Reagan" accused the county officials of shady dealings by hiring more men than were needed. "There is no crooked work going to be allowed," Jack vowed, and he threatened to cancel the entire project unless it was carried out as planned.[50]

Of course, Jack Reagan was not above some featherbedding of his own:

By early 1934, his own son Neil, who had graduated from Eureka less than a year before, was working as a statistician for the emergency relief project.[51] Dutch, by contrast, had no need to join the federal payroll. He had already, improbably enough, found a new career as a radio announcer even as so many other Americans were seeing their own professional aspirations shattered.

7

Radio Days

His quick tongue seemed to be as fast as the plays.

—*Quad-City Times*

The whole course of twentieth-century history might have been different if Ronald Reagan had been hired in 1932 to manage the sporting goods department of a new Montgomery Ward store that was opening in Dixon, Illinois. If he had decided to accept the position, one can imagine him staying in his hometown, marrying Margaret Cleaver, having a passel of kids, earning a few promotions, and living an utterly anonymous and ordinary existence. That would have been the normal thing—the expected thing—to do. As George Orwell wrote, "After the age of about thirty [the great mass of human beings] abandon individual ambition—in many cases, indeed, they almost abandon the sense of being individuals at all—and live chiefly for others, or are simply smothered under drudgery."[1]

If Reagan had taken that retail job and stayed in Dixon, someone else almost surely would have been elected president in 1980. And he might have taken the Montgomery Ward position if it had been offered; it would have been hard to turn down $12.50 a week in the middle of the Great Depression. At the very least, being offered the job would have presented a difficult dilemma to an impoverished young man: Should he pursue his improbable ambitions of stardom or follow the path of safety and security? In the event, he avoided what might have been a difficult choice. The salesman's position went to another former high school athlete, who would still be living in his hometown in the 1970s while Ronald Reagan was running for president.[2]

Not getting hired at Montgomery Ward left Dutch free to pursue his vaunted show business ambitions. He figured, correctly but improbably, that radio stardom could be his route to movie stardom. After all, there were plenty of radio stations in the area but not one film studio.

In 1920 the first commercial radio station in the country, KDKA in Pittsburgh, went on the air. By 1933 there would be 605 radio stations around the United States. Everyone, it seemed, was starting a radio station, often as an adjunct to an existing business. In New Lebanon, Ohio, a poultry farm started one; in Clarksburg, West Virginia, a hardware store; in Cleveland, a bank. In 1926, the Radio Corporation of America created the first radio network—the National Broadcasting Company (NBC)—to provide programming to affiliated stations. Soon it had a competitor: the Columbia Broadcasting System (CBS).[3]

Initially radio pioneers had high-minded aspirations of broadcasting uplifting lectures and classical music concerts without commercials—a sort of precursor of National Public Radio or the British Broadcasting Company. But by the 1930s the programming consisted mainly of lighter fare, such as comedy, dramas, variety shows, popular music, and sports—all interspersed with copious commercials. The most popular program was the comedy show *Amos 'n' Andy* featuring two white actors, often pictured in blackface, speaking in Black dialect—a racist trope that was still considered acceptable at the time. By 1934 more than 60 percent of American homes had a radio, and the entire country (including many Black Americans) seemed to stop and listen when *Amos 'n' Andy* was on.[4] The nationwide reach of radio did much to bind together and buoy a diverse nation during the depths of the Great Depression. For the first time, people from coast to coast could have shared experiences in real time. "Radio was magic," Reagan recalled. "It forced you to use your imagination. You'd sit in your living room and be transported to glamorous locales around the world, and eavesdrop on stories of romance and adventure brought to life by a few actors and vivid sound effects transmitted over the radio waves."[5]

Among the new professions created by radio was the sports announcer. The men—and they were exclusively men in those days—who called athletic events became as famous as the athletes they were describing. While still in college, Dutch began to dream of joining their ranks, thereby combining his love of drama with his love of sports. Coach Ralph McKinzie remembered him grabbing a broomstick after practice and pretending to broadcast a football game. "He got a kick out of that," Mac said. "Did a pretty good job too."[6]

But it was one thing to broadcast imaginary games. Getting paid for sportscasting was no easier in those days than it is today. In 1932 Dutch hitchhiked to Chicago looking for any kind of job in radio, only to return home defeated and dejected. The big-time radio stations had no interest in the neophyte. One kindly employee at the NBC station in Chicago suggested that he would be better advised to start in "the sticks."[7] Surveying the radio stations within easy driving distance of Dixon, he immediately stumbled upon WOC in Davenport, Iowa, only seventy miles away. Like Jack Reagan's hometown of Fulton, Illinois, Davenport was a bustling Mississippi River port located along the Iowa–Illinois border that had prospered in the nineteenth century as a conduit of the waterborne trade with St. Louis. In this modest-size town—part of the Quad Cities along with nearby communities— Dutch, against all odds, would take his first halting steps on the path to show-business success.

The Davenport station had been founded by one of those eccentric geniuses that America seems to produce in as much abundance as corn, automobiles, and bunkum. B. J. Palmer was a flamboyant grade-school dropout with a Van Dyke beard and shoulder-length hair that he infamously washed only once a year. His father, D. D. Palmer, was a fishmonger who had founded chiropractic medicine in 1895 on the theory that manipulation of the spine can cure most ills. D. D. Palmer was dubbed the "Discoverer of Chiropractic" by his acolytes, while B. J. Palmer was the "Developer." He turned the Palmer School of Chiropractic in Davenport into a flourishing, profitable enterprise, notwithstanding the skepticism of traditional physicians about the benefits of spinal manipulation. B. J. was so successful he bought a rambling, twenty-two-room mansion in Davenport and stocked it with bizarre bric-a-brac collected on his around-the-world trips, ranging from an elephant's foot to human spines. B. J. always slept with his head facing the North Pole because "he felt the currents of the earth must flow properly through his body."[8]

From the start, B. J., though spiritually driven in some matters, was a big believer in the newfangled discipline of advertising, offering Dutch an early lesson in the importance of marketing his work. Among the homilies Palmer scattered around his school campus was "Early to bed, early to rise; Work like hell—and advertise."[9] In 1922, the inveterately curious, always hustling B. J. Palmer became intrigued with a new medium for advertising. He purchased a tiny hundred-watt radio station, moved it to the Palmer School, and christened it WOC, for World, or Wonders, of Chiropractic. He installed his son Dave Palmer as business manager, expanded the station's signal power to five thousand watts, and promoted it as the voice of Davenport, which he dubbed, with trademark bombast, "Where the West begins in the state where the tall corn grows." Naturally, he organized contests for the tallest cornstalks.

In 1927 his station joined the newly organized NBC network, and in 1930 he also purchased WHO in Des Moines. Des Moines was Iowa's largest city (population 142,000), Davenport its second largest (population 60,000)—and both now were part of the growing audience for B. J.'s broadcasts. Together, the two stations helped link rural Iowa with the rest of the country by presenting popular programs such as the *Iowa Barn Dance Frolic* that offered its impoverished listeners a welcome, if fleeting, escape from the unemployment lines, foreclosures, and soup kitchens of Depression-era Iowa.[10]

In the fall of 1932, a cocky and handsome Eureka College graduate showed up at the Davenport station, located on the top floor of the Palmer School, inquiring about a job as an announcer. He immediately encountered a character almost as outrageous as B. J. Palmer. A Scottish immigrant, Peter MacArthur was an old vaudeville song-and-dance man who had come to Davenport seeking relief for crippling arthritis and had stayed on to become an announcer and then programming director at WOC. He used two canes to walk, had "twinkling eyes" and cheeks "the color of copper," spoke with a Highland burr "as thick as oatmeal," and had a "vocabulary that could crackle and scorch." He told Dutch that he was too late: The station had just filled an announcer's job and Dutch wouldn't have gotten it anyway because he had no experience. Reagan recalled that "the Irish in me kind of came to the fore," and so he responded with exasperation: "Well then, how was a guy to get experience if nobody would give him a chance?"

The crusty but kind-hearted Scotsman decided to give the desperate job seeker a shot. "Do ye perhaps know football?" he demanded. "Do ye think ye could tell me about a game and make me see it?" Dutch gulped and said yes to both questions. MacArthur marched him down the hall to a small studio draped in heavy blue velvet that provided makeshift soundproofing, pointed him at a microphone, and told him that when the red light went on, "Ye start talkin'."

It was a formidable challenge for any broadcaster, much less a neophyte: describe a game you cannot see. Employing his photographic memory, Dutch imagined the fourth quarter of an exciting game he had played in a year earlier, on October 10, 1931, against Western State Teachers College—a come-from-behind, thirteen-to-six victory for Eureka on a last-minute touchdown. Decades later Reagan recalled how his mock broadcast began: *Here we are in the fourth quarter with Western State University leading Eureka College six to nothing. . . . Long blue shadows are settling over the field and a chill wind is blowing up through the end of the stadium.* Those were not his exact words, of course, but the vivid imagery—"long blue shadows," "chill wind"—sounds like something he would have said. So, too, it makes perfect sense that Reagan, as he so often did, improved on real life. In the actual game he had missed a crucial block. In a postmodern twist to his imaginary broadcast, a player named "Dutch Reagan" threw a magnificent block that sprang the Eureka fullback for a sixty-yard gallop into the end zone.

Dutch got so caught up in the excitement of calling this imaginary contest that he was "weak and limp and a little hoarse" by the time he was done. "Ye did great, ye big SOB," MacArthur proclaimed. He told Dutch to report in two weeks' time to broadcast the big football game between the University of Iowa Hawkeyes and the University of Minnesota Golden Gophers. He would get five dollars and bus fare.[11]

On October 22, 1932—as the presidential campaign entered its final weeks with Democratic nominee Franklin Roosevelt blaming President Hoover for the Depression and Hoover delusionally insisting the recovery had already begun[12]—Dutch Reagan entered a press box for the first time at Iowa Stadium in Iowa City. Some ten thousand sodden fans were in attendance; it rained throughout most of the game. MacArthur was nervous enough about the newcomer that he brought a more experienced announcer to share play-calling duties, but Dutch acquitted himself admirably, even though the game was a blowout: Minnesota won twenty-one to six. The *Quad-City Times* raved about the broadcasting abilities of this "ex-gridiron gallant": "His crisp account of the muddy struggle sounded like a carefully written story of the gridiron goings-on and his quick tongue seemed to be as fast as the plays." MacArthur was impressed enough to hire Dutch to broadcast the Hawkeyes' final three local games for ten dollars a game. Dutch was not hired, however, to follow the team to Washington, DC, on October 28 to cover their thrashing at the hands of George Washington University.[13]

When the season ended on November 19—the same day that Hoover unveiled a misguided plan to cut a further $700 million from an already inadequate federal budget[14]—so did Dutch's job. By Christmas 1932, in the long interregnum between Roosevelt's election in November and his inauguration in March, Dutch was unemployed once again—and at the very same time that Jack Reagan was getting his pink slip from the Springfield shoe shop. This was quite possibly the hardest winter in US history, with a vacuum of leadership in Washington as bank failures, layoffs, and foreclosures accelerated. Literary critic Edmund Wilson wrote from Chicago, "There is not a garbage dump in the city which is not diligently haunted by the hungry," and when the Soviet trade office in New York asked for six thousand skilled workers to go to Russia, it received more than a hundred thousand applications.[15]

Yet, even as others were suffering so much misfortune, Dutch's luck seemed to hold. In early January 1933, Pete MacArthur called to tell him that staff announcer Hugh Hipple was leaving for a job at a Chicago radio station. Would Dutch be interested in auditioning? The answer was obvious. In early February, Dutch Reagan tried out for the spot along with seventeen other applicants. He was one of four finalists. On February 9, after passing another test, the job was his. He would earn a munificent salary of a hundred dollars a month at a time when relief payments in the city of Philadelphia amounted to less than seventeen dollars a month for a family of four. Dutch had enough money to help support Jack and Nelle in Dixon and Neil while he was finishing his studies at Eureka.[16]

———

As it turned out, Reagan was a natural at radio, but he was not instantly good at every aspect of the job. He struggled, for example, with reading scripts, as he had to do during commercials. As president he would become known as the master of the teleprompter, but at that time, he recalled, "I was plain awful." He improved with lots of help from Pete MacArthur, who gave him a "crash course on radio announcing." MacArthur became, like Reverend Cleaver and Coach McKinzie before him, another surrogate father. Before long, Dutch recalled, "I began reading over the commercials before airtime and practicing my delivery to get the right rhythm and cadence and give my words more motion."[17] He would do precisely the same thing decades later, sounding out his speeches and adding marks to his note cards for emphasis to get the cadences exactly right before delivering them.

Another lesson Reagan learned on the air was about the need to eliminate unnecessary verbiage. During station breaks, one of Dutch's fellow announcers would say, "This is radio station WHO Des Moines, Iowa." B. J. Palmer told him that "everything was superfluous except 'WHO Des Moines.'"[18] Dutch would become a master of the spare idiom of radio—and then apply the same technique to his political speeches, often striking out superfluous words from his speechwriters.

Later one of capitalism's most effective and ardent advocates, Dutch bridled, ironically, against the crass commercialism of the new medium. One day, only a month after starting, he was presenting a program of music sponsored by a mortuary. But he thought it was so incongruous to mention the mortuary before playing a romantic song ("Drink to Me Only with Thine Eyes") that he left out the sponsor. In B. J. Palmer's profit-driven operation, this was a firing offense. Someone—probably Dave Palmer—told Dutch he was out. The local newspaper even carried an announcement on March 1, 1933, that he was quitting and going home. But before he left, he was supposed to train his successor, a high school drama teacher named Burrens Robbins from Des Moines. When Robbins realized how quickly Reagan had been fired, he demanded security of employment, only to be informed coldly that Colonel Palmer did not give out contracts or job guarantees to his employees. Robbins left, and the more desperate Dutch returned to the microphone. As Mac McKinzie had noted, Dutch was cooperative and eager to please—and, with his "Midwestern ethic," he was willing to work even for an employer who might fire him on the spur of the moment. It beat being unemployed.[19]

As if Dutch needed any reminder of how badly he needed the job, he received it every morning on his walk to work in Depression-ravaged Davenport. As soon as he left his apartment on Perry Street, he passed panhandlers; he would make it a practice to give a dime to the first one who asked for a cup of coffee. Although barely out of college, he knew that he was already incomparably more privileged than most Americans. "I have never been richer," he recalled. "I bought a meal ticket to the Palmer School cafeteria—it was good for three meals a day, six days a week, total cost $3.65!"[20]

Soon Dutch Reagan, whose voice was praised by his hometown newspaper in Dixon for being "pleasing" and "well modulated," won an important promotion.[21] In June 1933—as President Roosevelt was concluding his first hundred days of attempting to enact "the measures that a stricken Nation in the midst of a stricken world may require"[22]—Dutch was transferred to the Palmers' other radio station, WHO in Des Moines, to serve as an all-purpose announcer and sportscaster. This was the largest city Reagan had lived in apart from his brief childhood stint in Chicago. Founded in 1843, Des Moines had developed into one of the chief metropolises of the Midwest, but, like the rest of the nation, it had suffered as a result of the Depression. Shantytowns were visible from the Renaissance-style State Capitol, some families were reduced to smashing their wooden furniture to fuel their stoves, and others even shared shoes (if one person went to town, the other stayed home), while enterprising homemakers were contriving dresses out of feed or flour sacks.[23] Even in the 1930s, however, Des Moines was a vibrant city that hosted annual events such as the Drake Relays (one of the world's largest track-and-field meets, held at Drake University) and the Iowa State Fair, which attracted hundreds of thousands of people every August with its livestock competitions, a famous cow sculpture molded of butter, food booths, and carnival-like attractions.

If this was not quite the big time, it was at least a bigger stage than Davenport or Dixon, and Dutch had money to spend on its attractions. He was now making $75 a week—a significant salary for those days—and he supplemented his income by writing a weekly column ("Around the World of Sports with 'Dutch' Reagan") for the *Des Moines Dispatch* and appearing in advertisements for local merchants such as Younkers department store ("The Christmas Store for All of Iowa").[24]

Dutch did all kinds of announcing, including spinning records, reading the news, and interviewing visiting celebrities such as boxer Jack Dempsey, actor Leslie Howard, and evangelist Aimee Semple McPherson. But sportscasting is what he loved the most and what he became most known for. He covered the Drake Relays, swim meets, auto races, and college football games, including one featuring the undefeated, national champion University of Michigan Wolverines, whose stars included linebacker and center Gerald Ford. He also called the games of Chicago's Major League Baseball teams, the White Sox and the Cubs, in broadcasts sponsored by General Mills, the makers of Wheaties cereal. It did not matter that he knew little about baseball and had never even been to a Major League game. Indeed, he covered hundreds of ball games without ever going to the ballpark.

This may seem bizarre to a later generation accustomed to sportscasters being present for the events they cover, but it was quite common until the 1950s for baseball announcers to "re-create" games based on nothing more than a terse telegraphic account, because it was cheaper than sending an announcer on the road. A Western Union operator at the ballpark would send out updates with notations such as "B1 LO OS" (ball one, low and outside) and "S1 S" (strike one, batter swung), and the distant radio announcers pretended they were seeing the action with their own eyes.[25]

One of Ronald Reagan's most cherished anecdotes—one that all who knew him heard so often they could practically recite it by heart—concerned what happened when he was told that the wire had gone dead while he was calling the ninth inning of a contest between the Chicago Cubs and the St. Louis Cardinals. On the mound was the Cardinals' ace pitcher Jay "Dizzy" Dean, a consummate showman known for boasting, Muhammad Ali–style, about his athletic prowess. "If ya do it," he liked to say, "it ain't bragging." The Cubs' star shortstop Billy Jurges—or was it left fielder Augie Galan?—was at the plate. (Dutch told the story both ways.) Reagan feared that if he told listeners the wire had gone dead, they would turn to a competing station. So, instead, he pretended that the batter was fouling off one pitch after another. The "foul balls" kept on going for seven agonizing minutes until the notification finally arrived that Jurges had popped out the first ball pitched. For days afterward, Reagan claimed, people would stop him on the street to ask "if Jurges had set a record for foul balls." "I never admitted a thing," he wrote with a wink.[26]

This story has often been cited, just like the tale of his radio audition, as a tribute to Reagan's active imagination—his ability to invent facts not in evidence. But he was not deceiving most listeners; the people who asked him about whether Jurges had set a foul-ball record were probably in on the joke. A 1934 *Des Moines Dispatch* article made clear how he worked: "Sitting in his studio in Des Moines, 'Dutch' builds a word picture of every detail of play, so vivid that hundreds of thousands of fans feel that they are almost 'seeing' the teams in action."[27] In a similar vein, a WHO press release noted, "So popular are his relived versions of the Chicago games that many people prefer listening to his accounts to broadcasts by eye witnesses of the game."[28] There was no secret about how Dutch called games. Listeners were eager participants in the illusion he was creating—just as so many would later be when he became a movie star and then a politician.

Dutch Reagan was so good at his job that he soon commanded more airtime at WHO. He hosted a twice-daily sports show, the *Teaberry Sports Review*, an early forerunner of ESPN's *SportsCenter*, every afternoon at 5:25 p.m. and every night at 10:10 p.m. And he was heard not just in Des Moines but all over the Midwest, because in April 1933 WHO had begun operating a fifty-thousand-watt transmitter—the most powerful then allowed by the government. Built at a cost of $250,000, the station's 532-foot broadcast tower was the tallest structure in Iowa. By August 1934, a little more than a year after he had started at WHO, the *Dixon Evening Telegraph* was reporting that Dutch had become "a daily source of baseball dope" for "millions of sports fans in at least seven or eight middlewestern states." The radio station was said to be receiving hundreds of letters of thanks and praise. "Reagan has been declared one of the leading sports announcers in the entire nation in the radio profession," the newspaper proclaimed.[29]

That was heady praise for a twenty-three-year-old just a couple of years out of college. He was becoming a big shot in Des Moines, just as he had been in Dixon and Eureka. By 1935, the year that FDR launched his Second New Deal, Dutch would be making the princely sum of $3,900 a year—not far from his stated goal of $5,000 a year.[30]

There is no indication that Dutch became conceited or arrogant as he grew more successful. "He was always just one of the guys, never stuck up," a friend from Des Moines recalled. One of his colleagues at WHO said that he was "delightfully personable"—someone that "everybody liked and enjoyed." Another colleague said, "He was an amiable, likeable, hail-fellow-well-met with a sense of humor, the gift of gab, and a high degree of competence as a sports broadcaster, especially at play-by-play."[31]

Dutch's appearance was as pleasing as his personality. One WHO press release gushed that "he is a handsome young chap over six feet tall, broad shouldered and slim waisted and carries himself like the born athlete that he is." Another WHO press release—apparently written by a publicist who thought the first one was too understated—described him as being six feet, one inch tall, with blue eyes, "wavy blond hair" (it was actually brown), and "a magnificent physique."[32]

Little wonder that a colleague recalled that the good-looking young radio star was "very popular with the young ladies" and had "pretty women" swarming all over him.[33]

* * *

Dutch was at last free to play the field, because in the spring of 1935 he was unceremoniously dumped by his fiancée Margaret Cleaver. The news arrived via a letter returning his fraternity pin and engagement ring. Mugs had gone on a trip to Europe with her sisters in the summer of 1934, and in Paris she had fallen for a US Foreign Service officer. A few weeks after Mugs broke off her engagement to Dutch, Nelle called to let her son know that the *Dixon Evening Telegram* had run an item announcing the engagement of this "charming and accomplished girl" to diplomat James W. Gordon Jr. The ceremony took place in June 1935 at the Disciples of Christ Church in Dixon with the Reverend Ben Cleaver presiding. Before long, the bridegroom would leave the Foreign Service and make a successful career as a lawyer in his hometown of Richmond, Virginia, where he and his bride would raise their children.[34]

Asked many years later why she had broken up with Dutch, Margaret told Edmund Morris, "I didn't want to bring up my children in Hollywood."[35] This was an indication of how strongly Dutch still dreamed of movie stardom—and how much his dreams clashed with hers. Her revulsion was perfectly understandable at a time when acting was still seen by many as a disreputable profession and Hollywood was often denounced as a breeding ground of depravity. It also made sense that their romance could not survive their long separation: It had been three years since their college graduation, and they had seen each other only sporadically during that time.

But that did not lessen Reagan's hurt. He told Morris, "I was kinda floored," and he wrote in his memoirs, "Margaret's decision shattered me, not so much, I think because she no longer loved me, but because I no longer had anyone to love."[36] His old high school drama teacher B. J. Frazer tried to console him with a letter, as did Nelle, who predictably told him that everything always works out for the best in the end.

This breakup set a pattern that Ronald Reagan would follow in his personal relationships throughout his life. He had trouble committing to a partner; both of his wives had to nudge him to the altar. But when he did commit, he assumed it would be for good. He valued stability and wanted to emulate the example of his parents' long-lasting marriage, even if theirs was hardly a joyous union. His engagement to Margaret Cleaver, just like his first marriage to Jane Wyman, would be dissolved over his baffled objections. A charmer with the ability to enchant almost anyone, at least for a time, Reagan would always be left crestfallen and bewildered to learn that for some people, even those closest to him, his appeal had simply worn off.

Dutch dated during his time in Davenport and Des Moines, but he did not find—or apparently seek—a serious relationship to replace the one that had just ended. A bookkeeper at WOC who went out with him while he lived in Davenport, usually as part of a group of friends, later claimed to have carried an "unrequited love" for him till the end of her days (she died in 2002 at age ninety-eight).[37] In 1936 he dated an attractive college senior, Jeanne Tesdell, from Drake University, a much larger Disciples college than Eureka. She understandably wondered how romantic his intentions were because whenever he came to pick her up at her family home, he kept delaying their dates "to lecture her father on the virtues of the Agricultural Adjustment Act."[38] That certainly sounds like Reagan—as do the descriptions of him from other former girlfriends in Des Moines as a "total extrovert"; "fun, glamorous, laughing, joking"; but always the courtly "gentleman."[39] He was not the kind of guy who got "fresh" if his date wasn't interested—and sometimes not even when she was.

Many of his male friends were current or former Drake students; many were also fellow members of his fraternity. Some of these Iowa friends would later follow him, as if anticipating the HBO show *Entourage*, to Los Angeles. One would be best man at his wedding to Jane Wyman. Even many decades later, Ronald Reagan easily recalled Hubert "PeeWee" Johnson, Donald Reid, Will Scott, and the rest of his Des Moines crew.[40] Many nights the whole gang wound up at Cy's Moonlight Inn, a bar owned by a former semi-pro baseball player, Lynn "Cy" Griffiths, that was famous for beer spiked with extra alcohol. There was also a dance floor known as the "passion pit" where patrons could dance to jukebox music. No doubt, it was playing big-band hits of the day, such as "Cheek to Cheek" performed by Fred Astaire, "Smoke Gets in Your Eyes" by Paul Whiteman and His Orchestra, and "I Get a Kick Out of You" by Ethel Merman. Like most people, Reagan had his musical tastes formed in adolescence and early adulthood, and big-band songs would remain his favorite music for the rest of his life.[41] Dutch became such a regular that a large picture of him at the WHO microphone was soon displayed behind the bar. But even if everybody else was getting snozzled, Dutch would stay sober enough to drive his friends home.[42]

Neil Reagan briefly came out to Des Moines in 1935. Dutch asked him to drive over a new, metallic brown Nash convertible he had just bought from a college friend who worked at an automobile dealership in central Illinois. Dutch then introduced Moon to Pete MacArthur, and before long another Reagan was on the air. The two brothers would appear together to argue about their predictions for the football games of the week, and Moon would deliver the Saturday-night football scoreboard. Moon only stayed a few months in Des Moines before being transferred to WOC in Davenport, where he became a sports announcer, then program director, and briefly station manager.[43]

By then Moon had already fallen in love with a Des Moines girl—and Drake graduate—named Bess Hoffman. Within two weeks of meeting each other, Moon and Bess decided to marry. Dutch thought that was much too fast; in his own romances, he was notoriously slow to commit. At Moon's wedding he even stage-whispered, "I'll give you two to one it doesn't last a year," a rare example of a cutting comment from Dutch and one that his brother overheard and never forgave. In fact, the marriage would last till Moon's death in 1996.[44]

One of Dutch's friends in Des Moines—a fellow announcer at WHO—had a reserve commission in the US Army Cavalry, which allowed him to ride horses at Fort Des Moines, the big army base outside of town. He convinced Dutch to join him. Army records contain an application from Ronald Wilson Reagan, dated February 27, 1935, for an appointment as a second lieutenant in the cavalry reserves.[45] "I had no particular desire to be an officer," Reagan later explained. "Like everyone else I thought we had already fought the last war."[46] The attraction was the horses that reserve officers could ride—just like his boyhood silent-screen idol, Tom Mix, one of the first movie cowboys. Dutch had learned to ride at Lowell Park, and he was eager to become a better horseman. This was the beginning of his lifelong passion for horses. He would often—very, very often—say throughout the rest of his life that "nothing is as good for the inside of a man as the outside of a horse."

But in order to get on a horse, he first had to pass a physical exam—no mean feat given how nearsighted he was. The army doctors recorded that he had only 20/200 vision in both eyes. Someone who is 20/200 is considered legally blind by the government. Dutch later claimed he had cheated on the eye exam to enter the army, but the army doctors simply recorded that his vision was correctible to 20/20 in both eyes with the use of glasses. On May 2, 1937, an army board met and, finding Reagan "physically, morally, generally and emotionally" qualified, recommended that he receive a second lieutenant's commission. On May 25, he was formally commissioned in the Fourteenth Cavalry Regiment.[47]

While taking on horseback riding as a new pastime, Dutch continued swimming. He regularly went to the giant public pool—at 350 feet by 150 feet, it was one of the largest in the country—located at Camp Dodge, the headquarters of the Iowa National Guard. During one of his outings, he saved two Girl Scouts who were drowning in the deep end of the pool. Those would be his seventy-eighth and seventy-ninth saves, even though he was no longer an actual lifeguard.[48]

Dutch's other notable act of heroism in Des Moines came one night around 11:00 p.m. while he was preparing for bed in the boardinghouse at 330 Center Street where he lived in the fall of 1933. A nursing student, Melba Lohmann, who was walking in front of the building, was accosted by a mugger who thrust an unidentified object into her back and demanded her money, purse, and suitcase. Reagan heard the commotion and leaned out the window to shout, "Leave her alone or I'll shoot you right between the shoulders!" He even brandished a pistol he owned. It was unloaded, but the robber did not know that; he dropped the purse and ran off. Reagan courteously came out in his pajamas, slippers, and robe to walk Miss Lohmann to the hospital where she worked half a block away.

As usual, Reagan was a self-effacing hero. He did not brag about what he had done and did not include this feat in either of his memoirs. After he talked about it in an interview with a hunting magazine in 1984 to make a gun-rights argument, Melba Lohmann King—as she was then known—confirmed his account. But then Tom Mix didn't brag after rescuing a damsel in distress either.[49]

———

The level of success that Dutch Reagan achieved in Des Moines would have satisfied most people. He was doing spectacularly well compared to most Americans in those penurious days. But beneath Dutch's modest demeanor continued to lurk a burning ambition. He had never abandoned his Hollywood aspirations and now took his first steps toward achieving them.

While shivering through the Iowa winter, Ronald Reagan got the bright idea of asking his bosses to send him to cover the Chicago Cubs in spring training. Since 1922, the Cubs, owned by the Wrigley chewing-gum dynasty, had taken up residence from roughly mid-February to mid-March off the coast of Los Angeles on Santa Catalina Island, also owned by the Wrigleys. (The family patriarch, William Wrigley Jr., was buried in a mountain mausoleum on Catalina befitting a monarch.) Accompanying the Cubs, Dutch argued to his bosses, would increase his knowledge of the team and make him a better broadcaster; wisely, he did not mention that he had an ulterior motive for making the trip. Somewhat surprisingly, the tightfisted B. J. Palmer signed off. So in the spring of 1935, Dutch packed "white buckskins, linen suits, [a] white sports coat, and, of course, swimming trunks" for his first visit to Southern California.[50]

Dutch traveled by train with part of the team. It was the first time he had never been west of Kansas City. One reporter onboard wrote from Flagstaff, Arizona, that "the rookies in the party all were up at 7 o'clock, most of them being lads from the south, north, and east, who had never seen sage brush and cactus in its native state." Dutch must have been as thrilled as the young ballplayers to see the unfamiliar sights. Leaving from Chicago on February 25, 1935, the traveling party led by manager Charlie Grimm reached Los Angeles on February 28 and immediately embarked on a boat for the choppy, twenty-two-mile ride across the San Pedro Channel to hilly Santa Catalina Island.[51]

Here they discovered "the golden sun of which southern California is the copyright owner," wrote a *Chicago Tribune* reporter. It was not hard to see why the newspaper boasted that its hometown team had the "finest training grounds in baseball": With a palm-lined main street, a "million-dollar hotel," a Moorish-style casino overlooking Avalon Bay, a rare-bird sanctuary, and a "beautiful and sporty golf course," Catalina—dubbed the "Magic Isle" or "the isle with a smile" by promoters—had "become one of the country's greatest summer resorts." In addition to fishing, yachting, golfing, tennis, gambling, hiking, swimming, and beachgoing, the recreations on offer included hunting quail, boar, and wild goats. "Santa Catalina Island has every vacation attraction," boasted a local journalist.[52]

Ocean and sun, hills and beaches, palm trees and chaparral—all of it was powerfully seductive to a young man who had spent his entire life in the frigid climes of the Midwest. Reagan's visit to the captivating Catalina Island would be the beginning of a lifelong love affair with Southern California that would not end until three-quarters of a century later amid the jacaranda trees and jasmine vines of Bel-Air.

———

As if its native charms were not enough, Catalina was tantalizingly close to the "film colony" in Hollywood. Indeed, the island was a frequent location shoot for movies, including *Mutiny on the Bounty*, *Treasure Island*, and *Captain Blood*. Film stars such as Charlie Chaplin, Joan Crawford, and Clark Gable were regular visitors, and many kept their yachts anchored in the harbor. In 1937, on his third visit to spring training, shortly after Franklin Roosevelt had delivered his second inaugural address lamenting that "one third" of the nation remained "ill-housed, ill-clad, ill-nourished," Dutch finally took advantage of Catalina's proximity to Hollywood.

The chronology is a little jumbled in Reagan's memoirs—and in biographies of him—but either at the beginning of the Cubs' spring training on March 9, 1937, or at the end of it on March 25, he snuck away to meet a Des Moines girl who had started off as a teenage singer at WHO and later moved to Los Angeles. A slim brunette with hazel eyes, Joy Hodges was singing with a big band at the nightclub of the Biltmore Hotel, one of the top venues in town, and performing bit parts for RKO Pictures. Between floor shows at the palatial hotel lavishly decorated in gold, marble, crystal, and bronze, she came out to join Dutch for dinner. No doubt she figured his intentions were romantic. He confessed the truth: He wanted to break into the pictures. "Take off those glasses," Joy told him. "Don't ever put them on again!" Seeing Dutch without those "awful horn-rimmed glasses," Joy decided he was handsome enough to be a matinee idol. She promised to connect him with her talent agent.

The next day, George Ward of the William Meiklejohn Agency would recall a tall Midwesterner striding into his office on Sunset Boulevard with "a 150-watt smile." Ward noted, "Built-up shoulder pads in the suit. Wide lapels. Close-cut hair. All standard for the year." With his vision blurry because he had taken off his glasses, Dutch Reagan gave the agent, he recalled, "a somewhat exaggerated description of my qualifications for movie stardom." Publicity material subsequently released by Warner

Brothers would falsely claim he had been part of a "small repertoire stock company playing in Peoria, Eureka, Ill., and Davenport, Iowa."[53] Dutch then asked, desperately, "Look, Joy told me that you would level with me. Should I go back to Des Moines and forget this, or what do I do?"

Without another word, or so Reagan later recalled, Ward picked up the phone and called Maxwell Arnow, a wunderkind casting director at Warner Brothers who would become known for discovering stars from Humphrey Bogart to Jack Lemmon. "Max, I have another Robert Taylor sitting in my office," Ward said with trademark Hollywood hyperbole, referring to the star of such pictures as *Magnificent Obsession* and *Camille*. Taylor was nicknamed the "Man with the Perfect Profile" and was one of the top leading men of the 1930s; he would later become one of Reagan's closest friends. Dutch supposedly could hear Arnow's booming retort on the phone: "God made only one Robert Taylor!" But he agreed to take a look at the newcomer.

A brief interview on the Warner lot left Reagan with "the impression of being apprised like a slab of beef." Arnow must have liked what he saw because he agreed to give Dutch a screen test. Joy Hodges later said that Dutch "really 'snowed' Max Arnow . . . with his fantastic gift of gab." Arnow gave the radio announcer a few pages to memorize from the script of a Broadway play. In one memoir, Reagan said it was *Holiday*, in another *The Philadelphia Story*. It's obvious why they would blur together in his mind: Both were romantic comedies, based on plays written by Philip Barry, that would be made into movies starring Cary Grant and Katharine Hepburn. Reagan was no Cary Grant, but he did develop a flair for this type of film. He rehearsed his lines with Joy Hodges, who "couldn't believe his ability to read a page and practically recite it back."

The screen test took place, according to a contemporaneous newspaper account, on Monday, March 29, 1937, the very day that the conservative Supreme Court, under pressure from a newly reelected President Roosevelt, upheld a minimum wage law in Washington after having previously overturned a similar law in New York.[54] (This became known as the "switch in time that saved nine" because it rendered moot the president's threats to expand the court's membership to win approval for New Deal programs.) Arnow did Dutch no favors by teaming him with a minor B movie actress—Helen Valkis—but at least let him audition with an experienced director and cameraman. Arnow promised to show the results to Jack L. Warner, the autocratic studio boss, and asked Reagan to stick around to hear the verdict. Dutch replied that he had to go back to work in Des Moines.

On the train ride back to Iowa, he kept kicking himself for not staying in Los Angeles, worried he had just blown his best chance at stardom. His worst fears seemed to be confirmed when by Thursday he had still heard nothing. Dutch was a bundle of nerves but couldn't tell anyone at the radio station why. He did not want to admit to having taken a screen test if the result was to be rejection and dejection.

On Friday morning, April 2, while fighting raged in the Spanish Civil War and sit-down strikes hit automobile plants in Detroit, Dutch came to WHO as usual and made straight for the mailroom. There he discovered a telegram that had arrived the night before. It was from George Ward: SCREEN TEST OKAY. MAILING $200-A-WEEK CONTRACT. Dutch was so excited he immediately threw the rest of his mail away, jumped about three feet in the air, and let out a whoop, startling those who were standing next to him. Once he calmed down a bit, he claims to have sent back a reply: SIGN BEFORE THEY CHANGE THEIR MINDS.

Joy Hodges dispatched a breathless telegram from Los Angeles to break the news to the *Des Moines Tribune*: YOU DO HAVE POTENTIAL STAR IN YOUR MIDST. . . . THEY CONSIDER HIM GREATEST GET SINCE TAYLOR WITHOUT GLASSES. The makers of Wheaties tried to convince him to stick around to call another season of the Cubs, but Dutch's mind was made up: He was California bound.[55]

Ronald Reagan had already achieved regional renown as a radio announcer in Des Moines. Now he had the opportunity to achieve much greater—and more lucrative—fame in Hollywood. But he knew perfectly well that lots of new talent was signed by the studios all the time and just as quickly jettisoned when they did not live up to the hype. The press was full of stories such as that of an actress who had been dropped by RKO and committed suicide by leaping off the HOLLYWOODLAND sign.[56] Simply because he had gotten his foot in the door did not mean he could get all the way inside. His potential was limitless, but his actual trajectory remained unknown.

He signed a seven-year contract, receiving a considerable boost from his announcer's salary of $75 a week, with potential built-in raises up to $1,000 a week in his final year. But for the first two years the deal was renewable every six months; thereafter it was renewable every year.[57] The studio bosses were only taking an "option" on him—not making a binding commitment. They could get rid of him anytime they wanted. This was merely a tryout, and he knew it. "I may be out there for only the six months," he admitted.[58]

Stardom still seemed improbable; the odds of being just a flash in the pan remained strong. But, at age twenty-six, Dutch Reagan was about to embark on the most exciting and nerve-racking gamble of his young life on the world's biggest stage. His father had singularly failed to achieve the American Dream—a term that first came into common usage in the 1930s when upward mobility appeared to be more myth than reality.[59] Now it was the son's turn to try.

ACT II

ACTOR

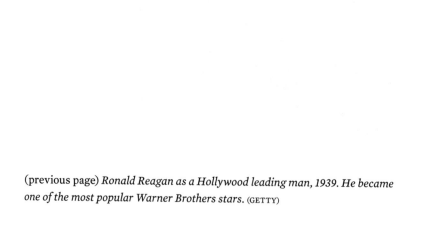

(previous page) *Ronald Reagan as a Hollywood leading man, 1939. He became one of the most popular Warner Brothers stars.* (GETTY)

8

Hayseed in Hollywood

I suppose when I get a little more accustomed to meeting celebrities at every turn, I'll get over the feeling of a small boy spending his first day in school.

—RONALD REAGAN

In heading out West, Ronald Reagan was joining one of the largest population migrations in American history. Between 1935 and 1938, roughly a quarter of a million people fleeing drought and dust would pack up all their belongings and relocate to California. Because so many came from Oklahoma, they became known as "Okies"—a term popularized in John Steinbeck's 1939 novel *The Grapes of Wrath*.[1] But, unlike the destitute and desperate Okies, the already well-off sportscaster from Des Moines was not heading to California to pick grapes or assemble aircraft. He was joining one of the most influential, indeed fabled, industries in the entire country—and one of the few to stage an economic rebound by the late 1930s. The movie studios, like the rest of the economy, had been battered by the Great Depression but had recovered faster than most other sectors. By 1936, average weekly attendance was up to eighty-eight million people a week, a new high, as moviegoers flocked to these "dream palaces" to escape the misery of their lives.[2] By 1939, the nation had more theaters (15,115) than banks (14,952), and Hollywood was producing 80 percent of all motion pictures in the world. Louis B. Mayer—head of the most successful studio, Metro-Goldwyn-Mayer (MGM)—was the highest-paid executive in the country, with an annual salary of $1.3 million.[3]

This era would later be acclaimed as the Golden Age of Hollywood, with 1939—the year of *Gone with the Wind*, *The Wizard of Oz*, *Stagecoach*, *Mr. Smith Goes to Washington*, and other classics—dubbed the "Greatest Year in Motion Pictures."[4] Even movies that seemed to have nothing to do with the Depression offered much-needed psychological balm to audiences of the 1930s. As noted by cultural critic Morris Dickstein, *The Wizard of Oz* included "plaintive longing for something better, that place at the end of the Yellow Brick Road," while *Gone with the Wind* reminded viewers that, however much adversity they faced, "tomorrow is another day."[5]

Hollywood's cultural cachet was immense: Tens of millions of Americans learned how they were supposed to look and behave while watching flickering images in the dark. When Clark Gable undressed to reveal that he was not wearing an undershirt in *It Happened One Night* (1934), sales of men's underwear were said to precipitously decline.[6] "It was directly through the movies that I learned to kiss a girl on her ears, neck, and cheeks, as well as on the mouth, in a close huddle," a male college student—a contemporary of Ronald Reagan's—wrote in 1929. Female students, meanwhile, recalled copying "Mary Pickford's curls and spunk," "Theda Bara's 'vamping' and man-killing star," and "Greta Garbo's languid walk," while their younger sisters would be equally influenced by Katharine Hepburn, Myrna Loy, Bette Davis, and other leading actresses of the 1930s.[7]

All of the film stars received vast numbers of fan letters from ordinary moviegoers and extensive, usually rapturous, coverage from fan magazines and powerful gossip columnists like Hedda Hopper and Louella Parsons—all carefully managed, of course, by studio press agents. Hortense Powdermaker, the first anthropologist to study the industry, wrote in 1950, "The star is not only an actor, but one of the gods or folk heroes in our society."[8] Summoned to Hollywood, Dutch would now be given the opportunity to find his own pedestal on this celluloid Mount Olympus of the cinematic deities.

Yet the stars, while objects of veneration for the moviegoing masses, were, like millions of Americans in other fields, simply salaried employees. The studio bosses, who would do so much to shape American culture, were themselves outsiders who were looked down upon by Eastern society and even by the Los Angeles business elite. Because so many of them were either Jewish immigrants from Eastern Europe or just one generation removed from the proverbial shtetl, they were denied entry to L.A.'s country clubs and so created their own in the Hillcrest Country Club. Many of them had found their way to the film business in the first place simply because it was so new that there were fewer barriers to entry and less antisemitism than in more established professions. As Neal Gabler wrote in his magisterial history *An Empire of Their Own: How the Jews Invented Hollywood*, the Hollywood Jews, denied a place at the *echt* American supper table, would fabricate on the screen an imagined, idealized coun-try "where fathers were strong, families stable, people attractive, resilient, resourceful, and decent."

Little wonder that Ronald Reagan would feel so at home in Hollywood: Having imbibed this fictionalized picture of America as a moviegoer him-self, he would propagate it in his own films and political campaigns. It was, Gabler noted acidly, "a fictive rehabilitation of the moguls' own lives—lives where fathers had been weak, families destabilized, people unattractive, doomed, impractical and indifferent." He might just as well have been describing the Reagan family, though they were decidedly not Jewish.[9]

The brothers Warner—Dutch's new employers—were typical of the movie moguls. Their father, originally known as Benjamin Wonsal, was a Jewish cobbler from Poland. Fleeing pogroms, he landed in Castle Garden, New York, in 1883, a quarter century after Ronald Reagan's family had arrived at the same port of entry, where, like so many other newcomers, they angli-cized their names. Eventually, the family settled in Youngstown, Ohio, with their nine surviving children. Four of the boys would eventually create a movie studio in which they would, in turn, change their ethnic actors' names to sound as quintessentially Anglo-American as their own. Like Jack and Nelle Reagan, they were not high school graduates. They had gotten into the film business in 1907 by purchasing a Kinetoscope, a primitive film projector invented by Thomas Edison, and renting a makeshift theater to display one of the first motion pictures, *The Great Train Robbery*, to Mid-western steelworkers and their families. Admission was five cents, and the chairs were borrowed from a neighboring funeral home.

From projecting motion pictures, it was only a short leap to making them. In 1912 the Warner brothers filmed their first "photoplays" at an abandoned foundry in St. Louis. That same year they opened their first office in Los Angeles near a neighborhood that would become synonymous with mov-iemaking. Hollywood already was drawing filmmakers with its Mediter-ranean climate, which made outdoor filming possible year-round, and its proximity to all sorts of locations—from downtown street scenes to moun-tains, deserts, oceans, beaches, and of course Catalina Island, which often served as a stand-in for the South Pacific. The movie industry would soon move largely outside of the geographical confines of Hollywood, but its roots would remain forever associated with the orange-grove locale of yore.

The Warners' first hit was an anti-German, wartime film, *My Four Years in Germany* (1917), based on the memoirs of a former US ambassador to Germany. In the 1920s, the apogee of silent films, the Warners' studio was considered a third-rate operation on Hollywood's "Poverty Row" far behind the industry leaders, Metro-Goldwyn-Mayer and Paramount. The Warners' biggest star was a German shepherd, Rin Tin Tin, who was rewarded with a salary of $1,000 a week, a diamond-studded collar, and T-bone steaks for dinner. *The Jazz Singer* changed all that. Released in 1927, it was the first motion picture with sound—but far from the first or last to feature a white actor in racist blackface. Its storyline—a Jewish immigrant, played by Al Jolson, eschewing a traditional way of life to make it in show business—struck close to home for the Warner brothers. Other moguls had dismissed sound as a passing fad—"a gimmick," scoffed Adolph Zukor of Paramount—but the Warners had seized on this untested new technology and reaped the rewards. After *The Jazz Singer* was released, Jack Warner boasted, in his characteristically uncouth way, that "the dough was rolling in faster than they could count it."

By the time a genial twenty-six-year-old radio announcer drove from Iowa in 1937 to join its stable, Warner Brothers had a hundred-acre lot in Burbank, and its constellation of stars included Jimmy Cagney, Edward G. Robinson, Paul Muni, Humphrey Bogart, Bette Davis, and Olivia de Havilland. Warner was known for "ripped from the headlines" gangster pictures, such as *Little Caesar*, *The Roaring Twenties*, and *The Public Enemy*, and socially conscious melodramas, such as *They Drive by Night* and *I Am a Fugitive from a Chain Gang*, featuring outcasts rebelling against an unjust American society. The Warner brothers were unusual among the Hollywood moguls in backing Franklin D. Roosevelt early on, although they reverted to the Republican fold in 1936 when Alf Landon challenged FDR, and many of their pictures displayed a New Deal sensibility. Warner Brothers would be the first studio to produce an anti-Nazi picture: *Confessions of a Nazi Spy* in 1939. But they also made frothy Busby Berkeley musicals such as *42nd Street* and *Gold Diggers of 1933*, notable for their surrealism and sensuality, and exciting Errol Flynn swashbucklers, such as *Captain Blood* and *The Adventures of Robin Hood*. In 1940 another demanding star would join the Warner Brothers roster: Bugs Bunny.

Overseeing this assembly line of dreams were Harry Warner, the company's genteel president based in New York, and his younger, more vulgar brother Jack L. Warner, the vice president and production chief in Los Angeles. The two men loathed each other. Harry once chased Jack around the studio lot with a lead pipe, screaming "I'll kill you, you son of a bitch," and Harry's widow later accused Jack of driving him to an early grave in 1958 by stealing the studio out from under him. (Jack did not attend Harry's funeral.)

They were, in fairness, very different personalities—even more different than Moon and Dutch Reagan. Harry was kind and honest, a devout Jew, and a devoted family man. He stayed married to the mother of his three children, and there was never a hint of scandal around his life. Jack, by contrast, was irreligious, foul-mouthed, and hedonistic. He wagered large amounts of money in the casinos of the French Riviera and scandalized Harry by divorcing his first wife and marrying his pregnant mistress. Like many of the movie moguls, he took advantage of the casting couch in ways that would be considered scandalous and even illegal today. One leading student of Hollywood has described Jack Warner, with his flashing white teeth, slicked-back hair, and pencil mustache, as "vain, ignorant, pretentious, deceitful, greedy, ruthless." When challenged, Jack had the ultimate retort: "Whose name is on the water tower?" The studio's iconic 133-foot water tower featured, of course, the famous WB logo.

With good reason, few of Jack Warner's employees liked or trusted him, and some of the studio's most prominent actors waged lengthy battles to get out of their contracts. Now Dutch would have to please this mercurial and disputatious tyrant to attain his most treasured ambition: movie stardom.[10]

On May 19, 1937, while a new recession was setting back the economic recovery—unemployment, which had fallen to 14 percent, would spike to 20 percent in 1937–1938[11]—radio station WHO threw an on-air goodbye party for Dutch Reagan. Among those paying tribute to him were the mayor of Des Moines and the state treasurer of Iowa—a sign of his prominence. "This sterling Dixon young man," his hometown newspaper reported, was "rendered speechless, as he admitted, for the first time in his life."[12] Four days later, Dutch hopped into his two-tone Nash convertible and headed west.

In *The Grapes of Wrath*, John Steinbeck captured the terror of tenant farmers in flight along Highway 66, seeking to reach California in rattling old jalopies piled high with mattresses and household goods, whose "ancient leaky radiators sent up columns of steam" and whose worn-out tires were liable to blow at any moment. As they pulled over to the side of the highway to repair their trucks or to sleep for the night, the Okies marveled at the "fine cars . . . cruising at sixty-five," going right by them on the way to California, so that *their* occupants could "sit in the lobby of the Beverly-Wilshire hotel" and "look at the Pacific Ocean" and say, "It isn't as big as I thought it would be."[13] Dutch Reagan wasn't going to California as a tourist, but he was in one of those big, fancy cars whizzing by, heading for an existence that would remain only a flickering fantasy to Steinbeck's subjects.

Reagan had initially intended to take it easy on the road but soon found himself pushing the gas pedal harder, driving faster and faster in his anxiety to open a new chapter in his life. He was stopped for speeding in Salt Lake City—he was doing sixty miles per hour in a twenty-five-mph zone—but the cop let him go after he explained he was heading for Hollywood to become an actor. He had to take out his contract to prove he wasn't kidding. The last stretch—the six hundred miles from Nephi, Utah, to Los Angeles—was "one awful ride," Reagan recalled, since he was "crossing the hot desert in the middle of the day." Finally arriving in Los Angeles, he made his way to the only hotel he knew: the Biltmore. He was bone tired but felt he "would have been lower than the underside of a snake" if he didn't express his appreciation to Joy Hodges for giving him his big break. He went to her show that night intending to do just that. The next thing he knew, Joy was shaking him awake, telling him, "Hey, Dutch, you can't sleep here. You'd better go upstairs and climb into the hay. Besides, that bowl of soup doesn't make a very good pillow." Yet, exhausted as he was, he was so excited that he tossed and turned all night.[14]

The next day, "dressed in [his] best bib and tucker," Dutch reported to Maxwell Arnow at Warner Brothers to launch his movie career. He immediately learned that, as a veteran costume designer was later to write, "A star was not born, but made." The first priority was to find him a name. Hollywood was notorious for changing the names of its stars: Frederic Austerlitz became Fred Astaire, Marion Morris became John Wayne, Emanuel Goldenberg became Edward G. Robinson, Archibald Leach became Cary

Grant. Arnow and several press agents sat around the table looking at Dutch and wondering, "What name does he look like?" As they were throwing out suggestions, Reagan interrupted to point out that he already had a lot of name recognition in the Midwest. One of them objected that they couldn't put "Dutch Reagan" on a marquee. So the newcomer said, "What about Ronald? . . . Ronald Reagan?" "Hey, that's not bad," someone replied. All he had to drop was his nickname. In Los Angeles, for the first time in his life, he would be known as Ron or Ronnie. "I walked out of the room with my own name," he chortled.[15]

But in other respects the newcomer had to undergo a makeover. "Where did you get that haircut?" one of the studio hairstylists demanded. "It looks like somebody cut it with bowl number seven." His hair was short and parted down the middle. From now on he would grow his hair longer, slick it back, and part it on the side.

Arnow took one look at Dutch's prized new white sport coat and told him, "You can't wear that outfit. The shoulders are too big—they make your head look too small." A tailor "ruthlessly attacked" his treasured jacket, Dutch recalled, taking all the looseness out and making the shoulders narrower. But Arnow was still dissatisfied: Reagan's neck looked too short for his head. Jimmy Cagney, one of Warner's biggest stars, had the same problem, so they sent him to Cagney's shirtmaker and told him to have all his shirts made with an extra-wide collar and to use a wide Windsor knot for his ties to reduce the gap between his lapels. He would wear Cagney-style, wide-collar shirts with a big Windsor knot for the rest of his life.[16]

The studio wasted no time in putting its newest contract player to work. His first part wasn't much of a stretch: He played a crusading radio announcer who uncovers racketeers in his small Midwestern town. When shooting started on stage eight on June 21, 1937, as the nation's steel industry remained shut by a monthlong strike, Reagan wrote, "I was as jittery as a June bride." But his stage fright faded when the director shouted "Action!" and the camera began to roll. He found himself "completely surrounded by a wall of light" that made it impossible to see anyone. "It gave me a feeling of privacy that completely dispelled any nervousness I might have experienced," he wrote. He was overjoyed when the director Nick

Grinde yelled "Cut!"—"I'd made my first movie scene," he exulted. "I was an ACTOR"—only to discover, to his dismay, that he had a dozen more takes in front of him.[17]

The movie, originally called *Inside Story* and released as *Love Is on the Air*, took three weeks to shoot and ran only sixty-one minutes. This was one of the short, low-budget, B pictures that the studios churned out to appear on a double bill alongside longer, more prestigious A pictures. A movies typically cost $200,000 to $400,000 to make, while Bs ran $50,000 to $100,000. These lesser efforts, produced at Warner Brothers by former child actor Bryan Foy, known as the "Keeper of the Bs," represented fully half of the studio's output in the 1930s. Churned out at the rate of more than one a week, they provided a steady stream of revenue and allowed the studio to try out new talent like Ronald Reagan.[18] "They were movies the studio didn't want good," Reagan later wrote, "they wanted 'em Thursday."[19]

But even (or perhaps especially) on the most minor of films, there was no slacking off. "Hollywood is engaged in the mass production of prefabricated daydreams," wrote Hortense Powdermaker, and, just like workers in a garment or steel plant, movie-industry employees enjoyed little downtime because of the relentless production quotas.[20] Many actors sought solace from the unrelenting pressure in drinking, pill-taking, or bed-hopping. "I find myself, amazingly enough, up at 6 A.M. in order to be on the job, ready and made-up by nine, when work starts promptly," Reagan wrote in a column for the *Des Moines Register*. "We rarely finish for the day before 7 P.M., and after an intensive nine or 10 hours under the hot lights, Mrs. Reagan's boy Ronald is ready, willing and able to hit the hay. . . . Radio work is a cinch by comparison. I used to consider two hours at the broadcasting station a long day."[21]

The world-weary Warner Brothers production chief Hal B. Wallis, who would be best known for producing *Casablanca*—only to have Jack Warner elbow him out of the way to claim the Best Picture Oscar for himself[22]—initially referred contemptuously to the newcomer as a "hick radio announcer."[23] Reagan himself later half-heartedly denied having ever been an "Iowa hayseed," but he sure came across as one. He was both in awe of the industry and "a little bit scared" of it; he worried that his good fortune "seems too good to last." A year later, he admitted to having been "scared stiff" when he first arrived in Hollywood.[24]

Reagan expected a lot of ribbing because he was the new kid on the set, but he was pleasantly surprised to find what he imagined to be a supportive, small-town-like atmosphere. He wrote that "everyone has been helpful and friendly and I have yet to encounter the slightest trace of ill-will or jealousy among my fellow workers." A cynic might reply that the backbiting would start when he became more successful—but Reagan's good nature ensured that seldom happened. He was impressed by everything from his colleagues' professionalism ("The efficiency of the crew is remarkable. . . . Everything works with clock-like precision") to the generous box lunches provided on location: "Each box, I discovered, contained half a fried chicken, a jelly and cheese sandwich, an apple or a banana, a piece of cake, pickles, a hard-boiled egg and a candy bar."[25]

When Reagan went out to dinner at a Polynesian restaurant on Vine Street called The Tropics with his *Love Is on the Air* costar June Travis, he gushed about meeting Pat O'Brien and his "charming wife." "Pat has been a favorite of mine for years," Reagan wrote of the Irish American actor who often costarred in pictures such as *Ceiling Zero* and *Angels with Dirty Faces* with his good friend James Cagney. Reagan was delighted to discover that "Pat is a great guy, just as you'd imagine him to be after seeing him on the screen. He's always got a good story on tap and he's one man who doesn't have to depend on smut to put a yarn over."[26] This was one of Reagan's highest accolades—he described his father the same way.

Dutch's dispatches to the *Des Moines Register*—he had agreed to write a column chronicling the start of his movie career—detailed all the other stars he met and how impressed he was by them. Here's Olivia de Havilland in the dressing room with her face smeared in cold cream. There's Errol Flynn in the commissary having lunch with a former boxer. He could hardly believe that the matinee idols "seemed to be just like ordinary humans." "I suppose when I get a little more accustomed to meeting celebrities at every turn," he acknowledged, "I'll get over the feeling of a small boy spending his first day in school."[27]

Reagan's initial, indiscriminate enthusiasm for all things Hollywood was naive, but it was also charming and unaffected. He had yet to experience the seamy side of the industry exposed in novels such as Budd Schulberg's *What Makes Sammy Run?* (1941), whose protagonist, the youthful striver Sammy Glick, proclaims that "going through life with a conscience is like driving your car with the brakes on."[28]

Reagan was in awe not just of Hollywood but of the whole city of Los Angeles. It was already the nation's fifth-largest metropolis, with more than 1.5 million residents, and growing fast. The architecture was a dizzying hodgepodge of styles very different from Dixon, Des Moines, or any other city. Middle-class residents lived in modest stucco bungalows or low-rise apartment houses, while movie stars, noted the journalist Margaret Talbot, built "imitation French chateaux, sprawling Spanish-style haciendas, columned replicas of stately plantation homes, Moorish castles with pointed arches." Adding to the air of unreality—many observers remarked that parts of Los Angeles looked like a movie set—some stores and restaurants were built to resemble the products they were selling. The original Brown Derby restaurant on Wilshire Boulevard, for example, was constructed in the shape of a big brown derby. The soundtrack to the city was provided, Talbot observed, by the nonstop "swish-swish of sprinklers" that kept lawns green in this desert-by-the-sea. There was, of course, also a down-and-out side of town that was all but invisible to the insulated denizens of the "film colony"—unless they went "slumming" in some *au courant* dive—chronicled by such authors as John Fante, Nathanael West, and Raymond Chandler.[29]

Reagan was most impressed by all "the facilities for exercise and sport" in Southern California. "A person who doesn't spend nine-tenths of his leisure time out of doors here," he lectured, "is either senile or just plain lazy." Before long he was surfing—not a sport he could have learned on the Rock River.[30] Yet, while he was far from the heartland, he was constantly surrounded by fellow transplants from the Midwest. Some wits even referred to Southern California as the "Iowa coast."[31] The very newness of Los Angeles—hardly anyone, it seemed, had been born there—made it much easier for newcomers like Dutch to blend in. "I'm a midwesterner (Illinois) but I became a westerner after a short time," Reagan later wrote. "I guess the poet Robert W. Service said it when he wrote the line, 'The land of gold held him as if in a spell.' "[32]

Once his Des Moines buddies joined Dutch in Los Angeles, they formed a proto–"Rat Pack" that was often out on the town together. One night in July 1937 they discovered a restaurant on the Sunset Strip called Bit o' Sweden with an all-you-can-eat buffet featuring "bits of ham, pickled fish, spice meat and goodness knows what else." They ate so much, Dutch wrote, that "you purr like a cat and don't give a whoop."³³ Another night, he and his buddies went out to dine at the Brown Derby and then moved on to a dance hall called the Palomar, where they met some girls and "sang several Iowa songs." "We had a swell time," he reported, employing his favorite adjective of approbation.³⁴

Before long the gang had a hangout of their own—a beer and hamburger shack on Santa Monica Boulevard called Barney's Beanery—to replace Cy's Moonlight Inn. Given the homophobic attitudes of the day, they saw nothing wrong with the crude, misspelled, hand-painted wooden sign displayed behind the bar: "Fagots—Stay Out!"³⁵

Reagan's first movie, *Love Is on the Air*, finally came out in September 1937. Seeing it for the first time at a preview in Huntington Park, California, he wrote, "I almost died.... I tried to appear nonchalant but I am sure I only looked sick." It was only a B picture, so it didn't get many reviews, but the *Hollywood Reporter*, a trade newspaper, commended its star as a "natural" who was—no surprise—"completely at home" in his role as a radio announcer. *Film Daily* was less impressed, writing that the picture "was not much of anything."³⁶

Unsurprisingly, the film received its "world premiere" in Des Moines, complete with klieg lights arcing into the sky. The 1,700 moviegoers in the cavernous Paramount theater roared their approval for the "handsome movie newcomer." According to a reporter, Nelle Reagan "with a lace-trimmed handkerchief poked at tears that coursed down her lined cheeks" and whispered, "That's my boy. That's my Dutch." Jack Reagan's laconic verdict: "Mighty good show."³⁷

By then their son had already filmed bit parts in two A movies and was the leading man in another B picture, *Sergeant Murphy*, playing a cavalryman who was devoted to his horse. Reagan enjoyed riding during the location shoot on the Monterey Peninsula in Northern California but had the bruises to show for it. "I'm wearing a lump as big as a goose egg where my bump of knowledge ought to be," he wrote in August 1937.³⁸

By September 1937—just three months after his arrival in Hollywood—Reagan was already acting like a jaded veteran of the industry. "It's a tough racket," he wrote, doing his best approximation of one of Warner Brothers' hard-boiled heroes, "but when you consider the rewards you're shooting at—fame such as couldn't be won in any other profession and wealth that amounts to dizzying heights—it's worth the chances you take."[39]

Those rewards were now drawing tantalizingly near. On October 3, Reagan exulted in his last column for the *Des Moines Register*: "MY OPTION'S BEEN TAKEN UP."[40] He would be employed for at least six more months— and with a pay raise. He was drawing closer to the pantheon of movie stars— and closer too, although he did not yet suspect it, to matrimony.

9

The White Knight

*[Jane Wyman] did the chasing, and doesn't
give a hoot who knows it.*

—*Modern Screen*

I t is a story as old as Hollywood: A newcomer with virtuous, hometown values attains stardom and loses his or her bearings amid the temptations of Tinseltown. Even in 1937, when the first version of *A Star Is Born* came out (with Janet Gaynor and Fredric March), it was already a cliché. By then the "film colony" had acquired a notorious reputation because of one scandal after another among its overpaid, oversexed stars—beginning with the 1921 manslaughter trial of comedian Roscoe "Fatty" Arbuckle after a showgirl died at a raucous party to celebrate his newly signed contract with Paramount. It didn't matter that Arbuckle was ultimately acquitted. His career was ruined, and Hollywood's reputation as the "Babylon of the West" was established. Soon, censorious journalists and politicians were denouncing, like modern-day Savonarolas, "the debaucheries, the looseness, the rottenness of Hollywood."[1]

Little wonder that Nelle Reagan was initially nervous about her boy going to "such a wicked place as Hollywood." Pete MacArthur, the program director at WHO, reassured her by telling her that he had spied Dutch in one of the radio station's studios, praying alone and on his knees. "I feel I can trust him anywhere, he has never lost his high ideals of life," Nelle wrote to the Reverend Ben Cleaver and his wife. "He does love God, and he never forgets to thank him for all his many blessings."[2]

Nelle need not have worried. Dutch's "Midwest ethic" would remain largely unaffected by his years in Hollywood. Ronald Reagan remained a straight arrow long before he was advertising Arrow shirts. His old-fashioned values, evident in his concern for his parents, would soon attract an ambitious and talented actress—Jane Wyman—who would supplant Nelle as the most important woman in his life.

Jack Reagan had suffered a heart attack and been forced to leave the federal payroll in June 1936. Ever since, Dutch had been sending $120 a month home to his parents. In the days before Social Security—which did not issue its first benefit check until 1940—his remittances had become their main source of support. When he finally got settled in Hollywood, he promised to bring them out. "Thinking that makes me so happy," Nelle told the Cleavers. "He thinks I can live my last days, making a home for him, it's almost more happiness than I ever expected in this life."[3]

Dutch was as good as his word. As soon as his contract was renewed, he moved his parents to Los Angeles in the fall of 1937.[4] Initially, he rented them an apartment near his own. He was living at 6650 Franklin Avenue in the ten-story, Art Deco Montecito apartment building, which still stands, and which counted many other actors among its residents. It was located conveniently close to the landmark Musso & Frank Grill, a movie-industry haunt known for its dark paneling, red booths, and perfectly mixed martinis. Then, in 1940, when he was making even more money, Reagan bought his folks the only home they would ever own, a bungalow at 9031 Phyllis Avenue in West Hollywood. Jack, who was often short of breath and did not have long to live, loved puttering around the backyard garden.[5]

Nelle immediately became active in the Hollywood-Beverly Christian Church, visiting prisons and medical institutions to comfort the afflicted just as she had done back in Dixon. To give Jack something to do besides tending his rosebushes, Ron arranged with the studio for his dad to be in charge of answering his fan mail—which was increasing commensurate with his larger roles.

With his uncomplaining dedication to learning his lines and hitting his marks, Ronald Reagan was pleasing his demanding bosses—Jack Warner and Bryan Foy—and they kept casting him in one picture after another. He appeared in eight films in 1938, eight in 1939, and six in 1940. Most are long-forgotten B pictures, but he was usually the star.[6] In 1938 he was even cast in his own series of action pictures as Secret Service agent Brass Bancroft—an obvious attempt to cash in on the popularity of movies glamorizing the FBI, such as the 1935 Warner Brothers picture *G-Men* starring Jimmy Cagney.

The first Brass Bancroft picture—*Secret Service of the Air*—came out in 1939. The publicity department, with its trademark understatement, announced it as "the first out-rider of a veritable cavalcade of thrilling and absorbing screen entertainment" and described its star as "tall, good-looking, charming, and intensely virile."[7]

Reagan would star in four Brass Bancroft movies in all. In truth, they were not that thrilling. The *New York Times* called *Secret Service of the Air*—the first and best of the series—"an uninspired reworking of the old story about smuggling aliens across the border."[8] For a modern viewer, used to the special effects of the computer age, they are virtually unwatchable. But however ludicrous their plots and low-rent their props, they would inspire recruits for the Secret Service—including a future agent named Jerry Parr, who would one day save President Reagan's life.[9] Ronald Reagan was the 1930s version of an action hero; although never nearly as famous as Tom Cruise or Jackie Chan, like them he did many of his own stunts. His hearing problems began when a blank .38 cartridge was fired too close to his ear on the set of *Secret Service of the Air*.[10] His growing success could be attributed more to his all-American looks and earnest demeanor than to acting skill. "I became the Errol Flynn of the B's," he recalled. "I was as brave as Errol, but in a low-budget fashion."[11]

The Australian-born Flynn, one of the biggest draws in Hollywood, had charisma to burn, but he was also a notorious sybarite in lifelong rebellion against the strictures of polite society. He was often hungover on the set and the subject of lurid tabloid headlines off of it; he would be tried (and acquitted) on statutory rape charges in 1942. So great was his reputation as a rake that men were known to brag after a sexual conquest that they were "in like Flynn." During a typical production, an exasperated Warner executive wrote that Flynn continually complained, did not study his lines, and refused to work past the afternoon—"his attitude has been that of the typical star."[12] Reagan was not nearly as talented an actor as Flynn, as he was the first to admit, but he was a lot easier to work with and never got into any trouble. Vincent Sherman, a veteran moviemaker who directed Reagan in *The Hasty Heart* (1949), described him in terms similar to those employed by his college coach Mac McKinzie: "He was easy to work with, always knew his lines, was conscientious and took direction." That assessment was echoed by the director Fred de Cordova. Before going on to a long career in television (*Leave It to Beaver, My Three Sons, The Tonight Show*), he directed Reagan in

Bedtime for Bonzo (1951) and later said, "He was a director's delight—always on time, always totally prepared, and extremely cooperative."[13]

That may have been faint praise coming from hard-bitten Hollywood professionals, but Ronald Reagan's growing legions of fans, especially female fans, were more exuberant in singing his praises. *Motion Picture* magazine billed Reagan in 1939, only two years after his arrival in Hollywood, as the "New Answer to Maidens' Prayers." The fan magazine reported, alongside a hunky picture of the new star—in swim trunks and shirtless to show off his "bronze body"—that girls had been "casting wistful eyes" on the "tall, lithe, well-muscled" former lifeguard who "seems to lack the usual actor-ego. . . . He seems just like the boy you knew in high school or college, the boy you didn't know very well, but the one you wished you knew better."

"The amazing thing to us is not that he is twenty-nine," the magazine gushed, "but that he is twenty-nine and still single. How has he escaped marriage so long?"[14]

Jane Wyman, a fellow Warner Brothers actor, was wondering the same thing—and she was intent on doing something about it. Although six years younger than Reagan (she was born on January 5, 1917), Wyman was vastly more experienced in the movie industry and considerably more cynical about it.

Like Reagan, she was from the Midwest—in her case, St. Joseph, Missouri, a town of a hundred thousand people known for its stockyards—and, like him, she had had a difficult childhood. Her birth name was Sarah Jane Mayfield. Her parents divorced when she was three, and her father died when she was five. Her mother, a secretary, felt unable to take care of the child on her own. Sarah Jane was taken in by Richard and Emma Fulks, a couple in their sixties who had already raised four of their own children. Richard was a former police detective turned local tax collector; Emma was, like Nelle Reagan, a frustrated would-be actress who bequeathed her stage dreams to her child. Emma wanted to make Sarah Jane into a star—and that meant, after the death of her husband in 1928, moving to Los Angeles where two of her older children already lived. Wyman later recalled that she was all too happy to leave a town that both she and her adopted mother viewed as "oppressive, straight-laced, hypocritical." Not for her Reagan's idealization of small-town life; she did not disguise her desire to escape.

Wyman was only fifteen when in 1932 she made her first appearance in a motion picture as part of the chorus line, alongside future stars Betty Grable, Paulette Goddard, and Lucille Ball, in *The Kid from Spain*, a lavish MGM musical. Performing brought Jane out of her shell; like Dutch, she had been a shy, withdrawn child. Discovering that "a good shield for shyness is a bold exterior," she put on enormous false eyelashes, dyed her chestnut brown hair blonde, and adopted a loud and brassy manner. By the time she turned eighteen in 1935, the "apple-cheeked" actress "with a pert little nose and big doe eyes framed by perfectly arched brows" had appeared as an extra in at least eight more pictures. She was signed by Warner in 1936, the year before Reagan joined the studio, and cast as a wisecracking blonde in a series of B pictures. While Ron received top billing in B pictures from the start, Jane started off as a minor player. His starting salary was $200 a week; hers was only $66, reflecting the unequal pay scale between men and women that pervaded American society at the time (and still does). One of her first movies for Warner was the Busby Berkeley musical *Stage Struck* (1936), in which the star, Dick Powell, asks the chorus girl played by Wyman her name. Her memorable reply: "My name is Bessie Fufnick. I swim, dive, imitate wild birds, and play the trombone."

The new Warner "player" was known as Jane Wyman because of a short-lived, early marriage to salesman Eugene Wyman. He was twenty-seven, she only sixteen, when they tied the knot in 1933, although she made herself out to be three years older—a lie that would trail her for the rest of her life. They divorced within two years. In 1937, at age twenty, she married another older gentleman—clothing manufacturer Myron Futterman, who was thirty-five. It seems safe to conclude that Wyman was in search of a father figure to replace her biological and adopted fathers, both now dead. Her second marriage ended in late 1938; in the divorce proceedings, Jane testified that Futterman was jealous of her dealings with other men and her movie career and that she wanted a baby and he didn't (he had children from a prior marriage). By that time Jane had already met Ronald Reagan; his presence in her life probably contributed to her desire to escape from Futterman, although they denied dating while she was still married.

After two bad marriages and five years spent fighting off countless casting-couch Lotharios, Wyman was cynical, jittery, and distrusting of men. She had even suffered a nervous breakdown in 1937. "She was a jumpy one!" recalled her first agent, William Demarest, better known as an actor in Preston Sturges's screwball comedies. "She couldn't stand any man even touching her. Help her down the steps—just a light touch on her arms—and she'd jump sky-high! I guess she got some rough treatment before I met her."

Demarest—a fatherly figure who was known for *not* putting the make on female clients—was just what she was looking for in an agent. Ronald Reagan was just what she was looking for in a husband: a consummate gentleman who would treat her respectfully. As she later said, he was someone she could truly trust. Demarest said that, from Jane's perspective, Ronnie was "the knight on the white charger . . . the dream of true, perfect manhood."[15]

Reagan was often pictured on the town with sexy, up-and-coming starlets such as Susan Hayward and Lana Turner on dates arranged by Warner Brothers publicists to generate news coverage.[16] Such outings were a "fringe benefit to which I usually didn't object," he wrote.[17] Ila Rhodes, his blonde costar in *Secret Service of the Air* (1939), later claimed that their romance had been more serious and, following "lunch-break trysts and weekends out together," he had even given her an engagement ring. But, she added, they broke up after he began to see Jane Wyman more seriously.[18]

That Reagan and Wyman were spending time together was mainly her doing. "She did the chasing, and doesn't give a hoot who knows it," *Modern Screen* magazine reported.[19] "She was the aggressor, the intent pursuer, from the start," Demarest confirmed. Although younger than Reagan, "she was far more worldly and experienced than he was."[20]

They first met when she asked him to sit at her table in the Warner Brothers commissary—reportedly giving him "the full benefit of her big brown eyes." "I liked Ronnie the first time I ever saw him," she recalled. "'He is no fop,' I thought."[21] She tried to convince the Warner publicity department to fix them up only to be told that each of them needed to date bigger names. The romance finally blossomed when they were on location in San Diego making their first movie together in July and August 1938. Based on a Broadway comedy, *Brother Rat* was set at the Virginia Military Institute, where new cadets are called "rats." Jane played the commandant's demure, bookish daughter who falls in love with a "rat" played by Ron. In a classic, corny screen moment, he begins to see how attractive she is when she removes her glasses, leading to their first kiss.

The real-life Reagan, not ready to try another lasting relationship after the pain of his breakup with Margaret Cleaver, was not so easy to snare. Taking the initiative, Jane found out that Ron spent most of his free time swimming, golfing, and horseback riding with his four buddies from Des Moines. Normally her preferred activity was nightclubbing; "athletics," she confessed, "held no charm for me."[22] But, reported *Modern Screen*, "All of a sudden she was a bug for outdoors. Ronnie started hearing what a swell scout the Wyman kid was. Before he knew it, she was one of them."[23]

Ronald Reagan was undoubtedly smitten with the newest member of his gang, and by the spring of 1939, as war was looming in Europe, they were living in the same Art Deco apartment building, at 1326B Londonderry View Drive just north of the Sunset Strip. They may even have been secretly cohabitating in the same apartment at a time when such arrangements were considered scandalous. But he still remained reluctant to marry the twice-divorced, fiery and fragile, insecure and emotionally scarred actress. "She swears she had to work to get him to ask her to say yes," a movie magazine reported. "He liked her fine, but he wasn't awfully quick at falling in love."[24]

In 1989, Nancy Reagan told Edmund Morris that Jane only convinced Ron to marry her by threatening to kill herself if he didn't—and then taking an overdose of pills to show that she was serious. The gossip of a second wife who had no love lost for a predecessor is not, of course, proof of anything. But the overdose story fits the known facts. It was reported at the time that Reagan and Wyman became engaged while she was in the hospital. A movie-industry reporter wrote that, before her hospitalization in October 1939, Wyman was suffering from a bad case of the "nerves" because "Ronnie's male imperviousness was getting her down. If he loved her, why didn't the lunkhead say so? If not, why didn't he quit dating her? She worked herself into such a state that the doctor shipped her to the hospital." Jane's affliction was said to be a "spastic stomach," something that could have been caused by a drug overdose. Lending further credence to this theory is the fact that she was admitted to Hollywood Receiving Hospital where, according to Morris, one young doctor had a reputation as "stomach pumper to the stars."[25]

On November 1, 1939, shortly after Jane's discharge from the hospital, Hollywood's reigning gossip columnist, Louella Parsons, reported the engagement of "two of Hollywood's very nicest young people." Ron had given his bride-to-be a fifty-two-carat amethyst engagement ring (amethyst was his birthstone). "We hope to stay married forever," Wyman gushed to a reporter a few days later.[26]

The wedding ceremony took place before a small group of friends and family, including Jack and Nelle Reagan, on January 26, 1940. The setting was the Wee Kirk o' the Heather, a popular movie-industry chapel modeled on a medieval Scottish church immortalized by Sir Walter Scott. It was located, somewhat incongruously, at Forest Lawn Memorial Park in Glendale, California, so it was often used both for "matches" and "dispatches." The pastor of the Hollywood-Beverly Christian Church officiated at the wedding—Reagan's first and Wyman's third. The bride wore "ice blue satin," sported a sable hat, and carried a "muff to match" with a corsage pinned on it. The groom wore a dark, three-piece suit with a large pocket handkerchief and boutonniere. His best man was Will Scott, one of his Des Moines buddies; Jane's maid of honor was her adopted sister. Since both Jane's biological and adopted fathers were dead, she was given away by Harry Martin, the boozy "clap doctor" to the stars who was married to Louella Parsons. "Docky," as Parsons called her third husband, had a flourishing practice discreetly performing abortions and treating sexually transmitted diseases.[27]

The fifty-nine-year-old gossip columnist had previously taken "Ronnie" and "Janie," along with four other studio up-and-comers, on a two-month, cross-country series of live shows billed as *Hollywood Stars of 1940*.[28] Now she hosted a wedding reception for them at her Beverly Hills home. The newlyweds then went for a brief honeymoon at the El Mirador hotel in Palm Springs, California, before returning to work on the Warner lot.[29] Almost exactly a year later, on January 4, 1941, their first child—Maureen Elizabeth Reagan—was born.

Parsons's role in the nuptials was indicative of the outsize part she played in Reagan's life. It was a monumental stroke of luck for him that the most powerful—and feared—woman in Hollywood happened to come from Dixon, Illinois, too. Being childless, she began to take a maternal interest in his well-being. Just as Reagan had previously benefited from the support of a series of surrogate fathers—the Reverend Ben Hill Cleaver, high school drama teacher B. J. Frazer, college football coach Ralph McKinzie, radio program director Peter MacArthur—so now he benefited from her mentorship. Maureen Reagan was to write that the woman she knew as Aunt

Lolly "was pretty much a fixture in our household during the early years of my childhood."[30]

The actor David Niven described Parsons, cruelly but not inaccurately, as "short, dumpy and dowdy, with large brown eyes and a carefully cultivated vagueness of smile and manner." He noted that she and her hated rival, Hedda Hopper, who together reached seventy-five million readers (plus millions of radio listeners), wielded "power out of all proportion to their ability and a readership out of all proportion to their literacy": "They could help careers and they could hinder careers and they could make private lives hell."[31] The queens of gossip often resorted to blackmail to fill their daily columns. Movie stars who fed them tidbits got favorable treatment; those who refused to cooperate were savaged. Hedda Hopper once quipped that her memoir should be titled "Malice in Wonderland" and called her Beverly Hills manse "the house that fear built."[32] Near the end of her long career, *Life* magazine described Parsons as "narrow, semi-literate, and often moved by blubbering sentimentality" but also as "shrewd," "tough," "wildly generous" to those she liked, and possessed "of inexhaustible energy and a passion for work."[33]

Many actors, David Niven included, chafed at the gossip columnist's incessant, heavy-handed demands and her unctuous pretenses of intimacy. (*Life* noted that Parsons would resort to "tears or temper tantrums in breaking the spirit of an evasive news source.")[34] Ronald Reagan, by contrast, never showed the slightest bit of pique. He was learning an important, early lesson in how to handle the press. "He lent himself to the press, he understood what they wanted and, consequently, they could always get a story from him," recalled a Warner Brothers publicist who worked with him during this period.[35]

Reagan received a considerable boost to his career by becoming one of Parsons's favorites. They shared not only a hometown but also a sensibility. Parsons, dubbed the "First Lady of Hollywood," was a moralistic Catholic convert who saw herself as the guardian of the industry's public image. The liberal playwright Arthur Miller scornfully described the conservative Hedda and Louella as "the police matrons planted at the portals to keep out the sinful, the unpatriotic, and the rebels against propriety."[36] Although she was a gossip columnist, Parsons often played down or even buried scandals in favor of presenting the stars as normal folks who were just as down-to-earth and devoted to their families as her readers. "Popular conception visualizes Hollywood as a place of lace-lined limousines, jewel-inlaid bathtubs, and Bacchanalian banquets," she had written in 1929. "These exotic ideas of what constitute the average film star's daily routine are so directly opposed to the truth that some inspired soul must have invented this fiction."[37] The libertine Errol Flynn flouted her fictionalized image of Hollywood; the straitlaced Ronald Reagan embodied it.

In a revealing article "as told to" writer Gladys Hall for a movie magazine in 1942, Reagan described himself as a "plain guy with a set of homespun features and no frills." "I hold that all of this business about making yourself important by means of externals is no good," he said. "Clothes, being seen in the Right Places, show, swank—No!" He insisted, "Nor do I believe you have to be a standout from your fellow men in order to make your mark in the world. Average will do it. Certainly, if I am to serve as my own guinea pig for this little homily, it will have to do it. For I'm no Flynn or [Charles] Boyer and well I know it. . . . Mr. Norm is my alias, or shouldn't I admit it?" He then listed some of his favorite things:

> I like to swim, hike and sleep (eight hours a night). I'm fairly good at every sport except tennis, which I just don't like. My favorite menu is steaks smothered with onions and strawberry shortcake. I play bridge adequately, collect guns, always carry a penny as a good luck charm and knock wood when I make a boast or express a wish. I have a so-so convertible coupe which I drive myself. I'm interested in politics and governmental problems. My favorite books are "Turnabout" by Thorne Smith, "Babbitt," "Tom Sawyer," "Huckleberry Finn" and the works of Pearl Buck, H. G. Wells, Damon Runyon and Erich Remarque. I'm a fan of Bing Crosby. My favorite actress is my wife. I like things colored green and my favorite flower is the Eastern lilac. I love my wife, baby and home.[38]

It is hard to imagine a better encapsulation of the mid-twentieth-century tastes and mores of Middle America. Note his revulsion toward tennis—a sport then largely limited to the upper class—and his omission of horseback riding, another rich person's pursuit. This article was a pure expression of the egalitarian "Midwestern ethic" he had learned as a child in small-town Illinois, even if one of the entries on the list (*Babbitt*) was mocking those very values. The whole list could have been scripted by a focus group.

Indeed, Reagan cited as his favorite authors the top-selling novelists of the day—authors of such books as *The Good Earth* and *All Quiet on the Western Front* that every middle-class American would have read, or at least pretended to. The singer he was fond of—Bing Crosby—was, by no coincidence, the most popular performer of the 1930s. With the obvious exception of "my favorite actress is my wife," it is a list that could have been compiled by millions of ordinary moviegoers. And that was precisely the point. Interviews like this, whether conducted with Parsons or Hopper or lesser-known journalists, were a key mechanism that studio publicity machines used to secure the allegiance of fans.

With many of the masters of movieland—who really did live bacchanalian lives—such image-making rang false. But not with Ronald Reagan. He owed much of his success—first in show business and then in politics—to his ability to credibly project a "regular guy" image even as he was ascending to heights of success that ordinary people could barely imagine. He would always, in some sense, remain a "hayseed" from the heartland who would avoid being corrupted by Hollywood and, later, Sacramento and Washington. As he wrote in a 1939 article for the *Des Moines Tribune*, "I am mighty grateful—that I haven't gone Hollywood, or actorish, or stuck up." In publicity material released in connection with his first Brass Bancroft picture that year, he said, in that genuine, aw-shucks way of his, "It's still a kick to me to get letters from all over the world. I can't get over the surprise."[39]

Yet the temptations of fame were about to get headier. In 1940 he not only got married. He also finally broke out of the B list.

10

The A List

[Reagan is] a very talented artist . . . and undoubtedly
a star in his own right.

— R. J. OBRINGER

There was a striking asymmetry to the year 1940: chaos and conflict in Europe and Asia, peace and tranquility in America. Although World War II had broken out on September 1, 1939, with Adolf Hitler's invasion of Poland, there followed a period of relative quiet on the western front. The "phony war" ended on April 9, 1940, with the German invasion of Denmark and Norway. Belgium, the Netherlands, and France were the next victims of the German blitzkrieg, leaving Britain, by the summer of 1940, to stand alone against the Nazis. Meanwhile, Japan invaded French Indochina and continued its brutal assault on China. Yet, in the United States, an eerie calm prevailed, and isolationism remained the order of the day.

While Europeans and Asians were trying to survive in the midst of cataclysmic conflicts, Americans remained focused on their families and careers. Ronald Reagan was no different from anyone else. As an avid consumer of news, he was closely following the disturbing developments abroad, but his attention as 1940 began was riveted not on the fate of Europe but on the fate of a film he had long wanted to make.

"Growing up in Illinois," Reagan later explained, "I was influenced by a sports legend so national in scope, it was almost mystical. It is difficult to explain to anyone who didn't live in those times. The legend was based on a combination of three elements: a game, football; a university, Notre Dame; and a man, Knute Rockne. There has been nothing like it before or since."[1] Reagan wanted to make a motion picture about Rockne, the legendary Notre Dame football coach who had tragically died in an airplane crash in

1931. Rockne was so famous that his funeral was broadcast nationwide by CBS Radio. Reagan had even fooled around trying to write a screenplay, all so he could get the role he really wanted—playing George Gipp, a supremely talented halfback, quarterback, and punter who had died in 1920, at age twenty-five, of pneumonia and a throat infection.

Reagan was excited to read in *Variety* early in 1940 that Warner Brothers had acquired the rights to Rockne's life story from his widow, Bonnie, but dismayed that other actors were already being tested for the part he wanted. Executive producer Hal Wallis had a hard time envisioning the one-time radio announcer as a gridiron great. So Reagan rushed home and brought back to the studio his Eureka College yearbook showing him in uniform. Pat O'Brien, the veteran actor slated to play Rockne, whom Reagan had been cultivating ever since their chance meeting in the summer of 1937, also put in a word for the eager newcomer. O'Brien even volunteered to come in and do a screen test with Ron. He got the part and thoroughly enjoyed filming the football scenes at Loyola University in Los Angeles. "The entire picture was a sentimental journey and a thrilling experience," Reagan wrote of what became known as *Knute Rockne, All American,* the film that, perhaps more than any other, would define his career.[2]

Indeed, it would be one of Ronald Reagan's iconic roles. Even though Gipp is only a small part of the story, the movie's emotional high point is a deathbed scene where Gipp tells his coach, "Some time, Rock, when the team's up against it, when things are wrong and the breaks are beating the boys, ask them to go in there with all they've got and win just one for the Gipper. I don't know where I'll be then, Rock, but I'll know about it, I'll be happy." Near the film's end, when Notre Dame is on the verge of losing to Army, Rockne motivates his players to a come-from-behind win by urging them to "win one for the Gipper."

Every line of the film was subject to approval by Rockne's widow and the University of Notre Dame, and the depiction of Gipp bore little relation to reality. He was hardly the clean-cut, all-American boy shown on-screen. At one point, Reagan-as-Gipp commends Rockne for teaching him and his teammates the "right way of living." The real-life Gipp regularly skipped class to spend his time hustling pool, playing poker, gambling, smoking, and drinking in the fleshpots of South Bend, Indiana, and Chicago. He was even a World War I draft dodger. There is no evidence that the touching deathbed scene between Gipp, who was seldom called "the Gipper" in his lifetime, and Rockne actually occurred. The first time Rockne recounted the supposed request to "win one for the Gipper" was eight years later during a pre-game pep talk to his team before they faced a powerhouse Army squad. Rockne had a history of fanciful orations: He had once motivated his team before a game against Georgia Tech by telling them that his six-year-old son Billy was very sick and had just sent him a telegram: PLEASE WIN THIS GAME FOR MY DADDY. After they won, the players returned to South Bend to find Billy Rockne waiting for them along with other fans on the train platform. "You never saw a healthier kid in your life," one of the Notre Dame players commented.[3]

But what did reality matter? In the 1962 film *The Man Who Shot Liberty Valance*—the story of a successful politician (played by Jimmy Stewart) whose career is built on a false claim of having killed a notorious outlaw in the Old West—a newspaper editor learns the truth but refuses to print it. "This is the West, sir," he explains. "When the legend becomes fact, print the legend." Hollywood had precisely the same "fiction over fact" ethos, and it would be a hallmark of Reagan's life as well. His identification with the fictionalized George Gipp would become so complete that he would become known as "the Gipper" himself. As president he would routinely implore people, including his vice president, to "go out there and win one for the Gipper."[4] A mediocre football player in real life, Reagan, with one stirring screen performance, appropriated the identity of one of the all-time greats of the college game. When people think of "the Gipper" these days, the face they are likely to see is Ronald Reagan's—not George Gipp's.

A sentimental bonus of making *Knute Rocke, All American* was that it offered Ron's ailing, Irish American father one last hurrah. The film's stars went on a publicity junket via train to open the picture in South Bend, Indiana, on October 4–5, 1940, and Ron received permission to bring Jack to a university that had become practically synonymous with the Irish in America. He was nervous that Jack would embarrass him by going on a bender, but everything went smoothly, even though Jack couldn't stay away from all the alcohol on offer. Jack Reagan thoroughly enjoyed the trip and bonded with the movie's genial star. "He thought Pat O'Brien was the greatest man since Al Smith," his son wrote.[5]

On returning home to Los Angeles, Jack proclaimed "that he wouldn't mind now if his faulty heart did call it quits: he had had the most wonderful time of his life."[6] A chain-smoker and binge drinker plagued by cardiac problems, he died of a heart attack a few months later, on May 18, 1941. He was fifty-seven years old. Nelle would survive until 1962, but her last years would be spent in a mental fog of dementia, mostly likely caused by Alzheimer's disease.

The *Los Angeles Times* reported that, with the release of *Knute Rockne, All American,* critics were saying "their first favorable word for Ronald Reagan." The *Chicago Daily News,* for example, wrote that "Reagan gave a superb portrait of a nonchalant athletic genius."[7] The *Los Angeles Daily News* reported that Jack Warner was so impressed by the positive comments of theatergoers at a preview screening in July 1940 that he "decided to give Reagan another rich dramatic opportunity" by immediately casting him in *Santa Fe Trail* alongside Errol Flynn and Olivia de Havilland, two of his top stars. The part had originally been offered to and rejected by John Wayne, who didn't want to play second fiddle to Flynn, but for Reagan it was a step up.[8]

Written by Robert Buckner, who also wrote the Knute Rockne movie, *Santa Fe Trail* was set in Kansas before the Civil War, and it was even more inaccurate than the football film. "I don't give . . . a damn about 'strict historical accuracy,'" Buckner wrote to Jack Warner, and it showed.[9] The picture was a historical mishmash that presented the fiery abolitionist John Brown (played by Raymond Massey) as a deranged and duplicitous "foe of the human race" reminiscent of Adolf Hitler. Army officers J. E. B. Stuart (Flynn) and George Armstrong Custer (Reagan)—future enemies in the Civil War who never met in real life—were shown as West Point classmates who work together to track down Brown. The film's outlook was sympathetic to the Southern cause; the suffering of enslaved people was never shown.

Flynn, an insecure megastar, paid Reagan the implicit compliment of being jealous of the handsome newcomer's screen time. In one scene, Flynn demanded that the Hungarian American director Michael Curtiz, who would go on to greater fame with *Casablanca,* move Reagan away from Flynn and behind a couple of other actors. In self-defense, Reagan quietly scraped together a mound of earth with his feet so that when he delivered his line, he could be clearly seen by the camera.[10] "Sometimes I could get so mad at him I wanted to hit him over the head with a camera," Reagan later wrote of Errol Flynn. "Physically he was a magnificent piece of machinery," and he was "one of the most instantly likable people I have ever met," yet "with all this going for him he had no confidence in his acting ability."[11] Reagan had less ability but more self-confidence.

For all of the implausibility of its storyline, *Santa Fe Trail* was an A picture (it cost $1.1 million[12]), and Reagan had a prominent part in it. "Ronald Reagan as General Custer has his best chance to date," the *Des Moines Register* wrote, "and makes the most of it."[13] Its success made possible his casting in the most acclaimed film of his career.

T hat *Kings Row* was made at all was a minor miracle given that Hollywood pictures of the period had to win the endorsement of Joseph I. Breen, the Catholic scold and notorious antisemite who ran the movie industry's Production Code Administration. Breen's job was to act as an internal censor so that the film industry could avoid outside censorship by prudish municipalities and boycotts by pressure groups such as the Catholic Legion of Decency. The first tenet of the motion picture code was, "No picture shall be produced which will lower the moral standards of those who see it. Hence the sympathy of the audience shall never be thrown on the side of crime, wrong-doing, evil or sin."[14]

That would be a major problem in adapting Henry Bellamann's bestselling 1940 novel *Kings Row*—a lurid melodrama, a proto–*Peyton Place*, set in a fictional turn-of-the-century town that was based on the author's hometown, Fulton, Missouri. Its message was the opposite of the one that small-town boosters such as Ronald Reagan liked to deliver. In his first memoir, Reagan whitewashed the story by describing it as "a slightly sordid but moving yarn about the antics of a small town."[15] A Warner executive was more accurate in writing, "The quintessence of the author's ideas is an accusation against the hypocrisy, the narrow-mindedness, and the cruelty of the typical midwestern rural town or if you will, of American society as a whole."[16]

After reading a proposed script, Breen wrote to Jack Warner on April 22, 1941:

> The novel, from which this screen play is taken, deals with a group
> of people in a small mid-western town, many of whose minds are
> warped and crooked, some of them by a dynamite suggestion of incest,

perversion, illicit sex, sadism, murder, and general lust. To attempt to translate such a story to the screen, *even though it is pre-written to conform to the provisions of the Production Code* is, in our judgment, a very questionable undertaking from the standpoint of the good and welfare of this industry.[17]

Warner, who knew that salaciousness sold tickets, forged ahead anyway. He assigned a top director to the project—Sam Wood, a Cecil B. DeMille protégé who had directed such classics as the Marx Brothers' *A Night at the Opera* (1935) and *Goodbye, Mr. Chips* (1939). The script was toned down to receive Breen's grudging sign-off. The movie, for example, eliminated the book's suggestion of a homosexual attraction between Reagan's character Drake McHugh and his best friend Parris Mitchell, played by Robert Cummings, another rising star of the era who was also from the small-town Midwest that was the movie's setting. And Reagan had to exclaim "for Pete's sake!" rather than, as in the novel, "for Christ's sake!"

Reagan's most difficult and important scene occurred after his character, who had been injured in a railroad accident, had his legs amputated by a sadistic doctor (played by the veteran Broadway actor Charles Coburn), who was furious at him for courting his daughter. Once again, just as in *Knute Rockne*, Reagan's best acting occurred in bed. When he awakened to discover that his legs were gone, he was supposed to scream at his future wife Randy Monaghan, played by Ann Sheridan: "Randy . . . where's the rest of me?"

Portraying "total shock" in just six words, Reagan wrote, was "the most challenging acting problem in my career." He spent weeks rehearsing on his own, consulting psychiatrists, and even talking to disabled people to "brew in myself the cauldron of emotions a man must feel who wakes up one sunny morning to find half of himself gone." While setting up the scene, Reagan hid his legs in a hollowed-out mattress. "As I lay there looking down the length of the bed," he wrote, "it really looked like my body ended at my hips. From there on, the bed covers were smooth and hollow." The illusion of losing his legs became so powerful that he "experienced a shock." The longer he looked, the more "horror" he felt. "Gradually," he wrote, "the affair began to terrify me." When Sam Wood yelled "Action," he was ready to do full justice to his powerful line.[18]

"Perhaps I never did quite as well again in a single shot," Reagan proudly wrote. "The reason was that I had put myself, as best I could, in the body of another fellow."[19] Such empathy did not come naturally to him. As the columnist Mark Shields was to write after Reagan's death, "Reagan was a man of enormous sympathy, yet little empathy." While he was "capable of frequent acts of personal generosity to friends and acquaintances down on their luck"—or even to complete strangers—Shields argued that he did not truly understand the feelings of those hurt by his policies, whether AIDS victims, homeless people, or Black South Africans, when they were very different from him.[20] Unlike the more emotional and outgoing Bill Clinton, the intensely reserved and private Reagan did not feel other people's pain. Nor did he truly understand how critics saw him or his agenda; he was usually puzzled by their opposition to what he viewed as his common-sense solutions. He often did not even understand what his own children were going through. While that lack of empathy did not hurt his political career, it was a hindrance during his movie career because the whole premise of acting is to turn yourself into someone else.

The noted film critic Richard Schickel, in an astute appraisal of Reagan's acting, wrote that he did "his famous line [in *Kings Row*] unimprovably—anguish and panic in his voice, in his facial expression, in his thrashing movements under the covers. Hard to ask for anything more from any actor." Schickel added that Reagan's shortcomings as an actor were more evident earlier in the movie, before the amputation, when his character was still "a careless womanizer and ne'er-do-well heir to a small fortune." "At this stage of the movie Drake McHugh is not a nice guy, and Reagan is visibly uncomfortable, straining, in these passages," Schickel noted. "He does not exhibit the born actor's relish at playing a heel. Instead, he exhibits the born public figure's discomfort at being mistaken for one. He has no technique to help him get under the character's skin or to distract us from his own discomfort."[21]

Being a nice guy himself, Reagan was only comfortable playing nice guys on the screen. The same problem had been evident in the Bette Davis vehicle *Dark Victory* (1939). Reagan flubbed his part because he could not bring himself to play an alcoholic, closeted homosexual who "could sit in the girls' dressing room dishing the dirt" while they dressed in front of him, as demanded by director Edmund Goulding. "I had no trouble seeing him in that role," Reagan wrote peevishly of the bisexual director, "but for myself I want to think that if I stroll through where the girls are short of clothes, there will be a great scurrying about and taking to cover." This was one of the few times Ronald Reagan, normally the most obliging of thespians, came into open conflict with his director. Goulding's biographer was to write that Reagan's "refusal to take chances make him appear insecure both as an actor and as a man."[22]

Reagan's inability or unwillingness to play parts far removed from his own personality would eventually help bring his Hollywood career to a premature and inglorious end—although he would always blame others, principally studio executives and federal antitrust enforcers, for his own failures. But in 1942 Reagan was still on the ascent in Hollywood. He received the best reviews of his career for *Kings Row,* and it was nominated for three Academy Awards, including Best Picture. *Dark Victory* also was nominated for three Oscars, including Best Picture, but, like *Kings Row,* did not win any. The *New Yorker* wrote that watching *Kings Row* "will give you that rare glow that comes from seeing a job done crisply, competently, and with confidence." Reagan, the magazine added, "capably breezes through the part of the town sport who becomes a victim of Dr. Gordon." The *Des Moines Tribune* was even more effusive, pronouncing that "Des Moines' own Dutch Reagan is swell as the rich kid gone to pot."[23]

Reagan always said that *Kings Row* was his best movie. He would regularly screen it for after-dinner guests, and he would use the line "Where's the rest of me?" as the title of his first autobiography. "I must have seen it 85,000 times," chuckled a screenwriter who knew him for thirty-five years.[24] Those screenings quickly became neuralgic for Jane Wyman; the film carried too many reminders of her repressive and sanctimonious small-town upbringing.[25] But Reagan failed to discern his wife's feelings, thereby providing more evidence of his empathy deficit.

Once it was released in 1942, *Kings Row* catapulted the boy from Dixon onto the Hollywood A list. He was no longer merely a "contract player" like so many others. After five years in Hollywood, he was a star at last—a veritable demigod in a movie-mad world. The next time he did a picture with Errol Flynn—*Desperate Journey* in 1942—the two men received equal billing. He was even briefly penciled in as the lead, alongside Ann Sheridan and Dennis Morgan, in a potboiler called *Everybody Comes to Rick's.* By the time the film came out in 1942 as *Casablanca,* it starred Humphrey Bogart,

Ingrid Bergman, and Paul Henreid. Reagan apparently had been slated for the Victor Laszlo role.[26] But losing out on one of the greatest motion pictures ever made—a status that the film would never have attained if the original casting had remained intact—did not prevent Reagan from cashing in on his newfound career success.

Warner Brothers agreed on July 29, 1941, to a new, seven-year contract that initially paid him $1,650 a week—more than eight times what he had been making when he first arrived in 1937. If Warner picked up his option after three years, his salary would nearly double again to $3,000 a week. The final year would be for $5,000 a week. The total value of this deal over seven years was more than $750,000.[27] This generous pay raise was negotiated by his powerful new agent, Lew Wasserman of the Music Corporation of America (MCA), a fast-expanding entertainment conglomerate that had bought out the William Meiklejohn Agency and many other small talent agencies. MCA would soon become a dominant force in Hollywood that would become known as "the Octopus." Being represented by its ruthless agents boosted the careers of many of its clients, including both Ronald Reagan and Jane Wyman.

By the middle of 1941, a Gallup survey ranked Reagan among the top one hundred stars in the movie industry. A 1942 survey found him tied for seventy-fourth place with Laurence Olivier, and he was receiving more fan mail than any Warner Brothers actor except Errol Flynn.[28] Reagan, a Warner executive wrote in an internal evaluation, was "a very talented artist who had started at a meager salary of $200 per week and rapidly developed in artistic ability and box office value until he was assigned to top productions . . . and was undoubtedly a star in his own right."[29] Those who would in later life denigrate him as merely a B-movie actor—an accusation that would generally be accompanied by a chuckle and a mention of *Bedtime for Bonzo* (1951)—were not quite being fair. For one brief, shining moment, before America's entry into the war, Reagan had become an A-list star.

Then, on December 7, 1941, came the Japanese attack on Pearl Harbor. The world would never be the same again—and neither would Ronald Reagan's acting career.

11

Fort Wacky

No twentieth century president, with the exception of Dwight
D. Eisenhower, has been seen in uniform by more people.

—STEPHEN VAUGHN

In a torrent of patriotic fervor, millions of American men rushed to enlist after the Japanese sneak attack on Pearl Harbor. Ronald Reagan was not one of them. He would eventually be drafted but only after receiving several studio-arranged deferments. His military service would be limited to the silver screen. He had already played military men in *Sergeant Murphy* (1937) and *Santa Fe Trail* (1940). He then twice played a Yank in the Royal Air Force—in *International Squadron* (1941) and *Desperate Journey* (1942)—even though in real life he had developed a phobia of flying and only took the train.[1] He would go on to make many military training and propaganda films, but, unlike many of his fellow actors, he would never get anywhere close to the front lines.

Yet, by war's end, Reagan, along with numerous other rear-echelon servicemen—including Navy Lieutenant Richard M. Nixon and Navy Reserve Lieutenant Commander Lyndon B. Johnson—would share in the warm, refracted glow of the far greater sacrifices and risks incurred by heroic combat veterans such as John F. Kennedy, who saved his surviving crew members after his patrol boat (PT 109) was sunk by a Japanese destroyer; George H. W. Bush, one of the youngest pilots in the Navy, whose torpedo bomber was shot down by Japanese antiaircraft fire; Gerald R. Ford, a naval officer aboard an aircraft carrier damaged by a typhoon during the Pacific campaign; and Bob Dole, who was severely wounded as a young Army officer fighting in Italy.

One of the closing commercials of Ronald Reagan's 1980 presidential campaign boasted that he was "a peacetime volunteer army officer, and with the outbreak of World War II, he signed on for active duty."[2] In truth, records kept both by Warner Brothers and the War Department make clear that the studio went to considerable lengths, with Reagan's help, to keep him out of uniform for as long as possible. Not only did studio executives write directly to the military, but they also put a "fixer" on the case who might have stepped out of one of James Ellroy's noir crime novels: William Guthrie, a shady former FBI agent who had been dismissed from the bureau for dishonesty and corruption. He, in turn, enlisted a retired officer who had been a technical adviser for the studio to personally lobby a West Point classmate who was now the commanding general of the Presidio.[3]

In late August 1941, the studio was notified that Reagan, as a reserve cavalry officer, could be called up in two weeks' time. Warner Brothers general counsel Roy Obringer immediately telegraphed the adjutant general of the US Army requesting a deferment because Reagan was filming *Kings Row*, a picture in which Warner had invested "a huge sum of money." A few days later, Obringer telegraphed the assistant secretary of war, requesting that Reagan not be called up "by reason of the importance of his position as an actor."[4] In mid-November 1941, Jack Warner's assistant, Steve Trilling, exulted that he had been told by Bill Guthrie that "due to Reagan's poor eye sight, he is being permanently deferred." But, realizing that it would be harmful to Reagan's image as an all-American actor if his attempts to evade military service were to become public knowledge, Trilling added, "As we unquestionably will want no publicity, I am telling Reagan and Guthrie not to discuss it with anyone."[5] Unfortunately for the studio, the military decided that, while Reagan was "not physically qualified for extended active duty as Visual Defects are beyond the minimal requirements laid down in the Army Regulations," he was still eligible for "limited service" in a rear-area unit.[6]

Reagan got into the act himself, sending a letter to the Southern California Military District on November 29, 1941, just a week before the Pearl Harbor attack, pleading for a delay in being called up "until War is actually declared." He cited not only his poor vision but also his obligations as a family man. "I have four dependents that are totally depending on me for a living," he pleaded, as if he were the only potential serviceman with dependents. "The pay and allowances of a Second Lieutenant would be insufficient to meet their needs."[7] The four dependents must have been his wife, daughter, mother, and aunt—one of Nelle's sisters having moved in with her after Jack's death six months earlier. But while Jane Wyman was not yet earning as much as her husband, she was making a lot more money ($750 a week) than the wives of most men called up for military service—or, for that matter, most of the men themselves.[8] Together, Jane and Ron were earning at least $96,000 a year, or $1.6 million in 2024 dollars.

The Reagans had genuine financial concerns, but they were far removed from those of average Americans. They had just built a seven-room, so-called dream house in the Hollywood Hills modeled on one they had seen in *This Thing Called Love*, a 1940 romantic comedy with Rosalind Russell and Melvyn Douglas: truly a case of life imitating art. It had a magnificent view of the city and cost $15,000—not a lot by movie-industry standards but five times more than the median American home at the time. (In 2022, the extensively remodeled house at 9137 Cordell Drive would sell for $70 million.)[9] Wyman, a free spender in her single days, had been deeply in debt. Now Ron, a stickler for paying bills before they were due, insisted on putting them on a tight budget and saving half of what they earned.[10] Taxes took another big chunk of their income: The top marginal tax rate for couples filing jointly in 1941 with an income between $90,000 and $100,000 was 83 percent.[11] So money was not flowing with typical film-colony abandon even before Ron's military service would cut his monthly pay from $6,660 to $250.[12]

Reagan managed to cushion the blow a bit by negotiating with Jack Warner to have the studio pay his mother $75 a week to handle his fan mail, taking over the job once done by his late father. He promised to repay her salary when he rejoined the studio payroll after the war. (In the end, Warner would forgive his $3,900 debt.)[13] But little wonder that Wyman was not happy about the prospect of her husband's impending military service—even if she faithfully played the part of the dutiful wartime wife in her dealings with the press.[14]

The studio pressure campaign succeeded in winning Reagan several deferments. He would not report for duty until April 19, 1942, the day after Jimmy Doolittle's daring bomber raid on Japan and shortly after finishing work on *Desperate Journey*. But even then, his preferential treatment continued. He spent only five weeks as a liaison officer at Fort Mason, the San Francisco port facility that shipped troops out to the Pacific theater. In late May 1942, shortly before the far-off, pivotal battles of Midway and El Alamein, Reagan was transferred back to Los Angeles after months of lobbying from Jack L. Warner and his minions.[15] Reagan was to serve in the First Motion Picture Unit being formed, at Warner's urging, by General Henry "Hap" Arnold, the chief of staff of the US Army Air Forces. Reagan was only one of many Warner Brothers employees sent to the unit; informants told the FBI that Bill Guthrie, the studio fixer, had dozens of blank army commissions and handed them out "on a large scale for his friends and those of Jack Warner."[16]

Jack Warner became a lieutenant colonel and took command of the new unit, initially stationed at the dilapidated old Vitagraph Studios in Hollywood and then at the more modern Hal Roach Studios in Culver City, where the Laurel and Hardy and *Our Gang* films had been made, jocularly referred to as Fort Roach or Fort Wacky.[17] Warner got to say that he did his part in the war effort before returning to civilian life in late 1942; his employees would address him as "Colonel" for the rest of his life. In turn, Hap Arnold would receive invaluable publicity in his struggle to turn the air force into a separate military service. As Warner, the architect of dreams, told him, "The more that is done now to publicize the Air Corps the sooner you will come to seeing your plans and dreams realized."[18]

Naturally, Reagan's two autobiographies gave no hint of these behind-the-scenes machinations. He merely quoted one of the army physicians who tested his eyesight as saying, "If we sent you overseas, you'd shoot a general," and another adding the punchline as if in a movie script, "Yes, and you'd miss him."[19] He depicted his transfer from Fort Mason as if he were a pawn of a distant, impersonal War Department bureaucracy over which he had no influence.

In his 1965 autobiography, written in anticipation of his first political race, for governor of California, Reagan was sensitive to accusations that he and the other members of the First Motion Picture Unit were "draft dodgers avoiding danger." "The Army doesn't play that way," he lectured critics. "There was a special job the Army wanted done and it was after men who could do that job. The overwhelming majority of men and officers serving at our post were limited service like myself or men who by reason of family, age, or health were exempt from normal military duty. Nonetheless, some people can't resist looking for ulterior motives."[20]

All true, but the fact remains that some Hollywood stars made strenuous efforts to get to the front lines, even though they might easily have been disqualified "by reason of family, age, or health." So, for that matter, did John

F. Kennedy, the son of a wealthy former ambassador who pulled strings to command a PT boat despite his debilitating back pain.[21] Reagan himself claimed to have cheated on his eye exam so he could join the cavalry and ride horses in Des Moines, but he made no comparable effort to seek out overseas service in World War II. He never left the country during the war, unlike fellow actors such as Bob Hope, Bing Crosby, and Pat O'Brien, who traveled to combat zones on USO tours. Henry Fonda, a well-known liberal who served in the Navy, was quoted as saying, "I don't want to be in a fake war in a studio."[22] Reagan, by contrast, did not seem to mind being a "Culver City commando"—although, in fairness, even if he had minded, it is far from clear that he could have gotten any closer to the action.

There was nothing dishonorable about his wartime service—but there was nothing heroic about it either. Like roughly 40 percent of all US military personnel, Reagan served in a noncombat assignment, and like roughly 30 percent, he did not serve overseas.[23] Few others, however, were regularly able to commute home or had their risk-free service glorified by a reverential press corps.

The First Motion Picture Unit had 1,300 officers and men—almost all of them, as Reagan noted, "film-cutters, wardrobe men, prop men," and other motion picture workers. The only qualified pilot in the bunch was stunt flier Paul Mantz, who was commissioned a major and made commanding officer after Lieutenant Colonel Warner's departure. Reagan began as the personnel officer. In early 1945, he became the adjutant, the number-two officer on the post, after having been promoted from second lieutenant to captain. He later claimed to have turned down a promotion to major because he did not feel he should be given higher rank without "hearing a shot fired in anger," but army records indicate that the promotion was denied because "higher grade is not considered appropriate for the position in question."[24]

Few of the men of the First Motion Picture Unit had any military training, and few military formalities were observed. Some officers tried to emulate the spit and polish of regular army outfits but not for long. Seeing soldiers march by in parade-ground formation, Reagan quipped, "Splendid body of men—with half this many I could conquer MGM."[25]

Contrary to one author's claim that Reagan was "a stickler for following rules and respecting rank,"[26] the men who served with him recalled that he was always telling jokes and stories, contributing to the post's reputation as Fort Wacky. He did not condescend to the lower ranks, made up of movie-industry craftsmen. A sergeant in the unit recalled, "He was a non-GI guy. He was one of the boys. He was personable, he didn't play GI, he didn't play tough stuff, so everybody liked him." Another sergeant said, "He was the most popular officer on the post, and he was very unceremonious, I mean, you didn't feel every time he came in that you had to stand at attention or whatever. It was pretty loose, and he was really a nice guy." "He was just Mister Charm," a third enlisted man said. "We loved the way he did his job."[27]

The First Motion Picture Unit would crank out more than three hundred major pictures in three years while also training combat camera crews who fanned out around the world to record the fighting in the air.[28] Reagan served as either an actor or a narrator in a number of short propaganda films.

In *Rear Gunner* (1942), Reagan played a bomber pilot, Lieutenant Ames, who convinces an enlisted man, "Pee Wee" Williams (played by Burgess Meredith, the renowned stage actor and future *Batman* villain), to become a rear-gunner on a B-24 bomber—a "modern knight of the air." At the end of the film, Pee Wee saves the crew from a Japanese fighter and receives a medal. The intent, an Air Force officer noted, was to "counteract publicity that the life of an Air Force gunner is very short" and to convince more men to enlist.[29]

In *Recognition of the Japanese Zero Fighter* (1943), Reagan played a fighter pilot, Lieutenant Saunders, who struggles to tell the difference between a US P-40 fighter and a Japanese Zero fighter. The film employed an actual Zero airplane that had been captured intact and shipped to California. This time the audience was more specialized—actual pilots at air bases in the Pacific who had to be trained to avoid "friendly fire" casualties.

In *For God and Country* (1943), Reagan played Father Michael O'Keefe, a Catholic army chaplain and former football star at Loyola University. His two best friends were Protestant and Jewish chaplains, and he died while trying to save a soldier who was Native American.[30] This was typical of the way wartime movies sought to promote national unity by showing GIs from different ethnic and religious backgrounds working together. One of the films that Reagan narrated was *Wings for This Man* (1945), a tribute to the Tuskegee Airmen—the Black pilots who, as Reagan noted, had to overcome "misunderstanding, distrust and prejudice" to serve their country.

Among the other short films Reagan narrated, the most notable was *Beyond the Line of Duty* about Captain Hewitt T. "Shorty" Wheless, a B-17 pilot who was sent to bomb Japanese ships off the Philippines shortly after Pearl Harbor. The twenty-two-minute film won an Academy Award for best short subject (two reel) in 1943. While Reagan appeared in eleven films that were nominated for Academy Awards, mainly in technical categories, this was as close as he ever came to acting in an Oscar winner for Best Picture.[31]

The most important movie made by the First Motion Picture Unit had the smallest audience. Special-effects wizards used plaster, foam, and paperboard to construct a sixty-by-ninety-foot scale model of Tokyo on a sound stage rigged with a crane and camera mount. They were then able to intersperse shots of the model with actual photographs of Tokyo and film from earlier bombing raids to provide B-29 bomber pilots with a realistic view of what they could expect to see over Japan's capital. As usual, Reagan was the narrator, delivering lines such as "Gentlemen, you are approaching the coast of Honshu on a course of three hundred degrees. You are now twenty miles offshore. To your left, if you are on course, you should be able to see a narrow inlet." The whole project was so sensitive, he noted, that "the entire sound stage was put under twenty-four-hour guard."[32]

The one full-length motion picture Reagan made during his military service was *This Is the Army* (1943), a Technicolor musical based on a hit Broadway show featuring the songs of Irving Berlin. It reprised a similar morale-boosting show that Berlin had staged during World War I. Reagan played the producer of a show-within-a-show, an army private working with his father, played by song-and-dance man George Murphy, to entertain the troops. Reagan's role was largely to provide the segues from one musical number to another—including a cringeworthy performance in blackface. *This Is the Army* won an Oscar for Best Music and became a considerable hit for Warner Brothers, with the profits going to the Army Relief Fund for needy service members. It may, in fact, have been the biggest box-office hit Reagan ever made—and he did it on a first lieutenant's salary of $250 a month.[33]

While Reagan spent the war in Culver City, the movie magazines treated him as if he were off to combat like fellow actors Jimmy Stewart (a bomber pilot who flew over twenty combat missions over Germany), Clark Gable

(an observer-gunner on five bombing missions over Germany), or his
Brother Rat costar Eddie Albert (coxswain of a landing craft during the
invasion of Tarawa).

Modern Screen reported in 1942 that Reagan had joined the army with
the headline "So Long, Button-Nose," his nickname for Jane Wyman. The
article quoted Wyman describing "Ronnie's sick face bent over a picture of
the small swollen bodies of children starved to death in Poland. 'This,' said
the war-hating Reagan between set lips, 'would make it a pleasure to kill.'"
It also quoted "Ronnie" saying, "Like ten million others, I'm sorry that such
a thing has come to the world. . . . Now it's a job that has to be done—the job
of ten million others and yours truly." The article went on to describe Reagan's wrenching departure for the war: Wyman, "who hasn't shed tears in
five years," found her "eyes grew blind with them." "But what business have
I got to squawk?" she asked stoically. "Every woman who's losing her guy
feels the same way."[34]

A 1943 story in *Modern Screen*, "My Soldier," featured a cover drawing
of Jane in a fur coat and Ron in his uniform, updating the story now that
nine months had passed since Reagan "went off to join his regiment." "His
movie career is something that happened in another life, laid away, like
the [riding] boots and breeches in mothballs," the magazine reported. "He
acts, says Jane, as if the responsibility for this whole war rests on his shoulders. He works with a quiet faith and intensity, feeling that every ounce of
effort he gives the job brings the end a little nearer." This article compared
Wyman's tribulations—at a time when she was raising a single child with
the help of a cook and a maid—to those of any other woman: "You don't want
to have fun while he's having trouble. . . . She's sure every wife and sweetheart feels the same."[35]

When Reagan was photographed visiting the Hollywood Canteen—a
USO center for visiting servicemen where Jane and other movie stars volunteered their time—*Movie Life* reported that he was home "on a short
leave."[36] "I remember that during the war, when he was stationed right here
in town, we would run articles as if he were 3,000 miles away," an editor of
Modern Screen recalled.[37]

Ronald Reagan cannot, of course, be held responsible for the content of
fan magazines, even if the articles were cooked up in collaboration with the
Warner Brothers publicity department. But he and Jane did cooperate with
the reporters, and he furthered the impression left by the articles that he

had become a grizzled war veteran. He wrote in his 1965 autobiography, "By the time I got out of the Army Air Corps, all I wanted to do—in common with several million other veterans—was to rest up awhile, make love to my wife, and come up refreshed to a better job in an ideal world."[38] He even claimed, implausibly, that "Hollywood . . . seemed as far away as another planet" when he was stationed at the Hal Roach Studios. A press release prepared by his first political campaign in 1966 claimed that he was on "Active Duty" during World War II and that he served on a "base of 1300 men and officers directly under the command of Air Force Intelligence," without any hint of that base's location or purpose.[39]

Reagan never lied about what he did in the war, but the media's overheated descriptions of his war service—combined with countless photos of him in uniform—left a deceptive impression with millions of Americans. "No twentieth century president, with the exception of Dwight D. Eisenhower, has been seen in uniform by more people," wrote historian Stephen Vaughn in the best account of the future president's movie career.[40] That imagery would prove of great value to Reagan after the war. He would have had trouble forging a political career in postwar America if he had avoided service altogether.

When he was at Fort Roach, Ronald Reagan was still "very liberal" and a "staunch Democrat," the men who served with him noted.[41] He loved debating with those who were more conservative, including fellow actors Dick Powell and George Murphy and his own brother, Neil, the family Republican, who had also moved to Los Angeles and had even gotten a few bit parts in movies before launching a career in advertising. "Argument is meat and drink to them both," a fan magazine wrote of the battling Reagan brothers. Jane Wyman grew so tired of their never-ending debates that she would push Moon out the door when he stayed too long at their house.[42]

Reagan's wartime experiences reinforced some of his liberal beliefs. In 1945, the First Motion Picture Unit received some of the first films shot by combat cameramen of liberated Nazi death camps. "None of us . . . will ever forget the horrors we saw—the living and the dead," he wrote decades later.[43] He was so haunted by those films that he kept a duplicate for himself and would later show it to his children and even occasional visitors so that they would never doubt that the Holocaust had really happened. (His daughter Patti recalled seeing the horrifying footage when she was nine years old.)[44] At a Beverly Hills cocktail party in 1943, according to the FBI, Reagan "almost came to blows with a man who made anti-Semitic remarks." He resigned from the posh Lakeside Country Club in 1946 once he learned it did not admit Jews and instead joined the Hillcrest Country Club, which had many Jewish members, including Jack Warner.[45]

In other ways, however, Reagan began to reassess his political beliefs during the war. As a US Army officer, he was part of a force of more than 12 million service members supported by 2.6 million civilian employees of the War and Navy Departments.[46] This was a vast bureaucracy that exhibited many of the maddening characteristics of any large organization. One of Reagan's fellow US Army Air Force veterans, after all, was to coin the phrase "catch-22" to describe a problem whose solution was rendered impossible by bureaucratic rules.

Reagan was to remember with particular exasperation the 250 civil service civilians who arrived at Fort Roach: "Their rules and regulations filled shelves from floor to ceiling, around virtually the four walls of a barrack-sized building."[47] While in uniform, he later wrote, "I saw empire building and was disgusted by the smug, 'business as usual' attitude of the bureaucrat—the professional government career man at a time when young men were dying all over the world."[48]

This was the beginning of his lifelong animus toward bureaucrats and big government that stood in marked contrast to his sympathy, which had lasted until the mid-1940s, for the New Deal programs that had employed his father and so many others during the Great Depression. But the Depression was over, and his father was dead. Even his idol, Franklin D. Roosevelt, died on April 12, 1945. Ronald Reagan was moving on.

In this new era, a significant influence pushing him to the right was the nation's most popular magazine. One of the men stationed at Fort Roach— the novelist and screenwriter Irving Wallace—recalled that Reagan "was not an incisive or original thinker, but he was interested in everything, a great magazine reader and clipper. I remember that somehow he managed to get his copy of Reader's Digest earlier than everyone else on the post. He would read it cover-to-cover overnight and come in the next day and tell everyone about everything he'd read. When we finally got our copies, we'd already heard the whole damn issue from Reagan."[49]

Founded in 1922, Reader's Digest had a decidedly right-wing propensity. Its articles overwhelmingly reflected the personal philosophy of its Minnesota-born publisher, DeWitt "Wally" Wallace, who in the 1930s believed, as his biographer John Heidenry put it, that "Nazi Germany ought to be appeased, that labor unions were corrupt, [and] that President Roosevelt wished to assume dictatorial power." Even when the United States was allied with the Soviet Union, Wallace remained a fervent anti-Communist who in January 1945 ran an influential article unfavorably comparing life in Russia with life in the Kansas state penitentiary. Heidenry wrote that Wallace and *Time-Life* publisher Henry Luce were more instrumental than "any other two people in the private sector . . . in persuading the American public to look upon the Soviet Union as not only the enemy but something very like the Antichrist."

Reader's Digest actually had a larger circulation than *Time* or any other magazine. The *New Yorker* wrote in 1945, "Except for the Scriptures, nothing ever published has been circulated more widely than the *Digest*." Highbrow readers disdained the *Digest*—Washington Post columnist Mary McGrory was to call it "the monthly for people who hate to read"—but Reagan not only read it; he imbibed it and believed it. You might say that during World War II he was beginning to digest its conservative outlook. The *Digest*, in turn, would become a major booster of his political career.[50]

Ronald Reagan was already primed, then, for a turn to the right by the time he left the US Army Air Forces on September 10, 1945, just eight days after the Japanese surrender. This speedy demobilization, far ahead of most servicemen, had been arranged, like Reagan's draft deferments in 1941–1942, by the Warner Brothers fixer Bill Guthrie. The studio, in fact, had been lobbying for Reagan's release even before the war's end, assuring the Army Air Forces that it was "engaged in the production of several motion pictures which are believed to be of vital interest to the war effort and it is our intention to use Captain Reagan in these pictures if he is released from the service."[51]

Because Reagan had not gone within thousands of miles of the front lines, his memories of World War II, while vivid, were often inaccurate, derived from his movie-viewing rather than from firsthand experience. As president, he became so overenthusiastic in describing what a profound impact the Holocaust had made on him that he gave both Israeli Prime Minister Yitzhak Shamir in 1983 and Nazi hunter Simon Wiesenthal in

1984 the impression that he had visited the death camps himself.[52] In his speeches, meanwhile, he later claimed that segregation in the armed forces had ended during World War II, with the impetus provided by heroes such as the "Negro sailor" at Pearl Harbor who "cradled a machine gun in his arms . . . and stood on the end of a pier blazing away at Japanese airplanes that were coming down and strafing him." As dramatized in the 1970 movie *Tora! Tora! Tora!*, a Black mess steward aboard the battleship *West Virginia* did man an antiaircraft machine gun during the attack on Pearl Harbor—although he did not cradle it in his arms—and he was credited with shooting down at least two enemy aircraft. But military segregation did not formally end until 1948.[53]

A story Reagan would tell even more regularly in the years ahead concerned a B-17 bomber limping back to base after being shot up over occupied Europe. Most of the crew parachuted to safety, but the ball-turret gunner was trapped and crying out in fear. The pilot stayed behind and comforted him by saying, "Never mind, son. We'll ride it down together." Reagan often insisted that the pilot had been posthumously awarded a Medal of Honor, his voice usually breaking as he said it. But if the pilot and gunner both died, who told the story? The story most likely derived from the 1944 film *Wing and a Prayer* starring Don Ameche and Dana Andrews.[54] Yet even telling the tall tale for the umpteenth time four decades later, Reagan would still get so "choked up" he "could hardly finish."[55]

If Reagan had gotten closer to the action and seen bloated corpses and maimed GIs for himself—or smelled the burning flesh of Japanese civilians incinerated in B-29 fire-bombing raids—his memories of World War II might have been more ambivalent and less nostalgic. At the very least, like most combat veterans, he would have been reticent to speak about the war at all. But seeing the war on black-and-white film reinforced his Manichaean, black-and-white view of the world. Admittedly, a war against the Nazis lent itself more than most conflicts to a good versus evil narrative. Reagan was inclined to see Americans as the good guys under almost all circumstances. This time they really were.

After three years and four months in uniform, Ronald Reagan was looking forward to reclaiming his post–*Kings Row* standing in the motion-picture business and to spending more time with his growing family. To go along with four-year-old Maureen, the Reagans had adopted a baby boy shortly after his birth to an unwed mother in Los Angeles on March 18, 1945. They named him Michael Edward Reagan, Michael and Edward both being common names in the Reagan family. Why adopt? Maureen wanted a brother and Ron a son, but Jane apparently did not want to go through another pregnancy.[56] To round out the clan, the Reagans acquired two adorable dogs: Scottish terriers, the same breed as FDR's beloved Fala, that they named Scotch and Soda.[57]

Reagan had never been at the slightest risk of sacrificing his life for his country, but he had sacrificed his salary and his stardom, while actors who had not served—such as John Wayne, an uber-patriot who won one dubious draft deferment after another—saw their careers flourish during the war. Now he wanted to pick up where he had left off in early 1942. He had no idea that, instead of getting back to moviemaking, he was about to play a starring role in Hollywood's hothouse politics in the rancorous and tumultuous postwar era.

12

The Strike

The CSU cannot exist together with the IATSE in Hollywood.
It has got to be destroyed.

—ROY BREWER

As early as October 19, 1945—only ten weeks after two atomic bombs had obliterated Hiroshima and Nagasaki—George Orwell warned that the world was going to be divided between "two or three monstrous super-states, each possessed of a weapon by which millions of people can be wiped out in a few seconds." He predicted a "permanent state of 'cold war,'" a term that was soon being used to describe the growing clash between the two postwar superpowers: the United States and the Soviet Union.[1] By the end of the decade, all of Eastern Europe had fallen behind what Winston Churchill dubbed the "Iron Curtain," and fears were growing that the Cold War could turn hot.

Harry S. Truman—the feisty former haberdasher from Missouri thrust unexpectedly into the presidency following Franklin D. Roosevelt's sudden death—had no desire to fight the Soviet Union, but he did want to curb its aggression. In 1947, he unveiled the Truman Doctrine (sending military aid to Greece and Turkey) and the Marshall Plan offering economic assistance to Europe. In 1948, Truman sent cargo aircraft to keep West Berlin supplied during a Soviet blockade that would last eleven months. In 1949, the United States, Canada, and ten European nations announced the creation of a new defensive alliance, the North Atlantic Treaty Organization (NATO).

This was all part of what American diplomat George F. Kennan dubbed containment—a "long-term" strategy requiring "the adroit and vigilant application of counterforce at a series of constantly shifting geographical and political points," with the eventual goal of forcing "either the breakup or the gradual mellowing of Soviet power."[2] That ultimate objective would not begin to be achieved until decades later during the presidency of a former actor who in 1945 was just getting out of the Army Air Forces.

In the meantime, the Communist advance appeared inexorable. In 1949, the Soviet Union tested its first atomic bomb, and China fell to a Communist revolution led by Mao Zedong. In June 1950, Communist North Korea invaded South Korea, drawing the United States into another bloody conflict. In October 1950, following the advance of US troops to the Yalu River, hundreds of thousands of Chinese troops streamed into North Korea, sending American forces reeling with heavy losses. In desperation, General Douglas MacArthur called for striking back with atomic bombs. Truman reflected the "jittery situation facing the country" when he grimly wrote in December 1950, "It looks like World War III is here."[3]

As fear gave birth to paranoia, America's domestic politics became disfigured by ugly suspicions that the Communist advance abroad was being facilitated by traitors on the home front. Those concerns were fueled by a series of high-profile Soviet espionage cases involving atomic spies Julius and Ethel Rosenberg, Treasury official Harry Dexter White, and former Roosevelt adviser Alger Hiss. Even before Republican Senator Joseph McCarthy of Wisconsin falsely claimed in 1950 that there were 205 Communists in the State Department, setting off the national hysteria that would become known as McCarthyism, the country was in the grip of a Red Scare. Truman issued an executive order in 1947 mandating that all federal employees sign a loyalty oath, while the House Un-American Activities Committee was hauling in witnesses to demand, "Are you now or have you ever been a member of the Communist Party?" The tentacles of the Communist conspiracy were said to extend all the way to Hollywood—the center of an industry whose products influenced the fears and fantasies of untold tens of millions. In the United States alone, eighty-five million to ninety million people a week were going to the movies in the late 1940s.[4]

Ronald Reagan was initially skeptical of the Red hunters and supportive of an idealistic foreign policy to foster world peace, but by decade's end he had morphed into a zealous, right-wing cold warrior who would be described by the FBI as "extremely anticommunist."[5] The period from 1945 to 1950 would prove pivotal not only to the country's political development but also to his own.

Reagan had a lot of time to think about politics after returning to civilian life in September 1945 because—contrary to what Warner Brothers told the War Department in trying to arrange his discharge—he found no immediate use for his services at his old studio. Having made only one full-length commercial motion picture between 1942 and 1945, he was no longer a bright, rising star, no longer as popular with audiences as he had been when he put on a uniform. Thus, Warner Brothers did not rush to cast him in new pictures.

The studio was paying Reagan $150,000 a year (equivalent to $2 million in 2024) but did not assign him to his first postwar movie—*Stallion Road*—until 1946. He was looking forward to this picture, in which he would play a veterinarian who competes with a novelist for the hand of a woman who owns a horse farm. It would allow him to ride a horse, it would costar Humphrey Bogart and Lauren Bacall, and it would be in glorious Technicolor. But shortly before filming began in April 1947, "Bogie" and "Betty," two of Hollywood's biggest stars, pulled out. They were replaced by Zachary Scott and Alexis Smith, two lesser lights, and the picture was downgraded from color to black and white.

The only good thing that came out of *Stallion Road* was a horse named Baby. Reagan was able to buy the black thoroughbred, which he rode in the movie, from its trainer, former Italian cavalry officer Nino Pepitone. Ronald Reagan and Jane Wyman bought a small, eight-acre ranch in then-rural Northridge, California, where he could keep Baby and breed other horses in partnership with Nino and his wife. They named the ranch Yearling Row, a mash-up of movie titles—Ron's *Kings Row* and Jane's forthcoming *The Yearling*. This was the very first ranch Reagan owned but far from the last. As with future spreads in Malibu and Santa Barbara, he reveled in doing much of the work himself, including building fences.[6]

But the ranch was scant consolation for the fact that Ron's movie career was idling, even as his wife's career was in overdrive. In 1945, Jane Wyman had gotten a role that changed her life: She played the fiancée of the alcoholic writer in *The Lost Weekend* directed by Billy Wilder. This was a critically acclaimed drama about the ravages of dipsomania that won Ray Milland an Academy Award for Best Actor and also earned plaudits for Wyman. "Suddenly," the *Los Angeles Times* wrote, "after more than seven years as a comedienne in pictures, Jane Wyman is being lauded as a dramatic actress." Good parts led to even better parts as Jane's talent became apparent to studio executives. When Ron left the army in September 1945, Jane was at Lake Arrowhead, ninety miles east of Los Angeles, filming *The Yearling*, in what the *Times* described as "a mother role, wearing burlap, using no make-up, and letting her eyebrows grow out."[7] This was a color film about a boy's love for a baby deer, costarring a young Gregory Peck, for which Wyman would receive her first Academy Award nomination in 1946.

Reagan joined his wife at Lake Arrowhead for a few weeks but had nothing to do save for boating on the lake and building model ships. Full of unchanneled energy, he became a regular public speaker at events all over Southern California. He spoke at what a newspaper described as a "super-colossal-terrific show" at the Los Angeles Coliseum, illuminated by fifty army searchlights, to celebrate victory in World War II.[8] He joined actor Robert Young and General Joseph W. "Vinegar Joe" Stilwell, one of the best-known, if most controversial, generals of World War II, in a "plea for civic unity and tolerance of American minority groups" at a United America day rally in Orange County. During this event, Reagan paid tribute to Japanese American GIs, saying, "The blood that has soaked into the sand is all one color."[9] He spoke to the Los Angeles Area Council of the Boy Scouts of America, using "first-hand information" derived from his "service as a captain in the Army Air Forces" to pay a "great tribute" to scouting.[10] Drawing on his experience as a sportscaster, he was master of ceremonies at the annual banquet of the Association of Professional Baseball Players of America.[11] And on and on. "Ronald Reagan is becoming one of the town's leading spokesmen," a Los Angeles newspaper noted in May 1946. "He has addressed 25 gatherings since Jan. 1."[12]

With unaccustomed self-reflection, Reagan later admitted, "I became an easy mark for speechmaking on the rubber-chicken and glass-tinkling circuit. It fed my ego, since I had been so long away from the screen. I loved it."[13]

I t also fed his idealism: He brimmed with well-intentioned desire to build a better postwar world and to avoid another conflict whose devastation could easily eclipse that of the two world wars. Many of the events where Reagan spoke were on behalf of the American Veterans Committee, a liberal counterpart to the more conservative American Legion and the Veterans of Foreign Wars. The American Veterans Committee advocated international control of atomic energy, an end to racial discrimination at home, and decolonization abroad. Reagan also supported the Citizens Committee on Displaced Persons and joined in calling for the United States to admit four hundred thousand refugees over four years.[14] He became active in yet another liberal group, the Hollywood Independent Citizens Committee of the Arts, Sciences and Professions (HICCASP), which advocated "universal disarmament," supported minority and labor rights, and opposed Truman's attempts to "get tough" with the Soviet Union for fear of triggering World War III.[15]

Reagan was an ardent activist, playing to the hilt the self-cast part of a war-weary veteran who had seen enough bloodshed to last a lifetime. "Like most of the soldiers who came back, I expected a world suddenly reformed," he was to write in his first autobiography, begging the question of *where* he "came back" from—Culver City? "Now that I have seen what war means," he told a reporter in January 1946, "I am more than ever determined that my son won't have to fight a third world war."[16]

Reagan later described himself as "a near hopeless hemophilic liberal" who "bled for 'causes'" and continued to faithfully support the Democratic Party. Two decades later, preparing to seek the Republican nomination for governor of California, he excoriated his younger self for having been "unusually naïve" and "not sharp about Communism: the Russians still seemed to be our allies."[17] There is no evidence, however, to corroborate the fanciful claim that the ex-Communist novelist Howard Fast made to Edmund Morris in 1990 that Reagan had flirted with joining the Communist Party before the war and was rejected by the party as a "flake." Reagan had been a New Deal liberal, not a Communist "fellow traveler," and he was never considered a "flake."[18]

By early 1946, Reagan was certainly no fan of Communism, but he was no Red-baiter either. When his pastor at the Hollywood-Beverly Christian Church urged him add to his speeches condemnation not only of fascism but also of Communism, he agreed to do so, even though, as he later wrote, he "hadn't given much thought to the threat of Communism." He would be appalled to find in early 1946 a progressive audience applauding his attacks on fascism but not on Communism.[19]

As he began to grow more concerned about the Communist threat, Reagan grew disenchanted with HICCASP ("pronounced like the cough of a dying man"), whose board he briefly joined in 1946. Although he would later denounce HICCASP as a Communist front, it would more accurately be described as a popular front organization bringing together Communists

and mainstream liberals. Its executive secretary, George Pepper, a violin-
ist forced to stop playing because of crippling arthritis, was a Communist
Party member, and its board included Communists or fellow travelers, such
as the highly paid screenwriters John Howard Lawson and Dalton Trumbo,
the "$2000-a-week proletarians." But most of the organization was made
up of anti-Communist liberals, such as Frank Sinatra, Gene Kelly, Olivia de
Havilland, Humphrey Bogart, and even Albert Einstein. Its chairman was
FDR's long-serving Interior secretary, Harold Ickes, a progressive Republican. Historians who have studied HICCASP's internal files have concluded
there is "no evidence" that it "was under Soviet influence."[20]

While HICCASP was neither pro-Soviet nor anti-Soviet, it was deeply
divided at a time when there was no middle ground to be found in the
emerging Cold War. At the first board meeting that Reagan attended on July
5, 1946, FDR's son, James "Jimmy" Roosevelt II, argued that such organizations must be "vigilant against being used by Communist sympathizers"
and demanded that the board sign a "declaration of principles" repudiating Communism. Reagan took to the floor to endorse Roosevelt's motion
and found himself, he recalled, "waist-high in epithets such as 'Fascist'
and 'capitalist scum' and 'enemy of the proletariat' and 'witch hunter' and
'Red baiter.'"[21]

As the meeting broke up in acrimony, the liberal film producer Dore
Schary invited Reagan to a meeting at Olivia de Havilland's apartment,
where twelve of HICCASP's leading liberals engaged in exactly the kind of
factional plotting that they accused the Communists of doing. They were
pleased by the day's events, Reagan later wrote, "because the whole thing
had been a preconceived plot to smoke out the 'others.'" Those present at de
Havilland's apartment agreed to present to the board a resolution stating,
"We reaffirm our belief in free enterprise and the democratic system and
repudiate Communism as desirable for the United States." In his memoirs,
Reagan made it sound as if the board would not back either free markets or
free elections. In fact, the board passed an alternative resolution that, while
it barely mentioned Communism, did affirm HICCASP's support for "our
democratic system of free enterprise, with government encouragement and
aid whenever and wherever it is necessary."[22]

But Reagan's mind was made up. He was convinced that HICCASP
was a Communist front organization, and he resigned from its board less

than a month after joining it. Many of the other liberals followed him out the door, leading HICCASP to reorganize as a more unapologetically leftist lobby lacking mainstream political credibility. Ironically, it was the departure of Reagan and the other liberals that turned HICCASP into a Communist-dominated organization.

While Reagan was engaged in the battle over HICCASP, he received a fateful visit at his home in the Hollywood Hills from three FBI agents. The FBI had already been in contact with him in 1943 about an actor who was a suspected Nazi sympathizer. Now they wanted to talk to him about Communists in Hollywood. "Instinctively," Reagan recalled, "my old liberal reaction popped up before I could think and almost by rote I found myself saying, 'Now look, I don't go in for Red baiting.'" "We don't either," one of the agents replied, casting it as a matter of rooting out "spies and saboteurs."

The agents got Reagan's attention by claiming that an informant reported a Communist Party member in Los Angeles asking, "What the hell are we going to do about that son-of-a-bitching bastard Reagan?" Presumably this was a sign of the party's displeasure with his actions within HICCASP. Reagan later recounted the rest of the conversation: "They confided in me that FBI investigations had shown the Party was attempting not only to gain control of the Hollywood work force but striving to influence the content of movies through the work of several prominent film writers and actors who were party members or sympathizers. They asked if they could meet with me periodically to discuss some of the things that were going on in Hollywood. I said of course they could."[23]

Reagan's brother, Neil, who was now working for the McCann-Erickson advertising agency in Los Angeles, was already an informant for the FBI. He recalled being asked to "lay in the bushes and take down the car numbers" parked outside a gathering in Bel-Air.[24] Now Reagan, who had once played a "T-man" in the Brass Bancroft movies, became FBI informant T-10. A leading student of Reagan's film career has even suggested that he may have acted "as an informant and provocateur for the FBI" in helping to precipitate the breakup of HICCASP.[25]

After leaving HICCASP, Reagan joined Americans for Democratic Action (ADA)—a more centrist organization whose leaders included

anti-Communist liberals such as Arthur Schlesinger Jr., Eleanor Roosevelt, and Hubert Humphrey. While HICCASP's successor organization,
the National Council on Arts, Sciences, and Professions, backed Henry Wallace's quixotic, left-wing campaign for president in 1948, the ADA endorsed
Harry Truman and his containment strategy. Reagan led the Labor League
of Hollywood Voters for Truman, even though he found FDR's plebeian successor "as inspiring as mud."[26] That did not, however, prevent the professional Red hunters at the FBI from attaching the "pinko" label to the ADA
too.[27] Indeed, in later years, Reagan himself claimed—wrongly—that the
ADA had been taken over by "the little Red brothers" and the "Pink ones."[28]

While Reagan served on the ADA's national board for a year, he was not
particularly prominent in that organization. He was more focused on his
work in the Screen Actors Guild (SAG), the actors' union. He had first joined
the board of what he called a "damned noble organization" in 1941 as an
"alternate" member—filling in for a regular board member who could not
attend—and, after a wartime interregnum, he resumed his role as an alternate in February 1946. He was elected a full-time board member as SAG's
third vice president in September 1946.[29]

That put him in a position to help arbitrate a labor dispute that was
tearing Hollywood apart just as studio moguls—like executives in other
industries—were eager to return to peacetime production. Labor unions,
desperate to recover from the austerity of the Depression and the war years,
had other ideas. The immediate aftermath of World War II would see the
greatest wave of strikes in US history in industries from automaking to steel
manufacturing, and the movie business was hardly exempt.

Two unions—the scrappy, upstart Conference of Studio Unions (CSU)
and the larger, better-established International Alliance of Theatrical
Stage Employees (IATSE)—were in a heated competition over which one
would represent Hollywood technicians and, therefore, collect their union
dues. The movie studios favored IATSE, which won them over with fear
and favors. Because IATSE represented movie projectionists, it could shut
down the industry at any time. But IATSE's corrupt leaders were willing
to take studio payoffs to keep labor peace and low wages. The studios each
paid $50,000 a year and never complained to law enforcement.[30] In 1941,
two IATSE leaders linked to the Chicago mob—William "Willie" Bioff and

George E. Browne—were convicted in a federal court on charges of extortion and sentenced to lengthy terms in prison. Bioff turned state's witness and after getting out of prison died in a car-bomb explosion presumably arranged by his old organized-crime associates. Joseph Schenk, the chairman of Twentieth Century Fox, who was the producers' liaison to Bioff and Browne, was also convicted and sentenced to a year in prison. Mafia influence in IATSE continued even after the downfall of Bioff and Browne, which merely elevated their associates in the union hierarchy.[31]

The studio bosses wanted IATSE—pliable and corrupt—in control of the craftspeople rather than the more militant CSU, which was led by a pugnacious former set painter and boxer named Herbert K. Sorrell, who sported a busted nose and cauliflower ears. Sorrell was intent on battling the "gangster interests" and getting a better deal for the studio workers.[32] IATSE and the studios, in turn, accused Sorrell of being a "Red" and the CSU of being a Communist-dominated union. The charge was as specious as it was potent in those days when the specter of Communist subversion loomed over American politics. Sorrell was a militant unionist but hardly a Communist, even if the House Un-American Activities Committee later claimed to have found a photostat of a party membership card for Herbert K. Stewart, Stewart being his mother's maiden name. Sorrell said it was a forgery, and he testified under oath to a congressional committee that he never belonged to the Communist Party, knowing that he could be charged with perjury if he was lying. No charges were ever brought. The Los Angeles Police Department "Red Squad," which closely surveilled the local Communist Party, never listed Sorrell as a party member or even a fellow traveler. The most prominent left-wing labor leader in the country—Harry Bridges, the Australian-born president of the International Longshoremen's and Warehousemen's Union, who was himself often accused of being a Communist—said that Sorrell was "totally apolitical and totally lacked leftist grounding." Even the producers' chief labor negotiator, Pat Casey, testified that Sorrell was not a Communist.

Sorrell, for his part, was willing to take support from the Communists or anybody else, but he was critical of both the Soviet Union and the Communist Party. "If I had my way," he said, "no Communist would be an officer or an organizer or a business agent of the union, because he would spend all his time organizing Communists instead of spending it organizing the workers."[33]

As if any further proof were needed that Herb Sorrell wasn't a Communist, it came in CSU's decision to stage a strike in March 1945 after the studios refused to recognize a federal arbitrator's ruling that the CSU rather than IATSE could bargain on behalf of set decorators. The Communist Party was intent on keeping labor peace during the war—it wanted America to help the Soviet Union defeat the Nazis—and its leaders denounced Sorrell's actions as "highly individualistic and irresponsible." "For National Unity—End the Film Strike" blared the Communist Party newspaper *People's World*. Sorrell later said that members of the Communist Party had "begged" him "to call off the strike," but he ignored them and kept ten thousand workers on strike through much of 1945.[34]

Much of America was being convulsed by labor disputes, leading to a conservative backlash from a Congress where, following the 1946 elections, Republicans were suddenly in control of both chambers. But few strikes were as violent as the one in Hollywood. In October 1945, hundreds of CSU picketers fought with police officers, studio security guards, and Teamster goons in front of the Warner Brothers studio in Burbank. On October 8, in a scene that could have inspired Elia Kazan's 1954 film *On the Waterfront*, "a wild melee" broke out "in which fists, knees, and weapons, including flares, were used . . . with scores of battlers going to the ground in grim combat."[35] Herb Sorrell was not one to shy away from a fight. "We met fist for fist and slug for slug," he later said.[36] The fighting continued on and off throughout October. At month's end, the executive council of the American Federation of Labor (AFL) told strikers to return to work while it arbitrated the dispute between the CSU and IATSE.

Unfortunately, the AFL arbitrators—the presidents of a postal workers' union, a barbers' union, and a railroad workers' union—knew nothing of the film industry and issued a series of rulings that only further confused the issue of which union would represent which workers. IATSE and the studios had no interest in compromising with CSU. "The CSU cannot exist together with the IATSE in Hollywood," declared Roy M. Brewer of IATSE. "It has got to be destroyed."[37] Brewer and the studio bosses concocted a plan to force out twelve hundred CSU carpenters and painters and replace them with IATSE workers. On September 23, 1946, the CSU workers were fired on a pretext. The CSU predictably responded by throwing up pickets in front of the studios. It was billed as a union strike, but it was really a management lockout.

The outcome of this violent labor conflict ultimately hinged on the position of the actors, whose union was the most influential in Hollywood. The studios could always replace carpenters and set decorators. They could not replace the stars who made people buy movie tickets: There was only one Bing Crosby, one Ingrid Bergman, one Gary Cooper. That made the views of the Screen Actors Guild of critical importance. Ronald Reagan was appointed as part of a small committee to decide whether SAG should support the CSU strike or not. Reagan and other SAG representatives, including Jane Wyman, traveled to Chicago in early October 1946 to meet with the AFL arbitrators, where they gathered information and came back to make a report to the SAG board and membership. It soon became clear that Reagan's mind was mind up: The CSU strike, as he later wrote, was part "of the Communist putsch for control of motion pictures."[38]

Where did Reagan get this idea, which was based on little more than hearsay and innuendo? He was heavily influenced, for one thing, by the FBI. Decades later, he wrote of the strike, "The truth is the F.B.I. let me know who were communists—not the other way around."[39] While Reagan credulously took whatever the FBI told him at face value, the bureau was rather promiscuous in accusing individuals and organizations of Communist sympathies. The paranoid FBI director, J. Edgar Hoover, saw the "red hand of communism" everywhere, even—or perhaps especially—behind the burgeoning civil-rights movement.[40] Hoover's outsize reputation has deflated over the years as his infringements on civil liberties have become widely known, but in the late 1940s, after the FBI's well-publicized battles against gangsters and Nazi saboteurs, he was at the apogee of his influence. While Harry Truman privately worried that the FBI was becoming a "Gestapo or Secret Police" that was "dabbling in sex life scandals and plain blackmail," even he did not dare to publicly challenge the bureau or try to rein it in.[41] No matter how extreme and unfounded, Hoover's accusations were accepted as gospel by most Americans—including not only Reagan but also other influential Hollywood figures.

Both Louella Parsons and Hedda Hopper were rabid Red-baiters whose views were shaped by their friendship with Hoover. A committed Republican, Hopper even urged Hoover to run for president. She claimed that "the Commies are trying to destroy the faith of the American people in the institutions and principles of the United States" and warned that labor unions were riddled with "Communistic elements." Parsons—"Aunt Lolly" to the Reagan children—vowed, "I shall continue to fight all subversive elements as long as I have a breath of life in my body."[42]

Also friendly with Hoover was Harry Warner, the president of Reagan's own studio; the two men would go together to the Del Mar Racetrack near San Diego every year to play the ponies. Like the other studio moguls, both Harry and Jack Warner were eager to help Hoover root out "Commies." They were terrified of having their own loyalties to America questioned given that, like many of the Hollywood Communists, they were Jewish and either immigrants or the children of immigrants.[43]

Another major influence on Reagan's thinking was the IATSE leader Roy Brewer, a fellow FBI informant from the Midwest with whom he became very close. Brewer was a former movie projectionist from Nebraska and a "gung-ho anti-Communist" who, in the words of SAG's executive secretary John "Jack" Dales Jr., "saw Communists under every bush."[44] Decades later, in the mid-1980s, when Reagan was president of the United States, Brewer would still be writing conspiratorial—and previously unreported—"Dear Ron" letters, claiming that Communists were "calling the shots in the campaign to defeat the nomination" of Judge Robert Bork to the Supreme Court and that the "underground communist movement . . . centers around three persons, Bradley, Cranston, and Willie Brown."[45] Needless to say, Los Angeles Mayor Tom Bradley, US Senator Alan Cranston, and California Assembly Speaker Willie Brown—all mainstream Democrats—were not part of any Communist cabal. Nor were Communists responsible for Bork's defeat. Yet President Reagan invited Brewer to the White House and naively wrote to his pal George Murphy, by then retired from the movie business and the US Senate, that "I've been keeping in touch with our old friend Roy Brewer, and he comes up with some darn good information."[46] No doubt Ron was equally credulous in the 1940s about the "darn good information" provided by his Red-baiting friend.

Just a few years earlier, Ron had argued with his Republican brother when Moon Reagan claimed that certain actors were Reds. "That's the trouble with you guys," Ron told him. "Anybody who voted for Roosevelt is a communist."[47] Now Ronald Reagan was becoming one of those "guys" himself—someone who, eliding the difference between liberals and Communists, saw Reds everywhere.

Father George H. Dunne, a scholarly but steely Jesuit who was a professor of economics at Loyola University in Los Angeles, left a revealing account of a meeting he had with Reagan during the CSU strike. Dunne, a former missionary in China who had previously been sent to Los Angeles from the University of St. Louis for his outspoken support for civil rights, had been asked in 1946 by the Catholic magazine *Commonweal* to report on the labor dispute in Hollywood. After investigating the matter, he concluded that Herb Sorrell was "a man of honesty and integrity," that the CSU was a symbol of "democratic and honest trade unionism," and that "the Red Menace was manifestly a red herring." Speaking at a strike meeting, Father Dunne said that "the strike could be settled within twenty-four hours if the actors and actresses would refuse to cross picket lines."[48] This brought him a nighttime visit to his modest quarters at Loyola University, just north of what was then called Los Angeles Municipal Airport (now Los Angeles International), from an angry SAG delegation consisting of Ronald Reagan, Jane Wyman, and George Murphy. Reagan later wrote that he was convinced Dunne was the "victim of a snow job" and wanted to set him straight.[49]

Dunne recalled that neither Wyman nor Murphy said much. Reagan did most of the talking. "This was not a labor dispute," Dunne remembered him saying. "It was a Communist conspiracy first to disrupt and then to take control of the motion picture industry." Reagan insisted that the Catholic priest "was being used by the communists." Dunne replied that there were Communists in every union—including SAG and IATSE—but "communism was not the issue here."

The dialogue "ended," Dunne wrote, "where it had begun, in complete disagreement." He was learning what many others would find out over the years: Once Reagan's mind was made up, it was nearly impossible to change it, even if he was presented with evidence that he was wrong. Dunne was left with the impression that Reagan was "a dangerous man, because he is so articulate, and because he's sharp. But he can also be very ignorant, as he clearly was, in my judgment, interpreting everything in terms of the Communist threat." The Jesuit later wrote, "It probably never occurs to Reagan that he is lying. He believes his own untruths. He lives in a world of fantasy which becomes for him reality."[50]

Dunne paid the price for his outspokenness: Under pressure from the studios, the Los Angeles archdiocese abruptly exiled him to Phoenix in 1947. In his 1965 memoir, Reagan vindictively exulted at Dunne's transfer to what he described, inaccurately, as "the other side of the country."[51] Years later, Reagan regaled fellow world leaders at the 1981 Group of Seven summit in Ottawa with tales from his Screen Actors Guild days, telling them that the KGB had sent a priest "to spread discord among the actors." The world leaders were puzzled. "What planet is that man living on?" French President François Mitterand asked Canadian Prime Minister Pierre Trudeau. But while his fellow G-7 leaders had no idea what he was talking about, Reagan was undoubtedly referring to Father Dunne, who by then was affiliated with Georgetown University. The Jesuit priest had been transformed in Reagan's febrile imagination into a Soviet agent.[52]

Reagan was displaying the same capacity to oversimplify a complex dispute that he had shown at Eureka College. Recall how he had reduced a confrontation that had multiple dimensions—including a personality clash between the college president and the dean and a dispute over whether dancing should be allowed on campus—into a simple, black-and-white morality play over budget-cutting without mentioning that the budget was still cut even after his side prevailed. "His grasp of particulars was sketchy because he thought them unimportant," Garry Wills wrote. "He quickly isolated a symbolic moral point, and devoted all his energies to enforcing that."[53] Reagan was now engaged in the same sort of moralistic oversimplification by presenting the IATSE–CSU dispute as a battle over whether Communists would take over Hollywood. Only now the stakes were much higher.

While the labor battle was raging, Reagan was working on his second postwar film, *Night unto Night*. He was playing, not very convincingly, a suicidal, epileptic biochemist who falls in love with a widow haunted by the death of her husband. The female lead was the striking Swedish newcomer Viveca Lindfors, who was engaged in a passionate affair with the film's director, Don Siegel. The picture was completed in January 1947, but it was such a clunker that it was not released by Warner Brothers until 1949. *Time* wrote, "Reagan plays the role of an epileptic with the abstract air of a man who has just forgotten an important telephone number."[54]

While Reagan was on the set in late 1946, he reported receiving an anonymous phone call. "There's a group being formed to deal with you," the caller told him. "They're going to fix you so you won't ever act again." The Burbank police took the threat seriously enough that Reagan was issued a license to carry a gun and took to wearing a .32 Smith & Wesson in a shoulder holster. A police officer was even stationed in front of the Reagans' seven-room house in the Hollywood Hills. He later claimed that someone, presumably affiliated with CSU, had been planning to throw acid in his face.[55] He also said that a bus he was about to ride into the Warner Brothers lot along with other studio employees, past the picketers, was bombed and burned just before he got on it.[56]

Reagan often cited such threats as the price of opposing Communism in Hollywood, even though there was no evidence that the violence—or threats thereof—was perpetrated by Communists. In truth, there is no way to tell who was responsible for threatening him. Yet he would later claim that not only had he been a victim of Communist plots but that he had been "number one on their hate list," thus piling one dubious claim on top of another.[57]

What Reagan did not mention was that Herb Sorrell also received a phoned-in threat—but the union leader could not count on the police to protect him. He was tied up, pistol-whipped, and dumped in the Mojave Desert by three assailants, one of them wearing a police uniform. He showed up at the next CSU meeting covered in bruises and bandages. On another occasion, Sorrell was nearly gunned down in a drive-by shooting in front of his house in Glendale.[58] Both sides in the labor dispute were guilty of violence—not just the CSU, as Reagan suggested in his memoirs.

As the world would later discover, Ronald Reagan was always a compelling speaker whether or not he had the facts on his side—and, with all the speeches he had been making, his oratorical skills had greatly improved since he had addressed a student strike meeting at Eureka College in 1928. He convinced SAG's conservative board not to honor the CSU picket lines on the grounds that it was locked in a jurisdictional dispute with IATSE. More than three hundred of SAG's more liberal members—including Katharine Hepburn, Edward G. Robinson, and Hume Cronyn—signed a petition disagreeing with the board's findings.

This led to a tense and contentious meeting on December 19, 1946, at a packed Hollywood Legion Stadium, a boxing venue, before eight hundred SAG members. CSU strikers rallied outside with signs that proclaimed

"Don't Wreck Our Union," while, inside, strong-arm squads of conservative stuntmen patrolled the aisles. Herb Sorrell spoke from the boxing ring, as did Roy Brewer and actors on both sides of the dispute. But it was Reagan who proved the most persuasive. Even those at odds with him were impressed by his speech; Edward G. Robinson, a fellow Warner Brothers star of such movies as *Little Caesar* and *Double Indemnity*, "marveled at [Reagan's] clear and sequential presentation."[59]

Persuaded by Reagan and his board colleagues, the SAG members overwhelmingly endorsed the board's decision to stay out of the IATSE–CSU dispute. They wanted to keep working. Without the actors' support, the CSU had no chance of prevailing. By 1947 the union began to dissolve "like sugar in hot water," as Reagan's memoir put it, and by the end of 1948 the lockout was over. While Herb Sorrell was on his way to a bitter defeat, Reagan was on the verge of a major triumph. Reagan's "overwhelming" and "masterful" performance at the strike meeting—as described by SAG executive secretary Jack Dales—helped propel him to the organization's presidency.[60]

The president of SAG, Robert Montgomery, famous for such films as *They Were Expendable* and *Mr. and Mrs. Smith* (and also the father of future *Bewitched* star Elizabeth Montgomery), was forced to resign in March 1947 when he decided to become a producer. Being both a union leader and a producer was considered a conflict of interest. The board chose Reagan to replace him. He was elected to a full, one-year term in November 1947 and reelected in 1948, 1949, 1950, 1951, and 1959, becoming one of the longest-serving presidents in the union's history during a series of critical turning points for the postwar film industry. That unpaid position, in turn, gave Reagan a front-row seat, quite literally, at the next major drama in the fight over Communism in Hollywood.

13

The Blacklist

Intelligent Ronald Reagan stole the show from
his better known colleagues.

—QUENTIN REYNOLDS

While Hollywood was being convulsed by the violent battles between its trade unions, it was also being probed by the House Un-American Activities Committee (HUAC). The movie industry was a natural target for HUAC—which had been created in 1938 to investigate political subversion and alleged disloyalty—not only because of its fame and influence but also because of the many Jews who were prominent in its affairs. Committee member John Rankin, Democrat of Mississippi, snarled that "alien-minded communistic enemies of Christianity and their stooges . . . are now trying to take over the motion-picture-industry . . . to spread their un-American propaganda, as well as their loathsome, lying, immoral, anti-Christian filth."[1]

The committee, with clandestine help from J. Edgar Hoover's FBI, decided to stage a show trial in October 1947 and subpoenaed forty-three members of the film community to testify—twenty-four as friendly, cooperating witnesses and nineteen as "unfriendly" witnesses who were accused of Communist sympathies.

The "capital's biggest show of the year," as one historian labeled it, opened on October 20 in an ornate hearing room in the marble-and-limestone, Beaux Arts–style Old House Office Building (now the Cannon House Office Building). Presiding was Chairman J. Parnell Thomas, Republican of New Jersey, a former stockbroker with a bald head, a beefy build, and a pug nose. Like most politicians, Thomas was ravenous for publicity, and by investigating the movie industry, he had found it. The hearings took place, the *New York Times* noted, "before 30 microphones, six newsreel cameras and blazing klieg lights." To make sure that the cameras would capture him in his pinstriped finery, the diminutive chairman discreetly sat on a red pillow resting atop a phone book.[2]

Reagan appeared before the committee on October 23, 1947, along with two past presidents of SAG, George Murphy and Robert Montgomery, and lanky screen icon Gary Cooper—"several hundred thousand dollars' worth of screen talent," as the *Los Angeles Times* put it. Movie fans—"chiefly women, from bobby-soxers to grandmothers"—packed the four hundred seats in the hearing room, the newspaper noted. "There was a long drawn out 'ooooh' from the jam-packed, predominantly feminine audience," the *New York Times* reported, at the appearance of "the tall Mr. Reagan, clad in a tan gabardine suit, a blue knitted tie and a white shirt." The Clark Kent–like horn-rimmed glasses he wore—a rarity in public—gave his remarks additional gravitas. He came across as earnest and idealistic—and, at age thirty-six, still very youthful.[3]

As a "friendly" witness, Reagan was briefly and decorously questioned by HUAC's chief investigator, Robert E. Stripling, who had provided him the questions in advance and even visited his hotel room the night before to rehearse his lines.[4] The SAG president walked a careful line between condemning Communism and defending Hollywood. He claimed there was a "small clique" within the Screen Actors Guild that "has been suspected of more or less following the tactics we associate with the Communist Party," but refused to say whether they were, in fact, Communists: "I have no investigative force, or anything, and I do not know." He agreed that Communists had tried to infiltrate the industry but insisted that they were not successful: "I do not believe the Communists have ever at any time been able to use the motion-picture screen as a sounding board for their philosophy or ideology."[5]

Reagan refused to name names of suspected Communists, and he refused to say whether the Communist Party should be outlawed. He was at odds, in this respect, with his fellow witness Robert Montgomery, who not only said that the party should be banned but added, to loud applause, that all Communists should all be "sent back to Russia or some other unpleasant place."[6] Reagan's answer to the question of whether the party should be legal was painstakingly noncommittal:

> As a citizen I would hesitate, or not like, to see any political party outlawed on the basis of its political ideology. We have spent 170 years in

this country on the basis that democracy is strong enough to stand up and fight against the inroads of any ideology. However, if it is proven that an organization is an agent of a power, a foreign power, or in any way not a legitimate political party, and I think the Government is capable of proving that, if the proof is there, then that is another matter.[7]

He even ended his testimony by expressing concern that the Red Scare would lead to violations of civil liberties:

I detest, I abhor [the Communists'] philosophy, but I detest more than that their tactics, which are those of the fifth column, and are dishonest, but at the same time I never as a citizen want to see our country become urged, by either fear or resentment of this group, that we ever compromise with any of our democratic principles through that fear or resentment. I still think that democracy can do it.[8]

Reagan's performance earned rave reviews. "Intelligent Ronald Reagan stole the show from his better known colleagues," wrote a liberal columnist, Quentin Reynolds, adding, presciently, that the actor might "have a future beyond show business."[9] His testimony had something for both the committee and its critics and offended neither side.

Little did the public know that—contrary to his later boast that he did not "point a finger at any individual"—Reagan, during a private meeting with FBI agents on April 10, 1947, gave the bureau the names of at least ten actors and actresses that he suspected of being Communists.[10] Among those he named was the Canadian actor Alexander Knox, star of a 1944 movie about Woodrow Wilson, who had aroused Reagan's ire by effectively mocking his anti-CSU speech at the Hollywood Legion Stadium. Nearly twenty years later, Reagan was still chagrined that Knox had induced an audience of his peers to laugh at him.[11] Knox would not be able to make another movie in the United States until 1967.

Subsequently, the SAG's executive secretary, Jack Dales, on July 31, 1947, named to the FBI fifty-four SAG members, including Lloyd Bridges and Lee J. Cobb, who were suspected of being Communists and provided the bureau with their internal SAG records. It is unlikely that he would have acted without the concurrence of his boss, SAG President Ronald Reagan.[12] Many of those identified as Communists by Reagan and Dales, whether rightly or wrongly, were either blacklisted or more informally "graylisted." The latter were usually denied work by the major studios but could still find employment at lesser production houses. The former had to leave the country to make a living.

The blacklist, which eventually included hundreds of movie-industry workers, was an outgrowth of the HUAC hearings in October 1947. The committee cited for contempt of Congress ten of the uncooperative witnesses, who became known as the Hollywood Ten. All of them were eventually sent to prison for terms of six months to a year. After the HUAC hearings, the motion-picture producers convened at the luxurious Waldorf-Astoria hotel in New York and decided that they would fire the Hollywood Ten and refuse to "knowingly" employ any Communists. Even liberal organizations such as the National Association for the Advancement of Colored People (NAACP) and the United Auto Workers were purging suspected Communists in those years, so the studios' action, while seen later as trampling on civil liberties, was typical of the paranoid early years of the Cold War.[13]

Ronald Reagan initially worried about how the movie industry could prove who was a Communist and who wasn't, but he did not publicly criticize the blacklist until decades afterward. Indeed, for many years, he denied the Hollywood blacklist even existed.[14] Not only did it exist; he participated in implementing it. In December 1947, Reagan proudly told FBI agents that he was involved in "purging the motion picture industry of Communists." He also said, reversing the public position he had taken at the HUAC hearing just two months earlier, that "Congress should outlaw the Communist Party."[15] Before long, he would be publicly describing all Communists as Russian "fifth columnists" and "traitors practicing treason."[16] No doubt some of his Red-hunting zeal was motivated by his desire to prove that he was not one of "them"—an impression that had been fostered in some quarters by his previous liberal activism between 1945 and 1947. Any taint of "pinko" sympathies could have killed his career.

Under Reagan's leadership, the Screen Actors Guild refused to protest the blacklist. The union defended HUAC and required that all SAG officers and committee members sign affidavits attesting that they were not Communists. The union spurned a 1951 appeal for help from Gale Sondergaard, an Academy Award–winning actress and wife of the director Herbert Biberman, one of the Hollywood Ten, who planned to plead the Fifth Amendment before HUAC. "If any actor by his own actions outside of union activities has so offended American public opinion that he has made himself unsaleable at the box office," SAG responded, "the Guild cannot and would not want to force any employer to hire him." (Sondergaard would not work again in the movies for twenty years.) In 1953, after Reagan stepped down as president but while he still remained on the board, SAG barred Communists from membership altogether. This was tantamount to preventing them from working in motion pictures.[17]

As a member and eventually president of the Motion Picture Industry Council, a labor-management group founded by his friend Roy Brewer in 1948, Reagan played an integral role in administering the blacklist. He promised to clear the names of movie workers accused of Communist ties—but only if they would "publicly declare their opposition to Communism" and "volunteer to appear before the FBI and the House Un-American Activities Committee." This meant, of course, not only undergoing ritual humiliation in public but also informing on friends and colleagues who would be exposed to obloquy and ruin. Dozens of individuals paid a severe personal and professional price for being blacklisted; a few may even have been driven to an early grave. Many observers, for example, blamed the stress of being blacklisted, along with his existing heart problems, for the tragic death of the liberal actor John Garfield, star of *The Postman Always Rings Twice* and *Gentlemen's Agreement*, at age thirty-nine in 1952.[18]

Decades later, in 1997, SAG and the other talent guilds apologized for their involvement in the blacklist. Jack Dales, who worked closely with Reagan in running SAG, expressed his own remorse about "what we did," which resulted, he admitted, in some people being "terribly mistreated."[19] Reagan, by contrast, never expressed any regrets or remorse about his own role in the Hollywood blacklist. While many workers in the movie industry were having their careers ruined by the Red Scare, Reagan's was being made.

Ronald Reagan was, for the time being, still a liberal New Dealer on economic issues. In 1948, for example, he shared a Los Angeles platform with Harry Truman and made a radio broadcast for Hubert Humphrey's Senate campaign in Minnesota. Humphrey was the mayor of Minneapolis and a liberal icon for his advocacy of civil rights against the Southern wing of the Democratic Party. In words that eerily anticipated the very criticisms he would hear from Democrats in the 1980s, Reagan complained that the Republican Congress elected in 1946 had passed "tax reduction bills . . . to benefit the higher income brackets alone"; "snatched away" Social Security benefits "from almost a million workers"; and "in the false name of economy, millions of children have been deprived of milk once provided through the federal school lunch program." "This is why we must have new faces in the Congress of the United States—Democratic faces," he implored listeners.[20] When the plucky president won a come-from-behind victory over Thomas Dewey, Reagan exulted: "I'm sure Truman with a Democratic Congress will do lots to make things better every way."[21]

But Reagan was now a hard-liner on Communism, and that stance was leading him to the right in general, even though he could have remained a liberal anti-Communist like Humphrey or Truman. Nineteen-forty-eight would be the last time he would vote for a Democratic presidential nominee, although he still supported the 1950 Senate campaign of Democrat Helen Gahagan Douglas, an actress and the wife of movie star Melvyn Douglas, against the Republican nominee, Richard Nixon, whom he astutely described as "less than honest" and an "ambitious opportunist."[22]

When Reagan became an outspoken advocate for conservative causes in the 1960s, he often cited as his chief credential his battle against Communism in Hollywood. "It must seem presumptuous to some of you for a member of my profession to stand here and attempt to talk on problems of the nation," he told the Illinois Manufacturers Association in 1961, sounding very much like a political candidate. "However, a few years ago a 'funny thing happened to us on the way to the theatre.' Ugly reality came to our town on direct orders of the Kremlin. Hard core party organizers infiltrated our business. . . . The aim was to gain economic control of our industry and then subvert our screens to the dissemination of Communist propaganda." He went on to explain that "under the guise of a jurisdictional strike, they made an open effort to destroy the guilds and unions who remained free from their control," but they had not counted on the effective opposition they received: "After the first shock, the people of the movie colony rallied quickly. . . . The studios had remained open thanks to the refusal of management and the majority of our people to be intimidated."[23]

Obvious but unsaid was that Reagan, as president of the Screen Actors Guild, had led the battle to stop the Communist takeover of one of America's most important industries. Note that in presenting his anti-Communist credentials, he shrewdly focused on the CSU strike, which few of his listeners would have known anything about, and not the infamous Hollywood blacklist, which by that point had been discredited and discontinued.

It was a nice story—and one accepted at face value by most of Reagan's chroniclers—but it wasn't true. The mythology concerning Reagan's postwar fight against Communism was even further detached from reality than the mythology concerning his wartime service—and far more important in his subsequent political rise.

Reagan was simply fantasizing when he wrote in his post-presidential memoir that "several members of the Communist Party in Hollywood who had been involved in the attempted takeover went public and described in minute detail how Moscow was trying to take over the picture business."[24] That never happened.

In both his 1965 and 1990 books, Reagan proudly cited the testimony of the dashing actor Sterling Hayden, the star of John Huston's *The Asphalt Jungle* and Stanley Kubrick's *The Killing*, who had been a member of the Communist Party for six months in 1946 and later testified before HUAC. Here is how Reagan recounted it: "Testifying under oath on the Communist maneuvers to take over Hollywood, Sterling Hayden was asked what tripped them up. His reply: 'We ran into a one-man battalion named Ronnie Reagan.'"[25] This quote has been faithfully repeated by Reagan hagiographers as evidence of his effectiveness in stopping the Kremlin from dominating the US film industry.[26] But it is ripped out of context. As anyone who bothers to read the actual transcript of the April 10, 1951, HUAC hearing can see, Hayden did not say that Reagan stopped a Communist takeover of Hollywood. He merely said that Reagan was a "one-man battalion" to prevent SAG from endorsing the CSU strike.[27]

Only if you believe, as Reagan did, that the CSU was a Communist front would you conclude that his opposition to the strike—or, more accurately, his support for the management lockout—stymied a Communist takeover of Hollywood. But there was no credible evidence then, and none has emerged in the many decades since, that the CSU strike was directed by, rather than simply supported by, the Communist Party. It's true that a former Communist leader said in 1954 that the party had been "very much interested in the success of the Conference of Studio Unions," because it wanted to establish a "progressive center in Hollywood."[28] But CSU leader Herb Sorrell did not follow the Communist line—if he had, he would not have launched a strike while World War II was still on—and a local Communist leader later told a historian that the party was not "actively involved" in the strike. So, too, the studios' chief negotiator with the CSU conceded that the conflict was not "communistic inspired."[29]

More broadly, while there were certainly Communists in Hollywood—a maximum of roughly three hundred party members worked from the 1930s to the 1950s in a movie industry employing thirty thousand to forty thousand people at a time—there is no evidence that Moscow attempted to hijack the film colony.[30] There is certainly no support for Reagan's fanciful assertion in 1951 that "the Russians sent their first team, their ace string, here to take us over" or his 1957 assertion that "Red infiltration of Hollywood was under direct orders of the Kremlin."[31]

The Soviet organization known as VOKS (a Russian acronym for All-Union Society of Cultural Contacts with Abroad), which served as a front for Soviet intelligence, was active in Los Angeles, and its files do show that Soviet intelligence officers and diplomats based at the Los Angeles vice-consulate (which closed in 1948) maintained "personal contact" with some "prominent Hollywood progressive figures . . . friendly to the Soviet Union." Many of these Soviet contacts—for example, Communist Party members Dalton Trumbo and John Howard Lawson—would become infamous as members of the Hollywood Ten.[32] But the files do not reveal that the Soviets made any great inroads in the US movie industry or plotted to take it over.

Edward Dmytryk, the director of *The Caine Mutiny* and *Murder, My Sweet*, was the first of the Hollywood Ten to admit to having been a Communist. He said after he broke with the party that he had seen no evidence of "secret plans" or "high treason." Party members, like their counterparts in many other political organizations, he said, "spent most of their time wrangling over . . . by-laws," "writing speeches," "trying to elect candidates favorable to communism," and beseeching members for donations.[33] Likewise, Sterling Hayden said, "I never heard anything that was subversive."[34]

Indeed, a leading account of the Red Scare in Hollywood concludes that while the movie-industry Communists were "apologists for the crimes of a foreign power," they were not "subversives": "There is no evidence to indicate that the Hollywood Reds ever, in any way, conspired, or tried to conspire, against the United States Government, spied for the Soviet Union, or even undermined any social institution in this country."[35] Nor is there any evidence that the Communists exercised much influence in the film industry. The Communists made the greatest inroads in the Screen Writers Guild, but they did not control even this union.[36] Their presence in the blue-collar unions was negligible.

Despite the FBI's extensive infiltration of the Communist Party USA, the G-men were never able to show that the Reds had inserted propaganda into any movies—or even tried to. The only pro-Soviet movies the studios made, such as Warner Brothers' *Mission to Moscow* (1943), were produced during the war with the encouragement of the Roosevelt administration to bolster support for the US-Soviet alliance. As soon as World War II ended and the Cold War commenced, Hollywood movies turned predictably anti-Soviet. Hunting for Communist influence, the FBI was reduced in its secret files to indicting popular movies such as *The Best Years of Our Lives* ("portrayed the 'upper class' in a bad light"), *Death of a Salesman* ("very unflattering portrayal of American life"), and *It's a Wonderful Life* ("a rather obvious attempt to discredit bankers").[37] The allegations were ludicrous and self-refuting. The G-men had uncovered liberal, not Communist, messaging. While trying to show the extent of Communist influence in Hollywood, they actually demonstrated its absence.

The Communists' lack of success in subverting this highly profitable and thoroughly capitalistic enterprise should have been no surprise. As the actor David Niven—a decorated British officer in World War II and a close friend of conservative icon William F. Buckley Jr.—was to note, "It was quite impossible for a tiny group of writers, directors, and actors to subvert for Communist propaganda the Motion Picture Industry when the whole business was in the hands of a dozen men."[38] And those dozen or so men— the studio moguls—were mostly Republicans who had conspired together to crush Upton Sinclair's Socialist campaign for governor of California in

1934. It strains credulity to imagine that even if Communists had controlled the Conference of Studio Unions (which they did not), and even if the CSU had controlled all of the craft unions (which it never came close to doing), that the studios could have been forced to produce pro-Communist movies that would have been box-office poison.

Reagan himself argued—in a 1960 letter to, of all people, *Playboy* publisher Hugh Hefner—that the blacklist was forced on Hollywood by "millions of moviegoers" who would "not pay to see pictures made by or with these people we consider traitors."[39] Yet somehow he imagined that the studios would churn out Communist propaganda on command—and moviegoers would watch it—if Herb Sorrell controlled the craft unions.

Reagan was right to see Communist regimes, and in particular the Soviet Union, as a serious danger to what was then known as the Free World, even though many anti-Communist regimes themselves were hardly democratic. He was wrong, however, to see Communist subversion as a major threat *within* the United States. Most Soviet spies were caught by the FBI, thanks to the US military's Venona intercepts of encrypted Soviet communications beginning in 1943, and the Communist Party USA declined in membership and influence following the war. But while Reagan in common with many Americans, especially politicians of the day, exaggerated the internal Communist threat, he was at least clever enough—and pragmatic enough—to avoid coming across as a shrill Red-baiter.

That was more than could be said for the nattily attired actor Adolphe Menjou, well known for his appearances in films such as *The Front Page* (1931) and *Paths of Glory* (1957), who, like Reagan, was a "friendly" HUAC witness. Menjou was a John Birch Society member who proudly admitted that he was a "witch hunter" and "red baiter": "I make no bones about it whatsoever."[40] Nor was Reagan as monomaniacal on the subject of Communism as *Kings Row* director Sam Wood, yet another HUAC witness, who made his heirs swear that they "are not now, nor have they ever been, Communists" as a condition of inheritance.[41]

By the end of the 1940s, Reagan came to share the paranoia of reactionaries like Menjou and Wood about Communist infiltration of American society, but, as with his later role in the 1960s' white backlash against civil rights, he would act his part more subtly and less provocatively than the most perfervid partisans of the far right. Indeed, his 1947 HUAC testimony was acclaimed as a model of middle-of-the-road good sense. From 1945 to 1950, Reagan established himself as an anti-Communist labor leader with a national profile, laying the groundwork for his future political career without necessarily being conscious that he was doing so.

But the period was hardly an unalloyed triumph for him. While he was fixated on the imaginary Communist plot to take over Hollywood, he was losing sight of all-too-real problems closer to home.

14

The Divorce

I tried to go to bed with every starlet in Hollywood.
And I damn near succeeded.

—RONALD REAGAN

The idealized and sanitized images propagated by Hollywood publicists and their journalistic collaborators created an impossible expectation for movie stars to live up to—especially when, as was evidently the case with Ronald Reagan, they came to believe their own publicity. The disconnect between image and reality would make it all the more painful for him to deal with the twin failures of his marriage and his acting career in the late 1940s.

Ever since the Wyman-Reagan wedding in 1940, the Warner Brothers public-relations machine had portrayed theirs as "the perfect marriage"—one that "will last forever and ever." They were proclaimed "Hollywood's nicest couple," and their love was said to grow by the year, creating a "non-stop honeymoon." They were depicted as perfect complements—she "hot-tempered" and "distrustful" of others, he "equable" and "instinctively friendly." "We've never had a quarrel," Wyman told one magazine, "because he's just too good-natured." In keeping with 1940s gender norms, their union was reported to be one in which the man was firmly in charge—and the "little lady" liked it that way. *Modern Screen* wrote in 1942, "Before the marriage [Wyman] was used to handling her own problems. 'Snarling plenty of them up,' she adds. Now she lays them like a trusting infant in Ronnie's lap."[1]

Pictures were even more powerful than words: The couple was regularly photographed with their children, Maureen and Michael, beaming for the cameras, often while sitting around their backyard pool. "She calls Ronnie her Wild Irishman and the children are Irishers," reported a fan magazine. As late as September 1947, shortly before Reagan's testimony to the House

Un-American Activities Committee, a newspaper was reporting, "They are very happy together."[2]

But trouble had long been developing beneath the idyllic surface as the couple's interests diverged. Jane devoted herself to her acting career, Ron to his volunteer work as a union leader. Ron was fascinated by politics, Jane bored by it. A glowing, but unintentionally revealing, profile in December 1946 reported Ron coming to the breakfast table eager to share the news of the world. "I've got news for you," Jane pointedly replied. "I'm not interested." The actress June Allyson, who was married to Reagan's friend and fellow actor Dick Powell, later wrote that Jane "seemed . . . upset with her husband's obsession with politics"—and with his long-windedness. "Don't ask Ronnie what time it is because he will tell you how a watch is made," Jane complained. Don Siegel, who directed Reagan in *Night unto Night*, reported an even more scabrous put-down from Jane. One night, while they were all going to dinner together, Ron "spouted off endlessly" until Jane snapped at him: "Hey, 'diarrhea-of-the-mouth,' shut up! Maybe we can get in a word edgewise." But, Siegel wrote, "Ron continued soliloquizing."[3]

While Ron was talking politics, Jane's acting career was fast eclipsing his own. This must have been difficult for him to accept in the more overtly sexist society of the 1940s when the man was expected to be the main, even sole, source of financial support for the family. One Hollywood reporter wrote at the time, "No man can watch his wife become important without trying to save face," and went on to portray Reagan's immersion in labor activism as his attempt to "save face" because his acting career was faltering in comparison with Wyman's.[4]

The couple's diverging paths were evident on March 13, 1947, when, just a few days after Ron had been elected president of the Screen Actors Guild, he attended with Jane the glittering Academy Awards ceremony where she was a nominee for best actress for *The Yearling*. She didn't win, but the movie was a big box-office hit. By contrast, his first two postwar movies, *Stallion Road* and *Night unto Night*, were flops, and he wasn't getting the parts he wanted. Reagan had sought a small role in John Huston's *The Treasure of the Sierra Madre*. Instead, in 1947, Jack Warner cast him in *The Voice of the Turtle*, a romantic comedy based on a hit Broadway play. It wasn't a bad role or a bad picture, but it lacked star power; Ron's costar was Eleanor Parker, who was not a big box-office draw.

Even worse was Ron's next assignment. *That Hagen Girl* was Shirley Temple's first adult role, but the public still saw the nineteen-year-old actress as a child star. The thirty-six-year-old Reagan was cast as a much older man who romances her, even though he is wrongly suspected of being her father. It was a cringe-inducing bit of miscasting that might have led another actor to simply refuse the part even at the cost of being suspended by the studio. But after protesting the assignment, Ron agreed to accept it. "Only did it to accommodate Warner Bros.," Reagan grumbled to one of his biggest fans. "I knew it wouldn't do anything for me but they were desperate, so you know 'old easy going' Reagan."[5]

In one of the scenes, Reagan was supposed to jump into a lake to save a drowning Shirley Temple. The director offered to use a stunt double, but Ron volunteered to do it himself. The next day, he felt as if he had been stabbed in the chest. It was more pain than he had ever experienced. On June 19, 1947, his condition worsening, he was taken by ambulance to Cedars of Lebanon Hospital where he was diagnosed with viral pneumonia. His temperature spiked to 106 degrees Fahrenheit. "Days and nights went by in a hazy montage in which I alternately shivered with chills or burned with fever," Reagan recalled.[6] The doctors were not sure he would make it.

Jane Wyman was understandably distraught. She was also five months pregnant. She had overcome her qualms about another pregnancy in the hope of expanding their family—and bringing them closer together. Under stress from Ron's alarming condition, however, she began to go into premature labor on June 25, 1947. She was rushed from their home to Queen of Angels Hospital, where she delivered a premature girl weighing only a pound and a half. Despite a press report that the baby "is given a good chance of survival," the infant, named Christine, died nine hours later.[7]

Jane had to endure this devastating blow by herself, while her husband was fighting for his life in another hospital. Her sobbing was uncontrollable, and she was inconsolable. She went into a "profound depression" that lasted for weeks.[8]

By mid-July 1947, Reagan was out of the hospital and, after missing nearly a month of filming, back on the set of *That Hagen Girl*. But Jane was still reported to be "terribly depressed." Their marriage would never recover from this ordeal. As a newspaper summed it up at the time, "Six months ago they were the happiest of couples. . . . She was nominated for an Academy award and he was elected president of the Screen Actors Guild. . . . Everything seemed to be going their way. . . . Then he got pneumonia and she lost her baby and in about three or four days those sunny skies turned grey."[9]

When Jane and Ron were finally reunited at home, they found they had little to say to one another as each dealt privately with the trauma of losing a child. "Ronnie felt she was remote and indifferent to him and his interests," said a reporter who knew them. "Jane felt that he didn't appreciate her and still neglected her."[10]

Like many couples whose marriage is in trouble, they threw themselves into their work. In Ron's case, that was the Hollywood labor struggle; not only was he dealing with accusations of Communist infiltration of the movie industry, but he was taking the lead in negotiating a new ten-year labor contract for the actors. Between shooting *That Hagen Girl* during the day and attending SAG meetings at night, Reagan had little time left for his family. "I think I can sleep standing up," he wrote.[11]

In Jane's case, work meant the film *Johnny Belinda*. She had been cast in a starring role as a deaf girl in Nova Scotia who is raped and impregnated by a neighbor. Her character, Belinda McDonald, gives birth to a boy she names Johnny Belinda. Jane immersed herself in the part by studying sign language and lip reading, even sealing her ears with wax to blot out all sound. Her devotion to the demanding part would pay off with an Academy Award for Best Actress in 1949.

In early September 1947, a few weeks before he was due to travel to Washington to testify to HUAC, Ron drove Jane to the location shoot on California's rugged Mendocino coast—a stand-in for Nova Scotia located 170 miles north of San Francisco. Then he returned home to his SAG business. The film company would spend the next month shooting in the wilderness.

With little to do after the cameras stopped rolling, the actors became unusually close. Jane spent much of her free time with her handsome costar, Lew Ayres. He played a kindly physician who befriended and defended her character. Ayres had become a star by playing a German soldier in the antiwar classic *All Quiet on the Western Front* (1930), an experience that converted him to a pacifist philosophy. He went on to star in the *Dr. Kildare* movies for MGM. Drafted in 1942, he shocked the nation by declaring himself a conscientious objector and refusing to fight. The resulting backlash almost ruined his career. But he redeemed himself with the public by serving heroically as a combat medic in the Pacific theater. Spiritual, sensitive, and soulful, Ayres was everything that Reagan was not. He was interested in art, books, philosophy, music, religion—not in politics.[12] Jane found that, while Ronnie was a good talker, Lew was a better listener. She denied rumors of an affair on the set, but even if their relationship remained platonic for the time being, it became intimate and emotionally intense. By 1949, she would be declaring, "Lew Ayres is the love of my life."[13]

A Hollywood journalist later described the impact of Jane's relationship with Lew: "When a girl is already emotionally at odds with her husband, close association with another man, attractive and considerate, might cause her to view her mate with an even more critical eye." This reporter noted that at a dinner at Le Papillon on the Sunset Strip shortly after *Johnny Belinda* finished shooting, Ron and Jane "weren't laughing at all, and their few smiles were pretty wooden. Once or twice Ronnie went into long dissertations, and I gathered from Jane's expression that she was pretty uninterested in what he was saying." The icy interactions between Ron and Jane contrasted with the way Jane and Lew related to one another at a party thrown by Errol Flynn: "They were having lots of laughs and both seemed very intent on what the other was saying."[14]

Shortly after the dour dinner with Ron on the Sunset Strip, Jane decided to head off for a vacation in New York—by herself. While there, she was tracked down by a gossip columnist. She told him that she was considering a separation from her husband: "There is no use in lying. I am not the happiest girl in the world." At around the same time, she told a friend, "We're through. We're finished. And it's all my fault."[15]

The news shook the film colony. No one was more surprised than Ronald Reagan, who must have believed the fairy-tale picture of his marriage painted by the pliant movie-industry press. He had no idea that his wife was so unhappy. The news hit him, he admitted, "like a ton of bricks." "I'm looking forward to a happy life with Jane for as long as we live," he told reporters.

"We've had tiffs before, as what married couple hasn't."[16] (So much for fan magazine claims that they never fought!) Privately, he wrote to the head of his fan club: "Janie is still a pretty sick girl, in my mind, but I'm still hoping that things will be different when she gets over this nonsense, so don't listen to the things you hear, please. I know she loves me, even though she thinks she doesn't."[17] The reference to Wyman's sickness probably referred to her severe depression after losing their daughter.

His statements simply reflected his lack of understanding of Wyman—and his stubborn tendency, rooted in the pain of growing up an alcoholic's son, to deny grim realities. Reagan was used to charming everyone he met. Just as he could not fathom why Margaret Cleaver would break off their engagement, now he could not understand why Jane Wyman might want to divorce him. His parents had stayed together, despite their evident unhappiness, until his dad's death. Why not he and Jane? "I suppose there had been warning signs, if only I hadn't been so busy," Reagan later admitted, "but small-town boys grow up thinking only other people get divorced. The plain truth was that such a thing was so far from even being imagined by me that I had no resources to call upon."[18]

It fell to Ron to have a difficult conversation with their seven-year-old daughter, Maureen; Michael, at age three, was too young to know what was going on. Like any other parent in a similar situation, he dutifully told her that the divorce was "the best thing" (which he did not, of course, believe), that he would always remain her father, and that he would still be around when she needed him. "Just remember, Mermie, I still love you," she remembered him saying, his voice cracking. "I will always love you." It was all a "blur" to Maureen, who cried at the news. Like the moviegoing public, she had heard no "rumblings" that a divorce was in the works.[19]

At the end of June 1948, after a failed attempt at reconciliation, the official divorce decree was set in motion stipulating that Ronald Reagan would pay $500 a month in child support. In a court hearing, Jane Wyman blamed the rift on politics. It wasn't that they differed in their views (she eventually became a conservative Catholic convert); her complaint was that he forced her to take part in political activities despite her own lack of interest and then did not consider her own ideas to be "important." "Finally," she told the court, "there was nothing in common between us, nothing to sustain our marriage."[20]

Reagan wasn't the only one heartbroken by the breakup. So was much of Hollywood and the moviegoing public. "Perfect marriage ends," blared a typical headline.[21] Louella Parsons, the unctuous queen of gossip who had taken a proprietary interest in their relationship and even hosted their wedding reception, wrote,

> It is unfortunate, but true, that Hollywood can shrug off most marriage crack-ups.... But when they are Jane Wyman and Ronald Reagan—well—we just can't take that! No marital separation since the [1936] story that Mary Pickford, America's sweetheart, was leaving Douglas Fairbanks has had the effect of the parting of the Reagans. Just as Mary and Doug stood for all that is best in this town, so have Ronnie and Janie.... To those of us who are close friends, they were an ideal Mr. and Mrs. That's why this hurts so much.[22]

Like most observers, Parsons assigned much of the blame for the divorce not on easygoing "Ronnie" Reagan but on his high-strung wife, who had become emotionally enmeshed with her costar and devoted so much of her attention to her demanding role. Reagan himself quipped, "If it comes to a divorce, I think I'll name *Johnny Belinda* co-respondent!" "Hollywood sympathy in this case is one hundred per cent with Ronnie, who is a prince," wrote one reporter. "Jane is a moody person, temperamental, ambitious, restless and seeking; furthermore, she is not now and hasn't been well for some time." Hedda Hopper joined in the pile-on, blaming Wyman—"sullen, rude and jittery"—for letting "a wonderful guy like Ronald Reagan slip out of her life."[23]

And it was true that Jane Wyman had trouble staying married. Having been married twice before, after divorcing Reagan she twice married and twice divorced the same man: a handsome studio composer and bandleader named Frederick "Freddie" M. Karger. After her second divorce from Karger in 1965, Wyman stayed single for the final forty-two years of her life. (She had expressed interest in marrying Lew Ayres following her divorce from Ronnie, but after two failed marriages of his own—to actresses Lola Lane and Ginger Rogers—Ayres was not willing to march down the aisle with her.) "Some women just aren't the marrying kind—or anyway, not the permanently marrying kind," she later said, "and I'm one of them."[24]

But there is plenty of blame to go around when most marriages unravel, and this one was no exception. If Wyman was a typical moody, emotional artiste, Reagan was a typical career man who paid more attention to his work than to his family. In particular, he showed a crippling lack of empathy for, and understanding of, his spouse. Reagan has sometimes been credited with displaying "emotional intelligence" or "interpersonal intelligence" in lieu of conventional intellect,[25] and it is true that he could be highly skilled in reading a whole crowd or even an entire nation, but his emotional intelligence often failed him in interpersonal relations—particularly with those closest to him. As his son Ron Reagan told me, "There were a lot of gaps in his emotional intelligence."[26]

Ronald Reagan showed little comprehension of what either his first fiancée or his first wife was thinking or experiencing. He was often equally oblivious about his own children and their challenges or about the squabbles and struggles of his senior aides in Sacramento and Washington. An introvert and a loner, he could relate brilliantly to almost anyone on a superficial level of shared bonhomie fostered by jokes and stories, but he seldom attained a deeper knowledge of those closest to him—and thus wound up losing first Margaret Cleaver and then Jane Wyman, the first two loves of life, while having strained and distant relationships with his own children.

He plainly needed a wife who would offer him total and unconditional love and understanding while expecting only limited empathy and little understanding in return. Such a woman would not be easy to find.

Ronald Reagan, age thirty-seven, was dazed and devastated by his divorce. He felt lonely and unloved. Both he and Jane moved out of the Hollywood Hills "dream house" they had built. He moved initially into an apartment building notorious for Hollywood high-life—the Garden of Allah—before renting the same apartment, at 136B Londonderry View, where he had lived before his marriage. He had to continue working—with commitments both to Warner Brothers and the Screen Actors Guild—and spending time with his two children while also starting to date for the first time in nearly a decade.

He later described his predicament:

> Picture a reasonably young man working with and among the most
> beautiful girls in the world—plenty of money in his jeans, a Cadillac
> convertible [a present from Jane], and an apartment. Sounds like an
> adolescent's daydream come true, doesn't it? The only trouble was, I
> wasn't an adolescent and I didn't exactly know how to be a bachelor all
> over again. Actually I had very little previous experience at being a gay
> blade around Hollywood. In my early Hollywood days I was too busy
> and scared to collect phone numbers.[27]

He would eventually get over his hesitancy about collecting phone numbers, but first he would have to get over his attachment to Jane Wyman and give up his hopes of a reunion, which he continued to harbor even after their divorce.

Going to England in the fall of 1948 seemed like the perfect opportunity to take his mind off the divorce. Reagan had never been to Europe before, and now he had his chance after being cast in *The Hasty Heart*, a film about a group of soldiers in a wartime hospital in Burma. Reagan was to play the token Yank. Richard Todd, a former British officer who had parachuted into Normandy on D-Day, played a dying Scottish corporal. Patricia Neal, a beautiful, twenty-two-year-old American actress, played the nurse who took care of them. The film was to be made on a soundstage in London because Jack Warner wanted to use frozen studio funds that the British government, battling a currency crisis, would not allow out of the country.

After a cross-continental train trip, Reagan set sail from Canada on November 20, 1948, aboard the Cunard steamship *Britannic*. He looked upon "the entire trip" as a "grand adventure to be savored, swallowed, and digested," but he found life in postwar Britain to be indigestible—literally. Patricia Neal noted that, with wartime rationing continuing, "the food was ghastly": "Cardboard fish covered with soggy bread crumbs and exhausted vegetables was a regular menu." "What they do to food we did to the American Indian," Reagan wrote in a jocular letter of complaint to Jack Warner. "The average meal should go from 'kitchen to can' thus avoiding the use of a middleman."

A wealthy man, Reagan took action to improve his diet. Neal wrote that "Ronnie adored steak and had them flown in a dozen at a time from '21' in

New York." Some of the steaks disappeared in the kitchen of the Savoy, the stately Victorian hotel near Trafalgar Square where they were staying; they were supposedly "spoiled." But the rest he shared with Neal.[28]

The inedible food was only the beginning of Reagan's complaints about life in postwar London, where the film company stayed for four months over the harsh fall and winter of 1948–1949. Everything from petrol to tobacco was in short supply. The only thing that was abundant was fog. Reagan discovered that the famous London fog was "almost combustible" and "so thick . . . with soft-coal smoke" that "it was a shock to my smog-sensitive sinuses." He also found that because of continuing "austerity under the Labor-Socialist government," "no billboards, window displays or marquees were permitted lighting. The only outdoor illumination came from dim and inadequate street lamps. A city can be pretty dreary under those circumstances."[29] The film's director, Vincent Sherman, wrote in early 1949, "Living conditions here are none too cheerful."[30]

Reagan was visiting Britain during a painful period of transition while Clement Attlee's Labour government was creating a welfare state that went far beyond America's New Deal by nationalizing steel, coal, railroads, electricity, and the medical system. Reagan focused only on the problems postwar Britain was experiencing—particularly all of the shortages of consumer goods—and unfairly blamed them entirely on the Labour government. He showed no recognition that the country had been bled dry by the cost of World War II. And, while focusing on the costs of expanded government, he ignored the benefits of providing a greater social safety net for the impoverished and elderly. He later described his time in England as one of the ideological turning points—after his wartime disgust with bloated bureaucracy and his postwar fight against Communists in Hollywood—that made him into a conservative. Looking back on his British sojourn, he wrote, "I shed the last ideas I'd held about government ownership of anything."[31]

His time in the United Kingdom wasn't all misery, of course. Reagan was able to tour the English countryside in a chauffeur-driven Rolls Royce and to take a brief vacation on the French Riviera. He also formed a friendship with Pat Neal, who lived next door to him in the swank Savoy hotel. This would have seemed like the perfect venue for a post-divorce fling, but, in Neal's account, it never happened. He regaled her with his views on politics—"it was not a conversation but a monologue"—but he never made a pass. "I sensed that he was still carrying a torch for Jane Wyman," she later wrote.[32] (Neal, who would win the 1964 Academy Award for Best Actress for *Hud*, married the British children's writer Roald Dahl in 1953.)

Indeed, Ron sent his ex-wife a model ship from London as a peace offering, with a note indicating that he still hoped to patch things up. She returned the gift with a note of her own: "Give me something I want."[33]

By the time he returned home in 1949, Reagan's torch for Jane Wyman was dimming—reduced to a "feeble flame" in the words of one movie magazine.[34] He began to date actively. "I tried to go to bed with every starlet in Hollywood," he recalled a quarter of a century later to the journalist Robert D. Novak. "And I damn near succeeded."[35]

One of his girlfriends reported, "He liked the all-American girl type. . . . He liked that outdoor, blond Pasadena Rose Bowl parade type of clean, California woman."[36] There was an almost limitless supply of such women around the studios—with, as a magazine writer noted, "a fresh supply of pulchritude arriving on every train."[37] The actresses he was seen with included Betty Underwood (said by a magazine to have "one of the six best figures in America"), Doris Day, Ann Sothern, Monica Lewis, Adele Jergens, Rhonda Fleming, and Ruth Roman. Edmund Morris later counted "at least sixteen different young and beautiful actresses" that he dated during this period.[38]

One of the few non-actresses he went out with was the witty gossip columnist Doris Lilly, who in 1951 published *How to Marry a Millionaire*, which became a hit movie starring Marilyn Monroe, and who would be cited as the model for Holly Golightly in Truman Capote's *Breakfast at Tiffany's*. Many years later Lilly described Reagan as "truly the all-American boy, never a lothario," and not a "come-on-strong type of man." "He behaved himself beautifully," she said.[39] But then that may have been because they had a serious, on-and-off relationship. Like many men, Reagan could be crueler with passing flings.

Piper Laurie, the future star of *The Hustler* and *Carrie*, left in her memoir an unflattering account of a one-night stand with the future president. (She conveyed to me, shortly before her death in 2023, that she had nothing to add beyond what she had written.) She was just eighteen and still living with her parents when she met Ronald Reagan in 1950 on the set of her first film—the comedy *Louisa*. He was playing her father, but it soon became obvious that his interest in her was far from paternal. One night, he invited her out to dinner; after getting her mother's permission, she agreed to go. En route in his car, Ron suggested that, instead of going to a restaurant, he could cook dinner at his apartment. She was just old enough to know what that meant. She discovered that the apartment was "rather small and seemed crowded with too much furniture"—furniture, of course, that had been removed from the marital manse. After making a "very nice" dinner of "hamburger steak and salad," the forty-year-old movie star proceeded to seduce his barely legal costar.

Laurie gave her enthusiastic consent; she later told him, "I'm very honored that such a respected and admired person was my first lover." But while she found that "Ronnie was more than competent sexually," she complained that he missed "the obvious clues of my inexperience, even to the small traditional stain on the sheet." He criticized her performance while bragging about how long "he had been 'ardent.'" "He was a bit of a show-off," she wrote. Laurie later concluded that "his insensitivity had been wounding and, in retrospect, even cruel" and turned him down when a few months later, during a publicity junket in Chicago, he tried to enter her hotel room for an encore.[40] Her criticism that Ron was overly self-centered would not have surprised Jane Wyman, but his aggressive behavior, while far from abnormal in Hollywood then or now, would have shocked fans who believed the fan-magazine portrait of the morally upright actor.

Celebrity biographer Kitty Kelley accused Reagan of even greater sordidness—including the "date rape" of the actress Selene Walters and refusing to take responsibility for the pregnancy of actress Jacqueline Park, leading her to get an abortion. Such allegations are impossible to verify, and Kelley was often accused of passing along unverified rumors and gossip, but Walters and Park stood behind their stories when questioned by *People* magazine in 1991.[41] If accurate, their accounts cast a fresh and unflattering light on Reagan's character. This was the sort of conduct one might associate with notoriously priapic presidents such as John F. Kennedy, Bill Clinton, and Donald J. Trump—not with Ronald Reagan, the happily married paragon of "family values."

In fairness, this kind of behavior was hardly typical of the long sweep of Reagan's life, and it occurred while he was unmarried. There has never been any evidence that he ever cheated on either of his wives; in his son Ron's words, "It's absurd to even consider the possibility."[42] The period following his divorce was a low point in his adult life—the one time he was truly lost and adrift. No one should be judged solely on how they behave during a bad day, and Reagan was having a lot of bad days in those years. It was not just that his marriage had ended against his will for reasons he did not comprehend or accept. His movie-making career was also decelerating, even stalling out.

For the first time in his career, Ronald Reagan was feuding with his boss Jack Warner. He even gave an interview complaining about having to always play "a screen goody-good." "If only I could play a scoundrel, or a murderer, or get a good case of madness," he wistfully speculated, as if such parts were in his dramatic range. He particularly yearned to do more Westerns; despite his association with cowboys in the popular imagination, he only starred in five pictures set in the Wild West during his whole career—fewer than 10 percent of all the features he made—and none was a big hit.[43] He thought that Jack Warner had reneged on an agreement to cast him in a Western called *Ghost Mountain,* and he was upset about it. The film was released in 1950 as *Rocky Mountain* starring Errol Flynn.[44] "I have come to the conclusion that I would do as good a job of picking [roles] as the studio has done. At least I could do no worse," he groused to another reporter. "With the parts I've had, I could telephone my lines in and it wouldn't make any difference."[45]

But the uncomfortable truth was that he was cast in undemanding roles, particularly in romantic comedies, because that was what he did best. He lacked the acting ability for more challenging character parts, and he did not project the frisson of danger, virility, and sheer animal magnetism conveyed by such leading men as Gary Cooper, William Holden, and John Wayne. As director Don Siegel said, Reagan was "inclined to be stiff as an actor" and was too "self-conscious" to "really let himself go," but "within the limits of his talent . . . he was quite good."[46]

Those limits, however, were now becoming apparent.

In the past, the studios could have kept a lesser "player" like Ronald Reagan—who had briefly tasted stardom and then lost it—working in B pictures, but the economics of the business were changing. In 1944, in response to a lawsuit against Warner Brothers by Olivia de Havilland, a California state court ruled that the studios could not commit actors to indefinite contracts. Four years later, in response to a Justice Department antitrust action, the Supreme Court ruled in *United States v. Paramount* that the studios had to sell their movie theaters, which had provided a steady stream of income and a captive market for their products.

The *De Havilland* and *Paramount* decisions, followed shortly thereafter by the rise of television, marked the beginning of the end of the old studio system. Most of the studios would survive, but they would not churn out as many pictures as they once had or provide guaranteed employment for so many actors, directors, writers, and technicians. Weekly attendance at the movies dropped from ninety million people in 1946 to sixty million in 1950, while studio profits plunged 70 percent in those years. In response, the studios had no choice but to cut costs. Actors went from employees on long-term contracts to free agents who were never certain where or when they would work next. As workers in other industries would discover in the decades ahead, transitioning from being "organization men"—and women—to being part of what today would be called the "gig economy" could be a bewildering process that produced a sense of dislocation.[47]

Ironically, given Reagan's later espousal of the free market, he was one of the casualties of the more cutthroat, less-coddled movie business, which offered greater rewards for the top stars, including profit sharing, and fewer opportunities for lesser lights like him. Yet he would blame "our government" for the movie industry's "economic distress"—and his own.[48] If you seek the roots of the Reagan administration's relaxed enforcement of antitrust laws, they can be found in a studio actor's anger over the *Paramount* decree.

As part of a general downsizing, which led to the release of such top stars as Bette Davis, James Cagney, and Humphrey Bogart, Warner Brothers reworked Reagan's contract in 1949. "Warner's have turned me out," he complained to the head of his fan club. "They decided I wasn't a very big drawing card and are afraid to risk giving me good parts."[49] His new, three-year deal called for only one picture a year rather than three and paid him only half of his previous salary, which had been $150,000 a year. The only benefit was that he would be free to work for other studios.

His agent Lew Wasserman arranged a deal calling for him to make one movie a year for five years at Universal Pictures, with each movie paying him $75,000. But he turned down two of the scripts he was offered and made only three pictures at Universal: the comedies *Louisa* (1950) and *Bedtime for Bonzo* (1951) and the Western *Law and Order* (1953).[50] He also did a few other movies as a freelancer for Paramount, MGM, RKO, and Columbia. But these were hardly the kind of roles he was yearning for. In *Bedtime for Bonzo,* an intermittently amusing romp, he portrayed a psychology professor who tries to raise a monkey like a human child to settle a "nature versus nurture" debate. His role—essentially playing straight man to a chimpanzee—would be mocked by his political opponents for decades to come.

Reagan suffered the cruelest blow of all on June 20, 1949. Playing in a baseball game for charity at a Minor League ballpark in South Central Los Angeles, he bunted and tried to beat out the throw but was blocked from the bag by the first baseman. They had a violent collision, and he came up in pain, initially thinking he had torn a ligament. A trip to the hospital emergency room revealed he had suffered six fractures of the right thigh bone.[51]

He later wrote that he was "headed for two months of traction, more months of cast, then a steel and leather brace, crutches, canes, and almost a year of therapy." As if that weren't awful enough, he developed an allergic reaction to the bandages wrapped around his leg. "Twenty-four hours later," he wrote, "my eyes were swollen shut, my teeth hurt at even the touch of my tongue, and I itched and peeled all over." Massive doses of histamines kept him "only semi-conscious" for a whole week. After that, he simply had to endure "weeks of discomfort because there was no removing the bandages."[52]

These were the harshest years of Ronald Reagan's adult life, and he tried to find solace in a series of meaningless liaisons. He realized his life was out of control when his nightclub bills were totaling $750 a month, and he was sleeping with so many women that one morning he didn't know whose head was on the pillow next to him.[53]

This was the vulnerable moment when a little-known actress named Nancy Davis entered his life via a clever ruse.

15

The Winning Team

Without Nancy Reagan, Ronald Reagan would never
have been elected to anything.

—THOMAS C. REED

lmost nothing in Ronald Reagan's upbringing and background
gave any hint that he was destined for Hollywood. Almost everything in Nancy Davis's upbringing and background pointed in
that direction.

She was born Anne Frances Robbins on July 6, 1921, making her a decade
younger than her future husband. Her father, Kenneth Robbins, was the
unambitious scion of a genteel New England family that had fallen on hard
times. Her mother, Edith Luckett—known as Lucky, Edie, or DeeDee—was
a high-school dropout from Virginia who had become a successful stage
actress. Their short-lived union was over in all but name by the time Anne
Francis, whose nickname was Nancy, was born in Flushing, Queens.

Once Nancy was out of diapers, Edith left her in the care of her sister and
brother-in-law, who lived with a daughter of their own in Bethesda, Maryland, while she pursued her stage career in companies that toured the East
Coast. Between the ages of two and eight, Nancy seldom saw her mother; her
best memories of those years were of being taken by her aunt to see Edith
perform on Broadway and getting to visit with her backstage, imbibing the
heady smell of greasepaint. Nancy later expressed chagrin "at the armchair
psychologists who claimed that I was 'abandoned' by my mother, when she
brought me to live in Bethesda," while acknowledging that "I missed her
terribly." When Nancy came down with pneumonia at age five, she recalled,
"I was angry that Mother was a thousand miles away in a touring company."
"It was," she wrote, "a painful period for both of us."[1]

Nancy was not to know a normal family life—something she desperately
desired—until, on a ship headed to England, her mother charmed an ambitious younger neurosurgeon from Chicago. The meeting occurred in 1927,

when Edith was thirty-nine and still technically married to Kenneth Robbins. Dr. Loyal Davis was only thirty-one and married with a two-year-old son. But his marriage was in the process of dissolution; his wife, a former nurse, was not supportive of his career, and he suspected her of cheating on him with one of his friends. A shipboard fling with a blonde, blue-eyed actress with an exuberant personality provided Loyal an escape from his failing marriage. Both Edith and Loyal soon divorced and then married each other in 1928. The following year, while "Dutch" Reagan was starting his second year at Eureka College, they moved with eight-year-old Nancy to the fourteenth floor of a luxury Lake Shore Drive apartment building on Chicago's Gold Coast facing Lake Michigan.

The Davis family was cushioned from the hardship of the Great Depression in a way that most American families—including the Reagans—were not, which may help explain why Loyal remained a staunch Republican throughout the 1930s. Edith did not give up her career—she would continue to act in Chicago-based radio soap operas—but she gave up touring and was reunited full-time with her daughter. Nancy was so happy to have a real home at last, after having been all but abandoned by her mother, that she pretended Kenneth Robbins had never existed and insisted Loyal Davis was her real father. She even pretended to have been born in Chicago. Many decades later, she would be furious when a reporter referred to Loyal Davis as her stepfather.[2]

"Dr. Loyal," as she called him, may have been demanding and prickly—Patti Davis recalled him as an "intimidating man" with a "thin unsmiling mouth and steely eyes"[3]—but Nancy was in awe of him. She described him as "a man of the highest principles" and "considered it a great privilege" to watch him operate on patients. He was, for many years, chief of surgery at Passavant Memorial Hospital in Chicago and chairman of the department of surgery at Northwestern University Medical School. "My father seemed to perform miracles and I was deeply proud of him," Nancy wrote, while adding that she considered her mother "the ideal doctor's wife."[4] As a teenager, she finally convinced Loyal to formally adopt her. Thus, Nancy Robbins became Nancy Davis.

Nancy Reagan was to write that Edie and Loyal "had a wonderful marriage, despite—or perhaps because of—their obvious differences. My father was tall and dark; my mother was short and blond. He was a Republican; she was a Democrat. He was often severe; she was always laughing. He was an only child; she came from a large family. He was reserved; she knew every-body."[5] In this case, the differences complemented each other rather than clashing. Loyal provided Edith with stability, financial support, and social standing; she provided him with adoration, emotional support, and a glit-tering social life, characteristics she would pass on to her daughter. Edith's friends from theater days included celebrated actors Spencer Tracy, Lil-lian Gish, Walter Huston, Colleen Moore, and Alla Nazimova—a silent film and theater star who was Nancy's godmother; the founder of the Garden of Allah, where Ronald Reagan lived after his divorce; and one of Hollywood's most prominent lesbians. All of them became regular visitors to the fami-ly's Chicago apartment; Loyal would even help the hard-drinking Spencer Tracy dry out from time to time. Nancy's son Ron said that Loyal was "a stick-up-the-ass kind of guy naturally" and Edith "really loosened him up."[6]

Nancy, in many ways, was quite different from her mother. Edith was bawdy and fun-loving, with a penchant for dirty jokes and four-letter words. Edith's friend, the newsman Mike Wallace, who worked in Chicago radio before World War II, later recalled that Nancy, by contrast, was a prim and proper young lady with a "Peter Pan collar and the black patent leather shoes and the white gloves and the pearls."[7] But while Nancy rebelled against her mother's wild, unconventional ways and took more after the staid and stodgy style of her stepfather, she did imbibe Edith's lessons for how to keep a husband happy. "Now, Nancy," Edith would say, "when you get married, be sure to get up and have breakfast with your husband in the morning. Because if you don't, you can be sure that some other woman who lives around the corner will be perfectly happy to do so."[8]

Young Nancy Davis also learned from her mother important lessons in social climbing. Edith overcame the handicap of being a thespian—still a disreputable profession to the old monied elite—to ingratiate both herself and her husband into the highest levels of Chicago society. She achieved this feat by becoming a prodigious fundraiser for charities such as the Red Cross, the Finnish Relief Fund, Passavant Memorial Hospital, and the Chi-cago Community Fund. She and Loyal even became close to Chicago Mayor Edward J. Kelly and his wife, Margaret, with Edith evidently serving as a sub rosa image consultant to the working-class politician in return for a city salary as a "temporary policewoman."[9]

Her mother's life taught Nancy the importance of family stability and how to achieve it: by slavishly catering to, and ceaselessly promoting, her husband. Nancy's stepbrother, Dr. Richard Davis, told me that "Nancy's marriage and Edith's were sort of parallel."[10]

As a child of privilege after her mother's second marriage, Nancy Davis attended much more elite schools than her future husband—Chicago's University School for Girls, followed by the still more prestigious Chicago Latin School for Girls, and then Smith College in Northampton, Massachusetts, one of the "Seven Sisters" liberal arts colleges—but she was no more accomplished academically. "I remember when she'd come back from Smith over the Christmas holidays, I'd have to do her physics test for her, not that that makes me look good," said Richard Davis, who was five years younger than Nancy. A neurosurgeon in later life, like his father, Dick remembered his stepsister as being a "very animated, outgoing teenager"—"full of life," in contrast to the "withdrawn," "very protective," and "sensitive" first lady that she became—but he added, acerbically, "Edith was not the brightest bulb on the tree. As a matter of fact, Nancy wasn't either."[11]

Like Ronald Reagan, Nancy Davis had no pretensions of scholarship and was more focused on her social life and extracurricular activities. She was not athletic, but she acted in school plays, even playing a president's wife on one occasion, and was repeatedly elected to student council positions. She later quipped that at Smith College, "I majored in English and drama—and boys."[12]

Like many young ladies in the 1940s, Nancy was hoping to graduate with a "Mrs.," but it did not work out. Her first serious boyfriend was Frank Birney, a handsome Princeton student and son of a Chicago banker. But only eight days after the Japanese attack on Pearl Harbor, Frank was struck and killed by a train in what was almost certainly a suicide. "It was the first time that anybody I was close to had died," Nancy wrote, "and it was a tremendous shock."[13] A romance followed with a wealthy Amherst College student named James Platt White Jr. who had joined the Navy. In 1944 they announced plans to marry, but Nancy abruptly canceled the engagement shortly thereafter. Her stepbrother told biographer Karen Tumulty, author of the definitive account of Nancy's life, that, when White came home on leave, Nancy discovered he was gay.[14]

A drama major, Nancy graduated from college in 1943 while World War II was still raging. Without a husband to support her, she had to figure out what to do with herself. One of her mother's friends, the actress ZaSu Pitts, star of Erich von Stroheim's 1924 silent-film epic *Greed*, offered her a small part in a touring play that wound up on Broadway. She stayed in New York after the play closed with financial support from her parents, experiencing the excitement of America's largest city during its postwar boom. "I don't think I would have had much work as a stage actress if it hadn't been for Mother," Nancy acknowledged. "There was just too much competition, and I didn't have the drive that Mother had."[15]

Her mother's friends not only provided Nancy Davis with a few parts on Broadway but even set her up in 1948 with Clark Gable when the screen idol was visiting New York. Gossip columnists imagined a competition for the "King of Hollywood" between a "slim, brown-eyed, brown-haired beauty named Nancy Davis" and the actress Ann Sheridan, who had been dubbed the "Oomph Girl" by the Warner Brothers publicity department.[16] But, frankly, the aging star of *Gone with the Wind* did not, so to speak, give a damn. Apparently still grieving over the loss of his third wife, Carole Lombard, in an airplane crash in 1942, Gable showed no desire to get serious with either woman.

Of greater importance to Nancy's career was Benjamin "Benny" Thau, the MGM vice president for talent, a middle-aged bachelor who was notorious for using the casting couch to select starlets for film roles. He later claimed that he got Nancy a screen test at MGM, and she was widely presumed to have been one of his many girlfriends—a charge she denied, albeit not very persuasively.[17]

Once Nancy's screen test was secure, her mother called Spencer Tracy, one of MGM's biggest stars, and he made sure that the test would be overseen by celebrated director George Cukor. Though the "gentleman director" concluded that she had "no talent,"[18] the most prestigious studio in Hollywood signed Nancy Davis in early 1949 to a $250-a-week contract. She was twenty-eight, old by the standards of Hollywood starlets, so the studio biography shaved a couple of years off, creating lasting confusion about her true age.[19]

Nancy Davis would act in roughly a dozen films and never achieve stardom, but she professed not to mind. Lacking Jane Wyman's acting talent, she was certainly not driven to career success as Wyman was. "I was always interested in falling in love with a nice man and getting married," she acknowledged, in words that would not endear her to feminists.[20] Her attitude toward marriage, indeed, was identical to that of the marriage-obsessed actress Julie Gillis, played by Debbie Reynolds, in the 1955 film *The*

Tender Trap. "A career is just fine, but it's no substitute for marriage," she says. "A woman isn't a woman until she's been married and had children."[21] Such sentiments were hardly uncommon in the 1950s.

It took the Hollywood blacklist—a nightmare for so many—for Nancy Davis to realize her matrimonial dreams. She read an article in 1949 listing her among the supposed Communist sympathizers in Hollywood; apparently, she had been mistaken for another actress with the same name. To straighten out a potentially career-ending mistake, she contacted the renowned director and producer Mervyn LeRoy, a friend of her mother's who was responsible for hits from *Mister Roberts* to *The Wizard of Oz.* He, in turn, called Ronald Reagan, the president of SAG and, as a member of the Motion Picture Industry Council, an arbiter of the blacklist. Reagan had the SAG staff check into Davis's background and told LeRoy that they would give her a clean bill of ideological health.

But that was not sufficient for an actress nervously nearing her thirties. Davis had already tried to catch Reagan's eye at a couple of social events and was now determined to meet him in person.[22] "I had seen some of his pictures," she later wrote, "and on screen, at least, he seemed nice and good-looking—someone I thought I'd like to meet."[23]

One afternoon in November 1949, Ronald Reagan called Nancy Davis and offered to allay her concerns about the blacklist over dinner. "How about seven thirty?" he asked. "It can't be a late night, because I have an early call in the morning." This was an old actor's dodge for blind dates: An early call offered an easy out if the evening fizzled. "Fine," Nancy replied, "I have an early call too." In truth, neither one of them was working much at the moment.

Two hours later, "Ronnie" Reagan, still recovering from his baseball injury and hobbling on crutches, appeared at Nancy Davis's Westwood apartment door. Her first impression: "This is *wonderful.* He looks as good in person as he does on the screen!" His first impression: "The door opened— not on the expected fan magazine version of a starlet, but on a small, slender young lady with dark hair and a wide-spaced pair of hazel eyes that looked right at you and made you look back."

They headed to dinner at La Rue, a fashionable French restaurant on the Sunset Strip. He suggested a simple solution to her problem: change her name as so many other actors did. Having worked so hard, however, to become Nancy *Davis*—rather than Robbins—she had no intention of changing her name now. The conversation soon moved on to the kind of mutual résumé-swapping that normally occurs on first dates. As usual, Reagan did most of the talking. "He told me about the Guild, and why the actors' union meant so much to him," she recalled. "He talked about his small ranch in the San Fernando Valley, about horses and their bloodlines; he was also a Civil War buff, and he knew a lot about wine." Jane Wyman would have been bored by Reagan's lengthy monologue, but Nancy Davis—a new and eager listener—was enthralled. Reagan, in turn, found her interest in him, her deep gaze, enchanting. "I discovered her laugh," he recalled, "and spent most of my time trying to say something funny."

The evening went so well that, after dinner, Ronnie invited Nancy to Ciro's nightclub to see the singer Sophie Tucker, known as the "Last of the Red Hot Mamas" because she sang so freely—and unusually for a female performer in those days—about her carnal desires. Their fibs about early-morning calls long forgotten, they stayed for two shows. Nancy did not get home until around 3:00 a.m.[24]

If this had been a typical 1950s screen romance, the next scene would have shown them getting married and living happily ever after. Things did not work so neatly in real life. Nancy Reagan claimed in her memoir that it was "pretty close" to "love at first sight," but, while that may have been true for her, it was not the case for Ron, a late-thirties divorcé who was still reeling from a marriage gone sour. "Bells didn't ring," he confessed, "or skyrockets explode."[25] Nancy herself had to concede, "I wish I could report that we saw each other exclusively, and that we couldn't wait to get married. But Ronnie was in no hurry to make a commitment. He had been burned in his first marriage, and the pain went deep. Although we saw each other regularly, he also dated other women."[26] She, in turn, dated other men, such as the actors Robert Walker and Robert Stack, if only to put pressure on Ronnie.[27]

Much like Jane Wyman had done a decade earlier, Nancy Davis had to undertake a campaign to convince Ronald Reagan to marry her. Following in her predecessor's footsteps, she feigned an interest in outdoorsy activities. In 1951, Reagan had traded in his small, eight-acre ranch in Northridge for a sprawling 360-acre spread in Malibu Canyon that was also named Yearling Row. "It's a honey, a great big ranch, nearer the ocean, swimming pool & everything," he exulted. "I feel like a big kid with a new toy."[28] Nancy Davis knew she had passed a big test when she was invited to the ranch on the weekends along with Ron's kids, Maureen and Michael. She was the first girlfriend he had introduced them to, and they would sing songs and play silly games together in the station wagon on the way to the ranch.

The ranch house was ramshackle and rundown—nothing fancy. But Ronnie loved it. He taught Nancy to ride, and she gamely painted fences, hardly her idea of a good time. "She spent as much time as she could out at his valley horse ranch, working, and she'd go home at night dog tired but happy," a movie magazine reported. It added with considerable exaggeration, "Although she had never had much experience with rural matters, she began to study the care and breeding of horses and soon became quite an authority on the subject."[29] In truth, Nancy became much more of an authority on Halston and other fashion designers than on horses. "I never became a great rider," she admitted. "But Ronnie rode, so I did too."[30]

And, like Jane Wyman, Nancy joined the SAG board—but, unlike Wyman, she also feigned a fascination with politics and labor disputes. "Ronnie's interest in the Guild and in politics had been a source of irritation in his first marriage," Nancy wrote, "and Jane had said publicly that she was bored by all of his talking. But I loved to listen to him talk, and I let him know it."[31]

One fan magazine noted, "Wherever they are, Ronnie is talking earnestly, and Nancy is drinking in every word."[32] In short, she was already practicing the reverential gaze that would later become so familiar to political reporters. Lou Cannon would write in 1969 that when her husband was giving a speech, "Nancy composes her features into a kind of transfixed adoration more appropriate to a witness of the Virgin Birth."[33]

Yet, despite Nancy's best efforts, once again Ronald Reagan was displaying frustrating, if entirely typical, indecisiveness. He was reluctant to both enter and exit relationships. There were hints even at this late date—nearly four years after their divorce—that Ron was still dreaming of a reunion with Jane Wyman. At the very least, he had apparently promised Jane not to remarry before she did.[34] His mother, Nelle, who approved of Nancy more than Jane, asked her, "You're in love with him, aren't you?" Nancy said, "Yes. Yes, I am." "Well," Nelle counseled, "you'll have to learn to be patient."[35] But with Nancy having entered her thirties in the summer of 1951, her patience was running out. With no proposal in sight, she decided to "give things a push" in January 1952 by announcing that she had asked her agent to find a part for her in a play in New York. This was an obvious nudge for Reagan to propose if he wanted her to stay in Los Angeles.[36]

The marriage got a "push" in another way that Nancy did not mention in her memoirs: She got pregnant. Patti Davis was conceived in mid-January 1950. Her parents' engagement was announced five weeks later—possibly just enough time for them to have received the result of a pregnancy test, which in those days was conducted by injecting a woman's urine into a frog. (A pregnant woman's urine contained hormones that triggered egg-laying in frogs.)[37] Did Nancy know about the pregnancy before their engagement was announced? Did she, in fact, tell Ronnie about it to convince him to marry her? Might she even have gotten pregnant in order to trap him into marriage? Patti Davis was later to write that she strongly suspected her mother had deliberately gotten pregnant to force her father into finally marrying her.[38] No one will ever know; Nancy Reagan took that secret to the grave.

All we can say for sure is that the marriage proposal occurred one evening in February 1952 at Chasen's, a movie-industry haunt in West Hollywood known for its chili and celebrity sightings. "I think we ought to get married," Ronnie told Nancy in a matter-of-fact way while they were sitting in their usual booth. "I think so too," she answered, trying to keep the excitement out of her voice.[39]

The engagement was announced on February 21, 1952, and the wedding took place just twelve days later on March 4, at the Little Brown Church, a small, out-of-the-way Disciples of Christ congregation in the San Fernando Valley. Why the rush? Presumably the couple found out that Nancy was pregnant either just before or just after the engagement, and, because "shotgun weddings" and out-of-wedlock births were considered scandalous in those days, they were eager to get married as quickly and quietly as possible in order to pass off the baby as a premature delivery. The pregnancy most likely accelerated the marriage but did not cause it. The newlyweds were genuinely in love.

The groom was forty-one, still youthful and handsome; the bride was thirty, petite and attractive in a gray wool suit with a white collar and a small hat and veil. So eager were they to avoid press attention—Reagan had been traumatized by all the publicity attendant to his divorce—that the only witnesses were their friends William Holden, one of the biggest stars of the decade, and his wife, Ardis, who acted under the stage name Brenda Marshall. Nancy was in such a "happy fog" that she didn't notice Bill and Ardis sitting at opposite sides of the church because they had just had an argument. (They would later divorce.) No family members were in attendance. Ron's daughter, Maureen, who was then ten years old, later wrote that she and her six-year-old brother Michael felt "a little weird" about being told their dad had remarried rather than being invited to the ceremony.[40] This was an early indication of how self-sufficient Ron and Nancy's relationship would be, with little space even for their own children, especially Reagan's two children with Jane Wyman.

The wedding reception consisted of dinner for four, complete with cake and champagne, at the Holdens' Toluca Lake house, located near the Warner Brothers studio in the San Fernando Valley. Then the newlyweds drove sixty miles west in Ron's Cadillac convertible to Riverside, California, to spend their wedding night at the historic, Spanish-style Mission Inn, the same hotel where Pat and Dick Nixon had spent their wedding night in 1940. Nancy was thrilled to see Ron sign the register "Mr. and Mrs. Ronald Reagan."[41]

The next day, they drove on to the Biltmore Hotel in Phoenix, where Nancy's parents spent the winters. Ron had already spoken to them on the telephone, but this was his first time meeting them. Nancy claimed that Ron had called Loyal Davis "to ask him for my hand in marriage—the old-fashioned way."[42] But her stepbrother Richard Davis said that his father wasn't notified of the marriage beforehand and was "very upset" and "very bitter about that."[43]

The new groom was understandably nervous about meeting Nancy's parents—and in particular his formidable father-in-law. But it turned into a veritable lovefest. Ron and Edith were soon cracking each other up with risqué jokes. "Edith really fell in love with him," Richard Davis remembered. "They became very close."[44]

Some later attributed Ronald Reagan's growing conservatism to Loyal Davis's influence. The wealthy surgeon had been bitterly critical of the New Deal and was adamantly opposed to Democratic proposals to have the government pay for medical care for the aged and indigent, which he denounced—in words that Reagan would echo—as "socialized medicine." Loyal was also accused by some writers of antisemitism and racism, but the former charge was almost certainly false—his best friend was Jewish, and he battled bigots to hire a Jewish physician at Northwestern—while the evidence for the latter claim is inconclusive.[45]

Richard Davis dismissed suggestions that his father shaped Ronald Reagan's political views or even encouraged him to go into politics as "totally false."[46] Loyal was not very active politically (he was laser-focused on his profession), and his own wife remained a Democrat, albeit of the conservative Southern variety. Moreover, Ron and Loyal did not see eye to eye on every issue: Ron never lost his faith in God, while Loyal had been a nonbeliever since childhood.

Even before he met Loyal Davis, Ronald Reagan was already moving to the right, although he was not yet as doctrinaire as he would become, particularly on economic issues. In 1952, the year he married Nancy, he was active in a group of Democrats campaigning for the Republican nominee, Dwight D. Eisenhower, even though he had no love lost for Ike's running mate, Richard Nixon. When Ike won, Reagan wrote to a college friend that he was "praying for the health and long life of Eisenhower because the thought of Nixon in the White House is almost as bad as of 'Uncle Joe' [Stalin]."[47]

Nancy and Ronald Reagan would enjoy a famously close and harmonious union. She provided the unstinting support he needed without being distracted, as Jane Wyman had been, by her own career ambitions. She was his perfect partner—and became, by the end of his days, not only his best but his only true friend. Ron and Nancy really were "an ideal Mr. and Mrs." in a way that Ron and Jane had never been. "Sometimes, I think my life really began when I met Nancy," Ronald Reagan later wrote. "From the start, our marriage was like an adolescent's dream of what a marriage should be. . . . Nancy moved into my heart and replaced an emptiness that I'd been trying to ignore for a long time."[48] Three years after their marriage, on Nancy's birthday, he telegrammed her mother:

DID YOU KNOW THAT WHAT YOU WERE DOING JULY 6, 1921
WOULD MAKE ME THE HAPPIEST MAN IN THE WORLD?
LOVE,
RONNIE[49]

Remarkably, that mutual passion would never wane over the decades to come. President Reagan's personal secretary, Kathleen Osborne, recalled how transparently happy he was to see the first lady after having been away a few days at an economic summit. "I don't think I've ever seen such a happily married man," she said. "It's like they were courting all their life. And they just never stopped."[50]

Nancy was much more than a devoted and loving wife, although she was that above all. She was also a tough infighter and a shrewd judge of people, who possessed, in the words of a family friend, "X-ray vision for character."[51] Ronnie was trusting and optimistic to the point of being Pollyannaish and a pushover. Nancy, by contrast, worried incessantly and trusted almost no one. She also confronted unpleasant issues and personality conflicts head-on rather than, as Ronnie did, evading them and wishing them away. As her son Ron Reagan noted, Nancy's presence "allowed my father to avoid the things he wanted to avoid, like interpersonal conflict, and provided him with safe space to think his thoughts and just be himself." "It wasn't like she controlled him," Kathy Osborne said. "She just looked out for him. And that was good for him because he was such a sweet, kind-hearted man that people would try to take advantage of him."[52]

Stuart Spencer, who would become Reagan's first and most enduring political consultant, was convinced that his client would never have risen to the heights of power if he had remained married to Jane Wyman: "Ronald Reagan would never have become governor of California without Nancy Reagan. He would never have become president of the United States without Nancy Reagan, period." Thomas C. Reed, one of Reagan's senior political aides in the late 1960s, said he "strongly disliked" Nancy, but he agreed: "Without Nancy Reagan, Ronald Reagan would never have been elected to anything." Spencer described her as not only "the love of his life" but also "the personnel director, the Human Resources Department," the one who hired and fired on his behalf. "She understood his strengths and weaknesses as well as anybody," Spencer said. "A lot of wives can't, but she did. She developed a profile of the type of people that should be around Ronnie. The only consistent thing it would say in that profile was that he had to have Ronnie's agenda."[53]

Nancy's ultimate strength, as her son Ron told me, was that she had no political views or ambitions of her own. She was completely and wholeheartedly dedicated to tirelessly and shrewdly promoting the interests of her husband—just as her mother had promoted *her* husband.

In 1952, Ronald Reagan costarred with Doris Day in a pedestrian if perfectly pleasant movie called *The Winning Team*—his last at Warner Brothers—about the Hall of Fame pitcher Grover Cleveland Alexander. The plot was hard to follow because the film glossed over its subject's epilepsy, but Reagan enjoyed the opportunity to play sports on-screen, something he hadn't done since *Knute Rockne, All-American*. Ron and Nancy ultimately formed their own "winning team," but little in their early years of marriage was indicative of their later success. The newlyweds' income was fast dwindling even as their expenses piled up.

A few months after returning from their short honeymoon in Arizona, the couple paid $42,000 for a Cape Cod–style, three-bedroom house with a sandbox and rosebushes in the backyard and an olive tree out front.[54] It was located at 1258 Amalfi Drive in Pacific Palisades, a secluded Los Angeles neighborhood nestled in the hills near the ocean between Santa Monica and Malibu. Founded by Methodists in 1922, Pacific Palisades came to attract many movie-industry figures along with intellectual German refugees, such as the author Thomas Mann, whose presence led to the enclave's nickname, "Weimar by the Sea."[55] The mortgage payments on this house, combined with those for the $85,000 ranch in Malibu, added up fast.

A little more than seven months after their wedding ceremony, their first child, Patricia Ann, arrived via cesarean section on October 21, 1952, and Nancy stopped working. They hired an English nanny to take care of the baby. When Patti was old enough, she was sent to fancy private schools: first the Brentwood Town and Country School and then John Thomas Dye School in Bel-Air, both favored by the Hollywood elite. In 1958, following two miscarriages, Nancy would have her second and final child: Ronald Prescott Reagan, known initially as "the Skipper" and later as "Ron." He would also attend John Thomas Dye. Michael Reagan and Maureen Reagan did not live with them, but Ronnie was responsible for paying child support. The kids from his earlier marriage also attended expensive private schools, beginning with the Chadwick School, a boarding school in Palos Verdes.[56]

Ronald Reagan had had a successful movie career, but he wasn't being offered many scripts anymore, and the ones he was seeing were, in his view, "hopeless." He blamed his misfortune not on his own artistic limitations or changing audience tastes but on trust-busters in Washington who broke up the studio system and on producers who supposedly could not see him in any role other than union negotiator. He even claimed, with no evidence, that a Communist whispering campaign was hurting his career.[57] The future politician who would preach the necessity of personal responsibility for people on welfare or in prison was ducking responsibility for the "rough sledding" in his own life.[58]

Reagan always remained proud of his work in fifty-four feature films and took umbrage whenever anyone demeaned him as a B-movie actor, claimed (erroneously) that he never got the girl in his pictures, or mocked movies such as the comedy *Bedtime for Bonzo*. "It touches an exposed nerve," he later said.[59] But his film career was increasingly in the rear-view mirror, and it was not clear what lay ahead.

Although Ronald Reagan had been earning considerable money right after World War II, his savings were dwindling. "Ronnie had been well paid for some of his movies," Nancy Reagan wrote, "but he was in the 91 percent tax bracket when he made his money—which certainly influenced his views later on taxes."[60] Reagan generalized his discontent with high taxes into a conclusion that the whole income-tax system was unfair and should be replaced by a flat tax. But in 1956, the 91 percent rate applied only to income over $200,000 (equivalent to more than $2 million in 2024); someone making a median income of $3,400 would have paid only a 20 percent tax rate.[61] Moreover, Reagan's woes were aggravated by his ill-advised decision to defer paying income taxes during World War II. Now he owed a hefty bill: In 1957, the Internal Revenue Service would file a lien against him for back taxes of $24,911.[62] Times were so tough that Ron and Nancy couldn't afford to furnish their new living room.[63]

While Nancy Reagan had household help to take care of cooking, cleaning, and child care, she considered marriage "a full-time job."[64] She feared that if she kept on acting, she would lose Ronnie as Jane Wyman had done. But financial necessity impelled her to go back to work. In 1953, she costarred in a low-rent, black-and-white science-fiction film called *Donovan's Brain* with Jane's former flame Lew Ayres, who played a scientist possessed by a dead man's brain. Four years later, in 1957, Ron and Nancy made their only picture together: *Hellcats of the Navy*, a rote World War II yarn in which he played a submarine skipper and she a navy nurse. The screenplay, ironically, had been secretly rewritten by a blacklisted writer.[65]

Just to stay afloat, Ron took to doing guest appearances on TV shows—at that time considered beneath the dignity of a movie star. He was so desperate for work that his new agent at MCA, Arthur "Art" Park, suggested that he appear in a lounge act in Las Vegas. His initial reaction was "You must be kidding!" But the pay was good: In two weeks he could earn as much as for his most recent movie, *Prisoner of War*, about American POWs in North Korea. And he was encouraged to assent by reading Carroll Righter's syndicated astrology column in the newspaper; both he and Nancy were devotees and personal friends of Righter's, who was the "guru to the stars." "I would not say that I am a great believer," Ronald Reagan later wrote of astrology, "and, yet, at the same time, I cannot deny evidence that would indicate that there might be something to it." On the morning Ron was to meet with MCA to discuss the Las Vegas offer, he recalled that the horoscope read, "This is a day to listen to the advice of experts." So he said yes—a decision that "caused many a raised eyebrow in moviedom," a newspaper columnist wrote. Ron did not hide his distaste for an assignment that he felt was beneath him. "The studios are driving us into other mediums," he complained to a reporter, making an unwitting pun. "Few actors are supported by the studios alone."[66]

Reagan did not sing or dance, so he served mainly as a joke-cracking master of ceremonies and participated in some skits with a male quartet called the Continentals. The show ran the last two weeks of February 1954 at the Western-themed Hotel Last Frontier ("The Early West in Modern Splendor"). He felt initially as if he were "going over Niagara Falls in a tub," but shortly after opening, he was bragging that "the show is going over real big and the whole thing is really a grand experience."[67] Ron was the quintessential trouper, and he knew how to serve as an emcee. But once again, just as in *Bedtime for Bonzo* two years earlier, he was upstaged by a monkey—or, rather, by a troop of chimpanzees.

One of the other acts on the bill was Gene Detroy and the Marquis Chimps. The chimpanzees were trained to perform each night at the same time. One night, however, the show was running late. By the time the chimps entered the room, they thought their work was already done and playtime had begun. George Schlatter, then a young booker for the Last Frontier, recalled, "All hell broke. I mean, they're in the lights, they're riding bicycles. One of the chimps was flirting with the bandleader. One of them sat down at a table and drank some Jack Daniels. They played and ran around the room. It was absolute pandemonium." The audience loved it, but the headliner was not so thrilled. "Ronald Reagan never really quite forgave me for having him work with the chimps," said Schlatter, who went on to become a successful Hollywood producer.[68]

Las Vegas nightlife held little appeal for Ron—or Nancy, who accompanied him. (There was no chance she was going to leave her new husband to spend two weeks by himself in a city full of comely chorus girls.) The couple brought a lot of books with them and spent their free time in their suite or by the pool. They avoided the gaming tables because they wanted to make money, not lose it. Ron said he had offers from other nightclubs in other cities, but after the two-week run, they went home to Los Angeles, convinced, as Nancy put it, "The nightclub life was not for us."[69] Ron later cited his Las Vegas lounge act as "the lowest point in his life."[70]

But if Ronald Reagan was not destined to become a nightclub performer, it was unclear how he would support his growing family. It was during this professional crisis, when he had few prospects and his career—like his father's—was in danger of ending in failure, that his agents at MCA came to him with an offer that would prove his financial salvation.

16

"Progress Is Our Most Important Product"

They were all slappin' him on the back saying,
'That's the way, Ron.' "

—EARL DUNCKEL

elevision spread through the cities and hinterlands of America with a force that would turn the 1950s into the first television decade. The technology of television—essentially adding pictures to radio transmissions—had been developed well before the onset of World War II, with the primary advances credited to the Russian émigré scientist Vladimir Zworykin and the Utah-born autodidact Philo T. Farnsworth, but it was not commercialized until after the war. In 1950 just 9 percent of households owned a television set. By 1960, 90 percent of households had one—and it was on for an average of more than three hours a day. Just as Ronald Reagan and other members of the so-called "greatest generation" had been the first to grow up listening to radio and going to the movies, so now their offspring—the baby boomers—were the first to grow up in front of a flickering cabinet, transfixed by shows such as *Howdy Doody, The Mickey Mouse Club, The Lone Ranger,* and *Dragnet.* The two principal networks initially were NBC and CBS; ABC did not become a serious competitor until the late 1950s, following its merger with the long-forgotten DuMont network. NBC was dominant at first, but by 1955, after raiding many of its rival's top talents, CBS began a long reign as number one—the "Tiffany Network." While programming initially had been shown live from New York featuring such comedians as Milton Berle and Sid Caesar, by the mid-1950s, shows such as *I Love Lucy* and *Perry Mason* were being taped on Los Angeles soundstages.

As early as 1951, a *New York Times* writer noted, "Television, in commercial use for a little more than five years, is influencing the social and economic habits of the nation to a degree unparalleled since the advent of the automobile." For the first time ever, a majority of Americans could experience the same sights and sounds at the same time. With more and more white, middle-class Americans buying homes and moving to suburbs where they hardly knew their neighbors, television created a new national community in which people felt closer to Ozzie and Harriet Nelson or Lucy and Ricky Ricardo—or, soon, Ronald and Nancy Reagan—than to whoever lived down the block. The new medium was, from the start, a powerful force for conservatism that reinforced the white, middle-class mores of the Eisenhower era. In TV land, couples slept in twin beds, pregnancy was unmentionable, homosexuality did not exist, criminals always faced justice, cops were humane and honest, nuclear families with hardworking dads and stay-at-home moms were the norm, and minorities were largely invisible save as servants or "savages" battling cowboys.[1]

Movie stars such as Ronald Reagan were aghast at the decline of the big screen and perplexed by the rise of the small screen, but he would turn out to be one of the biggest beneficiaries of the new medium—financially, professionally, and, ultimately, politically. As the host of *General Electric Theater*, he became one of the most recognizable faces during television's first decade. His road to television stardom, however, was paved with conflicts of interest and suspect deals involving the Music Corporation of America (MCA)—the conglomerate that swallowed Hollywood.

MCA was started in 1924 by Chicago ophthalmologist Julius Caesar Stein, who found it more profitable to book bands into nightclubs and music halls than to examine patients' eyes. The Chicago nightclub scene was dominated in those days by Al Capone and his organized-crime outfit. Stein was widely suspected of going into business with the mob—all the more so when he branched out into selling liquor to nightclubs. "Jules had to be with Capone," one of his associates later said, "or be shot in the head."[2] MCA also developed the dubious practice, known as "block booking," of forcing clubs that wanted to book high-profile acts, such as Tommy Dorsey or Guy Lombardo, to also book unknown bands. A judge who ruled against MCA in an antitrust suit concerning its booking of musicians called it "the Octopus . . . with tentacles reaching out to all phases and grasping everything in show business," and the nickname stuck.[3]

By 1934, MCA managed 90 percent of America's dance bands.[4] Having attained dominance in the live-music business, Stein's firm next went into radio, producing shows featuring its clients. This was a blatant conflict of interest, but, because of Stein's close alliance with the head of the American Federation of Musicians, he received a waiver from union rules forbidding the practice. Next in MCA's sights was the film business. In 1936, MCA opened a 25,000-square-foot headquarters in Beverly Hills, full of antique English furniture handpicked by Jules Stein. MCA's agents were serious, sober, college-educated men who dressed like FBI agents in dark suits, narrow ties, and white shirts—a far cry from the fast-talking "flesh peddlers" of old with their cigars and garish plaid suits.[5]

In 1938, a tall, gaunt new agent named Lew R. Wasserman arrived at MCA's Beverly Hills office. Like Stein and so many of the movie and television moguls, he was an impoverished offspring of Jewish Russian immigrants who was so desperate to succeed that he was willing to work harder than anyone else. A high school dropout who had gotten his start as a theater usher, Wasserman showed a genius for structuring deals and negotiating contracts while working sixteen-hour days, seven days a week. Soon he was running MCA's Hollywood business, which he vastly expanded by attracting new clients and buying other talent agencies. It was one of these acquisitions—of the Meiklejohn Agency in 1939—that turned Ronald Reagan into Lew Wasserman's client. By the end of 1946, MCA was by far the largest talent agency in Hollywood, and Wasserman was its president at age thirty-three, the older Jules Stein having made himself chairman of the board.[6]

In 1949, an MCA subsidiary called Revue Productions began producing TV shows. There was only one problem: SAG rules prohibited talent agencies from producing movies, a ban that was soon extended to television shows. It was considered a conflict of interest for one company to both represent and employ actors. Wasserman did not want to come begging to SAG every time Revue produced a new show. He demanded a blanket waiver—something that had been granted to no other company—and he secured one in July 1952 with the help of MCA client and SAG president Ronald Reagan. The waiver was made permanent in 1954 when Reagan was no longer president of SAG but still a board member.

As part of the negotiations, MCA broke with other producers in Hollywood by agreeing to give the actors reuse payments (or residuals) when their television programs were shown more than once. But there was still a great deal of opposition on the SAG board to the agreement. The beloved character actor Walter Pidgeon, of *Mrs. Miniver* and *How Green Was My Valley* fame, was another MCA client who would soon become SAG's president, and he turned the tide by telling fellow board members that letting MCA go into television production could keep actors' jobs in Los Angeles. Of course, if the goal was to promote employment for actors, why grant a waiver only to MCA? Why not encourage other talent agencies to get into the production business too?[7]

The waiver did benefit actors—but not as much as it benefited MCA. The firm was now able to put its own clients into its own shows, although it was prohibited from collecting a 10 percent fee from clients working in MCA productions. By the end of the 1950s, Revue was the largest producer of TV shows in America, with hits such as *The Jack Benny Show*, *Wagon Train*, and *Leave It to Beaver*. This, in turn, generated the revenues that allowed MCA in 1958 to acquire the 367-acre Universal Pictures backlot and in 1962 the whole studio. By 1962, MCA was producing more than 40 percent of all prime-time television, and the shrewd and ruthless Lew Wasserman had become known as the new "King of Hollywood."[8]

Ronald Reagan's fifth term as SAG president ended in November 1952. Decades later, he would cite his union work as "pretty good training" for the presidency of the whole nation. "Sitting at the table in Geneva," he wrote in 1985 after his first summit with Mikhail Gorbachev, "was a lot like those old days across the table from the studio heads in Hollywood."[9] But Reagan was glad to give up the leadership of SAG; he felt that union activities were distracting from his movie career and hurting his relations with producers, even though he was the most management-friendly of union bosses.

Reagan was lured back in 1959 for an unprecedented sixth term as SAG president to manage the union's dispute with the studios over residual payments to actors for airing old movies on television. He was reluctant to get back into the fray, and by then he was already a producer himself, so the conflicts of interest were piling up. But Lew Wasserman, with an unerring sense for how to promote his own interests, encouraged him to climb back into the saddle.[10] MCA had recently purchased Paramount Pictures' backlist of pre-1948 pictures for $50 million, so it had a substantial stake in this dispute.

The actors went out on strike in 1960 for six weeks. In April, SAG and the producers reached a deal that required a large concession by the actors: They agreed to relinquish any payments for television showings of movies made before 1960. In return the studios agreed to pay actors for television showings of movies made after 1960 and to start an actors' pension fund with an initial payment of $2.6 million. The SAG membership approved the deal, but many called it the "Great Giveaway" and grumbled that Reagan had caved once again to MCA. Even Bob Hope, who considered himself a friend of Reagan's, complained: "The [pre-1960] pictures were sold down the river for a certain amount of money, and it was nothing."[11]

The Justice Department opened an antitrust investigation of MCA in 1959. The Antitrust Division suspected the company of, among other offenses, engaging in a "conspiracy with the Screen Actors Guild to monopolize TV film program production."[12]

On the afternoon of February 5, 1962, the day before his fifty-first birthday, Ronald Reagan joined a long parade of Hollywood stars and executives who were questioned by Justice Department lawyers before a twenty-three-member grand jury meeting on the tenth floor of the rectangular Art Moderne federal building in downtown Los Angeles. Prosecutors clearly suspected that he had received a payoff for negotiating cushy deals with MCA. One of the grand jury members ran into Reagan in the elevator and thought he looked "very nervous." Reagan was as evasive on the stand as he would later be during the Iran-Contra affair, often insisting that his memory was "a little bit hazy." He claimed to have been out of town making *Cattle Queen of Montana* with Barbara Stanwyck in 1952 while the MCA waiver was being negotiated; in fact, that movie was filmed in 1954. Reagan later complained of having to spend "a long, unhappy afternoon being interrogated by a federal lawyer who'd seen too many Perry Masons" and accused the government of waging a "campaign against a private business concern."[13]

Both Wasserman and Reagan denied there was any corrupt bargain behind MCA's blanket waiver, and the government's attempt to uncover collusion between MCA and SAG was ultimately stymied by Wasserman's secretive ways. He said little and put even less down on paper. Wasserman was famous for valuing loyalty above all and for being both vindictive and well connected (his best friend was the infamous mob lawyer Sidney Korshak), so no one was willing to risk his wrath by testifying against MCA. The consensus of the grand jury, one juror later told journalist Dennis McDougal, "was that Lew Wasserman paid Ronald Reagan to help him maneuver this deal." But they could not prove it beyond a reasonable doubt. "I just know that the whole thing smelled," another juror said, "but there was nothing definite you could put your finger on."[14] The case was settled later that year with MCA announcing that, while it was acquiring Universal Pictures, it would divest its less-lucrative talent-agent business to end the ongoing conflict of interest between employing and representing actors.

Even if the dealmaking was not illegal, it was still unseemly and rife with conflicts of interest. The appearance of impropriety would only grow when Reagan received a life-altering business proposition from MCA.

In 1954, Taft Schreiber, the head of MCA's television business and a prodigious Republican fundraiser, offered Ronald Reagan the opportunity to host *General Electric Theater*. (Corporations in those days commonly attached their names to television shows.) This was a half-hour weekly series, featuring scripted comedies and dramas, that CBS had been running at 9:00 p.m. every other Sunday for the past year. Now the network wanted to make the show weekly. It was sponsored by General Electric and produced by its advertising agency, Batten, Barton, Durstine and Osborn (BBD&O), in cooperation with MCA. Reagan would be paid a starting salary of $120,000 a year—soon to be increased to $150,000—and all he had to do was say a few words at the beginning and end of each episode. He would also get to act in a few episodes, as would Nancy Reagan. Eventually he would be given the opportunity to produce as well.

Reagan was "gun-shy of television," as he put it, but he did not hesitate.[15] As he later described it during his grand jury testimony, he had had practically no motion-picture work for the past fourteen months. The only offers he was getting were for live television shows in New York, but he had no desire to move across the country. And then, he said, "This television show came riding along, the cavalry to the rescue."[16]

Reagan first appeared on *General Electric Theater* on September 26, 1954, and before long the program became one of the most popular on television, going as high as number three in the 1956–1957 season. Its popularity was due, in part, to being surrounded by other top-rated shows (*The Ed Sullivan Show* from 8:00 to 9:00 p.m. and *Alfred Hitchcock Presents* at 9:30 p.m.) on the Sunday-night lineup of the "Tiffany Network," but MCA also enlisted high-profile clients, such as Jimmy Stewart, Henry Fonda, Fred Astaire, and Jack Benny, to be guest stars. Reagan gave the series continuity and identity. Not wanting to wear glasses on TV, he would memorize his lines and repeat them flawlessly, hitting his marks down to the second with no need for a timer. His sign-off was always the same: "Here, at General Electric, progress is our most important product."[17]

Running for eight years, from 1954 to 1962, *General Electric Theater* introduced Ronald Reagan to millions of television viewers as a genial corporate spokesman and everyman—"the actor in the gray flannel suit," as one CBS press release called him, in tribute to Sloan Wilson's best-selling novel about the costs of corporate careerism, *The Man in the Gray Flannel Suit.*[18] The show provided him with financial security and then some. Starting in 1959, he no longer had to pay MCA an agent fee because he became a producer, that is, a part owner of the show, entitled to a quarter of all proceeds from reairings.[19] (This, of course, made his return as president of the Screen Actors Guild in 1959 even more problematic.) By 1958 the show was reaching twenty-five million viewers a week, and he was one of the most recognized men in the country.[20]

Reagan's small-screen stardom occurred just as television was first making an impact on politics. Vice-presidential nominee Richard Nixon, facing accusations of corruption during the 1952 campaign, saved his career by delivering on television his mawkish "Checkers speech" (named after a dog his daughter had received as a present), while the snarling Senator Joe McCarthy destroyed his career with his buffoonish and bullying performance during the televised Army–McCarthy hearings in 1954. With his mangled syntax and bald pate, President Eisenhower was awful on TV but, realizing he had to improve, hired the actor Robert Montgomery as a White House image consultant. John F. Kennedy, the young and handsome senator who won the Democratic presidential nomination in 1960, was more closely attuned to the demands of the new medium, right down to adjusting his own lighting and camera angles. His telegenic style, in fact, was credited for winning his lone debate with Nixon, who appeared decidedly unattractive with his five o'clock shadow and ponderous diction.[21]

Henceforward, the ability to perform well on television would be indispensable for any candidate for national office. With his experience on *General Electric Theater*, Reagan was at least the equal of JFK and far ahead of any Republican competitor in this regard. He would become the only president prior to Donald Trump who had hosted his own national television show before entering politics.

***

The GE job not only demanded that Ronald Reagan appear on television every week. It also called for him to travel the country visiting GE plants as part of the company's Employee and Community Relations Program. The travel was especially time consuming because he refused to fly and went instead by train.

Reagan would take the Super Chief ("the Train of the Stars") from Union Station in Los Angeles to Dearborn Station in Chicago and then switch to the Twentieth Century Limited ("the Most Famous Train in the World") to Grand Central Terminal in New York.[22] These were billed as the fastest trains in the world, but the journey was still a lengthy one: thirty-seven hours to Chicago and another sixteen hours to New York. Yet the travel was no hardship. The Super Chief, richly paneled in exotic woods, came equipped not only with a dining car but also a "Pleasure Dome" lounge car, a cocktail lounge, and Pullman sleeping cars. Passengers dined on steak and lobster and were waited on by a small army of almost exclusively Black porters, waiters, cooks, bartenders, stewards, barbers, maids, and valets.[23]

Reagan's contract initially called for him to be on the road sixteen weeks a year. Eventually this was whittled down to twelve weeks a year and then to six weeks, but he still wound up traveling a total of two years over the eight years he worked for GE. Many men, especially those with a young family, would have balked at this demanding schedule. But Reagan embraced the opportunity to travel thousands of miles to meet 250,000 GE employees working at 135 plants scattered across the country.[24]

Reagan was accompanied on his early tours by a public relations man from GE named Earl Dunckel and then by a former FBI agent named George Dalen, both of whom shared his increasingly conservative views. Dunckel recalled that he did not look forward to meeting the actor for the first time in New York in August 1954. "My limited previous exposure with Hollywood types left me with a general feeling of distaste," Dunckel said. "They tend to be arrogant, down-the-nose looking, full of themselves. So it was a great and pleasant surprise when this tall, slim, handsome (but not irritatingly handsome) fellow shook hands with me and smiled and was not posturing and was as natural as anyone else you would ever meet. . . . There was nothing of the posturing, nothing of the 'I am a star'—he was a regular guy."[25]

Dunckel recalled that during their first outing at a turbine plant in Schenectady, New York, women came rushing up to Reagan with "mash notes, autographs, and all that kind of thing." By contrast, he noted, "The men would all stand over here, all together, looking at him, obviously very derogatory. 'I bet he's a fag' or something like that. He would carry on a conversation with the girls just so long. He knew what was going on. Then he would leave them and walk over to these fellows and start talking to them. When he left them ten minutes later, they were all slappin' him on the back saying, 'That's the way, Ron.' "[26]

Sometimes Reagan had testy exchanges, but he invariably kept his good humor and never raised his voice. Often he had a snappy comeback. For example, when a hostile worker asked, "How much are they paying you for this shit?" he shot back, "They haven't got enough to make me put up with you."[27] But such confrontations were rare. "It was pretty hard to heckle Ron, because he is so obviously such a damned nice guy," Dunckel observed.[28]

Dunckel remembered that on a typical trip he and Reagan would disembark from a train at 6:30 a.m., and local company representatives would whisk them away in a car for a full day of meetings. They would not reach their hotel until after midnight. "Boy, we walked our legs right down to stumps," Dunckel said, but Reagan "bore up beautifully and never failed to deliver. . . . He never laid an egg." Another GE publicist called him "a veritable bionic man, all stamina and drive."[29] Reagan himself recalled, "The trips were murderously difficult. I could lose ten pounds in three weeks and eat anything I wanted. . . . *But I enjoyed every whizzing minute of it*. It was one of the most rewarding experiences of my life."[30]

As part of its community relations program, GE managers would ask Reagan to speak not only to their employees but also to local organizations such as a Chamber of Commerce, Rotary Club, or Elks Club. His talks in the early days were primarily a defense of Hollywood. He would often argue that denizens of the film colony were just as devoted to their families as any other Americans—and even more unlikely to get a divorce. He was not dissuaded from delivering this homily either by his own divorce or by government statistics that showed the divorce rate in Hollywood was actually far higher than the national average.[31]

But he also demonstrated he was more than just a spokesman for the film industry. Early on, there was a convention of high school teachers in one of the towns he was visiting, and the scheduled speaker fell ill. Reagan was asked to step in at the last minute and speak about education. Dunckel initially refused on his behalf, thinking, "My God, this is an area outside of my expertise. I would have to do a lot of research. I haven't got time to write a speech." But Reagan reassured him: "Dunk, let's give it a try. Don't worry." Dunckel was astonished the next day: "He got up there and gave a speech on education that just dropped them in the aisles! He got a good ten-minute standing applause afterward. . . . It was an amazing tour de force. It really was."[32] All of Reagan's reading of *Readers' Digest* and other publications seemed to have paid off. The run-of-the-mill actor turned out to be a superlative public speaker.

This was when Reagan first began to write down an outline of his speeches, along with relevant facts and anecdotes, on three-by-five-inch cards, employing abbreviations of his own devising. He knew that his appearances would not be effective if he delivered a canned talk. So he would constantly update and shuffle his cards based on the audience he was speaking to—and what he had just read in a newspaper or magazine. If a line worked particularly well, he would repeat it; if it fell flat, he would drop or revise it. His applause lines became finely honed, and some would stay in his repertoire for decades.

There were no speechwriters for him in those days; Reagan's talks were all his own devising. He learned to start, he later explained, with an "audience catcher"—"appropriate humorous remarks or jokes fitting the audience, the occasion, or the subject." He would then employ "parables or examples" to make his points in easy-to-understand fashion. Finally, he would finish with a "get-off line" that "is truly a climax to the entire address," rather than allowing his speech to "drift away" with "pleasantries about how nice it has been to be there."[33] From the start, he displayed what Dunckel described as "an almost uncanny ability to sense the mood of an audience."[34]

Reagan's work for GE was not intended to lay the groundwork for a political career, but it did just that. Not only did he gain nationwide visibility—both on TV and in person—but he also gained familiarity with the views of many different voters in many different parts of the country, including the South, where GE was locating new plants in conservative states that were hostile to union organizing. In the process, he figured out how to communicate effectively with individuals ranging from blue-collar workers to PhD researchers and in settings ranging from personal encounters to speeches in front of large audiences. He later credited his turn away from New Deal liberalism not to any "mentor or someone coming in and talking me out of it. I did it with my own speeches."[35]

Few novice candidates would ever be as well qualified to hit the campaign trail. By the time Reagan first ran for public office in 1966, he had already been campaigning for GE for years, constantly revising his speeches, responding to questions, and glad-handing audiences just as political candidates do. He even learned politicians' tricks, for example, drinking a fifty-fifty mix of white wine and water served in a martini glass so he could stay sober at cocktail parties while everyone else was "half-sozzled."[36]

"Those GE tours became almost a postgraduate course in political science for me," Ronald Reagan later wrote.[37] Now he just had to apply what he was learning.

17

Family Values

They were just totally preoccupied with his career.

—RICHARD DAVIS

Working for General Electric, whose slogan was "Live better electrically," came with some bright and shiny perks. In 1955, Ronald and Nancy Reagan decided to build a bigger, five-thousand-square-foot house at 1669 San Onofre Drive in Pacific Palisades. GE stuffed the mid-century modern house "with every imaginable electric gadget," as Ronald Reagan later noted.[1] These included a projector for movie screenings, a heated swimming pool, a dishwasher, a refrigerated wine cellar, self-closing curtains, mood lights in the dining room, an electronic eye security system in the driveway, intercoms in every room, and much more. Reagan jokingly described the house as having "everything electric except the chair."[2] These devices required so much power that a three-thousand-pound switch box had to be installed. Before the house was finished, Reagan drew a heart with his initials and Nancy's in the wet concrete on the patio outside their bedroom. This would be their home for the next quarter century.[3]

Of course, helping to build the house was not an act of altruism on GE's part. The whole family had to go on TV to show off the house and extol the virtues of all their electric appliances, from the toaster to the electric grill, even though Nancy Reagan, depicted as a paradigmatic, middle-class homemaker of the 1950s, did not actually cook. The production crews would bring in piles of food that Nancy had supposedly cooked, Patti recalled, but the kids were told not to eat any of it because no one knew where it had come from.[4] "I wasn't wild about having my home turned into a corporate showcase," Nancy admitted, "but this was Ronnie's first steady job in years, so it was a trade-off I was more than happy to make."[5]

While Ronald Reagan's work for General Electric made possible this luxurious house, it also necessitated his frequent and lengthy absences from home. He dearly missed Nancy while on the road, as he made clear in heartfelt love letters. The man who had always called his own parents by their first names now referred to his wife as "Mommie" or "Mommie Poo Pants"; she called him "Daddie Poo Pants" or simply "Daddie." One time, during his GE travels, he telegrammed her: WHAT AM I DOING HERE WHEN I WANT TO BE THERE. I MISS YOU & LOVE YOU.[6] On another occasion, he sent her a telegram while he still had a month on the road: DARLING: ONLY TWENTY EIGHT DAYS MORE OF EMPTINESS. I LOVE YOU—POPPA.[7] The program supervisor at *General Electric Theater*, Bill Cotworthy, noted that Ron ended every call with Nancy, no matter how short, with "I love you." Reagan upbraided Cotworthy for not doing the same with his wife.[8]

No one could doubt Ronnie's devotion to Nancy—as attested to by five archival boxes at the Reagan Library stuffed full of love letters, telegrams, and Hallmark greeting cards, which he faithfully sent her, often accompanied by flowers, for every anniversary, every Mother's Day, every Easter, every Christmas, every birthday over the course of their fifty-two-year marriage.[9]

Indeed, Ronald Reagan's devotion to his wife often seemed to exceed his devotion to his children. After being told that Patti had been born following a difficult pregnancy that culminated in a cesarean section (in those days fathers were not allowed in the delivery room), he wrote, "At that moment her arrival didn't impress me much. The only word I wanted concerned her mother." Regarding their son Ron's birth (also via C-section), he wrote, "Personally I would have settled for the three of us: I grew frightened every time I remembered that long night when Patti was born, and didn't want to take chances with a happiness already so great I couldn't believe it."[10]

There was little doubt that his primary source of happiness was his wife, not his children.

Ronald Reagan's travels left child-rearing largely to his wife, as was common in those days. It was not an easy task, particularly with their rebellious daughter. "My relationship with Patti has been one of the most painful and disappointing aspects of my life," Nancy Reagan admitted in her surprisingly frank memoir. "Somehow no matter what I do, we seem to square off. And it's been this way from the start." Nancy's stepbrother Richard "Dick" Davis recalled that for years Nancy would call Loyal Davis "almost every day and drive him half-crazy with ideas about how to handle Patti." She would also call Dick every two weeks or so on the same subject. "Her total obsession was with Patti," he said.[11]

In anger and frustration, Nancy would sometimes lash out at her daughter. Patti recalled that her mother began hitting her when she was eight years old "on a weekly, sometimes daily" basis. Patti, in turn, wrote that she "became intimately familiar with what would set my mother off, and I would push those buttons, even though I knew it would end up with her hand aimed at my face."[12] As Patti grew older, Nancy didn't like her daughter's choice of hairstyles or clothes or her decision to pierce her ears with help from her school friends. These seemingly trivial matters assumed a larger symbolic importance for both mother and daughter, and their battles came to define their stormy relationship in a dynamic that was hardly unique to the Reagan clan.

Patti was not the only person in the house who set Nancy off. She kept hiring and firing maids, gardeners, and nannies. "I remember sitting in my bedroom with my hands over my ears because I could hear my mother's voice in the kitchen, yelling at the maid about dishes in the wrong cupboard or something not being prepared right," Patti wrote. "I would sing to myself to block out the sound." Patti discovered that Nancy, like many housewives of the *Mad Men* era, regularly took the sedative Seconal and the tranquilizer Miltown for her "nerves."[13] But the pills didn't dispel Nancy's congenital jitteriness and apprehension, and her anger all too often was directed at her daughter.

Ron Reagan, who as a young boy was called "the Skipper"—a nickname he grew to detest—said that he only saw his mother slap his sister on a few occasions and that Nancy was "not physically abusive in a Joan Crawford kind of way." But he added, "My mother was very difficult. She could be emotionally and psychologically abusive." He remembered his mother being particularly prone to fits of anger and anxiety when her husband was on the road. He surmised that Nancy was worried that Ronnie would either suffer some sort of accident or cheat on her. She would calm down a bit when he returned home, only to dial up her agitation again when he began another trip.[14]

Skipper, the baby in the family, was a happy, easygoing child and his parents' favorite. He got along better with their parents than his sister did, but he caused his share of heartache too. In 1970, at age twelve, he announced that he did not believe in God and did not want to go to church. This was literally blasphemy given Ronald Reagan's religious upbringing—and an embarrassment given his newfound status as one of the country's leading champions of conservatism. By then, following the death of Nelle Reagan in 1962 from a cerebral hemorrhage, the family had left the Disciples of Christ. In 1965, they began attending the more socially prestigious Bel-Air Presbyterian Church whose charismatic pastor, Donn Moomaw, was a former college football star at UCLA and a family friend. (Reverend Moomaw was forced out of the church in 1993 by a scandal involving sexual improprieties with women in the congregation.)[15]

Ronald Reagan was disappointed by his son's atheism but never tried to compel his church attendance. Ron remembers his father telling him, "Well, I'm just afraid that one day you'll find that there's a big emptiness in your life and that only God can fill it. Only the man upstairs is the answer to that, and I'm just concerned that you're going to be very unhappy when you're without God and Jesus." Ron tested his parents' patience in other ways too: He would be kicked out of one high school and, as a teenager, would launch into an affair with an older, married woman with children of her own. Later, he would further exasperate his parents by dropping out of college to pursue his dreams of becoming a ballet dancer.[16]

Patti had an even more turbulent adolescence that included sexual relationships with a handsome dishwasher and a married, thirty-something English teacher whom she met at a remote, ranch-style boarding school in Arizona. She had been sent to the Orme School at age thirteen after frequently getting into trouble at her previous school. Her plan to run away with the dishwasher to Alaska was only spoiled when she asked her older brother, Michael Reagan, to sign her out of school and he notified their parents. Although Patti's parents blamed her for misbehaving, from the present-day vantage point we can see that this troubled teenage girl, reeling from strife at home, was taken advantage of and even sexually abused by a series of older men. Much later, Davis would describe being sexually assaulted by a music industry executive in the late 1970s.[17]

The trauma of her youth led Patti, as she later recounted, to abuse diet pills and other drugs, suffer from eating disorders, and attempt suicide.[18] After getting her high school diploma in 1970, she entered Northwestern University and then transferred to the University of Southern California but dropped out before graduation. "I've spent too many years being angry at my parents," Patti wrote in 1992, noting that "mostly I was angry at my mother." In later years, she would achieve a "tentative reconciliation" with Nancy.[19]

While Ron and especially Patti fought with their parents, at least they, for better or worse, had their parents' attention—Nancy's in particular. That was something that Maureen and Michael Reagan—Jane Wyman's children—did not enjoy. Nancy had done her best to win them over when she was wooing Ronnie but froze them out after she was married and had children of her own. Nancy Reagan and Jane Wyman could not stand one another, and Nancy forbade any mention of her husband's first wife at their home.[20] (Wyman was entirely omitted from the first draft of Reagan's post-presidential autobiography; a mention of her was only added at the editor's insistence.)[21] Patti recalled she was seven years old when she first learned that she had a half-brother and half-sister. This occurred in 1959 when fourteen-year-old Michael temporarily moved into their house to try to escape his escalating conflicts with his mother. "This family turned secrecy into an art form," Patti would later write.[22]

Jane Wyman's focus remained on her career, not her family. She moved often and did not stay in a relationship with any man for long. Like Nancy, she, too, went through a lot of maids and nannies—and she had an even more violent temper. She would beat Michael, her adopted son, with a riding crop. Both Michael and Maureen were packed off to boarding school in Palos Verdes early on—Michael when he was five and a half, Maureen when she was seven—and only saw their parents a few days a month. Michael remembered being so "miserable" that he cried himself to sleep every night. No one in the family knew that he was sexually molested by a camp counselor at age eight. Ronald and Nancy Reagan did not find out Michael's secret until 1987 when he was about to disclose it in a book.[23]

Michael, who had found out at age four that he was adopted—Maureen told him out of spite—had no source of stability in his life. He was desperate to be accepted as a member of Ron and Nancy's nuclear family: "I thought that at last I would be living with a family unit just like a normal kid," he wrote. When he moved in, Nancy discovered that he had a dozen cavities and almost no clothes outside of school uniforms. She took him clothes shopping and to the dentist—something Jane had not bothered to do.

But even when Michael was finally allowed to live with his father and stepmother, he was sent to a boarding school during the week—a Catholic school he hated, chosen because Jane had converted to Catholicism—and was only at the house on the weekends. In a sign of how peripheral he was to his own family, he slept on the living-room couch. Michael was excited when the family added an extra bedroom onto the house, figuring he would finally get his own room. Instead, the new bedroom went to the Skipper's nurse. "It nearly killed me," Michael recalled. "I was devastated. I felt that if Dad and Nancy didn't want me, I didn't want them either."[24]

By then a teenager, Michael engaged in self-destructive behavior such as doing poorly in school and picking up prostitutes to affirm his heterosexuality after having been molested by a male counselor. Nancy Reagan would upbraid him for his misconduct, telling him he was not living up to the Reagan name and that, unless he improved his behavior, he should change his name and leave the house. He, in turn, would resist his stepmother's attempts to discipline him, telling her, "You are not my mom."[25] Nancy Reagan later wrote, "Michael and I had such rough times during that period that there were days when I could have killed him." According to Richard Davis, Nancy "couldn't stand Michael."[26] Unlike Nancy's relationships with Maureen and Patti, her relationship with Michael never really improved over the years, culminating in her refusal to summon Michael to his father's deathbed in 2004.

Maureen was older than Michael and even further removed from the family, at least initially. On her infrequent visits to Pacific Palisades, she wrote, "I felt like I didn't belong there. . . . I always felt like I was imposing." She did not get along any better with Nancy than Michael did; Maureen called her stepmother the "Dragon Lady," and they would not establish a warmer relationship until the 1980s when Maureen came to live temporarily in the White House. As a high school sophomore, Maureen was sent to a Catholic boarding school in the suburbs of New York City, where she was far removed from her brother—the person she was closest to in the world. Feeling alone and unable to fit in, she began to overeat. By the time she returned home for Christmas she had gained thirty-five pounds. This horrified the

The re-created living room from Reagan's modest birthplace in Tampico, Illinois. There was a bar downstairs when he was born in 1911. (*Photograph by Max Boot*)

The Reagan family, circa 1916 (l. to r.): Jack, Neil, Dutch (age five), and Nelle. Dutch experienced an itinerant, poverty-stricken childhood, but his mother taught him to look on the "sunny side." (*RRPL*)

Reagan as a lifeguard at Dixon's Lowell Park, 1927. He saved seventy-seven people from drowning and became a local hero. (*RRPL*)

Reagan learned to act in high school and college. Here he is sitting in the middle of a Eureka College play. His sweetheart Margaret Cleaver is at far left. (*EC*)

Reagan was a sportscaster at WHO radio in Des Moines from 1933 to 1937. "His quick tongue seemed to be as fast as the plays," one newspaper marveled. (*RRPL*)

Reagan as George Gipp in *Knute Rockne, All American*. It was one of his iconic film roles, even though the heroic portrayal of Gipp bore little relation to reality. (*RRPL*)

Reagan with wife Jane Wyman and their children, Maureen and Michael, in 1946. Before their divorce in 1948, Hollywood publicists portrayed their marriage as idyllic. (*Alamy*)

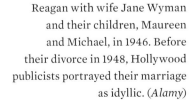

Captain Reagan at "Fort Wacky" in Culver City, California, circa 1943. The fan magazines made it sound as if he was going off to the front lines even though he never left Los Angeles. (*RRPL*)

In 1945–1946, studio technicians represented by the Conference of Studio Unions went on strike. It was a standard management-labor dispute, but Reagan claimed it was part of a "Red" plot to take over Hollywood. (*AP*)

Reagan, as president of the Screen Actors Guild, testifying to the House Un-American Affairs Committee, October 23, 1947. He earned rave reviews for his moderate stance. But behind the scenes he was integral to the blacklist in Hollywood. (*Getty*)

A date with Nancy Davis prior to their 1952 marriage. A reporter later wrote that when Reagan spoke, "Nancy composes her features into a kind of transfixed adoration more appropriate to a witness of the Virgin Birth." (*RRPL*)

Reagan on the set of *General Electric Theater*. Running from 1954 to 1962, the popular show rescued his failing acting career and made him one of the first TV stars. (*RRPL*)

Reagan rose to political prominence supporting Barry Goldwater's 1964 presidential campaign. He was a more effective orator than the actual candidate. (*RRPL*)

The 1965 Watts riot provided a political opening for Reagan to take advantage of a growing white backlash against civil rights legislation, which he opposed. (*RRPL*)

California governor Pat Brown was a well-meaning, middle-of-the-road Democrat who by 1966 had lost touch with a white middle class fed up with the breakdown of law and order. (*Getty*)

The newly elected governor leaves his residence in a wealthy Sacramento neighborhood. Nancy refused to live in the decrepit governor's mansion downtown. (*RRPL*)

Reagan was a prodigious but indiscriminate reader. Many of his favorite news sources (*Reader's Digest, Human Events, National Review*) peddled misinformation that he repeated for decades. (*RRPL*)

the charge in a conversation with his daughter Patti, telling her, "We were happy. Just look at the home movies," as if flickering images of the family cavorting for a few minutes at the beach or by the pool were more real than all that happened when the camera was off.[44]

Richard Davis, Nancy's stepbrother, had a simple explanation for why Ron and Nancy's family life was so difficult. "I don't think it was that complicated," he told me. "They were just totally preoccupied with his career."[45] This might have been a problem for someone who was about to launch a political career during which he would regularly extol traditional family values. But somehow Ronald Reagan would never suffer politically despite the disconnect between the traditional ideals he championed and his own messy home life.

Much as Reagan came to be associated with patriotic service and manly, martial virtues by dint of being pictured in uniform, so too the trappings of family, displayed in photographs and videos, conveyed the right image even if they were dissociated from the underlying reality. His experience in film and television taught Reagan the power of pictures, and he and his team exploited that power to the hilt as he began, in the mid-1960s, to make the transition from show business to politics. What he may not have fully appreciated was that his new career would place even greater strains on his family than the old one.

ACT III

"CITIZEN POLITICIAN"

(previous page) *The Reagans celebrating his election as governor of California, November 8, 1966, at the Biltmore Hotel in Los Angeles.* (RRPL)

18

The Right Man

They equate the Democratic Party with the welfare state, the
welfare state with socialism, and socialism with communism.

—JOHN F. KENNEDY

"'O ld easy going' Reagan," as he sardonically called himself,[1] had
always been eager to please authority figures, ranging from his
high school and college football coaches and drama teachers to
his employers at the WHO radio station and the Warner Brothers studio.
Now he extended the same willingness to please to his bosses at General
Electric—a company so conservative that its outlook was likened by one of
its own executives to that of the John Birch Society.[2] In the process, the former labor leader developed a new identity as a pro-business conservative.
The more he spoke out on the issues, the further right he moved—and he
was speaking out a good deal as the 1950s gave way to the 1960s, thereby
turning himself into a conservative idol.

The fourth largest company in America in the 1950s, General Electric
had long prided itself on being a benevolent employer; it had been a leader
in providing pensions, health insurance, and profit-sharing to its work-
force. It was, therefore, shaken to the core when its plants were hit by the
great strike wave of 1946 that also affected Hollywood. Ralph Cordiner, the
company's president from 1950 to 1958 and then chairman and chief executive until 1963, was determined to prevent a repeat of those labor troubles by undermining the power of the unions. He was, *Time* noted, a "short
(5 ft. 7½ in.), power-packed man with restless eyes" who lived a spartan
existence, seldom socialized, and was obsessed with time management. His
political views were "far to the right."[3]

To lead his antiunion offensive, Cordiner hired Lemuel "Lem" Boulware, a tall, dapper, and genial Kentuckian who had been captain of the
baseball team at the University of Wisconsin before beginning a long
career in business. As GE's vice president in charge of employee relations,

public relations, and community relations, he decided to go over the heads of union leaders by appealing directly to union members—essentially the same strategy that President Reagan would later employ to overcome union opposition to his agenda. This was surely no coincidence: Reagan greatly admired both Cordiner and Boulware and sought to emulate them. Cordiner was also noted for decentralizing authority and giving a great deal of autonomy to GE's operating units. As governor and president, Reagan would emulate this practice of delegating authority—sometimes effectively, sometimes disastrously—that he had learned from a man he always referred to as "Mr. Cordiner" even when he was on a first-name basis with fellow heads of state.[4]

Boulware's multifaceted public relations campaign, known as Boulwarism, encompassed everything from company publications and advertisements to educational programs. He hired more than a hundred writers to produce in-house propaganda. He also strongly encouraged GE managers to read conservative publications, such as the well-established *Wall Street Journal* along with new magazines such as the *Freeman* and *National Review*, and to study books by conservative authors such as Henry Hazlitt and Lewis Haney, who extolled the virtues of free markets and warned about the nightmarish consequences of government regulation.[5]

One of Boulware's assigned readings was John T. Flynn's alarmist and conspiratorial 1949 tract *The Road Ahead: America's Creeping Revolution*, which warned, ominously, that "we are being drawn into socialism on the British gradualist model." A journalist who had been active in the America First Committee, which had promoted isolationism before the Japanese attack on Pearl Harbor, Flynn suggested that socialism would soon give way to Communism. The cause of America's imminent ruin, in his view, was the "hordes of Socialist doctrinaires, ranging from dark red revolutionaries to mild-mannered pink conversationalist reformers," who had infiltrated the government during the New Deal and now had the Democratic Party at their "mercy."[6]

The premise of this book—that Britain had taken a wrong turn toward socialism in the late 1940s and that the Democratic Party was repeating that mistake—would have been appealing to the increasingly conservative Ronald Reagan, given his own negative memories of postwar Britain in 1948. GE's pitchman certainly had a lot of time to read its educational materials—along with such influential conservative texts as Friedrich Hayek's *The*

Road to Serfdom (1944) and Whittaker Chambers's *Witness* (1952)—on his long, cross-country train rides.[7] He also became a charter subscriber to *National Review* when it was launched in 1955. Reagan met the magazine's urbane, wealthy, Yale-educated editor, William F. Buckley Jr., when asked to introduce him in 1961 before he delivered a speech in Los Angeles. Ron and Nancy Reagan would become close to Bill Buckley and his socialite wife, Patricia, even asking Buckley to counsel their wayward children.[8]

W hat was happening at GE was only a microcosm of a larger political ferment that was leading to the resurgence of conservatism in the 1950s. Cordiner and Boulware were at the forefront of this development: Boulware was an early donor to *National Review,* and Cordiner became finance chair of the Republican National Committee during Barry Goldwater's campaign in 1964. The prewar Old Right had been discredited by its close association with the isolationism of the 1930s and Herbert Hoover's failed economic policies. The postwar New Right, by contrast, while still suspicious of foreign aid and the United Nations, generally favored an interventionist US foreign policy to battle the threat of Communism; many conservatives were even willing to risk nuclear war with the Soviet Union to liberate the "captive nations" of Eastern Europe.

The right's ideologues viewed everything from social welfare legislation to desegregation as part of a global Communist conspiracy to destroy the American way of life. There was a pronounced undercurrent of racism—or at least indifference to racial discrimination—in their arguments. Flynn's book *The Road Ahead,* for example, asserted in a chapter titled "The War on the South," "It is a fact that almost all of the publicity about the outrages against Negroes in the South has originated in the propaganda agencies of the Communist trouble-makers."[9]

National Review, which quickly became Reagan's favorite magazine, was also an unyielding opponent of the Supreme Court's *Brown v. Board of Education* ruling and of civil rights legislation. Its editorials mocked civil rights leaders such as Reverend Martin Luther King Jr. and supported the South's campaign of "massive resistance" to court-mandated school desegregation. One notorious 1957 editorial, "Why the South Must Prevail," written by Bill Buckley personally, argued that "the White community" was entitled to maintain political control of the South "because, for the time being, it is the advanced race." In a 1964 editorial, Buckley labeled the civil rights movement "Black Madness." Although Buckley was raised primarily in Connecticut, his family had Southern roots: His wealthy oilman father was from Texas, his mother was from New Orleans, and the family spent part of the year on a South Carolina estate staffed with Black servants.[10]

Much of the conservative movement was also sympathetic to Senator Joe McCarthy, a dangerous, dishonest demagogue who was terrorizing innocent people in the name of rooting out Communist subversives. Buckley even coauthored, with his brother-in-law L. Brent Bozell, a book defending McCarthy. It came out just a few weeks before the Army–McCarthy hearings in the spring of 1954 that finally brought down "Tailgunner Joe."[11] Undaunted, Buckley seven years later would publish a book-length defense of the long-discredited House Un-American Activities Committee.

These conservatives were outraged that President Eisenhower, the immensely popular Republican standard-bearer, was not enacting their hard-right agenda. While Eisenhower cut the defense budget and balanced the budget three times, he did not try to repeal the New Deal and in 1954 even expanded Social Security. Nor did he roll back Communist advances in Eastern Europe, as his 1952 campaign had irresponsibly promised, or repudiate FDR's supposed "betrayal" of American interests at the 1945 Yalta Conference. Eisenhower refused to intervene militarily to aid a Hungarian uprising against Soviet rule in 1956. He made peace in Korea in 1953, leaving the peninsula divided between the "Reds" and the "Free World" rather than expanding the war into China as General Douglas MacArthur, a right-wing icon, had advocated. Eisenhower did not intervene militarily to prevent the French defeat to Ho Chi Minh's Vietminh in 1954. He tried quietly to undermine Joe McCarthy. He also appointed the progressive Republican Earl Warren, a former governor of California, to lead the Supreme Court, and sent federal troops to Little Rock, Arkansas, in 1957 to uphold the court's *Brown v. Board of Education* ruling ending school segregation, which he privately thought premature.

From the conservative standpoint, therefore, Eisenhower's list of offenses was long and galling. Unlike most Americans, conservatives did not like Ike.

Eisenhower called his middle-of-the-road agenda "Modern Republicanism" and saw it as a continuation of the progressive Republican path charted by Theodore Roosevelt, Charles Evans Hughes, and Thomas Dewey. Barry Goldwater, a department store heir elected to the US Senate from Arizona in 1952, had a less kind description of Eisenhower's program. He called it a "dime store New Deal."[12] Members of the far-right John Birch Society— organized in 1958 by candy magnate Robert W. Welch Jr., maker of Junior Mints and Sugar Daddies—were even more virulently anti-Eisenhower. They accused the five-star general of being a "dedicated, conscious agent of the Communist conspiracy" whose controller was his brother Milton.[13] *National Review* publisher William Rusher later said that "modern American conservatism largely organized itself during, and in explicit opposition to, the Eisenhower Administration." The leaders of this bumptious new brand of conservatism saw themselves not as conservators of the status quo but rather, as Bill Buckley said, revolutionaries "against the present liberal order."[14]

The new conservatives were convinced that a majority of Americans shared their convictions, and all the GOP had to do to win was present an unflinchingly right-wing platform. They blamed all Republican defeats on insufficient adherence to conservative principles. Some zealots, such as the influential antifeminist leader Phyllis Schlafly, who would become known for her opposition to the Equal Rights Amendment in the 1970s, even suggested that GOP defeats were deliberately engineered by "a small group of secret kingmakers"—all hated members of the Eastern Establishment— who favored "a continuation of the Roosevelt–Harry Dexter White–Averell Harriman–Dean Rusk policy of aiding and abetting Red Russia and her satellites."[15] White was a Soviet agent; Roosevelt, Harriman, and Rusk were all liberal anti-Communists.

As a first step toward transforming American politics, the right was intent on purging liberals and moderates from GOP ranks to make the party monolithically and doctrinairely conservative. In place of the moderates, they wanted to wrest from the Democrats the loyalties of conservative white Southerners and Northern blue-collar, white ethnic voters. That dream seemed as unobtainable in 1960 as landing a man on the moon, but it was well on its way to becoming a reality by the time Reagan was elected president in 1980.

When the 1950s began, Reagan was already an anti-Communist hardliner. A decade later he had become a laissez-faire hard-liner too, repudiating the last traces of his previous faith in the New Deal. In 1976 he would even claim, bizarrely, that "fascism was really the basis for the New Deal."[16] He took to arguing, as discussed earlier, that it was the Democratic Party that had changed following Franklin D. Roosevelt's election in 1932—not him.[17] This was not only an inaccurate account of the 1930s, when he had enthusiastically supported New Deal programs like the ones that employed his father, but also a rewrite of more recent history that was intended to disguise his dramatic ideological transformation.

Contrary to Reagan's animadversions, the Democratic Party of the postwar years was far from radical. Harry Truman had fought a war to defend South Korea from a Communist invasion, risked another war to supply Berlin during a Soviet blockade, and put in place the containment and deterrence policies that eventually won the Cold War. The Democratic standard-bearer in 1952 and 1956, Governor Adlai Stevenson of Illinois, was reviled on the right as an "egghead" and an "appeaser" (Nixon shamefully said he had a "PhD from Dean Acheson's cowardly college of Communist Containment"), but on the issues, he was not much different from Eisenhower. The centrist Stevenson supported prosecutions of Communist Party leaders, opposed "socialized medicine," and did not advocate a full-throated civil rights platform. The two dominant Democratic congressional leaders of the 1950s—House Speaker Sam Rayburn and Senate Majority Leader Lyndon B. Johnson—were both moderates from Texas who strongly backed the free enterprise system, the defense budget, and the containment of Communism.[18]

In 1960, Democratic nominee John F. Kennedy actually ran to Richard Nixon's right by complaining about an illusory "missile gap" with the Soviet Union. After JFK won, he backed a proxy invasion of Cuba, tried to overthrow or kill Fidel Castro, and risked World War III to keep Soviet nuclear weapons out of Cuba; ramped up US military involvement in South Vietnam; increased defense spending by 20 percent; and advocated an 18 percent income tax cut to boost the economy that President Reagan would later cite as a precedent for his own agenda. At the time, some conservatives opposed Kennedy's tax plan as fiscally irresponsible. Granted, Kennedy also pursued more liberal initiatives, such as sending troops to desegregate state universities in Mississippi and Alabama and signing a Limited Nuclear Test-Ban Treaty with the Soviet Union. But judging by modern standards, he could have been considered practically a conservative—a case actually made in a 2013 book by a conservative journalist.[19]

As president, Reagan often cited Kennedy as a model, and he chided his 1984 Democratic opponent, Walter Mondale, for not following JFK's moderate example.[20] Yet in 1960 Reagan told his daughter that JFK was almost a fellow traveler: "Well, Patti, his views are very socialist and, you know, that's the first step to Communism."[21] He wrote to Nixon that same year, "Shouldn't someone tag Mr. Kennedy's *bold new imaginative* program with its proper age? Under the tousled boyish haircut it is still old Karl Marx— first launched a century ago. There is nothing new in the idea of a government being Big Brother to us all."[22]

In maligning John F. Kennedy as a closet Marxist, Reagan was detached from reality but very much in tune with the ultraconservative sentiments of the day. One right-wing pamphlet called Kennedy's proposal for a new cabinet department of urban affairs a "blueprint for the destruction of private property in the United States."[23]

Such venomous hatred was later blamed by many for the young president's assassination in Dallas on November 22, 1963. The charge was unfair. Although Kennedy was killed in a staunchly conservative city, his assassin was the left-wing, pro-Castro fanatic Lee Harvey Oswald, who had once defected to the Soviet Union. But there is no doubt that some conservatives were less than grief-stricken by JFK's demise, which occurred just as Reagan began making his final film, *The Killers*. He was playing, against type, a gangster who slaps around his girlfriend, played by Angie Dickinson, one of JFK's rumored paramours. Much to Patti's disgust, her parents refused to cancel a cocktail party they were hosting a few days after the assassination at a time when the whole nation was in shock and mourning.[24]

As Reagan's condemnations of JFK would indicate, he was moving far to the right by the early 1960s. The journalist Jonathan Darman, son of Reagan White House aide Richard Darman, discerned that uncompromising conservatism offered Nelle Reagan's son "the unqualified moral clarity and dramatic urgency he preferred."[25] Every complicated, hard-to-understand issue under the sun was subsumed into a larger, Manichaean struggle between Good and Evil, and Reagan was one of the Good Guys because he was so anti-Communist. Not for him the kind of nuanced, liberal anti-Communism espoused by fellow New Dealers Reinhold Niebuhr and Arthur Schlesinger Jr., who supported the welfare state at home while backing the containment of the Soviet Union. Reagan's speeches in the early 1960s became shrill and alarmist. They began, in fact, to display the influence not only of mainstream conservative thought but also—to an extent not properly appreciated by previous biographers—of the conspiratorial John Birch Society, a group so extreme that it denounced the fluoridation of water as a Communist conspiracy.

Typical of the talks that Reagan was delivering in this period was one called "Encroaching Control" that he gave on March 30, 1961, to the Phoenix Chamber of Commerce, on Barry Goldwater's home turf. He began with the apocryphal story of how he had stymied a Communist takeover of Hollywood and went on to argue that the danger to America was now more acute than ever: "The inescapable truth is that we are at war, and we are losing that war simply because we don't, or won't, realize that we are in it." He warned that America was falling victim to an insidious Communist plot: "We'll adopt emergency 'temporary' totalitarian measures, until one day we'll awaken to find we have grown so much like the enemy that we no longer have any cause for conflict."

What were these "temporary totalitarian measures"? This was Reagan's description of social welfare legislation and the growth of the federal government. "Traditionally," he warned, "one of the easiest first steps in imposing statism on a people has been government paid medicine." He also spied a creeping socialist takeover in federal aid to education and to farmers, the progressive income tax ("No nation in history has ever survived a tax burden of one-third of its national income"), and the growing number of federal regulations and federal employees. The federal bureaucracy, he argued, was "a permanent structure of government beyond the reach of Congress and actually capable of dictating policy. This power, under whatever name you choose, is the very essence of totalitarianism." The speech ended with an apocalyptic warning that "we have ten years . . . to win or lose—by 1970 the world will be all slave or all free."[26]

A highly dubious thesis even then, it looks completely wrong more than sixty years later, when the world is still neither "all slave or all free." In making his case, Reagan deployed many questionable and even demonstrably false statistics, quotations, and anecdotes that were undoubtedly accepted at face value by his audience. For example, he complained that the average family of four with an income of $3,500 had to pay a third of its earnings to the government. He must have been assuming that everyone else paid the same rate as high earners like him. In fact, the historian Robert Mann found the actual average tax burden, federal and state, for a family of four in 1960 was just 14 percent of income.[27]

Reagan was particularly enamored of quotes from Communist leaders conveniently revealing, like James Bond villains, their dastardly plots against America. For example, he quoted Vladimir Lenin as saying, "They would take Eastern Europe, next organize the hordes of Asia, then surround the United States and, he predicted, 'that last bastion of Capitalism will not have to be taken. It will fall into our outstretched hands like overripe fruit.'" He quoted Soviet defense minister Nikolai Bulganin as saying, "The American working man is too well fed; we cannot appeal to him, but when through inflation America has priced herself out of the world market and unemployment follows—then we will settle our debt with the United States." He quoted Soviet leader Nikita Khrushchev as saying, "We can't expect the American people to jump from Capitalism to Communism, but we can assist their elected officials in giving them small doses of Socialism, until they awaken one day to find they have Communism." And he quoted the American Socialist Party leader Norman Thomas as saying, "The American people would never knowingly vote for Socialism but . . . under the name of liberalism, they would adopt every fragment of the socialist program."[28]

These quotes all have something in common: They are all false. These made-up quotations were circulated by the John Birch Society and other right-wing extremists to impugn Democrats as closet Communists. For example, the faux quote from Lenin, claiming that the United States will "fall like overripe fruit," comes from page ten of *The Blue Book of the John Birch Society*, compiled in 1958 by Robert Welch.[29] It was prominently featured in John A. Stormer's best-selling, self-published 1964 paperback *None Dare Call It Treason*, which was accurately described as a "deliberate hoax and a fraud."[30] That Reagan was repeating so many of these canards shows how deeply he was influenced by the radical right during this period and how indifferent he was to fact-checking his assertions. His aspersions on Norman Thomas—a democratic socialist and staunch anti-Stalinist—were particularly grievous.[31]

There is a good reason why the right had to make up these quotes: They were at odds with the actual Communist strategy. Marxist-Leninists did not imagine that they would defeat capitalist societies by inducing them to adopt socialist reforms. Rather, they expected that the internal contradictions of capitalism would worsen, leading to a pitched battle between the owners of capital—the bourgeoisie—and the proletariat, resulting in a workers' revolution and the creation of a Communist paradise. Karl Marx specifically warned against "the petty bourgeois" plans for "better wages and security for the workers" and greater "welfare measures." He saw such legislation as simply an attempt "to bribe the workers with a more or less disguised form of alms and to break their revolutionary strength by temporarily rendering their situation tolerable."[32]

Indeed, Communist revolutions occurred in countries such as China, Russia, and Cuba that had corrupt ruling cliques, vast income inequalities, and virtually no social safety net. They did not have "government paid medicine," which Reagan warned was a precondition for totalitarianism. But every wealthy democracy save the United States did develop some version of universal health-care coverage, beginning with Britain in 1948 and swiftly spreading to the Scandinavian countries, Japan, Canada, and Australia. The United States never went as far, but Congress would create Medicare and Medicaid in 1965 without endangering the country's survival. Reagan's attempts to draw an equivalence between the expansion of the federal government in the United States and the imposition of totalitarianism in the Soviet Union were far-fetched at best. The federal government may have been growing, but it wasn't opening gulags to imprison dissidents.

There was also no validity in Reagan's oft-repeated assertion that a country cannot survive if the government consumes a third of the gross domestic product. Even in 1960, some European countries, including Austria, France, Germany, the Netherlands, and the United Kingdom, had governments that were spending a third or more of GDP without endangering their survival. By the time Reagan was elected president in 1980, the United States had joined their ranks. Today the 33 percent threshold has long been surpassed by nearly every wealthy democracy. In Belgium, Denmark, Finland, and France, the government actually spends more than 50 percent of GDP—and yet they remain wealthy and free.[33]

Reagan seemed to have missed a crucial distinction in one of his favorite books, Hayek's *The Road to Serfdom*. (An "underlined, annotated, dog-eared" copy sat on his bookshelf.)[34] The Austrian economist did not argue that greater welfare spending would necessarily "lead to totalitarianism." He was warning *only* about "the abolition of private enterprise, of private ownership of the means of production, and the creation of a system of 'planned economy' in which the entrepreneur working for profit is replaced by a central planning body."[35] Hayek was unperturbed by such government interventions as curbing pollution and providing social security and even a guaranteed minimum income, but such nuances were removed from the *Readers' Digest* version of his book that reached millions of American readers.[36]

Social democracies in Europe had already shown by 1961 that a free market was perfectly compatible with a robust welfare state and progressive rates of income taxation. In fact, by reducing poverty and income inequality, a social-welfare state could increase support for capitalism and stave off a Marxist revolution. This was a critical distinction that Reagan missed but that his erstwhile hero Franklin Roosevelt had intuitively grasped.

And yet, no matter how often his false assertions, statistics, and quotations were rebutted, Reagan continued to perseverate them—and listeners continued to believe them. As president, he regularly trotted out the "overripe fruit" quote—itself overripe by then—which he used to warn of the dangers of Communist advances in Central America. It was even included in his 1990 memoir, prefaced by the phrase "I was told that Lenin once said," presumably so that the ghostwriter (a former *New York Times* reporter) would not have to vouch for its veracity.[37] Reagan's first national security adviser, Richard V. Allen, who had written his dissertation on Marxism-Leninism, said that Reagan was addicted to "spurious quotations from Lenin."[38]

On the rare occasions when Reagan was challenged about the sources of his dubious assertions, he was evasive and unconvincing. Asked in 1965 by a graduate student about his oft-repeated claim that "no nation in history has ever survived a tax burden of one-third of its national income," Reagan replied, "I'm sorry—this was from a summation on the history of past empires and first used by me 10 years ago—I just plain don't have that source any longer."[39] Yet as president he was still citing this faux fact, which he attributed to some unnamed economist.

Reagan had a disturbingly cavalier attitude toward factual accuracy that, arguably, helped to inure the Republican Party to "fake news." It was the relentless accumulation of vivid facts, apposite quotations, and colorful anecdotes that gave his speeches such specificity and power, yet he felt no duty to fact-check or correct himself when shown to be wrong. He was convinced his larger moral point was correct and that was all that mattered. The gibe he aimed at liberals—"It isn't so much that Liberals are ignorant. It's just that they know so much that isn't so"[40]—described him perfectly. In 1984, Democratic House Majority Leader Jim Wright complained, "He can utter the most monstrous falsehoods, in the sweetest tone of voice and with the most innocently pleasant look on his face, [so] that people who do not know the dimension of the lie would be tempted to think it so."[41] That same tendency was evident twenty years earlier.

Another consistent thread throughout Reagan's career was that reporters seldom held him to account for his falsehoods. In the mid-twentieth century, reporters were more deferential to powerful figures, especially to individuals such as Reagan whom they personally liked, and they usually bent over backward to avoid expressing any personal opinions in their writing. Few "fact checkers" existed. Most media uncritically repeated whatever a public figure said. Some journalistic accounts would note in passing that no source had been found for one of Reagan's claims but usually without drawing the obvious conclusion: that he was not telling the truth. Reporters and readers alike gave Reagan credit for sincerity even when he was wrong. As George Skelton, the longtime *Los Angeles Times* bureau chief in Sacramento, said, "He wasn't purposely lying to anybody. He actually believed the stuff."[42] Even when reporters did call Reagan out, however, they found that most readers did not care. As a result, the Right's man paid no price for so often being wrong.

Some of the apocryphal stories that Reagan kept repeating (for example, the one about a pilot aboard a disabled B-17 bomber telling his trapped turret gunner "we'll ride it down together") were inspirational and innocuous.[43] But his use of false quotations to associate social-welfare reforms with a Communist plot to take over the United States was far more insidious—and also far more central to his message. He was doing just what President Kennedy, during a 1961 speech in Los Angeles, accused many right-wingers of doing: "They equate the Democratic Party with the welfare state, the welfare state with socialism, and socialism with communism."[44] This rhetorical pattern, of course, continues to the present day.

President Kennedy may have hated it, but conservatives—including conservative Southern Democrats—loved Reagan's message, precipitating a vast transformation in American political power as Southern Democrats began to renounce their previous allegiances and flock to the Republican Party. Reagan was telling right-wing audiences what they wanted to hear, and he was doing so in a folksy, nonthreatening manner. He spoke "with the staccato delivery of the sportscaster and the ringing conviction of a film star," wrote a reporter who covered one of Reagan's speeches in 1962, adding that he was gaining a reputation as "a Right Wing oracle."[45]

In his new role, Reagan recorded a widely distributed record in 1961 for the American Medical Association, "Ronald Reagan Speaks Out Against Socialized Medicine," that began with the faux quote about creeping socialism from Norman Thomas and went on to warn that government-provided health insurance would lead to the total destruction of freedom in America. This record was intended to be played by doctors' wives at social gatherings under the aegis of the AMA's Operation Coffee Cup—part of a larger lobbying campaign that helped stymie the passage of Medicare and Medicaid for years.

Reagan also joined the board of Young Americans for Freedom, whose songbook featured catchy lyrics such as "Deck the halls with Commie corpses" and "Adlai the bald-headed Com-Symp." He raised money for California Republican Congressman John Rousselot, a member of the John Birch Society. He chaired a right-wing primary challenge in 1962 to California's liberal Republican senator Thomas Kuchel by Jane Wyman's former divorce lawyer, Loyd Wright, who advocated a "preventative war" against the Soviet Union. "If we have to blow up Moscow," Wright said, "that's too bad." He spoke at rallies for right-wing groups including the Christian Anti-Communist Crusade, which drew tens of thousands of people to its highly profitable "schools of anti-communism," and Project Prayer, which was dedicated to overturning a Supreme Court decision banning prayer in public schools.[46]

In 1960, Reagan enthusiastically endorsed for president the same Dick Nixon he had described a decade earlier as an "ambitious opportunist." Nixon hadn't changed, but Reagan had. Two years later, he backed Nixon in a losing campaign for California governor; by this time, the two men were on a first-name basis.[47] In 1962, years after he had ceased voting for Democrats, Reagan finally decided to end his formal affiliation with the Democratic Party and register as a Republican. He had only delayed taking that step as a favor to Nixon, who thought it was more politically effective for Reagan to endorse him as a Democrat.[48] But Reagan's ideological fervor transcended party lines. He also supported notorious Democratic segregationists such as Governor Orval Faubus of Arkansas and Governor Ross Barnett of Mississippi, and they gave him awards of appreciation that he proudly hung in his Pacific Palisades home.[49]

Yet, while catering to the far right, Reagan was pragmatic enough to avoid being publicly tarred with some of its worst excesses. He knew how to avoid looking like a kook. He did not make any claims that African Americans were intellectually unqualified to exercise their political rights, as segregationists did, even while he opposed all civil rights legislation and denounced federal interference in issues of race. And while echoing the John Birch Society's warnings about the creeping communization of America, he did not attribute this alarming development to a cabal of traitors—much less accuse Eisenhower ("whose love of country is beyond question"[50]) of being a Red. Reagan usually accepted the good faith of "our well-meaning liberal friends" and warned that it would be "the height of folly to infer the liberals are less patriotic than ourselves."[51]

"No responsible person can imply that people of a liberal philosophy are engaged in a conspiracy or are pro-communist," he said in 1962, conveniently forgetting that he had hurled just such accusations at labor leader Herb Sorrell, among many others in Hollywood. But Reagan was generally smart enough to limit his accusations of disloyalty to private chats with FBI agents so that he did not gain a reputation as a McCarthyite witch-hunter. While granting that liberals "are sincerely motivated by the most humanitarian of ideals," he added in his 1962 speech, "If someone is setting fire to the house, it doesn't really matter if he is a deliberate arsonist or just a fool playing with matches, the damage will be the same."[52]

This was the dividing line in the early 1960s between mainstream conservatives and right-wing extremists: The former were willing to grant that their opponents were delusional if well meaning; the latter insisted that they were traitors and Communist agents. In this divide, Reagan fell squarely on the side of the mainstream—but he was still very far to the right at a time when a liberal consensus prevailed in US politics.

General Electric had never previously told Reagan what to say, but its executives began to get worried about what he was saying in the early 1960s—especially when he began attacking the Tennessee Valley Authority (TVA), a major GE customer to the tune of some $50 million a year. In a conversation with CEO Ralph Cordiner, Reagan, ever the pragmatist at least when it came to his own self-interest, agreed to stop mentioning the TVA in his speeches, but this did not mollify his critics.[53]

GE found itself in a vulnerable spot because it was under Justice Department investigation for price-fixing in the electrical industry. The case began at the end of the Eisenhower administration and picked up momentum under Kennedy. Three GE executives were convicted of price-rigging and sentenced to prison. Subsequent civil suits cost the company hundreds of millions of dollars in damages. Ronald Reagan had nothing to do with these violations, but it is ironic that the company he worked for—and held up as the epitome of the free market system at its best—was actually a corporate scofflaw.

The government investigation hastened the departure of Lem Boulware and Ralph Cordiner from the company. Cordiner remained as chairman and CEO until 1963, but even he was now concerned about having the company pitchman taking such a partisan and controversial stance against the Democratic administration. Although Reagan was a former union leader, by 1962 the AFL-CIO was referring to him as a "right-wing zealot," and a Minnesota high school canceled one of his speeches because he was considered "too controversial."[54]

An executive at BBD&O, GE's ad agency, called Reagan to ask him to limit his speeches to "commercial pitches about GE products." He refused, he later said, because he couldn't imagine giving a "spellbinding" oration about "the new 1963 coffee pot." "I told this gentleman," he wrote, "that if the speeches were an issue I could see no solution short of severing our relationship."[55]

Firing Reagan was no longer unthinkable because his show was no longer the ratings winner it had been in the 1950s. In 1962, *General Electric Theater*, still a half-hour black-and-white show, was losing audience share to *Bonanza*, NBC's hour-long, color Western. (Reagan himself was one of its avid viewers.) *General Electric Theater* wasn't even among the top thirty shows in the 1961–1962 season.[56] The widow of Charles Bower, who was then the head of BBD&O, told Edmund Morris that Reagan tearfully begged Bower to keep him on as he demanded, "What can I do, Charley? I can't act anymore. I can't do anything else. How can I support my family?"[57] Reagan denied this story. Whether he pleaded for his job or not, it did no good. In March 1962, after an eight-year run, the show was canceled. Having rebuffed suggestions that he might alter the show's format or remain a GE spokesman without the show, Reagan found himself out of a job.

A former GE executive later told Lou Cannon that Reagan's firing was based solely on his poor ratings.[58] But Reagan blamed Attorney General Robert F. Kennedy for forcing him out as supposed retribution for his support for Nixon in 1960. Patti Davis, then nine years old, recalled her father telling her, "Robert Kennedy is behind this attack on me." In his 1965 memoir, Reagan accused the Justice Department of using "force and coercion" to get him fired.[59] In his post-presidential memoir, he even claimed, preposterously, that the Kennedy administration had sent cabinet members or some other "high official" to rebut his speeches in every city where he spoke. That simply was not so.[60]

These far-fetched claims were indicative of Reagan's lifelong tendency to imagine that he was the victim of conspiracies by his political foes—whether Communists in Hollywood or Democrats and moderate Republicans in Washington. In 1979, for example, he would tell liberal columnist Jack Germond that two attempts on President Gerald Ford's life in 1975—as well as the arrest of a derelict with a starter's pistol in his pocket during a Jimmy Carter speech in 1979—might have been a "put up job . . . arranged for political purposes." "He was always a man with a very loose hold on the real world around him," Germond commented.[61]

Reagan's grievances, even if unsubstantiated, played a powerful role in shaping his Weltanschauung. His firing from GE was one more item he could add to his accumulating list of grievances against a federal government that, in his view, had already victimized him by breaking up the studio system, subjecting his income to unfairly high rates of taxation, and investigating his dealings with MCA. His antipathy toward the federal government was not just theoretical or ideological. It was visceral and deeply personal.

Even after losing his job as host of *General Electric Theater*, Ronald Reagan did not give up hope of making a living by acting. He not only accepted

Lew Wasserman's offer to appear in the 1964 film *The Killers*—the only time in his entire career he played a villain—but he also agreed in 1964 to host another anthology TV show, the long-running, Borax-sponsored Western series *Death Valley Days*. This job was arranged by his brother Moon, who was working as an ad executive on the Borax account.[62]

Despite his new television role, Reagan was increasingly focused on politics, not show business. Being fired from GE did not dissuade him from the right-wing trajectory he was on. All of the attention and opposition he was getting only further convinced him of how, well, right he was. And now, freed of his GE duties, he had even more time for politicking. Indeed, he had little else to do beyond working at his Malibu ranch—which could hardly satisfy someone in his early fifties still seething with energy and barely concealed ambition.

Even without GE's patronage, Reagan continued to travel the country delivering anti-Communist, antigovernment speeches, which had become an all-consuming passion—and another way for him to make money. He was advancing his conservative vision and also making himself its star spokesman. A TV interviewer who spoke with him told viewers that he was "on a constant crusade and a man on soap box."[63]

Just as in the 1930s Ronald Reagan had made the transition from sportscasting to acting, and then in the 1950s from movies to television, so now in the 1960s he was making the transition from show business to political activism—and doing so just as a conservative crusade was transforming American politics.

19

The Speech

The Reagan personality has a soothing effect, like a warm bath.

—JOSEPH ALSOP

Barry Goldwater had looked forward to a race in 1964 against John F. Kennedy, whom he liked and respected. But, after JFK's death, he had no illusions about his ability to defeat President Lyndon Johnson, whom he loathed. Johnson was a skillful and unscrupulous politician who had just succeeded a martyred president. A Gallup poll in March 1964 found Johnson getting 78 percent of the vote to just 13 percent for Goldwater.[1] Goldwater later wrote, "I didn't want to run for the presidency. . . . I knew, and said privately from the start, that I would lose."[2]

Yet he calculated that he could still advance the conservative cause even in a losing campaign, and, either foolishly or courageously, he refused to make any compromises to expand his popularity beyond his base. "We'll offer a choice, not an echo," he famously vowed—the line that inspired Phyllis Schlafly's paranoid book. In his memoir, Goldwater approvingly quoted a Johnson aide who described his campaign as "right out of the Old Testament—the blood of the sacrificial lamb—Barry and the true believers. I never believed Barry Goldwater wanted to become President. Instead, he was on a modern crusade—blood shed in what he and the conservatives believed was a sacred cause."[3]

Ronald Reagan, by then a washed-up actor making the transition to political activism and part-time ranching in Malibu, was one of many conservatives who was eager to enroll in the Goldwater crusade. He had become friendly with Goldwater in the late 1950s after they were introduced by Nancy's parents, who lived near the senator in Phoenix. Reagan wrote that he "admired [Goldwater] greatly. . . . He is a truly humble man and utterly incapable of doing an unkind or dishonorable thing."[4] He thought that Goldwater was making "a lot of the same points I'd been making in my speeches and I strongly believed the country needed him."[5]

As it happened, most voters did not think they needed Goldwater—but, by campaign's end, a lot of Republicans concluded they needed Reagan. He would wind up benefiting from the 1964 campaign more than anyone else. The failed Goldwater campaign would propel Reagan toward the successful launch of his own political career.

Goldwater was, in some ways, a JFK of the right. With his deep tan, square jaw, silver hair, and distinctive black, horn-rimmed glasses, the Arizona senator was a handsome man who in 1964 was fifty-five years old. His war record was not quite as good as that of the hero of PT-109, but it was good enough: He had piloted transport aircraft over the eastern Himalayas, a dangerous region known as the "Hump." Like JFK, he was wealthy (his family owned a chain of department stores), and he had overcome his somewhat suspect social origins (Goldwater's father was Jewish but his mother was Protestant, while he was Episcopalian) to become firmly entrenched in the upper-class society of his home state. Goldwater liked to dash around the country piloting his own airplane and tool around Washington in a two-seat Ford Thunderbird convertible. As one admiring newspaper wrote, "Like Kennedy, he has a devastating impact on the ladies; he also projects an aura of rugged masculine competence with which men like to identify."[6]

With his cowboy conservatism, Goldwater became the darling of the New Right in the 1950s by attacking organized labor—and the insipid Eisenhower administration. In 1957 he had denounced Ike for embracing "the siren song of socialism" and practicing "government by bribe" for proposing a $71.8 billion budget.[7] He was filling a leadership void on the right that had been left by the death in 1953 of Senator Robert A. Taft of Ohio, a Midwestern isolationist known as "Mr. Republican."

In 1960 Goldwater issued a best-selling manifesto called *Conscience of a Conservative* at the urging of Clarence Manion, a member of the John Birch Society and the host of a popular conservative radio show. Manion, who had been hoping to draft Goldwater to run for the Republican nomination in 1960, hired as a ghostwriter William F. Buckley Jr.'s brother-in-law, L. Brent Bozell Jr., a hard-line Catholic convert who had previously worked for

Senator Joe McCarthy and was such an admirer of Spanish dictator Francisco Franco that he would soon move to Spain.[8] The ghostwritten tome made clear that Goldwater was not offering up the kind of tepid tap water that Eisenhower and his "modern Republicans" had been pouring. This was two-hundred-proof firewater that the right found intoxicating.

With federal spending now approaching $100 billion a year, Goldwater denounced the federal government as a "Leviathan" that was "out of touch with people, and out of their control." Like many Western conservatives, he did not mention that his state received far more in federal funds than it paid in taxes. Although Goldwater was not personally racist—as a major general in the Air Force Reserves, he had desegregated the Arizona National Guard, and he hired African Americans for his Senate staff—he made common cause with racists by endorsing "state's rights," the Southern slogan for resisting desegregation. Denouncing *Brown v. Board of Education*, he insisted that "the federal Constitution does not require the States to maintain racially mixed schools" and expressed support for "all efforts by the States, excluding violence of course, to preserve their rightful powers over education." He denounced the graduated income tax as "confiscatory" and the welfare state as an "instrument of collectivization."

While demanding fiscal conservatism, Goldwater called for an expansion of military spending to achieve "victory over Communism." He wrote that if another uprising occurred behind the Iron Curtain, such as in Hungary in 1956, "we would invite the Communist leaders to choose between total destruction of the Soviet Union, and accepting a local defeat." Might this confrontational approach not lead to World War III? Goldwater advised readers not to worry—and to overcome their "craven fear of death."[9]

Goldwater did not soften his bellicose tone during his presidential campaign. In May 1964, he called for the use of low-yield nuclear weapons to defoliate the jungles in Vietnam. He even joked about lobbing a nuclear bomb "into the men's room of the Kremlin."[10] Little wonder that his opponent in the general election, President Lyndon Johnson, was able to paint him as a reckless warmonger, most memorably through a devastating commercial showing an adorable young girl plucking daisy petals followed by a mushroom cloud. Goldwater's campaign slogan was, "In your heart, you know he's right." Democrats responded, "In your guts, you know he's nuts."[11] Ironically, even as he was portraying his opponent as a warmonger, Johnson was preparing—with Goldwater's support—to escalate the war in Vietnam based on the sweeping authority granted to him by the Gulf of Tonkin Resolution passed by Congress on August 7, 1964.

Goldwater dealt another self-inflicted blow to his campaign on June 10, 1964, when he became one of only six Senate Republicans to join with Southern Democrats to support a filibuster to block the 1964 Civil Rights Act—making it impossible for Black voters and white moderates to support him. Goldwater had a twisted constitutional rationale for opposing civil rights legislation that had been provided to him by conservative scholars William Rehnquist and Robert Bork: He claimed it trampled on "our God-given liberties" and entailed the "creation of a federal police force of mammoth proportions." Goldwater did not vote for crass political reasons—he did not do anything, as Jonathan Darman noted, for crass political reasons—but his vote had seismic political repercussions.[12]

The party of Lincoln had traditionally been the party of civil rights, and even in 1964 a higher percentage of congressional Republicans than Democrats voted for the civil rights bill. By opposing civil rights legislation, Goldwater won the allegiance of many Southern Democrats—and further alienated Black voters who had already been migrating to the Democrats since the days of FDR. He was "transforming the Republican Party into the White Man's Party," political reporter Robert D. Novak wrote in 1965.[13] This was the origin of the "Southern strategy" that Nixon would employ so successfully in 1968 and 1972. The Democratic and Republican parties were essentially switching positions on civil rights, leading to a slow-motion political realignment that would take the "solid South" from the Democratic Party to the GOP.

The irony of 1964 was that the very positions that made Goldwater unacceptable to the general electorate—his opposition to civil rights, his apparent warmongering—actually solidified his standing with the Republican Party's increasingly conservative base.

The battle for the Republican nomination between Goldwater and the moderates' standard-bearer, Governor Nelson Rockefeller of New York, came down to the California primary on June 2, 1964. Reagan stumped relentlessly for Goldwater—often more effectively than the candidate himself. Goldwater frequently read his speeches with little emotion and came across as uninterested, ornery, even angry. He would respond to prolonged shouts from the audience of "We Want Barry! We Want Barry!" by growl-ing, "If you'll shut up, you'll get him."[14] He was, wrote the political columnist Joseph Alsop, "God's angry man."

Reagan was much more genial and effective. After hearing the actor address the Los Angeles Lions Club, Alsop marveled at his speaking skill:

> Reagan's tone is infinitely sincere, his timing and modulation impeccable. . . . In a purely technical sense—in terms of delivery, tim-ing, entertainment value—"the speech" was more effective than any political speech I have heard in years. . . . He not only tells his conser-vative audiences what they want to hear—he does so with such profes-sional expertise that even the three-Martinis-before-lunch men stay awake. . . . The Reagan personality has a soothing effect, like a warm bath. . . . Ronald Reagan is the television Good Guy come to life, and his answers to even tough questions are about as harsh as Pablum.[15]

The contrast between Goldwater and Reagan was so great that at one San Francisco fundraiser featuring both men, a waitress wondered, "I'm con-fused. Which one was the candidate?"[16]

Reagan's relentless speechifying helped his candidate eke out a narrow victory in California by spurring a strong turnout in Los Angeles County, San Diego County, and especially Orange County. This was the new con-servative heartland of American politics—the home of the activists who had been dubbed "little old ladies in tennis shoes" by a critic. As far back as 1921, the poet John Steven McGroarty had written, "Los Angeles is the most celebrated incubator of new creeds, codes of ethics, philosophies and near philosophies of thought, occult, new and old."[17] Now Southern California was giving birth to a new conservative creed. Many of its adherents were, like Ronald Reagan, white migrants from the rural Midwest—men and women who lived in single-family, suburban homes; owned automobiles; had a radically individualistic outlook with little allegiance to any party; and were fired up by evangelical Protestantism and militant anti-Communism. This area would be dubbed "Reagan country" by the conservative polit-ical scientist James Q. Wilson, who grew up there. In an influential 1967 *Commentary* article, Wilson neglected, however, to mention one of the key tenets of this burgeoning political faith: a desire to keep suburbs lily-white in order to avoid the ills (crime, disorder, falling property values) that many white voters associated with having African American neighbors.[18] However much his supporters might attempt to gloss over it, Goldwater's opposition to civil rights legislation was a major part of his appeal—as it would later be for Reagan.

Nelson Rockefeller, by contrast, was anathema in Southern California not only because of his support for civil rights and denunciations of the John Birch Society but also because of his association with Eastern moneyed interests and his recent divorce and marriage to a much younger woman who gave up custody of her four children to be with him. Indeed, the birth of his first son with his new wife, Margaretta "Happy" Rockefeller, a few days before the primary election in California may have sealed his fate by reminding voters of his divorce. One conservative activist declared that Rocky was "socialist, monopolist, internationalist, pro-communist . . . he is a licentious person politically and economically—not fit for any political office."[19]

By the time the Republican national convention was held on July 13–16, 1964, just south of San Francisco in the Cow Palace—built, ironically, by FDR's Works Progress Administration—the outcome was not in doubt. The only question was whether the Goldwater forces could heal the rift with more liberal Republicans.

The moderate wing proposed amendments to the platform calling on the federal government to exercise its "Constitutional responsibility" to defend voting rights and "equal protection under the law" for all Americans and denouncing attempts by "irresponsible extremist groups such as the Communists, the Ku Klux Klan, the John Birch Society and others" to infiltrate the party. Both planks, moderate as they sounded, were overwhelmingly voted down by a convention hall of Goldwater supporters in a chilling indication of the party's future direction, although the final platform did pledge "full implementation and faithful execution of the Civil Rights Act of 1964, and all other civil rights statutes." When Rockefeller rose to warn of the "extremist threat," he had to struggle to make himself heard above the catcalls, hisses, and jeers. One delegate noted that "the venom of the booing and the hatred in people's eyes really was quite stunning."

In another bellwether of what was to come for the GOP, the conservatives' ire was directed not just at their more liberal rivals but also at the news media covering the convention. Reagan was one of many Goldwater supporters who saw a "conspiracy in the Eastern liberal press" to "discredit" their candidate. Even mild-mannered Dwight Eisenhower, in his address to the convention, denounced the efforts of "sensation-seeking columnists and commentors" to foster division within GOP ranks. At this, a reporter noted, "the Convention exploded in applause, shouts, boos, catcalls, horns, klaxons." Some attendees shook their fists at the hated press, and some reporters felt compelled to flee the Goldwater galleries for their own safety. The baseball star Jackie Robinson, one of the few Black delegates, warned that his party had been taken over by the "high priests of hatred, many of them committed to the sheeted Ku Klux Klan or the suited John Birch Society."

Yet on accepting the nomination, Goldwater endorsed rather than restrained the zeal of his supporters. "I would remind you that extremism in the defense of liberty is no vice," he thundered. "And let me remind you also that moderation in the pursuit of justice is no virtue."[20]

The Republican convention, broadcast to the nation on television, did to the Goldwater campaign what an iceberg did to the *Titanic*. As the influential political chronicler Theodore H. White noted, all of the televised "wrath and fury" left an "indelible impression of savagery which no Goldwater leader or wordsmith could later erase."[21]

That was not, however, an impression shared by Ronald Reagan. He attended the convention as an alternate delegate (Nancy was there too), and he did not record his disapproval of anything he saw. That fall, he served as cochair of the Goldwater campaign in California, traveling around the state raising funds and speaking for the candidate. His brother, Neil, also worked on behalf of the campaign as a vice president at the McCann-Erickson advertising agency, which had the Goldwater account.

Shortly after the convention, Ron lamented in a letter to a fan that the "assault against [Goldwater] has now reached such a point of desperation that there seems to be no conscience whatsoever with regard to ignoring things he has actually said." Accusations of racism against Goldwater were particularly unfounded, he insisted, because "Barry has a fantastic record of personal involvement in behalf of negroes."[22] This ignored the distinction drawn by Martin Luther King Jr.: "While not himself a racist," he said, "Mr. Goldwater articulates a philosophy which gives aid and comfort to the racist."[23]

Reagan himself always insisted, "I just am incapable of prejudice."[24] As evidence, he cited his father's admonitions against bigotry, his college friendship with Black football teammates, and even his imaginary efforts as a radio broadcaster in the 1930s to integrate baseball.

For years he would claim, as he did while speaking at his daughter Patti's school in 1970, "The opening line of the official [Major League Baseball] guide read: 'Baseball is a game for Caucasian gentlemen.' Many of us covering sports editorialized and fought to change that." Most accounts of his life have uncritically repeated this assertion. In fact, as noted by historian Rick Perlstein, there was no such line in the official baseball guide; segregation in baseball was the result of an informal conspiracy among team owners, not a written policy. What no previous account has noted is that newspaper databases do not turn up any evidence of Reagan criticizing baseball segregation until long *after* it had ended. A history of the battle to break the color line in baseball makes no mention of any involvement on his part, while crediting other white journalists of the 1930s—such as Heywood Broun, Westbrook Pegler, Jimmy Powers, and Shirley Povich—for their outspoken efforts. There is, in short, no evidence that Reagan ever did anything to battle segregation in baseball, or anywhere else, while it was going on. This was yet another legend about his own life—like his role in stopping a supposed Red takeover of Hollywood—that Reagan repeated so many times over the years that he probably convinced himself it was true.[25]

In fairness, Reagan did inveigh against racial bigotry while raising his own children.[26] Whatever his private feelings, however, Reagan, like Goldwater, was more than capable of catering to white racists. "I was opposed to the Voting Rights Act from the beginning," he later acknowledged, describing it as "humiliating to the South."[27] He also opposed the Civil Rights Act from the start. Writing to a fan in 1964, Reagan denounced this landmark civil rights law as "purely an emotional bill based on political expediency." "Under this new bill," he complained, "any individual can charge the proprietor of a café, or bar, or hotel, or any employer with discrimination, and the man accused is guilty as charged until and unless he can prove the charge is false. I personally believe the danger in this far overshadows the evil we are trying to correct."[28]

Far overshadows? Reagan did not acknowledge the extent of the evil actually suffered by African Americans, who were denied the right to vote; excluded from education, housing, public transportation, stores, and restaurants; and assaulted and killed with impunity. Between 1882 and 1968, there were 4,743 lynchings in the United States along with many other outbursts of racial violence such as the 1921 Tulsa Race Massacre.[29] Reagan could hardly plead ignorance of this ugly history; as discussed earlier, his hometown of Dixon, Illinois, saw considerable Ku Klux Klan activity during his adolescence, and Chicago, only a hundred miles away, was the scene of a bloody race riot in 1919.

Yet Reagan, shamefully, was more concerned about the impact of civil rights laws on white Southerners than about the impact of Jim Crow laws on Black Southerners. While denouncing the supposed abuses of the federal government, he said not one censorious word about the egregious abuses committed by the Southern states, which were ignoring judicial rulings and unleashing police dogs, club-swinging policemen, and murderous, white-sheeted terrorists on peaceful civil rights demonstrators in order to maintain an American version of apartheid. Reagan took at face value white Southerners' incredible protestations that denying them the right to oppress their Black neighbors was an infringement on *their* freedom.[30]

While Reagan convinced himself and his many fans that, like Goldwater, he was free of racial animus, he inadvertently hinted at his own prejudice when he defended Goldwater's attacks on the United Nations. "No one in the beginning even contemplated a U.N. in which some sixty new and very uneducated Nations such as the African States, with a total population between them less than that of the United States, could outvote the United States sixty to one," he complained in a 1964 letter. "The U.N. could today actually demand the right to move into the South and take action on our racial problems."[31]

The political world would be shocked in 2019 when historian Timothy Naftali uncovered a tape-recorded October 1971 conversation in which Reagan complained to President Richard Nixon about African delegates in the United Nations General Assembly breaking with the US position to support seating a delegation from mainland China rather than Taiwan: "To see those, those monkeys from those African countries—damn them, they're still uncomfortable wearing shoes!"[32] But Reagan had already made the essence of the complaint in his 1964 letter, albeit without the incendiary word "monkey" in reference to Black people, which was not a normal part of his vocabulary. Reagan's children Ron Reagan and Patti Davis, along with his former campaign manager Stuart Spencer and his former Sacramento aide George Steffes, told me that they never heard him use racial epithets even in private, but it is doubtful that the only time he ever did so was when he was recorded by Nixon's Oval Office taping system.

Why complain about African states voting against the United States when there were plenty of non-African states doing so as well? In fact, Naftali writes, Nixon's own "State Department blamed factors other than African voting, including maneuvering by the British and French behind the scenes, for the [1971] loss." Blaming US setbacks in the United Nations on supposedly uncivilized Africans reflected racism on the part of Nixon—and Reagan— even if their personal views were less noxious than those of unapologetic white supremacists such as George Wallace or Strom Thurmond.

That impression was only reinforced by a joke Reagan told in 1965 to Massachusetts attorney general and future US senator Edward Brooke. In some African countries, he quipped, "When they have a man for lunch, they really have him for lunch." Brooke, the highest-ranking elected Black Republican in the country, was not amused.[33]

While stumping for Goldwater in California, Reagan repeatedly delivered what came to be called "The Speech"—a version of the same antigovernment, anti-Communist plaint he had been making for years leavened with dubious quotes and statistics. Employing his ever-present note cards, he would deliver it multiple times a day, usually to "spellbound" audiences.[34] When he gave The Speech on October 1 before some five hundred people packed into the Cocoanut Grove nightclub at the Ambassador Hotel in Los Angeles for a thousand-dollar-a-plate Goldwater fundraiser, the audience was wowed by his well-rehearsed yet seemingly spontaneous words.[35] Two of the men present that night—Ford dealer Holmes Tuttle and oilman Henry Salvatori—insisted that Reagan repeat his speech on a national television broadcast. "He was electrifying," Salvatori said of the former *General Electric* spokesman.[36]

Goldwater and his aides initially were not enthusiastic; they feared that Reagan's attack on Social Security—he called for making it voluntary— would alienate older voters and that his eloquence could upstage the candidate. But after listening to a tape of Reagan's speech, Goldwater found himself in full agreement and gave his go-ahead. The money to buy a half hour of airtime on NBC was provided not only by Tuttle, Salvatori, and other Los Angeles supporters but also by the Goldwater campaign's national finance chairman, former GE president Ralph Cordiner.

The Speech was taped, at Reagan's insistence, in front of an invited audience of Republicans at an NBC studio in Burbank on October 12, 1964; he knew that having spectators react to his words would heighten their impact. It aired nationally on NBC a week before the election, at 9:30 p.m. on October 27 opposite ABC's melodrama *Peyton Place* and CBS's situation-comedy *Petticoat Junction*. Billed by the announcer only as a "thoughtful address," it came to be called "A Time for Choosing." This was a finely honed compendium of zingers and one-liners from Reagan's previous speeches—minus the phony quotes he routinely used to decry a purported Communist plot to take over America. His appeal was populist: "This is the issue of this election," he said. "Whether we believe in our capacity for self-government or whether we abandon the American revolution and confess that a little intellectual elite in a far-distant capitol can plan our lives for us better than we can plan them ourselves."

Reagan complained not only about Lyndon Johnson's Great Society but also about New Deal programs such as farm subsidies and Social Security that he had avidly supported as a young man. "A government can't control the economy without controlling people," he warned, darkly. "And they know when a government sets out to do that, it must use force and coercion to achieve its purpose."

Dollops of humor made the hard-line message more digestible. For example, he quipped, "A government agency is the nearest thing to eternal life we'll ever see on this earth." But some of his attempts at humor were glaringly insensitive. "We were told four years ago that 17 million people went to bed hungry each night," he said, referring to John F. Kennedy's justification for launching a Food Stamps pilot program. "Well, that was probably true. They were all on a diet." This gratuitous mockery of the poor in America drew some laughs from the well-off audience but was, to say the least, in poor taste.

Reagan did not explicitly mention civil rights legislation, an issue where he was at odds with most of the country. (A Gallup poll in 1964 showed the public supporting the Civil Rights Act by two to one.)[37] But he did allude to civil rights obliquely in the speech by arguing, "It is time we realized that socialism can come without overt seizure of property or nationalization of business. It matters little that you hold the title to your property or business if government can dictate policy and procedure and holds life and death power over your business." This would have resonated with conservative listeners who viewed laws forbidding racial discrimination as an impingement on the rights of white homeowners and businessowners.

Reagan was more explicit in his televised address in attacking the United Nations and foreign aid—both popular right-wing targets—relying, as usual, on fictionalized examples. He claimed, for instance, that US taxpayers had bought a $2 million yacht for the emperor of Ethiopia, Haile Selassie. He was referring to an old, decommissioned US Navy seaplane tender, the USS *Orca*, that had been loaned to the Ethiopian navy as a training ship—not an imperial yacht. This misinformation had apparently come from a *National Review* article bemoaning waste in foreign aid.[38] He also attributed to Democrats statements they had not made—for example, claiming that Senator J. William Fulbright of Arkansas had said that "the Constitution is outmoded" and that Senator Hubert Humphrey of Minnesota had accused Goldwater of seeking "to eliminate farmers." In fact, Fulbright had defended presidential authority over foreign policy despite the constraints of the Constitution, and Humphrey had accused Goldwater of wanting to eliminate farm *subsidies*—which was accurate.

A graduate student who studied the speech concluded that it contained seven false or exaggerated statements and thirteen unconfirmed statements that were almost certainly false as well. But these falsehoods were seldom if ever noted in either journalistic or historical accounts.[39]

Goldwater was largely an afterthought in Reagan's remarks, while President Johnson was not mentioned even once. He did deny that Goldwater was a "trigger-happy man," while calling for tough action against the Soviet bloc: "We cannot buy our security, our freedom from the threat of the bomb by committing an immorality so great as saying to a billion human beings now enslaved behind the Iron Curtain, 'Give up your dreams of freedom because to save our own skins, we're willing to make a deal with your slave masters.'" It was a rousing appeal, even if he did not explain how he would free the people of the Communist bloc without risking a world war.

Like most effective political oratory, the whole speech was long on exhortation and short on specifics. As John F. Kennedy had done in his 1961 inaugural address ("We shall pay any price, bear any burden"), Reagan was rhetorically summoning listeners to join him in the fight for freedom, only he saw the enemy not just as tyrants abroad but also as America's own government.

To win over skeptical viewers, Reagan stressed that he was a former Democrat who was disenchanted with his old party. Its leadership, he said, was "taking the Party of Jefferson, Jackson and Cleveland down the road under the banners of Marx, Lenin and Stalin." This was a grotesque slur, straight out of the John Birch Society playbook, given that Democratic administrations had done just as much as Republicans, if not more, to resist the expansion of Communism around the world. Nor were Democrats trying to confiscate private property or to impose Five Year Plans on industry. Indeed, earlier that year, President Johnson had signed a massive tax cut, reducing the top income-tax rate from 90 percent to 70 percent, that would later be cited by Reagan as a precedent for his own supply-side economics.

Ironically, after attacking Franklin Roosevelt's legacy and seeking to dismantle it, Reagan ended with a line borrowed from FDR: "You and I have a rendezvous with destiny." While Roosevelt had used this phrase as a call to service in the depths of the Great Depression, Reagan used it as a prelude for an apocalyptic ultimatum that echoed Abraham Lincoln's 1862 message to Congress in the middle of the Civil War. "We'll preserve for our children this, the last best hope of man on earth," he said, "or we'll sentence them to take the last step into a thousand years of darkness."[40]

Patti Davis, Reagan's precocious twelve-year-old daughter, was one of the few people in the studio audience who was not impressed. "People around me were clapping and crying, blowing their noses and wiping their eyes," she recalled. "My mother's face was streaked with tears." Patti later wrote that she was "completely confused": "Was my father suggesting that the only hope for man on earth was Barry Goldwater?"[41]

He was, and his appeal struck a powerful chord with Goldwater supporters. Reagan was inundated with enthusiastic telegrams. YOUR SPEECH GREATEST EVER DELIVERED, said one. Even Dwight Eisenhower chimed in that the speech was "excellent."[42] Not only were people sending congratulations; they were sending money. Reagan's claim that the speech raised $8 million was wildly exaggerated (TV for Goldwater-Miller, the committee that sponsored the address, raised a total of $2.51 million that fall), but its actual haul—$600,000 to $700,000—was impressive enough. That would be $5.3 million to $6.1 million in 2024 dollars.[43]

Goldwater still suffered one of the worst drubbings in US political history. He carried only six states—his home state of Arizona and five states of the Deep South. In a sign of a looming racial realignment, however, while he won only 6 percent of the Black vote nationally—compared to Richard Nixon's 40 percent in 1960—he garnered a majority of the white vote in every Southern state except LBJ's Texas. This would be the last time that a Democratic ticket would win the majority of the white vote in a presidential election—a historic shift that would have greater consequences in coming decades.[44]

While Goldwater had lost, Reagan had won. The political observers David Broder and Stephen Hess would describe the "Time for Choosing" speech as "the most successful national political debut since William Jennings Bryan electrified the 1896 Democratic Convention with the 'Cross of Gold' speech."[45] Indeed, many Republicans concluded that Reagan would have been a more effective candidate than the man they had actually nominated. "When Reagan spoke," a Florida man wrote, "everyone said, 'Why didn't [Goldwater] say it that way?'"[46]

The fading actor had suddenly morphed into a political star. But could he reach beyond the Republican base to win an election in what was now the nation's most populous state? The political world was about to find out.

20

The Friends of Ronald Reagan

Reagan articulated the things they felt.

—ROBERT TUTTLE

Not only did Lyndon Johnson win in a historic landslide in 1964, but Democrats picked up two seats in the Senate and thirty-six in the House. The Republican drubbing had many learned students of politics penning obituaries for the conservative movement and even the Republican Party. *New Yorker* correspondent Richard Rovere wrote, "The election has finished the Goldwater school of political reaction." *Time* proclaimed the country "On the Fringe of a Golden Era" in which ideological disagreements would recede. Johnson himself—never one for understatement—said that "these are the most hopeful times in all the years since Christ was born in Bethlehem."[1]

Johnson's hubris would set him up for a fall of Shakespearean proportions. But in 1965 his sanguineness appeared to be merited as he marched from one legislative accomplishment to another. In the space of just six months, Congress approved federal funding for low-income schools and low-income housing, created Medicare and Medicaid, passed the Voting Rights Act, and revamped the nation's immigration system to allow the admission of more newcomers from Asia and Latin America. It was a dazzling array of achievements that rivaled FDR's first hundred days.

Yet LBJ's domestic achievements would soon be overshadowed by the looming war in Vietnam. The United States had only 23,300 troops in South Vietnam at the beginning of 1965. By year's end that number would grow to 184,300, and it would continue increasing until it topped out at 536,100 troops in 1968.[2] The expanding war effort brought more draft calls and protests on college campuses and beyond, with the University of California, Berkeley, emerging as the epicenter of student protest. "Hey, hey, LBJ! How many kids did you kill today?" demonstrators poetically chanted. And that, in turn, intensified a right-wing backlash against antiwar advocates who were viewed by many older Americans as overprivileged and unpatriotic.

As coats and ties, dresses and heels gave way among the young to bell-bottom jeans, miniskirts, sandals, and tie-dyes, the World War II generation grew increasingly disenchanted with their baby boomer offspring. The spread of drugs, promiscuity, foul language, and rock 'n' roll only widened the generational chasm. "The times they are a-changin'," Bob Dylan sang in 1964, but few Americans over the age of thirty appreciated the changes. Former president Dwight D. Eisenhower, one of the greatest products of the Great Generation, spoke for many when he wrote to a friend in 1965 lamenting "lack of respect for law, laxness in dress, appearance and thinking, in conduct and in manner," which he believed reflected "a lack of concern for the ancient virtues of decency, respect for law, and elders, and old-fashioned patriotism."[3]

Alongside the older generation's backlash against the young was a white backlash against African Americans' continuing demands for equality. This was evident in the two-to-one margin by which California voters in 1964 passed Proposition 14 to repeal the 1963 Rumford Fair Housing Act, a state law that had banned racial discrimination in the sale or rental of most single-family homes and apartments. (The law would be restored in 1966 by the California Supreme Court.)[4] While many white people outside the South might support the passage of the Civil Rights Act or the Voting Rights Act, that did not mean they wanted a Black family moving in next door. A 1965 Gallup poll found that 69 percent of respondents were likely to move "if colored people came to live in great numbers in your neighborhood."[5]

White apprehension only grew after a riot broke out in the summer of 1965 in Watts, a Black neighborhood in South Central Los Angeles whose residents struggled with high rates of unemployment, inadequate housing, few stores or public services, and tense relations with the city's notoriously racist police department. The violence was triggered by a confrontation on August 11, 1965, between a white highway patrolman and a Black motorist who had been pulled over for drunk driving. By the time thirteen thousand National Guard troops restored order on August 16, thirty-four people had been killed, more than four thousand arrested, and a thousand buildings had been damaged or destroyed. Suburbanites were terrified by televised images of arson, looting, and rock-throwing accompanied by chants of "Burn, baby, burn."[6]

Coming shortly after the passage of the Civil Rights and Voting Rights Acts, the unrest in Watts soured a large number of white Americans on the whole civil rights movement by suggesting that, as the political commentators Thomas and Mary Edsall later wrote, the new laws, rather than leading to Black assimilation into white society, were bringing "to the surface grievances so intense that they found expression only in violence."[7] White fear would only increase as further Black uprisings followed in other cities, most notably Detroit and Newark in 1967. As the violent crime rate increased—it went up 126 percent between 1960 and 1970[8]—so did the white backlash. Many white Americans blamed crime on "Negro" criminals and "bleeding heart" liberal judges.

The brief era of good feelings heralded by the dawn of Johnson's Great Society was rapidly dissipating, leaving fear and loathing in its wake—and creating an opportunity for a has-been actor who had remade himself into an eloquent champion of conservative causes.

———————————

Edmund G. "Pat" Brown, the well-meaning if bumbling Democratic governor of California, was as unprepared as Lyndon Johnson for the shifting public mood. Brown—as his son and future California governor Jerry Brown noted to me—had a "similar upbringing" to Reagan's. Like Jack Reagan, Brown's father was an impoverished, hard-drinking descendant of Irish immigrants from County Tipperary. His mother was a German immigrant and a Unitarian who, like Reagan's parents, taught her children to oppose bigotry. More echoes of Reagan: Brown adored the outdoors, was not renowned for his intellect, and changed his political affiliation as an adult. Having been raised in San Francisco when it was a Republican bastion, Brown switched to the Democrats in 1934, at age twenty-nine, because of his devotion, shared by Dutch Reagan at the time, to Roosevelt and the New Deal. Unlike Reagan, however, Brown never lost his belief in the power of government to improve people's lives.

Brown had gone to night school to become a lawyer and in 1943 was elected district attorney of San Francisco. He was elected state attorney general in 1950 and reelected in 1954 as the nominee of both the Democratic *and* Republican parties. Brown was not charismatic, eloquent, or telegenic, but neither was he partisan or polarizing.

In 1958, Brown won the governorship by a margin of a million votes over his formidable, right-wing opponent, US Senator William Knowland, on a platform of "responsible liberalism." Over the next eight years, working with legislators of both parties, Brown vastly expanded California's infrastructure, building new dams and aqueducts, schools and universities, bridges and freeways for a rapidly growing population. Buoyant and optimistic, Brown seemed the perfect governor for a state that was seen by millions as a promised land of limitless sunshine and infinite opportunity. In 1962, California became the nation's most populous state with nearly eighteen million people. That same year, Brown turned back a well-funded challenge from former vice president Richard Nixon. "You won't have Nixon to kick around anymore," the losing candidate told the press.

By 1966, however, Pat Brown was increasingly out of touch with an electorate whose concerns could be symbolized, as Brown family chronicler Miriam Pawel noted, in two loaded words: Berkeley and Watts. He tried to stake out middle-of-the-road positions on both issues—supporting the right to peaceful protest while opposing any illegality—and thereby pleased no one. He defended the Rumford Act and did not hesitate to brand its opponents as bigots, thereby alienating many white voters. But he never went far enough for the radicals of the New Left because he refused to criticize an unpopular war in Vietnam or to break with Lyndon Johnson. In the struggle between the establishment and the counterculture ("There's battle lines being drawn," Buffalo Springfield sang in 1966), Brown was stranded in a political no-man's-land.

A "good but uninspiring governor," in the words of one reporter, Brown found himself abandoned by many on both the left *and* right and denigrated as a hopeless square by the youthful avatars of the "new age." The New Deal coalition was splintering, and American politics was being transformed by forces beyond his control or understanding.[9]

Brown's cascading woes created an opening for a Republican challenger in 1966, when he was stubbornly determined to seek a third term despite warnings that he would be better advised to gracefully retire.[10] And after the success of the "Time for Choosing" speech, it was obvious which potential challenger had seized the imagination of California conservatives.

A conservative activist who visited California in late 1965 listed in the right-wing newspaper *Human Events* all the reasons why Ronald Reagan was an "ideal candidate" for governor and "also, perhaps, a future President of the United States." These included his charm, his eloquence, his mastery of television, his ability as a former Democrat "to cross party lines," his "financial backing" and "organizational muscle," and, finally, "that quality ever present in winners—luck." He was someone, in short, who could sell conservative ideas far more successfully than Barry Goldwater had done. As the headline put it, "Principle Is His Most Important Product."[11]

Given Ronald Reagan's passion for politics, there had long been talk of him running for office. He had set his sights as high as they could go. Bill Cotworthy, who worked with him on *General Electric Theater*, recalled suggesting around 1956 that he run for mayor of Los Angeles. He remembered Reagan's reply: "President or nothing."[12]

Reagan had turned away entreaties from right-wing businessmen to run for governor or senator in 1962. He kept insisting that he was no politician—"The farthest thing from my mind was running for political office," he always claimed—but his interest was growing. In 1963, with the aid of a ghostwriter, he began working on an autobiography, *Where's the Rest of Me?*, that would be released in 1965. It read a lot like a campaign book; it even ended with one of his typical speeches.[13]

Just days after Goldwater's 1964 defeat, California's Republican secretary of state, Frank Jordan, touted Reagan as a candidate for governor. "I've never had any political aspirations as a candidate," Reagan insisted, while refusing to rule out a run.[14] His coyness fooled no one. By the end of November 1964, the *Los Angeles Times* was touting him as the Republicans' "hottest—and newest—prospect." His potential primary opponent was San Francisco's "middle of the road" former mayor, George Christopher, who had supported Nelson Rockefeller in 1964. Both men, the newspaper reported, "have sent out quiet feelers to political sources, inquiring what steps might be taken in the months ahead to get a gubernatorial campaign in shape for 1966."[15]

The most obvious problem any candidate running for office in a giant state like California faced was raising the funds to advertise and organize. But money would be no issue for Reagan in those days before serious limitations on campaign financing. He had the enthusiastic support of a group of wealthy, right-wing Southern California businessmen. These tycoons, who eventually became known as the Kitchen Cabinet, had been getting to know Ron even before his star turn during the Goldwater campaign. That had been largely Nancy Reagan's doing. As her mother had done with Loyal Davis, Nancy was using her social-climbing skills to advance not only her social life but also her husband's career.

Vanity Fair correspondent Bob Colacello, who enjoyed Nancy Reagan's enthusiastic cooperation, offered the most insightful dissection of her social climb during the 1950s and early 1960s in his book *Ronnie and Nancy: Their Path to the White House—1911 to 1980.* He even acquired the menus of dinner parties the Reagans attended; one soirée in 1962, hosted by Alfred and Betsy Bloomingdale, featured "beef Wellington, zucchini, limestone lettuce with two cheeses, strawberry sherbet, fresh raspberries, fresh strawberries, apricot sauce, oatmeal cookies, and Chateau Cheval Blanc."[16]

Colacello noted that the Reagans were not really part of the Hollywood A list. In the 1950s, they preferred to socialize quietly at home with their good friends Dick Powell and June Allyson, Bill and Ardis Holden, and Robert and Ursula Montgomery. Robert Montgomery may have been Reagan's closest friend in the 1950s—quite possibly the last close male friend he had aside from his future ranch hands. Patti Davis's godfather, Bill Holden, best known for his role as Norma Desmond's kept man in the 1950 classic *Sunset Boulevard*, would fade from their circle as he divorced and took to drinking heavily and dating much younger women. Patti would not see him again until she happened to run into him in a restaurant shortly before his death in 1981.[17] But while the Reagans' friends were big shots in the "film colony," they were far removed from the elite downtown Los Angeles social set that looked down on movie people.

Nancy Reagan set out to change their social isolation by forging friendships with the wives of successful executives who were not in the film industry. The Reagans' new friends included Marion and Earle Jorgensen, whose company sold steel and aluminum; Betty and William Wilson, whose business interests ranged from the oil industry to real estate; Betsy and Alfred Bloomingdale, who was an heir to a department store fortune and had started the Diners Club credit card (Betsy would become Nancy's closest friend); Lee and Walter Annenberg, the publisher of the *Philadelphia Inquirer*, *TV Guide*, and *Seventeen* magazine; Anita and Tom May, chairman of the May Company department stores; Harriet and Armand Deutsch Jr., a former MGM executive and heir to a Sears, Roebuck fortune;

and Mary Jane and Charles Z. Wick, who had started a nationwide chain of nursing homes.

Ronald Reagan dutifully socialized with the "fellas"—he was always happy to share his political philosophy and his tales of Hollywood—but the real relationships were forged by Nancy. As their son Ron noted, "He really didn't care too much about that. You had to kind of blast him out of the house. Five o'clock came, and the PJs and the robe were on, and he was ready to settle in, and maybe do a little reading, watch the news, have dinner."[18] A loner by nature, he would have been just as happy to stay home. Nancy was the one who cared about building relationships—and she easily bent her good-natured husband to her steely will. "I think it meant a lot to her to be an accepted member of a group that was privileged, exclusive, and snobbish, and she valued all her superficial status symbols," wrote the celebrity astrologer Joan Quigley, who would become close to Nancy in the 1980s.[19]

In 1962, Nancy knew that she had been admitted to the inner sanctum of Los Angeles society when she was invited to join the Colleagues, an exclusive charitable group that limited its membership to fifty women. Nancy and her posh new friends had not only their own charity but also their own fashion designer, their own hairdresser, their own flower arranger and party planner, their own interior decorator, and their own hangout—a new Beverly Hills restaurant called The Bistro. If, as a friend told Colacello, "Nancy cherry-picked her friends," she did so in a way that elevated not only her husband's social standing (and her own) but also his nascent political career.[20]

N ancy Reagan's social network overlapped in significant ways with Ronald Reagan's political network. The early leaders of the political effort were Holmes Tuttle, an Oklahoma native who had gotten his start working at a Ford assembly plant and now owned a string of automobile dealerships in California and Arizona; Henry Salvatori, an Italian immigrant who founded an oil exploration firm; A. C. "Cy" Rubel, a geologist from Kentucky who had retired as president of Union Oil Company; and Edward Mills, a son of Dutch immigrants who had worked his way up from stock boy to president at the giant Van de Kamp Bakeries. These were mostly "self-made men," said Holmes's son Robert Tuttle. They had hated FDR and worried about the future of the country. They had backed Goldwater—Tuttle and Salvatori, and their wives, had attended the 1964 GOP convention with the Reagans—and now they naturally transferred their allegiance to their friend Ron. "For them, Reagan articulated the things they felt," Robert Tuttle said.[21]

Their immediate goal was to elect Reagan as governor of California, but the ultimate destination was always 1600 Pennsylvania Avenue. The group became known as the Kitchen Cabinet—originally a term of derision applied to President Andrew Jackson's informal advisers in the 1830s. "They hooked their star to Ronnie," said Arthur Laffer, an economist close to drugstore magnate Justin Dart. "Every one of them loved Ronnie and Nancy."[22]

The Kitchen Cabinet's support for Reagan has usually been depicted as a selfless act on the part of idealistic believers in the free market. And that was certainly how they saw themselves. "We didn't have any selfish interest," Ed Mills said, while Holmes Tuttle insisted that "they didn't want anything from the governor" aside from "good government."[23]

The reality, however, was that these multimillionaires stood to greatly benefit from electing a staunch conservative as governor and eventually president. Their political investment would pay off handsomely when Reagan as president would lower the top rate on federal income taxes from 70 percent to 28 percent—with most of the benefits accruing to the top one percent of earners. That's not to suggest that the Kitchen Cabinet's support for Reagan was simply a matter of crass self-interest, but it wasn't entirely altruistic either. This would seem like an obvious point, but it is missing in most accounts of Reagan's rise.

Acting as emissaries on behalf of the other money men, Holmes Tuttle and his wife, Virginia, visited the Reagans' Pacific Palisades house in late 1964 and early 1965 to convince Ron to run for governor. He did not say yes on the spot, but he did not say no either. In February 1965, Reagan called Tuttle and told him that he would run if they "still felt the same way." But he did not want to announce a campaign right away. He preferred to "just kind of put feelers out" and keep up the pretense that he was not an actual candidate—that he would only run if the people demanded it.[24]

Indeed, Reagan kept up a public stance of uncertainty throughout 1965 even as he privately told friends, "I'm fairly certain I will—run that is."[25] Putting off a formal campaign announcement allowed him to continue appearing on *Death Valley Days,* his primary source of income. Meanwhile, Tuttle, Salvatori, Rubel, and Mills set up a group called Friends of Ronald Reagan to raise money for the undeclared campaign.[26]

The old movie star was about to take on a new role as a political candidate. Rescuing California from the turmoil of the mid-1960s would form the perfect storyline. The Kitchen Cabinet would be the producers. Now, for the show to be a hit, they just needed to find the right director.

21

The Backlash Candidate

The majority of Californians were ripe for a radically
different type of Governor.

—PAT BROWN

ntil the mid-twentieth century, American political campaigns
were run by political bosses who employed patronage networks to
mobilize party loyalists. But those methods no longer applied in a
mega-state such as California where party organizations were weak and the
only way to reach millions of voters was by mail, radio, or television. That
required a new breed of political professional—the campaign consultant—
who was expert in advertising, polling, direct mail, fundraising, turnout
operations, and other arcane arts. These guns for hire worked not for a
party organization but for whichever candidate or cause could afford their
hefty fees. As party bosses lost power, the political consultants became the
new kingmakers.

In searching for a consultant to run his nascent campaign, Ronald Rea-
gan reportedly asked Barry Goldwater if he had any recommendations.
Goldwater's campaign had had a near-death experience during the 1964
California primary when Nelson Rockefeller had come from thirty points
down to nearly win. "Rocky's" California campaign had been managed by
Stuart K. Spencer, a former small-town parks and recreation director, and
William Roberts, a former television salesman. They had become active in
the Los Angeles Republican Party and, putting up five hundred dollars each,
had gone into business together in 1960. Theirs was only the third political
consulting firm in the whole state, and they enjoyed an attention-getting
win early on with liberal Republican Thomas Kuchel's 1962 US Senate campaign. That led to getting hired by Rockefeller.

"We never thought much of the Spencer-Roberts team," Goldwater later
wrote. "They ran a rotten, underhanded campaign against me in California."[1] But when asked in 1965 by Reagan to recommend a consultant, he

supposedly said, "Hire those sons of bitches Spencer-Roberts." Or so Stu Spencer later told anyone who asked, including this author.

The Friends of Reagan committee did decide to hire Spencer-Roberts & Associates, and Reagan voiced no objection despite the bitterness he and other Goldwater supporters still harbored against the Rockefeller campaign. That testifies to his supreme pragmatism when it came to matters of self-interest. Spencer-Roberts had developed a reputation, in the words of the *Saturday Evening Post*, as "the shrewdest political image-makers in the business,"[2] and, if Reagan was going to run, he wanted to win. It did not matter to him that Spencer and Roberts were no ideologues. As Spencer noted, "He was a ferocious competitor."[3]

But did Spencer-Roberts want to take him on as a client? Reagan's prospective opponent, former San Francisco mayor George Christopher, had already asked to hire them. This moderate ex-mayor appeared to many to be a better bet than a right-wing actor. "Not one in ten thousand takes the Reagan movement seriously," a liberal Republican assemblyman said in 1965. Pat Brown himself wrote of Reagan that year, "He doesn't worry me." A joke attributed to Jack Warner made the rounds: "Reagan for governor? No, Jimmy Stewart for governor, Ronnie Reagan for best friend."[4]

From their first meeting with Reagan at the Caves du Roy club in Los Angeles in April 1965, Stu Spencer and Bill Roberts discovered that he was "nice," "relaxed," and "pleasant," Spencer said. But they didn't know too much about him. Was he, for example, a member of the John Birch Society? Spencer-Roberts had run John Rousselot's House campaign in 1960 and came to regret it once they found out he was a Bircher. Was Reagan also a "right-wing nut"? And what about Reagan's divorce? Rocky's remarriage had helped to sink his campaign. Would Reagan's private life be a problem?

The consultants spent weeks investigating Reagan, talking to him and to people who knew him. They became convinced that he was not a member of the John Birch Society and that his divorce would not be a problem. Jane Wyman told them she wasn't surprised by his new political career, wished him well, and would not say a word against him. "Don't worry," Spencer recalled her saying with a laugh, having already downed a couple of morning cocktails, "I won't tell the world he's a lousy lay."

Spencer and Roberts concluded that, in Spencer's words, Reagan was a viable candidate with a "serious belief system" and a superb ability to communicate. Working for him was a risk, but at least he wasn't dull like Christopher. Dull was deadly in California politics. Reagan was "hot, spicy, new." And he had plenty of money behind him: no small consideration for consultants who described themselves as "mercenaries."

Reagan was getting tired of Spencer and Roberts' equivocating and questioning. Finally, in May 1965, he asked them point blank, "Now goddamnit, I want to get some answers from you guys. Are you going to work for me or not?"

The partners said yes. They were in.[5]

<hr />

Spencer and Roberts found Reagan an easy candidate to manage; he was used to being directed. Their real challenge was in dealing with the demands of the candidate's wealthy backers, his brother (whose ad agency produced ineffective campaign commercials), and especially his wife. All had their own ideas about how the campaign should be run.

Stu Spencer soon learned to expect a call from Nancy Reagan every day at 10:00 a.m.—"you could set your watch"—after she had talked about the state of the campaign with six or seven confidantes who could range from the Kitchen Cabinet (or their wives) to the actor Jimmy Stewart or the producer A. C. Lyles. Invariably her friends claimed the campaign was screwing up something and Nancy, "a classic worrier," relayed their concerns. "Some of it was good," Spencer said. "Some of it was bad . . . gossip, trivia, crap." Another campaign operative, Tom Reed, complained, "Nancy was difficult on the phone and a pain in the butt."[6]

Spencer, a savvy political pro, was smart enough to listen patiently, realizing he had to humor the candidate's wife to stay on the candidate's good side. One of the campaign's telephone operators showed less patience: She once put through Nancy's call to Bill Roberts by announcing, "The bitch is on the line," without realizing that Nancy could hear what she said.[7]

Nancy was of one mind with Spencer-Roberts about how to handle her husband's divorce: by drawing as little attention to it as possible. Reagan's adult children with Jane Wyman—twenty-five-year-old Maureen Reagan and twenty-one-year-old Michael Reagan—were banished from the campaign. Maureen, who was becoming active in Republican politics, was asked to introduce her father before a speech only once—and Nancy was "livid" when she found out. Maureen, in turn, was "humiliated" when she was told to read a campaign biography that declared, "Ronald Reagan and his wife Nancy have two children, Patti and Ronnie."

While "Mermie" and Mike had been edited out of the picture like irksome extras, fourteen-year-old Patti and eight-year-old Ron were used as props in photo shoots. The campaign managed to suppress any news about Patti's rebellious ways, which already included pot smoking and trying to run away from her boarding school in Arizona with a kitchen worker.[8]

Spencer-Roberts knew just how to handle Reagan's lack of experience: He would campaign as a "citizen politician" while attacking Pat Brown as a "professional politician." "I am an ordinary citizen with a deep-seated belief that much of what troubles us has been brought about by politicians," Reagan often said, "and it's high time that more ordinary citizens brought the fresh air of common sense thinking to these problems."[9] Audiences, predisposed to believe that politics was the only professional field where inexperience was a virtue, ate it up.

Rather than being defensive about his show-business background—another potential negative—the candidate joked about it. When asked what he would do as governor, he would quip, "Gee, I don't know. I've never played a governor before."[10] Given that California voters in 1964 had elected his fellow thespian George Murphy to the US Senate, it was obvious that coming from Hollywood was no disqualification for high office in the Golden State.

The accusation that Reagan was a right-wing extremist was harder to handle. Denouncing the John Birch Society, as Nixon had done in 1962, would cost him votes. It might even cost him the Republican primary, given that California alone had more than ten thousand Birchers and they were politically active.[11] But not denouncing the Birchers would make him look like a kook and alienate more moderate voters.

There was no disguising that Reagan was sympathetic to the John Birch Society's mission and was an avid consumer of its propaganda—more so than previous biographers have realized. Many of his claims about a Communist plot to take over America—buttressed by imaginary quotes from Communist leaders—had their origins in Bircher publications. As late as the early 1970s, he admitted in previously unreported letters to having read two of the nutty tracts published by John Birch Society members: W. Cleon

Skousen's *The Naked Capitalist* and Gary Allen's *None Dare Call It Conspiracy*. Both books accused shadowy "insiders," "secret power manipulators," and the "super-rich"—namely, the Rothschilds, the Rockefellers, the Morgans, the Council on Foreign Relations, the Bilderberg Meeting, the big banks, and all the other Bircher bugbears—of conspiring for some reason (did they have a death wish?) to bring Communism to America.

"Have you read Skouson's [sic] new book, *The Naked Capitalist*?" Reagan asked his old Red-baiting friend Roy Brewer in 1971. "He presents a frightening new aspect to the whole left movement."[12] Referencing both *The Naked Capitalist* and *None Dare Call It Conspiracy*, he told another correspondent that he could not "properly evaluate the charges contained in both the . . . books," while suggesting that they could well be accurate: "Of course, no one can deny there are some people of great wealth who seem to be unusually attracted by left-wing causes."[13] Stuart Spencer said he wasn't aware of Reagan reading Bircher publications, but he wasn't surprised: "He read everything he could."[14]

Reagan resisted calls to denounce the Birchers as a violation of their "civil rights," arguing that it would unfairly deny "an entire group" the opportunity to "participate in the normal electoral process."[15] His concern for the "civil rights" of these political extremists was disingenuous—they could still participate in politics even if he denounced them—and stood in stark contrast to his opposition to legislation to redress actual civil rights violations against African Americans. Reagan also claimed, ironically, that repudiating the Birchers "smacks of a kind of McCarthyism," even though the Birchers themselves were avid McCarthyites.[16] "I . . . am acquainted with members of the Society who are fine upstanding citizens," he told one voter, "and I'll be most proud to have their support."[17]

One of the Birchers Reagan was friendly with was former (and future) congressman John Rousselot, the society's public relations director. "Johnny Rousselot is a terrific fellow," Reagan told a group of San Francisco conservatives in July 1965. "He called Stu Spencer and offered all his help in my campaign. In fact, he said he would do anything from calling me names in public to endorsement—whatever we want." Spencer told me this accurately reflected a conversation he had had with Rousselot, a childhood friend and former client.[18]

Two months later, in September 1965, the *Los Angeles Times* created an uproar by reporting Reagan's remarks about Rousselot. The candidate was finally forced to distance himself from the Birchers. As *National Review* had already done, Reagan tried to separate the rank-and-file Birchers from their leader. He criticized Robert Welch, the conspiratorial candymaker, for casting "utterly reprehensible" aspersions on former president Eisenhower's patriotism and making other "reckless and imprudent statements," but he defended members of Welch's organization from charges of subversion and extremism, pretending that they might not agree with their lunatic leader. The true genius of his response was this statement: "If anybody decides to vote for me, he has bought my philosophy; I haven't bought his."[19]

It was as deft a sound-bite as any politician has ever concocted. In just sixteen words, Reagan managed to distance himself from the Birchers without actually repudiating them. This cynical maneuver was representative of the New Right as a whole. Historians have recently dispelled the myth that William F. Buckley Jr. cast the Birchers out of the conservative movement by showing that they remained in the "vanguard" of the Republican coalition, often pioneering conspiratorial claims that soon seeped into the mainstream.[20] Reagan did just enough in 1966 to prevent the society from dragging down his campaign without risking a backlash from his right-wing base. It was clever but not courageous.

Besides his lack of political experience and his associations with the far right, the other problem that Reagan immediately encountered was his lack of knowledge of state government. He had been giving speeches for years assailing the Red menace, but he didn't know much about mundane issues closer to home and that made him gaffe-prone.

Speaking to a meeting of the wood products industry in San Francisco on March 12, 1966, Reagan responded to a question about preserving California's redwood forests by saying, "A tree is a tree. How many more do you have to look at?" A few months later, during a July 29 campaign event in a rural part of Northern California, he was asked about a planned diversion of the Eel River through Clear Lake. He replied, "You've got me on this one; I'll have to bone up," even though he was standing next to Clear Lake.[21] As so often happens, these flubs were magnified in the retelling. Reagan was often quoted as having asked, "Where's the Eel River?" and being told that he was standing next to it, while the tree comment was often rendered as

"If you've seen one redwood, you've seen them all." But, even without the embellishments, what he actually said was embarrassing enough.[22]

The Kitchen Cabinet tried to address Reagan's obvious deficiencies by spending $33,000 in early 1966 to hire a firm run by two college professors to tutor him on the issues. Kenneth Holden and Stanley Plog were behavioral psychologists who had created a company called the Behavior Science Corporation (BASICO) that consulted for companies and schools. "He knew zero about California when we came in," Plog recalled. "I mean zero."

The BASICO team of political scientists, sociologists, statisticians, and other experts made a list of more than thirty important issues that included transportation, agriculture, water, and the economy. For each issue, Plog said, they compiled relevant facts, summarized opposing views, and offered "potential positions that might be assumed by Mr. Reagan," focusing on "which position is most defensible and consonant, in our opinion, with the philosophy of Mr. Reagan." They then stuffed black binders with hundreds of five-by-eight-inch index cards, creating "a cross reference file of facts and figures" for the candidate and his staff.

With his photographic memory, Reagan was as quick to digest what BASICO produced as he had once been to commit movie scripts to memory. Just to be sure he never faced a question he couldn't answer, one of the BASICO principals always traveled with him.[23]

Reporter Jack Germond observed how the process worked. Reagan was asked at one campaign stop about the workman's compensation system. In reply, he delivered a "long, rambling response about the unemployment insurance law"—a separate issue. Afterward, one of the BASICO representatives gave him a thirty-minute briefing on both the workman's comp and unemployment insurance systems. At the next stop, he "dazzled listeners" by discussing both subjects "with equal facility." Germond was impressed: "In a half hour, Reagan could absorb enough to speak with easy authority. Not a bad quality for a candidate."[24]

Reagan spent the last six months of 1965 crisscrossing California on the pretense of finding out whether the people wanted him to run for governor. Not surprisingly, everything he saw supported his instinct to run.[25] But in truth he was generating an enthusiastic reaction at the Republican grassroots. There was, Stu Spencer said, "a prairie fire out there that was starting."[26] Reagan remained surprisingly reticent in dealing with voters one-on-one—he was, as his future aide Michael Deaver noted, "painfully shy"[27]—but in his speeches and his handling of questions he was already showing why he would come to be known as the Great Communicator. Crowds were cheering his remarks, volunteers were signing up, and donations were pouring in. Even a Democratic operative had to concede that Reagan "was quite articulate and makes [an] excellent impression."[28]

Not everyone Reagan met on the road was friendly, but, just as he had done when touring General Electric plants, he showed a deft touch in dealing with hecklers. When demonstrators mocked his salesmanship for Boraxo, the sponsor of *Death Valley Days*, he quipped, "That may be only soap to you, but it was bread and butter to me."[29]

Reality did not comport with the superficial image of Reagan as a dumb actor simply reciting lines fed to him by his handlers. He didn't need a script; he was fast on his feet. In those days, he wrote all his own speeches; Stu Spencer later called him "the best speechwriter I've ever seen." Spencer noted how, when the introverted Reagan was about to take the stage, he would stand up a little straighter, thrust out his chest, and appear to grow larger before his eyes, like Clark Kent turning into Superman. "I never forgot that sight," he said. "I've been through four hundred campaigns and never saw that before in my life."[30]

In his post-presidential memoir, Reagan wrote that after months of listening to voters ask, "Why don't you run for governor?" he finally gave in and said to Nancy, "How do you say no to all these people?" And, in an oral history, he claimed to have decided to run only at the end of November 1965—whereas his private letters make clear that he had actually made up his mind at the beginning of the year, *before* launching his listening tour.[31]

It was all a pretense to camouflage his fierce ambition. He was cultivating a "Mr. Reagan Goes to Sacramento" image as someone who was seeking office out of a sense of duty and obligation rather than ego and ambition. In truth, like most politicians, he was driven by both selfish and selfless motives.

———

Reagan's formal candidacy, by now a foregone conclusion, was announced on January 4, 1966, in a half-hour televised appeal followed by a press conference and dinner for donors at the sprawling Statler Hilton hotel in downtown Los Angeles. The fifty-four-year-old candidate, looking dapper in a mid-1960s way with his dark suit and narrow tie, spoke of fostering a "creative society" that called "on the genius and power of its people."[32] His vapid slogan, the brainchild of a radio evangelist and John Birch Society member who advised the campaign, was designed to counter LBJ's "Great Society" by suggesting that Republicans, too, had a positive agenda, even though there were few specifics attached.[33] Like most challengers, Reagan was more comfortable tearing down the incumbent than offering his own plans.

In his announcement speech, Reagan complained in his usual folksy way that unemployment and taxes were too high, but he focused much of his fire on the issues of crime and campus unrest, which his travels had taught him were uppermost in the minds of voters. Libertarians would later be disappointed that Reagan did not do more to reduce the size of government in either Sacramento or Washington, but from the start his electoral appeal—like that of the New Right as a whole—was based mainly on social and cultural issues rather than on free-market economics.[34]

In his campaign launch, Reagan complained that universities no longer "teach self-respect, self-discipline and law and order" and lamented that "a great university" could be "brought to its knees by a noisy, dissident minority." In other campaign events and commercials, he was more explicit in denouncing "beatniks and advocates of sexual orgies, drug usage and filthy speech" and demanding that student radicals be expelled for breaking the law. He blamed leftist professors for the campus turmoil, demanding to know "why some instructors are able to use the classrooms to indoctrinate and propagandize his children against the traditional values of a free society in this country."[35]

He also spouted bogus claims that undergraduate applications to the University of California, Berkeley, which he called "a refuge for communism and immorality," had dropped 20 percent and that professors were leaving at three times the normal rate.[36] He never mentioned that, in a 1966 survey, Berkeley was ranked the top university in the country for graduate education, ahead of Harvard, Yale, and Stanford.[37] One of Pat Brown's aides noted that Reagan's "facts" were a "bunch of junk, but they're awfully hard to deal with or refute."[38] There was an anti-intellectual undertone to Reagan's incessant attacks on the University of California: He was mobilizing resentment against ivory-tower elitists among voters who had not been lucky enough to attend college. (Eighty-nine percent of the state's population lacked a university degree in 1960.)[39]

The Vietnam War did not play a major part in Reagan's message—he was running for governor, not president—but when he did comment on it, he did so in ways that resonated with conservative voters and reinforced his complaints about campus radicals. "We should declare war on North Vietnam," he said. "We could pave the whole country and put parking stripes on it, and still be home by Christmas."[40] This was a bumper sticker, not a foreign policy. His plans to win the war never got much more specific than that, but it didn't matter: he was making clear which side of the ideological and generational divide he was on. Two years later, in 1968, Reagan would write to his fellow conservative John Wayne, praising his gung-ho, widely panned Vietnam War movie *The Green Berets*: "Every American should see this picture to learn who the enemy really is and see him revealed in all his savage barbarism."[41]

Reagan's campaign, not surprisingly, was much more focused on fighting crime than on fighting the Vietcong. Reagan said that it was time to "untie the hands of our local law enforcement officers"—by this he meant overturning US Supreme Court and California Supreme Court decisions protecting the rights of criminal suspects—because "our city streets are jungle paths after dark." There was nothing subtle about the racial imagery of "jungle paths," which he repeated many times during the campaign. This was a tamer version of the kind of "law and order" appeal Alabama's segregationist governor, George Wallace, was making in more lurid terms. Reagan also expressed confidence in Los Angeles's brutal and racist police chief William H. Parker, who had compared rock-throwing protesters in Watts to "monkeys in a zoo."[42]

The appeal to working-class and middle-class white voters was reinforced by Reagan's complaints about "a segment of society capable of caring for itself but which prefers making welfare a way of life, free-loading at the expense of more conscientious citizens." Reagan's audiences would have understood that the freeloaders he was calling out—"welfare queens," he would later call them—were mainly African Americans. The year before, in March 1965, Assistant Labor Secretary Daniel Patrick Moynihan had issued a "widely discussed and quoted" report blaming the expansion of welfare caseloads on "the steady disintegration of the Negro family structure," and newspapers and magazines were increasingly illustrating stories about poverty with pictures of Black people, even though most poor people were white.[43] As a Democratic campaign operative later pointed out in an internal memorandum, "Welfare is a Reagan issue. People are opposed to welfare and everything it represents," from "lazy black mothers drinking beer and having babies" to "a swollen bureaucracy of social workers and administrators."[44]

Combined with his opposition to the Rumford Fair Housing Act, which he denounced as an infringement on *"our* freedom" (a turn of phrase that implicitly excluded minorities), Reagan was sending out an unmistakable dog whistle to white bigots while insisting that he was no racist. "I would not consciously patronize any business that discriminated against any human being on the basis of prejudice," he insisted. But, he added, "If an individual wants to discriminate against Negroes or others in selling or renting his house, he has the right to do so." He called the Rumford Act an attempt "to give one segment of our population rights at the expense of the basic rights of all our citizens."[45]

Reagan would become associated with a sunny style of politics, but there was nothing uplifting about the manner in which he was launching his political career. Far from claiming it was "Morning in America," he was suggesting that it was ten minutes to midnight, because California and the country were being destroyed by liberal policies. He resisted the label, but he was widely and correctly perceived as the "white backlash" candidate.[46] That was a winning if morally fraught strategy at a time when non-Hispanic white people made up roughly 80 percent of California's population—a figure that by 2020 had fallen to just 39 percent.[47]

Reagan was offering voters, as Pat Brown later noted with a hint of jealousy, "a clear good guys–bad guys distinction."[48] The "bad guys" were lazy welfare recipients (mainly Black), dangerous criminals (also mainly Black), and subversive beatniks (privileged, white ingrates). The "good guys" were the law-abiding, tax-paying, put-upon, white, middle-class homeowners who yearned for simpler days—and he was their champion.

Reagan was trying to have it both ways—appealing to bigots while insisting on his opposition to bigotry—and it caught up with him on March 5, 1966, during an appearance with other Republican primary candidates before the National Negro Republican Assembly in Santa Monica.

He was tired from having missed his afternoon nap and traveling nonstop for three days while battling the flu, and he was not as sharp as usual when he was asked how he could appeal for Black votes given his opposition to the 1964 Civil Rights Act. Reagan tried awkwardly to explain that he supported the goals of the civil rights law but that it was "a bad piece of legislation"—something he often said to camouflage his opposition to all new civil rights legislation, no matter how it was drafted. A minor gubernatorial candidate, William P. Patrick, called his position "indefensible." Former San Francisco mayor George Christopher, his main primary opponent, said that he would have voted for the Civil Rights Act and argued that Barry Goldwater's opposition "did more harm than any other thing to the Republican Party.... Unless we cast out this image, we're going to suffer defeat now and in our future." Of course, all present knew that Reagan had joined Goldwater in opposition to the Civil Rights Act.

Reagan was normally mild-mannered. But on this occasion, he blew his top. Nobody had called him a racist, but he acted as if they had. "I resent the implication that there is any bigotry in my nature. Don't anyone ever imply I lack integrity," he said, his face flushing. "I will not stand silent and let anyone imply that—in this or any other group." He then angrily muttered, referring apparently to Christopher, "I'll get that son of a bitch," crumpled up the program, threw it into the audience, and stalked off the stage. Some observers even spotted tears in his eyes. "Any insinuations he was a racist, he took personally," Stu Spencer said.

Reagan's driver took him back to his home on San Onofre Drive. His press secretary, a perpetually disheveled former reporter named Lyn Nofziger, witnessed the scene in horror. He drove to Pacific Palisades and begged Reagan to go back, lest the assembled African Americans interpret his walkout as a snub. Reagan dutifully returned and tried to smooth things over during a cocktail reception.

This was the low point of the campaign, producing scathing headlines about Reagan's "explosion" and "stormy exit." His outburst might well have been the sign of a guilty conscience on the part of Jack Reagan's son who had been taught he should be better than that. From a political standpoint, the issue wasn't alienating Black voters; Reagan was not going to win their support in any case. The problem was that his behavior raised concerns about his mental stability. The *Los Angeles Times*' liberal cartoonist Paul Conrad drew an image of a decapitated Reagan holding his head under his right arm and asking, "Where's the rest of me?" Reagan was so irate he wanted to call the owner of the newspaper and demand *Conrad's* head; Nofziger talked him out of it.

After his meltdown in Santa Monica, Reagan's lead in the polls over Christopher shrank. Kitchen Cabinet member Henry Salvatori was worried enough that he unsuccessfully implored former Republican governor Goodwin Knight to enter the race. Stu Spencer and Bill Roberts warned Reagan that one more outburst could finish him. But his aides took greater care to ensure that he was well rested, and Reagan managed to stay calm for the rest of the campaign.[49]

Ironically, the blowup in front of the Black Republicans ultimately redounded to Reagan's benefit by convincing the Brown campaign that, as one of its strategists put it, "We have to screw Christopher, because he's gonna be tough in November and we can roll through Ronald Reagan."

Has a more colossally mistaken political judgment ever been rendered? In attempting to "screw" Christopher, Brown screwed himself. His campaign tipped off the national columnist Drew Pearson that George Christopher, a dairy owner, had been convicted of a misdemeanor in 1940 for violating milk-price controls. The story hurt not only Christopher but also Brown when he was forced to admit that his campaign had spread the smear. Reagan stayed above the fray and reaped the rewards.[50]

Reagan easily won the Republican primary on June 7, 1966, with 65 percent of the vote. Brown won a lower percentage of the Democratic vote—52 percent—in turning back a strong primary challenge from the conservative Democratic mayor of Los Angeles, Sam Yorty, who had supported Nixon in 1960. Many of Yorty's white, working-class supporters—the original Reagan Democrats—would back the Republican nominee in the fall.[51] Reagan could win crossover support because, as a reporter who covered him noted, "Reagan wasn't a scary conservative like Goldwater."[52]

Reagan certainly did not make the mistake Goldwater had made in 1964 of failing to reach out to moderate Republicans. He successfully courted Christopher supporters—such as former San Francisco assemblyman Caspar Weinberger, MCA executive Taft Schreiber, and drugstore magnate Justin Dart—and rebuffed Barry Goldwater's offers to campaign on his behalf. The Republican state party chairman, Gaylord Parkinson, a Reagan supporter, helped unite the party around his candidacy by propounding what became known as the Eleventh Commandment: "Thou shalt not speak ill of another Republican."[53]

In the fall campaign, Reagan overcame his fear of flying to barnstorm Northern California in an old DC-3 owned and flown by a supporter. It was called the Turkey Bird because it had once been used to ferry live turkeys to market; the campaign staff and reporters would sometimes make gobble-gobble noises on landing. In Southern California, Reagan campaigned on a Greyhound bus loaded with coffee and rolls for breakfast, sandwiches and fried chicken for lunch, and whisky and gin for the long drive home at night. The bus, with journalists and aides already on board, picked him up at home in the morning and always made a stop at a motel in the afternoon so that he could take a nap and be fresh for a dinnertime speech. By 10:00 p.m., he was usually home and in bed.

Pat Brown worked longer hours—he campaigned from 7:00 a.m. to midnight—but with less success. Jerry Brown later lamented to me that his father was so focused on policy that he never grasped the "theatricality of politics" in the way that Reagan did.[54]

"I think brother Brown has some good, juicy, muddy ones to throw at me," Reagan wrote apprehensively to his friend Bill Buckley in July 1966.[55] Brown did try to make an issue of Reagan's inexperience and his ties to extremists. But nothing stuck to a good-natured candidate who appeared to be sheathed in Teflon long before becoming president. Former president Dwight D. Eisenhower spoke for many when he rejected accusations that Reagan was "an extremist of any kind." Ike described him as "a man of real courage and integrity and, I think, of common sense."[56] Meanwhile, a fresh riot that broke out in the Hunters Point section of San Francisco six weeks before the election, after police shot and killed a Black teenager, reinforced Reagan's law-and-order message among scared white suburbanites.

Brown sabotaged himself in the homestretch by airing a half-hour documentary on his life. Part of it featured him talking with elementary school students. "You know I'm running against an actor," he told the kids. "Remember this, you know who shot Abraham Lincoln, dontcha?" It was intended as a joke but landed with a thud. It was widely seen as a low blow and cost Brown support in Hollywood.

Reagan played it perfectly. When asked by reporters about Brown's comment, he feigned shock: "Pat said that? Why I couldn't believe that. Pat wouldn't say anything like that." It was a bravura acting job. Reagan had cast himself as Mr. Nice Guy, and Pat Brown, a nice guy himself, had inadvertently assumed the role of the heavy. As the *New York Times* noted, "Reagan Handles His Role as a Political Amateur Like an Old Pro."[57]

On election day, November 8, 1966, at the same time that the Pentagon indicated US troop numbers in Vietnam might swell from 345,000 to 500,000 by the end of 1967,[58] Reagan trounced Brown by nearly a million votes. Republicans won five of six statewide offices and cut into the Democratic majorities in the State Assembly and Senate. Across the country, the GOP picked up forty-seven House seats, three Senate seats, and seven governorships. The Republican Party was fast recovering from the nadir of 1964 as the political pendulum swung to the right.

In hindsight, Reagan's victory could appear inevitable. "The majority of Californians were ripe for a radically different type of Governor and immensely receptive to the personality, style and philosophy of Reagan," Pat Brown reflected in 1970.[59] But in 1965 few would have predicted that a washed-up actor who had never before held office, knew next to nothing about state government, and was widely viewed as an extremist could defeat a successful, two-term governor so decisively.

Reagan's rise was improbable—and could not be explained entirely by the support of the Kitchen Cabinet or the machinations of Spencer-Roberts. They were the producers and the directors, respectively, of the Reagan show. But he was the star—and the scriptwriter. He was elected because of his own pragmatism and personality. He made himself the right man at the right moment to take advantage of California—and the nation's—shifting politics.

In the process, he pioneered the white-backlash playbook that would be employed by Richard Nixon to win the White House in 1968 by using racially loaded but seemingly neutral language to appeal to what Nixon dubbed the "silent majority." Many observers later would write that, in 1980, Reagan was implementing Nixon's "Southern strategy," but in truth Reagan himself had pioneered the strategy in 1966. "In retrospect," wrote a California reporter in 1968, "1966 was clearly a dress rehearsal for the Presidential election of 1968."[60]

Now at age fifty-five, Ronald Reagan was embarking on a demanding new job as the governor of the nation's most populous state—and the world's fifth-largest economy. Just before the campaign launch, Nancy Reagan had already wondered, "Good God, what have we gotten ourselves into?"[61] That feeling would only have intensified now that her husband actually had to govern.

22

The Amateur

I made lots of mistakes because of inexperience.

—RONALD REAGAN

Ronald Reagan's tenure as California's thirty-third governor got off to a bizarre start. He took the oath of office in an unprecedented midnight ceremony before a small crowd of guests and reporters assembled in the neoclassical State Capitol rotunda, underneath its soaring, hundred-foot dome, at 12:15 a.m. on January 2, 1967. "Well, George, here we are on the late show again," Reagan quipped to Senator George Murphy. Nancy Reagan shed a tear of joy as the oath was administered by a State Supreme Court justice using a four-hundred-year-old Bible that had belonged to the Spanish missionary Junipero Serra. A white marble statue of Christopher Columbus kneeling before Queen Isabella—which stood in the rotunda from 1883 to 2020—bore mute witness to the unusual proceedings three days ahead of his formal inauguration.[1] "At that hour of the night, the whole thing seemed unreal, almost like a dream," wrote Maureen Reagan, who was present along with the other Reagan children, except for Michael. "Remember, less than two years earlier Dad had still been hosting 'Death Valley Days' on television."[2]

Reagan aides told reporters that the reason for the midnight swearing-in was to prevent outgoing Governor Pat Brown from making any more appointments, but the defeated incumbent had already had nearly two months since his election defeat to select judges and other officeholders. The widely whispered explanation—denied by the new governor and first lady—was that the alignment of the planets had dictated the move. Reagan, in his 1965 autobiography, had made no secret of the couple's reliance on celebrity astrologer Carroll Righter. "Every morning," he wrote, "Nancy and I turn to see what he has to say about people of our respective birth signs."[3]

The normal inaugural ceremony on January 5, a chilly but sunny day, proceeded as if the earlier swearing-in had not occurred. The new governor delivered his inaugural address before fifteen thousand people from the West Front of the white granite State Capitol. He reprised many of his familiar campaign bromides about crime, student radicals, high taxes, big government, and other issues before concluding with a populist plea: "For many years now, you and I have been shushed like children and told there are no simple answers to the complex problems which are beyond our comprehension. Well, the truth is that there are simple answers—there are just not easy ones."[4]

Ronald Reagan would soon find that most of the issues that came across his desk had neither simple nor easy solutions. His early days in office would amount to a crash course in the substantial differences between campaigning and governing. Even finding a place to live would turn out to be harder than it looked.

The governor's mansion was a Victorian Gothic pile built in 1887 by a hardware magnate at 16th and H Streets in downtown Sacramento. The Addams Family would have felt right at home there, but Nancy Reagan did not. The upper floors were a fire hazard, and the building was located next to a busy intersection across the street from a motel and a gas station. This was not the kind of place where the offspring of Chicago's Gold Coast was used to living. After touring the mansion with the outgoing governor's wife, Bernice Brown, Nancy returned home to Pacific Palisades and burst into tears. "I'm sure I made Ronnie feel awful," she wrote, "but that house was so depressing that I just couldn't stand the thought of living there." Not surprisingly, her obliging husband soon echoed her views, describing the mansion as "that old beat-up trap" and "the most dreary, dismal place in the world," even though the middle-class Browns had been perfectly content to live there.[5]

The Reagans' dissatisfaction with their new home was magnified by their unhappiness with the whole city of Sacramento. Located at the confluence of the American and Sacramento Rivers in the northern part of the vast, agricultural Central Valley, it had become a boomtown during the 1849 Gold Rush and then grown as the western terminus of the first transcontinental railroad. In 1854 California legislators had located the state capital there. By 1970, despite a spurt of postwar growth, Sacramento still had a population of just 250,000 people compared to 2.9 million for Los Angeles—and, of course, there was no neighborhood of Sacramento remotely comparable in opulence to Beverly Hills or Bel-Air.[6] There were only a handful of decent restaurants where lobbyists wined and dined legislators, and there was little to recommend the city to a pair of film colony transplants. As a visiting journalist wrote in 1968, it was "just one more example of the great featurelessness of modern America": "a vast urban sprawl of motels, supermarkets, used car lots, and suburbs built yesterday, surrounding a center of nondescript two- and three-story structures, shabby hotels, and the domed white capitol building."[7]

Sacramento native Joan Didion was to say, "It kills me when people talk about California hedonism. Anybody who talks about California hedonism has never spent a Christmas in Sacramento."[8] The Reagans were no fan of Didion—she wrote a scathing *Saturday Evening Post* piece in 1968 called "Pretty Nancy" that derided the first lady as a "woman who seems to be playing out some middle-class American woman's daydream, circa 1948"[9]—but her assessment of Sacramento was one they would have shared.

The Reagans made little attempt initially to socialize with legislators and their wives, which the lawmakers took as evidence that the governor and first lady looked down on them. There was certainly an element of condescension, particularly on Nancy's part, but the explanation was actually simpler: Ronald Reagan was not the kind of guy to go out carousing at night. He had seldom done it in Los Angeles, and he wasn't going to start in Sacramento. He was, as columnists Rowland Evans and Robert Novak wrote in 1967, "naturally aloof." "He didn't need a lot of buddies," his aide Edwin Meese III noted.[10] He preferred to come home by 5:30 p.m., change into his pajamas, have dinner, read a bit, and watch one of his favorite TV programs such as *Bonanza* or *Mission: Impossible*. In Los Angeles, Nancy pushed Ron to socialize with her wealthy friends, but she wasn't going to force him to hang out with low-rent legislators in Sacramento. That reticence cost Reagan the opportunity to build a rapport that would have made it easier to achieve his agenda.

"Those first days were very dreary, very dark," Ronald Reagan recalled. "First of all, January and February in Sacramento are dreary and dull. Those damn tule fogs!" Adding to his winter of discontent was Nancy's decision to stay in Los Angeles until their eight-year-old son, the Skipper, had finished his semester of school. She would commute up on weekends or Ron would commute down to Los Angeles.[11]

Things improved somewhat when, after three months of misery in the governor's mansion, the Reagans risked criticism for extravagance by moving to a spacious, if generic, Tudor-style house at 1341 45th Street in a leafy, upscale neighborhood called the "Fab 40s" that more closely resembled Pacific Palisades. The Reagans leased the six-bedroom house with a swimming pool for $1,250 a month, with their housing cost reimbursed by the state. When the homeowner decided to sell in 1969, the Reagans worried they could not afford to buy it. So fifteen wealthy backers put up $5,000 apiece to buy the "executive residence" and continue renting it to the first couple of California. To decorate the house, Nancy solicited $125,000 in loans of art and furnishings, including an English-style mahogany dining table that could seat twenty-four and a French Regency fruitwood cabinet, from wealthy supporters.[12] She would later use a similar strategy to refurbish the White House—and pay a price in public criticism as a latter-day Marie Antoinette.

The first lady also redecorated the governor's rundown corner office on the first floor of the State Capitol, where the unpretentious Pat Brown had left a dented desk and a patched-up carpet. She put in new red carpets (red being her favorite color), old prints of California, and a large jar of jellybeans. The governor had started snacking on jellybeans when he had given up smoking, and they would soon become his trademark.[13]

The new house had a spacious front yard where their dogs, Lady and Fuzzy, could run around, and there were lots of kids in the neighborhood for the Skipper to play with. A half century later, Ron Reagan, having long ago outgrown his childhood nickname, would still have fond memories of asking his father to join him and his friends to play football on the front lawn. Nancy would insist that he was busy doing "governor things," but the former Dixon High School and Eureka College letterman could never resist the lure of the gridiron. "He was just a big kid, he just wanted to play football," Ron said. "His only condition being that he be the quarterback of both teams. He would switch sides, whoever was on offense." On weekends, when they were usually in Pacific Palisades, father and son would tune in to watch the UCLA Bruins football team and the Los Angeles Rams—and they would occasionally attend a game in person. Ron was thrilled one year to go with his dad to a Rams practice and receive an old jersey, shoulder pads, and helmet from quarterback Roman Gabriel.[14]

The Friends of Ronald Reagan purchased a plot of land near the American River where they built a twelve-thousand-square-foot home that was supposed to be occupied by future governors of California. But by the time it was completed, Ron had left office and his successor, Pat Brown's son, Jerry, had no intention of living in the "taj mahal." So it was sold and never housed a single governor.[15] During his second stint as California's governor from 2011 to 2019, Jerry Brown became the first governor to move back into the mansion that the Reagans had vacated in 1967.

Although Ronald Reagan had been a movie star, he was not all that wealthy when he was elected. He felt the pinch of trading in his six-figure paycheck as host of *Death Valley Days* to become governor at an initial salary of just $44,000. That simply was not enough for them to live, as Nancy expected, like her far-wealthier friends. According to Michael Reagan, his father nevertheless angrily turned down a bag full of tens of thousands of dollars in cash offered to him in 1965 by Kitchen Cabinet member Justin Dart. "When you're running for governor, you're not able to go out and make a living," Dart reportedly said. "So this is a little something for you and Nancy." But, while honorably rejecting what appeared to be an outright bribe, the newly elected governor gladly accepted a far larger, less obvious windfall arranged by MCA's Taft Schreiber and Lew Wasserman. They convinced Twentieth Century Fox—run by staunch Republican Darryl F. Zanuck and his son Richard D. Zanuck—to buy the Reagans' Malibu ranch, Yearling Row, at a hefty premium.

Back in 1951, Reagan had bought the Malibu ranch for just $85,000, or $275 an acre. In December 1966, shortly after his election, Twentieth Century Fox paid him $8,178 an acre, far above the assessed price, providing a windfall of $1.93 million (equivalent to $15.6 million in 2024). This sale represented a return on investment of more than 2,000 percent and made Reagan a millionaire for the first time. "I could not have run for office unless I sold the ranch," he told Lou Cannon in 1968.

Reagan used part of the proceeds from the sale of Yearling Row to buy 778

acres in Riverside County, west of Los Angeles, for $347,000. He intended
to turn this land into his next ranch, but he couldn't obtain water or power
service at the remote desert location, so in 1974 he bought a 688-acre spread
near Santa Barbara for $527,000. In 1976 he sold the Riverside County prop-
erty to a developer for $856,000, turning another hefty profit.

Twentieth Century Fox never made use of the Reagan ranchland in Malibu and allowed him to keep his horses stabled there. In 1974, shortly before
Reagan left the governorship, the studio cut its losses by selling its holdings
to the state for $4.8 million. The State Parks and Recreation Department
wanted to turn the land into a state park and bought all of the studio's property in the area for $1,800 an acre—less than a fourth of the cost per acre the
studio had paid Reagan in 1966.

Like the deals that Reagan negotiated with MCA in 1952 and 1960, his
agreement with Twentieth Century Fox in 1966 was highly suspect ethi-
cally even if it was perfectly legal. The inflated price paid by the studio
clearly represented a generous subsidy from his wealthy supporters to the
former actor to underwrite his transition to public life. The executives who
took over Fox in 1971 after Darryl Zanuck was ousted by the board could
not figure out why the purchase had been made; it wasn't needed as a tax
shelter, a production facility, or a development opportunity. One of Richard
Zanuck's closest friends told journalist Connie Bruck, "It was a sweetheart
deal." Critics alleged that the studio earned a handsome return when in 1968
Reagan signed a bill, which had been vetoed by his predecessor, changing
the way that films were valued for state tax purposes. Tax liability would
now be calculated not on a film's potential market value but on the physical
cost of the reels and film. This provided a major tax windfall to the studios.

In 1968, the giant Kaiser Aetna corporation bought another fifty-four
acres of land that Reagan owned next to his ranch for $165,000—five times
the assessed value—and promptly turned around and sold it to a shell company incorporated in Delaware and based in New York. That entity, the 57th
Madison Corporation, was controlled by none other than Jules Stein, the
founder of MCA, a trustee of Reagan's blind trust, and a principal beneficiary of the deals that Reagan, as head of the Screen Actors Guild, had negotiated with MCA.[16]

Reagan's deals were not all that different in spirit from the shady arrangements that Lyndon B. Johnson and Richard Nixon used to enrich themselves
through their political supporters. Reagan actually made far more from the

sale of his ranch than Nixon, his fellow California Republican, did from the $18,000 "slush fund" that he had accumulated by 1952 while a US senator and from the $205,000 loan he secretly received in 1956 from industrialist Howard Hughes to buy a house in Washington. Nixon, who was poorer than Reagan, suffered real political damage from his attempts to enrich himself. He had to give the maudlin "Checkers" speech in 1952 to stay on the presidential ticket after news of the slush fund leaked, and the Hughes revelations hurt him in the 1960 presidential election.[17]

Reagan, by contrast, would suffer no such damage, even though his dealings with MCA and Twentieth Century Fox were no secret; indeed, the very openness of these transactions, in contrast to Nixon's secretive dealings, somehow suggested they were not all that tawdry. Perhaps because he appeared so guileless and good-natured, Reagan would avoid the taint of sleaziness that hung over Johnson and Nixon like a noisome body odor. The newly elected governor became known, in *Time*'s words, as "Mr. Clean."[18]

Ronald Reagan counted on the Kitchen Cabinet not just for financial support but for help in governing. "I had not actually thought beyond November," he admitted. "I guess I thought more about winning the election than about the job to follow."[19] He largely turned over the staffing of his new administration to his campaign fundraisers—in particular, Henry Salvatori and Holmes Tuttle—in spite of their total lack of government experience. Operating under the dubious but popular conceit that businessmen could run the government better than experienced politicians, they scoured the private sector looking for executives willing to take a hefty pay cut to help implement their conservative agenda.

The results were decidedly mixed. Some of the initial appointments— for example, rancher and lawyer William P. Clark Jr. as cabinet secretary, prosecutor Edwin Meese III as legal affairs secretary, and lumberman and environmentalist Norman "Ike" Livermore as natural resources administrator—were solid choices who would have long careers in government. But two of the most important appointees were serious misfires: Philip Battaglia, an ambitious thirty-two-year-old attorney who had run the Reagan campaign in Southern California, became executive secretary (that is, chief of staff) after Stu Spencer declined the job, and Gordon Paul Smith, a management consultant from Booz, Allen and Hamilton, became finance director. Both Battaglia and Smith were confident, verging on arrogant, but did not have the background or judgment to perform their critical jobs.

Lacking government experience of his own and uninterested in details, Reagan was in even greater need than most officeholders of competent staffers. Unfortunately, Battaglia and Smith magnified rather than masked his deficiencies. "We were not only amateurs, we were novice amateurs," lamented the governor's new press secretary, Lyn Nofziger, whose power vastly exceeded his modest title.[20] (He was, a reporter noted, "more of a policy maker than a disseminator of information" because he was the aide that the governor knew best—the only one to address him as "Ron.")[21]

A Republican assemblyman recalled, "Governor Reagan initially exhibited a total lack of comprehension of the system." Reagan himself later conceded, "I made lots of mistakes because of inexperience."[22]

Out of those early stumbles would emerge an administration considerably different from the one his critics had feared—and that his most fervent supporters had hoped for. Ronald Reagan's on-the-job training would prove painful but ultimately more successful than his many detractors among both Republicans and Democrats could have imagined.

23

The Moderate

Was [Reagan] blackmailed—or did he ever believe what
he told us in 1964 and 1965?

—JOHN SCHMITZ

Passing a budget is one of the most critical tasks that any chief executive can accomplish. As President Joe Biden liked to say, "Don't tell me what you value. Show me your budget—and I'll tell you what you value."[1] Ronald Reagan, on becoming governor in 1967, knew what he valued, but he had little idea of how to translate those values into detailed fiscal documents. The only budgets he had ever managed were the ones for his own household and the actors' union. His inexperience and that of his team left them ill-prepared to deal with the budget crisis they inherited.

The state was facing a budget deficit of $386 million that Pat Brown had hidden with accounting gimmicks.[2] California, unlike the federal government, could not legally run a deficit. The budget had to be balanced before the new fiscal year began on July 1, 1967. "We really had a tough situation financially," Ed Meese acknowledged.[3]

Reagan initially proposed an across-the-board budget cut of 10 percent for all state agencies along with one-off savings, such as selling the state airplane and asking state employees to come in voluntarily on Lincoln's and Washington's birthdays. (The state later leased an executive aircraft for Reagan's use that cost $200,000 a year to operate—the same cost as the one he had sold.)[4] The 10 percent cutback was impractical—it imposed a one-size-fits-all solution on agencies confronting vastly different challenges—and was never implemented.

Instead, Reagan and his advisers decided to swing the budget axe at the Department of Mental Hygiene, because, thanks to the development of psychiatric drugs, the number of patients in its hospitals had been declining. The result was an increase in the number of mentally ill people on the streets. Reagan would be forced to reverse course in 1969 and support a $28 million increase for that department.[5]

Overall, Reagan's first budget called for more expenditures than Pat Brown's last budget. Reagan's blueprint, put together by Gordon Smith and Phil Battaglia, contained $5.06 billion in spending for the 1967–1968 fiscal year, up from $4.6 billion in 1966–1967. To pay for these expenditures, the Reagan budget boosted taxes by $1.05 billion. It was the largest spending plan and the largest tax hike in the history of California—or any other state—until that point. "Reagan was, and always, remained a pragmatist," his aide Thomas C. Reed explained. "The tax increase was contrary to his belief system, but that was the price of avoiding a fiscal disaster."[6]

The substance of the budget was negotiated by the governor's representatives with the powerful speaker of the assembly, an old-school Democrat named Jesse Unruh who had assumed the post in 1961. His Texas childhood as a sharecropper's son had been even more impoverished than Reagan's in Illinois, and, like Lyndon Johnson, Unruh was a master of the legislative process who saw his mission as helping those who could not help themselves. He was an outsize figure who weighed nearly three hundred pounds, with thick lips and bulldog jowls, and he was renowned for his Brobdingnagian appetites for food, liquor, and women.

Unruh had a near-absolute hold on the lower house because of his close connections with business lobbyists, which allowed him to direct campaign donations—often paper bags full of cash—to favored candidates. He was famous for two aphorisms: "Money is the mother's milk of politics," and—in reference to lobbyists—"If you can't eat their food, drink their booze, screw their women, and then vote against them, you've got no business being up here." His nickname, which he detested, was "Big Daddy" after the domineering patriarch in Tennessee Williams's *Cat on a Hot Tin Roof*.[7]

It was hard to imagine a politician more different from Reagan, and the speaker often grated on the governor with his acerbic criticisms. While Reagan almost always avoided personal invective, his frustrations did sometimes show through. Reagan's legislative director, George Steffes, said that Reagan once joked at a meeting, "Jesse would have liked to be here today, but he's busy out walking his pet rat."[8]

Yet the governor and the assembly speaker found it relatively easy to strike

a budget deal in much the same way that Lyndon Johnson, as Senate majority leader, had been able to work effectively with President Eisenhower—or
as President Reagan would later work with House Speaker Tip O'Neill.
Unruh agreed that taxes had to be hiked to cover the budget shortfall and
figured that Reagan, as an antitax conservative, would suffer political damage as a result. Unruh, who had long been chafing to move up, calculated
that a right-wing backlash would allow him to unseat Reagan in 1970.

Even as a neophyte, however, Reagan understood the politics of the budget better than the wily old legislative veteran did. Reagan shrewdly appre-
hended that by passing the tax increase so soon after taking office, he could
blame it on his predecessor for bequeathing him a budget deficit. He also
took care to include a modicum of property tax relief for two hundred thousand low-income, elderly homeowners as a sweetener to offset the bitterness
of the tax hikes. Moreover, when the tax hike produced a surplus, Reagan
provided taxpayers with a 10 percent income-tax rebate in 1970—the year,
not so coincidentally, he faced reelection.[9]

The one issue where Unruh and Reagan strongly disagreed was on
whether income taxes should automatically be withheld from paychecks or
whether, as was then the case, taxpayers should be forced to write checks to
the state. "Taxes should hurt," Reagan said. He got his way in 1967, keeping
withholding out of the budget, but in 1970, once his aides explained to him
how much revenue the state was missing by not withholding tax payments,
he changed his mind. The governor had previously said that his feet were
set in concrete on this issue. When questioned about his change of heart, he
replied, with a smile, "The sound you hear is the concrete cracking around
my feet."[10]

Reagan's successor as president, George H. W. Bush, would suffer politically from raising taxes. But Reagan paid no political price as governor—or,
for that matter, as president—for his acceptance of higher taxes. While criticizing taxes for being too high, he had never issued an explicit "no new
taxes" pledge, and this was a less polarized time when the Republican Party
was less conservative. All but one Republican in the State Legislature voted
for the governor's budget, and it passed by large, bipartisan majorities that
insulated Reagan from any political blowback.

The only Republican "nay" vote was cast by State Senator John G.
Schmitz of Orange County, a former Marine fighter pilot who was the only
John Birch Society member in the legislature. (He once joked that he had

joined the society to court the moderate vote in Orange County.) Schmitz called the budget "indefensible" and denounced Reagan as a "betrayer."[11]

"Schmitz strikes me as a guy who jumps off the cliff with flags flying," Reagan told a reporter. "I'm willing to take what I can get and go out and get some more next year."[12] The public appreciated the governor's willingness to compromise and thereby incur the wrath of the right-wing extremists. By July 1967, his approval rating stood at 74 percent.[13]

There would be other examples during Reagan's early months of his unexpected moderation. He had campaigned against the Rumford Fair Housing Act; indeed, his opposition to this legislation was one of the major reasons he beat Pat Brown. After the California Supreme Court overturned the 1964 initiative repealing the Rumford Act, the issue was back in the legislature. Conservative Republicans and Democrats pushed in 1967 for repeal of the legislation, but they were stymied by liberals of both parties. (In those days, "liberal Republican" was not an oxymoron.) Reagan might have tilted the legislature toward repeal if he had highlighted the issue in his public appearances—particularly on his favorite medium, television— but he did not. He made it clear that he was open to modifying rather than repealing the Fair Housing Act, and when even that did not occur, he did not make it an issue.

In 1968, when repeal of the Rumford Act came up again, Reagan revealed that he had had a change of heart after finally talking with Black leaders who explained why the law was needed—something he had apparently not bothered to do during the 1966 campaign. He admitted at a press conference that he had not previously understood the extent to which the legislation was an important "symbol" to minorities and threatened to veto any bill repealing it. Reagan tried to pretend he had not changed his mind by claiming he had never supported outright repeal unless there was "something in its place." But that was nonsense. The *Los Angeles Times* was right to note, "The statement was a radical departure from earlier positions held by the governor in connection with this controversial measure."[14] Reagan won office in no small part by appealing to bigots, but in this important instance he refused to cater to their prejudices while in office—no doubt because he understood that, in order to be a successful governor, he had to appeal to more than a narrow, right-wing constituency.

Reagan's Rumford Act reversal, coming after his massive tax hike, brought another withering rebuke from Schmitz. "I find it hard," he said, "to express the depth of my resentment at the twisted politics of a man who would promise millions of people to help wipe out a law they had already voted down 2 to 1, and then, after 15 months as governor, suddenly announced he intends to use all the powers of his office to preserve the law."

Schmitz gave full vent to the John Birch Society's conspiracy-mongering by demanding to know, "Was he blackmailed—or did he ever believe what he told us in 1964 and 1965?" He suggested that Reagan should "go back to the party he started out with."[15] He even cooperated with a right-wing activist who published a book-long anti-Reagan screed in 1968 accusing the governor of being a *conscious* liberal with a pattern of deliberate lying."[16]

Reagan was initially irate at the over-the-top attacks and privately vowed to veto the first Schmitz-authored bill that came across his desk. But when a bill sponsored by the Orange County Republican was finally passed, Reagan told his legislative director, George Steffes, "I can't veto this bill. It's a good bill." "That's Ronald Reagan," Steffes said. His boss was the anti-Nixon: He was too good-natured to hold a grudge.[17]

As for Schmitz, his political career would end in 1982 when it was revealed that this married champion of family values had fathered two children with his mistress. His daughter Mary Kay LeTourneau, a married teacher, would subsequently earn notoriety and go to prison for repeatedly having sexual relations with an elementary school student.[18]

A s if right-wingers needed yet another reason to be disenchanted with Reagan, he provided it during the debate over a more liberal abortion law shortly after he took office. Abortion in California was only legal if necessary to save the mother's life, but many women were receiving abortions anyway either in the state or across the border in Mexico—often at risk to their own lives.

A newly elected Democratic state senator from Beverly Hills, Anthony C. Beilenson, introduced in 1967 the Therapeutic Abortion Act to allow abortions in the case of rape or incest or if the pregnancy threatened a woman's physical or mental well-being. A Harvard Law School graduate and future congressman, Tony Beilenson had worked in the law firm of his cousin, Larry Beilenson, who had represented the Screen Actors Guild, Ronald

Reagan, and MCA. His legislation had the support of women's groups, medical associations, and 72 percent of the state's voters. The opposition was led by the Catholic Church, which held that abortion was murder. A Right to Life League was formed to oppose the bill, and it engaged the services of Reagan's campaign consultants, Spencer-Roberts.

A bitter, emotional battle ensued first in the State Senate and then the State Assembly. In both chambers the legislation passed narrowly but in bipartisan fashion. Many Republicans supported the bill on libertarian grounds, while many Catholic Democrats opposed it on moral grounds.

Reagan's advisers were divided on the issue—and so was he. This was a pattern that would be evident throughout Reagan's governorship and presidency: He found it hard to choose among dueling advisers and, thus, often turned indecisive when there was no internal consensus about what he should do. The primary opponents of the bill were Bill Clark and Phil Battaglia, both Catholics, while Lyn Nofziger supported it. Spencer-Roberts arranged for the governor to talk to the Catholic cardinal of Los Angeles. His father-in-law, Loyal Davis, favored the legislation and urged him to sign it.

Reagan sent conflicting signals about his intentions, with aides quietly trying to prevent the legislation from reaching his desk, even though the governor, when asked by the press, indicated he would sign it. "I probably did more studying and more soul searching on this issue than anything that has happened," Reagan later told an interviewer. He finally signed the bill on June 15, 1967, but he was not happy about it. Tony Beilenson noted that the governor was "frosty" at the bill-signing until the TV lights were turned on, and then he turned into his usual genial, joking self.

Reagan almost immediately regretted his decision—one of the few mistakes he ever admitted—and later claimed that he had not realized how many abortions would occur under the vague "mental health" standard, even though he had been warned about the consequences before he signed the bill. The number of legal abortions in California skyrocketed from 518 in 1967 to 199,089 in 1980. A similar increase in abortion numbers across the nation occurred after the Supreme Court overturned state abortion bans in its landmark 1973 *Roe v. Wade* ruling.

Reagan subsequently declared himself an opponent of abortion. "I am of the firm belief," he wrote in 1974, "that the fetus is a living human being and an abortion is the taking of HUMAN life. I can justify the taking of that life only on the basis of self defense, i.e., if the mother's life is in physical danger by carrying the child to full term."

However, abortion was never a major issue for him; as his aide Peter Hannaford noted, he would answer questions about social issues but "not bring them up gratuitously in his speeches." As governor, Reagan made no attempt to repeal the Therapeutic Abortion Act, and as president he appointed two Supreme Court justices who preserved *Roe v. Wade*.

Whatever Reagan's personal misgivings, in 1967 he did more than any previous politician in US history to expand the availability of abortion. Beilenson wrote that supporters of his bill "were probably lucky that Mr. Reagan was governor," because Pat Brown, a devout Catholic, might have vetoed it.[19]

Besides abortion, the governor agonized the most during his first term over another life-and-death issue. Reagan had campaigned as a supporter of capital punishment, but he found it no easier than his predecessor to decide on petitions for clemency from death row inmates. In 1967, time ran out on appeals for Aaron Mitchell, a Black man who had killed a police officer during a botched robbery in Sacramento. Mitchell wrote to the governor pleading, "I just think that I could do more with my life than to occupy a hole in the ground." A clemency committee headed by Reagan's legal secretary, Ed Meese, carefully examined the case, found no extenuating factors, and recommended that the execution go forward.

Reagan accepted that conclusion, but he did not do so lightly. On the night of April 12, 1967, protesters held a silent, all-night vigil in front of the Reagans' house on 45th Street. The next morning Mitchell was duly executed in the gas chamber at San Quentin penitentiary. Afterward, Reagan's private secretary, Kathy Davis, found him brooding in his private study, "visibly exhausted from the strain," with a lump in his throat and tears in his eyes.[20]

The next death penalty case to reach Reagan's desk, two years later, concerned another Black man, Calvin Thomas, who had been convicted of hurling a firebomb into the home of his girlfriend, killing her three-year-old son. This time Meese concluded there were grounds for clemency—Thomas had suffered severe brain damage as a child—and Reagan jumped at the chance to commute the death sentence.[21]

This was the last death penalty case that Reagan would confront. In 1972 the state Supreme Court ruled, six to one, that the death penalty was unconstitutional under the state and federal Constitutions as "cruel and unusual punishment." The decision was written by Chief Justice Donald R. Wright, who had been appointed in 1970 by none other than Governor Reagan.

A longtime critic of the Warren Court, Reagan was also eager to restrain the California Supreme Court, which had become known for its own rulings protecting the rights of criminal defendants. He nominated Wright, a highly respected judge from Los Angeles originally appointed by then-governor Earl Warren, after his judicial selection committee assured him that Wright would follow a "policy of judicial restraint." The governor did not seem to notice or care that Wright was no conservative ideologue. Former Republican congressman Donald Rumsfeld, then head of Richard Nixon's Office of Economy Opportunity, wrote to White House domestic policy adviser John Ehrlichman, "Governor Ronald Reagan has appointed as his Chief Justice of the State of California, a man who supports the Legal Services Program. Will wonders never cease."

Wright caused considerable consternation with his death penalty opinion, which prevented the execution of more than a hundred convicted murderers and led the chief justice to be dubbed "Reagan's Earl Warren." "I am deeply disappointed," Reagan said, and "somewhat shocked." He later called it "the most illegal, Mickey Mouse decision yet." William French Smith, a corporate attorney from Los Angeles who had joined the Kitchen Cabinet, insisted that Wright had obtained his appointment "through deceitful means" by telling Smith "that he was in favor of the death penalty." "That was really a double-cross," Ed Meese fumed. Wright, however, denied ever discussing the issue with Reagan or any of his aides.[22]

To Reagan's credit, despite his often intemperate and untruthful rhetoric, he governed more on the merits of the issues rather than on ideology or politics. He told his cabinet, "The politics in this doesn't count—what's right and wrong is the main thing."[23] Although this could be seen as self-serving posturing, and politics did occasionally intrude, the minutes of his cabinet meetings—held in a birch-paneled cabinet room around a rectangular table with a leather-covered box of jellybeans in the middle—make clear that he really was struggling to make the right decisions rather than simply make decisions that would please the right.[24]

In 1968, for example, the governor was confronted with the issue of over-crowding in state prisons: Should the state respond by releasing inmates a few months early or by building more prisons? For many conservatives, this would have been an easy call. Not for Reagan. The cabinet minutes record him telling aides, "It seems to me the whole consideration should not be whether to build new buildings—but rather what is best for the people of California. If less crime through early release—then fine. But our consideration should not be on building space—just on what is best."[25]

Indeed, despite his law-and-order image, Reagan made some surprisingly progressive penal decisions, such as allowing conjugal visits for inmates after prison officials convinced him this would reduce tensions in the system and reward good behavior. The Los Angeles Times praised Reagan's views on penology as "among the most enlightened in the nation."[26]

Reagan even turned out to be an unexpected advocate of gun control. On May 2, 1967, the governor was on the West Lawn of the Capitol complex about to start a lunch event with a group of eighth graders when he witnessed an alarming spectacle: A group of thirty African Americans—twenty-four men and six women—marched by in black bomber jackets, berets, and sunglasses, openly carrying shotguns, rifles, and pistols. The camera crews and reporters who had been covering the governor immediately made a beeline for the newcomers, who called themselves the Black Panthers.

This group of Black Power militants from Oakland had vowed to protect their community from police brutality. They were in Sacramento to protest a bill sponsored by a conservative Republican assemblyman from Oakland, Don Mulford, to repeal the right to openly carry firearms in public. The Panthers, led by Bobby Seale (later one of the Chicago Eight charged with disrupting the 1968 Democratic convention) walked right into the Capitol; no metal detectors or security guards barred their way in those more relaxed times. After getting the media attention they sought—"CAPITOL IS INVADED" screamed the front-page headline in the Sacramento Bee—they calmly walked out and drove away. The police (or "pigs," as the Panthers called them) later stopped their vehicles and arrested twenty-five of them for misdemeanor offenses, such as disturbing the peace, for which they served short prison sentences.

The governor's staff responded to this alarming intrusion by installing bulletproof glass in Reagan's office and setting up a buzzer system for his outer doors, which had previously been unlocked. The legislature passed the Mulford Act, banning the carrying of loaded firearms without a permit, with the support of the National Rifle Association, which in those days was neither as powerful nor as opposed to gun control as it later became. Reagan signed the law, saying he saw "no reason why on the street today a citizen should be carrying loaded weapons."

Opposition to gun regulation was not yet a Republican passion—and, of course, white politicians were far more alarmed by gun-toting African Americans than they would have been by gun-toting whites. Under Reagan, California had some of the strictest gun control laws in the nation—including a five-day waiting period and a mandatory background check before a gun dealer could deliver a weapon to a customer. In the future, when he would court gun owners, Reagan would attempt to rewrite his own history. In 1979, he wrote that the Mulford Act only made it "unlawful to bring a loaded gun into the Capitol Building" and claimed, "I hardly think it was gun control." In reality, the bill prohibited carrying loaded firearms anywhere in public—and it was most definitely a gun control measure.[27]

The governor was turning out to be far more liberal than his opponents had feared and his most fervent supporters had hoped—or than he would later admit—because, unlike many other ideologues, he understood the difference between campaigning and governing. A pragmatist on many issues, he intuited the need to appeal to voters who did not necessarily share his conservative convictions. Moreover, in office, he was exposed to a wider range of views than when on the right-wing speaking circuit. Always impressionable, Reagan was influenced by more moderate advisers and his own wife to veer toward the center.

His gubernatorial record would turn out to be far removed from his far-right rhetoric of the early 1960s, with its obvious John Birch Society influences. Indeed, many of his early decisions, from raising taxes to supporting the Rumford Act to legalizing abortion to tightening gun laws, could just as easily have been made by his Democratic predecessor. "When Reagan got all the facts, he would much more often than not make the right decision," said his legislative director, George Steffes. "His great strength was he didn't measure if it was a conservative principle or whatever. He measured it by 'Is it the right thing to do?'"[28]

Reagan's weakness, Steffes added, was that "he relied on staff to bring him the facts as opposed to really saying, 'Hey what about this?' and 'What about that?'" If his staffers were ill-informed or pushing a private agenda, Reagan would be at their mercy. That made it even more problematic that, as aide Tom Reed said, "Ronald Reagan would not search out good people. It was whoever was outside the door."[29]

Reagan's first few months in Sacramento had been nerve-racking. "Each morning began with someone standing before my desk describing another newly discovered disaster," he recalled. "The feeling of stress became unbearable."[30] He was overwhelmed with difficult decisions on matters of which he knew little, and he was relying primarily on staff members who were still strangers to him. He often had a gnawing feeling, recognizable to anyone who has ever started a new job, that he did not quite know what he was doing; he had the same feeling when he first arrived in Hollywood thirty years earlier. Hence his anguished reversals on the abortion bill. For the first time in his life, Reagan developed ulcers, which he regarded as "evidence of weakness" and blamed on the "problems we ran into during that first year."[31] (We now know that, while the symptoms can be worsened by stress, ulcers are usually caused by bacteria or anti-inflammatory drugs.)

Nancy Reagan's transition was even rougher. As a movie star's wife in the pre-TMZ days when fawning press coverage was the norm in Hollywood, she was not used to being criticized—or seeing her husband criticized. A press aide, Nancy Reynolds, remembered accompanying the first lady on a Pacific Southwest Airlines flight from Sacramento to Los Angeles when they overheard two passengers who were sitting in the row directly behind them loudly criticizing the governor's budget. Rather than ignoring them, the first lady abruptly flipped her seat back and told the startled men, "That's my husband you're talking about, and you don't know any of the facts. You don't know anything about this subject. You don't know what you're talking about."

"I was astounded," Reynolds recalled. "I thought to myself, this is a first lady to be reckoned with."[32] Many other staffers reached the same conclusion and gave her a wide berth. The governor's secretary Helene von Damm, who had a tense relationship with the first lady, wrote that while Reagan "always gave people the impression that he liked them, she, probably without knowing it, gave the opposite impression. Everyone tensed when she came into the office." Few saw the first lady the way her husband did—as, in von Damm's words, "the sweetest, gentlest, most wonderful person in the world."[33] Nancy Reagan was widely viewed in Sacramento, and later in Washington, as a schemer and a snob obsessed with social standing, money, fashion, and her own image. Those perceptions colored news coverage of her.

Thin-skinned and insecure, Nancy would never learn to accept criticism of either herself or Ronnie gracefully. Joan Didion's savage 1968 article "Pretty Nancy," which mocked her for conventionality, insincerity, and inauthenticity—the great sins of the 1960s—reduced her "almost to the point of tears of anger."[34] Nancy became so irate at the critical editorials in the liberal *Sacramento Bee* that she insisted on canceling their subscription; her husband continued to read it at the office. "She bleeds pretty good," the governor said with a laugh in 1968. "Sometimes I come home and find she's pretty sore about something I laugh off."[35] He would only get sore if his wife, who had devoted her whole life to his well-being, was the one being attacked.

Gradually, after this bruising crash course in governance, the Reagans began to feel more at home in Sacramento and more confident in carrying out their duties. They began to invite legislators to their home and establish more links with the Sacramento crowd, even if they still went back to Pacific Palisades almost every weekend. At one social event for the governor's staff in 1969, Reagan even dove into the pool to save a seven-year-old girl, the daughter of a file clerk, from drowning. Once a lifeguard, always a lifeguard.[36]

In 1979, Ronald Reagan looked back and reflected, "There were a few months there in which, oh, yes, I was very uncomfortable. Because [there was] always the controversy about everything." He recalled being attacked "constantly" and dealing with the crushing weight of expectations—"you know, we're *supposed* to solve the problems." But, he added, "Things got better.... There came a day when the tension just left and, don't ask me why, it was just entirely different and I enjoyed going to the office instead of dreading it, and I knew that we had a handle on it. Things could be done." Nancy, for her part, later wrote, "I was struck by how much Ronnie had taken to politics."[37]

At some point, Ronald Reagan said, "Nancy and I looked at each other and said that this made anything else we'd ever done in our lives seem dull as dishwater. It was the most personally fulfilling experience I've ever felt. Some nights you come home feeling ten feet tall."[38]

But even as the Reagans were finally settling into Sacramento, their new-found sense of confidence and security was about to be subverted by the biggest scandal of his gubernatorial tenure.

24

The "Homosexual Ring"

I refuse to participate in trying to destroy human beings
with no factual evidence.

—RONALD REAGAN

Walter Jenkins had gone to work for Lyndon B. Johnson in 1939 when Johnson was a member of the House of Representatives, and for the next quarter century there was no aide who labored more faithfully or industriously on his behalf. He even named one of his sons Lyndon. But after Jenkins was caught on October 7, 1964, by District of Columbia police having sex with another man in the changing room of a YMCA—and the news was leaked to the *Washington Evening Star*—Johnson cut his trusted aide loose with no hesitation. "I think that the presidency is something that we've got to protect, and you can't protect it by procrastinating," Johnson told a confidant.[1]

Homosexuals in those days were looked upon, and diagnosed by the medical profession, as sufferers from a mental illness—and as potential security risks because they were subject to blackmail. "The sexual pervert's . . . lack of emotional stability and weakness of moral fiber make him susceptible to the blandishments of foreign agents," a government report warned.[2] There were few more potent accusations against a government worker in those days than that of "sexual perversion."

That was a vulnerability for Philip Battaglia, Ronald Reagan's staff secretary, or chief of staff, that his bureaucratic rivals ruthlessly exploited in the summer of 1967. This was, as it happens, "the summer of love," when tens of thousands of hippies who had not forgotten to wear some flowers in their hair (to paraphrase Scott McKenzie's contemporary song) were converging on San Francisco's Haight-Ashbury neighborhood for a massive "be-in," whatever that was supposed to mean. While long-haired young people in a "riot of costumes" were dropping acid, smoking weed, protesting the war, enjoying easy access to sex ("free love"), and grooving to the sounds of the

Grateful Dead, Jimi Hendrix, and Jefferson Airplane,[3] the State Capitol, located but ninety miles away, was in the grip of an internecine struggle among ambitious power brokers who, with their dark suits, narrow ties, and short haircuts, might have stepped out of a different epoch. The skullduggery in state government would come to haunt Reagan and sabotage his hopes of making a quick move from the statehouse to the White House just when he was gaining nationwide recognition as a bulwark of the embattled white middle class against the counterculture's inchoate challenge.

The balding, nattily attired Battaglia had made lots of enemies with his high-handed ways. Some reporters privately referred to him as the "acting governor" or the "deputy governor." He was described as both "a brilliant tactician and an arrogant upstart."[4] Many felt he patronized Reagan, and he was blamed by other members of Reagan's inner circle for early stumbles, such as proposing that state employees voluntarily work on a holiday, for often missing important meetings, and for not doing his homework.

In early August 1967, Cabinet Secretary William P. Clark Jr. heard from the governor's representative in Washington, DC, that Battaglia and his top aide had engaged in homosexual activity while visiting the nation's capital. Several other men connected with the governor's office and campaign were also implicated. All were deeply closeted, and for good reason, in those homophobic days. Battaglia, for example, had a wife and two adopted children.[5]

Bill Clark quickly shared his information with press secretary Lyn Nofziger; Tom Reed, an aide who had just left the governor's staff; legal secretary Ed Meese; and others who had no love lost for the domineering chief of staff. They hired a private detective who, in searching for evidence of homosexuality, lost Battaglia while trailing him and tried, but failed, to bug Battaglia's office and enter his aide's apartment. "We made the Keystone Cops look good," Nofziger admitted.[6]

Yet, despite their inability to find any proof, the "coup plotters," as Reed called them, decided that Battaglia had to go before rumors of a "homosexual ring" in the governor's office became public. Two members of the Kitchen Cabinet—auto dealer Holmes Tuttle and attorney William French Smith—were alerted to the existence of a "Walter Jenkins situation" and agreed to help oust Battaglia. Reed insisted that he and most of the other plotters were libertarians and didn't care if Battaglia was gay; they just "used Battaglia's personal lifestyle as the vehicle to get rid of him."[7]

Ronald Reagan, with his extremely hands-off management style, was blissfully unaware of these backroom machinations. In August 1967, the Reagans were enjoying a beach holiday at the storied Hotel del Coronado near San Diego—a massive, wooden Victorian resort that had been a location for the 1959 gender-bending comedy *Some Like It Hot*. The governor was recuperating from prostate surgery to fix a urinary tract infection. With no notice, all of the conspirators converged on the Reagans' hotel suite on August 25. They found the governor and first lady in beach robes. Seeing eleven of his most trusted aides and supporters show up unannounced, Reagan quipped, "Golly, are you all quitting at once?"[8]

As soon as they had all settled into the sunny sitting room with its rattan upholstered furniture, Tom Reed handed Ronald and Nancy Reagan a lengthy memorandum laying out the case against Battaglia and the others. "The Reagans' faces turned white, and tears welled in Nancy's eyes," Reed noted. "There were a few questions along the lines of, 'Are you sure?'"[9]

The Reagans were hardly shocked by homosexuality per se; both had known gay people in Hollywood, and Nancy had been surrounded by gay men and women all her life. Her closest male friend from the late 1960s on was Jerome "Jerry" Zipkin, the wealthy, "acid-tongued Park Avenue bachelor" who was a frequent companion (or "walker") for society ladies whose husbands could not be bothered to attend their social events. Ted Graber, the interior decorator favored by Nancy and her friends, was also gay, and he and his boyfriend would be the first same-sex couple to openly stay overnight at the White House.[10] Indeed, there were more homosexuals around them than they realized: William Roberts, one half of the Spencer-Roberts firm that had run Reagan's 1966 campaign, was a closeted gay man. He was not connected to the so-called "homosexual ring" in the governor's office, but another one of the Spencer-Roberts partners was caught up in the scandal: Fred Haffner, who ran the firm's San Francisco office, was more flamboyant and less discreet. He would lose his job as a result of the scandal.[11]

A decade later, in 1978, even while seeking the support of social conservatives for his presidential campaign, Reagan would courageously oppose a California ballot initiative, Proposition 6, an unsuccessful attempt to bar gay men and lesbian women from working in public schools. In a newspaper op-ed, he refuted the canard that homosexuals were likely to be child molesters. "Whatever else it is, homosexuality is not a contagious disease like the measles," he wrote. "Prevailing scientific opinion is that an individual's sexuality is determined at a very early age and that a child's teachers do not really influence this."[12]

Reagan was no model of consistency and no gay rights crusader. He also referred to homosexuality as a "tragic illness" and worried that his son Ron might have caught it when he decided to become a ballet dancer. But his views were more progressive than that of many Americans at the time. His "basic attitude," wrote his aide Peter Hannaford, was "live and let live." He was certainly not obsessed with the supposed evils of homosexuality as many of his supporters on the religious right were. "Reagan didn't have any animosity toward gay people at all," said George Skelton, a reporter who covered him for decades.[13]

Despite their own relatively tolerant views, however, the Reagans understood the political damage he would suffer if news of homosexuals working in his office were to leak out. "This is terrible," Nancy Reagan said. "Yes, we must act," the governor agreed. "Phil must go."[14] Or so Tom Reed remembered him saying; others who were present recall him deferring the decision until the next day.

Ronald Reagan, who had been conflict-averse since childhood, refused to deliver the news personally. The job of firing Battaglia and his top aide was delegated to Holmes Tuttle.[15]

Battaglia's replacement as chief of staff was thirty-five-year-old William Clark, who had taken the lead in ousting Battaglia and who had already accumulated considerable power as cabinet secretary. The governor viewed his own role as that of the chairman of the board and relied on an inner circle of six cabinet members, coordinated by Clark, to run the government.[16] Now Clark took on even greater responsibility as, in effect, the deputy governor.

The courtly, quiet Clark may not have been as intelligent as Battaglia, but he was more self-effacing and effective, and he came to enjoy an almost mystical mind-meld with the governor, a fellow rancher and horse enthusiast. Clark introduced an important innovation—the mini-memo. This was a one-page document summarizing any issue that the governor had to decide, listing arguments pro and con, and concluding with a recommendation for action. Often, Reagan would sign off with a quick scrawl: "OK RR."

Sometimes he would object or demand more information. Pat Brown, with his more details-oriented style, may have scoffed at it, but the "mini-memo" proved the perfect device for Reagan's approach to management and would be continued in the White House.[17]

As his deputy chief of staff, Clark installed another newcomer who would occupy a central place in Reagan's rise: Michael Deaver, a twenty-nine-year-old former state Republican Party operative who worshipped the governor. He would take on the Nancy Reagan portfolio, dealing with the difficult and demanding first lady so that other staff members, who were "scared to death" of her, did not have to. He established such a close rapport with both Ronald and Nancy Reagan that he became practically a member of their extended family.[18]

Another important staff change also improved the effectiveness of the governor's operation: In early 1968, Gordon Paul Smith—who, Deaver recalled, "had no political experience and was a disaster"—was ousted as director of finance.[19] He was replaced by the prominent San Francisco attorney Caspar W. "Cap" Weinberger, who had served in the assembly and had better political instincts than Smith. Weinberger had previously been vetoed by the Kitchen Cabinet for supposedly being too liberal—he had supported Nelson Rockefeller in 1964—but now the governor turned to him for help. "Cap" proved so capable that President Nixon would lure him away at the end of 1969 to assume a series of high-level posts in Washington.

The reason for Battaglia's departure was kept strictly secret both for his protection and the governor's. In a press release, Reagan lamented the resignation of "a good personal friend" and "a trusted adviser" and falsely claimed, "I have known from the beginning that his service would be limited."[20] Press speculation ran rampant about the real reasons for the early exit—the *Sacramento Bee* called Battaglia's departure the "Capitol's 1967 Puzzlement"[21]—but few knew the real story. This cover-up allowed Battaglia to use his administration contacts to set up shop as a Sacramento lobbyist—much to Nancy Reagan's annoyance. She did not want him cashing in on his brief stint working for Ronnie. "Why doesn't someone do something about Phil?" she demanded, as if she were King Henry II asking, "Will no one rid me of this turbulent priest?" in reference to Thomas Becket.[22] Her words would have fateful consequences.

Her complaint motivated Lyn Nofziger to tell the real story, off the record, to a select group of journalists over drinks while attending a national governors' conference aboard a cruise ship. He had no idea that any of the reporters would write up his revelations; he thought they would be too hot to handle by the staid press standards of the day. Nofziger did not realize that the story would draw the attention of Washington's version of Louella Parsons and Hedda Hopper. Drew Pearson had been writing his nationally syndicated "Washington Merry-Go-Round" column, a combination of gossip and muckraking, since 1932. One of the most feared journalists in America—he was nicknamed the "Scorpion on the Potomac"—the liberal Pearson was lauded for standing up to Joseph McCarthy but also reviled for his scurrilous lambasting of the first defense secretary, James Forrestal, which some blamed for driving Forrestal to commit suicide in 1949.[23]

By reporting on George Christopher's history of violating milk-price controls, Pearson had inadvertently helped elect Reagan as governor. He now moved to ensure that Reagan would not become president. On October 31, 1967, Pearson and his younger associate Jack Anderson published a column that began, "The most interesting speculation in the key state of California is whether the magic charm of Gov. Ronald Reagan can survive the discovery that a homosexual ring has been operating in his office." They cited Nofziger's bar-room banter with reporters as the source of the revelations.[24]

Pearson and Anderson wrote that eight men had been implicated. They did not name the culprits, perhaps fearing a libel suit, but it was easy for insiders to figure out who they were referring to. They mentioned, for example, "one athletic adviser on youth activities who has since gone on leave for the fall athletic season." This was a thinly veiled reference to Buffalo Bills quarterback Jack Kemp, a thirty-two-year-old conservative who had been working as an intern in Reagan's gubernatorial office during the off-season and was now back leading his football team to a dismal four-to-ten record. Battaglia, also thirty-two, had struck up a friendship with the handsome quarterback and may have had a crush on him. They had even bought a vacation home together in Lake Tahoe. Pearson wrote that Reagan's chief bodyguard, Art Van Court, had "come up with a tape recording of a sex orgy which had taken place at a cabin near Lake Tahoe, leased by two members of Reagan's staff." No such tape existed, and there was no evidence that Kemp was gay, but Pearson and Anderson's column would dog the future congressman throughout his political career. Stu Spencer said that the allegations took Kemp out of consideration as a potential running mate for Reagan in 1980.[25]

Pearson and Anderson also falsely asserted that "Reagan, though given this evidence last winter, did not move to clean up his office until last August when certain members of his staff were abruptly dropped." They unfavorably contrasted Reagan's supposed inaction with the speed with which LBJ had dumped poor Walter Jenkins, ignoring that in Battaglia's case there was no police involvement. In any case, Reagan had not learned about the allegations until August.

Pearson and Anderson were known for their sometimes cavalier attitude toward fact-checking, and the whole column was a mixture of fact and fiction. But the core of it—the news that two of Reagan's aides had been fired for homosexuality—was accurate.[26]

Wanting to protect his former aides and their families, Reagan immediately and foolishly denied the whole thing. He called Pearson a "liar" at his weekly press conference and said, "This is just absolutely not true." Seeing Nofziger standing nearby, Reagan turned to him and said, "Want to confirm it, Lyn?" Nofziger was put in the unenviable position of either lying or publicly contradicting his boss. "Confirmed," he said, even though several of the reporters he had talked to were in the room.[27]

These unconvincing lies compounded the problem for Reagan by damaging his credibility and giving newspapers that had refused to print the salacious Pearson column an excuse to cover the story. "Reagan Denies 'Homo' Rumor," blared the *San Francisco Examiner*. Pearson taunted the governor, accusing him of lying and daring him to sue for libel. "Drew Pearson better not spit on the sidewalk when he comes to California," Reagan fumed to reporters, making a clumsy threat to arrest the columnist if he did anything wrong in the state.[28]

A couple of weeks later, at another press conference, Reagan had to admit he was suffering from a "credibility gap" but insisted, plausibly, that his lack of candor was for the best of reasons: "I refuse to participate in trying to destroy human beings with no factual evidence . . . and if that means it is a credibility gap, then so be it, there's a credibility gap."[29]

Nancy Reagan was irate about this debacle and blamed it on Nofziger, ignoring the way she had goaded him to destroy Battaglia. She began agitating for her husband to fire the rotund press secretary, who had already offended the elegant, immaculately turned-out first lady with his uncouth ways—he was known for his disheveled appearance, cheap cigars, bad puns, and a general air of don't-give-a-damn insouciance. Nofziger got wind of her machinations and went to the governor to submit his resignation. Much to his surprise, Reagan, who regretted putting Nofziger on the spot, refused to let him leave. Nofziger hung on for another year, until October 1968, and would later return to the Reagan fold. This was an indication that Reagan, no matter how much he loved Nancy, did not always do what she wanted.[30]

The scandal faded over time because no new revelations were forthcoming. But the damage had been done. Indeed, so potent was the charge of homosexuality in US politics that Battaglia's downfall inspired Richard Nixon's unscrupulous political consultant Murray Chotiner to pass along a rumor to Drew Pearson that Chotiner's rival Nixon aides, H. R. Haldeman and John Ehrlichman, were lovers. Asked to investigate, J. Edgar Hoover quashed the false allegation.[31] But there was no undoing the news about Battaglia. Breaking in the fall of 1967, the "homosexual scandal" undercut Reagan's long-shot chances of snaring the Republican presidential nomination in 1968. Ironically, given how much Pearson and Anderson loathed Nixon, he would be the chief beneficiary of their reporting on the "homosexual ring" in his quest for the 1968 Republican nomination.

25

The Forgotten Campaign

How—or perhaps more accurately, why—did all of this campaigning slip the future president's recall?

—THOMAS REED

The normal expectation of the political establishment is that newly elected governors or senators will, in the hoary phrase, "pay their dues" and gain some governing experience before seeking the nation's highest office. Only a few candidates have defied those expectations, and even fewer have done so successfully, most notably Woodrow Wilson, who was elected president just two years after being elected governor of New Jersey, and Barack Obama, who won the presidency while still in his first Senate term.

Some of Ronald Reagan's aides in Sacramento wanted him to emulate Woodrow Wilson's example and seek the White House in 1968. The primary impetus came from Lyn Nofziger and Tom Reed. Both men were convinced that Lyndon Johnson would be vulnerable and that Reagan should take advantage of his status as the hottest property in the party to go after the nomination without waiting his turn. Other aides, including Bill Clark and Phil Battaglia, then still in everyone's good graces, thought that Reagan needed to concentrate on governing rather than running for president. But Reagan was listening to the men with White House dreams because he harbored those ambitions as well. After all, in 1956, he had turned down a GE coworker's suggestion to run for mayor of Los Angeles by saying, "President or nothing."

On November 17, 1966, only nine days after beating Pat Brown, Reagan sat down with his campaign brain trust in the living room of his Pacific Palisades house to talk about a presidential run. After a lengthy discussion, Reagan gave the go-ahead to hire Spencer-Roberts and F. Clifton "Clif" White, the political wizard who had helped Barry Goldwater secure the GOP nomination in 1964.[1]

For a newly elected governor to immediately and publicly set his sights on higher office would have looked unseemly. So the team settled for quietly lining up conservative support for Reagan, particularly in the South, where his opposition to civil rights legislation made him attractive to white voters—the "greatest thing to come along since cornpone and hog jowls," as one reporter wrote.[2] In the meantime, they hoped, none of the leading candidates—former Vice President Richard Nixon, Michigan Governor George Romney, New York Governor Nelson Rockefeller—could assemble enough delegates to win a first-ballot victory at the Republican convention. As a "favorite son," Reagan would hold the votes of the California delegation and, they hoped, prevail on subsequent ballots.

The shadow campaign immediately hit a big snag: Reagan was an ambivalent candidate. He was not sure that 1968 was his year, and, unlike Barry Goldwater, he was too practical to commit himself to a quixotic campaign. When Republican delegates from across the country came to him and demanded to know if he was running, he would say cryptically, "Fate takes a hand in these things. The office often seeks the man."[3]

"I looked him right in the eye and I said, 'That's bullshit,'" Stu Spencer recalled. "If you want to be president of the United States, you've got to go get it and you've got to fight for it."[4] But Reagan held back. Many Republicans walked away confused and frustrated. They refused to commit to a man who wasn't committed to running.

Most conservatives rallied around Nixon because they hated the liberal Rockefeller and thought the former vice president gave Republicans the best chance of winning. Senator Strom Thurmond, the arch-segregationist former Democrat who controlled the South Carolina delegation, told Reagan (who was only nine years younger), "You'll be president someday, young man, but not this year."[5] Even Barry Goldwater, who resented Reagan for trying to take away his mantle as the leader of the conservative movement, backed Nixon. The "homosexual scandal" further derailed a campaign that was hardly on track to begin with. "From this blow," wrote campaign chronicler Theodore H. White, "the Reagan campaign never recovered."[6]

Yet, despite his ambivalence and the heavy odds against him, Reagan continued campaigning. Throughout 1967 and 1968, even as he was dealing with multiple crises in California, he maintained a grueling schedule of out-of-state fundraising and speaking. His daunting challenge in 1968 was to harness to his own political advantage the nation's worst civil disturbances since the Civil War, as he had previously taken advantage of the unrest in Berkeley and Watts to defeat Pat Brown.

Nineteen-sixty-eight was one of the most tumultuous—and nightmarish—years in US history. The country appeared to be collapsing in a miasma of nihilistic bloodletting that made a mockery of the high ideals of a decade that had begun with John F. Kennedy imploring his "fellow Americans" to "ask not what your country can do for you—ask what you can do for your country."

The year began with the North Korean capture on January 23 of a US Navy intelligence ship, the *Pueblo*, whose crew was held hostage. Then on January 30, the Vietcong launched the Tet Offensive across South Vietnam, unexpectedly striking cities from Hue to Saigon. A group of black-clad fighters even infiltrated the heavily fortified US Embassy compound. This massive uprising, although eventually defeated, brought home to Americans that their country was not winning the war. CBS anchorman Walter Cronkite, reputedly the most trusted man in America, sonorously proclaimed that the war was stalemated, and only 26 percent of the public expressed confidence in President Johnson's handling of the conflict after the Tet Offensive.

On March 12, an antiwar candidate, Senator Eugene McCarthy, came within a whisker of beating Johnson in the New Hampshire primary. Four days later, Senator Robert F. Kennedy, the heir of Camelot who loathed his brother's successor, announced his own campaign for the Democratic nomination. Seeming to crack under the unrelenting pressure of the world's most powerful post, an exhausted and dejected Johnson told a stunned television audience on March 31, "I shall not seek, and I will not accept, the nomination of my party as your president."[7]

Bobby Kennedy automatically became, along with Vice President Hubert Humphrey, one of the front-runners for the Democratic nomination—and that in turn increased Reagan's interest in running. He hated Bobby with a passion and blamed him for getting fired from *General Electric Theater*. (One of the books prominently displayed in the governor's office was a venomous attack on the senator from a right-wing polemicist that was described as a "collage of every fact, innuendo, rumor and slander ever whispered about R.F.K.")[8] With his superb communications skills, Reagan had already bested RFK in a 1967 CBS town hall about the Vietnam War; Kennedy's press secretary recalled that whenever "Bob Kennedy was annoyed with something I had done . . . he would turn to me accusingly and say, 'You're the guy who got me into that debate with Ronald Reagan.'"[9] Now Reagan saw 1968 as an opportunity for further "retribution" against RFK, Tom Reed wrote.[10]

On April 4, 1968, Ronald and Nancy Reagan flew to Washington, DC, as part of the campaign to expand his national exposure.[11] They landed to the calamitous news that Martin Luther King Jr., the nation's premier civil rights leader and a moral beacon in the battle against segregation, had just been slain by a sniper's bullet in Memphis, Tennessee. Washington and other cities were soon engulfed in rioting, leading to the dispatch of federal troops to restore order.

The next day, April 5, Reagan proceeded with a planned luncheon address to the Women's National Press Club at the Hilton Hotel, even while other politicians were canceling their appearances and government offices were shuttering in the assassination's aftermath. A reporter noted that, after a "charming, witty introduction," Reagan spent twenty minutes joking "about movie stars and governors" before he mentioned King's death at the very moment when groups of Black teenagers from Southeast DC were breaking windows and looting stores nearby. "Whatever your opinion of Martin Luther King—whether you approved or disapproved—our nation died a little, too," Reagan said.[12] A few days later, he called King's assassination "a great tragedy that began when we began compromising with law and order and people started choosing which laws to obey," thereby implying, as historian Daniel S. Lucks noted, that "King was somehow responsible for his assassination by embracing civil disobedience to unjust laws."[13]

The curious wording of Reagan's statements was an implicit acknowledgment that most of his supporters viewed the slain civil rights leader as a dangerous radical, even a Communist, and that Reagan shared that assessment. Indeed, while King would later come to be revered as one of the greatest figures in America's history, at the time he was not popular with many white Americans, who blamed him for civil unrest, or even with many Black radicals, such as Stokely Carmichael, who thought his nonviolent methods were no longer applicable. In 1966, Gallup reported that only 32 percent of respondents had a positive view of King compared to 63 percent with a negative view.[14]

After his speech to the women's press club, Reagan headed to Southeast Washington for a meeting with Black leaders designed, as Nofziger said, to "soften Reagan's image." But only a few minutes into the already tense gathering, a police officer poked his head into the room and said, "The city's going up. You'd better get out of here." Reagan headed back to the Madison Hotel, jammed into a car with two bodyguards and two aides. "As we drove you could almost taste the panic as people attempted to flee the city," Nofziger recalled. "We saw young blacks smashing windows and grabbing the contents."[15]

Traffic gridlock eventually stalled their progress. Four blocks from their hotel, they decided to walk the rest of the way. Security man Art Van Court was nervous that Reagan would be recognized, so he made the governor put on a pair of sunglasses, which he normally never wore. The disguise didn't work. A young African American who was running by stopped and stared. "Hey, man, ain't you Ronald Reagan?" he demanded. "It was just classic," press aide Nancy Reynolds said. "Reagan tore the glasses off and that was the last time he ever wore sunglasses."[16]

Back at their luxurious hotel, an oasis of calm amid the bedlam gripping the capital, the Reagans could see from their penthouse suite fires burning all over the city. Heading to the Baltimore airport for a flight home, they passed convoys of National Guard vehicles entering the capital.[17]

Unlike other leading Republicans, including Richard Nixon, George Romney, John Lindsay, and Nelson Rockefeller, Ronald Reagan did not attend Martin Luther King Jr.'s funeral on April 9 in Atlanta. He did not walk with tens of thousands of other mourners, "black and white, the lowly and the powerful," in a funeral procession as King's mahogany casket was carried through the streets on a crude farm wagon pulled by two Georgia mules. Nor was he present in the packed pews of King's own Ebenezer Baptist Church to hear the Reverend Ralph Abernathy, King's successor as president of the Southern Christian Leadership Conference, describe the murder as "one of the darkest hours of mankind."[18]

That Reagan skipped King's funeral was an omission that was, to say the least, curious, given that his security concerns were no greater than those of the many other public figures who attended. But it was, as Daniel Lucks showed in an examination of Reagan's record on race, part of a troubling pattern. In 1983, President Reagan would express opposition to turning King's birthday into a national holiday, only reluctantly signing the bill after it passed both houses of Congress by veto-proof majorities. In a private letter, Reagan described King as "immoral" and derided the public's veneration of him as "based on an image, not reality."[19]

No doubt, Reagan's opinions were heavily influenced, as they had been in the days of the Hollywood blacklist, by the reactionary views of J. Edgar Hoover, who engaged in a surveillance and smear campaign against King. The FBI director was convinced that, as he told reporters, the civil rights leader was "the most notorious liar in the country" and that he was being manipulated by Communists.[20] As governor of California, Reagan remained in close contact with the FBI, just as he had been as president of the Screen Actors Guild, relying on the G-men for information not only on "the Berkeley situation" but also on his own wayward offspring.[21] And, just as in the past, Reagan remained remarkably credulous in accepting the FBI's often paranoid assessments.

The madness of 1968 did not end with Martin Luther King's death. On June 4, Robert F. Kennedy, who had urged Americans after the King assassination "to tame the savageness of man and to make gentle the life of this world," won the South Dakota and California primaries, bringing him closer to Hubert Humphrey in the delegate count. But, shortly after midnight in Los Angeles, as Kennedy was walking out of his victory party at the Ambassador Hotel through the hotel kitchen, a mentally unstable Palestinian immigrant named Sirhan Sirhan, who hated RFK for supporting Israel, began indiscriminately firing a .22 caliber revolver. Kennedy, hit in the head, died a day later and was buried with full honors alongside his older brother at Arlington National Cemetery. The haunting photograph of a seventeen-year-old busboy cradling a dying Kennedy, lying in a pool of his own blood, became one of the defining images of this ill-starred year.

Perhaps because it occurred in his own state, indeed in his adopted hometown, Reagan seemed more shaken by Robert F. Kennedy's death than he had been by John F. Kennedy's, despite his antipathy toward the senator. The next day, his secretary Kathy Davis wrote, the governor was "dazed, depressed, and sickened." "Even though I disagree with him on political matters and even though I disapprove of him and his approach to these problems," Reagan wrote to Patti at her boarding school in Arizona, "I still feel very deeply the tragedy of this young man taken from his family in this way."[22]

In response, President Johnson decreed that all serious candidates for president—Ronald Reagan included—would receive Secret Service protection for the first time. On one occasion, the agents scared away two men who were trying to toss a Molotov cocktail into the Reagans' Sacramento house while they were sleeping.[23] "It was clear to me that my mother loved having Secret Service protection," Patti Davis later wrote. "She never drove anymore; she was, instead, driven."[24] Two of the agents assigned to the governor would forge a lasting relationship with him: Edward Hickey would leave the Secret Service to become Reagan's chief of security in Sacramento, a logistical aide in the Reagan White House, and chairman of the Federal Maritime Commission, while John Simpson would stay in the Secret Service and be appointed its director by President Reagan.[25]

While Reagan was now more secure against attack, his prospects of winning the Republican nomination were fast fading. Clif White had been convinced that the GOP would never nominate Nixon to run against another Kennedy. But with Bobby Kennedy dead, the Democratic nominee by default was Hubert Humphrey. He was a powerful orator who had bravely stood up to the segregationist wing of his own party, but he lacked Kennedy's glamour and he was saddled with Johnson's unpopular war, which he privately criticized but felt compelled to support in public. Like Pat Brown two years earlier, Humphrey was a middle-of-the-road candidate at a time when the middle ground in American politics was fast disappearing. Humphrey's ascendancy made it more likely that Nixon could win, leading the Republican establishment to rally behind him.

The 1968 Republican convention was held from August 5 to August 8 in Miami Beach. It was a more sedate affair than the chaotic Democratic convention a few weeks later in Chicago, where Mayor Richard Daley's police officers would go on a violent rampage against demonstrators that would confirm the general impression of a country out of control. In Chicago, delegates and the news media could witness the wild brawls outside the convention hall and hotels; indeed, many were caught in the street fighting. During the Republican convention, by contrast, delegates and media gathered at the Miami Beach Convention Hall were barely aware that, just eight miles away on the other side of Biscayne Bay, a riot had broken out in the African American neighborhood of Liberty City, leading to the deaths of three unarmed Black men in a fusillade of police bullets.[26] "The atmosphere was crackling with tedium," reported *New York Times* correspondent Russell Baker from the convention hall, noting the insiders' consensus that Nixon had locked up the nomination weeks earlier.[27]

One unexpected jolt of excitement came on the opening day when Reagan impetuously and unwisely announced, at the urging of former Republican Senate leader William F. Knowland, that he wasn't just a favorite-son candidate—he was a full-fledged contender. So much for his "noncandidate" strategy of the past eighteen months. Even Nancy was surprised.[28] Reagan then worked around the clock in the remaining forty-eight hours to woo delegates who were brought to him either at his sixteenth-floor suite at the Deauville Hotel or at his campaign trailer parked outside the convention center. "He was still meeting with members of the Mississippi delegation when the roll call began at 1:19 a.m. [on August 8]," noted Clif White.

It was all for naught. Nixon won a first-ballot victory with 692 delegates in a remarkable comeback following his 1960 defeat for president and his 1962 defeat for governor of California. Nelson Rockefeller was second with 277, and Reagan a distant third with 182. Neither "Rocky" nor Reagan received the vice-presidential nod, as many had expected. Instead, it went to Spiro Agnew, the combative and corrupt conservative governor of Maryland.[29]

"I'm not disappointed that I didn't get the nomination," Ronald Reagan insisted to Nofziger, trying to put the best face on his defeat. "I wasn't ready for it." Nancy Reagan was less able to hide her pique. Patti Davis noted, "My mother, upon her return, took her anger out on the maids." The cook confided in Patti: "She's really on the war path since he lost."[30]

In subsequent years, Ronald and Nancy Reagan were to all but erase any memories of the failed campaign, even though it helped prepare him for future, more successful presidential contests. In a 1985 letter, Reagan would deny that he had ever been "a real candidate."[31] In his 1990 memoir, he wrote that in 1968 "running for president was the last thing on my mind. . . . I said I didn't want to run for the presidency and I meant it." He claimed to be "surprised to learn quite a few delegates had pledged their support to me," as if this had been a freak of nature and not the product of his own campaign.[32]

Tom Reed recalled being "stunned" when he "first read those words":

> *Whose campaign had I been running?* I had met with Reagan over one hundred times in the company of others, often his wife, to discuss this project. We also consulted privately on another 21 occasions for one-on-one talks about the most sensitive aspects of our drive. I accompanied Reagan on dozens of politically funded flights on a chartered Jet Commander to meet with backers in our intended primary states. . . . When Lyndon Johnson withdrew from, and Bobby Kennedy entered the Democratic contest in March 1968, we moved up to a chartered 727 jet to accommodate over 40 members of the traveling press. How—or perhaps more accurately, why—did all of this campaigning slip the future president's recall?[33]

The explanation could be found in Reagan's habit, going back to childhood, of blotting out unwelcome news and rewriting reality in adherence to his mother's dictum, "The sunny side's the only side." There was nothing sunny about bungling and losing a presidential campaign, so Reagan decided it had never happened.

For the same reason, Philip Battaglia, who returned to the practice of law and a quiet post-government existence, was entirely missing from Reagan's memoir, as was any mention of the "homosexual scandal." So too did Gordon Paul Smith, another misbegotten selection, disappear from Reagan's recollection; as far as Reagan was concerned, Cap Weinberger was the only budget director he had ever had. He remembered his life story as he wanted it to be, not as it actually was.

If there was a silver lining to his failed presidential campaign, it was that Ronald Reagan did not have to manage the nation's myriad problems in 1969: He did not have to figure out how to extricate the United States from the Vietnam War and to calm a nation in the throes of revolutionary ferment. But California's problems loomed large enough at a time when student protests in Berkeley and beyond were reaching new heights of vociferousness and violence.

26

Battles in Berkeley

If it takes a bloodbath, let's get it over with.
—RONALD REAGAN

Berkeley is a small city of less than eighteen square miles with a population of slightly more than a hundred thousand inhabitants perched between the gritty metropolis of Oakland and the murky waters of San Francisco Bay. For years it had been a prosperous and conservative suburb that was known as the "Athens of the West" because of the presence of the University of California, which by the 1950s had more than twenty thousand students and more Nobel laureates than any other university in the world. As late as 1961, the city's voters had been evenly divided between Democrats and Republicans.[1] But in the coffeehouses, funky shops, and secondhand bookstores of Telegraph Avenue, a bohemian, beatnik culture had blossomed in the 1950s, while a spirit of liberal idealism had been sparked among students by President John F. Kennedy's speech to more than eighty-eight thousand people at Berkeley's Memorial Stadium in 1962.

This previously placid college town would become the epicenter of student protest in America, and indeed the world, beginning with the 1964 Free Speech Movement, whose members committed acts of civil disobedience to end a ban on political organizing on campus, and its comical 1965 sequel, the Filthy Speech Movement, whose members demanded the right to say "fuck" in public. Fraternity and sorority membership declined, and Berkeley became a hippie mecca. "Dropouts and visionaries and hustlers—sometimes all three in a single skin—found a place to drop into," wrote sociologist Todd Gitlin, one of the leaders of the radical Students for a Democratic Society. "The radicals were hipper in Berkeley, the hippies more combative, and there were enough of each, and all the possible hybrids, to feed any utopian vision imaginable."[2]

As the 1960s progressed, the New Left's tactics and goals became more extreme. "We cannot be coopted because we want everything," Yippie leader Jerry Rubin said. Many radicals were inspired by the Black Panthers, Malcolm X, Ho Chi Minh, and Fidel Castro to take up arms against "the system." In 1968 and 1969 there were more than a hundred actual or attempted bombings and acts of arson on campuses across the nation, and Berkeley was at the forefront of this trend too. Protests in Berkeley first turned violent in 1968, with demonstrators throwing rocks at police, and police—a.k.a. "the pigs"—responding with tear gas. Reflecting the more combative ethos of youthful radicals, a newspaper in Richmond, next door to Berkeley, ran a headline in 1968 proclaiming, "Today's Pig Is Tomorrow's Bacon."[3]

Ronald Reagan had become governor at the "dawning of the Age of Aquarius" (to quote the Fifth Dimension song from 1969) in no small part by turning "that mess in Berkeley"—which he blamed on radical professors and professional agitators—into a symbol of all that was going wrong in the country. His solution was simple: As a bronze and walnut plaque above the door to his Sacramento office proclaimed, "Observe the Rules or Get Out."[4] This was the right-wing answer to such popular 1960s slogans as "Make love, not war" and "Don't trust anyone over thirty."

Among those advocating a hard-line approach were two members of Reagan's staff who were personally invested in pacifying Berkeley. Edwin Meese III, the governor's legal secretary and later chief of staff, had grown up in a politically active, if hardly wealthy, family in a white enclave of Oakland, a city with a rapidly expanding Black population. A devout Lutheran, Meese had graduated from Yale University and the University of California's Boalt Hall Law School and become an officer in the Army Reserves. He was disarmingly nice and gentle in person, but he was also a strong "law and order" man who decorated his office with porcelain pigs in honor of the police and liked nothing better than to ride in a patrol car.[5] As an Alameda County deputy district attorney, Meese had orchestrated the mass arrest of Free Speech Movement members in Sproul Plaza on the Berkeley campus in 1964. Alex C. Sherriffs, the governor's education adviser—and an FBI informant—had been fired as UC Berkeley's vice chancellor of student affairs after precipitating the confrontation with the Free Speech Movement. He was angry, resentful, and eager for revenge against leftist students whose disrespect for authority he attributed to overly permissive parenting.[6]

Meese and Sherriffs advocated a crackdown on disruptive protests; as Meese told the University of California Regents, "The chaotic situation must be brought to termination by aggressive action on the part of the University."[7] But both the governor and his radical adversaries would find that accomplishing their objectives—quelling the protests for him, changing society for them—would prove a great deal harder than coining catchphrases.

A̲t the very first meeting of the University of California Regents that Reagan attended on January 19, 1967, the regents voted to dismiss University of California President Clark Kerr. Like Pat Brown, Kerr found himself occupying a rapidly shrinking center: He was criticized by conservatives for being too weak on radical agitators and by leftists for being too tough. Reagan was widely held responsible for Kerr's firing, but he was a largely passive participant in the meeting; the motion to fire Kerr was actually made by a Brown appointee. Kerr's dismissal stirred controversy but did little good. Even with Kerr gone and Reagan in the governor's office, the tide of protest continued to engulf college campuses in California.[8]

Supposedly privileged college radicals in love beads and tie-dyes—widely disliked by ordinary, middle-class voters—made a perfect foil for the quick-witted governor. While attending a Regents meeting at the University of California, Santa Cruz, in 1969, Reagan was surrounded in his limousine by angry students, including one bearded demonstrator shouting, "We are the future!" Reagan reportedly took out a piece of paper and scrawled his reply: "I'll sell my bonds." This was a spontaneous quip, but many of his one-liners were well rehearsed, if also usually written by him. He often said, "Their signs said, 'make love, not war,' but it didn't look like they could do either," and "For those of you who don't know what a hippie is, he's a fellow who dresses like Tarzan, has hair like Jane, and smells like Cheetah."[9]

The only thing better, for Reagan's political purposes, than tangling with student radicals was taking on Black militants. In 1968 the governor pressured the Regents to cancel a series of sociology lectures that the Black Panthers' minister of information Eldridge Cleaver—a convicted criminal, presidential candidate, and best-selling author who was out on bail after a shootout with police—had been planning to deliver to Berkeley students for school credit. "If Eldridge Cleaver is allowed to teach our children, they may come home at night and slit our throats," Reagan said, not realizing that his own daughter Patti had Cleaver's book *Soul on Ice* by her bed.[10]

Cleaver responded by calling the governor "a punk, a sissy, and a coward" and challenging him to a "duel to the death or until he says Uncle Eldridge." As weapons, he suggested "a baseball bat, a knife, a gun or a marshmallow." "I will beat him to death with a marshmallow 'cause he's a punk," Cleaver quipped.[11]

Nancy Reagan was outraged and alarmed; aides overheard the governor telling her, "But, honey, I can't have him arrested just because he says those things."[12] Reagan, for his part, could barely conceal his delight. Responding to Cleaver's challenge, he said at a Republican fundraiser that his weapon of choice was "words of not more than four letters each." The crowd roared with laughter.[13] Regarding Cleaver, who would soon flee the country to avoid going back to prison, Reagan told his cabinet, "You only have to make a reference saying 'stand firm'—and people will come to their feet with [an] ovation."[14]

There was no doubt that events on some campuses were spinning out of control, but Reagan did not make any attempt to build, in the words of a 1970 Simon and Garfunkel song, a "bridge over troubled waters." Rather, in giving expression to a conservative backlash, he seldom missed an opportunity to exacerbate an already tense situation. With his fiery rhetoric, he was a provocateur, not a peacemaker.

In 1968, for example, Reagan blamed Robert F. Kennedy's assassination—a crime that had nothing to do with student protests—on "our educational institutions." He claimed, with little logic, "A sick campus community in California in many ways is responsible for a sick community around those campuses."[15] In early 1969, Reagan repeatedly claimed that a group of Black students armed with "switchblade knives" had forced the dean of admissions at San Francisco State College to admit forty minority applicants. "I don't know what the hell he's talking about," the dean replied.[16] In early 1969, during a strike at San Francisco State by minority students demanding the creation of a Black Studies Department, Reagan said, "I say that this confrontation must be won, and I don't care what force it takes, that force must be applied. Those who want to get an education, those who want to teach should be protected at the point of bayonets if necessary."[17] In 1970, when asked what it would take to restore order on campus, he snapped, "If it takes a bloodbath, let's get it over with. No more appeasement."[18]

When criticized for his militaristic rhetoric, Reagan insisted his reference to a "bloodbath" was "just a figure of speech" and that anyone who took him seriously was being "neurotic."[19] But what government leaders say matters, and Reagan's uncompromising words set the stage for a violent showdown that turned Berkeley into a virtual war zone. Radicals wanted to play the part of guerrillas fighting a colonial army of occupation, and the governor was all too happy to oblige.

As 1969 began, a group of Berkeley students of color calling themselves the Third World Liberation Front was agitating for the creation of departments of Asian, African American, Mexican American, and Native American studies. Ethnic studies departments are now taken for granted, but in those days it was a revolutionary demand that was resisted by the educational establishment. When on January 17, 1969, the governor came to Berkeley for a Regents' meeting, he was greeted by chants of "Fuck Reagan," and his limousine was pelted with eggs and rocks.[20] A few days later, on January 22, the Third World Liberation Front called a student strike. Vowing to "close this goddamn place down," they chanted "get your asses out of classes—join the masses." That day, fire gutted a lecture hall—an act of arson widely blamed on the protesters.

Few white students or faculty joined the walkout, so the Third World Liberation Front tried to keep them off campus by force. Strikers, many carrying sticks labeled "student power," locked arms and blocked the main entrance to campus at Bancroft and Telegraph Avenues. Some students who tried to enter anyway were beaten. When plainclothes police officers tried to make arrests, the strikers fought back, eschewing Martin Luther King Jr.'s gospel of nonviolent resistance.

In response, Chancellor Roger W. Heyns, a moderate liberal, summoned help from nearby police departments. Alameda County sheriff's deputies in blue jumpsuits became known as "Blue Meanies" after the villains in the Beatles' animated film *Yellow Submarine*. They would charge into the crowd attempting to arrest suspected ringleaders, employing a tactic encouraged by Deputy DA Ed Meese in 1964. Protesters responded by throwing tomatoes, cans, and rocks. On February 5, 1969, citing "the acts of violence, disorder and intimidation caused by a coalition of dissidents and criminal anarchists," the governor proclaimed a "state of extreme emergency" and dispatched fifty Highway Patrol officers to campus.

By February 23, 1969, Berkeley increasingly felt like a war zone, with more than seven hundred police officers deployed in this compact city, augmented for the first time by fifty National Guard troops. One Berkeley professor estimated that "something on the order of 90 or 95 percent of the violence that took place on campus was initiated by the police." The confrontation finally, if only temporarily, ended in March when Chancellor Heyns agreed to create a Department of Ethnic Studies.[21]

Violent as the battle with the Third World Liberation Front had been during the winter of 1969, it was a mere prelude to the battle royale over People's Park in the spring of 1969.

The university had been planning to build first a dormitory and then a soccer field near the corner of Telegraph Avenue and Dwight Way, but the development stalled, and for ten months it was little more than a dirt lot. Local activists decided in April 1969 to create a communal park. Hundreds of people of all ages showed up with picks and shovels to plant flowers, trees, and bushes; lay out brick paths; build a stage for musical performances; and install swings and play equipment. After someone hung a sign proclaiming "Power to the People," it became known as People's Park. Soon it became a draw for hippies and radicals, many smoking marijuana, cooking soup in trashcans, and banging bongo drums.

University administrators fumed over what one local conservative described as a "Hippie Disneyland freak show" and another called "a human cesspool." In 1969 the Regents and the university administrators decided to proceed with plans for an athletic field primarily to provide an excuse to evict the hippies. One of Reagan's aides advised him that the state could "ill afford" to cede "one inch of property" to the "parasites known as 'street people of Berkeley.'"

In the early morning hours of May 15, 1969, in a maneuver undertaken with quasi-military precision and planning, the park was surrounded by a large force of California Highway Patrol officers and Berkeley police in riot gear. Meeting no resistance, they evicted everyone sleeping there. Workers then used a bulldozer to destroy most of the landscaping and erected an eight-foot cyclone fence around the park. The operation went smoothly, but just after noon, at a rally on the steps of Sproul Hall, student body president-elect Dan Siegel took the microphone and urged the crowd to "go down there and take the park." Chanting "we want the park," thousands of people surged down Telegraph Avenue. Running into police lines a block west of the park, demonstrators broke up into small groups, smashing windows and hurling rocks and bottles and opening a fire hydrant. Police responded with tear-gas canisters. A Berkeley police car was overturned and set on fire; one of the officers who had been inside had to draw his pistol to escape. Highway Patrol officers pursuing demonstrators had the windows of their cruiser smashed.

The police were scared, outnumbered, and unprepared. The Alameda County sheriff, Frank Madigan, who was part of the old, conservative Oakland establishment, authorized his men to use pump-action shotguns loaded with either birdshot (a very small pellet that usually doesn't kill people) or buckshot (a larger round used for hunting deer that can be fatal to people). The choice, he said, was between using shotguns or "abandoning the City of Berkeley to the mob." Ed Meese, who was in Berkeley that day, may also have been involved in this decision; he served as the governor's on-the-ground coordinator.

In the early afternoon, the helmeted deputies opened fire with their shotguns seemingly at random. They were "shooting at anything that moved," one student said. The police were also clubbing and arresting people without cause and firing tear gas indiscriminately using machines that resembled leaf blowers. As had occurred in Chicago during the Democratic convention the previous year, many bystanders and journalists were caught up in a "police riot." People were staggering around blindly, coughing and retching. Some had blood streaming down their faces.

There had been violence in Berkeley before, but nothing on this level. At least fifty people were shot with birdshot or buckshot, some in the back. William Donovan Rundle Jr., a first-year student who had done nothing to provoke the police, had his intestines perforated by buckshot and required multiple surgeries to save his life. At one point, someone atop a Telegraph Avenue apartment building threw a couple of rocks at the police below without hitting anyone. Several deputies wheeled and opened fire through the tear-gas clouds toward the rooftops of adjacent buildings where spectators were standing. One of the men on the rooftop, carpenter Alan Blanchard, lost his sight, while James Rector, a former Air Force enlisted man, was fatally wounded; he died four days later. In all, 58 civilians and 111 police officers were injured in the melee. All of the police officers had superficial injuries, while 15 civilians required hospitalization.

Governor Reagan called the dispute over People's Park a mere "excuse for a riot," and ordered 2,500 National Guard troops into Berkeley. The governor imposed a curfew between 10:00 p.m. and 6:00 a.m. All marches and rallies were prohibited; it became illegal for more than three people to congregate. The college town was under de facto martial law. National Guard troops carrying bayonet-tipped rifles would occupy Berkeley for the next seventeen days; some pitched their tents in People's Park.

The troops proved more disciplined and professional than the police, but their arrival hardly brought peace. On May 20, about three thousand people, many wearing black armbands, gathered in Sproul Plaza to commemorate James Rector's death. An olive-drab National Guard H-19 helicopter appeared overhead, spraying the crowd with highly noxious CS tear gas, a chemical weapon so potent that its use in war was later outlawed. People tried to flee but found the plaza exits blocked by soldiers and police in gas masks. The wind carried the gas to a nearby hospital, recreational facilities, and schools, sickening people who had nothing to do with the protests. One young girl came home from school saying, "Mommy, Mommy, we've been gassed."

Two days later, on May 22, some 1,500 protesters marched through downtown Berkeley. Police and National Guard troops boxed them into a trap, where they were arrested for unlawful assembly. Sheriff's deputies verbally and physically abused many of the arrestees. Eventually, all 482 arrests made that day were dismissed in court, and Alameda County would pay out more than a million dollars ($7.5 million in 2024) to settle lawsuits brought by victims of police brutality.

In early June 1969, the National Guard was finally withdrawn from Berkeley, and a semblance of peace returned. But more than a half century later, People's Park remained an empty, university-owned lot without landscaping, full of homeless people and hippies. The counterculture won in Berkeley, while the rest of the country was turning more conservative.[22]

Many critics condemned the governor's excessive use of force. San Francisco Mayor Joseph Alioto, a Democrat, called it "amateur night in Berkeley" and said "that's not professional police work." The *Los Angeles Times*, which had endorsed Reagan, inveighed against the "overreaction by police and National Guardsmen" with their "indiscriminate use of tear gas and buckshot," arguing that "they played into the hands of the revolutionaries by a use of repressive force beyond any order of magnitude required." Democratic Assemblyman John Burton of San Francisco said Reagan had turned Berkeley into "his own Vietnam" and castigated him for trying to use "armed force" to solve "the great social problems of our time."[23]

The governor was unapologetic. He met in Sacramento on May 21, 1969, with a group of Berkeley professors who pleaded with him to withdraw the National Guard. When one of the scholars accused him of stoking tensions, the governor, his face "pale with fury," shouted, "You are a liar!" "Once the dogs of war have been unleashed," he insisted, "you must expect things will happen, and that people, being human, will make mistakes on both sides." He thanked the National Guard and police for a "job well done" and commended them for the "remarkable restraint they displayed in the face of extreme provocation." In a press conference, he wrongly insisted that the police were "forced to defend themselves ... only after police officers and citizens were seriously hurt." He even falsely claimed that the tear-gassing of Sproul Plaza on May 20 had been necessary to stop an "imminent assault" on the National Guard—an assault that existed only in his mind. With his combative performance as governor, Ronald Reagan seemed far removed from the days when he had played a genial TV pitchman for General Electric.[24]

Just as Reagan had once falsely concluded that a labor strike in Hollywood was part of a Communist conspiracy to take over America, so now he hinted that the violence in Berkeley was also part of a larger radical plot—a charge that the FBI might have been expected to support but actually refuted in its own investigation. "It should be obvious to every Californian," Reagan said, "that there are those in our midst who are bent on destroying our society and our democracy and they will go to any ends to achieve their purpose—whether it be a so-called park or a college curriculum." He even went so far as to blame James Rector's death on university administrators such as Clark Kerr, who was no longer in office. "The police didn't kill the young man," he said. "He was killed by the first college administrator who said some time ago it was all right to break the law in the name of dissent."[25]

Ed Meese was even more unrepentant. In 1980, he would tell a reporter that James Rector "deserved to die" because he had been trying to "kill a policeman"—a claim refuted by numerous witnesses. A quarter century later, Meese insisted to me that Rector had been "hurling these sharpened steel spikes at the police, trying to kill the police."[26] Like the governor, his legal secretary was prone to stick with a story no matter how often it was debunked.

Reagan's mishandling of the Berkeley protests, even more than the Phil Battaglia scandal, was a low point of his governorship—and one that has been glossed over by most of his biographers. For a man who had long warned against the threat to freedom posed by the government, Reagan was remarkably indifferent to actual infringements on civil liberties—and even loss of life—committed by his own government. His mindset was that of a wartime commander in chief determined to crush the enemy at all costs—he said there was no "room for appeasement" of campus radicals[27]— when he should have been trying to defuse a volatile situation. Nothing frustrated militants more than restraint by the police. When in 1966 campus police arrested only six leaders of a large Sproul Plaza sit-in, a woman who was not arrested screamed at the cops, "You fucking male supremacists, arrest me too!"[28]

President Nixon's 1970 Commission on Campus Unrest, chaired by former Republican governor William W. Scranton of Pennsylvania, concluded that overly harsh tactics were counterproductive: "The use of force by police is sometimes necessary and legal, but every unnecessary resort to violence is wrong, criminal, and feeds the hostility of the disaffected." The Scranton commission declared it "urgent that Americans of all convictions draw back from the brink."[29] The governor of California wasn't listening then—or later. In an Oval Office meeting with President Jimmy Carter after the 1980 election, Reagan expressed envy of South Korea's military dictator Chun Doo-hwan for the way he handled student protests: "He closed all the universities and drafted the demonstrators into the army." Reagan told a startled Carter he wished he had such authority.[30] (Chun Doo-hwan also sent his military to massacre protesters in the Gwangju uprising, resulting in as many as two thousand deaths.)

Calm was eventually restored to California college campuses during the 1970s—not, as Reagan later claimed,[31] because of his deployment of the National Guard but because of changing public sentiments. After Nixon withdrew US troops from Vietnam in 1973, much of the impetus for campus demonstrations dissipated.

Far from suffering politically from his mishandling of the Berkeley protests, however, Reagan saw his poll numbers soar.[32] A typical telegram from a "citizen and taxpayer" following one of his televised jeremiads against "anarchy on campus" cited a term coined by Nixon: THE "SILENT MAJORITY" IS DISGUSTED WITH VIOLENT MINORITIES. Another proclaimed, THANK GOD SOMEBODY HIGH UP FINALLY SAID IT.[33] Drew Pearson wrote in early 1969 that "Reagan is a shoo-in as Governor for a second term—thanks to his enemies, the students."[34]

Reagan was employing a strategy similar to that of the Nixon White House—and one that earlier had been pioneered by his own 1966 gubernatorial campaign. John Ehrlichman, Nixon's domestic policy adviser, explained to a reporter in 1994, "The Nixon campaign in 1968, and the Nixon White House after that, had two enemies: the antiwar left and black people. You understand what I'm saying? We knew we couldn't make it illegal to be either against the war or black, but by getting the public to associate the hippies with marijuana and blacks with heroin, and then criminalizing both heavily, we could disrupt those communities. We could arrest their leaders, raid their homes, break up their meetings, and vilify them night after night on the evening news."[35] Reagan was not as cynical as Nixon and his henchmen. But, as governor, Reagan targeted the same groups—"the antiwar left and black people"—and reaped the same political benefits as Nixon did.

The unprovoked National Guard shooting at Kent State University on May 4, 1970, which killed four students and wounded nine others who had been protesting Nixon's invasion of Cambodia, provided a sobering warning of where a militaristic approach to campus unrest could lead. The governor of California, of course, had nothing directly to do with the events in Ohio, but less than a month earlier he had vowed "a bloodbath" if necessary to defeat campus radicals, and now the bloodbath had occurred, albeit in a different state.

Even after Kent State, Reagan remained unapologetic about his militaristic approach. Saying that "death is not very selective when the violence of a mob is confronted by the force necessary to contain it," he implicitly blamed demonstrators for bringing this tragedy upon themselves.[36] His daughter Patti, who was herself a college student at the time, remembered that he sympathized with the troops at Kent State and never acknowledged the shootings as "a tragedy or a crime."[37] Patti's errant ways only contributed to her father's frustration with college students. "She is typical of the generation gap, finds much wrong with the world and can't really see that some of us are trying to help," Reagan complained to his old Dixon mentor, the Reverend Ben Cleaver. "I'm afraid I'm something of an embarrassment to her."[38]

But, even if Ronald Reagan was unperturbed and unrepentant, the American public was profoundly shaken by what had happened at Kent State. The Pulitzer Prize–winning picture of a kneeling girl in jeans screaming in anguish over the prone body of a Kent State student became one of the iconic images of this turbulent era.[39] In protest over the shooting, millions of high school and college students walked out of class in the largest student strike in US history. Put on the defensive, Reagan was forced to close all of California's public universities for a four-day "cooling off" period while pleading in a televised address for "dissent without disorder."[40]

Tom Reed, one of the strategists running Reagan's 1970 reelection campaign, found that "resentment of unruly students was evaporating" and opposition to the Vietnam War was growing. After Kent State, Reed wrote, "Parents did not want to hear any more about 'getting tough with those kids.'"[41] The old themes of "law and order" and "campus unrest" were losing salience. The campaign would have to focus on other issues—find other applause lines—if Reagan was to secure another term.

27

A Quieter Term

I think he was a pretty good governor.

—JERRY BROWN

Ronald Reagan was preternaturally lucky in his choice of political opponents. In 1966, he had defeated Pat Brown, who was easily caricatured as a liberal career politician out of step with an increasingly conservative electorate. Now in 1970, to win reelection, he would face an even less attractive foe.

Jesse Unruh was no longer California Assembly speaker since the Democrats had lost control of the chamber in 1968, and he was desperate to shed his "Big Daddy" image. He went on a crash diet and lost a hundred pounds. He had his teeth straightened by an orthodontist. He even slimmed down his first name from "Jesse" to "Jess."[1] But those cosmetic changes could not undo his reputation as an uninspiring power broker and political bully. One observer wrote that he combined "the bulk of Falstaff" with "the political cunning of Richard III," but neither of those Shakespeare characters was likely to win a race for public office in America.[2]

Ironically, even though Reagan was the self-proclaimed "citizen politician" and Unruh was the professional, the Reagan campaign was better funded and better run. Spencer-Roberts pioneered the use of computers to analyze demographics and voting patterns, spent extensively on television commercials, and conducted daily tracking polls to calibrate the campaign's message. To assist them, they brought in pollster Richard Wirthlin, a Mormon bishop's son with a PhD in economics from the University of California, Berkeley, who would work on all of Reagan's subsequent campaigns. Bill Roberts, suffering from diabetes and depression, was too distracted to be an effective campaign manager, but Tom Reed was a capable replacement, and Stu Spencer continued to offer shrewd strategic guidance.

Reagan was a more polished candidate in 1970 than he had been in 1966.

Even Pat Brown, still nursing a grudge from the 1966 campaign, had to admit, "Reagan is . . . for all his expressed contempt for politics and politicians . . . an instinctively talented and increasingly skilled politician." The governor was almost robotically on message. *New York Times* reporter Steven V. Roberts, who interviewed him in his Sacramento office adorned with old hunting prints, discovered, to his dismay, "that most of what he said had come practically word-for-word from old speeches."[3] Reporters did not like such well-rehearsed answers, but most voters couldn't have cared less.

Unruh was more spontaneous than Reagan and better informed about state government but not nearly in his league as a public speaker and campaigner. He was dull and uncharismatic—deadly sins in the age of television. Willie L. Brown Jr., a Democratic Assembly colleague, noted that Unruh had a "gifted intellect" and superior "tactical, operational, and strategy skills" but that "his social skills were not equal to the rest of his ability. . . . If he'd had better social skills he would have been governor."[4] Having alienated so many of his fellow Democrats with his high-handed ways, Unruh had trouble assembling a campaign team and tapping into the "mother's milk of politics." His campaign was constantly strapped for cash. He raised just $1.2 million compared to Reagan's $3.5 million, and he had to use part of the money to beat a primary opponent.[5]

The contrast between the two candidates in the battle of televised images was dramatic—and deeply unflattering to Unruh. The *New York Times* noted, "The Governor is handsome, seemingly younger than his 59 years, and self-assured from a lifetime of stepping easily from one pinnacle to the next." By contrast, "The challenger is a short man condemned to constant fasting by an unhappy combination of appetite and metabolism rate. . . . His face often looks far older than his 47 years."[6] If this had been a movie, it would have featured a clean-cut hero like Jimmy Stewart or Henry Fonda running against a conniving, corrupt political boss played by Broderick Crawford, of *All the King's Men* fame, cackling over his misdeeds while smoking a fat cigar. Unruh had actually quit smoking cigars in an unsuccessful effort to avoid that particular stereotype.[7]

Reagan benefited from the fact that, even after four years in office, many voters still treated him more like a movie star than a politician. At a Labor Day picnic in 1970 at the Orange County Fairgrounds, one man shouted, "I remember your pictures, Ron," while a mother nudged her daughter and said, "He used to be in the movies." Another admirer gushed, "How come

you never get old? You just get better looking." Even a woman wearing a
"huge Unruh button" asked for his autograph.[8]

————

Drawing on his hardscrabble roots in Texas, Unruh decided to campaign
as a populist, casting his opponent as a captive of the "Daddy Warbucks"
crowd that financed his campaign and arranged for the lucrative sale of his
ranch.[9] But Unruh overplayed his hand when, at the kickoff of the general
election campaign on September 7, 1970, he parked his campaign bus in front
of the Bel-Air home of Henry and Grace Salvatori. Unruh wanted to use
their mansion as a backdrop for arguing that a Reagan proposal for property
tax relief would disproportionately benefit his wealthy supporters. But he
had not counted on the Salvatoris being home. Both Salvatoris, with Henry
in tennis togs from having just played on their backyard court, marched out
to the front gate and denounced Unruh. "Oh you ass you," Henry shouted.
"You're a liar, Mr. Unruh." "We worked for the money to pay for it," Grace
said, referring to their sprawling property. "This is what you call cheap
politics." The publicity stunt backfired, reinforcing the old impression that
Jesse Unruh was a low-class bully. When Unruh subsequently showed up in
front of the Reagans' house in Sacramento—the Reagans, unlike the Salvatoris, were not home—he became a laughingstock among political insiders.[10]

But in the final two months of the campaign, as the state's economy
slowed and the unemployment rate ticked up, Unruh's populist appeal began
to resonate with the blue-collar Democrats who had defected to Reagan in
1966. Reagan, who until then had been trying to ignore his opponent, went
on the attack, focusing on Unruh's shady ties with lobbyists. Eschewing his
previous emphasis on "law and order" and campus unrest, Reagan spent
much of the campaign talking about less incendiary subjects, such as getting smog under control and creating jobs. Naturally, attacks on government
still formed a central part of his message; as his aide Mike Deaver noted,
"He campaigned as if he had not been part of it for four years."[11]

As in 1966, Reagan's message once again was aimed squarely at working-
class and middle-class white voters. Minorities made only brief appearances in his speeches, typically as welfare cheats or criminals. The furthest
he would go in criticizing George Wallace's segregationist campaign for
governor of Alabama was to remark, "Well, let's just say I wouldn't have
campaigned that way." Despite his volte-face on repealing the Rumford Act,

he continued to campaign against civil rights measures such as school busing. In his dream world, the problems of racial discrimination would simply
fade away as African Americans and Latinos gained "the economic means
to follow the trend to the suburbs."[12]

Much of Reagan's appeal lay in his soothing promises to make intractable
problems such as crime, poverty, and civil strife magically vanish. He implicitly offered a return to an earlier, largely imaginary age of comity and conformity without demanding any sacrifices from the well-to-do. His white,
middle-class supporters appreciated his leadership in fighting for "the survival of our system" in a world gone mad. He was defending the American
Dream while the country seemed to be living through a nightmare. And he
did it all with a smile—not a snarl like Spiro Agnew or George Wallace.[13]

Unruh, campaigning on bread-and-butter issues, could not make nearly
as potent an appeal to voters. But while he didn't win, he did considerably better than Pat Brown had done. Brown had lost to Reagan by a million votes; Unruh cut the margin in half. In 1970 Democrats also unseated
Republican Senator George Murphy and regained control of the State
Legislature, meaning that for six of his eight years as governor, Reagan
would have to work with a legislature dominated by the opposition party.
Not that it made much difference: The Republicans who ran the State Senate and Assembly were nearly as liberal as the Democrats. The important thing, from Reagan's perspective, was that he had won the validation
of reelection.

The skies were clear blue and the temperature chilly at Ronald Reagan's
second inauguration on January 4, 1971. The proceedings were interrupted
by hecklers chanting obscenities and waving Vietcong flags. (The governor
remained a staunch supporter of the increasingly unpopular war in Vietnam; his only complaint was that America wasn't doing enough to win.)
Someone even threw an orange at him that was deftly caught in midair by
State Controller Houston I. Flournoy.[14]

Notwithstanding this tumultuous beginning, Reagan's second term
would be much less fraught than the first. He receded from the national
spotlight once it became clear he had no intention of mounting a quixotic primary challenge in 1972 against Richard Nixon, even though many
conservatives, upset by Nixon's opening to China and his liberal domestic

initiatives, urged him to do so. Temporarily putting on hold intoxicating dreams of national office, Reagan was left to concentrate on the prosaic reality of governing his state.

By now the governor's chief of staff, Bill Clark, had moved on. Reagan had appointed him as a state trial-court judge at the end of 1968, even though Clark had dropped out of both college and law school without graduating. Later Reagan would elevate him to the court of appeals and then the state Supreme Court, making a mockery of his frequent boasts that there was no cronyism or politics in his judicial selections.[15] Clark had been replaced as chief of staff by Ed Meese—Clark's choice, not Reagan's. Whether as governor or president, Reagan invariably relied on others to make personnel decisions.

Meese's selection worked out relatively well. Although notoriously disorganized, he was self-effacing, loyal, cheerful, and hard-working. He was an amiable loner, much like his boss, and knew how to simplify complex issues for a hands-off governor. He would later develop a reputation in the White House as a right-wing ideologue. But in dealing with most issues that crossed his messy desk in Sacramento, Meese was known as a bland bureaucrat with a talent for synthesizing discordant views to reach a consensus. He made Reagan's cabinet style of government—with all but the biggest decisions delegated to subordinates—work smoothly. He later said that he saw his role as being "an honest broker" presenting the governor with "full information" and then faithfully implementing whatever decision was made.[16]

Like most of the governor's staffers, the chief of staff was devoted to his boss. Unlike some other politicians, Reagan's "nice guy" persona in public wasn't just an act. "His language, his demeanor was not that different when he was speaking to two or three people or giving a speech to ten thousand," Ed Meese said. "He was probably the most genuine and non-self-serving or non-self-promoting individual I've ever met." Reagan's legislative director, George Steffes, who would go on to a long career as a Sacramento lobbyist, said that "the finest human being I've come in contact with is Ronald Reagan. I never saw him disrespect another human being, and he made the people around him better than they would have been otherwise. You always had the feeling he had your back."[17]

These were not just sentimental views rendered in a nostalgic haze. A reporter in 1971 profiled Reagan's top aides—a group of "extremely polite," "very competent" "squares" who toiled "quietly in a maze of green-carpeted first-floor offices in the Capitol"—and found that they were bound together by "an apparent case of virtual worship for Reagan."[18] Certainly that was true of Reagan's longtime secretary, Austrian-born Helene von Damm, who described herself as "completely enthralled by Ronald Reagan." She raved in 1974, "He's a dream as a boss and possesses all [the] qualities a secretary treasures—a pleasant personality, good sense of humor, the ability to delegate and make your job as challenging as you can handle and, as an extra bonus, never takes me for granted or demands what he can get through asking."[19]

Reagan was invariably considerate of his staff. He did not kill himself with hard work—he got to the Capitol by 9:00 a.m. and left by 6:00 p.m. at the latest—and he did not want his staff to do so either. He would stick his head in his aides' offices around 5:00 p.m. and say, "Hey fellows, it's time to go home to your wives and families."[20]

Yet Reagan never became all that close to any of his aides; he always maintained a certain distance, preserved his privacy, and never sought, as Reagan's other longtime secretary, Kathleen Osborne, observed, "to be anyone's buddy." "No one could say that they really knew the Reagans," she wrote. Lyn Nofziger told an interviewer that "my personal relationship with him was very good," but "I'm not sure he knew my children's names." Reagan was not just remote. He was also, as Ed Meese noted, "not awfully generous with praise." Verne Orr, who in 1970 succeeded Caspar Weinberger as finance director, later recalled, "He never called me in and criticized me. He never called me in and complimented me."[21]

Paradoxically, because Reagan asked so little of his aides, they were eager to do everything possible to help him. "He inspired those around him to do their best," wrote Peter Hannaford, the director of public affairs.[22] The fierce loyalty that Reagan would engender among his staff as both governor and president would be one of the secrets of his success.

Reporters, naturally, were less smitten with Ronald Reagan than his aides were, but most of them also came to like him. As governor, Reagan was not shielded from the press nearly as much as he would be as president. He held a news conference every Tuesday, and, according to a veteran statehouse reporter, "Reagan usually sparkled at these sessions."[23] Even though Reagan seldom remembered reporters' names, he nevertheless charmed them. Reagan's press secretary typically introduced a reporter by saying, "You remember *Jack*, don't you Governor?" leading reporters to joke that when Reagan went home at night, his press secretary went with him to say, "You remember *Nancy*, don't you Governor?"[24]

"He was always gracious, completely gracious, always smiling," said George Skelton, longtime Sacramento bureau chief of the *Los Angeles Times*. He gave Reagan credit for "listening to people," being "pretty practical," and being "willing to change his mind." It also didn't hurt that he called Skelton's mother on her eighty-fifth birthday. Or that he regaled reporters with "show biz stories, many of them unprintable and all of them swell," in Lou Cannon's words. "You never heard anybody [in the press corps] say they disliked Ronald Reagan," Skelton said. The national political reporter Jack Germond, who regularly visited California, noted that "it was clear he never took any of us very seriously, but neither was he hostile or contemptuous, as Nixon had been." He did not "take offense at persistent or skeptical questioning."[25]

Reagan had learned in Hollywood, when he had benefited from Louella Parsons's patronage, that it was better to cooperate rather than fight with the press. That was a lesson he applied in both Sacramento and Washington. The goodwill he engendered contributed to his rise: Whether they admit it or not, journalists will pull their punches when writing about someone they like. Thus, journalists were seldom harshly critical of Reagan even when he pandered to bigots or propagated falsehoods.

The top priority in Reagan's second term was welfare reform. Indeed, at the beginning of 1971, Reagan wrote to Tom Reed, "I think my whole political life has come to its reason for being with our proposals for welfare reform."

The number of Californians receiving welfare benefits—primarily Aid to Families with Dependent Children—had soared from 620,000 in 1963 to 2.3 million in 1970, a rate of increase even faster than the national average. "The state is on a collision course with bankruptcy," Reagan warned in 1970. In a memo to his staff that same year, Reagan declared "all-out war on the tax taker" on behalf of the "tax-payer." But he also recognized a duty to help the less fortunate. "I always say that it is right to do what we can for those who really are in need," he told his cabinet. "It would seem to me that here are the people to whom we recognize our responsibility." Thus, he pursued a much more balanced approach to welfare reform than his campaign rhetoric about freeloaders would have suggested.

A welfare overhaul was drafted by a task force led by state welfare director Robert Carleson in 1970 and 1971, but the proposed changes required the support of the Democratic-controlled legislature. While many liberal Democrats were hostile, Reagan found a negotiating partner in the new Assembly speaker Robert Moretti, a tough-talking, working-class, thirty-four-year-old, Italian American accountant who represented a suburban district in Los Angeles. "I don't like you particularly and I know you don't like me," Moretti told Reagan, "but we don't have to be in love to work together."

At first, Moretti said, "He pounded his fist on the table and cussed a little. I suggested something that was physically impossible and that cleared the air." Meeting for a week straight, from early in the morning until late at night, the governor and the speaker, along with their aides, hammered out the principles of a bill that both parties could support. While Reagan later tried to claim that he had simply forced the Democrats to capitulate to his demands by mobilizing public opinion, he had, in fact, engaged in backroom bargaining, with plenty of give and take, just as he had once done as a union negotiator in Hollywood. Moretti later said that he and the governor had "developed a grudging respect for each other."

The California Welfare Reform Act, which passed in 1971, was Reagan's most important legislative achievement as governor. The bill raised grants for 80 percent of welfare recipients, as demanded by Democrats, while also giving Reagan what he wanted by tightening eligibility for aid and launching a small pilot "workfare" program to force able-bodied people without young children to seek jobs. By the time Reagan left office in 1975, welfare caseloads were on the decline. The legislation allowed Reagan to claim credit for the declining caseloads, even though other factors, such as a rising abortion rate and an improving economy, contributed to the decrease. Indeed, welfare caseloads had actually started declining even before the bill was passed. Reagan was particularly proud of the "workfare" provision, but only 9,600 workfare participants found jobs before the program was discontinued in 1975, and a state study concluded that it "did not prove to be administratively feasible and practical."

The California legislation represented a very different approach to welfare from the one pushed by President Nixon. He had introduced a plan, at the urging of Milton Friedman and Daniel Patrick Moynihan, among others, to replace existing welfare programs with a guaranteed annual income for all families with children. But Nixon's plan ran into resistance from both liberals and conservatives; Reagan, for one, complained that it would "weaken the moral fiber and fiscal integrity of the nation; and it would drain the productive wellspring of America." He wrote to the president to express "deep philosophical antipathy toward a government-guaranteed income."

This was the only major issue on which Reagan, a loyal Nixon supporter, broke ranks with the president—and he carried the day. While the House passed Nixon's plan in 1970 and again in 1971, Reagan actively lobbied against it, and the Senate rebuffed the legislation on both occasions. Instead, Congress created the Supplemental Security Income program to help the aged, disabled, and blind.

Many states emulated the California "workfare" program, and it would become the model for national legislation signed by President Bill Clinton in 1996. That it was possible to trim spending on welfare "without diminishing the benefit payments to any needy family—and actually increasing benefits in some states—is a tribute to the approach to welfare reform that was pioneered in California by Governor Reagan," the *Sacramento Union* wrote in 1974.[26]

Given Ronald Reagan's criticisms of welfare programs for being too generous, liberal critics found it easy to caricature him as someone who did not care about the poor. But, in his personal life, he was generous in responding to appeals for help by writing a small check or doing something else to help people with a tale of woe. In the case of Bertha and Samueline Sisco—two middle-aged, unmarried sisters in the Sonoma Valley wine country town of Healdsburg who took care of a brother, Joseph "Buzzy" Sisco, with cerebral palsy—Reagan developed a long-term epistolary relationship that showed his capacity for compassion.

Their correspondence began on October 6, 1972, when the two sisters wrote a six-page letter to the governor complaining about a reduction in Buzzy's Social Security and welfare benefits and asking for help in rectifying the situation as well as in acquiring a rocking chair for him. Reagan wrote back sympathetically and sent them not only a check but also his own rocking chair, while directing his aides to see if there could be some way to increase Buzzy's benefits. The sisters, who styled themselves Miss Bertha and Miss

Sam, then wrote to the governor wondering if he would help them sell their leatherwork and arrange for them to write newspaper columns about "the common folk" to augment their meager income. "Bertha and I are desperate and I mean desperate to get a 'livable paying job,'" Sam Sisco wrote in 1973.

Many other officeholders would have ignored this continual importuning as an annoying imposition. But not Reagan. He actually had his aides contact newspapers such as the *San Francisco Chronicle* to see if they would be interested in running the Siscos' column. When they got back a no, he tried to interest executives in Hollywood in producing a Western film based on a script the sisters had written and to get leather goods stores to carry their products. He even bought some of their belts and hatbands as presents for Nancy and others. When the Siscos made a belt for Richard Nixon, Reagan sent it to the president with an explanation about the sisters—"an amazing pair."

Reagan maintained this heartfelt epistolary relationship until at least 1987 without ever making any effort to publicize his efforts to assist the Siscos. Reagan could be callous in promulgating policies or making sweeping statements that harmed large groups of people, whether welfare recipients or student protesters, but he was invariably thoughtful and humane when confronted with individual hard-luck stories. "He's the softest touch around," Nancy Reagan said.[27]

Besides welfare reform, another signal achievement of Reagan's governorship was in the environmental realm. This might seem counterintuitive in light of his infamous 1968 comment, "A tree is a tree. How many more do you have to look at?" But Reagan administration policy, whether in Sacramento or Washington, was hugely dependent on the preferences of his appointees, and he had gotten lucky with his choice for executive director of natural resources. Norman "Ike" Livermore had been in the lumber business, but he was also a dedicated, Teddy Roosevelt–style conservationist, an avid outdoorsman, and a longtime member of the Sierra Club. Reagan hit it off with Livermore, as he did with Bill Clark, in no small part because Ike rode horses. Livermore became the only cabinet member to serve all eight years of Reagan's tenure in Sacramento, and he made his influence felt. He was so persistent that his colleagues joked, "The sun never sets on a Livermore argument."

Reagan, moreover, had an unerring sense of the public mood, and he could tell by the early 1970s that even Republican voters were worried about the environment. Smog, in particular, had become a severe problem in Southern California, ground zero of America's car culture, where noxious fumes were trapped by the San Gabriel Mountains to the east. Voters' desire to reduce air pollution soon extended to a more general commitment to clean up the environment. The first Earth Day took place in 1970, the same year the Environmental Protection Agency (EPA) was created.

Reagan initially had been skeptical of the creation of a Redwood National Park along the northern coast of California to preserve the world's tallest trees, but he wound up supporting congressional legislation to create the park in 1968. He contributed state land for the project while also winning concessions that saved jobs in lumber towns.

Reagan achieved another unexpected victory for environmentalists—and a defeat for powerful farming and development interests—in the battle over a dam that the state Department of Water Resources and the Army Corps of Engineers were planning to build at Dos Rios on the Eel River. This was part of Pat Brown's plan to provide for the water needs of a growing state. But the cost of the Dos Rios dam would have been high: It meant flooding the Round Valley, located in the eastern part of the state near the Nevada border, which was home to hundreds of farms, ancient archaeological sites belonging to the Yuki people, and a freshwater habitat used by steelhead trout. Reagan had shown his ignorance of the Eel River during the 1966 campaign, but the more he learned about the issue, the less he liked the dam.

On December 10, 1968, Livermore recalled receiving a phone call from the governor. "Ike," he said, "I hate to see a beautiful valley destroyed." Reagan's opposition strengthened after meeting a delegation of the Yuki people. "We've broken too many damn treaties," he punned.

Reagan's efforts stopped the dam and saved the valley. In 1972, he vetoed a bill sponsored by State Senator Randolph Collier, a pro-business Democrat known as the "father of the California freeways" for supporting a massive expansion of the state's road system, that would have reopened the door to an Eel River dam. Instead, to the "exultation of environmentalists," he signed a rival bill authored by Peter Behr, a liberal Republican state senator from Marin County, to protect California's northern coastal rivers.

The same year, Reagan stopped a planned federal highway that would have cut through some of the most picturesque parts of the Sierra Nevada.

Reagan went to inspect the terrain for himself on horseback, riding for three hours along steep trails, as if appearing in another of his beloved Westerns, wearing a pearl-gray cowboy hat, jeans, and long-sleeve shirt. Fifty state officials and reporters—mainly tenderfeet—struggled to keep up with him.

In a meadow with a dramatic view of the 9,200-foot Minaret Summit, Reagan dismounted and gave a dramatic speech announcing that he had convinced the Nixon administration to suspend construction of the highway. "The cavalry came galloping over the hill just in time," he said. Sore after so much riding, the governor was limping by the time he boarded a plane back to Sacramento, hosannas from the grateful Sierra Club ringing in his ears, as if he were a cowboy hero heading into the sunset after vanquishing the bad guys.

Reagan was no Teddy Roosevelt, but he compiled a solid environmental record at a time when environmental issues were rising in importance. Lou Cannon was to write that if only President Reagan had made Ike Livermore his first secretary of the Interior, he would have been remembered as not just a conservationist governor but also a conservationist president. Instead, Reagan chose the egregious James Watt, who proceeded to make an enemy of environmentalists with his callous determination to open wilderness areas to economic exploitation.[28]

Reagan's last major initiative as governor—a constitutional amendment to cut taxes—was not nearly as successful as his effort to save redwoods or reform welfare. It was the brainchild of Lewis K. Uhler, a former member of the John Birch Society who had gone to work for the governor as director of the Office of Economic Opportunity. In 1972, Ed Meese, a law school classmate of Uhler's, selected him to head a task force on reducing taxes. Uhler came up with a confoundingly complex state ballot initiative that would have gradually reduced state taxes over the next fifteen years from 8.3 percent of personal income to 7 percent while also establishing tax limits for local governments. The whole bill ran to 5,700 words and was nearly impossible to decipher, yet Meese and Uhler convinced Reagan to back this sweeping change as Proposition 1 in a special election in November 1973.

The strategists who had directed Reagan's 1970 gubernatorial campaign—Stu Spencer and Tom Reed—had drifted away and wanted nothing to do with this project, so Mike Deaver, Reagan's young deputy chief of staff, was put in charge of selling Proposition 1. Meese and Deaver raised a substantial amount of funds, and Reagan worked hard to pass the initiative, but they faced an even more effective campaign against the measure orchestrated by Assembly Speaker Bob Moretti with the help of the California Teachers Association. Opponents warned that Proposition 1 would cut resources for education and for low- and middle-income people.

Ultimately the proposition was undone by its own complexity. Just eleven days before the election, Reagan was asked in a TV interview, "Do you think the average voter really understands the language of this proposition?" "No," Reagan replied. "He shouldn't try. I don't, either." The incomprehensible initiative lost, 54 to 46 percent.

Presciently, Reagan had anticipated the antitax fervor that would grip the state in the years ahead: In 1978 voters would approve Proposition 13 to cap property taxes. But Howard Jarvis and Paul Gann, the populists behind that proposition, were smarter than Uhler and Meese in crafting their initiative: They kept it simple. As usual, Reagan was at the mercy of his staff. If they were subpar, as was the case with Proposition 1, the result was a failure.[29]

During his first campaign in 1966, Reagan had told Stuart Spencer, "Politics is just like show business. You have a hell of an opening, coast for a while, and then have a hell of a close."[30] The failure of Proposition 1 meant that he wasn't closing his run as governor on a high note, but he still remained popular, with 71 percent of poll respondents in August 1974 rating his job performance as "good" or "fair."[31]

Ronald Reagan rejected entreaties by his Kitchen Cabinet to seek a third term; he was tired of being governor. Republicans nominated Houston Flournoy, the centrist state controller, and he lost narrowly to the Democratic nominee—Pat Brown's son, Edmund G. "Jerry" Brown Jr. In the post-Watergate 1974 election, Democrats swept every statewide office save for attorney general. But while the GOP in California—and across America—was reeling, Reagan was leaving office in fine form. Not only was he exiting with a high approval rating, he also had found that he enjoyed governing. "These last several years have been the most challenging and most inwardly rewarding that I have ever known," he wrote in 1974.[32]

Even his political opponents were generally complimentary. "I think he was a pretty good governor," Jerry Brown told me. "I think in some ways he was a better governor than president." Willie L. Brown, a powerful San Francisco Democrat who had first been elected to the State Assembly in 1964, agreed that "he was quite a person" and "ended up being a pretty good governor." Brown remembered Reagan as a "friend" and a "delightful host." As the chairman of the Assembly Ways and Means Committee, he recalled going to the governor's house once a month for dinner with other legislative leaders. "He and I would ditch the other guests," Brown recalled. "He was into toy trains. We'd go downstairs and run the trains while the rest of the people were finishing dinner."[33]

Those accolades from Democrats hint at an uncomfortable reality for Reagan's legions of conservative admirers: His record as governor was not all that conservative. He was most right-wing, and arguably least successful, in his heavy-handed law-and-order agenda, which failed to quell campus protests or reverse a rising crime rate. The homicide rate doubled during his eight years in office, and the number of armed robberies went up even faster despite legislation that lengthened prison sentences.[34]

Both taxes and spending went up during Reagan's tenure. Corporate taxes rose by more than 60 percent, and the top tax rate on personal income climbed by nearly 60 percent, while his introduction of withholding made taxes easier to collect.[35] Notwithstanding three tax rebates made possible by budget surpluses, state income-tax collections almost tripled as a share of personal income.[36] Reagan inherited a state budget of $4.6 billion from Pat Brown and bequeathed to Jerry Brown a $10.2 billion budget—a 121 percent increase over eight years, for an average growth rate of 15 percent a year. Pat Brown's budgets had grown by a nearly identical rate during his eight years in office.[37] Reagan did succeed in reducing the growth of the state work-force, and he did veto $1.5 billion in additional spending, but the boast in his memoir that "we made the state government less costly, smaller, and more businesslike" rang hollow.[38] A conservative state senator was closer to the mark when he griped in 1975, "When you come down to it, we have a hell of a lot more government in California than before Reagan came in."[39]

Reagan's tenure was quite liberal in ways that went beyond his fiscal policies. After all, he legalized abortion, introduced progressive penal reforms, strengthened gun controls, inadvertently helped bring about the temporary end of the death penalty, and added 145,000 acres to the state's parks. While bemoaning the radicalization of higher education, he still increased funding for the state's universities by 136 percent.[40] He explained to supporters who wanted him to defund the universities, "You don't punish good students and good teachers because of the irresponsible actions of a small number of students, faculty members and non-students."[41]

This is a part of the Reagan story that didn't fit neatly into narratives that labeled him as a hard-line conservative, something that both the right and the left were wont to do—the former to celebrate him, the latter to condemn him. He was more complicated than such simplistic labels would suggest.

What accounted for the disconnect between Reagan the campaigner and Reagan the governor? A lot of the explanation, as Lou Cannon shrewdly discerned, lay in the different feedback that Reagan received in different environments. As a speaker on the "mashed potato circuit," he received information almost exclusively from his favorite conservative publications (*Reader's Digest, Human Events, National Review*) and talked almost exclusively to right-wing audiences. Ever since his start performing for audiences as a boy in small-town Illinois, Reagan always liked to please, and he learned that he would be rewarded for saying what conservatives wanted to hear—no matter how misleading or even false. In Sacramento, by contrast, he had to deal with Democrats who were usually in control of the legislature, and he received competing perspectives on major issues. The pressure as governor was to do deals and get legislative results—and Reagan showed an unexpected talent for doing just that. He was the ultimate pragmatist. Having entered office as an untested conservative crusader, he was leaving it as a seasoned and skilled governor.[42]

Any other politician with a record like Reagan's would have lost Republican support. "Conservatives would run him out of the country today," Willie Brown told me in 2019 during the third year of the Trump administration.[43] But Reagan remained the darling of the right in 1975, just as he had been when first elected in 1966. Right-wingers sensed that he was on their wavelength, and they took comfort from his words while ignoring many of his deeds. Throughout his governorship, as one California newspaper noted in 1974, "Ronald Reagan has continued his annual ritual of decrying expenses as if Governor Reagan had no part in the affair."[44] Because Reagan constantly talked about the virtues of "cutting the cost of government," many voters gave him credit for at least trying to pare it back.[45] In a way, conservatives condescended to him just as liberals did, with both sides assuming he was not really in control of his own administration.

Thus, Reagan managed the difficult feat during eight years as governor of mainly acting as a centrist while remaining a conservative heartthrob. Now he just had to figure out what to do for an encore once he left office. The Sacramento show was closing. He still wanted to be a headliner, but he needed a new stage. There was only one logical destination, but it was already occupied by a Republican incumbent. Would he dare challenge President Jerry Ford in the 1976 primaries? That was the question confronting him as he exited the governor's office at the beginning of 1975.

28

The Primary Gambit

*If I don't do it, I'm going to be the player who's always been
on the bench but never got into the game.*

—RONALD REAGAN

When Richard M. Nixon was launching his political career in Southern California in the 1940s by expertly and unscrupulously catering to the resentments and fears of the white, suburban middle class, Ronald Reagan was still a progressive New Dealer who had nothing but scorn for "Tricky Dick." But by the time Nixon ran against John F. Kennedy in 1960, Reagan was a staunch supporter, and so he remained until the bitter end of the Nixon presidency in 1974—and beyond.

While other conservatives fumed over President Nixon's opening to China, his détente with the Soviet Union, and his liberal domestic initiatives—for example, the creation of the Environmental Protection Agency and the Occupational Health and Safety Administration—Reagan remained staunchly loyal. As an employee of Warner Brothers and General Electric, he had faithfully followed the company line—and now, as a Republican officeholder, he extended similar allegiance to the head of his party. He invariably answered letters from conservatives critical of the president with some version of the words he wrote to a woman in early 1970: "I strongly believe in giving President Nixon our full support to end the Vietnam conflict for I have great confidence in his judgment. He has all the facts before him, many of which we do not have."[1]

Although Reagan would become an outspoken critic of détente with the Soviet Union as practiced by President Ford, he was far more supportive when the policy was initiated by President Nixon. Only minutes after Nixon announced on July 15, 1971, his intention to go to Beijing to meet with Mao Zedong, National Security Adviser Henry Kissinger telephoned the governor at his Sacramento residence to win his support.[2] The Nixon White House knew how critical it was to keep such a prominent conservative on board. Sure enough, Reagan defended Nixon's diplomacy to conservative critics. "We are seeing an American President dealing realistically and calculatingly with the enemy—Chinese and Russian—as no American President has dealt for many, many years," Reagan wrote following Nixon's trips to Beijing and Moscow in 1972. He assured another letter-writer that "I still believe the president has the same conservative philosophy he always had."[3]

In a 1972 speech, Reagan did warn "that every nation in history which has sought peace and freedom solely through negotiations has been crushed by conquerors bent on conquest and aggression."[4] Of course, he offered no evidence for this dubious assertion: Which nation had ever entrusted its security *solely* to negotiations without making any attempt to defend itself? But, contrary to one author's claim,[5] he wasn't criticizing Nixon, whom he praised in that same speech as a farsighted leader pursuing a "grand design" for "peace" and "prosperity." He was attacking Democratic proposals to cut defense spending. The following year, Reagan joined other movie stars in attending a glitzy poolside reception hosted by Nixon for Leonid Brezhnev—a fan of Hollywood Westerns—when the portly Soviet leader visited the Western White House in San Clemente, California.[6]

Remarkably, Reagan's faith in Nixon was not shaken by the Watergate scandal. He ignored his friend William F. Buckley Jr.'s warning in the fall of 1973 that "Our Leader is in deep trouble" and that "a patient, cautious dissociation would appear to be prudent."[7] Almost until the day of Nixon's resignation, Reagan naively insisted that the president was innocent. He even said that the president's men were "not criminals at heart," giving them a benefit of the doubt he never extended to welfare cheats or street criminals.[8] "I still have confidence that when the smoke clears we will find the President was not involved," Reagan wrote in June 1973 of the Watergate burglary and cover-up. He reasoned, wrongly, that Nixon was just as hands-off a manager as he was: "If my staff wanted to keep something of this kind from me, it would be very easy for them to do so."[9]

Reagan was just as supportive of Vice President Spiro Agnew, the snarling point man in the administration's populist culture wars who was known for denouncing intellectuals as an "effete corps of impudent snobs." After Agnew's resignation amid charges of corruption and tax evasion, Reagan complained, "It's really so sad and so unfair, what happened to him."[10]

Nixon's private opinion of Reagan was a good deal lower than Reagan's opinion of him. In an Oval Office tape recorded on November 17, 1971, Henry Kissinger described Reagan as a "pretty decent guy" with "negligible" brains. Nixon readily agreed, calling the California governor "pretty shallow" and "a man of limited mental capacity" who "simply doesn't know what the Christ is going on in the foreign area."[11]

While he had nothing but contempt for Reagan's intellect, Nixon had a healthy respect for Reagan's political skills. "Only two governors we need to keep happy—Reagan and Rocky," a White House political aide noted in 1970.[12] Nixon was paranoid about Reagan challenging him in 1972 and made sure to keep the governor loyal by employing him as an international envoy—complete with an official airplane, Secret Service protection, and all the other trappings. Periodically, Nixon would instruct his aides, "It's time to stroke Ronnie. Find somewhere for him to go on a presidential mission."[13]

Reagan, who had seldom traveled abroad before, became Nixon's de facto envoy to a bevy of right-wing dictators: the Philippines' Ferdinand Marcos (September 1969); South Korea's Park Chung-hee, Singapore's Lee Kuan Yew, Taiwan's Chiang Kai-shek, and South Vietnam's Nguyen Van Thieu (October 1971); Spain's Francisco Franco (July 1972); and Indonesia's Suharto and Singapore's Lee Kuan Yew again (December 1973). One of the highlights of these trips for Reagan was meeting the pope; one of the lowlights was having to listen to Imelda Marcos sing.[14]

Although he styled himself as a champion of freedom, Reagan effusively praised the strongmen he was meeting because of their anti-Communism. He even absurdly compared Thieu, a military dictator, to George Washington because both men won elections unopposed.[15] Reagan never seemed to notice the tension between his impassioned denunciations of Communist tyranny and his embrace of anti-Communist tyrants—a discrepancy he would struggle to reconcile in the White House.

No one was more shocked and surprised than Reagan by the release of the "smoking gun" tapes on August 5, 1974, proving Nixon's complicity in the Watergate cover-up. Reagan would tell his family that Nixon "should have destroyed the damn tapes."[16] Ignominiously, Nixon was forced to resign just four days later and Vice President Gerald Ford, an amiable former House minority leader, became president. Reagan saw himself as Nixon's natural heir and had already begun to plot a presidential campaign, but now his future was in doubt.

Declaring "our long national nightmare is over," Ford entered office riding a wave of popularity, but his support plummeted when, on September 8, 1974, he pardoned Nixon for any crimes he might have committed. Few Americans agreed with Ronald Reagan that Nixon had "suffered as much as any man should."[17] The genial new president also alienated the right by appointing Nelson Rockefeller as vice president, offering a limited amnesty to draft resisters, keeping Henry Kissinger as secretary of state, and continuing Nixon's policies toward China and the Soviet Union. Ford's reputation was further battered by North Vietnam's conquest of South Vietnam in April 1975 and the dismal performance of the economy. A brief recession ended in 1975, but the unemployment rate was still 8.2 percent, and inflation was running at 6.9 percent—hardly the ideal conditions in which to seek another term.

Ford enjoyed a brief surge of popularity after he ordered a military raid in May 1975 to free US sailors from the merchant ship *Mayaguez*, seized by Cambodia's Khmer Rouge, even though forty-one US service members died in the botched assault. ("It shows we've still got balls in this country," Barry Goldwater said.)[18] But although a skilled athlete—Jerry Ford had been a football star at the University of Michigan while Dutch Reagan had barely made Eureka's varsity squad—the president was developing a reputation as an ineffectual bumbler. Comedians such as Chevy Chase regularly mocked him for stumbling down the stairs of Air Force One. Reagan joined in, later joking, "I bumped my head, I'm getting like Jerry Ford."[19]

Now a private citizen, Reagan watched developments in Washington closely from his old home in Pacific Palisades and his new office on Wilshire Boulevard in Westwood near the UCLA campus. Two of his aides, Michael Deaver and Peter Hannaford, had arranged a cushy, post-gubernatorial livelihood for Reagan—and for themselves. They formed a public relations firm, Deaver & Hannaford Inc., with Reagan as their major client. They arranged for him to write a syndicated weekly newspaper column, to deliver daily radio commentaries, and to give lucrative speeches on the "mashed potato circuit." Before long, Reagan was being heard on 350 radio stations and read in 150 newspapers, reaching an estimated twenty million people a week—roughly 10 percent of the population.[20]

His columns were mainly written by Hannaford, with help from other ghostwriters such as Pat Buchanan and Lyn Nofziger, but Reagan wrote most of his own radio commentaries, taping three weeks' worth in one sitting. CBS, the onetime home of *General Electric Theater*, asked him to become a weekly television commentator, but he turned down the offer for fear of "wearing out my welcome."[21] He didn't want to overexpose himself on TV. Radio had been his preferred medium ever since his days as a sportscaster in the Midwest in the 1930s, and so it would remain. His income shot up from $49,100 as governor in 1974 to as much as $800,000 in 1975.[22]

All the while, a potential presidential run loomed in the background. Ed Meese recalled that a "conscious decision" was made that nothing Reagan did in his post-gubernatorial life would endanger a presidential campaign. That meant "not taking any corporate boardships or doing anything that would be inconsistent with running."[23]

"There were many, many people urging him to run for the presidency," Meese recalled. But many other supporters, he noted, were "very upset" about the prospect of challenging a sitting Republican president in a divisive campaign that could open the way for Democrats to regain the White House. Reagan himself had echoed such concerns when he had refused to challenge Nixon in 1972. "To go after an incumbent President literally guarantees the election of our opponents," he had written back then in a previously unreported letter. "There would be no way to come out of a divided convention with a unified Party."[24]

Yet while Reagan had been unfailingly loyal to Nixon and Agnew, those sentiments did not extend to the new president. He viewed Ford as too liberal, too weak—and too much of an impediment to his own ambitions. "I just don't think Jerry can do it," he told Mike Deaver. "And if I don't do it, I'm going to be the player who's always been on the bench but never got into the game."[25] He knew how badly that felt during his freshman year at Eureka College.

With his long experience in Washington and extensive knowledge of government, Ford had as little respect for Reagan as Reagan had for him. Thus, he was not concerned when his staff told him that the former governor was preparing to challenge him. "I hadn't taken those warnings seriously because I didn't take Reagan seriously," Ford admitted in his memoirs.

During their few meetings, Ford had found Reagan pleasant but inscrutable. "He was one of the few political leaders I have ever met," he observed,
"whose public speeches revealed more than his private conversation."[26]
(Nancy Reagan came across very differently: Betty Ford, who felt far more
free to unburden herself in public than the tightly wound former first lady of
California, noted that "off camera" Nancy was icy but "on camera," warm.)[27]
In private, Ford was even more scathing. "He considered Reagan a superficial, disengaged, lazy showman who didn't do his homework and clung to a
naïve, unrealistic and essentially dangerous world view," wrote a journalist
to whom Ford unburdened himself near the end of his life.[28]

So Ford made only minimal attempts to head off a Reagan primary challenge. He did not offer to make Reagan vice president, as advocated by Reagan's Kitchen Cabinet. Instead, he offered to make him ambassador to the
Court of St. James or secretary of transportation or commerce—all jobs
that Reagan perceived as beneath him. The only appointment that Reagan
accepted was a part-time role on a presidential commission investigating
Central Intelligence Agency (CIA) abuses.

This was neither the first nor last time that Reagan would be
underestimated—and Ford, like so many others, would pay a steep price for
his condescension.

As 1975 progressed, the sixty-four-year-old former governor edged closer
to a presidential run while holding off a formal announcement as long as
possible so as not to endanger his earnings from radio and newspapers. An
exploratory committee called Citizens for Reagan was announced on July
15. Nevada's new Republican senator, Paul Laxalt, who had become friendly
with Reagan when the two men were governors of adjoining states, agreed
to chair it. A centrist former New Hampshire Republican governor, Hugh
Gregg, signed up as the head of the New Hampshire campaign. Many of the
Kitchen Cabinet members were initially opposed to challenging a Republican president, but most of them—with the notable exception of Henry
Salvatori—eventually came around.

The campaign manager was John P. Sears III, a thirty-four-year-old
political wunderkind from Washington with prematurely gray hair who
had played an important role in Richard Nixon's 1968 campaign and had
been slated to run Spiro Agnew's 1976 presidential campaign. He was hardly

a staunch conservative, and he was reserved "almost to the point of shyness," but he had a reputation as a political mastermind.[29] Few realized he also had a serious drinking problem. Reagan barely knew Sears, but he went along with the judgment of his advisers that they needed a campaign manager from "back East" with credibility among the national press corps. Stuart Spencer, the California strategist behind both of Reagan's gubernatorial campaigns, was little known in Washington and had tense relations with Deaver and Meese. So he was cut out—and would help Ford stave off the Reagan challenge.

Averse as always to making difficult personal decisions, Reagan never actually told his aides he was running. They just assumed he was, and he did not contradict them. "Every step of the way where we had to make a decision that would take him closer to being a candidate, he always said, 'Yes, go ahead and do it," Peter Hannaford recalled, "but he never said, 'I'm going to run.'"[30]

The Reagans did not sit down to talk with their children about the looming campaign until October 31, 1975, just three weeks before the formal announcement, when the decision had already been made. The aspiring president treated his family as another campaign audience. Convening the children at their Pacific Palisades home, he gave a little speech arguing that he had a duty to run because he was being urged to do so by every hotel bellhop and chambermaid he met on the road. "So the grassroots response is out there, and I feel I have a good chance to win." Nancy was not enthusiastic about another campaign but was supportive of his ambitions. The reaction among the children was more mixed.

Maureen Reagan was thirty-four years old, twice divorced, and living with song-and-dance man Gene Nelson, who was nearly as old as her father and had once appeared in a picture with him. This May–September romance did not please her father and stepmother. After trying and failing to make it as an actress, Maureen was seeking without much success to build a new career as a radio and television host. She urged her dad to stay out of the race, calculating (correctly) that 1976 would not be a Republican year following the debacle of the 1974 midterm elections.

Michael Reagan was then a thirty-year-old speedboat racer and boat salesman who was deeply in debt, recently divorced (his first wife had left him while she was pregnant), and newly engaged. He and his fiancée, Colleen Sterns, were more enthusiastic about the announcement, at least outwardly. In private, however, Michael was terrified that the campaign would expose the sexual abuse he had experienced as a child.

Ron Reagan was a rebellious, long-haired, seventeen-year-old high school senior who regularly skipped class to go bodysurfing, smoked pot, and was carrying on an affair with thirty-year-old Kris Harmon Nelson, a mother of four and the wife of teen idol Ricky Nelson, a son of television stars Ozzie and Harriet Nelson. Having been expelled from a fancy boarding school by a headmaster who deemed him a bad influence, Ron was now attending the Harvard School for Boys, an elite day school in Los Angeles, and living "uncomfortably" at home. He would enter Yale University in the fall of 1976, only to drop out in his first semester, over his parents' objections, to pursue a career as a ballet dancer. "I was at that age disenchanted with politics and certainly not a Republican," he remembered. "While I supported my father personally, we did not see eye to eye politically. And I felt no need to suck up by pretending otherwise."

Missing entirely from the family meeting was Patti Davis, already an outspoken liberal who had changed her last name to avoid association with her conservative father. A twenty-four-year-old college dropout and aspiring actress and songwriter, she was, much to her parents' disapproval, living with her boyfriend, Eagles' guitarist Bernie Leadon, in Topanga Canyon, and growing her own pot. "Living together without the benefit of marriage is a sin in the eyes of God," her father lectured her. She did not attend the family meeting because she had not been invited. She felt "far removed from the looming reality of 1976."

At one point, Michael expressed hope that the impending presidential campaign would bring the disunited family closer together. His father was puzzled. "But the family *is* close," Ronald Reagan insisted.[31]

———

The formal campaign announcement took place at the National Press Club in Washington on November 20, 1975, followed by campaign swings on a chartered jet through Florida, New Hampshire, and other early primary states. Thus began the long, exhausting grind of campaigning—"an endless series of hotels and motels, buses and cars," as Nancy Reagan noted, with one place blurring into another. "You fall into bed at midnight, and the next day you're up at dawn to do it all over again."[32]

In his campaign announcement, the challenger did not attack Ford by name. Instead, he blamed Washington generically for the stagnating economy, the expansion of the federal government, and the supposed erosion of US military superiority over the Soviet Union. For a master of the one-liner, Reagan's core complaint was surprisingly clunky: "Our nation's capital has become the seat of a 'buddy' system that functions for its own benefit—increasingly insensitive to the needs of the American worker who supports it with his taxes." The phrase "buddy system"—unlike so many other Reaganisms—was not destined to roll off the tongue and would soon be discarded.[33]

On the campaign trail, the challenger reverted to familiar complaints about federal excesses and boasts about his own record that were usually exaggerated and sometimes downright false. Reagan's most excusable and understandable hyperbole concerned his tenure as governor. Like most politicians, he was prone to aggrandizing his achievements and ignoring his failures. He claimed, for example, that "we lopped 400,000 off the welfare rolls," whereas the actual figure was 232,070. He also bragged about delivering tax rebates and property-tax decreases without mentioning that he had also signed record-breaking tax increases.[34]

Reagan also continued to repeat dubious statistics to attack the federal government that usually came from *Reader's Digest, Human Events,* or *National Review.* He routinely said, for example, that "no other country in the world puts so many taxes on its businesses." In fact, Canada, France, West Germany, and many other countries had higher corporate tax rates. He also asserted that the Environmental Protection Agency had forty-one congressional lobbyists instead of the actual six, and that the Food and Drug Administration had killed forty thousand patients who had tuberculosis by refusing to approve a drug widely available in Europe. In fact, the drug had been on the market, with the FDA's blessing, since 1971—and fewer than twenty-eight thousand Americans died of tuberculosis during the entire decade.[35]

The most noxious Reagan falsehoods were ones that touched on incendiary matters of race. As during his 1966 gubernatorial campaign, he was not subtle in 1976 about tapping into white fear and resentment of minorities, employing racist dog whistles at the very least. "If someone set out to design a welfare program that wouldn't work, they couldn't do better than food stamps," he often said. "You've probably had the same idea when you were standing in the checkout line at the market with your package of hamburger, watching the strapping young fellow in line ahead of you buying T-bone steaks with food stamps." While campaigning in Florida, he altered the script to denounce a "strapping young buck." Reagan insisted the phrase was innocuous, but "buck" had long been used in the South to refer to Black men who defied white authority.

Another example he often cited to illustrate the supposedly excessive generosity of the welfare state was the Taino Towers—subsidized, high-rise housing for the poor, mainly Puerto Rican and Black residents, in New York's East Harlem. "If you are a slum dweller," Reagan complained, "you can get an apartment with 11-foot ceilings, with a 20-foot balcony, a swimming pool and gymnasium, laundry room and play room, and the rent begins at $113.20 and that includes utilities." In reality, only 92 out of 656 units had eleven-foot ceilings, and they were intended for large families. The going rate was $450 a month, not $113.20. And the pool, gymnasium, and other amenities were public facilities shared with two hundred thousand residents of the neighborhood.[36]

No Reagan story attracted more attention than the one about the "welfare queen" who appeared to be Black. "There's a woman in Chicago," Reagan would often say. "She has 80 names, 30 addresses, 12 Social Security cards, and is collecting veteran benefits on four nonexistent deceased husbands. And she's collecting Social Security on her cards, she's got Medicaid, getting food stamps and is collecting welfare under each of her names. Her tax-free cash income alone is over $150,000."[37]

This was a garbled account of a story that originally ran in the *Chicago Tribune* and that was picked up by *Human Events* concerning a woman named Linda Taylor, a mixed-race child of itinerant Southern sharecroppers whose mother was white and father Black. While reporters criticized Reagan for exaggerating Taylor's misdeeds—she was estimated to have stolen around $40,000, not $150,000—he had also left out even more damning details. Josh Levin, a journalist who wrote a book about Taylor, found that she was a lifelong grifter who was guilty not just of welfare fraud but, likely, also of murder and kidnapping. Reagan left out that part of the story, even though it had been reported, presumably because mentioning it would have made it harder to paint Taylor as a typical example of a welfare cheat.

While the specifics of Taylor's life remain a matter of dispute, Reagan's larger message—that welfare fraud was rampant—was clearly false. The US Department of Health, Education and Welfare estimated in 1978 that only 1 percent of its annual spending was lost due to fraud and most of that occurred in Medicaid and other health-care programs—not in Aid to Families with Dependent Children, the program with a heavily African American caseload that Reagan often denounced.[38]

Naturally, when Reagan was called out for catering to bigots, he resorted to familiar falsehoods to defend himself—including his oft-repeated fiction that as a sportscaster in the 1930s he had campaigned to end segregation in Major League Baseball. "Traveling with him on the campaign trail was a never-ending excursion into fantasy," wrote veteran reporter Jules Witcover.[39]

Jeffrey Bell, a young and idealistic Reagan aide, worried that the candidate's speeches lacked intellectual heft. He wanted Reagan to advance a program of his own rather than merely denounce Washington, so he wrote a speech calling for many federal social-welfare programs to be devolved to the states. John Sears, Peter Hannaford, Mike Deaver, Lyn Nofziger, and Reagan himself all liked his draft speech but did not subject it to much critical scrutiny. Reagan duly delivered the address before the Executive Club of Chicago on September 26, 1975, promising that the "transfer of authority" to the states "would reduce the outlay of the federal government by more than $90 billion."[40]

The press at first ignored Reagan's speech, but, on November 21, 1975, he was asked on ABC's *Issues and Answers* whether New Hampshire would have to increase state taxes to pay for programs that had previously been administered at the federal level. Reagan did not deny it—and thereby did fatal injury to his chances of beating Ford.

This blunder was instantly seized on by Ford's political director—none other than Stuart Spencer, who had been brought in by the young White House chief of staff, Dick Cheney. Spencer realized that Ford wasn't taking Reagan seriously. No one thought the old "B-movie actor" could defeat a sitting president. *New York Times* columnist James "Scotty" Reston spoke for the Establishment when he dismissed Reagan's candidacy as an "amusing but frivolous ... fantasy" that "makes a lot of news" but "doesn't make much sense." Spencer, the shrewd consultant from California, knew better. "I'd run his two governor's races," he said. "I knew this guy was for real."[41]

Rather than assuming that Reagan wouldn't gain any traction, Spencer realized that the Ford campaign would have to go on the attack. The $90 billion proposal proved the perfect cudgel. New Hampshire had no state sales tax or state income tax, and most voters wanted to keep it that way. Reagan was now on the defensive in a must-win state.

A week before the February 24, 1976, New Hampshire primary, internal polling showed that Reagan's lead over Ford, which had been in double digits, had shrunk to just four points. Yet Sears had Reagan campaigning in Illinois in the two days before the New Hampshire vote because local operatives in the Granite State told him that having the candidate on the ground would interfere with their get-out-the-vote operations. Campaign pollster Richard Wirthlin was apoplectic; he was convinced that Reagan could have won New Hampshire with one more day of in-person campaigning. Wirthlin became even more irate when he found out that Sears had not bothered to tell Reagan that his early lead had evaporated.[42]

Reagan, as was his wont, had not second-guessed Sears's decision to send him to Illinois. He still had the mindset of an actor who did whatever his director wanted. "My husband, who is very trusting, never imagined that anything was being kept from him," Nancy Reagan wrote.[43]

Sears's miscalculation, coming after the "$90 billion blunder," resulted in a costly near miss.[44] Ford won New Hampshire by a mere 1,317 votes out of 108,328 cast; the little-known former governor of Georgia, Jimmy Carter, won by a much larger margin in the Democratic primary. A switch of just 659 votes would have cost Ford the primary—and quite possibly the nomination.

Reagan had done better in New Hampshire than Democrats Eugene McCarthy in 1968 or George McGovern in 1972, and their strong showings had led to the ouster of the front-runners. But because the Reagan campaign had leaked polls showing its candidate ahead, he was seen as the loser. "Expectations got out of control in New Hampshire," said Charlie Black, one of Sears's lieutenants. "We were expected to win." Jeff Bell told me he got blamed for the loss.[45]

In truth, the fault lay with the candidate who had signed off on the "$90 billion blunder" and failed to campaign till the final day. As Harry Truman said, the buck ultimately stops with the president—or, in this case, the presidential candidate. The beginning of the 1976 campaign, for neither the first nor the last time, had illuminated Reagan's political strengths—particularly his ability to tell Republican voters what they wanted to hear in a way that did not scare non-Republicans—but also his political weaknesses—namely, his inattention to detail and his tendency to defer to aides who did not always know what they were doing. He would not have long to recover from the agonizing defeat in New Hampshire—if recovery was possible.

29

"I Shall Rise and Fight Again"

Even though we lost, we won.

—JOHN SEARS

Ronald Reagan was hardly innocent of the adversity of human existence—witness his impoverished upbringing, his painful divorce, and the end of his film career—but, on the whole, he had led a charmed life. Taking advantage of his film and television stardom, he skipped over the lower rungs of the political ladder and entered the arena by running for, and winning, the governorship of the nation's most populous state. Reelection followed four years later. He did fail in his first presidential campaign, in 1968, but he simply pretended it never happened. In 1976, however, no such pretense was possible. He had entered the primaries against an incumbent president, fought hard, and suffered a defeat—all the more crushing for being so close—in New Hampshire.

With the momentum swinging against him, Reagan lost the next four primaries—in Massachusetts and Vermont (March 2), Florida (March 9), and even in his native state, Illinois (March 16). The campaign was running out of money—and hope. Republican leaders were demanding that Reagan pull out and endorse Ford; even Barry Goldwater backed the president. "For Reagan," the *Los Angeles Times* editorialized, "the real question ought not to be *whether* to bow out, but *when*."[1] Without telling Reagan, John Sears went to meet secretly with Ford's campaign chairman to see if a deal could be brokered for a graceful exit. Nancy Reagan thought her husband was being humiliated and wanted him to quit.

However, when Lyn Nofziger went to talk to Reagan at Nancy's behest about pulling out, the candidate remained defiant. "I'm not going to quit," said Reagan, displaying his innate stubbornness. "I'm going to stay in this thing until the end. I still think we can win, but even if we don't, I can't let down all those people who believe in the things we believe in and who want me to be president."[2] Charlie Black said that "Reagan's resolve to keep fighting on caused everybody to keep working."[3]

The next primary was on March 23 in North Carolina, and it would be Reagan's last stand. Win here, and he could keep going to the other Southern primaries. Lose, and the campaign would be finished, making another presidential run unimaginable. At this critical juncture, with his entire political career on the line, Reagan found a new issue—and a new patron.

Naturally, as a governor, despite his four trips abroad on behalf of Nixon, Reagan had not been much concerned with foreign affairs. In 1973, Bill Buckley warned Reagan that a "well-wisher" had told him "that it will have to be Rockefeller in 1976 because you 'refuse to wrap your mind around foreign policy.'"[4] Yet beginning with the 1976 Florida primary, Reagan began to emphasize foreign policy, hitting hard at President Ford and Secretary of State Kissinger for the alleged weakness of their détente policy—which he had never criticized when Nixon was president.

This is a shift that gets overlooked in the conventional Reagan narrative because of the erroneous assumption that, like many other conservatives, he had been a consistent and outspoken critic of détente from the start. In fact, as noted previously, he had supported the policy while Nixon was in office. It's possible that Reagan had turned into a vociferous foe of détente once he saw its consequences. After the humiliating fall of South Vietnam in 1975, Reagan complained that the North Vietnamese would never have attacked "had its leaders believed we would respond with B-52's."[5] It was Ford's decision not to bomb North Vietnam, although congressional opposition gave him little choice.

Reagan was also incensed by Ford's refusal to meet with the Soviet dissident Aleksandr Solzhenitsyn—described by Reagan as "one of the great moral leaders of our time"—in the summer of 1975 for fear of derailing détente. Indeed, Senators Strom Thurmond and Jesse Helms had demanded that the president receive the émigré writer for precisely this purpose.[6] Reagan's views were shaped more by anecdotes and stories than by philosophical concepts, and the snub to Solzhenitsyn may have helped to crystallize his opposition to détente. As president himself, Reagan would invite Solzhenitsyn to the White House in 1982 only to have the cantankerous novelist refuse to come.[7]

But there are also more cynical explanations for Reagan's newfound opposition to détente: that he had largely kept quiet about his doubts earlier out of loyalty to Nixon and in the hope of being anointed Nixon's successor, and that his criticisms now were mainly motivated by his rivalry with Ford. It was noteworthy that Reagan published a column attacking Ford's handling of Solzhenitsyn just three days after announcing on July 15, 1975, the formation of his Citizens for Reagan campaign committee, suggesting that his critique was at least as much about politics as principles.[8]

Whatever his motivation, Reagan's attacks on Ford's foreign policy were dire—and deceptive.

He often warned that the United States was losing its military superiority to the Soviet Union—"a nation that has never made any effort to hide its hostility to everything we stand for."[9] It was true that the Soviet Union, which had always had larger conventional forces than the United States, was now approaching nuclear parity as well. But the qualitative US military advantage was growing with the introduction of computer technology. In any case, as Henry Kissinger said, "Military superiority has no practical significance . . . under circumstances in which both sides have the capability to annihilate one another."[10]

In response to attacks from Reagan and other conservatives, Ford's CIA director, George H. W. Bush, brought in a Team B of hawkish outside analysts who criticized the CIA for underestimating Soviet military strength, warning that within ten years the Soviets would have such an overwhelming military advantage that they could achieve their "hegemonic objectives" without firing a shot. In fact, history would show that even the CIA's analysts were substantially *overestimating* Soviet capabilities. Moscow was actually slowing the rate of increase in its defense spending during this period.[11]

Reagan also excoriated the 1975 Helsinki Accords—signed by the United States, the Soviet Union, and almost all of the nations of Europe to reduce tensions on the continent—for supposedly recognizing Soviet hegemony over Eastern Europe. In fact, the treaty did not involve any Western concessions and was later seen as a contributing factor in the collapse of the Soviet bloc because Soviet leaders pledged to respect human rights. By 1981, even Reagan was criticizing the Kremlin's failure to allow emigration as a "direct violation of the Helsinki pact."[12]

Reagan's most potent foreign policy issue was Ford's attempt to renegotiate the 1903 treaty, a product of Theodore Roosevelt's gunboat diplomacy, that had given the United States near-total control of the Panama Canal Zone "in perpetuity." Fears were growing of a violent upheaval in Panama if the United States did not undo this relic of early twentieth-century American imperialism. Talks to transfer the canal had been going on for years, with little controversy, until conservative Republicans such as Strom Thurmond and Jesse Helms seized on the issue. They claimed, in the face of all evidence to the contrary, that Panama's military dictator, Omar Torrijos, was a closet Marxist and that turning over the canal to Panama would hand it to the Soviet bloc. The John Birch Society charged that it was "treason" to relinquish the canal.

"We own it. We bought it. It is ours," Strom Thurmond proclaimed in 1974. Reagan had "never thought" about the issue, Mike Deaver recalled, but he now took up the slogan with gusto and found it was a sure-fire crowd pleaser. Much of what Reagan said about the canal, like much of what he said about the US-Soviet arms race, was not, strictly speaking, true. The Ford administration wasn't engaged in "secret negotiations"; they were widely publicized. The canal zone wasn't "sovereign United States territory just as much as Alaska is"; "Zonians" did not automatically become US citizens at birth as Alaskans did. And handing over the canal would not, as history was to show, endanger US security. Even some right-wing stalwarts, such as John Wayne (who was married to a Latin American actress), Barry Goldwater, and Bill Buckley, supported the negotiations, because they understood that the likely alternative was Latin American resentment, rioting, and even guerrilla warfare.

Whatever the merits of the issue, however, the Panama Canal controversy resonated among conservatives upset about the humiliating defeat in the Vietnam War, the Arab oil embargo, and the general decline of US prestige after Watergate. Control of the canal came to symbolize American strength and patriotism. Reagan's jingoistic riff—"We built it! We paid for it! And we should keep it!"—"prompted his audiences to go practically berserk," observed political reporter Fred Barnes.[13]

Another part of the Reagan appeal to North Carolina Republicans—one that has not been sufficiently emphasized by most previous writers—concerned the candidate's opposition to civil rights legislation. Reagan won over many white voters with his support for legislation or even a constitutional amendment to outlaw school busing; his excoriation of "welfare queens"; his opposition to the federal government trying to force all-white private schools that received federal funds to admit minority students; and his condemnation of a recent extension of the Voting Rights Act as an act of "pure cheap demagoguery" that would lead to "a new wave of carpetbaggers to look over the shoulder of your local officials, just as Reconstruction did in 1865." He even castigated the lunch-counter sit-ins that civil rights activists had mounted against Jim Crow laws on the grounds that "there can never be any justification for breaking the law," while never censuring white Southerners' unlawful campaign of "massive resistance" to the Supreme Court's school desegregation decision. Reagan's double standard recalled Martin Luther King Jr.'s admonition in his 1963 "Letter from Birmingham Jail" that the biggest obstacle to racial progress was not "the Ku Klux Klanner but the white moderate who is more devoted to 'order' than to justice."

All those semisublimated appeals to bigotry were mighty pleasing to Senator Jesse Helms, the ultraconservative former television commentator and born-again Baptist who had become the dominant political figure in North Carolina. Reagan had endorsed Helms's first Senate campaign in 1972 and had spoken at his fundraisers. Helms, in turn, promised over lunch at the governor's Pacific Palisades home in August 1973 to support Reagan's presidential ambitions. In 1974, Reagan wrote to John Wayne, "I know the Senator very well and certainly approve of his philosophy."

Helms's philosophy troubled many other people, if not Ronald Reagan. Unlike most other white Southern politicians, Helms never recanted his opposition to civil rights or his support for segregation. He also backed right-wing dictatorships, including apartheid South Africa, while denouncing, inter alia, abortion, foreign aid, homosexuality, and modern art. Although personally congenial and unpretentious—"the soul of Southern courtesy"—Helms was a master of slash-and-burn politics. He and his chief strategist, Thomas F. Ellis, had created their own political action committee, the North Carolina Congressional Club, which became part of the New Right juggernaut.

In addition to his political work for Helms, Tom Ellis also served on the board of the Pioneer Fund, which funded pseudoscientific research intended to show that Black people were genetically inferior to white people. Ellis had once warned that integration would lead to miscegenation and the disappearance of the white race. His bigoted views would force him to withdraw his nomination to the Board for International Broadcasting in 1983—he was nominated, of course, by President Ronald Reagan—after opposition from senators such as Joe Biden, who said, "You are by my definition a racist." But Helms's own views, which were disturbingly similar to Ellis's, did not hinder—and, in fact, made possible—his long career as a Republican kingmaker.

Like other conservative activists such as Richard Viguerie (dubbed the "King Midas of the New Right"), Howard Phillips, and Paul Weyrich, Helms and Ellis pioneered the use of direct-mail fundraising that kept donations coming in by frightening the faithful about purported Democratic plots to destroy America. "The shriller you are," one fundraiser noted, "the easier it is to raise money." In North Carolina that meant catering to the bigotry of many white voters. The Reagan campaign objected to a newspaper story reprinted by the Helms organization suggesting that Ford might appoint Senator Edward M. Brooke, a Black Republican, as his running mate. But there was evidence that the flier continued to circulate anyway. In any case, Helms and Ellis remained in complete control of Reagan's North Carolina campaign, and Reagan never criticized their retrograde racial views.

Ellis's masterstroke was to air on North Carolina TV stations, over John Sears's objections, an old-fashioned, half-hour videotape of Reagan speaking straight to the camera, repeating his shopworn warnings that "to continue on the present course is to recognize the inevitability of a Socialist America," as if the McCarthy-like rhetoric of the early 1950s needed only a bit of refurbishment in the 1970s. That resonated with GOP voters. So did Reagan's ability, in response to a question from a rural voter, to easily recite a favorite Bible verse (Second Chronicles 7:14), signaling that he was in tune with the religious sensibilities of the "Jessecrats."

The Ford campaign had assumed Reagan was finished and eased off in North Carolina. Even the Reagan campaign did not expect to win. Both sides were shocked by the outcome: Reagan, 52 percent; Ford, 46 percent. Ebullient Reagan aides aboard the campaign plane broke out champagne and vanilla ice cream and sang, "Nothing could be finer than to give Ford a shiner." A *New York Times* headline proclaimed a "Whole New Ballgame." The Reagan campaign had a new lease on life—and it had been granted by one of the most racist and right-wing members of the Senate.[14]

The battle now shifted to Texas, which held its primary on May 1, 1976. Reagan had a major advantage there because independents and Democrats could vote in the Republican primary. By now, it was clear that George Wallace, who had been left paralyzed after an assassination attempt in 1972, was going to lose the Democratic nomination to Jimmy Carter, so Wallace partisans were up for grabs. With help from Jesse Helms and Tom Ellis, the Reagan campaign went all out to appeal to supporters of the racist demagogue who had once vowed "segregation now, segregation tomorrow, segregation forever." One of Reagan's commercials, produced by New York media consultant Arthur Finkelstein, featured a "blue collar and down home" Democrat from Fort Worth saying, "As much as I hate to admit it, George Wallace can't be nominated. Ronald Reagan can. He's right on the issues. So for the first time in my life I'm gonna vote in the Republican primary. I'm gonna vote for Ronald Reagan."

Henry Kissinger, who was then visiting Africa, inadvertently helped the Reagan cause by proclaiming US opposition to white minority rule in South Africa and Rhodesia. "Conservatives hit the ceiling," Ford ruefully noted. As if he didn't have enough problems, the president was photographed in San Antonio trying to eat a tamale without removing the inedible husk. "The great tamale incident," as it became known, was a sign that Ford wasn't from 'round these parts.[15]

Reagan won with more than 66 percent in Texas on the strength of the crossover Democratic vote and then, on a streak, prevailed in the next three primaries—Georgia, Indiana, and Nebraska. He was now catching up in the delegate count, and it became obvious that the battle was going to play out all the way to the convention. Ford tried to use all of the advantages of incumbency, including lavish pork-barrel spending, to prevail. Reagan cracked that, when the president arrived in a primary state, the band didn't know "whether to play 'Hail to the Chief' or 'Santa Claus is Coming to Town.'"[16] But Ford remained a dull, plodding candidate who compared poorly on the stump to his silver-tongued challenger. "It was a heavyweight fight between one guy who is a huge person that if he ever hits you with his right, you're dead," Sears recalled. "That was the president. You're lighter but you can move quicker and you jab him to death and you hope you can wear him down. That was us."[17]

Reagan might actually have knocked out his heavyweight opponent if he hadn't kept tripping over his own feet. He hurt himself in the Florida primary by suggesting that some Social Security funds could be invested in the "industrial might of the nation's economy," allowing the Ford campaign to use one of Reagan's own tropes against him by complaining that this was a "blueprint for back-door socialism." Reagan then cost himself the Tennessee primary and probably the Kentucky primary too by suggesting, in response to a question, that he would have to "look at" privatizing the Tennessee Valley Authority.

And, six days before the California primary, Reagan said he would be open to sending US troops as peacekeepers to Rhodesia, where the white minority government was fighting a Black insurgency. Stu Spencer immediately rushed out commercials warning voters, "*Governor* Ronald Reagan couldn't start a war. *President* Ronald Reagan could." "It was quite a while before I could forgive Stu for that one," Nancy Reagan wrote. Even her easygoing husband got red in the face when he heard about the Ford commercial, muttered "That damn Stu Spencer!" and slammed his fist against the airplane bulkhead.[18]

Reagan still won the California primary by a large margin on June 8, 1976, but Ford bested him that day in New Jersey and Ohio.

With the primaries over, Ford was slightly ahead of Reagan, but neither candidate had the 1,130 delegates needed to secure the nomination. Both campaigns spent the next six weeks trying to win delegates in states that allotted them in caucuses and conventions, while trying to lure delegates from the other side and keep their own delegates from being poached. Ford was able to secure a narrow majority with the help of his chief delegate wrangler—a blue-blood attorney from Houston, James A. Baker III, who had been undersecretary of commerce. Ford took full advantage of the trappings of office by inviting the chairman of the Mississippi delegation to a state dinner for Queen Elizabeth II and taking uncommitted delegates with him to view the nation's bicentennial celebrations from the deck of an aircraft carrier in New York Harbor.

John Sears knew that the Reagan campaign was finished unless he did something dramatic. So he suggested announcing in advance of the convention that Senator Richard S. Schweiker from Pennsylvania would be

Reagan's running mate. Schweiker was considerably more liberal than Reagan: He had supported civil rights legislation, Medicare, and Medicaid; advocated federal rent subsidies for the poor; and criticized the Vietnam War. Oh, and he was a Ford delegate. All these facts were positives in Sears's mind. Picking Schweiker would combat the perception that Reagan was a right-wing extremist. "It licked our number one problem," Sears said. "We were no longer George Wallace. George Wallace would never have picked Schweiker."[19]

Those who knew Reagan only by reputation as a conservative ideologue might have expected him to be aghast at the prospect of running with a Rockefeller Republican. But he was serenely unperturbed. Sears recalled that Reagan's first question about Schweiker was simply, "Do you think he'll do it?" Sears had already checked with Schweiker and knew he was amenable.[20] The governor and senator hit it off, and on July 26, 1976, the campaign stunned the political world by unveiling the Reagan-Schweiker ticket. The *New York Times* hyperbolically compared this "daring gamble" to "the recent Israeli raid to free hostages at the Ugandan airport at Entebbe," as if Sears were rescuing Reagan from conservative captivity.[21]

Reagan's willingness to run with Schweiker was more evidence that he was, as Sears said, "a principled pragmatist." "The whole image of Reagan as this dyed-in-the-wool, never-violate-my-principle, never-go-against-anything conservative was not quite correct," Sears noted.[22] But many Reagan supporters were considerably more doctrinaire than he was, and they greeted the news of Schweiker's selection with horror. Jesse Helms called it "the shock of my life."[23] The Reagan campaign was inundated with letters from outraged voters labeling him a "sellout."[24]

Sears had hoped that Schweiker could shake loose some delegates from the Pennsylvania delegation and prevent Ford's coronation. But it was not to be. By the time the Republican National Convention opened amid the usual hoopla at Kemper Arena in Kansas City on August 16, 1976, Ford had an insurmountable lead. The Reagan campaign tried a few final, desperate ploys. A resolution demanding that Ford announce his running mate in advance was voted down. A resolution sponsored by Jesse Helms implicitly upbraiding Ford's foreign policy and championing "morality in foreign policy"—an odd position for a supporter of so many right-wing dictatorships—was adopted after the president shrewdly decided not to fight it.

Ford won with 1,187 delegates to Reagan's 1,070. It was hardly a landslide.

In fact, it was the closest any president has ever come to losing his party's nomination since the advent of the primary system after World War II. Reagan's near miss was a sign of how much the combination of his sunny personality and his hard-edged politics resonated with the Republican grassroots. He had nearly unseated Ford, a staid, middle-of-the-road Republican, by appealing to conservative voters who thought the United States was losing too much power abroad while minority groups were gaining too much power at home. Reagan's surge was a sign that the New Right was nearly in control of the Republican Party. Nearly, but not quite.

After the conclusion of the convention roll call, Ford came to Reagan's suite at the Alameda Plaza at 1:30 a.m. on August 19, 1976, to try to make a show of unity. It wasn't easy. The two men held each other in abject contempt. Lyn Nofziger wrote that "Reagan, who is seldom bitter, went to California a bitter man, convinced that Ford stole the election from him."[25] Ford, for his part, "never forgave Reagan" for his primary challenge and Reagan's failure to campaign harder in the fall, which he believed doomed "his dreams of being an elected president."[26] As if that weren't bad enough, their strong-willed wives—Nancy Reagan and Betty Ford—also feuded with each other. Betty Ford horrified conservatives by endorsing *Roe v. Wade* and the Equal Rights Amendment while condoning premarital sex and marijuana smoking. Nancy Reagan, by contrast, never publicly disagreed with her husband on any issue.[27]

Despite the importuning of the Kitchen Cabinet, Reagan refused to be considered for vice president. "Only the lead horse gets a change of view," he liked to say.[28] Ford should have asked him anyway. Reagan later said he would have accepted ("my conscience would have haunted me had I refused")—and Ford might have won the election. Instead, Ford picked Senator Bob Dole of Kansas, a decorated and wounded war veteran noted for his barbed wit, who had solicited Reagan's private endorsement.[29]

Ford's acceptance speech on the night of Thursday, August 19, 1976, was widely acclaimed as the finest of his career. He was interrupted by applause fifty-nine times as he defended his record and challenged the Democratic nominee, Jimmy Carter, to a debate. At the end of his remarks, he asked for "my good friend, Ron Reagan, to come down and bring Nancy." The delegates began cheering, applauding, chanting "We want Reagan! We want Reagan!" and "Speech! Speech!" The Reagans had no choice but to accede to the president's request, and they began to make their way down to the stage, escorted by their Secret Service detail, "through a labyrinth of back halls, stairwells, tunnels and corridors." As they were fast-walking, practically running, down the corridor, Reagan turned to his wife and asked, "What am I going to say? I don't know what to say!" "Don't worry," Nancy replied. "You'll think of something." He always did.

In truth, the Ford campaign had alerted Mike Deaver that morning that the president might ask his defeated challenger to speak. Reagan did not have a speech written for the occasion, but he did have an idea of what he would say. His speechwriter Peter Hannaford had asked him the day before whether he should work on an acceptance speech. "Don't bother, Pete," Reagan replied. He went on to recount a recent drive home from his new ranch near Santa Barbara, with the Pacific Ocean on one side and the Santa Ynez Mountains on the other, when he had been thinking about a letter he had been asked to write for a time capsule. There would be no acceptance speech now, but that story would form the backbone of the unscripted remarks he was about to deliver from the crowded convention stage. He looked tanned, handsome, and resplendent in a dark suit, white shirt, and burgundy tie, a white handkerchief nattily peeking out of his breast pocket. Nancy stood beside him in an elegant white skirt and sweater.

After a few words of thanks, Reagan began by telling the fifteen thousand people in the arena—and the tens of millions watching at home—about being asked "to write a letter for a time capsule that is going to be opened in Los Angeles a hundred years from now." He realized he would be writing "for people a hundred years from now who know all about us" while "we know nothing about them." In particular, "We don't know what kind of world they'll be living in."

He then mentioned two "challenges confronting us": First, "the erosion of freedom that has taken place under Democrat rule in this country, the invasion of private rights, the controls and restrictions on the vitality of the great free economy that we enjoy." Second, the threat posed by "nuclear weapons that can in a matter of minutes . . . destroy virtually the civilized world we live in." He continued in dramatic fashion:

And suddenly it dawned on me; those who would read this letter a hundred years from now will know whether those missiles were fired. They will know whether we met our challenge.

Whether they will have the freedom that we have known up until now will depend on what we do here. Will they look back with appreciation and say, Thank God for those people in 1976 who headed off that loss of freedom? Who kept us now a hundred years later free? Who kept our world from nuclear destruction?

And if we fail they probably won't get to read the letter at all because it spoke of individual freedom and they won't be allowed to talk of that or read of it.

This is our challenge and this is why we're here in this hall tonight.

His implication was clear: Democrats were leading America to socialist tyranny and nuclear annihilation. Republicans had to save the country—and the world. He concluded, "We must go forth united, determined, that what a great general said a few years ago is true: There is no substitute for victory." He and Nancy left the stage to thunderous applause and the strains of "California, Here I Come."

While it ended with a quotation from Douglas MacArthur, Reagan's six-minute oration bore faint echoes of Winston Churchill's famous speech on June 18, 1940, when the wartime prime minister had said, "Let us therefore brace ourselves to our duties, and so bear ourselves that, if the British Empire and its Commonwealth last for a thousand years, men will still say, 'This was their finest hour.'" Churchill was speaking as Nazi armies were marauding across Europe. Reagan spoke at a far less fraught moment—superpower tensions in 1976 were much reduced from the early years of the Cold War thanks to the policy of détente he so often denounced—but he nevertheless adopted a characteristically apocalyptic tone that lifted his brief remarks out of the realm of standard campaign rhetoric and gave them historical resonance. It was true that the threat of nuclear annihilation never went away during the Cold War, but it was also true that Reagan's supporters never tired of being told that the final showdown between freedom and tyranny was at hand—even though, like a doomsday preacher, he had been delivering that same message since the 1950s.

Reagan held his listeners rapt. The vast hall was entirely silent save for the lachrymal sighs of some of his more emotional supporters. Once again, as in 1964, his oratory had outshone that of the Republican nominee. Once again, many Republicans were left with the sinking feeling they had nominated the wrong man. "In a way he won," John Sears said. "Even though we lost, we won."[30]

Few, however, thought there would be another chance to nominate the man who had captured the delegates' hearts. After all, as the *New York Times* noted the next day, Reagan was sixty-five—"too old to seriously consider another run for the presidency." His future, the newspaper was convinced, lay as a "commentator on national affairs."[31]

If Reagan was finished as a political figure, however, nobody had bothered to notify him. At an emotional farewell to the California delegation the morning before his convention speech, the candidate, "blinking back tears, his voice choking with emotion"—"I've got to stop talking," he said at one point, "I've got a baseball in my throat"—assured his teary-eyed supporters that he wasn't planning to retire to a "rocking chair on the front porch." He quoted an English ballad about a sixteenth-century privateer that he had memorized as a schoolboy in Dixon:

Lay me down and bleed a while.
Though I am wounded, I am not slain.
I shall rise and fight again.[32]

The tribulations of Jimmy Carter—who went on to defeat Jerry Ford in a closer-than-expected election—would provide the opening that Reagan sought to "rise and fight again."

30

The Santa Claus Campaign

The Republicans, traditionally the party of income growth, should be the Santa Claus of Tax Reduction.

—JUDE WANNISKI

Jimmy Carter was a fine man—"perhaps as admirable a human being as has ever held the job," one of his aides wrote[1]—and he made a good first impression. But, as the electorate became more familiar with him, admiration in many cases turned to disappointment and even contempt. The former peanut farmer from Plains, Georgia—a town so small it made Dixon, Illinois, seem like a major metropolis—entered office riding a wave of popularity as an honest, smart, unpretentious newcomer to Washington with a toothy grin and a handsome family. His approval rating hit a high of 75 percent during his political honeymoon in late March 1977. Thereafter, it began a long, calamitous descent until it hit a low of just 28 percent in early July 1979—Nixon in Watergate territory—as the public came to see him as an arrogant, humorless, sanctimonious micromanager with a charisma deficit.[2] He was his own worst enemy, failing to win over even his party's liberal base, thus setting up a primary challenge in 1980 from Senator Edward M. Kennedy of Massachusetts.

In retrospect, Carter's four years in office appear more impressive than they did at the time. In domestic policy, he deregulated trucking and airlines to spur competition, pushed for renewable energy (he installed solar panels on the White House roof that were subsequently taken down by Ronald Reagan), doubled the size of the national park system, appointed more women and minorities to the federal bench than all of his predecessors combined, and appointed in Paul Volcker a Federal Reserve chairman who cracked down on inflation. In foreign and defense policy, he launched high-tech weapons systems such as the Stealth bomber and cruise missile, agreed to deploy intermediate-range missiles to Europe to counter a Soviet buildup, championed human rights, aided Afghan guerrillas fighting a Soviet invasion, established diplomatic relations with China, negotiated the Panama Canal Treaties (thus removing a source of tension with Latin America), and—his most impressive achievement—personally negotiated the 1978 Camp David Accords that brought peace between Israel and Egypt. His defense buildup and economic deregulation actually anticipated his successor's more conservative agenda.[3]

Yet, for contemporaries, Carter's failures loomed much larger than his achievements. Critics blamed Carter's supposed weakness for the seizure of sixty-six American hostages at the US Embassy in Tehran on November 4, 1979, and for the Soviet invasion of Afghanistan on December 24, 1979. The president only compounded the impression of ineffectuality when the military operation he had ordered to rescue the hostages, Operation Eagle Claw, ended in ignominious failure on April 24, 1980, at a rendezvous point known as Desert One. Eight US service members were killed, and no hostages were released.

The president's popularity actually rebounded after the seizure of the hostages, as the nation rallied around its leader. But he could not survive the travails of the economy. In 1976, Carter had popularized the "misery index"—a combination of the unemployment and inflation rates—to attack Gerald Ford. Now the "misery index" was to make Carter's own life miserable. Between 1976 and 1979, it climbed from 12.7 percent to more than 19 percent.[4] The nation was in the grip of "stagflation," with high unemployment and inflation and low economic growth. Energy prices were skyrocketing, leading to gasoline shortages and long lines at the pump, and Carter seemed to have no answer other than donning a cardigan sweater and urging everyone to join him in turning down the thermostat.

Carter compounded his problems with an Oval Office address on July 15, 1979, that contrasted markedly with Ronald Reagan's more upbeat speaking style. Instead of rallying the country, the president hectored it in puritanical tones. "Too many of us now tend to worship self-indulgence and consumption," he lectured, adding that "piling up material goods cannot fill the emptiness of lives which have no confidence or purpose." "There is simply no way to avoid sacrifice," he concluded. Carter's pollster, Patrick Caddell, told reporters that the speech was about the "malaise" gripping the country, and the phrase stuck, even though Carter never actually used the word.[5]

"The immediate public response to the speech was actually somewhat favorable," Reagan's pollster Richard Wirthlin later wrote. "But the instant

I heard it I knew Carter had stepped on a strategic land mine."[6] A couple of land mines, actually: Carter seemed to be blaming the American people for the country's problems, and he sounded pessimistic about the future. "People didn't like it," acknowledged Democratic House Majority Leader Jim Wright of Texas. "Carter was just being Carter: painfully honest and disdainful of flattering language."[7]

Reagan, by contrast, did not always tell the truth, but he never castigated the American people and always projected the unerring optimism with which he had armored himself since his difficult childhood. Carter challenged the American people; Reagan reassured them. In retrospect, Wirthlin was to write, the "malaise speech" was "the exact moment I knew Ronald Reagan could beat Jimmy Carter."[8]

By then—with eighteen months to go before the 1980 election—the Reagan campaign was already in high gear. Indeed, it had never really stopped after his loss to Jerry Ford. There was still $1.5 million left over in campaign funds from 1976. Reagan could have done anything he wanted with the money, including depositing it in his own bank account, but he chose to create a new political action committee called Citizens for the Republic. Lyn Nofziger, who was tapped to run the new organization based in Santa Monica, suggested the name because it was so similar to the old campaign organization Citizens for Reagan. They initially called it CFR for short, but right-wingers complained that it shared the same initials as the Council on Foreign Relations, a pillar of the Eastern Establishment and a focus of John Birch Society conspiracy theories. So the abbreviation was hastily changed to CFTR.[9]

Nofziger initially thought Reagan would be "too old" to run in 1980, and the organization would focus on building "a political power base that would effectively carry on the Reagan philosophy long after he had retired."[10] "It would have been hard," Peter Hannaford noted, "to find anyone in the Reagan circle who believed he would be a candidate again."[11]

Yet the former governor showed no sign of slowing down in his late sixties. As soon as his 1976 campaign ended, he returned to delivering radio commentaries, producing a newspaper column, and maintaining a steady schedule of public speaking while also engaging in back-breaking labor to fix up his ramshackle new ranch near Santa Barbara. His personal appearances were partially designed to make money (he was charging $5,000 a speech) and partially to build up political chits. CFTR became one of the top Republican fundraising machines in the country, collecting donations through direct-mail appeals and doling out millions of dollars to candidates.

Twice a month, it sent out a newsletter to donors featuring a commentary called "Ronald Reagan Speaks Out." Each warned about some Carter initiative in alarmist tones that would anticipate the output of conservative talk radio and the Fox News Channel decades later. A typically strident commentary in 1977 said that a White House staffer's call for schools to educate students about energy conservation was tantamount to "Big Brotherism" or "*Mein Kampf.*" Another commentary advocated "medical freedom of choice" and called for taking away the FDA's power to ban drugs for being ineffective. This was part of a right-wing lobbying campaign to approve an alternative cancer treatment called Laetrile whose benefits were unproven.[12]

The brain trust of the 1976 campaign reassembled at the Reagans' comfortable but far from ostentatious Pacific Palisades home, still outfitted with GE appliances, on December 20, 1977. John Sears was back as the presumptive campaign manager despite growing tension between him and the clique of Californians—Ed Meese, Mike Deaver, Lyn Nofziger, and all the rest—around the former governor. As usual, Reagan never said outright that he was running, but "nobody could mistake Reagan's desire for a last try," reported the well-sourced columnists Rowland Evans and Robert Novak. They quoted one of Reagan's "top political operatives" telling fellow Republicans, "I wouldn't have thought it possible, but, believe me, this guy is running."[13]

Martin Anderson, an economist from the Hoover Institution who had worked on the 1976 Reagan campaign, signed on as chief domestic policy adviser. The post of foreign policy adviser was filled by Richard V. Allen, an international trade consultant who had advised Richard Nixon in 1968 and briefly served on the staff of the National Security Council (NSC) before falling out with Henry Kissinger. The two men assembled a vast network of informal, unpaid advisers with impressive credentials, including former Treasury secretaries George Shultz and William Simon and former defense secretaries James Schlesinger and Donald Rumsfeld, along with a plethora of intellectuals—many of them Democratic defectors known as neoconservatives—such as Jeane J. Kirkpatrick, Fred Iklé, Irving Kristol, and Milton Friedman.

Dick Allen remembered that during his first on-on-one conversation with Reagan at his Pacific Palisades home in January 1977, the former governor said, "Do you mind if I tell you my theory of the Cold War? My theory is that we win, they lose. What do you think about that?"[14] The hawkish foreign policy adviser thought it sounded just fine, but he was careful to keep Reagan from saying something so provocative in public. He knew it would get Reagan branded as a "warmonger" at a time when the consensus within the foreign policy establishment was that the United States had to learn to coexist with the Soviet Union.

For the same reason—a desire to keep from frightening mainstream voters—the campaign was careful to keep out of sight another of Reagan's convictions that was reinforced during a visit on July 31, 1979, to the North American Aerospace Defense Command (NORAD) headquarters inside Cheyenne Mountain, Colorado. Reagan came away disturbed that there was still nothing the United States could do to stop a Soviet nuclear missile attack. He told Martin Anderson on the flight home, "We should have some way of defending ourselves against nuclear missiles," a subject to which he had first been exposed during a 1967 visit to the Lawrence Radiation Laboratory (now the Lawrence Livermore National Laboratory).[15] Anderson subsequently circulated a campaign memorandum calling for the United States to "develop a protective missile system" and for an endorsement of the "vigorous research and development of an effective anti-ballistic missile system"— but not a deployment—that made it into the 1980 Republican platform.

But the candidate never mentioned missile defense during the campaign because his advisers feared, Anderson wrote, that discussing "radical changes in nuclear weapons policy" would leave him "wide open to demagogic attacks from his Democratic opponent."[16] Deploying missile defenses, after all, would have been a violation of the 1972 Anti-Ballistic Missile Treaty and would have been seen by the Soviet Union as an attempt by the United States to gain "first strike" capability, thereby undermining the doctrine of mutual assured destruction that kept an uneasy peace. Nor would it have been helpful for Reagan to publicly express his private concern that "that man in the White House makes me wonder if Armageddon isn't just around the corner."[17] A candidate expecting the end times? That would simply have made a lot of voters wonder about Reagan's mental stability.

The campaign, at John Sears's direction, was determined to avoid any-thing too provocative and to present Reagan as a leader who projected "strength, maturity, decisiveness, resolve, determination and steadiness." Sears was desperate to assuage public concerns, reflected in Dick Wirth-lin's polls, that Reagan was "too simplistic and naïve," "rash," "too ideolog-ical," "inflexible," and "dumb and dangerous," with a "shoot from the hip approach to international affairs." Another campaign document noted that many independents and conservative Democrats viewed Reagan as "a lit-tle 'trigger happy.'" The campaign goal was to "hold the right-wing conser-vatives while broadening the appeal to the moderate and soft Republican vote, Independents, swing voters and soft (disenchanted) Democrats." Dick Allen advised Reagan that he had "to (re)package the consistent positions you have taken" and "soften the delivery of your message" to attract "poten-tial new supporters."

Accordingly, Allen arranged two major foreign trips for the candidate—to Japan, Taiwan, Hong Kong, and Iran in April 1978 and to Britain, France, and Germany in November 1978—to establish "Reagan's credentials as a world leader."[18]

The prime minister of Britain, James Callaghan of the Labour Party, would not see the conservative former governor, pawning him off on his foreign secretary, David Owen. The two men had a half hour of desultory conversa-tion on November 27, 1978, but, Allen recalled, Reagan's appearance was of more interest to the "tea ladies" who served afternoon tea and cakes to the mandarins. One of the women asked, "Mr. Reagan, is it? Mr. Reagan from Hollywood?" He said, "Why, yes." She turned to the other tea ladies and said, "It's him, girls!" Half a dozen excited women in blue smocks instantly converged on the former Hollywood heartthrob to ask him questions about his movie career. Allen was impatient to move on to their next appointment, but Reagan said, "Take it easy, Dick. These are my fans." Reagan was that rare political figure who had fans, not just supporters.[19]

Another of his fans was the leader of the Conservative Party, Marga-ret Thatcher, who would become prime minister the following year. They had already met in 1975, during an earlier Reagan trip to London, and now eagerly renewed their acquaintance over lunch. "I liked her immediately—she was warm, feminine, gracious, and intelligent—and it was evident from our first words that we were soul mates when it came to reducing government and expanding freedom," Reagan later wrote.[20]

After a few, fruitless days in France, whose supercilious leaders snubbed the former governor, the trip concluded with Reagan making his first visit to West Germany. As they were driving along the Autobahn in a Mercedes limousine, Reagan asked Allen about a road sign he had seen: "When are we getting to this place called Ausfahrt?" Revealing the little boy behind his aging exterior, Reagan thought the name was hilarious. Allen had to explain that it simply meant "exit." Reagan spent the rest of the trip asking Allen for other examples of "fart" words in German.[21]

Reagan won an audience on November 30, 1978, with Chancellor Helmut Schmidt, a Social Democrat.[22] "Reagan," Allen acknowledged, "probably wasn't certain of the difference between a Social Democrat and a socialist." He also met the same day with the leader of the Christian Democrats, Helmut Kohl, who would become chancellor in 1982. This was Reagan's first opportunity to see the Berlin Wall, the ugly concrete edifice topped with barbed wire and watchtowers that had divided the city since 1961. Allen remembered Reagan standing next to the wall, his jaw set, saying, "Dick, we've got to find a way to knock this thing down." Allen told me, "His precise words were burned in my memory."[23] But, like winning the Cold War or building missile defenses, knocking down the Berlin Wall was too provocative a position for a serious presidential candidate to espouse in the late 1970s.

When Reagan returned home, his foreign policy speeches concentrated on calling for more defense spending and castigating Carter for allegedly weakening America's defenses while painting an alarming—and exaggerated—picture of Soviet military capabilities. "America cannot afford to be number two," he often said.[24] The Panama Canal Treaties were ratified by the Senate in 1978 with the support of many Republicans, effectively taking that issue off the table. Instead, Reagan concentrated much of his foreign policy fire on SALT II—the Strategic Arms Limitation Talks. This was a treaty to limit the growth of "strategic" (that is, long-range) nuclear weapons that President Carter and Soviet leader Leonid Brezhnev signed in Vienna on June 18, 1979.

Even when Reagan urged the Senate to reject the pact, he did so in a speech that the New York Times described as "moderately worded . . . to reflect efforts by his advisers to make him appear less vehement on issues that arouse high emotions among conservatives." Little did the reporters know that the candidate was privately assuring his supporters "that Ronald Reagan is not moderating his position in any way." Eschewing the "rousing partisanship" of the past, Reagan made clear that while he opposed SALT II, he would support a new treaty that "finally, genuinely reduces the number of strategic nuclear weapons." His theory was that only a US military buildup could induce the Soviets to seriously negotiate arms-control agreements. Few, in those days, could have imagined he would make good on his promise.[25]

When it came to domestic policy, Reagan understandably did not revive the disastrous proposal from his 1976 campaign to devolve many of the federal government's functions to the states—the "$90 billion blunder." Instead, he made the centerpiece of his 1980 campaign support for the Kemp-Roth Act. This legislation—introduced in 1978 by Delaware Senator Bill Roth and Reagan's former intern in Sacramento, Jack Kemp, who had survived the "homosexual scandal" and was now a Republican congressman from Buffalo, New York—called for a one-third cut in personal income-tax rates phased in over three years, with the top marginal rate falling from 70 percent to 50 percent.[26]

The entire Republican Party soon embraced this legislation, with varying degrees of fervor. The passage in 1978 of California's Proposition 13, an initiative cutting property taxes, made clear that a tax revolt was roiling American politics as inflation pushed many taxpayers into higher income brackets. Congress, by bipartisan majorities, cut the maximum rate of capital gains taxes in 1978 from 49 percent to 28 percent, and the Kemp-Roth bill nearly passed too.

Economist Arthur Laffer, author of the famous "curve" claiming that revenue would decline if tax rates were too high, said that Reagan decided to make tax cuts a centerpiece of his 1980 campaign because of Proposition 13's success, despite the reservations of some fiscally conservative Kitchen Cabinet members. "I remember Holmes Tuttle at my house screaming at me," Laffer said. "'How the hell can you cut taxes when you're running a goddamn deficit?'"[27] Embracing the Kemp-Roth bill also ensured that Jack Kemp did not challenge Reagan in the 1980 primaries, as he had contemplated doing.

You did not have to be a "supply-sider" to support tax cuts to stimulate an anemic economy or argue that excessively high tax rates could discourage economic activity. Even British economist John Maynard Keynes, the conservatives' *bête noir*, had anticipated the Laffer curve when he wrote that "taxation may be so high as to defeat its object."[28] But the supply-siders—principally eccentric economists Robert Mundell of Columbia University and Art Laffer of the University of Southern California and perfervid polemicists Jude Wanniski and Robert L. Bartley of the *Wall Street Journal* editorial page—made claims that struck mainstream economists as farfetched. They argued that tax cuts would obviate the need to raise interest rates—and thus the unemployment rate—to get inflation under control; that massive tax cuts would pay for themselves by stimulating the economy and generating more tax revenue; and that the largest tax cuts should go to the wealthiest taxpayers on the theory that their spending and savings would stimulate the entire economy. Critics branded this the "trickle-down" theory.[29] In their more messianic moments, the supply-side evangelists talked as if tax cuts, combined with a gold standard and deregulation, could cure every ill of society from poverty to racism. They spoke of "converting" to the supply-side "faith" as if it were a religion—which for some it was.

Mainstream economists, by contrast, warned that tax cuts, while undoubtedly stimulating the economy, risked exacerbating inflation and budget deficits, and they viewed the gold standard as anachronistic and unworkable. Even academic economists who were conservative tended to write off the supply-siders as "charlatans and cranks," in the words of Harvard's N. Gregory Mankiw, a future adviser to President George W. Bush. Wanniski, an autodidact with no formal economics training, hardly dispelled such concerns when he argued that tax rates were the major driving force behind virtually every historical event or, later, when he championed Louis Farrakhan, Slobodan Milošević, and Saddam Hussein.[30] Wanniski's megalomania was legendary; he wrote that "God had chosen me, of all people, to bring the good news of supply-side economics to mankind, thereby saving the world from perpetual economic decline."[31] Even Art Laffer considered Wanniski "freaky" and a "nut case" (albeit a "brilliant nut case") and acknowledged, "He scared the shit out of me."[32] But supply-side views soon came to dominate the GOP because of their appeal to voters—and to wealthy Republican donors eager for a big tax cut.

REAGAN

Reagan was first introduced to the views of the supply-siders in 1975 when Art Laffer said at a meeting of Reagan's economic advisers, "If you cut taxes, revenues may go up."[33] Laffer was particularly influential with Reagan because he lived in Los Angeles and was a protégé of Kitchen Cabinet member Justin Dart. But Reagan had been a supply-sider *avante la lettre*. Indeed, his aversion to the high tax rates he had been forced to pay as a movie star—with a top rate in 1945 of 94 percent on income over $200,000 ($3.3 million in 2024 dollars)—helped spur his conservative conversion.[34] As far back as the 1950s, he had claimed (falsely) that graduated income taxes were invented by Karl Marx and argued that "confiscatory" tax rates led to unemployment in the motion-picture business and caused "a loss of tax revenue to the Government."[35] He never seemed to notice that the economy had rapidly recovered from the Great Depression during World War II when personal income-tax rates and federal spending as a percentage of GDP were higher than they had ever been before or since, suggesting that high taxes were not necessarily an impediment to economic growth.[36]

Yet Reagan never became a consistent supply-sider and hardly ever used the term. His team of economic advisers included many conventional economists, such as Alan Greenspan, a former chairman of Ford's Council of Economic Advisers, who wanted to focus on cutting spending rather than taxes. His future budget director, David Stockman, a young, fervent convert to this new economic creed, complained that Reagan "had only the foggiest idea of what supply side was all about."[37] Unlike some of the supply-siders, Reagan had always worried about budget deficits. In 1959, he had said, "We must end deficit spending and reduce the fodder upon which government has fed and grown beyond the consent of the governed," and he continued to hold that view until the end.[38]

Reagan's platform, a product of disparate influences, came to include not only a massive cut in personal income taxes but also a massive increase in defense spending and a pledge to balance the budget by 1983. How could he possibly do all three at once? It wasn't by promising to eviscerate social spending. He was astute enough not to attack popular programs such as Social Security, Medicare, veterans' benefits, or farm subsidies, as he had done so often in the past. Indeed, in laying out his economic agenda in Chicago on September 9, 1980, two months before the election, he vowed to protect "the integrity of the Social Security system," thereby distancing himself from his call in the 1964 "Time for Choosing" speech to make the program voluntary. He made it sound as if the federal budget could be balanced painlessly simply by eliminating "waste, extravagance, abuse and outright fraud" while waiting for an economic boom, stimulated by his cuts in taxes and regulations, to shower the Treasury with newfound revenues.[39]

Reagan's more sober-minded economic advisers indignantly denied that they expected tax cuts to pay for themselves; the campaign, Marty Anderson wrote, "conservatively estimated that only a little over 17 percent of the tax cut would be recovered over the five-year period." (The actual figure would turn out to be a third.)[40] But nobody bothered to tell the candidate—or, more likely, they did tell him and it didn't register. Reagan continued to insist that tax cuts would pay for themselves immediately with the encouragement of ardent supply-siders. Republican Senator Howard Baker of Tennessee said that Reagan was "absolutely mesmerized by the idea."[41]

Indeed, Reagan's very first endorsement of a 30 percent personal income-tax cut in a 1976 radio broadcast included the claim that "history shows that government would increase its revenues, thus reducing the deficit" by cutting taxes.[42] In 1980, he said that every time personal tax rates were cut, "there was such an increase in prosperity that the government, even in the first year, got *increased* revenues, not less."[43] He would keep repeating this false claim for his whole presidency; in 1985, for example, he told incredulous members of Congress during a White House meeting, "You cannot show me a single time in history when a major tax cut did not result in greater revenues."[44]

Showing that he was no systematic thinker, however, Reagan also argued that tax cuts would force spending cuts—the "starve the beast" theory popular among conservative intellectuals—without acknowledging that this could happen only if the tax cuts *reduced* revenues.[45] Reagan wanted to cut high taxes, which he viewed as immoral and counterproductive. His justifications varied.

As evidence that tax cuts would increase revenues, Reagan cited the tax cuts proposed by John F. Kennedy, whom he had once reviled as a closet Marxist. He kept insisting that Kennedy had cut personal taxes by 27 percent and that this had stimulated the economy and paid for itself. In fact, the Kennedy tax plan—enacted after his death by Lyndon Johnson in 1964—cut individual income taxes by only 18 percent and, unlike Reagan's plan, it was highly progressive; the top income-tax rate, while reduced from 90 percent, remained at 70 percent. The nonpartisan Congressional Budget Office (CBO) found that the immediate impact of LBJ's tax cut was a $12 billion *reduction* in tax revenue. After a couple of years, the CBO estimated, the government recovered between $3 billion and $9 billion of this lost revenue, but most of the resurgence in revenue "was due to economic growth that would have taken place even without the tax cut."[46]

Such sober analysis helped explain why many of Reagan's Republican rivals in 1980 mocked what came to be known as Reaganomics. "The only way Reagan is going to cut taxes, increase defense spending, and balance the budget at the same time is to use blue smoke and mirrors," scoffed Congressman John Anderson of Illinois, while former CIA director George H. W. Bush called Reagan's plan "voodoo economics."[47] They were right. Indeed, the only way the Reagan campaign could make its hastily assembled budget blueprint add up was by relying on outlandishly optimistic economic growth projections.

But it turned out that most voters did not care all that much about budget deficits. They wanted both tax cuts *and* spending increases. Jude Wanniski was onto something, politically if not economically, when he argued that both parties needed to play Santa Claus: "The Democrats, the party of income redistribution, are best suited for the role of Spending Santa Claus. The Republicans, traditionally the party of income growth, should be the Santa Claus of Tax Reduction."[48]

By embracing the supply-side gospel, Reagan metamorphosed into Santa Claus—rather than, as Republicans had been in the past, Scrooge. And who doesn't love Santa Claus?

31

Sears Agonistes

Well, you sons of bitches, the best guy we had just left.
—RONALD REAGAN

E ven before the Iran hostage crisis or the Soviet invasion of Afghanistan, Jimmy Carter's litany of woes drew a long line of eager Republican challengers, visions of the Oval Office dancing in their heads. They included not only John Anderson and George H. W. Bush but also former Texas Governor John Connally, Senator Bob Dole, Senate Minority Leader Howard Baker, and Congressman Phil Crane of Illinois. But the candidate who, according to the polls, might have been the most formidable contender—former President Gerald Ford—chose not to enter the race.

That left the 1976 runner-up as the clear favorite for the nomination. A poll in July 1979, a year before the convention, found that Ronald Reagan had the support of 37 percent of Republican voters, Connally was second with 15 percent, and Baker third with 13 percent.[1] The Carter campaign was delighted by this turn of events; his political advisers believed Reagan was the "weakest candidate" in the GOP field. As Carter later wrote, "It seemed inconceivable that he would be acceptable as President when his positions"—for example, "an enormous tax cut for the rich" and "slashes in . . . programs for the poor and aged"—"were clearly exposed to the public."[2] Once again, as in 1966 and 1976, Reagan benefited from being underestimated by his adversaries.

Following the same plan as four years earlier, Reagan announced the formation of an "exploratory" committee on March 7, 1979—little more than a month after the Ayatollah Khomeini had returned to Iran from exile to take charge of its Islamic revolution and just a few weeks before the most serious nuclear accident in US history, at Three Mile Island in Pennsylvania—to allow him to continue making money while campaigning. (The *Wall Street Journal* reported that he was earning $45,000 a month.)[3] The presidential campaign was formally announced on November 13, 1979, in New York City, a week after American hostages had been seized in Tehran and a few weeks before the Soviet invasion of Afghanistan. Unlike Reagan's 1976 announcement, when only Nancy joined him in Washington, this time all four of the Reagan children were present. Even Patti showed up, although, as she later wrote, "I disagreed with my father's politics" and "I did not want him to be president."[4] The East Coast location was chosen to signal that Reagan was not a flaky, Left Coast candidate and to tap into the fundraising largesse of Wall Street. Campaign chairman Paul D. Laxalt wanted everyone to understand, "You're not talking about a right-wing nut with horns growing out of his ears. You're talking about a responsible conservative."[5]

Reagan employed his favorite FDR phrase—"you and I have a rendezvous with destiny"—three times in a thirty-minute speech as part of his attempt to appeal to disenchanted Democrats. In keeping with his characteristic distaste for personal attacks, he did not mention Carter by name but blamed "leaders in our government" for a "crisis of confidence" and vowed to restore America's luster as a "shining city on a hill." This was another of his favorite quotations—from Puritan leader John Winthrop in 1630. The headline proposal was hardly right-wing red meat: He called for a "North American Accord" to allow "people and commerce" to "flow more freely" across the borders between the United States, Canada, and Mexico. This idea would eventually blossom into the North American Free Trade Agreement, which a future Republican president—Donald Trump—would denounce as the "worst trade deal ever." Even in 1979, the conservative newspaper *Human Events* was not impressed; it wrote that the "foreign policy portion of the Reagan speech had a rather pathetic quality to it."[6]

But Reagan had long ago won over the right; now he needed to appeal to the center. He knew he could win if he could "convince people I'm not some combination of Ebenezer Scrooge and the Mad Bomber." Sears saw the North American Accord as a way to demonstrate the candidate's "statesmanship," but the proposal was so anodyne it would soon fade out of the stump speech.[7]

One of the biggest issues that John Sears had worried about—Reagan's age—was easily dispelled with a few wisecracks because the candidate looked so trim and vigorous. On the eve of Reagan's announcement, a *Washington Post* reporter noted, "The face is outdoorsy, ruddy, like an apple just shined. Up close, you see the lines and creases and crow's feet: leather finely cracked, like a saddle or the seat of an old Jaguar. These lines seem indigenous; they don't detract." His hair was still thick and dark, as it would remain for the rest of his life. (Reagan always denied using hair dye, but tabloid biographer Kitty Kelley claimed that Nancy's hairdresser, Julius Bengtsson, had been secretly dying his gray roots since 1968.) Reagan's remarkable communication ability was certainly unimpaired by the passage of years; as the *Post* noted, he was a "natural on the speaking platform," his voice "a sibilant whisper, breathy, talking just to YOU."[8]

Yet, at Nancy's urging, the campaign was careful not to exhaust the retirement-age candidate. He campaigned just fifteen to eighteen days a month and received three days' rest after every four- to five-day campaign swing. Traveling west to east particularly took it out of him. "He's not so good in the second meeting," admitted press secretary Jim Lake.[9]

Sears was running, as Lyn Nofziger noted, "a Rose Garden strategy without a Rose Garden." He wanted Reagan to look presidential and stay above the fray.[10] The front-runner did not take part in a January 19, 1980, Republican debate in Iowa. He disingenuously defended his absence on the grounds that he wanted to avoid "friction within the party."[11] In truth, the last time he had debated a campaign opponent was the 1966 Black Republican primary forum in Santa Monica that had ended in a mortifying meltdown after Reagan heatedly denied he was a racist and stormed out. Sears was nervous that Reagan would go off script and commit a costly gaffe, so he chose to keep the candidate in controlled settings, giving the same old speech decrying big government. The California crowd complained that Sears had contempt for the candidate and wasn't letting "Reagan be Reagan." The campaign manager did not exactly dispel such doubts when he compared Reagan to a "champion thoroughbred" and said, "I'm not going to take this beautiful horse out of the stable and risk breaking his leg."[12]

There were, however, dangers to staying in the stable, as the Reagan campaign discovered on January 21, 1980. That was the date of the Iowa caucus, and the results were shocking. George H. W. Bush, the Connecticut preppy turned Texas oilman, pulled off an improbable come-from-behind win after practically moving to the state where young "Dutch" Reagan had first made a name for himself as a radio broadcaster. Bush got 32 percent of the vote to Reagan's 30 percent. He came out of Iowa boasting of his momentum—"the

Big Mo"—and shot up to near-parity with Reagan in nationwide polls. If Reagan lost on February 26 in New Hampshire, he would be finished, written off as another early favorite who just didn't connect with voters. Yet Bush suddenly had a six-point lead in New Hampshire.

The Iowa defeat brought to a head growing dissatisfaction in the Reagan campaign with John Sears. Marty Anderson complained that Sears—a "somewhat shy, brilliant man with a self-mocking sense of humor"—had developed "a touch of what one might call megalomania" and that he had "suddenly turned into a secretive stranger who bristled at the slightest opposition to any of his ideas."[13] Ed Meese groused to me that "John thought he was smarter than Ronald Reagan" and was trying to transform Reagan into a "more middle-of-the-road" candidate.[14]

Coming into conflict with the Californians surrounding Reagan, Sears began to purge them one by one. Lyn Nofziger was the first to go. Sears gave him a job—fundraising—for which he was poorly suited. When Nofziger predictably failed, he was forced out of the campaign in August 1979. Next, Sears decided, "Deaver's got to go."[15] On November 26, 1979, a few days after Thanksgiving, Deaver was summoned to the Reagans' Pacific Palisades house. As he walked in, he saw that Sears and his top lieutenants, Charlie Black and Jim Lake, were already present. He was asked by Nancy Reagan to wait in a bedroom, but after about twenty minutes he got impatient and walked into the living room, demanding, "What's going on?"

"Mike," Reagan explained, "the fellows here have been telling me about the way you're running the fund-raising efforts, and we're losing money. As a matter of fact, they tell me I have to pay thirty thousand dollars a month to lease my space in your office building." In fact, the campaign was in dire financial shape mainly because of Sears's big spending, but Deaver did not try to defend himself. "If these gentlemen have convinced you that I am ripping you off, after all these years, then I'm out," he said. "I'm leaving." Reagan protested that wasn't what he wanted, but Deaver walked out, feeling "hurt," "crushed," and "stabbed in the back." In frustration, Reagan snapped, "Well, you sons of bitches, the best guy we had just left."[16]

Marty Anderson also resigned in disgust, returning to the Hoover Institution, after Sears set up a costly new policy apparatus in Washington to make Reagan sound more centrist. That left Ed Meese as the only

Sacramento hand left in the campaign—and before long Sears was scheming to remove him, too. Ed Meese later likened the purge to "an Agatha Christie mystery: the original Reaganites kept disappearing."[17] Yet Reagan still denied with a straight face "that a power struggle was going on" or that Nofziger, Deaver, and Anderson had left "because of Sears' pressure."[18] In reality, the campaign was wracked by divisions that would prefigure the staff turmoil of the Reagan White House.

Many years later, Sears told me that forcing out Deaver—the aide closest to Nancy Reagan—was a fatal error. "She didn't have her eyes and ears out there anymore," he said.[19] In truth, an even bigger mistake was Sears's failure to cultivate the candidate and his wife, as Deaver had done so assiduously. The irony is that Reagan and Sears had somewhat similar personalities. Both men—one the son of an alcoholic, the other a closet alcoholic himself—were aloof and distant. Nancy Reagan's description of Sears—"he was inscrutable and rarely showed emotion"—applied equally well to her husband. But Reagan was much better than Sears about hiding his shyness behind a mask of bonhomie. Ronnie complained to Nancy about his campaign manager: "John doesn't look you in the eye," he said. "He looks you in the tie."

"The chemistry between the two of them wasn't good to begin with," Nancy declared, and after the Deaver firing, it got even "worse."[20]

With the campaign's front-runner status in doubt, Reagan undertook in New Hampshire the kind of intensive, retail campaigning he had not done in Iowa. There was no longer any question of avoiding debates. Reagan acquitted himself admirably in a forum with the six other candidates in Manchester on February 20, 1980. The voters surveyed by Dick Wirthlin picked Reagan as the clear winner, allowing him to pull nearly even with Bush.[21]

The second and final debate was to take place at Nashua High School on February 23, the Saturday before the primary. Initially Sears had been eager to have Reagan debate Bush one-on-one, confident he would outshine a lackluster opponent. The Bush campaign was happy to cooperate to separate their candidate from the pack. The *Nashua Telegraph* agreed to sponsor the debate, but Bob Dole complained to the Federal Election Commission that this would constitute an illegal campaign contribution to Reagan and

Bush. Sears offered to split the costs with the Bush campaign, but they refused to ante up, so he picked up the entire tab.

But then Sears changed his mind about the two-man debate. The campaign's internal polls were now showing Reagan with newfound momentum after the Manchester debate, and Sears didn't want to jeopardize it. "A two-man debate gives us a fifty-fifty chance of losing or winning," he told press secretary Jim Lake. "If we have a six-man debate, we've got only a one in six chance of blowing it."

With Reagan's blessing—he had thought all along it was unfair to exclude the other candidates—Sears and Lake called the also-rans and invited them to Nashua. All except Connally showed up. The Bush campaign had no idea what was happening until they got to the high school and found that Howard Baker, Bob Dole, John Anderson, and Phil Crane were also there. Yet Bush's campaign manager, James A. Baker III, insisted on sticking with the agreed-on format, and so did the *Nashua Telegram*'s editor, Jon Breen, who was moderating the debate. In the classroom where all the candidates but Bush were milling around before the debate, there was uncertainty about what to do. Nancy Reagan settled the issued by saying, "You should *all* go on out." And so they did.

Reagan marched into the gymnasium tailed by the five other candidates, "like little boys following their scout leader," and began to make the case for including them. Exasperated by this deviation from the rules, Breen ordered the sound man to turn off Reagan's microphone, not realizing that the technician was in the employ of the Reagan campaign. The sound remained on. Reagan flushed and said indignantly, "I am paying for this microphone, Mr. Green!" The audience of 2,400 erupted in cheers while Bush sat frozen in his seat, not knowing what to do. In that dramatic moment, the campaign had essentially ended.

Reagan may have mangled the editor's name, and he may have been citing a line delivered by Spencer Tracy in Frank Capra's 1948 film *The State of the Union*—about a tycoon's quest for the Republican presidential nomination—but he showed that he was quick on his feet and forceful in a crisis. By contrast, Bush, by his own admission, looked "terrible." "What can I say?" one of his advisers acknowledged. "He choked up." Bush later explained his failure by saying that he had been taught from childhood to "play by the rules." John Sears had essentially ended his candidacy by changing the rules in the middle of the game.

Jim Baker's premonition while watching his candidate onstage—"I thought we were in deep shit," he told me—was borne out. Film of Reagan grabbing the microphone was played nonstop on television during the next forty-eight hours as his lead in the polls soared from seven or eight points to twenty-seven points. Bush's complaints that he had been "sandbagged" only made him sound whiny. Reagan won New Hampshire with 51 percent to just 22 percent for Bush. The primary campaign was all but over. With his clever gambit in Nashua, John Sears had helped put Reagan on the path to the presidency. But for the mercurial campaign manager, the journey was to end in the Granite State.[22]

Ronald and Nancy Reagan were determined to oust Sears; as early as the beginning of February, the candidate had been "joking" with reporters about needing a new campaign manager.[23] They decided to make the switch on the afternoon of the New Hampshire primary, February 26, 1980, so that Sears's departure would not look like a reaction to the election outcome. Nancy had already summoned William J. Casey—a gruff New York corporate lawyer, Republican fundraiser, and former chairman of the Securities and Exchange Commission with droopy jowls, owlish glasses, and an incomprehensible mumble—to conduct a "management audit" of the campaign in January 1980. "Ronald Reagan hasn't got a campaign organization," Casey told the Kitchen Cabinet. "He's got a civil war." He now agreed to take over from Sears and try to instill some management rigor despite his lack of political experience or a relationship with the candidate, whom he had first met in 1979. When he was offered the job, Casey called his friend Paul Laxalt to ask what the Reagans were like. "Nancy is the strong one," Laxalt explained. "Ron will take direction."[24]

At 2:30 p.m. on February 26, 1980, while the polls were still open, John Sears, Jim Lake, and Charlie Black were summoned to the Reagans' suite at the Manchester Holiday Inn. With Nancy Reagan, Bill Casey, and other staff members looking on, the candidate handed Sears a one-page press release announcing that the three of them were resigning to return to private life. "We had seen it coming enough that we weren't surprised or depressed," said Charlie Black.[25] Both Black and Lake would work with Reagan again. Sears never would.

This was an exceedingly rare event in Reagan's life—one of the few times he ever fired anyone. Having lived through the Great Depression, he had "a traumatic feeling about unemployment."[26] But he seldom hired anyone either; Charlie Black remembered that the only person Reagan ever asked him to be put on the payroll was an eighteen-year-old pen pal from suburban Philadelphia who went to work on the 1980 campaign.[27]

Reagan's peculiar management style was a product of his childhood aversion to conflict. As Marty Anderson described it, "He made no demands, and gave almost no instructions. . . . He made decisions like an ancient king or a Turkish pasha, passively letting his subjects serve him, selecting only those morsels of public policy that were especially tasty. Rarely did he ask searching questions and demand to know someone had or had not done something."[28] For Reagan to confront Sears in person was an indicator of how much the campaign manager had gotten under his skin.

Years later, Canadian Prime Minister Brian Mulroney told me that he asked his good-natured friend Ron Reagan whether he had any enemies—whether he hated anyone after all those years in politics. Reagan couldn't think of anyone at first. "Well, if you push me," he continued, "I was mad as hell at one guy one time because I thought he let down the troops. Does the name John Sears mean anything to you?"[29]

With Sears gone, the Californians—Marty Anderson, Mike Deaver, Lyn Nofziger—came back into the fold, and Ed Meese became campaign chief of staff. While Casey cut the payroll and returned the campaign to solvency, Meese, Nofziger, Deaver, and Wirthlin jointly managed campaign strategy. It was an unwieldy arrangement, but, with Reagan far ahead of the primary field, it did not matter at first. George Bush kept battling, arguing that Reagan was too right-wing to defeat Carter, and he won a few primaries, notably in Massachusetts, Pennsylvania, and Michigan, but by the end of May he pulled out and endorsed Reagan.

Republicans assembled for their convention at Joe Louis Arena in the heavily Black city of Detroit on July 14, 1980, with the presumptive nominee dodging uncomfortable questions about whether he had any senior Black staffers. (He did not.)[30] The only suspense concerned who would be his running mate. Bush was the obvious choice: As a moderate with ample Washington experience, he would balance out the conservative newcomer from California. But Reagan was rankled by Bush's description of his economic agenda as "voodoo economics," and he thought that Bush's pro-choice views on abortion were unacceptable. Moreover, even though Bush nearly died piloting a torpedo bomber during World War II while Reagan was making movies at Fort Wacky, Reagan thought that Bush was a bit of a wimp: He lacked "spunk" and "just melts under pressure," the governor complained to associates.

Dick Wirthlin's polls suggested that, besides Bush, the person who would help the ticket the most was Jerry Ford. Reagan and Ford had reconciled—in Detroit, Reagan even gave his former foe a Native American peace pipe—and aides to the two men spent several days negotiating over the terms of an unwieldy and unprecedented power-sharing arrangement. Ford wanted Henry Kissinger as secretary of state and Alan Greenspan as secretary of the Treasury. Although Reagan aides later denied it, a deal was close to being concluded, and it would have been welcomed by many moderate Republicans who lacked faith in Reagan's ability to govern.

With rumors rife that a "dream ticket" was in the offing, CBS News anchor Walter Cronkite interviewed Ford at Joe Louis Arena on the night of Wednesday, July 16. Ford insisted he would not be a "figurehead vice president," and when Cronkite said, "It's got to be something like a co-presidency," Ford did not disagree. Watching on television in his suite on the sixty-ninth floor of the Detroit Plaza Hotel, the Republican nominee could not believe what he was hearing. "Did you hear what he just said about a co-presidency?" Reagan said incredulously. Deaver said Reagan "almost choked on whatever he was eating." Other aides recalled Reagan was "aghast" and "perturbed."

It was dawning even on Ford that a co-presidency would not be feasible. He came to Reagan's suite at 11:30 p.m. to tell the nominee, "This isn't going to work." As soon as Ford left, Reagan asked his assembled aides, "Well, what do we do now?" Dick Allen replied, "We call Bush."

By now, Bush had resigned himself to being passed over in favor of Ford. After giving his own convention speech, he was relaxing with his wife and kids in his Pontchartrain Hotel suite, wearing khakis and a tennis shirt, beer in hand. At 11:37 p.m., the telephone rang. Jim Baker answered. "Is Ambassador Bush there?" a voice asked. "Who's calling?" Baker asked. "Governor Reagan," the caller said. Bush assumed that this was just a perfunctory call to let him know Ford had been selected. But after a minute on the telephone, Bush flashed his crooked grin and raised his thumb to his family. "Well, yes, sir," they could hear him saying, "I think you can say I support the platform—wholeheartedly!"[31]

The Reagan-Bush ticket was set.

———————

The next night, Thursday, July 17, Reagan gave his acceptance speech with, in one reporter's words, "ease and polish." He delivered his standard, slightly self-contradictory complaints that the government was too weak abroad and too strong at home. "For those who have abandoned hope," he vowed, "we'll restore hope, and we'll welcome them into a great national crusade to make America great again," reiterating his campaign slogan.

The speech ended with a quotation from Franklin D. Roosevelt's 1932 Democratic convention acceptance address complaining that government "costs too much." This was part of Reagan's continuing attempt to rewrite history to suggest that it was Democrats who had changed ideologically—not him. The New York Times editorial board praised this as an "audacious, even brilliant" gambit to remind listeners that he had once been a Democrat and to signal that he was not "content to be the darling of narrow ideology."[32]

And yet within weeks of the convention he was back to appealing to narrow ideology.

32

What It Took

I believe in states' rights.

—RONALD REAGAN

While Republicans came out of their convention united and optimistic about their chances of reclaiming the White House—"The G.O.P. Gets Its Act Together," the *New York Times* pronounced[1]—Democrats were again proving the validity of Will Rogers's old quip, "I'm not a member of any organized political party. I'm a Democrat." Indeed, on the very day that Republicans convened in Detroit, the president's grasping younger brother, Billy Carter, responded to a threat of legal action from the Justice Department by registering as a lobbyist for Libyan dictator Moammar Qaddafi, forcing the president to issue a statement denouncing his own sibling.[2]

The follies continued during the Democratic convention at Madison Square Garden in New York City from August 11 to 14. The president's teleprompter malfunctioned during his acceptance speech, leading him into some strange ad-libs (he referred to the late Hubert Humphrey as "Hubert Horatio Hornblower"), and a balloon drop at the end dribbled out in a symbolic failure, with only a few balloons floating to the floor. More significantly, efforts at reconciliation between Carter and his defeated rival, Senator Ted Kennedy, went haywire. Kennedy delivered a barnburner of an oration—vowing that "the work goes on, the cause endures, the hope still lives, and the dream shall never die"—that hardly sounded like a concession speech. Then he failed to join with Carter in the expected gesture of raising and clasping their hands together in unity. "The optics on television were emasculating for Carter," noted his biographer, Kai Bird.[3]

Still, for all the Democrats' blunders, the race tightened up considerably after the conventions as voters continued to harbor doubts about a former actor's suitability for the nation's highest office. An Associated Press–NBC News poll in mid-August showed that Carter had cut Reagan's lead from twenty-five points to only seven. A Gallup poll found that Carter was even closer—only a point behind Reagan in a three-way race with independent candidate John Anderson, a white-haired, middle-of-the-road Republican.[4] The Reagan campaign could hardly afford to relax in the three months remaining before the judgment of the voters was rendered on November 4, 1980. Those months, they knew, could determine the country's direction for decades to come—and, given the power of the American president in those tense Cold War days, even the fate of the entire world.

In *What It Takes: The Way to the White House*, a classic account of a later presidential race—the one in 1988—Richard Ben Cramer wrote that in order to win a candidate had to show that "here was a guy who'd do what it took." "The system," he explained, "demanded totality." For all its manifest flaws—"it was spendthrift, exhausting, hurtful, and it savaged its protagonists"—it was "a stress test that was a match for the job." A winning candidate had to understand "what the forest-gods demanded, what the people wanted in a chief: his enemies felled and bleeding, drawn limb from limb and thrown to earth for the people to dance, in blood-roar. America defiles its losers."[5]

In the 1980 general election, Ronald Reagan was willing to do what it took to win. Despite his nice-guy image, the Gipper hated to lose. Many of his aides, from Bill Casey to Roger Stone, were even more ruthless. The 1980 Reagan-Bush campaign would be dogged by controversy involving a stolen debate book, an alleged payoff to ensure a victory in New York State, a reputed conspiracy to delay the release of American hostages from Iran—and appeals to bigoted voters who had very different ideas about civil rights than Jack Reagan had taught to little Dutch in the early twentieth-century Midwest, when *The Birth of a Nation* was playing at the picture show and the Ku Klux Klan was marching in their white finery through Dixon.

Ronald Reagan's first postconvention campaign stop in 1980 was at the Neshoba County Fair in Philadelphia, Mississippi—a decision that would come to haunt his historical reputation. The fairgrounds, long a forum for white supremacist rabble-rousers such as Mississippi governors Theodore

Bilbo and Ross Barnett (who, as noted earlier, had once given actor Ronald Reagan a certificate of appreciation), were located only a few miles from the spot where, in 1964, civil rights workers James Chaney, Michael Schwerner, and Andrew Goodman had been murdered and buried in an earthen dam by Ku Klux Klan members whose ranks included the local sheriff.

Reagan went to Neshoba County, near the center of Mississippi, at the request of his state cochair, Representative Trent Lott, who got around resistance from Reagan's national campaign staff by personally asking the candidate to come. "I'd waged a stirring battle to bring the candidate to this century-old event," Lott later boasted. A former University of Mississippi cheerleader and future Senate majority leader with a "well-lacquered helmet of hair," Lott was eager to woo Southern whites away from Jimmy Carter and over to the Republican fold. According to state party officials, he insisted that the way to do it was for Reagan to come to Mississippi and utter a two-word incantation: *states' rights*. This was the slogan that Southern segregationists had been using to resist federal civil rights efforts for decades. (In an interview for this book, Lott denied that he had told Reagan to use "states' rights" and insisted, implausibly, that he had no idea that it was such a "loaded phrase.")

When the campaign pollster Dick Wirthlin heard that Reagan was planning to start his general election campaign in Neshoba, he was aghast, fearing this was a misstep that would produce terrible headlines. Although he had made appealing "to the White Southern Protestants and the populist voters in the South" a key campaign objective, Wirthlin tried to talk Reagan out of the trip because he was also eager, as one of his strategy documents said, to convince "white suburbanite ticket-splitters" that Reagan was no racist. His objections were seconded by regional political director Ken Klinge, who urged the campaign to "cancel Neshoba" because it was not "acceptable politically." According to Lyn Nofziger, even "Nancy was mad as hell about that. She didn't think we should go there."

Those objections ran into the buzzsaw of the candidate's stubbornness. Reagan could show surprising flexibility on issues such as taxes, but he hated to go back on a promise to an individual. Now he insisted on going to Mississippi because he had given his word to Trent Lott, who in 2002 would resign as Senate majority leader after praising Strom Thurmond's 1948 segregationist campaign for president. "Dick," Reagan said to Richard

Wirthlin, "one thing I've learned as an actor was that once the billing is set, you don't pull out." When Wirthlin kept pressing his case, Reagan lost his temper, shouting, "I'm giving this speech!" and throwing the pages of his speech into the air in frustration.

On Sunday, August 3, 1980, Ron and Nancy flew from Los Angeles to the Magnolia State on a chartered jet and then traveled by motorcade to the fairgrounds, whose attractions included livestock shows, concession stands selling cotton candy and fried pickles, country music acts, pie-eating contests, and the only legal horseracing track in the state. They were greeted at the capacious grandstand by more than ten thousand fans sweltering under the brutal Southern summer sun. A band played "Dixie" and supporters chanted "We want Reagan!" While Neshoba County was one-third Black, the fairgoers were almost exclusively white. Even decades later, no African Americans owned any of the 350 cabins, many decorated with Confederate flags, where well-heeled visitors stayed for a week of revelry fueled by gallons of beer and whiskey, lemonade and iced tea, during "Mississippi's giant house party." A Black resident of Philadelphia said a decade after the Reagans' visit, "My father told me, 'The Neshoba County Fair is no place for black folks.'"

After telling the good folks how glad he was to be there ("Nancy and I have never seen anything like this, because there isn't anything like this any place on earth"), Reagan moved on to his standard attacks on the incumbent ("People have been telling me that Jimmy Carter has been doing his best—and that's our problem"), before delivering what historian Rick Perlstein called "the payload." "I believe in states' rights," Reagan said. "I believe in people doing as much as they can for themselves at the community level and at the private level. And I believe that we've distorted the balance of our government today by giving powers that were never intended in the Constitution to that federal establishment." Almost as significant as what he said was what he did not say: There was not a word about civil rights.

The cheering audience got the message. *He was one of them.* Jimmy Carter, in spite of being from the South, clearly was not. Why, his IRS was trying to take away a tax deduction from South Carolina's Bob Jones University just because it prohibited interracial dating—a decision that the Reagan Justice Department would try to reverse. After Reagan won, John Bell Williams, a segregationist former congressman and governor of Mississippi, declared, "I'm happy to say we have a president now who talks our language."[6]

A few days after Reagan's speech, Carter's former United Nations ambassador, Andrew Young, a friend of the late Martin Luther King Jr., recalled his own experiences with violent "nightriders" in Neshoba County and wrote in the *Washington Post* that he found Reagan's words "chilling": "One must ask: Is Reagan saying that he intends to do everything he can to turn the clock back to the Mississippi justice of 1964? Do the powers of the state and local governments include the right to end the voting rights of black citizens?"[7]

Notwithstanding Young's angry, anguished article, the backlash that Wirthlin had feared never truly materialized. Speaking on September 16, 1980, at the Ebenezer Baptist Church in Atlanta, Carter said, "You've seen in this campaign the stirring of hate. And the rebirth of code words like 'states' rights' in a speech in Mississippi.... Hatred has no place in this country! Racism has no place in this country!"[8]

The Black congregation cheered the president on, but the overwhelmingly white national press corps jeered. "With Reagan, this was something that simply would not play," tut-tutted Jack Germond and Jules Witcover, the prominent liberal columnists who both shaped and reflected the conventional wisdom. "The Republican candidate might have been vulnerable to accusations of naivete, ideological rigidity, or intellectual sloth, but there was no evidence he was a racist."[9]

Their whitewash, of course, ignored the way that, ever since Reagan's first campaign in 1966, he had repeatedly used code words such as "jungle paths" and "welfare queens" while consistently denouncing civil rights legislation. In 1980, Reagan added loaded new terms to his lexicon—not only "states' rights" but also "The War Between the States," the preferred term for the Civil War among partisans of the Lost Cause, which he used in the South.[10] He told a reporter in 1980 that the Voting Rights Act had been "humiliating to the South."[11] Reagan likely would never have won public office in the first place if he had not opposed civil rights legislation such as the Rumford Fair Housing Act in California. It was no coincidence that his 1976 campaign— and therefore his subsequent political career—had been saved by the old segregationist, Senator Jesse Helms of North Carolina. Whatever Reagan's private views, his public record was one of courting white backlash voters even while avoiding explicitly racist language.

That reality was not changed by Reagan's willingness to meet with civil rights leaders Reverend Jesse Jackson and Vernon Jordan, to address the National Urban League, and to visit the South Bronx—all of which he did in August 1980 immediately after his appearance at the Neshoba County Fair. Jesse Jackson told Reagan during a contentious meeting in Chicago that the phrase "states' rights" was "seen by blacks as localized oppression."[12]

Instead of savaging Reagan, however, the press corps went after *Carter*, arguing that his accusations showed that the president had a "mean streak" that was at odds with his goody-goody image. "Do you think that Governor Reagan is running a campaign of hatred and racism?" demanded a journalist at a White House press conference. "And how do you answer allegations that you are running a mean campaign?" Carter realized that his accusations were backfiring and tried to backtrack. "I do not think he is running a campaign of racism or hatred," he insisted, unconvincingly. "And I think my campaign is very moderate in its tone."[13]

The "meanness" issue would dog Carter throughout the fall. During one interview, Barbara Walters told him, "Mr. President, in recent days you have been characterized as mean, vindictive, hysterical, and on the point of desperation."[14] What do you—what can you—say to that? As Carter biographer Jonathan Alter noted, Carter was a "Velcro politician, while Reagan was usually coated with Teflon."[15]

While the national news media preemptively absolved Reagan of racism, one of his campaign operatives later told a more nuanced story.

Lee Atwater was a product of Strom Thurmond's South Carolina political machine. He worked on the 1980 Reagan campaign running operations in South Carolina, and then went to work in the Reagan White House. He became deputy campaign manager of Reagan's 1984 campaign, campaign manager for George H. W. Bush in 1988, and then chair of the Republican National Committee before dying of brain cancer at age forty in 1991. Speaking anonymously to a political scientist in 1981, Atwater insisted that the 1980 Reagan campaign "was devoid of any kind of racism," but his description of the "coded racism" of the Southern strategy was awfully familiar to anyone who studied the 1980 election:

You start out in 1954 by saying, "N——, n——, n——." By 1968 you can't say "n——"–that hurts you, backfires. So you say stuff like, uh, forced busing, states' rights, and all that stuff, and you're getting so abstract. Now, you're talking about cutting taxes, and all these things you're talking about are totally economic things and a byproduct of them is, blacks get hurt worse than whites. . . . "We want to cut this," is much more abstract than even the busing thing, uh, and a hell of a lot more abstract than "n——, n——."[16]

Reagan, of course, was not as crude or cynical as Lee Atwater. He never, as far as we know, used the "n-word" even in the 1950s. He was, however, as noted earlier, caught on a White House tape-recording in 1971 referring to African diplomats as "monkeys," and it's doubtful that was the only time he ever used such epithets. Reagan often cited his antiracist bona fides as the son of Jack Reagan and recalled how, during his undergraduate years, he took two Black football teammates to sleep at his house. But he also said that growing up he never knew there was a racial problem in America, implying that the whole issue had been exacerbated or possibly created by civil rights activists.

"Frankly, I don't believe Reagan ever fully understood the multilayered nuances of the 'image politics' that surround race in America," Dick Wirthlin wrote, while Trent Lott insisted that in using "states' rights" Reagan wasn't referring to civil rights battles at all: "As a former governor, he felt under the Constitution that states have certain delegated authorities."[17] That was a whitewash.

True to his reputation for blunt candor, Stu Spencer acknowledged, "Race played a role in every election, and there were words and events that delivered the message without saying it. 'States' rights' was a big one. When you said 'states' rights,' that told the guy in Mississippi or Alabama that we can take care of the 'n——.'" Did Reagan realize that? "I think he probably knew it," Spencer said, "but we never discussed it."[18]

Indeed, there were limits even to Reagan's legendary naivete. He seldom, if ever, used the phrase "states' rights." It was not a standard part of his stump speech. It beggars belief that he could have used it at the Neshoba County Fair, of all places, while remaining ignorant of what those two noxious words connoted. "He wasn't a dummy," Spencer noted, and Wirthlin had warned how his speech would be perceived.[19] But Reagan did not care. This was the dark side of his pragmatism: He was willing to tap into dangerous and disreputable prejudices to win the presidency while insisting to everyone, even himself, that his intentions were pure.

———

While giving Reagan a pass for his Neshoba County Fair speech, political reporters spent much of August 1980 castigating him for a series of gaffes that pleased his base but displeased centrist voters and depressed his poll numbers.

August 16: Reagan said at a news conference that the United States should still maintain an "official relationship" with Taiwan, even though Carter had extended diplomatic recognition to the People's Republic of China. His remarks caused a backlash from Beijing, but they played well with conservatives who were unhappy about what they viewed as Carter's abandonment of Taiwan.

August 18: Reagan suggested, in a speech to the Veterans of Foreign Wars in Chicago, that the Vietnam War had been a "noble cause," which led the media to excoriate him for bringing up such a divisive topic, even though many Americans were eager to see America's lost war in a heroic light.

August 22: Reagan told a convention of evangelicals in Dallas that there were "great flaws" in the theory of evolution and that schools should teach "creationism" as well. That led to media criticism that he was breaching the wall between "church and state," but it helped to win over a key constituency—white evangelical Christians—who had voted for Carter, himself a pious Southern Baptist, in 1976. Reagan cleverly told the evangelicals, "Now I know this is a non-partisan gathering, and so I know that you can't endorse *me*, but I only brought that up because I want you to know that I endorse *you* and what you're doing." In fact, the evangelicals were only nominally nonpartisan. The Reverend Jerry Falwell, a Baptist preacher from rural Virginia who was host of the *Old-Time Gospel Hour* on TV and head of a new group called Moral Majority, referred to the Republican platform as "exactly what we believe," and his group went on to produce commercials demonizing Carter, who supported the Equal Rights

Amendment and wanted to deny tax exemption to educational institutions that were guilty of racial discrimination, as a "traitor to the South and no longer a Christian." The support of the Christian Right would prove critical to Reagan's success while alarming more moderate voters who agreed with Carter's private assessment that Falwell and his followers were "religious nuts."

August 27: Reagan said the country was in a "severe depression," even though it was actually a recession. This was an embarrassment to the campaign's economic team, but Reagan turned it to his advantage by coining a quip that he would repeat throughout the fall: "A recession is when your neighbor loses his job. A depression is when you lose your job. Recovery is when Jimmy Carter loses his job."[20]

Surveying these blunders, the *New York Times* noted a pattern of "apparently shaky staff work, Reagan plunging ahead on instinct, and making strong statements that provided ammunition for his critics."[21] As a result of the challenger's missteps, the incumbent was rapidly catching up in the polls.

A myth was to arise in conservative circles that, after the firing of John Sears, Reagan was successful because he was finally freed of his handlers. "Bill Casey and I . . . had the common sense to allow Ronald Reagan to be himself—something the previous management had not done," Ed Meese later wrote.[22] In truth, the gaffes of August showed the risks of "letting Reagan be Reagan" as so many of his admirers, but not the candidate himself, demanded.

Mike Deaver and Nancy Reagan, the most influential voices of moderation among Reagan's advisers, decided they needed a new handler to take charge of a faltering campaign. They already had asked Stuart Spencer—described by one reporter as "short, banty in his body language in the manner of James Cagney characters, fond of liquor, cigarettes, and rough humor"—to come back as a consultant shortly before the convention. Now they moved to expand his role.[23] The Reagans, ever pragmatic, were able to put aside their animus toward Spencer for his hard-edged tactics on behalf of Ford in 1976, because they realized they once again needed him. In fact, Spencer would play a prominent role in all four of Reagan's successful political campaigns dating back to 1966.

Spencer recalled getting on the Reagan campaign airplane for the first time on the way to Detroit and sitting down next to the candidate: "I was prepared for a lot of crap in my ear—'Why did you do this? Why did you do that?'" He did get an earful from Nancy but not one word of reproach from Reagan. "It was like we had a conversation seven years ago, and we were just continuing the conversation," Spencer recalled. "Never raised 1976 one iota. Not one. It was eerie. We had a great conversation, and I was back in."[24]

Following the gaffes of August, Spencer's role was elevated. He would manage the rest of the campaign working with Mike Deaver, Lyn Nofziger, Marty Anderson, press secretary Jim Brady, and former Nixon speechwriter Ken Khachigian from the campaign's Boeing 727, dubbed LeaderShip 80. Bill Casey—derided behind his back as "Spacey"—was largely limited to overseeing administrative matters at the campaign headquarters in Arlington, Virginia. "We lived on the plane. We were gone six days out of every week," Spencer said. "It was a tight team. We all got along. No knifing and no back-stabbing. It was one of the most fun campaigns ever."[25]

The formal kickoff of the fall campaign was at a Labor Day picnic at Liberty State Park in New Jersey on September 1, 1980, with a stunning view of the Statue of Liberty in the background—and, according to a campaign press release, "ethnic bands and dancing groups" providing entertainment.[26] Looking tanned and wearing a white cotton shirt without a jacket, his normally coiffed hair tousled by the sea breeze, Reagan paid tribute to "the millions of men and women who first stepped foot on American soil right there, on Ellis Island, so close to the Statue of Liberty." As Nancy Reagan looked on with her characteristically rapturous gaze, he vowed to "make America great again" and to vindicate the dreams of all those immigrants who made "this refuge the greatest home of freedom in history."[27]

While willing to cater to the prejudices of white voters who resented the gains made by African Americans, Reagan was consistent in rejecting the siren song of nativism. He supported Puerto Rican statehood if the people of Puerto Rico voted for it and refused to speak of "illegal aliens"; he preferred the term "undocumented immigrants."[28] Earlier, during a primary debate with George H. W. Bush in Houston, the candidates had been asked whether the "children of illegal aliens should be allowed to attend Texas public schools for free, or do you think their parents should pay for their education?" Both Republicans passed up an opportunity to appeal to xenophobes. Reagan advocated opening "the border both ways" and said, "Rather than talking about putting up a fence, why don't we work out some recognition of our mutual problems, and make it possible for them to come here legally with a work permit?"[29]

Hard as he tried, Stu Spencer could not eliminate all of Reagan's gaffes. On October 8, 1980, the candidate wrongly suggested that "growing and decaying vegetation" was producing 93 percent of nitrogen dioxide pollution. This led to quips, including from Reagan's own staff, about "killer trees," and undermined the campaign's efforts to demonstrate, as one aide wrote, that "the Governor is not a berserk strip miner and air polluter."[30] But Spencer cut back the candidate's press availabilities and gave the campaign sure-handed direction down the stretch. He even tried to prevent Reagan from reading the conservative weekly *Human Events*—the apparent source of many of his erroneous claims.[31]

When Spencer saw polls in early October showing a big "gender gap"—Reagan was much weaker with women voters than with men because of his opposition to abortion and the Equal Rights Amendment and his reputation as a warmonger—he came up with an idea.

Rousing Reagan out of bed early in the morning, Spencer proudly announced, "I've solved your problem!"

"How?" The groggy candidate wondered.

"Would you have any problem," Spencer asked, "telling the American public that your first appointment to the Supreme Court is going to be a woman?"

"Not if she's qualified," Reagan replied.

"Christ," Spencer said, "there's thousands of women judges out there, they've got to be qualified."

"No problem," Reagan said.[32]

And so, on October 14, 1980, at a press conference in Los Angeles, Reagan announced he would appoint the first woman to the Supreme Court. This pledge would result in the selection the following year of Sandra Day O'Connor.[33]

In September 1980, the country was in considerable economic pain, with unemployment running at 8 percent, inflation at 13 percent, and interest rates at a whopping 14 percent. Reagan should have had an easy path to victory by promising to get the economy moving again. Yet the electorate harbored enough doubts about his qualifications for the presidency that, by October 11, his lead was down to one point in the campaign's internal tracking poll. On that day, Dick Wirthlin warned Reagan that "we have not been able to capitalize fully on Carter's unattractiveness" and that your "lead is a mere shadow of what it was following the Republican convention."[34]

The unexpectedly tight race may have prompted some Reagan campaign aides to go to unscrupulous extremes to ensure victory. Roger Stone, who was the New York, New Jersey, and Connecticut regional political director for the Reagan-Bush campaign, told me—confirming a story he had first recounted to journalist Matt Labash in 2007—that, with the election "very close," he worked with the notorious attorney Roy Cohn, Joe McCarthy's former henchman, to arrange for the New York Liberal Party to endorse John Anderson's third-party candidacy to split the Carter vote in that state.[35] According to Stone, Cohn gave him a suitcase full of cash to pass along to a well-connected lawyer in the Bronx, and, a few days later, on September 7, 1980, the Liberal Party endorsed Anderson. Stone said he never opened the suitcase, but Cohn had discussed a fee of roughly $125,000 (nearly $500,000 in 2024 dollars).[36]

The story—which Stone waited to relate until the statute of limitations had expired—is entirely plausible if difficult to verify. Joel McCleary, who ran the Carter campaign in New York, said that the Liberal Party's longtime boss Raymond B. Harding had come to him demanding to know what the Carter campaign would offer for his endorsement. "Harding was strictly cash and carry," McCleary said. "We weren't in that game. Carter was clean—maybe too clean." He added that "it was always our assumption from what we were hearing" that the Reagan campaign offered Harding a better deal.[37]

Stu Spencer said that he wasn't shocked to hear what Roger Stone and Roy Cohn—whom he described as "terrible people"—might have done, but he stressed that their actions were "not sanctioned by the Reagan campaign."[38] Sanctioned or not, the ploy appeared to pay off. With the Liberal

Party nod, Anderson would go on to win 7.5 percent of the vote in New York—far more than the narrow margin between Carter (43.9 percent) and Reagan (46.6 percent) in that state.

Roy Cohn would be disbarred in 1986 for unethical conduct; Ray Harding would plead guilty in 2009 to corruption charges (funneling bribes to a state official); and Roger Stone would be convicted in 2019 on multiple felony counts for obstructing a congressional investigation probing Donald Trump's ties to Russia before being pardoned by then-president Trump.[39] Prior to his death from AIDS in 1986, Cohn would enjoy entrée into the Reagan White House: He brought his client Rupert Murdoch to the Oval Office in 1983 in a bid to win administration support for Murdoch's media empire, and Murdoch would later benefit from the Federal Communication Commission's relaxation of media ownership rules.[40]

If these machinations occurred in his New York campaign, Reagan should have known about them, but, of course, he did not. He simply did not delve very deeply into what his subordinates were doing—a habit that would carry over to the White House. He assumed his coworkers—whether film-production crews or campaign aides or government officials—were doing their jobs. So he focused on doing *his* job: selling himself to the public.

Reagan had already debated John Anderson on September 21, 1980. Now, despite some staffers' fears that he might commit a campaign-ending gaffe, he would have to debate Carter: a much higher-risk proposition. Carter's campaign operatives were eager to get him onstage with Reagan because they were convinced their candidate was smarter and more knowledgeable. The debate was hastily scheduled for Cleveland on October 28, 1980—a week before the vote. A serious mistake by either candidate could cost him the election because there would be so little time to recover.

Reagan prepared for the debate at Wexford, a mansion in the Virginia hunt country about an hour south of Washington owned by Bill Clements, a former governor of Texas. The campaign set up a studio in an old garage, complete with klieg lights and television cameras, to replicate the feel of a debate stage. David Stockman, a bright young Republican congressman from Michigan, took the role of Carter while other aides played reporters asking questions.

The Reagan debate team, led by Bush's former campaign manager, James

A. Baker III, had a secret advantage: a stolen copy of Carter's debate briefing books. Author and conservative activist Craig Shirley concludes that the
likely thief was a Kennedy family loyalist named Paul Corbin who hated
Carter for defeating Ted Kennedy. He allegedly gave the purloined briefing books to Bill Casey, who in turn handed them over to Baker.[41] When
the story of "debategate" broke in 1983 (in a book by *Time* correspondent
Laurence Barrett), Baker swore under oath that he had gotten the briefing books from Casey. Casey denied it, but few believed him. Whether this
briefing material, which consisted primarily of quotations from Reagan's
own pronouncements, was important remains a matter of, well, debate. "I
didn't see anything of value there," Stu Spencer recalled.[42]

But it was telling that the Reagan camp never bothered to notify the
FBI or to return the materials. Instead, they made use of the stolen briefing books, foreshadowing the Reagan administration's casual approach
to ethics.

The actual debate, which would be seen by more than a hundred million
people, or almost half of the population, turned on three key moments. Carter was widely ridiculed for saying, "I had a discussion with my daughter,
Amy, the other day, before I came here, to ask her what the most important
issue was. She said she thought nuclear weaponry and the control of nuclear
arms." In a clumsy attempt to suggest that his opponent was a warmonger—an echo of LBJ's "Daisy" commercial from 1964—the president had
made it sound as if a thirteen-year-old girl was his national security adviser.

Even more consequential was an exchange that occurred near the end of
the debate. Carter noted that "Governor Reagan began his political career
campaigning around this Nation against Medicare" and attacked him for
now opposing "national health insurance." As Carter spoke, Reagan had
an incredulous look on his face. With a smile and a shake of his head, he
shot back, "There you go again." He went on to explain, "When I opposed
Medicare, there was another piece of legislation meeting the same problem
before the Congress. I happened to favor the other piece of legislation and
thought that it would be better for the senior citizens and provide better
care than the one that was finally passed. I was not opposing the principle of providing care for them. I was opposing one piece of legislation as
versus another."[43]

"There you go again," a phrase that Reagan had stumbled on during a debate rehearsal, turned into a signature line. The audience laughed with Reagan because it shared his assumption that, as the media so often said, Carter was too mean.

What has gotten lost—both at the time and subsequently—was that Carter was right on the facts and Reagan was wrong. As discussed earlier, Reagan had been part of an American Medical Association lobbying campaign in 1961 against Medicare, which he derided as "socialized medicine." In place of Medicare, which would provide universal health-insurance coverage for seniors, Reagan had advocated a slight expansion of the 1960 Kerr-Mills Act, which offered federal financing for interested states to subsidize private health insurance for the aged. Three years after its passage, the law covered fewer than 1 percent of older Americans. Reagan made it sound as if he had supported another plan comparable in scope to Medicare. He hadn't. Contrary to what he said on the debate stage, he had not accepted the principle that the government should provide medical care for all senior citizens. Indeed, he warned that accepting this very principle would lead to a total loss of freedom in America.[44]

But, for practical political purposes, the facts did not matter. Reagan had just landed a knockout blow—and he did not let his opponent get off the mat. His masterful closing statement began with another memorable line: "Are you better off than you were four years ago?" This was the third critical point of the debate. In just ten words, Reagan encapsulated his core message: *Time for a change.* He had turned the election into a referendum on the incumbent—and that was an election Carter could not win.

The debate, pollster Richard Wirthlin concluded after conducting four surveys in its aftermath, had been a "smashing success. . . . It neutralized to a large extent Carter's effort to paint Ronald Reagan as radical and reckless."[45] Reagan aides were now convinced they would win—as long as Carter did not spring an October Surprise.

Americans were obsessed by the Iran hostage crisis in 1980. Yellow ribbons sprouted across the country in honor of the hostages, and the nightly news offered a running count of how many days America itself had been "held hostage." Coming after the fall of South Vietnam, this appeared to be the latest humiliation for a crippled giant.

The term "October Surprise" originated in the Reagan campaign in the spring of 1980 to describe the possibility that Carter would engineer the release of the remaining fifty-two American hostages shortly before the election. Wirthlin's polling indicated that if the release occurred before the end of October, it could swing the election by adding ten points to Carter's total.[46] "That was a big concern," Ed Meese recalled.[47] Dick Allen, Reagan's chief foreign policy adviser, said that the campaign deliberately publicized the prospect of an October Surprise to make any hostage release seem like a cynical political ploy.[48] The campaign set aside hundreds of thousands of dollars to air commercials in the event of a last-minute hostage release and tabbed a retired reserve admiral, Robert Garrick, to recruit military friends to keep an eye on any movements at major US air bases that might signal the hostages were about to be freed.[49] Campaign manager Bill Casey, in particular, "was obsessed by the October Surprise," Stu Spencer recalled. "A day didn't go by that he didn't call me and talk about his army out there watching every airport."[50]

Did the Reagan campaign go beyond planning for the hostages' release to trying to avert it? Was the Iranian decision not to release the hostages until after Reagan's inauguration on January 20, 1981, even though the outlines of a deal were evident months before, due to the mullahs' animus toward Carter—or to a secret bargain struck with the Reagan-Bush campaign?

Gary Sick, a former naval intelligence officer and the Iran expert on Ford's and Carter's National Security Council, began to investigate rumors of a deal in the late 1980s. In 1991, he published a book called *October Surprise* laying out his conclusion that there had been a backroom arrangement. He noted that, immediately after the hostages were released, Israel sold about $300 million in military equipment to Iran, much of it spare parts for US-made equipment. The Reagan administration could have blocked the arms transfers but chose not to do so, raising suspicions of a quid pro quo.[51]

Both the Senate and House launched investigations into these charges, with the House October Surprise Task Force led by Democratic congressman Lee Hamilton of Indiana and Republican congressman Henry Hyde of Illinois doing the more thorough job. Their report, released on January 3, 1993, concluded, in Hamilton's words, "We found little or no credible evidence of communications between the 1980 Reagan campaign and the Government of Iran and no credible evidence that the campaign tried to delay the hostages' release."[52]

And yet credible evidence has emerged since the task force's investigation to suggest that its conclusions may have been premature.

First, in 1996, Palestinian Liberation Organization chairman Yasser Arafat told Jimmy Carter in the presence of historian Douglas Brinkley, "Mr. President, you should know that in 1980 the Republicans approached me with an arms deal if I could arrange to keep the hostages in Iran until after the election. I want you to know that I turned them down."[53]

Second, Ben Barnes, a wealthy real estate developer and former Democratic lieutenant governor of Texas, told historian H. W. Brands (and subsequently confirmed to the *New York Times*) that in the summer of 1980 he accompanied John Connally on a tour of the Middle East in which the former Texas governor and US Treasury secretary told top officials in five Arab countries that it would "not be helpful" to the Reagan campaign for the hostages to be released before the election. A Democrat turned Republican, Connally hoped to become secretary of state or defense in a Reagan administration and was in constant contact with the campaign. After returning from the Middle East, he briefed Bill Casey about his trip.[54]

Third, Mark Bowden, a distinguished journalist who wrote the definitive history of the Iran hostage crisis, talked to Iranian officials and hostage-takers who confirmed to him that there had been outreach from Casey and the Reagan campaign, while adding that it "had little bearing" on Iran's decision-making about the hostages.[55]

Fourth, Bill Casey's alibi began to fall apart. Iranian businessman Jamshid Hashemi testified before the House task force under oath that he and his brother Cyrus had orchestrated two meetings on the weekend of July 26–27, 1980, in Madrid between Casey and a representative of the Iranian regime. Jamshid told ABC's *Nightline*, "Casey said the Iranians should hold the hostages until after the election . . . and the new Reagan administration would feel favorably towards Iran, releasing military equipment and the frozen Iranian assets."[56]

The task force accepted the assurances of Casey's family that the campaign chairman, who died in 1987, had been at the Bohemian Grove in California that weekend and then in London on Monday and Tuesday, July 28 and 29, 1980, for a conference on World War II history. Significantly, however, Casey's passport was missing along with his calendar entries for those dates. Investigative reporter Robert Parry, who covered the story for the Associated Press, *Newsweek*, and PBS's *Frontline*, subsequently uncovered evidence that Casey had visited the Bohemian Grove in August, not July. Moreover, Parry discovered at the George H. W. Bush Presidential Library reference to a long-buried State Department cable from the Madrid embassy that stated "Bill Casey was in town, for purposes unknown" on July 26 and 27, 1980. Casey did not show up at the conference in London until the afternoon of July 28, leaving plenty of time to meet Iranian emissaries in Madrid.[57]

Yet the cable was never turned over to the House task force because Bush aides viewed its work as "partisan" and a threat to the president's 1992 reelection. Bush was accused, and exonerated by the task force, of meeting with Iranian representatives in Paris in October 1980. The Bush White House was determined, as one staffer wrote, to "kill/spike this story."[58] Lee Hamilton subsequently criticized the Bush administration for impeding the House investigation.[59]

With the emergence of the Madrid memo and the statements of Yasser Arafat, Ben Barnes, and Iranian officials, the evidence for the October Surprise theory is substantial and credible if still circumstantial. Many of those who said they were privy to the details were, like the future perpetrators of the Iran-Contra affair, shady operators and proven prevaricators. Dick Allen denied there was any attempt to delay the hostage release; he called that theory "unremitted bullshit."[60] Retired admiral Bobby Ray Inman, who was director of the National Security Agency (NSA) from 1977 to 1981 and then deputy CIA director from 1981 to 1982, insisted that if Bill Casey, with whom he often clashed, or other Reagan aides had contacted Iranian officials, he "would have seen evidence of it" from NSA intercepts of Iranian government officials. Not seeing any such evidence, he concluded that "it did not occur," even while acknowledging that the NSA did not collect intelligence on Americans such as Casey.[61]

Few who knew Casey, an inveterate schemer and risk-taker, doubted that he was capable of such a ruthless gambit. "He always lived on the edge," Secretary of State Alexander M. Haig Jr. later said.[62] When asked whether Casey could have connived to keep the hostages in captivity, Jim Baker replied, "There is nothing about Casey that would surprise me. He was a piece of work."[63] In a similar vein, Stu Spencer said, "I have an easy time believing it.... Casey was nuts. He was the personification of a spook. Everything with him was spooky, spooky, spooky."[64] Indeed, as Reagan's CIA director, Casey would become a prime architect of the covert effort to sell missiles to Iran in return for freeing US hostages while illegally funneling the proceeds to Nicaraguan rebels. His machinations in 1980 may have served as a prelude to future arms deals with Iran.

There was no suggestion that Reagan himself was aware of any efforts by his campaign to prolong the imprisonment of the hostages—any more than he was aware of a stolen debate book or a scheme to pay off the New York Liberal Party—and he surely would have disapproved had he known. Even if Casey had told him, which was unlikely, the hard-of-hearing candidate might have missed it. As Stu Spencer noted, "Casey was such a mumbler that Reagan couldn't understand him half the time."[65] But just as the captain of a ship is ultimately responsible for everything that happens aboard, whether he is aware of it or not, so too a presidential candidate is ultimately responsible for whatever his campaign does.

John Limbert, one of the diplomats held hostage in Tehran, told me, "If the cynical bastards kept us in our cells, betraying us, our families, and the nation—which is highly likely—then they could not escape Karma. Five years later, during Iran-Contra, Iran would return to bite them in the ass. Their dubious, noxious 'success' in 1980 made them think they were smarter than they were, and lost in their delusions, they nearly destroyed Reagan's presidency."[66]

Ultimately, the October Surprise was that there was no surprise. When the hostages were not released before the election, Jimmy Carter's fate was sealed. With Reagan's lead growing in the campaign's final days, as more voters concluded he could be entrusted with the nation's highest office, there was little suspense about the outcome. The day before the vote, the Carter campaign pollster, Patrick Caddell, mournfully told the White House chief of staff, Hamilton Jordan, "The sky has fallen in. We are getting murdered. . . . It's the hostage thing."[67]

The Reagans were at home in their "General Electric house" in Pacific Palisades on Election Day, November 4, 1980, when, a little after 5:00 p.m. on the West Coast, Nancy heard news anchor John Chancellor announce on NBC that her husband would win in a landslide. Ron was taking a shower, so Nancy banged on the shower door, and he stepped out, dripping wet, to hear the good news. A few minutes later the phone rang. The president was on the line congratulating the president-elect. Carter had not even waited for the polls to close on the West Coast. He knew he had suffered "an overwhelming defeat."[68]

In the nation's historic shift to the right, Reagan won 51 percent of the popular vote to 41 percent for Carter and 7 percent for John Anderson. The Electoral College outcome was even more lopsided: 489 electoral votes for Reagan, only 49 for Carter. The incumbent won just six states. Reagan had not been greatly hurt by his numerous gaffes and falsehoods—nor by the difficulty of making his economic plans add up. With the country mired in malaise, his indictment of Jimmy Carter's stewardship resonated—as did his promises to "make America great again" by cutting taxes, boosting defense spending, and standing up to the Soviets.

Reagan won almost a third of the Democratic votes and ran nearly even with Carter in union households, thanks to his success in courting blue-collar, white voters in the Midwest and Northeast—the "Reagan Democrats." He won 56 percent of white votes compared to 37 percent of Latino and only 14 percent of Black votes. His Faustian bargain had paid off. By endorsing "states' rights" and embracing the religious right, he won all but one state of the South—Carter's own Georgia—and thereby advanced the project that Goldwater and Nixon had launched: the realignment of American politics. By the 1990s, the South, once solidly Democratic, would be solidly Republican, giving the party a decided Southern tinge and a large base of support not only in the Electoral College but also in Congress.[69]

Appeals to white bigotry were hardly front and center in Reagan's campaign; he was no George Wallace, and he actually took a liberal position on immigration. But his criticism of civil rights legislation, busing, affirmative action, and welfare programs that disproportionately aided minorities helped spur Southern and Northern white voters, particularly white men, to abandon their previous allegiance to a Democratic Party that was increasingly identified with the interests of women and minorities. "For Reagan," concluded political analysts Thomas and Mary Edsall, "conservative racial policies were more important in his appeal to white Democrats than they were in securing his Republican base."[70] Of course, it was those white Democrats who made possible Reagan's 1980 landslide given that Democrats still outnumbered Republicans.

On top of winning the White House, Republicans, in a stunning reversal, won the Senate for the first time since 1952 and picked up thirty-three seats in the House. Reagan would ride into the White House not only with a mandate but also with a working conservative majority in Congress that presaged the country's ideological direction for decades to come.

———————

Ronald Reagan had reinvented himself many times, rising from an impoverished, small-town upbringing to become a well-known radio announcer, then a movie star, corporate pitchman, right-wing firebrand, governor of the nation's most populous state, and a three-time presidential candidate. Now, shortly before turning sixty-nine, he was about to assume the most difficult post in the world under the most trying circumstances imaginable, with America's standing, economically and internationally, in a disconcerting slump—indeed, at a post–World War II low.

The previous four presidents were seen as failures. The last president who had served two full terms was Eisenhower. The country was viewed as virtually ungovernable, the presidency as unmanageable. Could a former actor who was already past retirement age do any better? Many had their doubts. Tip O'Neill, the powerful speaker of the House, sternly warned the president-elect after the election, "The governor of a state plays in the minor leagues. When you're president, you're in the big leagues."[71]

The speaker had a point. The challenge of occupying the Oval Office was infinitely greater than the challenge of occupying the California governor's office—and that had been difficult enough. Yet if Ronald Reagan had any doubts about his ability to bat in the big leagues, he never revealed them. Possessed of a preternatural self-confidence, he appeared oddly undaunted by the formidable challenges that lay ahead.

ACT IV

MR. PRESIDENT

(previous page) *Telephoning members of Congress to lobby them on legislation from the* Resolute *desk in the Oval Office, August 5, 1986. Reagan seldom called anyone unless asked to do so by his staff.* (RRPL)

33

Assembling an Administration

Every president knows, when he's picking his chief of staff, my God, he'd better get the right man in that job or he'll be ruined.

—THEODORE SORENSON

I t is axiomatic that every president seeks to distinguish himself from his predecessor. And Ronald Reagan, more than most, had an incentive to do that, given that the man he had defeated was leaving office with a job approval rating of just 34 percent.[1] White House staff documents from the first few years of the Reagan administration are filled with horror at the prospect that *their* president might be "Carterized," that is, seen as an unsuccessful and ineffectual leader.[2] The fear of Carterization helped to explain the post-election blitz that the Reagans mounted to win over their new neighbors in Washington. As an anonymous Reagan aide told the *Washington Post*, "We want to avoid Jimmy Carter's fatal mistake. He never met the power brokers in this city. He never had any real friends here. Gov. Reagan not only wants to know them, but he needs them to get this place working again."[3]

In wooing the capital's permanent establishment, the newly elected president, a fading movie star who looked his best on a horse, had his work cut out for him since most of the old-time Washingtonians were Democrats who greeted his ascension with incredulity and derision. He was seen as "an amiable dunce," in the words of Democratic Party elder statesman Clark Clifford. The liberal journalist Nicholas von Hoffman wrote in *Harper's* that it was "humiliating to think of this unlettered, self-assured bumpkin becoming our President." "Washington was beside itself," conservative columnist George F. Will recalled. "It was the barbarians coming over the gate."[4]

The Reagans' social blitz consisted of three initial events: a dinner they hosted at the tony, old-line F Street Club on November 18, 1980; another dinner hosted by George Will at his Chevy Chase home on November 20; and finally—the *pièce de résistance*—a dinner hosted by *Washington Post* publisher Katharine Graham, the supreme arbiter of Washington society, at her Georgetown mansion on December 11. When Nancy Reynolds, a former Reagan aide who was now a lobbyist in Washington, called with invitations for the F Street soirée, some of the guests replied, "Are you sure this is serious? It's not a practical joke? I'm a Democrat."[5]

Casting their doubts aside, more than fifty guests showed up to the F Street dinner alone, and even the city's Democratic mayor, Marion Barry, professed himself charmed by his host. The invitees were so "captivated" by the new president's old stories that they hardly noticed students from the nearby George Washington University heckling the newcomer with shouts of "Bonzo! Bonzo! Bonzo!" If truth be told, many of the liberal power brokers were glad to be rid of the holier-than-thou scold Jimmy Carter. With the more glamorous Reagans about to occupy the White House, there was a sense that the good times could roll again. One guest was heard passing on wine with dinner and saying to a waiter, "Oh, make it Scotch and water! The Carters are gone."[6]

At George Will's dinner, the bow-tied columnist presented the president with a walking stick topped with a likeness of President William McKinley's bald pate. On receiving the gift, Reagan said appreciatively, "I always liked McKinley. He freed Cuba." Will recalled saying to himself, "Boy, am I glad there aren't any cameras in here. The president-elect wants to free Cuba, you can just see the headlines!"[7] (Of course, McKinley did not really free Cuba—after kicking out the Spanish, he made the island an American dependency.)

This charm offensive was engineered by Nancy Reagan, who, like her mother, had a shrewd appreciation of how to use social ties to advance her husband's interests—and her own. She would develop friendships with George Will and Kay Graham, among other influential Washingtonians. "Kay and Nancy formed this partnership that was really, really important," said David Gergen, communications director in the Reagan White House. He noted that the first lady was never "particularly ideological" and simply wanted her husband "to be a really good president."[8]

The hard right was not happy to see the Reagans' outreach to many of the people who had been on Richard Nixon's enemies list. As Kay Graham noted in her memoir, a photograph showing her hugging the president-elect might have "upset arch-conservatives almost as much as the famous one of Jimmy Carter bussing Leonid Brezhnev at the Vienna summit."[9]

Conservatives would have been even unhappier if they had realized that, while clinking glasses with the limousine liberals in Washington, the Gipper had stiffed his old friends at *National Review*. Back in the spring of 1980, William F. Buckley Jr. had asked the candidate to headline his magazine's twenty-fifth anniversary dinner in New York City on December 5. Reagan replied that he would put the date on his calendar but warned that events might intervene. The normally imperturbable Buckley was upset when he found out, a few weeks before the event, that Reagan wasn't coming. After Reagan apologized for "an enormous goof-up on my part," Buckley assured him "that all is forgiven."[10]

The president-elect did not have any competing events on December 5; he simply preferred to spend the day in his Pacific Palisades home while he still could.[11] (After winning the White House, the Reagans decided to sell their old "General Electric house.") Reagan did attend two *National Review* events during his presidency, but his choice of dinner engagements after the 1980 election made clear that the new president's team was intent on broadening his appeal far beyond the straitened conservative base.

That same pragmatic impulse—the desire to succeed in Washington—was responsible for what may have been the most important decision of Reagan's entire presidency: the choice of his first White House chief of staff. Dwight Eisenhower, with his military background, had been the first president to install a chief of staff. Since then, the position had grown in importance such that it was second in power only to the president himself. "Every president knows, when he's picking his chief of staff," said John F. Kennedy adviser Theodore Sorenson, "My God, he'd better get the right man in that job or he'll be ruined."[12] Carter had shown what happens if you don't have a strong chief of staff: He had favored a "spokes on a wheel" system in which far too many staffers had direct access to him. The result was an administration that was often spinning its wheels.[13]

About ten days before the November 4, 1980, election, the old California hands Stuart K. Spencer and Michael K. Deaver discussed who might fill the all-important position of chief of staff in a Reagan White House. They understood that Reagan was no hands-on manager and needed someone who was. They agreed that Ed Meese was the wrong man for the job, even though he had held that very position in Sacramento. While an improvement over Phil Battaglia, the governor's first chief of staff, Meese was notoriously disorganized and had no experience in Washington. "Ed's bottomless brief-case" was a joke of long standing among Reagan staffers, who would see their proposals disappear forever into Meese's paper pile.

Spencer and Deaver decided that Houston attorney James A. Baker III would be a far better choice. He was smart, disciplined, and hardwork-ing, and he understood how Washington functioned. While conservative, he wasn't ideological. He was the ultimate pragmatist who wanted to get things done. What made Baker such an unconventional choice was that he had worked *against* Ronald Reagan twice: first as campaign chairman for Gerald Ford in 1976 and then as campaign manager in 1980 for his best friend and tennis doubles partner, George H. W. Bush. Presidents do not normally appoint a political opponent to the most important job in the entire admin-istration. But that's just what Spencer and Deaver proposed.[14]

They found an indispensable ally in Nancy Reagan. She had never cared for Meese and in fact had called him a "jump-off-the-cliff-with-the-flag-flying conservative."[15] As Jim Baker's biographers Peter Baker and Susan Glasser noted, Baker made a much better impression: "He was handsome, debonair, and carried himself well." Baker had also impressed Nancy with how smoothly he ran debate preparation in the fall of 1980. The final test came when Spencer and Deaver slipped Baker onto the campaign plane in the days before the election, and he quickly established a personal rapport with the first couple. "Ronnie had been leaning toward Ed Meese," Nancy Reagan wrote, "but Mike [Deaver] prevailed." Of course, it was the first lady, not Mike Deaver, who exercised the decisive influence.[16]

Ronald Reagan broke the bad news to Ed Meese over a tuna-fish salad lunch on election day in Los Angeles. Meese was "totally devastated," Deaver recalled. This was a job he had assumed he would get. After all, he had already taken charge of the transition. Reagan, always eager to avoid interpersonal conflict, offered the post to Baker the next day but told him to "make it right with Ed." "I will certainly try, Mr. President," Baker replied diplomatically.[17]

The two lawyers met for lunch that very day, November 5, at the Century

Plaza hotel in Century City to hash out a deal as if they were negotiating a corporate merger. Meese had been working on elaborate plans for "cabinet government" and wanted to become counselor to the president with cabinet rank. He would supervise, at least in theory, both domestic policy and foreign policy. The national security adviser, Richard Allen, would report to him rather than directly to the president, as other holders of that position had done. Meese would take over the West Wing office traditionally assigned to the national security adviser while Allen would be relegated to the White House basement.

Baker took for himself the title of chief of staff and the spacious corner office—the biggest in the West Wing after the Oval Office—that came with it. He also shrewdly won control of, as their agreement stipulated, "all in and out paper flow to the President and of presidential schedule and appointments" along with "hiring and firing authority over all elements of White House staff." In addition, he would be in charge of the press office and legislative affairs.[18]

Baker knew that real power lay in controlling the paper flow to the president, legislative and press relations, and appointments to key positions—not in supervising "cabinet councils" that accomplished little. In any case, Baker would be a member of the cabinet too. He had just run circles around Meese, and Meese did not even know it. This was the first of many instances when Baker would show that he was a negotiator nonpareil. He became known as the "velvet hammer" and would be acclaimed by many as the best White House chief of staff in history.[19]

The senior leadership team was rounded out with Mike Deaver, who was appointed deputy chief of staff and given a prime office right next to the Oval Office in what had been the presidential study. The balding and bespectacled Deaver had little interest in, or knowledge of, policy. "I didn't have a clue . . . how it all worked," he later admitted. "It was a pretty awesome and intimidating, for me, experience."[20] His background was in public relations, and his chief asset was a close personal relationship with the Reagans, who regarded him as practically a son.

Deaver would take charge of the president's schedule and the optics of the presidency. He understood that the key to driving news coverage was producing arresting "visuals" for television that would communicate the president's message without a word being said. His motto: "Television elects presidents."[21] But his most important job might have been as Nancy Reagan's designated handler. He dealt with the strong-willed first lady, whose rare appearances in the West Wing sent the staff scurrying in terror.

Baker, Deaver, and Meese become known as the "Troika" or the "Big Three," and stories of their rivalry became as much a part of Washington chatter as the fate of the Redskins, as the local NFL team was then known. Their internecine rivalry led to dueling press leaks and bad feelings on both sides, with most White House staffers seeing themselves as part of either the Meese or Baker factions—the "prags and the wingers," as Baker's deputy Richard Darman irreverently dubbed the pragmatists and the right-wingers. The wingers viewed the prags as sellouts; the prags viewed the wingers as "nutcases," in Jim Baker's words. "You never knew when in the middle of the night something would flash and you'd have a dagger in your back," said communications director David Gergen, who was one of the prags.[22]

Initial press speculation suggested that Meese was the first among equals, but that turned out to be wrong. With supreme confidence and sublime bureaucratic skill, Baker accumulated power while Meese proved just as ineffectual as his detractors had expected. One of Baker's advantages was that his lieutenants were more experienced in the ways of government than Meese's more ideological hires. "They didn't have a clue how the White House worked," Baker aide Margaret D. Tutwiler recalled. "They were left in the dust."[23]

Baker's right-hand man was Dick Darman, the White House staff secretary. A liberal Republican with sharp elbows, great intellect, and considerable self-esteem, he took charge of the paper flow to and from the president at Baker's behest, making himself into one of the most powerful people in the entire government. "Dick Darman had the final say on a [presidential] speech," White House speechwriter Peggy Noonan later complained. "Now I came in here assuming it was the president, but it was really Dick, for all intents and purposes. . . . I was astonished by his authority and power." By contrast, Noonan recalled, the speechwriters had little contact with Meese's shop and could "sometimes ignore them."[24]

Mike Deaver threw his considerable influence behind Jim Baker, not Ed Meese. "They saw eye to eye on almost everything," Gergen noted.[25] A poor boy from Bakersfield who had worked his way through San Jose State as a lounge piano player, Deaver was a closet alcoholic with a taste for fine wines who suffered from a deep sense of personal inadequacy. He was dazzled by the older, taller, wealthier man who had attended Princeton University and came from one of the first families of Houston. "Baker is everything that Deaver would like to be," said Lyn Nofziger, the White House political director.[26] "There was some truth to that," Deaver conceded. But he also said that it was "great to have somebody like Baker who knew how it all worked."[27]

Deaver's desire to attain Baker-level wealth would ultimately bring him down. After leaving the White House and opening up a public relations shop, he would be convicted on perjury charges while skirting lobbying rules. But as long as he was in the government, he was an expert overseer of Reagan's image. ABC's White House correspondent Sam Donaldson said Deaver was such an effective salesman, he "could have saved the Edsel."[28]

The job of selecting cabinet officers was handed over to the Kitchen Cabinet, as it had been when Reagan became governor. A Transition Advisory Committee, chaired by Reagan's longtime lawyer William French Smith, was formed in Los Angeles. Other prominent members included drugstore magnate Justin Dart, Ford dealer Holmes Tuttle, land developer William Wilson, and beer mogul Joe Coors. Influential advisers such as Vice President George Bush and Senator Paul Laxalt also had considerable input. Laxalt was called the First Friend by those who did not realize that, as George Will quipped, Ronald Reagan was married to his only true friend.[29]

The influence of the Kitchen Cabinet did not last long. Following the inauguration, Bill Wilson and Justin Dart tried to establish a base in the Old Executive Office Building next to the White House. But the Troika had no intention of letting these wealthy dilettantes meddle in policy. White House counsel Fred Fielding presented the donors with a thick ream of financial disclosure forms that they would have to fill out if they wanted to serve in government. "They don't want us here," Dart realized. "I'm going home." Nancy Reagan did not lift a finger to save her old friends; she understood that Ronnie was playing for bigger stakes now. The only Kitchen Cabinet member to serve in the government would be Charles Z. Wick, a movie producer and owner of nursing homes, whose wife, Mary Jane, was one of

Nancy's best friends. He took a subcabinet position as director of the US Information Agency.[30]

Much to the consternation of New Right firebrands such as Jesse Helms, most of those selected for the cabinet were not particularly ideological; they were mainly standard-issue, middle-of-the-road Republicans who could have fit just as comfortably in a Nixon or Ford administration. "Although his Cabinet is second-rate, Reagan has not gone too ideological in his choice of secretaries, choosing for the most part managerial types to whom he can delegate," noted Barber Conable, a moderate Republican congressman from Rochester, New York.[31]

That description certainly fit William French Smith, who became attorney general; Malcolm "Mac" Baldridge, a corporate executive and friend of George Bush who became commerce secretary (Reagan liked him because he was a rodeo rider); Donald T. Regan, the CEO of Merrill Lynch, who became Treasury secretary after the two top candidates withdrew; business executive and longtime Republican operative Drew Lewis, who became secretary of transportation; veteran school administrator Terrel "Ted" Bell, who became secretary of education; Illinois hog and corn farmer John Block, whose appointment as secretary of agriculture was championed by Senator Bob Dole; William E. Brock III, a former senator from Tennessee and Republican National Committee chairman who became the US trade representative despite his support for Jerry Ford and the Panama Canal Treaties; and Richard Schweiker, Reagan's old running mate from 1976, a centrist senator from Pennsylvania who was appointed secretary of health and human services.

Besides Schweiker and Brock, the other veteran of Congress in the cabinet was the white-haired, chain-smoking wunderkind David Stockman, only thirty-four years old when he took office. Brash and brilliant, ambitious and idealistic, naive and erratic, he became director of the Office of Management and Budget after impressing Reagan by playing the role of Jimmy Carter in his debate preparation. Stockman would emerge as the dominant player on economic policy in the first year.

The cabinet also included a large number of duds. James Watt, a right-wing public interest attorney, was appointed Interior secretary after the first choice—a former senator from Wyoming—dropped out of contention over financial issues. Watt would stir up a storm of controversy with his embarrassing gaffes, his ideological zeal, and his unseemly eagerness to open up wilderness areas to economic exploitation. Another fallback choice was James B. Edwards, a dentist and former governor of South Carolina, who became secretary of energy notwithstanding his near total ignorance of energy issues after the front-runner, an oilman from Texas, declined to disclose his finances. When the Canadian ambassador called on Edwards, he got the distinct impression that the new secretary had never heard of a major US-Canada gas pipeline.[32]

Other cabinet members would be dogged by accusations of unethical conduct. Labor Secretary Raymond J. Donovan, a construction company executive from New Jersey and a prodigious Republican fundraiser, would be forced to resign in 1985 after becoming the first sitting cabinet member ever indicted on criminal charges. After being acquitted of fraud by a jury, he was left to plaintively demand where he could go to get his reputation back.[33] Secretary of Housing and Urban Development Samuel R. Pierce Jr., the only African American in the cabinet, would preside over one influence-peddling scandal after another; sixteen of his subordinates would be convicted of corruption.[34] A corporate lawyer from New York, Pierce had been recruited by Kitchen Cabinet member Alfred Bloomingdale, who had been tasked with finding "a black for the Cabinet."[35]

The Environmental Protection Agency was not a cabinet-level agency in the Reagan administration, but its administrator Anne Gorsuch—mother of future Supreme Court Justice Neil Gorsuch—presided over mismanagement at the Superfund toxic-waste clean-up program and was forced out of office after being cited for contempt of Congress. Her subordinate, EPA Assistant Administrator Rita Lavelle, went to prison for lying to Congress.[36]

The president-elect did not play much of a role in most of these appointments. During the campaign he had promised to eliminate the Departments of Education and Labor. They survived, but he was not overly concerned with who ran them or with most other domestic agencies for that matter. In June 1981, at a White House meeting with mayors, the president greeted Sam Pierce as "Mr. Mayor" and asked, "How are things in your city?" Reagan tried to laugh it off, but Pierce was mortified.[37] The president was just as confused about whom he had appointed to run the EPA: In a 1984 meeting, he twice addressed Anne Gorsuch's well-respected successor, William

Ruckelshaus, as "Don," apparently confusing him with Middle East envoy Donald Rumsfeld.[38] That same year, at the annual Gridiron Club dinner, the president gave no indication of recognizing Agriculture Secretary John Block when he stopped to chat.[39]

Reagan's inattention to management and his general hostility to government allowed chaos and corruption to run rampant at many agencies. By one count, there would be more officials indicted in the Reagan administration than in the Nixon administration, although the Nixon indictments brought down more senior officials.[40] Reagan's appointees showed the danger of imagining that people who were successful at business would invariably be successful in government. Some of them simply looked at their government posts as another opportunity for peculation—or appointed associates who did. Many Reaganites looked on their mission as being, in the words of Lyn Nofziger, to "dismantle" the government.[41] The Reagan team was not consciously trying to appoint incompetent or corrupt leaders, but it frequently did—and thereby helped discredit the government it loathed.

Foreign policy positions were considered more critical than those in domestic policy, but Reagan's initial record of appointees was just as spotty in that area. Dick Allen would turn out to be a weak national security adviser who would last less than a year. Bill Casey, the campaign manager, wanted to be secretary of state but, given that he was a chronic mumbler and tie-chewer, he was thought by Nancy Reagan, among others, to lack the requisite qualities to represent the United States on the world stage. He was appointed, instead, to run the CIA because of his background as an OSS officer in World War II. Washington wags joked that Casey didn't need a "scrambler" phone because no one could understand what he was saying anyway. To sweeten the deal, the CIA director was elevated for the first time to the cabinet. A zealous cold warrior and devout Catholic whose politics were described by a friend as "to the right of Attila the Hun," Casey would rebuild and revitalize the spy agency after the scandals of the 1970s but also display a dangerous contempt for congressional oversight and cut far too many ethical corners in covert operations.[42]

The position Casey coveted—secretary of state—went to retired general Alexander M. Haig Jr., a former White House chief of staff and NATO commander with a hair-trigger temper and a face that looked as if it had been carved from granite. He had been recommended by Richard Nixon, who assured the new president that Haig was "intelligent, strong and generally shares your views on foreign policy" and that "he would be personally loyal to you and would not backbite you on or off the record."[43] In fact, Haig would turn out to be thin-skinned, turf-conscious, and self-aggrandizing. He would begin the administration by trying unsuccessfully to take charge of all crisis management and publicly proclaiming himself the "vicar" of foreign policy. Haig made clear he did not believe that any other official—especially the president—had enough experience or wisdom to shape foreign policy, and he clashed in particular with the powerful secretary of defense, Caspar Weinberger.

Weinberger, admittedly, had little background in national security policy beyond his World War II service as a junior officer on General Douglas MacArthur's staff. But Weinberger had a long-standing relationship with Reagan, which Haig lacked, although it would be a stretch to describe Weinberger as one of Reagan's "oldest friends"; they were old colleagues, not old friends.[44] Weinberger had served not only as state finance director in Sacramento but also as chairman of the Federal Trade Commission, director of the Office of Management and Budget, and secretary of the Department of Health, Education and Welfare. As OMB director in the Nixon administration, he had been such a zealous budget cutter that he had earned the nickname "Cap the Knife." He was appointed secretary of defense with the expectation that he would serve as a prudent steward of a growing defense budget. Indeed, many conservatives criticized his appointment because they did not think he was hawkish enough. But, acting like a lawyer representing a client, he became a zealous defender of every last penny of Pentagon spending.

The final cabinet member in foreign policy was Jeane J. Kirkpatrick, the only woman and only Democrat in the group. She was a "neoconservative" professor at Georgetown University who had caught Reagan's eye by writing a *Commentary* article, "Dictatorships and Double Standards," excoriating the Carter administration for being too tough on right-wing dictatorships and too soft on Communist ones. That earned her an appointment as United Nations ambassador. But, while she would achieve celebrity on the right for her staunch defense of US interests at the United Nations, she would exercise little influence in actual decision-making. "Many people think a woman shouldn't be in high office," she complained of her administration colleagues.[45]

Even President Reagan, the soul of gentility, could be belittling about women in public life. Betraying his age and upbringing, he privately referred to Republican congresswoman Margaret Heckler of Massachusetts, whom he appointed in 1983 as secretary of the Department of Health and Human Services, as "a good little girl."[46] Such comments may have been unexceptionable in 1920s Dixon, but they were considered patently offensive in 1980s Washington. Haig was even more openly sexist. He bridled at Kirkpatrick's elevation and reportedly fumed, "I don't know how anybody expects that I will work with that bitch."[47]

It was not much commented on at the time, but the cabinet had little ethnic or gender diversity. There was one Black member and one woman. There were no Jews, Hindus, Muslims, Latinos, or Asian Americans. Women and minorities were no better represented on the White House staff. The only woman in a senior White House policy role was Elizabeth Dole, who was in charge of mobilizing outside interest groups, and Reagan did not have a Black member of his inner circle until Colin Powell became national security adviser in 1987. Most of the Black and brown faces in the executive mansion belonged to the household staff. A few African Americans were appointed to other agencies, most prominently future Supreme Court justice Clarence Thomas first as assistant secretary of education and then chairman of the Equal Employment Opportunity Commission.

This was, admittedly, an era when American society was much more heavily white and male-dominated and "diversity" much less of a priority. But Jimmy Carter had made strenuous efforts to promote women and minorities.[48] Diversity simply was not as much of a priority for Ronald Reagan, whose administration would seek to repeal affirmative action programs. "Although the Reagan people are not strongly biased against women and blacks, they seldom realize the need to bring women and blacks into their operation," said Lyn Nofziger.[49]

The priority for the Reagan White House was filling subcabinet posts with reliable conservatives, not women or people of color. This led to regular clashes between White House personnel director E. Pendleton "Penn" James, a close ally of Ed Meese, and cabinet secretaries who were intent on appointing experienced pragmatists rather than conservative ideologues to their teams.[50]

W hile Reagan was largely aloof from staffing his own administration, he was more intently focused on what he would say when it began. The inaugural address was crafted by the former Nixon wordsmith Kenneth Khachigian, who been recruited to write speeches during the general election campaign. Reagan began the process on December 16, 1980, by talking with Khachigian for about twenty minutes and giving him a pile of four-by-six-inch cards he had been using to deliver speeches. The key points that Reagan stressed: "Careful not to take a crack at previous administration. Spiritual element is important. Reach out to disaffected. Not a laundry list. Grand themes—speak to history. 20 minutes outside—aim at 15." Khachigian then composed a draft that Reagan heavily revised. The president-elect wrote out the final version in longhand on a yellow legal pad.

The speechwriter did not want to include any quotations. "Nobody quotes great men quoting other great men," he told Reagan. But quotations—many of dubious provenance—had always been an integral part of Reagan's speeches. He was particularly eager to include a quote, sent to him by a supporter, from a soldier named Martin Treptow who had died in World War I. Treptow had kept a diary and on the flyleaf were written the words, "My Pledge: America must win this war. Therefore I will work. I will save, I will sacrifice, I will endure, I will fight cheerfully and do my utmost, as if the issue of the whole struggle depended on me alone."

This would be the first inaugural ceremony that would be held on the Capitol's West Front rather than the East Front; the choice was not, as widely reported, made by the new president but, rather, had been made the year before by the inaugural committee of Congress. Since the West Front faced out onto the Washington Mall and, beyond it, to Arlington National Cemetery, Reagan thought this would be an ideal opportunity to showcase Private Treptow's stirring words. Khachigian nearly spoiled those plans when he came back on January 18, 1981, to say that he had taken out the quotation because his researchers were having trouble verifying Treptow's words and had discovered he was buried in his hometown in Wisconsin. Reagan told him to put Treptow back in. The final speech implied, but did not state outright, that Treptow was buried at Arlington.

This was indicative of Reagan's devotion to emotional rather than literal truth. Only now that he was in the White House, he would have a team of writers and researchers scrubbing his utterances to try to take out some of the apocryphal stories and faux facts that he had been relying on for years. Such falsehoods would become rare in prepared speeches but would still pop up regularly in Reagan's extemporaneous remarks.[51]

The specter hovering over the inauguration was the fate of the US hostages in Iran. Jimmy Carter had gone without sleep in his final two days in office while working out the details of a deal to release them. He called Reagan, who was staying at Blair House, at 6:47 a.m. on January 20 to update him on the hostage negotiations. To Carter's astonishment, Reagan was still asleep. He returned the call after awakening at 8:31 a.m.[52]

A few hours later, the two men observed a tradition that would not be broken until 2021 by riding together in the presidential limousine to the inauguration. There wasn't much to say. The atmosphere, Reagan recalled, was "chilly." Ever the entertainer, he tried to fill the time with stock stories of Hollywood. "He kept talking about Jack Warner," Carter later said to an aide. "Who's Jack Warner?" Later, while the two men were waiting for the inaugural ceremony to start, Carter complained that Reagan "told a series of anecdotes that were remarkably pointless," including a joke about the Ayatollah Khomeini's long beard.[53]

Carter had been sworn in wearing a business suit. Reagan—or, more precisely, his wife—chose a more formal charcoal gray "stroller" jacket, with dove-gray waistcoat, striped gray trousers, and gray four-in-hand tie.[54] Nancy Reagan was typically resplendent in a red Adolfo dress, coat, and hat. That evening the president would don white tie and tails and the first lady a one-shouldered white gown from her favorite designer, James Galanos, to attend ten glitzy inaugural galas. Frank Sinatra, a Reagan family friend, planned the opulent festivities, which cost nearly five times what Carter's inauguration had. So many well-heeled supporters flocked to Washington that National Airport ran out of space for private aircraft and local rental companies ran out of stretch limousines. Liberal scolds denounced the lavish spectacle as "a bacchanalia of the haves," but the country was ready for a break from the austerity of the Carter years.[55]

The weather was unseasonably warm for January—in the fifties Fahrenheit—when at noon on January 20, Ronald Wilson Reagan rose to take the oath of office from Chief Justice Warren Burger using a patched-together old Bible handed down from Nelle Reagan. As the oath was being administered, the clouds dissipated, as if scripted by Hollywood, and the new president felt "an explosion of warmth and light" on his face, giving the religious chief executive the distinct impression that fortune was shining down on him.[56]

Reagan began his inaugural address by enumerating the "economic ills we suffer," including "one of the worst sustained inflations in our national history" and "idle industries" that "have cast workers into unemployment, human misery and personal indignity." In a similar vein, his erstwhile hero, Franklin D. Roosevelt, had begun his 1933 inaugural address with acknowl-edgment of "the dark realities of the moment." FDR had then promised gov-ernment action to lift the nation from misery.

Reagan took a very different approach. His most memorable line was, "In this present crisis, government is not the solution to our problem. Gov-ernment is the problem." He thereby heralded the most radical attempt to downsize spending and taxes since the advent of the New Deal a half cen-tury earlier. "It is my intention to curb the size and influence of the Federal establishment," he announced, and that very day he would sign executive orders decontrolling oil and gas prices and freezing some civilian hiring in the federal government. The Reagan Revolution had begun.

Reagan was making clear that he would not be dissuaded from attack-ing the government simply because he ran it; he would always act as if he were an outsider even while becoming the ultimate insider. That would make Reagan an oddly passive chief executive who would fail to effectively oversee his own subordinates. Populists had normally complained about "elites" in big business and big banks. Reagan redirected populist anger against big government. Yet, at the same time he reviled the American gov-ernment, Reagan celebrated America's achievements: "Here in this land we unleashed the energy and individual genius of man to a greater extent than has ever been done before." Left unanswered was how Americans could have accomplished so much if their government was so awful.[57]

Later that year, a longtime federal worker would write to the president complaining, "Your administration has made me feel ashamed to be a civil servant. You, Mr. President, have needled us in nearly every speech, all but calling us lazy." Reagan would sheepishly reply that "I have stated many times that the majority of government workers are ... good public servants," but "such lines are seldom if ever quoted."[58] This was another triumph of the imagination; the only federal workers he regularly lauded were soldiers and astronauts.

Reagan's incessant attacks on the federal government not only undermined the morale of some government workers and encouraged some corrupt officials to take advantage of their positions but also further intensified the suspicion of Washington that was already rife in America after Watergate and the Vietnam War. Public trust in the government had declined from 68 percent in 1968 to just 32 percent in 1980.[59] Jimmy Carter and Jerry Brown, among others, had tapped into similar anti-Washington sentiments, but Reagan took the argument further than they did and did more to undermine confidence in public institutions.

The inaugural speech drew a pointed if unspoken contrast with Carter's arguments that Americans had to accept a new age of limits. In calling for an "era of national renewal," the new president insisted, with his trademark sanguinity, "It is time for us to realize that we're too great a nation to limit ourselves to small dreams. We're not, as some would have us believe, doomed to an inevitable decline."[60] Reagan certainly had not limited himself to small dreams in his own life, having risen in sixty-nine years from an apartment above a saloon in Tampico to the White House. Ignoring the daunting obstacles that held others back, he imagined that everyone else in America was just as free to pursue their dreams as he had been.

Just a few minutes after finishing his speech, as he was about to address an inaugural luncheon in the Statuary Hall of the Capitol, President Reagan received word that the airplanes carrying the American hostages had finally left Iranian airspace. His presidency was already off to an auspicious start—and he had not yet done a thing. Now he would have to figure out how to address the far more intractable problems facing the nation.

In the White House

I enjoyed the ceremonial aspects that go with being president.

—RONALD REAGAN

W hen newly inaugurated presidents move into the White House, they know their lives have changed forever. They are no longer ordinary mortals. They are, proverbially speaking, walking with history. In almost every room are reminders of their predecessors: the Lincoln Bedroom where Abraham Lincoln signed the Emancipation Proclamation; the Oval Office originally built by William Howard Taft and moved to the side of the building by Franklin D. Roosevelt; the basement Situation Room constructed by John F. Kennedy. The White House is a museum, an office building, and a five-star hotel all in one. Some ninety butlers, stewards, cooks, maids, electricians, carpenters, florists, gardeners, and other household staff tend to the needs of the First Family. Newly elected presidents always appreciate the obsequious and efficient service, but they soon learn that it comes with a stiff price.

Most presidents find it hard to adjust to a life in which they are not allowed to drive or shop for themselves—or even to walk the streets anytime they feel like it. Their movements are tightly constricted by the demands of security; their every public utterance, no matter how prosaic, is instantly transcribed and treated as news. Bill Clinton described 1600 Pennsylvania Avenue as "the crown jewel of the federal penitentiary system," and Barack Obama complained, "It's like a circus cage, and I'm the dancing bear."[1]

Although he had lived much of his life in the public eye, Ronald Reagan was hardly immune to feelings of frustration about what he described as a "bird-in-a-gilded-cage sense of isolation." More than once he would stare out the window, envying the freedom of ordinary people walking by on Pennsylvania Avenue. In early February 1981, he wanted to continue his usual practice of going to a store to buy Nancy a Valentine's Day card. His

Secret Service detail took him to a nearby gift shop. The result, as an aide
wrote, was "total pandemonium, as stunned customers milled around and
a crowd of onlookers formed." "That was just about my last shopping expe-
dition outside the White House," Reagan ruefully wrote. "It caused such a
commotion that I never wanted to do that to a shopkeeper again." He did
not go to church regularly for the same reason: He claimed not to want to
inconvenience the congregation at nearby St. John's Church ("the church of
the presidents") by forcing them to pass through metal detectors, although
Stuart Spencer told me the president simply preferred to read the funnies
on Sunday morning.[2]

Despite some inevitable difficulties—"the first few days were long and
hard," Reagan noted in his diary[3]—he settled into the presidency easier and
faster than many of those who have occupied that august office. That was in
part because he was so easygoing, in part because he had been used to taking stage directions ever since his days in Hollywood, and in part because
he had already been the governor of the most populous state and a three-
time presidential candidate. Although he was a former movie and television
star who railed against "professional politicians," he was an experienced
politician himself by the time he assumed the nation's highest office. His
first taste of politics had come, after all, more than three decades earlier as a
leader of the Screen Actors Guild during the Hollywood Red Scare.

Nothing really prepared you to be president—a job that came with a
laminated wallet card, called "the biscuit," that contained the authenti-
cation codes needed to launch a nuclear strike that could kill hundreds of
millions of people—but Reagan had more preparation than many others
for the job's daily demands. "My first morning in the Oval Office had a
surprising ring of familiarity to it," he later wrote. "It reminded me a lot
of my job as governor. On my desk was a schedule of appointments for the
day; there were meetings with the cabinet, staff and legislators; and outside my door were Ed Meese, Mike Deaver and others who had been with
me in Sacramento."[4]

———

Ronald Reagan's life, of course, was far more tightly circumscribed
and regimented in the White House than it had been in the State Capitol. The Troika dictated that only a small number of people—a handful of
family members, the vice president, the Secret Service, his physician, his

secretary—could directly reach the president on the telephone. Anyone else, including cabinet members, the chairman of the Joint Chiefs of Staff, foreign heads of state, members of Congress, and old Hollywood friends, had to have their calls cleared by one of the Troika.[5]

Few if any presidents have ever been so totally isolated even from their most senior cabinet members. Secretary of State Alexander Haig was driven nearly to distraction by his inability to get a one-on-one meeting with the president.[6] Donald Regan took it more in stride, but he also found it bewildering. "In the four years that I served as Secretary of the Treasury," he wrote, "I never saw President Reagan alone and never discussed economic philosophy or fiscal and monetary policy with him one-on-one. From first day to last at Treasury, I was flying by the seat of my pants. The President never told me what he believed or what he wanted to accomplish in the field of economics. I had to figure these things out like any other American, by studying his speeches and reading the newspapers."[7]

Many presidents would call friends or allies to blow off steam or get an outside perspective. That is what Nancy Reagan did; Ron sometimes good-naturedly grumbled, in the years before email and texting, that she had a telephone glued to her ear all day long. But the president, as his personal aide Jim Kuhn noted, "was far more comfortable writing letters than talking on the telephone."[8] He happily devoted time to answering the thirty to fifty letters forwarded to him every week by the White House Correspondence Office out of the thousands they received every day. This was a practice that went back to his time answering fan mail in Hollywood. He regularly told his aides, Kuhn recalled, to "listen to the people, as they know what is best"; the letters were his way of communing with the vox populi.[9] While Reagan occasionally sent letters without his staff's knowledge, he almost never placed phone calls unless instructed to do so by the Troika—usually to seek support from a member of Congress or convey a message to a foreign leader. He would not even call his supposed First Friend, Senator Paul Laxalt, unless told to do so by the staff.[10]

Reagan would dutifully carry out his assignments, often writing "mission accomplished" on the call sheet, but it would never occur to him to seek an independent perspective on what the Troika was telling him. Dismissing numerous danger signs, the president was always convinced that "we have a darn good team" and that "the fellas," as he generically referred to his aides because he was always bad at remembering names, would take care of things. In fact, as Dick Darman noted of the fractious White House, calling it a " 'team' turned out to be more aspiration than description."[11]

Every phone call, every personal appearance, every meeting, no matter how perfunctory, now came with a script—or "talking points" as they were called in Washington. This was the case even for a ten-minute visit to the White House Map Room by a teacher and her students from the Chadwick School in Palos Verdes, California, which Maureen and Michael Reagan had attended. Before the Chadwick group arrived on March 18, 1981, the responsible staffer, Elizabeth Dole, dutifully sent the president a standard memorandum listing the meeting's purpose, background, participants, press plan, sequence of events, and talking points. She suggested the president tell the visitors, "Your devotion to education, in general, and to Chadwick School, specifically, has been much admired by many. Even before Mike and Maureen joined Chadwick, I was aware of your outstanding reputation. I am delighted to have the chance to greet you on this, your last Chadwick tour. Your retirement will be a great loss to Chadwick."[12]

The president undoubtedly enlivened his remarks with one of his trademark jokes or stories. But he often stuck to his talking points so robotically that some visitors came away thinking he did not really know what he was talking about or to whom he was talking. Eight years later, Canadian Prime Minister Brian Mulroney would be shocked on January 19, 1989, to receive a courtesy call from George H. W. Bush in which the president-elect was clearly "speaking extemporaneously." By contrast, he noted, "Ronald Reagan always followed a script, even in these conversations."[13]

Jimmy Carter received a wakeup call as early as 5:30 a.m., arrived at the Oval Office at 6:00 a.m., and often did not retire until 11:00 p.m. or even later.[14] The new president turned seventy on February 6, 1981—a milestone celebrated with a black-tie bash at the White House whose guest list included Frank Sinatra, Jimmy Stewart, and the tycoons of the Kitchen Cabinet—and in May he would become the oldest man ever to occupy the presidency up to that point.[15] He had no interest in working long hours, which in his view had not done Carter much good.

On a fairly typical day in Reagan's new life—Thursday, February 12, 1981, when he was shadowed by *Time* correspondent Laurence Barrett—he received a wakeup call at 8:00 a.m. There was a small TV set in his bathroom that he could watch while he shaved. He was a fast dresser who required, Dick Darman noted, "little time in the morning after arising to get prepared." His closet, located in a dressing room next to the spacious bedroom he shared with Nancy, was spare and uncluttered—reflecting, aide James Rosebush wrote, "a man of simple Midwestern tastes." He had exactly twenty-seven dress shirts, Reagan's personal assistant Jim Kuhn discovered, and he prided himself on getting two days' wear out of each shirt. Of course, most men of simple tastes do not have a valet to help them get dressed; the president usually did—a Navy steward from the Philippines.

On February 12, as usual, Ron had a light breakfast with Nancy in their second-floor family quarters full of familiar furniture from their old Pacific Palisades home. Normally, he ate "cereal and fruit, skim milk, and decaffeinated coffee." Both Reagans prided themselves on staying fit, and the petite first lady, in particular, had a horror of gaining a dress size. The president glanced over the news summary prepared by his press office and the newspapers the office sent up, looking for his favorite conservative columnists: William F. Buckley Jr., George F. Will, and James J. Kilpatrick. Invariably, like many of his contemporaries, he began with the comics section. "I am a comic strip reader from way back and still consider it a major crisis if I have to start a day without them," the president wrote to Chester Gould, the creator of *Dick Tracy*. "I rarely do." Highbrows scoffed; he didn't care.

Trailed by Secret Service agents, who transmitted his every movement by talking into microphones hidden in their sleeves, the president took his personal elevator to the first floor and crossed the Rose Garden colonnade to the Oval Office, arriving at 9:00 a.m. sharp. He dropped off a thick folder of papers he had read and signed with his secretary, Helene von Damm, saying proudly, like a student turning in his homework, "Look what I did last night." After the first lady complained about her husband having to stay up late to complete his nightly assignments, Dick Darman grumbled about "Nancy's bullshitting" but took care to regulate the reading packets so that the president had "a couple of hours work nightly—enough but not too much."

Reagan then walked into the most famous office in the world. The Oval Office did not look all that different than it had when Jimmy Carter worked there. It had the same tan carpet with blue flowers, the same couches and armchairs, the same *Resolute* desk built from the timbers of an old British warship that had been used by most presidents since Queen Victoria gave it

to Rutherford B. Hayes in 1880. Reagan had trouble fitting his knees under
the desk because the large rolling chair he brought from California was too
high, so he sat sideways, but he refused to complain to anyone. (Later that
year, an aide would arrange, on his own initiative, to have the desk raised by
two inches.) Displayed on a stand near the bookcase were miniature Western saddles in bronze—a gift from the publisher Walter Annenberg. On the
walls were portraits of George Washington, the first president, and Andrew
Jackson, the first Western populist president, along with a painting depicting Union troops in prayer during the Civil War. On the coffee table sat a jar
of jellybeans. Atop his desk was a hand-tooled leather plaque proclaiming
his managerial philosophy: "There is no limit to what a man can do or where
he can go, if he does not mind who gets the credit."

The president's staff arrived at work long before he did—and left much
later. Jim Baker was typically picked up by a White House car at 7:10 a.m.
and had bacon and eggs in his spacious West Wing corner office with Ed
Meese and Mike Deaver at 7:30 a.m. Baker then presided over a senior staff
meeting with two dozen people in the Roosevelt Room at 8:00 a.m. These
two meetings set the day's priorities and the "line of the day" to shape
news coverage. At 9:00 a.m., the Big Three briefed the president on what
lay ahead. The National Security Council's Richard Pipes was surprised
by "how little deference Deaver and Baker showed Reagan—they seemed
to treat him rather like a grandfather whom one humors but does not take
very seriously."

Every meeting with Reagan had to begin with at least one joke. Jim
Baker, who prepared with maniacal intensity for every assignment, came
in with fresh comedic material every day. The president, for his part, had
a seemingly inexhaustible supply of gags—many so off-color (at least by the
standards of the 1920s small-town Midwest) that he would never tell them
if a woman were present.

At 9:15 a.m., Vice President Bush and his chief of staff, Admiral Dan Murphy, arrived for an intelligence briefing from National Security Adviser
Dick Allen, who handed Reagan the President's Daily Brief (PDB), a top-
secret compendium of the latest intelligence. Sitting in a peach-colored
wingback chair by the crackling fireplace, Reagan asked a question about
the situation in Poland, where the Communist government was threatening to crack down on the Solidarity labor movement. While most presidents
insist on alterations in the PDB to suit their own style—some wanting more

detail, others less—Reagan was so unassuming and passive that he was content to receive pretty much the same briefing book as Carter. One of the few changes Allen insisted on was to have a larger, easier-to-read typeface. Reagan was a diligent reader of the PDB, as he was of most documents in his inbox. The PDB was "more like *Reader's Digest* than *War and Peace*," Meese noted, and the president, after all, was a longtime *Reader's Digest* subscriber.

Allen, Bush, and Murphy left fifteen minutes later, while press secretary James Brady and chief congressional liaison Max Friedersdorf came in to discuss economic issues. The Troika didn't go anywhere. Baker, Deaver, and Meese were all afraid to leave one of their number alone with the president or to leave Reagan on his own. "They were all busy keeping their eyes on each other, making sure no one was whispering in the President's ear about the other," noted David Stockman.

The rest of the president's morning included a meeting of the cabinet's Budget Working Group to consider budget cuts (Reagan often got bored at such gatherings and doodled), a meeting with the chairman of the Council of Economic Advisers, Murray L. Weidenbaum, and a brief statement to the press about the economy. Since it was Lincoln's birthday, the president traveled by motorcade shortly after noon to lay a wreath at the Lincoln Memorial. The day was frigid despite a "brilliant winter sun," wrote *Time*'s Larry Barrett. Reagan, after waiting outside in a thin topcoat for nearly fifteen minutes, was practically shaking by the time he delivered a brief tribute to the first Republican president.

The president preferred to eat lunch alone, usually soup and salad, although on Thursdays he liked to have the Mexican plate from the White House mess—"tacos, enchiladas, beans, rice, the works." On February 12, however, he had a working lunch with representatives from twenty Hispanic organizations in the second-floor dining room. On the menu were shellfish soup, filet mignon, artichoke salad, fruit compote, and California wine. He told them that five Hispanic appointments at the subcabinet level were "in the pipeline."

"By 2:15 p.m.," Larry Barrett noted, "he [was] back at his desk, making phone calls and signing papers." At 3:00 p.m., Dick Allen returned to the Oval Office with an NSC staffer to prepare for the president's next meetings. Half an hour later Reagan received the Italian foreign minister for a "courtesy call." As they exchanged stilted pleasantries via translators, Barrett noted, "a herd of photographers and TV crews bursts into the room, cameras blazing, and leaves a few moments later." Next in was the foreign minister of Oman for a similar session, focusing on how to resist Soviet advances in the Middle East. Reagan assured him that, whatever human rights violations his government might commit, "our policy was not to interfere in the domestic affairs of Oman." Reagan's staff tried to build in an hour of "office time" in the morning and afternoon when he could read or write or simply decompress. But today the schedule was a blur.

Between 4:40 p.m. and 5:10 p.m., the president sat down for a discussion with Baker, Deaver, Meese, Bush, and E. Pendleton James, the White House director of personnel, about appointments to ambassadorships and presidential boards. When the meeting ended, Reagan headed down to the tiny White House barber shop intending to get his weekly trim from barber Milton Pitts—a staunch Republican who cut the hair of Nixon and Ford but not Carter. He changed his mind about the haircut, however, and returned for his normal, fifteen-minute, end-of-the-day wrap-up session with Baker, Meese, and Deaver. He then spent twenty minutes talking to the reporter who had been tailing him all day. "It's very funny how quickly you settle in and your habits are formed, living habits and all the rest," he told Larry Barrett. "It's strange, but it has happened."

At 5:50 p.m., the president returned to the family quarters—living "above the store," he called it. He took with him color-coordinated folders full of his nightly homework: orange folders for telephone calls, blue for unclassified information, yellow for signatures, and the like. He enjoyed nothing more at this point than to change into his pajamas and eat dinner with "Mommy" off trays in front of the television. But this evening he and Nancy had to go to the vice president's residence at the Naval Observatory, where George and Barbara Bush were hosting them at dinner. "Just the 4 of us & most enjoyable," Reagan noted politely in his diary. They arrived back at the White House at 9:38 p.m. At 10:50 p.m., after some bedtime reading of government documents, he retired for the night.

While some presidents were notorious for operating by their own clock, Reagan was meticulous about following his schedule down to the minute and got annoyed when others were late. "His session started on time. . . . He focused on the specific agenda, and he dismissed us promptly," Education Secretary Terrel Bell noted of cabinet meetings. Peter Wallison, the White House counsel in 1986–1987, got used to seeing Reagan's eyes "kind of glaze over" five minutes before a meeting was scheduled to end. Wallison took that as a sign that the president was thinking of a joke to end the meeting in a good mood and get to the next one on time. Reagan was always acutely conscious that if one of his meetings ran late, then he would be inconveniencing those waiting to see him next. It never occurred to Reagan to deviate from his daily schedule, any more than it would have occurred to him to deviate from his shooting script in Hollywood.[16]

Reagan was often mocked for starting work later and returning to the White House residence earlier than other presidents and even for napping during the day (which he rarely did). He deflected such attacks with one of his typically disarming quips: "It's true that hard work never killed anybody, but I figure why take the chance?"[17] In reality, the criticism got to him. "The press keeps score on office hours," he complained in his diary, "but knows nothing about the never ending desk & paperwork that usually goes on 'till lights out."[18] And he wrote indignantly to a student, "I don't take daily zzzz's. That's another distortion of the press."[19] Dick Darman confirmed that the president was diligent about going through all of his assigned paperwork: "He was a clean desk man."[20]

As his daily schedule showed, in fact, Reagan did work hard, even if not as hard as many other presidents. "He was the most civilized president I've worked for in terms of work hours," said John Negroponte, who was Reagan's deputy national security adviser from 1987 to 1989. "He was a real American. He believed in working nine to five."[21]

But while Reagan had serious flaws as a chief executive—even CIA Director Bill Casey complained "about the President's lack of interest in specifics, his unwillingness to take hard decisions (especially between feuding cabinet members) and his rather simplistic view of the world"—these shortcomings would not have been fixed simply by arriving at the Oval Office an hour earlier or staying an hour later.[22] Losing sleep, however, might have impaired his greatest assets: his ability to communicate and to charm.

Weekends brought a welcome respite from the daily grind of the White House. Typically, around 3:00 p.m. on Friday, the Reagans would board a limousine or the Marine One helicopter for the trip to Camp David. Nestled in the heavily wooded Catoctin Mountains of Maryland about sixty miles outside Washington, the presidential retreat had been built in 1942 on the site of an old Works Progress Administration camp. Franklin Roosevelt dubbed it "Shangri-La" after a fictional Himalayan paradise. President Eisenhower thought the name was "just a little fancy for a Kansas farm boy" and renamed it after his grandson David. Numerous presidents had added various improvements over the years, but it remained rustic in the style of a summer camp or hunting lodge. There were twenty cabins, a recreation center, a pool, a gym, a health clinic, and various other facilities to take care not only of the First Family and their visitors but also of the Navy personnel who ran the site.

The presidential cabin was called Aspen, and it was described by one of the camp commanders as "very much like your grandparents' longtime home—dated but comfortable furniture, aged-stone fireplaces, bookshelves filled with leather binders containing press clippings and articles of historic events." By the time the Reagans first arrived on the weekend of January 30, 1981, Aspen was not looking its best: "The bathrooms were old, with wheezing pipes and aging tile, and the room had a hodgepodge feeling." The furniture looked as if it had been "purchased at a garage sale" and "the TV in the bedroom sat on a tubular metal stand with gold paint flaking off."

Having found the White House too rundown, Nancy Reagan was in the process of an extensive and costly renovation of the living quarters that attracted controversy for its extravagance, even though all the money was privately raised. She might have been repulsed by the condition of Camp David, which was in far worse shape than the White House. Instead, she was charmed by its rusticity. She convinced the Navy to make some minor upgrades and was content with that.[23]

"I had a tremendous feeling of release when we got to Camp David," Nancy Reagan later wrote.[24] Her husband felt the same way. A natural introvert, he found that "the days I hated most were those with nonstop meetings, one after another, with no time to collect my thoughts." While the president would always bring "a pile of homework" to Camp David and tape his Saturday-morning radio address from there, the retreat also provided plenty of time to relax. Because the grounds were so secure—the complex was hidden behind heavy woods and an electrified fence patrolled by Marines and Secret Service agents—he could walk outside anytime.[25] His favorite recreational activities, as always, were swimming and horseback riding. "I guess it is the old lifeguard in me, or maybe I still like to show off for Nancy, but I still enjoy doing a swan dive and a jack knife now and then," he wrote.[26] He also enjoyed simply reading a book by the fireplace.

During their eight years in the White House, the Reagans visited Camp David more than any other First Family had, for a total of 517 days, or almost a year and a half.[27] When they didn't have time to go back to their own ranch near Santa Barbara, this Maryland retreat was where they came to escape the rigors of the White House. "The president and first lady really loved Camp David," said military aide Peter Metzger.[28]

Of course, a president never really goes anywhere alone. Although the Reagans seldom invited guests to Camp David, they were always accompanied by their Secret Service detail and the president's personal assistant, physician, a military aide carrying "the football" (the aluminum and leather satchel with nuclear strike options), their Marine helicopter pilots, and a few other aides. Ever considerate, Ronald Reagan felt guilty about dragging all these people away from their families on the weekends and sometimes invited spouses and children to join them. In the second term, Rex, a Cavalier King Charles spaniel given to the First Family by William F. Buckley Jr. for Christmas 1985, usually accompanied them, too. Their other dog, Lucky, a Bouvier des Flandres given to them in December 1984, was so rambunctious that he was exiled to the California ranch.[29]

On Friday and Saturday nights, the Reagans would ask their staff to join them to watch a movie. Ron and Nancy would sit together on the couch, often holding hands, while the rest of the audience gathered around them in armchairs. Then a motorized movie screen would descend from the ceiling and a film—either a recent release or an oldie—would be projected. A steward would pass out popcorn and drinks. If a horse appeared on the screen, Rex would often bark, and the president would tell him to be quiet.[30]

When the lights went on, the president would ask everyone what they thought. Naturally if the film being screened was one he had acted in, as it sometimes was, everyone was careful to praise it. Reagan still took great pride in his movie career, as he did in his athletic prowess, and was genuinely hurt if anyone criticized his pictures—even *Bedtime for Bonzo*, which he screened at Camp David on June 22, 1984. The notoriously blunt Stu Spencer was the only Reagan aide who had had the temerity to tell the president that playing second banana to a chimpanzee had not been a good idea.[31]

As a movie professional himself, Reagan would sometimes deliver film criticism that would never occur to a normal viewer. After Steven Spielberg screened *E.T. the Extra-Terrestrial* at the White House in 1982, the president, who cried during E.T.'s brush with death, pulled the director aside and complained that the closing credits, at three minutes, were too long. "In my day, when I was an actor, our end credits were maybe fifteen seconds long," he said. Spielberg politely ignored the president's advice to truncate the credits.[32]

Generally, however, Reagan was an indulgent, appreciative movie fan who often remarked that what he had just seen was "darn good." The only exception was when a picture transgressed the mores of the early twentieth-century Midwest where he had grown up. On Valentine's Day 1981, for example, the Camp David audience screened *9 to 5*, a satire about three secretaries—played by Jane Fonda, Lilly Tomlin, and Dolly Parton—who get revenge on their sexist boss by kidnapping him and running the business themselves. Reagan thought it was "funny," but he was "mad" about a scene that showed the stars smoking marijuana. "A truly funny scene if the 3 gals had played getting drunk but no they had to get stoned on pot," he fumed in his diary. "It was an endorsement of Pot smoking for any young person who sees the picture."[33] Nancy Reagan would make her signature initiative a campaign to discourage drug use under the slogan "Just Say No," and the Reagans extended their stern disapproval to marijuana, which they associated with the radicals and hippies in Berkeley.

The president expressed an even greater dislike of *The Big Chill* (about a reunion of old college classmates suffused with the sex, drugs, and rock 'n' roll ethos of the 1960s) and *Kiss of the Spider Woman* (about the friendship in a Brazilian prison between a leftist revolutionary and a transgender woman).[34] "It was dreadful," Nancy Reagan complained of *Kiss of the Spider Woman*, which starred William Hurt and Raul Julia. "We turned it off halfway through the reel." The Reagans, said Mike Deaver, who had recommended the film, were "still clinging to the values of the 1950s."[35] The nation would pay a high price for the president's old-fashioned sensibilities after a new virus called the human immunodeficiency virus (HIV) was identified in 1981. It primarily afflicted gay men and intravenous drug users, two groups that were invisible in the smalltown Midwest where he grew up. The Reagan administration was tragically slow to mobilize a federal response even as the victims piled up.

The president's worldview had been formed long ago in an America very different from the one he led in the 1980s. He liked movies like John Huston's rousing *Victory*, starring Sylvester Stallone, about a soccer match between Allied prisoners of war and their German captors during World War II. "The pic. is good & will be good for people to see," he wrote in his diary. "It has a flag-waving finish."[36]

Flag-waving was very important to Ronald Reagan—and to his presidency. On April 14, 1981, after the *Columbia* completed the first space shuttle mission with a flawless touchdown at Edwards Air Force Base in California, he wrote in his diary, "Our astronauts landed and what a thrill that was. I'm more & more convinced that Americans are hungering to feel proud & patriotic again."[37]

His administration set out to feed that palpable hunger with a series of rousing, patriotic extravaganzas that might have been scripted by Cecil B. DeMille or Busby Berkeley. These spectacles began even before he was inaugurated. The inaugural committee staged an "opening ceremony" on January 17, 1981, at the Lincoln Memorial that was attended by fifteen thousand people despite temperatures hovering around twenty-five degrees Fahrenheit. The Mormon Tabernacle Choir sang "God Bless America" and the "Battle Hymn of the Republic," and the Army band boomed out Aaron Copland's "Fanfare for the Common Man" and John Philip Sousa's "Stars and Stripes Forever," while red, white, and blue fireworks exploded overhead and emerald-green lasers illuminated the night sky.[38] The next day, Reagan told speechwriter Ken Khachigian that he had found the whole spectacle so moving ("I've never been filled with such a surge of patriotism") that he had been "crying frozen tears"—and, Khachigian recorded, "Even as he was telling me this story, his eyes filled up again. He looked at me and said it was going to be hard to keep his eyes dry."[39]

The newly sworn-in president was just as moved eleven days later when, on January 28, he hosted a televised welcome-home ceremony on the South Lawn of the White House for the fifty-two American hostages freed from Iran. A quarter of a million Washingtonians turned out to welcome the hostages and their families as they were transported in buses from Andrews Air Force Base to the White House for a ceremony featuring military honor guards amid a sea of flags and yellow ribbons. The ceremony was designed to "send chills up your spine," wrote a reporter. "Everything was done to

maximize the dramatic effect—and that objective was accomplished."[40]
The president and first lady watched the hostages and their families arriving from a second-floor window "with tears in their eyes." Reagan initially
began shaking hands with the dazed former hostages but then said, "Oh, I
can't stand this!" and began to hug and kiss them.[41] "I've had a lump in my
throat all day," he wrote in his diary.[42]

———————

After seeing how quickly their years in Sacramento passed in a whirl of
activity, both Reagans, at Nancy's suggestion, kept handwritten diaries
during the presidency in order to remember their time at the top. After
allowing her ghostwriter to make use of it for her memoirs, Nancy ordered
her diary destroyed before her death. But her husband's diary was published. It was a fairly perfunctory chronicle, really an annotated version
of his daily schedule, which was devoid of introspection, self-doubt, astute
psychological insights, or acerbic put-downs—all the things that make other
diaries entertaining reading. "It was pretty banal, frankly," the president's
son Ron said. And yet senior White House aide Craig Fuller said that the
intensely private president expressed more of his feelings in the diary than
he ever did in person.[43]

While the diary revealed Reagan's intellectual limitations, it also show-
cased the strength of his character: He was a patriot who was utterly dedicated to the country and an optimist who was almost always cheerful in
the performance of his duties. There was no hint in his diary—or anywhere
else—of any cynicism or self-serving motives. (Of course, he may have been
composing his diary with one eye on history, knowing that it would be read
by historians, but subterfuge was hardly his style.) Reagan told his appointees that "every decision" they made "should be based only on the criterion
of what is best for the United States of America" and not on any short-
term political calculation.[44] That is not to say politics was ever absent from
administration deliberations or even from Reagan's own calculations, but
those who knew him generally agreed that he was less cynical and less self-
serving than many other politicians. "I certainly didn't agree with a lot of
the Republican agenda," said White House photographer Pete Souza, "but
I always felt that he honestly was trying to do what he thought was best for
the country."[45]

Reagan was constantly tearing up during patriotic occasions: "Somehow the Star Spangled Banner when you hear it in another country brings a tear to the eye," he wrote on March 11, 1981, during a brief trip to Canada. And he never took his high office for granted. In New York on March 13, 1981, on their way to see their son Ron dance with the Joffrey Ballet, the Reagans took a motorcade from LaGuardia Airport to the Waldorf-Astoria hotel in midtown Manhattan along a route lined with clapping and cheering crowds. "I wore my arms out waving back to them," the president wrote in his diary. "I keep thinking that this cant [sic] continue and yet their warmth & affection seems so genuine I get a lump in my throat. I pray constantly that I wont [sic] let them down."[46]

As commander-in-chief, Reagan felt a special responsibility to the troops—and, like his erstwhile hero FDR, he made expert use of the "bully pulpit" to inspire them. The new president made a big impression on the armed forces by journeying to the Pentagon on February 24, 1981, to award a Medal of Honor to Master Sergeant Roy P. Benavidez, a Green Beret hero from the Vietnam War. Reagan even read the sergeant's citation personally, something that presidents did not normally do. "The military services had been restored to a place of honor," wrote Brigadier General Colin Powell, who was then working in the Pentagon.[47]

Such shows of presidential support combined with big defense-budget increases to help the military recover from its post-Vietnam nadir. *Baltimore Sun* reporter Robert Timberg, a battle-scarred Vietnam veteran, wrote that, while he was no Reaganite, he was grateful to Reagan because he "portrayed servicemen not as persons to be feared and reviled—ticking time bombs, baby-killers, and the like—but as men to whom the nation should be grateful, worthy of respect and admiration."[48]

For many presidents, making hortatory speeches, greeting delegations, and presiding over ceremonial events was a distraction from the real work of governing. From Reagan's perspective, having come from show business, symbolism and speechmaking *were* the main business of the presidency. "I . . . enjoyed the ceremonial aspects that go with being president," he acknowledged. As for the actual management of the government, he said modestly, "I have three guys who mostly run things for me."[49]

That was no exaggeration. White House spokesman Larry Speakes noted that Reagan "really did have little interest in details. . . . Nor did he choose to involve himself in many points of substance." Reagan would say of his aides, "They tell me what to do," as if he were not the ultimate boss.[50] Reagan saw his job as being the salesman for the policies that his aides formulated based on the vague guidance offered by his speeches and private comments. When it was not clear what the president wanted, his aides often acted on their own preferences while claiming they were channeling his innermost desires—and they usually got away with it.

While Reagan's critics would accuse him, with some legitimacy, of living in a land of "make-believe," they could not deny that his presidential performance was effective—and therapeutic for a nation battered by the traumas and the loss of confidence of the 1970s. He arguably made more effective use of television than any other president. Prime Minister Mulroney of Canada marveled, "He never took a bad picture or gave a bad speech."[51] He did, however, have many bad press conferences; without a script, he often stumbled in addressing complicated issues he did not truly understand. The White House press office would regularly issue "clarifications" of Reagan's off-the-cuff statements.

It was no insult to say that Ronald Reagan was the "acting president." All presidents have to act. Reagan just did it better than most—his only rivals in the twentieth century being Theodore Roosevelt, Franklin D. Roosevelt, and John F. Kennedy. As the end of his presidency neared, he remarked, "There have been times in this office when I wondered how you could do the job if you hadn't been an actor."[52]

All good actors convey emotional truths to their audiences, and Reagan proved more effective at this task in Washington than he had been in Hollywood. He was far more of a natural as the president than as the caddish playboy Drake McHugh in *Kings Row* or even the dying gridiron great George Gipp in *Knute Rockne, All-American*. His decency and good humor shone through every public appearance. He wore the burden of office lightly, and that inspired confidence in his leadership—at least among most white Americans. Most African Americans, in contrast, remained resistant to the Reagan charm because of his long history of catering to bigots, which did not end in the White House.

"Part of his personality was not to look like he had the weight of the world on his shoulders," Ed Meese said. "He didn't think that was the picture he should present to the public." Pete Souza remarked that Reagan's "even keel disposition" was similar to Barack Obama's: "It would take a lot to get them riled up. They didn't get very high, didn't get very low." Souza did find, however, that it was a lot harder to get to know Reagan than Obama, who was more of a "regular guy."[53]

One of Reagan's speechwriters, Peggy Noonan, wrote that "what always struck me was his friendly grace, his enjoyment of the moment and of other people and his intuitive understanding of the presidential style." Some occupants of the office learn how to behave presidentially, she noted; others never do. "Reagan always comported himself as if he got it so easily, so effortlessly, that he didn't even notice that he had it."[54] He was a natural at the symbolism, if not the substance, of the presidency.

And yet his presidential performance almost ended just sixty-nine days after it had begun.

35

Finest Hour

Honey, I forgot to duck.

—RONALD REAGAN

Monday, March 30, 1981, dawned gray and overcast in Washington.[1] Ronald Reagan began the day with an 8:30 a.m. pep talk in the East Room to subcabinet appointees "to personally welcome you to our team," followed by the usual meeting with the Troika in the Oval Office and the intelligence briefing with National Security Adviser Dick Allen.[2] Also scheduled that morning were a telephone call with German chancellor Helmut Schmidt and a gathering with Latino supporters. At 12:25, the president had lunch with Ted Graber, the interior decorator from Beverly Hills whom Nancy had hired to redo the family quarters. At 2:00 p.m., the president was due to speak to the AFL-CIO's Building and Construction Trades Department at the Washington Hilton Hotel. This was part of his continuing outreach to blue-collar households, which, despite the hostility of union leaders, had given him nearly half of their votes in 1980.

At 1:45 p.m., the president's armored Lincoln Continental limousine, code-named Stagecoach and weighing more than ten thousand pounds, pulled away from the White House. Reagan, who was known as Rawhide to the Secret Service (Nancy was Rainbow), was joined for the four-minute ride to the hotel by Labor Secretary Ray Donovan. Sitting in the front passenger seat was Jerry Parr, the lead agent on the presidential detail. A former electrical company lineman who had joined the Secret Service in 1962 and looked a bit like the actor Walter Matthau, Parr had decided to take the trip to get to know the new president a little better. At the wheel was Agent Drew Unrue.

Ahead of the presidential limousine were Metropolitan Police outriders on motorcycles, a police cruiser, and a decoy limousine carrying the president's physician Dr. Daniel Ruge, a onetime colleague of Nancy Reagan's stepfather, Dr. Loyal Davis. Close behind Stagecoach was an armored Cadillac code-named Halfback carrying six heavily armed Secret Service agents, including a former college football player named Tim McCarthy and shift supervisor Ray Shaddick. Following Halfback was the "control car" carrying a military aide with the "nuclear football," the president's personal assistant David Fischer, and Mike Deaver. A senior White House staffer almost always traveled with the president, and today it was Deaver's turn. Next was a staff car with the burly press secretary, Jim Brady, along with speechwriter Mari Maseng and a photographer. Trailing behind were two vans carrying the press pool. In all, the motorcade comprised fifteen vehicles.

Traveling down streets closed to traffic, Stagecoach reached the Hilton's VIP entrance at 1:52 p.m. The president stepped out, waved to some spectators and reporters behind a rope line, and went inside to meet the union leaders. Sixty-six Secret Service agents, along with police backup, deployed around the hotel and grounds to safeguard him.[3]

The speech before four thousand union members went as well as could be expected, ending in polite applause. At 2:24 p.m., Reagan walked out of the VIP entrance. A clutch of reporters and spectators—about thirty people in all—was clustered behind a rope line just fifteen feet away. None of them had been cleared through a metal detector. The reporters were shouting questions, and Mike Deaver told Jim Brady to go deal with them. As Reagan approached the limousine, surrounded by Secret Service agents, Tim McCarthy opened the back door for him. A woman caught Reagan's attention by shouting "Mr. President! President Reagan!" Reagan turned and waved.

Suddenly there was a pop, and the smile disappeared from Reagan's face to be replaced by a look of terror. Then another pop and another. Six in all. The Secret Service agents knew immediately that they were hearing gunshots. Jerry Parr grabbed the president by the back of his belt and pants and, with help from Ray Shaddick, shoved him into the limousine's backseat, landing on top of him. "Let's get out of here! Haul ass!" he shouted at the wheelman. The limousine squealed away from the hotel driveway, leaving a scene of carnage in its wake.

Jim Brady, who was standing close to the rope line and in front of the president, was hit first; a bullet smashed into his skull. Police officer Thomas Delahanty was struck in the back. "I'm hit!" he screamed as he fell. Tim McCarthy did what Secret Service agents are supposed to do under the circumstances: Rather than ducking, he spread his arms to make himself as large a target as possible to shield the "protectee." He was hit in the chest and knocked to the ground near Brady and Delahanty. The fifth bullet struck the bulletproof window of Stagecoach and ricocheted just as Reagan and Parr were getting inside. The third and sixth shots went harmlessly by. Only 1.7 seconds elapsed from first shot to last.

A phalanx of Secret Service agents and police officers quickly overpowered a young man in a tan jacket who had been firing a .22 caliber revolver loaded with exploding Devastator rounds. The gunman turned out to be a mentally disturbed twenty-six-year-old, John Hinckley Jr., who had decided to shoot Reagan out of a demented desire to impress the actress Jodie Foster. He had become obsessed with her after seeing the 1976 movie *Taxi Driver* at least fifteen times. The main character in the film, Travis Bickle (played by Robert De Niro), was an angry, alienated veteran who, after being spurned by a beautiful campaign worker (played by Cybill Shepherd), decides to assassinate her boss, a candidate for president. His plot thwarted by the Secret Service, Bickle sets out to violently liberate a child prostitute (played by Jodie Foster) from her pimp.

As so often seemed to happen with Ronald Reagan, real life was imitating reel life. A president who had spent much of his life promoting flickering fantasies was now trapped in a celluloid-induced nightmare. His only salvation lay in Jerry Parr, who, as a boy, had been inspired to join the Secret Service by one of Reagan's own Brass Bancroft movies: 1939's *Code of the Secret Service*.[4]

Inside the presidential limousine, Reagan was slumped over, "almost paralyzed by pain," he recalled.[5] "Were you hit?" Parr asked him. "No, I don't think so," Reagan replied. "I think you hurt my chest when you landed on top of me." Parr didn't see any blood, so initially he decided to head back to the White House. But then Reagan started having trouble breathing, his face turned gray and his lips blue, and blood began to appear on his lips. It was obvious he was hurt, but it wasn't clear what had happened. Maybe he had broken a rib falling into the limousine?[6]

Parr decided to head at top speed, sirens screaming, straight to the nearest trauma center, at George Washington University Hospital. It was 2:30 p.m. when they reached the hospital, just three minutes having elapsed since the shooting. No one was waiting to receive them, even though the Secret Service had tried to radio ahead. Reagan got out of the vehicle and started walking toward the sliding glass doors. He did not get far before his legs buckled. Parr and Shaddick grabbed his arms to prevent him from falling. The agents and medical personnel then lifted the president and carried him to the emergency room, where he was placed on a gurney.

His blood pressure was rapidly dropping. His pulse was faint. He was going into shock. Many of the medical personnel present did not expect him to survive. "Am I dying?" the president asked one of the physicians who first reached him. "I can't breathe, my chest hurts."[7]

The medical personnel cut off the president's new suit and found a small slit below his left armpit where Hinckley's fifth bullet had penetrated. There was no exit wound, which meant the bullet was still inside. He had a collapsed lung and a chest cavity filling with blood. One of the surgeons inserted a tube into his chest to relieve some of the pressure and started a blood transfusion. Feeling momentarily better, Reagan spotted Jerry Parr from his gurney and said through his oxygen mask, "I hope these guys are Republicans," meaning the doctors.[8]

While the doctors raced to save the president's life, Mike Deaver used a hospital telephone to call Jim Baker's office and break the terrifying news. "He's taken a shot in the back," Deaver said. "Jesus," said Meese. "Shit," said Baker, writing down on a slip of paper "P hit/fighting."[9] Baker and Meese, along with Lyn Nofziger and Larry Speakes, jumped into a White House car and raced to the hospital. When they arrived, the news was grim: The doctors said they feared Reagan was "bleeding to death" and "we're going to lose him."[10]

The first lady had panicked the second she heard there had been a shooting, even though she was initially informed that her husband had not been hit. The Secret Service didn't want to take her to the hospital—they didn't know if there were still assassins at large—but she told them she would walk if necessary. Arriving amid the "bedlam" of the emergency room, the distraught first lady demanded to see her husband. She was "near hysterics,"

Deaver observed.[11] The doctors were reluctant to let her in, not wanting to interfere with the medical care and fearing she would be traumatized by what she saw. But she insisted.

She walked in, as she wrote, to "a horrible scene—discarded bandages, tubes, blood." Ronnie looked "pale and gray." When he saw her, he pulled up his oxygen mask and repeated a line that heavyweight champion Jack Dempsey had used after losing a title fight in 1926: "Honey," he whispered, "I forgot to duck." Fighting back tears, she told him, "Please don't try to talk."[12]

At 2:57 p.m., thirty minutes after the shooting, the president was wheeled out of the trauma bay toward the operating room. Nancy walked alongside the gurney, and he held her hand. They passed by Jim Baker, Ed Meese, and Mike Deaver waiting anxiously nearby. Spotting them, Reagan quipped through his oxygen mask, "Who's minding the store?" and they responded with a nervous laugh.[13] Nancy Reagan went to the hospital chapel to pray, joined by Jim Brady's wife, Sarah.

As he was being put to sleep by an anesthesiologist, Reagan again used the line he had first employed in the trauma unit: "I hope you're all Republicans." Even strapped onto an operating table, he was doing what he always did: putting others at ease. This time, he got a laugh. The surgeon, Dr. Joe Giordano, was a Democrat, but he said, "Today, Mr. President, we're all Republicans."[14]

Back at the White House, National Security Adviser Dick Allen was convening senior officials in the windowless, cramped, wood-paneled Situation Room in the basement. Secretary of State Al Haig hurried to the White House as soon as he heard the news. He telephoned other cabinet secretaries and told them to do the same. He also called Vice President George Bush, who was on an airplane over Texas, to tell him to turn around and head back to Washington. But until Bush returned, it was not clear who was running the government.

Along with Allen and Haig, Defense Secretary Caspar Weinberger, Treasury Secretary Don Regan, CIA Director Bill Casey, White House counsel Fred Fielding, Attorney General Bill Smith, Bush's chief of staff Dan Murphy, and other officials assembled around the long table in the Situation Room. Allen had a duplicate "nuclear football" at his feet. Aides kept entering to update their bosses as the room filled with cigarette smoke and the table became littered with overflowing ash trays and Styrofoam coffee cups.[15]

This was one of those moments so traumatic and historic that most Americans would remember where they were when they heard the news. (This author was in an elementary school classroom in Riverside, California.) Even the hardened reporters in the city room of the *Los Angeles Times* "were momentarily immobilized by the awful rush of events," and some were choking back tears while others were silently praying at their typewriters. "Gone was the studied cynicism in which reporters customarily indulge," noted veteran reporter Larry Stammer.[16]

In the White House press room, reporters were clamoring for news, but no one was sure what to tell them. Larry Speakes, who had just come back from the hospital, hardly allayed their concerns. Asked who was running the government, Speakes said, "I cannot answer that question at this time." Watching on a television set in the Situation Room, Al Haig could not believe what he was hearing. "He's turning this into a goddamn disaster," he fumed.[17]

At 4:14 p.m., Haig charged upstairs to try to set the record straight, dragging Dick Allen with him. Gripping the wooden podium, he told the media, "Constitutionally, gentlemen, you have the president, the vice president and the secretary of state, in that order. And should the president decide he wants to transfer the helm to the vice president, he will do so. He has not done that. As of now I am in control, here in the White House, pending the return of the Vice President."[18] He was wrong: The secretary of state was not second in line to the presidency but, rather, fourth—after the speaker of the House and the president pro tempore of the Senate.

While Haig was trying to instill confidence in the nation, his words had the opposite effect. It sounded as if a power-mad general were seizing control of the government. It was not just what he said but how he said it: The secretary of state, who had had double heart bypass surgery the previous year, was perspiring and short of breath after his dash upstairs. Dick Allen, who was standing next to him, was afraid he would collapse. "He was a little off," Allen later said. "He had a Napoleonic vision of himself."[19]

Haig would never live down this rash statement about being in control of the government—the most famous utterance he would ever make.

Downstairs, the rest of the cabinet was incredulous at his words. Cap Weinberger let Haig know in no uncertain terms that the secretary of state was not in the military chain of command. Haig's days were now numbered. A few days later, Stu Spencer, an influential outside adviser, told Mike Deaver, "Haig needs a keeper; we have to be prepared for his replacement."[20]

There was still the matter of the Twenty-Fifth Amendment to the Constitution, which had been passed after John F. Kennedy's assassination. It provided that the vice president and a majority of the cabinet could pass power to the vice president if they signed a "written declaration" that the president was "unable to discharge the powers and duties of his office." White House counsel Fred Fielding had previously prepared the necessary documents to invoke the Twenty-Fifth Amendment and now brought them out for discussion. Alarmed at what he was hearing, Dick Darman grabbed the papers and locked them in his office safe. He did not want the group in the Situation Room—which, he noted, "had shown itself capable of chaotic, emotional, half-informed discussion"—to do anything rash in this hour of crisis. He knew there was no immediate national security emergency and that Bush would return before long.[21]

Bush landed at Andrews Air Force Base at 6:30 p.m. and reached the Situation Room a half hour later by motorcade. He could have gotten there faster by taking a helicopter to the White House lawn but that was normally a privilege reserved for the president; Bush did not want to be seen as usurping power or disturbing Nancy Reagan by landing right outside her window. With the even-keeled vice president now in the Situation Room, the situation calmed down a bit pending news from the hospital.[22]

At George Washington University Hospital, in Operating Room 2, the fight to save Reagan's life went on. He lost 3.5 liters of blood, more than half of his total blood volume. The surgeons were trying to extract the bullet, but they were having trouble finding it. Finally, at 5:40 p.m., Dr. Benjamin Aaron, the senior thoracic surgeon, discovered the flattened Devastator round, about the size of a dime, in the left lung and removed it. It had ricocheted off a rib and missed the president's heart by an inch. The surgeons stitched a damaged artery shut and began to sew up the patient at 6:00 p.m. The president's vital signs were strong, and the doctors became optimistic about his chances of recovery. He was in remarkably good shape for a man of his age.[23]

At 7:15 p.m., after having been moved to the recovery room, the president began to emerge from anesthesia. Everything he saw was white—the sheets, the walls, the coats of the medical personnel—making him wonder, like Jimmy Stewart in *It's a Wonderful Life*, if he was in heaven surrounded by angels.[24]

All four of the Reagan children were on their way to the hospital, but Patti, Mike, and Maureen, along with Michael's wife, Colleen Reagan, and Maureen's husband, Dennis Revell, would not arrive from California on a National Guard cargo aircraft until the next morning. Even when they were together, they remained isolated from each other. "What kind of family is this?" Patti wondered. "Even a bullet can't bring us together."[25]

The Secret Service chartered a Lear jet to fly Ron Reagan and his wife, Doria, from Lincoln, Nebraska, where he was traveling with a Joffrey Ballet touring company, and only Ron—his parents' favorite—arrived on the afternoon of the shooting. He and his mother went into the recovery room together. Seeing her husband with "his face drained of color, a tube in his throat to help him breathe, and all that equipment attached to his body," Nancy started to cry. "It was bad," Ron recalled. "It was much worse than people knew at the time."[26]

"I can't breathe," the president wrote on a pad. His son tried to explain to him that the ventilator was like scuba gear; it would help him breathe. They left him to try to rest, but, with nurses having to roll him over every four hours and pound him violently on the back to prevent a buildup of fluids in his lungs, he couldn't get any sleep. It sounded like butchers pounding a side of beef.

The breathing tube made it hard for Reagan to talk, so he asked the nurses for a pencil and paper. His first message was a paraphrase of W. C. Fields: "All in all, I'd rather be in Phil[adelphia]." More messages, mostly lighthearted, followed: "What happened to the guy with the gun? Was anyone else hurt? . . . Could we rewrite this scene beginning about the time I left the hotel? . . . If I had this much attention in Hollywood I'd have stayed there." And to an attractive nurse who was tending him, "Does Nancy know about us?"[27]

This was Ronald Reagan's finest hour. He had survived the shooting with his sense of humor intact. If, as Ernest Hemingway said, "Courage is grace under pressure," Reagan had exhibited impressive courage. Ironically, Al Haig, a four-star general, had buckled under the stress, but the former actor who had been shot had not. A Culver City Commando during World War II, Reagan was doing a credible imitation of the way stoical, wisecracking tough guys behaved in war movies. Only this was no movie; the blood was real and so was the pain. "Getting shot hurts," he wrote matter-of-factly in his diary.[28] His conduct after he was nearly killed at age seventy was his most impressive display of heroism since he had pulled seventy-seven people from the Rock River as a teenage lifeguard. "He was really magnificent," said his brother-in-law, Dr. Richard Davis, who visited him in the hospital. "His attitude was absolutely marvelous."[29]

This was Lyn Nofziger's finest hour too. Reagan's portly, perpetually disheveled former press secretary from Sacramento, now the political director in the White House, would not last long in Washington. But he performed one last, vital service for Ronald Reagan when Jim Baker asked him to go out and brief the press at George Washington University Hospital.

Nofziger announced that Reagan was undergoing surgery and so was Jim Brady. As he was stepping away from the microphone, a reporter asked, "Did he say anything?" "Oh, yes," Nofziger said. "I almost forgot." Taking out his notes, he recounted some of the president's best quips, such as "I hope you're all Republicans" and "Honey, I forgot to duck." This information convinced the nation the president was going to make it. More than that, it transformed Ronald Reagan from a politician into a legend. In that instant a bond was forged between the president and the American people that transcended party lines. It would be strained but never broken. Even many of those who disagreed with his policies admired his sangfroid in a life-threatening crisis.[30]

Jim Baker, Mike Deaver, and Ed Meese were eager to convince the nation that Ronald Reagan was still in charge, so the day after he was shot, they arrived at the hospital with a dairy support bill he needed to sign. "I should have known I wasn't going to avoid a staff meeting," the patient joked, before affixing a shaky signature.[31]

Despite the attempt to show a president working as normal, his path to recovery was hardly straightforward. Five days after being shot, Reagan began coughing up blood, and his temperature spiked because of an infection. Maureen Reagan wrote that "he was as close to death's door as I'd ever care to see him."[32] After seeing how awful he looked, Mike Deaver went home "and totally broke down."[33] But the president rallied yet again.

The doctors found that Reagan was not only resilient but also easy to deal with—unlike some other celebrities they had treated. He never complained, never imposed. Once he went into the bathroom, insisting he was well enough to wash himself, and did not come out for a long time. The nurse finally went in to discover him on his hands and knees cleaning up a spill he had made. "I made a mess and didn't want you to have to clean it up," he explained with typical consideration.[34]

On Saturday, April 11, 1981, twelve days after being admitted, Ronald Reagan was discharged from the hospital. The doctors wanted him to take a wheelchair, but he insisted on walking. A crowd of several hundred cheering supporters and aides greeted his return to the White House. He was wearing a red cardigan over a bulletproof vest.

Reagan had come closer to dying than his handlers were willing to admit, and he was still in bad shape. When Dick Darman went upstairs to the residence to see Reagan on the morning of April 12, he wrote, "I was shocked by his appearance. He was obviously uncomfortable walking. In the bright morning sunlight, his face looked deathly pale. His skin had a pallid, see-through quality. His distinctive smooth voice—the voice that had soothed listening audiences since his early days in radio—was lost. In its place was a low, raspy substitute. He had to strain visibly to ease himself into a deep sofa." Al Haig was also dismayed by the president's appearance: "He was a shell of his old self."[35]

Darman feared that Reagan might still suffer the fate of Woodrow Wilson, who became so disabled that others, including his wife, had to govern in his name. But "within a few weeks," he noted, "the President seemed to have been miraculously transformed. His color was back along with the bounce in his step." However, his son Ron Reagan noted that the shooting "aged him," and "he never quite had the energy that he had before."[36]

To aid her husband's recovery, Nancy Reagan had a gym installed on the second floor of the White House complete with exercycle, treadmill, hand weights, and weight machines for both legs and upper body work. Every day, Reagan would do ten minutes of warmups and fifteen minutes of exercises. "After a long day I genuinely look forward to jumping into my gym shorts and working out," he wrote in 1983. Before long he was boasting of all the muscles he had added to his chest and arms: "I am starting to worry some of my suits may split a seam," he wrote proudly.[37]

Agent Tim McCarthy and Officer Thomas Delahanty made a full recovery. Jim Brady was not so lucky; he would never return to work. His deputy, Larry Speakes, would take over his duties, but Brady would keep the title of press secretary and the salary that went with it as long as Reagan was president. Brady and his wife, Sarah, would become prominent advocates for gun control. When he died in 2014, the 1981 shooting was ruled as the cause of death.[38]

For the first two weeks after returning to the White House, Ronald Reagan did a bare minimum of work, briefly meeting with his top advisers upstairs while wearing pajamas and slippers. Vice President Bush filled in for him at most events. On April 24, Reagan returned to the Oval Office for the first time. "Whatever happens now I owe my life to God and will try to serve him in every way I can," he vowed in his diary.[39] He felt a particular calling to avert nuclear Armageddon.

Always brittle, Nancy Reagan was more emotionally scarred by the ordeal than her resilient husband. She was in a "state of shock" for a long time afterward and had trouble eating or sleeping. For months she couldn't even refer to the "shooting" or "assassination attempt." She called it "the thing that happened to Ronnie."[40] "For the rest of Ronnie's presidency—almost eight more years—every time he left home, especially to go on a trip, it was as if my heart stopped until he got back," she wrote.[41] For solace, she began paying a celebrity astrologer, Joan Quigley of San Francisco, for advice on how to adjust Ronnie's schedule to keep him out of danger. She took the fact that he was never again shot as vindication of her efforts.[42]

President Reagan emerged from the shooting stronger not only physically but also politically. On April 9, 1981, pollster Dick Wirthlin told Mike Deaver and Stu Spencer that there had been a 10 to 11 percent spike in the president's approval ratings since the shooting. Spencer noted that "RR is now perceived as a martyred surviving hero." These strategists began plotting, in Spencer's words, "to use the shooting incident to help jawbone a satisfactory economic package."[43]

Just a few days before the shooting, Dan Rostenkowski, the Democratic chairman of the powerful House Ways and Means Committee, had said there was no chance of passing the president's plan for a 30 percent cut in personal income taxes.[44] Now there was every chance in the world.

36

"The Whip Hand"

Appalled by what seems to me a lack of depth,
I stand in awe nevertheless of [Reagan's] political skill.
I am not sure I have seen its equal.

—JIM WRIGHT

In a letter to Ronald Reagan written after the election, in which he recommended Alexander Haig for secretary of state, former president Richard Nixon also offered some strategic advice for the administration's early days: "I am convinced that decisive action on the inflation front is by far the number one priority. Unless you are able to shape up your home base it will be almost impossible to conduct an effective foreign policy."[1]

The Reagan team hardly needed the advice. They understood that, with both inflation and interest rates in double digits, the public focus was on the economy. Richard Wirthlin reported that in his polls only 8 percent of respondents saw foreign policy as "the number one national problem."[2] Much to Haig's consternation, foreign policy was relegated to the back burner throughout the first year, with the president only taking brief foreign trips to Canada and Mexico. Social issues—which Reagan never liked to deal with and which Jim Baker liked even less—were even further down on the administration's priorities. "Our one hundred day plan says we are to have three priorities," said Senate Majority Leader Howard Baker, "and those three priorities are economic recovery, economic recovery, and economic recovery."[3]

During the campaign, Martin Anderson, the Hoover Institution economist, had been in charge of formulating an economic plan with input from outside advisers ranging from mainstream economist Alan Greenspan to impassioned supply-sider Jack Kemp. In the new administration, the driving force on economic policy would be David Stockman, who had a better grasp of the budget than anyone else in the White House. "He is the only person I ever met who actually read all of the federal budget," Anderson marveled.[4] Stockman was a fervent ideologue whose ideology had changed radically over the years. At Michigan State University in the 1960s, he had been, by his own description, a long-haired "neo-Marxist." As a graduate student at no less than the Harvard Divinity School, he had become a babysitter for the children of Daniel Patrick Moynihan, a former Harvard professor who was then domestic policy adviser in the Nixon White House, and he adopted Moynihan's centrism. This had led to a staff job with Congressman John Anderson of Illinois that turned him into a Republican.[5]

During his time in Washington, Stockman became a committed free-marketer. He ran on a conservative platform and won a House seat in Michigan in 1976. In the House he came under Jack Kemp's influence and became a supply-sider with quasi-theological devotion; he later said that Jude Wanniski's batty book *The Way the World Works* "hit me with the force of revelation."[6] With help from Jack Kemp and friendly columnist Robert D. Novak, Stockman secured the crucial position of director of the Office of Management and Budget. His calling card was a thirty-five-page memorandum warning of "an economic Dunkirk during the first 24 months of the Reagan administration," with another recession likely in 1981, unless the administration got inflation and spending under control.[7]

While Stockman wanted to cut taxes, he did not share Kemp's, or Reagan's, naive faith that tax cuts would pay for themselves. He jokingly described himself as only a "half-breed supply-sider" who was also a "kind of recidivist Hooverite." While Reagan kept insisting that "a cut in tax rates can very often be reflected in an increase in government revenues," Stockman was convinced that "the only way to pay for the massive Kemp-Roth tax cut" was with "a frontal assault on the American welfare state."[8]

Stockman's determination to cut spending went well beyond anything that Reagan had advocated as a candidate. There was no popular mandate or plan for a "Reagan revolution" to downsize government. The president was amenable to spending cuts, but, as Stockman noted, "he had no blueprint for radical governance." That was what Stockman supplied.[9] In cabinet meetings, Reagan focused on trivial budget savings—for example, making government motor pools run more efficiently.[10] Stockman knew that balancing the budget required slashing tens of billions of dollars from popular programs. Spare change from motor pools wouldn't cut it.

The Reagan team, as part of their desire to avoid being "Carterized," was determined to make rapid progress on its economic plan. Jim Baker's papers contain a blueprint for the start of the administration that called for a "decisive break with past, fresh hope for future," "emphasis upon new leadership," and setting a "brisk but not frantic pace."[11] The president's advisers were acutely aware that no president's honeymoon lasts long, and they were determined to strike while Democrats were still reeling from the 1980 election results. "We needed to hit the ground running," Ed Meese said.[12] Accordingly, the president was scheduled to address a joint session of Congress on February 18, 1981, only a month after taking office, to lay out his "Program for Economic Recovery." Stockman did not have long to come up with the actual program.

Beginning with his appointment on December 2, 1980, Stockman later wrote, he "began cranking up the budget-cutting machinery on a frantic schedule."[13] That wasn't easy to do because massive entitlement programs such as Social Security, veterans' benefits, and Medicare, which accounted for more than half of domestic spending, were off the table. That left only 17 percent of the budget—domestic discretionary spending—to absorb all the cuts.[14]

Much depended on what economic forecasts governed the budget. A faster rate of economic growth would produce more revenues and thus necessitate fewer painful budget cuts. So, too, a higher rate of inflation, while deleterious to the economy, was beneficial for budgeting because it swelled government revenues, at least on paper. Murray Weidenbaum, an economics professor who was chairman of the Council of Economic Advisers, obligingly agreed to base the 1982 budget on an assumption of 5.2 percent real growth and 7.7 percent inflation. When Stockman asked how he generated his projections, the rumpled economist slapped his belly and said, "It came out of here—my visceral computer." This became known as the "Rosy Scenario," and it bore no relation to reality. The actual figures for 1982 would turn out to be *minus* 1.8 percent growth and inflation of just 3.8 percent.[15]

Even with highly unrealistic assumptions, Stockman still struggled to come up with enough cuts to balance the budget by 1984. (During the campaign Reagan had promised a balanced budget by 1983, but Stockman quietly moved the goal by a year.) His task was complicated by the massive increases in defense spending he inadvertently agreed to. During the campaign, Reagan had promised to raise defense spending by 5 percent a year. But the outgoing Carter administration, in its final budget, had already promised 5 percent a year growth, so the new administration felt compelled to top that.

On January 30, 1981, Stockman went to Caspar Weinberger's palatial Pentagon office to reach agreement on the defense budget. The budget director suggested a 7 percent annual increase. The defense secretary, after grumbling that this was a "pretty lean ration," agreed. But Stockman, who had been up since 4:30 a.m., neglected to specify the "baseline" from which the spending increase would be calculated. The campaign's math had been based on Carter's 1980 defense budget of $142 billion. But following the hostage-rescue debacle at Desert One, Congress had already accelerated defense spending to $222 billion by fiscal year 1982. Stockman unwittingly accepted 1982 spending as the new baseline, meaning that the Reagan defense budget increases would be layered on top of the Carter increase. By 1989, the defense budget would reach $300 billion in constant dollars—66 percent higher than when Reagan took office. This was an unprecedented defense buildup for peacetime. But by the time Stockman realized what he had agreed to, it was too late: Weinberger refused to budge, and Reagan refused to intercede.[16] As a senior military officer noted, the defense secretary was "stubborn" and "fiercely ideological."[17]

Other cabinet members also tried to protect their budgets, but Stockman managed to override most of them. "All I could do was play a damage control game.... My power base was too feeble to do much else," wrote Education Secretary Terrel Bell. "I knew I had to accept the Stockman cuts."[18]

While he could not touch defense or popular middle-class entitlement programs, Stockman was able to make real, painful cuts in domestic programs that helped the needy, including Aid to Families with Dependent Children, Food Stamps, child nutrition, mental health services, housing assistance, aid to low-income students, and job training. His reductions were particularly steep when measured against projected outlays before Reagan came to office. While overall federal spending would continue to grow in the 1980s, domestic discretionary spending would decline as a percentage of GDP.[19] But animated by the free-market zeal of a convert, Stockman seemed to give little thought to what his cuts would mean for individual recipients of aid.

To his credit, Stockman did want to balance cuts to lower-income families with cuts to various corporate welfare programs—for example, farm subsidies, the oil depletion allowance, highway spending, and the Export-Import Bank—but he was usually stymied by proponents of those programs in the cabinet and Congress. Even the most right-wing Republicans would defend spending that benefited their constituents. Jesse Helms, for example, made it clear that there would be no reductions in subsidies for tobacco farmers, while Strom Thurmond insisted on safeguarding the Rural Electrification Administration long after rural areas had already been electrified. "You take good care of those REAs," he told Stockman in that honey-glazed accent of his. "Them's some real fine people."[20] In the Reagan administration, the wealthy and the middle class had their interests protected. The poor, by contrast, lacked effective champions.

Where was Reagan while his budget was being formulated? He was, as usual, a genial, aloof presence. Budget plans were presented to Reagan "in several hour-long blizzards of paper," Stockman noted. Reagan signed off but had little idea of the specifics. "When he was later called on to justify the cuts," Stockman noted, "he would remember only that he was making the cut, not why."[21]

By early February 1981, Stockman had compiled $47 billion in budget cuts to take effect by 1984. It was a lot of money—the most substantial rollback of federal spending since the advent of the New Deal—but still fell well short of balancing the budget. Indeed, with the economic outlook weakening and defense spending increasing, deficit projections were soaring. So Stockman invented what came to be known as the "magic asterisk": He promised to find $44 billion of additional savings . . . *somewhere*.[22] Ed Rollins, the deputy White House political director and no fan of the budget director, recalled, "With Stockman, the numbers changed every day. He bullshitted the president in many, many instances."[23] Stockman basically acknowledged that was the case. The president, he wrote in his memoir, had no idea that "his architect had been frenetically designing a fiscal house of cards."[24]

Reagan's major input was to preserve big tax cuts and big defense spending increases; on almost everything else, he was flexible. He saw his job primarily as salesmanship: "The fellas" formulated the program, and he sold it to the nation. He did his job well, giving a prime-time speech from the Oval Office on February 5, 1981, and an address to a Joint Session of Congress on February 18. But the whole structure was built, as John Anderson had warned, on "smoke and mirrors." It was, as Howard Baker said, "a riverboat gamble."[25]

The premise behind the economic program was even more questionable than David Stockman realized. The assumption of the president's team—and of many economists—was that curbing inflation required massive spending cuts to reduce the budget deficit, win the confidence of Wall Street, and bring interest rates down. But in subsequent years inflation and interest rates went down while the budget deficit went up. How could this be? It turned out that the deficit was less important than many believed. The economists with the best handle on inflation were not the supply-side tax cutters or the traditional fiscal conservatives but, rather, monetarists such as Milton Friedman who argued that inflation was a monetary phenomenon. It was caused by too much money in circulation and could only be reduced by reducing the growth of money supply. That meant the most powerful economic policymaker was not the president of the United States but the chairman of the Federal Reserve Board, the quasi-independent agency that controlled the money supply.

Inflation had gotten out of control in the 1960s and 1970s in large part because, under pressure from the White House, two previous Fed chairmen, William McChesney Martin and Arthur Burns, had refused to clamp down on money supply and slow the economy. Combined with two Middle East oil shocks (in 1973–1974 and 1979–1980), the result was "stagflation": a combination of high inflation and sluggish economic growth.

Jimmy Carter finally began to break that inflationary spiral in 1979 when he eased out the Fed chairman, G. William Miller, and appointed in his place Paul A. Volcker, the head of the New York Federal Reserve Bank. Volcker was an intellectual and physical giant: He stood six feet, seven inches, and had spent most of his career working for the government. Nonpartisan and highly competent, he exemplified the very best of the federal bureaucracy that Reagan so often derided. He was as frugal in the conduct of his own affairs as he was in the nation's: He smoked cheap cigars and stayed in Washington in a tiny, one-bedroom apartment in a building favored by college students, while his wife rented out a room in their New York apartment and worked as a part-time bookkeeper to make ends meet.[26]

Shortly after his appointment in October 1979, Volcker made clear that the Fed would be restricting money supply as tightly as necessary to get inflation (then at 12.1 percent) under control. His actions resulted in massive hikes in interest rates without immediately bringing down either inflation or unemployment. Carter lost the 1980 election after the Fed hiked the federal funds rate by three percentage points in the final six weeks before the election.[27]

The question now was whether Reagan would continue Carter's hands-off policy toward the Fed or whether he would try to pressure Volcker to bring down rates, as Lyndon Johnson and Richard Nixon had done, in order to boost the economy and his poll numbers. Many Republicans were hostile to the Fed, with some even questioning whether it should exist. Volcker, a Democratic appointee, had considerable trepidation about the attitude of the incoming Republican administration.

Reagan's aides wanted to arrange an early meeting between the Federal Reserve chairman and the president, but Volcker refused to come to the White House for fear of appearing to compromise his independence. He did not want the president coming to the Fed's ornate headquarters either. They decided on a neutral venue: the Treasury building. On January 23, 1981, Reagan insisted on walking from the White House. It was a short walk but one that, for security reasons, he would never again make. He brought his whole economic team: Ed Meese, Jim Baker, Martin Anderson, David Stockman, Murray Weidenbaum, and, of course, Don Regan, who hosted the lunch.

They had barely been seated when the president asked an unexpected question: "I've had several letters from people who raise the question of why we need the Federal Reserve at all. They seem to feel that it is the Fed that causes much of our monetary problems and that we would be better off if we abolished it. Why do we need the Federal Reserve?"

Marty Anderson was sitting across the table and thought the look on Volcker's face was "priceless": "His face muscles went slack and his lower jaw literally sagged a half-inch or so as his mouth fell open. For several seconds he just looked at Reagan, stunned and speechless." But the unflappable Fed chairman quickly recovered and went on to give a brief lecture about why the Fed, which had been created in 1913, "has operated well and has been very important to the stability of the economy." Reagan seemed to accept

that explanation and expressed support for the Fed's efforts to fight inflation. Volcker breathed "a sigh of relief."[28]

Most of their future meetings would be held in the Oval Office. Volcker
would do most of the talking, reporting on the state of the economy, and
Reagan would reply with his standard talking points: "I, and all members
of my administration, appreciate the cooperation we've received from the
Federal Reserve in working to reduce inflation. We will stand firm in the
fight against inflation."[29]

A rapport developed between the two men, leading Reagan to reappoint
Volcker to another four-year term in 1983. The White House "figured that
Volcker was an extraordinarily capable individual, who if we treated him
decently, would probably conduct himself in a professional, nonpartisan
manner," Marty Anderson wrote.[30]

And that was just what happened, but it still took considerable courage
and perspicacity for Reagan to continue backing Volcker even while the
Fed's assault on inflation took a severe, short-term toll on the economy and
on the president's own popularity. "I am certain that his people, every time
there was a press conference, would say this is your chance now to go out
and attack the Federal Reserve, but he never did," Volcker told me. "That
was obviously very helpful from my standpoint. That helped us to do what
we needed to do."[31]

Prospects for the Reagan budget had appeared uncertain before the president was shot but improved along with his health during his recovery. The
Troika adopted Richard Wirthlin's suggestion a few days after the shooting:
"The first time RR is on TV must be a block-buster. How about a joint session of Congress 3–4 days before floor vote. This would throw Democrats
for a loop."[32] That is just what happened when Reagan gave his first post-
shooting speech before a Joint Session of Congress on April 28, 1981. His
remarks were interrupted at least fourteen times by applause. "We've just
been outflanked and out-gunned," House Majority Leader Jim Wright of
Texas conceded in his diary.[33]

The most powerful Democrat in the nation was House Speaker Tip
O'Neill. With his substantial belly, bulbous nose, white hair, and backslapping manner, the cigar-smoking House speaker was no match on television for the smooth and handsome president. O'Neill looked like a caricature

of a big-city machine politician—which is just what he was. He had entered Congress, representing John F. Kennedy's old district centered on Boston, in 1953, when Reagan was still pursuing his acting career, and the two men had little in common besides their shared Irish ancestry, love of a good story, and unwillingness to study too hard for their jobs. Like former California Assembly Speaker "Big Daddy" Jesse Unruh, an earlier Reagan adversary, O'Neill maintained the New Deal faith that Reagan had long ago shed: He believed that a substantial federal government was needed to protect the underprivileged. He was, in short, the very personification of the "tax and spend Democrats" that Reagan so often denounced.

A legend has developed that Reagan and O'Neill were friends.[34] In truth, Ed Meese said, "there was a certain feeling of respect" but not "actual friendship."[35] In his memoirs, O'Neill wrote, "I've known every president since Harry Truman, and there's no question in my mind that Ronald Reagan was the worst."[36] Jim Wright noted in his diary that during a typical meeting over budget cuts, "Tip gave Reagan the toughest going over I've ever heard a president subjected to." When the speaker accused him of not caring about the poor, Reagan grew red in the face and exclaimed, "God damn it, Tip, we do care about those people!"[37]

While opposed to Reagan's agenda and worldview, O'Neill was, above all, a practical politician who knew how to count votes. He understood that, with some forty conservative Democrats in the House, mainly from the South, he had lost control of his own caucus. The White House was assiduously courting the "boll weevils," as the conservative Democrats were called, and there was nothing O'Neill could do to stop them from defecting.

O'Neill could have tried to use parliamentary maneuvers to prevent Reagan's budget from coming to the floor, but he felt the American people would not forgive him if he did. "I know when to fight and when not to fight," he said. Making the best of a bad hand, he shrewdly calculated that if the economy did not improve after the passage of "Reaganomics," the president would get the blame—and Democrats could rebound in the 1982 elections.[38]

The White House orchestrated a masterful lobbying campaign to push its budget over the finish line. Those efforts were overseen by the Legislative Strategy Group, which convened several afternoons a week in Jim Baker's corner office. The eight regular members included Ed Meese, Mike Deaver,

The governor meeting with his cabinet. Natural resources director Norman "Ike" Livermore is on the left (next to Reagan). Finance director Caspar Weinberger on the right (closest to camera). Reagan delegated most of the management of state government. (*RRPL*)

Governor Reagan with his first chief of staff, Philip Battaglia, who was forced out after other Reagan aides discovered he was gay. The resulting scandal hurt Reagan's first presidential campaign in 1968. (*RRPL*)

The National Guard patrols Berkeley, 1969. Reagan's heavy-handed response to campus unrest simply led to more violent confrontations. (*Getty*)

Reagan was a die-hard defender of President Nixon and Vice President Spiro Agnew. He hoped to succeed Nixon in 1976, but those plans were foiled when Nixon was forced to resign, making Gerald Ford president. (*Getty*)

The Reagans with their children at home in Pacific Palisades, 1976: l. to r., Patti, Michael, Maureen, Ron. The family was not close, and Reagan did not inform his children that he was running for president until just before making the announcement. (*RRPL*)

The support of Senator Jesse Helms in North Carolina saved Reagan's 1976 primary campaign from a premature end. Helms was a notorious segregationist, but Reagan said, "I know the Senator very well and certainly approve of his philosophy." (*Getty*)

The Iran hostage crisis made President Jimmy Carter look weak. New evidence has emerged that Reagan aides tried to prevent Iran from releasing the hostages before the 1980 election. (*Getty*)

The energy crisis contributed to "stagflation"—slow growth combined with high inflation and unemployment—which further eroded Carter's popularity. (*Getty*)

Reagan won his lone debate with Carter with a killer line—"There you go again"—after Carter accused him of having opposed the creation of Medicare. No one seemed to care that Carter was right. (*Getty*)

President Reagan with his first cabinet. Two bitter rivals—Al Haig (l.) and Caspar Weinberger (r.)—are in the front row. The cabinet, which Reagan played little role in choosing, was full of duds such as Raymond Donovan, Samuel Pierce, and James Watt (back row). The lone woman, UN Ambassador Jeane Kirkpatrick, is in the middle. (*RRPL*)

The troika—(l. to r.) Jim Baker, Ed Meese, and Mike Deaver—ran the White House. A master of bureaucratic politics, Baker emerged as first among equals. He ran rings around the more doctrinaire and disorganized Meese. (*RRPL*)

The most powerful player on economic policy in the first term was the wunderkind budget director, David Stockman. (*RRPL*)

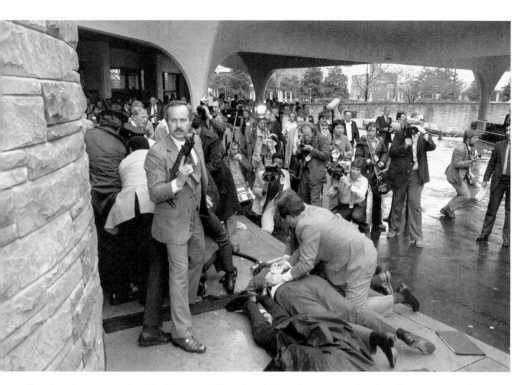

The chaotic scene at the Washington Hilton hotel, March 30, 1981, shortly after Reagan and three others were shot. The president came closer to dying than his aides revealed at the time. (*RRPL*)

Contrary to legend, Reagan and House Speaker Thomas "Tip" O'Neill were hardly friends. But, despite their political differences, they were able to work together. (*RRPL*)

The Group of Seven summit in Williamsburg, Virginia, May 29, 1981. Other heads of state were at first befuddled by Reagan, but he won them over with charm and humor. He was closest to British prime minister Margaret Thatcher (second from right). (*RRPL*)

legislative director Max Friedersdorf, cabinet affairs director Craig Fuller, communications director David Gergen, and staff secretary Dick Darman. Don Regan and David Stockman often sat in as well. Jim Baker, a stern and unrelenting taskmaster, was in charge. He handed out assignments and followed up incessantly to make sure they were completed.[39] "Those were the most effective meetings I've ever been to in any White House," David Gergen, a veteran of four administrations, recalled. "It was where the thinking got done. It was like the cockpit of the White House."[40]

The Reagan White House staff were much more solicitous of members of Congress than the Carter White House had been: for example, they handed out passes to the president's box at the Kennedy Center for Performing Arts and even made sure to offer Tip O'Neill his favorite brand of cigar. "We worked each and every member," said Kenneth Duberstein, deputy director and then director of legislative affairs. "We had them down to the White House. The president was on the phone. We had meetings galore. We coopted a bunch of ideas."[41]

Jim Baker was legendary for returning all calls at the end of the day, whether from lawmakers or journalists; he often called after business hours, knowing he would get an answering machine but the recipient would be grateful for the callback.[42] Indeed, Education Secretary Terrel Bell marveled that "the busiest man in the White House was the promptest in returning his phone calls."[43] Baker, Darman, Fuller, and Gergen also regularly provided background briefings to reporters and floated trial balloons to test reaction to proposals or drive media coverage. This was something that the Meese faction, which was suspicious of the mainstream press, did not do nearly as well. "Nobody in my long experience was more skillful in manipulating reporters than Baker," wrote columnist Robert Novak.[44]

Reagan was the lobbyist-in-chief—not only in his public speeches but also in frequent conversations with members of Congress. "Reagan has many more meetings with Congressmen than any other President I have served with," Representative Barber Conable, who had joined the House in 1965 and was now the ranking Republican on the Ways and Means Committee, wrote in his diary. "He seems to enjoy receiving reports from Congress and although says comparably little and at that of a general nature clearly has the intelligence to understand what is going on."[45]

Democratic congressman Richard Gephardt of Missouri recalled that the president would begin by reading from his index cards and then, if members of Congress asked detailed questions, would "disengage" and let his staff answer. While Conable lamented that Reagan did "not have detailed knowledge of anything" and too often segued into stories that "do not appear to have great relevance to the issues at hand," he got "the strong impression that [Reagan] is completely in control at the White House . . . and that he is the President in fact as well as in appearance. He surprises me with his vigor and his absolute decisiveness."[46]

The White House made only one mistake that spring—and that was to touch the "third rail" of American politics. Stockman was eager to cut Social Security because it was heading for insolvency, and he needed additional savings to balance the budget. Social Security accounted for 21 percent of federal spending. Ever since the 1960s, workers had been able to retire early, at sixty-two, by paying a 20 percent penalty on their expected Social Security benefits. Stockman proposed to more than double the early-retirement penalty to 45 percent and to implement the new rules immediately.

The budget director presented his plan during an hour-long meeting with the president on May 11, 1981, focusing on the cost of early retirements. "I've been warning since 1964 that Social Security was heading for bankruptcy," Reagan agreed, "and this is one of the reasons why." This was one of the few times the president approved a proposal on the spot. But Stockman never mentioned that the changes would be implemented with no advance notice, and Reagan never asked.

Alarmed, Dick Darman ran off to notify Jim Baker. Baker, in turn, convened the Legislative Strategy Group to minimize the damage. He decided that the plan would be released by Dick Schweiker, the secretary of health and human services, not by the White House. "This isn't Ronald Reagan's plan," Baker declared. "It's Dick Schweiker's." Schweiker was not happy, but everyone understood that Baker's decisions were usually final because Reagan hated to overrule his subordinates. As chief of staff, Baker was in effect the prime minister; he easily outranked a mere domestic cabinet secretary.

Even Baker's last-second maneuver, however, was not enough to avert disaster. The Democrats finally had an opening, and they exploited it to the hilt. Tip O'Neill told the press that the White House plan was breaking faith with Social Security recipients and called it "rotten" and "despicable." Florida congressman Claude Pepper, the eighty-year-old chairman of the House

Committee on Aging, described it as "cruel and insidious." Republicans ran for the hills. The Senate voted ninety-six to zero to condemn any plan to "precipitously and unfairly penalize early retirees." "We blew it," David Gergen admitted.

Social Security still needed to be reformed to stay solvent, but this episode taught the administration the dangers of pursuing changes without Democratic buy-in. At the end of 1981, at Baker's initiative, the White House convened a bipartisan commission, chaired by Alan Greenspan, to push this explosive issue past the 1982 midterm elections.[47]

The president's first big victory came on May 7, 1981, when the House voted, 270 to 154, to approve his budget blueprint, known as Gramm-Latta, after Democratic congressman Phil Gramm of Texas and Republican congressman Delbert Latta of Ohio. Not only did Republicans hold all 190 of their House members, but they also won over 63 conservative Democrats.[48] "We never anticipated such a landslide," Reagan wrote in his diary. "It's been a long time since Repubs. have had a victory like this."[49] More victories would follow as spring turned to summer. At the end of June, the House and Senate approved a spending plan that called for roughly $38 billion in savings in 1982, at least on paper.[50]

"I'm getting the shit whaled out of me," Tip O'Neill complained.[51] In his diary, Jim Wright pondered the paradox of Ronald Reagan: "It's odd. In conversations over programs, he has seemed terribly shallow, albeit charming. He isn't able—nor willing—to discuss programs in detail. His philosophical approach is superficial, overly simplistic, one-dimensional. . . . Yet so far the guy is making it work. Appalled by what seems to me a lack of depth, I stand in awe nevertheless of his political skill. I am not sure I have seen its equal."[52]

Attention now turned to the tax bill, the Economic Recovery Tax Act, known as Hance-Conable after Democratic congressman Kent Hance of Texas and Republican congressman Barber Conable of New York. Many of the moderate Republicans ("gypsy moths") and conservative Democrats ("boll weevils") who had voted for the Reagan budget were reluctant to support massive tax cuts that would send the deficit soaring. The administration had initially proposed three annual 10 percent cuts in personal income taxes. Reagan was willing to modify that only slightly to a

5 percent cut on October 1, 1981, followed by 10 percent cuts on July 1, 1982, and July 1, 1983. The top marginal tax rate would still plummet from 70 percent to 50 percent. In addition, congressional Republicans insisted on indexing taxes to inflation starting in 1985, thereby providing another tax break for taxpayers—and another revenue cut for the Treasury. "I'll hail it as a great bipartisan solution," Reagan wrote in his diary. "H—l! It's more than I thought we could get."[53] (He never spelled out curse words, even mild ones, in his diary.)

Pro-business Republicans believed it was essential to cut not just individual but also corporate taxes, so they insisted on a much more favorable depreciation schedule, known as 10-5-3, that would greatly reduce companies' tax liabilities. Democratic leaders proposed an alternative package with smaller tax cuts and more deficit reduction. To win votes for its plan, the White House had to load up Hance-Conable with all sorts of special-interest tax breaks. Major wins for the wealthy included a tripling of the estate-tax exemption and a cut of almost one-third in capital gains taxes, even as impoverished families were about to be pushed from welfare rolls. The vote-buying bazaar was in full swing. As House Minority Whip Trent Lott said, "Everybody else is getting theirs, it's time we got ours."[54]

The Reagan tax cut had now ballooned well beyond the original Kemp-Roth plan to reduce personal income taxes, which was estimated to cost the government $983 billion in lost tax revenues between 1982 and 1990. The new business-depreciation schedule cost another $402 billion in lost revenue, while the special-interest tax breaks added $468 billion. So now the total tax package would cost more than $1.8 trillion over eight years. Any hope for balancing the budget had just disappeared.[55]

Dick Darman had never expected, he confessed, "that a tax cut of that magnitude would actually be enacted." He had assumed Congress would pare it back—not expand it. He told Stockman, "I don't know which is worse, winning now and fixing up the budget mess later, or losing now and facing a political mess immediately." Political expediency won out. "We win it now," Darman said, "we fix it later."[56]

The president pressed for passage of the Economic Recovery Tax Act with an Oval Office speech on July 27, 1981, in which he portrayed the issue as being whether members of Congress were for or against him.[57] After he urged supporters "to contact your Senators and Congressmen," congressional offices were inundated with letters and phone calls. "Clearly," Barber

Conable noted in his diary, "Reagan has the whip hand."[58] Opposing such a popular president so early in his term was seen as political suicide even by lawmakers who harbored grave doubts about the legislations. Senator Paul Laxalt said in 1982, "If there had been a secret ballot in the Senate last year, there wouldn't have been more than 12 votes for the tax cut."[59]

On July 29, 1981—with Ronald Reagan feeling "d——n lonesome" in the White House while Nancy was in London attending the wedding of Prince Charles and Lady Diana Spencer—the tax bill sailed through Congress.[60] The margin in the House was 238 to 195, with forty-eight Democrats voting aye. In the Senate the vote was even more lopsided: 89 to 11. The following morning, a front-page story in the *New York Times* marveled, "In 190 days President Reagan has not only wrought a dramatic conservative shift in the nation's economic policies and the role of the Federal Government in American life but also swept to a political mastery of Congress not seen since Lyndon B. Johnson."[61]

The administration was only halfway through its first year, but the Reagan Revolution had just reached its high-water mark. Now the nation would have to reckon with the consequences.

37

"Vacation!"

He just loved getting dirty and working with his hands.
—DENNIS LEBLANC

With his economic program moving through Congress, Ronald Reagan was eager to escape from Washington for the month of August 1981 to his rustic "ranch in the sky" in the dun-colored mountains outside Santa Barbara, California, within sight of the sparkling waters of the Pacific Ocean. But before he could get away, he had to deal with some pressing business.

In June 1981, Potter Stewart, a centrist justice appointed by President Eisenhower, announced he was retiring from the Supreme Court. Attorney General William French Smith had known since March about his intention to step down, giving the administration plenty of time to choose a successor. The hard-core conservatives at the Justice Department wanted to choose a conservative legal giant such as Robert Bork. But since Ronald Reagan had promised during the 1980 campaign, at Stuart Spencer's instigation, to appoint a woman, he was intent on honoring that pledge. Justice William Rehnquist may have been the first to suggest the name of an old flame from Stanford Law School: Sandra Day O'Connor, a centrist Republican who had been majority leader of the Arizona State Senate and was now serving on Arizona's appeals court.

Two of the leading antiabortion Republicans in Congress—Congressman Henry Hyde of Illinois and Senator Don Nickles of Oklahoma—called White House legislative director Max Friedersdorf to "protest the possible appointment of the Connor woman from Arizona to the Supreme Court." They warned that she had voted six times for "unlimited abortion," supported the Equal Rights Amendment, and would "cause a firestorm among Reagan supporters."

But O'Connor was championed by such influential figures as Senator

Barry Goldwater, Chief Justice Warren Burger, and Nancy Reagan's stepfather, who was now living with Nancy's mother in Phoenix. William P. Clark, Reagan's old chief of staff in Sacramento and a former California Supreme Court justice, now serving incongruously as deputy secretary of state, read over all the appellate opinions O'Connor had authored and pronounced himself "impressed with the Judge's work." "While I would be disinclined to label her a conservative," Clark wrote to Ed Meese, "I think it is clearer that she is not a liberal."

On June 23, Reagan met with the Troika and the attorney general to discuss a Supreme Court nominee. O'Connor was the only candidate to receive serious consideration. Bill Smith told the president she favored judicial restraint and was from the West. As for abortion, O'Connor finessed the question when it came up as part of the vetting by saying that "she considered abortion personally abhorrent" and that the courts should be open to reversing old decisions—thereby raising unwarranted hopes among conservatives that she might vote to overturn *Roe v. Wade*.

When O'Connor met with Reagan in the Oval Office, abortion was never mentioned. Instead, they chatted about ranch life, O'Connor having grown up on the Lazy B cattle ranch in Arizona. She stole Reagan's heart when she told him, "As far as I'm concerned, the best place to be in the world is on a good cutting horse working cattle." His sentiments exactly!

On July 7, 1981, O'Connor was formally nominated. The religious right predictably attacked her, but she knew how to turn on the charm, and with an expert application of flattery and humility, she won over such skeptics as Jesse Helms and Strom Thurmond. O'Connor was confirmed ninety-nine to zero on September 21, 1981. She would go on to enrage conservatives by refusing to overturn *Roe v. Wade*, even though she was willing to curb its scope slightly. But Ronald Reagan, a pragmatist who never cared much about social issues, was unperturbed. He gave no evidence of ever deviating from his original judgment: "I think she'll make a good Justice."[1]

———

Only one more major issue loomed before the Reagans could return to their refuge in California: a strike by the Professional Air Traffic Controllers Association (PATCO).

PATCO's membership—mainly middle-class white men who lived in the suburbs and had served in the military—was full of Reagan supporters. It had been one of the few unions, along with the Teamsters, to endorse his 1980 candidacy. PATCO's leaders hoped their political support would be reciprocated by generous contract terms. Transportation Secretary Drew Lewis did put a massive $40 million package on the table, including a substantial salary boost and a reduction in working hours. But it was not good enough for PATCO. By the end of July 1981, the union was threatening to strike, even though it was illegal for federal employees to walk off the job. PATCO's leaders gambled that the administration would cave if they threatened to shut down airline travel and announced a walkout beginning on Monday, August 3, 1981.

The union underestimated the president, who was determined to send a "don't mess with me" message of resolution during this crisis early in his presidency. He spent the weekend of August 1 at Camp David, "loafing by the pool & swimming." After conferring with his advisers, Reagan decided that those who went on strike would lose their jobs if they did not return to work within forty-eight hours. "Damnit the law is the law and the law says they cannot strike," Reagan told aides. He was channeling one of his heroes: The flinty, small-town New Englander Calvin Coolidge, whose portrait now hung in the Cabinet Room, had as governor of Massachusetts emerged as a leading advocate of "law and order" during the post–World War I Red Scare by breaking a Boston police strike in 1919. "There is no right to strike against the public safety by anybody, anywhere, any time," Coolidge had proclaimed, and now Reagan said pretty much the same thing.

The president announced his decision in the Rose Garden at 11:00 a.m. on August 3. PATCO leaders still hoped to negotiate an end to the walkout, but Reagan refused to talk. "You can't sit and talk with a union that's in violation of the law," he snapped. Some 90 percent of the strikers—more than eleven thousand men and women—refused to return to work by the August 6 deadline. The nation's air traffic fell by half that week. But 3,291 supervisors and 4,669 nonstriking controllers, along with military controllers and even furloughed pilots, worked long hours to keep the system functioning. None of the strikers ever got their jobs back, and PATCO had to dissolve. This was the second union—after the Conference of Studio Unions in postwar Hollywood—that Ronald Reagan, the only former labor leader to become president, had helped destroy.

Firing the air-traffic controllers was a high-stakes gamble that might have gone horribly wrong. If there had been an airplane crash in those weeks, the public might have blamed the president, and PATCO might have prevailed. But aircraft continued to take off and land safely. Only one crash could have been linked to the strike, and it occurred months later: Amid a snowstorm on January 13, 1982, an Air Florida flight taking off from Washington's National Airport crashed into the Potomac River, killing seventy-eight people. While PATCO insisted the crash was caused by inexperienced controllers who wrongly gave the icy airplane permission to take off, the National Transportation Safety Board and the Federal Aviation Administration concluded that the controller's instructions were not a factor in the crash. Far from being politically hurt by this fatal accident, Reagan turned it to his advantage. In his 1982 State of the Union Address, he celebrated Lenny Skutnik, a young federal worker who dove into the icy Potomac to rescue one of the passengers and was sitting in the congressional gallery during the speech. This began a tradition of presidents bringing notable guests to the State of the Union.

"The PATCO strike helped make Ronald Reagan's presidency," wrote labor historian Joseph A. McMartin, by showing his steely resolve in a crisis. Future secretary of state George Shultz said that Reagan's handling of the strike put foreign leaders on notice that he was a president to be reckoned with. "This was his first important foreign policy decision," Shultz said.

The breaking of PATCO struck a substantial blow against organized labor in the United States, much as Reagan's compatriot Margaret Thatcher, the "Iron Lady," would later do in Britain by crushing a coal miners' strike in 1984–1985. The United States had averaged 286 major work stoppages a year between 1960 and 1980. During the 1980s the number sank to 83 and continued to fall thereafter. Public-sector strikes plummeted even more dramatically. Union power was in decline because of many factors, particularly advances in transportation and technology that made it easier and cheaper to manufacture products in lower-income countries and export them to the United States. But Reagan's handling of the PATCO strike legitimized the use of replacement workers and undercut union bargaining power. Employers found it easier to force workers to accept lower wages. This helped bring inflation under control while leading to long-term income stagnation for the working class, a hollowing out of the middle class, and a widening of income inequality, producing an increasingly alienated white working class with profound and unsettling repercussions for the American political system.

Ironically, firing the air-traffic controllers proved much more expensive than simply giving in to their demands. It cost an estimated $2 billion to train new controllers, and airlines lost a billion dollars a month in the immediate aftermath of the strike. But while the breaking of the PATCO strike had consequences both good and bad for the country, the impact on the Reagan presidency was undeniably positive. The liberal columnist Meg Greenfield wrote that, by "showing that he meant what he had warned and was willing to take the political consequences," Reagan "gave himself a huge infusion of presidential credibility, even among some people who deplored the act itself."[2]

Ronald Reagan felt a palpable sense of relief in early August once his economic package had passed, the strikers had been fired, and a state dinner for Egyptian president Anwar Sadat had concluded. "Vacation!" he wrote in his diary on August 6, 1981, as if he were a small boy being let out of school.

That afternoon, the president flew with the first lady aboard Air Force One to Point Mugu Naval Air Station and from there switched to a helicopter for the half-hour flight to their 688-acre ranch northwest of Santa Barbara in the rain-starved Santa Ynez Mountains, with their chapparal, grasslands, and oak trees and their mountain lions, coyotes, rabbits, lizards, and squirrels. The helipad they landed on was one of many recently constructed facilities that allowed the president to carry out his duties at the "Western White House." Temporary buildings were tucked away all over the property to house the Secret Service agents and aides who accompanied the president whenever he traveled. In all, there were roughly 175 people at the ranch at any one time.[3] Along with rattlesnakes and rabbits, dogs and horses, the property was now roamed by Secret Service sniper teams. "But," as Reagan noted in his diary, "it is all temporary & . . . minimal in its effect on appearance."[4] The ranch remained extremely rustic, primitive, and isolated—just as the president wanted it.

The Reagans had bought this property in November 1974 for $527,000 near the end of his second term as governor at the suggestion of financier William Wilson, who owned his own spread nearby.[5] (Reagan would appoint Wilson, a devout Catholic, as ambassador to the Vatican.) If one did not take a helicopter, getting there required a jolting drive on a one-lane road over seven miles of twists and turns from the Pacific Coast Highway before you finally reached a sun-kissed meadow. Here stood a tiny adobe house that had been built in 1872 and a small lake that provided its water supply. There were few amenities, but Reagan immediately fell in love with the property, which, sitting atop a 2,240-foot mountain, offered sweeping views all the way to the Pacific Ocean.

The previous owner had called it Tip Top Ranch. The Reagans renamed it Rancho del Cielo, or Ranch in the Sky, and Ron set about making it livable with help from two former state police bodyguards who became close friends: Willard "Barney" Barnett and Dennis LeBlanc. Working with a contractor, they expanded the house, replaced the roof, added a patio, and built a wooden fence around it.

When they finished in early 1977, the house was still modest: It had only five rooms totaling just 1,500 square feet, and the downscale Western furniture and décor—which looked as if it had been scavenged from a flea market—would never pass muster with *Architectural Digest*. On one wall were a pair of jokey mounted "jackalope" heads: jackrabbits with antelope antlers attached. The appliances were made by Reagan's old employer General Electric—not a fancier brand like Thermador or Sub-Zero favored by wealthy homeowners. The countertops were Formica, not marble. The bookshelves were full of well-thumbed volumes Reagan had read rather than the unread, leather-bound books favored by interior decorators.

Reagan was always determined to do much of the work on his property personally—and the work never ended. His son Ron recalled an episode in the late 1970s when, as a teenager, he was enlisted to help his dad build a patio. Reagan wanted to fashion it out of native sandstone, so the two of them hopped in an old red jeep with a trailer attached and set off to a pile of rocks that Reagan had scouted on horseback. The two men grunted and groaned as they filled the trailer with as many rocks as it could carry, then headed back to the house.

But rather than going along the flat, winding road they had taken there, Reagan decided to return via a shortcut straight over a hill. After getting about halfway up, the jeep began to groan and strain. It wouldn't go any farther even with his foot all the way down on the gas pedal. Then it began to roll backwards, propelled by the heavy load of stones. As they picked up speed going in the wrong direction, the younger Reagan "was fighting to maintain sphincter control," while his dad "looked almost psychotically unconcerned."

Somehow Reagan managed to maneuver the jeep back to level ground, and, rather than admit defeat, he insisted with characteristic stubbornness on going back up the hill. It took "four lip-chewing, throttle-grinding, pant-sharting attempts before we finally conquered the ridge," Ron wrote. But it was worth it. "To this day," he conceded, "the stone patio gives the old house a handsome, rough-hewn look."[6]

When Reagan was at Rancho del Cielo, he spent most of his time either horseback riding or doing ranch work. Riding was a new challenge for the Secret Service, which had to set up a riding school for its agents. John Barletta was one of the few agents who was already proficient on horseback; he had learned from the Boston Mounted Police, where his father had been a police officer. He earned Reagan's respect by keeping up with him on horseback; the president was an excellent rider in the English style (he usually wore Dehner riding boots, jodhpurs, and a long-sleeve shirt). Reagan treasured his solitude, but that wasn't really possible for the president even on horseback. Trailing behind him would be a Humvee carrying Secret Service agents, a doctor, a military aide with the nuclear football, and secure communications equipment.[7]

To keep the president safe, Barletta convinced him to stop jumping his horse over obstacles such as fallen trees. But horseback riding remained one of the most dangerous sports one could engage in—more dangerous than motorcycling, skiing, or football—and Reagan refused to wear a helmet. He also refused to stop using a chainsaw, much to the consternation of his security detail.[8]

While Barletta was often at Reagan's side during morning horseback rides, the president's companions in afternoon ranch work—cutting firewood, clearing brush, repairing the fence, pruning trees—were Barney Barnett and Dennis LeBlanc. The white-haired Barnett, who was close to Reagan's own age, was retired from the California Highway Patrol and in Reagan's employ. LeBlanc was a younger man who, after leaving the state police, had worked as a Reagan advance man. He then became a Pacific Telephone lobbyist; his boss thought it was in the heavily regulated company's interest to loan him to the leader of the Free World for ranch interludes.

Reagan had long been a regular at ritzy black-tie events, but he preferred getting sweaty and just being "one of the guys," LeBlanc told me. "No matter what the day was, we'd be cutting or building something. He didn't have any other down-to-earth, working, get-dirty type friends. He just loved getting dirty and working with his hands."

What did they talk about while working? "No politics," LeBlanc said. "All we did was talk ranch stuff or family stuff." But they were just as happy to pass the time in companionable silence.[9] When asked by a journalist what he "really" thought about while "chopping all that wood," Reagan replied with a two-word answer worthy of the famously taciturn Calvin Coolidge: "The wood."[10]

After a hard day's labor, all three men would be exhausted and head back to the house for dinner with the first lady. "Man, I could eat a house," LeBlanc would think to himself. But the actual menu was stingy. Nancy Reagan never cooked, so the food was prepared by their longtime housekeeper, Ann Allman. The petite first lady watched her figure (she was a size 2) and made sure Ronnie did too. There was only one plate of food per person, and the men would get up almost as hungry as when they sat down, but the unassuming president never complained or asked for seconds.[11] His son Ron did recall his father's dismay at one pre-Christmas family dinner at the White House where, at Nancy's direction, he was served skinless chicken breast, braised celery, and soda crackers. The president endured "this mingy meal" hoping for a satisfying dessert. His frustration finally found expression when he was presented, at meal's end, with a broiled grapefruit. "That's not dessert," he said, dejectedly, "that's a grapefruit."[12]

After dinner, all four of them—Ron and Nancy, Barney and Dennis— would settle down in the living room to watch a television show like *Murder, She Wrote* starring the redoubtable Angela Lansbury. By 9:00 p.m., the three men were usually so exhausted that they fell asleep in front of the set. Nancy would gently tap Dennis on the foot to let him know it was time to go to bed. He and Barney would shuffle out the door; sometimes, if they were lucky, the housekeeper would sneak them a few cookies to take back to their trailer. The president and first lady then headed to their modest bedroom.

Dennis LeBlanc said that Barney Barnett "was the president's best buddy": "They were one year apart and their birthdays were the same day—February 6. He was the only guy that I knew that could say, 'God damn it, Governor, you can't do it this way,' in regard to building something if the governor wasn't doing it correctly. And the governor would say, 'Yeah, okay, Barney, you're right.' How many other friends could talk to him like that?" (Barnett still called Reagan "governor" even when he was president.) LeBlanc, too, became closer to Reagan than just about anyone. He was so torn up when his old friend died in 2004 that he couldn't bear to go to the funeral. He simply sat at home, watching the television coverage and sobbing.[13]

A man who always remained down-to-earth no matter how high he climbed, Ronald Reagan arguably had a more intimate relationship and a truer friendship with his blue-collar buddies at the ranch than he did with all the grandees, such as Walter Annenberg or Alfred Bloomingdale, with whom he hobnobbed at glittering galas. That was Nancy's circle. Barney and Dennis—those were Ron's guys. "They were, in my opinion, his best friends," said Reagan's long-serving secretary Kathy Osborne.[14]

Ronald Reagan never felt happier or more relaxed than when he was engaged in back-breaking labor at Rancho del Cielo. Nancy Reagan, by contrast, preferred to spend time in Beverly Hills and rode horseback only reluctantly, but she tolerated the visits because she knew how good it was for her husband physically and spiritually.

Few outsiders were ever invited to the ranch; Nancy even kept the kids away most of the time save for a family Thanksgiving celebration, because she knew that her introverted husband treasured his isolation. Only a few world leaders—notably Queen Elizabeth II, Margaret Thatcher, Brian Mulroney, and Mikhail Gorbachev—ever made it to this treasured hideaway. If Rancho del Cielo wasn't heaven, Reagan often said, it "probably has the same zip code."[15]

Reagan was often criticized for taking too many vacations, especially compared to Jimmy Carter, who took only 97 days off during his four years in office. But, while Reagan spent more time on holiday or at a second home (335 days) than Bill Clinton (174) or Barack Obama (235), he spent fewer days vacationing than George W. Bush (533). Donald Trump, who spent at least 277 days in Palm Beach and Bedminster, New Jersey, during his single term, was also on a pace to far exceed Reagan (although Trump spent far less time at Camp David).[16]

And it was not as if Reagan could entirely escape the duties of office even in his secluded, mountaintop retreat. During his August 1981 vacation, for example, he signed the newly passed spending and tax bills in a brief ceremony while sitting at a patio table in jeans and cowboy boots. White House staff always accompanied the president to California, staying at a hotel in

Santa Barbara and remaining in regular contact by secure telephone. On the property itself, there was a White House communications team to ensure the president had secure links to the outside world.

It was while staying at the ranch, indeed, that Reagan received word on August 20, 1981, of the first military action of his presidency—a dogfight between US and Libyan warplanes. It was a reminder that however much the administration might want to focus on domestic priorities and the president on his ranch getaway, the world had a way of intruding.

38

The Cold War Heats Up

*Those early Reagan years in Washington were the most difficult
and unpleasant I experienced in my long tenure as ambassador.*

—ANATOLY DOBRYNIN

While Republicans had depicted Jimmy Carter as soft on Communism, the Soviet leadership had come to loathe him. With his emphasis on democracy and human rights, Carter challenged the very basis of Soviet power. He had also launched a military buildup and imposed harsh sanctions on the Soviet Union after the invasion of Afghanistan, including a boycott of the 1980 Moscow Olympics and an embargo on grain sales. *Pravda*, the official Kremlin organ, described him as an "atomic maniac" engaged in a "chimerical" attempt "to remake the world in America's own image" and wrote that the American people must have "sighed with relief when they learned that he will be returning to his native Plains to grow peanuts once again." Despite Ronald Reagan's long history of anti-Communism, the Soviets hoped he would turn out to be a dealmaker in the Nixon mold.[1]

Eventually they would be proved right, but it would take four years and three changes of leadership in the Soviet Union for that to happen. In the meantime, the Kremlin's expectations for a renewal of détente were brutally upended. At his very first news conference, on January 29, 1981, President Reagan said, "So far, détente's been a one-way street that the Soviet Union has used to pursue its own aims . . . the promotion of world revolution and a one-world Socialist or Communist state." He added, echoing one of the faux Lenin quotes circulated by the John Birch Society, that they "have openly and publicly declared that the only morality they recognize is what will further their cause, meaning they reserve unto themselves the right to commit any crime, to lie, to cheat, in order to attain that."[2] On May 17, 1981, in a speech at Notre Dame University, Reagan said, "The West won't contain communism, it will transcend communism . . . as some bizarre Chapter in human history whose last pages are even now being written."[3] Ten days later, at West Point, he told the cadets that they were "holding back an evil force that would extinguish the light we've been tending for 6,000 years."[4] Privately, he told aides that the Soviets were pursuing "world domination" just like Hitler.[5] He had been expressing similar sentiments since the 1950s. But they had a distinctly different impact now, coming from the president of the United States rather than from an actor or a corporate spokesman or even a governor.

Matching actions to words, Reagan launched a massive military buildup that included submarine-launched Trident missiles, land-based MX intercontinental ballistic missiles (despite the lack of a basing plan for them), two strategic bombers (the B-1 and the stealthy B-2), three ground-attack aircraft (the AV-8B, the A-10, and the stealthy F-117), four fighter aircraft (the F-14, F-15, F-16, and F-18), two types of nuclear-powered submarines (the *Ohio* class and the *Los Angeles* class), three nuclear-powered aircraft carriers (at $3 billion each), multiple army helicopters (the AH-64 Apache, UH-60 Black Hawk, and CH-47 Chinook), thousands of Abrams tanks and Bradley Fighting Vehicles, and much else besides. Most of these systems were developed in the 1970s but procured in the 1980s.

As important as all of the hardware Reagan bought was the change he helped bring about, with his pro-military rhetoric, in how the armed forces were perceived by society. The bumbling military misfits of Goldie Hawn's 1980 movie *Private Benjamin* and Bill Murray's 1981 *Stripes* gave way to the supremely skilled action heroes of Sylvester Stallone's Rambo movies beginning in 1982, Tom Clancy's novels starting with *The Hunt for Red October* in 1984, and Tom Cruise's 1986 film *Top Gun*, made with extensive support from the Department of Defense, which knew a public relations windfall when it saw one.

Reagan also declared his intention to carry out a NATO decision, reached in December 1979, to deploy 464 US cruise missiles and 108 Pershing II missiles to Europe in 1983 to match a Soviet deployment of medium-range SS-20 ballistic missiles that threatened Western Europe. He continued, and even expanded, another Carter policy by providing aid to the Afghan mujahideen battling the Red Army and, soon, to rebels fighting the Nicaraguan Sandinistas and to the government of El Salvador fighting leftist guerrillas. He also focused, as Carter had done, on human rights, demanding that the Soviets release political prisoners such as Anatoly Sharansky and Andrei

Sakharov and allow the immigration of seven Pentecostals who had taken refuge in the US embassy in Moscow.

Yet even as Reagan continued to maintain that the world could not long remain "half-slave, half-free," he also spoke of his desire for "an honest, verifiable reduction in nuclear weapons by both our countries to the point that neither of us represented a threat to the other."[6] He advanced, in the fall of 1981, a "zero plan" for both superpowers to eliminate all of their medium-range missiles in Europe. This was a lopsided proposal since the Soviets had already deployed 250 SS-20s while the United States had not yet fielded a single Pershing II or cruise missile. It was intended by Pentagon hard-liners as merely a ploy "to capture world opinion," in Defense Secretary Caspar Weinberger's words. He explained to the NSC that, while the Soviets "will certainly reject" this proposal, "they would be set back on their heels" and "we . . . would be shown as the White Hats."[7] But most Western European leaders, including Prime Minister Margaret Thatcher, were horrified by the "zero plan" because they feared it would leave them defenseless against the Red Army.[8]

Reagan, perhaps alone in the administration, took the plan seriously: "Even 1 nuclear missile in Europe was too many," he wrote in his diary, and he told a college president that "our ultimate goal must be the elimination of nuclear weapons."[9] The way to achieve that objective, he believed, was to bargain constructively with the Soviets—an impulse at odds with his public demonization of their regime as "an evil force." Reagan explained his bargaining philosophy to the National Security Council: "One should ask for the moon, and when the other fellow offers green cheese, one can settle for something in between."[10]

As a sign of his desire to improve relations, Reagan overrode the objections of his foreign policy team and on April 24, 1981, kept a campaign promise intended to win the support of farm states by lifting the grain embargo on the Soviet Union. He notified the doddering Soviet leader Leonid Brezhnev, an old-style, hard-line apparatchik, of his decision in a handwritten letter penned while recuperating from his shooting, pleading for "meaningful and constructive dialogue which will assist us in fulfilling our joint obligation to find lasting peace."[11] When NSC hard-liner Richard Pipes read Reagan's draft, he was dismayed that "it was so maudlin and so at odds with Reagan's public stance."[12] Secretary of State Al Haig convinced Reagan not to tell Brezhnev that his goal was "a world without nuclear weapons" and to allow the State Department to append a formal letter denouncing the Soviet military buildup. It would be up to the Kremlin to figure out which letter spoke for the administration: the handwritten missive from the president or the typed one ghostwritten by the State Department.[13]

Brezhnev's reply, Reagan noted, was "icy," and no wonder: The Soviet leadership did not understand his mixed signals. Moscow's ambassador to Washington, Anatoly Dobrynin, noted that the Kremlin "viewed Reagan with great indignation and suspicion" and "regarded his actions as adventurism." "Those early Reagan years in Washington were the most difficult and unpleasant I experienced in my long tenure as ambassador," wrote Dobrynin, who had been in Washington since 1962. "We had practically no room for really constructive diplomatic work."[14]

While most Americans saw the Soviets as the aggressors, the Soviet leaders saw themselves as the ones threatened by the United States. KGB chief Yuri Andropov became so worried about a preemptive US nuclear attack that in March 1981 he launched Operation RYAN, a Russian acronym for "nuclear missile attack," instructing KGB officers all over the world to be on high alert for any signs of such a strike. "The origins of RYAN," wrote KGB defector Oleg Gordievsky and historian Christopher Andrew, "lay in a potentially lethal combination of Reaganite rhetoric and Soviet paranoia." While Andropov feared that "nuclear apocalypse" was nigh, Marshal Nikolai Ogarkov, chief of the Soviet general staff, warned that "the beginning of the Reagan Presidency calls to mind the Fascist seizure of power"—which, of course, led to the Nazi invasion of the Soviet Union.[15]

Reagan's dual messages of confrontation and conciliation—designed to set the stage for productive arms-control talks—were not getting through. Only the confrontation part was clear in Moscow. The result was to ratchet up East-West tensions and Cold War paranoia to their highest levels since the 1962 Cuban Missile Crisis, leading to a dangerous series of crises that could have resulted in a nuclear war that neither side wanted.

Because Ronald Reagan talked about ending—or, per Dick Allen, winning—the Cold War and the Cold War actually ended shortly after he left office on America's terms, there has been an understandable tendency to ascribe greater perspicacity to him than was often the case. He did understand the Soviet Union's economic weakness better than most, and he was one of the few people who believed there was hope of ending the Cold War. The CIA found that the Soviet economy, after a period of rapid industrialization, was stagnating by the early 1980s. As Reagan discerned, the West had the opportunity to increase the pressure through economic sanctions if he could overcome the opposition of European allies and America's own business lobby. "The Soviet Union is economically on the ropes—they are selling rat meat on the market," he told the NSC on December 30, 1981. "This is the time to punish them."[16]

While correctly assessing the Soviet Union's economic weakness, however, Reagan greatly exaggerated its military strength and geopolitical ambitions. His view echoed Defense Department propaganda: Every year the Pentagon issued bombastic booklets, called *Soviet Military Power*, giving a vastly inflated assessment of Soviet military capabilities to justify more US defense spending.[17] Reagan had been raising the alarm about the Soviet threat since the late 1940s, and he made little effort initially to adjust his mindset to changing realities, even though there was a vast difference between Joseph Stalin and Leonid Brezhnev.

Reagan, in particular, showed no awareness that the corruption and inefficiency that beset the Soviet economy were also undermining the Soviet military. He depicted the Soviet armed forces as supermen akin to the fictional boxer Ivan Drago (played by Dolph Lundgren) who killed Apollo Creed with one mighty blow in the 1985 film *Rocky IV*. Reagan remained convinced that America was losing the arms race even when his military buildup was in full swing. "There's no question," the president said in 1982, "but that they have a superior military force than we do now." In 1983, he wrote in his diary, "We are still dangerously behind the Soviets & getting farther behind."[18]

Reagan was overly alarmist not just about Soviet strength but also about Soviet intentions. "They seek a superiority in nuclear strength that, in the event of a confrontation, would leave us with a choice of surrender or die," he wrote in the draft of a speech he gave in Chicago on August 18, 1980. The final version was slightly softened, changing "surrender or die" to "submission or conflict."[19] These beliefs were echoed by administration hawks, such as the Harvard historian Richard Pipes, who joined the NSC staff in 1981. He had been a member of Team B, which had criticized the CIA in 1976 for supposedly underestimating Soviet strength and intentions, and in 1977 he had published an influential *Commentary* article, "Why the Soviet Union Thinks It Could Fight and Win a Nuclear War," which was based on Team B's alarmist, exaggerated conclusions.[20]

Carter's outgoing CIA director, Stansfield Turner, tried to set President-elect Reagan straight shortly before the inauguration. Turner told Reagan that "the USSR had no advantage over the United States" and that "even after a Soviet first strike, the U.S. would have enough strategic nuclear weapons to destroy all Soviet cities with populations over 100,000." Reagan responded with stony silence because this ran so counter to his own beliefs about an American "window of vulnerability" created by Ford's and Carter's policies.[21] (CIA briefers would find that Reagan "knew what he thought about everything" and rejected intelligence assessments at odds with his beliefs.)[22]

Yet history would show that Turner was right and Reagan wrong.

When American experts visited Soviet military installations after the end of the Cold War, they found decrepit systems, outdated technology, and dysfunctional organizations. "There was no sign of the war machine the Reagan administration had conjured up," noted journalist David Hoffman.[23] For example, the Pentagon had claimed that, by the end of the 1980s, the Soviets could field a prototype of a space laser to shoot down satellites. But, in 1989, an American delegation found the Soviets' most powerful laser could generate only a two-kilowatt beam—"roughly the intensity of a sunbeam."[24]

After the end of the Cold War, the CIA conducted an overview of its Soviet assessments with the benefit of newly released Soviet documents and found that "virtually all of Team B's criticisms ... proved to be wrong": "While Team B was estimating a relentless, continuing buildup at a growing pace, it was learned that, in fact, Soviet leaders had just cut back the rate of spending on their military effort [in 1976] and would not increase it for the next nine years." Indeed, Soviet defense spending would remain relatively constant at 14 to 16 percent of GDP from 1960 to 1990. And, even after a Soviet strategic arms buildup in the 1970s, the United States in 1980 still enjoyed a large lead in nuclear warheads—9,200 US warheads versus 6,000 Soviet ones. Moreover, US missiles, with their superior guidance systems, were far more accurate than the Soviet models. Far from achieving military superiority, as Reagan warned, the Soviets never even achieved parity. The CIA concluded that "the Soviet leaders never had capabilities that could give them confidence in surviving and winning a nuclear war," as Reagan feared, and that "the Soviet leadership did not believe the strategic balance had shifted in its favor or that its hands were freed to be more bold and aggressive in its initiatives."[25]

While the United States did need to modernize its arsenal and improve military morale, discipline, and training, the size of the Reagan buildup was disproportionate to any actual Soviet threat. Why, for example, did the United States need a six-hundred-ship navy to fight a land power like the Soviet Union? Or why did it need fifty MX missiles—a new land-based intercontinental ballistic missile (ICBM)—even when it already had roughly two thousand ICBMs and ten thousand nuclear warheads?[26] Or why build a non-stealthy B-1 bomber, which could be easily targeted by Soviet air defenses, in addition to two Stealth aircraft, the F-117 and B-2? Carter, for good reason, had canceled the B-1; Reagan, for no good reason, revived it.

It made little sense, yet Cap Weinberger—like Ronald Reagan—never questioned the desires of the service chiefs. Rather, Weinberger pushed the generals to ask for more and more. "His view," Assistant Secretary of Defense Richard Perle said, "was that if we threw enough money at the problem, we would succeed in rebuilding our defenses. He wasn't as focused on the specifics of how we spent it."[27] The Joint Chiefs of Staff, wrote Colin Powell, "went from their wish lists to their dream lists, pulling out proposals they never expected to see the light of day."[28]

More quietly, the administration also made a major investment in civil defense and continuity of government planning designed to ensure the nation's leadership would survive World War III—a very real concern amid the heightened superpower tensions of the early 1980s. The money was buried in the budget of the Federal Emergency Management Agency, which was planning, implausibly, to evacuate nearly 150 million Americans from major cities in the event of nuclear war.[29] Reagan thought the costly American effort was necessary because Team B had claimed that the Soviets were investing in their own civil defense in the expectation of winning a nuclear war. But this was another right-wing myth. The CIA ultimately concluded that the Soviets did not "have a highly optimistic view about the effectiveness of their . . . civil defense."[30]

While Reagan kept warning of a Communist offensive to secure world domination, in reality the two major Communist powers—the Soviet Union and China—were now at odds. China was drawing closer to the United States to contain Soviet power, and the Soviet leaders themselves had long ago given up any hope of global revolution. "No Soviet leader after Khrushchev had seriously thought of the creation of Communist systems in the Western world as a policy goal," wrote the eminent Sovietologist Archie Brown of Oxford University.[31] By the early 1980s, the Kremlin was led by tired, sick, fearful old men who simply wanted to coexist with the United States and die in their beds. Even the hard-liner Richard Pipes noted of a Brezhnev speech in February 1981, "Brezhnev was in some respects surprisingly defensive: he no longer spoke of 'world revolution' as an objective but emphasized the mounting foreign and domestic problems facing his country."[32]

Contrary to Reagan's beliefs, the Soviet military buildup was not the result of any fantastical Soviet plan to destroy the United States or turn it into a Soviet satellite state; it was driven by the internal imperatives of the Soviet military-industrial complex and by the paranoia of Soviet leaders who feared their country would be attacked again, as it had been in the Napoleonic Wars, World War I, and World War II. The Red Army had not invaded Afghanistan to secure a warm-water port on the Indian Ocean or to seize the Middle East's oil—as hawks like CIA Director Bill Casey imagined[33]— but to topple an overly independent Communist leader who, the Kremlin feared, was going to align Afghanistan with the United States. (This was similar to the Soviet rationales for the brutal invasions of Hungary in 1956 and Czechoslovakia in 1968.)[34] The overthrow of the Somoza regime in Nicaragua was the result of a popular revolution, not Soviet subversion. Outside support for leftist movements in Nicaragua and El Salvador was driven primarily by Fidel Castro, a difficult ally that the Kremlin leadership distrusted, with the Soviets dragged reluctantly along primarily as a way to distract Washington. "We cannot fight in Cuba because it is 11,000 kilometers away," Brezhnev told Fidel's brother Raul Castro. "If we go there, we'll get our heads smashed."[35]

Yet Reagan was firmly convinced that the Kremlin was carrying out a plot to take over the world—and doing so with increasing success because of supposed American weakness under his old adversaries Jerry Ford and Jimmy Carter. Just as he had once blamed Communists for labor troubles in Hollywood based on scant evidence, so now, with just as little factual foundation, he blamed them for all the political instability across the entire Third World—as if poverty, oppression, corruption, income inequality, tribalism, and other problems did not exist. "Let's not delude ourselves," Reagan said in 1980. "The Soviet Union underlies all the unrest that is going on. If they weren't engaged in this game of dominoes, there wouldn't be any hot spots in the world."[36] In fact, he was the one who was deluded in blaming the Kremlin for every hot spot. The number of regional crises actually increased after the collapse of the Soviet Union, which had been a stabilizing factor in some areas.

Convinced (rightly) that the Soviet Union was weak economically and (wrongly) that it posed a growing military and political threat, Ronald Reagan launched from the beginning of his administration an ambitious effort to end what he viewed as America's losing streak in the Cold War. In many ways, Reagan was reverting to the foreign policy of one of his heroes, Dwight Eisenhower, who had attempted, with little success, to "roll back" Communist advances via covert action in the 1950s. The Cold War had already been heating up ever since the reckless and ill-fated Soviet invasion of Afghanistan in 1979. Now it was about to get even hotter—and more dangerous.

39

The Reagan Doctrine

We can't afford a defeat. El Salvador is the place for a victory.

—RONALD REAGAN

To the extent that the Reagan administration focused on foreign policy in its first year, much of its attention was riveted on two hot spots—Poland and Central America—where the president and his team spied opportunities for Cold War victories. Both areas had historic resonance for generations of American policymakers.

Ever since the promulgation of the Monroe Doctrine in 1823, US leaders had been determined to dominate Central America, leading to numerous small-scale interventions by US Marines in the nineteenth and early twentieth centuries. As for Poland, two of its most illustrious sons, Casimir Pulaski and Tadeusz Kościuszko, had become heroes of the American Revolution, and ever since then, many Americans had been well-wishers of the struggle for freedom in Poland—none more so than Americans of Polish ancestry, nine million strong in 1980. President Reagan and his aides espied the best opportunity in generations to free that long-suffering nation from Soviet domination, while also raising shrill alarms about the supposed advance of Communist subversives in Central America.

Yet, however much the Reagan administration was determined to focus on Poland and Central America, it would also find itself dragged into the quagmire of the Middle East—showing that even the most powerful policymakers are often at the mercy of distant events.

In Poland, the Communist regime was struggling to contain the growing power of the Solidarity labor movement led by Lech Wałęsa, a charismatic electrician from Gdansk. The Reagan administration spent much of 1981 trying to dissuade the Soviet Union from invading Poland and the Polish government from declaring martial law. The White House had excellent information on what was happening behind the scenes thanks to a well-placed Polish army colonel spying for the CIA. In the event, the Soviet Union never invaded; the Kremlin, less reckless in those days than in 2022 when Russia invaded Ukraine, feared the blowback from such a drastic move. But, under Soviet pressure, Polish leader Wojciech Witold Jaruzelski did declare martial law on December 13, 1981, rounding up Wałęsa and other Solidarity leaders.

Reagan was excited by the Polish revolt. "This is the first time in 60 years we have had this kind of opportunity," he exclaimed in an NSC meeting eight days later. "There may not be another in our lifetime. Can we afford not to go all out? I'm talking about a total quarantine on the Soviet Union. No détente!" As evidence of the "kind of strength" he wanted to display, the president bizarrely cited the 1939 Warner Brothers movie *Confessions of a Nazi Spy*, the first anti-Nazi movie made by a major Hollywood studio, which had come out while he was working there. Showing the strong grip that his Hollywood career continued to exert over his thinking, Reagan noted that pro-German interests wanted to buy the movie "to prevent it from being shown . . . but Warner Brothers refused to do it. The film was run and had as much impact as anything in alerting world opinion."[1] Yet Warner Brothers, having already been banished from the German market in 1934, risked little by releasing a movie that would aggravate the Nazis. US government action against the Soviet Union ran the risk of far more significant geopolitical repercussions.

Eventually Reagan backed away from his plans to wreak havoc on the Soviet economy when aides pointed out that America's European allies would not go along and that a complete break with the Soviet Union would be dangerous politically. "We don't want to get into a World War III scenario," Al Haig cautioned at the December 21, 1981, NSC meeting.[2] Even allowing the Polish regime to default on its debt, which it would have done without financial aid from the West, was rejected because it would simply inflict misery on the Polish people—and on the Western banks that had lent the money.

Sitting at one of the NSC meetings where the discussion focused on how to respond to martial law in Poland, Richard Pipes noticed that the president rarely spoke and seldom listened attentively. "RR totally lost, out of his depth, uncomfortable," Pipes wrote in his diary. "All this—both the substance and human conflict—is above and beyond him. He has not enough of either knowledge or decisiveness to cut through the contradictory advice that is being offered to him." Yet Pipes concluded that "Reagan understood remarkably well—intuitively rather than intellectually—the big issues."[3]

In the end, the measures Reagan took in response to martial law were modest, such as blocking US companies from exporting oil and gas equipment to the Soviet Union and revoking landing rights in the United States for the Soviet airline Aeroflot, but they nevertheless ratcheted up Cold War tensions. A year later, on November 4, 1982, Reagan would approve a CIA covert action program code-named QRHELPFUL to provide Solidarity with nonlethal assistance, such as money to print materials, conduct radio and video transmissions, and organize demonstrations. QRHELP-FUL, building on an effort begun under the Carter administration, helped undermine Communist control in Poland without risking a direct superpower confrontation.[4]

Reagan wanted to stop all Western technology and financing for the construction of a 3,500-mile natural gas pipeline from Siberia to Western Europe that would deliver a hard currency windfall for the Kremlin and make Western Europe dependent for energy on the USSR. But Haig pointed out, "We are smoking opium if we think we can get Allied agreement."[5] European leaders argued that the United States would be promoting a double standard if it allowed its farmers to sell wheat to the Soviets but tried to prevent the Europeans from selling pipeline components. "To say the least there was a certain lack of symmetry," complained Prime Minister Margaret Thatcher.[6] While the CIA conducted a few covert actions to try to sabotage the pipeline—none of which resulted, contrary to myth, in a massive pipeline explosion in Siberia[7]—the administration initially decided to let it go ahead for fear of a rupture with the Europeans.

Hard-line Reaganites were distraught over the president's relatively restrained approach. In a long indictment of Reagan's supposedly dovish foreign policy published in the *New York Times*, *Commentary* editor Norman Podhoretz complained that Reagan "could not bring himself to go even as far as Carter had gone. One remembers easily enough that Carter instituted a grain embargo and a boycott of the Moscow Olympics, but one is hard-pressed even to remember what the Reagan sanctions were."[8] As was his wont, Reagan shrugged off such criticism. Once again, for all of his bellicose rhetoric, he was acting more pragmatically and cautiously than many of his supporters wanted or his opponents feared. There were always sharp limits on how far he was willing to go in confronting a nuclear-armed superpower.

———————

While treading cautiously in Soviet-dominated Eastern Europe, the United States had always been more aggressive in Central America, a region it had long regarded, with imperial condescension, as "its own backyard." By the 1980s, US policymakers no longer cited the Monroe Doctrine but remained just as concerned about foreign interference in the region, with their fears focused on the tiny nations of Nicaragua and El Salvador, whose combined population of 7.8 million people was roughly the same as New Jersey's. In 1979, the dictator of Nicaragua, Anastasio Somoza, had been overthrown in a popular revolution that led to the rise of the Sandinista regime supported by Cuba and the Soviet bloc. That same year, a coalition of leftist groups known as the Farabundo Martí National Liberation Front (FMLN) launched an uprising against the military junta in El Salvador, employing weapons from Cuba and Nicaragua.

President Reagan did not perceive these insurgencies as reactions to injustice and income inequality in countries ruled by corrupt oligarchies, but rather imagined they were part of a comprehensive Soviet plot to take over all of Latin America. In an NSC meeting, he fretted about "this hemisphere becoming an extension of the Warsaw Pact" and naively fantasized about how much "North and South America" could accomplish together "if we were all buddies."[9] While Margaret Thatcher claimed in her memoir to have been the first foreign head of state to visit the United States after Reagan's inauguration,[10] in fact the honor had gone to Jamaica's new conservative prime minister Edward Seaga—an indication of the importance that Reagan assigned to Latin America. "I think we can help him & gradually take back the Caribbean which was becoming a 'Red' lake," Reagan wrote in his diary on January 28, 1981, after meeting Seaga.[11] Thatcher did not arrive in the United States until a month later.

That the Caribbean could ever become a "Red lake," given America's overwhelming military might in the region, was, of course, preposterous, but it was indicative of the paranoia in the Reagan administration's early days, when many senior officials from the president on down were in thrall to a mindset little changed from the early days of the Cold War. Al Haig was particularly combative. A Vietnam veteran, he imposed a dated 1960s ideology on the 1980s, viewing Cuba as another North Vietnam drawing the United States into another unwinnable guerrilla war, and he advocated going "to the source of the problem" in Havana just as Vietnam hawks had once advocated bombing or even invading North Vietnam.[12]

When a task force appointed by Haig reported there was no feasible option to overthrow Castro, the secretary of state exploded at what he called "limp-wristed, traditional cookie-pushing bullshit." He then began drawing up plans to blockade Cuba. In one NSC meeting, Haig reportedly growled, "You just give me the word and I'll turn that fucking island into a parking lot." In another meeting, he broached the idea of "air strikes" on Cuba.[13] "That struck horror in our hearts because we were trying to focus on the economic stuff," Jim Baker recalled.[14] Haig sneered at the "caution" of the White House staff, while lamenting that "there was no other advocate for what I would call the more vigorous approach."[15]

Reagan had no desire to be "bogged down" in a ground war in Central America, but he was convinced, as he told the NSC, "We can't afford a defeat. El Salvador is the place for a victory."[16] Reagan revived the discredited "domino theory" that had once been employed to justify US involvement in the Vietnam War, claiming that El Salvador had "become the stage for a bold attempt by the Soviet Union, Cuba, and Nicaragua to install communism by force throughout the hemisphere."[17] He kept trotting out his favorite faux Lenin quote about the United States falling into Communist hands "like overripe fruit" if they took Latin America.[18]

Brian Mulroney recalled Reagan later telling him over lunch in the White House, "You know, Brian, if we're not firm here, these fellows are going to wind up challenging us in Brownsville, Texas." Mulroney was incredulous that a tiny, impoverished Central American country could threaten the mighty Colossus of the North. "Ron," he replied, "there's not a chance these guys can challenge you anywhere."[19] But Reagan wasn't listening. He was mesmerized by the Communist threat in Latin America.

The president gave no sign of having absorbed what his own national security professionals were saying about Cuba. An NSC analysis from February 1981 argued that Castro's interventions abroad were actually "a defensive tactic during periods of greatest pressure from the US" to "'defend' Cuba by diverting US attention to other areas." Another NSC analysis warned that "the Castro regime's traditional paranoia, fed by the deterioration in relations with the US after 1978, increased markedly following the November elections in the US."[20] In other words, the Reagan administration's bellicose words and actions were leading Castro to step up support for left-wing movements in Central America and even Africa, where he had deployed troops in both Ethiopia and Angola. This, in turn, led to more aggressive US threats against Cuba, more US support for anti-Communist movements, and more death and suffering for the people of Central America. It was a vicious cycle.

The chief political objection to doing more in Central America was fear of "another Vietnam." That led the administration to focus on aiding local forces rather than sending US combat forces—and that, in turn, gave rise to concerns about US complicity in the repression carried out by the unsavory regimes it was supporting. The Carter administration had briefly cut aid to El Salvador after its National Guard troops raped and murdered three American nuns and a Catholic lay worker on December 4, 1980. But Carter resumed assistance on January 14, 1981, after the FMLN launched a "final offensive" to topple the government that soon fizzled out.[21]

Early in his tenure, Reagan was far less concerned than Jimmy Carter about the human rights violations of anti-Communist regimes. The same indifference was displayed by members of his cabinet; until George Shultz replaced Al Haig as secretary of state in mid-1982, there would be no high-level advocate of applying the same standards to right-wing regimes as to left-wing ones. "We must change the attitude of our diplomatic corps so that we don't bring down governments in the name of human rights," Reagan told the NSC on February 6, 1981. "None of them is as guilty of human rights violations as are Cuba and the USSR. We can't throw out our friends just because they can't pass the 'saliva test' on human rights. I want to see that stopped."[22]

Meeting the following month with General Roberto Viola, the new leader of the Argentinian junta, Reagan assured him that "there would be no public scoldings and lectures," even though Viola's regime was responsible for killing some thirty thousand civilians in the so-called Dirty War against left-wing political opponents who were indiscriminately labeled as terrorists and Communists; the regime's victims, known as "the disappeared," were often machine-gunned or pushed out of airplanes into the sea. In a virtual endorsement of the regime's brutality, which also included the widespread use of torture, Reagan said that "he understood that firm actions need to be taken to curb violence."[23] After the downfall of the junta in 1983, Viola would be sentenced to sixteen years in prison for crimes such as torture and kidnapping.

On February 27, 1981, Reagan fired the first salvo in what would later become known as the "Reagan Doctrine" (a term coined by columnist Charles Krauthammer) of supporting anti-Communist fighters around the world: He approved $25 million in military aid for El Salvador, more than that country had received in total since 1946, and increased the number of US military advisers from twenty-eight to fifty-four.[24] This was an expansion and update of the 1947 Truman Doctrine, which had focused on aiding countries such as Greece and Turkey that were under threat of Communist subversion. The Reagan administration was determined to aid not only anti-Communist governments seeking to suppress leftist insurgencies but also anti-Communist rebels trying to overthrow socialist regimes.

US aid to El Salvador was enough to avert a rebel victory, but, as in earlier aid efforts to regimes from Congo to Chile, it also implicated the United States in terrible human rights abuses; the San Salvador regime was killing far more civilians than the guerrillas were. The worst atrocity of all, a Central American version of the 1968 My Lai massacre in South Vietnam, occurred on December 11, 1981, when the elite, US-trained Atlácatl Battalion murdered at least eight hundred civilians, including many women and children, in the village of El Mozote. Reagan administration officials such as Assistant Secretary of State Thomas O. Enders denied that a massacre had occurred and tried to undermine the credibility of American journalists on the scene.[25]

Reagan, for his part, falsely claimed that "the radical rightwing forces in El Salvador . . . operate without government sanction" and demanded to know, "Why is it that every murder is purported to be the work of the so-called death squads?"[26] The president would have known better if he had ever had a candid conversation with Deane R. Hinton, the US ambassador to El Salvador from 1981 to 1983. The veteran diplomat privately admitted to Deputy Secretary of State Ken Dam "what he could not put in cables: namely, that there are death squads who go around killing people in El Salvador and that we are dealing with some very intractable problems with regard to the morality of some of the people in the military just below the top level."[27]

But while the Reagan administration tried to cover up Salvadoran military abuses, it also worked to curtail them. A March 1981 NSC analysis cautioned, "Unless root social, economic and political causes are effectively addressed, insurgency will remain an ever-attractive alternative for the alienated populations."[28] Pollster Richard Wirthlin, meanwhile, advised the White House that the best way to rally public support for its unpopular El Salvador policy would be to support "free elections."[29] Vice President George H. W. Bush traveled to El Salvador in 1984 to warn the government that "if these death squad murders continue, you will lose the support of the American people."[30]

The Reagan administration threw its support behind the relatively moderate center-right leader José Napoleón Duarte and his Christian Democratic Party, whose land-reform proposals were anathema to wealthy landowners. The United States spent more than $4 million to help the Christian Democrats win the 1982 legislative election and the 1984 presidential election, defeating the far-right National Republican Alliance (ARENA) party led by the notorious death-squad leader Roberto D'Aubuisson.[31]

The bloodthirsty and brutal D'Aubuisson, who was described by the CIA as a "psychopath" and "mentally unstable," was widely blamed for the murder of Archbishop Oscar Romero in 1980 and was implicated in a plot to murder US ambassador Thomas Pickering, who succeeded Deane Hinton in 1983. Yet D'Aubuisson was the favorite candidate of American conservatives such as Jesse Helms, who claimed that the principles of ARENA "are the principles of the Republican Party in the United States." When D'Aubuisson visited Washington in the 1980s, conservative luminaries belonging to such New Right organizations as Young Americans for Freedom, the Moral Majority, and the National Pro-Life Political Committee gathered to toast him as a "freedom fighter."[32] Once again, Ronald Reagan was showing himself to be considerably more moderate than many of his supporters—in no small part because he was surrounded by moderate advisers.

For all the understandable controversy attendant to US support for the El Salvadoran government and its brutal military, it was a policy that had begun under Carter and enjoyed bipartisan support in Washington, if not in the country at large. Even under Democratic control, Congress never stopped aid to El Salvador. It was a different story in Nicaragua, where the

Reagan administration was politically isolated in its fervent support of anti-Sandinista forces.

Carter had suspended economic aid to Nicaragua shortly before leaving office, but the US ambassador to Managua told the Sandinistas that aid would resume if they cut off support for the FMLN. By the end of February 1981, Nicaraguan arms shipments to the El Salvador rebels had finally stopped. Yet, perversely, Reagan administration hard-liners insisted on cutting off aid to Managua anyway on April 1, 1981. The arms pipeline from Nicaragua to El Salvador resumed shortly thereafter, thereby providing the Reagan administration with an excuse to throw its covert support behind overthrowing the Sandinista regime as part of a broader anti-Communist crusade.[33]

On March 9, 1981, in a seemingly small but highly significant step, President Reagan authorized covert action to interdict the flow of weapons to El Salvador. Argentina was already training and arming former Nicaraguan National Guardsmen and other regime opponents in Honduras. They became known as Contras (short for *contra-revolucionarios*), and the CIA joined in supporting them. CIA director Bill Casey recruited flamboyant CIA officer Duane "Dewey" Clarridge to take over the agency's Latin American operations, even though he had no background in the region, because he shared both Casey's willingness to run big risks and his contempt for congressional or press oversight. Clarridge's priorities were simple: "1. Take the war to Nicaragua. 2. Start killing Cubans."[34]

On December 1, 1981, Reagan signed a new presidential finding authorizing support for a thousand Contras. This was justified by stopping illegal arms smuggling to El Salvador, but Dick Allen secretly recommended to Reagan that the "ultimate goal" should be "to 'liberate' the country." That was exactly what Reagan had in mind. He made clear that he wanted this operation to be "truly disabling and not just flea bites."[35]

The president was convinced that Nicaragua was becoming a "base for the communizing of all of Central Am," much as US policymakers in the 1960s claimed that Vietnam would be a base for communizing all of Southeast Asia. Bill Clark, who replaced Allen as national security adviser in early 1982, was even more alarmist. He told an NSC meeting that "the Nazi threat in the 1930s and 1940s" was "much more limited in scope, with fewer resources being expended" than the Communist threat in the "Caribbean region."[36] It sometimes seemed as if there were a game of one-upmanship in the upper reaches of the Reagan administration to see who could be the most hysterical about Communist threats in Latin America. Such rhetorical grandstanding allowed senior policymakers, from Reagan on down, the moral certitude they craved: They could depict themselves as righteous crusaders against evil and paint opponents of their policies as, at best, dupes who were being manipulated by Communists.

One day in 1982, CIA Deputy Director Bobby Ray Inman walked into a meeting where Bill Casey and Dewey Clarridge were plotting to overthrow the Sandinista regime—a goal that far exceeded the more modest covert action the president had authorized and that Congress had been briefed on. Inman decided to resign rather than become party to any illegal activity, and he privately notified the appropriate congressional committees of why he was leaving. The news media also reported that the CIA's secret war in Nicaragua was expanding into a regime change operation.[37]

These revelations led to the passage in December 1982 of the Boland Amendment, sponsored by Congressman Edward Boland of Massachusetts, the moderate Democratic chairman of the House Intelligence Committee, forbidding the use of taxpayer funds "for the purpose of overthrowing the government of Nicaragua." Casey barely noticed, much less cared. By the middle of 1983, the Contra army was nearly ten thousand strong, and CIA assets were attacking Nicaraguan infrastructure and mining Nicaraguan harbors without the now-rogue CIA bothering to notify Congress. Once they found out, members of Congress, even Republicans, were "pissed off," as Senator Barry Goldwater, the chairman of the Senate Intelligence Committee, put it in a letter to Casey.[38]

"For reasons I never fully comprehended, Bill Casey became obsessed with Central America," his aide Robert Gates later wrote.[39] John Negroponte, who as US ambassador to American ally Honduras from 1981 to 1985 had a front-row seat to the secret US war in Central America, said it was never clear to him whether Reagan shared Casey's dream of overthrowing the Sandinistas or whether the president was just trying to pressure the Sandinistas into negotiating: "There was a lack of strategic clarity."[40] In any case, neither Reagan nor his revolving cast of national security advisers kept an effective check on Casey, ensuring that his obsession—which was Ronald Reagan's obsession, too—would drag the administration into its worst scandal.

Europe and Central America were the top foreign policy priorities for the Reagan administration. The Middle East ranked much lower. Ronald Reagan had only visited the region once—a trip to Iran in 1978—and never would do so again; Nancy Reagan was afraid he would be assassinated if he did. "For him," the journalist Patrick Tyler was to write, "the Middle East was terra incognita."[41] He was about to go on a steep learning curve.

In 1981, the Middle East was in flames: Iran and Iraq were at war; Lebanon was being torn apart by a multisided civil war that drew in Israel, Iran, and Syria; and, in October, Egyptian President Anwar Sadat was assassinated by Islamist militants. The Reagan administration sent a special envoy to mediate in Lebanon, but its attention was often riveted further west: Libyan ruler Moammar Qaddafi, a designer dictator known for his flashy wardrobe and trademark sunglasses, would become a Reagan obsession, his very own supervillain, playing the role of Lex Luthor to his Superman.

In his memoirs, Reagan demonstrated how little he understood about Libya's ruler by claiming that Qaddafi "was trying to unify the world into a single nation of fundamentalists under rigid religious control—a theocracy, like Iran."[42] In fact, Qaddafi was a secular nationalist who had almost nothing in common with the ayatollahs beyond a shared animus toward Israel and America. But he did use his oil wealth to destabilize his neighbors and sponsor terrorism, he had invaded Chad in 1980, and he was accused of killing an opposition leader in the United States. He also claimed the entire Gulf of Sidra as his territorial waters far beyond the internationally recognized twelve-mile limit. Qaddafi was in many ways an ideal adversary for a president eager to reassert US power: He was strong enough to be menacing but weak enough to be attacked with relative impunity.

At an NSC meeting on June 1, 1981, Reagan approved a plan to send two aircraft carrier battle groups into the Gulf of Sidra despite—or because of—the obvious risk of a military confrontation. In a subsequent meeting, he stressed that "we will respond instantly, should we be shot at" and chase Libyan aircraft "right into the hangar" if they try to escape. "He's a madman," Reagan wrote of Qaddafi in his diary. "He has been harassing our planes out over international waters & it's time to show the other nations there Egypt, Morocco, et al that there is different management here."[43]

On August 19, 1981, two Libyan Su-22 fighter aircraft challenged a pair of F-14 Tomcats flying about sixty miles off the Libyan coast. One of the Libyan planes fired a missile at the US aircraft. The F-14s took evasive maneuvers and brought down both Libyan aircraft with Sidewinder missiles; the pilots parachuted to safety. It was the first US military action since the Desert One debacle in 1980 and represented a small step toward recovering America's confidence in its military might. Reagan exuded pride two days later when he visited US military personnel aboard the aircraft carrier *Constellation* for what a later generation would call a "mission accomplished" moment.

R eagan was at Rancho del Cielo when, at 11:05 p.m. Pacific time on August 19, 1981, Ed Meese was informed by Cap Weinberger of what had happened. Meese waited five-and-a-half hours, until 4:24 a.m., to wake the commander-in-chief. After hearing the news, Reagan went back to sleep.[44] There was arguably little that Reagan could have done, but the long wait led to scathing news stories suggesting that he was out of touch. Jim Baker and Mike Deaver, always acutely sensitive to press coverage, were horrified. This gaffe fed their growing sense that the current setup—with National Security Adviser Dick Allen reporting to Ed Meese—was not working. They began looking for a way to oust the prickly, ineffectual Allen and install a more influential successor who would have direct access to the president.[45]

Allen provided the instrument of his own downfall when he left in his office safe a thousand dollars in cash. A Japanese reporter had tried to give the money to Nancy Reagan before an interview, as was customary in Japan, and Allen intercepted it and put it away. When the money was discovered in December 1981, it provided the perfect pretext to ease Allen out pending an investigation. He never got his job back, even though there was no finding of any wrongdoing.

Allen recalled that he was "infuriated to tears, practically," watching the media besmirch his reputation. He asked Reagan for his job back but was turned down. In his diary, Reagan blamed a media "lynch mob" for Allen's ouster, thereby evading responsibility for cashiering his own national security adviser. This was typical behavior for a president who often acted as if he were a bystander in his own administration.[46] Allen was a Reagan loyalist who had worked on both the 1976 and 1980 campaigns, but, ultimately, like every other staffer, he was expendable. "People could become emotionally attached to Ronald Reagan," Allen told me bitterly, "but that didn't mean that he was emotionally attached to them."[47]

Baker and Deaver decided, with Reagan's blessing, to install his affable old crony Bill Clark as national security adviser. Judge Clark, as he liked to be called, admitted to knowing next to nothing about foreign policy during his confirmation hearings for deputy secretary of state in early 1981.[48] But he had a much closer relationship with Reagan than Allen had—the two men shared a passion for horses—and, having once been Ed Meese's boss in Sacramento, Clark would not defer to the White House counselor. So that made him the best candidate available in the eyes of Baker and Deaver. It was a decision they would soon have cause to regret.[49]

While Reagan was a supporter of Israel and never seriously tried to pressure the Israelis into making concessions to the Palestinians, he found himself at loggerheads with Israeli leaders more than did many subsequent presidents, particularly fellow Republicans George W. Bush and Donald Trump. On June 7, 1981, US-made Israeli aircraft bombed the Osirak nuclear reactor in Iraq on the orders of the conservative Israeli Prime Minister Menachem Begin. A Polish Jew who in the 1940s had resisted the Nazis and Soviets and then the British colonialists in Palestine, Begin, by virtue of his own history and his people's, was as dour, intense, and gloomy as Reagan, the California transplant, was sunny, laidback, and optimistic. The prime minister argued the Osirak operation was necessary to save his country from "another Holocaust" and noted that he had warned the Carter administration about his growing concern over Iraq's nuclear program. But somehow those concerns had never been communicated to the Reagan administration. When Reagan heard about the Israeli air strike, he was shocked. "I swear I believe Armageddon is near," he wrote in his diary.[50]

There was a division in the administration over how to respond. Cap Weinberger, a former executive of the oil services giant Bechtel, which did business with Arab states, wanted to freeze all US aid to Israel. "He was anti-Israel," said Robert "Bud" McFarlane, then a State Department adviser. Al Haig was more pro-Israel, and Reagan sided with Haig. While the president was "surprised and dismayed" by the strike, he was also convinced that Iraqi leader Saddam Hussein was "a 'no good nut'" who was "trying to build a nuclear weapon." Reagan settled on a perfunctory punishment by voting to condemn Israel's actions at the United Nations, limiting Israel's access to US satellite data, and delaying the delivery of four F-16s to Israel. Begin, prickly and proud, was irate over the US response. When the US ambassador to Israel, Samuel Lewis, criticized the bombing, Begin responded with "ninety minutes of cold fury."[51]

Reagan tried to mollify Begin by negotiating a strategic cooperation agreement between the United States and Israel. But he suspended the accord almost immediately, in December 1981, to protest Begin's sudden annexation of the Golan Heights, which Israel had captured from Syria in 1967, in violation of international law.[52]

"Whereas the President originally had been very positive on Israel during the campaign," noted Deputy Secretary of State Ken Dam, "as he actually came face to face with the practical difficulties of dealing with Israel, particularly in the Begin/Sharon period, he came to believe that it would be necessary to use U.S. leverage on Israel." Press secretary Larry Speakes later wrote that Begin was "one of the few people that Reagan genuinely disliked."[53]

Further exacerbating US-Israeli relations was America's growing closeness with Saudi Arabia. Early in his tenure, Bill Casey journeyed to Riyadh and struck a de facto deal with the royal family: The Saudis would fund secret operations to roll back the Soviet empire, and in return the United States would do more to defend the kingdom.[54] This understanding resulted in generous Saudi support for anti-Communist guerrillas in Afghanistan, Nicaragua, and Angola, among other places. For its part, the administration moved forward with a Carter-era agreement to sell F-15s to the Saudis along with a sophisticated AWACS airborne-control aircraft.

The AWACS sale was opposed by the Begin government and Israel's formidable lobby in Washington, which feared that these systems would pose a threat to Israeli security. A majority of senators initially shared those concerns and signed a letter opposing the sale. Dick Allen had been put in charge of selling the deal on the Hill, but the task proved beyond him. "It was a job I really shouldn't have had," he told me, while adding that he couldn't make the AWACS deal a priority until the economic program was passed. In the fall of 1981, after the budget had been enacted, Jim Baker took over the lobbying for the AWACS sale personally with the help of the Legislative Strategy Group.

Wheeling and dealing as only he could, Baker pushed the deal across the finish line by providing assurances to skeptics that the planes would not be used against Israel. The administration also played LBJ-style hardball by threatening to cut off cooperation with senators who voted against the sale. "We just beat his brains out," one White House aide said of Iowa Republican Senator Roger Jepsen, who switched from "nay" to "aye." Reagan came in to lobby senators personally with a softer sell; he didn't do LBJ-style arm twisting. As for Israel's objections, Reagan said, "It is not the business of other nations to make American foreign policy."

The sale squeaked by the Senate, fifty-two to forty-eight, on October 28, 1981. Reagan privately compared his relief to "shitting a pineapple." The next cover of *Time* magazine showed the smiling president holding a vote tally—with no pineapple in sight. The headline proclaimed, "He Does It Again!"[55]

This was the last of the major legislative victories that the administration won in 1981. The president and his aides could take comfort from what appeared to be a phenomenally successful first year. Ronald Reagan had achieved all of his urgent priorities—major tax cuts, domestic spending decreases, and defense budget increases—while establishing his bona fides as a tough leader who was not afraid to take on Libya or Israel, the Soviet Union or the Sandinistas, PATCO or Tip O'Neill. He had even scored a historic first by appointing Sandra Day O'Connor to the Supreme Court. Just as significant, if harder to pin down, was the way Reagan had changed the atmospherics of the presidency with his optimistic, can-do ethos.

By being "easy with himself and confident of the rightness of what he was doing," wrote *Washington Post* editorial page editor Meg Greenfield, Reagan was breaking the "spell of a series of doomed presidencies." Another liberal journalist, Mark Shields, wrote that Reagan was dispelling the notion "that our problems were probably beyond both our control and our comprehension and that permanent presidential-congressional stalemate would be the future norm." "In less than a year . . . ," he continued, "Ronald Reagan has redefined the presidency in the words of President Kennedy as 'the vital center of action in our whole scheme of government.'" Washington "wise man" Bryce Harlow privately told a Reagan aide, "I have known personally, often intimately, every President from (and including) Roosevelt on, excepting Carter. Reagan's start is by far the most impressive, except for Roosevelt who had economic collapse to handle."[56]

But the president's second year was to prove more politically fraught than the first. By the end of 1981, his approval rating was cratering along with the economy, rapidly dispelling the good feelings engendered by so many early achievements and leading to a mood of apprehension and even dread in the White House as the country became mired in its worst recession since the 1930s.

40

The Fairness Issue

What to do to counter the trend toward characterization of
this administration as pro-rich, pro-bigness, do-nothing-for-
the-little guy, etc.?

—DICK DARMAN

In American politics, a president's fate is usually linked to that of the economy. That spelled bad news for Ronald Reagan during his first two years in office. He had claimed that his economic package, with its tax and spending cuts, would lift the economy out of its doldrums. Instead, the passage of Reaganomics coincided with the start of the worst recession since the Great Depression. With the Fed keeping interest rates high to bring down inflation—the Fed funds rate remained in double digits until September 1981—the economy went into recession in July 1981.[1] The unemployment rate, already high at 7.4 percent in July, swelled to over 10 percent in September 1982 and stubbornly stayed above that level until July 1983. Inflation was finally beginning to abate—it would fall from 9.3 percent in January 1982 to 4.5 percent in December—but that was scant comfort to a country mired in an economic crisis.[2]

"The recession of 1981–1982 was a watershed in America's social history," notes historian Doug Rossinow.[3] The deindustrialization of the Midwest and Northeast, which had already begun in the 1970s, now accelerated. Battered by growing foreign competition, numerous US factories shuttered, eliminating large numbers of union jobs in what became known as the Rust Belt. "It's been total devastation," lamented a union leader in Youngstown, Ohio, a blue-collar town that had long been a center of steel production.[4] The US automobile industry was particularly hard hit, leading the Reagan administration to pressure Japan into imposing "voluntary" quotas on its automobile exports to avoid congressionally mandated tariffs. In all, the economy lost 1.9 million jobs during the 1981–1982 recession—and, while new jobs were eventually created, many of the old ones never came back.

Presidents are insulated from the suffering of ordinary people, but Ronald Reagan was exposed to heartrending complaints, many from his own supporters, in the cross-section of letters forwarded to him weekly by the White House Correspondence Unit. The president of a metal company in Bridgeview, Illinois, wrote to complain that "two weeks ago the bank thrust us into Chapter 11 by calling our loan. . . . What single issue has killed us? The interest rates. . . . I've been a 'DuPage County Republican' for 29 years, but now I am shaken deeply." The co-owner of a small excavation business in Texarkana, Arkansas, wrote, "My husband and I are starving slowly to death. We have no money for food. . . . Do you have any idea what it feels like to see everything you've worked hard for fall right through your hardworking callused hands, to not be able to pay your bills, feed your family or heat your home?" The president of a flooring company in Chicago wrote, "My sales are off approximately 70%, my number of employees down from 105 to 34 and my hopes for the future entirely smashed. I am in the process of trying to sell my home in order to pay some of my creditors."[5]

In his replies, Reagan invariably pleaded for patience; sometimes, he would even write a small check to help someone in need or ask his aides to see if the government could do something to assist. He often spoke of his empathy for the unemployed after having lived through the Great Depression. "I think that any of us who experienced that have a traumatic feeling about unemployment," he told an interviewer. "That's why today it isn't ice water, it's real blood that I bleed for the unemployed."[6]

But the president's own agenda—with large tax cuts for the wealthy and spending cuts for the poor—fostered an impression that, as a woman in Kentucky wrote to him, "your present plan [is] robbing from the poor and giving to the rich."[7] Because of the 1981 budget cuts, as many as five hundred thousand families lost their eligibility for the main welfare program, Aid to Families with Dependent Children, and another three hundred thousand families had their benefits reduced; a million people lost Food Stamps; and only 45 percent of the jobless in 1982 received unemployment benefits compared to 76 percent during the recession of 1975.[8]

To cope with a 40 percent cut in funding for the National School Lunch Program, the Department of Agriculture in September 1981 shrank milk servings from six ounces to four ounces and, in an infamous gaffe, let schools count ketchup and relish as vegetables. This led to withering criticism, with *New York Times* columnist Russell Baker writing, "This is an idea by one of Oliver Twist's workhouse bullies, isn't it?" The president disavowed the ketchup decision, blaming it on "bureaucratic sabotage," but he had to retreat from that accusation after an angry response from Agriculture Secretary John Block, who pointed out he was merely implementing the president's budget.[9]

There were growing numbers of homeless people in major cities in part because the 1981 budget eliminated federal funding for community mental-health services and replaced it with block grants to the states at a lower level. That made it nearly impossible to provide help to the vast numbers of patients with chronic mental illnesses who were being "deinstitutionalized" as states closed old-fashioned mental hospitals. By 1988, the National Institutes for Mental Health estimated that between 125,000 and 300,000 mentally ill people were homeless.[10]

The media began to fill up with stories of the homeless and the impoverished, leading Reagan to vent his frustration. "Is it news," he demanded, "that some fellow in South Succotash someplace has been just laid off, that he should be interviewed nationwide?" It *was* news, and the news coverage only got more brutal. In April 1982, CBS News correspondent Bill Moyers, a former press secretary to Lyndon Johnson, appeared in a documentary called *People Like Us* showcasing the stories of a few families that had been hurt by Reagan budget cuts. "It is a thoroughly dishonest demagogic, cheap shot," Reagan fumed in his diary, but the CBS program reached, and resonated with, a wide audience.[11]

It did not help Reagan's cause when the architect of his budget disavowed his own creation. Throughout the budget battles of 1981, David Stockman had been talking with great candor to journalist William Greider on the understanding that Greider would not publish anything until the budget was passed. That moment arrived in the fall of 1981. On November 10, 1981—Stockman's thirty-fifth birthday—the *Atlantic* released Greider's article, "The Education of David Stockman." It quoted the budget director lamenting that the budget math did not "add up" and saying, "None of us really understands what is going on with all these numbers." Stockman even said that supply-side economics was really "'trickle-down' theory."[12]

Reaganites were aghast, Democrats delighted. "On each point the architect of the Administration's economic program is admitting exactly what I and other critics have been saying for six months," Tip O'Neill chortled.[13]

Most of the senior White House staff, and even the first lady, wanted Stockman fired, but Jim Baker viewed him as an indispensable budget savant and intervened to save his job. He told Stockman to go into the Oval Office for lunch with the president: "The menu is humble pie. You're going to eat every last mother-fucking spoonful of it. You're going to be the most contrite sonofabitch this world has ever seen. . . . When you go through the Oval Office door, I want to see that sorry ass of yours dragging on the carpet." Stockman was in shock. "Never in my life had I been treated to such a rude, unsparing humiliation," he complained. When Stockman published his account of the conversation in 1986, Baker's mother, a proper Southern belle, was also shocked. "Jimmy, darling," she demanded, "you didn't say those things, did you?" "Oh no," he told her. "Of course not, mother." But he confirmed to me that Stockman's account was so accurate the budget director might as well have been wearing a wire.[14]

Ronald Reagan himself was gentler than his chief of staff. After a lunch of soup and tuna salad on November 12, 1981, the president turned to his budget director, who had never been alone with him before, and asked more in sorrow than anger, "Dave, how do you explain this? You have hurt me. Why?" Stockman gave a lengthy explanation, trying to convince the president that his quotations were not all that bad and that they were supposed to be off the record. (In fact, according to Greider, Stockman had never asked him not to publish anything he said.) Always a soft touch, Reagan decided that Stockman had been "a victim of sabotage by the press" and asked him to stay on. Stockman agreed to do so in the hope of clearing up the "shambles" he had created.[15]

But while Stockman would remain in office until 1985, "he was much diminished from the days of his veritable godhood in early 1981," noted another White House aide.[16] The erstwhile whiz kid was now seen by many as a flim-flam artist, and the White House was perceived to have lost its way. Reagan did not exactly dispel those concerns when he wrote to the supply-side apostle Jude Wanniski in December 1981, "Please believe me, there is less disarray among our family here than the press would lead you to believe."[17]

Another denizen of the White House was also undermining the president's response to the recession, but she would not receive even the mild rebuke given to Stockman. Nancy Reagan had always lived well ever since her upbringing on Chicago's Gold Coast, and she saw no reason to change despite the nation's economic struggles. For the inaugural balls, she wore a designer gown that cost more than $10,000 and a diamond necklace and earring set from Harry Winston that cost nearly $500,000.[18] Thus began her habit of "borrowing" expensive jewelry and gowns that were not always given back.

She then launched into an extensive renovation of the White House, focusing on the rundown family quarters on the second and third floors, paid for by $822,641 in donations from campaign contributors.[19] "I had always been a nester," she wrote in her memoirs, but her luxe nesting habits were now subject to a degree of public scrutiny she had never known before. The criticism became even more heated when she unveiled plans in September 1981 to buy a new set of White House china for more than $200,000 on the very day the Department of Agriculture announced that ketchup would be counted as a vegetable. "I was called more names than I can remember," she complained. "Queen Nancy. The Iron Butterfly. The Belle of Rodeo Drive. Fancy Nancy. The Cutout Doll. On *The Tonight Show*, Johnny Carson quipped that my favorite junk food was caviar."[20]

Ronnie complained in his diary that Mommie was getting "a bum rap . . . from a few bitchy columnists." But while he could shrug off criticism, she could not. Nancy was traumatized by all the attacks; her stepbrother, Richard Davis, recalled that she often complained that "Washington is a mean-spirited town." "She wanted to be popular, but just couldn't pull it off," Davis said. Instead, she became "more withdrawn, very protective, and very sensitive to any type of criticism. . . . I didn't see her laugh that much."[21]

Nancy's press secretary Sheila Tate suggested that the best way to fight back would be with a good-humored appearance at the annual dinner of the Gridiron Club on March 27, 1982, attended by Washington's movers and shakers. Nancy agreed to take part in a skit singing new lyrics, written by White House speechwriter Landon Parvin, for an old Fanny Brice tune, "Second Hand Rose." Wearing an ensemble that made her look like a bag lady, the first lady brought down the house with a song that began, "I'm wearing second-hand clothes, / Second-hand clothes, / They're quite the style / In Spring fashion shows. / Even my new trench coat with fur collar, / Ronnie bought for ten cents on the dollar."[22]

"The smash of the evening was Nancy," her doting husband enthused. "Maybe this will end the sniping."[23] By suggesting that the first lady could joke about herself, this performance certainly helped repair her reputation in Washington if not in the rest of the country.

Also helpful was her adoption of the antidrug cause. Nancy Reagan would make the slogan "Just say no" famous, even though, as documented by biographer Karen Tumulty, she herself had been "dependent on prescription medications" (uppers and downers) ever since the 1950s.[24] But that dependency would not be revealed to the public until the publication of daughter Patti Davis's memoir in 1992. While some sophisticates may have sneered at the "Just say no" campaign, it helped burnish the first lady's image. She was finally making headlines for something other than her fashion, jewelry, and decorating choices.

Like most presidents, Ronald Reagan blamed the media for his political struggles, with his approval rating in the Gallup poll falling from 68 percent in May 1981 to 35 percent in January 1983. "The press has done a job on us & the polls show its effects. The people are confused about ec.[onomic] program," Reagan complained in his diary. "They've been told it has failed & it's just started."[25]

White House aides strategized about how to address the administration's central political problem: "What to do," in Dick Darman's words, "to counter the trend toward characterization of this administration as pro-rich, pro-bigness, do-nothing-for-the-little guy, etc?" Another senior White House aide, Richard S. Williamson, expressed concern that "we are not presenting the nice side of Ronald Reagan, but rather the harsh side of the budget cutter who takes food away from children and will take away pension benefits from the elderly." Ultimately, wrote deputy political director Lee Atwater, "The Achilles Heel of this Administration is the 'fairness issue.'" United States Information Agency director Charles Z. Wick warned Reagan that "your adversaries are generating an image of you as 'Hoover-like,' caring only for your rich friends, insensitive to the needs of the poor and less fortunate." Communications director David Gergen likewise lamented the widespread impression "that RR just doesn't give a damn about people on the lower end of the ladder."[26] White House aides thought this was an unfair criticism purveyed by the liberal news media, but it was grounded in reality: While the bottom 50 percent of taxpayers saw a decline in after-tax income from 1980 to 1983, the top 1 percent saw a 22.7 percent increase.[27]

Cabinet secretary Craig Fuller warned in May 1982, with midterm elections looming in the fall, that "we need to be doing far more to build and maintain the support for the President from the populist voter—the blue collar worker, the farmer, the steel worker, etc. We also need to . . . demonstrate that the administration is concerned about the plight of people who are having difficulty coping with the recession: unemployed, poor, minorities, and the blue-collar workers." Fuller suggested that the solution was for Reagan to deliver speeches aimed at the working class, while Gergen urged a "broad-scaled new offensive . . . before we are overrun and lasting, negative impressions are formed about the President."[28] But there was only so much that a communications strategy could achieve amid double-digit unemployment and interest rates.

There was no interest in the White House in creating a federal jobs program or expanding unemployment benefits—the traditional remedies during a recession—because such steps conflicted with free-market orthodoxy. The defense buildup and tax cuts provided some stimulus but not enough. And, to Reagan's credit, he was not willing to pressure the Fed to prematurely cut interest rates at the risk of allowing inflation to fester. "The current economic downturn and the projected increases in '82–'84 deficits *do not call for any basic change in economic policy*," the White House Legislative Strategy Group concluded in December 1981.[29] That left the White House with few policy options to deal with the deep downturn.

The White House tried to blame the recession on "past policy mistakes," but after a year in office, President Reagan had ownership of the economy even if he did not control it.[30] This was the Reagan Recession. "Our problem," Gergen wrote in March 1982, "is that recession—deep, numbing, almost frightening to some—has given the other side a wide opening to attack us on every conceivable front."[31]

Democrats took full advantage of the opening, with Tip O'Neill telling the press in early 1982, "I don't believe the President appreciates the depth of what is going on. Generally, I like the fella. He tells a good Irish story.

But he has forgotten his roots. He associates with the country club-style of people." Reagan angrily retorted, "Well, I have only played golf once since I have been President, and he is an inveterate golfer, and I am sure he must go to a country club to play golf." O'Neill did play at a country club, but that didn't take the sting out of his accusation. The "Teflon president," as he was nicknamed by Democratic Representative Patricia Schroeder of Colorado, was losing some of his ability to deflect criticism.[32]

Despite their differences, O'Neill was willing to work with Reagan, in that less polarized age, to address the ballooning budget deficit. By early 1982, with federal revenues shrinking along with the economy, the deficit was projected to exceed $100 billion the following year. "We who were going to balance the budget face the biggest budget deficits ever," Reagan noted ruefully in his diary. This was particularly embarrassing given that he had long been blaming the nation's economic ills on "almost forty years of deficit spending."[33] His own administration's experience—with the economy reviving while the deficit continued to grow—would provide the ultimate refutation of that theory.

Still adhering to mainstream rather than supply-side economics, most congressional Republicans were, as Senate Majority Whip Ted Stevens said, "in a state of shock" about the skyrocketing deficits. There was little appetite in Congress for more cuts in domestic spending, particularly spending on the poor, so the only practical ways to reduce the deficit were either through tax increases or defense cuts or both. White House pragmatists and the first lady urged the president to adopt this advice only to run into his intransigence—a sign, depending on your perspective, of his stubbornness or his devotion to principle. In November 1981, Reagan defiantly told a group of money managers, "I don't have any reverse gear—I'm not going to retreat one inch.... Damn the torpedoes, full speed ahead!" In January 1982, he wrote in his diary, "I told our guys I couldn't go for tax increases. If I have to be criticized I'd rather be criticized for a deficit than for backing away from our Ec. program."[34]

But gradually, as the expected tax revenues did not materialize and the budget projections worsened, Reagan relaxed his opposition to what his aides took to calling "revenue enhancements." As he had previously demonstrated in Sacramento on issues from fair housing to tax withholding, he did have a reverse gear after all. He allowed Jim Baker and Dave Stockman to negotiate an agreement with congressional leaders that would result in the largest peacetime tax increase in US history—$98.3 billion over three years (more than $300 billion in 2024 dollars). What made it politically palatable for the president was that the bipartisan bill didn't undo his 25 percent cut in personal income taxes. Rather, the Tax Equity and Fiscal Responsibility Act (TEFRA) closed some of the tax loopholes that had been added during the frenzy to pass the budget in 1981 while raising corporate taxes and excise taxes on cigarettes, telephone calls, and airline travel. In his memoir, Reagan wrote that the bill only did "limited loophole-closing," which was not accurate.[35]

The Troika, backed by Nancy Reagan and Senate Republican leaders such as Bob Dole and Howard Baker, argued that the tax hike was necessary to assure the bond markets that the deficit was coming under control—which, in turn, would reduce interest rates and increase economic activity. Reagan finally gave in, saying, "All right, goddamn it, I'm going to do it, but it's wrong," and throwing his glasses on the desk in frustration. "He was really pissed when he finally agreed," Jim Baker recalled.[36]

Reagan mollified himself with assurances from his budget negotiators Jim Baker and Dave Stockman that the Democrats would deliver three dollars of spending cuts for every dollar of tax increases, but the Democrats never agreed to any such formula. All the talk of budgetary savings was vague and aspirational. Martin Feldstein, chairman of the White House Council of Economic Advisers from 1982 to 1984, wrote that "the administration's negotiators knew that the spending reductions would never be achieved but preferred to maintain the fiction to get the president's support for tax increases."[37] Reagan was so convinced this fictional deal existed that he spent the rest of his life complaining that the Democrats had reneged on their promises of spending cuts. Once again, Reagan had fallen prey to his own inattention to detail, his extreme delegation of authority, and his penchant for wishful thinking.

Tip O'Neill promised to pass the tax hike only if Reagan convinced at least a hundred House Republicans to support it over the opposition of conservative firebrands such as Jack Kemp and Newt Gingrich. Reagan's heart wasn't in it, but he dutifully undertook a "tax blitz," telling Republicans that, while "raising taxes is a very unpleasant task, one which none of us likes doing," it had to be done.[38] His personal popularity, though reduced since

1981, was still sufficient to sway many Republicans, and, like Nixon going to China, he had more credibility than a Democrat to sell a tax increase.

In August 1982, TEFRA passed with bipartisan support by narrow margins in both the House (226 to 207) and the Senate (53 to 47). Right-wingers blamed what they saw as a betrayal of Reaganite principles on the president's moderate advisers. Conservatives gathered by direct-mail king Richard Viguerie were, in the words of Jude Wanniski, "foaming at the mouth" about Jim Baker and Dave Gergen.[39] Privately, conservative White House aides were equally apoplectic; Ed Meese called TEFRA a "debacle" and "the greatest domestic error of the Reagan administration."[40] Jim Baker came under public attack from conservative die-hards—"the nutcases," he called them—who demanded that Reagan fire him.[41] But Reagan staunchly defended his chief of staff and disdained the "ultra pure conservatives."[42] "Those bastards will never be satisfied," he scoffed.[43]

While the conservatives' battle cry was "Let Reagan be Reagan," they did not grasp that he was not a rigid ideologue but a pragmatic idealist. "I'm in charge," Reagan wrote to one of Baker's critics, "and my people are helping to carry out the policies I set."[44] Yet however often he said it, conservatives continued to believe Reagan was the unwitting dupe of what one of their magazines called the "moderate Eastern liberal-Republican Big Business establishment."[45] Many of them had just as low an estimation of his intelligence as liberals did.

TEFRA did not come close to stanching the flow of red ink. The 1983 budget deficit, estimated at around $100 billion at the time the bill was passed, actually exceeded $200 billion—a level considered frighteningly high at the time. But the law assured financial markets that something was being done to address deficits, which undoubtedly would have been even higher without it.

The passage of TEFRA was part of a pattern in the Reagan administration, which raised taxes more often than it cut them. This should hardly be surprising since Reagan had done the same thing when he was governor of California. The supply-side economist Bruce Bartlett calculated that the administration cut taxes four times and raised them eleven times.[46] The year after TEFRA, Reagan signed legislation to more than double gasoline taxes to pay for highway improvements and also increased payroll taxes to keep Social Security solvent. The bipartisan Social Security agreement, which included benefit reductions and tax hikes on a fifty-fifty basis, was negotiated by Jim Baker with Tip O'Neill's representative after the 1982 midterm election.

Overall, the Treasury later calculated, the value of Reagan's major tax cuts in 2012 dollars ($111.7 billion) exceeded the value of his major tax increases ($78.1 billion), but that there were so many tax increases provided further evidence of Reagan's willingness to deviate from supply-side dogma.[47] Reagan, in particular, showed a willingness in 1982 to correct the excesses of his halcyon first year in office, when tax-cut legislation had grown considerably larger than anyone had anticipated during its passage in Congress.

The early Reagan budgets not only increased the deficit; they also increased income inequality. Most of the benefits of the 1981 tax act flowed to wealthy households, and many of the later tax hikes—such as increases in excise taxes and payroll taxes—fell disproportionately on the poor because they were paid at a flat rate regardless of income. "From 1980 to 1985," wrote journalists Thomas and Mary Edsall, "the combined effective tax rate—including federal income, Social Security, excise, and corporate taxes—rose sharply for the bottom 20 percent of all households, going from 8.4 to 10.6 percent; and dropped most precipitously for those in the top 20 percent, from 27.3 to 24 percent."[48]

It was no coincidence that in the 1980s the top 1 percent of families saw their income grow by 75 percent while the bottom 90 percent saw their income grow by just 7 percent.[49] This was not completely, or even primarily, the result of federal tax policy—there were also sweeping changes occurring in the economy that were benefiting college-educated, white-collar workers—but President Reagan's policies contributed to a growing divergence between high-income and middle- and low-income households that would only grow more extreme in succeeding decades. Fifty-nine percent of Americans belonged to the middle class in 1981, but by 2020 the figure had declined to 50 percent. Measured another way, while the income gap between the ten poorest and the ten richest counties in the country grew by 39 percent from 1980 to 2020, the gap in the death rate, reflecting disparities in health care and healthy habits, grew by a shocking 570 percent. By 2020, nearly four decades after the launch of "Reaganomics," income inequality in the United States was wider than in almost any other developed democracy.[50]

That trend would have profound social and political consequences, leading to the rise of populist movements on both the left and the right and creating a widespread sense that the political system did not work for ordinary Americans.

The country had to grapple not only with the mixed consequences of Reagan's tax and spending agenda but also with his deregulatory agenda. On October 15, 1982, little more than a month after signing TEFRA, Reagan went to a Rose Garden crowded with savings-and-loan executives to sign the Garn–St. Germain Depository Institutions Act. Sponsored by Republican Senator Jake Garn of Utah and Democratic Representative Fernand St. Germain of Rhode Island, it had passed both houses of Congress by overwhelming margins and sounded like an innocuous piece of legislation; Reagan noted in his diary that "it had to do with untangling & removing some of the restriction regulations on these institutions."[51]

But, in fact, the bill would turn out to be a ticking time bomb underneath the entire savings-and-loan industry. The Garn–St. Germain Act tried to help S&Ls that were suffering losses because of rising interest rates and declining home sales by loosening restrictions on the interest rates they could offer consumers and the lines of business they could enter. Because S&Ls remained federally insured, the legislation encouraged irresponsible risk-taking such as investments in junk bonds. By the end of the 1980s, more than a third of all S&Ls had failed, necessitating a bailout that would cost taxpayers a staggering $132 billion. It would be the biggest financial bailout in US history to that point. Business journalist Martin Mayer called this "the worst public scandal in American history. . . . The S&L outrage makes Teapot Dome and Credit Mobilier seem [like] minor episodes."[52]

The S&L crisis was a bipartisan mess, but it did happen on Reagan's watch and was a consequence of the kind of deregulation that he advocated along with his administration's carelessness about ethical standards. Some of the S&L operators used political influence to escape regulatory oversight from the Federal Savings and Loan Insurance Corporation. The most notorious example was Charles Keating, owner of Lincoln Savings and Loan in California, who in the 1980s donated heavily to five senators of both parties who became known as the Keating Five. Reagan was hardly the main culprit, yet he refused to accept *any* responsibility, wrongly blaming it all on bank regulators in California and Texas, two of the states that saw the highest number of S&L failures.[53]

At the behest of business interests, Reagan's administration also cut back spending for the Environmental Protection Agency that was needed to enforce clean air and clean water regulations, restricted enforcement of safety rules by the Occupational Safety and Health Administration, and expanded the lease of public lands to mining and energy companies.

The administration justified its deregulatory initiatives with the claim that they would generate economic growth without harming the public. That was certainly true in some instances, particularly when it came to deregulation of the energy, telephone, and airline industries—efforts that had begun under Jimmy Carter to foster greater competition and lower prices. But there was no justification for allowing the savings-and-loan industry to run amok with federally insured funds. While Reagan would ultimately claim credit for the return of economic growth in the 1980s, he could not escape blame for some of the decade's debacles.

Reagan's hope was that by cutting taxes, spending, and regulations, he would jump-start the economy. But in 1982 there was no economic growth to be seen. Democrats campaigned on the "fairness issue" and accused Republicans of wanting to cut Social Security. (There was no hint that, after the election, Tip O'Neill would agree to Social Security cuts.) That Reagan was losing control of the debate became evident in September 1982 when both the House and Senate voted to override his veto of a $14.1 billion appropriations bill that included $2 billion less for defense and $1 billion more for social spending than he wanted. It was his first veto override.[54]

On Election Day, November 2, 1982, Republicans lost twenty-six House seats and seven governorships while maintaining an eight-seat majority in the Senate. "Democrats Victors in Key Races in a Wave of Reagan Discontent" ran the *New York Times* headline.[55] The House losses were about average for a president's party, but they broke the de facto control exercised by a conservative coalition. While Reagan characteristically put the best gloss on a bad situation—"had to expect that & it could have been worse," he wrote in his diary about the loss of House seats—there was no disguising the reality that Tip O'Neill and the liberals were back in charge.[56]

As it happened, the recession technically ended the same month, signaling better days ahead. The Fed was convinced that inflation (down to 5 percent) had finally been tamed, and it was allowing interest rates to fall in tandem. But the unemployment rate was still 10.8 percent. The recovery would not make itself felt until late 1983.

As if the news was not grim enough, Loyal Davis, Nancy Reagan's revered stepfather, died of congestive heart failure at age eighty-six on August 19, 1982. Ronald Reagan had pleaded with Davis, a lifelong atheist, to accept God, and Davis did speak to a chaplain two days before his death, but that hardly cushioned the blow.[57] Nancy was in tears, and Ronnie wrote in his diary, "I wish I could bear her pain myself."[58] Although Loyal had stipulated in his will that his remains should be cremated without any memorial service, Nancy (taking charge in place of her infirm mother) not only buried him but also held a religious service attended by sixty mourners, including the president.[59] Her stepbrother, Richard Davis, was so aghast by her actions, he didn't attend the service or speak to the Reagans for eighteen months. "She disobeyed him," he said, "and I wasn't going to put up with it."[60]

The loss of Loyal Davis wasn't the only family drama in 1982. The president's youngest son, Ron Reagan, was briefly furloughed from his job as a dancer at the Joffrey Ballet and collected unemployment insurance, creating some embarrassing headlines for the White House.[61] After finally being elevated from the Joffrey II junior ensemble to a secondary role in the senior dance troupe, he would leave ballet dancing for good the following year to pursue a journalism career. He was proud of having gotten as far as he did after a late start in a demanding discipline akin to professional sports, but his $300-a-week salary was hardly enough for him and his wife to live on in New York, and it was obvious he would never be another Baryshnikov.[62]

Meanwhile, Maureen Reagan decided to enter the Republican primary for an open US Senate seat in California, ignoring the advice of her father's aides and supporters to launch her political career by seeking a lower office first. Asked by a reporter whether Maureen would run, her father replied, "I hope not." She accepted his disingenuous explanation—"having campaigned myself, it's not something I would wish on anyone"—but she was furious that her uncle Neil "Moon" Reagan made a commercial for another candidate, saying, "We Reagans urge you to support Pete Wilson." When the notoriously unfiltered White House political director Ed Rollins told a reporter, "She has the highest negatives of any candidate I've seen," Maureen tried to get him fired. But the president told Rollins, "Hell, Ed, don't worry about it. I know she shouldn't be in this race."

San Diego Mayor Pete Wilson won the primary and the Senate seat; Maureen came in fifth with only 5 percent of the vote. Her ill-fated campaign exposed the continuing discord in the first family. "Mermie" would spend more time at the White House in the years ahead, sleeping in the Lincoln Bedroom, as her father tried to find a role for her. She would serve as a part-time consultant on women's issues, an unofficial goodwill ambassador to Africa (she and her husband, who had no biological children, adopted an African girl), and cochair of the Republican National Committee. Her relations with Nancy Reagan, which had been hyperborean for decades, would warm up so much that she would start to refer to the first lady as "Mom," much to Nancy's delight.[63]

A few weeks after the midterm election, on November 20, 1982, President Reagan ad-libbed a sound check before delivering his weekly radio address from Camp David. "My fellow Americans, I've talked to you on a number of occasions about the economic problems and opportunities our nation faces," he said. "And I am prepared to tell you, it's a hell of a mess."[64] He didn't think his microphone was live, but his unexpected outburst of candor was heard by the press corps.

By early 1983, polls were showing Reagan trailing badly in trial heats against the most likely 1984 Democratic nominees—losing forty to fifty-two to former vice president Walter Mondale and thirty-nine to fifty-four to Ohio senator and former astronaut John Glenn. Winning reelection looked like a long shot, and some conservative activists were urging the president, who was in his seventies, not to run again.

In January 1983, the *New York Times* editorialized, "The stench of failure hangs over Ronald Reagan's White House." *Washington Post* columnist David S. Broder wrote that "Reaganism" ended in 1981 and that "what has been occurring ever since is an accelerating retreat from Reaganism, a process in which he is more spectator than leader." Dick Darman agreed with Broder but put a positive spin on it. Reagan, he later wrote, was showing a willingness to "sacrifice the purity of his ideology for the practical necessities of governance."[65]

By the end of 1982, the triumphs of 1981 already seemed, like glowing embers, as if they belonged to the distant past. The year had been a difficult one for the country economically and for Reagan politically. Could he do any better abroad? Reagan's plan had always been to revive the nation's economy and spirits to strengthen America's standing abroad. Now he was facing the challenge of projecting power while dealing with the weakest economy since the Great Depression—and a foreign policy team riven by self-destructive infighting.

41

The Ash Heap of History

It's tempting to go back and say, "You know, we had this great strategy and we had all these things figured out," but I don't think that's accurate.

—GEORGE SHULTZ

The National Security Council was created in 1947, in the earliest years of the Cold War, as part of the same legislation that also birthed the CIA and the Department of Defense. Located in the grand Victorian pile known as the Old Executive Office Building next to the White House, its small staff—roughly thirty-five professional staff members in the early days of the Reagan administration—was tasked with supporting the president in the conduct of foreign policy and coordinating among executive branch departments.[1] Confusingly, the abbreviation "NSC" was also colloquially applied to the regular meetings of national security decision-makers. (In the Reagan administration, the most senior gathering of "principals"—the president, vice president, the secretaries of state and defense, the CIA director, the chairman of the Joint Chiefs of Staff, and the national security adviser—was dubbed the National Security Planning Group, or NSPG.)[2] The NSC had a low profile until the advent, starting with the Kennedy administration, of a series of intellectual and influential national security advisers, among them McGeorge Bundy, Walt Rostow, Henry Kissinger, and Zbigniew Brzezinski. The office shrank to insignificance during Dick Allen's troubled tenure in 1981 but grew in influence once again in January 1982 when William P. Clark—the former California Supreme Court justice and Reagan chief of staff in Sacramento—succeeded Allen.

The new national security adviser had little knowledge of foreign policy in spite of his recent service as deputy secretary of state, but he did have a close relationship with the president—a prerequisite for wielding power in the White House. Both Reagan and Clark defined themselves as Western ranchers. This was an identity that the new appointee emphasized with the stockman's hat and hand-tooled, black cowboy boots he wore along with his expensively tailored, blue pinstripe suits. He even kept in his office a US Marshal's badge and a Colt .45 worn by his grandfather, a lawman in Ventura County, California, in the 1920s and 1930s. One journalist thought that Clark looked "like a Norman Rockwell version of a judge," while another wrote that he had a "winning modesty and a willingness to listen that is unusual for a high government official."[3] Dick Allen had been insecure and jealous of his limited authority; he lamented to me that he was constantly undermined by bureaucratic rivals.[4] By contrast, his more self-effacing, if less knowledgeable, successor was more willing to have NSC staffers brief the president and to receive credit for their own work.

To run the NSC's day-to-day operations, Clark brought in as his deputy a tightly wound former Marine officer, Robert "Bud" McFarlane, a protégé of Henry Kissinger's who most recently had been an adviser to Al Haig. McFarlane later noted that "the popular judgment on Ronald Reagan's approach to foreign affairs was not favorable: it was being said that he had none. The first year had been one of drift, of reacting to events."[5]

One the first priorities of Clark and McFarlane was to try to bring some coherence to the administration's ad hoc approach to the Soviet Union, which had veered from tough measures, such as the massive defense buildup and the imposition of sanctions following martial law in Poland, to attempts at conciliation, such as the lifting of the grain embargo and Reagan's mawkish letters to Leonid Brezhnev. This became a job primarily for two NSC staffers: Tom Reed, the former Reagan campaign operative from California who had served as Ford's air force secretary, and the Polish-born historian Richard Pipes, who was on leave from Harvard to serve as the NSC's chief Soviet expert. Both men were dedicated cold warriors who were determined to apply their own thinking—which they assumed was shared by the president—to the administration's policy toward the Soviet Union.

The NSC's labors resulted in two National Security Decision Directives, or NSDDs, signed by the president, that attempted to shift US policy from merely containing and deterring the Soviet Union to trying to undermine the Soviet empire. NSDD 32, authored primarily by Reed and issued on May 20, 1982, called on the United States to "discourage Soviet adventurism . . . by forcing the USSR to bear the brunt of its economic shortcomings, and to encourage long-term liberalizing and nationalist tendencies within the Soviet Union and allied countries." NSDD 75, written primarily by Pipes and issued on January 17, 1983, further elaborated on the need "to promote, within the narrow limits available to us, the process of change in the Soviet Union toward a more pluralistic political and economic system in which the power of the privileged ruling elite is gradually reduced."[6]

Tom Reed summarized the new approach by saying, "We believe the free world can prevail." This echoed Ronald Reagan's 1977 comment to Dick Allen about winning the Cold War. At other times, however, Reagan spoke of ending, not winning, the Cold War—an objective that could be accomplished by cooperation, not confrontation. Because the Cold War ended in 1989 and the Soviet Union collapsed in 1991, there is an understandable tendency to draw a direct connection between these epochal events and the policies enunciated in NSDDs 32 and 75. These were "the directives that won the Cold War," wrote Clark's admiring biographers Paul Kengor and Pat Clark Doerner.[7]

The truth is considerably more complicated. In the first place, while introducing a new emphasis on undermining Soviet power, the two national security directives did not entirely eschew attempts to cooperate with the Soviet Union. NSDD 75 called on the United States "to engage the Soviet Union in negotiations to attempt to reach agreements which protect and enhance U.S. interests," while NSDD 32 advocated "equitable and verifiable arms control agreements." These lines were a result of pressure from the State Department, which always emphasized the importance of diplomacy and could never be sidelined entirely even by a hawkish staff at the NSC.

While many Reagan admirers have suggested that NSDDs 32 and 75 amounted to a declaration of "economic warfare" against the Soviet Union,[8] in November 1982 the president lifted the US embargo on the Siberian gas pipeline to preserve comity with America's European allies without getting any meaningful concessions in return. Hawks such as Richard Pipes were frustrated by the president's willingness to renounce one of America's most powerful economic weapons and to engage in dialogue with the Soviets. They thought the president was being naive in trying to reach an accommodation with the Kremlin.[9]

"It's tempting to go back and say, 'You know, we had this great strategy and we had all these things figured out,' but I don't think that's accurate,"

George Shultz, who would become secretary of state in 1982, told me. "What is accurate was that there was a general 'peace through strength' attitude."[10]

There were, in reality, sharp limitations on the extent to which *any* written strategy could govern policy decisions made years in the future. Dick Pipes, after leaving the NSC at the end of 1982, concluded that "the process of decision-making ... is not the result of careful weighing of data and all the pros and cons." Instead, decisions were "usually made ad hoc, on the basis of intellectual predispositions and the mood of the moment," with "personalities" playing an "enormous role."[11]

This was certainly true in the case of Ronald Reagan who, as even his admirers had to admit, was no systematic thinker and had trouble sorting out the conflicting advice he received from aides. Pipes found that the president "was altogether incapable of thinking abstractly; his mind worked either emotionally or in reaction to individuals whom he could visualize."[12]

Thus, in dealing with the Soviets, Reagan was constantly torn between two opposing images. On the one hand, there was the suffering of people behind the Iron Curtain—as described in an emotional Oval Office meeting on May 28, 1981, with Avital Sharansky, wife of imprisoned Soviet dissident Anatoly Sharansky, and Yosef Mendelevich, a recently released political prisoner. "D——n those inhuman monsters," the president wrote that night in his diary. "[Sharansky] is said to be down to 100 lbs. & very ill. I promised I'd do everything I could to obtain his release & I will."[13]

On the other hand, there was the specter of nuclear destruction—a constant concern throughout the Cold War—if the US–Soviet confrontation ever spun out of control. This danger was brought home to Reagan when he participated in a nuclear war game, code-named Ivy League, on March 1, 1982. While Reagan watched from the White House Situation Room, the entire map of the United States turned red to simulate the impact of Soviet nuclear strikes. "He looked on in stunned disbelief," Tom Reed noted. "In less than an hour President Reagan had seen the United States of America disappear.... It was a sobering experience."[14]

Reagan's meetings with Soviet dissidents pushed him toward confrontation with the USSR. But his knowledge of what a nuclear war would entail pushed him toward cooperation—and toward hopes of creating a defense against ballistic missiles. Ultimately, he wanted to end the Cold War in order to lift the dual threats of totalitarianism and nuclear annihilation, but the specifics always remained to be determined based on circumstances. NSDDs 32 and 75 encapsulated the president's vision early in his first term, but his actual policies would undergo considerable modifications in the years ahead. He was too pragmatic, and too easily influenced by a changing cast of advisers, to consistently pursue any strategy laid out in any document.

The primary significance of these NSC directives—one just issued, the other already in preparation—may have been their influence on one of the most important speeches of Reagan's presidency: the one delivered at the Palace of Westminster on June 8, 1982.

During his first year and a half in office, with his team determined to keep the focus on the economy, Ronald Reagan never left the Western Hemisphere; he only traveled to Canada, Mexico, Barbados, and Jamaica. But on June 2, 1982, he arrived in Paris for a meeting with French president François Mitterrand followed by a Group of Seven summit at Versailles with the leaders of West Germany, Italy, France, Britain, Canada, and Japan. This was actually his second G-7 summit—the first had been in Canada in July 1981—and by now his fellow world leaders were becoming accustomed to a president like no other.

At first, other heads of state were puzzled by the former actor with a fondness for long digressions about his movie career and little grasp of the nuances of policy. Canada's liberal prime minister, Pierre Trudeau, was dismayed by Reagan's conduct at the 1981 G-7 summit, which he hosted at Quebec's rustic Montebello hotel, billed as the world's largest log cabin. Trudeau's biographer John English recounted,

> Things started off badly when Reagan expressed shock on his arrival that most of the staff spoke a foreign language to each other. Then, at the first meeting, he stunned the others when he pulled out note cards for the discussion and read from them. Frustrated, Trudeau insisted on informality, and Reagan switched to telling his favorite stories— during which the Japanese prime minister Zenko Suzuki dozed off and Trudeau played studiously with his rose. When East-West issues came up, for instance, Reagan, in Trudeau's recollection, "launched into one of his anecdotes about his time as president of Actors Equity in Hollywood in the 1940s." He claimed that the KGB sent a priest to

"spread discord among the actors in the union." In a private conversation about the Middle East that had occurred when Reagan visited Ottawa in March, Reagan had mused that religion was the answer. Puzzled, Trudeau tried to draw him out. Reagan explained that religion was the key to driving out communist influence from the Middle East because everyone there was religious—Muslims, Christians, and Jews—but the communists were atheists. Everyone else therefore had a common interest in fighting the communists. As Reagan spun out his tale, Trudeau humored him, slyly eyeing Reagan's embarrassed assistants as he focused his full attention on the president. Reagan's anecdotes amused and troubled Trudeau simultaneously.[15]

Yet, like so many other people, Trudeau was gradually won over by Reagan's disarming charm and good humor. Trudeau was to write in his memoirs, "Later, in my final term, I even got along quite well with Ronald Reagan, even though we were about as far apart in outlook and personality as two people could be."[16]

West Germany's Social Democratic chancellor, Helmut Schmidt, had a similar change of heart about the American president. At first, he dismissed Reagan as a made-for-television populist who trafficked "in the simplest, most vivid, most posterlike formulas." But after his first state visit to the Reagan White House in May 1981, he announced, "I like this man." He told Reagan that "you are not the sort of fellow who is depicted, namely, a cowboy or one who appears only in cowboy films." He even found that he preferred Reagan to Jimmy Carter, who was closer to him ideologically. "I was relieved," Schmidt later wrote, "and believed that after four years of insecurity I was once again dealing with a consistent and therefore reliable American president."[17] Reagan would get along even better with Schmidt's successor, Helmut Kohl, a Christian Democrat who took office in October 1982.

One of Reagan's strengths was that he did not seem to care about—or even notice—the condescension with which he was treated by everyone from his own aides to fellow world leaders. He was armored in obliviousness. This was in many ways a virtue because he utterly lacked the kind of insecurity and resentment that had disfigured the presidencies of Lyndon Johnson and Richard Nixon—and later that of Donald Trump. Reagan was able to get along even with those who subtly—or not so subtly—derided him.

In his diary, for example, he sunnily described the Montebello G-7 meeting as a "successful summit" and had not a disparaging word about anyone.[18]

"What Reagan brought to the presidency was a sense of serenity about himself and a sense of unconcern about what the critics may or may not say," said Brian Mulroney. "That only comes from a tremendous degree of self-assurance that you don't have when you're in your forties. As it turns out, the fact that Reagan was seventy when he was inaugurated was a great advantage to him. He was a fully grown man."[19]

Ed Meese said he could not think of any foreign leaders Reagan *didn't* like, but there were some he liked more than others.[20] After taking office in 1984, Mulroney, another genial conservative of Irish descent and small-town, working-class origins, would become one of Reagan's closest friends in the elite club of world leaders. During a 1985 meeting in Quebec City known as the Shamrock Summit, the two men even joined in a rendition of "When Irish Eyes Are Smiling" that brought down the house. Reagan felt free to let loose with mild expletives around Mulroney that he would never utter in public—or if a woman were present. For example, when the two leaders were waiting for both of their delegations to enter a meeting room before they could go in, Reagan told Mulroney with a grin, "Brian, it's protocol—spelled bullshit."[21]

The other world leader that Reagan was closest to was Margaret Thatcher, whom he had first met in 1975 during a trip to London. They were very different people: Thatcher was difficult and demanding, Reagan genial and easygoing. She was immersed in policy details; he was oblivious to them. But they shared a similar laissez-faire ideology. Her adviser Charles Powell said that "she adored him, and he certainly liked her. It was far beyond the level of intimacy that you would normally find in the relationship between heads of government. . . . On almost everything they saw eye to eye." Reagan himself wrote in his diary, "I believe a real friendship exists between the P.M. her family & us—certainly we feel that way & I'm sure they do." He also wrote that "Margaret Thatcher is a tower of strength and a solid friend of the U.S." She, in turn, was "struck by his warmth, charm and complete lack of affection."[22]

At international gatherings such as the G-7 summits, Thatcher, a chemist and barrister who had graduated from Oxford University, often defended the US position far more forcefully and cogently than the Eureka College graduate could do himself. Having been schooled in the cut and thrust of parliamentary debate, she had no need of note cards to make her case. As Charles Powell recalled, "He was a brilliant communicator in a way that she was not, and she was a great debater, which he certainly wasn't." Historian Richard Aldous, in his astute study of their relationship, noted that "Reagan was anecdotal, Thatcher policy-driven and analytical."[23]

Despite her admiration for Reagan, Thatcher was hardly blind to his limitations. Recalling Thatcher's first visit to the Reagan White House in February 1981, British Foreign Secretary Peter Carrington (Lord Carrington) told Thatcher's official biographer Charles Moore, "After the arrival ceremony we went into the Oval Office and I remember Reagan saying: 'Well of course, the South Africans are whites and they fought for us during the war. The blacks are black and are Communists.' I think even Margaret thought this was rather a simplification. . . . She came out and she turned to me, and pointing at her head, she said, 'Peter, there's nothing there.'" Another Thatcher aide, Robin Butler, remembered that after international gatherings she often lamented that Reagan "didn't know anything" about the subject under discussion.[24]

Yet even though Thatcher remained doubtful about Reagan's intellect, she always appreciated his political instincts because they tallied so closely with her own on most issues. Even when they disagreed on policy, as they regularly did, they maintained a fast political friendship with an undertone of chaste flirtation. Like most postwar prime ministers, Thatcher was convinced that Britain had to maintain its "special relationship" with the United States to maximize its influence after the dissolution of the British empire.

By the time of the 1982 Versailles summit, other Western leaders had become used to Reagan, but that did not mean they were always willing to go along with him. The Europeans were united in their desire to see the United States deploy Pershing II and cruise missiles to the continent despite massive protests, but they refused to support US sanctions on the Soviets' Siberian gas pipeline, and they complained about the Fed's high interest rates, which were hurting their own economies. Thatcher, the most pro-American of Europeans, joined with the others to oppose the administration position on the pipeline. The Europeans were particularly incensed by proposals to block European subsidiaries of US companies from selling oil and gas equipment to the USSR.

Even Reagan, who had always walked on the "sunny side of the street" since his troubled childhood, conceded in his diary, "There were differences over East-West trade, Global negotiations and credits to Soviet U. plus how to stabilize currency exchange rates." Yet, true to character, he felt compelled to add an optimistic spin—"We more than held our own and believe came out on top"—which belied the reality that he had not won over the Europeans on the pipeline sanctions.[25]

From Versailles, Reagan traveled on June 7, 1982, to Vatican City for an audience with Pope John Paul II in the gilded papal library. The two men had much in common: Both were visceral anti-Communists who had survived assassination attempts in 1981. (The pope had been shot less than two months after the president.) In a private meeting lasting nearly an hour, Reagan reportedly told John Paul, "Look how the evil forces were put in our way and how Providence intervened." The two men agreed they had been spared by God for a purpose and that "atheistic communism lived a lie that, when fully understood, must ultimately fail."[26] But the most widely reported news from their meeting was that the jet-lagged, seventy-one-year-old president fell asleep in full view of television cameras while the pope was delivering public remarks. Nancy Reagan would insist on future trips that aides schedule more downtime to make sure her aging husband could stay awake.

A myth has developed that the American president and the Polish pope cooperated to support Solidarity and bring down the Soviet empire. In their biography of John Paul II, journalists Carl Bernstein and Marco Politi claimed that the two men formed a "holy alliance," with the church working closely with devout Catholics such as Bill Clark and Bill Casey to free Poland. But national security scholar Seth Jones, who has written the definitive account of the Reagan administration's policy toward Poland, concluded that "U.S. and Vatican officials did not develop a joint strategy or conduct mutual planning to undermine Communism in countries like Poland, nor did the CIA significantly utilize Catholic officials in QRHELPFUL [the CIA program to aid Solidarity]."[27] The Catholic Church and the Reagan administration worked along parallel lines to aid Solidarity, but there were also significant differences, with some church officials opposing any sanctions on Poland and trying to cooperate with the Communist regime to lessen the suffering of the Polish people. John Paul's biographer, George Weigel, agreed that "the claim that the two men entered into a conspiracy to affect the downfall of European communism is journalistic fantasy."[28]

<hr />

From Reagan's perspective, the highlight of his European tour was his next stop: Windsor Castle. On the evening of June 7, 1982, Queen Elizabeth II and Prince Philip hosted a black-tie dinner for the president and first lady. The next morning, June 8, in a carefully choreographed photo op, the president and the queen rode horses together while Nancy Reagan and Prince Philip trailed behind in a carriage drawn by four horses. (There had been weeks of haggling between the White House and Buckingham Palace over such details as what horse the president would ride and what saddle he would use.) "This was a fairy tale experience," wrote the boy from Dixon who had never exhibited any of the anti-English animus common in Irish American families.[29]

Reagan then helicoptered to London to address Parliament. In his diary, he recorded, "I addressed Joint session of Parliament. First Pres. ever to do so."[30] That was an exaggeration. He had initially been scheduled to address a joint session of Parliament in Westminster Hall, which would have made him only the second foreign leader after Charles de Gaulle to do so. But opposition from the Labour Party and even from some Conservative members of Parliament who considered him a "cowboy" and a "warmonger" led to the speech being moved to the Royal Gallery of Westminster Palace, where a number of foreign leaders had spoken before. Most Labour MPs, no fans of the right-wing American president, boycotted his speech, so the audience was composed mainly of Tories. It was nevertheless a dramatic setting, with Beefeaters in scarlet flanking the president, portraits of British monarchs on the walls, and stained-glass windows and murals depicting the battles of Trafalgar and Waterloo. The three US television networks broadcast his remarks live.

While the speech was later seen as one of Reagan's most important because it prophesied the end of the Cold War, its significance was not widely recognized at the time. The audience reaction was tepid. The MPs were most impressed not by *what* the president said but by how smoothly he said it. They were amazed to discover he was reading his speech from a teleprompter—an American invention many had never seen before, even though it had been in use since the 1950s.[31]

Much of the impetus for Reagan's speech was a desire to allay concerns that his policies were dragging the world to war. Vast numbers of protesters were mobilizing across Europe and the United States to demand a "nuclear freeze" and the cancellation of US missile deployments to Europe. On June 12, 1982, just four days after Reagan's Westminster speech, nearly a million people descended on New York's Central Park to support a nuclear freeze in the largest peace rally in US history.

Even the president's own daughter Patti Davis had become an antinuclear activist; her Toyota sported a bumper sticker warning "One Nuclear Bomb Can Ruin Your Whole Day." Later that year, she brought the well-known Australian antinuclear campaigner Helen Caldicott to the White House for a contentious meeting with her father. Reagan was convinced, based on what he read in *Reader's Digest* and *National Review* rather than in his intelligence reports, that the whole nuclear freeze movement was a tool of the KGB. Caldicott was incredulous. He also told Caldicott that the Soviets were "godless monsters" and that "treaties mean nothing to them." The physician and peace activist walked out of the White House more frightened than when she had entered. But her concerns may have reinforced his own growing fears of nuclear war.[32]

Indeed, to a far greater degree than almost anyone appreciated at the time, Reagan shared the freeze movement's "horror of nuclear weapons." With hopes of "eliminating all such weapons" rather than simply freezing them at current levels, he actually went further than most peace campaigners.[33] He simply favored mutual rather than unilateral disarmament.

Reagan realized that, if he were going to defeat the freeze movement, he had "to demonstrate that [he] wasn't flirting with doomsday." The nuclear freeze, warned a White House aide, was "rapidly gaining a momentum . . . more than almost any issue in recent times."[34] The Westminster speech was designed to arrest that momentum before it became irreversible.

In his Westminster address, Reagan assured the world that it was possible "to preserve freedom as well as peace." Adopting a suggestion from Dick Pipes, he turned the Marxist dialectic on its head: "In an ironic sense," he said, "Karl Marx was right. We are witnessing today a great revolutionary crisis, a crisis where the demands of the economic order are conflicting directly with those of the political order. But the crisis is happening not in the free, non-Marxist West, but in the home of Marxist-Leninism, the Soviet Union." He then went on to detail the economic difficulties of the Soviet system before predicting that "the march of freedom and democracy...will leave Marxism-Leninism on the ash-heap of history." Given that the Soviet Union collapsed less than a decade later, this would be seen in hindsight as astonishingly prescient.

Beyond prophesying the Soviet system's ultimate collapse, the speech also outlined a plan of action for the United States that extended beyond a military buildup. Citing democratic transitions around the world, Reagan said, "We must be staunch in our conviction that freedom is not the sole prerogative of a lucky few, but the inalienable and universal right of all human beings." He proposed "to foster the infrastructure of democracy" and mentioned that Democratic and Republican leaders were studying "how the United States can best contribute as a nation to the global campaign for democracy."

The president was referring to a proposal from Al Haig, which was viewed skeptically by Bill Clark and hard-line NSC staffers, to create an Institute for Democracy to "support democratic change." The following year, Congress would create the National Endowment for Democracy to promote freedom around the world, working with organizations affiliated with the Democratic and Republican parties, labor unions, and the Chamber of Commerce.

But while the Reagan administration would eventually become a champion of democratic reform in both Communist and non-Communist dictatorships, in his Westminster speech Reagan was only focused on the threat to freedom posed by Soviet-supported movements. He did not criticize a single right-wing dictatorship. The administration would only grow concerned about holding right-wing regimes to a higher standard after a change of secretaries of state—a transition that was almost at hand as Reagan spoke.

The Westminster speech had many authors, primarily speechwriters Aram Bakshian and Anthony Dolan, with contributions and edits from Dick Darman, David Gergen, Bill Clark, and even columnist George Will. According to two scholars who have studied the drafting of the address, Reagan himself wrote about 14 percent of the paragraphs and made changes on another 45 percent. Not surprisingly, given Reagan's skill as a communicator, the most memorable line—the "ash heap of history"—was of his own devising.[35]

While Reagan invariably displayed pellucid moral clarity about Communism—an issue that had obsessed him for decades—he struggled to figure out how to respond to conflicts that did not fit neatly into the familiar template of the Cold War. Yet he had to deal with two such conflicts that very year.

42

Allies—and Aides—at War

Here on our television, night after night, our people are being
shown the symbols of this war and it is a holocaust.

—RONALD REAGAN

A s a superpower, the United States had allies all over the world. Ordinarily this was a source of strength in the Cold War struggle with the Soviet Union, which had many satrapies but few true friends. But there was also a considerable downside to this web of relationships: Allies had a tendency to draw the United States into their quarrels and conflicts, sometimes imposing heavy costs on the distant superpower. In 1982, two prominent US allies—Britain and Israel—separately went to war, and the Reagan administration was forced to play a significant role in both conflicts much against its will. The British war started first, but the Israeli one would last far longer. The US intervention in Britain's conflict would pay unexpected dividends, while its intervention in Israel's conflict would lead to unexpected tragedies. These conflicts only intensified the growing turmoil on the president's foreign policy team as his senior advisers found themselves at odds over how to respond—leading to a critical change at the top of the State Department.

One of Ronald Reagan's few applause lines in the Westminster speech was his tribute to British troops fighting to evict Argentinean invaders from the Falkland Islands in the South Atlantic. Although located only three hundred miles off the Argentine coast, the Falklands had been settled by Britons as early as 1765 and ruled by Great Britain since 1833—and Margaret Thatcher's government was determined to keep it that way. "Those young men aren't fighting for mere real estate," Reagan said in endorsing the British position. "They fight for a cause—for the belief that armed aggression must not be allowed to succeed, and the people must participate in the decisions of government—the decisions of government under the rule of law."

Many of the MPs who applauded his remarks probably had no idea how much acrimony the Falklands War had engendered within the Reagan administration. The invasion of the Falkland Islands began on April 2, 1982. Argentinean troops quickly overpowered the small British garrison and took control of the islands, which they called the Malvinas, with their 1,800 inhabitants and 400,000 sheep. Thatcher immediately assembled a formidable naval armada and sent it steaming to the South Atlantic. The conflict started, an American diplomat wrote in his diary, as a "comic opera" war like something out of "Gilbert and Sullivan as told to Anthony Trollope by Alistair Cooke." But it soon turned "not only quite serious, but exceptionally nasty."[1]

Reagan had phoned the president of Argentina, General Leopoldo Galtieri, to dissuade him from launching the invasion, but his arguments failed to move the macho military dictator, who, in the view of US officials, sounded inebriated and spoke "in broken mafioso-type English."[2] The question now was whether the United States would observe a strict neutrality or favor one of the combatants. UN Ambassador Jeane Kirkpatrick, whose doctoral thesis had been a sympathetic portrayal of Juan Perón's rule of Argentina in the 1950s, was the most pro-Argentinian voice in the administration's senior circles. In an NSC meeting, she argued the importance of preserving the "Inner American System," which drew a sharp rebuke from Admiral Bobby Ray Inman, the deputy CIA director who was sitting in for an absent Bill Casey. "I couldn't disagree more with Jeane's statement," he interjected. "It's the most wrongheaded thing I've heard!"[3]

Reagan at first leaned toward Kirkpatrick's position, dispatching Al Haig for a fruitless round of shuttle diplomacy between London and Buenos Aires. But Inman, who worked closely with his British counterparts, and Secretary of Defense Caspar Weinberger, a staunch Anglophile, mobilized the vast resources of the intelligence community and the Defense Department, respectively, to aid the British with weapons deliveries, intelligence sharing, and the use of an American military base on Ascension Island midway between Britain and the Falklands. The president, the ultimate hands-off manager, did not seem to have any idea of what Weinberger and Inman were doing; in his diary, he claimed that an accurate *Washington Post* article about US aid to the British war effort was "false."[4]

Driven by Churchill-like determination to secure a resounding military victory, Thatcher had no patience with US efforts to end the fighting with a negotiated compromise. During a phone call on May 13, the British prime minister bulldozed the American president. "The negotiations have not stopped military action nor can they, because the fact is, Ron, we're only getting somewhere as the military pressure builds up," she lectured him. She then repeated her arguments that British settlers had been in the islands for generations and that one day the Argentinean junta would fall and be replaced by leftist Peronistas. "I thought the last thing anyone wanted was the Russians in Cuba and Russians controlling the Falklands . . . a tremendous strategic point," she told him, appealing to his reflexive anti-Communism. The only thing missing was her regular suggestions that any compromise with Buenos Aires would be appeasement akin to Munich 1938. Reagan could hardly get in a word edgewise as the willful prime minister was in full oratorical flight. The transcript shows him saying little more than "Yes, yes," "yep," "I, I—," and "No, no, I can't quarrel with that."[5]

This was a microcosm of the Thatcher-Reagan relationship in which the strong-minded Iron Lady often tried to impose her will on the amiable leader of the much larger country who was much more concerned than she was with being liked. "I believe Maggie Thatcher was the only person who could intimidate Ronald Reagan," Senator Howard Baker said. An NSC staffer who listened to one of the Reagan-Thatcher calls thought "the President came off sounding like even more of a wimp than Jimmy Carter." His hesitancy to back Britain in the Falkland Islands dispute infuriated Thatcher, and she let him know it.[6]

Once negotiations failed, Reagan shifted to a more pro-British posture—hence his comments in Westminster on June 8, 1982. British troops, acting as if this were a Victorian colonial skirmish, landed in the Falklands on May 21, and the Argentinean defenders surrendered on June 14. Galtieri resigned three days later, and the next year Argentina transitioned to democracy. The new president was not a Peronist radical in league with the Soviet Union, as Thatcher had feared, but a centrist lawyer. The British prime minister reaped a political windfall for briefly reviving her country's martial glory on these remote South Atlantic islands at a time when the British economy was in bad shape. Headline writers hailed Britain's victory by invoking the title of a popular 1980 movie: "The Empire Strikes Back."

Even as the Falklands War was ending, another US ally was launching a far more brutal conflict that would draw the United States into a tragic quagmire. This war had its genesis in the expulsion of the Palestinian Liberation Organization (PLO) from Jordan following an attempted coup in 1970. The PLO set up camp in Lebanon, upsetting that country's delicate sectarian balance and triggering a civil war in 1975 that drew in both Israel and Syria. The PLO used southern Lebanon as a base from which to attack Israel. In 1982, Prime Minister Menachem Begin and his defense minister, General Ariel Sharon, decided on a daring gambit: They would send the Israeli Defense Forces (IDF) to destroy the PLO and place into power the Christian Phalange militia leader Bashir Gemayel. He would then sign a peace treaty with Israel, transforming Lebanon from foe to friend.

Begin had floated the plan for an Israeli incursion into Lebanon in October 1981 to Al Haig while both men were attending the funeral of Egyptian President Anwar Sadat. Haig told Begin, "Unless there is a major, internationally recognized provocation, the United States will not support such an action." Sharon, separately, warned Haig of Israeli plans to "rewrite the political map of Beirut" after the next Palestinian provocation.[7] Yet neither Haig nor his boss made much effort to head off the looming war. "Reagan's benign neglect was catastrophic," wrote Patrick Tyler in a history of US dealings with the Middle East.[8]

The provocation that Begin and Sharon were waiting for occurred on June 3, 1982, when the Israeli ambassador to London was shot and wounded by terrorists. The attackers were not from the PLO—they were part of the renegade Abu Nidal Organization supported by Iraq and opposed to Yasser Arafat—but Begin and Sharon were not concerned about such details. On June 6, while Reagan was meeting with G-7 leaders at Versailles, twenty-five thousand Israeli troops crossed the Lebanon border. Begin told Reagan that they were only clearing out a safe zone extending twenty-five miles into Lebanon, but their actual destination was Beirut. On June 12, Israeli forces reached the outskirts of the capital. George H. W. Bush, Bill Clark, and Michael Deaver were all furious at the Israeli assault and recommended cutting off US security aid in protest. But Al Haig, Bill Casey, and Jeane Kirkpatrick argued for backing the Israelis on the grounds that the Syrian regime and the PLO were aligned with the Soviet Union. Haig believed in letting Begin "go into Beirut and finish the job."[9]

This struck a chord with a president who, like many Americans, was instinctively supportive of Israeli and hostile to the PLO, then seen simply as a terrorist organization. Reagan was not overburdened by knowledge of the region and its complexities. He had remarked to Helmut Schmidt that "the notion that a Palestinian state has to be located in Israel is somewhat confusing, especially since when the land of Palestine was divided, 80 percent of it was in Jordan and 20 percent in Israel." On another occasion, Reagan said of Arafat that "someone should tell him to shave" and wondered, "Is it conceivable that he would be chosen by [the Palestinians] to lead them if they were given some place to live?" Dick Allen jumped in to explain that "Arafat had a bad skin condition and avoided shaving."[10]

But Reagan was always strongly affected by images of suffering, and he was repulsed by what he saw on television while Israeli troops encircled and assaulted West Beirut, the Shiite Muslim neighborhood where Arafat and many of his PLO fighters were located. Normally the most placid of men, Reagan was angry when he talked on the telephone from the Oval Office with Begin on August 12, 1982. "Here on our television, night after night, our people are being shown the symbols of this war and it is a holocaust. A little seven-month-old baby with its arms blown off, two five-year-old twins dead—and this goes on night after night," Reagan complained to Begin. "Mr. President, I know all about a Holocaust," snapped Begin, who had lost both parents and a brother to the Nazis. But he listened as Reagan argued that "the massive shelling and bombing has been so out of proportion . . . that it has been a simple blanket barrage against an area that is populated by civilians." Reagan warned that the US-Israeli relationship was at stake and demanded an immediate cease-fire.[11]

To end the siege, the administration endorsed a proposal for both the PLO and the Israelis to leave Beirut. The plan called for evacuating six thousand PLO fighters from Beirut to other Arab countries in return for a promise that Palestinian refugee camps, which had been protected by PLO gunmen, would be safe from attack. The whole process would be overseen by an international peacekeeping force that included US troops. Under American pressure, Begin on August 19 ended a ten-week siege of Beirut. On August 23, Israel's ally, Bashir Gemayel, who was also covertly supported by the CIA, was elected president by Lebanon's national assembly. On August

25, eight hundred US Marines began landing in Beirut as part of a Multi-national Force, also composed of eight hundred Italian and four hundred French troops, to oversee the evacuation of PLO fighters.

On September 10, 1982, with the PLO evacuation complete, Cap Weinberger ordered the Marines to leave without checking with the White House, even though the US envoy Philip Habib had promised the Marines would stay for up to thirty days to oversee the transition. Bud McFarlane called Weinberger's move "criminally irresponsible."[12]

Within days, everything went catastrophically wrong. On September 14, a massive bomb demolished the Phalange headquarters in Christian East Beirut, instantly killing President-elect Gemayel. The bomb was planted by Syrian operatives, but Gemayel's followers blamed the Palestinians. Phalange gunmen took a grisly revenge by murdering hundreds of innocent Palestinian civilians in the Sabra and Shatila refugee camps; survivors reported children with slit throats, fetuses torn out of pregnant women, decapitations, and other horrors. Israeli troops surrounded the camps but did nothing to stop the slaughter. An Israeli commission of inquiry later found that Ariel Sharon bore indirect responsibility for the massacre, and he was forced to resign as defense minister in 1983. Reagan was "deeply shaken" by the indiscriminate killing, which he knew might have been prevented if the Multinational Force had remained in Beirut. "What could move people to do something like this?" he wondered in horror.[13]

Wanting to bolster the weak Lebanese government—now led by Bashir's playboy brother Amin Gemayel—and prevent further atrocities, Reagan ordered the Marines to return to Beirut. In his diary, he wrote with typical wishful thinking that "apparently there was no disagreement" about this decision.[14] In fact, the Marine redeployment was supported by the National Security Council and the State Department but opposed by the Defense Department. Weinberger called the mission too risky and insisted, "We shouldn't be the Beirut police department."[15] He was right, but Reagan went ahead anyway. On September 29, 1982, the Marines established a base at the Beirut airport as part of an amorphous and dangerous peacekeeping mission in a country where there was no peace to keep. Opposed to the deployment in the first place, Weinberger kept it as limited as possible, hampering the Marines' ability to accomplish their mission or even to defend themselves.

When the Israeli invasion had begun, Iran's Islamic Revolutionary Guard Corps had dispatched its fighters to Lebanon's Bekaa Valley to begin training and organizing Lebanese Shiites to carry out terrorist attacks against the "Zionist imperialists" and their supporters from the "Great Satan," that is, the United States.[16] This was the origin of what became known as Hezbollah (Party of God), the militant Shiite organization whose signature tactics would be suicide bombing and hostage-taking. Reagan's ill-advised decisions had put all Americans in Lebanon—military and civilians alike—in the crosshairs of one of the world's most ruthless terrorist organizations.

One of the foremost champions of the Marine deployment was the new secretary of state, George Shultz, a Marine veteran of World War II. He had taken over in July 1982 after Al Haig had completed his spectacular self-immolation.

From the start of the administration, Haig had grated on the easygoing president. At NSC meetings, Richard Pipes noted, Haig "flatters the president but RR feels very uncomfortable with him, especially when caught in a crossfire between Haig (on his right) and Weinberger (on his left)." Haig's behavior at NSC meetings, Pipes observed, "alternates between impassioned and often accusatory outbursts and sneering silence." Less than two months into the administration, Reagan noted that Haig was complaining about "being undercut by other agencies" and worried "that he has something of a complex about this." On June 14, 1982, following the president's return from his European trip, he wrote, "The Al H. situation is coming to a head. I have to put an end to the turf battles we're having & his almost paranoid attitude."[17]

By now the power-hungry secretary of state had no defenders left in the White House—and no understanding of how it operated. "To me," he admitted in his memoirs, "the White House was as mysterious as a ghost ship; you heard the creak of the rigging and the groan of the timbers and sometimes even glimpsed the crew on deck. But which of the crew had the helm? Was it Meese, was it Baker, was it someone else? It was impossible to know for sure."[18]

Whoever it was, they were annoyed by Haig's high-handed ways. Mike Deaver took a sneaky revenge—for example, consigning Haig to an inferior seat on the Air Force One flight to Europe for the economic summit and to a separate helicopter from the president's on a subsequent flight from London to Windsor Castle. "Haig felt a lack of respect," said the deputy national security adviser, Bud McFarlane. In his memoir, he noted that "the White House staff, notably Jim Baker and Mike Deaver, returned from Europe with a white-knuckled animus toward Al Haig." Fatally for his chances of survival, the secretary of state had even alienated the powerful first lady, who was to write in her own memoir, "Haig represented Ronnie's biggest mistake in the first term."[19]

During the administration's first year, the deputy secretary of state, Bill Clark, had partially shielded Haig from the wrath of the White House, but when Clark became national security adviser, he joined Haig's legions of critics. During the June 1982 trip to Europe, the two men clashed over the Siberian pipeline, with Clark demanding tougher sanctions than Haig thought prudent. The *New York Times* reported that they engaged in shouting matches—and while this was typical behavior for the high-strung general, it was out of character for the mellow national security adviser.[20]

After initially siding with Haig, Reagan now came down on Clark's side of this dispute. He abruptly decided to apply sanctions on the European subsidiaries of US companies selling oil and gas equipment to Moscow, and he did so, McFarlane concluded, "chiefly" to put the imperious secretary of state "in his place" even at the cost of alienating US allies. "I was appalled when I learned of the decision," Margaret Thatcher wrote. "I condemned it in public. The reaction of the Europeans generally was still more hostile."[21]

Haig offended Clark one time too many when on June 12, 1982, he insisted on sending instructions to US envoy Philip Habib, who was trying to negotiate a cease-fire in Lebanon, without clearing them first with the White House. This was a red line. Haig had just arrogated to himself the powers of the presidency. Only the senior White House staff was supposed to have that privilege![22]

On June 24, 1982, Reagan met in the Oval Office with Haig, who presented a long list of grievances enumerating all the ways he had been prevented from playing his self-appointed role as the "vicar" of foreign policy. "If it can't be straightened out, then surely you would be better served by another secretary of state," he said, hinting that he might resign but hoping that Reagan would not take him up on his offer. The next day, when they met again, Reagan surprised Haig by handing him a sealed envelope with a single typed page: "Dear Al, It is with the most profound regret that I accept your letter of resignation." This was the first time since the downfall

of John Sears in 1980 that Reagan had fired anyone in person; Haig, like
Sears, had gotten under his skin.

Haig was dumbfounded: "The President was accepting a letter of resignation that I had not submitted." He returned to the State Department and
hastily drafted a letter complaining that the administration's foreign policy
had gotten off track. In his diary, Reagan scoffed at the notion that they had
had "a disagreement on foreign policy." "Actually," he wrote, "the only disagreement was over whether I made policy or the Sec. of State did."[23]

Even before Haig "resigned," Reagan had telephoned George Shultz, who
was traveling in London, to ask whether he would be willing to become secretary of state. Shultz, president of the engineering giant Bechtel and an
outside economics adviser to the president, said yes. Thus, at the very same
afternoon press conference where Reagan announced Haig's departure,
he also announced Shultz's nomination to replace him. The response was
"excellent," Dick Darman noted, because of "Shultz's outstanding intellectual quality, character, balance, reassuring poise and record of team play."[24]

The phlegmatic Shultz did not have as much foreign policy experience as
his mercurial predecessor. He was an economist by training and a former
dean of the University of Chicago Business School who had served President Nixon as labor secretary, budget director, and Treasury secretary.
But he was calmer than Haig, more thoughtful, and less egotistical. Shultz,
too, clashed with other cabinet members, in particular his former subordinate Cap Weinberger (former general counsel of Bechtel and deputy OMB
director), but, unlike Haig, he understood the need to cultivate the president
and senior White House staff. He was even shrewd enough to develop ties
with Nancy Reagan to influence her husband. "Nancy and I were friends,"
Shultz recalled.[25]

While Shultz was not as ardently pro-Israel as Haig or as obsessed with
the threat from Cuba, on issues such as dealing with the Soviet Union the
two men were actually in substantial agreement. Working with Jim Baker,
Mike Deaver, George H. W. Bush, and even Nancy Reagan, Shultz would
be in a much stronger position than his prickly predecessor to advocate a
less confrontational approach with the Soviets. An early sign of his growing
clout was his success in November 1982 in convincing the president to lift the
Siberian pipeline sanctions that had been enacted over Haig's protests—and

those of the European allies—even though martial law remained in effect in Poland. The Soviet gas pipeline was completed two years later, making Western Europe dangerously dependent on Russian-supplied energy.[26]

Yet, while the "pragmatists" had a powerful new player on their team, the conservative purists—Clark, Casey, Kirkpatrick, Meese, and Weinberger—retained considerable influence. Each side would win on some issues and lose on others; Reagan, who was always loath to pick among competing aides, tried to placate both camps. This jockeying for power would play out for the highest stakes in 1983 when superpower relations would enter what may have been their most dangerous phase since the 1962 Cuban Missile Crisis.

43

The Year of Living Dangerously

Damn those Russians. Damn them.

—RONALD REAGAN

eonid Brezhnev, the supreme leader of the Soviet Union since 1964, had long been sickly and senescent. He had suffered minor strokes and a heart attack in the 1970s but continued to drink and smoke prodigiously. A doctor at George Washington University Medical Center judged that the Soviet leader would never have survived if he had been shot like his American counterpart. By the early 1980s, Brezhnev was slurring his words and falling asleep at Politburo meetings or avoiding them altogether.[1] He finally died at age seventy-five on November 10, 1982. His replacement was KGB chief Yuri Andropov, who was a few years younger but no healthier; he would spend much of his fifteen-month tenure in and out of hospitals seeking treatment for diabetes and kidney failure. The old KGB man had been fearful since early 1981 that Ronald Reagan was preparing for nuclear war with the Soviet Union. "Reagan is unpredictable," Andropov told Anatoly Dobrynin, the Soviet ambassador in Washington. "You should expect anything from him."[2]

The new secretary of state, George Shultz, realized that US-Soviet relations had gone into a "deep freeze" since the invasion of Afghanistan in 1979, and he thought that was a dangerous place to be. Like Ronald Reagan, Shultz was confident that the inefficiencies of the Communist system would eventually bring it down—"the Soviet system is incompetent and cannot survive," he had said in 1979—but he was more cognizant than Reagan of the risks of conflict "through fear or missed opportunities to resolve outstanding problems."[3]

On January 19, 1983, at the beginning of a year that would bring a series of crises with the Kremlin, Shultz sent the president a proposal for "an intensified dialogue with Moscow to test whether an improvement in the US-Soviet relationship is possible"—culminating, "if relations warrant," in a presidential summit. National Security Adviser Bill Clark accused the State Department of "wishful thinking . . . about the nature of the Soviet system and its willingness to compromise" and warned that "if we follow its recommendation for intensified dialogue . . . we will be sending all the wrong signals to the Soviets." But Reagan gave Shultz permission to engage with the tough but charming Dobrynin, a fixture in Washington since 1962.[4]

A blizzard that hit Washington, DC, on Friday, February 11, 1983, just as Shultz was returning from a trip to China, provided a serendipitous opportunity to go further. Because of all the snow, which had Washingtonians skiing through the streets, the Reagans could not make it to Camp David for the weekend. So, on Saturday morning, February 12, Nancy Reagan called the secretary of state and invited him and his wife, Helena "O'Bie" Shultz, to the White House for dinner with just her and Ronnie. This wasn't a purely social call: Nancy liked Shultz ("George reminded me of a big teddy bear," she wrote, "but underneath that soft exterior was a tough negotiator with enormous energy"), and she was eager to bolster his influence at the expense of the hard-liners whom, she feared, would draw her husband into a war.

During a free-wheeling conversation in the family quarters, Shultz discovered that the president "had never had a lengthy session with an important leader of a Communist country, and I could sense that he would relish such an opportunity." Reagan took pride in his negotiating skills from his years leading the Screen Actors Guild and was confident he could be as successful dealing with Communist bosses as he had been with studio bosses. Shultz mentioned that he would be meeting Dobrynin again on Tuesday and asked, "What would you think about my bringing Dobrynin over to the White House for a private chat?" "Great," Reagan responded.

When he found out about the planned meeting, Bill Clark objected ("Clark's nose is out of joint," noted a Shultz aide), but he did not succeed in stopping it. This was Shultz's first intimation, he told his biographer Philip Taubman, that the NSC's hard-line views did "not reflect Reagan's true feelings." Indeed, Reagan wrote in his diary a few months later, "Some of the N.S.C. staff are too hard line & don't think any approach should be made to the Soviets."

Mike Deaver, who was all in favor of dispelling the popular caricature of Reagan as a warmonger, arranged to smuggle Dobrynin into the White House family quarters on the afternoon of February 15, 1983. Dobrynin and Reagan spoke for nearly two hours over coffee, with Shultz mostly listening. No interpreter was needed; Dobrynin spoke English fluently.

The president began by telling the ambassador, "Probably people in the Soviet Union regard me as a crazy warmonger. But I don't want a war between us.... We should make a fresh start." He then asked in all innocence whether "the Soviet Union indeed believed the United States posed a threat to the Soviet Union." Reagan was so convinced of America's good intentions—and was so ignorant of the paranoia among Soviet leaders who had lived through a Nazi invasion—that he could not conceive that they might genuinely perceive his country as a threat. Then the two men engaged in a wide-ranging discussion on issues from arms-control talks to human rights. "Sometimes," Reagan noted, "we got pretty nose to nose."

As a test of goodwill, Reagan proposed that the Kremlin allow the emigration of seven Pentecostals who had taken refuge in the US Embassy in Moscow in 1978, promising that if they were allowed to leave the country, the Kremlin would not be embarrassed by "undue publicity." Dobrynin duly relayed the message to his masters in Moscow. The Soviet leadership was puzzled by the importance Reagan attached to these seven individuals but decided to humor him. By July 18, 1983, all the Pentecostals had left the country. True to his promise, Reagan did not claim credit for this Kremlin concession.[5]

The release of the Pentecostals might have provided an opening to improve relations, but by then Ronald Reagan was again ratcheting up his anti-Soviet rhetoric. On March 8, 1983, speaking to the National Association of Evangelicals in Orlando, Florida, he referred to the Soviet Union as the "evil empire" and "the focus of evil in the modern world."

The speech was regarded as a minor one, and it was primarily devoted to domestic issues such as abortion and prayer in school, so it had not been carefully vetted by the national security bureaucracy. The phrase "evil empire" had been inserted by speechwriter Anthony Dolan—a staunch conservative, like most of his fellow White House wordsmiths—to warn white evangelicals, by then an important Republican constituency, not to endorse a nuclear freeze as other religious groups were doing. Another speechwriter, Aram Bakshian, realized that "the State Department would have conniptions," so he "made a point of not flagging it."

White House communications director David Gergen did see the early drafts, and he found them alarming. "Listen," he told Deputy National Security Adviser Bud McFarlane, "we've got this red-hot speech. We can go with this, but it's going to raise holy hell on the international side." McFarlane agreed, and the two men "started pulling it back some." They tamped it down to the point where, Gergen recalled, "Dolan thought it was too weak. But we left in 'the evil empire,' because that was the least provocative of what they had written." The speech was actually more nuanced than it appeared—Reagan also defended talking with the Soviets to reach "an understanding with them"—but it was the incendiary phrase "evil empire" that garnered all the attention.

The official Soviet TASS news agency denounced the address as evidence of Reagan's "bellicose, lunatic, anti-Communism"; *New York Times* columnist Anthony Lewis called it "outrageous" and "primitive"; and historian Henry Steele Commager labeled it "the worst presidential speech in American history." Soviet dissident Anatoly Sharansky, who heard about the speech in the gulag, had a more positive reaction. He called it "the brightest, most glorious day. . . . President Reagan had from that moment made it impossible for anyone in the West to continue closing their eyes to the real nature of the Soviet Union."[6]

What few knew at the time was that, only two days after delivering this belligerent speech, Reagan privately told Shultz to continue meeting with Dobrynin as part of a dual-track campaign of pressure and persuasion. "The contradictions between words and deeds . . . greatly angered Moscow, the more so because Reagan himself never seemed to see it," Dobrynin wrote. "In his mind such incompatibilities could coexist in perfect harmony, but Moscow regarded such behavior at that time as a sign of deliberate duplicity and hostility."[7]

The Politburo was even more alarmed by Reagan's next major speech, just fifteen days later, announcing a new plan to defend against ballistic missiles—and thereby potentially upsetting the delicate balance of deterrence between the two superpowers.

———

Ronald Reagan had been interested in missile defense at least since his 1967 visit to Lawrence Radiation Laboratory, a leading center of missile defense research located in his home state. Even as governor he had told aides that America needed a defense against nuclear attack.[8] His interest in the subject had been reawakened by his 1979 tour of the NORAD headquarters in Colorado. Some journalists attributed his interest to movies, including his own 1940 Brass Bancroft film *Murder in the Air,* featuring directed-energy weapons shooting down aircraft, but this is largely speculative. Of greater importance was Reagan's religious conviction that Armageddon was imminent, and that it was his job to avert it. He saw missile defense as a major step toward the abolition of all nuclear weapons.

Reagan's interest was nurtured by an eccentric group of outside advisers, far outside the scientific or military mainstream, who assured him that a defense against ballistic missiles had become practical. This was similar to the way that he became an enthusiast for supply-side economics, another doctrine disdained by most experts in the field. In both cases, there was a germ of truth to the arguments of the true believers—tax cuts *could* stimulate economic activity, defensive systems *could* eventually shoot down some missiles—but Reagan had a tendency to take each argument to the extreme. Just as he had argued that tax cuts would pay for themselves, which no serious economist believed, so he took to arguing that missile defenses could create an impermeable shield against nuclear attack, which no serious scientist believed.

In *Way Out There in the Blue: Reagan, Star Wars, and the End of the Cold War,* the journalist Frances Fitzgerald traced the lobbying campaign by various conservatives to convince Reagan to embrace missile defense despite a 1981 Defense Science Board study which concluded that "today ballistic missile technology is not at the stage where it could provide an adequate defense against Soviet missiles."[9]

Republican Senator Malcolm Wallop of Wyoming, working with a young Senate staffer named Angelo Codevilla, imagined that a Manhattan Project–type effort could lead to the launch of two dozen orbiting chemical lasers by the end of the 1980s capable of shooting down a thousand missiles simultaneously. (A Defense Department study concluded that it would actually take nearly fifteen hundred orbiting lasers to accomplish this mission.) Retired Army lieutenant general Daniel O. Graham, an adviser to Reagan's campaigns in 1976 and 1980, envisioned unmanned space vehicles firing projectiles that would destroy Soviet missiles. Then there was Edward Teller, the renowned Hungarian American physicist known as the "father of the hydrogen bomb" who had hosted Reagan during the governor's 1967 visit to Lawrence laboratory. Teller imagined a constellation of nuclear-powered X-ray lasers safeguarding America from space, even though the X-ray laser was still in the research phase. He was to missile defense what Robert Mundell was to supply-side economics: a well-respected expert who gave his imprimatur to outlandish ideas.[10]

In 1981, Daniel Graham and Edward Teller were involved in setting up an organization called High Frontier to agitate for greater spending on missile defense. It came to be lodged at the Heritage Foundation and had financial support from members of the Kitchen Cabinet. The Air Force, after studying its plans, concluded "that the High Frontier proposals are unrealistic," had "no technical merit," and "should be rejected." But that did not stop these influential advocates from meeting with senior administration officials to advance their ideas. At a meeting with the president on January 8, 1982, the leaders of High Frontier warned that the Soviets were deploying "powerful directed energy weapons" that would allow them to "militarily dominate both space and the earth" unless the United States acted first. (No such weapons were ever deployed.) Martin Anderson wrote that "as I left the Roosevelt Room, I was personally convinced that President Reagan was going ahead with missile defense." Yet little happened in 1982, in part because of the skepticism of the White House science adviser, George "Jay" Keyworth, a protégé of Teller's who understood how difficult it would be to implement his mentor's dreams.[11]

Missile defense was given fresh life at the beginning of 1983 by Bud McFarlane and Rear Admiral John Poindexter, Bill Clark's military assistant. They were frustrated by a defeat in the House on December 7, 1982, for the administration plan to build a hundred MX missiles. The House refused to authorize the giant ICBMs because the Pentagon could not figure out how to deploy them to survive a Soviet first strike. McFarlane pushed for the appointment of a bipartisan commission led by former national security adviser Brent Scowcroft to come up with an MX deployment plan that could win congressional backing. In the meantime, to undercut support for the nuclear freeze and strengthen the US hand in the strategic arms negotiations with the Soviets in Geneva (known as the Strategic Arms Reduction Talks, or START), McFarlane asked Poindexter to study the feasibility of missile defense. "It was my opinion at the time that we were never going to be able to get a new land-based ballistic missile approved," Poindexter said. "In my opinion, I thought it was time to start thinking about defense."[12]

Poindexter, in turn, went to Admiral James Watkins, the chief of naval operations, a devout Catholic who was uneasy about the morality of mutual assured destruction. Watkins reported that "improvements in computational speed and directed energy systems could give us a foundation for moving gradually away from an offensive to a defensive strategy within our lifetimes." McFarlane noted that "Jim was more motivated by moral considerations than military ones," but the admiral managed to bring along the other chiefs of staff. All the services, after all, stood to benefit from additional missile defense spending.[13]

The chiefs presented missile defense as a possible option in a meeting with the president in the windowless Roosevelt Room, only steps from the Oval Office, on February 11, 1983, another snowy day in Washington. "Wouldn't it be better to protect the American people rather than avenge them?" asked Army General John W. Vessey Jr., the chairman of the Joint Chiefs. The chiefs did not endorse any particular plan for missile defense and warned that it was only a possibility, not a probability.

Reagan, however, seized on their endorsement while ignoring their caveats. In his diary, he wrote that a "super idea" came out of the meeting: "What if we tell the world we want to protect our people not avenge them; that we [a]re going to embark on research to come up with a defensive system that could make nuclear weapons obsolete? I would call upon the scientific community to volunteer in bringing such a thing about." In truth, no one had said anything about making nuclear weapons obsolete. The chiefs had made clear that missile defense would be only a supplement, not a substitute, for nuclear deterrence.[14]

The military brass expected their vague suggestions would be subject to more study, and McFarlane thought it was imperative to work with Congress, the Defense Department, the State Department, and US allies to forge support for this radical idea. Both Cap Weinberger and George Shultz were skeptical of the feasibility of the ambitious and potentially destabilizing project—one of the few times they were in accord. "Shultz and Weinberger went through the roof," Poindexter recalled. But Reagan was so enthusiastic that he would brook no delay. He directed Bill Clark and Bud McFarlane to prepare the missile-defense proposal as an insert in a nationally televised defense budget speech on March 23, 1983, and he directed them to "keep this tightly under wraps" to prevent opposition from mobilizing.[15]

The result of all the secrecy was that it was impossible to subject the plan to scientific scrutiny or to build support in either NATO or Congress. George Shultz only found out about the plan two days before it was to be announced, and he was appalled. From what he knew of missile defense research, "it seemed to present huge, perhaps insuperable problems": It was no simple matter to hit an ICBM traveling up to 15,000 miles per hour. Richard "Rick" Burt, the assistant secretary of state for European and Canadian affairs, called "a nuclear-free world a pipe dream" and warned that "a speech like this by the president will unilaterally destroy the foundation of the Western alliance."[16]

The defense secretary eventually would become a supporter of the missile defense program in no small part because it offered a way to block arms-control agreements with the Soviets. But initially he, too, was skeptical, telling Reagan, "We have not studied this." Even the Joint Chiefs "were stunned by how fast Reagan moved and how he had overstated their ideas," wrote the well-connected *New York Times* correspondent Hedrick Smith. General Vessey and Admiral Watkins recommended that the president not give the speech.[17]

But Reagan, normally deferential to the views of advisers, would not be dissuaded. He felt at least as passionately about missile defense as he did about tax cuts, and he wasn't interested in hearing any dissenting views. "He was terribly excited," McFarlane said, and "he was less worried about the details."[18]

"The pragmatists were basically cut out," David Gergen recalled. "They just sort of popped that out on us the morning of the speech, without anybody knowing what the hell it was. Then it was sort of a mess, but on that one the conservatives prevailed."[19]

On March 23, 1983, near the end of a televised speech from the Oval Office devoted to touting his defense buildup, Reagan made a grandiose announcement: "My fellow Americans, tonight we're launching an effort which holds the promise of changing the course of human history." He spoke of plans to "intercept and destroy strategic ballistic missiles before they reached our own soil or that of our allies." His ultimate goal, he said in a line that he had personally inserted, was "rendering these nuclear weapons impotent and obsolete."[20]

In fact, Reagan's goal—of constructing a reliable defense against a large-scale nuclear missile attack—still has not been achieved more than forty years later despite the expenditure of hundreds of billions of dollars.[21] Efforts to field limited, ground-based missile defenses long predated Reagan's speech—the Patriot air-defense system had been under development since the early 1960s and entered full-scale production in 1980—and they have proven their worth in numerous conflicts beginning with the 1991 Gulf War.[22] But ground-based missile defenses have not come close to rendering ICBMs obsolete or lifting the threat of nuclear annihilation. The idea of a "space shield" shooting down missiles with directed-energy blasts remains confined to the realm of science fiction.

This lack of success in achieving Reagan's lofty objectives was entirely predictable. Hans Bethe, a Nobel laureate in physics who helped design the atomic and hydrogen bombs, spoke for much of the scientific community when he warned the president, "I consider the chances of success of an effective defense to be incredibly small."[23] Almost no government officials believed that Reagan's vision was achievable in any realistic timeframe. Even most of those who backed what became known as the Strategic Defense Initiative (SDI)—a name suggested by Poindexter—viewed it, in Bud McFarlane's words, as merely "a useful negotiating chip in arms control talks."[24]

America's European allies were aghast and against the entire project. Margaret Thatcher feared that missile defense would not work and that, if it did, it would render the British nuclear deterrent obsolete. "She wouldn't let us hear the end of it," McFarlane recalled, although her opposition softened once the Pentagon awarded missile-defense contracts to British firms. Brian Mulroney, who became Canada's prime minister in 1984, also opposed SDI because he "found the thought of the weaponization of space and the creation of another costly arms race extremely disconcerting." Senator Ted Kennedy called the plan "a reckless 'Star Wars' scheme," and the name stuck, much to Reagan's chagrin.[25]

Reagan was unmoved by all the criticism. His devotion to the "space shield" was based on fear (of nuclear war) and faith (in American ingenuity) rather than on facts. He had been worried about the cost of war ever since his boyhood in the aftermath of World War I, and his religious beliefs had convinced him that Armageddon was looming. His diary was peppered with references to the Apocalypse, and he kept bringing up his fears with visitors until Mike Deaver told him to stop because "it scares the hell out of people."[26] The onetime lifeguard imagined he could save the entire world from nuclear destruction.

For the Soviet Union, the Strategic Defense Initiative was a nightmare, not a dream. Yuri Andropov had no illusions about the practicality of a "space shield," but he warned that the United States was embarked on "an extremely dangerous path" that would escalate the arms race.[27] The more ICBMs each side had, after all, the greater the chances that at least some would get through, and it would not take many nuclear missiles to kill millions of people. Reagan tried to assuage such concerns by suggesting that the United States could share defensive technology with the Soviet Union—evidently not realizing that to do so would be to render the system ineffective by allowing the Soviets to exploit its vulnerabilities. In any case, Soviet leaders never believed that the United States would share such sensitive technology.

Reagan aides and supporters, even those who had been skeptical initially, would later argue that SDI helped bankrupt the Soviet Union and convinced the Kremlin that it could not win the Cold War. McFarlane told me, with mock precision, that SDI "accelerated the Soviet collapse by about five years." In fact, an émigré Russian researcher concluded in 2017, after examining once-classified Soviet documents, that "the SDI program ... did not help bring the Cold War closer to the end." Rather, it was "an impediment to the disarmament process" and only emboldened "those in the Soviet Union who defined security in confrontational terms and benefitted from continuing the arms race."[28]

Indeed, the immediate impact of the SDI speech, coming shortly after the "evil empire" speech, was to heighten Soviet paranoia. "Moscow regarded Reagan's decision primarily as a move to destabilize the strategic situation ... in order to deprive the Soviet Union of the chance to retaliate in case of a nuclear war," Dobrynin wrote.[29]

Soviet fears were further heightened by US military actions—some public, others not. Publicly, the United States began deploying nuclear-armed Pershing II missiles and cruise missiles to Europe in the fall of 1982—missiles that could hit Moscow within six minutes of launch. Secretly, the Defense Department launched what an official National Security Agency (NSA) history later described as "a campaign of psychological military warfare" against the Soviet Union. US Air Force aircraft "probed East Bloc borders in increasingly provocative flights," with the Strategic Air Command sending B-52s "over the North Pole to see what the Soviet reaction would be." At the urging of the brash young Navy secretary, John Lehman, the US Navy was even more "daring": "Two huge naval exercises—one near the Murmansk coast in 1981, the other in the Sea of Okhotsk in April of 1983—served notice that Allied naval forces would intrude into what the Soviets had come to regard as their own private lakes."

The latter naval maneuver, which occurred shortly after the "evil empire" and SDI speeches, was the Pacific fleet's biggest exercise since World War II. It involved three aircraft-carrier battle groups operating off the Kamchatka Peninsula and the Kuril Islands, which had been occupied by the Soviets from Japan in 1945. On April 4, 1983, six F-14 Tomcats flew at low altitude over a Soviet naval base on the Kuril Islands. "These actions were calculated to induce paranoia," the NSA wrote, "and they did." The Soviets knew exactly what the US Navy was up to—although the American public did not—because they had a spy aboard the aircraft carrier *Enterprise*, a member of the spy ring run by former naval petty officer John Walker.

After the violation of Soviet airspace, Major Gennady Osipovich, one of the Soviet pilots stationed in the Kurils, recalled, "A commission flew out to the regiment and gave us a dressing down. They really berated us." Soviet pilots were put on notice that they needed to be more aggressive in protecting their skies.[30]

Korean Air Lines Flight 007, a Boeing 747 carrying 269 passengers and crew from New York to Seoul, made a routine refueling stop in Anchorage, Alaska, on August 31, 1983. The veteran pilot and copilot made a fatal error shortly after takeoff from Anchorage at 4:00 a.m. local time: They set the autopilot on a constant magnetic heading that would take the jumbo jet off its scheduled flight path, heading straight for the Soviet Union's sparsely populated Kamchatka Peninsula, located between the Sea of Okhotsk and the Pacific Ocean, in the very area where the US Navy exercises had taken place in the spring. The Korean Air pilots had no idea they would be flying close to a RC-135 Cobra Ball, a four-engine US Air Force intelligence-gathering aircraft used for monitoring ballistic missile launches. From below, the RC-135 resembled a 747, which also had four engines. Soviet radar had been monitoring the RC-135, but after it crossed paths with KAL 007 and then flew away, the radar operators made a critical mistake: Not realizing there were two aircraft in the sky, they began tracking KAL 007 as if it were a US Air Force plane.

When the Korean airliner headed straight for Soviet airspace, fighter aircraft were scrambled to intercept it. "The target is military," ground controllers told Major Osipovich, one of the Soviet pilots streaking toward the lumbering aircraft in a Su-15 fighter. He was ordered to flash his lights as a warning and to fire his cannon, but there was no response to these attempts to signal the aircraft. Nor did the airplane respond to his attempts to reach it via an international emergency radio frequency.

At 3:24 a.m., when KAL 007 was near Sakhalin Island and heading out of Soviet airspace, a Soviet ground controller ordered Osipovich, "Approach target and destroy target!" A minute later, the fighter pilot fired two air-to-air missiles. He saw an explosion and then the airplane began to descend, hurtling with increasing speed toward the pitch-dark sea below. "The target is destroyed," he reported. All 269 people aboard died, including 62 Americans. The most prominent victim was Congressman Larry McDonald, a right-wing Democrat from Georgia who was the chairman of the John Birch Society.[31]

Ronald Reagan received the horrific news at Rancho del Cielo in the early-morning hours of Thursday, September 1, 1983. Nancy Reagan heard him saying to Bill Clark on the telephone, "My God, have they gone mad? What the hell are they thinking of?" Secret Service agent John Barletta recalled that later in the day, as they were riding, "He was really pissed. I never saw him that way." "Damn those Russians," the president said. "Damn them."[32]

Reagan, nevertheless, resisted his aides' entreaties to cut short his Labor Day weekend at the ranch and return to Washington. "It was heartbreaking—I had really looked forward to those last 3 days," he lamented in his diary. He was so reluctant to leave his ranch, in fact, that he did not budge until he received a call from Stuart Spencer—one of the few outside advisers the Reagans respected. "I got on the phone and chewed him up one side, down the other, telling him to get his ass off the hill," Spencer said.[33]

When Reagan got back to the White House the next day, September 2, 1983, he found an internal debate over what had happened and how to respond. A secret NSA listening station in Japan had recorded the conversations between Osipovich and ground control. His words—"the target is destroyed"—seemed damning enough that the administration played snippets of the tape for congressional leaders and the public. Soviet leaders, by lying about what had happened and trying to cover it up—they claimed KAL 007 had deliberately flown into Soviet airspace on a CIA mission—made themselves look even guiltier. Yuri Andropov was privately irate at this "gross blunder" by "those blockheads of generals" but felt compelled to defend the military in public.[34]

Hard-liners in the Reagan administration were convinced, as NSC staffer John Lenczowksi wrote, "The only possible motive for this crime was to commit an act of terrorism to instill ever more fear in the hearts of the people of the free world." But US intelligence quickly realized that a US spy plane had also been in the area and that the shootdown had been a tragic accident—"a case of mistaken identity," not a deliberate massacre. "Possible Soviet uncertainty about the identity of the airplane was known to everyone in the Reagan administration within twenty-four hours," the CIA's Robert Gates wrote. Yet "the administration's rhetoric outran the facts that were known to it."[35]

Ronald Reagan spent much of Labor Day, September 5, 1983—when he would rather have been back at the ranch—sitting in his wet trunks near the White House swimming pool rewriting a speech about KAL 007 after getting two drafts from the speechwriters that he did not like. When he appeared on television that night, he called the shootdown a "crime against humanity." He mentioned the RC-135 but only to dismiss its importance: "At no time was the RC-135 in Soviet airspace. The Korean airliner flew on, and the two planes were soon widely separated." There was, of course, no mention of US Navy aircraft having recklessly violated Soviet airspace in this same area just four months earlier—something the Soviets knew but

Reagan probably did not. In his memoirs, Reagan wrote that the Soviets "cold-bloodedly" shot down KAL 007 and cited this as evidence that the USSR really was an "evil empire."[36]

In blaming the Soviets for deliberately carrying out what he called the "Korean Airline Massacre," Reagan channeled the fury of the American public and stood squarely with administration hard-liners. But when it came to the response, he shifted, as he so often did, to the pragmatic camp. Cap Weinberger argued for cutting off all arms-control negotiations. Don Regan advocated economic sanctions. Senator Strom Thurmond suggested, in a move he thought was clever, expelling 269 KGB agents from the United States—one for each victim of KAL 007. Reagan brushed aside all these proposals and told Shultz to keep a scheduled appointment with Soviet foreign minister Andrei Gromyko in Madrid, although the meeting turned out to be so contentious that it ended early.[37] The responses Reagan announced were limited to modest steps such as demanding an apology and reparations. Even grain sales to Russia continued.

The *Los Angeles Times* editorial board, along with many other commentators, commended Reagan for his "forceful restraint" and "statesmanship." However, the ultraconservative *New Hampshire Union-Leader,* owned by the irascible Elizabeth "Nackey" Loeb, called his statement "mealy-mouthed mush," and the conservative columnist George Will labeled Reagan's policy "pathetic," leading the president to complain that he was "really upset" with Will for becoming "very bitter and personal in his attacks."[38] When a conservative wrote a letter demanding retaliation, Reagan replied personally:

> I can understand the frustration of those who want some kind of punishment imposed on the perpetrators of the Korean airline massacre. No one is more frustrated than I am. Do you believe that I and my advisers . . . did not review every possibility? There were things that might have sounded good on the TV news but wouldn't have meant a thing in reality. Send their diplomatic people home? They would send ours home. And, believe me, there is no time for us to be without eyes and ears in Moscow.[39]

This was an abrupt shift. After Reagan the True Believer had denounced the "evil empire," ordered a missile-defense crash program, and distorted the facts about KAL 007, now Reagan the Pragmatist was acting, in the face of conservative criticism, to damp down rising superpower tensions. Reagan's restraint was admirable but also baffling both to his own supporters and to the leaders of the Soviet Union. "If anyone had the illusion about the possibility of an evolution for the better in the policy of the present administration, recent events [have] dispelled them completely," Andropov, then in his final months of life, said bitterly.[40]

Thus, the KAL 007 shootdown, despite Reagan's restrained response, further exacerbated Cold War tensions.

Just three weeks after the downing of KAL 007, at 12:15 a.m. on September 27, 1983, an alarm began to blare in a bunker known as Serpukhov-15 about seventy miles southwest of Moscow. This was the Soviet equivalent of the US early warning center in Cheyenne Mountain, Colorado, and it was receiving satellite signals that the United States had just fired ICBMs at the Soviet Union. The Russian words for "launch" and then "missile attack" flashed in red on a giant screen. A few minutes later the electronic system warned of a second missile launch, then a third, fourth, and fifth. If the system was accurate, the Soviet Union was only minutes away from destruction—and had to launch its own missiles immediately.

Luckily, the watch commander, Lieutenant Colonel Stanislav Petrov, did not want to risk unleashing World War III if there was any chance of a false alert. He carefully checked the feed from reconnaissance satellites that should have recorded the contrails of American missiles arcing into space. No ICBMs were visible. Petrov wasn't sure what was happening, but he erred on the side of caution and told his superiors that this was a false alert.

It would later emerge that Soviet early-warning satellites had picked up reflections from clouds passing over a US Air Force base in Wyoming. By taking his time to verify the launch alert, Petrov became known as the "man who saved the world."[41]

Yet the "year of living dangerously" (to borrow the title of a 1982 movie) was not yet over. In November 1983, the United States and its NATO allies staged an extensive war game called Able Archer 83. It was designed to simulate the outbreak of a nuclear war with the Soviet Union and involved an unusually large number of troops and weapons systems, including nuclear-armed submarines and B-52 bombers. The Soviets were carefully monitoring the NATO movements and responded by putting fighter-bombers based in East Germany on heightened alert. Some of the aircraft were even loaded with nuclear munitions. Oleg Gordievsky, the KGB's deputy chief of station in London and a British mole, warned his MI6 handlers that the Soviets were genuinely afraid the United States might launch a preemptive war under cover of an exercise. Fortunately, a senior US Air Force officer in Europe, Lieutenant General Leonard H. Perroots, was cognizant of the risk of miscalculation and refused to elevate NATO's alert level. Like Stanislav Petrov, Perroots was one of the anonymous heroes who may have helped avert World War III.

In 1990, the President's Foreign Intelligence Advisory Board issued a top-secret study of this incident and concluded that the Soviets were genuinely alarmed about "the US launching a nuclear first strike." This conclusion, which was echoed in numerous journalistic and historical accounts, was challenged in 2020 by historian Simon Miles. He concluded that "although Soviet policymakers saw Washington as a threat, at no point did they envision a U.S. surprise attack akin to Pearl Harbor." He argued that while some lower-level Soviet officials may have thought the risk of an American first strike was real, the most senior leaders in the Kremlin knew better. Indeed, a NATO employee spying for the East German Stasi had reassured his handlers that Able Archer was just an exercise. Yet, even if reports of Soviet concerns about a preemptive strike were exaggerated, they would have an important influence on how Ronald Reagan viewed the Cold War. [42]

The president already had been growing concerned about the risks of World War III. Always influenced by Hollywood, he had seen on October 10, 1983, a preview of a powerful ABC television movie, *The Day After*, about the impact of a nuclear strike on Lawrence, Kansas. "It's very effective & left me greatly depressed," he wrote in his diary. It wasn't clear when he learned of reports that the Soviets were worried about the United States launching a preemptive war, but on November 18, 1983, just a few days after the conclusion of Able Archer, Reagan wrote, "I feel the Soviets are so defense minded, so paranoid about being attacked that without being in any way soft on them we ought to tell them no one here has any intention of doing something like that." [43]

The president had come a long way since the beginning of the year when he had expressed incredulity to Ambassador Dobrynin that the Soviets could possibly see the United States as a threat. He had come even further from the beginnings of his political career when he had campaigned for a Republican presidential nominee who had joked about lobbing a nuclear bomb "into the men's room of the Kremlin."

The crises in the fall of 1983 over KAL 007 and Able Archer were the beginning of an epiphany for Reagan—that the United States could not simply continue ratcheting up the pressure on the Soviet Union without running the risk of World War III. That concern found public expression in a major speech on East-West relations that he delivered on January 16, 1984.

The address had been initially scheduled for mid-December 1983 but was pushed back at the insistence of Nancy Reagan's astrologer. The first draft had been written by the NSC's new Soviet expert, Jack Matlock, a career Foreign Service officer who had replaced the more hawkish Richard Pipes. But the most famous part of the speech was added by Reagan himself in a handwritten insert at the end. The president imagined two typical Soviets— "an Ivan and Anya"—spending time with two typical Americans—"a Jim and Sally"—and finding that they had much in common. Matlock had to tone down the sexism: Reagan, a product of 1920s America, had the men chatting about work and the women about recipes and children. The speech concluded, "If the Soviet Government wants peace, then there will be peace. Together we can strengthen peace, reduce the level of arms, and know in doing so that we have helped fulfill the hopes and dreams of those we represent and, indeed, of people everywhere. Let us begin now."

A cynical White House staffer who read the addition to the text, without knowing where it had come from, reportedly demanded, "Who wrote this shit?" The "Ivan and Anya speech" was undoubtedly sentimental and perhaps naive, but it was also the beginning of a major shift in Reagan's approach toward the Soviet Union that made a mockery of later claims that he had pursued a consistent hard-line strategy. He followed, instead, a zig-zag course. After ratcheting up tensions in 1983 with his "evil empire" and "Star Wars" speeches, provocative military exercises, and harsh (and inaccurate) rhetoric about the shootdown of KAL 007, Reagan was now offering an olive branch to the country he had denounced as the "focus of evil." But was there anyone on the other side strong enough to receive it?[44]

After a mere fifteen months in office, Yuri Andropov—who had tried with little success to get the Soviet economy moving again by cracking down on malingerers—died on February 9, 1984. One of his last acts was to order Soviet negotiators to walk out of nuclear arms-control talks in Geneva to protest the US deployment of Pershing II and cruise missiles to Europe. Reagan refused to go to Andropov's funeral, saying, "I don't want to honor that prick."[45] Vice President Bush went in his place.

Andropov was replaced by Konstantin Chernenko, another infirm hardliner who represented the Communist old guard. He had been born the same year as his American counterpart but was much less vigorous: He suffered from shortness of breath and coughing fits, often appeared confused, and could barely read a prepared text. Reagan wanted to arrange a summit with him—"It was time for the lion and the lamb to lie down together," he said during an Oval Office meeting with Brian Mulroney in 1984[46]—but Chernenko, too, would die before that could happen. With both the Soviet Union and the United States still set on their Cold War course, the risk of conflict remained dangerously high as 1984 began.

If anyone needed a reminder of Cold War tensions, Reagan provided it by cracking an ill-advised joke before his weekly radio address on August 11, 1984: "My fellow Americans, I'm pleased to tell you today that I've signed legislation that will outlaw Russia forever. We begin bombing in five minutes." He didn't realize the microphone was on, and his remarks were overheard by the press corps, thereby creating what he ruefully called an "international incident."[47] It was only a jest—but one that reflected the jittery tenor of the times.

44

The Thrill of Victory . . . and the Agony of Defeat

The president's face turned ashen. . . . All the air seemed to go out of him.

—ROBERT "BUD" MCFARLANE

If there was any position that turned over even more rapidly than the leader of the Soviet Union in the early 1980s, it was that of US national security adviser. Ronald Reagan went through national security advisers more often than any other president save for Donald Trump—and the frequent personnel changes made it much more difficult to shape a coherent foreign policy or to deal with sudden crises of the kind that inevitably test any president.

Bill Clark, the second of Reagan's six national security advisers (not counting one "acting" adviser), was worn down by constant battles with administration moderates. With his hard-line approach to the Soviet Union, he ran afoul of what he described as "the real troika, frankly, in the White House": Nancy Reagan, Jim Baker, and Mike Deaver. "They were so anxious that Ronald Reagan be shown as the Peace President," he complained, that they felt confronting the Soviets "was not the way to go."[1]

From the standpoint of the pragmatic faction, Clark was a foreign policy novice who was in over his head and was blocking attempts to improve relations with Moscow. They felt, moreover, that he abused his relationship with the president to do an end run around the normal policy process—for example, by approving covert actions to overthrow the Nicaraguan government and by sending his deputy, Bud McFarlane, as an envoy to the Middle East without notifying the State Department.[2] George Shultz, who often clashed with Clark, told an aide, "There is a management crisis in foreign affairs here. It's not easy to accomplish anything. . . . It's the worst organization I've ever seen."[3]

The two sides clashed not only over policy and personnel decisions but also over leaks of secret information that Clark blamed on the Baker faction. In fact, one of the biggest leakers was Casey himself; he was regularly and secretly meeting with journalist Bob Woodward. Not knowing about the Casey-Woodward conversations, Bill Clark and Ed Meese proposed to the president that the most senior officials be polygraphed as part of a leak investigation and that anyone who refused be fired. Reagan was about to sign an executive order on September 14, 1983, authorizing the lie-detector tests when, at the last minute, Deaver found out and notified Baker. The two men, who were on their way to lunch at the Madison Hotel, raced back to the White House and stormed into the Oval Office where Reagan was having lunch with George Shultz and George Bush. The secretary of state threatened to resign if he were asked to take a polygraph, and Reagan backed off. "Bill shouldn't have done that," the president blurted out. Mike Deaver recalled that Meese and Clark "were very, very unhappy."[4]

Clark told McFarlane that "things were very bad at the White House" and "working with the Baker-Deaver crowd . . . was becoming impossible." Deaver agreed: "There just wasn't any trust at all. You can't operate that way, and I think the president knew it."[5]

An opportunity for Bill Clark to exit gracefully arose on October 10, 1983, when Interior Secretary James Watt was fired. Watt had become politically toxic because of his desire to open federal lands to economic exploitation. "We will mine more, drill more, cut more timber," he vowed, thereby arousing strong opposition from environmental groups and lawmakers of both parties.[6]

Watt compounded his woes by repeatedly shooting himself in the foot. On April 7, 1983, he announced that rock groups such as the Beach Boys would not be invited to play at a Fourth of July concert on the Mall because they weren't "wholesome" enough. "A ban on apple pie couldn't have brought a stronger reaction," the Washington Post noted. The outraged Beach Boys fans included George H. W. Bush and Nancy Reagan.[7]

Watt completed his self-destruction on September 21, 1983, when he described the membership of a commission to review coal leases: "We have every kind of mix you can have. I have a black, I have a woman, two Jews and a cripple." He wrote an abject letter of apology to the president for his "unfortunate remarks," but it wasn't enough to save his job. Nancy Reagan, Jim Baker, and Mike Deaver—the "real troika"—had no desire to go into an election year saddled with such an unpopular cabinet member.[8]

Ronald Reagan wrote in his diary that Watt had "done a fine job" despite his "unfortunate way of putting his foot in his mouth" and that he was "the victim of a 2½ year lynching."[9] But he bowed, as he usually did, to political reality, and Bill Clark, a rancher at heart, jumped at the chance to take a less demanding job by replacing the gaffe-prone Watt.

Jim Baker was also weary of his grueling job; as far back as early 1982, he had been talking about leaving. In his memoir, he described a "barely civil war within the White House." "The first term, quite honestly, was a rat fuck," he told me.[10] Those constant internecine battles among the staff were the price of having a frequently disengaged chief executive. Clark's departure offered Baker an opportunity to get a new post of his own as national security adviser, which he saw as a stepping stone to becoming secretary of state or defense—maybe even president. He suggested that Mike Deaver replace him as chief of staff, and Deaver agreed to take the job. They ran it by the president, and he casually consented.

Clark only found out about the planned moves on Friday, October 14, 1983—the day Baker's and Deaver's appointments were to be unveiled—from a casual conversation with Reagan. He was startled that the president was about to make such a "major appointment" without first having "round-tabled" it with the "principals." Clark mobilized his conservative allies Cap Weinberger, Bill Casey, and Ed Meese to implore the president not to appoint Jim Baker. They viewed him as "the biggest leaker in Washington," an unprincipled self-promoter who refused to "let Reagan be Reagan," and a political operative lacking in foreign policy experience.[11]

The president was displeased to discover, as he confided in his diary, "great division & resistance in certain quarters," and he backed off the planned appointments to assuage the conservative faction. Baker took the news gracefully, but Deaver was "pretty upset," as the president noted.[12] From Deaver's perspective, this was the second time he had been betrayed by someone who was practically an adopted father to him; the first time had been when Reagan had acceded to John Sears's demand to fire him in 1979.

That left the question of who would become national security adviser—a decision Reagan had to make over the weekend at Camp David. The conservatives pushed for one of their own, Jeane Kirkpatrick; Bill Casey thought "she had balls." She was eager for the job, but the moderates vetoed the tart-tongued UN ambassador. Shultz was particularly opposed because of her habit of doing end runs around him and her reputation as a "terrible administrator" who was "cantankerous" and "difficult to work with." As Reagan wrote in his diary, if he appointed Kirkpatrick, "there would be bad chemistry with Geo. S & State." The one nominee who was least objectionable to both the conservative and pragmatic factions was Bud McFarlane, so, on Monday, October 17, he got the job.[13]

This was another example of how Reagan's inability to manage and his desire to avoid personal conflict led him into trouble. McFarlane, although he appeared steady and solid, was too volatile, too insecure, and too lacking in the judgment necessary for such a sensitive position. Press secretary Larry Speakes called him "one of the most bizarre characters I ever met." Haunted by feelings of intellectual inferiority compared to such storied predecessors as Henry Kissinger and Zbigniew Brzezinski, McFarlane had a tendency to use "twenty-five-dollar words" in an unsuccessful bid to impress people, Speakes noted. "This job is way beyond me," the new national security adviser confessed to a friend.[14] Further aggravating the disarray at the NSC, McFarlane appointed as his deputy Rear Admiral John Poindexter, a nuclear physicist who had no feel for politics and could not make up for McFarlane's deficiencies.

The Iran-Contra affair in all likelihood would never have happened if Baker had simply gotten the job he wanted. In his memoirs, Reagan was to concede, "My decision not to appoint Jim Baker as national security adviser, I suppose, was a turning point for my administration, although I had no idea at the time how significant it would prove to be."[15]

Bud McFarlane had no time for on-the-job training. As soon as he took office, two new crises blew up—one of them literally. On Friday, October 21, 1983, he traveled with the president and first lady to Augusta National Golf Club in Georgia, the home of the Masters tournament, for a weekend of golf with George Shultz, Don Regan, Republican Senator Nick Brady of New Jersey, and their wives. Reagan was not much of a golfer ("I guess you have to play more than 4 times in almost 3 yrs.," he wrote in his diary), but he enjoyed spending time with this "fun group."[16]

The very first night at Augusta, while the Reagans were sleeping in the same cottage once occupied by President Eisenhower, McFarlane received a call at 3:00 a.m. from Vice President Bush, who was chairing a crisis-management group in Washington. He notified McFarlane that Dominica's formidable prime minister, Eugenia Charles, had requested on behalf of the seven-member Organization of Eastern Caribbean States (OECS) that the United States intervene militarily to restore democracy in Grenada.

That tiny Caribbean island had just ninety thousand inhabitants. Ruled since 1979 by a Marxist party known as the New Jewel Movement, it had just been convulsed by a coup. Prime Minister Maurice Bishop had been overthrown and murdered on October 19 by an even more radical faction led by Deputy Prime Minister Bernard Coard. Some of Grenada's neighbors were worried by the growth of a Cuban-aligned regime in their midst. Even more alarmed were Reagan administration hard-liners who decided that this would be a perfect opportunity to bring about regime change at gunpoint. Administration officials had nudged the OECS states to "provide cover for the [US] intervention," acknowledged Duane "Dewey" Clarridge, the CIA's Latin America Division chief. The administration turned to the tiny OECS to bless an invasion because the larger Caribbean Community, known as CARICOM, which represented nearly twice as many nations, advocated a diplomatic solution.[17]

Back on March 23, 1983, in his "Star Wars" speech, Reagan had warned that Cuban construction workers were helping Grenada build a new airfield with a ten-thousand-foot runway (it was actually nine thousand feet). "Grenada doesn't even have an air force," he said, ominously. "Who is it intended for?" The implication was that this would be a Soviet air base—one that, he later claimed, would be used for long-range bombers capable of hitting the United States.[18]

In fact, the airport was intended to facilitate tourism. A dozen other Caribbean islands already had airports with nine-thousand-foot runways capable of handling a fully loaded Boeing 747, and Grenada wanted to catch up. There was no indication, such as the construction of underground fuel storage or hardened aircraft shelters, that the airfield was to be used for military purposes. Grenada had only turned to Cuba to help build the airport after the US government had refused to do so. Yuri Pavlov, a veteran

Soviet diplomat who in 1983 was ambassador to Costa Rica, later said, "No one in his right mind was thinking in Moscow . . . along the lines of any possibility of turning Grenada into yet another Cuba."[19]

Margaret Thatcher came to the same conclusion about Grenada, which was part of the British Commonwealth. She wrote in her memoirs that her friend Ron Reagan was exaggerating "the threat which a Marxist Grenada posed": "Our intelligence suggested that the Soviets had only a peripheral interest in the island" and that, while the new airfield could be useful for the transit of Cuban troops to and from Africa, Grenada's "main purpose" in building it "was, as they claimed, a commercial one."[20]

But the president was convinced that Grenada was part of a Soviet plot to turn the entire Caribbean into a "Red lake," and he was not listening to alternative views. In his memoir, he even suggested fancifully that, because Grenada was a major producer of nutmeg, the Soviets might be scheming to "steal Christmas" by seizing control of the spice used in eggnog.[21]

Now, following the coup in Grenada, there was added concern about the fate of six hundred American citizens studying at St. George's University School of Medicine, a for-profit institution founded by American investors in 1977. The medical students and school administrators did not think they were in any danger, and the new Grenadian government said they were free to leave. The medical school administrators refused to request a US military rescue (Dewey Clarridge complained that they were being "uncooperative"), but Reagan and his aides were obsessed with the possibility that the students could be taken hostage, reprising the nightmare of the Iranian hostage crisis that had helped bring down Jimmy Carter.[22] It did not seem to occur to them that launching a major military operation would put the students in even greater danger. Or perhaps it simply did not matter. The supposed plight of the medical students was only a pretext to finally overthrow a Marxist regime, however tiny and inconsequential.

As soon as McFarlane heard about the request from the OECS for US military action early on the morning of October 22, he notified Shultz, and they went to wake up the president. McFarlane couched the decision as a test of American leadership: "For us to be asked to help and to refuse would have a very damaging effect on the credibility of the United States and your own commitment to the defense of freedom and democracy," he told the president. Sitting in his robe, pajamas, and slippers in the Eisenhower cottage, Reagan did not hesitate. Probably unaware that the OECS request had been engineered by his own aides as a pretext for a US invasion, Reagan told McFarlane, "You're dead right. There's no way we can say no to this request." He thereby set in motion plans that would lead to the invasion of Grenada three days later.[23]

Shultz strongly supported the operation while Weinberger was more skeptical. In dealing with the Soviet Union, the defense secretary was the hard-liner and the secretary of state was the advocate of diplomacy, but when it came to the use of force, the roles usually reversed. Reagan himself was largely a bystander in these debates, with few firmly fixed views of his own. As a State Department historian noted, the president "did not so much make decisions on the use of force as allow himself to be swayed by the counsel of his more opinionated advisors"—often based on whichever option seemed the most "politically expedient" at the moment.[24] In the case of Grenada, a successful military operation could be depicted as a Cold War victory after a long string of defeats, while the risks of fighting such a puny adversary were minimal. So it was a relatively easy call for Reagan to make, even if his rationale for the operation—which has been faithfully echoed in most accounts of his presidency—was largely bogus.

Prime Minister Thatcher, normally Reagan's staunchest ally, was appalled by the decision and saw no danger to US or British citizens. In her view, the US invasion would be a regime-change operation comparable to the Soviet interventions in Hungary and Czechoslovakia. "The Americans are worse than the Soviets," she fumed. Knowing how she felt, Reagan made no attempt to consult Thatcher or even to notify her until *after* the decision had already been made, even though Grenada was a former British colony whose head of state was still Queen Elizabeth II. Reagan later explained that he did not consult Thatcher in advance "because I didn't want her to say no."

When she found out about his decision, she was "extremely agitated," according to Deputy Secretary of State Ken Dam. "That man!" she exclaimed of Reagan. "After all I've done for him, he didn't even consult me!" Reagan, in turn, was upset by her lack of support.[25]

The Grenada crisis represented the worst rupture in the Anglo-American "special relationship" during the administration. After the invasion had started, Reagan telephoned Thatcher to apologize for keeping her in the dark, saying with old-fashioned gallantry, "If I were there, Margaret, I'd throw my hat in the door before I came in."

"There's no need for that," the no-nonsense prime minister gruffly replied.[26]

A few hours after deciding to invade Grenada, Reagan was on the Augusta National golf course when his game was rudely interrupted by a genuine hostage crisis closer to home. A deranged gunman named Charles Harris, who had recently been laid off from a paper mill, took five hostages, including two White House aides, at the Augusta pro shop. He was demanding to speak to the president to complain about American jobs going overseas. The Secret Service immediately hustled the president into his armored limousine and evacuated him. Reagan tried phoning Harris to calm him down, but that didn't work. A few hours later, however, the hostages escaped and Harris surrendered.[27]

The president insisted on remaining at Augusta and carrying on with his schedule. But at 2:27 a.m. on Sunday, October 23, 1983, McFarlane was awakened by another middle-of-the-night phone call. This time it was the White House Situation Room calling to notify him that a truck loaded with twelve thousand pounds of explosives, driven by a suicide bomber, had leveled the four-story US Marine barracks in Beirut. "The casualties were high . . . and climbing," McFarlane was told. Eventually the death toll would reach 241 Americans—the worst Marine losses in a single day since the invasion of Iwo Jima in 1945. At the same time, another truck bomb struck the French military barracks in Beirut, killing 58 French troops. Buried in the rubble, along with all of the French and American victims, were the remnants of the Reagan administration's ill-advised Lebanon policy.

McFarlane was a former Marine who had recently visited the leathernecks in Beirut. "I felt as though I had been stabbed in the heart," he wrote. When McFarlane awakened Reagan to tell him the tragic news, "the president's face turned ashen. . . . He looked like a man, a 72-year-old man, who had just received a blow to the chest. All the air seemed to go out of him." The president responded to the news in disbelief: "How could this happen? How bad is it? Who did it?"[28]

The short answer was that Iranian-sponsored terrorists were responsible, and it had happened because the president had recklessly sent the Marines on a perilous, ill-defined peacekeeping mission with scant hope of success. "The Marines were sitting ducks," said McFarlane, who had helped place them in that position. Even Shultz, the primary advocate of the mission, conceded, "I think it's fair to say that we stayed too long."[29]

This was actually the second tragedy the United States had suffered in Lebanon that year. On April 18, 1983, a truck bomb had struck the US Embassy in Beirut, killing sixty-three people, including seventeen Americans, the CIA's top Middle East expert, Robert Ames, among them. Yet, in spite of that attack, the Marines remained deployed in an exposed position while under rifle, rocket, and mortar fire. In September, US warships had begun shelling Syrian and militia positions in the hills around Beirut that were threatening the Marines and the US-backed Lebanese army. Far from deterring further attacks, the naval bombardment had only convinced the Syrians, and their Iranian allies, that the United States was now a party to this conflict and that its troops needed to be driven out so they could overthrow the Christian-dominated, Israeli-backed government. Iran had even further cause for anti-American and anti-French animus because both Washington and Paris were covertly supporting Iraq in its war with Iran.[30]

Reagan had previously insisted on sticking to his schedule so as not to tip off anyone to the impending invasion of Grenada. But now the Beirut barracks bombing gave him the perfect excuse to return to Washington early on Sunday, October 23, 1983. "It was a somber morning—cold, bleak and rainy," recalled a White House staffer. "The weather matched everyone's mood."[31]

The White House would spend the next few days simultaneously managing the two crises: Grenada and Beirut. Reagan even tried to argue implausibly in a televised address that the two events were "closely related" because Moscow supposedly "assisted and encouraged the violence in both countries . . . through a network of surrogates and terrorists."[32] (There is no evidence that the Soviet Union had anything to do with either the coup in Grenada or the Beirut bombing.) McFarlane described this period as "intense, frenzied, exhausting, stressful, solemn and significant."[33] The administration was about to experience, in the words of a then-popular TV sports program, "the thrill of victory . . . and the agony of defeat."

On October 26, 1983, a day after the invasion of Grenada, Reagan wrote in his diary, "The Marines, the A.F. [Air Force] & the Army & Navy planned beautifully and executed even better."[34] In truth, planning was virtually nonexistent, intelligence was poor, and the execution botched. The whole operation might have turned into a disaster if the US forces were not facing inconsequential opposition from just 500 to 600 Grenadian soldiers and 2,000 unsalaried, unmotivated Grenadian militiamen supported by 43 Cuban military advisers and 636 Cuban construction workers. Most of the Cuban workers had prior military training and AK-47s, but they were hardly the "1,000 well-trained and equipped Cuban soldiers" described by the administration.[35] "They were more mechanics than soldiers," admitted General Vessey.[36] The defenders' heaviest weapons were a few armored vehicles and vintage antiaircraft guns. They had no missiles, no artillery, no tanks, no aircraft, no ships: in short, none of the equipment of a modern military force.[37]

This was no Bay of Pigs—the humiliation that had launched the Kennedy presidency in 1961—when ragtag Cuban exiles trained by the CIA had unsuccessfully tried to storm ashore in Cuba without air cover or armored vehicles against Fidel Castro's better-equipped military. This time, the invaders had an insuperable military advantage. Operation Urgent Fury, as the Grenada operation was code-named, was closer in spirit to Lyndon Johnson's one-sided invasion of the Dominican Republic in 1965 or to Woodrow Wilson's interventions in Haiti in 1915 and the Dominican Republic in 1916.

Yet US forces stumbled repeatedly. All four military services, plus the recently formed Joint Special Operations Command, wanted a piece of the action, and all wound up being sent into battle despite their inexperience at joint operations. Because the invasion was deemed urgent, there was insufficient time for preparation or coordination.

Things went wrong from the start. On Sunday, October 23, a team of sixteen Navy SEALs were supposed to parachute from Air Force C-130 transport planes into the waters off Grenada and then infiltrate the island using a pair of Boston Whaler boats rigged for parachute drops. But the Air Force officers who planned the drop had neglected to note, because of confusion over time zones, that the sun set in Grenada an hour ahead of the eastern United States. So an airdrop that was supposed to happen in daylight occurred at night—and in heavy seas and high winds. Four SEALS drowned.[38]

On October 25, the first full day of the invasion, Black Hawk helicopters carrying the Army's elite Delta Force were mauled by point-blank antiaircraft fire in a disastrous daylight raid on Richmond Hill Prison. The commandos were supposed to be liberating political prisoners but discovered, to their dismay, that the prison had been abandoned. Meanwhile, the Navy's SEAL Team Six found itself besieged while trying to "rescue" the British governor general, Sir Paul Scoon, who did not feel he was in any danger because he had "very good" relations with the new regime. Once in US custody, however, he did agree to sign a letter retroactively requesting the invasion. The twenty-two lightly armed SEALs were surrounded by Grenadian infantry supported by a single armored personnel carrier. The SEALs had no weapons that could take out an armored vehicle and needed air support. Having no radios that could communicate with the Air Force, they had to use a calling card to telephone Fort Bragg in order to reach an AC-130 gunship.[39]

For all the US blunders, there was never any doubt of the outcome of Ronald Reagan's first and only ground war. The island was fully secured within three days, democracy was restored, and all the American students were safely evacuated. The administration pointed to eleven thousand captured weapons supplied by the Soviet Union, Cuba, and North Korea to buttress Reagan's claim that "we got there just in time" to prevent Grenada from becoming "a major military bastion to export terror and undermine democracy." But a secret CIA assessment, declassified twenty-five years later, concluded that the weapons (mainly light machine guns, shotguns, and sidearms) "were intended to insure internal security and to defend Grenada against attack"—not, as Reagan claimed, to "supply thousands of terrorists."[40]

The official toll was 19 US service personnel killed in combat and another 125 wounded, but, if Special Operations forces were added in, the real number of wounded rose to at least 157. (This was a time when the army did not even publicly acknowledge the existence of Delta Force.)[41] Operation Urgent Fury suffered from many of the same dysfunctions as Operation Eagle Claw, the failed 1980 attempt to rescue the hostages in Tehran. As an internal Defense Department history noted, "The success of Operation URGENT FURY was marred by the consequences of inadequate time for planning, lack of tactical intelligence, and problems with joint command and control."[42] The shortcomings of both operations would provide impetus for the passage in 1986 of the Goldwater-Nichols Department of Defense Reorganization Act mandating greater joint training and coordination among the military services.

But, despite all the stumbles along the way, the invasion of Grenada was a political triumph for Reagan, much as the Falklands War had been for Thatcher. Clint Eastwood, a Republican, would even make a testosterone-laden movie about the Marines in Grenada—*Heartbreak Ridge* (1985)—in the same mold as World War II epics such as John Wayne's *The Sands of Iwo Jima*. The only controversy involved complaints from reporters that they had been misled about the operation by the White House and not allowed to accompany the invasion force, but the public did not much care about the media's concerns. That the entire invasion had been undertaken based on false pretexts—a runway that was not intended for Soviet military aircraft, medical students who had not been taken hostage—and that the operation had been botched in many ways seemed to largely escape public notice. Urgent Fury's ultimate success precluded too many hard questions about its origins or conduct.

One of the first medical students returning to the United States dropped to his knees at a military airfield in Charleston, South Carolina, and kissed the ground. As soon as the acting White House press secretary, Larry Speakes, saw that image on television, he shouted, "That's it! We won." Mike Deaver later told journalist Mark Hertsgaard, "This country was so hungry for a victory, I don't care what the size of it was, we were going to beat the shit out of it." Indeed, the United States had not had a single clear-cut military victory since 1945, but, as Canadian Ambassador Allan Gotlieb wrote tartly in his diary, "Any country that needs the invasion of Grenada to restore its national pride is not too well."[43]

No such victory was forthcoming in Lebanon. The attack on the Marine barracks cast a "pall . . . over the White House," McFarlane wrote. "All of us were numbed by shock and horror that wouldn't recede." On November 4, 1983, a grief-stricken president and first lady traveled to Camp Lejeune, North Carolina, for a memorial service honoring the fallen Marines. "It was a dreary day with constant rain which somehow seemed appropriate," Reagan noted in his diary. "It was a moving service & as hard as anything we've ever done. At the end taps got to both of us." Reagan would spend months responding to grief-stricken relatives such as an Arkansas man who wrote, "I do not like to sound mean but I have two brothers but now I only have one. You sent my 19 year old brother over to beruit [sic], and his dead now what are you doing."[44]

The anguished commander in chief vowed vengeance. "The first thing I want to do is to find out who did it and go after them with everything we've got," he told an NSC meeting on October 23, 1983, just hours after receiving news of the bombing. The US intelligence community quickly identified the culprits: a shadowy terrorist group called Islamic Amal, a precursor of Hezbollah, which was controlled by Iran's Islamic Revolutionary Guard Corps. "Bill Casey had the goods," McFarlane recalled. Indeed, the National Security Agency had intercepted a phone call from the Iranian ambassador in Damascus to Tehran a month before the attack referring to a "spectacular action against the U.S. Marines." The intercept was too vague to act on before the attack, but afterward it helped to establish culpability.[45]

The administration launched discussions with François Mitterand's government about a joint US-French air strike on the Sheikh Abdullah Barracks, the Revolutionary Guard base in Lebanon's Bekaa Valley. On October 28, 1983, Reagan signed a National Security Decision Directive that stated, "Subject to reasonable confirmation of the locations of suitable targets used by elements responsible for the October 23 bombing, attack those targets decisively, if possible in coordination with the French."[46]

McFarlane claimed that Reagan, after returning from a weeklong trip to Japan and South Korea, gave oral authorization for air strikes at a November 14 National Security Council meeting. (The Reagan Library archives do not contain any minutes of this meeting.)[47] Two US aircraft carriers off the Lebanese coast stood ready to launch aircraft, but the launch order never came. The French attacked on their own and were bitter about being left in the lurch by their allies. According to McFarlane, Cap Weinberger on his own authority decided not to proceed with the air strikes because he didn't want to be drawn deeper into the Lebanese quagmire. McFarlane was furious and went to Reagan to protest, but the president refused to call his secretary of defense on the carpet. Thus, in McFarlane's telling, Weinberger got away with "his insubordinate behavior." In his own memoir, Weinberger labeled McFarlane's account "absurd" and insisted "I had received no orders or notifications from the President."[48]

Which man was right? In his history of Reagan's foreign policy, William Inboden concludes that Weinberger's story was more plausible than McFarlane's. Even John Poindexter, no fan of Weinberger, agreed that no "execute" order had been signed by the president, and no such order has been found in the archives.[49]

What seems to have happened was that Reagan was furious about the bombing and initially eager to retaliate but started to have second thoughts. Then he was paralyzed by indecision because of the irreconcilable differences between McFarlane and Shultz, who advocated bombing, and Weinberger and General Vessey, who opposed it. Vice President Bush was sympathetic to the hard-liners, while Jim Baker and Ed Meese, with their eyes on the 1984 election, urged caution. Knowing little about the Middle East, Reagan could not sort out this conflicting advice, so in the end he opted to do nothing while giving both the pro- and anti-retaliation factions the impression that he agreed with them.

While the White House promoted the image of a take-charge chief executive—"a tough and decisive leader," in Ed Meese's words, who "never flinched . . . in defense of U.S. interests"—the indecision over Lebanon was typical of Reagan's foreign policy deliberations. As Richard Pipes observed after one NSC meeting, "He has not enough of either knowledge or decisiveness to cut through the contradictory advice that is being offered to him." Another NSC aide, Geoffrey Kemp, noted that the president "made very few decisions" and "was an extraordinarily passive participant" in the policy process.[50]

In his memoirs, Reagan masked his policy paralysis by claiming that he had canceled the planned air strikes because "our intelligence experts found it difficult to establish conclusively who was responsible for the attacks on the barracks" and "I didn't want to kill innocent people." In fact, Bill Casey had told him that the intelligence community had proof positive of Iranian responsibility and that there were no civilians at the Sheikh Abdullah Barracks.[51]

The United States did finally launch an airstrike in Lebanon on December 4, 1983, but this was in retaliation for Syrian missile attacks on patrolling US aircraft—and it was a disaster. Syrian air defenses shot down two US Navy jets, with one crewman killed and another captured. To the administration's embarrassment, a Democratic presidential candidate, the Reverend Jesse Jackson, won the release of the African American aviator imprisoned by Syria. The impression of American military might fostered by the Grenada invasion was being undermined by the agony and ineffectuality of US forces in Lebanon.

Always stubborn, Reagan was adamant about not being driven out of Lebanon by the Marine barracks bombing. He wrote to his friend William F. Buckley Jr. on January 5, 1984, that "there has been progress" because of the Marines' presence and that withdrawing them would lead to "instant chaos." In a February 2 interview with the *Wall Street Journal*, Reagan rejected calls by House Speaker Tip O'Neill to end the mission: "He may be ready to surrender but I'm not."[52]

But, while Schultz was traveling in Latin America, Cap Weinberger, with support from George Bush, Jim Baker, Ed Meese, Mike Deaver, and Bud McFarlane, finally convinced the president to cut his losses before the Lebanese imbroglio imperiled his reelection chances. Lebanon, as Dick Darman noted, "was not likely to be a popular war."[53] On February 8, less than a week after the defiant *Wall Street Journal* interview, the White House announced the "redeployment of the Marines from Beirut airport to their ships offshore"—"redeployment" being a euphemism for "retreat." This recalled the way the pragmatic president had agreed in 1982 to tax increases after claiming "I'm not going to retreat one inch" or the way that, as governor of California, he had reversed course on tax withholding ("the sound you hear is the concrete cracking around my feet").

To cover the withdrawal, the battleship USS *New Jersey* lobbed shells the size of Volkswagens into the hills around Beirut. That final, futile gesture could not disguise the dismal reality: 269 service personnel had died for nothing. "It was," as McFarlane noted in his book, "one of the worst defeats of the Reagan administration." He told me in 2013 that "we're paying a price for it to this day," because the perception of America as a "weak horse" had incited more attacks from Islamist extremists such as Al Qaeda.[54]

The Reagan administration had sent a signal of weakness and indecision that encouraged further aggression from the Iranian regime and its Lebanese proxies. On January 18, 1984, Malcolm Kerr, president of the American University of Beirut and father of future basketball star Steve Kerr, was murdered in Beirut. Then the kidnappings started. On February 10, American University professor Frank Regier was seized by Shiite gunmen in Beirut. On March 7, CNN bureau chief Jeremy Levin. On March 16, CIA station chief William Buckley (not to be confused with the conservative journalist

THE THRILL OF VICTORY . . . AND THE AGONY OF DEFEAT   585

and Reagan friend). On May 8, the Reverend Benjamin T. Weir. "The image of America's fate in the Middle East was now a blindfolded captive," noted historian Patrick Tyler.[55] For a White House so concerned about being "Carterized," this had disquieting echoes of the hostage crisis that had dominated the previous presidency.

As if to underscore American helplessness, on September 20, 1984, another Hezbollah suicide bomber with a car bomb struck the US Embassy annex in East Beirut where US diplomats had relocated after the destruction of the original embassy building in 1983. Twenty-four people died, including two Americans. Once again, the US intelligence community had proof the attack was carried out from the Sheikh Abdullah Barracks; satellite imagery showed that the terrorists had practiced on a mockup of the annex. But once again Weinberger "was strongly against retaliation," and once again "the President decided not to retaliate," noted Ken Dam.[56]

George Shultz was so frustrated by the failure to strike back that on October 25, 1984, a month after the Beirut annex bombing, he gave a speech at a synagogue in New York arguing that the United States had to launch a "war against terrorism." "We may never have the kind of evidence that can stand up in an American court of law," he argued. "But we cannot allow ourselves to become the Hamlet of nations, worrying endlessly over whether and how to respond."

A month later, on November 28, Cap Weinberger countered with a speech of his own at the National Press Club, arguing that force should only be used as a last resort when defending "our vital national interests"—and then only with clearly defined objectives, overwhelming military power, public support, and the "intention of winning." This became known as the Weinberger Doctrine; Shultz criticized it as a "counsel of inaction bordering on paralysis." The differences between the secretary of state and the secretary of defense were both personal and philosophical.[57]

Bud McFarlane told the president that the constant feuding was producing "paralysis within your administration" and that he should jettison either Shultz or Weinberger. Reagan refused. "They are both my friends," he replied. "I don't want to fire either one of them." He told McFarlane to "make it work."[58]

One way to "make it work" was by employing covert action to circumvent Weinberger's opposition to the use of military force. On November 10, 1984, Reagan signed a presidential finding authorizing the CIA to create secret units of foreign nationals in the Middle East to carry out preemptive strikes against terrorist groups. With this authority in hand, Bill Casey, who was anguished over the torture and murder of the CIA's William Buckley, arranged for the assassination of Sheikh Sayed Mohammed Hussein Fadlallah, a prominent Lebanese Shiite cleric who was mistakenly held responsible by the administration for the anti-American terrorism in Lebanon despite his uneasy relations with Tehran. On March 8, 1985, a massive car bomb exploded near Fadlallah's residence in Beirut. He escaped unharmed, but at least eighty civilians were killed and two hundred injured. The president subsequently rescinded the finding that had made this fiasco possible.

There are differing accounts of how this operation worked. Bob Woodward wrote that the bombing was arranged by the Saudis with CIA financing and carried out by mercenaries led by a former British commando. Israeli author Ronen Bergman wrote that the CIA directly paid Lebanese Phalangist militiamen to carry out the attack. And a retired CIA officer told historian David Crist that the Saudis contracted with Lebanese army intelligence to maintain CIA deniability. Whatever the mechanics, there was no disputing the essential point: In trying to fight terrorism, the Reagan administration had become implicated in terrorism itself. This was one of the administration's most shameful, if least known, episodes.[59]

Despite all these debacles, Ronald Reagan paid no political price for his tragic mishandling of Lebanon. The shootdown of two Libyan jets, the invasion of Grenada, the defense buildup, and the president's hawkish rhetoric insulated him from criticism for failing to defend American interests, and most Americans did not care much about Lebanon to begin with. Removing the Marines from Beirut was popular even if it came at the cost of reduced American credibility and security. By exiting this Middle East quagmire, Reagan cleared the decks to seek reelection without the risk of more body bags coming home. There would not be "another Vietnam"—a political obsession at the time, less than a decade after the fall of Saigon. Indeed, by the time Reagan was ready to launch his final campaign, the dark clouds of war and recession were lifting, and sunny political skies could be glimpsed ahead.

45

The Haves and Have-Nots

Most Black and many White Americans now view
Ronald Reagan as a clear and present danger to the civil
rights of minority Americans.

—DAN J. SMITH

"Had it been up to me," Nancy Reagan later wrote, "Ronald Reagan might well have been a one-term president." The first lady missed her life of leisurely lunches and sumptuous dinner parties with her friends in California and remained concerned about her husband's safety. "She was scared to death because of the assassination, and I don't blame her," Stuart Spencer said. But when she brought up the subject in 1983, she quickly discovered that her husband was intent on seeking a second term. "There were still things he wanted to do," she wrote. "He also thought it had been too long since an American president had served two full terms in office."[1]

Seeking reelection was not, of course, an entirely altruistic undertaking, even if Reagan genuinely believed that he was serving the country he loved. He also had a fierce drive to succeed that was only partially camouflaged by his genial, relaxed manner. "He was a ferocious competitor," Spencer noted. That ambition had carried him from the small-town Midwest to the White House—and he wasn't about to leave without one final win for "the Gipper" that could secure his legacy as a truly great president. "If you feel that strongly, go ahead," Nancy finally told him. "You know I'm not crazy about it, but okay." Of course, true to form, the president never told even his closest aides that he was actually running; they just assumed it, and he did not contradict them.[2]

Fittingly, for a president who was a master of the medium, Reagan announced his reelection campaign in a nationally televised speech from the Oval Office. His campaign paid for his announcement to air on all three major networks at 10:55 p.m. on January 29, 1984. Wearing a formal dark blue suit, white shirt with cufflinks, and a red tie, with family photos visible in the background, he began his four-minute address with a reminder of how far the country had come since 1981: "When I first addressed you from here, our national defenses were dangerously weak, we had suffered humiliation in Iran, and . . . we were on the brink of economic collapse from years of government overindulgence and abusive overtaxation."

Now, he could proudly boast, "Things have changed." The recovery from the 1981–1982 recession was gathering speed as 1984 began. That year would see economic growth spike to 7.2 percent, the highest rate since 1951, when the United States had also been in an economic recovery. The unemployment rate was still stubbornly high at 7.5 percent, but inflation had fallen below 4 percent. "America is back and standing tall," Reagan said. "But our work is not finished. We have more to do in creating jobs, achieving control over government spending, returning more autonomy to the States, keeping peace in a more settled world, and seeing if we can't find room in our schools for God."[3]

The Reagan reelection pitch would never get much more specific than that. But the president did not need an agenda for his second term when he could point to such impressive results in his first term—even if they were not, for the most part, of his own doing. As Treasury Secretary Donald Regan wrote, "The President himself had very little to do with the invention and the implementation of the policies and mechanisms that encouraged this remarkable increase in the nation's wealth and general well-being."[4]

Reagan was lucky that, to the frustration of supply-siders, Congress had insisted on phasing in his tax cuts over more than two years, with only a 5 percent reduction in income taxes in 1981. By the time his final 10 percent cut in taxes took effect in October 1983, inflation had already been tamed. If all the tax cuts had been implemented at once in 1981, they might have sent inflation, which was starting to fall, soaring once again. As it was, Fed chairman Paul Volcker's harsh anti-inflation remedy worked: The 1981–1982 recession purged high inflation, and the business cycle did the rest. A fall in global oil prices helped, too. The cost of crude oil topped out, in inflation-adjusted terms, at $147 a barrel in April 1980. By October 1984, it was down to $84 a barrel and by March 1986 just $28 a barrel.[5] Falling energy prices further reduced inflation and boosted the economy. Reagan's primary contributions were to lift people's spirits and not impede the Fed's anti-inflationary campaign. He wisely disregarded the counsel of, among others, Don Regan, who argued that Volcker "should be encouraged to loosen monetary policy"—advice that might have proven disastrous if prematurely applied.[6]

Reagan's partisans would attempt to make his economic performance seem more impressive than it actually was by absolving him of any responsibility for the 1981–1982 recession, which they blamed on Jimmy Carter, while crediting Reagan for all of the economic gains between 1983 and 1990 ("the seven fat years," *Wall Street Journal* editor Robert L. Bartley called them), when another recession started eighteen months after he left office.[7] In point of fact, average annual GDP growth under Reagan (3.49 percent) was about the same as under Nixon (3.5 percent), slightly higher than under Carter (3.25 percent), and below the rate under Bill Clinton (3.89 percent), Lyndon Johnson (5.3 percent), John F. Kennedy (4.37 percent), and Franklin D. Roosevelt (9.3 percent).[8] In other words, there was nothing particularly impressive or unusual about the Reagan economic record. But nor was "Reaganomics" as damaging to the economy as critics made it out to be. While budget deficits did soar—from $79 billion in 1981 to $185 billion in 1984— they proved only a minor impediment to the recovery and were far smaller than future deficits under presidents beginning with George W. Bush.[9]

Reagan benefited from an accident of timing because the economy, in its comeback from a particularly severe recession, hit a transitory peak in an election year. In a regression to the historical mean, economic growth would slow in 1985 to 4.2 percent and then in 1986 to 3.5 percent. In politics, as in show business, timing is everything—and Reagan's timing was always impeccable.

Prosperity, even hedonism, was in the air in 1984. Investment bankers were becoming "masters of the universe," as Tom Wolfe dubbed them in his 1987 novel *Bonfire of the Vanities*. Dealmakers such as Carl Icahn, Donald Trump, and T. Boone Pickens were becoming celebrities, while Wall Street titans Michael Milken and Ivan Boesky were heading to prison on insider-trading charges. "Yuppies" (young urban professionals) were gentrifying decrepit urban neighborhoods, and "preppies" were wearing the uber-Waspy Polo clothing line designed by Ralph Lauren. The jet set was going to discos and snorting cocaine, as depicted in the best-selling "brat pack" novels *Less Than Zero* and *Bright Lights, Big City*. TV viewers were watching consumption porn on Robin Leach's *Lifestyles of the Rich and Famous*. And Madonna was singing in her 1984 breakout hit "Material Girl," "You know that we are living in a material world."

The idealistic ethos of the 1960s, which disdained money-making for its own sake, gave way to a new ethos of professional advancement in the 1980s as surely as sandals, tie-dyes, and bellbottoms gave way to bouffant hairdos, Spandex leotards, and shoulder-padded suits. As historian Doug Rossinow shrewdly observed, the mood of the decade was captured in the 1981 comedy *Arthur* when the title character, a wealthy drunk played by Dudley Moore, is asked, "How does it feel to have all that money?" After a moment's reflection, Arthur replies, "It feels great." Another iconic line of the decade was delivered by Michael Douglas as the financier Gordon Gekko in Oliver Stone's 1987 movie *Wall Street*: "Greed, for lack of a better word, is good."

But while there was considerable excess, bad taste, and even criminality in the 1980s, there were also technological and entrepreneurial developments that would lead the country to new heights of well-being and global influence. The 1980s saw the spread of personal computers pioneered by IBM (*Time*'s "man of the year" in 1982 was a computer) and the emergence of two iconic American companies: Apple and Microsoft. Their leaders, Steve Jobs and Bill Gates, would become two of the most admired executives in the world.

Ronald Reagan both reflected and encouraged the materialistic mood of the 1980s by celebrating the achievements of American business, cutting taxes, and relaxing antitrust enforcement to enable a wave of mergers and acquisitions that destroyed some companies while allowing others to expand. Nancy Reagan, with her designer clothes, pricey china, and posh friends, did her part to encourage the conspicuous consumption of the decade. Reagan's critics would deride the 1980s as the "decade of greed," while his defenders would give him credit for engineering an economic expansion and laying the foundation for even greater affluence in the future.[10]

Prosperity, of course, was far from universal. Most of the gains in the 1980s went to the wealthy. The middle class stagnated, and those in poverty fell further behind, leading to a dramatic expansion of income inequality, a hollowing out of the middle class, and a growing political polarization between the haves and have-nots. In the 1980s, the after-tax incomes of the top 1 percent rose by 87.1 percent, while the incomes of the bottom decile fell by 10.4 percent.[11]

African Americans were one of the most prominent groups left behind. While the white unemployment rate in 1984 was just 6.5 percent, among Black workers it was 14.4 percent.[12] This was not all, or even mainly, the fault of the Reagan administration, but its cuts to social welfare programs disproportionately hurt the Black community. Twenty-six percent of Black households received Food Stamps, for example, compared to only 2 percent of white households.[13] So policies that removed half a million families from the welfare rolls, a million people from Food Stamps, and 2.6 million children from school lunch programs hit minorities especially hard.[14]

If Reagan was worried about the impact of these cutbacks, he gave little evidence of it. One of his paradoxes was that he could care about individuals he knew personally while being callous about larger groups that remained an abstraction to him. From 1984 to 1988, for example, he regularly corresponded with, and visited, his pen pal Rudolph "Rudy" Lee-Hines, a Black elementary school student in Southeast Washington, DC.[15] But he showed little awareness of the toll that his social spending cutbacks were taking on Rudy's community.

In one of his mental pirouettes, Reagan actually convinced himself that he was helping Black Americans by cutting government programs that benefited them. He subscribed to the views of conservative writers such as Charles Murray and George Gilder, who argued that welfare programs only made life worse for the "underclass" by encouraging single motherhood and discouraging work—creating what Reagan described as "a permanent culture of poverty."[16] This ignored evidence of the dramatic progress in reducing poverty achieved by LBJ's Great Society. Reagan was simply wrong to state, as he often did, that Johnson had declared "War on Poverty" and "poverty won the war." Of course, Johnson did not eliminate poverty. But the percentage of Americans living below the poverty line declined from 20 percent in 1968 to 12 percent in 1978.[17] Then came the recessions of 1980 and 1981–1982 and the Reagan cutbacks in social welfare reforms. The number of Americans living below the poverty line increased by 27 percent from 1979 to 1988, and homelessness became a national problem.[18]

The 1980s also witnessed the rise of a significant Black middle class, as portrayed on *The Cosby Show*, which began airing in 1984, but African Americans had much less cause than their white neighbors to celebrate Reagan's achievements. Many were angry over what they viewed as his attempts to roll back civil rights. "We do not admire their president," the Black novelist Alice Walker, author of *The Color Purple*, wrote in 1984. "We know why the White House is white."[19] A 1984 Gallup poll showed that 72 percent of Black voters thought Reagan was racially prejudiced compared to only 31 percent of white voters.[20]

Reagan always reacted indignantly to such accusations. He wrote, for example, to NAACP President Benjamin Hooks in 1983, "Ben, if only it were possible to look into each other's hearts and minds, you would find no trace of prejudice or bigotry in mine."[21] But no other person could possibly know what was really in Reagan's "heart and mind." African Americans judged the president by his actions and words, and those sent a more disturbing message than his impassioned avowals of colorblindness.

Ronald Reagan, after all, had risen to power by opposing civil rights legislation and embracing the white backlash—a strategy that culminated in his 1980 endorsement of "state's rights" in Philadelphia, Mississippi, near the site where three civil rights workers had been murdered by white-supremacist terrorists. The administration's point man on civil rights was William Bradford Reynolds, a conservative white ideologue and corporate lawyer who was appointed assistant attorney general for civil rights in spite of his lack of background in civil rights law. Reynolds's father was a country lawyer from Tennessee, and his mother was a DuPont heiress. He had attended Phillips Academy, Yale College, and Vanderbilt Law School, and showed little empathy for the concerns of the underprivileged. He later said, with astonishing insularity, that he did not realize that "civil rights is such an emotional subject for so many people."[22]

Reynolds insisted that he was seeking "the high moral ground of true nondiscrimination."[23] But his legions of critics had a less charitable description of his agenda. "During Reynolds' tenure, under the banner of color blindness," wrote journalist Ari Berman, "ending busing became more important than desegregating schools, dismantling quotas became more important than integrating the workforce or academia and preventing proportional representation became more important than achieving a multiracial government. Seemingly overnight, the priorities of the Civil Rights Division shifted dramatically."[24]

Solicitor General Charles Fried recalled that his Justice Department colleague "Brad" Reynolds had an "extreme emotional attachment" to "extreme positions." When Fried told him he would not argue before the Supreme Court that a consent decree requiring the Alabama State Police to hire African Americans was unconstitutional, the normally unemotional Reynolds "actually wept," Fried said. William Weld, a future governor of Massachusetts who ran the Justice Department's Criminal Division from 1986 to 1988, said that Reynolds was "so smart that he always thought of sixteen reasons why he wasn't a racist in doing something"—but Weld always suspected that his true motivations were rooted in bigotry.[25]

With senior White House aides distracted by other concerns and the attorneys general he served (in the first term William French Smith, in the second Ed Meese) sympathetic to his conservative outlook, Brad Reynolds managed to embroil the administration in one controversy after another. His lax record of civil rights enforcement would lead the Republican-majority Senate Judiciary Committee to narrowly reject his nomination in 1985 to the number-three position at Justice. Delegates at an NAACP convention in Dallas broke out in cheers when they heard the news. In response to the committee vote, Reagan issued a statement whose full import he may not have grasped: "Let me emphasize that Mr. Reynolds' civil rights views reflect my own," he said.[26]

While Brad Reynolds's hard-line views on civil rights came wrapped in a veneer of race-neutral language, others in the administration were more openly bigoted. Education Secretary Terrel Bell, who was labeled "Comrade Bell" by some administration conservatives for defending vigorous civil rights enforcement in education, reported that he heard mid-level White House staffers sneering at "Martin Lucifer Coon," calling Arabs "sand n——s," and referring to Title IX as "the lesbian's bill of rights."[27]

The administration's first civil rights contretemps occurred over the extension of the Voting Rights Act, which was set to expire in 1982. Reagan had opposed the legislation when it originally passed in 1965 and when it was first extended in 1975. The conservative Supreme Court had, by a five-to-four ruling, eviscerated the law in a 1980 decision which held that plaintiffs would have to prove discriminatory intent to prevail rather than simply discriminatory effects. There was bipartisan support in Congress for overturning the "intent" standard, which would have made it virtually impossible for the Justice Department to win voting rights cases. But Brad Reynolds and a brilliant young special assistant to the attorney general, future Supreme Court justice John G. Roberts, convinced Bill Smith to endorse the "intent" standard. Smith, in turn, won over his former client, Ronald Reagan, to the hard-line position.

Administration opposition did not prevent the Democratic-controlled House from overwhelmingly passing an extension of the Voting Rights Act that would overturn the "intent" standard. In the Senate, Bob Dole engineered a compromise, overturning the "intent" standard while making clear that lack of proportional representation was not itself a violation of the law. The Dole compromise passed with the support of eighty-five senators after a filibuster by Jesse Helms was broken. Reagan bowed to reality and in 1982 signed a twenty-five-year extension of the Voting Rights Act, knowing that a veto would have been overridden. But Reagan's reluctance to support the bill ensured that he received no political credit for it in the Black community.[28]

The Reagan administration faced another backlash after the Treasury and Justice Departments announced on January 8, 1982, that the IRS would no longer deny tax-exempt status to educational institutions such as Bob Jones University in South Carolina that engaged in racial discrimination. This move, reversing a policy that had been in effect since 1970, pleased South Carolina Senator Strom Thurmond and Mississippi Representative Trent Lott, who had lobbied to overturn the policy, but it outraged a wide spectrum of public opinion. "With its decision to grant a federal tax exemption to segregated private schools, the Reagan Administration has moved from a lack of interest in fighting racial discrimination to active promotion of it," charged the *New York Times* columnist Tom Wicker.[29]

Mike Deaver had been caught by surprise by the move, and he scrambled to find Black staffers who could explain to the president why this was such a bad decision. The best he could do, given the lack of high-level African American representation in the White House, was to round up two junior aides who normally had no contact with the president. They explained to Reagan how much outrage this decision had generated among Blacks. "The president was astounded," Deaver said. "Until that moment he didn't fully realize how this was being viewed." Reagan immediately said, "We can't let this stand. We have to do something."[30] On January 12, 1982, just four days after the initial announcement, the president endorsed legislation to deny tax exemption for schools that discriminated while claiming, wrongly, that the IRS did not have the authority to revoke Bob Jones University's tax exemption under current law.

At Brad Reynolds's insistence, the Justice Department refused to defend the IRS's previous ruling denying tax-exempt status to discriminatory institutions in a lawsuit filed by Bob Jones University. The Supreme Court had to appoint an outside attorney to argue on behalf of the IRS's long-standing policy.[31] Eventually, in 1983, the high court ruled eight to one that discriminatory schools were ineligible for tax exemption. The lone dissent was from Justice William Rehnquist, who as a Supreme Court clerk in 1952, two years before *Brown v. Board of Education*, had supported *Plessy v. Ferguson* and opposed mandating school desegregation under the Fourteenth Amendment. He later denied that the 1952 memorandum reflected his own views, but it clearly had; even into the 1990s, he continued to deny that the Fourteenth Amendment required integration in education.[32] In 1985, following the retirement of Warren Burger, Rehnquist would be elevated by President Reagan to the position of chief justice. Once again, in the Bob Jones case, the Reagan administration found itself on the wrong side of an incendiary racial issue.

It happened yet again in 1983 during the debate over whether the Reverend Martin Luther King Jr. should be honored with a national holiday. Efforts to celebrate the slain civil rights leader had long been stymied by conservative lawmakers who viewed him as a closet Communist and a philanderer to boot. Reagan, who had not attended King's funeral in 1968, tried to tread a middle path by publicly expressing admiration for King while claiming that a holiday would be too expensive. Privately, he shared the right-wing view of King as a dangerous subversive. But, despite the president's opposition, the House approved the holiday on August 2, 1983, by 338 to 90. Jesse Helms filibustered the bill in the Senate, but, on October 19, 1983, it was approved by the upper chamber, 78 to 22. All but four of the no votes in the Senate were cast by Republicans, showing how the two parties had effectively switched positions on racial issues since Barry Goldwater's 1964 campaign. Goldwater, of course, was one of the no votes.

Reagan had no choice but to sign the bill—it had passed by veto-proof majorities—but he was not happy about it. When asked by Sam Donaldson of ABC News about King's supposed Communist ties, he gave credence to the smear by cracking, "We'll know in about thirty-five years, won't we?"— meaning when FBI files would be declassified. ("Thirty-five years later," notes King biographer Jonathan Eig, "when the FBI released thousands of pages from its secret files on King, no evidence emerged to suggest that communist operatives controlled or manipulated King.")[33] Former New Hampshire governor Meldrim Thomson Jr., a member of the John Birch Society, compounded the damage by releasing a letter in which Reagan referred to King as "immoral." Reagan tried to quell the furor by phoning King's widow, Coretta Scott King, just before jetting off for his fateful golf weekend—the one where he decided to invade Grenada and learned of the Beirut bombing. He was playing, of course, at the all-white Augusta National Golf Club, which did not accept its first Black member until 1990.[34]

Little wonder, then, that the president had so little African American support. Dan J. Smith, a Black former White House staffer, wrote to one of Jim Baker's assistants in a previously unreported 1984 letter to explain why "most Black and many White Americans now view Ronald Reagan as a clear and present danger to the civil rights of minority Americans." Smith insisted that the president was no bigot but complained that "throughout our Administration civil rights has not been deemed a 'Presidential issue,'" that "there has been gross insensitivity at the Civil Rights Division of Justice," that there was "an apparent senior White House staff belief that outreach to Black America is illegitimate," and that many in the West Wing viewed "the very nature of the Reagan Administration . . . as fundamentally at odds with Black America."[35]

It was a damning indictment—all the more so coming from a Reagan loyalist—but there was little hope that Dan Smith's concerns would ever be adequately addressed. While a few centrist White House aides wanted to "make civil rights a *GOP* priority," it never happened.[36] "We're in such a deep hole on this one that it's hard to know what to do," David Gergen acknowledged.[37] From a purely political perspective, Ronald Reagan's handlers had long ago given up hope of winning a substantial number of Black votes. The campaign's chief interest in combating the image of him as a racist was to avoid alienating moderate white voters.

The core of the Reagan reelection strategy, as deputy campaign manager Lee Atwater explained, was to target "populists in the South and West" and "Archie Bunkers in the East and Midwest" who were suspicious of big business and big government. "These people are mostly former Democrats, typically blue-collar workers and small farmers," he wrote to Jim Baker. Campaign manager Ed Rollins acknowledged that while, "at its best, populism stands for self-reliance, decentralization, and open and responsive government . . . at its worst, populism is chauvinistic, xenophobic, paranoid, and racist." As Rollins noted, George Wallace was "the ultimate populist," and the Reagan campaign was again determined—just as in 1976 and 1980—to win over Wallace voters.[38]

It went without saying that this target group was not only white but also primed for coded racial appeals on issues such as crime, which was continuing to rise at an alarming rate in the 1980s. New York vigilante Bernhard Goetz, who in 1984 shot four Black teenagers who confronted him on a subway train, became a folk hero to many white Americans and served only eight months in prison.

During the 1980s, a bipartisan coalition of Democrats and Republicans passed, with Reagan's enthusiastic endorsement, a series of tough-on-crime bills such as the 1984 Comprehensive Crime Control Act and the 1986 Anti-Drug Abuse Act that lengthened prison sentences and militarized law enforcement. The number of incarcerated Americans nearly doubled during the Reagan years—from 315,974 in 1980 to 603,372 in 1988—and more than 40 percent of all new prisoners were Black at a time when Blacks made up only 12 percent of the population.[39] Part of the reason for the disparity was that Reagan-era laws meted out far harsher penalties for the possession of crack cocaine, used primarily by inner-city Blacks, than for more expensive powdered cocaine, used primarily by white Yuppies. Later, white opioid addicts would be regarded with a popular sympathy that had not been extended to Black crack addicts of the 1980s.

While many African Americans viewed the "war on crime" and the "war on drugs" as a war on their whole community, Reagan's tough-on-crime approach resonated with white voters terrified of crime. Employing the coded racial language he had used to appeal to white backlash voters since his first campaign in 1966, Reagan told police chiefs in 1981, "We must never forget *the jungle* is always there waiting to take us over. Only our deep moral values and our strong social institutions can hold back that jungle and restrain the *darker impulses* of human nature. . . . I commend you for manning the thin blue line that holds back a *jungle* which threatens to reclaim this clearing we call civilization" (italics added).[40]

Both white and Black voters got the message without the president employing any blatantly racist rhetoric. "The racial stuff was all sublimated, but it was there," David Gergen said. "You just sort of knew."[41] Reagan's toxic relations with the Black community would not impede the campaign juggernaut his team was assembling in 1984, but it would mar his presidential legacy. He missed a chance to demonstrate that he was the president of all Americans, not just white Americans.

46

"Don't Screw Up":
The 1984 Campaign

I was awful.

—RONALD REAGAN

The 1984 election was the ultimate referendum on the Reagan presidency. Win, and Ronald Reagan would earn the affirmation of becoming a two-term president. Lose, and he would be consigned to the political purgatory of one-term presidents, such as Jimmy Carter and Herbert Hoover, who had been humiliatingly repudiated by the voters.

The task of averting a premature end to the Reagan presidency was entrusted to the Reagan-Bush '84 committee. It was run from a plush Capitol Hill office building—much nicer, campaign staffer John B. Roberts II noted, than the "downright gritty" headquarters of the 1980 campaign in Arlington, Virginia.[1] But then an incumbent president found it much easier to raise money than a challenger.

Day-to-day operations were run by campaign manager Edward J. Rollin, a combative former boxer, and his ambitious and unscrupulous young deputy, Lee Atwater—a task complicated by their rivalry and lack of mutual trust.[2] Richard Wirthlin and Robert Teeter did the polling. Jim Baker, with the aid of his deputies Dick Darman and Margaret Tutwiler, provided oversight from the White House. Overall strategy was devised by the political consultant Stuart Spencer, the old pro from California who had the confidence of the Reagans and regularly shuttled between the campaign headquarters and the White House.[3]

The candidate himself had essentially no involvement in campaign decision-making. He met only briefly with the campaign's all-star Tuesday Team of advertising executives, popping into a meeting to announce, with his usual self-deprecating charm, "I figured if you're going to sell soap, you ought to see the bar."[4] Ronald Reagan wasn't one of those presidents, like Lyndon Johnson, Richard Nixon, or Bill Clinton, who was fascinated by political minutiae. He set the tone for both campaigning and governing with his speeches and expected his staff to do the rest. "You're sort of my director," he told Ed Rollins. "You tell me where you want me to be and what you want me to say and I'll say it."[5] From a political operative's perspective, he was a perfect candidate because he was, as his bosses had previously found in the entertainment industry, so docile and diligent. Unlike so many other stars in both Hollywood and Washington, his ego was firmly in check.

With the economy booming and the nation at peace, no candidate could have run for reelection in more favorable circumstances than Reagan encountered in 1984. While many in Washington saw Reagan as "a second-rate monarch," Canadian Ambassador Allan Gotlieb noted in his diary, "He has fouled up little.... The U.S. domestic scene is at peace, and Americans sense that they stand taller in the world, after Carter, Iran, and Watergate."[6] Reagan's job approval rating was over 50 percent at the beginning of 1984, up from just 35 percent a year earlier. The president had not drawn a primary challenger. The GOP was entirely and enthusiastically united behind him.

Meanwhile, the Democratic front-runner, Walter "Fritz" Mondale, an uncharismatic, old-fashioned liberal who had been Jimmy Carter's vice president, was facing unexpectedly stiff challenges from Gary Hart, a younger senator from Colorado with Kennedyesque good looks and "new ideas," and Jesse Jackson, a preternaturally eloquent civil rights activist who was mobilizing a "Rainbow Coalition" of minorities and white progressives. The candidate the Reagan team most feared—Ohio Senator John Glenn, a former astronaut who could tap into the same wellsprings of patriotism as the incumbent—flamed out early on. The Reagan campaign could husband its resources for the fall while the Democrats spent the first half of 1984 mauling each other.

The Reagan hands knew that all the indicators were in their favor. "The whole motto was, 'Don't screw this up,'" Stu Spencer remembered. "We knew we were gonna win if we didn't screw up. But win by the margin we did? I never imagined that was going to happen." That did not, however, stop Nancy Reagan from worrying. She drove Ed Rollins and Stu Spencer "crazy" with her nonstop questions and concerns.[7]

When Spencer was trying to figure out what the theme of the campaign should be, he asked Dick Darman what issues the administration was planning to focus on in a second term. "Issues?" Darman said. "We milked it dry. We got nothing." The administration had already achieved its top priorities—cutting domestic spending and taxes and increasing defense spending. "There was no second-term agenda," Ed Rollins acknowledged. So, without a policy platform to campaign on, Spencer realized "we had to capitalize on the good feelings Reagan had created. People were happy. People were doing well. We didn't have to throw new crap on the table."[8]

In lieu of new policy proposals, the campaign emphasized age-old themes of patriotism and nostalgia. "We should remember that President Reagan was elected to make America great again," Lee Atwater advised, citing the 1980 campaign slogan that would be recycled decades later by Donald Trump.[9]

The campaign's most famous commercial, created by the Tuesday Team, showed gauzy pictures of America—farmers working the fields, executives heading to work, a couple getting married—to the strains of sentimental music while a folksy narrator (the legendary ad man Hal Riney) intoned, "It's morning again in America, and under the leadership of President Reagan, our country is prouder and stronger and better. Why would we ever want to return to where we were less than four short years ago?" From the vantage point of forty years later, when the country has become considerably more diverse, it is striking that nearly all the people depicted were white, but this was not considered controversial at the time.[10] Dick Darman argued for a more forward-looking campaign, but nostalgia won out.[11]

In 1976, Reagan had criticized Jerry Ford for harnessing the power of the presidency for political purposes. In 1984, he did the same thing. Even his foreign travel that year was harnessed for electoral advantage. With the Soviet Union undergoing another leadership transition, the time wasn't right to visit Moscow, but in April 1984 the Reagans made a widely praised trip to Communist China to demonstrate that he was a peacemaker, not a warmonger. The president was relieved to be able to handle chopsticks after some tutoring; amazed to discover that China had mountains, forests, and lakes just like America; and wowed by his visit to the Great Wall—"a tremendously emotional experience." He returned from his six-day trip "heartened by some of the things that we saw," he said. "The Chinese have begun opening up their economy."[12]

Then in June it was off to Europe. The Reagans visited his ancestral homeland in Ireland (all the better to appeal to Irish American voters), a Group of Seven meeting in London, and commemorations in Normandy of the fortieth anniversary of D-Day. The backdrops were chosen, a White House document noted, to "be colorful and dramatic" for television coverage.[13]

The highlight of the trip—indeed, one of the highlights of his entire presidency—was Reagan's speech at Normandy. With sixty-two aging former Army Rangers sitting before him and the gray English Channel looming behind him, Reagan paid tribute to "the boys of Pointe du Hoc" who had stormed ashore on D-Day: "These are the men who took the cliffs. These are the champions who helped free a continent. These are the heroes who helped end a war."[14] Many, including some of the former Rangers, wept as the president spoke.

The event was designed to be "emotional, stirring, and personal," and it delivered. A former actor who had spent World War II on a studio backlot thus effectively identified himself with some of the greatest heroes of his generation. The words were written by Peggy Noonan; it was her "first really big speech," she recalled, and she went through fifteen drafts to make it "really good." The visuals were arranged by Mike Deaver; he ensured that the "trip photo" would be a carefully staged shot of the president and first lady walking among the tombstones at Normandy's American military cemetery. But the performance was quintessentially Reagan. He had a power to evoke patriotic sentiments with well-chosen words and pitch-perfect delivery rivaled by few other leaders.[15]

At the Mondale campaign office in Washington, policy director William Galston was one of those crying as he watched Reagan's Normandy address on television—and as he looked around the office, he saw others brushing away tears as well. With victories over Gary Hart in the New Jersey and West Virginia primaries, Mondale had secured the nomination that very day—normally a cause for celebration. But, Galston said, "It was at that moment that I understood that our candidate was up against an irresistible force—a talented politician and superb orator, backed by a staff that knew how to present his strengths to best advantage—and that our cause was probably lost."[16]

The following month, on July 28, 1984, Reagan traveled to his adopted hometown, Los Angeles, to open the Summer Olympics. The Soviet bloc boycotted the games to retaliate for the US boycott of the 1980 Moscow Olympics. But that simply allowed the US team, led by sprinter Carl Lewis and gymnast Mary Lou Retton, to top the medal count for the first time since 1968. That, in turn, created a patriotic frenzy that carried over into the Republican National Convention in Dallas in August. Country-music star Lee Greenwood sang "God Bless the USA," and the delegates interrupted Reagan's acceptance speech with Olympic-style chants of "USA! USA! USA!" "First the Olympics, now this," one delegate told a reporter. "I'm just OD'ing on pride in America."[17]

If Reagan needed any more help, it was provided by Mondale himself. At the Democratic convention in San Francisco in July, the Democratic nominee blundered in trying to capitalize on the record budget deficit—one of Reagan's few vulnerabilities. "By the end of my first term I will cut the deficit by two-thirds," he vowed. "Let's tell the truth. Mr. Reagan will raise taxes, and so will I. He won't tell you. I just did." Even Tip O'Neill couldn't believe what he was hearing. "It was a terrible mistake," he acknowledged. Ed Rollins chortled, "We might as well have written that part of his speech ourselves."[18] In truth, Reagan had raised taxes repeatedly and would do so again—but he only spoke of cutting, not raising, taxes. Mondale had violated the first rule of Tax Club: Never talk about Tax Club.

Mondale, a cautious, career politician, was so far behind that he tried an uncharacteristically bold gamble by selecting Representative Geraldine Ferraro of Queens, New York, as the first woman to be a major party vice-presidential nominee. "Mondale blindsided us with his choice of Ferraro," a Reagan campaign operative admitted. An opposition-research team at the Reagan campaign scrambled to unearth—and leak to the news media—information showing that Ferraro had inaccurately filled out congressional financial disclosure forms and that she and her husband had organized-crime ties. Roy Cohn—the soon-to-be-disbarred lawyer who represented mobsters and had helped the Reagan campaign in 1980 by allegedly paying off the New York Liberal Party—first brought the mafia allegations to the campaign. But the effort to bring down Ferraro, although demanded by a perpetually nervous Nancy Reagan, turned out to be entirely unnecessary.[19] Her selection provided only a fleeting boost to the Democratic ticket. An NBC News poll in mid-August 1984, a month after the Democratic Convention, showed Mondale-Ferraro trailing Reagan-Bush by twenty-three points.[20]

Mondale's last chance to catch up would come in the two presidential debates scheduled for the fall. Incumbent presidents often do badly in their initial debate because they have gotten out of practice, and Reagan was no exception. At the first debate in Louisville on October 7, Ed Rollins conceded, "He came across as old, tired and bit befuddled. He groped for words, lost his train of thought, and mangled his closing soliloquy." At one point, Reagan even said, "I'm all confused now." "He was lost," Mondale thought. "It was actually a little frightening."[21]

To Reagan's credit, he was clear-eyed about what had happened. When he asked Stu Spencer how he had done, Spencer answered diplomatically, "Well, you didn't do bad." "You're crazy," Reagan replied. "I was awful." In his diary, he conceded, "I have to say I lost. . . . I didn't feel good about myself."[22]

While the president accepted responsibility for the debate disaster, the first lady tried to pin the blame, as she was wont to do, on his aides, claiming they had overprepared him. After talking with Nancy Reagan, Paul Laxalt told reporters, "The president was . . . brutalized by his own aides." In truth, Spencer recalled spending the previous weekend with the Reagans at Camp David. Every time Spencer entered their cabin, he saw the debate briefing book in the same place. "He hadn't touched the briefing book," Spencer said. "He hadn't done his damn homework."[23]

But Nancy wanted a scapegoat, and she tried to fire Dick Darman, who had been in charge of debate preparation. Darman insisted he had only given the president what he wanted—Reagan kept demanding more "factual material" to rebut all of Mondale's "accusations"—and that it was the president's own fault for not practicing his closing statement. As if he were a player in a real-life episode of *House of Cards*, Darman, who knew all the White House secrets, went to Laxalt and threatened to cause serious embarrassment if he were fired. "Paul," he recalled saying, "I want you to know that I'm happy to make my fair responsibility for this, and then some.

But there's a limit. . . . If somebody tries to go beyond the limit I'm not going to respond too well."[24]

Darman kept his job. But could Reagan keep his?

Reagan's poor performance in the first debate revived the "age issue": At seventy-three, was he too old and too out of it to be president? At the final debate, in Kansas City on October 21, Henry Trewhitt of the *Baltimore Sun* artfully raised this issue by asking whether Reagan would have the stamina to go "days on end with very little sleep" as John F. Kennedy had done during the Cuban Missile Crisis. "Is there any doubt in your mind that you would be able to function in such circumstances?" he asked.

"Not at all, Mr. Trewhitt," Reagan replied with a trademark shake of his head, the hint of a smile on his lips. "And I want you to know that also I will not make age an issue in this campaign. I am not going to exploit, for political purposes, my opponent's youth and inexperience."[25]

The audience broke into loud laughter and applause. Even Mondale had to laugh at "one of the great lines in the history of presidential debate." "I knew in that moment that we were in trouble," he later wrote.[26]

The killer quip was crafted personally by a candidate who had a history of winning debates with perfectly timed ripostes of his own devising. (The prepared one-liners that Jim Baker suggested before the debate—for example, "Soviet conduct seems to baffle Mr. Mondale, but it doesn't baffle anyone else"—were not nearly as effective.)[27] Reagan had done it in 1980, after all, with "I am paying for this microphone, Mr. Green" and "There you go again." Even in his mid-seventies, Ronald Reagan was still the "Great Communicator."

Sixteen days later, on November 6, 1984, Reagan won in a historic landslide. He took nearly 59 percent of the vote, 525 out of 538 electoral votes, and 49 of 50 states. Mondale only won his native Minnesota and the District of Columbia. Reagan got just 10 percent of the Black vote but 66 percent of the white vote—and white voters made up 86 percent of the electorate. He even won among union households.[28]

It was one of the most lopsided margins in US history, ranking with his erstwhile hero Franklin Roosevelt's 1936 defeat of Alf Landon. Reagan got an even higher percentage of the electoral college votes than Richard Nixon had in 1972 or Lyndon Johnson in 1964. But the candidate's coattails were short: While Republicans picked up sixteen House seats, they lost two Senate seats. Control of the two chambers remained unchanged, with Republicans in charge of the Senate and Democrats of the House. Some Republicans wondered if more of their candidates might have been elected if the president had campaigned harder on the issues rather than turning the election into a referendum on his personal popularity.

The Reagans watched the election returns, as they had in the past, at the Bel-Air mansion of steel magnate and Kitchen Cabinet member Earle Jorgensen and his wife, Marion. This was followed by a victory party at the modernist, arc-shaped Century Plaza hotel, the favored hostelry of Los Angeles Republicans. A few days later, the newly reelected president was able to put politics behind him, at least temporarily, and do what he loved best. He and Nancy went to their sprawling, spartan ranch on November 8, 1984, and he merrily spent three days doing chores such as "cutting up a couple of downed Oak Trees & splitting the wood," sweating alongside his blue-collar pals Barney Barnett and Dennis LeBlanc.[29]

When he returned to the nation's capital, the president would have the momentous task of figuring out what to do next, cognizant that a second term had proven the undoing of the last two presidents to win one—Johnson and Nixon. The campaign had provided few clues to either voters or aides of how the administration would handle the next four years. But if the reelection campaign was relatively placid and uneventful, the second term would be anything but. No one could have anticipated the soaring highs and extreme lows to come in the next four years—most of them in the realm of foreign policy, which the White House had been so careful to steer clear of in the administration's early years.

47

Hail to the Chief (of Staff)

Regan never understood that the job of chief of staff
is to be chief of staff, not chief of everything.

—JIM BAKER

onald Reagan was entering into a second term in a nation transformed in a multitude of ways over the past four years. By 1985,
the traumas of the 1970s—the Vietnam War, Watergate, gasoline
lines, "stagflation," the Iran hostage crisis—seemed to belong to the distant
past, and even the severe recession of 1981–1982 was fast fading into history. American-backed insurgents were battling Soviet-supported regimes
in Afghanistan, Angola, and Nicaragua, but US troops were not fighting
anywhere in the world, and the threat of nuclear war was receding after
the multiple crises of 1983, "the year of living dangerously." The country
had regained its confidence and swagger, thanks in part to the policies and
pageantry orchestrated by the genial former actor who had made the job of
being president look deceptively easy.

Due to factors beyond the White House's control, however, Reagan's
second inaugural ceremony did not deliver the pomp and production values the nation had come to expect after four years of made-for-television
extravaganzas. Because January 20, 1985, fell on a Sunday, Chief Justice
Warren Burger, a white-haired Nixon appointee with an air of gravitas,
administered the oath privately to the president and vice president at the
White House just a few hours before the San Francisco 49ers defeated the
Miami Dolphins in the Super Bowl. The massive inauguration ceremony
planned for the next day on the West Front of the Capitol was scrapped
because of arctic weather. It was just seven degrees Fahrenheit at noon—
the coldest temperature ever recorded for an inauguration.[1] If the sunlight that shone on Reagan during his first inaugural was symbolic, so, in
a different way, was the deep chill that greeted his second term. He delivered his second inaugural address inside the Capitol rotunda before 1,000

select guests rather than the 140,000 scheduled to be present outside. The planned parade down Pennsylvania Avenue was moved to the Capitol Centre in Landover, Maryland, home to Washington's professional basketball and hockey teams.

The inaugural address itself unveiled no new policies but had all the patriotic, feel-good chords that Reagan could strike as expertly and effortlessly as Louis Armstrong could play the trumpet. As usual, he expressed reverence for America ("In this blessed land, there is always a better tomorrow") combined with abhorrence of its government, which he would lead for four more years. "We must never again abuse the trust of working men and women," he said, "by sending their earnings on a futile chase after the spiraling demands of a bloated Federal Establishment." Reagan ended with a paean to "the dream of freedom," claiming that America was called by God "to pass that dream on to a waiting and hopeful world."[2] He would have far more success, far faster, in turning that dream into reality at the global level than any of his listeners could reasonably have expected on that frigid day in early 1985.

The end of a president's first term marks a natural dividing line when there is usually a substantial turnover of personnel as burned-out aides exit for the private sector to be replaced by energized newcomers drawn to power. This can often result in the "A team" giving way to the second string. That was certainly the case in the Reagan administration: By the beginning of his second term, the president's team was substantially weaker than it had been at the end of the first term.

Treasury Secretary Donald Regan had been chafing throughout the first term at the ascendancy of the White House staff over the cabinet. "I've sat over here for four years being ordered around by assholes like you at the White House," he told White House political director Ed Rollins. "I've learned that's where the power is."[3] Having previously been a CEO on Wall Street—he had enjoyed a long and successful run at Merrill Lynch—Regan now wanted to be the chief executive in Washington as well.

He knew that Jim Baker was burned out, so shortly after the 1984 election he suggested they swap jobs. Knowing that the top cabinet posts were more prestigious and less grueling than being White House chief of staff, Baker jumped at the chance to become Treasury secretary. He enlisted

Mike Deaver to sell the idea first to Nancy Reagan and then, once they had her blessing, to her husband.

When they finally brought the idea to the Oval Office on January 7, 1985, Deaver quipped, "Mr. President, I've finally found you a playmate your own age."[4] (Don Regan was about to turn sixty-six.) Regan was stunned by the president's passivity: He asked almost no questions and approved the momentous job switch in a meeting that lasted all of thirty minutes. "He seemed to be absorbing a *fait accompli*, rather than making a decision," Regan marveled.[5] He would soon learn that this was typical of Reagan's hands-off management style.

Bud McFarlane, who stayed on as national security adviser, had already learned he would not get much feedback from the president. After the election, he had his staff prepare twelve extensive studies on possible foreign policy priorities for the second term. He asked the president "to select the most important issues for us to focus on." But he couldn't get Reagan to focus. Finally, while flying on Air Force One, the president told him, "I think these are just terrific ideas. Let's do them all!"[6]

The president was amenable to the Baker-Regan job swap because he had always gotten along well with the Treasury secretary, who had a nearly identical last name. Both of their families came from Ireland, and they speculated that they were related. "Reagan and I hardly knew each other as men," Regan observed, but the new chief of staff, the son of a Boston cop, was precisely the kind of conservative, self-made millionaire with whom the president, himself a Horatio Alger character come to life, liked to associate. The Kitchen Cabinet was full of such self-made men. The two of them swapped Irish jokes and complaints about high taxes. "Even on the basis of our limited personal contacts," Regan wrote, "Reagan and I had developed an easy rapport."[7]

While Regan got along well with the president, he lacked any of the essential qualifications for the second most important position in the entire government. He certainly did not possess Jim Baker's sure political instincts and talent for cultivating both lawmakers and the press—two of the most powerful constituencies in Washington. Regan, in fact, held both reporters and members of Congress in contempt because they were not nearly as wealthy as he was. He liked to brag that he was worth $30 million and sneered that Senate Majority Leader Bob Dole, a career politician, "would starve to death on the outside." Regan, Ed Rollins said, "had the worst political instincts that anybody ever had." The president's son Ron Reagan put it this way: "My own feeling about Don Regan is that he may have been very capable at all sorts of things, but that he was a bit of a prick. Don Regan had to be the smartest guy in the room. Don Regan had to be the boss. Don Regan had to tell you how it was."[8]

Don Regan would turn out to be the most abrasive and unpopular chief of staff since H. R. "Bob" Haldeman in the Nixon White House. And Regan was not smart enough or secure enough to hire strong, smart aides who could make up for his deficiencies. Instead, he surrounded himself with loyal, low-profile subordinates he brought over from the Treasury. They were nicknamed "the mice" because of the way they scurried around carrying out "the chief's" diktats, often causing offense to staunch Reaganites. Speechwriter Peggy Noonan was irate about "the mice" nibbling away at her prose: "I'm a good speechwriter," she complained. "I write interesting speeches. I think a boring speech is an insult. I understand rhetoric. [David] Chew, [Dennis] Thomas, [Thomas] Dawson, et al, do not have sufficient literary and communications talents to edit my speeches adequately."[9]

Regan disbanded the Legislative Study Group, which had guided the Reagan agenda through Congress in the first term, and turned over the crucial job of communications director, once occupied by savvy centrist David Gergen, to former Nixon speechwriter Patrick J. Buchanan, who was far more combative and conservative.[10] No ideologue himself, Regan apparently hoped that Buchanan would shield him from the kind of right-wing blowback Jim Baker had endured.[11] Besides Buchanan, the only other high-profile staffer in the West Wing was Bud McFarlane, and Regan undercut him relentlessly, even spreading false rumors that the national security adviser was having an affair with NBC News correspondent Andrea Mitchell.[12]

There would be no more clashes among the Troika—but also no check on the erratic judgment of the White House chief of staff. "People chafed at having Don as the majordomo," Regan's aide David Chew recalled. "They were used to having more than one channel to try to get their ideas across."[13]

Regan's arrogance was monumental, his understanding of politics minimal. It was a bad combination. "Regan never understood that the job of chief of staff is to be chief of *staff*, not chief of everything," Jim Baker told me.[14] Regan became the first White House chief of staff to demand his own Secret Service detail, and he became notorious for elbowing his way into pictures with the president. When Reagan entered the naval hospital in Bethesda,

Maryland, in July 1985 for the removal of a cancerous polyp, Regan insisted on flying there by helicopter, while everyone else, including the first lady, went by car. He even had a new flagstone patio installed outside his office that was bigger than the one outside the Oval Office.

His presumptuousness grated on the first lady, and Regan made no effort to cultivate her—a fatal mistake in this administration. "He was an old-fashioned guy," said Regan aide Peter Wallison. "He didn't think much of women being involved in politics or defense policy or things like that."[15]

Dealing with Nancy Reagan had been the job of Mike Deaver, but he, too, was on the way out. He was exhausted after the first term and eager to make more money than his modest White House salary of $60,662 a year. (After leaving the White House, he opened a public relations shop and triggered an influence-peddling scandal.) He was also suffering from alcoholism that he hid from all those around him. By the end of his time in the White House, he was putting away a fifth of Scotch a day. At the end of January 1985, he would land in the hospital with kidney failure aggravated by hypertension and heavy alcohol consumption. "I had to get out of there," Deaver said. "I was a sick guy."[16]

A few weeks before being hospitalized, Deaver informed the president that he was going to leave in the spring. Now that he was almost out the door, this was the first time he ever called his boss "Ron" to his face rather than "Governor" or "Mr. President."[17] Yet the president did not reach out to buck up Deaver in his struggles with alcoholism and the legal system.[18] Outwardly affable, Reagan was remote even from those closest to him. "Ed, you've got to understand," longtime aide Joe Holmes explained to Ed Rollins, "Ronald Reagan can get along without anybody. Probably not Nancy but anyone else."[19]

Only as he was leaving did Deaver confide in Don Regan one of the most closely guarded secrets in the White House: that Nancy Reagan, terrified of any harm coming to her Ronnie after the assassination attempt, consulted with a mysterious personage in San Francisco whom she referred to only as "my friend" in scheduling the president's personal appearances. This was the astrologer Joan Quigley, a Vassar graduate with scientific pretensions, who was paid for her service as if she were a therapist or attorney.

While Nancy later tried to play down the court astrologer's carefully concealed influence, Quigley boasted, "I was responsible for timing all press conferences, most speeches, the State of the Union addresses, the takeoffs and landings of Air Force One."[20] It was far-fetched for Quigley to claim credit for changing "the relations between the superpowers" and other policy achievements, but she did know more about the president's movements well in advance than all but a few top aides—and she did not have a security clearance. The Secret Service would have been apoplectic if they had known. It would now be Don Regan's job to reconcile the demands of the presidency with the signs from the stars. Unfortunately, he lacked Deaver's patience for the first lady's foibles.

"My departure marked a virtual clean sweep of the original Reagan management team," Deaver noted.[21] Ed Meese had been nominated to be attorney general, and, after having his nomination delayed by a special counsel investigation into his financial dealings, he was finally confirmed in 1985 after the prosecutor decided not to press charges. Dick Darman was heading with Jim Baker over to Treasury as deputy secretary. David Stockman left after completing his final budget in August 1985 and, like so many other ambitious people in the 1980s, went into investment banking. Legislative director Max Friedersdorf and political director Ed Rollins departed in the fall of 1985. Even Bill Clark, who had been serving as Interior secretary, was heading home to California. The only person left in the White House who was close to the president was the first lady. He would begin his second term surrounded by virtual strangers.

By no coincidence, the second term began with what Don Regan described as "an appalling public relations disaster."[22] Its origins lay in a November 1984 meeting between Reagan and Germany's conservative chancellor Helmut Kohl. Kohl asked Reagan to visit a German military cemetery as a gesture of reconciliation on the fortieth anniversary of the end of World War II. Reagan agreed to do so while on a visit to Germany in spring 1985 to attend the Group of Seven summit in Bonn. In February 1985, Deaver led an advance team to scout the Bitburg cemetery, which was chosen by the German government for the presidential visit. "We literally could not see the pitfalls," Deaver wrote. "It was February. The graves, most of the markers, were covered by blankets of snow."[23]

On April 12, 1985, one day after the president's trip was announced, the media reported that buried at Bitburg, along with regular Wehrmacht soldiers, were forty-seven members of the notorious Waffen SS. This triggered outrage from veterans' and Jewish groups. The renowned writer Elie Wiesel, a Holocaust survivor, denounced the planned visit while at the White House to receive a Congressional Gold Medal from the president. "That place, Mr. President, is not your place," he said. "Your place is with the victims of the SS."[24]

A majority of the House and Senate, many White House aides, and even the first lady urged Reagan to find another site to visit. "I pleaded with Ronnie to cancel the trip," Nancy wrote. But Kohl implored Reagan to keep his promise, warning that if he backed out, it would be, as Reagan recorded in his diary, "a disaster in his country & an insult to the German people." Reagan, who could be stubborn as a mule and loyal to a fault, refused to budge. "There is no way I'll back down & run for cover," he insisted.[25] He had, of course, backed down on a number of policies, but he hated to break his word once he had given it to a friend or ally.

Deaver did his best to manage the fallout during his final days in the White House. As a first step, Deaver made sure "to keep Pat Buchanan the hell out of it." The communications director was arguing, he recalled, "for a harder line" and "virtually an amnesty for the Third Reich" to show that Reagan wasn't "succumbing to the pressure of the Jews," as Buchanan scribbled on a note. Buchanan, who regularly protested the deportation of accused Nazi war criminals, even told a Jewish delegation to start thinking like Americans rather than Jews. Reagan, unlike Buchanan, was untainted by any charges of antisemitism, but he did little to rein in his communications director—or any other staff member. [26]

Deaver worked to minimize the damage by organizing a presidential visit to the Bergen-Belsen concentration camp, where Anne Frank had died, on the same day as Bitburg. Reagan would speak at the concentration camp and later at the US air base in Bitburg, and he would be accompanied by a German general and an American general who had fought on opposite sides.

As was so often the case, Reagan salvaged something positive from the controversy with a powerful speech, this one penned by Ken Khachigian, the wordsmith called in from California for special occasions such as the first inaugural address. At Bergen-Belsen, Reagan struggled to keep his composure while reading a snippet from Anne Frank's diary. "Here, death ruled," he said, "but we've learned something as well. Because of what happened, we found that death cannot rule forever, and that's why we're here today. We're here because humanity refuses to accept that freedom of the spirit of man can ever be extinguished."[27]

Richard Nixon, never one to worry about morality in foreign policy, commended Reagan's handling of the controversy. "The real test of the skipper of the ship of state is how he navigates the rough seas—not the smooth ones," the thirty-seventh president wrote to the fortieth. "You have passed that test superbly."[28]

It was not exactly a political triumph, but it was at least a credible job of limiting the damage from a political blunder that had needlessly paralyzed the White House for a crucial month at the start of the new term. The Bitburg controversy revealed Reagan's stubbornness—or, from another perspective, his devotion to principle—in standing by an unpopular decision. But his relations with the Soviet Union beginning that same year would show an impressive and unexpected willingness to adapt his thinking to changing circumstances.

48

"We Can Do Business Together"

[We] had truly made a start.

—MIKHAIL GORBACHEV

Konstanin Chernenko, the infirm leader of the Soviet Union, breathed his last on March 10, 1985, after little more than a year in office. Within twenty-four hours, the Politburo chose a far more youthful, vigorous, and intelligent replacement from its own ranks. The fifty-four-year-old Mikhail Sergeyevich Gorbachev would turn out to be that rarest of leaders, a true "black swan": He rose to the top of a totalitarian system yet would lose faith in that system and go on to dismantle it. He would, in fact, turn out to be the last leader of the USSR. The only comparable leader in modern history was F. W. de Klerk, who dismantled apartheid in South Africa. By contrast, dictators such as North Korea's Kim Jong Un or Venezuela's Nicolás Maduro, who maintained the repressive systems they inherited, are commonplace.

Those who argue that Ronald Reagan brought down the "evil empire" usually focus on Gorbachev's ascension as the turning point, crediting the American president and his defense buildup with the selection of a reformer as secretary general of the Soviet Communist Party. "In a very real sense," asserted the conservative polemicist Peter Schweizer, "Gorbachev owed his selection to the pressures Reagan was exerting on the Soviet system."[1] The problem with this theory is that no one in early 1985—not even Gorbachev himself—knew how radical a reformer he would turn out to be. If his colleagues on the Politburo *had* known, they likely would not have selected him. They had no desire to end the Soviet empire—or their own power and privileges.

While Gorbachev privately told his stylish wife, Raisa, "We can't go on living like this anymore," he remained a dedicated Leninist and generally concealed his reformist impulses from his comrades. In taking power, he told the Politburo, "We must not change our policy. It is a true, correct and genuinely Leninist policy. We have to raise the tempo, move forward, expose shortcomings and overcome them, and see our bright future clearly."[2] In other words, Gorbachev presented himself as someone who would run the existing Soviet system more effectively—not transform it radically. "Thus," wrote the eminent Sovietologist Archie Brown, "his colleagues in the Soviet leadership had very little notion of the policies he would pursue, and in foreign policy least of all. The idea, sometimes mooted, that the Politburo consciously picked a 'soft-liner' because they were so worried by Reagan's hard-line policy is devoid of substance."[3] Indeed, two scholars who have studied Soviet archives have concluded that Reagan's first-term pressure on Moscow was actually counterproductive "by providing opponents of reform with arguments against better relations with the West and relaxation of internal controls."[4]

Gorbachev was not driven to reform the Soviet system because he wanted to compete more effectively with the Reagan defense buildup. Just the opposite. He was genuinely worried about the dangers of nuclear war, and he was appalled by how much money the Soviet Union was spending on its military-industrial complex—an estimated 20 percent of GDP and 40 percent of the state budget. He wanted to end the arms race to lessen the risk of nuclear annihilation and to redirect defense resources to improve the living standards of ordinary Soviet citizens.[5]

This was not a reflection of a Reagan-induced crisis that threatened the bankruptcy of the Soviet Union but rather a product of his own humane instincts. "When Gorbachev became general secretary in 1985," wrote historian Chris Miller, "the Soviet economy was wasteful and poorly managed, but it was not in crisis." The Soviet regime, having survived Stalinist terror, famine, and industrialization, followed by World War II and de-Stalinization, could have survived the stagnation of the mid-1980s, as did other Communist regimes such as China, Cuba, Vietnam, and North Korea, all of which were poorer than the USSR. Indeed, from 1985 to 1989, the Soviet Union was able to borrow from Western capital markets at rates similar to those of Portugal, Belgium, and Canada, suggesting that investors were not worried about its staying power.[6]

There was nothing inevitable about the Soviet collapse, and it was not the product of Reagan's efforts to spend more on the military and to curb Soviet expansionism abroad. It was the unanticipated and unintended consequence of the increasingly radical reforms implemented by Gorbachev over the objections of his more conservative comrades, who finally tried to overthrow him in 1991. The Soviet Union would break up not because it was economically bankrupt but because Gorbachev recognized that it was morally bankrupt, and he refused to hold it together by force. If any other member of the Politburo had taken power in 1985, the Soviet Union might still exist and the Berlin Wall might still stand, as does the DMZ dividing North Korea from South Korea.

How did Gorbachev become so radicalized? What led him to undertake bold experiments in restructuring the state-run economy (*perestroika*) and opening the political system to dissent and eventually democracy (*glasnost*)? The short explanation is that he was an unusually decent and intelligent person who perceived the failures of the Soviet system and was determined to do something about them even if it meant diminishing his own power. He was, however, deluded in thinking initially that the Leninist system could survive his radical reforms.

Like Ronald Reagan, Gorbachev came from a small town in an agricultural region whose inhabitants were often looked down upon by big-city sophisticates. "Misha" had been born into a peasant family on March 2, 1931, in southern Russia, with a port wine–colored birthmark on his head (in Russian folklore, a sign of the devil). Both of his grandfathers were arrested on spurious charges during the Stalinist purges of the 1930s, and his maternal grandfather was tortured into a confession that he was a Trotskyite counterrevolutionary. So Misha grew up with a visceral awareness of the injustice of the Stalinist regime.

Gorbachev was reared in far greater poverty and privation than even Dutch Reagan had known. His family initially lived in a two-room adobe hut, shared with his paternal grandparents, that had earthen floors and no running water. The children slept atop a big stove. Unlike Tampico, Illinois, the Gorbachevs' village, Privolnoye, had no electricity, no radio, no telephone. There was not even enough to eat: Famine struck in 1932, 1944, and 1946. And the Germans came in 1941, when Misha was just ten years old.

Privolnoye was occupied for nearly five months by the Nazis. Misha's father, Sergei, a tractor driver with only four years of formal education, was away from home fighting for four years and was seriously wounded. Indeed, for a year the family thought he was dead. Yet Gorbachev, like Reagan, emerged from a difficult and bleak childhood with a sunny, optimistic outlook—and, also like Reagan, an aversion to war. Dutch had been deeply affected by World War I, Misha by World War II.

Misha's strong-willed mother, Maria, was illiterate but insisted, like Nelle Reagan, that her son get an education. Misha was a better student and harder worker than Dutch; he would grow up to be an intellectual. But in other ways, the two men were alike. Like Dutch, Misha showed leadership potential early on—in his case as a leader in the Komsomol, or Youth Communist League—and a flair for acting in school plays. Both men also won acclaim as teenagers. While Dutch earned headlines in his hometown newspaper for saving lives on the Rock River, Misha earned the Red Banner of Labor, one of the USSR's highest awards, for helping his father break harvesting records.

Dutch left the Midwest for Los Angeles in 1937. Misha made a similarly momentous move to the big city thirteen years later. In 1950, he enrolled at Moscow State University, the Yale, Harvard, and Princeton of the Soviet Union all rolled into one. There he earned a law degree, became close friends with one of the future leaders of the 1968 "Prague Spring," and married Raisa Titarenko, a fellow student who eventually earned a doctorate and became a social scientist. Mikhail and Raisa would have a famously long and contented marriage similar to Ronald and Nancy Reagan's. And just as Nancy was Ronnie's closest adviser, so too was Raisa to Misha.

Gorbachev became a full member of the Communist Party in 1952 and enthusiastically embraced Khrushchev's de-Stalinization efforts. After graduation, he returned to his native Stavropol region where he steadily rose as a party functionary while also acquiring a second university degree in agriculture. Unlike many other party officials, he was not a backslapper— but neither was he corrupt nor a drunkard.

By 1970, he had become first secretary of Stavropol at the age of just thirty-nine. In 1978, he moved to Moscow as a secretary of the Central Committee dealing with agriculture. In 1979 he became a candidate member of the Politburo—the top decision-making body—and in 1980 a full member. He was a protégé of KGB boss Yuri Andropov, who was also from Stavropol and admired the younger man's vigor and intelligence. The secret police chief had some desire to reform the economy, but he was no liberal; he certainly would never have dissolved the Soviet empire as Gorbachev was to do.

Andropov had wanted Gorbachev to succeed him but died before he could make it happen. But, after missing out on the top spot in 1984, Gorbachev became de facto second secretary and successor in waiting to the sickly Chernenko. It was his seniority within the Soviet leadership, even as a relatively young man, that ensured his takeover—not pressure from the Reagan administration.

Gorbachev's privileged status allowed him to read subversive books and periodicals not normally available to Soviet citizens and to make foreign trips that others could not. He became enchanted by the greater freedom and higher standard of living he found in Western Europe during five trips in the 1970s. Those impressions were reinforced by trips to Canada in 1983 and to Italy and Britain in 1984. In Britain, Gorbachev spent more than five hours meeting with the Iron Lady at the prime minister's country residence, Chequers. Thatcher was impressed by how different Gorbachev was from the usual run of robotic apparatchiks. That Gorbachev traveled with Raisa was itself unusual; Soviet officials customarily left their wives at home. Gorbachev showed Thatcher a map of Soviet missile targets in Britain and said, "Prime Minister, we need to stop with all this, as soon as possible." Thatcher emerged with a surprising judgment: "I like Mr. Gorbachev. We can do business together."[7]

Now Thatcher just had to convince her fellow anti-Communist, Ronald Reagan, that Gorbachev was a different kind of Communist. Many within the US administration and at the CIA were skeptical. Hard-liners such as Caspar Weinberger and Jeane Kirkpatrick refused to believe that a genuine reformer could have risen to the top of the Soviet system. But Thatcher, because of her friendship with Reagan and her conservative credentials, was a powerful advocate for the opposing viewpoint. A few days after meeting Gorbachev, "Margaret" traveled to Camp David in December 1984 to share her impressions with "Ron." She praised Gorbachev as "an unusual Russian in that he was much less constrained, more charming, open to discussion and debate, and did not stick to prepared notes." "Basic Soviet policy has not changed," she emphasized, but she implied that it could if Gorbachev took over.[8]

Gorbachev's ascension gave the upper hand in the Reagan administration to the pragmatic faction that was anxious to thaw Cold War tensions. "For more than a year," Bud McFarlane wrote, "George Shultz, George Bush and I—and, for different reasons, Mike Deaver and Nancy Reagan—had been nurturing a change in President Reagan's attitude toward engaging with the Soviet Union." The first fruits of that effort had been evident in the "Ivan and Anya" speech in January 1984. Reagan had long been eager to meet a Soviet leader, but, as he complained to Nancy, "How am I supposed to get anyplace with the Russians, if they keep dying on me?" The best he could manage was an Oval Office meeting in September 1984 with the "stern and forbidding" Soviet Foreign Minister Andrei Gromyko, a champion of the old order who had been in office since 1957, when Reagan had still been a GE pitchman.[9]

With a vigorous, younger leader now in charge of the Soviet Union, Reagan wasted no time in proposing a summit. In a letter delivered by Vice President Bush and Secretary of State Shultz when they attended Chernenko's funeral, he invited the new Soviet leader "to visit me in Washington" for "serious negotiations." Gorbachev responded with a "positive attitude" toward a summit, but he did not want to make it appear as if he were "paying court to Reagan," so rather than coming to America, he suggested meeting at a neutral site. By July 1985, they had agreed to meet in Geneva in the fall.[10]

Reagan was so determined to improve relations that he refused to be knocked off course when on March 24, 1985, Soviet sentries in East Berlin shot and killed a US military officer, Major Arthur Nicholson, who was photographing Soviet military equipment, as he was legally allowed to do under a US-USSR agreement. Asked by a reporter if Nicholson's death would "prevent a summit meeting," Reagan replied, "No, it would make me more anxious to go to one."[11]

The outlook for the summit further improved when on July 2, 1985, Gorbachev sacked Andrei Gromyko, the dour old cold warrior. His unexpected replacement as foreign minister was the reform-minded party boss of Georgia, Eduard Shevardnadze, an affable, white-haired foreign policy neophyte who shared Gorbachev's discontentment with the status quo. Shevardnadze and Shultz quickly established a rapport. To prepare for the summit, Shevardnadze traveled to Washington and Shultz to Moscow.

Yet there was still considerable skepticism in Washington as hard-liners and pragmatists waged what House Majority Leader Jim Wright described as "a battle for the president's soul." CIA Director Bill Casey insisted that Gorbachev and his aides "are not reformers and liberaliz-ers either in Soviet domestic or foreign policy," and his skeptical outlook was initially shared by many others, including Defense Secretary Caspar Weinberger, who thought Gorbachev was trying to trick America into reducing its defense spending. A National Security Council aide, John Lenczowksi, warned that Gorbachev was "a quintessential Communist Party man" who would not "radically change the character of Soviet pol-icy." A senior State Department official even sniped that Gorbachev's "ugly purple birthmark" made him look like Luca Brasi, the mob enforcer in *The Godfather*. White House communications director Pat Buchanan encour-aged Reagan to stand firm by sending him articles such as one from the *National Review* headlined "Arms Control: Three Centuries of Failure"—precisely the same view long espoused by Reagan's old friend and attor-ney Laurence Beilenson, who had written a book called *The Treaty Trap* that the president often cited.[12]

Reagan himself was skeptical of the new Soviet boss. "I believe that Gor-bachev will be as tough as any of their leaders. If he wasn't a confirmed ideo-logue he would never have been chosen by the Politburo," he wrote in his diary. Told by the oil magnate Armand Hammer, a frequent visitor to Mos-cow, that "'Gorby' is a different type than past Soviet leaders & that we can get along," Reagan retorted in his diary, "I'm too cynical to believe that."[13]

Reagan spent months preparing for the upcoming summit by meeting with Soviet experts, reading background papers, and even watching informa-tional videos made by aides who realized this would be an effective way to communicate with the former movie star. The NSC's Jack Matlock likened the preparation to a college course, "Soviet Union 101," designed to make up for what Bud McFarlane described as "the president's spotty command of historical facts."[14]

One of Reagan's favorite teachers was the American writer Suzanne Massie (he called her "the greatest student I know of the Russian people"), who had a romantic view of Russia and rhapsodized about Russian culture.

She told him, as Reagan wrote in his diary, that "the Russians are going through a spiritual revival and are completely tuned out on Communism." (In fact, while Russians were tuning out Communism, there was scant evidence of any religious revival.) She also taught him a Russian phrase, translated as "trust but verify," that he would repeat "until the General Secretary was tired of hearing it," as he noted.[15]

But Reagan found it hard to give up the right-wing shibboleths about the Soviet Union that he had been repeating for decades. In a remarkable memorandum to himself that the president wrote shortly before the summit to distill his own thinking, he insisted, "The Soviets are planning a war. They would like to win without it and their chances of doing that depend on being so prepared we could be faced with a surrender or die ultimatum."[16] This was, in hindsight, an epic misreading of Gorbachev; not even his more hardline predecessors entertained such grandiose ambitions. In fairness, however, it was not yet clear how radical the Soviet leader would become. Soviet foreign policy had barely changed since his ascension; the war in Afghanistan only intensified, and Soviet support continued for "fraternal" regimes from Nicaragua to Angola.

Yet while initially suspicious of Gorbachev, Reagan rejected the extremes of both hawks who argued that any agreement with the Soviets was worthless and doves who believed that the United States had to make major concessions to achieve an agreement. These were roughly the views of the Pentagon and State Department, respectively. As usual, Reagan had trouble picking between the competing advice of George Shultz and Cap Weinberger, so, ever pragmatic, he tried to split the difference. He did not rule out an agreement with the Soviets—but only as long as it was "in the long-term interest of the United States."[17] The question was whether the Geneva summit could produce such an agreement.

The Reagans arrived in Geneva on Saturday, November 16, 1985, three days ahead of the summit to allow plenty of time to get over jet lag. They were accompanied by their son Ron who had ended his ballet career and was on assignment for *Playboy* to write about the meeting. The president and first lady stayed at Le Maison de Saussure, an eighteenth-century, gray stone chateau with a lovely view of Lake Geneva, where Prince Aga Khan

IV, one of the world's wealthiest royals, lived with his wife and son. The boy left Reagan a note asking him to feed his goldfish, and the president faithfully complied, but one of the fish died anyway. The chagrined president dispatched an aide to a Geneva pet store to get two replacement goldfish and left a note of apology signed "Your friend, Ronald Reagan."[18]

Reagan was suffering from nerves, like an athlete before a big game or an actor before a big scene. "Lord," he wrote in his diary on November 18, "I hope I'm ready & not overtrained." Nancy surprised him that afternoon with a masseuse; the president fell asleep repeatedly on the massage table. Gorbachev, who did not arrive in Geneva until November 18, also approached the meeting with "high anxiety." He did not know what to expect from a president whose entire political career had been characterized by "virulent anti-Sovietism."[19]

Tuesday, November 19, 1985, was the big day: the start of the first summit between Soviet and American leaders since 1979, when Carter and Brezhnev met in Vienna. A lengthy motorcade whisked the president to the Chateau Fleur d'Eau, a nineteenth-century villa owned by a Swiss businessman. It sat on a seven-acre park located five miles outside Geneva and offered privacy for the historic occasion. Reagan arrived before Gorbachev; the plan was for him to greet the Soviet leader on the steps. The weather was bitterly cold, and Reagan was wearing a blue cashmere overcoat and white scarf over his blue suit. But Reagan's personal aide Jim Kuhn became convinced that the overcoat would convey the wrong image, and he implored Reagan to take it off.

A few minutes later, a wail of sirens signaled the arrival of the Soviet leader in his ZiL limousine. Gorbachev was wearing a dark overcoat and fedora. Reagan was twenty years older than Gorbachev but looked more youthful and energetic as he bounded down the steps without a topcoat to welcome the Soviet leader. "You're lightly dressed," Gorbachev quipped. "Don't catch cold, or I won't have anyone to hold talks with."[20]

"We ended up rolling the Soviets big time," Kuhn exulted. He rather missed the point: Reagan was intent not on "rolling the Soviets" but on reaching an accommodation with them. "Let there be no talk of winners and losers," Reagan had written to himself prior to the summit. His aides had not gotten the memo—quite literally. (Reagan kept it to himself.) Gorbachev also did not want the summit to become a "great propaganda battle" but rather a "springboard to develop new relations with Reagan."[21]

The summit was scheduled to start with a fifteen-minute meeting between Reagan and Gorbachev with only a translator on each side. The actual session lasted an hour, from 10:20 a.m. to 11:20 a.m. As the two men kept talking in a small blue parlor, the American delegation waiting outside grew increasingly agitated. "A palpable concern floated that maybe, behind those closed doors, [Reagan] was being savaged," wrote the president's official biographer, Edmund Morris, who was standing with the US team. At Don Regan's prompting, Jim Kuhn asked George Shultz if he should go in and break it up. "Look," Shultz snapped, "if you're dumb enough to do that, you don't deserve your job."[22]

While the Soviet and US teams were initially in the dark, we now know exactly what was happening behind those closed doors as the two leaders were meeting alone, thanks to the declassification of the "MemCons" (memorandums of conversation) prepared by the American and Soviet translators. Reagan began this first get-acquainted session by trying to find common ground. He noted that both men came from "a small farming community" and now had "the fate of the world in their hands." He argued that their "primary aim" should be "to eliminate the suspicions which each side had of the other," with the "resolution of other questions" naturally following if the two men developed a level of trust.[23]

Gorbachev reciprocated Reagan's warm opening by saying he too "was convinced" that they "could begin to change our relations for the better" and that "in the USSR there was no enmity toward the United States or its people." Gorbachev sought to convince Reagan that he was willing "to take a new political approach" and "was not playing a two-faced game."[24]

Reagan repeated his old belief that it was hard to trust the Soviet Union because its leaders believed "that the Marxist system should prevail." Gorbachev sought to allay these concerns: "The U.S. should not think that Moscow was omnipotent and that when, he, Gorbachev, woke up every day he thought about which country he would now like to arrange a revolution in. This simply was not true." He was speaking the truth, but Reagan remained unconvinced.[25]

Gorbachev closed their private meeting with a gesture of friendship: He told Reagan that Soviet scientists had concluded there would be a major earthquake in California and Nevada in the next three years. Reagan did not

act surprised. Like a typically fatalistic Californian, he said that "he realized that such an earthquake was considered to be overdue."[26]

The talks turned more acrimonious in the next two sessions, held before
and after lunch, where the two leaders were joined by their delegations—
seven aides on each side—around a large wooden table in the ornate salon.
The US delegation pointedly did not include Defense Secretary Caspar
Weinberger, who did not think the summit should have taken place at all
and had tried to sabotage it. Gorbachev objected to suggestions from American conservatives, specifically citing the Heritage Foundation, "that the
United States should use the arms race to . . . weaken the Soviet Union." He
insisted that this was a "delusion" and that the central priority should be
"to halt the arms race and to disarm." He feared Reagan's plans for ballistic
missile defense would simply expand the arms race to space and enable a US
first strike on his country.[27]

In his response, Reagan wrongly insisted that the United States lagged
militarily behind the Soviet Union and blamed the Soviets for rejecting past US arms-control proposals, conveniently forgetting that he
himself had opposed SALT II. Reagan defended the Strategic Defense
Initiative by arguing that it could protect against an attack from a "madman . . . with a nuclear weapon" such as Moammar Qaddafi, and he promised to share the system with the Soviet Union. Gorbachev replied that
the two sides should ban space weapons. Reagan kept insisting that SDI
did not constitute "the militarization of space" because it was intended to
be a defensive system.[28]

They also touched on regional issues, with Gorbachev offering to pull
Soviet troops out of Afghanistan as part of a political settlement negotiated
by the United Nations. This was a major new concession. But Reagan did
not seem to understand what Gorbachev was saying and reverted to his prepared talking points denouncing the Soviet invasion of Afghanistan, which
Gorbachev had privately opposed. For good measure, the president added
complaints about the Soviet role in Cambodia and Nicaragua.

By 3:40 p.m., the talks had reached an impasse, and voices were being
raised on both sides. As Gorbachev later noted, the two leaders sometimes
sounded "like the 'No. 1 Communist' and the 'No. 1 Imperialist' trying to
out-argue each other."[29] Reagan suggested that the two leaders take a walk

by themselves—accompanied, of course, by interpreters—down to a nearby boathouse where the US advance team had a log fire burning. Although this was presented as an impromptu gesture, it had been carefully planned; Reagan assumed he could make more progress with Gorbachev one-on-one.

The atmosphere instantly lightened during the stroll down the gravel walkway. Reagan jocularly told Gorbachev that he should inform one of the Soviet Union's top experts on America "that he had made not only grade-B movies but also a few good ones." Gorbachev mentioned that he had seen *Kings Row*, the president's most critically acclaimed movie, "and had liked it very much." There was no surer way to Reagan's heart than to praise his athletic or acting prowess—as the KGB undoubtedly had informed the wily general secretary.[30]

Once they were seated by the cozy fireplace, Reagan handed Gorbachev a previously mooted proposal, written in both English and Russian, for a 50 percent reduction in strategic nuclear missiles and the complete elimination of intermediate-range missiles in Europe. Gorbachev received this plan positively, but the meeting, which lasted more than an hour, quickly veered into a debate about SDI. Gorbachev said the Soviet Union had no reason to "believe the President's statement about sharing results of the research" and not taking advantage of a missile defense system to attack his country. The Soviet position was that a cut in missiles needed to be accompanied by a ban on space weapons; otherwise, the arms race would only get worse. Reagan responded with an analogy to nations banning chemical weapons but keeping a supply of gas masks to suggest that it would be possible both to cut offensive weapons and build defensive systems at the same time.[31]

As would happen every time they broached the subject, the debate went nowhere because both leaders were locked into their opposing positions. Reagan could be supremely stubborn about one of his *idées fixes*, and Gorbachev's adamant opposition only convinced him that SDI must be truly valuable if the Soviets feared it so much. In fact, Gorbachev's concern was not that SDI would work but that it would make it hard for him to reduce the number of nuclear missiles. But on the walk back to the chateau, they did reach an agreement to hold two more summits—one in the United States, the other in the Soviet Union. That was significant progress. Indeed, Reagan later remembered their fireplace chat as the turning point of the Cold War. In his memory, he omitted the presence of translators to make the scene seem even more dramatic.[32]

That evening, Mikhail and Raisa Gorbachev hosted a dinner for Ronald and Nancy Reagan at the Soviet mission in Geneva. "What a dinner," the normally abstemious president wrote in his diary. "They must be influenced by the Orientals. Course after course & for half of them I thought each one had to be the entrée."[33] (Reagan had been feted at lengthy banquets the previous year during his trip to China, hence his reference to "Orientals," a pejorative term only then beginning to fall out of popular usage.) Seated next to Gorbachev, Nancy Reagan tried to make her own personal connection by asking about the Soviet film industry, drug abuse in the Soviet Union, and the Soviet leader's family. Sounding like a Republican, Gorbachev pronounced himself an advocate of "family values" and expressed concern that too many couples were living together without benefit of marriage. Nancy couldn't have agreed more.[34]

The first lady of the United States did not, however, get along so well with the first lady of the Soviet Union. The chronically insecure Nancy Reagan felt that the more intellectual Raisa Gorbachev lectured and condescended to her. Instead of discussing safe subjects like their families, Raisa insisted on talking about Marxist-Leninist philosophy. "Her conversational style made me bristle," Nancy later wrote. It did not help that Raisa attracted more media attention because it was so unusual to see a Soviet leader's wife on the world stage, much less one who was so well dressed. At one point, Nancy fumed, "Who does that dame think she is?" Luckily, their husbands got along better, even if they too had some "rough moments," as Nancy described her meetings with Raisa.[35]

Each leader said something extraordinary in his dinner toast that the other would long remember. Gorbachev quoted the Book of Ecclesiastes "to the effect that there is a time to throw stones and there is a time to gather them" and that "now is the time to gather stones which have been cast in the past."[36] Reagan was impressed to hear a "godless Communist" quoting the Bible. A week or so later, he told his former aide Michael Deaver, "I don't know, Mike, but I honestly think he believes in a higher power."[37]

Reagan, for his part, impressed Gorbachev by saying "that if the people of the world were to find out that there was some alien life form that was going to attack the Earth approaching on Halley's Comet, then that knowledge would unite all the peoples of the world." He was implying that nuclear weapons were that alien presence that should lead to global unity. The American president also showed sensitivity to Soviet perceptions by noting that it was forty-three years to the day since the Soviet counterattack at Stalingrad had turned World War II "around" and that it was time for "yet another turning point for all mankind—one that would make it possible to have a world of peace and freedom."[38]

The second day of the summit, Wednesday, November 20, 1985, began with the two leaders meeting by themselves at the Soviet mission from 10:15 a.m. to 11:25 a.m. They spent much of the time sparring over human rights. Reagan urged Gorbachev to allow more emigration of Soviet Jews and to make other human rights improvements. In return, just as with the release of the Pentecostals, he "would never boast that the Soviet side had given in to the U.S." Gorbachev replied that he was "willing to look at specific cases," but he objected that Reagan was bringing up the issue to score political points at the Soviet Union's expense. "I myself spent time trying to fend off accusations of human rights abuses," Gorbachev later acknowledged, "even though I was not always convinced that these were not justified."[39] In the time-honored fashion of Soviet leaders, he pointed out that the United States had its own problems. Reagan defended the American record by pointing out that US laws forbid discrimination against "hiring women, blacks and so forth," without mentioning that he had opposed for years the enactment of those very laws.[40]

This tête-à-tête was followed by another "plenary session" with both delegations, at which Reagan and Gorbachev rehearsed their already familiar arguments about SDI while agreeing that they should reduce strategic missiles by 50 percent. Both leaders became angry as they debated SDI; at one point, Reagan "exploded," Shultz noted. Gorbachev finally cut off the discussion, realizing it was going nowhere, but giving Reagan credit for sincerity. "The stuff really hit the fan," Reagan noted in his diary. "He was really belligerent & d—n it I stood firm."[41]

At the final plenary session on the afternoon of November 20, the leaders haggled over what to say in a joint statement. Reagan had refused to follow the normal pattern of having a communiqué drafted in advance because he didn't want striped-pants diplomats to put words into his mouth. The final statement was not ironed out until 4:30 a.m. on November 21 after

Gorbachev personally intervened to tell the chief Soviet negotiator to stop quibbling about wording. The final communiqué declared that "nuclear war cannot be won and must never be fought," which Gorbachev viewed as a significant achievement.[42]

The two-day summit culminated on the evening of November 20 with a dinner at the Aga Khan's sumptuous chateau hosted by the Reagans, featuring California wines and lobster soufflé served on Nancy Reagan's red-bordered White House china, all flown over for the occasion. Both leaders struck a conciliatory note. Gorbachev said that "he felt that he and President Reagan had truly made a start" even if they had not made "great progress right away." Reagan agreed, saying, "This is a beginning. No matter what it was we failed to agree on, the important thing was that the two of them would continue to meet."[43]

Thursday, November 21, 1985, may have been the longest but most satisfying day of Ronald Reagan's life. In the morning, with light snow showers falling outside, Reagan and Gorbachev delivered brief statements to the vast press throng gathered at the international conference center in Geneva to cover the summit. In the afternoon, the Reagans flew to Brussels so the president could brief NATO leaders. He told them that he found the private discussions "especially useful" and that Gorbachev was committed to dispelling "mutual suspicions and distrust."[44] Then back to Washington. Air Force One took off from Brussels at 6:00 p.m. Central European Time and landed at Andrews Air Force Base at 8:35 p.m. Eastern Daylight Time. The president flew by Marine One straight to the Capitol to deliver a triumphant, prime-time speech to a rapturous, jam-packed joint session of Congress.[45] "I haven't gotten such a reception since I was shot," he exulted. "The gallerys [sic] were full & members wouldn't stop clapping & cheering." It was 4:00 a.m. in Switzerland by the time he got to bed at the White House with a feeling of immense and well-deserved satisfaction.[46] "They were on a tremendous high," Nancy's stepbrother Richard Davis said of the first couple, "not having slept much or eaten much."[47]

It was not obvious at the time, but in hindsight the Geneva summit would be seen as the beginning of the end of the Cold War. In two days of meetings, the leaders of the United States and the Soviet Union had begun to clear away decades of conflicts and misunderstandings—and thereby to change the course of history. "Once Reagan met Gorbachev, he did not need an intelligence officer to tell him whether he was a guy he could deal with," said Jack Matlock, the NSC's Soviet expert. "He felt it instinctively."[48]

In a similar vein, Gorbachev told his ambassador to Washington, Anatoly Dobrynin, on the plane ride home that, while he found Reagan to be "stubborn and very conservative," he still "found it possible to establish contact with him and discovered a man who was not as hopeless as some believed." "I realized by the end of our two-day meeting," Gorbachev later wrote, "that Ronald Reagan too was a man 'you could do business with.'"[49]

49

Despotism and Terrorism

South Africans certainly don't need us to tell them how to solve
their race problems.

—RONALD REAGAN

Nineteen-eighty-five was a triumphant year for Ronald Reagan, beginning with his second inauguration and culminating in the summit with Mikhail Gorbachev. It could not have worked out better if scripted by Hollywood. Indeed, Reagan would later cite the Geneva summit as the high point of his entire presidency.[1]

Nineteen-eighty-six would be a decidedly more difficult year as he dealt with Middle Eastern terrorism, South African apartheid, and a "people power" uprising in one of America's closest Pacific allies before attending an ill-starred summit with Gorbachev and, finally, becoming mired in the worst scandal of his presidency. When asked what was the most troubling problem he faced, the British Prime Minister Harold Macmillan was reputed to have replied, "Events, my dear boy, events." After 1986, Ronald Reagan might have said something similar.

Fittingly, given what was to follow, the year began with a disaster literally from the blue.

NASA had planned an ambitious schedule of launches in 1986 for its fleet of space shuttles, the reusable space planes that had first flown in 1981. The first mission of the year, launched on January 12, went flawlessly. After traveling 2.5 million miles in space, the *Columbia* landed at Edwards Air Force Base in California on January 18. Just four days later, another shuttle, the *Challenger*, was scheduled to roar into space with its seven crew members from Cape Canaveral, Florida. During the six-day mission to follow, it was supposed to deploy a communications satellite and instruments to observe Halley's comet. On board, in addition to the usual assortment of astronauts, was Christa McAullife, a high school teacher from New Hampshire who had been selected from among eleven thousand applicants for NASA's Teacher in Space Project.

On the morning of January 28, after six days of delays, the crew finally boarded the *Challenger*. Engineers warned that the unexpectedly cold temperatures overnight might have stiffened the O-ring seals designed to contain the hot gases produced by the shuttle's two rocket boosters. But NASA managers, eager to avert any more delays, chose to proceed with the launch. The shuttle lifted off at 11:38 a.m. For the first minute or so, everything seemed to go smoothly. But seventy-three seconds into the flight, the shuttle exploded in a massive fireball that could be seen on television screens around the world. All seven crew members were killed instantly. An investigation later revealed that the O-rings had been breached, igniting the external fuel tank, which was full of more than half a million gallons of rocket fuel.[2]

President Reagan received the news from his distraught communications director, Pat Buchanan, shortly before noon in the Oval Office, where he was preparing for that night's State of the Union Address. The president and a few aides then adjourned to his small study next to the Oval Office—Mike Deaver's old office—to watch television replays of the tragedy. "The president looked stricken," his aide Jim Kuhn noted. "Hands clasped, the president watched in pain." It was the most emotion press secretary Larry Speakes had ever seen him display. In his diary, Reagan described it as a "day we'll remember for the rest of our lives. . . . There is no way to describe our shock & horror."[3]

The president and his senior staff made a decision to postpone the State of the Union and have him deliver, instead, a short address from the White House on the disaster. Don Regan knew who to call when an emotional speech had to be prepared. "Get that girl . . . you know, have that girl do that," he instructed his aides. He was dismissively referring to Peggy Noonan, a former writer for Dan Rather at CBS Radio who had already distinguished herself with the "Boys of Pointe du Hoc" speech in 1984. Noonan thought what had happened was akin to an entire nation seeing a terrible car crash: "It's very frightening, and you need somebody to sort of calm you down. . . . It's very important to put these things in context again, and say terrible things happen to pioneers, but the trek does not stop there."[4]

The short address—just 650 words—that the president delivered to the nation at 5:00 p.m., little more than five hours after the tragedy, magnificently accomplished those objectives. "Nancy and I are pained to the core by the tragedy of the shuttle *Challenger*," Reagan began. "We know we share this pain with all of the people of our country. This is truly a national loss." The speech ended with words from a poem written by an airman killed in World War II that Noonan had remembered reading in seventh grade. "We will never forget them," Reagan said of the space shuttle crew, "nor the last time we saw them, this morning, as they prepared for their journey and waved goodbye and 'slipped the surly bonds of earth' to 'touch the face of God.' "[5]

Even the president's political opponents had to concede he had risen to the occasion as few others could. That very morning, Tip O'Neill had had a bitter argument with Reagan in the Oval Office after the president had suggested that so many people were unemployed (the unemployment rate was still 7 percent) because they didn't really want to work. "Don't give me that crap," the grizzled Irish American politico snapped. "Those stories may work on your rich friends, but they don't work on the rest of us. I'm sick and tired of your attitude, Mr. President."

When O'Neill left the White House, he wrote, "I was still genuinely angry at this man, who seemed blind to the suffering of so many people. This, without a doubt, was Ronald Reagan at his worst." Yet later that day, in the *Challenger* speech, he saw "Ronald Reagan at his best." "As I listened to him," O'Neill wrote, "I had a tear in my eye and a lump in my throat." He concluded that "with a prepared text he's the best public speaker I've ever seen. . . . I'm beginning to think that in this respect he dwarfs both Roosevelt and Kennedy."[6] It was, of course, a different matter in press conferences where Reagan often stumbled around.

Certainly, few other presidents have been as expert in using their platform to rally and inspire the nation in adversity. "He has managed to become the flag," Canadian Ambassador Allan Gotlieb marveled in his diary. "He transcends politics."[7]

A president, of course, must do more than speak. He must also make tough decisions. One of the toughest—and most agonizing—decisions that Reagan made that year concerned the fate of Philippine President Ferdinand Marcos, an American ally who had turned increasingly corrupt and repressive during his three decades in power. In 1983, opposition leader Benigno "Ninoy" Aquino Jr. had been shot dead on his return to the Philippines, and the evidence indicated that Marcos's forces were responsible. In 1984 the opposition made significant gains in National Assembly elections despite Marcos's cheating.

Marcos's days appeared numbered, but Reagan had a soft spot for the corrupt strongman and his flamboyant wife, Imelda. In 1969 then-governor Reagan and Nancy Reagan had been feted by the Marcoses in Manila. In 1982, President Reagan had reciprocated by hosting them for a state visit to the United States. When asked about Marcos during a presidential debate in 1984, Reagan endorsed the dictator: "I know that there are things there in the Philippines that do not look good to us from the standpoint right now of democratic rights. But what is the alternative? It is a large Communist movement to take over the Philippines."

Reagan blamed Jimmy Carter for not doing more to support Somoza in Nicaragua and the shah in Iran, and he didn't want to repeat that purported mistake in the Philippines. Secretary of State George Shultz, however, had a different viewpoint. "I became increasingly convinced that Marcos was the problem, not the solution," he wrote. Now he would just have to convince the famously stubborn president that US interests would be better served by pushing Marcos out of office.

Shultz persuaded Reagan to send his close ally, Senator Paul Laxalt, to Manila in October 1985 to tell Marcos to reform—or else. Laxalt informed Marcos that many members of Congress felt he had lost the support of his people. In response, the dictator decided to move up the date of the next presidential election by more than a year, to February 7, 1986, expecting that he would win in a landslide over Benigno Aquino's widow, Corazon "Cory" Aquino. She was the mild-mannered product of a wealthy, landowning family whose identity, up to that point, had been that of a dutiful wife and mother— not a political leader in her own right. Marcos's own election commission claimed he won, but independent observers, including Senator Richard Lugar of Indiana, the influential chairman of the Senate Foreign Relations Committee, reported massive fraud by Marcos. No fraud, by contrast, was detected on the part of the opposition. Yet Reagan claimed in a February 11, 1986, press conference that there "could have been" fraud by both sides. This was a sign of how much trouble he was having in giving up Marcos.

On February 16, Cory Aquino called for nonviolent "people power" protests to prevent Marcos from stealing the election. Millions of Filipinos took to the streets. On February 22, the armed forces' deputy chief of staff and the defense minister resigned, pledged loyalty to Aquino, and holed up with supporters at a military base on the outskirts of Manila. Marcos mobilized loyal troops to attack the rebels.

Violence seemed imminent as Shultz convened the administration's foreign policy team at his home on Sunday, February 23, 1986. Those in attendance included Defense Secretary Caspar Weinberger and National Security Adviser John Poindexter, who had replaced a burned-out Bud McFarlane in December 1985. "Everyone was in agreement that the U.S. position had to be for Marcos to leave," recalled Paul Wolfowitz, the assistant secretary of state for East Asia. That view was reinforced by Senator Lugar and other influential members of Congress.

The only dissent came later that day from Don Regan, an incorrigible sexist who was convinced that a housewife like Cory Aquino was incapable of running a country. But President Reagan was finally persuaded that Marcos had to go. "The brilliant thing that Shultz did," Wolfowitz observed, "was to tell Reagan that, 'You need to make clear that this isn't Carter dealing with the Shah—that Marcos is welcome to come to the United States.'" Offering Marcos asylum in America assuaged Reagan's guilt about abandoning an ally.

On February 24, 1986, Laxalt delivered the bad news to Marcos, urging him in a telephone call to "cut and cut cleanly." After a painfully long pause, the dictator replied, "I am so very, very disappointed." The next day, Ferdinand and Imelda Marcos, along with dozens of relatives and retainers, left the Philippines on a US Air Force jet bound for a gilded exile in Hawaii. When federal prosecutor Rudolph Giuliani subsequently decided to indict the Marcoses on racketeering and fraud charges, Reagan ignored the deposed dictator's pleas to be "merciful" and quash the investigation.[8]

At virtually the same time, the Reagan administration was facilitating the exit of another ruthless and unpopular, but pro-American, dictator: On February 7, 1986, Jean-Claude "Baby Doc" Duvalier left Haiti aboard a US Air Force plane for exile in France.

The ouster of Marcos and Duvalier marked a major inflection point in the administration's foreign policy. Previously, Reagan had been almost exclusively concerned with human rights abuses in Communist countries and inclined to reflexively support anti-Communist dictators. His first secretary of state, Al Haig, reinforced those prejudices. But Shultz and his neoconservative subordinates Paul Wolfowitz and Elliott Abrams had a more nuanced view. Their advocacy for democracy promotion gradually prevailed in the second term. The administration would facilitate democratic transitions not only in the Philippines and Haiti but also in Chile, Paraguay, Taiwan, and South Korea.

In 1988, the *New York Times* would celebrate Reagan's "human rights conversion":

> When Ronald Reagan took office in 1981, his aides viewed human rights concerns as a bleeding-heart legacy of the Carter years. The new attitude was stated by Secretary of State Alexander Haig in his first news conference: fighting terrorism, he said, "will take the place of human rights." . . . Now look. The Reagan Administration is winding up remarkably close to the once-scorned Carter view. The State Department issues candid annual reports on human rights. Every U.S. embassy has a human rights officer who routinely asks questions of host governments. And in countries like South Korea, Chile and Paraguay, Washington has made useful trouble with "friendly" dictators.[9]

This highly significant, if often overlooked, shift toward a more evenhanded application of human-rights standards—pushed by George Shultz and the State Department—began in 1986. It laid the foundation for the Republican Party, which in the past had been associated with the realpolitik outlook of Richard Nixon and Henry Kissinger, to eventually embrace what George W. Bush was to call the "freedom agenda"—and that, in turn, would bring a fresh set of difficulties.

Yet Ronald Reagan's support for human rights was hardly consistent. He took a very different approach when it came to dealing with the white minority government of South Africa, then the subject of impassioned anti-apartheid protests across America, thereby providing further evidence of his troubling insensitivity on racial issues.

Conservatives such as Reagan had long accused liberals of overlooking or making excuses for Communist crimes. But they did precisely the same thing with the crimes of apartheid. As journalist Jacob Heilbrunn has documented, one of Reagan's favorite magazines, *National Review,* had a long history of defending South Africa, just as it had defended Jim Crow in the United States. Back in 1960, *National Review* had opined that "the whites are entitled, we believe, to pre-eminence in South Africa." The magazine routinely claimed that the African National Congress (ANC), the main anti-apartheid organization, was a Communist front—just as so many on the right claimed that Martin Luther King Jr. was a Communist dupe. When in 1964 Nelson Mandela and other ANC leaders received long prison sentences, *National Review* applauded the punishment of "admitted terrorists." While conservatives argued for isolating the Soviet Union, they argued for engagement with South Africa. "If the outside world really wants to shake apartheid," *National Review* wrote in 1968, "the only practical way is to sup with the devil: step up trade, increase all forms of contact."[10]

The Reagan administration point man on South Africa, Assistant Secretary of State Chester Crocker, was a leading proponent of "constructive engagement" with Pretoria. So was his boss, George Shultz, even though there was little evidence that US economic dealings were actually improving the lot of most Black South Africans or hastening the end of apartheid. Another faction within the administration—composed of Don Regan, Pat Buchanan, John Poindexter, and Bill Casey—argued for simply embracing South Africa as an anti-Communist ally without worrying about its apartheid policies. Buchanan, who was often accused of bigotry, described South Africa to Reagan as "the most progressive and advanced nation in a fearfully retarded continent" and wrote in his memoir that "as leader of the West, America's place should be at South Africa's side." But while they approached the issue of sanctions from different directions, both camps wound up in opposition to strict sanctions: Shultz and Crocker on the grounds that they would hurt Black South Africans, the others on the (contradictory) grounds that they would undermine the Pretoria regime.[11]

President Reagan embraced the language of Shultz and Crocker about the need to end apartheid—"All of us find apartheid repugnant," he assured a letter-writer—but in practice he was closer to the views of the hard-liners. In 1980, Reagan said, "South Africans certainly don't need us to tell them how to solve their race problems," although he felt no such compunction about lecturing Communist regimes on their human-rights problems. "All

Reagan knows about southern Africa," Crocker told a reporter in October 1980, "is that he's on the side of the whites."[12]

South African Anglican Archbishop Desmond M. Tutu, a powerful advocate of nonviolent protest and racial reconciliation and a recipient of the Nobel Peace Prize, bitterly criticized the administration's "constructive engagement" policy as "immoral, evil, and anti-Christian." Reagan met with Tutu in December 1984, only to dismiss him as "naïve." "The Bishop seems unaware, even though he himself is Black, that part of the problem is tribal not racial," Reagan wrote in his diary. "If apartheid ended now there still would be civil strife between the Black tribes." Reagan revealed his paternalism and condescension by suggesting that he knew more about South Africa—a country he had never visited—than its most prominent religious leader.[13]

In fact, Reagan knew so little about South Africa that in an August 1985 radio interview he asserted, outrageously, that it had "eliminated the segregation that we once had in our own country." That simply was not so, as he subsequently had to admit. Nor was it true, as Reagan said in 1986, that the P. W. Botha government had "expressed its desire to rid the country of apartheid." Just a few months earlier, President Botha had said, "If we respect minority rights, we won't have black majority rule."[14]

The antiapartheid movement in the United States had been building since the 1970s. By 1986, as the Pretoria regime cracked down on internal critics, it had become a major force across the country. Student activists were building shantytowns and demanding that universities and companies divest from South Africa. Celebrities were getting arrested protesting apartheid. The singer and actor Sammy Davis Jr., a member of Frank Sinatra's "Rat Pack" who had entertained at Reagan's 1985 inaugural celebrations, telegrammed the White House: AS MY FRIEND AND MY PRESIDENT, PLEASE DO SOMETHING ABOUT SOUTH AFRICA.[15] A bipartisan group of lawmakers, with the Congressional Black Caucus in the forefront, was intent on doing just that by enacting tough new sanctions on South Africa. Opposing them were many Reaganites, including an aide to Pat Buchanan who warned that "wimping out" and acceding to the agenda of the "Boer Bashers at State" would "alienate conservatives."[16]

Pollster Richard Wirthlin warned the White House that it was on the wrong side of public opinion on this issue.[17] But, reflecting the hard-right views of Don Regan and Pat Buchanan, Reagan opposed the sanctions bill. In a July 22, 1986, speech, he acknowledged that apartheid was "morally wrong" and "must be dismantled." But he called sanctions "immoral" and "utterly repugnant" because they would supposedly victimize Black workers. He insisted that the way to end apartheid was by fostering "prosperity and growth," even though America's own postwar boom had not improved conditions for African Americans until the passage of civil rights laws. He also denounced the ANC in harsh and inaccurate terms: "The South African Government is under no obligation to negotiate the future of the country with any organization that proclaims a goal of creating a Communist state and uses terrorist tactics and violence to achieve it."[18]

Canadian Ambassador Allan Gotlieb summed up the general reaction when he called it the worst speech he had heard Reagan give: "He sounded complacent, unconvincing and a bit like father knows best." But Pat Buchanan, who oversaw preparation of the speech to the horror of the State Department, passed along to Reagan praise from the white South African press, assuring him, "While the South Africa address may not have played well in Georgetown, we certainly swept the boards in Jo'burg." That was precisely the problem. Even most Republicans did not want to be seen as supporting the repugnant South African regime. Reagan's "strident pro-Pretoria tilt," as Chet Crocker termed it, backfired by driving more lawmakers to support legislation banning US loans and investment in South Africa. Congress passed the Comprehensive Anti-Apartheid Act by an overwhelming margin and then, on October 2, 1986, overrode Reagan's ill-advised veto.[19]

South Africa turned out to be one of the few countries in modern history where international sanctions helped bring about regime change. Under intense pressure, F. W. de Klerk, the scion of a prominent Afrikaaner family who became South Africa's president in 1989, dismantled apartheid and freed Nelson Mandela, the world's most celebrated political prisoner. Elected president in 1994, Mandela, a towering moral figure who radiated dignity and decency, championed an agenda of unity and reconciliation that was utterly at odds with the conservative caricature of him as a terrorist and Communist.

The pellucid moral clarity that Ronald Reagan displayed when confronting the "evil empire" deserted him in dealing with the evils of apartheid. "Unlike what he did in Poland, where he lit a candle for the victims of Soviet oppression," Chester Crocker said, "he didn't light a candle for the victims of apartheid."[20]

This was the foreign policy analogue to Reagan's failure to support civil rights legislation at home. His soft-on-South-Africa stance can be explained by a combination of anti-Communist paranoia and barely concealed bigotry. He viewed all leftist insurgencies, from Africa to Latin America, as made-in-Moscow, and he did not see Black South Africans as ready to rule themselves in the same way as, say, Poles or East Germans. Reagan deserved credit for hastening democratic transitions in the Philippines and other countries and criticism for not doing the same in South Africa. He—or at least Nancy Reagan—may have realized in hindsight that this was not a position to be proud of; there was no mention of South Africa in his presidential memoir.

President Reagan was no paragon of morality or model of consistency when it came to dealing not only with apartheid but also with terrorism. Sometimes he engaged in appeasement, sometimes in military action.

On June 14, 1985, Hezbollah terrorists backed by Iran hijacked TWA Flight 847 carrying 153 passengers and crew, including 135 Americans, from Athens to Rome. The terrorists diverted the airplane first to Beirut, then to Algiers, and then back to Beirut while demanding the release of 766 Lebanese Shia imprisoned in Israel. On the ground in Beirut, the hijackers shot one of the passengers, US Navy petty officer Robert Stethem, and dumped his body on the tarmac. The White House put the Army's Delta Force on standby to stage a hostage rescue, but mounting such an operation in Beirut was judged too perilous. Over the next few days, the terrorists freed the women and children while spiriting forty American men to captivity in the southern suburbs of Beirut.

After meeting the families of the remaining hostages in Chicago Heights, Illinois, on June 28, Reagan became consumed by a desire to free them at any cost. The president pressured Israel to free its prisoners, reasoning that somehow it wasn't "dealing with terrorists"—it was just a mutual release of "hostages" held in both Israel and Lebanon. Syrian dictator Hafez al-Assad also helped by offering to provide Iran with Scud missiles in return for a US promise not to attack Lebanon or Syria in retaliation for the hijacking. The hostages were released on June 30, thereby avoiding a reprise of the Iran hostage crisis but only at the cost of convincing the Iranian government that hostage-taking paid—and the US administration that arms could be traded for hostages. The administration's handling of the Flight 847 crisis made a mockery of a 1984 National Security Decision Directive signed by the president, which declared, "State-sponsored terrorist activity or directed threats of such action are considered to be hostile acts and the U.S. will hold sponsors accountable."[21]

The administration was tougher a few months later in responding to the hijacking on October 7, 1985, of the Italian cruise ship *Achille Lauro* in the Mediterranean by Palestine Liberation Front (PLF) terrorists. Demanding the release of fifty Palestinian prisoners from Israel, the pirates shot a wheelchair-bound American Jewish passenger, Leon Klinghoffer, and dumped his body in the sea. The ship made its way to Port Said, Egypt, where the country's president, Hosni Mubarak, negotiated the release of the four hundred hostages with PLF leader Muhammad Abu Abbas. All the hostages left the ship on October 9. Mubarak, who had promised the hijackers safe passage, publicly announced they had already left Egypt. But, with help from Israeli intelligence, the White House discovered they were still in the country and would take off on October 10 aboard a chartered EgyptAir flight to Tunisia.

John Poindexter, recently promoted to vice admiral but still the US deputy national security adviser, and two NSC staffers, Navy Captain James Stark and Marine Lieutenant Colonel Oliver L. North, hatched an audacious plan to have US Navy F-14s intercept the EgyptAir Boeing 737 and escort it to a NATO airbase in Sicily. Weinberger was opposed to the use of force as usual, but Reagan approved the plan on the spot when he was briefed on it by Bud McFarlane.

It worked perfectly: The F-14s directed the plane to follow them, and as soon as it landed at Sigonella air base in Sicily, Navy SEALs surrounded the aircraft on the runway. But they, in turn, were immediately surrounded by Italian soldiers and police. In order to avoid a shootout with a NATO ally, the SEALs were forced to stand down. The Italians took the terrorists into their own custody.

Reagan bragged that the airplane intercept had sent a "message to terrorists everywhere: 'You can run but you can't hide.'" That was only partially true, however. While the Italians prosecuted four hijackers, they let the leader, Abu Abbas, go as part of a nonaggression pact with Palestinian militants. True victories in the war on terrorism were few and far between.[22]

President Reagan would be reminded of that lesson again in 1986 when dealing with terrorism sponsored by Libya. While the administration appeased Iran in order to save US hostages, it adopted a harder line against Moammar Qaddafi—who could have, but did not, take hostages among the fifteen hundred Americans in Libya (mostly oil-field workers and public-works contractors). Libya remained a major state sponsor of terrorism but also was weak enough to be easily attacked. That again made it an inviting target for an administration eager to display toughness against terrorism, even if the 1981 shootdown of two Libyan warplanes over the Gulf of Sidra had done little to alter Libyan behavior. Indeed, the CIA reported that the 1981 clash had simply led Qaddafi toward "a closer relationship with Moscow."

In 1985, the CIA began supplying weapons to anti-Qaddafi groups, and the Reagan administration unsuccessfully pressured Egypt to invade Libya and overthrow Qaddafi. Meanwhile, Qaddafi's support for international terrorism continued. Abu Nidal, a Palestinian renegade backed by Libya, hijacked an EgyptAir flight in November 1985. His men shot two Israelis and three Americans. Sixty more passengers died after Egyptian commandos stormed the plane in Malta. Then, shortly before Christmas 1985, the Abu Nidal organization attacked the Rome and Vienna airports, killing a total of twenty people, including five Americans.

In a predictable pattern, George Shultz and John Poindexter urged US air strikes on Libya, while Cap Weinberger and the new chairman of the Joint Chiefs of Staff, Admiral William J. Crowe, resisted. They argued that the evidence linking Qaddafi to the airport massacres was not ironclad and worried that he could take Americans hostage. As usual, Reagan, when not sure what to do, tried to find a compromise between the competing factions, in this case by imposing stricter economic sanctions and ordering large-scale naval maneuvers in the Gulf of Sidra.

Qaddafi rose to the bait offered by the US Navy, which positioned three aircraft-carrier battle groups near his "line of death" in the Gulf of Sidra. Libyan air defenses fired on US aircraft, and US aircraft retaliated on March 24 and 25, 1986, destroying a Libyan missile site, sinking two Libyan patrol boats, and damaging another. Libyan agents, in turn, retaliated on

April 5, 1986, by setting off a bomb in a popular discotheque in West Berlin frequented by American GIs. Two American soldiers and a Turkish woman were killed, and 229 people were wounded. Having intercepted Libyan communications ordering the terrorist attack, the administration now had the "'smoking gun' evidence" the president wanted to justify retaliation.

On April 9, 1986, Reagan approved Operation El Dorado Canyon, using carrier-based A-6E strike aircraft and British-based F-111F bombers to strike regime targets, including Qaddafi's own compound in Tripoli. Recalling the way that LBJ had selected bombing targets in North Vietnam, Reagan personally signed off on each target in Libya while looking at maps spread out over the Oval Office. In a televised news conference, he vowed to "defend ourselves" from "this mad dog of the Middle East."

European allies, which had flourishing commercial ties with Libya, opposed the US plan. Even Margaret Thatcher declared that retaliatory strikes were "against international law" and worried about triggering "a cycle of revenge and counter-revenge." She only reluctantly granted the United States permission to use airfields in the United Kingdom to avoid another Grenada-style row, leading snarky British critics to call her "Reagan's poodle," but France and Spain refused overflight rights. (The French remembered how the United States had left them in the lurch in Lebanon.) That forced the F-111s to fly a circuitous, six-thousand-mile round trip around the Iberian Peninsula with four in-flight refuelings.

El Dorado Canyon took place on the night of April 15, 1986. The operation was designed to minimize both US casualties and civilian damage, and it largely succeeded. Flying low to evade radar, US aircraft struck most of their targets around Tripoli and Benghazi. Only one aircraft, an F-111 with two crew members, was shot down by Libyan air defenses. US intelligence agencies had trouble tracking Qaddafi's movements (he "moves quickly, secretly and often," an intelligence assessment noted), and he survived the attack, although he claimed that his adopted daughter was killed and two sons injured at his compound. Oliver North, who was involved in planning the strike, wrote that killing Qaddafi—which would have violated an executive order against political assassinations—"was never part of our plan," but "nobody would have shed any tears" if he had died.

The American public overwhelmingly approved of El Dorado Canyon—the only time the Reagan administration ever retaliated militarily for a terrorist attack—even though Admiral William J. Crowe, the chairman of the

Joint Chiefs of Staff, was concerned it did not "hurt Qaddafi meaningfully." Along with the invasion of Grenada in 1983, the bombing of Libya in 1986 gave the impression that the US military was "winning" and helped offset the image of ineffectuality created by the 1983 bombing of the US Embassy and Marine barracks in Beirut, the 1984 attack on the US Embassy annex in Beirut, the hostage-taking in Lebanon beginning the same year, and the 1985 hijacking of TWA Flight 847. Reagan was so cautious about the use of force, which was almost always opposed by Cap Weinberger, that when he did unleash the military, it was usually in low-risk situations where a public-relations victory, at the least, was virtually assured.

The cost of El Dorado Canyon, however, turned out to be higher than it initially appeared. European governments had opposed the bombing in the belief that, as a US intelligence assessment noted, "retaliatory raids against Libya will simply goad Qadhafi and other radical Arabs into further ter-rorist actions." The Reagan administration had insisted, "That's simply not true." But European fears were vindicated when, on December 21, 1988, a bomb destroyed Pan Am Flight 103 over Lockerbie, Scotland, killing 259 people onboard, including 189 Americans, and 11 people on the ground. Investigators blamed Libya for one of the worst terrorist attacks in history and theorized that this was Qaddafi's revenge for the US bombing in 1986.[23]

Libyan responsibility for the Lockerbie bombing did not become clear, however, until 1990. By then, Reagan was gone from office. Thus, as presi-dent, he got to bask in the reflected glory of bombing Libya while sidestep-ping the ugly fallout. In similar fashion, the "Teflon president" would avoid much historical blame for his now-discredited position on South Africa sanctions and his appeasement of the TWA Flight 847 hijackers, while reap-ing well-deserved credit for forcing Ferdinand Marcos out of power, cap-turing the *Achille Lauro* hijackers, and bringing the nation together after the *Challenger* explosion. Reagan's usually sure handling of public opinion cushioned the impact of policy lapses, while maximizing the political wind-fall from undoubted achievements.

50

The Surprise Summit

It's too bad we have to part this way.

—RONALD REAGAN

The political atmosphere of the 1980s, though often contentious, was not nearly as partisan or polarized as American politics would become in future decades. This was a time when members of both political parties still ran the gamut from liberal to conservative, when there was still a tradition in Congress of bipartisan cooperation on major issues, and when the major media organs were still centrist in orientation. There were no conspiracy-mongering websites or partisan cable news channels in those days, and even political talk radio was in its infancy. The lower-decibel environment made it possible for Ronald Reagan to rack up a series of substantial legislative achievements in 1986, even as he was grappling with multiple foreign crises from the Philippines to Libya—and attending, as we will see, an unexpected summit with Mikhail Gorbachev.

The Goldwater-Nichols Act restructured the Defense Department to foster greater "jointness" among the military services. The Simpson-Mazzoli Immigration Reform and Control Act imposed penalties on employers for knowingly hiring undocumented immigrants while providing a path to legal residency for millions of migrants who had arrived without documentation before 1982. And the Tax Reform Act undertook the most comprehensive reform of the tax code since the creation of the income tax in 1913.

All three bills passed with large bipartisan majorities—something that would have been difficult to imagine in a later age of extremes—and all three were signed by Reagan in the fall of 1986. Admittedly, he did not take an active role in crafting any of them, but a more doctrinaire president could have impeded efforts to achieve bipartisan consensus. He did try unsuccessfully to stop the South Africa sanctions bill, but in other instances he supported rather than stymied the dealmaking instincts of his shrewd aides.

The tax reform bill was the administration's top second-term domestic priority. Its goals were, as Jim Baker wrote, "to simplify the tax code, broaden the tax base, and reduce rates while maintaining 'revenue neutrality'— neither increasing nor decreasing the overall tax revenues of the U.S. Treasury."[1] Reagan had almost nothing to do with formulating the complicated plan, which was heavily modified from a politically unrealistic draft put together by Don Regan when he was at Treasury. When the new draft was unveiled at a cabinet meeting, the president "seemed remarkably uninterested in the details" while being confident "it will be very popular," noted Deputy Secretary of State Ken Dam. Even Jim Baker, in Dam's judgment, "did not seem to control the material fully."[2]

But the president did use his unparalleled communication skills to sell a plan he did not understand any better than he had understood Proposition 1, the tax-cutting initiative rejected by California voters in 1973. Reagan backed Baker's proposal in a national address from the Oval Office on May 28, 1985. "Death and taxes are inevitable," he said, "but unjust taxes are not." House Ways and Means Chairman Dan Rostenkowski of Illinois delivered the Democratic response, essentially endorsing Reagan's message and promising to work with him to craft a bipartisan bill. "Dan likes to cut deals with Senator Bob Dole or with the White House," the more partisan House majority leader Jim Wright noted with disapproval.[3]

Conservative Republicans were just as unhappy with the tax compromise as some liberal Democrats because it contained tax increases as well as decreases. In a test vote on December 11, 1985, only fourteen House Republicans supported an early version of the bill sponsored by Rostenkowski. Tip O'Neill announced he would not advance the legislation unless it had at least fifty Republican supporters. Jim Baker urged the president to get personally involved, telling him, "This is your number one domestic priority. Are you going to let it go down the tubes because you're not willing to tell the House Republicans to pass the Democratic bill, so we can fix it in the Senate?"[4] The savvy Baker even persuaded Nancy Reagan to nudge her husband into action to avoid an embarrassing defeat.

Like a rancher looking for stray cattle, Reagan went to Capitol Hill on December 16, 1985, to round up Republican votes after having attended a memorial service at Fort Campbell, Kentucky, for 248 US soldiers killed when their chartered aircraft crashed in Canada while returning from peacekeeping duty in the Sinai Peninsula. Reagan began with an off-the-cuff tribute to sacrifice and patriotism that touched the hearts of his audience. He then convinced 70 House Republicans to join with 188 Democrats to back the bill. "Apparently my meeting with the Repub. Conf. yesterday had an impact," Reagan wrote with quiet satisfaction in his diary. After nearly another year of wheeling and dealing, the sweeping tax reform legislation was finally approved in its final form by huge majorities at the end of September 1986 and signed into law on the South Lawn of the White House on a "gloriously sunny autumn day" in October.[5]

It was truly a model of bipartisan compromise. The bill reduced the top personal tax rate from 50 percent to 28 percent and increased the bottom rate from 11 percent to 15 percent, removed four million low-income taxpayers from the tax rolls, lowered the top corporate tax rate from 50 percent to 35 percent, raised capital gains taxes from 20 percent to 28 percent, and eliminated many business tax breaks. Overall, the legislation raised taxes on businesses while cutting them for individuals. Thus, the legislation helped alleviate some of the growing income inequality exacerbated by the administration's previous tax and spending cuts.[6]

That same year—1986—the United States and Canada launched negotiations for a free trade agreement, an idea first broached by Reagan during the 1980 campaign. The US-Canada agreement would be signed on January 2, 1988, just eighteen days before Reagan left office. Five years later, in 1993, Mexico would join the accord, fulfilling Reagan's original vision and creating the North American Free Trade Agreement, or NAFTA. It would provide a boost for all three economies while contributing to painful dislocations in US blue-collar manufacturing communities—and sparking vitriolic criticism from protectionists such as Donald Trump, who called it "the worst trade deal ever made." Canadian Prime Minister Brian Mulroney would have less success in convincing Reagan to limit pollution that was causing acid raid in Canada—an environmentalist initiative that was anathema to pro-business Republicans. A treaty to address that problem would not be signed until 1991 during George H. W. Bush's presidency.[7]

Neither the US-Canada negotiations nor all the domestic legislation that Reagan signed occupied nearly as much of his attention as his dealings with

Mikhail Gorbachev in 1986. Following the superpower summit in Geneva in November 1985, the Soviet leader had delivered a speech on January 15, 1986, laying out a radical plan to abolish all nuclear weapons by the turn of the century that few Americans other than Reagan took seriously. The deadly accident on April 26, 1986, at the Chernobyl nuclear reactor in Soviet Ukraine, which spewed radiation across the region and forced the evacuation of hundreds of thousands of people, further convinced Gorbachev of the necessity to abolish nuclear weapons—and reform the sclerotic Soviet system. In an exchange of letters, Reagan wrote that Gorbachev's proposal was "significant and positive," while laying out a counterproposal to eliminate all ballistic missiles followed by the deployment of missile defenses.[8]

Yet the two leaders were largely talking past one another while the superpower relationship continued to be strained. The Soviets were still waging a brutal war in Afghanistan and still arming Moammar Qaddafi, Fidel Castro, the Sandinistas, and other despotic leaders. The Reagan administration, in turn, was increasing support for the Afghan mujahideen, with much of the aid flowing through Pakistani channels to Islamist extremists who would come back to haunt America. In 1986, the administration made the momentous decision to supply the Afghan rebels with Stinger antiaircraft missiles. These portable, high-tech weapons took a heavy toll on low-flying Soviet aircraft and increased the pressure on Gorbachev to finally stanch this "bleeding wound" by withdrawing Soviet troops—as he had already resolved to do.[9]

After Congress in 1985 repealed the Clark Amendment prohibiting US military aid to any faction in the Angolan civil war, the Reagan administration in 1986 also began to supply Stingers and other military aid to the South African–supported UNITA rebels fighting a Marxist government in Luanda backed by Cuba and the Soviet Union. While anathematizing the ANC's heroic leader Nelson Mandela, Reagan idealized UNITA leader Jonas Savimbi, a brutal warlord who repeatedly demonstrated that he had no interest in reaching a peace settlement. Savimbi, who had initially trained in guerrilla warfare in Maoist China before recasting himself as an anti-Communist fighter to gain Western support, was twice received by the president in the White House.[10]

The summer of 1986 brought a fresh superpower crisis: On August 23, the FBI arrested a Soviet official at the United Nations in New York on charges of espionage. A week later, the KGB retaliated by arresting on trumped-up espionage charges *U.S. News and World Report* correspondent Nicholas Daniloff in Moscow. Reagan was "hopping mad"—he viewed Daniloff as another American hostage—but Gorbachev refused to release the reporter until the United States agreed to release the UN official. A swap was duly arranged, even though Reagan indignantly and unconvincingly denied any quid pro quo.[11]

Gorbachev was frustrated that arms-control progress wasn't being made as rapidly as he wanted, but he did not want to travel to Washington until agreements were ready to be signed. On September 15, 1986, he proposed to Reagan "a quick, one-on-one meeting, let us say in Iceland or in London," to break the impasse.[12] Reagan accepted this sudden invitation, and, with far less preparation than usual, the two leaders traveled to Reykjavik, the capital of Iceland, for talks less than a month later, on the weekend of October 11–12, 1986.

Reagan left Nancy behind in the expectation that Gorbachev would do the same with Raisa, but, to the Americans' surprise, the Soviet first lady showed up, *New York Times* reporter Maureen Dowd noted, "in her stiletto-heeled suede boots to sell the charms of the Soviet Union to a fascinated public." Once Nancy Reagan found out Raisa was coming, she contemplated changing her plans but decided she wasn't going to be "jerked around" by her Russian rival. Nancy spent the weekend seething while watching television coverage showing Raisa visiting with children.[13]

A lonely Reagan stayed by himself at the US ambassador's modest residence in Reykjavik, while the Gorbachevs lodged on a Soviet cruise ship moored in the harbor. The setting for their talks would be much less sumptuous than the ornate Maison de Saussure in Geneva. They met in Hofdi House, a simple, two-story wooden structure built in 1909 on the windswept shore of the North Atlantic. It had once housed foreign consuls before becoming a government reception house. It was reputed to be haunted and was so small that when Reagan aides needed to work in privacy they had to retreat to the bathroom. Cold rain and wind lashed the building for most of the weekend, broken up by short periods of blinding sunlight. Through the windows, the delegations could glimpse the turbulent gray waves in the distance.

The meetings at Hofdi House were not supposed to rise to the level of a summit, but they turned out to be one of the most dramatic and least scripted summits of the entire Cold War. "There was a unique sense of uncertainty in the air," Shultz wrote. "The meeting had come about so suddenly. Nothing seemed predictable."[14]

While Reagan and Gorbachev began their first session, at 10:40 a.m. on October 11, they were alone save for two translators and a notetaker. Gorbachev was dismayed to see that Reagan was mainly reading or consulting notes written on index cards and not engaging in the specifics of competing arms-control proposals. At one point, the cards fell on the floor, and, after picking them up, Reagan shuffled them, trying to find the right ones.[15] Hoping for more substantive discussions, Gorbachev asked their foreign ministers, Eduard Shevardnadze and George Shultz, to join them. For the rest of the sessions, the four men sat together around a rectangular table in a small, first-floor room.

As soon as Shevardnadze and Shultz came in, Gorbachev—described by Shultz as "brisk, impatient, and confident"[16]—put his dramatic proposals on the table: He wanted to cut "strategic offensive arms," meaning land-based ICBMs, submarine-launched ballistic missiles, and heavy bombers, by 50 percent and dismantle all US and Soviet intermediate-range missiles in Europe, while adhering for at least ten years to the 1972 Anti-Ballistic Missile Treaty prohibiting deployment of missile defenses.[17]

Gorbachev emphasized that he was making considerable concessions. For example, he was excluding the British and French nuclear arsenals from his proposal to eliminate intermediate-range missiles in Europe, and he was willing to allow development and testing of the Strategic Defense Initiative in the laboratory but not deployment in space. Reagan was surprised by the generosity of the Soviet proposals. "We are very encouraged by what you have presented here," he said. Yet, while he agreed with the plan to reduce nuclear weapons, he refused any limits on testing and deployment of his beloved SDI. White House aide Marlin Fitzwater noted that when the president was talking about his dream of a space shield to make nuclear weapons obsolete, "his eyes would light with that sparkle normally reserved only for riding horses and chopping wood."[18]

After the first day of meetings, technical experts from the two delegations worked all night to try to come up with workable proposals that bridged the gap between the two leaders. The Soviets again made more concessions: They agreed not just to cut ballistic missiles by 50 percent, which would still have left their country with an advantage, but to reduce the number of warheads and delivery vehicles to the same level for both sides. This important achievement presaged the START Treaty that Gorbachev would sign with President George H. W. Bush in 1991. The two leaders also reached agreement on dismantling intermediate-range missiles in Europe while, as an interim measure, keeping a hundred missiles on each side—based, respectively, in Soviet Asia and the continental United States. This made possible the Intermediate Nuclear Forces (INF) Treaty that Gorbachev and Reagan would sign in 1987.

But the two men spent most of their meetings in an increasingly acrimonious and futile argument about SDI. This was not, as so many Reagan supporters later claimed, because Gorbachev thought that SDI would work. The general secretary was well aware, based on reports from Soviet experts, that what Reagan was proposing wasn't practical. Indeed, the Soviet Union never tried to field its own SDI; Gorbachev rejected the pleas of the Soviet military-industrial complex to match the US program. But Gorbachev feared that if the United States proceeded with SDI, he would face inexorable pressure from his own military-industrial complex to maintain high levels of defense spending. He preferred to reallocate those funds to the civilian sector.[19]

As in Geneva, Gorbachev protested to Reagan that "SDI would mean a transfer of the arms race" to space, while Reagan insisted it was only a defensive system. He again raised the prospect of a madman like Qaddafi acquiring nuclear weapons and argued that "when the use of chemical weapons was prohibited after World War I, we did not reject gas masks." Gorbachev was irritated. "Yes, I've heard all about gas masks and maniacs, probably ten times already," he snapped. "But it still doesn't convince me."[20]

Reagan again tried to assuage Gorbachev's concerns by offering to make a commitment "to share with you the defensive weapons we are able to create." "Excuse me, Mr. President," Gorbachev replied, "but I do not take your idea of sharing SDI seriously. You don't want to share even petroleum equipment, automatic machine tools or equipment for dairies." Indeed, the Joint Chiefs of Staff and other US officials adamantly opposed sharing cutting-edge technology with the Soviets.[21]

"We have brought far-reaching proposals," Gorbachev insisted. But, he

continued, "As the American saying goes, 'It takes two to tango.' . . . Therefore, I invite you to a male tango, Mr. President." But the tango never quite
came off. Reagan was not willing to limit SDI testing to laboratories, and he
insisted on the right to deploy missile defenses after all ballistic missiles had
been eliminated in ten years.[22]

Getting frustrated, Reagan began complaining about the Soviet Union's
historic conduct and trotting out his favorite phony Lenin and Marx quotes.
In reply, Gorbachev borrowed one of Reagan's own lines: "There you go
again, talking Marx and Lenin."[23]

Undeterred, Reagan continued delivering his historically shaky indictment of the Soviet Union. "Even during World War II, when we were fighting together," he said, "you did not want to allow Allied bombers flying from
England to land in your country before making the return flight." US aircraft had actually flown 2,207 sorties from airbases in Soviet Ukraine in
1944. But instead of trying to set Reagan straight—an impossible task, as
Gorbachev had already discovered—the Soviet leader tried to keep their discussion focused on arms control. ("Many times I would try to correct the
president on particular facts of a favorite story," George Shultz lamented.
"It rarely worked.")[24]

A t the very last session, in the late afternoon on October 12, the two leaders came tantalizingly close to an agreement to eliminate *all* nuclear weapons by 1996 along with all their launchers. This was a radical proposal that,
once it became known, scandalized both European and American officials
who feared that a Europe bereft of nuclear weapons would be at the mercy
of the Red Army. It would also have been difficult, verging on impossible,
to convince other nuclear nations to disarm. Nuclear abolition within ten
years was a grandiose but impractical goal. Margaret Thatcher was "totally
appalled" by this "pie in the sky" scheme; the chairman of the Joint Chiefs
of Staff, Admiral William Crowe, described it as a "huge mistake"; and
National Security Adviser John Poindexter "strongly recommend[ed]" that
the president "step back from" this position.[25]

Even if nuclear abolition was impractical, the two leaders could have
reached more limited—but still landmark—agreements eliminating all
of their intermediate-range nuclear missiles and half of their strategic
nuclear missiles were it not for the president's stubborn refusal to accept

any limitations on testing of SDI. In fact, Reagan's own Soviet expert, Jack Matlock, was to write, "Ten years in laboratories would not have killed SDI. . . . There was at least that much research needed to determine what technologies were most promising."[26]

As darkness fell on Reykjavik, prospects dimmed for a breakthrough. "All right, then, let's end it here," Gorbachev said. "What you propose is something we cannot go along with. I've said all I can."

"Are you really going to turn down a historic opportunity for agreement for the sake of one word in the text?" an incredulous Reagan asked, referring to "testing" of missile defenses.

"You say that it's just a matter of one word," Gorbachev said. "But it's not a matter of a word, it's a matter of principle."

Finally, just before 7:00 p.m., Reagan dramatically closed his briefing book and stood up to go. "It's too bad we have to part this way," he said. "I don't know when we'll ever have another chance like this and whether we will meet soon."

"I don't either," Gorbachev replied.[27]

Both leaders walked into the frigid night air dejected and disappointed. Reagan wrote in his diary, "I was mad—he tried to act jovial but I acted mad & it showed." Press secretary Larry Speakes noted that "Reagan's teeth were clenched, his lips were drawn tight, his face had lost much of its color." White House aide Jim Kuhn observed that Reagan seemed truly "distraught" and unsure what to do next. "I had never seen him this upset before," Kuhn recalled. Gorbachev was also agitated and later spoke of the "truly Shakespearean passions" that had been aroused in Reykjavik. A few days later, still angry, he described Reagan to the Politburo as "extraordinarily primitive, troglodyte, and intellectually feeble."[28]

The summit was widely written off as a failure. While Republicans applauded Reagan for standing up to Gorbachev—speechwriter Anthony Dolan told Reagan that "the American people are bursting with pride at your courage and decisiveness"—Democrats lamented his inflexibility on SDI. "This is a sad day for mankind," said Senator Claiborne Pell, the ranking Democrat on the Senate Foreign Relations Committee.[29]

As it turned out, however, the failed summit contained the seeds of later success. On the flight back to Moscow, Gorbachev stressed the progress made on missile cutbacks despite the continuing disagreement over SDI. "We need not fall into despair," he told aides. "Everybody saw that agreement is possible. . . . That is why I am even more of an optimist after Reykjavik."[30]

A myth was to develop about the surprise summit in Iceland. As White House aide James Rosebush later wrote, "When Reagan refused to give up SDI at the 1987 Reykjavik, Iceland, summit with Gorbachev, his Soviet counterparts knew their country would never win the Cold War as long as Reagan was in charge."[31] Therefore, in this telling, Gorbachev decided to end the Cold War because he knew the Soviet Union could not match SDI.

The flaw with this reasoning is that Gorbachev already had been intent on ending the Cold War long before the Reykjavik summit. Reagan's stubborn refusal to make concessions on SDI was actually an impediment to that goal—but not a fatal one. Once tempers cooled, both sides got back to work, making possible a dramatic reduction in nuclear weapons and superpower tensions. But at the time, the summit added to a perception that 1986 was ending in a series of defeats for the administration, notwithstanding the passage of the important immigration, tax reform, and defense reorganization bills.

On September 29, less than two weeks before Reagan went to Reykjavik, Congress voted to override his veto of the Comprehensive Anti-Apartheid Act. On November 4, less than a month after his return from Reykjavik, Democrats capitalized on disenchantment with the Reagan presidency to pick up eight Senate seats in the midterm elections and regain control of the Senate for the first time since 1980. Now Reagan, who had made fifty-four appearances in twenty-two states while campaigning for GOP candidates,[32] would have to deal with a Democratic Senate for the final two years of his administration.

That was a hard blow, but even worse was a revelation the day before the midterms. On November 3, an obscure Lebanese magazine reported that the former national security adviser Robert McFarlane had recently visited Tehran to barter weapons for the release of US hostages held by Iranian proxies. Reagan dismissed it three days later as "a story that . . . has no foundation."[33] But within a few months, McFarlane would be contemplating suicide, and Reagan would be embroiled in a scandal that threatened to end his presidency in disgrace and possibly impeachment.

51

"A Dark and Hurtful Time"

*I just heard something that makes this whole thing
sound like Watergate.*

—DONALD REGAN

The worst scandal of Ronald Reagan's sixteen years in elected office began on a typically hot and muggy summer day in Washington. On July 3, 1985, David Kimche, a former Mossad officer turned director general of the Israeli foreign ministry, came to see National Security Adviser Robert "Bud" McFarlane at the White House. He let McFarlane know that Israel, which was eager to resume the close ties with Tehran that had prevailed under the shah, had identified an opposition movement in Iran that needed support. As evidence of the Iranian moderates' sincerity, they were offering to release the Americans taken hostage in Beirut since Iranian-backed terrorists had begun kidnappings of Westerners in 1982 to pressure Israel and its foreign backers to pull out of Lebanon. Five Americans, including CIA station chief William Buckley, were then being held by Iranian-backed terrorists—a number that would fluctuate over the next few years as some were killed or released and new hostages were kidnapped.

McFarlane was instantly interested—for two reasons. First, as a protégé of Henry Kissinger, he had worked on the Nixon administration's opening to China and now dreamed, as a policymaker in his own right, of a similar opening to Iran. Second, as McFarlane noted in his memoir, "Everyone who worked with Ronald Reagan was acutely aware of his great concern for the fate of the . . . men held hostage in Beirut in the summer of 1985." A "deeply sentimental man," Reagan had been shaken by meeting the families of hostages. He told McFarlane, "I have a responsibility to these people, and I just can't ignore their suffering." Presidential aide Jim Kuhn noted, "Their plight just tore him apart." Reagan himself said, "Those hostages are never out of my mind. I'll never rest until their ordeal is ended."[1]

So now McFarlane rushed to tell the president about the Israeli outreach.

"Gosh, that's great news," Reagan replied. He wanted to know how soon the hostages could be released.[2]

But a few days later there was a complication. A shady Iranian businessman named Manucher Ghorbanifar told the Israelis that, in return for the hostages, the Iranians wanted to receive a hundred US antitank TOW missiles. The Israelis were willing to supply the missiles, but they needed assurances that the Pentagon would replace whatever they sent to Iran. McFarlane briefed the president on July 18 and 19 at Bethesda Naval Hospital, where he was recuperating from surgery to remove a cancerous polyp from his colon. ("I didn't have cancer," Reagan later said in a typical bit of wishful thinking. "I had something inside of me that had cancer in it, and it was removed.") Reagan was initially hesitant about sending weapons to Iran, but, after thinking about it overnight, he asked McFarlane if there wasn't some way "to help these guys."[3]

In the weeks that followed, the Iranian offer—"a very fraught proposition," as McFarlane later described it to me—became the subject of heated debate within the administration.[4] Defense Secretary Caspar Weinberger and Secretary of State George Shultz, normally at odds, were united in their opposition to sending any weapons while Iran was under a US arms embargo for its support of terrorism. Weinberger even warned the president that the transaction would be illegal unless Congress received notification under the Arms Export Control Act. Bud McFarlane, Vice President Bush, and Chief of Staff Don Regan were in favor of exploring the opportunity further. So too was CIA Director Bill Casey, and he didn't bother to tell the other "principals" that the CIA had previously dealt with Ghorbanifar and had issued a "burn notice" on him, meaning that he was so dishonest he could not be trusted.

As usual, when confronted with differing opinions among his top advisers, Reagan did not announce a decision in a National Security Council meeting. "He didn't want to disappoint anyone to his face," McFarlane explained. But on the afternoon of August 3, 1985, McFarlane recalled, Reagan called him into the Oval Office and said, "Well, I've thought about it, and I want to go ahead with it. I think it's the right thing to do."[5]

The Iran initiative was run by Oliver North, a square-jawed Marine lieutenant colonel straight out of Central Casting who had served on the NSC staff since 1981 and had acquired a reputation for hard work and zeal. Both North and McFarlane were Naval Academy graduates and Vietnam War veterans. McFarlane looked on the younger man almost as a son, but he did not realize that his protégé, while patriotic and dedicated, was also self-aggrandizing and manipulative. North himself would later admit to making false statements to Congress, and a fellow NSC staffer described him as a "habitual liar." A CIA official who dealt with North put it more colorfully: "God, the man could speak a blue haze of bullshit." North, for example, repeatedly claimed to have had private meetings with Reagan, yet White House records showed he was never alone with the president. Having him work with another fantasist—Manucher Ghorbanifar—would turn out to be a spectacularly bad idea.[6]

On August 20, 1985, an Israeli-chartered aircraft delivered ninety-six TOW missiles to Tehran. No hostages were released, and the missiles were immediately taken by the hard-line Islamic Revolutionary Guards, not by any Iranian "moderates." Ayatollah Khomeini, the supreme leader, was aware of the dealings with the Americans and approved of them to bolster Iran's war effort against Iraq—not to improve ties with the "Great Satan."[7]

Ghorbanifar told the Reagan administration that the United States and Israel needed to ship another four hundred TOW missiles to get even one hostage back. "The price," North told McFarlane, "went up." McFarlane called Reagan, and Reagan authorized the transaction. On September 15, 1985, the Israelis delivered 408 TOW missiles to Iran. Iran reciprocated by freeing one hostage—the Reverend Benjamin Weir.[8]

The Iranian demands kept going up: They started asking not just for TOW missiles but also for Hawk antiaircraft missiles, Harpoon antiship missiles, and Phoenix air-to-air missiles. "I should have ended it," McFar-lane later admitted.[9] But he didn't. Acting on McFarlane's recommendation, Reagan approved the shipment of eighty Hawk missiles from Israel's inventory. They were ultimately delivered, at North's request, on a CIA aircraft on November 25, 1985. But the Iranians were irate that the missiles were not the latest model and came stenciled with the Star of David. They refused to release any hostages.

After this botched transaction, the president, wearing pajamas and a bathrobe, met on Saturday morning, December 7, 1985, in the family quarters of the White House with his most senior advisers to review the Iran initiative. McFarlane had stepped down a few days earlier as national security adviser—a decision he instantly regretted—because he was tired of Don Regan's relentless sniping, but he attended the meeting because he was still working on the Iran project as a White House consultant. Also present was his successor as national security adviser, John Poindexter, an aloof nuclear engineer who loved to suck on his pipe and tinker with computers but did not like to engage in the hurly-burly of politics. He had been picked, like McFarlane before him, because he was the lowest common denominator acceptable to all the major players in the administration.

Both Shultz and Weinberger again argued vociferously against trading arms for hostages, and again they were ignored by the president. Reagan would later insist that he had no idea he was doing anything wrong, but his comments at this meeting give a different impression. The president said that "he could answer charges of illegality, but he couldn't answer the charge that 'big strong President Reagan passed up a chance to free hostages.'" He insisted the public would not understand if hostages died because "I wouldn't break the law." "They can impeach me if they want," Reagan said defiantly, adding, "Visiting Days are Wednesdays." "You will not be alone," Weinberger shot back.[10]

At the request of nervous CIA officials, Reagan had already signed a covert action finding on December 5, 1985, retroactively approving Israeli arms transfers to Iran. On January 6, 1986, he signed a new finding directing the CIA to deliver arms directly to Iran *without notifying Congress* so as to preserve the secrecy of the sensitive operation.[11] While Reagan would later claim that his primary focus had been on improving relations with Iran, his own words tell a different story. On November 22, 1985, the day after returning from the Geneva summit, he wrote in his diary, "Back to the office for a brief NSC. Subject was our hostages in Beirut. We have an undercover thing going by way of an Iranian which could get them sprung momentarily."[12]

———

At the recommendation of Bill Casey, Ollie North brought in retired Air Force Major General Richard Secord, who had become an international arms dealer, to handle the missile sales to Iran. North envisioned shipping four thousand TOWs and fifty Hawk missiles to secure the release of the remaining US hostages. Ghorbanifar was selling the missiles to Iran for $10,000 each—far above the actual cost of $3,469. Even after various middlemen took their cut, the arms sales would generate millions of dollars in profit that, by law, should have gone back to the US Treasury. Instead, North decided to send the money to a private group called the Enterprise, started by Secord and Iranian American businessman Albert Hakim, that was buying weapons and supplies for the Contras. North called the diversion of funds "a neat idea," and Poindexter agreed.[13]

North later said he assumed that Reagan was familiar with the diversion, but Poindexter, normally a stickler for hierarchy and protocol, insisted he never briefed the president. "I knew very well that it was very controversial," Poindexter told me, "but from my long association with the president I was sure that he would approve. . . . I wanted to give him plausible deniability."[14]

Poindexter knew how devoted Reagan was to the Nicaraguan guerrillas. He rhapsodized about the Contras as "freedom fighters" who were "the moral equal of our Founding Fathers." (One of North's own aides, who dealt closely with the Contra leaders, had a less idealistic view: "They are not first-rate people, in fact they are liars, and greed and power motivated.") Reagan was deeply upset when Congress cut off funding for the Contras in 1984 after learning of the CIA's secret mining of Nicaraguan harbors. "I want you to do whatever you have to do to help these people keep body and soul together," he instructed McFarlane. "Do everything you can." Like the Marine that he was, McFarlane saluted and set out to do his commander in chief's bidding.[15]

There was only one problem: The second Boland Amendment, which took effect on October 12, 1984, had forbidden the CIA, Defense Department, or "any other agency or entity of the United States involved in intelligence activities" from providing any support for "military or paramilitary operations in Nicaragua." But Poindexter and North convinced themselves that the law did not apply to the NSC because it wasn't an intelligence agency.[16]

To circumvent Congress's cut-off of Contra funding, North tapped into the same network of conservative fundraisers depicted in the 2007 film *Charlie Wilson's War* (about parallel efforts to fund the Afghan mujahideen) to raise $10 million for the Enterprise. He implored wealthy "patriots" to keep the "spark of liberty" alive "in the darkness of Nicaragua." Reagan helped by glad-handing some of the donors. On one occasion, Pat Buchanan told Don Regan that former Treasury secretary Bill Simon "has a Canadian friend who will contribute $7 million to his efforts to aid Nicaraguan Refugees," provided "they get an endorsement for their cause and campaign from the President." The White House duly produced a letter signed by the president endorsing Simon's efforts to aid "the Democratic Resistance in Nicaragua." McFarlane went to the Saudis, and they secretly kicked in $32 million. Taiwan donated another $2 million, and Brunei wired $10 million that never reached the Contras. North's assistant Fawn Hall, whose appearance before a congressional committee would later rivet TV audiences, had apparently typed the bank account number incorrectly.

Before long, the Enterprise's Swiss bank accounts were also swollen with $3.8 million in profits from the Iran arms sales in violation of the Boland Amendment. By 1986, the Enterprise was operating its own fleet of aircraft and even a cargo ship to deliver weapons to the Contras. The effort to circumvent the congressional ban on funding the Contras had become a big business—and, for the middlemen, a lucrative one.[17]

In April 1986, the unctuous Ghorbanifar proclaimed a breakthrough: The Iranians, he said, were prepared to receive an American delegation to discuss relations between their two countries. This set the stage for one of the strangest trips in the annals of American diplomacy.

At 7:20 a.m. on May 25, 1986, in a plot twist out of a spy novel, an unmarked Israeli aircraft with CIA pilots at the controls landed in Tehran after flying a circuitous route from Tel Aviv. Aboard were Bud McFarlane and Ollie North along with NSC staff member Howard Teicher, retired CIA operative George Cave, Israeli counterterrorism adviser Amiram Nir, and a CIA communications technician. All were traveling under phony Irish passports. North, naively, had brought a chocolate cake with a brass skeleton key on top as a symbol of their desire to "unlock" the US-Iran relationship. Also aboard was a pallet of Hawk spare parts as a down payment to the Iranians. If they released the US hostages, more spare parts were in Israel ready to be delivered.

Nobody greeted the new arrivals at the airport. After they sat in the VIP lounge for a couple of hours, an apologetic Ghorbanifar showed up with a minor government official whose "breath could curl rhino hide" and an escort of bearded, young Revolutionary Guards who happily ate the cake.[18] They took the visitors to the old Hilton hotel, now the Independence hotel, where they were isolated on the top floor. From there they could see through the muggy haze the sprawl of downtown Tehran and the majestic, snow-capped Elburz Mountains.

Ghorbanifar had assured McFarlane they would meet with top-level Iranian officials, but he had been fibbing as usual. The most senior Iranian official they saw, a foreign affairs adviser to the speaker of the Parliament, Akbar Hashemi Rafsanjani, told them they could have all the hostages in exchange for all the Hawk spare parts, but McFarlane insisted on the hostages being freed before any more missile parts were delivered. They were at an impasse, and, as Howard Teicher noted, "An atmosphere of mistrust enveloped the talks."[19]

After a couple of days of fruitless haggling as if in a bazaar, McFarlane decided enough was enough. He announced they were leaving on the morning of May 28. The delegation escaped Iran safely, thereby avoiding another hostage crisis, but with nothing to show for it. "This was a heart-breaking disappointment for all of us," President Reagan wrote in his diary that evening after being briefed on the latest developments. But instead of giving up, the president stubbornly kept trying to reach a deal with the Iranian officials he privately referred to as the "rug merchants."[20]

Two months later, on July 26, 1986, Hezbollah finally released another hostage: the Reverend Lawrence Martin Jenco, a Catholic aid worker from Illinois. In return, Reagan agreed to ship twelve pallets of Hawk spare parts to Iran.[21] Once intended to win the freedom of all the hostages, the spare parts were now enough to ransom only one.

Even North was starting to realize that Ghorbanifar was not a trustworthy intermediary. So he found another channel to Tehran: Rafsanjani's nephew Ali Hashemi Bahramani, an Islamic Revolutionary Guards officer. In an episode that might have come straight out of the 1985 satire *Spies Like Us* starring Chevy Chase and Dan Aykroyd as inept intelligence agents, the earnest and naive North on September 19, 1986, brought Bahramani to the White House, along with two other bearded Revolutionary Guards, and even gave them a personal tour of the West Wing. This led to a meeting in Frankfurt the next month between North and the Revolutionary Guards' intelligence chief. In a move that seemed too outlandish to be true—fact again proving stranger than fiction—North presented him with a Bible that Reagan had signed at Poindexter's request. Once again, they dickered about the terms of a hostage release.[22]

On October 28, 1986, five hundred more TOW missiles arrived in Tehran. Five days later, Hezbollah released hostage David P. Jacobsen, director of the American University Hospital in Beirut. Reagan's secretary Kathy Osborne recalled that he was so "thrilled" when he found out, "he was almost kind of skipping through my office."[23] But although Hezbollah had released three American hostages, it seized three more hostages as additional collateral in Beirut in September and October 1986. All the US arms transfers—2,004 TOW antitank missiles, 18 Hawk antiaircraft missiles, and 240 sets of Hawk spare parts—had not changed the number of Americans held hostage. Indeed, five more US hostages would be kidnapped in Beirut between 1987 and 1988.[24]

The whole disreputable initiative now began to unravel. The covert supply effort for the Contras was blown on October 5, 1986, when a Sandinista soldier in Nicaragua used a shoulder-fired antiaircraft missile to bring down a C-123 cargo plane belonging to the Enterprise that was ferrying supplies to the rebels. The Sandinistas captured the lone survivor, Eugene Hasenfus, a former Marine who claimed he was working for the CIA. Bill Casey told Ollie North to "shut it down and clean it up," but it was too late.[25] On November 3, the Lebanese magazine *Al-Shiraa* revealed McFarlane's travel to Tehran, apparently at the behest of Rafsanjani's rivals in the Iranian government. The next day, Rafsanjani publicly confirmed the magazine report and even revealed that the Americans had brought a cake. The two dimensions of the scandal had broken into public view, but their connection was not yet known, and the news was temporarily overshadowed by headlines about Democrats regaining control of the Senate in the November 4 midterm election.

Reagan's first instinct was to deny everything and continue dealing with the Iranians. "We will never pay off terrorists," he insisted, "because that only encourages more of it." Reagan was not just saying this for public consumption. He genuinely believed it, even though it wasn't true. In the privacy of his own diary, he denounced a "wild" and "unfounded story" that "we bought hostage Jacobsons [sic] freedom with weapons to Iran," again displaying his lifelong proclivity to reshape reality to his own liking.[26] If he had just leafed back a few pages—for example, to the previously noted diary entry on November 22, 1985, about an "undercover thing" to get the hostages "sprung momentarily"—he would have seen evidence of just how central the release of the American captives was in his dealings with Iran.

Poindexter encouraged him in the belief that the primary purpose of the outreach to Iran had been to improve relations, not to release the hostages. The admiral was, and remained, unrepentant; years later, Poindexter told me that the only mistake they made was "we didn't have a public affairs plan for when it leaked." (By contrast, McFarlane cried during an interview while recalling, nearly three decades later, how he had "failed the country" and the president, "a man I loved.") George Shultz questioned the Poindexter narrative and called for the entire initiative to be shut down. When he returned to the State Department, he complained that White House aides were "distorting the record" and "taking the president down the drain. . . . It's Watergate all over."[27]

Reagan shared the concern about "another Watergate," but in his imagination, as a last-ditch Nixon defender, the similarity was that both scandals had been concocted by the liberal news media. "The whole irresponsible press bilge about hostages & Iran has gotten totally out of hand," Reagan fumed in his diary on November 12, 1986. "The media looks like it's trying to create another Watergate."[28]

The next day, November 13, Reagan gave a prime-time address from the Oval Office to defend his "secret diplomatic initiative to Iran." He insisted that he had only "authorized the transfer of small amounts of defensive weapons and spare parts" to forge "a new relationship" with Tehran; that "these modest deliveries, taken together, could easily fit into a single cargo plane"; and that "the actions I authorized were, and continue to be, in full compliance with Federal law, and the relevant committees of Congress are being, and will be, fully informed." His bottom line: "We did not—repeat—did not trade weapons or anything else for hostages, nor will we."[29] Reagan may have believed all those statements, but none of them were true.

A week later, at a November 19 press conference, the president delivered an even more mendacious and unconvincing performance. He not only repeated many of his earlier falsehoods but added a few new ones—insisting, for example, that "we weren't giving [weapons] to the Ayatollah Khomeini" and that "we did not condone and do not condone the shipment of arms from other countries." Less than a half hour after Reagan denied that any other countries (meaning Israel) had been involved, the White House corrected his statement.[30]

In an attempt to get the story straight, Attorney General Ed Meese launched an informal inquiry. Rather than calling on the FBI, he sent two of his confidants—his chief of staff John Richardson and civil rights chief William Bradford Reynolds, described as "Ed's Roy Cohn" by a senior Justice Department official—to the White House on the weekend of November 22, 1986. They asked one of Ollie North's assistants to bring them the relevant documents from the NSC files. One of those documents, written in April 1986, noted that $12 million in "residual funds" from the Iran arms sales would "be used to purchase critically needed supplies for the Nicaraguan Democratic Resistance Forces."

"Holy cow!" Reynolds exclaimed. When he told Meese what they had found, the attorney general's reaction was more graphic: "Oh, shit."

The discovery of the diversion raised the prospect that federal funds had been misappropriated. Someone could go to prison. Yet Meese, acting more as the president's confidant rather than as the nation's top law-enforcement officer, did not try to secure the potential crime scene. At 11:00 p.m. on Sunday, November 23, Ollie North went to his office and, with his secretary Fawn Hall, spent five hours shredding, stealing, and altering documents to cover his tracks. John Poindexter also destroyed crucial documents, including the findings Reagan had signed to authorize arms sales to Iran.[31]

On Monday, November 24, 1986, Ed Meese went to see the president in the Oval Office and told him about the diversion of funds carried out by Ollie North, with John Poindexter's blessing, to keep the Contras going despite a congressional aid cutoff. Don Regan, the only other person present, recalled,

> The President, in person, is a ruddy man, with bright red cheeks. He blanched when he heard Meese's words. The color drained from his face, leaving his skin pasty white.
>
> The President wore a stern, drawn expression that was new to me—and just as new, I suspect, to Meese, who had known him for more than twenty years. Nobody who saw the President's reaction that afternoon could believe for a moment that he knew about the diversion of funds

before Meese told him. He was the picture of a man to whom the inconceivable had happened.[32]

Don Regan was just as shocked by the news—or so he said. White House counsel Peter Wallison recalled that the chief of staff was "white as a sheet" when he told him: "I just heard something that makes this whole thing sound like Watergate."[33]

The next day, November 25, 1986, the White House announced the diversion to the world along with Poindexter's resignation and North's dismissal. (Still trusting to the end, Reagan wrote of Poindexter in his diary, "I wouldn't refuse his resignation but regretted it.")[34] "IRAN PAYMENT FOUND DIVERTED TO CONTRAS; REAGAN SECURITY ADVISER AND AIDE ARE OUT," screamed a banner headline in the next morning's *New York Times*. Thus was born what became known as the Iran-Contra affair.

When Meese laid out the diversion of funds at a White House press conference, with the president by his side, he insisted that Reagan had known nothing about it. But since Watergate, the public and the press had grown skeptical of assurances that presidents had nothing to do with the wrongdoing of their subordinates. "You could hear people all suck in their breath," said *Newsweek's* White House correspondent, Eleanor Clift. "It was that kind of story."[35] Democrats and the press corps, having previously failed to make any accusations stick against the Teflon president, were publicly concerned, privately elated. At a dinner party in Georgetown at the end of 1986, Canadian Ambassador Allan Gotlieb found "unadulterated glee all around at the anticipated fall of Reagan."[36]

Such gloating was premature—and in poor taste. But the scandal would paralyze the Reagan administration and dominate US politics for the next year. Eventually it would be grouped by historians alongside the Grant administration's Whiskey Ring and Credit Mobilier affairs, Warren Harding's Teapot Dome, Nixon's Watergate, the Bill Clinton–Monica Lewinsky affair, and Trump's two impeachments as among the most serious presidential scandals in US history.

Poindexter's replacement as national security adviser was Frank Carlucci, a former Foreign Service officer who had served as deputy CIA director and deputy defense secretary. When Carlucci asked Reagan why he was picked, the president candidly told him, "You're the only person George [Shultz] and Cap [Weinberger] could agree on." "Hardly a flattering start," Carlucci recalled, but he would become Reagan's best national security adviser to date. He was, as Gotlieb noted, "a pro's pro."[37]

As his deputy, Carlucci brought in another pro—Lieutenant General Colin Powell, who had been his senior military assistant at the Pentagon. Powell had just taken over command of the Army's V Corps in Germany and had no desire to be dragged back to Washington to clean up the political mess. Carlucci had to ask Reagan to call Powell to importune him to take the job. "I could almost see him reading the talking points over the phone," Powell told me.[38]

Carlucci and Powell, taking over amid dysfunction and scandal, quickly cleaned up the NSC. "I fired 60 percent of the NSC staff," Carlucci recalled, "and I said we weren't going to have any more Ollie Norths." That meant ensuring that the NSC would be only "a coordinating body" and would not meddle in operations. One of Powell's first assignments was to review all ongoing covert actions and to put a stop to any that, if revealed in the next day's Washington Post, would embarrass the administration. "We changed the way the National Security Council was working to make sure it functioned properly," Powell said. When Manucher Ghorbanifar had the audacity to call Powell in 1988 and once again offer his services to release hostages "cost free," Powell firmly rebuffed him.[39]

The president gave the newcomers carte blanche to do what they wanted—just as he had done with their predecessors. Reagan, in fact, was even more hands-off than usual because he was so distracted by the scandal. "It was hard for him to focus," Carlucci said. In his memoir, Powell wrote, "The President's passive management style placed a tremendous burden on us. Until we got used to it, we felt uneasy implementing recommendations without a clear decision."[40]

While overhauling the NSC could prevent future scandals, it would not make the present one go away. Both houses of Congress voted to form select committees to investigate and, if needed, to recommend articles of impeachment. In charge would be two moderate, level-headed Democrats: Senator Daniel Inouye of Hawaii and Representative Lee Hamilton of Indiana. Meese also requested the appointment of an independent counsel to investigate potential law-breaking. On December 19, 1986, a judicial panel chose Lawrence Walsh, a former federal judge and deputy attorney general in the Eisenhower administration.

But Meese understood that the president was under a cloud and could not wait for Congress or the independent counsel to complete their work. He convinced Reagan to appoint on December 1 a Special Review Board—composed of former Republican senator John Tower, former Ford administration national security adviser Brent Scowcroft, and former Democratic senator and secretary of state Edmund Muskie—to launch its own inquiry on a much faster timetable. Meese hoped their findings would exonerate Reagan.

All these investigations were complicated by the massive stroke that Bill Casey suffered on December 15, 1986, as a result of a brain tumor. The CIA director was intimately involved in the whole affair—many would later conclude that he had been Oliver North's de facto case officer—but he was no longer able to testify and would die five months later, on May 6, 1987. Bob Woodward claimed that Casey, on his deathbed, confessed with a nod of his head to knowing about the diversion of funds to the Contras.[41]

An additional obstacle was Reagan's uncertainty about what had transpired, making it nearly impossible to answer the Watergate question: "What did the president know and when did he know it?" "The president had it all mixed up," Poindexter recalled.[42] Years later, after Reagan's Alzheimer's diagnosis was revealed, many wondered whether he was already starting to suffer from memory loss in 1986 and 1987. His cognitive abilities were definitely declining with age, but there is no evidence that he had dementia while in office.

One of the key issues was whether the president had approved in advance the first shipment of TOW missiles from Israel to Iran in August 1985, months before he had signed a finding legally authorizing such transfers. Bud McFarlane told the Senate Intelligence Committee that he had. Don Regan, by contrast, testified that the president had not known about the shipment until after the fact. This was widely seen as an attempt by Regan to shield not only the president but also himself and to shift all the blame to McFarlane and the Israelis. McFarlane, a prickly and proud man who was prone to depression, cited this as a major factor in his unsuccessful February 8, 1987, attempt to commit suicide with an overdose of valium.[43]

At his first interview with the Tower Commission on January 26,

1987, Reagan said he had probably approved the August 1985 shipment in advance. But later, at a White House meeting, Don Regan said he recalled that the president had been surprised by the shipment, and Reagan readily agreed. White House counsel Peter Wallison told him that if this was what he remembered, he should say so to the Tower Commission. He even gave Reagan a memorandum to refresh his memory: "If that is your recollection and if the question comes up at the Tower Board meeting, you might want to say that you were surprised."

On February 11, 1987, at Reagan's second interview with the Tower Commission in the Oval Office, the question *did* come up. When it did, Reagan got up and walked to the massive wooden *Resolute* desk, whispering to Wallison, "Peter, where is the piece of paper you gave me this morning?" Finding the paper, he shocked everyone by reading from it: "If the question comes up at the Tower Board . . ."

"I was horrified," Wallison said. "Tower's jaw went slack, the faces of Scowcroft and Muskie drained, and my heart skipped," wrote David M. Abshire, the US ambassador to NATO, who had been brought in as the White House crisis manager. This incident, which was leaked to the press, gave the impression that a senile president was being manipulated by his aides, conjuring up parallels for the historically minded of how Woodrow Wilson's wife had run the government after he was incapacitated by a stroke in 1919.[44]

This was a low point in Ronald Reagan's charmed life and presidency. Ever since he arrived in Hollywood nearly a half century earlier, he had established a bond with the public. He had invariably played good guys in the movies, and he had always cast himself as the white hat in the political dramas that convulsed the country. Now his bond with the American people was at the breaking point. His Gallup approval rating plummeted from 63 percent in late October 1986 to 43 percent in early March 1987. In another survey, only 14 percent said they believed the president's story. Reagan was bewildered. "I just don't understand why they don't believe me," he complained to his new press secretary, Marlin Fitzwater. "I wasn't trying to trade arms."[45]

Instead of grappling with his own mistakes, Reagan was consumed by King Lear–like feelings of anger, helplessness, and self-pity. He referred to the scandal as "our own 'Dreyfus' case"—as if he were the victim of an antisemitic witch hunt like the French officer Alfred Dreyfus—and complained he "was being lynched" by the press. He stubbornly insisted "there were mistakes in the implementing of policy but not in the policy itself." And he still called Oliver North a "national hero."[46]

The administration was paralyzed by the scandal, and the political vultures were circling. "There is a smell of death around the White House," Arthur L. Liman, chief counsel of the Senate Iran-Contra committee, wrote in his diary. "It is almost as if the professionals feel that the administration is drawing to an end, and they want to be sure their reputations are intact for the next. The president seems to be almost a bystander in the whole investigation."[47]

The situation was so alarming that Ron Reagan, still pursuing a career in journalism, made a rare trip to Washington in early 1987 to convince his father to snap out of it. "I found my father lost in a fog of depression and denial," Ron wrote. He later explained, "I think that was very difficult for him psychologically, to come to grips with the fact that people around him had been doing stuff that he didn't really necessarily know about, and that, by denying this at first, he had lied to the American public. The idea that lots of people thought he was being dishonest was just a real blow to him. It was shocking to him, and very disturbing and depressing to him."[48] The blow was all the greater for someone who had been taught from an early age to always look on the "sunny side" of life, and it helped lead him deeper into a fog of depression and confusion.

"It was a dark and hurtful time, and it lasted for months," wrote Nancy Reagan. She was so personally traumatized she found herself losing weight. "In eight years in Sacramento and six more in Washington," she noted, "we had never experienced anything like this. The entire government seemed to grind to a halt, and only Iran-contra mattered."[49]

The Tower Commission released its eagerly awaited report on February 26, 1987. It was the only news story anyone—Reagan most especially—was interested in. The president, Jim Kuhn noted, "seemed preoccupied, uneasy and even nervous" all day. He was "off his stride," Kuhn later concluded, in the same way he was on only two other occasions during his administration: at the end of the 1986 Reykjavik summit and during Nancy Reagan's operation for breast cancer in October 1987.[50] Reagan knew his presidency was on the line.

The commission concluded that the dealings with Iran had been an arms-for-hostages swap, and it faulted the president for his hands-off "management style" that had made it possible. But it found "no evidence" that Reagan had been aware of the unlawful diversion of funds to the Contras—potentially the only impeachable offense. The president could exhale. The three commissioners reserved their most stinging criticism for Don Regan, who "more than almost any chief of staff of recent memory . . . asserted personal control over the White House staff and sought to extend this control to the national security adviser." Regan, the commission found, "must bear primary responsibility for the chaos that descended upon the White House."[51]

Even before the Iran-Contra scandal, Nancy Reagan had been convinced that Don Regan was not serving her husband's interests. But Ronnie would not act on her suggestions to get rid of the imperious chief of staff. "Get off my back!" he snapped. This was one of the few times that their staff saw open conflict between the president and first lady.[52]

Now the conflict between Nancy Reagan and Don Regan escalated into an epic feud, a Washington version of the 1989 film *The War of the Roses,* which starred Michael Douglas and Kathleen Turner as battling spouses. On February 8, 1987, Regan tried to schedule a press conference for the president only a month after he had had prostate surgery. Nancy Reagan thought he needed more time to recover—and her astrologer agreed. Regan got so frustrated that he hung up on her. That was a fateful mistake. "You didn't want to get on her bad side," her son Ron Reagan said. "That was the wrong place to be."[53]

As if to illustrate the point, her special assistant, Jane Erkenbeck, told me that after state dinners, the first lady would review all the pictures taken by the White House photographer, and if any happened to feature someone she did not like, she would tear off a corner to signal that no prints should be made. All the other attendees would receive a photo showing them at the dinner—but not the people who had incurred Nancy's wrath. "Just tell them," Nancy instructed Erkenbeck, "that it's just too bad, that the photographer ran out of film." A crueler fate would be reserved for administration appointees who ran afoul of the first lady. "If Nancy didn't like someone, they were basically fired or shunted aside," said her stepbrother, Richard Davis.[54]

Now Nancy Reagan used all her considerable powers of guile and persuasion to get rid of Don Regan. The news about the chief of staff hanging up on her was leaked to NBC newsman Chris Wallace, the son of Nancy's old friend Mike Wallace, from "a source very close to Mrs. Reagan"—that source being former Reagan staffer Nancy Reynolds, now a lobbyist in Washington. The first lady knew that seeing it reported on *NBC Nightly News* would get her husband's attention. Maureen Reagan, who alone of the Reagan children was spending considerable time in the White House, also told the president that Regan had snapped at her, calling her "a pain in the ass." To press her case, Nancy called in influential outside advisers Mike Deaver and Stuart Spencer. But the president remained loyal to his chief of staff. "I'll be god-damned if I'll throw somebody else out to save my own ass," he said.[55]

The crushing denouement came at a staff meeting when Don Regan tried to blame Nancy Reagan for the unfortunate choice of a replacement for Pat Buchanan as communications director—a news executive born in Germany who was revealed to have been a member of a Nazi youth group as a boy. (He had been recommended by USIA Director Charles Wick with Nancy's support.) When Regan's comment was reported in the next day's *Washington Post*, the president was irate. "That does it—I guess Mon. will be show down day," he wrote in his diary on Saturday, February 21, 1987, as if he were a Western lawman strapping on his six-guns.

"If I don't stand up for my wife, who will?" he asked his vice president. "A certain honor is at stake."[56] It was telling that Reagan—a chivalrous husband but a poor administrator—was finally firing Don Regan not for leading his administration astray but for insulting his wife.

On a snowy Monday, February 23, 1987, Reagan told his embattled chief of staff that, with the Tower Commission report coming out on Thursday, "it would be appropriate" for him "to bow out now." "If I go before that report is out," Don Regan protested, "you throw me to the wolves. I deserve better treatment than that." He demanded that his departure be delayed until some point after the commission report. The president—who, Regan noted, "dislikes confrontations more than any man I have ever known"—agreed to hold off. But on Thursday, February 26, Vice President Bush gingerly approached Regan and told him that the president "asked me to find out what your plans are . . . about leaving." Regan raged about "being fired like a shoe clerk"—in a presumably unconscious echo of the actual fate that had befallen the president's father—but eventually offered to submit his resignation on Monday, March 2.[57]

He did not have the chance. The very next day—Friday, February 27—CNN, the new cable news network, reported that the chief of staff had just resigned and would be replaced by former Senate Majority Leader Howard Baker. Presumably Nancy Reagan had leaked the news to hasten Regan's departure.

Frank Carlucci got a call that afternoon from Robert Tuttle, the director of presidential personnel and son of Kitchen Cabinet member Holmes Tuttle, asking if he had seen the report. "Bob, why are you calling me?" Carlucci asked. "I'm the national security adviser."

"Because," Tuttle replied, "you're the next ranking person in the White House and I'm not sure the president has said anything to Don Regan."

"Well, OK," Carlucci said. "I'll do what I can."

The national security adviser telephoned Reagan, who was in the family quarters, and said, "Mr. President, this news is all over TV. Have you talked to Don Regan?"

He would never forget Reagan's reply: "Uh-oh."

"Okay," Carlucci sighed. "Let me try."

He walked over to Regan's corner office and broke the bad news. "Well, with that, Don Regan erupted like a volcano," Carlucci recalled. "He dictated in my presence a one-sentence letter saying, 'Mr. President, I hereby resign as Chief of Staff to the President of the United States.'" Press secretary Marlin Fitzwater found the tough-guy chief of staff a few minutes later in his office crying, his eyes swollen, his face red "in a wild combination of anger and sorrow." The president called shortly thereafter to tell Regan he was sorry it was ending this way. Regan would not accept his apology. "There's been a deliberate leak, and it's been done to humiliate me," he said. "I deserved better treatment than this."[58]

Regan, the titan of Wall Street and Washington, now reduced to a self-described shoe clerk, was furious about his unceremonious dismissal, and he didn't care who knew it. His papers, now at the Library of Congress, contain a folder labeled "Revenge, 1986–1989." He was as good as his word. In his memoir, published in 1988 while the Reagans were still in the White House, he revealed Nancy Reagan's reliance on an astrologer. Nancy was "shocked and humiliated" by the resulting media mockery; she would never forgive Regan for turning her into a "national laughingstock."[59]

While Nancy Reagan paid a considerable price for mishandling Don

Regan's departure, she was right to force him out. She thereby confirmed her indispensable role as de facto chief personnel officer for her conflict-averse husband. Don Regan had been, as Ed Rollins noted, "a disaster from start to finish."[60] The only way that the administration could conceivably recover from the Iran-Contra scandal was to bring in a new team. But in that "dark and hurtful time," it was not clear whether even a new chief of staff could save a presidency crippled by the worst scandal since Watergate.

Howard Baker was Reagan's third choice as chief of staff after former transportation secretary Drew Lewis and Senator Paul Laxalt turned him down. First elected to public office in Tennessee in 1966, the same year as Reagan in California, Baker had risen to fame on the Senate Watergate committee as a dogged investigator of Nixon's misconduct. He had a reputation for integrity and was well respected on both sides of the aisle, while being distrusted by conservatives for his moderation. He had left the Senate in 1985 after eighteen years, the last eight of them as Republican leader. "I'd probably take some lumps from our right wingers but can handle it," Reagan wrote in his diary about choosing Baker.[61]

The former senator was on a family vacation in Florida when the president phoned him on February 26, 1987, a day before Don Regan was ousted. Howard's wife, Joy, told the president he was at the zoo with their grandchild. "Wait until he sees the zoo I have in mind for him," Reagan chortled.[62] Even though he was contemplating his own presidential run, Baker felt he couldn't say no to a president in such deep trouble. He flew up to Washington and assembled a team of his trusted former Senate aides to salvage the Reagan presidency. As deputy chief of staff, he appointed Kenneth Duberstein, a skillful lobbyist who had been director of legislative affairs in the first term and knew the first couple better than Baker did.

There was no time to waste. Howard Baker's first day on the job would be Monday, March 2, 1987. His confidant James M. Cannon spent much of Friday evening and Saturday talking to White House staffers in a scouting mission to figure out what they were dealing with. Cannon was a gray-haired veteran of Washington who had previously worked for Nelson Rockefeller and Gerald Ford, so he thought he had seen everything. But he was stunned by what he found: "The staff system had just broken down. It had just evaporated." Looking at the staff's paperwork, he concluded they were "rank amateurs." Even worse was what they told him about the president: He was "inattentive," "inept," "lazy"; "he wasn't interested in the job"; "he wouldn't read the papers they gave him"; "they felt free to sign his initials on documents without noting that they were acting for him."[63]

Jim Cannon did not know it, but Don Regan had said something similar to George Shultz about the president: "He's not really working at the job and not in touch with reality." Those complaints were not new; at the beginning of the administration, Bill Casey had said of Reagan, "He barely works at the job."[64] But the problems were getting worse: Reagan was slowing down as he aged, and the White House no longer had a staff capable of making up for his deficiencies.

That Sunday, Cannon sat down and typed a memorandum to Baker suggesting they might have to invoke the Twenty-Fifth Amendment, ratified in 1967, which allows the president to be removed from office if a majority of the cabinet concludes that he "is unable to discharge the powers and duties of his office." Cannon presented his memorandum to Baker on Sunday night. The incoming chief of staff was skeptical. "Well, it doesn't sound like the Ronald Reagan I just saw," he said in his soft Tennessee drawl, "but we'll see tomorrow."[65]

On Monday, Baker and his top aides observed the president carefully for signs that he was unable to do his job. He appeared to be his usual, genial, wisecracking self. "Boys," Baker told his staff, "this is a fully functioning and capable president and I don't want to hear any more talk about that." Then they rolled up their sleeves and got on with trying to dispel the widespread impression that, as Duberstein recalled, the president was a "lame duck" or even a "dead duck."[66]

―――――――――

The Iran-Contra scandal continued to preoccupy public attention until the fall of 1987, with televised congressional hearings, featuring a star turn by Oliver North, riveting the nation. "It consumed our lives for the next six months," incoming communications director Thomas Griscom remembered.[67]

The new White House counsel, A. B. Culvahouse, and his deputy conducted thirteen separate interviews with the president to get as much of the story from him as possible. "We did not want to put our credibility on the line if it turned out that, essentially, the president was lying," Culvahouse said. But he became convinced the president was telling the truth when he said he hadn't known about the diversion of funds. Reagan, unfortunately, remained stubbornly convinced that he had not traded arms for hostages. "I don't think the president, to his dying day, understood what happened," Frank Carlucci said. "We never succeeded in getting him to understand what really happened." But the new White House team understood that to put the scandal behind him, Reagan would have to accept responsibility. A show of repentance had to precede public forgiveness.[68]

The president was scheduled to give a speech to the nation on March 4, 1987, about the Tower Commission findings, but it was unclear what he would say. Nancy Reagan smuggled Stuart Spencer and John Tower into the White House to shape the message. "I told him to just *mea culpa* the thing and get the hell out of it," Spencer said. "I remember saying, 'You can withstand the heat. You will survive the heat.'" Reagan was finally convinced to read a speech artfully crafted by outside speechwriter Landon Parvin, one of the first lady's favorites.[69]

"A few days ago," he said, "I told the American people I did not trade arms for hostages. My heart and my best intentions tell me that was true, but the facts and the evidence tell me it is not.... There are reasons why it happened, but no excuses. It was a mistake." Journalists applauded the speech and compared it to John F. Kennedy's 1961 remarks taking responsibility for the Bay of Pigs debacle—exactly the model the White House staff had used. The president's job approval rating immediately jumped by nine points in one poll.[70]

Even after this well-received speech, dangers still lurked. What if the congressional committees or the independent counsel discovered some new and damning evidence? In particular, what if John Poindexter testified that Reagan had approved the diversion of funds? White House staff were fearful of what Poindexter would say, but Reagan was serenely unperturbed. He told aides, "John Poindexter is an honorable man. He's a Naval Academy graduate. I spent a lot of time with him. He will not lie."[71] Sure enough, when it was Poindexter's turn to testify to Congress on July 15, 1987, he insisted Reagan had not been told about the diversion of funds. Many wondered if the dutiful admiral was simply falling on his sword, like a disgraced samurai, for the commander in chief. In any case, the man who had embroiled the president in scandal now saved him from its worst consequences. In his personal correspondence, Reagan referred to the hearings as "the lynching that failed"; he never tired of equating himself with the Black victims of racist violence.[72]

While Poindexter was the most important witness from the standpoint of Reagan's legal exposure, the most dramatic was Oliver North. Testifying between July 7 and 14 in his uniform replete with decorations, North presented himself as a patriot who was "proud" of all he had done to help the Contras and free the hostages. He was a powerful public speaker, and his testimony led to an outbreak of "Olliemania" that put the congressional committees on the defensive. "North took the Hill with a mixture of straight-arrow toughness, flag-wrapped piety and macho swagger," noted *Newsweek*. Reagan himself marveled that North "has captured the heart of America" and seemed to hold no grudge over the former NSC aide's catastrophic missteps. Nancy Reagan was not so forgiving. She would help to defeat North—"who lied to my husband and lied about my husband"—during his 1994 campaign for the US Senate in Virginia.[73]

The final report of the Democratic majority (joined by three moderate GOP senators) was released in November 1987. It reached what A. B. Culvahouse described as "harsh conclusions": "The ultimate responsibility for the events in the Iran-Contra Affair must rest with the President . . . ," the report found. "It was the President's policy—not an isolated decision by North or Poindexter—to sell arms secretly to Iran and to maintain the Contras 'body and soul,' notwithstanding the Boland Amendment."[74] But the committee did not find evidence that Reagan knew of the arms diversion and did not recommend impeachment. There was no evidence he had acted for personal gain or ordered a Nixon-like cover-up. He had not even invoked executive privilege. This wasn't another Watergate after all.

Independent counsel Lawrence Walsh concluded that Reagan had known about the diversion of funds, as claimed by Oliver North, but he could never prove it.[75] During the course of an investigation lasting more than six years, he would secure fourteen indictments and eleven convictions—including of Poindexter, North, McFarlane, Elliott Abrams, and Richard Secord. Reagan refused to pardon any of them to avoid suspicion of complicity in a cover-up. But the convictions of Poindexter and North were overturned by appeals courts because they had received limited immunity for their testimony before Congress.

Just four days before the 1992 election and nearly four years after Reagan had left office, Walsh indicted former secretary of defense Caspar Weinberger on charges of making false statements, perjury, and obstruction of justice. Even though Weinberger had opposed the Iran initiative, he had known more about it than he let on. A part of the indictment alleged that President Bush also had known more about the Iran arms sales than he claimed. After Bush lost his reelection bid, he pardoned Weinberger along with McFarlane, Abrams, and three former CIA officers.[76] Republicans would vilify Walsh for Javert-like prosecutorial abuses and for "criminalizing policy differences." The dogged and upright Walsh, for his part, was convinced that a cover-up had succeeded.

The Iran-Contra affair was the worst but far from the only scandal of the Reagan years. The roll call of dishonor was long and ignominious: Grant-rigging at the Department of Housing and Urban Development (HUD) resulted in sixteen convictions, including of former Interior secretary James Watt, two assistant HUD secretaries, and two aides to HUD Secretary Samuel Pierce. The FBI's Illwind corruption probe at the Department of Defense, named after an old English proverb, resulted in, among others, an assistant navy secretary and deputy assistant navy secretary going to prison for taking bribes. The Wedtech affair, in which a New York company used bribes to win federal contracts, resulted in two Democratic congressmen going to prison and Attorney General Ed Meese, whose best friend was a consultant for Wedtech, resigning in July 1988. The misuse of funds at the EPA led to the agency's administrator, Anne Gorsuch, resigning and the assistant EPA administrator, Rita Lavelle, going to prison. The attempts by former White House aides Michael Deaver and Lyn Nofziger to cash in on their government service resulted in their convictions for violating lobbying rules.

These scandals were all part of the cost the nation paid for a disengaged president who had little interest in, or aptitude for, running the federal government. Even the conservative columnist James Jackson Kilpatrick, a self-described "pro-Reagan Republican," had to admit, in writing about the HUD scandal, that "the primary responsibility for this debacle lies squarely in the lap of President Reagan. The buck stopped there. For the eight years of his administration, it now seems evident, the president paid virtually no

attention to this huge, costly department."[77] Reagan was not personally corrupt, even if he did cut a few ethical corners in his dealings with MCA in
the 1950s and 1960s, but he failed to set or enforce an expectation of ethical
behavior by his appointees. Indeed, by constantly denigrating the federal
government and acting as if he were not its chief executive, he may have
inadvertently encouraged misbehavior by officials who were more interested in peculation than the public good.

But of all these scandals, Iran-Contra was the most significant. It was
the only one that directly implicated the president and, therefore, the only
one that threatened his political survival. The damage was severe and self-
inflicted but, as it emerged, ultimately survivable. By the fall of 1987, it was
obvious that Ronald Reagan would serve out his term of office. But he was
left a much-diminished figure, and it was far from clear how much he could
accomplish in the scant months he had left in office.

Ronald Reagan was a seventy-six-year-old man who had suffered a
shooting that might have ended his life and a scandal that might have ended
his career, and he was starting, for the first time, to reflect his advanced
age. After years of making the job of being president seem surprisingly easy,
he increasingly appeared overwhelmed and disoriented by the demands
of high office. His energy was fading, and old Washington hands could see
power ebbing away from him as surely as floodwaters receding on the Potomac. The next presidential contest was already in full swing with a dozen
major contenders—six Republicans and six Democrats—positioning themselves for the 1988 primaries of both parties. All the journalistic excitement
was about who would become president next and not what the president
still in office would do next.

The aging lion in the Oval Office, licking his wounds after a long and savage political mauling, would have to summon every last reservoir of energy,
intellect, and determination to avoid becoming prematurely transmogrified
into the most contemptible of Washington creatures: the lame duck.

52

Culture Wars

Robert Bork's America is a land in which women would
be forced into back-alley abortions.

—TED KENNEDY

Ronald Reagan had spent much of his life in Hollywood—Babylon
on the Pacific—and he had gone through a womanizing phase
between his marriages to Jane Wyman and Nancy Reagan. But he
always retained the old-fashioned, moralistic outlook he had formed while
growing up in the 1920s in the Disciples of Christ Church in Dixon, Illinois.
He approved of prayer in school and of going to church regularly—although
he seldom went to church as president and did not start cabinet meetings
with an invocation.[1] He disapproved of abortion, drug use (even marijuana),
"living in sin" (that is, out of wedlock), homosexuality, pornography, and
even swearing in "mixed company" (meaning when women were present).
While he remained unwavering in his views, however, he was characteristically pragmatic in their application.

Alfred Kingon, one of Don Regan's top aides, recalled one time when he
was walking out of the White House with President Reagan to board the
Marine One helicopter on the South Lawn. "He's carrying on about how
much he abhors women having abortions," Kingon recounted. "He's talking
and talking and talking. I said, 'Well, if you feel so strongly about it, why
don't you do something?' He stopped dead in his tracks, turned around
and looked me in the eye, and said, 'Al, there's a limit to what you can do
in politics.'"[2]

There's a limit to what you can do in politics. With that statement, Reagan
showed that he was a pragmatic politician who was all about getting results,
not a grandstander interested in making futile gestures to please the Republican base. In his first term, Reagan prioritized reviving the economy and
the armed forces; in his second term, ending the Cold War. Social issues
were always a lesser concern. They were too controversial, and there was

little potential for victories in a Congress where Democrats held the House majority and even the Republican caucus still had many moderate and even liberal members. Symbolic of Reagan's arm's-length approach to social conservatives was his aides' decision not to have him address the annual March for Life—a giant antiabortion rally in Washington—until 1985, when he would never have to face voters again, and then only by telephone.[3] His image-makers did not want him too closely associated with an issue as divisive as abortion, and he did not insist on acting on his convictions, as he did with SDI or tax cuts—the two issues closest to his heart.

The conservative White House speechwriters tried to inject abortion into presidential speeches, but, during the first term, Jim Baker and Dick Darman routinely cut those passages out or at least severely truncated them. When chief speechwriter Bentley "Ben" Elliott succeeded in getting the president's approval to keep three paragraphs on abortion in a March 6, 1984, speech to the National Association of Evangelicals, Darman was "furious" and threatened to fire him. Elliott and fellow speechwriter Peter Robinson protested that they were only doing what the president wanted. Darman memorably retorted, "We second-guess the President a hundred times a day. It's our job to protect Ronald Reagan from himself." (That Elliott could even plead his case to the president personally was a rare occurrence. Given how routinely the speechwriters were overruled by the president's senior aides and how little access they had to the president, Robinson groused that their "morale has ranged from low to abysmal.")[4]

But no president, no matter how hard he (or his aides) tried, could entirely avoid the culture wars that from the early days of the republic have defined and divided the country, pitting traditionalists against modernists, conservatives against liberals, religious believers against the secular, country folk against city slickers. In 1987, Reagan would assume a higher profile on those contentious issues because of the spread of the AIDS pandemic and the nomination of Robert Bork to the Supreme Court.

In June 1981, the Centers for Disease Control (CDC) reported that five young men in Los Angeles, all homosexuals, had contracted a rare form of pneumonia. Two of them died. Two months later, the CDC reported that a hundred gay men had been infected either with the same pneumonia or an unusual cancer, Kaposi's sarcoma, and nearly half had died. It was unclear what was causing these infections, but cases were growing exponentially. Victims could go for months without showing any symptoms, allowing them to infect many others.

In 1982, the disease was given a name: acquired immunodeficiency syndrome, or AIDS. By 1984, French and American researchers had identified the human immunodeficiency virus (HIV) that caused AIDS and determined that it could be transmitted through sexual contact, intravenous drug use, transfused blood, in utero contact, or breastfeeding between an AIDS-infected mother and her infant. In the next four decades, more than eighty-four million people around the world would become infected with this virus and more than forty million would die of it, including approximately seven hundred thousand Americans.[5]

As early as 1983, a White House aide cautioned, "It is important that it not appear we are only now becoming concerned about AIDS." Yet White House spokesman Larry Speakes treated AIDS as a joke when asked about it in 1982. "I don't have it," he told a reporter amid the laughter of the White House press corps. "Do you?" Ronald Reagan, for his part, did not mention AIDS publicly until 1985 and then only in response to a question at a press conference. That year, Rock Hudson, one of the biggest Hollywood heartthrobs of the 1950s and 1960s and a closeted gay man, became the first celebrity to die of AIDS. Hudson was an acquaintance of the Reagans, and Reagan called him at a hospital in Paris, where he was dying of what his publicist initially described as liver cancer. Reagan's diary indicates he was aware that Hudson had AIDS even before the actor announced it on July 25, 1985. And yet the only "aids" that would be mentioned in the president's diary for the next two years would be the hearing aids he wore. The next mention of the epidemic would not occur until March 31, 1987.[6]

Reagan was less homophobic than many straight men of his generation because he had known so many gay men in Hollywood and Nancy Reagan had so many gay friends (for example, the New York socialite Jerry Zipkin and the Beverly Hills decorator Ted Graber), but he still harbored old-fashioned prejudices. He told Edmund Morris in 1987 that "maybe the Lord brought down this plague" because "illicit sex is against the Ten Commandants." For humorous effect, Reagan would sometimes adopt a lisp to act out the part of an effeminate homosexual, saying something like, "If those fellows don't leave me alone, I'll just slap them on the wrist."[7]

The president's son, Ron Reagan, recalled that his mother, who was a doctor's daughter and had been around gay people all her life—beginning with her godmother, the silent screen star Alla Nazimova—was more progressive than his father on social issues. So was Ron, who had gotten to know many LGBTQ people in New York. He and his mother "started talking to him about it," Ron said, trying to convince his dad to make the fight against AIDS a greater priority.[8]

There were, however, strong countervailing forces within the conservative movement and the White House. Many on the right shared the president's prejudice that AIDS was divine punishment for homosexuality. Pat Buchanan wrote in 1983, two years before becoming White House communications director, "The poor homosexuals—they have declared war on nature and nature is exacting an awful retribution." *Commentary* editor Norman Podhoretz described AIDS research as "giving social sanction to what can only be described as a brutish degradation." William F. Buckley Jr. even suggested in 1986, "Everyone detected with AIDS should be tattooed in the upper forearm, to protect common-needle users, and on the buttocks, to prevent the victimization of other homosexuals."[9]

Reagan never echoed such offensive sentiments in public, but nor did he heed the pleas of AIDS activists, such as the playwright Larry Kramer, to speak out about a disease that was taking a grim toll. He kept almost entirely silent about AIDS until 1987. "Reagan was not inclined to be too sympathetic," Don Regan said, because he did not want to "make the world safe for immoral practices."[10]

While Reagan ignored the AIDS epidemic, his administration did not. By 1983, when only 1,450 AIDS cases had been reported, the US Public Health Service had already declared AIDS its number-one priority. By 1988, federal spending on AIDS research and treatment was up to $925 million ($2.4 billion in 2024 dollars). AIDS, writes historian Jonathan Engel, "was drawing the most federal money per patient of all contagious diseases."[11] This funding made possible the development in 1985 of a reliable blood test for HIV. Reagan did not provide any leadership, but nor did he impede the efforts of civil servants to address the epidemic. The primary movers in the administration were a trio of physicians: Edward N. Brandt Jr., a medical school administrator who was assistant secretary of health; Anthony Fauci, the chief AIDS researcher at the National Institutes of Health; and the surgeon general, C. Everett Koop, a pediatric surgeon from Philadelphia.

These officials, in turn, worked with members of Congress from both parties to fund the federal response. Democratic Representative Henry Waxman of Los Angeles was a leader in the House, and Senator Lowell Weicker, a liberal Republican from Connecticut, took the lead in the Senate while Republicans retained control. The House and Senate appropriated twice as much money for AIDS research and treatment as the Reagan administration requested. Unfortunately, conservatives in the administration prevented the government from spending all the money. After the Democratic takeover of the Senate in 1987, the liberal lion, Ted Kennedy of Massachusetts, took the lead. He forged an unexpected partnership with Republican Senator Orrin Hatch, a Mormon from Utah, to overcome the obstructionism of Senator Jesse Helms, who insisted that educational materials should promote "abstinence outside of a sexually monogamous marriage" while forgoing any instruction on safe sex.[12]

C. Everett Koop, with his throwback bowties and Abraham Lincoln–style beard, turned out to be one of the biggest surprises of the administration. A devout Presbyterian, he had been chosen primarily because of his conservative views on abortion, but he earned the ire of conservatives by addressing the AIDS crisis in a clinical, nonjudgmental manner. "Tony" Fauci was "Chick" Koop's personal physician and helped educate him about the new disease.[13]

Koop later complained of how frustrated he was that, because of turf battles, "for an astonishing five and a half years I was completely cut off from AIDS." That changed in 1986 when, during a visit to the Department of Health and Human Services, Reagan announced—at the urging of advisers who realized he could not continue to ignore this crisis—that the surgeon general would produce a report on AIDS. This was a surprise to Koop, but it was common for the president to offer direction to his subordinates in his speeches.[14]

Koop wrote the report himself at his stand-up desk in the basement of his house on the National Institutes of Health campus. He was determined to allow no political interference, presenting his thirty-six-page report as a fait accompli to the cabinet just before it was released. "I had to skate fast on thin ice, to get by political appointees who placed conservative ideology above saving lives," he recalled, noting that social conservatives "attempted to thwart my efforts to educate the public about AIDS and tried to stir up hostility toward its victims."[15] To the horror of many on the right, Koop's report advocated condom use and AIDS education starting "at the lowest grade possible," while rejecting mandatory testing or quarantining of HIV carriers. "We can no longer afford to sidestep frank, open discussions about sexual practices—homosexual and heterosexual," Koop declared.[16]

Koop released the "unusually explicit" report on October 22, 1986, causing a media sensation. "Suddenly," he wrote, "I found myself praised by my former liberal adversaries and condemned by my former conservative allies." Right-wing activist Phyllis Schlafly accused him of wanting to teach "safe sodomy" to third graders. White House aides pressured him to "update" the report to take out the word "condom," but he refused. In 1988, Koop would oversee the mass mailing of a shorter pamphlet called *Understanding AIDS* to a hundred million households over the opposition of social conservatives who argued, in the words of White House domestic policy adviser Gary Bauer, that "the clinical details in the brochure violate family privacy. . . . It discusses anal sex, sex organs, semen, condoms."[17]

The problem, Koop later wrote, was that the president was not "offering the leadership that only he could provide. At least a dozen times I pled with my critics in the White House to set up a meeting between the president and me so he could hear my concerns about America and the AIDS epidemic. And for months I had tried to cover for the embarrassing silence of the Oval Office on the scourge of AIDS."

The first Reagan speech to mention AIDS did not come until April 1987, more than halfway through his second term, and his comments were brief and superficial. TV anchorman Tom Brokaw reported that Reagan had not even read his own surgeon general's report on AIDS.[18]

The following month, Reagan was due to deliver a longer speech on AIDS at the invitation of movie star Elizabeth Taylor, whom Nancy Reagan had known since their long-ago days as young actresses at MGM. Now the national chairwoman of the American Foundation for AIDS Research, Taylor invited the president to address the group's fundraising dinner in Washington on May 31, 1987. By then AIDS had already killed more than sixteen thousand Americans and infected many more. Its high-profile victims included fashion designer Perry Ellis, the pianist Liberace, right-wing attorney Roy Cohn, and conservative activist Terry Dolan (whose brother Tony Dolan succeeded Ben Elliott as the chief White House speechwriter).[19]

Wanting to make sure that conservatives in the White House speechwriting office did not put words in the president's mouth, Nancy Reagan brought in Landon Parvin, who in March had crafted Reagan's Iran-Contra *mea culpa*, to write the speech. As with most major presidential addresses, what emerged was a compromise, with Parvin having to balance the scientific advice of Koop and Fauci with the political and religious views of social conservatives such as Gary Bauer and Education Secretary William Bennett. Bauer recalled that the conservatives did not want the president to address AIDS at all: "On the conservative side, there was more of a sense, you know, this is why we have a surgeon general." The only message the conservatives wanted to send, Koop noted, was that the answer to AIDS was a return to "traditional morality."[20]

Reagan never mentioned homosexuality in his speech, but he did issue a plea for tolerance of AIDS patients: "It's . . . important that America not reject those who have the disease, but care for them with dignity and kindness." He also did his best to dispel "unfounded" fears "based on ignorance," saying that "the Public Health Service has stated that there's no medical reason for barring a person with the virus from any routine school or work activity. There's no reason for those who carry the AIDS virus to wear a scarlet A. AIDS is not a casually contagious disease."

Among AIDS activists, the most controversial part of the speech was his call to expand testing and deny entry to the United States to AIDS patients. Those sections of the speech were greeted with boos and cries of "no" from some in the audience. Activists wanted laws passed to prevent discrimination against AIDS patients before mandating testing. Koop—described by the author Randy Shilts as a "certifiable AIDS hero"—supported such legislation. Reagan did not. But Elizabeth Taylor said afterward that, "while there are differences of opinion on AIDS testing," Reagan's remarks were "basically in concurrence with what we all hope and pray for."[21]

The month after delivering his speech to the AIDS research foundation, Reagan responded to political pressure by forming the President's Commission on the HIV Epidemic to investigate the disease and make policy recommendations. The list of eleven members drawn up by the White House

included leading social conservatives with no medical or scientific expertise, such as Cardinal John O'Connor of New York and California sex therapist Theresa Crenshaw, who had called for quarantining AIDS patients
and expelling them from schools. The chairman was retired Admiral James
Watkins, a devout Catholic who, as a member of the Joint Chiefs of Staff,
had played a major role in launching "Star Wars" in 1983. There was only
one openly gay member—a professor of medicine from New York—and even
his inclusion led to criticism on the right. Gary Bauer fumed to Reagan, "For
you to appoint a known homosexual to a Presidential Commission will give
homosexuality a stamp of approval. . . . If you feel we must appoint a homosexual, I would recommend a 'reformed' homosexual—that is someone not
currently living a gay life style."[22]

Despite the pressure exerted by social conservatives, the Watkins commission report, released in 1988, turned out to be much less doctrinaire than
expected. It argued against mandatory testing and reporting and called
for new legislation forbidding discrimination against people with the HIV
virus. The White House response was "muted," but the report was welcomed by AIDS activists.[23]

Reagan became more sensitized to the toll of AIDS after Reagan family
friend Douglas Wick—a movie producer and son of US Information Agency
director Charles Z. Wick—arranged a meeting in 1988 for the president
and first lady with museum director Elizabeth Glaser. The wife of actor
Paul Michael Glaser (one of the stars of television's *Starsky and Hutch*), she
had contracted AIDS during a blood transfusion and had infected her two
infant children, one of whom had already died. A wealthy, white, heterosexual woman from a show-business family—now this was an AIDS suf-
ferer with whom Reagan could identify. Wick noted that "he was riveted"
while she told her story. She implored the president "to be a leader in the
struggle against AIDS." After this "intense," hourlong meeting in the White
House family quarters, Glaser left convinced "that we were on the threshold of major and significant political change." But she soon realized she was
wrong: "Time went by and nothing happened." She herself would die of
AIDS in 1994.[24]

It is damning with faint praise to say that President Reagan's record on
AIDS was not as bad as it could have been; he was no Jesse Helms. But his

record was not nearly as good as it could have been or should have been given the magnitude of the crisis. Nearly fifty thousand Americans died of the disease while he was president, and yet it was never a priority for him. "Ronald Reagan made me an AIDS activist," Act Up founder Larry Kramer said. "On this issue, and on anything having to do with homosexuality, Reagan was just dreadful."[25]

The journalist Randy Shilts, in his best-selling book *And the Band Played On* about the early years of AIDS, argued that "Ronald Reagan would be remembered in history books for one thing beyond all else: He was the man who had let AIDS rage across America."[26] That was an understandable exaggeration from an author who would himself become one of the epidemic's many casualties. In reality, scientific understanding of this mysterious new disease would have taken time no matter who was president. But the development of treatments and vaccines could have been accelerated with more federal support early on.

Historian Jonathan Engel delivered a more measured but still scathing verdict: "In the end, Reagan's record on AIDS was middling to poor. Although he eschewed the vitriolic gay-baiting rhetoric of the far right, his reluctance to fully embrace the disaster in all of its magnitude exposed his latent homophobia, or disengagement, or both."[27] And yet Reagan disappointed his social conservative allies by not taking an even more callous and censorious approach to what they called the "gay plague."

Reagan finally delivered for social conservatives in the summer of 1987 when Justice Lewis Powell, a courtly Southern centrist appointed by Richard Nixon, retired from the Supreme Court. He was the pivotal fifth vote providing a working majority to the liberal bloc, so his replacement would be crucial in determining whether conservatives would finally seize control of the high court, as they had been trying to do ever since the 1954 *Brown v. Board of Education* decision. Organizations such as the Federalist Society, the Free Congress Foundation, and the Heritage Foundation strategized with Attorney General Ed Meese and his top aides to place "movement conservatives" on the bench.

Right-wing legal activists had been disappointed with Reagan's first choice for a high court seat—Sandra Day O'Connor—but they had been much happier with Reagan's decision in 1986, following the retirement of Chief Justice Warren Burger, to elevate Associate Justice William Rehnquist to chief justice and to nominate Antonin Scalia, a brilliant appeals court judge, as an associate justice. Both Rehnquist and Scalia were hard-core conservatives who generally could be counted on to oppose abortion, pornography, civil rights, gay rights, and criminal defendants' rights while defending the death penalty, gun rights, religion in public life, campaign financing, and economic freedoms. Their judicial philosophy was known variously as "originalism," "judicial restraint," or "strict constructionism," and it was premised on the notion that judges should not read any more into the Constitution than the Founders had intended. They looked with scorn on more liberal judges who saw the Constitution as a living document meant to be interpreted in light of changing circumstances. The same conservative view was shared by many of the nearly four hundred federal judges appointed by Reagan—nearly half of the entire federal judiciary and more than any other president in history.[28]

Those appointments were engineered by conservative activists in the Justice Department and the White House. The president had little knowledge of, or interest in, their abstruse legal theories. Nor, contrary to what so many imagined, was he determined to put justices on the bench with the single-minded goal of overturning *Roe v. Wade*, the landmark 1973 decision recognizing a right to abortion. Ever since his days as governor of California, his primary interest in the courts had been in their handling of criminal cases. He did not want to appoint any more judges in the mold of Donald R. Wright, the California State Supreme Court chief justice who had voted to overturn the death penalty. White House counsel A. B. Culvahouse recalled that "there were never any *Roe v. Wade* instructions" from the president: "He just said he wanted to pick judges who would not invent new ways to turn guilty criminals free."[29]

Judge Robert H. Bork seemed like the perfect choice. Highly intelligent and exceedingly erudite, he was a conservative legal superstar: a former solicitor general in the Nixon administration and former Yale law professor now serving on the federal appeals court for the District of Columbia. His criticisms of antitrust law had influenced the Justice Department's decision to drastically scale back antitrust enforcement. As far back as 1981, Reagan had been privately assuring conservatives upset about O'Connor's selection that "the person highest on the list for the next appointment, which I hope will be soon, is Bob Bork." When Lewis Powell announced his retirement on June 26, 1987, Reagan told Culvahouse, "I believe it's Bob Bork's turn."[30]

The White House was lulled into a false sense of complacency by the unanimous confirmation of the congenial Scalia, while ignoring the danger signs from Rehnquist's bruising confirmation battle: Thirty-three senators had opposed his promotion to chief justice. Administration aides seemed to imagine that Bork, a Falstaffian figure with a scraggly beard and a love of talk, drink, food, and cigarettes, could win without a serious fight. They touted him as "one of the most qualified individuals ever nominated to the Supreme Court." But he had a long, troubling record that provided ample ammunition for his critics.

In 1963, he had written an article condemning civil rights legislation to ban discrimination in restaurants, hotels, and other public accommodations because it meant the government telling private businesses what to do. He called this "a principle of unsurpassed ugliness," ignoring—as Ronald Reagan also did—the even greater ugliness of Jim Crow segregation. In a 1971 article, he excoriated the Supreme Court's 1965 ruling in *Griswold v. Connecticut*, which cited an expectation of privacy in the Constitution to overturn a ban on contraception. He then vilified *Roe v. Wade*, which grew out of *Griswold*, as an "unconstitutional decision." What's more, as solicitor general in 1973, Bork had gained a reputation as a right-wing hatchet man by following Richard Nixon's order to fire special counsel Archibald Cox in the "Saturday Night Massacre" after the attorney general and deputy attorney general had resigned rather than do so.[31]

Ted Kennedy, a former chairman of the Senate Judiciary Committee, was well briefed—and considerably alarmed—about Bork's views. He was ready to strike as soon as the nomination was announced on July 1, 1987. In his distinctive Boston accent, he thundered,

> Robert Bork's America is a land in which women would be forced into back-alley abortions, blacks would sit at segregated lunch counters, rogue police could break down citizens' doors in midnight raids, school children could not be taught about evolution, writers and artists

could be censored at the whim of the government, and the doors of the federal courts would be shut on the fingers of millions of citizens for whom the judiciary is—and is often the only—protector of the individual rights that are at the heart of democracy.[32]

Kennedy's scathing indictment distorted and exaggerated Bork's views—the nominee had never opposed the teaching of evolution, for example—but Bork was fooling himself in thinking that "not one line of that tirade was true."[33] There was enough truth in what Kennedy said that his words stung and had staying power.

The chairman of the Senate Judiciary Committee, Senator Joe Biden of Delaware, soon joined Kennedy and other liberals in opposition to the Bork nomination. Biden waited an unusually long time—two-and-a-half months—between the nomination and the start of confirmation hearings to give liberal activists time to mobilize. Kennedy worked all summer to marshal a coalition of civil rights groups, women's rights groups, labor rights groups, and others. "Those opposing the Bork nomination have been effective and are very organized," A. B. Culvahouse warned Howard Baker.[34]

Bork and his camp, by contrast, did not mount a similar campaign. The nominee thought that would be unseemly. He and his supporters imagined that his intellectual brilliance would shine through and win over the senators. Rather than try to defend Bork's views, the administration argued that the Senate had no right to reject him over a mere difference of opinion because he was qualified to sit on the court. "We really touched a nerve in the ultra-liberal community," Reagan wrote to his fellow conservative actor Charlton Heston a week after nominating Bork, "but he doesn't deserve the abuse he's taking."[35]

The pro-Bork forces were at a critical disadvantage in the battle for public opinion because in 1987 most Americans still got their news from mainstream news organizations—in particular, the three major broadcast networks—that were dominated by journalists of the center left. Among the major newspapers, only the *Wall Street Journal*'s conservative editorial page championed Bork's cause, and even its news side offered more critical coverage.

While there were some conservative talk-radio hosts around the country, Fox News Channel and most of the conservative media that would spring up in the decades ahead did not yet exist. Reagan's Federal Communications Commission (FCC) was bringing them into being that very year—1987—by repealing the Fairness Doctrine, which had forced broadcasters to present both sides of controversial issues. FCC chairman Mark S. Fowler, a Reagan appointee, was a libertarian who believed that television is "just another appliance ... a toaster with pictures," and he argued that federal oversight of its content was unnecessary. Congress tried to reinstate the Fairness Doctrine in June 1987, but the former radio sportscaster in the Oval Office vetoed the bill, which was opposed by the broadcasting industry. "It shouldn't take the force of law to compel broadcasters to be fair," Reagan said. Maybe it shouldn't have, but the law's absence would create a free-for-all in broadcast media that would make it possible for the *Rush Limbaugh Show* to premiere in national syndication in 1988 and for Fox News Channel to make its cable debut in 1996.[36]

These and many other outlets, including social media sites that were unimaginable in the 1980s, would give conservative activists powerful tools to shape public opinion without the necessity to be fair—or accurate. But all that lay in the future. In 1987, the high-profile battle over Bork was fought on mainstream media terrain unfavorable to the hard right.

The confirmation hearings began on September 15, 1987, in the spacious and ornate Senate Caucus Room in the Russell Senate Office Building. This had been the setting of numerous historic showdowns, including the Army-McCarthy hearings and the Watergate hearings. Just two months earlier, in this very room, Oliver North had scored an unexpected public relations victory over the Iran-Contra committees. The Democratic Senate Judiciary Committee staff were determined not to allow a replay of that debacle; they even lowered the height of the platform from which the senators were speaking so they did not appear to loom over the witnesses.

In truth, they need not have worried. Bob Bork was no Ollie North. "I did not have the histrionic talents of North," the nominee acknowledged, "and, if I had, would not have employed them."[37] Rather than emotional, flag-waving appeals, Bork preferred to stick to cold legal logic. This time it would be the Democratic senators who would rouse the public. Prickly and persnickety, Bork acted as if he were in a law school colloquium rather than fighting for his life in the political colosseum. When Ted Kennedy brought up his 1963 opposition to the Civil Rights Act, for example, Bork said he had modified his views but did not apologize for his past statements or show any empathy for the suffering Black Americans had endured.

Bork's most damaging replies were to supposedly easy questions from his own supporters. Senator Orrin Hatch wanted him to explain that his opposition to a 1966 Supreme Court decision striking down literacy tests for voting—a ploy used in the South to disenfranchise Black voters—did not mean that he was in *favor* of literacy tests. "I have, in matter of fact, no view of literacy tests," Bork replied woodenly. "I have not looked at how they operate." Republican Senator Gordon Humphrey of New Hampshire asked him to discuss the responsibility of judges "to protect society and individual citizens from criminals." Again, Bork passed up the opportunity, saying, "I am not an expert on criminal law." Worst of all, Republican Senator Alan Simpson of Wyoming asked Bork why he wanted to be on the Supreme Court. Rather than talking about how much he wanted to serve the country, Bork replied, "I think it would be an intellectual feast." That would be the only line most people would remember from the hearings. He thereby gave the impression that he was an egghead far removed from the concerns of ordinary citizens.[38]

Reagan was clearly not paying close attention to the hearings because he claimed in his diary that Bork's opponents "never laid a hand on him." In fact, they knocked him out—and Bork had no one but himself to blame. "It was apparent," White House communications director Tom Griscom noted, "that Judge Bork looked at some of these senators asking questions and felt like they were asinine. He was going to show them he was smarter than they were." That was an understandable but self-destructive impulse.[39]

By the end of the twelve days of hearings, the impolitic nominee had lost the conservative Southern Democrats and liberal Northern Republicans whose support he needed. Bork and his backers blamed the White House for not doing more to champion his cause—in part, they suspected, because Chief of Staff Howard Baker was not overly enthusiastic about the nomination. A. B. Culvahouse acknowledged to me that conservative critics were right: "I think the White House was still back on its heels from Iran-Contra. We felt like we had just survived. . . . The whole White House was not leaning in like they could have."[40] But no amount of White House lobbying could have saved Bork from himself. He was simply not an effective advocate for his own cause.

By October 9, 1987, Bork's defeat was a foregone conclusion. He nevertheless went with his family to the White House that day to ask President Reagan not to pull his nomination. Deputy Chief of Staff Ken Duberstein recalled Bork saying, "I want the sons of bitches to vote up or down." "He believed he was railroaded," Duberstein explained, "and he was trying to restore his own reputation."[41] But Bork was merely prolonging the agony. On the afternoon of Friday, October 23, the Senate voted fifty-eight to forty-two to reject his nomination—the biggest margin of defeat for any Supreme Court nominee in history. It was a stinging loss for the Reagan administration and the conservative legal movement. The hearings gave birth to a new term among Republicans—"borking"—for the calumny they believed the nominee had suffered.

If Reagan was as hurt by Bork's defeat as many of his supporters were, he gave little sign of it. He phoned Bork to express, as he wrote in his diary, "my very real regret and reiterated my great respect and admiration for him." He also complained to conservative supporters about the "disgraceful . . . shenanigans." But he showed little real anger. Bork—a *cause célèbre* on the right—warranted only one brief mention in Reagan's memoir. The perpetually sunny president, unlike so many of his supporters, was not one to nurse grievances. He preferred, in fact, to erase defeats (for example, his 1968 campaign for president) from his memory banks.[42]

In any case, Ronald Reagan had greater worries that autumn than the fate of the Bork nomination. On October 5, 1987, Nancy Reagan was diagnosed with breast cancer; twelve days later, on October 17, she had a mastectomy. The president had taken the initial diagnosis in his usual, optimistic stride, but, according to Jim Kuhn, the morning of the surgery he "looked hollowed out, nervous, even frightened," because he was so fearful of anything happening to his "roommate." When the pathology report confirmed that the removed tumor had been malignant, the president wept.[43]

Two days after the successful surgery, on October 19, 1987, the stock market experienced its biggest one-day drop since the Great Depression as part of a worldwide financial contagion that highlighted the risk of "globalization." Many worried that the stock market crash presaged troubles for the larger economy. It didn't, but it would take nearly two years for stocks to recover from "Black Monday" and finally surpass their pre-crash high.[44]

And then, a week after Black Monday, Nancy's mother, Edith Luckett Davis, died of a stroke at age ninety-nine. (Obituaries reported she was ninety-one because she had lied about her age.) Ronnie looked "just stricken" when he told Nancy, "Honey, Edie is now with Loyal." The first lady, only days after her own surgery, was in a "daze" as she flew to Phoenix for the funeral and the same might be said of her grief-stricken husband. Even a death could not, however, dispel the Reagans' difficult family dynamics. Nancy was irate when her daughter Patti skipped the funeral. Patti later apologized but never told Nancy the reason why: Edith had traumatized her, when Patti was just entering adolescence, by making crude comments and roughly grabbing her.[45]

There is nothing like personal heartbreak to put professional disappointment into perspective. October 1987 was, as Nancy wrote, "a terrible month" for reasons that had nothing to do with a judicial nomination. So Bork's defeat did not weigh nearly as much on the president as it did on many of his supporters. In any case, one of Reagan's great strengths, Howard Baker noted, "was that he almost never—sometimes but almost never—held any sort of grudge or lingering regret about things. He just moved [on]."[46]

As soon as Bork was defeated, Ed Meese pushed for the appointment of another staunch conservative from the District of Columbia Circuit Court of Appeals: Judge Douglas H. Ginsburg. Reagan was amenable. "There's no way I'd go for a touch of liberalism to win over the lynch mob," he assured his old conservative comrade, retired senator and actor George Murphy.[47]

Described by White House vetters as an "extremely intelligent and able man with outstanding academic and professional qualifications," Ginsburg was much younger than Bork and had served only a year on the bench. His lack of a paper trail made him, in theory, more confirmable. Before joining the court in 1986, Ginsburg had served as an assistant attorney general for antitrust. "We don't have to vet him, he's one of us," Meese assured the White House staff.[48]

That turned out to be a fatal miscalculation. Days after his nomination on October 29, 1987, reporters discovered that Ginsburg had used marijuana while on the Harvard Law School faculty in the late 1970s. This was

considered a graver issue in those days than it would be today and cost Ginsburg support among social conservatives who were wary of him to begin
with. He was forced to withdraw his nomination after a mere nine days.[49]

The president and his team had struck out twice. They could not afford to
fail again or else they would reinforce the impression created by the Iran-
Contra affair of an administration that had lost its way. By now the White
House wasn't looking for a conservative fire-breather; they just wanted
"somebody who's confirmable," Ken Duberstein recalled.[50]

Anthony Kennedy, a soft-spoken federal appeals court judge from Sacramento, fit the bill. Unlike Bork, he had a consensus-building style and a
bland public image. White House aides described him as "somewhat of an
enigma," which would make him hard to attack. And, unlike Ginsburg, he
did not have any blemishes in his private life. When A. B. Culvahouse and
Ken Duberstein sat down to interview him, Kennedy said, "You know, you're
in for a very boring Sunday morning," which was just what they wanted
to hear. "I probably vetted Kennedy harder than I've vetted anyone else,
because we had no margin for error," Culvahouse said. In the future, when
Tony Kennedy and his wife would run into Culvahouse, the justice would
turn to her and say, "Mary, you remember A.B. He was the lawyer that asked
me if you were pregnant when we got married."[51] Kennedy breezed through
his confirmation hearing and was confirmed ninety-seven to zero—the last
justice to be confirmed unanimously.

He would go on to confirm the worst fears of conservatives by becoming part of a centrist Supreme Court bloc that voted to uphold *Roe v. Wade*.
It would be another thirty-five years—not until 2022—before conservatives
could muster a Supreme Court majority to overturn the abortion decision.
That result might have been achieved decades earlier if Bork had prevailed
in 1987. But there was little sign that Ronald Reagan was personally troubled by that failure. He just wasn't the pro-life crusader that so many of his
followers desired. The president was concentrating on different matters in
his final years in office. His focus was primarily on foreign policy, specifically on working with Mikhail Gorbachev to end the Cold War.

Tear Down This Wall

He was a master at putting out the right rhetoric that would
ensure his base of support would stay with him and at the same
time proceeding down a more pragmatic path.

—FRANK CARLUCCI

After the 1985 Geneva summit and the 1986 Reykjavik summit, President Reagan and his top advisers remained unsure how seriously to take Mikhail Gorbachev's talk of peace and cooperation: Was he genuinely intent on transforming the Soviet system, or was this merely a ploy to sucker the United States into letting down its guard? As so often happened, Secretary of State George Shultz and Secretary of Defense Caspar Weinberger were on opposite sides of the internal debate.

Shultz visited Moscow in April 1987 and had productive meetings with Gorbachev and Foreign Minister Eduard Shevardnadze. They were much less defensive than their predecessors had been about the Soviet human rights record, and Gorbachev was eager to hear from Shultz about how the spread of computers was transforming the global economy. Shultz felt he was establishing a relationship of mutual respect and trust with both men. The secretary of state also saw for himself that Gorbachev's bold reforms, *glasnost* (openness) and *perestroika* (restructuring), were beginning to transform Soviet society. He came away convinced, as he later wrote, "that we now had broken through to new ground with the Soviets."[1]

Weinberger, by contrast, remained an unreconstructed cold warrior. "Gorbachev to this day is a committed Communist and still believes that what is necessary is to strengthen communism," he told an interviewer in 2002. "I didn't, frankly, ever trust Gorbachev." Weinberger was joined in his skepticism by CIA Deputy Director Robert Gates, who wrote to the president in late 1987, "It is hard to detect fundamental changes, currently or in prospect, in the way the Soviets govern at home or in their principal objectives abroad."[2]

The division among Reagan's advisers mirrored the division in his own head. On the one hand, he had met Gorbachev twice and found that he was amiable, someone he could work with. On the other hand, it was hard to jettison the anti-Soviet ideology he had been espousing for forty years. Moreover, it was politically advantageous to sound like a hard-liner to rally conservatives during the Iran-Contra crisis. In his State of the Union Address on January 3, 1987, Reagan cited the presence of Soviet military advisers all over the developing world and demanded, "Can anyone still doubt their single-minded determination to expand their power?" Speaking privately to the National Security Council on March 13, 1987, he trotted out his favorite fake Lenin quote about how, once the Communists seized control of Latin America, the United States would "fall into their hands like overripe fruit." "I'm still the R.R. I was, and the evil empire is still just that," Reagan assured Elizabeth "Nackey" Loeb, the ultraconservative publisher of the *Manchester Union-Leader* in New Hampshire.[3]

Yet Reagan rejected the advice of hard-liners like Weinberger to cut off contact with the Soviets after a spy scandal at the US Embassy in Moscow in the spring of 1987: The KGB was found to have suborned one of the Marine guards and to have planted listening devices in a new US embassy building that was under construction. Despite the outrage this generated in the United States, Reagan gave Shultz permission to continue talking with the Soviets.

The president's competing impulses could be seen in his celebrated speech in Berlin on June 12, 1987. Standing before a picture-perfect backdrop, with the Berlin Wall and the Brandenburg Gate looming behind him, Reagan noted evidence of change in the USSR—"Some political prisoners have been released. Certain foreign news broadcasts are no longer being jammed. Some economic enterprises have been permitted to operate with greater freedom"—but he expressed uncertainty about their significance: "Are these the beginnings of profound changes in the Soviet state? Or are they token gestures, intended to raise false hopes in the West, or to strengthen the Soviet system without changing it?" Then came the rhetorical hammer blow: "There is one sign the Soviets can make that would be unmistakable, that would advance dramatically the cause of freedom and peace. General Secretary Gorbachev, if you seek peace, if you seek prosperity for the Soviet

Union and Eastern Europe, if you seek liberalization: Come here to this gate! Mr. Gorbachev, open this gate! Mr. Gorbachev, tear down this wall!"[4]

The speech—one of the most notable of the entire presidency, ranking alongside the Westminster speech in 1982, the D-Day speech in 1984, and the *Challenger* speech in 1986—would become so famous that it would spark quarrels about its gestation. Reagan himself had almost no input in preparing the address, which was primarily written by speechwriter Peter Robinson, beyond approving the memorable phrase "Mr. Gorbachev, tear down this wall!"; the seventy-six-year-old president was slowing down by 1987 and wasn't as active a participant in speechwriting as he had once been.[5] The State Department expressed misgivings about so openly challenging Gorbachev when relations with the Soviet Union were finally improving, but with the president's blessing the phrase stayed in—and the rest was history.

Or was it? Some Reagan admirers like to draw a straight line from the words he spoke in 1987 to the collapse of the Berlin Wall two-and-a-half years later. But, in fact, there is scant evidence of any connection. Gorbachev did not need Reagan to tell him that the wall should come down; he had already said as much to East German leader Erich Honecker the previous month. Reagan's speech, by alarming Soviet hard-liners, may actually have made that goal harder to achieve. Brent Scowcroft, who would be national security adviser when the wall fell, told author James Mann that the speech was "irrelevant," and George Shultz never mentioned it in his 1,183-page account of his tenure as secretary of state.[6]

Reagan himself seemed to walk back the speech a little more than a year later: On September 23, 1988, he told Eduard Shevardnadze in the Oval Office that "it had perhaps been unrealistic to have suggested then that the Berlin Wall be torn down in its entirety" and suggested that he would be satisfied if "the two parts of Berlin" could simply "work together."[7] That conciliatory message, so at odds with the confrontational rhetoric at the Brandenburg Gate, is missing from Reagan hagiography.

The primary significance of the Berlin Wall speech would turn out to be the way it, along with the "ash heap of history" speech, added to the legend of Ronald Reagan as an oracle prophesying the end of the Cold War. But, contrary to so much mythologizing from Reagan supporters (but not from Reagan himself), the Cold War ended not because of Reagan's confrontational approach but because of his willingness to cooperate with Gorbachev. Frank Carlucci suggested in an interview for this book that the "Tear Down

This Wall" speech was essentially a feint to keep conservatives happy: "He was a master at putting out the right rhetoric that would ensure his base of support would stay with him and at the same time proceeding down a more pragmatic path."[8]

The path to peace was cleared by the fortuitous removal of hard-liners on both sides. On May 28, 1987, a German teenager named Matthias Rust stunned the world by flying a small Cessna aircraft from Helsinki to land in Moscow's Red Square. His flight greatly embarrassed the Soviet military by so easily penetrating their air defenses. Gorbachev took advantage of this debacle to sack 150 senior officers, including the minister of defense, who were hostile to his reform agenda. With this bloodless purge, Gorbachev removed a major obstacle to ending the arms race.[9]

In 1987 Gorbachev not only offered to get rid of all medium-range missiles on both sides but also abandoned his demands to keep SDI in the laboratory as the price of a deal; he was willing to allow testing while maintaining a ten-year delay before any deployment. Much to the consternation of Russian generals, he also agreed to include among the missiles to be eliminated the short-range SS-23, which technically did not meet the definition of a "medium-range" missile. He even offered intrusive on-site inspections that neither the Soviet nor US militaries were comfortable with. This allowed Soviet and American negotiators to complete work by the end of the year on an Intermediate Nuclear Forces (INF) Treaty.

The Reagan administration, in turn, was more willing to deal with Gorbachev because of the departure of Cap Weinberger from the Defense Department in November 1987. The official explanation was that he was leaving to spend more time with his sick wife—a story Jane Weinberger publicly denied—but there was a general sense that Weinberger was now the odd man out in an administration that was no longer bound by the old dogmas of the Cold War that had prevailed since the late 1940s.[10] The military buildup was over; now it was time for arms reductions that Weinberger could not stomach. Frank Carlucci took over as defense secretary and Lieutenant General Colin Powell replaced him as national security adviser, becoming the first African American ever to hold that post.

Both men would find a congenial partner in Chief of Staff Howard Baker—and, after Baker's departure in July 1988 (also to take care of a sick wife), with his replacement, Ken Duberstein. Powell and Duberstein were both from New York—Powell from the Bronx, Duberstein from Brooklyn—and they would become particularly close friends. Duberstein effectively ran the White House long before receiving the title of chief of staff. "[Howard] Baker's forte had never been in administration," his biographer noted. He delegated those responsibilities to Duberstein, who recalled that Baker lost interest in the job once he realized that Reagan had his faculties "in great shape" and that "he was president, not Howard."[11]

Shultz and Carlucci did not always see eye to eye; Carlucci was more skeptical of Gorbachev. But Weinberger's departure meant that the administration for the first time had a reasonably cohesive foreign policy team composed of pragmatists. Shultz, Powell, and Carlucci met at 7:00 a.m. every day when they were in Washington for coffee and doughnuts in Powell's West Wing office. Not getting much useful guidance from the president, they decided to simply run foreign policy on their own. "No staff, no fixed agenda, but we made a lot of decisions," Carlucci recalled. "The three of us decided that we would sort out the different conflicts and make the decisions, because if the three of us agreed, the president would agree."[12]

The foreign policy team also had excellent relations with Baker and Duberstein and with communications director Tom Griscom and press secretary Marlin Fitzwater. "We were really good as a team," Powell said. "We were all knitted up. The reason it worked was because we all got along."[13]

———

Reagan had long been anxious to bring Soviet leaders to America to convince them of the superiority of capitalism: "I'd . . . like to ask when, if ever, they think their systems can produce anything like what we have here." He finally got his chance. While Mikhail Gorbachev turned down White House offers for "the grand tour" of America, he arrived with Raisa on December 7, 1987, in Washington, DC.[14]

Normally a treaty was signed at the end rather than the beginning of a summit. But Ken Duberstein insisted to Colin Powell that the INF Treaty would have to be signed on December 8 at precisely 1:45 p.m. Powell demanded to know why the timing was so important. Duberstein hemmed and hawed but eventually revealed that the first lady's astrologer had insisted. (Duberstein had inherited Michael Deaver's old job of liaison with Nancy Reagan.) At the appointed hour, Reagan and Gorbachev sat side by side in the East Room at a table once used by Abraham Lincoln to sign the first US-Soviet treaty that did not just limit the growth of missile stockpiles but actually eliminated an entire class of missiles. As a result of the INF Treaty, the United States would scrap 859 missiles and the Soviet Union 1,752.[15]

In the conversations between the two leaders that day and the next, Gorbachev tried to accelerate agreement toward ending the Cold War, but Reagan had trouble following exactly what Gorbachev was saying or seizing the opportunities on offer. Colin Powell noted that Gorbachev, who spoke through a translator, was "bright," "fast," "vigorous," and that he was "tossing off terms like 'MIRV' and 'depressed trajectories' and the throw weights of SS-12s, -13s, 18s, and 24s, like one of Ken Adelman's wonks in the Arms Control and Disarmament Administration."[16]

By contrast, the aging president let George Shultz do most of the talking for the US side, and when he did interject, the results were embarrassing. That afternoon, during a meeting in the Oval Office, Reagan trotted out one of his stock anti-Soviet jokes: An American professor takes a taxi to the airport on his way to the Soviet Union and the taxi driver tells him he is trying to make money to finish his education. When the professor asks what he wants to be, he replies, "I haven't decided yet." On arriving in the Soviet Union, the professor has a similar conversation with a Russian taxi driver. When asked what he wants to be, the Russian replies, "They haven't told me yet."

"As he finished the story," Powell observed, "the Americans wanted to disappear under the table, while Gorbachev stared straight ahead." Reagan did not seem to notice how his offensive joke fell flat; he was so proud of it, in fact, that he included it in his memoir.[17]

Reagan's first-day performance seemed to vindicate Richard Nixon's private judgment after meeting with him in the family quarters of the White House a few months earlier: "I must regretfully observe that Reagan looks far older, more tired, and less vigorous in person than in public. There is no way he can ever be allowed to participate in a private meeting with Gorbachev." Powell realized that "the President's performance continued to reveal his thin preparation," and ordered the NSC staff to work all night if necessary to prepare better talking points for the next day.[18]

The next morning, December 9, 1987, the president got off to a better start by reading a lengthy opening statement from note cards. But he barely responded when Gorbachev proposed that the two superpowers work together to end regional conflicts in countries such as Angola, Afghanistan, and Nicaragua. Gorbachev proposed that both sides cut off arms supplies to their proxies and pressure them into political settlements. This would have achieved what Reagan wanted—getting the Soviets to stop supporting wars of "national liberation" in the Third World. Indeed, Gorbachev had already made clear in private that the Red Army was going to leave Afghanistan—a commitment he would publicly announce in February 1988. The withdrawal was completed a year later.

Rather than seize the opportunity, Reagan complained that if the United States cut off support for the Afghan "freedom fighters," they would be at the mercy of the government's army. He ignored well-founded warnings that the overthrow of the Soviet-supported Najibullah regime would lead to a takeover by Islamic extremists. As for Nicaragua, Reagan simply complained that "Soviet supplies" made the Sandinistas "the most powerful military force in the area," seemingly without understanding that Gorbachev had just offered to cut off the Sandinistas.[19]

Predictably, the two leaders also talked past one another on SDI. Gorbachev tried to get firm agreement on what had tentatively been agreed to at Reykjavik: a 50 percent cut in strategic nuclear weapons along with a delay of at least ten years in deploying missile defenses. He had since made a concession by agreeing that the United States could test SDI systems, but there was no comparable concession from the US side. Instead, Reagan proposed that both sides deploy missile defenses. Gorbachev replied with obvious exasperation that "Moscow had no intention of developing its own SDI." Unlike Reagan, Gorbachev was listening to the scientists—in particular, to his scientific adviser Evgeny Velikhov—who were warning that a space shield was a costly fantasy.[20]

But the disagreements behind closed doors were overshadowed by the theatrics of the summit—the first time a Soviet leader had come to the United States since Leonid Brezhnev's visit in 1973. The Reagans hosted a glittering state dinner for the Gorbachevs at the White House on December 8, with entertainment provided by the American pianist Van Cliburn, who was beloved in Russia. The next night, the Gorbachevs reciprocated the Reagans' hospitality at the Soviet Embassy. A who's who of capitalist society—movie stars, athletes, authors, musicians, religious leaders, industrialists,

and many others—eagerly showed up to meet the world's most powerful Communist. Joe DiMaggio even asked both leaders to sign a baseball
for him, and they obliged. Not even Nancy Reagan's continuing feud with
Raisa Gorbachev could put a damper on events. Nancy, resplendent at the
state dinner in a black, floor-length James Galanos gown, was offended that
Raisa lectured her, failed to offer condolences on her mother's death, did not
inquire about her recent breast cancer surgery, and held up the receiving
line at the state dinner by talking with each guest.[21]

On the morning of December 10, 1987, "Gorbymania" reached new
heights when the Soviet leader ordered his ZiL limousine to stop unexpectedly at the corner of Connecticut Avenue and L Street NW so he could jump
out to press the flesh as if he were running for office. "If a spaceship had
landed in the middle of Washington, it could not have caused more commotion," *New York Times* correspondent Maureen Dowd wrote. "Pedestrians
quivered with excitement. The Secret Service looked terrified. The K.G.B.
looked stunned." Gorbachev's unscheduled stop caused him to be late to the
White House, making Nancy Reagan "really, really, really angry," recalled
Tom Griscom, because he was throwing off the carefully planned schedule.
But her good-natured husband shrugged it off.[22]

The summit ended that afternoon with agreement that Reagan would
visit Moscow in the spring with the goal of signing a START treaty to reduce
the number of strategic weapons on both sides. The two leaders wrapped up
their final meeting together by swapping jokes. This time, Reagan refrained
from anti-Soviet jests.[23]

Gorbachev's charm offensive won over most Americans, including Ronald Reagan, but left many conservatives decidedly unimpressed. *National
Review* compared the president to arch-appeaser Neville Chamberlain, and
right-wing activist Howard Phillips accused the president of becoming "a
useful idiot for Soviet propaganda." The right even made common cause
with their old foes Henry Kissinger and Richard Nixon—the architects of
détente—to oppose an INF Treaty they all feared would undermine deterrence. Kissinger was "privately hyper critical" and told the White House
that the INF Treaty was the "worst thing since World War II."[24]

But while Reagan was pained by these attacks from his own side, he was
not swayed; he shot back that critics were uninformed and had accepted the
inevitability of war. It was an argument he won handily. The Senate ratified
the treaty by ninety-three to five in May 1988.

While making peace with the Soviet Union, Reagan once again found himself mired in conflict in the Middle East. Beginning in 1986, the administration agreed to reflag Kuwaiti oil tankers and provide them with naval escorts through the Persian Gulf to protect them from Iranian attacks that were an outgrowth of the Iran-Iraq War. On April 14, 1988, the frigate USS *Samuel Roberts* hit an Iranian mine that damaged the ship and injured ten sailors. US naval forces retaliated four days later in Operation Praying Mantis by sinking two Iranian oil platforms and six Iranian ships. Reagan approved the operation but, belying his trigger-happy image, insisted on warnings being issued to Iranian sailors so they could escape before their ship or platform was sunk.[25]

It would take a tragic accident, with echoes of the shootdown of KAL 007 in 1983, to finally end the tanker war: On July 3, 1988, the guided missile cruiser USS *Vincennes* detected what its crew believed was an inbound Iranian fighter aircraft and blew it out of the sky with a missile, only to learn that it was a civilian Iranian airliner carrying 290 people to Dubai. Wrongly believing that the shootdown had been deliberate, Iranian leaders decided to end their war with Iraq—and hence also their attacks on Persian Gulf shipping—before the US military became more heavily involved. On July 20, 1988, Ayatollah Khomeini announced an end to the eight-year Iran-Iraq War, which had cost half a million lives. Somehow, the Reagan administration had stumbled into unexpected success in its dealings with Iran after years of failure, heartbreak, and scandal.[26]

Even as US forces were at war in the Persian Gulf, Ronald Reagan remained far more focused on superpower relations. He was due to make his first visit to the Soviet Union in the spring of 1988, even though a START treaty reducing the number of strategic weapons was not ready for signing. The stumbling blocks were on the American side. The US Navy, for example, resisted Soviet demands to cut sea-launched nuclear cruise missiles or to verify compliance with on-site inspections. "On this issue the American position was absurd," wrote Jack Matlock, now the US ambassador to Moscow. "It was motivated not by U.S. national interests, but by the perceived parochial interest of a military service." A stronger, better-informed president might have broken through the bureaucratic inertia, but, as Richard Nixon discovered after meeting with him, "Reagan, candidly, did not seem to be on top of the issues—certainly in no way as knowledgeable as Gorbachev."[27]

Reagan's priority was preserving SDI, even though there was no sign of any impending technological breakthrough that could turn his vision of a space shield into reality. The Soviets had already dropped a link between stopping SDI and eliminating intermediate nuclear forces, but they were not willing to drop the link with strategic weapons reductions. Gorbachev also tried to interest the American side in massive cutbacks in conventional forces, but Shultz and Reagan did not seize the opportunity, preferring to leave that issue to negotiators in Vienna.[28]

Thus, the Moscow summit would be more about symbolism than substance—but, oh, was the symbolism significant. "If someone had told me when Ronnie and I were first married that we would eventually travel to Moscow as president and first lady and would be the honored guests of the Soviet leadership," Nancy Reagan wrote, "I would have suggested that he get his head examined."[29] And yet that is just what happened.

After four nights in Helsinki to adjust to jet lag, the Reagans landed on May 29, 1988, a sunny spring day, at Moscow's Vnukovo International Airport. Gorbachev having vetoed their plan to go to the apartment of a Jewish dissident couple, the Reagans proceeded straight to the Kremlin for a lavish welcoming ceremony and the first talks between the two leaders. Reagan and Gorbachev revisited many of their old disagreements but without the rancor of the past. "The two were like actors wearily reciting a familiar script," Matlock wrote. Gorbachev had become resigned to Reagan's discursive speaking style, his reliance on tired old anecdotes and jokes, and his inability to engage in the specifics of arms control. He told Nancy that they had developed a "chemistry," and he wished her husband could stay in office for four more years.[30]

At the end of the first day, the Reagans decided to go out and meet ordinary people as Gorbachev had done in Washington. To the consternation of both the KGB and the Secret Service, they took a ten-minute stroll through the Arbat, a pedestrian mall where they were enthusiastically greeted by shoppers. Tom Griscom described this as Nancy Reagan's revenge on Gorbachev for "the Connecticut Avenue deal." The KGB agents accompanying the president and first lady were not used to this sort of retail politicking, and they began elbowing and punching people to prevent them from getting too close to the Reagans. The Reagans had to intervene personally to prevent the security men from dragging away UPI reporter Helen Thomas.[31]

Notwithstanding this contretemps, the "friendliness and warmth" of ordinary Russians made a big impression on Reagan. "Where we went," he marveled, "they were massed on the curb, waving, smiling and cheering." When the president delivered a speech in praise of freedom to students at Gorbachev's alma mater, Moscow State University, Jack Matlock wryly noted, "The prolonged standing ovation he received was probably the most enthusiastic he had witnessed since the demonstration that followed his nomination at the Republican convention."[32]

While Reagan and Gorbachev strolled through Red Square, stopping to talk with small groups of people, Gorbachev picked up a small boy and told him, "Shake hands with Grandpa Reagan." Once the two leaders returned to the Kremlin, Sam Donaldson of ABC News asked, "Do you still think you're in an evil empire, Mr. President?" "No," Reagan replied. "I was talking about another time and another era."[33]

On his return to the United States on June 3, 1988, the president's focus shifted to other matters, in particular the election of a successor. He did not endorse his faithful vice president, George H. W. Bush, until after he had locked up the Republican nomination over a large field of rivals. While the two men got along well, they were not particularly close, and Nancy Reagan and Barbara Bush couldn't stand each other. (Bush's biographer Susan Page wrote that "Nancy was disdainful of Barbara for her sturdy figure, her matronly clothes, and her blunt manner," while "Barbara was disdainful of Nancy as brittle and shallow, and as a mother who failed to forge a close or even functional relationship with her children.")[34] Reagan was appreciative of Bush's loyalty but dubious about his political skills. "The problem with George on the campaign trail," Reagan told Brian Mulroney with a sad and wistful expression, "is that he doesn't seem able to generate gut enthusiasm for his cause."[35]

While lacking Reagan's political gifts, Bush made up an early poll deficit with a bare-knuckles campaign run by Reagan's 1984 deputy campaign manager, Lee Atwater, that was at odds with his gentlemanly mien. The Bush campaign played to white backlash politics just as Reagan had done so often in the past—in this case, with commercials lambasting the Democratic nominee, Massachusetts Governor Michael Dukakis, for a prison furlough program that released an African American criminal named Willie Horton who, while out of prison, raped a white woman and stabbed her boyfriend.[36] By depicting Dukakis as a soft-on-crime liberal and a "card-carrying member of the ACLU," while vowing never to raise taxes, Bush became the first sitting vice president since Martin van Buren in 1836 to win the presidency.

Bush made some attempts to differentiate himself from Reagan. In his convention acceptance speech, he promised a "kinder and gentler nation," implicitly acknowledging liberal critiques of the Reagan administration for being hard-hearted, and he adopted a more skeptical attitude toward Gorbachev's reforms in part to appeal to conservative voters. But in most respects, he ran as Reagan's heir. There could be no greater vindication of Reagan's tenure than to see his vice president winning what many saw as Reagan's third term. It was the first time since the days of Franklin Roosevelt that one party had won the White House in three straight elections.

—————

While American democracy continued to function much as it had for more than two centuries, Gorbachev was shaking up the Soviet Union, using Reagan's support as a cudgel against growing opposition from hard-liners in his struggle to create a more liberal system in his own country. Once-musty propaganda journals were reporting factual information and stirring passionate debate. The first competitive elections for the Soviet legislature, the Congress of People's Deputies, were scheduled for the following year. Soviet troops were leaving Afghanistan. A dictatorship was being transformed into a democracy—with profound implications for the Soviet Union's relations with the rest of the world.

Gorbachev came to New York to deliver a landmark address at the United Nations General Assembly on December 7, 1988, in the waning days of the Reagan presidency. Speaking at the familiar green marble desk used by so many world leaders over the decades, he heralded the emergence in the Soviet Union of a "socialist state based on the rule of law" and announced that he was unilaterally cutting the Soviet military by five hundred thousand troops while pulling fifty thousand troops and five thousand tanks out of Eastern Europe. He proclaimed a "new world order" in which "the rights and liberties" of all people would be recognized, every nation would be free to choose its own path, and "force and the threat of force can no longer . . . be instruments of foreign policy." This gave de facto permission to the nations of Eastern Europe to leave the Soviet bloc. The Iron Curtain was finally being lifted after more than four decades of repression. "Perhaps not since Woodrow Wilson presented his Fourteen Points in 1918 or since Franklin Roosevelt and Winston Churchill promulgated the Atlantic Charter in 1941 has a world figure demonstrated the vision Mikhail Gorbachev displayed yesterday at the United Nations," the *New York Times* wrote.[37]

Shortly after his UN speech, Gorbachev met with President Reagan and President-elect Bush at Governors Island in New York Harbor, with the city skyline providing a telegenic backdrop. Power had already been flowing to Bush during Reagan's last months in office in what Ed Rollins called "the greatest baton-pass in the history of American politics."[38] When cabinet officers such as Attorney General Ed Meese and Treasury Secretary James Baker resigned, Reagan allowed Bush to recommend their successors—Dick Thornburgh and Nicholas Brady, respectively. At Governors Island, Gorbachev tried to persuade Bush to follow his predecessor's foreign policy toward the Soviet Union. Bush was noncommittal, but Reagan was ecstatic. "I think the meeting was a tremendous success," he wrote in his diary. "A better attitude than at any of our previous meetings. He sounded as if he saw us as partners making a better world."[39]

George H. W. Bush would preside over the formal end of the Cold War during the next three years—a remarkable period beginning in 1989 with the unexpected fall of the Berlin Wall and culminating in 1991 with the equally surprising fall of the Soviet Union—but those epochal changes were already well under way when Ronald Reagan left office. Reagan did not initiate the changes sweeping the Soviet Union, but he was shrewd enough to support them. Thus, he helped to peacefully end a forty-year struggle that could have resulted in nuclear Armageddon.

That Reagan, who entered public life as a staunch anti-Communist in the 1940s and ran for the presidency in 1976 and 1980 as a critic of détente, was working so closely with a Communist leader was the ultimate tribute to his pragmatism. His long record as an anti-Communist hard-liner gave him flexibility to embrace Gorbachev that a Democratic president—who would have risked accusations from Republicans of being soft on Communism—would have lacked. And, unlike most ideologues of left or right, Reagan was willing to abandon the dogmas of a lifetime when it became evident they no longer applied to a changing world.

While many Reagan fans have suggested that he followed an unwavering policy toward the Soviet Union throughout his presidency, this was not the case. As George Shultz noted, "Ronald Reagan was not at the end of his presidency what he was when he started out."[40] Few other leaders have shown as much boldness or flexibility in changing with the times. That transformation was all the more remarkable coming from a famously stubborn and ideological president who was approaching his eighth decade of life.

ACT V

EX-PRESIDENT

(previous page) *Reagan salutes from the steps of Marine One on his final day in office, January 20, 1989.* (RRPL)

54

Fadeout

He just tried to kind of live his life the best way he could
at that point, and enjoy what he could enjoy, and gradually
just slip away.

—RON REAGAN

The last major speech of Ronald Reagan's presidency was a televised farewell address delivered from the Oval Office at 9:00 p.m. on January 11, 1989. Peggy Noonan, the celebrated author of the "Boys of Pointe du Hoc" and *Challenger* speeches, had already left the White House in 1986 after being passed over by Don Regan, that incorrigible sexist, for the job of chief speechwriter.[1] In 1988, she had written George H. W. Bush's acceptance speech at the Republican National Convention heralding civic organizations as a "thousand points of light" and vowing "Read my lips: no new taxes." But, at Reagan's personal request, she returned for one last hurrah to pen the valedictory for a man that, she had to admit, she—and the rest of the world—barely knew after eight years in office.

"They love you, Mr. President, but you're still a mystery man to them in some respects," Noonan wrote to Reagan. "We're going to reveal more of you than they've seen in the past, mostly by talking about big things in a personal and anecdotal way."[2] To craft the farewell address, Noonan met five times with Reagan—along with Chief of Staff Ken Duberstein and communications director Mari Maseng—on "mellow winter afternoons" in the Oval Office. But Reagan, an introvert who had kept the world at a safe remove ever since his painful childhood, predictably resisted her desire for a more personal approach. "When asked about policy, about great events, the answers seem rote," Noonan noted to her dismay. When asked about his most difficult day in office, he replied, "Oh well, I don't know." Noonan noted, "So many politicians resist introspection. But Reagan takes it farther than most." She concluded astutely, "I would never know him, but now I thought I knew why. He did not need to be known."[3]

The speech she produced was full of poetic reminiscences, but those largely came from her, not from him. ("This is a tonal speech—a tone poem aimed at subtly reminding the people of what a giant you are," Noonan had told Reagan.)[4]

"It's been the honor of my life to be your president," Reagan began his farewell address, and noted his mixed feelings about leaving: "'Parting is such sweet sorrow.' The sweet part is California and the ranch and freedom. The sorrow—the goodbyes, of course, and leaving this beautiful place."[5]

He then offered his own version of recent history, mentioning the Grenada invasion, the Washington and Moscow summits, the recession of 1981–1982, and the expansion that followed. "The way I see it, there were two great triumphs, two things that I'm proudest of," he said. "One is the economic recovery, in which the people of America created—and filled—19 million new jobs. The other is the recovery of our morale. America is respected again in the world and looked to for leadership."

Both were indeed major achievements, even if the president deserved more credit for the recovery of Americans' self-confidence than for the economic recovery. His role in raising military morale was particularly important. Tom Clancy, who had begun publishing best-selling military thrillers in 1984, would write to Reagan later that year: "When you took over, the people in the military had morale so low that it had to improve to hit bottom. It really was that bad. . . . [They] felt like orphans. You made them part of the family again."[6] Reagan's unrelenting optimism and growing list of accomplishments had helped the nation to move beyond Watergate, the Vietnam War, gasoline lines, double-digit inflation, the Iran hostage crisis, and all the other traumas of the 1970s. It was, in many ways, his most significant legacy.

Like other presidents, Reagan exaggerated the amount of credit he deserved for an economic expansion while ducking blame for a recession. In his farewell address, he said that "we cut the people's tax rates, and the people produced more than ever before," implying a cause-and-effect relationship that many economists would dispute. The "Reagan recovery"— more accurately described as *the nation's* recovery—was, in fact, typical of what happens when inflation has been tamed and the business cycle turns. As noted previously, average economic growth under Reagan was similar to other postwar presidencies and actually lower than under Bill Clinton, who raised taxes. Reagan's tax cuts undoubtedly contributed to the expansion, as did all of his defense spending, but they did not cause it. If any individual deserved credit, it was Fed Chairman Paul Volcker.

In his farewell speech, Reagan claimed to have carried out "the first revolution in the history of mankind that truly reversed the course of government." This was a considerable exaggeration. While Reagan undoubtedly embodied and encouraged public antipathy toward the federal government, the "Reagan revolution" always remained more aspiration than reality. Federal spending during his presidency had risen nearly as fast as state spending in California during his governorship: Budget outlays soared by almost 70 percent from 1981 to 1989, from $678 billion to $1.1 trillion. He reduced tax rates but not spending, causing the annual budget deficit to nearly double (from $79 billion in 1981 to $152.6 billion in 1989) and the total national debt to nearly triple (from $994 billion to $2.8 trillion). If you discount the effect of inflation, the increases were smaller but still significant: In constant dollars, spending under Reagan grew by 25 percent and the budget deficit by 40 percent. He practiced Keynesian, not supply-side, economics by financing an economic expansion with government borrowing. Gross government debt soared from 32 percent of GDP when he entered office to 52 percent of GDP when he left.[7]

The consequences of all the debt that Reagan accumulated were not nearly as "catastrophic" as critics claimed, according to the Nobel Prize–winning economist Paul Krugman; he called it "a modest drag on our economy, not a crippling burden."[8] And the breakneck growth of future deficits from the early 2000s on would make Reagan's then record-setting deficits seem almost puny by comparison. But the deficit did weigh on Reagan's legacy and his conscience, given that he had been decrying deficit spending since the 1950s and had repeatedly promised to balance the budget—originally by 1983. In his farewell address, Reagan admitted to only one regret, and that was the deficit. His successor would pay the price: George H. W. Bush would agree in 1990, breaking his imprudent pledge of no new taxes, to a budget deal with Democrats that would increase taxes, cut spending, and eventually help eliminate the deficit—but that would also help cost Bush the 1992 election.

Reagan's panegyric omitted a few undoubted accomplishments, such as his resilience after being shot, his appointment of the first woman to the Supreme Court, and his support—albeit grudging and under pressure—for democratic transitions in El Salvador, the Philippines, Taiwan, South Korea, and Chile. Nor did he claim credit for helping move the federal judiciary in a more conservative direction by appointing a record-setting number of federal judges. While considered a major achievement by his conservative supporters, this was a sore point for liberal critics and therefore went unmentioned in a valedictory address intended to be unifying.

More glaring were all the failures that went unmentioned. There was no mention of the bombings of the US Embassy, the embassy annex, and the Marine barracks in Beirut—or the paralyzing indecision that followed. No mention of the humiliating capture of American hostages in Lebanon—or of his attempts to ransom them with weapon sales to Iran. No mention, either, of the diversion of funds to the Contras that gave rise to the Iran-Contra affair. No mention of the scandals involving savings-and-loan regulators, the Department of Housing and Urban Development, and other government agencies. No mention of the attempted rollback of civil rights laws. No mention of the failed Bork nomination. No mention of the unfortunate visit to Bitburg cemetery. No mention of Jim Watt, Anne Gorsuch, and so many other embarrassing appointees. No mention of the disastrous Jim Baker–Don Regan job swap. No mention of growing income inequality, and the hollowing out of the middle class, exacerbated by the administration's cuts to taxes and social-welfare programs. No mention of the president's apathy toward the AIDS pandemic. No mention of his opposition to tough sanctions on South Africa. No mention, even, of the dangerous confrontation with the Soviet Union, which, in the early 1980s, had been exacerbated by his military buildup and his histrionic rhetoric.

Reagan's focus, understandably, was on the reduction of nuclear arsenals and Cold War tensions by the end of his second term. By a rhetorical sleight of hand, Noonan credited his defense buildup for the outbreak of peace: "So, we rebuilt our defenses, and this New Year we toasted the new peacefulness around the globe." In fact, the outbreak of peace was largely due to the serendipitous ascension of Mikhail Gorbachev. As previously noted, Gorbachev was not motivated to radically reform the Soviet Union because he wanted to keep pace with US military programs such as SDI. Gorbachev wanted to end the arms race altogether because he viewed it as a dangerous waste of resources—and not because the USSR was unable to keep up. The Soviet Union was far from bankrupt and could have bankrolled its massive military indefinitely, as the far poorer Cuba and North Korea have done for decades. The Soviet economy was stagnating, not collapsing, and that was because of the inefficiency of Communist central planning—not because of any secret Reagan administration plan to overthrow the "evil empire." In his farewell address, Reagan did at least pay tribute where it was due: "My view is that President Gorbachev is different from previous Soviet leaders," he said. "I think he knows some of the things wrong with his society and is trying to fix them. We wish him well."

Noonan beautifully evoked Reagan's modesty in the speech's most celebrated lines: "I won a nickname, 'The Great Communicator.' But I never thought it was my style or the words I used that made a difference: It was the content. I wasn't a great communicator, but I communicated great things, and they didn't spring full bloom from my brow, they came from the heart of a great nation." This was typical of Reagan's habit of deflecting praise— and of his populist faith in the wisdom of the American public. (He wanted to call his memoir *Trusting the People* until his publishers talked him out of it.)[9] But the truth was that he had been a masterful communicator and the author of many of his most effective lines, from "honey, I forgot to duck" to "the ash heap of history" to "there you go again."

There was no arguing with Reagan's conclusion: "My friends: We did it. We weren't just marking time. We made a difference." The debate over the impact of his policies would continue long after he left office—it goes on to this day—but no one could deny the consequential nature of Reagan's presidency. And even those who opposed him, as many did, had to concede that his two terms in office were seen as largely successful by most Americans. He was leaving office with a Gallup job approval rating of 63 percent, the second highest of any postwar president—behind only Bill Clinton at 66 percent. Senator Barry Goldwater was far from alone in concluding, as he wrote in his usual gruff way to Reagan, "You have done one hell of a good job."[10]

On his final day in office, January 20, 1989, Ronald Reagan got up earlier than usual and went down to the Oval Office for the last time, finding it "pretty bare," because his belongings were already boxed up and George H. W. Bush's had not yet been moved in. He walked around, touching the furniture for the last time, then sat down at the *Resolute* desk to write an encouraging note for his successor on a pad of paper with the heading, "Don't let the Turkeys Get You Down." As he was walking out, National Security Adviser Colin Powell told him, "The world is quiet today, Mr. President."[11] That was a far cry from the dire situation he had inherited on his first day in office following the takeover of anti-American regimes in Iran and Nicaragua, the Soviet invasion of Afghanistan, the US boycott of the Summer Olympics in Moscow, the looming threat of martial law in Poland, and the ripple effects from oil shocks and "stagflation." The world had changed dramatically and largely for the better over the past eight years.

Then at 11:00 a.m., it was off to the Capitol with the president-elect for the inauguration. By 12:40 p.m., all the ceremonies were finished. "George is now Pres. & I'm ex," Reagan noted laconically in his diary. From the Capitol, the Reagans rode in a helicopter—no longer Marine One, it was now dubbed Nighthawk One—to Andrews Air Force Base and the flight back to Los Angeles aboard what had formerly been known as Air Force One and was now called Special Air Mission 27000.

Various dignitaries and admirers, along with the University of Southern California and Salvation Army marching bands, were waiting to meet the Reagans on arrival at Los Angeles International Airport, just as their arrival in Washington eight years earlier had been heralded by a pre-inauguration laser light show and concert. When the music finally ended, at long last, the Reagans left the airport in a much-reduced Secret Service motorcade. "Then home & the start of our new life," the now former president wrote in his last diary entry.[12]

Nancy Reagan and the Reagans' staff had been carefully preparing for that new life long before the end of the presidency. Once again, as in Sacramento, the Kitchen Cabinet bought a house and leased it to the first couple. The donors paid $2.5 million in 1986 for a 17-room, 7,200-square-foot mansion in Bel-Air with a backyard pool for the old lifeguard to swim in. Now the house was fully furnished and ready for them to move in. The original address had been 666 St. Cloud Road, but the superstitious Reagans had the number changed to 668 because they viewed "666" as the mark of Satan.[13] The Reagans still had a small Secret Service detail, but they had to learn to live again without the massive White House staff. "As you well know," Ronald Reagan wrote to Richard Nixon, "we're having to learn or I should say re-learn a lot of simple things like turning off the lights etc. Just learning to find the light switches was a chore after living in that public housing on Pa. ave."[14]

That the Reagans needed help to buy a house showed that, while far from impoverished, they remained much less wealthy than most of their multimillionaire friends. Their income in 1987, the last year for which they released tax returns, was $345,359, with the largest contribution coming from the president's salary of $201,526. The ex-president set out to make more money in his retirement. He was roundly criticized for accepting a $2 million fee in 1989 from a Japanese media conglomerate for two twenty-minute speeches and some personal appearances in Japan. It was still considered unseemly for a former president to cash in, but when the check arrived, Reagan's secretary Kathy Osborne recalled, he was "extra happy," because, he told her, now Nancy wouldn't have to worry about house payments if anything happened to him.[15]

Both Reagans signed lucrative book deals, with the former president getting approximately $7 million from Simon and Schuster for a memoir and a collection of speeches and the former first lady receiving $2 million for her own memoir. Nancy's ghostwritten book, *My Turn*, came out first, in 1989. Surprisingly frank and indiscreet, it was full of payback against the objects of her scorn, including many of her husband's top lieutenants, and even contained scathing criticism of her own children, Patti in particular. It became known in Washington as "My Burn."

Her husband's memoir was less honest and less hurtful. Simon and Schuster hired former *New York Times* reporter Robert Lindsey to write the book, but Reagan had little interest in the project. Lindsey found—just as Peggy Noonan and Edmund Morris had—that it was nearly impossible to draw him out about his own life. He had no ability to be introspective or to evaluate events "in an analytical way," Lindsey noted. Reagan also "didn't want to hurt the feelings" of his former aides, declining to criticize anyone in print except Al Haig and Don Regan. He didn't even have harsh words for his would-be assassin John Hinckley ("a mixed-up young man from a fine family"). Beyond not hurting anyone's feelings, Reagan didn't much care what wound up in "his" book. "He virtually never changed anything I'd written," Lindsey noted.[16]

Simon and Schuster's legendary, English-born publisher, Michael Korda, part of an illustrious family of filmmakers, flew to Los Angeles in early 1990 to implore Reagan to be more forthcoming; an initial draft had not even mentioned his first wife, Jane Wyman, presumably in deference to Nancy's sensitivities. After initially resisting, Reagan reluctantly allowed the editorial team to insert two anodyne sentences about the mother of his first two children. Korda tried to tell Reagan that if he weren't more forthcoming, the book would be savaged by critics. "I never pay much attention to critics," Reagan shrugged. "Never have."

Like Noonan, Korda finally gave up. He concluded that "no amount of prodding could get the president to reveal what his thoughts, if any, had been" on various historic occasions. Korda was frustrated yet couldn't help liking the former president. "It would be hard to imagine a gentler, nicer, more natural, or more sincere person," he wrote in his own memoir. "The president was genial, lavish with the anecdotes that were his familiar repertoire, and appeared never to have met a person he didn't like."

When *An American Life* was published in the fall of 1990—to scornful reviews and smaller than expected sales—Reagan came to the Simon and Schuster offices in New York for a promotional event. "I hear it's a terrific book!" he jauntily told the staff (or so Korda claimed). "One of these days I'm going to read it myself."[17]

———

Korda's meeting with Reagan took place in the ex-president's office in the Fox Tower in Century City, near the Twentieth Century Fox studios. The publisher found that the offices were furnished "in the Williamsburg colonial style and staffed by clean-limbed, smiling young women and good-looking young men in suits. Both genders presented a perfect picture of wholesomeness."[18]

Frederick Ryan, a former White House aide who was now Reagan's post-presidential chief of staff—and one of those wholesome-looking young people—had rented the top-floor office because it came with sweeping views of the ocean and the city. The movie *Die Hard* had been filmed on the premises, and there were still blank gun shells on the floor when they moved in. Reagan was so eager to go to the office, even though he had little to do there, that he arrived before it was ready. At the end of the first day, he handed Fred Ryan a list of people he wanted to meet with. Looking at the list, Ryan was puzzled. He couldn't recognize any of the names. Who were they?

It turned out the phone lines had been hooked up improperly and the receptionist's phone was ringing at the ex-president's desk. Many of the callers were simply members of the public who wanted to meet him. Instead of telling them to get lost or complaining to his staff about the intrusion, Reagan politely answered the phone and took down their names, much as he had faithfully answered select letters from the public over the past eight years. Reagan had been changed remarkably little by his years at the pinnacle of power. He remained as modest, unaffected, and down-to-earth as ever. "He didn't put on airs or puff himself up," Ed Meese noted. "He was so humble," agreed his longtime secretary Kathy Osborne.[19]

The former president showed little interest in burnishing his legacy—"unlike Nancy," Michael Reagan noted, "Dad didn't spend a lot of time worrying about his image"[20]—but he gamely went along with plans, pushed by his wife and his supporters, for a presidential library and museum. It was originally slated for Stanford University, but, after protests from faculty and students, it wound up being situated in Simi Valley outside of Los Angeles on a hill with a sweeping view of the Pacific Ocean. The Spanish-style library, largely funded by campaign donors, opened in 1991 with a lavish event attended by all five living presidents—but only after the same kind of internecine infighting that had plagued the Reagan White House.

Three old Reagan loyalists—Ed Meese, Bill Clark, and Martin Anderson—were dropped from the Ronald Reagan Presidential Foundation board at the instigation of Nancy Reagan. She had never cared for the arch-conservatives and preferred to fill the board with tycoons—the successors to the old Kitchen Cabinet—capable of prodigious fundraising for the library. Another old Reaganite, Lyn Nofziger, went public with his disenchantment, writing in the *Washington Post*, "Ronald Reagan, you have broken my heart. . . . You appear to have forgotten old loyalties and to have walked away from old friends."[21]

Ronald Reagan, as usual, gave no indication of noticing or caring about the contretemps. He went right on doing what he enjoyed—visiting the ranch, playing golf, and meeting with world leaders. "My so-called retirement has taken on a kind of frantic or frenetic activity," he told Bill Buckley in 1989. "I'm . . . too busy out on the mashed potato circuit to think of myself as 'retired,'" he told Dick Nixon in 1990.[22]

Reagan spoke at the 1992 Republican convention in support of George H. W. Bush's reelection but generally steered clear of politics. One exception was his support for gun control: In 1991 he endorsed the Brady Bill imposing background checks on gun buyers (named after his former press secretary Jim Brady), and in 1994 he endorsed an assault-weapon ban. Both bills passed. This was a reminder that he was no more an absolutist about gun rights than he was about abortion or taxes. All the way back in 1967, after all, he had signed a bill, aimed at the Black Panthers, prohibiting Californians from carrying loaded guns in public. His pragmatic gun-control stance would have been unimaginable for later generations of Republicans who embraced an absolutist interpretation of the Second Amendment no matter the cost.[23]

Meanwhile, the world continued to go his way. The Berlin Wall came down in 1989, Germany reunified in 1990, the Soviet Union collapsed in 1991. Liberal democracies spread across Eastern Europe, and even Russia itself temporarily turned democratic. The Red Army left Afghanistan in 1989. The Marxist FMLN gave up its armed struggle and made peace with the government of El Salvador in 1992. The Nicaraguan Sandinistas, one of Reagan's obsessions, gave up power in 1990 after losing an election; US support for the Contras had not overthrown the regime but had pressured it to hold internationally supervised elections. Sandinista leader Daniel Ortega, however, would return to power in 2007, demonstrating, contrary to what Reagan had always believed, that his rule wasn't dependent on Soviet support.

With the end of the Soviet Union, America entered a period of unprecedented—if fleeting—primacy in the 1990s as the world's sole superpower. Soon, Russia would revert to dictatorship under Vladimir Putin and Afghanistan under the Taliban would become a staging ground for anti-American terrorists, but, in the early 1990s, history appeared to be going America's way.

Ronald Reagan was too modest to claim that these historic developments were all his doing. "I have been delighted to see all the wonderful changes in Eastern Europe and Poland and Nicaragua," he wrote to a congressman in 1990, "but certainly don't feel that I can take all the credit. It was a long process of so many dedicated and freedom-loving people who were determined to make a change for the better."[24] Reagan's many admirers were less reticent about giving him credit for the end of the Cold War. (Ironically, Reaganites usually praised him for confronting Gorbachev rather than cooperating with him.) His reputation soared while he played golf—something he had more time to do after leaving the White House—and chopped wood.

The former president, who turned seventy-eight shortly after leaving office, appeared to be his jaunty old self in his first few years of retirement. Michael Korda found in 1990 that Reagan's memory was "razor sharp" if he was talking about horses, a passion they both shared, while he was fuzzy on subjects he wasn't interested in, such as the savings-and-loan crisis.[25]

But by the early 1990s, Reagan was starting to have trouble delivering speeches. He appeared confused in public and sometimes could not recognize longtime aides and associates. Secret Service agent John Barletta noticed he was making "rookie mistakes on a horse that a person of his ability wouldn't make." Veteran diplomat John Negroponte, the deputy national security adviser from 1987 to 1989, recalled Reagan telling him over lunch in 1992: "I just forgot what I was going to say. That's been happening to me more and more often." The following year, Reagan lost his train of thought in the middle of a lunch with his good friend Brian Mulroney and his wife, Mila. "Mommy, where was I?" Reagan asked Nancy plaintively, while the Canadian couple looked down "sadly at the table."[26]

A team from the Mayo Clinic made the diagnosis in August 1994: Alzheimer's disease.[27] Reagan's brother, Neil, who would die in 1996, was showing similar symptoms, as had their mother Nelle before her death in 1962. Nancy Reagan tried to put off telling her husband the dispiriting diagnosis as long as possible, but, as their son Ron noted, "By November 1994 that sorry duty had become a necessity. His decline had become obvious even to a casual observer." The night before she broke the news, Nancy called to tell Dennis LeBlanc, her husband's ranch helper and quite possibly his closest friend. "She was crying, and I was crying," LeBlanc recalled.[28]

On Saturday, November 5, 1994, Fred Ryan came to the Bel-Air house with a doctor to help Nancy break the news. Ryan recalled that Reagan "listened very attentively" and asked a few questions about the progression of the disease. He wanted to know "what it would mean for Nancy as the caregiver" and "what his life would be like going forward," but, unlike Nancy, he showed little outward emotion.

His first thought, as always, was of his loyal followers—what in Hollywood had been his audience and in Sacramento and Washington his voters.

Bravely flouting the public stigma of admitting an Alzheimer's diagnosis, he sat down at a little round table in the library of their home and wrote out a short, eloquent, and unaffected letter in longhand telling his "fellow Americans" that "I now begin the journey that will lead me into the sunset of my life." As always, the man who had been taught by his mother "the sunny side's the only side" had to add an optimistic grace note: "I know that for America there will always be a bright dawn ahead."

Reagan told Ryan to get it typed up and distributed. "I don't think you want to type this up," Ryan replied. "This is in your own hand. This is as clear and powerful as the message could be." Reagan's press office faxed the handwritten statement to news organizations to make clear that he had authored it himself. "He didn't sit and commiserate or want to wallow in any negative way. He wanted to enjoy life and move on," Ryan said.[29]

A few months later, while doing ranch work, Reagan told Dennis LeBlanc, "You know, Dennis, this Alzheimer's really isn't that bad." "Really?" LeBlanc asked. "Yeah. Every day you meet new people." LeBlanc laughed and thought to himself, "That's Ronald Reagan. Turning something negative into a positive, funny moment."[30]

His son Ron recalled that the former president "did not really speak" about his affliction. "He just tried to kind of live his life the best way he could at that point, and enjoy what he could enjoy, and gradually just slip away."[31]

———

While Reagan did not want to speak about his condition, the rest of the world did. His diagnosis was front-page news and prompted speculation about whether he had suffered from Alzheimer's while in office. Dr. Ronald C. Petersen, a renowned Alzheimer's specialist at the Mayo Clinic who treated Reagan, told me that patients often develop the plaques and tangles in their brains that are characteristic of the disease many years before they show any symptoms.[32] So it is likely that Reagan did have undiagnosed Alzheimer's while in office. But many Alzheimer's patients are asymptomatic or show only mild cognitive impairment initially. I asked dozens of former Reagan aides and associates whether they saw any evidence of dementia while he was in office, and they all answered no—or, as John Barletta said, "no way in hell." "I never saw the Alzheimer's coming," Kathy Osborne insisted.[33] Their answers might be chalked up to personal loyalty. But that Reagan continued to write his diary and letters in the same clear hand from the beginning of his presidency to the end offers further evidence that he was not suffering from dementia as president. There is no doubt, however, that he suffered some cognitive decline during his years in office, as do most people in their seventies, particularly those who have suffered a severe trauma such as a gunshot wound.

"One of the most vexing questions that we have in our field is: Where does the forgetfulness of aging end and the forgetfulness of disease begin?" Petersen said. "It's really a complicated issue." It was all the more complicated in Reagan's case because, as Stuart Spencer noted, "Reagan never remembered anybody's name. I don't give a damn if he's fifty-five or eighty-five. He couldn't remember names. He'd remember your face, but he wouldn't remember your name."[34]

Beyond the question of whether Reagan had dementia in office was the issue of his overall intelligence. Initially, many critics doubted that he was smart enough to exercise the onerous duties of the presidency. The record shows he had sufficient intelligence to be a successful governor and president but that he also lacked intellectual curiosity or depth and that even his emotional intelligence was spotty—he was more attuned to the public's moods than to those of his family or closest aides. He had a few deeply rooted beliefs and simply cherry-picked information, often from dubious sources, in support of what he already believed. His mind was full of apocryphal stories and pseudo-facts—including a treasure trove of phony quotes attributed to Communist leaders by far-right conspiracy theorists—that could not be dislodged no matter how many times they were refuted. He was almost entirely at the mercy of his aides: If they gave him bad information, he made bad decisions.

Even many of those who most admired Reagan had to admit his intellectual limitations. Peggy Noonan, for example, wrote, "The battle for the mind of Ronald Reagan was like the trench warfare of World War I: Never have so many fought so hard for such barren terrain." Lyn Nofziger, while insisting Reagan wasn't "dumb," put him no higher than the top 20 percent in intelligence and acknowledged that he didn't have the "same analytical mind" as Jimmy Carter or Richard Nixon. "I don't think he's a genius," Nofziger said, while adding, "I don't think you want a genius for president."[35]

Yet Reagan accomplished more than many presidents who undoubtedly would have scored higher on an IQ test. The central paradox of his presidency was that, as Bud McFarlane said to George Shultz, "He knows so little and accomplishes so much."[36] The publication of Reagan's letters and radio scripts showed that he was more intelligent and better informed than many realized. Far from being an unlettered bumpkin, as some of his critics imagined, he was an avid reader and skilled writer who could almost always find *le mot juste*. He was also fast with a quip or comeback when speaking or debating, and his letters are a pleasure to read. But it would be a mistake to jump to the conclusion, as some of his most fervent followers have done, that he was some kind of genius and that only the purblindness of liberal elites prevented them from recognizing his towering intellect.

The revisionist view of Reagan was first played for laughs in a December 1986 *Saturday Night Live* skit. It began with a seemingly befuddled Reagan, played by Phil Hartman, telling a reporter that he didn't know anything about the Iran-Contra affair. Once she left, however, the president began barking orders to aides for secret arms transactions. When a Girl Scout was ushered in for a photo-op, he went back to acting genial and clueless, muttering, "The part of the job I hate." And then, as soon as she was gone, he again started giving detailed orders while talking on the telephone in both Arabic and German.[37] The skit's ironic title was "Mastermind" because that was the very opposite of how most people regarded the septuagenarian president.

Yet, as the years went by, and his record came to look better and better, many did come to regard Reagan as a kind of mastermind. One author, for example, wrote that Reagan was "a colossus . . . who operated to a logic, rhythm, and instinct almost unfathomable to those who watched him in action, save for the eyes of history."[38] That was as exaggerated as the earlier impression of him as an "amiable dunce." He was neither a demigod nor a dunce. He was a man of slightly above-average intelligence and limited knowledge of public policy who had a wonderful personality and a streak of pragmatism that took him far. Like his onetime hero Franklin Roosevelt, Ronald Reagan had "a second-class intellect but a first-class temperament."

Admittedly, he also benefited from large dollops of luck—particularly in having Paul Volcker as a partner in the economic recovery and Mikhail Gorbachev as a partner in peacemaking. "He was the luckiest politician I ever knew," Stu Spencer marveled.[39] But he was also shrewd enough to make the most of his luck—in no small part by appointing, with Nancy Reagan's indispensable help, so many experienced and pragmatic officials who helped him steer the ship of state. The ultimate success of his presidency owed much to such wise counselors as Jim Baker, Dick Darman, George Shultz, Colin Powell, Howard Baker, Ken Duberstein, and Frank Carlucci. Reagan, by contrast, floundered when he listened to advisers such as Al Haig, Bud McFarlane, John Poindexter, and Don Regan, who were not well fitted for the high posts they held.

The progression of Reagan's Alzheimer's disease was slow but inexorable and cruel. Dennis LeBlanc remembered being woken up by the Secret Service one night at the ranch because "the president had gotten dressed and was standing outside on the patio. It was four o'clock in the morning, but he thought it was sunrise, and he was ready to go work." The most jarring part of this story for LeBlanc? That Reagan, who had always been meticulous about his personal appearance, was unshaven.[40]

It fell to Secret Service agent John Barletta to tell the former president that he couldn't ride anymore—which was "like asking him to stop breathing." Barletta was in tears when he broke the news; "my heart's in my mouth," he said. But instead of protesting or acting hurt, Reagan put his hand on Barletta's shoulder and gently said, "It's okay, John. I know." "At probably one of his worst hours," Barletta marveled, "he was trying to comfort *me*."[41] Indeed, while many Alzheimer's patients turn cantankerous or unpleasant in the mind-altering grip of dementia, Reagan, no matter how senescent, never lost his essential sweetness and amiability.

By 1996, just two years after his diagnosis, the former president could no longer go to the ranch at all, and Nancy Reagan put it up for sale. In 2001, his mental and physical condition further deteriorated after he fell down and broke his hip. That year his Century City office closed. The sad but inevitable end for a tragically diminished giant finally arrived on June 5, 2004. Six days of national mourning followed, culminating in the state funeral in Washington and interment in Simi Valley.

By the time of his death at age ninety-three, Reagan was remembered fondly even by most of his political opponents. A president who had been polarizing while in office—the gap in his approval rating between Democrats and Republicans was the highest recorded to that point—he became more generally beloved after leaving it.[42] His policies of tax cuts and "peace through strength" became GOP gospel, even while his libertarian suspicion of big government lost sway. It was no coincidence that former House Speaker Kevin McCarthy displayed a giant portrait of Reagan in his office. Many Republicans had little affection for other Republican presidents such as Eisenhower, Nixon, Ford, and the two Bushes, but they revered Reagan. His presidential library became an obligatory shrine for Republican leaders to visit. His name adorned roads, buildings, schools, an airport, even an aircraft carrier. Ronald Reagan became the most unifying figure—indeed, arguably, the *only* unifying figure—in the Republican Party and the conservative movement.

Yet, by 2016, Reagan's party had left his seemingly genteel brand of politics behind for the harder-edged populism of Donald J. Trump. Many analysts wondered if Trump represented a repudiation of Reagan's legacy or a continuation of it. The truth, as with questions of Reagan's intelligence, was complicated.

There were many obvious differences between Trump and Reagan, both in their policies and their styles. Reagan was pro-immigration, pro-free trade, pro-democracy, and pro-NATO. He was also a consummate gentleman who never indulged in name-calling or acerbic put-downs. He was, moreover, a staunch believer in American democracy who would never have dreamed of instigating an insurrection to prevent a lawfully elected candidate from taking office. Reagan believed in compromising with Democrats, not in keeping them out of power by extra-constitutional means. All of those political and personal proclivities put him starkly at odds with Trump. And, indeed, the bombastic real estate developer had been harshly critical of Reagan's policies in the 1980s. Trump had taken out newspaper advertisements in 1987 to argue that "Japan and other nations have been taking advantage of the United States" and that "the world is laughing at America's politicians as we protect ships we don't own, carrying oil we don't need, destined for allies who won't help."[43]

But, despite their many differences, there were also some startling similarities between the two presidents who had been TV stars before taking office. Republican Senator Lindsey Graham of South Carolina, an admirer of both men, even described Trump as "a cross between Jesse Helms, Ronald Reagan and P. T. Barnum."[44] Reagan, after all, was a populist who

Libyan dictator Moammar Qaddafi was a perfect arch-villain for Reagan: strong enough to be menacing but weak enough to be attacked with relative impunity. (*Getty*)

The bombing of the Marine barracks in Beirut in 1983 killed 241 U.S. military personnel. Reagan was paralyzed by indecision and never retaliated, even though Iranian complicity was clear. (*AP*)

National Security Adviser Robert "Bud" McFarlane and Secretary of State George Shultz brief Reagan in the early morning hours of October 22, 1983, about a request (secretly orchestrated by the administration) from a few Caribbean governments to intervene militarily in Grenada. (*RRPL*)

U.S. forces quickly put down ragtag opposition in Grenada. Reagan claimed that Grenada was going to be a Soviet military base and that U.S. students were being held hostage. That wasn't true, but the operation was a success. (*Getty*)

Flag-waving was very important to Reagan—and to his presidency.
Here he welcomes American hostages home from Iran on January 27, 1981. (*RRPL*)

Reagan in 1983 at his beloved ranch near Santa Barbara, California, with ranch hands (and
former police officers) Dennis LeBlanc (l.) and Barney Barnett. They were probably his closest
friends after Nancy. (*RRPL*)

Reagan on Air Force One with campaign consultant Stuart Spencer (l.) and deputy campaign manager Lee Atwater, October 15, 1984. Spencer was the key architect of all of Reagan's winning campaigns going back to 1966. (*RRPL*)

At the start of his second term, Reagan casually agreed to let White House Chief of Staff Jim Baker (l.) and Treasury Secretary Donald Regan swap jobs. It was a disastrous miscalculation: Regan turned out to be utterly unfit for his new role. (*RRPL*)

Sitting with Soviet leader Mikhail Gorbachev at their first summit in Geneva, November 19, 1985. Reagan later cited this as one of the highlights of his presidency. The rapport the two men established helped to end the Cold War. (*RRPL*)

Receiving the Tower Commission report in the Cabinet room, February 26, 1987, from John Tower (l.) and Edmund Muskie. As Reagan's facial expression makes clear, the Iran-Contra affair was the low point of his presidency. (*RRPL*)

Reagan managed to salvage his second term with the help of new Chief of Staff Howard Baker (center) and National Security Adviser Colin Powell, shown at Rancho del Cielo. (*RRPL*)

In 1987, Reagan nominated the brilliant, but impolitic, Judge Robert Bork to the U.S. Supreme Court, leading to a Senate showdown that the administration lost. (*RRPL*)

Anti-apartheid protesters in New York's Central Park, June 14, 1986. A few months later, Congress overrode Reagan's veto of a South Africa sanctions bill—part of his pattern of insensitivity on racial issues. (*AP*)

Reagan's failure to do more to combat AIDS—an epidemic that claimed the lives of more than eighty-nine thousand Americans during his presidency—was one of the biggest stains on his record. He did not even give a speech devoted to AIDS until 1987. (*Getty*)

Reagan leaves the Oval Office on his last day in office, January 20, 1989. National Security Adviser Colin Powell told him: "The world is quiet today, Mr. President." *(RRPL)*

reviled the government he led—even if he did not call it the "deep state"— and denigrated expertise, even though he frequently consulted experts. He was proud of his dealmaking skills (learned as a union negotiator, not as a real estate mogul), and he promised to "make America great again." He displayed an often-shocking ignorance of public policy even if he knew far more, and read far more, than Trump. He often repeated false statements, even if he uttered fewer falsehoods than Trump. Early in his political career, he regularly accused Democrats of plotting to turn America into a socialist and even a Communist country, just as Trump later did. He mishandled a pandemic just as Trump did—AIDS in Reagan's case, Covid-19 in Trump's. And he catered to white bigotry to win office, even if he did so far more subtly than Trump.

In a sense, both Reagan and Trump were a product of the hard-right turn the GOP had taken in 1964 by nominating Barry Goldwater, an opponent of civil rights legislation and an advocate of waging nuclear war, if necessary, to free Eastern Europe. The party drifted steadily to the right for decades thereafter. Reagan was considerably to the right of Nixon and Ford, while Trump, in turn, was considerably to the right of Reagan. If Reagan had still been alive in 2016, he undoubtedly would have been derided by most Republicans as a RINO (Republican in Name Only) like the two Bushes, John McCain, and Mitt Romney; indeed, conservatives had frequently expressed their frustration with Reagan even during his presidency. Yet Reagan had helped set the GOP—and the country—on the path that ultimately led it to embrace divisive figures such as Donald Trump. Reagan's legacy included, after all, not only empowering the Christian Right and a growing white backlash against minority empowerment but also economic policies that helped hollow out the middle class, thereby creating the conditions for Trump's populist movement. (Of course, once in office, Trump's policies favored the well-off as much as Reagan's had.)

It was perhaps symbolic that, after Nancy Reagan's death in 2016, the Reagans' house in Bel-Air was bought by a neighbor who bulldozed it to enlarge his own estate. The ten-acre lot was then sold, along with a 25,000-square-foot mansion, to Lachlan Murdoch for $150 million. So, in a sense, the chief executive of Fox News—the network that had been integral to Donald Trump's rise—had literally erased part of Reagan's legacy, and yet he had done so while exemplifying the kind of extreme income disparity that Reagan's policies had accelerated.[45]

W̶hile Reagan's legacy continues to be debated, his place in history appears secure. He didn't have "the most successful presidency ever," as his devoted speechwriter Tony Dolan suggested in a 1989 fan letter. But a 2021 poll of historians ranked him ninth among the forty-five presidents. Only Abraham Lincoln, George Washington, Franklin Roosevelt, Theodore Roosevelt, Dwight Eisenhower, Harry Truman, Thomas Jefferson, and John Kennedy ranked higher. (Other surveys produced slightly different results.) Canadian Prime Minister Brian Mulroney's prediction, from a 1985 diary entry, appeared to be coming true: "RR may, 100 years from now, be revered as a truly great president because he made America feel good about itself again—made it throw off its self-doubt, accrued from Vietnam to Watergate, and become a more proud and unsullied nation, capable of providing strong leadership."[46]

Reagan did not inaugurate an era of lasting Republican power—Bill Clinton won the 1992 election and control of Congress regularly switched parties through the years—but he did inaugurate two decades of center-right governance while inuring the nation to the further-right populism still to come. Clinton paid a backhanded compliment to Reagan's influence when he proclaimed in 1996, "The era of big government is over." In 2008, Barack Obama said, "What Reagan ushered in was a skepticism toward government solutions to every problem, a suspicion of command-and-control, top-down social engineering. I don't think that has changed."[47] Henry Kissinger, who had clashed with Reagan in the 1970s, suggested to me that Reagan came along at exactly the right moment: "Ten years earlier it was not so necessary to remind the American public of its greatness. Ten years later, he might have looked exaggerated. By then the issues were becoming more complicated and did not require to the same extent his masterful ability to simplify the issues. But the period when he was in office was a great presidency."[48] The historian Sean Wilentz grouped Reagan along with Thomas Jefferson, Andrew Jackson, Abraham Lincoln, Theodore Roosevelt, and Franklin Roosevelt as one of the presidents "who for better or worse have put their political stamp indelibly on their time."[49]

That was a monumental achievement for the impoverished child from a troubled family who had been underestimated from the start of his political career. Reagan's life was, in a sense, the archetypal American success story:

poor boy makes good. It was no coincidence that so many other presidents—
from Andrew Jackson and Abraham Lincoln to Bill Clinton and Barack
Obama—could chart a similar, up-by-the-bootstraps trajectory. It made
Americans feel good to vote for someone who had started off with next to
nothing; it affirmed their faith in the American Dream of upward mobility
even when it was more aspiration than reality.

Reagan's ascent was an outcome that no one in Dixon, Davenport, or Des
Moines could have predicted, and yet he made it look effortless. Perhaps
his greatest achievement of all was that, no matter how far or how fast he
climbed, he never lost his trademark dignity, modesty, and grace or forgot
the "Midwestern ethic" that he had learned growing up. He was, and always
remained, a quintessential product of early twentieth-century, small-town
America, with all the strengths and blind spots inherent to that time and
place. The America into which he had been born—a laissez-faire land in
which the federal government had scant power to collect tax revenue, protect the rights of minorities, or cushion the toll of economic adversity—had
long vanished by the time of his death, yet he remained its faithful champion to the very end. Indeed, his success in embodying an idealized and sanitized image of America—an image that airbrushed out pervasive ills such
as racism and discrimination, corrosive poverty, and widening inequality—
made possible his rapid ascent and armored him against the many setbacks en route.

Reagan was far from ordinary, but he had an innate understanding of
ordinary Americans, at least ordinary white Americans, that carried him a
long way in his storybook life. He charmed the Japanese public during his
1989 speaking tour the same way he had charmed so many different audiences in so many different roles over so many decades—as, in a reporter's
words, "a larger-than-life symbol of what they see as the old America of
strength and can-do optimism."[50] The power of that symbolism remains
alluring and enduring even in the twenty-first century as the world continues to grapple with the impact of Reagan's complicated life and legacy.
Whether he changed the world for better or worse—or, more likely, some
of both—he undoubtedly left his "strong footprints in the sands of time," as
Jane Wyman told Nancy Reagan shortly after his death.

Acknowledgments

Since beginning work on this book in 2013, I have accumulated too many debts to count. My greatest debt is to the Council on Foreign Relations (CFR). This is a CFR book, and I am lucky to be a CFR fellow.[1] CFR's former president Richard Haass, director of studies James Lindsay, and deputy director of studies Shannon O'Neil supported this project from the start and provided the most congenial work environment imaginable. Michael Froman has been the ideal steward of CFR's august legacy since becoming its president in 2023—and an extremely sympathetic and supportive boss. So, too, I must thank the *Washington Post*—in particular, the late editorial page editor Fred Hiatt and his successor David Shipley—for employing me as a columnist. I am honored to be associated with the Council and the *Post*, two storied institutions full of impressive and accomplished people.

I do all my own research and writing, but I have been blessed with an extraordinary series of research associates at CFR who have helped me by tracking down books, contacting archives, making logistical arrangements, preparing budgets, and performing myriad other tasks. Thanks are due to the late Seth Myers (who died far too young), Greg Roberts, Harry Oppenheimer, Sherry Cho, Mallika Parlikar, and Vishnu Sriram. Ora Dreiser, a freelance researcher in Russia, helped me access material from the Russian archives.

I am grateful to all the archivists who have done so much to assist in this project—and none more so than Jennifer Mandel of the Ronald Reagan Presidential Library in Simi Valley, California. Ever since we first met in the reading room, Jenny has been endlessly patient and incredibly helpful in helping me navigate the vast Reagan archives. I am also grateful to the leaders of the Reagan Foundation for facilitating my research: in particular, chairman Fred Ryan, executive director John Heubusch, and chief administrative officer Joanne Drake. I have been inspired during my writing process by a brick that John sent me from the demolished Reagan house in Bel-Air!

Christopher Buckley kindly granted me access to the William F. Buckley Jr. papers at Yale University and Lou Cannon to his own papers at the University of California, Santa Barbara. Former Reagan aide John B. Roberts II provided invaluable interviews with fellow White House staffers conducted in the 1980s for a book that was never written. I thank Jane Mayer for putting me in contact with him.

A number of scholars have been extremely helpful during my research—in particular, Bob Spitz, who generously provided me with some of the research materials he had accumulated while writing his own Reagan biography; James Graham Wilson, who was kind enough, among other things, to provide me with a searchable version of the Reagan diaries; Junius Rodriguez, who filled me in on the history of Eureka College; Will Inboden, who sent me an advance copy of his book on Reagan's foreign policy; and Karen Tumulty, who provided an invaluable perspective on Nancy Reagan, the subject of her own superb biography. I am also grateful to all the Reagan family, friends, and aides who consented to sit down with me for often lengthy interviews. The full list is in the bibliography.

I am deeply grateful to all the scholars who read the manuscript and made many useful suggestions: Jim Lindsay, David Hoffman, Doug Rossinow, Robert Mann, and James Graham Wilson.

I have benefited from reading too many books to count, but, in addition to the authors cited above, I particularly commend the work of Anne Edwards, Garry Wills, and Edmund Morris on Reagan's early life; Stephen Vaughn on his movie career; Robert Mann, Rick Perlstein, and Jonathan Darman on his emergence as a conservative leader; Lou Cannon, Bill Boyarsky, and Seth Rosenfeld on his governorship; and Lou Cannon, Laurence Barrett, Del Wilber, Hedrick Smith, Peter Baker and Susan Glasser, Jane Mayer and Doyle McManus, Archie Brown, and James Graham Wilson on his presidency. Among the many memoirs, the most unvarnished—and thus the most valuable—were by Martin Anderson, David Stockman, Larry Speakes, Donald Regan, Jim Kuhn, Peggy Noonan, Terrel Bell, the Reagan children, and (surprisingly) Nancy Reagan. The most opaque, characteristically, were from Ronald Reagan himself.

It is a privilege to be represented by Tina Bennett, the best literary agent in the business, and to be edited by the supremely gifted and warmly encouraging Robert Weil. This is the fourth book Bob and I have collaborated on, and I cannot imagine writing a book without his brilliant guidance and unstinting support. His editing suggestions, as usual, were invaluable. Bob's assistants—first Haley Bracken, then Kadiatou Keita, and finally Luke Swann—have also been a pleasure to work with. The same is true of the whole team at Liveright (Peter Miller, Nick Curley, Pete Simon, Anna Oler, Steve Attardo, and Bill Rusin) and at Norton (Julia Reidhead, Brendan Curry, Steve Pace, Rebecca Homiski, and Don Rifkin). All of them care deeply about books, not just about the business of publishing, and I am grateful to be a Liveright author.

Finally, I am filled with gratitude to my family for their support, in particular Abigail Boot, William Boot, Alexander Vidra, Elle Vidra, Anna Golovchinsky, my late mother Olga Kagan, and, above all, to my beloved wife, Sue Mi Terry, my most ardent supporter and most perceptive critic. They have been living with this project for longer than Ronald Reagan was in the White House.

Notes

Prologue: Mourning in America

1. *Architectural Digest*, Aug. 18, 2016 (driveway); PD, *Goodbye*, loc. 2482 (jasmine); PD to author, email, March 12, 2021.
2. AI/FR.
3. MDOH, UVA.
4. PD, *Floating*, 44; RPR, *My Father*, 221.
5. PD, *Floating*, 118, 160.
6. DD, RRPL.
7. PD to author, email, March 12, 2021; RPR to author, email, October 20, 2021.
8. RPR, *Father*, 222.
9. PD, *Goodbye*, loc. 2555.
10. JW to NR, June 7, 2004, CN, RRPL.
11. Gallup poll, June 7, 2004.
12. Roosevelt to NR, CN, RRPL.
13. Rubisz to NR, June 11, 2004; Douglas to NR, June 7, 2004; Price to NR, June 8, 2004; Bush to NR, all in CN, RRPL.
14. *WSJ*, June 10, 2004.
15. *WP*, July 8, 2004.
16. PD to author, email, March 12, 2021.
17. Tumulty, *Triumph*, 555.
18. RPR to author, email, October 20, 2021. When I contacted MER, who gave me only one brief interview, to ask for his recollection of the funeral, he replied by email that he was too busy to talk to me.
19. Ibid.
20. AI/GJ.
21. Smith to NR, June 14, 2004, CN, RRPL.
22. *WP*, June 12, 2004.
23. AI/JD.
24. Baldridge to NR, July 19, 2004.
25. Al Jolson's words in *The Jazz Singer* were "Wait a minute, wait a minute, you ain't heard nothin' yet."
26. Unless otherwise specified, descriptions of the state funeral come from *LAT*, *WP*, and *NYT* news articles, June 11–12, 2004; from news videos available online; and from AI/GJ, AI/RPR, and AI/JD.
27. AI/GJ.
28. AI/RPR.

Introduction: The Pragmatist

1. Rosebush, *True*, 15.
2. AI/JABIII; AI/SS.
3. Historical Tables, Fiscal Year 2016, Budget of the United States; *WP*, April 26, 1980.
4. *WP*, Aug. 13, 1986.

5. Deaver, *Scenes*, 40; Von Damm, *Side*, 60.
6. "Republicans used to call Ronald Reagan the best president in US history. Now it's Donald Trump," You-Gov, Feb. 15, 2021; "Republicans view Reagan, Trump as best recent presidents," Pew Research Center, Aug. 22, 2023.
7. Darman, *Landslide*, 148; AI/JABIII.
8. Alter, *Best*, 148–165.

Chapter 1: Main Street

1. Sisson et al., *American Midwest*, xxii.
2. Ibid., 76, 69, 121.
3. Wood, *Revolt*.
4. Kelly, *Graves*, 2.
5. "New York, U.S. Arriving Passenger and Crew Lists (including Castle Garden and Ellis Island), 1820–1957," Ancestry.com.
6. Spitz, *Reagan*, 22.
7. Edwards, *Early Reagan*, 27.
8. Census Bureau, *Statistical Abstract 1999*, 876.
9. Edwards, *Early Reagan*, 32.
10. For Jack and Nelle's family backgrounds, see Spitz, *Reagan*; Reagan, *My Father*; Edwards, *Early Reagan*; Burke's Peerage, "Presented." For the birthplace, see "National Register of Historic Places Application Form—Main Street Historic District, Tampico"; *American Heritage*, Winter 2011.
11. *TT*, Feb. 17, 1911. For Tampico and Fulton population, see 1910 Census, "Statistics for Illinois."
12. *TT*, Feb. 4, 1910.
13. Census Bureau, *Statistical Abstract 1999*, 885.
14. *TT*, June 27, 1913.
15. *TT*, Feb. 4, 1910.
16. *TT*, Feb. 10, 1911.
17. Spitz, *Reagan*, 36–37.
18. *TT*, Feb. 10, 1911.
19. RR birth certificate, PF, RRPL.
20. RR, *Rest*, 3 ("noise"); RR, *Life*, 21 ("red-blooded").
21. NROH, UCLA.
22. McCullough, *Truman*, 38.
23. *San Diego Union*, May 10, 1981; Vaughan, "Inheritance," 118–119 (manual).
24. Kennedy, *Rise*, 202–203.
25. *U.S. Federal Government Revenues: 1790 to the Present*, UNT Digital Library.
26. 1940 Census, "Comparative Occupation Statistics, 1870–1940," 100.
27. Kennedy, *Freedom*, 16.
28. "African American Perspectives," Library of Congress.
29. "Swanee," Library of Congress.
30. RR to Mrs. John E. Reagan, Sept. 12, 1973, GP/CO, RRPL ("background"); *Parade*, April 12, 1981 ("roots"); RR to Donald B. Reagan, April 2, 1970, and RR to Donald A. Reagan, GP/CO, RRPL (misapprehension).
31. Lewis, "Defense."
32. RR, *Life*, 31.
33. Cannon, *Governor*, 119.
34. RR to Neil Reagan, June 21, 1984, box 3, HWF, Series II, RRPL; RR, *Life*, 374.
35. RR, "Address to the National Association of Evangelicals," March 8, 1983, RRPL.
36. AI/SS.
37. Cannon, *Ronnie*, 155.

Chapter 2: "The Sunny Side's the Only Side"

1. Garrison, *Religious Movement*, 99; Butler, *Religion*, 203.
2. Vaughan, "Inheritance."
3. Gardiner, "Nelle Reagan."
4. BJT, BSPP ("average"); *LAT*, May 10, 1981.
5. RR, *Rest*, 15 ("frustrated," "sheet"); NROH, UCLA (*Dust*).
6. Lindsey, *Ghost*, 159.

7. RR, *Life*, 22.

8. *DET*, April 9, 1927.

9. RR, *Life*, 21 ("purpose"); *Modern Screen*, May 1950 ("trust"); Cannon, *Governor*, 13.

10. NR, *Turn*, 107–108.

11. RR, *Rest*, 9.

12. *TT*, Sept. 13, 1907.

13. *DET*, April 10, 1926.

14. RR, *Rest*, 8–9; RR to Norman Cousins, July 17, 1984, HWF, Series II, RRPL.

15. *WSJ*, Oct. 8, 1980 ("thirst"); RR, *Rest*, 7–8 ("odor"); PD, *Dear Mom*, 33.

16. RR, *Rest*, 8 ("sickness"); RR, *Life*, 34 ("surly"), 25 ("disappeared"), 33 (Christmas); Lou Cannon interview with Neil Reagan, June 19, 1988, box 23, LCP, UCSB.

17. RPR, *My Father*, 68–69 ("dinnertime"); Deaver, *Scenes*, 40 ("unable"); RR, *Rest*, 7 (asleep).

18. RR, Rest, 9 ("burning"); *Star*, June 17, 1980 ("enemy"); Kennedy, *Freedom*, 17 (foreclosure).

19. *Inter Ocean*, Sept. 12, 1897.

20. RR, *Life*, 24.

21. Ibid., 28 ("government"); NROH, UCLA; RR, *Rest*, 40 ("tracks").

22. Lou Cannon interview with Neil Reagan, box 24, LCP, UCSB (clothes); RR, *Life*, 24 (cat); 29 (oatmeal).

23. Miller, *City*, 446.

24. RR, *Life*, 24.

25. Wilson, *Galesburg*, 113; Sandburg, *Prairie-Town Boy*.

26. RR, *Life*, 24.

27. RR, *Life*, 25 ("memorize"); Charles Bednar to RR, Aug. 23, 1989, KOPPP, RRPL (report card); Morris, *Dutch*, 28 (skipped).

28. AI/EMIII.

29. RR, *Rest*, 12; RR, *Life*, 24–25.

30. RR to Helen P. Miller, Sept. 3, 1981, PP, RRPL.

31. RR, *Rest*, 11.

32. BJT, BSPP ("outgoing"); *The Star*, June 17, 1980 ("serious"); RR, *Life*, 34 ("deficiency").

33. RR, *Life*, 31.

34. AI/SS; AI/EMIII; Rosebush, *True*, 62.

35. NR, *Turn*, 106.

36. Rankin, "1976."

37. RR, *Life*, 26.

38. Ibid.

39. PPP, RRPL; Skinner, *Hand*, 430–432.

40. RR, *Rest*, 13.

41. Wills, *Reagan's America*, 9.

42. RR, *Rest*, 13–14.

43. Ibid., 15.

44. Ibid., 16.

Chapter 3: "A Good, Clean Town"

1. RR, *Rest*, 17.

2. Lamb, *Dixon*, 68–132.

3. *DET*, April 14 ("expert") and Oct. 26 ("neat"), 1921.

4. Bellamann, *Kings Row*, 3.

5. RR to Helen P. Miller, Sept. 3, 1981, HWF, Series II, RRPL ("patron"); *DET*, March 19, 1921 ("games"); RR, *Rest*, 17 ("antics").

6. Gibler, *Dixon*, 97 (five thousand); "What Was Chautauqua?" University of Iowa Libraries ("American," "yokels"); BJT, BSPP.

7. *DET*, July 11, 1922.

8. BJT, BSPP.

9. RR, *Life*, 30.

10. Edwards, *Early Reagan*, 53.

11. Gordon, *Second Coming*, 2, 164–165.

12. *DET*, Jan. 17, 19, and 22, 1923.

13. *DET*, Sept. 19, 1924.

14. Cannon interview with RR, Oct. 26, 1968, box 25, LCP, UCSB.

15. "Chicago Race Riot of 1919," *Britannica*.

16. RR, *Life*, 27.

17. RR, "Remarks at Homecoming Birthday in Dixon," Feb. 6, 1984, RRPL.

18. For the government role in the development of a Midwestern town, see Morser, *Hinterland*.

19. Edwards, *Early Reagan*, 50.

20. NROH, UCLA.

21. AI/RPR; *WSJ*, Oct. 8, 1980 ("goody"); NROH, UCLA.

22. RR, *Life*, 29–30; Reagan, *My Father*, 94; RR to Anthony R. Dolan, April 7, 1981, HWF, Series II, RRPL.

23. *DET*, March 31, 1921.

24. *DET*, Dec. 6, 1924.

25. Wright, *Printer*, 111 ("deserving"), 319 ("Capitol").

26. RR to Jean B. Wright, March 13, 1984, in Skinner, *Letters*, 6.

27. Edwards, *Early Reagan*, 58.

28. RR to Jean Wright, March 13, 1984, in Skinner, *Letters*, 6.

29. RR to Rev. and Mrs. Ben H. Cleaver, Jan. 4, 1973, GP/CO, RRPL.

30. RR, *Life*, 36–37.

31. Edwards, *Early Reagan*, 52.

Chapter 4: The Lifeguard

1. Morris, *Dutch*, 695.

2. NROH, UCLA.

3. Miller, *Big Scrum*; Revsine, *Kickoff*.

4. "A Letter from Lee County," in LCHGS.

5. RR, *Life*, 32, 34.

6. 1926 *Dixonian* ("good"), 1927 *Dixonian* ("grit"), 1928 *Dixonian* ("Spirit"), all in LCHGS.

7. *DET*, Jan. 3, 1928 (race); RR to Trudy Feldman, Jan. 28, 1986, HWF, Series II, RRPL.

8. *Photoplay*, Aug. 1942.

9. RR, "School Spirit," Nov. 4, 1927, Series II, PPP, RRPL.

10. *DET*, Oct. 1, 1928.

11. *Reagan's Dixon*, in LCHGS.

12. *DMR*, Dec. 3, 1939.

13. Edwards, *Early Reagan*, 65.

14. 1928 *Dixonian*, in LCHGS.

15. *National Enquirer*, June 25, 1985.

16. *DET*, Feb. 28, 1981.

17. Eliot, *Reagan*, 20.

18. *National Enquirer*, June 25, 1985.

19. *DET*, July 23, 1932.

20. *National Enquirer*, June 25, 1985.

21. *Motion Picture*, Nov. 1939.

22. Reagan, *My Father*, 122.

23. 1928 *Dixonian*, in LCHGS ("clean," "grand").

24. "Rhapsody in Blue," *Encyclopedia Britannica*.

25. 1928 *Dixonian*, in LCHGS ("struggle"); RR, *Life*, 42 ("insecurity").

26. *DMR*, June 6, 1980.

27. RR, *Life*, 41 ("small man"); *DET*, Jan. 15, 1925 ("convulsed").

28. *Reagan's Dixon*, in LCHGS; Rockford *Register Star*, May 7, 1980 ("flubbed").

29. RR to Ben T. Shaw, May 31, 1973, GP/CO, RRPL.

30. *DET*, June 4, 1928.

31. RR, *Rest*, 22 ("sermons"); RR, *Life*, 40 ("intelligent").

32. 1927 *Dixonian*, in LCHGS.

33. Wills, *Reagan's America*, 22. RR's letters to Cleaver from the 1960s and 1970s may be found in GP/CO, RRPL.

34. Vaughn, "Inheritance," 112 ("Depression"); *DET*, Feb. 27, 1928 ("vigorous").

35. For Ben Cleaver's background and views, see Vaughn, "Inheritance," 112, 115, 120.

36. RR, *Life*, 41.

37. RR, *Rest*, 23.

Chapter 5: 'Neath the Elms

1. *The Singing Fool*, International Al Jolson Society.
2. "120 Years of American Education: A Statistical Portrait," US Department of Education, January 1993.
3. NROH, UCLA.
4. *DET*, April 3, 1928.
5. RR, *Life*, 54.
6. *DET*, June 30, 1931.
7. RR, *Life*, 45.
8. Edwards, *Early Reagan*, 83.
9. RR, *Life*, 45–46.
10. Adams, *Eureka*, 27–30.
11. A. C. Gray, "The Melting Pot" and "The New Immigration," *American Home Missionary*, in JRPP.
12. Rev. Fred W. Helfer, "A Christian Resolution," *Scroll* 33, no. 5 (January 1937), 149, reproduced in J. Bruce Fowlkes, "Brotherhood," Medium.com, July 30, 2015.
13. *Chicago Sun Times*, April 30, 1967 ("Grand Central"); RR, *Rest*, 56 ("gasoline"); RR, *Life*, 53 ("hangover"); *LAT*, April 23, 1967 ("playboy").
14. RR, *Rest*, 33–34; 1931 *Prism*, EC .
15. RR, *Life*, 51.
16. For the pregnancy theory, see Spitz, *Reagan*, 109–111. For a compelling refutation, see *American Spectator*, June 28, 2019.
17. For the origins of the strike, see Wills, *Reagan's America*, 48–49, 60–61; Boyarsky, *Rise*, 43–44; *DP*, Nov. 24 ($658,000) and Dec. 8, 1928; Adams, *Eureka*, 174.
18. *DP*, Nov. 28, 1928.
19. Wills, *Reagan's America*, 58.
20. Morris, *Dutch*, 698.
21. RR, *Life*, 48.
22. The best account of the student strike is in the *Peoria Journal Star*, April 23, 1967.
23. Adams, *Eureka*, 192, 200.
24. Junius Rodriguez to author, email, March 19, 2021.
25. *DP*, Dec. 8, 1928.
26. RR, *Life*, 49 ("seduced"); RR, "Remarks at Eureka College Pep Rally," Oct. 17, 1980, RRPL.
27. NROH, UCLA.
28. NROH, UCLA ("younger"); Lou Cannon interview with Neil Reagan, box 24, LCP, UCSB.
29. AI/RPR.
30. NROH, UCLA.
31. "RR and Eureka College," fact sheet, EC.
32. Reagan, *My Father*, 125. There is no contemporaneous record of an Olympic offer. But, in 1937, RR said that, when he was a high school junior, the Illinois Athletic Club had offered to pay him to join its swim team. He turned down the offer to go to college. *DMT*, April 3, 1937.
33. *LAECN*, Nov. 7, 1946. RR used virtually identical language thirty-five years later in *WP*, March 2, 1981.
34. Edwards, *Early Reagan*, 86; 1930 *Prism*, EC.
35. RR, *Life*, 47; 1930 *Prism*, EC.
36. RR, *Life*, 52.
37. 1931 *Prism*, EC.
38. 1930 *Prism*, EC.
39. *CT*, Sept. 17, 1985.
40. Box 11, HWF, Series II, RRPL.
41. RH, EC.
42. RH, EC; AI/JR.
43. RR, *Rest*, 63–64.
44. RR, *Life*, 52; RR, *Rest*, 64. Burghardt said that this incident occurred in LaSalle, Illinois: *WP*, March 7, 1981. However, Reagan and another classmate, Raymond Holmes, placed it in Dixon (see RH, EC). McKinzie said it occurred in Aurora (Cannon, *Reagan*, 38).
45. RR to Effie B. Porter, Sept. 13, 1982, box 4, HWF, Series II, RRPL.
46. *WP*, March 7, 1981.
47. 1932 *Prism*, EC.
48. RR, *Rest*, 44.
49. RR, *Life*, 58; 1931 *Prism* yearbook (for the 1929–1930 school year), EC; Morris, *Dutch*, 80–83.

50. RR Transcripts, EC, provided to author at the request of Patti Davis.

51. Wills, *Reagan's America*, 67.

52. RR, "Questionnaire for Alumni Project," Jan. 14, 1974, EC; RR to Tressie Kozelka, Jan. 10, 1991, EC.

Chapter 6: The New Dealer

1. *NYT*, June 8, 1932.

2. *DET*, June 7, 1932; RR, *Rest*, 40.

3. Wills, *Reagan's America*, 69.

4. Kennedy, *Freedom*, 41 (3 percent owned stocks), 77 (bank failures), 87 (unemployed), 163 (GDP).

5. Smith, *FDR*, 405; Egan, *Worst Hard Time*, 227.

6. Lowitt and Beasley, *One Third*, 55–61, 91.

7. Egan, *Worst Hard Time*, 5.

8. *WP*, April 13, 2020.

9. *DET*, 1951 Centennial Edition.

10. Kennedy, *Freedom*, 88.

11. *Motion Picture*, Nov. 1939.

12. RR, *Rest*, 45.

13. National Bureau of Economic Research, "Wages During the Depression," 1933.

14. RR, *Life*, 59.

15. Morris, *Dutch*, 79.

16. RR, *Life*, 55.

17. AI/EM; Wills, *Reagan's America*, 74.

18. RR, *Rest*, 41.

19. McElvaine, *Great Depression*, 90.

20. *NYT*, April 29, 1933.

21. RR, *Life*, 66.

22. NROH, UCLA (Neil); RR to Ben T. Shaw, Jan. 14, 1971, GP/CO, RRPL ("ardent"); MR, *First Father*, 117; RR, *Life*, 66.

23. FDR speech at Oglethorpe University, May 22, 1932, APP.

24. Kennedy, *Freedom*, 101.

25. Kennedy, *Freedom*, 109 ("amiable"), 101 ("pleasant," "boy scout"), 112 ("actor's"), 114 ("light"); Smith, *FDR*, 388 ("temperament").

26. Smith, *FDR*, 372.

27. Ibid., 11.

28. Leuchtenburg, *Shadow*, 209–213.

29. RR, *Life*, 66.

30. Leuchtenburg, *Shadow*, 211.

31. RR, *Life*, 67.

32. RR to Ben. T. Shaw, Jan. 14, 1971, GP/CO, RRPL.

33. Ibid.

34. Leuchtenburg, *Shadow*, 212.

35. RR, *Life*, 244.

36. Wills, *Reagan's America*, 129; *DMR*, Sept. 3, 1936; Leuchtenburg, *Shadow*, 213, 234.

37. Leuchtenburg, *Shadow*, 215.

38. "1932 Democratic Party Platform," APP.

39. FDR, "Address Accepting the Presidential Nomination," July 2, 1932, APP.

40. Smith, *FDR*, 490–492.

41. Ibid., 435–438; RR, *Life*, 66.

42. "Federal Budget Receipts and Outlays, Coolidge–Biden," APP.

43. *DET*, Nov. 4 and 10, 1933.

44. RR, *Life*, 68.

45. Ibid., 68–69.

46. FDR, "Annual Message to Congress," Jan. 4, 1935, APP.

47. *DET*, Dec. 16, 1933.

48. "Women and the New Deal," University of California, Berkeley.

49. *DET*, May 1, 1934.

50. *DET*, Jan. 16, 1934.

51. *DET*, Feb. 27, 1934.

Chapter 7: Radio Days

1. Orwell, "Why I Write," 1946, Orwell Foundation.
2. RR, *Life*, 20; Edwards, *Early Reagan*, 120.
3. Lewis, *Empire*, 163, 228.
4. Balio, *Design*, 14.
5. RR, *Life*, 59.
6. McKinzie interview, AEP, UCLA.
7. RR, *Life*, 61.
8. Palmer, *The Palmers*, 156.
9. Vaughn, *Hollywood*, 24.
10. For Palmer's background, I rely on Palmer, *The Palmers*, and my own visit to Davenport in 2019.
11. For Dutch's audition, see RR, *Rest*, 48–50 ("twinkling," "scorch"); RR, *Life*, 63–65 ("copper," "oatmeal"); *Motion Picture*, Nov. 1939 ("Irish"); *DP*, Oct. 11, 1931 (Western State game).
12. *NYT*, Oct. 23, 1932.
13. Iowa vs. Minnesota: RR, *Life*, 65–66; RR, *Rest*, 51–54; *Iowa City Press Citizen*, Oct. 24, 1932; Davenport, Iowa: *Quad-City Times*, Oct. 23, 1932 ("crisp"). Morris, *Dutch*, 112, and Spitz, *Reagan*, 122, erroneously claim that the first game that Dutch called was Iowa vs. Bradley on Oct. 1, 1932. *DET*, Oct. 7, 1932, confirms that the Iowa–Minnesota game was the first one—just as Reagan remembered. However, that game was two weeks after his audition and not, as Reagan recalled, the same week.
14. *NYT*, Nov. 20, 1932.
15. Smith, *FDR*, 405–406.
16. RR, *Rest*, 54; RR, *Life*, 69–70; *Davenport Daily Times*, Feb. 9, 1933; *DET*, Feb. 10, 1933; Smith, *FDR*, 406 ($4.23). Reagan left out the auditions from his own account, writing that MacArthur called to offer him the job in January. Biographers have repeated the error: see, e.g., Edwards, *Early Reagan*, 125; Eliot, *Reagan*, 30.
17. RR, *Rest*, 56 ("awful"); RR, *Life*, 71.
18. RR to W. J. Luttig, Aug. 24, 1989, KOPPP, RRPL.
19. RR, *Rest*, 56–57; RR, *Life*, 70; Wills, *Reagan's America*, 122–123; *Quad-City Times*, March 1–2, 1933.
20. RR, *Rest*, 55.
21. *DET*, April 12, 1933.
22. FDR, "Inaugural Address," March 4, 1933, APP.
23. Schwieder, *Iowa*, 268, 271–272.
24. *DMT*, Dec. 6, 1934.
25. Walker, *Crack*, 141–156.
26. RR, *Life*, 73, says it was Billy Jurges. RR, *Rest*, 66, says it was Augie Galan.
27. Quoted in *DET*, Aug. 11, 1934.
28. "Dutch Reagan: Sports Announcer," n.d., in "Manuscript Furnished by WHO—Des Moines," SHSI.
29. *DET*, Aug. 11, 1934.
30. Morris, *Dutch*, 116.
31. *DMR*, Nov. 5, 1980 ("guys"); Herb Plambeck interview, 1986, AEP, UCLA ("personable"); Jack Shelley interview, AEP, UCLA ("gab").
32. "Dutch Reagan: Sports Announcer" and "Dutch Reagan Gets Contract in Hollywood," April 9, 1937, both in "Manuscripts Furnished by WHO," SHSI.
33. Herb Plambeck interview, AEP, UCLA.
34. RR, Life, 76; *DET*, May 1, 1935.
35. Morris, *Dutch*, 121.
36. Morris, *Dutch*, 122; RR, *Life*, 76.
37. *Quad-City Times*, July 23, 2002.
38. Morris, *Dutch*, 123.
39. *DMR*, June 6, 1980.
40. Morris, *Dutch*, 134.
41. RR to Susan Nelson, Nov. 9, 1988, box 21, HWF, Series II, RRPL.
42. DMR, June 6, 1980; Edwards, *Early Reagan*, 141 (picture).
43. RR, Rest, 61; NROH, UCLA.
44. Edwards, *Early Reagan*, 143; McClelland, *Hollywood*, 2.
45. MSR, RRPL.
46. RR, *Rest*, 67.
47. MSR, RRPL.
48. *DMR*, Aug. 26, 2020, June 6, 1980.

49. *DMR*, Jan. 28, 1984; Morris, *Dutch*, 121; Wills, *Reagan's America*, 131–132; Boyarsky, *Rise*, 59–60.
50. RR, *Life*, 70.
51. *CT*, Feb. 28, 1935 ("rookies"), and March 1, 1935.
52. *CT*, Feb. 16, March 21, 1935 ("finest"); Ehrgott, *Wrigley's*, 154 ("magic"); *Wilmington* (Calif.) *Daily Press*, Nov. 12, 1936 (boar); *Fresno Bee*, May 16, 1934 ("attraction").
53. "Introducing Ronald Reagan," box 3, folder 687, RR, WBA.
54. *NYT*, March 30, 1937.
55. Reagan tells slightly differing versions of his signing in RR, *Rest*, 71–74, and RR, *Life*, 78–81. In both memoirs he mistakenly writes that he dealt directly with Meiklejohn (a claim echoed in, inter alia, Spitz, *Reagan*, 141), but in 1937 he had written a letter to thank Ward for discovering him. See *Time*, June 17, 1985 ("150-watt"). He also credited Ward in *DMR*, June 13, 1937. The best contemporaneous account, which suggests the screen test took place on March 29 and RR opened the telegram on April 2, is *DMT*, April 3, 1937 ("okay," whoop, "potential star"). For "recite it back," see Edwards, *Early Reagan*, 155. For General Mills's effort to keep him at WHO, see *Time*, June 17, 1984. For Joy Hodges's memories, see McClelland, *Hollywood*, 154–156 ("awful," "snowed").
56. Talbot, *Entertainer*, 131.
57. "History of RR's Contracts with Warner Bros.," Sept. 24, 1941, box 1, folder 2838A, RR, WBA.
58. *DMT*, April 3, 1937.
59. Dickstein, *Dancing*, xxi.

Chapter 8: Hayseed in Hollywood

1. Egan, *Worst Hard Time*, 235.
2. Balio, *Design*, 13–17, 30.
3. Friedrich, *Nets*, 20.
4. Balio, *Design*, 1.
5. Dickstein, *Dancing*, xiv, 232.
6. Balio, *Design*, 2.
7. Fuller, *Picture Show*, 185–189.
8. Powdermaker, *Hollywood*, 35.
9. Gabler, *Empire*, 13.
10. Warner: Sperling, *Brothers*, 81 (Rin Tin Tin), 142 ("dough"), 283–284 (lead pipe); Thomson, *Warner*; Gabler, *Empire*, 154–156 (Jack-Harry feud), 422 (FDR), xii ("water tower"); Bingen, *Warner*; Krist, *Mirage*, 237 ("gimmick").
11. "Recession of 1937–38," Federal Reserve History.
12. *DET*, May 20, 1937.
13. Steinbeck, *Grapes*, 90, 118–119, 154–156.
14. *DMR*, June 13, 1937.
15. Balio, *Design*, 164 ("made"); RR, *Life*, 83 ("not bad"); Lou Cannon interview with RR, Oct. 26, 1968, box 25, LCP, UCSB ("own").
16. RR, *Life*, 81–83; *DET*, June 17, 1937.
17. *DMR*, June 27 and July 4, 1937.
18. Balio, *Design*, 98–102.
19. RR, *Life*, 90.
20. Powdermaker, *Hollywood*, 39.
21. *DMR*, July 18, 1937.
22. Wallis, *Starmaker*, 92.
23. O'Brien, *Wind*, 207.
24. RR, *Life*, 84 ("hayseed"); *DMR*, June 19, 1938.
25. *DET*, Sept. 11, 1937, and July 16, 1937.
26. *DMR*, July 18, 1937.
27. *DMR*, June 27, 1937, and June 20, 1937.
28. Schulberg, *Sammy*, 63.
29. Talbot, *Entertainer*, 125–126 ("French chateaux," Brown Derby, "swish-swish"); McWilliams, *Island*, 344 (like a movie set).
30. *DMR*, Sept. 12, 1937 ("lazy"), and Sept. 5, 1937.
31. Krist, *Mirage*, 111.
32. RR to Dolores M. Ballchino, Dec. 2, 1986, series II, box 17, HWF, Series II, RRPL.
33. *DMR*, July 11, 1937.
34. *DMR*, June 20, 1937.

35. Edwards, *Early Reagan*, 178. The sign did not come down until 1985. See *AP*, Jan. 15, 1985.
36. *DMR*, Sept. 19, 1937 ("nonchalant"), and Aug. 22, 1937 ("natural"); box 3, folder H–34, RR, WBA ("anything").
37. *DMR*, Oct. 1, 1937 ("handsome"), and Sept. 17, 1937 ("boy").
38. *DMR*, Aug. 15, 1937.
39. *DET*, Sept. 11, 1937.
40. *DMR*, Oct. 3, 1937.

Chapter 9: The White Knight

1. Krist, *Mirage*, 187.
2. Nelle Reagan to Rev. and Mrs. B. H. Cleaver, May 26, 1937, RC/NR, RRPL.
3. Ibid.
4. *DMR*, Oct. 3, 1937.
5. RR, *Life*, 92–93; Edwards, *Early Reagan*, 206.
6. Vaughn, *Reagan*, 30.
7. Advance publicity, box 4, folder 688, RR, WBA.
8. *NYT*, March 2, 1939.
9. Parr, *Secret Service*, 24.
10. Vaughn, *Reagan*, 71.
11. RR, *Rest*, 81.
12. Bob Fellows to T. C. Wright, Sept. 10, 1940, in box 8, file 2226, RR, WBA.
13. McClelland, *Hollywood*, 160, 150.
14. *Motion Picture*, November 1939.
15. For Wyman, see Dick, *Ladies*, 7–21; Quirk, *Wyman*, 17 ("oppressive"), 14 (shy), 17 ("shield"), 19 ("rough"), 30 ("knight"); Morella, *Wyman*, 12 ("Bessie Fufnick"); "Why Don't We Talk about Jane Wyman Anymore?" Establishing Shot blog, March 22, 2022 ("pert"); Edwards, *Early Reagan*, 193 (trust); box 1, folder 2842, JW, WBA ($66); *LAT*, June 15, 1937 (breakdown).
16. *DMR*, Dec. 5, 1937.
17. RR, *Life*, 88.
18. *Lodi Sentinel*, Dec. 18, 1980; Eliot, *Reagan*, 72–73; Edwards, *Early Reagan*, 185.
19. *Modern Screen*, July 1947.
20. Quirk, *Wyman*, 31.
21. *DMR*, Dec. 3, 1939.
22. Morella, *Wyman*, 29.
23. *Modern Screen*, July 1947.
24. McClelland, *Hollywood*, 44.
25. Morris, *Dutch*, 162–163; *Modern Screen*, April 1943 ("nerves").
26. *Scranton* (Penn.) *Tribune*, Nov. 1, 1939 ("nicest"); *DMR*, Dec. 3, 1939.
27. Barbas, *First Lady*, 131.
28. Ibid., 213.
29. Dick, *Ladies*, 35; *Modern Screen*, April 1943.
30. MR, *First Father*, 27.
31. Niven, *Empty Horses*, 28–42.
32. Frost, *Hopper's Hollywood*, 1, 32.
33. *Life*, June 4, 1965.
34. Ibid.
35. *LAT*, Aug. 17, 1980.
36. Frost, *Hopper's Hollywood*, 1.
37. Barbas, *First Lady*, 128.
38. *Photoplay*, August 1942.
39. *DMT*, Aug. 10, 1939; RR, "My Business Is Acting," Advance Publicity, box 5, folder 688, RR, WBA.

Chapter 10: The A List

1. 1. RR, "Address at Commencement Exercises at the University of Notre Dame," May 17, 1981, RRPL.
2. RR, *Rest*, 94.
3. Cavanaugh, *The Gipper*.
4. RR, "Remarks at the Republican National Convention," Aug. 15, 1988, RRPL.
5. RR, *Rest*, 97.

6. Ibid., 99.

7. *LAT*, Oct. 30, 1940; box 5, folder 688, RR, WBA.

8. *Los Angeles Daily News*, July 15, 1940; Steve Trilling to Hal Wallis, June 24, 1940, box 8, folder 2226, RR, WBA.

9. Vaughn, *Reagan*, 89.

10. RR, *Rest*, 96.

11. RR to Peter R. Brooke, Dec. 2, 1970, GP/CO, RRPL.

12. R. J. Obringer to Ralph Lewis, Sept. 20, 1944, box 1, folder 2838A, RR, WBA.

13. *DMR*, Jan. 31, 1941.

14. Balio, *Design*, 48.

15. RR, *Rest*, 4.

16. Wolfgang Reinhardt to Hal Wallis, July 3, 1940, box 7, folder 2022A, RR, WBA.

17. Joseph I. Breen to Jack L. Warner, April 22, 1941, box 7, folder 2022A, RR, WBA.

18. RR, *Rest*, 4–5; RR, *Life*, 95.

19. RR, *Rest*, 6.

20. CNN.com, June 16, 2004.

21. Schickel, *Reagan*, loc. 198–213.

22. RR, *Rest*, 101; Kennedy, *Goulding*, 180.

23. *New Yorker*, Feb. 7, 1942; *DMT*, April 29, 1942.

24. *LAT*, Aug. 17, 1980.

25. Quirk, *Wyman*, 63.

26. *LAT*, Aug. 17, 1980; McClelland, *Hollywood*, 28; Sperling, *Warner*, 247.

27. "History of Ronald Reagan's Contracts with Warner Bros.," Sept. 24, 1951, box 1, WBA/RR.

28. Vaughn, *Reagan*, 36–37, 79.

29. R. J. Obringer to Ralph Lewis, Sept. 20, 1944, box 1, WBA/RR.

Chapter 11: Fort Wacky

1. RR's fear of flying developed during a turbulent flight to Catalina in 1937 and was exacerbated by an even rougher flight through a snowstorm to Chicago in 1939. See Edwards, *Early Reagan*, 199; Wills, *Reagan's America*, 135; Morris, *Dutch*, 130, 164.

2. Perlstein, *Reaganland*, 875.

3. Obringer to Wallis, Oct. 6, 1941, box 1, folder 2838A, RR, WBA; Rosenfeld, *Subversives*, 118.

4. Obringer to Adjutant General, Aug. 29, 1941, and Obringer to Assistant Secretary of War, Sept. 6, 1941, both in MSR, RRPL.

5. Trilling to Warner, Nov. 15, 1941, RR Personal Files, RR, WBA.

6. HQ, First Military Area, to Commanding General, 9th Corps, Jan. 24. 1942, MSR, RRPL.

7. RR to Executive, Southern California Military District, Nov. 29, 1941, MSR, RRPL.

8. JW contract, Aug. 25, 1941, box 1, folder 2842, JW, WBA.

9. *Real Deal*, Sept. 13, 2022. The median value of a home in 1940 was $2,938: CNBC.com, June 23, 2017.

10. *Screenland*, Nov. 1941.

11. "Federal Income Tax Brackets (Tax Year 1942)," Tax-Brackets.com.

12. Morella, *Wyman*, 52–53.

13. "History of Ronald Reagan's Contracts," Sept. 24, 1954, box 1, RR, WBA.

14. Claudette Colbert told Morris (*Dutch*, 727) that Wyman was "furious" with Ron for agreeing to military service.

15. W. L. Guthrie to Maj. Gen. George Kenney, May 5, 1942, MSR, RRPL (Jack Warner, Hal Wallis, and Howard Hawks spoke to Arnold about "arranging for the transfer of Ronald Reagan . . . to the Air Force"); Kenney to Commanding General, Fort Mason, May 10, 1942, MSR, RRPL.

16. Rosenfeld, *Subversives*, 119.

17. Betancourt, "World War II."

18. Cunningham, "Imaging."

19. RR, *Rest*, 107.

20. Ibid., 113.

21. Logevall, *JFK*, 322–326.

22. *Guardian*, Feb. 6, 2010.

23. "US Military by the Numbers," National WWII Museum, New Orleans.

24. RR, *Rest*, 117; Col. C. D. Bowen to officer in charge, Promotion Section, Officers' Branch, July 17, 1945, MSR, RRPL.

25. RR, *Rest*, 115.

26. Colacello, *Ronnie*, 154.

27. Interviews with Harry Harris, Howard Landres, and Eugene Marks, FMPUOH, RRPL.

28. Cunningham, "Imaging."

29. Vaughn, *Reagan*, 113; Lt. Col. Curtis Mitchell to Director, PR, Jan. 18, 1943, box 60, AEP, UCLA.

30. Vaughn, *Reagan*, 116.

31. Ronald Reagan's Filmography, RRPL.

32. RR, *Rest*, 118–119.

33. Ibid., 121.

34. *Modern Screen*, July 1942.

35. *Modern Screen*, Jan. 1943.

36. McClelland, *Hollywood*, 40.

37. *LAT*, Aug. 17, 1980.

38. RR, *Rest*, 138.

39. RR Biography, box 40, WFBP, YALE.

40. Vaughn, *Reagan*, 118.

41. Harry Harris, FMPUOH, RRPL ("liberal"); Howard Smit, FMPUOH, RRPL ("staunch").

42. *Modern Screen*, April 1944.

43. RR to Michael Carowitz, April 29, 1985, box 12, HWF, Series II, RRPL.

44. PD, *Dear Mom*, 42.

45. "Screen Actors Guild," May 23, 1951, RRFBI ("blows"); Morris, *Dutch*, 208–209; RR to David A. Altshuler, Sept. 20, 1966, box C1, GP/CO, RRPL.

46. "Executive Branch Civilian Employment since 1940," US Office of Personnel Management.

47. RR, *Rest*, 124–125.

48. RR to Ben T. Shaw, Jan. 14, 1971, GP/CO, RRPL.

49. *LAT*, Aug. 17, 1980.

50. Heidenry, *Kingdom*, 119 ("appeased"), 202 (penitentiary), 209 ("Antichrist"), 203 (Scriptures), 507 (McGrory).

51. R. J. Obringer to Whom It May Concern, July 23, 1945, MSR, RRPL; Vaughn, *Reagan*, 117.

52. *WP*, April 29, 1985.

53. Wills, *Reagan's America*, 196; Lucks, *Reconsidering*, 120.

54. *WP*, Jan. 1, 1984.

55. RRD, Feb. 2, 1982.

56. MER, *Outside*, 13–14; MR, *First Father*, 49–51.

57. Edwards, *Early Reagan*, 226–227.

Chapter 12: The Strike

1. Orwell, "You and the Atom Bomb," *Tribune*, Oct. 19, 1945.

2. X (George Kennan), "The Sources of Soviet Conduct," *Foreign Affairs*, July 1947.

3. Truman note, Dec. 9, 1950, Truman Library.

4. Patterson, *Expectations*, 12.

5. W. V. Cleveland to Mr. Gale, "Ronald Wilson Reagan," Jan. 18, 1967, RRFBI.

6. RR, *Rest*, 186–288.

7. *LAT*, Oct. 21, 1945.

8. *LADN*, Oct. 26, 1945.

9. *LADN*, Dec. 5, 1945; June Goto to RR, Nov. 19, 1987, box 2, KDP, RRPL.

10. *Whittier News*, Jan. 22, 1946.

11. *LAECN*, March 12, 1946.

12. San Pedro (Calif.) *News Pilot*, May 7, 1946.

13. RR, *Rest*, 141.

14. *NYT*, May 8, 1947.

15. Vaughn, *Reagan*, 123.

16. RR, *Rest*, 139; *LAECN*, Jan. 24, 1946.

17. RR, *Rest*, 139–141.

18. Morris, *Dutch*, 157–158. For a refutation of this "improbable accusation," see Lou Cannon's book review, *LAT*, Oct. 3, 1999.

19. RR, *Life*, 106; *LAECN*, March 21, 1946.

20. "RR, *Rest*, 166 ("cough"); Horne, *Class Struggle*, 21 ("proletarians"); Background/History, HDCR ("influence").

21. Rosenfeld, *Subversives*, 123 ("vigilant"); RR, *Rest*, 167.

22. RR, *Rest*, 168; Vaughn, *Reagan*, 131.
23. RR, *Life*, 111.
24. NROH, UCLA.
25. Vaughn, *Reagan*, 130.
26. Edwards, *Early Reagan*, 301.
27. Vaughn, *Reagan*, 166–169; FBI memo, May 23, 1951, RRFBI.
28. RR to Light Thompson, Jan. 9, 1985, box 11, HWF, Series II, RRPL.
29. "Ronald Reagan," SAG-AFTRA website. RR, *Rest*, 132 ("noble"), incorrectly states that he joined the board in 1938.
30. Bruck, *King*, 58–62, 204.
31. Horne, *Class Struggle*, 24–25.
32. Ibid., 22; Boyarsky, *Rise*, 78.
33. Sorrell not a Communist: Horne, *Class Struggle*, 17–20; Sbardellati, *Hoover*, 110; HKSM, UCLA; Friedrich, *Nets*, 406 (Casey).
34. Horne, *Class Struggle*, 18 ("irresponsible"); Ceplair and Englund, *Inquisition*, 218 ("unity"); HKSM, UCLA ("begged").
35. *LAT*, Oct. 9, 1945.
36. HKSM, UCLA, 156.
37. Dunne, *Pawn*, 149.
38. RR, *Rest*, 157.
39. RR to Roy Brewer, Sept. 25, 1985, box 13, HWF, Series II, RRPL.
40. Sbardellati, *Hoover*, 171.
41. Patterson, *Expectations*, 188.
42. Frost, *Hopper's Hollywood*, 111, 115; Barbas, *First Lady*, 264–266.
43. Gabler, *Empire*, 481.
44. JDOH, UCLA.
45. Brewer to RR, Sept. 8, 1987, box 19, and Feb. 25, 1986, box 15, HWF, Series II, RRPL.
46. RR to Murphy, Nov. 25, 1985, box 14, HWF, Series II, RRPL; RRD, Sept. 23, 1981 (Brewer at White House).
47. NROH, UCLA.
48. Dunne, *Pawn*, 148, 152, 154.
49. RR, *Rest*, 182.
50. Dunne, *Pawn*, 152–156; GHDOH, UCLA ("dangerous").
51. Dunne, *Pawn*, 161–162; RR, *Rest*, 182.
52. English, *Watch*, 571; Trudeau, *Memoirs*, 332 ("planet"); Attali, *Verbatim*, 86–87; Morris, *Dutch*, 442.
53. Wills, *Reagan's America*, 286.
54. Cannon, *Ronnie*, 40.
55. RR, *Rest*, 174; RR, *Life*, 108.
56. *LAT*, Jan. 14, 1954.
57. RR to Ronald Eldredge, May 11, 1982, box 3, HWF, Series II, RRPL.
58. Horne, *Class Struggle*, 207, 189; GDOH, UCLA; HKSM, UCLA.
59. Schwartz, *Writers' Wars*, 249–250; Horne, *Class Struggle*, 212–213 ("marveled").
60. RR, *Rest*, 157; JDOH, UCLA.

Chapter 13: The Blacklist

1. Gabler, *Empire*, 471.
2. Doherty, *Show Trial*, viii ("biggest"), 106 (pillow); *NYT*, Nov. 20, 1970 ("blazing").
3. *LAT*, Oct. 24, 1947; *NYT*, Oct. 24, 1947.
4. Doherty, *Show Trial*, 167.
5. HUAC 1947, 214, 217.
6. HUAC 1947, 170.
7. HUAC 1947, 217.
8. HUAC 1947, 218.
9. Doherty, *Show Trial*, 168–169.
10. RR, *Rest*, 158 ("point"); Rosenfeld, *Subversives*, 127.
11. RR, *Rest*, 183; Perlstein, *Invisible Bridge*, 378.
12. Rosenfeld, *Subversives*, 129–130.
13. Patterson, *Expectations*, 184–185, 193.
14. RR to Mrs. Hepner, July 4, 1960, PPP, RRPL; RR to Hugh Hefner, July 4, 1960, in Skinner, *Letters*, 149.
15. FBI report, May 23, 1951, RRFBI.

16. *Fortnight*, Jan. 22, 1951.

17. *LAT*, Jan. 15, 1948, and July 1, 1953; *NYT*, Nov. 18, 1947; Prindle, *Glamour*, 80 ("if any actor"); RR, *Rest*, 158; Vaughn, *Reagan*, 162, 217–218; SAG minutes, Sept. 29, 1947, AEP, UCLA.

18. RR, *Life*, 115 ("declare"); Ceplair and Englund, *Inquisition*, 359, 421.

19. *WP*, Nov. 23, 1997; JDOH, UCLA.

20. Pre-1966 speeches, RRSC, HI.

21. RR to Lorraine Wagner, Nov. 13, 1948, LW, RRRC.

22. RR to Sam Harrod, n.d., Series 00.10, RMC, EC.

23. RR, "A Foot in the Door," May 9, 1961, box G0200, Pre-1966 Speeches, RRPL.

24. RR, *Life*, 109.

25. RR, *Rest*, 174.

26. See, e.g., Schweizer, *Reagan's War*, 13.

27. HUAC 1951, 162.

28. *LAECN*, Jan. 14, 1954.

29. Horne, *Class Struggle*, 21, 176; Ceplair and Englund, *Inquisition*, 223; Wills, *Reagan's America*, 288–289.

30. Horne, *Class Struggle*, 20; Friedrich, *Nets*, 432; McWilliams, *Island*, 339.

31. *LAT*, July 17, 1951; Mann, *Becoming*, 101.

32. Vice Consul Toumantsev to VOKS chairman, June 25, 1947, Fond. 5283, op. 22a, file 28, VOKS, GARF.

33. *SEP*, May 15, 1951. See also Dmytryk, *Hell*.

34. Vaughn, *Reagan*, 212.

35. Ceplair and Englund, *Inquisition*, 243. This conclusion is confirmed in Theoharis, *Chasing*, 155.

36. Schwartz, *Writers' Wars*, 226.

37. Sbardellati, *Hoover*, appendix.

38. Niven, *Empty Horses*, 102.

39. RR to Hugh Hefner, July 4, 1960, in Skinner, *Letters*, 149.

40. Boyarsky, *Rise*, 90.

41. Wills, *Reagan's America*, 298.

Chapter 14: The Divorce

1. Quirk, *Wyman*, 45–46 ("perfect"); *Motion Picture*, April 1945 ("nicest"); *Modern Screen*, Feb. 1942 ("honeymoon"); *Photoplay*, Jan. 1942 ("distrustful"); *Silver Screen*, Aug. 1941 ("quarrel"); *Modern Screen*, Feb. 1942 ("infant").

2. *Motion Picture*, 1946 ("Irishers"); *LAECN*, Sept. 4, 1947.

3. *Photoplay*, Dec. 1946 ("news"); Allyson, *June Allyson*, 96 ("watch"); Siegel, *Siegel Film*, 114.

4. *Photoplay*, March 1949.

5. RR to Lorraine Wagner, n.d., LW, RRRC.

6. RR, *Rest*, 194–195; box 11, files 1489A, 2838A, RR, WBA; Edwards, *Early Reagan*, 325.

7. *LAT*, June 17, 1947.

8. Quirk, *Wyman*, 110.

9. *Valley Times*, July 17, 1947.

10. Quirk, *Wyman*, 110.

11. RR to Lorraine Wagner, Jan. 5, 1947, LW, RRRC.

12. Coffin, *Ayres*.

13. *Photoplay*, March 1949.

14. *Modern Screen*, June 1949.

15. *Greenville News*, Dec. 5, 1947 ("girl"); *Photoplay*, Feb. 1948 ("through").

16. Quirk, *Wyman*, 113 ("bricks"); *SB*, Dec. 5, 1947.

17. RR to Lorraine Markler, n.d., LW, RRRC.

18. RR, *Rest*, 201.

19. MR, *First Father*, 67–68.

20. *LAT*, June 29, 1948.

21. *Wilmington* (Calif.) *Daily Press Journal*, May 6, 1948.

22. *Photoplay*, April 1948.

23. *Modern Screen*, March 1948 ("co-respondent"); *Silver Screen*, April 1948 ("prince"); *Modern Screen*, March 1948 ("sullen") and Oct. 1948 ("slip").

24. Quirk, *Wyman*, 120.

25. See, e.g., Cannon, *President Reagan*, 111, and NPR interview, Aug. 5, 2014, with Rick Perlstein ("emotional intelligence").

26. AI/RPR.

27. RR, *Rest*, 203.

28. Food: RR, *Rest*, 203 ("grand"); Neal, *As I Am*, 111–112; RR to Warner, Dec. 1948, in Skinner, *Letters*, 137.

29. RR, *Rest*, 209.

30. Sherman to Steve Trilling, Jan. 13, 1949, Hasty Heart box, file 2749, WBA.

31. RR to Ben T. Shaw, Jan. 14, 1971, GP/CO, RRPL.

32. Neal, *As I Am*, 112.

33. AI/DR.

34. Kelley, *Nancy Reagan*, 88.

35. Novak, *Prince*, 270.

36. *CT*, Sept. 11, 1980.

37. Talbot, *Entertainer*, 125.

38. Morris, *Dutch*, 281.

39. *CT*, Sept. 11, 1980.

40. Laurie, *Learning*, 64–69.

41. Kelley, *Nancy Reagan*, 88, 92; *People*, April 29, 1991.

42. AI/RPR.

43. Reagan's Westerns were *Santa Fe Trail* (1940), *The Last Outpost* (1951), *Law and Order* (1953), *Cattle Queen of Montana* (1954), and *Tennessee's Partner* (1955). He also starred in some Western episodes of *General Electric Theater* and *Death Valley Days*.

44. January 1, 1950, clipping in box 21, folder 662, WBA; RR to Jack Warner, May 3, 1950, in Skinner, *Letters*, 137–138.

45. *Los Angeles Mirror*, Jan. 6, 1950, in box 1, file 2838A, WBA.

46. DS, MHL.

47. Schatz, *Boom*, 329–333; Lev, *Transforming*, 7.

48. RR, "Business, Ballots, Bureaus," *Landman*, Sep. 1960, PPP, RRPL.

49. RR to Lorraine Wagner, Sept. 21, 1949, LW, RRRC.

50. Vaughn, *Reagan*, 231–232; Edwards, *Early Reagan*, 432–433.

51. RR to Tressie Kozelka, Sept. 22, 1949, EC.

52. RR, *Rest*, 214.

53. RR, *Rest*, 233 ($750); Morris, *Dutch*, 282.

Chapter 15: The Winning Team

1. NR, *Turn*, 69–70.

2. PD, *Dear Mom*, 26.

3. Ibid., 97.

4. NR, *Nancy*, 29–31.

5. NR, *Turn*, 76.

6. AI/RPR.

7. Colacello, *Ronnie*, 121.

8. NR, *Turn*, 77.

9. Tumulty, *Triumph*, 45–51.

10. AI/RD.

11. Ibid.

12. NR, *Turn*, 82.

13. Ibid., 83.

14. Tumulty, *Triumph*, 61.

15. RR, *Turn*, 84.

16. *Modern Screen*, July 1949.

17. Tumulty, *Triumph*, 70–71; Colacello, *Ronnie*, 226–227, 235–236, 248; Kelley, *Nancy Reagan*, 74.

18. Levy, *Cukor*, 329.

19. In NR's first memoir, *Nancy*, she wrote that she was born in 1923 rather than the actual 1921 (p. 14). In her second memoir, *My Turn*, she was coy about her age: "When, exactly, was I born? I still haven't made up my mind" (p. 67).

20. NR, *Turn*, 90.

21. Patterson, *Expectations*, 364.

22. Tumulty, *Triumph*, 78.

23. NR, *Turn*, 93.

24. For closely coordinated his/hers versions of the first date, see NR, *Turn*, 94–96; NR, *Nancy*, 110–111; NR, *Love*, 10–11; RR, *Rest*, 235–236; RR, *Life*, 122–123.

25. NR, *Turn*, 97; RR, *Rest*, 235.
26. NR, *Turn*, 97.
27. Tumulty, *Triumph*, 95.
28. RR to Lorraine Wagner, March 21, 1951, LW, RRRC.
29. *Modern Screen*, March 1952.
30. NR, *Love*, 22.
31. NR, *Turn*, 100.
32. Tumulty, *Triumph*, 98.
33. Cannon, *Ronnie*, 161.
34. Tumulty, *Triumph*, 101; PD, *Dear Mom*, 80.
35. AI/RPR.
36. NR, *Love*, 24.
37. *Atlantic*, May 4, 2017.
38. PD, *Dear Mom*, 81.
39. NR, *Love*, 24.
40. MR, *First Father*, 94.
41. NR, *Turn*, 102.
42. NR, *Nancy*, 122.
43. AI/RD.
44. Ibid.
45. Tumulty, *Triumph*, 34–35; Colacello, *Ronnie*, 128–131. Richard Davis told me that accusations of antisem-itism and racism against his father were "absolute nonsense."
46. AI/RD.
47. RR to Sam Harrod, n.d., Series 00.10, RMC, EC.
48. RR, *Life*, 123.
49. RR to Edith Davis, July 6, 1955, box 1, Correspondence, NRP, RRPL.
50. AI/KO.
51. AI/DW.
52. AI/RPR; AI/KO.
53. AI/SS; AI/TR.
54. PD, *Dear Mom*, 59.
55. *NYT*, Nov. 25, 2007.
56. MER, *Outside*, 21.
57. Lou Cannon interview with RR, Oct. 26, 1968, box 25, LCP, UCSB.
58. RR, *Rest*, 241.
59. Eliot, *Reagan*, 5 (54 films); Lou Cannon interview with RR, Oct. 26, 1968, box 25, LCP, UCSB.
60. NR, *Turn*, 124.
61. Mann, *Becoming*, 101–103.
62. Rosenfeld, *Subversives*, 142.
63. NR, *Love*, 33; RR, *Rest*, 242.
64. NR, *Nancy*, 101.
65. Dick, *Ladies*, 147.
66. Colacello, *Ronnie*, 256 (Carroll Righter); RR to Belva Clement, April 16, 1980, box 5, 1980 campaign series I, RRPL ("believer"); NR, *Turn*, 248–249 ("experts"); *LADN*, Feb. 16, 1954 ("eyebrow"); Pomona (Calif.) *Progress Bulletin*, Feb. 15, 1954 ("mediums").
67. RR to Lorraine Wagner, Feb. 19, 1954, LW, RRRC.
68. AI/GSC. See also *Las Vegas Review Journal*, Jan. 29, 2010.
69. NR, *Turn*, 127.
70. Deaver, *Scenes*, 40.

Chapter 16: "Progress Is Our Most Important Product"

1. Edgerton, *Television*, 90 (1950), 217 (1962), 124 ("influencing"), 240 (minorities); Patterson, *Expectations*, 348–351.
2. Bruck, *King*, 32.
3. Moldea, *Dark Victory*, 20.
4. Bruck, *King*, 36.
5. Ibid., 50.
6. Ibid., 65–89.
7. Ibid., 119–121.

8. Wills, *Reagan's America*, 324.
9. RR to George Murphy, Nov. 25, 1985, box 14, HWF, Series II, RRPL.
10. RR, *Rest*, 276.
11. Moldea, *Dark Victory*, 184; McDougal, *Mogul*, 264–265.
12. Moldea, *Dark Victory*, 213.
13. McDougal, *Mogul*, 292–294; Moldea, *Dark Victory*, chap. 23 (grand jury transcript); RR, *Rest*, 287 (Perry Masons).
14. McDougal, *Mogul*, 294.
15. Lou Cannon interview with RR, Oct. 26, 1968, box 25, LCP, UCSB.
16. Moldea, *Dark Victory*, 245.
17. EDOH, UCB.
18. CBS press release, March 22, 1957, box 63, AEP, UCLA.
19. Wills, *Reagan's America*, 319, 329.
20. Raphael, *President Electric*, 188.
21. Edgerton, *Television*, chap. 6.
22. NR, *Love*, 55–56.
23. New York Social Diary, Aug. 15, 2010.
24. RR, *Rest*, 257.
25. EDOH, UCB.
26. Ibid.
27. Evans, *Education*, 63.
28. EDOH, UCB.
29. *CT*, July 13, 1960.
30. RR, *Rest*, 261.
31. Mann, *Becoming*, 94–96.
32. EDOH, UCB.
33. RR to Mrs. H. P. Shockey, April 2, 1971, file 3, GP/CO, RRPL.
34. EDOH, UCB.
35. Witcover, *Marathon*, 100.
36. *CT*, July 13, 1960.
37. RR, *Life*, 129.

Chapter 17: Family Values

1. RR, *Life*, 131.
2. Evans, *Education*, 62
3. NR, *Love*, 63.
4. PD, *Dear Mom*, 68.
5. NR, *Turn*, 128.
6. NR, *Love*, 71.
7. RR to NR, Sept. 23, 1956, box 1, Correspondence, NRP, RRPL.
8. WCOH, RRPL.
9. NRP, RRPL.
10. RR, *Rest*, 243, 274.
11. NR, *Turn*, 161; AI/RD.
12. PD, *Way*, 33.
13. Ibid., 29, 51.
14. AI/RPR.
15. *LAT*, April 16, 1995.
16. AI/RPR.
17. *WP*, Sept. 21, 2018.
18. PD, *Way*, 121–123, 131–134, 138–141, 144–145.
19. PD, *Way*, 13 ("angry"); PD, *Dear Mom*, 127 ("reconciliation").
20. PD, *Way*, 64.
21. Korda, *Life*, 469.
22. PD, *Way*, 29; PD, *Dear Mom*, 116.
23. MER, *Outside*, 33–34 (crop, "miserable"), 42–47 (molested); MR, *First Father*, 79–82 (boarding school).
24. MER, *Outside*, 71 ("normal"), 74 (cavities), 83 ("devastated").
25. Ibid., 81, 84.
26. NR, *Turn*, 156; AI/RD.

27. MR, *First Father*, 97, 139, 328, 103; MER, *Outside*, 84 ("Dragon").

28. Rosenfeld, *Subversives*, 148–149, 297.

29. MR, *First Father*, chap. 6.

30. PD, *Way*, 65.

31. AI/RPR.

32. Cannon, *Ronnie*, 158.

33. AI/RPR ("eyes"); MER, *Outside*, 90.

34. PD, *Dear Mom*, 46.

35. MER, *Lessons*, 11 (Disneyland); MER, *Outside*, 65 ("squirrels").

36. PD, *Dear Mom*, 50.

37. MER, *Outside*, 96.

38. MER, "Biographer Gets It Wrong on Me and My Dad," Newsmax, May 15, 2015.

39. MER, *Outside*, 112, 116.

40. Ibid., 122–124.

41. PD, *Dear Mom*, 173.

42. Ibid., 19.

43. AI/AL.

44. PD, *Dear Mom*, 17–18.

45. AI/RD.

Chapter 18: The Right Man

1. RR to Lorraine Wagner, n.d., LW, RRRC.

2. *CT*, July 13, 1980.

3. *Time*, Jan. 12, 1959.

4. Barrett, *Gambling*, 59.

5. *CT*, July 13, 1960; Philips-Fein, *Invisible Hands*, chap. 5; Evans, *Education*, chap. 3.

6. Flynn, *Road*, 10, 70, 93.

7. Mann, *Becoming*, 91–92.

8. Buckley, *Reagan*, 3–5.

9. Flynn, *Road*, 98.

10. Bogus, *Buckley*, 65–66, 158; Curtis, "Jungle."

11. Continetti, *The Right*, 108.

12. *NYT*, May 30, 1998.

13. *Harper's*, Nov. 1964.

14. Kabaservice, *Rule*, 13–15.

15. Schlafly, *Choice*, 112–113.

16. Leuchtenburg, *Shadow*, 219–220.

17. RR, *Life*, 134.

18. Patterson, *Expectations*, 253.

19. Stoll, *JFK*.

20. RR, "Remarks at a Rally in Macon, Georgia," Oct. 15, 1984, RRPL.

21. PD, *Way*, 46.

22. RR to Nixon, July 15, 1960, Series 320, box 621, PPP, RMNPL.

23. Perlstein, *Storm*, 153.

24. PD, *Way*, 82; Kelley, *Nancy Reagan*, 129–130.

25. Darman, *Landslide*, 139.

26. RR, "Encroaching Control," March 30, 1961, box GO200F, P1966, RRPL.

27. Mann, *Becoming*, 117.

28. RR, "Encroaching Control."

29. *NYT*, Oct. 8, 1985.

30. *NYT*, July 17, 2018.

31. Patterson, *Expectations*, 186.

32. Karl Marx, "Address of the Central Committee to the Communist League," March 1850, Marxists Internet Archive Library.

33. Schuknecht, *Public Spending*, 20–21.

34. Witcher, *Right*, 20.

35. Hayek, *Serfdom*, 54, 83.

36. Oreskes and Conway, *Myth*, 200.

37. Boller, *Never Said It*, 71–72; RR, *Life*, 474.

38. AI/RVA.
39. Hayes, "Thoughtful Speaker," cited in Mann, *Becoming*, 204.
40. RR, *Rest*, 306.
41. JWJ, Feb. 23, 1984.
42. AI/GS.
43. RR, commencement address, June 1952, box GO200, P1966, RRPL.
44. JFK, "Address to the California Democratic Party Dinner," Los Angeles, Nov. 18, 1961, JFK Presidential Library.
45. Santa Rosa (Calif.) *Press Democrat*, Oct. 10, 1962.
46. Dallek, *Right*, 38–39; Mann, *Becoming*, 124–140; Schlozman and Rosenfeld, "Long New Right," 17 (YAF); *Pasadena Independent*, Jan. 22, 1963 ("too bad"); "Ronald Reagan Speaks Out on Socialized Medicine," YouTube/Reagan Foundation.
47. RR to Nixon, March 26, 1962, in Skinner, *Letters*, 706.
48. RR, *Life*, 135.
49. *Look*, Nov. 1, 1966.
50. Mann, *Becoming*, 148.
51. RR, *Rest*, 311.
52. RR, "Losing Freedom in Installments," speech to the Fargo Chamber of Commerce, Jan. 26, 1962, box 61, AEP, UCLA.
53. RR, *Rest*, 269–270.
54. Evans, *Education*, 161–163.
55. RR, *Rest*, 273.
56. Mann, *Becoming*, 141.
57. Morris, *Dutch*, 321.
58. Cannon, *Governor*, 113.
59. Davis, *Way*, 67; RR, *Rest*, 339.
60. RR, *Life*, 137; Mann, *Becoming*, 143.
61. Germond, *Fat Man*, 151–152.
62. Edwards, *Early Reagan*, 478–479.
63. Darman, *Landslide*, 47.

Chapter 19: The Speech

1. Caro, *Passage*, 597.
2. Goldwater, *Goldwater*, loc. 3072.
3. Ibid., loc. 3075.
4. RR to Lorraine Wagner, Sept. 8, 1964, LW, RRRC.
5. RR, *Life*, 138.
6. Perlstein, *Storm*, 139.
7. Ibid., 33.
8. Ibid., 52–53.
9. Goldwater, *Conscience*, 12 ("Leviathan"), 20 ("racially mixed"), 38 (confiscatory), 41 (welfare state), 51 ("craven").
10. Ibid., 72.
11. Perlstein, *Storm*, 444.
12. Darman, *Landslide*, 169; Perlstein, *Storm*, 362–363.
13. Novak, *Agony*, 177.
14. Perlstein, *Storm*, 340.
15. *SEP*, Nov. 20, 1965.
16. Perlstein, *Storm*, 350.
17. Sitton and Deverell, *Metropolis*, 201.
18. James Q. Wilson, "A Guide to Reagan Country: The Political Culture of Southern California," *Commentary*, May 1967.
19. Kabaservice, *Rule*, 90.
20. GOP convention: Kabaservice, *Rule*, 112 ("responsibility"), 113 ("booing"); Mann, *Becoming*, 165 ("conspiracy"); White, *Making*, 201 ("exploded"); Jackie Robinson speech ("high priests"); Novak, *Agony*, 439–464; Perlstein, *Storm*, 382–383 ("irresponsible"); "Republican Party Platform of 1964," July 13, 1964, APP ("execution"); RNC, TMP (amendments to the platform).
21. White, *Making*, 211.

22. RR to Lorraine Wagner, June 16, 1964, LW, RRRC.
23. Lucks, *Reconsidering*, 34.
24. *Congressional Quarterly*, July 28, 1967.
25. RR speech, Orme School, June 1970, box 4, 1980 file, RRPL, and RR Q&A session with TV anchors, Feb. 7, 1983, RRPL ("Caucasian"); Perlstein, *Invisible Bridge*, 554; Lamb, *Conspiracy* (Broun et al.).
26. PD, *Dear Mom*, 44.
27. Barrett, *Gambling*, 426.
28. RR to Lorraine Wagner, Aug. 4, 1964, LW, RRRC.
29. "History of Lynching in America," NAACP.
30. Lucks, *Reconsidering*, 44; Cowie, *Dominion*.
31. RR to Lorraine Wagner, June 16, 1964, LW, RRRC.
32. *Atlantic*, July 30, 2019.
33. Carter, *From*, 64; *Newsweek*, Oct. 11, 1965.
34. Mann, *Becoming*, 169–170.
35. Date of speech: *LAT*, Sept. 30, 1964.
36. *NYT*, May 31, 1980.
37. Pew Research Center, Jan. 16, 2020.
38. Mann, *Becoming*, 185.
39. Hayes, "Thoughtful Speaker," cited in Mann, *Becoming*, 202–206.
40. RR, "A Time for Choosing Speech," Oct. 27, 1964, RRPL.
41. PD, *Way*, 97.
42. Mr. and Mrs. Robert L. Stevenson to RR, Oct. 24, 1964, box C35, GO/CO, RRPL; DDE Appointment Book, Oct. 30, 1964, box 1, PPP, DDEPL.
43. Mann, *Becoming*, 198; RR, *Life*, 143.
44. Patterson, *Eve*, 26; "Election Polls—Vote by Groups, 1960–1964," Gallup; *NYT*, Oct. 13, 1964.
45. Hess and Broder, *Republican Establishment*, 253.
46. Mann, *Becoming*, 200.

Chapter 20: The Friends of Ronald Reagan

1. Perlstein, *Storm*, ix; Patterson, *Eve*, loc. 56; *NYT*, Dec. 20, 1964.
2. "Vietnam War: Military Statistics," Gilder Lehrman Institute.
3. Patterson, *Eve*, loc. 83.
4. Brilliant, *Color*, 192.
5. Patterson, *Eve*, 121.
6. Ibid., 179–184.
7. Edsall and Edsall, *Chain Reaction*, 50.
8. Brennan Center for Justice, March 16, 2015.
9. AI/JB ("similar"); Brown: Pawel, *Browns*, 18–173 (165, Berkeley and Watts); Dallek, *Right*, chaps. 1, 3, and 5; Smith, *Who Is*, 84 ("uninspiring").
10. Dallek, *Right*, 150.
11. *Human Events*, Feb. 19, 1966.
12. WCOH, RRPL.
13. RROH, UCB ("farthest"); Ferhman, "Blockbuster." RR wrote to Lorraine Wagner, July 11, 1963, LW, RRRC: "I have a girl helping because I'm working on a book."
14. Charlotte (NC) *Observer*, Nov. 10, 1964.
15. *LAT*, Nov. 29, 1964.
16. Colacello, *Ronnie*, 304.
17. PD, *Dear Mom*, 61.
18. AI/RPR.
19. Quigley, *What*, 32.
20. Colacello, *Ronnie*, 285, 311–312.
21. AI/RT.
22. AI/AL.
23. KCOH, CSUF.
24. Ibid. (Tuttle).
25. RR to Lorraine Wagner, May 1965, LW, RRRC.
26. KCOH, CSUF (Tuttle).

Chapter 21: The Backlash Candidate

1. Goldwater, *Goldwater*, loc. 3285.
2. *SEP*, Nov. 20, 1965.
3. AI/SS.
4. *Ramparts*, Nov. 1965 ("seriously"); Brown to Lewis J. Miller, Dec. 17, 1965, carton 752, EGBP, UCB; Brown, *Reagan*, 41 ("best friend").
5. Spencer Roberts: AI/SS ("nice," "lay," "belief system," "hot"); SS, UVA; WEROH, UCB ("nut," "yes"); DeGroot, *Selling*, 129 ("mercenaries"); Lewis, *What Makes*, 108 ("answers").
6. AI/SS; AI/TR.
7. AI/SS; Nofziger, *Nofziger*, 46.
8. MR, *First Father*, 146–147 ("humiliated"); Tumulty, *Triumph*, 139–140 ("livid").
9. RR speech, "The Creative Society," April 19, 1966, box 40, WFBP, YALE.
10. Lewis, *What Makes*, 131.
11. Dallek, *Right*, 104.
12. RR to Roy Brewer, May 14, 1971, Hollywood file, GP/CO, RRPL.
13. RR to Mrs. H. A. Staples, Aug. 11, 1972, file 4, GP/CO, RRPL.
14. AI/SS.
15. RR to Mr. and Mrs. P. A. Agnew, June 15, 1966, box C1, GP/CO, RRPL.
16. RR to David M. Altshuler, Sept. 20, 1966, box C1, GP/CO, RRPL.
17. RR to Mrs. H. Albright, Oct. 13, 1965, box C1, GP/CO, RRPL.
18. *LAT*, Aug. 25, 1965; AI/SS.
19. Lewis, *What Makes*, 133; Dallek, *Right*, 124–125; "Statement of Ronald Reagan Regarding the John Birch Society," Sept. 24, 1965, box 40, WFBP, YALE.
20. Miller, *Conspiratorial*, 8–9; *New Republic*, March 8, 2021.
21. *Fresno Bee*, March 12, 1966; *SB*, July 31, 1966.
22. For the apocryphal versions, see Cannon, *Governor*, 299; Nofziger, *Nofziger*, 45, 48; Spitz, *Reagan*, 325.
23. SPOH, UCLA; BASICO contract, Feb. 1, 1966, box C33, GP/CS, RRPL.
24. Germond, *Fat Man*, 153.
25. RROH, UCB.
26. AI/SS.
27. Deaver, *Drummer*, 5.
28. Bernard Elias to Governor's Office, May 11, 1965, carton 752, EGBP, UCB.
29. SPOH, UCLA.
30. AI/SS.
31. RR, *Life*, 147; RROH, UCLA.
32. RR speech, "A Plan for Action," Jan. 4, 1966, box C30, GP/CS, RRPL.
33. DeGroot, *Selling*, 149; Smith, *Who Is*, 106–108.
34. Schlozman and Rosenfeld, "Long New Right," 8.
35. DeGroot, "Unrest"; RR commercial, "Berkeley," Sept. 28, 1966, box C30, GP/CS RRPL.
36. Dalzell, *Battle*, 16.
37. *LAT*, May 22, 1966.
38. DeGroot, *Selling*, 196.
39. "Higher Education in California," Public Policy Institute of California, San Francisco. Morris, *Dutch*, 348, wrongly claims that "80 percent of young Californians went to college."
40. Lewis, *What Makes*, 131.
41. RR to John Wayne, July 1, 1968, GP/CO, RRPL.
42. Dallek, *Right*, 142.
43. Levin, *Queen*, 89; *NYT*, Aug. 27, 1965 ("discussed").
44. Lu Haas to Jesse Unruh, July 28, 1970, 1970 campaign files, JMUP, CSA.
45. *NYT*, June 1, 1966 ("our"); Brilliant, *Color*, 222 ("patronize"); *LAT*, Oct. 21, 2020 ("right"); *Madera Daily Tribune*, Nov. 21, 1966 ("segment").
46. *NYT*, Sept. 28, 1966.
47. "California's Latino Plurality Brings a Sense of Déjà Vu," NPR, May 4, 2014.
48. Brown, *Reagan*, 19.
49. Blowup: *LAT*, March 6, 1966; Nofziger, *Nofziger*, 38–42; JBRPP, LNI; FCNOH, UCB; LNOH, UVA; AI/SS ("took personally"); Dallek, *Right*, 199–202; Lewis, *What Makes*, 114–116; Boyarsky, *Rise*, 148–149. Stanley Holden of BASICO claimed it was he, not Nofziger, who convinced Reagan to go back: DeGroot, *Selling*, 168–169.
50. Dallek, *Right*, 203–209; Ritchie, *Columnist*, 263.

51. Cannon, *Ronnie*, 84.
52. AI/GS.
53. Nofziger, *Nofziger*, 50.
54. Boyarsky, *Rise*, 150–152; Patrick, *Reagan*, I:13–20; AI/JB.
55. RR to WFB, July 11, 1966, box 4, WFBP, YALE.
56. DDE to Mrs. John P. Campbell, May 25, 1967, box 2, PPP, DDEPL.
57. Dallek, *Right*, 234–236; *NYT*, Oct. 2, 1966 ("Old Pro").
58. *NYT*, Nov. 9, 1966.
59. Brown, *Reagan*, 13.
60. Gentry, *Last Days*, 284.
61. NR to William F. Buckley Jr., Oct. 1965, box 36, WFBP, YALE.

Chapter 22: The Amateur

1. *SB*, Jan. 2, 1967; *LAT*, Jan. 3, 1967.
2. MR, *First Father*, 155–156.
3. RR, *Rest*, 249.
4. RR, "Inaugural Address," Jan. 5, 1967, RRPL.
5. NR, *Turn*, 137; RROH, UCB.
6. "1970 Census of Population," US Department of Commerce, April 1973.
7. *National Review*, Oct. 22, 1968.
8. *NYT*, June 10, 1979.
9. *SEP*, June 1, 1968.
10. *Life*, May 1967; AI/EMIII.
11. RROH, UCB.
12. KCOH, CSUF (Salvatori); Cannon, *Ronnie*, 139; Tumulty, *Triumph*, 163 ($125,000); Colacello, *Ronnie*, 362 (table).
13. Davis, *Really Like*, 6–7.
14. AI/RPR.
15. Didion, *White Album*, 69.
16. Ranch: MER, *Lessons*, 47 (Dart); Cannon, *Reagan*, 354 ("run for office"); Bruck, *King*, 266–267 ("sweetheart"); *NYT*, Aug. 13, 1976; Marvin S. Shapiro to Jess Unruh for Governor Committee, Oct. 7, 1970, JMUP, CSA; *Rolling Stone*, Aug. 26, 1976 (new Fox executives, "good deal," shell company); *Napa Valley Register*, July 24, 1968 (studio tax break).
17. Feldstein, *Poisoning*, 44, 61.
18. *Time*, Nov. 10, 1967.
19. RROH, UCB.
20. Cannon, *Governor Reagan*, 184.
21. *Oakland Tribune*, March 26, 1967.
22. Bagley, *Golden*, 118; RR, *Life*, 166.

Chapter 23: The Moderate

1. *NYT*, Sept. 15, 2008.
2. Cabinet minutes, Jan. 15, 1968, box 4, WPCP, HI.
3. AI/EMIII.
4. *SB*, Dec. 8, 1974.
5. Cannon, *Governor*, 189–194.
6. Reed, *Enigma*, 93.
7. Boyarsky, *Big Daddy*, 13–14, 112.
8. AI/GST.
9. "Governor Reagan: Action and Results," Dec. 1974, 1974 file, GP/CO, RRPL.
10. Boyarsky, *Reagan*, 156–159; Cannon, *Governor*, 334; Von Damm, *Sincerely*, 44 ("hurt").
11. Cannon, *Ronnie*, 153–154.
12. Lou Cannon interview with RR, Oct. 26, 1968, box 25, LCP, UCSB.
13. *Congressional Quarterly*, July 28, 1967.
14. *LAT*, April 3, 1968.
15. *SB*, April 3, 1968.
16. Steffgen, *Here's the Rest*, 129.
17. AI/GST.

18. *WP*, Jan. 12, 2001.

19. Abortion: Beilenson, *Looking*, 2.86–125 (113, "frosty"; 116, "lucky"); Cannon, *Governor*, 212–214; Cannon, *Reagan*, 128–132; RR interview with Robert Dornan, Aug. 1, 1970, JMUP, CSA, 1970 campaign files ("soul searching"); RR to Sally Lockwood, July 26, 1974, 1974 file, GP/CO, RRPL ("firm belief"); Boyarsky, *Reagan*, 121–124; Hannaford, *Reagans*, 183 ("gratuitously").

20. Death penalty: *SB*, April 12, 1967; Cannon, *Governor*, 214–217; Meese to RR, "Clemency hearing of Aaron Mitchell," April 11, 1967, box 222, EMP, HI; Aaron Mitchell to Gov. Brown, Dec. 27, 1966, box 222, EMP, HI; Boyarsky, *Reagan*, 188; Davis, *Really Like*, 47 ("exhausted").

21. Governor's press release, June 29, 1967, box 222, EMP, HI.

22. Wright: Cannon, *Governor*, 222–225 (223, "restraint"; 224, denied, "Reagan's Earl Warren"); Boyarsky, *Reagan*, 182–190; Rumsfeld to Ehrlichman, May 22, 1970, WHCF, RMNPL ("wonders"); *SB*, Feb. 18, 1972 ("shocked"); RR to MR, March 6, 1972, box 4, 1980 Campaign Series I, RRPL ("Mickey Mouse"); AI/ EMIII ("double-cross"); WFSOH, UCB ("deceitful").

23. Cabinet minutes, Feb. 13, 1968, box 4, WPCP, HI.

24. Hannaford, *Reagans*, 33.

25. Cabinet minutes, Feb. 16, 1968, box 24, GP/CU, RRPL.

26. Boyarsky, *Reagan*, 185.

27. Winkler, *Gun Fight*, 237–247; *SB*, May 2, 1967; RR to Lorraine Wagner, Feb. 15, 1979, LW, RRRC ("hardly").

28. AI/GST.

29. AI/TR.

30. RR, handwritten note, 1983, box 7, HWF, Series II, RRPL.

31. RR, *Life*, 167.

32. AI/NR.

33. Von Damm, *Side*, 70–71.

34. Cannon, *Reagan*, 143.

35. Lou Cannon interview with RR, Oct. 26, 1968, box 25, LCP, UCSB.

36. Cannon, *Governor*, 332.

37. RROH, UCB; NR, *My Turn*, 144.

38. RROH, UCB.

Chapter 24: The "Homosexual Ring"

1. CNN.com, Sept. 18, 1998.

2. Perlstein, *Storm*, 490.

3. Gitlin, *Sixties*, 215.

4. *Oakland Tribune*, March 26, 1967.

5. Reed, *Enigma*, 104–105.

6. Nofziger, *Nofziger*, 77.

7. AI/TR.

8. Reed, *Enigma*, 111.

9. Ibid., 112.

10. Colacello, *Ronnie*, 2, 396–400; RR to Jerome Zipkin, Feb. 11, 1917, box 2, GP/CO, RRPL (thanking "Jerry" for arranging Nancy and Patti's trip to New York).

11. AI/SS.

12. *Los Angeles Herald Examiner*, Nov. 1, 1978.

13. Perlstein, *Reaganland*, 375 ("tragic"); MER, *Outside*, 157–158 (ballet); Hannaford, *Reagans*, 184; AI/GS.

14. Reed, *Enigma*, 133.

15. AI/TR.

16. *San Jose Mercury News*, Feb. 13, 1967.

17. Kengor and Doerner, *Judge*, 63–64.

18. MDOH, UVA.

19. Ibid.

20. RR press release, Aug. 26, 1967, box 1, WPCP, HI.

21. *SB*, Sept. 3, 1967.

22. Nofziger, *Nofziger*, 79.

23. Ritchie, *Columnist*, 4, 118, 265; Feldstein, *Poisoning*, 35–36.

24. Tampa (Fla.) *Tribune*, Oct. 31, 1967.

25. AI/SS.

26. Feldstein, *Poisoning*, 82–85.

27. RR press conference transcript, Oct. 31, 1967, box 1, WPCP, HI.

28. Nofziger, *Nofziger*, 81.

29. RR press conference transcript, Nov. 14, 1967, box 1, WPCP, HI.

30. Nofziger, *Nofziger*, 82–83, 87; *SB*, Nov. 10, 1967.

31. Ritchie, *Columnist*, 264–265.

Chapter 25: The Forgotten Campaign

1. Cannon, *Governor*, 258; Reed, *Enigma*, 59–60.

2. Cannon, *Ronnie*, 264.

3. Reed, *Enigma*, 117.

4. SSOH, UVA.

5. Reed, *Enigma*, 120.

6. White, *President 1968*, 39–40.

7. Dallek, *Giant*, 528–529; Patterson, *Expectations*, 678–685.

8. Davis, *Really Like*, 15; *NYT*, April 23, 1967.

9. Frank Mankiewicz to RR, June 5, 1981, HWF, Series II, RRPL; *National Review*, May 22, 2007.

10. Reed, *Enigma*, 140.

11. Nofziger, *Nofziger*, 70.

12. *Shreveport Journal*, April 6, 1968; *WP*, April 6, 1968.

13. Lucks, *Reconsidering*, 89–90.

14. Gallup News Service, Jan. 16, 2006.

15. Nofziger, *Nofziger*, 70–71.

16. AI/NR.

17. Nofziger, *Nofziger*, 71.

18. *NYT*, April 10, 1968.

19. Lucks, *Reconsidering*, 188–193.

20. Eig, *King*, 456.

21. Rosenfeld, *Subversives*, 3–8.

22. PD, *Way*, 79–80.

23. NR, *Turn*, 143.

24. PD, *Way*, 136.

25. Nofziger, *Nofziger*, 72.

26. *WP*, Aug. 7, 2018.

27. *NYT*, Aug. 8, 1968.

28. Cannon, *Governor*, 268.

29. White and Gill, *Why Reagan*, 82–129.

30. Nofziger, *Nofziger*, 74; Davis, *Way*, 136.

31. RR to Dennis Puleo, March 5, 1985, box 12, HWF, Series II, RRPL.

32. RR, *Life*, 176–177.

33. Reed, *Enigma*, 179.

Chapter 26: Battles in Berkeley

1. Rorabaugh, *Berkeley*, 176.

2. Gitlin, *Sixties*, 353–354.

3. Rorabaugh, *Berkeley*, 91 ("everything"); Gitlin, *Sixties*, 342 (hundred), 287 ("Bacon").

4. Cannon, *Governor*, 295.

5. Von Damm, *Side*, 69.

6. Rosenfeld, *Subversives*, 187–191, 329–330; Cannon, *Reagan*, 151.

7. Regents minutes, Feb. 21, 1969, box GO156, GP/RF, RRPL.

8. Cannon, *Governor*, 175–178.

9. Ibid., 285.

10. Rosenfeld, *Subversives*, 425; PD, *Way*, 135–136.

11. *Los Angeles Free Press*, Oct. 1968, in box 2, WPCP, HI.

12. Cannon, *Reagan*, 145; Tumulty, *Triumph*, 152.

13. *Valley News*, Oct. 10, 1968.

14. Cabinet minutes, Sept. 25, 1968, box 4, WPCP, HI.

15. RR press release, June 11, 1968, box GO156, GP/RF, RRPL.

16. *SB*, Feb. 21, 1969.

17. *SB*, Jan. 6, 1969.

18. *SB*, April 9, 1970.
19. *San Bernardino County Sun,* April 17, 1970.
20. *Daily Californian,* Jan. 20, 1969.
21. Third World Liberation Front: Rosenfeld, *Subversives,* 418–446 (418, "goddamn"; 431, arson); *Daily Californian,* Jan. 20, 1969 (Reagan car pelted), Jan. 23, 1969 (fire), Jan. 29, 1969 ("student power"), Feb. 24, 1969 (seven hundred police); Rorabaugh, *Berkeley,* 84–85 ("asses"); *NYT,* Feb. 22, 1970 ("90 or 95 percent"); Governor's press release, Feb. 5, 1969, box GO156, GP/RF, RRPL ("extreme emergency").
22. People's Park: John T. Kehoe to RR, June 10, 1969, box GO157, GP/RF, RRPL ("parasites"); *Daily Californian,* May 16, 1969 ("freak show"), May 21, 1969 (helicopter), May 23, 1969 (482 arrests); Rosenfeld, *Subversives,* 447–466 (455, buckshot; 460, fifty people shot; 484, $1 million); Rorabaugh, *Berkeley,* 155–166; CNN.com, June 8, 2020 (tear gas); Dalzell, *Battle,* 4 ("cesspool"), 89 ("take the park"), 99 ("moved"), 120 (on this level), 134 ("mob"), 224 ("Mommy"); Governor's office, "The 'People's Park': A Report on a Confrontation at Berkeley, California," July 1, 1969, box GO157, GP/RF, RRPL.
23. *SB,* Aug. 6, 1969 (Alioto); Brown, *Reagan,* 148–149 (*LAT*); *Fresno Bee,* May 23, 1969 (Burton).
24. *Oakland Tribune,* May 22, 1969 ("dogs of war"); *Fresno Bee,* June 3, 1969 ("restraint"); RR press conference, May 20, 1969, box GO157, GP/RF, RRPL ("hurt"); RR, speech to the Commonwealth Club, June 13, 1969, box GO157, GP/RF, RRPL ("imminent").
25. Rosenfeld, *Subversives,* 468 (refuted); *SB,* May 21, 1969 ("destroying"); *Daily Californian,* May 23, 1969 ("young man").
26. *LAT,* June 26, 1980; AI/EMIII.
27. DeGroot, "Unrest."
28. Rorabaugh, *Berkeley,* 109.
29. "Report of the President's Commission on Campus Unrest," 1970, US Department of Education.
30. Carter, *Diary,* 187.
31. RR, *Life,* 182.
32. *NYT,* Feb. 28, 1969.
33. J. G. Forbes to RR, Dec. 9, 1968, and William Waterfield Jr. to RR, Dec. 9, 1968, box GO156, GP/RF, RRPL.
34. *WP,* March 28, 1969.
35. *Harper's,* April 2016.
36. *SB,* May 7, 1970.
37. PD, *Way,* 150–151.
38. RR to Ben H. Cleaver, Dec. 17, 1973, box 4, 1980 Campaign Series I, RRPL.
39. *WP,* April 19, 2021.
40. *SB,* May 7, 1970.
41. Reed, *Enigma,* 184–189.

Chapter 27: A Quieter Term

1. Boyarsky, *Big Daddy,* 13, 198.
2. *Time,* Sept. 14, 1970.
3. Brown, *Reagan,* 20; *NYT,* Oct. 25, 1970.
4. AI/WB.
5. Cannon, *Reagan,* 175; Boyarsky, *Big Daddy,* 199.
6. *NYT,* June 7, 1970.
7. *Time,* Sept. 14, 1970.
8. *NYT,* Oct. 25, 1970.
9. Jesse Unruh to "Daddy Warbucks," JMUP, CSA.
10. *LAT,* Sept. 8, 1970; Boyarsky, *Big Daddy,* 202.
11. Deaver, *Scenes,* 44.
12. *NYT,* Oct. 25, 1970.
13. Ibid.
14. *LAT,* Jan. 5, 1971; *NYT,* Jan. 5. 1971.
15. RR, *Life,* 175.
16. AI/EMIII ("broker"); Cannon, *Governor,* 327; *LAT Magazine,* May 4, 1984; Boyarsky, *Reagan,* 107–108; Hannaford, *Reagans,* 34 (synthesizing).
17. AI/EMIII; AI/GST.
18. *San Francisco Examiner,* May 9, 1971.
19. Von Damm, *Side,* 53; Von Damm to Harriet Johnson, June 14, 1974, 1974 file, GP/CO, RRPL.
20. LNI, JBRPP.

21. Davis, *Really Like*, 36; LNOH, UVA; AI/EMIII; Dec. 1, 1980, box 1, SFP, RRPL (Orr).
22. Hannaford, *Reagans*, 31.
23. Boyarasky, *Reagan*, 122.
24. Germond, *Fat Man*, 155.
25. AI/GS; Lou Cannon interview with RR, Oct. 26, 1968, box 25, LCP, UCSB ("swell"); Germond, *Fat Man*, 155.
26. Welfare reform: RR to Reed, May 9, 1972, file 2, GP/CO, RRPL ("political life"); Boyarsky, *Reagan*, 125–139 (130, 2.3 million); Cabinet meeting minutes, Feb. 13, 1968, box 4, WPCP, HI ("our responsibility"); RBOH, CSUF; Meese, *With Reagan*, 35–36 (negotiations with Morretti); Cannon, *Reagan*, 166 ("tax taker"), 180 ("in love"), 181 ("grudging"), 183 (9,600); AI/EMIII; Cannon, *Governor*, 350–362; RR, *Life*, 188–190; *SB*, Dec. 8, 1974 ("cussed"); *LAT*, April 12, 1980 (caseloads declining); *SF Chronicle*, April 13, 1976 ("feasible"); Crafton, "Incremental" ("moral fiber," "bankruptcy"); RR to Nixon, April 29, 1970, file 2, GP/CO, RRPL ("antipathy"); *Sacramento Union*, April 4, 1974 ("tribute"). Contrary to the bizarre claim in Morris, *Dutch*, 369, Moretti was never known as "Macho Bob."
27. The Sisco-RR letters can be found in boxes 4–5, 1980 Campaign Series I, RRPL, and other files of RR letters. For RR's rocking chair, see Edwin J. Gray to Charles Gould, April 13, 1971, box 4, 1980 Campaign Series I, RRPL. For RR's Nov. 21, 1974, letter to Nixon ("amazing"), see GP/CO, RRPL. "Softest:" *WP*, May 1, 1980.
28. Environmental policies: Cannon, *Governor*, 297–321 (312, "beautiful"; 313, treaties; 320, Watt); NBLOH, UCB (85, "never sets"); *Oakland Tribune*, June 29, 1972 (Minarets speech); *Fresno Bee*, June 29, 1972 (Minarets speech); *SB*, Dec. 29, 1972 ("exultation"); Boyarsky, *Reagan*, 166–176.
29. Prop. 1: Cannon, *Governor*, 368–379; Boyarsky, *Reagan*, 159–165.
30. Wilentz, *Age*, 127.
31. *LAT*, Aug. 27, 1974.
32. RR to Gen. William C. Westmoreland, Jan. 30, 1974, 1974 file, GP/CO, RRPL.
33. AI/JB; AI/WB.
34. Cannon, *Reagan*, 185; Cannon, *Governor*, 388.
35. Cannon, *Reagan*, 156–157.
36. *LAT*, April 12, 1980.
37. *WP*, April 26, 1980; *Riverside Press Enterprise*, June 18, 1974.
38. *SB*, Dec. 8, 1974; RR, *Life*, 191.
39. Lucks, *Reconsidering*, 114.
40. "Governor Reagan: Action and Results," Dec. 1974, box GO153, GP/RF, RRPL; Cannon, *Reagan*, 154.
41. RR speech, L.A. Rotary Club, Sept. 25, 1970, box GO156, GP/RF, RRPL.
42. Cannon, *Reagan*, 196.
43. AI/WB.
44. *Riverside Press Enterprise*, June 18, 1974.
45. *NYT*, Oct. 25, 1970.

Chapter 28: The Primary Gambit

1. RR to Vivian Young, Jan. 6, 1970, file 4, GP/CO, RRPL.
2. Buckley, *Reagan*, 52.
3. RR to Gaylord S. Parkinson, May 31, 1972, file 2, GP/CO, RRPL; RR to Mrs. H. R. Younginer, early 1972, in Skinner, *Letters*, 266.
4. RR speech, World Affairs Council, Oct. 12, 1972, in RR, *Time for Choosing*, 99–105.
5. Lettow, *Quest*, 26.
6. *NYT*, June 26, 1973.
7. WFB to RR, Oct. 24, 1973, box 227, Part II, WFBP, YALE.
8. *California Journal*, Nov. 1974.
9. RR to Lorraine Wagner, June 22, 1973, LW, RRRC.
10. Deaver, *Scenes*, 53.
11. *Mother Jones*, Nov. 16, 2007.
12. Dwight Chapin to H. R. Haldeman, April 27, 1970, WHCF, RMNPL.
13. Mann, *Rebellion*, 11.
14. AI/CD.
15. *San Diego Tribune*, Oct. 15, 1971.
16. PD, *Way*, 191.
17. *NYT*, Sept. 15, 1974.
18. Patterson, *Giant*, 101.

19. Speakes, *Speaking Out*, 103.
20. Skinner, *Hand*, xv.
21. MDOH, UVA.
22. Cannon, *Governor*, 399.
23. AI/EMIII.
24. RR to Jessie S. Neider, Nov 22, 1972, box 3, GP/CO, RRPL.
25. MDOH, UVA.
26. Ford, *Heal*, 294.
27. Kelley, *Nancy Reagan*, 218.
28. DeFrank, *Write It*, 122.
29. *NYT*, Aug. 2, 1976.
30. AI/PH.
31. Family meeting: MR, *First Father*, 227–229; MER, *Outside*, 126 (wife left), 129 (in debt), 142 (terrified), 143 ("grassroots"); AI/RPR; RPR emails to author, Jan. 26–27, 2022 ("uncomfortably," "disenchanted"); Davis, *Way*, 203 ("sin"), 209–212 (209, "removed"); PD, *Dear Mom*, 127 (pot); NR, *My Turn*, 181; Colacello, *Ronnie*, 434–436; Kelley, *Nancy Reagan*, 219–226.
32. NR, *My Turn*, 184.
33. *NYT*, Nov. 21, 1975; RR, "Announcement for Presidential Candidacy," Nov. 20, 1975, RRPL.
34. *Washington Star*, Feb. 4, 1976.
35. Ibid. (taxes, EPA); Perlstein, *Invisible Bridge*, 665–666 (FDA).
36. *Washington Star*, Feb. 4, 1976.
37. Ibid.
38. Levin, *Queen*, 87–88.
39. Witcover, *Marathon*, 388.
40. Hannaford, *Reagans*, 70–74.
41. *NYT*, Nov. 19, 1975; AI/SS.
42. Wirthlin, *Communicator*, 18–22.
43. NR, *My Turn*, 186.
44. Wirthlin, *Communicator*, 19–22.
45. AI/CB; AI/JB.

Chapter 29: "I Shall Rise and Fight Again"

1. *LAT*, March 18, 1976.
2. Nofziger, *Nofziger*, 179–180.
3. AI/CB.
4. WFB to RR, Oct. 24, 1973, Part II, box 227, WFBP, YALE.
5. *NYT*, June 2, 1975.
6. Shirley, *Revolution*, 142 ("great"); Link, *Righteous Warrior*, 141–143.
7. Pipes, *Vixi*, 184–186; *WP*, May 11, 1982.
8. RR column for release, July 18, 1975, box 39, RNP, GFPL. Shirley, *Revolution*, 44, notes the coincidence, while erroneously stating the RR column ran on July 15.
9. Perlstein, *Invisible Bridge*, 630.
10. Fitzgerald, *Blue*, 97.
11. Haines and Leggett, *Watching the Bear*, 159–163.
12. Helsinki: Morgan, *Final Act*, 5 (concessions); RR notation on James W. Nance to RR, Dec. 4, 1981, HWF, Series II, RRPL ("violation").
13. Panama Canal: Clymer, *Big Ditch*, 57 ("treason"), 29 ("secret," "sovereign"), 31 ("built it"); MDOH, UVA ("never thought"); Shirley, *Revolution*, xvi ("berserk").
14. North Carolina: Lucks, *Reconsidering*, 119 (sit-ins), 126 (busing, private schools, "carpetbaggers"); *NYT*, June 3, 1976 (busing); Link, *Righteous Warrior*, 3 (never recanted), 100 ("courtesy"), 146–147 (RR, Helms relationship), 148 ("demagoguery"), 152 (flier), 157 (Bible); RR to John Wayne, June 28, 1974, box 4, 1980 Campaign Series I, RRPL ("approve"); *Charlotte Observer*, July 27 and July 29, 1983 (Ellis nomination); Perlstein, *Reaganland*, 385 ("King Midas"); Kruse and Zelizer, *Fault Lines*, 96 ("shriller"); Novak, *Prince*, 274 ("Socialist"); Witcover, *Marathon*, 415 ("shiner"); *NYT*, March 25, 1976 ("Ballgame"); Shirley, *Revolution*, 158–176.
15. Texas: Lucks, *Reconsidering*, 125–128; Ford, *Heal*, 381 ("ceiling"); Garcia, *Comeback*, 61 ("down home"), 99–102 (tamale).
16. Witcover, *Marathon*, 411.
17. AI/JS.

18. Witcover, *Marathon*, 386–387 (Social Security), 427–428 (TVA), 431 ("war"); NR, *My Turn*, 191 ("forgive"); *NYT*, June 6, 1976 (red in the face); AI/CB ("damn," fist); Deaver, *Drummer*, 66 (fist).
19. AI/JS.
20. Ibid.
21. *NYT*, Aug. 2, 1976.
22. AI/JS.
23. Shirley, *Revolution*, 275.
24. Roger O. Blake to John Sears, July 28, 1976, box 75, CFRR, HI.
25. Nofziger, *Nofziger*, 206.
26. DeFrank, *Write It*, 122–123.
27. Tumulty, *Triumph*, 194–195.
28. MR, *First Father*, 231.
29. VP: Germond and Witcover, *Blue Smoke*, 168 (would have accepted); AI/BD; RR to Lorraine Wagner, Feb. 15, 1979, LW, RRRC ("conscience"); Nofziger, *Nofziger*, 203 (Dole).
30. RR speech: RR, "Republican National Convention Speech," Aug. 19, 1976, RRPL; NR, *My Turn*, 197–200 ("labyrinth," "don't worry"); AI/PH (acceptance speech); Shirley, *Revolution*, xix–xxiv, 330–334; Wirthlin, *Communicator*, 27–30; Deaver, *Scenes*, 72; Anderson, *Revolution*, 63–72; AI/JS ("we won"); AI/JL; MDOH, UVA; Hannaford, *Reagans*, 134–136.
31. *NYT*, Aug. 20, 1976.
32. California delegation: Nofziger, *Nofziger*, 205; *Bridgewater* (N.J.) *Courier-News*, Aug. 20, 1976 ("blinking"); *Charlotte Observer*, Aug. 20, 1976 ("baseball," "rocking chair"); *Ft. Worth Star-Telegram*, Aug. 20, 1976.

Chapter 30: The Santa Claus Campaign

1. *Atlantic*, May 1, 1979.
2. "Presidential Job Approval Center," Gallup News.
3. Alter, *Best*, 1–9.
4. "U.S. Real GDP Growth Rate by Year Compared to Inflation and Unemployment," The Balance.
5. Alter, *Best*, 456–472.
6. Wirthlin, *Communicator*, 36.
7. JWJ, Dec. 8, 1985.
8. Wirthlin, *Communicator*, 35.
9. Nofziger, *Nofziger*, 216.
10. Ibid., 215.
11. Hannaford, *Reagans*, 141.
12. CFTR newsletters, May 16, 1977 (energy), July 1, 1977 (Laetrile), box 38, 1980 Campaign Series I, RRPL; Drew, *Portrait*, 111.
13. Fredericksburg (Va.) *Free-Lance Star*, Jan. 17, 1978.
14. AI/RVA.
15. Lettow, *Quest*, 18–20.
16. Anderson, *Revolution*, 80–86.
17. RR to Walter Annenberg, April 16, 1980, box 5, 1980 Campaign Series I, RRPL.
18. Wirthlin et al., "Reagan for President Strategy, 1980," box 547, WJCP, HI ("strength," "too simplistic," "credentials"); Steve Cohen to Peter H. Dailey, "Marketing Plan," July 30, 1980, box 553, WJCP, HI ("trigger happy"); Allen to RR, "The 'Strategy for Peace' Theme," Aug. 25, 1978, box 51, JMP, HI ("soften").
19. AI/RVA.
20. RR, *Life*, 204.
21. AI/RVA.
22. "RR Schedule, Europe, November 25–December 3, 1978," box 178, 1980 Campaign Series, RRPL.
23. AI/RVA.
24. Hannaford, *Reagans*, 180.
25. *NYT*, Sept. 16, 1979; RR to Ruth V. Johnson, Jan. 3, 1980, box 5, 1980 Campaign Series I, RRPL ("moderating"); Hannaford, *Reagans*, 206–209 (buildup).
26. Collins, *More*, 177.
27. AI/AL.
28. Anderson, *Revolution*, 142.
29. Krugman, *Peddling Prosperity*, 90.
30. Chait, *Big Con*, 22 ("cranks"), 29 (Wanniski).
31. Wanniski, *Way*, xv.

32. AI/AL.

33. Anderson, *Revolution*, 166.

34. "Historical U.S. Federal Individual Income Tax Rates & Brackets, 1862–2021," Tax Foundation.

35. Witcher, *Right*, 17; Barrett, *Gambling*, 55; Meese, *With Reagan*, 122.

36. McElvaine, *Great Depression*, loc. 432.

37. Stockman, *Triumph*, 49.

38. Witcher, *Right*, 18.

39. RR, "Speech to International Business Council," Chicago, Sept. 9, 1980, APP.

40. Anderson, *Revolution*, 132; Bartlett, *Economy*, 120.

41. Feldstein, *Economic Policy*, 25; Lou Cannon interview with Baker, May 22, 1989, box 16, LCP, UCSB.

42. Hannaford, *Reagans*, 139.

43. Perlstein, *Reaganland*, 775.

44. JWJ, July 11, 1985.

45. Collins, *More*, 207.

46. Congressional Budget Office, "Understanding Fiscal Policy," April 1978, p. 25; *WP*, Dec. 7, 2017.

47. Anderson, *Revolution*, 126; Meacham, *Destiny*, 235.

48. *National Observer*, March 6, 1976.

Chapter 31: Sears Agonistes

1. *NYT*, July 29, 1979.

2. Carter, *Faith*, 552.

3. *WP*, Nov. 13, 1979.

4. PD, *Way*, 236.

5. *NYT*, July 29, 1979.

6. Inboden, *Peacemaker*, 16.

7. Germond, *Fat Man*, 158 ("Scrooge"); Hannaford, *Reagans*, 209 ("statesmanship").

8. *WP*, Nov. 13, 1979 ("outdoorsy," "sibilant"); Kelley, *Nancy Reagan*, 293 (Bengtsson).

9. *WP*, Nov. 13, 1979.

10. Meese, *With Reagan*, 7.

11. RR to Polly Nelson Hippler, Feb. 14, 1980, box 5, HWF, Series I, RRPL.

12. *NYT*, July 29, 1979.

13. Anderson, *Revolution*, 329.

14. AI/EMIII.

15. AI/CB.

16. Deaver, *Scenes*, 86–88; AI/CD ("crushed"); Cannon, Governor, 448–449.

17. Meese, *With Reagan*, 4.

18. RR to Ruth V. Johnson, Jan. 3, 1980, box 5, 1980 Campaign Series I, RRPL.

19. AI/JS.

20. NR, *Turn*, 180, 205.

21. Wirthlin to Meese, "Evaluation of Wednesday's Debate," Feb. 22, 1980, box 547, WJCP, HI.

22. Nashua: AI/JL ("one in six"); AI/SS; Hannaford, *Reagans*, 237 (Nancy); White, *Search*, 30–32 (31, "scout leader"); RR, "I am paying for this microphone," YouTube; AI/JB ("deep shit"); Meacham, *Destiny*, 230–233 (232, "terrible," "rules"); *NYT*, Feb. 29, 1980; Germond and Witcover, *Smoke*, 124–130 (129, "choked"; 130, twenty-seven points, "sandbagged"); Cannon, Governor, 460–463.

23. *WP*, Feb. 4, 1980.

24. Persico, *Casey*, 175, 178–179.

25. AI/CB.

26. RR interview with *U.S. News and World Report*, Oct. 7, 1982, box 4, HWF, Series II, RRPL.

27. AI/CB.

28. Anderson, *Revolution*, 289–290.

29. AI/BM.

30. *NYT*, July 15, 1980.

31. VP: Cannon, Governor, 472 ("spunk"), 473 ("melts"); Germond and Witcover, *Smoke*, 166–190 (182, "figurehead"; 183, "aghast"; 188 "yes sir"); Wirthlin, *Communicator*, 60 ("did you hear"); MDOH, UVA ("choked"); *NYT*, July 30, 2000 ("do now"); AI/JB; Hannaford, *Reagans*, 270–277; Meese, *With Reagan*, 43–45; Meacham, *Destiny*, 242–256; White, *Search*, 320–327.

32. RNC speech: RR, "Address Accepting the Republican Nomination," July 17, 1980, APP; *NYT*, July 18, 1980 ("ease"); *NYT*, July 20, 1980 ("audacious").

Chapter 32: What It Took

1. *NYT*, July 13, 1980.
2. Bird, *Outlier*, 542.
3. Ibid., 544–549.
4. *NYT*, Aug. 19, 1980.
5. Cramer, *What It Takes*, 145–146.
6. Neshoba: Lott, *Cats*, 75–76 ("stirring"); *WP*, Dec. 20, 2002 ("helmet"); AI/TL ("loaded"); Wirthlin et al., "Reagan for President Strategy, 1980," box 547, WJCP, HI ("populist voters"); Wirthlin and Jim Brady to RR, "Reagan Focused Impact," Aug. 11, 1980, 1980 Campaign Series IX, box 264, RRPL ("ticket splitters"); Ken Klinge to Bill Timmons, "Re: Neshoba County Fair," 1980 Campaign IX, box 264, RRPL ("cancel"); Wirthlin, *Communicator*, 64–69 ("don't pull out"); LNOH, UVA ("mad"); Watts, "House Party" (white, cabins, "no place"); Perlstein, *Reaganland*, 829–834 (833, "payload"); speech text, *Neshoba Democrat*, April 8, 2021; "Ronald Reagan Speaking at the Neshoba County Fair," YouTube; *New Yorker*, Oct. 2, 2023 ("our language"); Jackson (Miss.) *Daily News*, Aug. 4, 1980; Lucks, *Reconsidering*, 144–146.
7. *WP*, Aug. 11, 1980.
8. Perlstein, *Reaganland*, 859.
9. Germond and Witcover, *Smoke*, 225.
10. *WP*, Feb. 4, 1980.
11. Barrett, *Gambling*, 426.
12. McClaughry to Meese et al., "Re: Jesse Jackson Meeting, Chicago 8/5/80," Aug. 7, 1980, box 264, 1980 Campaign Series IX, RRPL.
13. Perlstein, *Reaganland*, 859.
14. Germond and Witcover, *Smoke*, 262.
15. Alter, *Best*, 585.
16. *Nation*, Nov. 13, 2012.
17. Wirthlin, *Communicator*, 66; AI/TL.
18. AI/SS.
19. Ibid.
20. Gaffes: *NYT*, Aug. 17, 1980 (Taiwan); *LAT*, Aug. 26, 1980 (Taiwan), Aug. 28, 1980 (depression); Germond and Witcover, *Smoke*, 214–218; Cannon, *Governor*, 479–481; Perlstein, *Reaganland*, 845 ("endorse"); Hackensack (N.J.) *Record*, Oct. 22, 1980 ("platform"); White, *Search*, 384–387; Bird, *Outlier*, 569 ("traitor," "nuts").
21. *NYT*, Aug. 27, 1980.
22. Meese, *With Reagan*, 9.
23. Barrett, *Gambling*, 101.
24. AI/SS.
25. Ibid.
26. Reagan-Bush news release, box 264, 1980 Campaign Series IX, RRPL.
27. RR, "Labor Day Speech at Liberty State Park," Sept. 1, 1980, APP; RR, "Remarks at Liberty State Park," YouTube.
28. White, *Search*, 309.
29. Perlstein, *Reaganland*, 774–775.
30. Germond and Witcover, *Smoke*, 223; Cannon, *Governor*, 495–498; John McClaughry to Meese et al., Oct. 6, 1980, box 264, Campaign Series IX, RRPL ("berserk").
31. AI/SS.
32. Ibid.
33. Ibid.; *WP*, Oct. 15, 1980. Maureen Reagan claimed her father, in response to her pleas, had already committed at the family Thanksgiving dinner in 1979 to choose a female justice: MR, *First Father*, 252–253. Michael Reagan wrote this was part of a deal for Maureen to stop supporting ERA during the 1980 campaign: MER, *Lessons*, 50.
34. Wirthlin to RR, Casey, "Status of the Campaign," Oct. 11, 1980, box 547, WJCP, HI.
35. *Weekly Standard*, Nov. 5, 2007.
36. AI/RS.
37. AI/JM.
38. AI/SS.
39. *NYT*, June 24, 1986, Aug. 9, 2012, and Nov. 15, 2019.
40. Cohn to Mike Deaver, Feb. 10, 1983, box 48, MDP, RRPL.
41. Shirley, *Rendezvous*, 420.
42. AI/SS.

43. "Presidential Debate in Cleveland," Oct. 28, 1980, APP; "Carter vs. Reagan: The Second 1980 Presidential Debate," YouTube.
44. Oberlander, *Medicare*, 30; Gritter, "Kerr-Mills."
45. Richard Wirthlin et al., "Campaign Chronicle," box 568, WJCP, HI.
46. Ibid.
47. AI/EM.
48. AI/RVA.
49. Germond and Witcover, *Smoke*, 10.
50. AI/SS.
51. AI/GS; Sick, *October Surprise*, 200.
52. *NYT*, Jan. 24, 1993.
53. AI/DB.
54. Brands, *Reagan*, 235–236; *NYT*, March 18, 2023.
55. Bowden, *Guests*, 627.
56. Bird, *Outlier*, 560.
57. Paul Beach, Memo, Nov. 4, 1991, CBGF, GHWBP ("unknown"); "Anglo-American Conference on the History of the Second World War," July 28–31, box 509, WJCP, HI; Bird, *Outlier*, 559–560; Parry, *Stolen Narrative*, 82–113.
58. "October Surprise Interagency Meeting" and Ron von Lembke to C. Boyden Gray, n.d., CBGF, GHWBP.
59. Brands, *Reagan*, 235.
60. AI/RVA.
61. AI/BRI.
62. Strober and Strober, *Reagan*, 449.
63. Bird, *Outlier*, 562.
64. AI/SS.
65. Ibid.
66. AI/JLIM.
67. Bird, *Outlier*, 580.
68. NR, *Turn*, 221; Carter, *Faith*, 579.
69. "How Groups Voted in 1980," Roper Center.
70. Edsall and Edsall, *Chain Reaction*, 164.
71. Anderson, *Revolution*, 282.

Chapter 33: Assembling an Administration

1. "Presidential Job Approval Center," Gallup News.
2. See, e.g., David Gergen to Jim Baker, "Public Affairs re: Airliner," Sept. 2, 1983, box 6, DGP, RRPL.
3. *WP*, Nov. 19, 1980.
4. *WP*, Dec. 15, 1983 ("dunce"); Barrett, *Gambling*, 15 ("bumpkin"); AI/GFW.
5. *WP*, Nov. 19, 1980.
6. Ibid.
7. AI/GFW.
8. AI/DG.
9. Graham, *Personal History*, 612.
10. WFB to RR, April 28, 1980, box 2 (anniversary dinner); RR to WFB, Dec. 9, 1980, box 70 ("goof-up"), and WFB to RR, Dec. 6, 1980 ("forgiven"), all WFBP, YALE; Felzenberg, *A Man*, 256–257.
11. Jennifer Mandel (NARA archivist) to author, email, June 10, 2022.
12. Whipple, *Gatekeepers*, 12.
13. Alter, *Best*, 288.
14. AI/SS; MDOH, UVA.
15. NR, *Turn*, 240.
16. Ibid.; Baker and Glasser, *The Man*, 131.
17. MDOH, UVA; AI/JABIII.
18. Meese and Baker memo, Nov. 13, 1980, box 60, series 6, JABIIIP, SML.
19. Baker and Glasser, *The Man*, 140.
20. MDOH, UVA.
21. Hertsgaard, *Bended Knee*, 17.
22. AI/JABIII; AI/DG.
23. AI/MT.
24. PNEI, RRPL.

25. AI/DG.
26. Strober and Strober, *Reagan*, 57.
27. Deaver, *Scenes*, 126; MDOH, UVA.
28. Hertsgaard, *Bended Knee*, 35.
29. *WP*, March 7, 2016.
30. *Vanity Fair*, May 29, 2009; Tumulty, *Triumph*, 252–253.
31. BCD, Feb. 10, 1981.
32. Gotlieb, *Diaries*, 22.
33. *NYT*, June 5, 2021.
34. *WP*, Nov. 4, 2000.
35. *Vanity Fair*, August 1998.
36. *WP*, Feb. 1, 2017; *NYT*, Jan. 10, 1984.
37. *NYT*, June 19, 1981.
38. Cannon, *President Reagan*, 470.
39. Germond, *Fat Man*, 160.
40. PolitiFact, Jan. 9, 2020.
41. Rollins, *Bare Knuckles*, 81.
42. Persico, *Casey*, 42.
43. Nixon to RR, Nov. 17, 1980, Reagan correspondence, RMNPL.
44. Tyler, *Trouble*, 257.
45. Collier, *Political Woman*, 119.
46. Barrett, *Gambling*, 4.
47. Collier, *Political Woman*, 118.
48. Alter, *Best*, 313; Wilentz, *Age*, 76–77.
49. Dec. 1, 1980, box 1, SFP, RRPL.
50. Bell, *Thirteenth*, 38–51.
51. Inaugural address: AI/KK; box 1, KKP, RRPL; handwritten draft, box 1, HWF, Series III, RRPL; Reeves, *President Reagan*, 4–5; Cannon, *President Reagan*, 73–77.
52. Johnson, *Sleepwalking*, 26; Carter, *Diary*, 512.
53. RR, *Life*, 225 ("chilly"); Reeves, *President Reagan*, 2 ("Jack Warner"); Carter, *Diary*, 513 ("beard").
54. *NYT*, Jan. 2. 1981.
55. Johnson, *Sleepwalking*, 19–23.
56. RR, *Life*, 226.
57. RR, "Inaugural Address 1981," RRPL; "Ronald Reagan's Inaugural Address," Jan. 20, 1981, YouTube.
58. J. P. Fox to RR, Sept. 30, 1981, and RR to Fox, HWF, Series II, RRPL.
59. "Public Trust in Government: 1958–2023," Pew Research Center.
60. RR, "Inaugural Address 1981."

Chapter 34: In the White House

1. *WP*, Nov. 9, 1993 (Clinton); Obama, *Promised Land*, 138.
2. RR, *Life*, 395 ("isolation," "last"); Weinberg, *Movie Nights*, 2 ("stunned"); AI/SS.
3. RRD, Jan. 20, 1981.
4. RR, *Life*, 230.
5. "Telephone Access to the President," Dec. 14, 1981, box 49, MDP, RRPL.
6. Haig, *Caveat*, 141.
7. Regan, *Record*, 142.
8. Kuhn, *In Private*, 157.
9. AI/JK.
10. AI/ER.
11. RRD, Feb. 11, 1981; Darman, *Who's in Control*, 41.
12. Dole to RR, "Meeting with Janet Collins and Chadwick School group," March 18, 1991, box 10, Series III, RGDP, RRPL.
13. Mulroney, *Memoirs*, 648.
14. See, e.g., Carter's daily diary for Feb. 13, 1981, JCPL.
15. *NYT*, Feb. 7, 1981.
16. Daily schedule: *Time*, Feb. 23, 1981 (source of all quotes unless otherwise noted); PDD, RRPL, Feb. 12, 1981; Speakes, *Speaking Out*, 112 (favorite columnists); RDI, JBRPP (fast dresser, "bullshitting," "enough," "color-coordinated," "clean desk"); RSOH, LC (valet); Fred Fielding to Bentley Elliott, "Presidential Article," Sept. 21, 1983, Articles-Books-Booklets file, HWF, RRPL ("cereal"); RR to Chester Gould, n.d., HWF,

Series II, RRPL ("comic strip"); Rosebush, *True*, 47 ("no limit"), 55 ("simple tastes"); JAB schedule, Feb. 25, 1981, box 3, JWCP, RRPL (Troika schedule); Fred F. Fielding to Bentley Elliott, "Presidential Article— How I Keep Physically Fit," Sept. 21, 1983, Articles-Books-Booklets file, HWF, RRPL (Mexican plate); Oval Office decorations, RRPL; *Christian Science Monitor*, March 20, 1981 (newspapers received); RRD, 1.19; AI/JABIII (jokes); Kuhn, *In Private*, 83 (desk), 149 (schedule); AI/JK (twenty-seven shirts, two days' wear); Pipes, *Vixi*, 176 ("deference"); Stockman, *Triumph*, 117 ("eyes"); AI/PW ("glaze over"); Bell, *Thirteenth*, 30 ("on time"); Priess, *Book of Secrets*, 150–189 (PDB); MemCon, "President's meeting with Omani foreign minister," Feb. 12, 1981, box 48, ES/NSC, RRPL ("domestic"); AI/PM ("store").

17. *WP*, April 27, 1987.
18. RRD, July 1, 1981.
19. RR to Joan Roberts, May 31, 1984, box 3, HWF, Series II, RRPL.
20. RDI, JBRPP.
21. AI/JN.
22. Gates, *Shadows*, 218–219.
23. Giorgione, *Camp David*, 36 ("fancy"), 9–11 (Aspen), 66 (wheezing).
24. NR, *Turn*, 255.
25. RR, *Life*, 397.
26. "Presidential Article," Sept. 21, 1983, Articles-Books-Booklets file, HWF, Series II, RRPL.
27. Doherty, "Presidential Travel," White House Transition Project.
28. AI/PM.
29. "Presidential Pets," RRPL.
30. AI/KO.
31. Weinberg, *Movie Nights*, 115–126.
32. Ibid., 69–83.
33. RRD, Feb. 14, 1981; Weinberg, *Movie Nights*, 1–12.
34. Kuhn, *In Private*, 140.
35. Deaver, *Scenes*, 101.
36. RRD, July 24, 1981.
37. RRD, April 14, 1981.
38. *WP*, Jan. 18, 1981.
39. Ken Khachigian, "Meeting with Governor Reagan," Jan. 18, 1981, box 1, KKP, RRPL.
40. Jan. 28, 1981, box 1, SFP, RRPL.
41. *NYT*, Jan. 29, 1981.
42. RRD, Jan. 27, 1981.
43. AI/RPR; AI/CF.
44. Briefing Paper, March 30, 1981, box 3, PBP, RRPL.
45. AI/PS.
46. RRD, March 11 and 13, 1981.
47. Powell, *Journey*, 249.
48. Timberg, *Song*, 17.
49. RR, *Life*, 387; Wilber, *Rawhide*, 211.
50. Speakes, *Speaking Out*, 67, 306.
51. AI/BM.
52. *WP*, Sept. 3, 2017.
53. AI/EMIII; AI/PS.
54. Noonan, *Character*, 312.

Chapter 35: Finest Hour

1. Wilber, *Rawhide*, 8.
2. Briefing Paper, March 30, 1981, box 3, PDP, RRPL.
3. Motorcade: Wilber, *Rawhide*, 64–68; Parr, *Secret Service*, 12.
4. Shooting: Wilber, *Rawhide*, 77–87; Parr, *Secret Service*, 215–219; RR, *Life*, 259–260; RRD, March 30, 1981; Assassination Report, box 28, EMP, RRPL.
5. RRD, March 30, 1981.
6. Wilber, *Rawhide*, 88.
7. Ibid., 109–110.
8. Parr, *Secret Service*, 223.
9. *WP*, April 3, 1981.
10. Speakes, *Speaking Out*, 6.

11. NR, *My Turn*, 5; Deaver, *Scenes*, 21.
12. NR, *My Turn*, 6.
13. Baker, *Work Hard*, 144; Deaver, *Scenes*, 21.
14. Parr, *Secret Service*, 223.
15. Wilber, *Rawhide*, 180.
16. Larry Starmer to Deaver, April 13, 1981, box 1, MDP, RRPL.
17. March 30 tape recordings, box 1, RVA, RRPL.
18. Ibid.
19. AI/RVA.
20. "Meeting on Long Term Strategy," April 9, 1981, box 26, MDP, RRPL.
21. Darman, *Who's in Control*, 54.
22. Assassination Report, box 28, EMP, RRPL; Untermeyer, *Things*, 41.
23. Wilber, *Rawhide*, 187–188.
24. NR, *My Turn*, 9.
25. PD, *Way*, 270.
26. NR, *Turn*, 9; AI/RPR.
27. Wilber, *Rawhide*, 201.
28. RRD, March 30, 1981.
29. AI/RD.
30. Nofziger, *Nofziger*, 294–295.
31. Deaver, *Scenes*, 24.
32. MR, *First Father*, 275.
33. Strober and Strober, *Reagan*, 112.
34. Parr, *Secret Service*, 233.
35. Darman, *Who's in Control*, 60; Strober and Strober, *Reagan*, 111.
36. Darman, *Who's in Control*, 61; AI/RPR.
37. "Presidential Article," Sept. 21, 1983, Articles-Books-Booklets file, HWF, RRPL.
38. *WP*, Aug. 8, 2014.
39. RRD, March 30, 1981.
40. Barrett, *Gambling*, 123.
41. NR, *My Turn*, 20.
42. Ibid., 46–49; AI/RQ.
43. "Meeting on Long Term Strategy," April 9, 1981, box 26, MDP, RRPL.
44. *NYT*, March 26, 1981.

Chapter 36: "The Whip Hand"

1. Nixon to RR, Nov. 17, 1980, box 1, PPC, RMNPL.
2. Wirthlin to RR, June 18, 1981, HWF, Series II, RRPL.
3. "Reagan," *American Experience*, PBS, 1998.
4. Anderson, *Revolution*, 245.
5. Stockman, *Triumph*, 19–47.
6. Ibid., 42.
7. "Avoiding a GOP Economic Dunkirk," box 1, KKP, RRPL.
8. Feldstein, *Economic Policy*, 275 ("half-breed"); Rossinow, *Reagan Era*, 34 ("reflected"); Stockman, *Triumph*, 9.
9. Stockman, *Triumph*, 10.
10. Darman, *Who's in Control*, 43.
11. "Working Schedule," box 60, JABIIIP, SML.
12. Meese, *With Reagan*, 119.
13. Stockman, *Triumph*, 89.
14. Rossinow, *Reagan Era*, 59.
15. Stockman, *Triumph*, 105.
16. Ibid., 114–116. For budget figures, see Historical Tables, Office of Management and Budget, White House.
17. Crowe, *Line of Fire*, 126.
18. Bell, *Thirteenth*, 67.
19. Feldstein, *Economic Policy*, 284; Palmer and Sawhill, *Reagan Record*, 185–186.
20. Stockman, *Triumph*, 153 (Helms), 161 (Thurmond).
21. Ibid., 119.
22. Ibid., 130–141.

23. AI/ER.
24. Stockman, *Triumph*, 135.
25. Farrell, *Tip O'Neill*, 548.
26. Silber, *Volcker*, 153–154.
27. Ibid., 193.
28. Anderson, *Revolution*, 250–251; AI/PV.
29. "Meeting with Paul Volcker," July 15, 1981, box 1, HWF, Series I, RRPL.
30. Anderson, *Revolution*, 252.
31. AI/PV.
32. "Meeting on Long Term Strategy," April 9, 1981, box 25, MDP, RRPL.
33. JWJ, April 30, 1981.
34. Matthews, *Tip and the Gipper*.
35. AI/EMIII.
36. O'Neill, *Man of the House*, 360.
37. JWJ, Jan. 31, 1983.
38. Farrell, *Tip O'Neill*, 555, 544–545.
39. *National Journal*, June 26, 1982.
40. AI/DG.
41. AI/KD.
42. Baker and Glasser, *The Man*, 159.
43. Bell, *Thirteenth*, 129.
44. Novak, *Prince*, 388.
45. BCD, July 1, 1980.
46. AI/RG; BCD, March 3 and 30, 1981.
47. Social Security: Stockman, *Triumph*, 192–205 (198, "warning"); Niskanen, *Reaganomics*, 36–39; Farrell, *Tip O'Neill*, 570–573 (572, "despicable"); May 20, 1981, SFP, RRPL ("blew it").
48. *NYT*, May 8, 1981.
49. RRD, May 7, 1981.
50. Stockman, *Triumph*, 240.
51. Farrell, *Tip O'Neill*, 558.
52. JWJ, June 11, 1981.
53. RRD, May 28, 1981.
54. Stockman, *Triumph*, 272.
55. Ibid., 282.
56. Darman, *Who's in Control*, 67, 90.
57. RR, "Address on Federal Tax Reduction Legislation," July 27, 1981, RRPL.
58. BCD, July 1, 1981.
59. *NYT*, Oct. 24, 1982.
60. RRD, July 26, 1981.
61. *NYT*, July 30, 1981.

Chapter 37: "Vacation!"

1. O'Connor: Based mainly on Evan Thomas's excellent biography of O'Connor, *First*, 122–145 (124, Rehnquist suggested; 127, June 23 meeting, "abhorrent"; 144–145, "best place"). "Protest": Max Friedersdorf to Jim Baker et al., July 6, 1981, box 2408, EMP, RRPL. "Not a liberal": Clark to Ed Meese, July 1, 1981, box 2408, EMP, RRPL. "Good Justice": RRD, July 6, 1981.
2. PATCO: Based mainly on McMartin, *Collision Course* (262, $40 million package; 389, "Damnit"; 292, "can't sit"; 297, 90 percent; 301, replacement workers; 326, crash; 328, "strike helped make"; 350, work stoppages; 349, "why can't"; 332, cost an estimated; 329, "infusion"). Reckoned with: AI/GS. "Credibility": *WP*, March 17, 1982. Coolidge: Johnson, *Sleepwalking*, 165.
3. Barletta, *Riding*, 9.
4. RRD, Aug. 6–Sept. 3, 1981.
5. Cannon, *Governor Reagan*, 437.
6. RPR, *My Father*, 168–170.
7. AI/JB.
8. Ibid.
9. AI/DLB.
10. Rosebush, *True*, 43.

11. AI/DLB.

12. AI/RPR.

13. AI/DLB.

14. AI/KO.

15. Cannon, *Governor Reagan*, 438.

16. Doherty, "Presidential Travel," White House Transition Project, 22.

Chapter 38: The Cold War Heats Up

1. Wilson, *Improvisation*, 42.

2. RR, "President's News Conference," Jan. 29, 1981, APP; Weisberg, *Reagan*, 89.

3. RR, "Address at University of Notre Dame," May 17, 1981, RRPL.

4. RR, "Address at US Military Academy," May 27, 1981, RRPL.

5. NSC minutes, July 6, 1981, box 2, ES/NSC, RRPL.

6. RR to Severin Palydowycz, June 1980, in Skinner, *Letters*, 374–375; RR, "Peace," Aug. 18, 1980, in Skinner, *Hand*, 484.

7. NSC minutes, Oct. 13, 1981, box 3, ES/NSC, RRPL.

8. Aldous, *Reagan and Thatcher*, 61.

9. RRD, Jan. 7, 1982; RR to Jill K. Conway, Oct. 25. 1982, HWF, Series II, RRPL.

10. NSC minutes, Nov. 12, 1981, box 3, ES/NSC, RRPL.

11. RR, *Life*, 273.

12. Pipes, *Vixi*, 194.

13. Morris, *Dutch*, 437–438.

14. Dobrynin, *In Confidence*, 478.

15. Wilson, *Improvisation*, 52–53; Andrew and Gordievsky, *Comrade*, 67.

16. NSC minutes, Dec. 30, 1981, box 6, ES/NSC, RRPL.

17. *National Interest*, Jan. 3, 2002.

18. RR remarks, Rockwell International, May 25, 1982, APP; RRD, March 7, 1983.

19. RR speech, Chicago, Aug. 18, 1980, in Skinner, *Hand*, 485; final version of speech, "Peace: Restoring the Margin of Safety," RRPL.

20. *Commentary*, July 1977.

21. Wilson, *Improvisation*, 23.

22. Priess, *Secrets*, 154.

23. Hoffman, *Dead Hand*, 321.

24. *NYT*, July 9, 1989.

25. Haines and Leggett, *Watching the Bear*, 33 (GDP), 160–161 ("Team B"), 163 (warheads), 170 ("balance").

26. Norris and Cochran, *Nuclear Forces*, Table 1.

27. AI/RP.

28. Powell, *Journey*, 249.

29. Graff, *Raven Rock*, 305.

30. Haines and Leggett, *Watching the Bear*, 167.

31. Brown, *Human Factor*, 135.

32. Pipes to Richard Allen, Feb. 26, 1981, box 30, JMP, RRPL.

33. Persico, *Casey*, 309.

34. Wilson, *Improvisation*, 46.

35. Ibid., 58.

36. *WSJ*, June 3, 1980.

Chapter 39: The Reagan Doctrine

1. NSC meeting minutes, Dec. 21, 1981, box 4, ES/NSC, RRPL.

2. Ibid.

3. Pipes, *Vixi*, 166–167.

4. Jones, *Covert Action*, 9–10.

5. NSC meeting minutes, Oct. 16, 1981, box 3, ES/NSC, RRPL.

6. Thatcher, *Downing Street*, 255.

7. Tom Reed, who served on the NSC in 1982, claimed in *Abyss* (269) that CIA "bugs" inserted into Siberian pipeline software resulted in "the most monumental non-nuclear explosion and fire ever seen from space," but he admitted to historian Will Inboden that he heard the story secondhand and had

"no documentation" (Inboden to author, email, April 4, 2022). In fact, as noted in *Wired*, March 1, 2020, there was no record of such a blast. A CIA historian, Nicholas Dujmović, writes that "policy discussions about such covert action went on for years, into 1986, but no decisions were made or findings signed, in large part because of the ethical implications"—meaning, presumably, that such sabotage would have resulted in civilian casualties and could have been seen as an act of war. See *Studies in Intelligence* 60, no. 1 (March 2016).

8. *NYT*, May 2, 1982.
9. NSC minutes, Feb. 10, 1982, box 3, ES/NSC, RRPL.
10. Thatcher, *Downing Street*, 158.
11. RRD, Jan. 28, 1981.
12. NSC minutes, Feb. 6, 1981, box 91282, ES/NSC, RRPL.
13. LeoGrande, *Backyard*, 82–83 ("limp-wristed," "parking lot"); MemCon, March 19, 1981, FRUS, III.83–85 ("air strikes"). Deaver is the only source for the "parking lot" quote. I have not been able to find those words in the NSC meeting minutes, but Haig did not deny saying it.
14. AI/JABIII.
15. "Caution": Haig, *Caveat*, 129. "Advocate": Lou Cannon interview with Haig, June 6, 1989, box 18, LCP, UCSB.
16. NSC minutes, Feb. 18, 1981 ("bogged down"), and NSC minutes, Feb. 6, 1981 ("victory"), both in box 91282, ES/NSC, RRPL.
17. D'Haeseleer, *Crucible*, 65–66.
18. NSC minutes, Feb. 10, 1982, box 3, ES/NSC, RRPL.
19. AI/BM.
20. "Cuban Foreign Policy and Activities Abroad," Feb. 5, 1981, and "Promoting Revolution in Latin America," Feb. 6, 1981, both in box 91282, ES/NSC, RRPL.
21. LeoGrande, *Backyard*, 70.
22. NSC minutes, Feb. 6, 1981, box 91282, ES/NSC, RRPL.
23. MemCon, RR and Viola, March 17, 1981, box 48, ES/NSC, RRPL.
24. LeoGrande, *Backyard*, 90; D'Haeseleer, *Crucible*, 25; *Time*, April 1, 1985 ("Reagan Doctrine").
25. D'Haeseleer, *Crucible*, 80–81; LeoGrande, *Backyard*, 154–155, 235.
26. RR to Harry Ide, May 31, 1984, box 3, HWF, Series II, RRPL.
27. June 8, 1983, KDM, SDVRR.
28. "US Policy in Central America and the Caribbean," March 24, 1981, box 1, ES/NSC, RRPL.
29. Wirthlin to Bill Clark, April 25, 1983, box 71, WPCP, HI.
30. LeoGrande, *Backyard*, 230.
31. D'Haeseleer, *Crucible*, 104.
32. LeoGrande, *Backyard*, 250–252; *LAT*, March 1, 1992.
33. LeoGrande, *Backyard*, 104–108.
34. Clarridge, *Spy*, 197.
35. Allen to RR, Nov. 13, 1981, and NSC minutes, Nov. 10, 1981, both in box 2, ES/NSC, RRPL.
36. RRD, Nov. 10, 1981; NSC Meeting, Feb. 10, 1982, box 3, ES/NSC, RRPL.
37. AI/BRI.
38. LeoGrande, *Backyard*, 308–309; Persico, *Casey*, 371–380.
39. Gates, *Shadows*, 242.
40. AI/JN.
41. Tyler, *Trouble*, 257.
42. RR, *Life*, 281.
43. NSC meeting minutes, July 31, 1981, box 2, ES/NSC, RRPL; RRD, June 1, 1981.
44. Barrett, *Gambling*, 95–96.
45. Fitzgerald, *Blue*, 138.
46. RRD, Dec. 27–Jan. 3, 1982.
47. AI/RVA.
48. *WP*, Feb. 15, 1981.
49. Barrett, *Gambling*, 231–233.
50. Begin to RR, June 8, 1981, box 5, GKP, RRPL; RRD, June 8, 1981.
51. AI/RM ("anti-Israel); "President's Meeting with Five Arab Ambassadors," June 11, 1981, box 48, ES/NSC, RRPL ("surprised"); RRD, June 11, 1981 (nut); AI/BRI (punishment); Lewis to Haig, July 6, 1981, box 5, GKP, RRPL ("fury").
52. Tyler, *Trouble*, 266–267.
53. April 22, 1983, KDM, SDVRR; Speakes, *Speaking Out*, 109.
54. Tyler, *Trouble*, 260–261.

55. AWACS: AI/RVA ("job"); Barrett, *Gambling*, 276, 445 ("pineapple"); DMR, Oct. 29, 1981 ("brains"); *Time*, Nov. 9, 1981; RR, "News Conference," Oct. 1, 1981, RRPL ("other nations").
56. *WP*, March 17, 1982 (Greenfield); *WP*, Dec. 11, 1981 (Shields); Bob Garrick to Ed Meese, Aug. 12, 1981, box 19, DGP, RRPL (Harlow).

Chapter 40: The Fairness Issue

1. "Recession of 1980–81," Federal Reserve History.
2. FRED (Federal Reserve Economic Data), St. Louis Federal Reserve Bank.
3. Rossinow, *Reagan Era*, 84.
4. Johnson, *Sleepwalking*, 116.
5. Bruce A. Petsche to RR, Nov. 17, 1982; Lorna Chandler to RR, Feb. 8, 1982; and David R. Ruble to RR, June 28, 1982, all in HWF, Series II, RRPL.
6. RR interview, *U.S. News & World Report*, Oct. 7, 1982, HWF, Series II, RRPL.
7. Bonnie M. Porter to RR, Oct. 1, 1981, ibid.
8. Palmer and Sawhill, *Reagan Record*, 190–192.
9. Rossinow, *Reagan Era*, 91–93.
10. Torrey, *American Psychosis*, 100.
11. *NYT*, March 18, 1982 ("South Succotash"); Rossinow, *Reagan Era*, 94 (Moyers); RRD, April 22, 1982.
12. *Atlantic*, December 1981.
13. *NYT*, Nov. 12, 1981.
14. AI/JABIII.
15. Stockman, *Triumph*, 1–8; RRD, Nov. 11–12, 1981; Greider, *Education*, xxvi.
16. Untermeyer, *Things*, 116.
17. RR to Wanniski, Dec. 17, 1981, box 2, HWF, Series II, RRPL.
18. Tumulty, *Triumph*, 247.
19. Ibid., 253–254.
20. NR, *Turn*, 23, 37.
21. RRD, Oct. 25, 1981; AI/RD.
22. NR, *Turn*, 42; Tate, *Lady in Red*, 42–49.
23. RRD, March 27, 1982.
24. Tumulty, *Triumph*, 319–320.
25. Presidential Job Approval Center, Gallup; RRD, Feb. 22, 1982.
26. Darman to Deaver et al., Feb. 1, 1982, box 1, RGDP; Williamson to Michael Deaker, Dec. 4, 1981, box 13, CFP; Lee Atwater to Craig Fuller, May 6, 1982, box 31, MDP; Wick to RR, April 15, 1982, box 23, DGP; and Gergen to Baker et al., n.d., box 8, DGP, all in RRPL.
27. Rossinow, *Reagan Era*, 64.
28. Fuller to Mike Deaver, May 5, 1982, box 31, MDP; and Gergen to Baker et al., n.d., box 8, DGP, both in RRPL.
29. "LSG Agenda," Dec. 5, 1981, box 1, CFP, RRPL.
30. "The Reagan Presidency: A Review of the First Year," White House Office of Public Affairs, box 55, MDP, RRPL.
31. Gergen to the Troika and Bill Clark, March 9, 1982, box 48, MDP, RRPL.
32. *Time*, Feb. 22, 1982.
33. RRD, Dec. 8, 1981; RR to Dorothy Walton, Sept. 1981, HWF, Series II, RRPL.
34. *Time*, Feb. 22, 1982 ("shock"); Wayne H. Valis to Elizabeth Dole, "President's Discussion at 11/5/81 Money Managers' Meeting," box 20, DGP, RRPL; RRD, Jan. 22, 1982.
35. RR, *Life*, 314.
36. AI/JABIII.
37. Feldstein, *Economic Policy*, 51.
38. "Meeting with California Republican Congressional Delegation," Aug. 5, 1982, box 1, HWF, Series I, RRPL.
39. Wanniski to Jim Baker, Jan. 29, 1982, box 52, Series 6, JABIIIP, SML.
40. Meese, *With Reagan*, 147.
41. AI/JABIII.
42. RRD, Aug. 19, 1982.
43. Barrett, *Gambling*, 25.
44. RR to Clymer L. Wright Jr., May 18, 1982, HWF, Series II, RRPL.
45. *Conservative Digest*, July 1982.
46. Bartlett, *American Economy*, 153.
47. "Revenue Effects of Major Tax Bills," US Treasury Department, Feb. 2013.
48. Edsall and Edsall, *Chain Reaction*, 159.

49. Ibid., 193.

50. "How the American Middle Class Has Changed in the Past Five Decades," Pew Research Center, April 20, 2022; *WP*, Oct. 3, 2023 (39 percent, 570 percent).

51. RRD, Oct. 15, 1982.

52. Mayer, *Bank Robbery*, 1.

53. Korda, *Life*, 472.

54. *WP*, Sept. 11, 1982.

55. *NYT*, Nov. 3, 1982.

56. RRD, Nov. 2, 1982.

57. *WP*, Sept. 14, 2018.

58. RRD, Aug. 9, 1982.

59. *Sun* (Flagstaff, Ariz.), Aug. 22, 1982.

60. AI/RD.

61. *NYT*, Oct. 15, 1982.

62. *WP*, Jan. 18, 1983; AI/RPR.

63. Maureen: MR, *First Father*, 283–291; Rollins, *Bare Knuckles*, 98–102; NR, *Turn*, 153–154.

64. *NYT*, Nov. 21, 1982.

65. *NYT*, Jan. 9, 1983; *WP*, Jan. 12, 1983; Darman, *Who's in Control*, 115.

Chapter 41: The Ash Heap of History

1. Rothkopf, *Running*, 222.

2. "History of the NSC, 1947–1997," White House.

3. Kengor and Doerner, *Judge*, 164, 145.

4. AI/RVA.

5. McFarlane, *Trust*, 193.

6. NSDD 32, May 20, 1982, and NSDD 75, Jan. 17, 1983, RRPL.

7. Kengor and Doerner, *Judge*, 169, 166.

8. See, e.g., Kengor and Doerner, *Judge*, 176.

9. Pipes, *Vixi*, 184.

10. AI/GSH.

11. Pipes, *Vixi*, 208–209.

12. Ibid, 166–167.

13. RRD, May 28, 1981.

14. Reed, *Abyss*, 244.

15. English, *Watch Me*, 571. Reagan's mention of a priest sent by the KGB was undoubtedly a garbled reference to Father George H. Dunne: see Chapter 12.

16. Trudeau, *Memoirs*, 220.

17. Schmidt, *Men and Powers*, 241, 245; MemCon, Schmidt and RR, May 21, 1981, box 48, ES/NSC, RRPL ("cowboy").

18. RRD, July 20–21, 1981.

19. AI/BM.

20. Strober and Strober, *Reagan*, 137.

21. Mulroney, *Memoirs*, 367–368.

22. AI/CHP ("adored"); RRD, February 27, 1981 ("friendship"), July 20–21, 1981 ("tower"); Thatcher, *Downing Street*, 157 ("warmth").

23. AI/CHP; Aldous, *Reagan and Thatcher*, 15.

24. Moore, *Thatcher: Grantham*, 576 ("simplification"); Moore, *Thatcher: Zenith*, 601 ("didn't know").

25. RRD, June 2–June 11, 1982.

26. Kengor and Doerner, *Judge*, 172.

27. Jones, *Covert Action*, 205.

28. Weigel, *Witness*, 441.

29. Aldous, *Reagan and Thatcher*, 111; RRD, June 2–June 11, 1982.

30. RRD, June 2–June 11, 1982.

31. Rowland and Jones, *Westminster*, 55–56 (not joint session), 14 (teleprompter).

32. PD, *Way*, 252, 294–296; PD, *Dear Mom*, 148–154.

33. RR to Mrs. Laurence Clark, December 14, 1983, box 8, HWF, Series II, RRPL.

34. RR, *Life*, 554; Red Cavaney to Mike Deaver, April 16, 1982, box 26, MDP, RRPL.

35. Westminster: RR, "Address to British Parliament," June 8, 1982, RRPL; speech drafts, box 4, HWF, RRPL; Rowland and Jones, *Westminster*, 46–49 (many authors); FRUS, 1.312–324 (Haig proposal).

Chapter 42: Allies—and Aides—at War

1. JRFD, MTF.
2. Ibid.
3. JRFD, MTF; AI/BRI.
4. RRD, April 14, 1982.
5. MemCon, Reagan-Thatcher, May 13, 1982, box 50, ES/NSC, RRPL.
6. HBOH, UVA ("intimidate"); JRFD, MTF ("wimp"); Aldous, *Reagan and Thatcher*, 106 (infuriated).
7. Haig, *Caveat*, 326, 335.
8. Tyler, *Trouble*, 276.
9. Ibid., 281.
10. MemCon, Schmidt and RR, May 21, 1981, box 48; and MemCon, Philip Habib and RR, July 28, 1981, box 49, both in ES/NSC, RRPL.
11. MemCon, Begin and RR, Aug. 12, 1982, box 7, GKP, RRPL; Strober and Strober, *Reagan*, 191.
12. McFarlane, *Trust*, 211.
13. Shultz, *Turmoil*, 105; McFarlane, *Trust*, 211.
14. RRD, Sept. 19, 1982.
15. Shultz, *Turmoil*, 108.
16. Crist, *Twilight War*, 122–123.
17. Pipes, *Vixi*, 148 ("outbursts"); RRD, March 19, 1981 ("complex"), June 14, 1982 ("paranoid").
18. Haig, *Caveat*, 84.
19. Barrett, *Gambling*, 240–241 (Deaver's revenge); AI/RM ("respect"); McFarlane, *Trust*, 199–200 ("animus") NR, *Turn*, 242 ("mistake").
20. *NYT*, June 22, 1982.
21. McFarlane, *Trust*, 204; Thatcher, *Downing Street*, 256.
22. Tyler, *Trouble*, 279.
23. Haig firing: Haig, *Caveat*, 314–315 ("straightened," "accepting"); RRD to Haig, June 25, 1982, box 3, WCP, RRPL ("regret"); RRD, June 24–25, 1982 ("disagreement").
24. Darman, "Scheduling Shultz," June 26, 1982, box 3, WCP, RRPL.
25. AI/GSH.
26. Shultz, *Turmoil*, 142.

Chapter 43: The Year of Living Dangerously

1. Taubman, *Gorbachev*, 171–172; *WP*, April 11, 1982.
2. Dobrynin, *In Confidence*, 523.
3. Shultz, *Turmoil*, 5–6.
4. FRUS, IV.1–5 ("test"), IV.57–59 (Clark memo); Shultz, *Turmoil*, 162; Clark to RR, March 9, 1983, box 41, JMP, RRPL ("wishful").
5. Dobrynin meeting: NR, *Turn*, 243 ("teddy bear"); Schultz, *Turmoil*, 163–165 ("chat"); Taubman, *Service*, 180 ("reflect"); Dobrynin, *In Confidence*, 517–522 ("warmonger"); RRD, Feb. 15, 1983 ("nose"), April 6, 1983 ("NSC staff"); MemCon, Feb. 15, 1983, FRUS, IV.30–32.
6. "Evil empire": Schlesinger, *Ghosts*, 326–329 ("conniptions"); RR, "Remarks to National Association of Evangelicals," March 8, 1983, RRPL; AI/DG ("red-hot," "too weak"); Inboden, *Peacemaker*, 200 (TASS, Lewis, Commager); *Weekly Standard*, June 21, 2004 ("glorious").
7. Dobrynin, *In Confidence*, 527.
8. Lettow, *Quest*, 12.
9. Fitzgerald, *Blue*, 120.
10. Ibid., 121–131.
11. Ibid., 142, 136; Anderson, *Revolution*, 96.
12. AI/JP.
13. McFarlane, *Trust*, 226.
14. Lettow, *Quest*, 98–99; Smith, *Power Game*, 598–599; RRD, Feb. 11, 1983.
15. AI/JP; McFarlane, *Trust*, 230.
16. Shultz, *Turmoil*, 246, 250.
17. Smith, *Power Game*, 594.
18. Ibid., 600.
19. AI/DG.
20. RR, "Address on Defense and National Security," March 23, 1983, RRPL.

21. Between 1985 and 2016, the Defense Department spent $239 billion (in 2016 dollars) on missile defense. *Mother Jones*, Jan. 27, 2017.

22. "Patriot," CSIS Missile Defense Project, Center for Strategic and International Studies.

23. Bethe to RR, March 29, 1983, box 11, GJKP, RRPL.

24. Strober and Strober, *Reagan*, 221; AI/RM.

25. McFarlane, *Trust*, 234; Mulroney, *Memoirs*, 349: *NYT*, Sept. 25, 1985 ("Star Wars").

26. MDOH, UVA.

27. Shultz, *Turmoil*, 260.

28. AI/RM; Podvig, "Soviet Response."

29. Dobrynin, *In Confidence*, 528.

30. Exercises: Johnson, *Cryptologic History*, 318 ("notice," "paranoia"); Hoffman, *Dead Hand*, 63–66 ("berated"); Inboden, *Peacemaker*, 206–207 (F-14s); Lehman, *Oceans*.

31. KAL 007 shootdown: Hoffman, *Dead Hand*, 72–79; Ambinder, *Brink*, 167–170; International Civil Aviation Organization, "Destruction of KAL 007 Boeing 747," July 16, 1993.

32. NR, *Turn*, 260; AI/JB.

33. RRD, Sept. 2, 1983; AI/SS.

34. Dobrynin, *In Confidence*, 537.

35. Lenczowski to Bill Clark, Sept. 3, 1983, box 3, WCP, RRPL ("terrorism"); Persico, *Casey*, 356 ("mistaken identity"); Gates, *Shadows*, 267–268 ("the facts").

36. RR, "Address to the Nation on the Soviet Attack on a Korean Civilian Airline," Sept. 5, 1983, RRPL; RR, *Life*, 582.

37. Shultz, *Turmoil*, 364–365; FRUS, IV.373–375.

38. *LAT*, Sept. 6, 1983; Nackey Loeb to RR, Sept. 7, 1983, box 10, HWF, RRPL; *WP*, July 18, 2014; RRD, Sept. 17, 1983.

39. RR to John A. Lindon, Sept. 19, 1983, box 7, HWF, Series II, RRPL.

40. Ambinder, *Brink*, 174.

41. Petrov: Hoffman, *Dead Hand*, 6–11; Ambinder, *Brink*, 178–184.

42. Able Archer: Jones, *Able Archer*, 56–57; Kaplan, *The Bomb*, 159–162; FRUS, IV. 455–461, 1420–1434; Inboden, *Peacemaker*, 246; Miles, "War Scare."

43. RRD, Oct. 10, 1983, and Nov. 18, 1983.

44. Ivan and Anya: Matlock, *Reagan and Gorbachev*, 80–83 (astrologer, sexism); Jones, *Able Archer*, 289–302; Gaddis, *Cold War*, 228; RR, "Address on United States–Soviet Relations," Jan. 16, 1984, RRPL; box 31, JMP, RRPL (speech drafts).

45. Mann, *Rebellion*, 151.

46. MemCon, RR and Brian Mulroney, June 21, 1984, box 12, ES/NSC, RRPL.

47. RRD, Aug. 11, 1984.

Chapter 44: The Thrill of Victory . . . and the Agony of Defeat

1. WCOH, UVA.

2. Deaver, *Scenes*, 170; MDOH, UVA.

3. Taubman, *Service*, 203–204, 212.

4. Leaks: Smith, *Power Game*, 438–440 ("done that"); Deaver, *Scenes*, 170; MDOH, UVA ("unhappy," Oval Office); Baker, *Work Hard*, 193–195; Meese, *With Reagan*, 111–113.

5. McFarlane, *Trust*, 254; MDOH, UVA.

6. Cannon, *President Reagan*, 469.

7. *WP*, April 7, 1983.

8. *WP*, Sept. 22, 1983; Watt to RR, Sept. 22, 1983, box 13, DGP, RRPL.

9. RRD, Oct. 8, 1983.

10. *Newsday*, March 14, 1982 (leaving); Baker, *Work Hard*, 195; AI/JABIII.

11. NSC: WCOH, UVA; Baker and Glasser, *The Man*, 213–216; Smith, *Power Game*, 318–321; Persico, *Casey*, 350–352; Meese, *With Reagan*, 114 ("biggest").

12. RRD, Oct. 14, 1983.

13. Persico, *Casey*, 305 ("balls"); KDM, SDVRR, June 22, 1983 ("administrator"); Speakes, *Speaking Out*, 83; RRD, Oct. 15–16, 1983 ("chemistry").

14. Speakes, *Speaking Out*, 271–272 ("bizarre"); Mayer and McManus, *Landslide*, 59 ("beyond me").

15. RR, *Life*, 448.

16. RRD, Oct. 21, 1983.

17. Clarridge, *Spy*, 249 ("cover"); Moore, *Thatcher: Zenith*, 123.

18. RR, "Address on Defense and National Security," March 23, 1983, RRPL; Menges, *Inside*, 63.

19. Kukielski, *Grenada*, loc. 3835–3963 (tourism), loc. 3990 ("no one"); Strober and Strober, *Reagan*, 236.
20. Thatcher, *Downing Street*, 329.
21. RR, *Life*, 457.
22. Clarridge, *Spy*, 250; Menges, *Inside*, 69.
23. McFarlane, *Trust*, 261–262.
24. Avshalom Rubin, *Passport* 46, no. 2 (Sept. 2015), 44.
25. Thatcher, *Downing Street*, 330 (no danger); KAOH, UVA ("say no"); KDM, SDVRR ("agitated"); Aldous, *Reagan and Thatcher*, 162 ("worse"), 163 ("consult").
26. MemCon, Reagan-Thatcher phone call, Oct. 26, 1983, MTF. The audiotape, recorded by NSC staff to aid in transcription, was released by the RRPL in 2014.
27. RR, *Life*, 452; *WP*, April 8, 2018.
28. McFarlane, *Trust*, 262–263.
29. AI/RM; AI/GS.
30. Tyler, *World*, 290–297.
31. Menges, *Inside*, 54.
32. RR, "Address on Events in Lebanon and Grenada," Oct. 27, 1983, RRPL.
33. McFarlane, *Trust*, 263.
34. RRD, Oct. 26, 1983.
35. McFarlane, *Trust*, 266.
36. Strober and Strober, *Reagan*, 263.
37. Kukielski, *Grenada,* loc. 743.
38. Ibid., loc. 737–688.
39. Ibid., loc. 1414 (prison), 1582, 1646 (Scoon), 2120 (calling card); Clarridge, *Spy*, 252, 256–257 (Scoon).
40. Kukielski, *Grenada,* loc. 4558–4571 (CIA); RR speech, "Address to the Nation on Events in Lebanon and Grenada," Oct. 27, 1983, RRPL ("terrorist").
41. Kukielski, *Grenada,* loc. 3651.
42. Cole, *Operation Urgent Fury*, 5.
43. Speakes, *Speaking Out*, 160 ("we won"); Hertsgaard, *Bended Knee*, 211 ("shit"); Gotlieb, *Diaries*, 259 ("pride").
44. McFarlane, *Trust*, 267 ("pall"); RRD, Nov. 4, 1983 ("dreary"); Kenneth Randolph to RR, Jan. 30, 1984, box 3, HWF, Series II, RRPL ("only one").
45. McFarlane, *Trust*, 267 ("everything"); AI/RM ("goods"); Crist, *Twilight War*, 135 ("spectacular").
46. NSDD 111, Oct. 28, 1983, RRPL.
47. Jennifer Mandel (NARA archivist) to author, email, Sept. 13, 2022.
48. McFarlane, *Trust*, 270–271; Weinberger, *Peace*, 161–162.
49. Inboden, *Peacemaker*, 255–256.
50. Meese, *With Reagan*, 14 ("tough"), 204 ("flinched"); Pipes, *Vixi*, 166 ("cut"); Strober and Strober, *Reagan*, 99–100 ("passive").
51. RR, *Life*, 463 ("conclusively"); Crist, *Twilight War*, 146 (proof).
52. RR to WFB, Jan. 5, 1985, box 2, WFBP, YALE; RR, "Interview with Bartley and Hunt of WSJ," Feb. 2, 1984, RRPL.
53. Schultz, *Turmoil*, 230–231; RDI, JBRPP.
54. McFarlane, *Trust*, 273; AI/RM.
55. Tyler, *Trouble*, 307.
56. Oct. 19, 1984, KDM, SDVRR; Naftali, *Blind Spot*, 140–145; Crist, *Twilight War*, 152.
57. Shultz speech, *Air Force Magazine*, Oct. 25, 1984; Weinberger speech, PBS *Frontline*, Nov. 28, 1984; Taubman, *Service*, 249 ("paralysis").
58. McFarlane, *Trust*, 286–287; Timberg, *Song*, 359.
59. Fadlallah: Crist, *Twilight War*, 157–158, 593; Bergman, *Secret War*, 72–73; Woodward, *Veil*, 393–398; Persico, *Casey*, 428–430.

Chapter 45: The Haves and Have-Nots

1. NR, *Turn*, 264; AI/SS.
2. AI/SS ("ferocious"); NR, *Turn*, 264 ("okay"); RDI, JBRPP (never told).
3. RR, "Address Announcing Candidacy for Reelection," Jan. 29, 1984, UVA.
4. Regan, *Record*, 143.
5. "Crude Oil Prices—70 Year Historical Chart," Macrotrends.
6. Regan, *Record*, 192.
7. Krugman, *Peddling Prosperity*, 110–111.

8. "GDP Growth by President," July 19, 2022, The Balance.
9. "Historical Tables," Office of Management and Budget, White House.
10. Rossinow, *Reagan Era*, chap. 7.
11. Edsall and Edsall, *Chain Reaction*, 23.
12. "Civilian Unemployment Rate, 1964–2010," Bureau of Labor Statistics.
13. Edsall and Edsall, *Chain Reaction*, 162.
14. Hinton, *Mass Incarceration*, 314.
15. Skinner, *Letters*, 747–748.
16. Hinton, *Mass Incarceration*, 314.
17. RR, "Radio Address on Welfare Reform," Feb. 15, 1986, RRPL; *WP*, May 17, 2014.
18. Hinton, *Mass Incarceration*, 315.
19. Rossinow, *Reagan Era*, 140.
20. *Suffolk News Herald*, Aug. 31, 1984.
21. Walsh, *Family*, 148.
22. *WP*, Jan. 10, 1988.
23. Reynolds to RR, July 9, 1985, box 13, HWF, Series II, RRPL.
24. Berman, *Ballot*, 143.
25. AI/CFR; AI/WW.
26. *WP*, June 28, 1985.
27. Bell, *Thirteenth*, 104.
28. Lucks, *Reconsidering*, 164–171; Berman, *Ballot*, 136–142.
29. *NYT*, Jan. 12, 1982.
30. Barrett, *Gambling*, 415–416.
31. *NYT*, May 25, 1983.
32. Berman, *Ballot*, 146; *Slate*, June 1, 2023.
33. Eig, *King*, 658.
34. Lucks, *Reconsidering*, 188–193.
35. Smith to James W. Cicconi, Dec. 14, 1984, box 6, JWCP, RRPL.
36. James W. Cicconi to Michael Deaver, Nov. 12, 1984, box 6, JWCP, RRPL.
37. Gergen to Baker et al., n.d., box 8, DGP, RRPL.
38. Atwater to Jim Baker, Nov. 11, 1982, box 12, CFP, RRPL; Edward J. Rollins, "Populism," March 23, 1983, box 4, RGDP, RRPL.
39. "Race of Prisoners Admitted to State and Federal Institutions," May 1991, Bureau of Justice Statistics; "Growth in Mass Incarceration," Sentencing Project.
40. RR, "Remarks at International Association of Chiefs of Police," Sept. 28, 1981, RRPL.
41. AI/DG.

Chapter 46: "Don't Screw Up": The 1984 Campaign

1. Roberts, *Cowboys*, 24.
2. Brady, *Bad Boy*, 128–129.
3. AI/JBR.
4. Roberts, *Cowboys*, 29.
5. AI/ER.
6. Gotlieb, *Diaries*, 195.
7. AI/SS; Rollins, *Bare Knuckles*, 137.
8. AI/ER; AI/SS.
9. Atwater to Jim Baker, Nov. 11, 1982, box 12, CFP, RRPL.
10. "Prouder, Stronger, Better" commercial, Reagan Foundation; *NYT*, May 7, 2016.
11. AI/JBR.
12. China: RR, *Life*, 369–370 (chopsticks, Great Wall); Germond, *Fat Man*, 159 (lakes); RR, "Remarks upon Returning from China," May 1, 1984, RRPL ("heartened").
13. "The President's Trip to Europe," April 16, 1984, box 3, RGDP, RRPL.
14. RR, "Remarks Commemorating 40th Anniversary of D-Day," June 6, 1984, Reagan Foundation.
15. "The President's Trip to Europe," April 16, 1984, box 3, RGDP, RRPL ("stirring"); PNEI, RRPL ("really big"); Roberts, *Cowboys*, 31, 52 ("trip photo").
16. AI/WG.
17. Germond and Witcover, *Wake Us*, 463.
18. Ibid. ("two-thirds"); O'Neill, *Man of the House*, 359 ("terrible"); Rollins, *Bare Knuckles*, 139 ("ourselves").

19. Roberts, *Cowboys*, 60–67.
20. *WP*, Aug. 17, 1984.
21. Rollins, *Bare Knuckles*, 144; Mondale, *Good Fight*, 300 ("frightening").
22. AI/SS; RRD, Oct. 6–7, 1984.
23. Darman, *Who's in Control*, 126 ("brutalized"); AI/SS.
24. RDI, JBRPP.
25. Germond and Witcover, *Wake Us*, 9.
26. Mondale, *Good Fight*, 302–303.
27. Baker to RR, Oct. 19, 1984, box 62, JABIIIP, SML.
28. "How Groups Voted in 1984," Roper Center.
29. RRD, Nov. 8–10, 1984.

Chapter 47: Hail to the Chief (of Staff)

1. *WP*, Jan. 18, 2021.
2. RR, "Inaugural Address 1985," Jan. 21, 1985, RRPL.
3. Rollins, *Bare Knuckles*, 158.
4. Mayer and McManus, *Landslide*, 24; Baker, *Work Hard*, 212.
5. Regan, *Record*, 228–229.
6. McFarlane, *Trust*, 288.
7. Regan, *Record*, 228, 190.
8. Rollins, *Bare Knuckles*, 162 ("starve"), AI/ER ("worst"), AI/RPR ("prick").
9. Noonan to Patrick J. Buchanan, Sept. 26, 1985, box 4, PJBP, RRPL.
10. AI/KD.
11. Speakes, *Speaking Out*, 87.
12. Mayer and McManus, *Landslide*, 132–133.
13. AI/DC.
14. AI/JABIII.
15. NR, *Turn*, 312–313; AI/PW.
16. MDOH, UVA.
17. Deaver, *Scenes*, 196; *NYT*, Jan. 4, 1985.
18. Timberg, *Song*, 287.
19. AI/ER.
20. Quigley, *What*, 12.
21. Deaver, *Scenes*, 209.
22. Regan, *Record*, 257.
23. Deaver, *Scenes*, 181.
24. *NYT*, April 20, 1985.
25. NR, *Turn*, 63 ("pleaded"); RRD, April 19, 1985 ("insult"), and April 5, 1985 ("cover").
26. Deaver, *Scenes*, 182 ("hell"); *LAT*, May 4, 1985 ("pressure"); Rollins, *Bare Knuckles*, 164 (like Americans); Buchanan to Ed Meese, Jan. 29, 1987, box 4, PJBP, RRPL (deportation).
27. RR, "Remarks at Bergen-Belsen," May 5, 1985, RRPL.
28. Nixon to RR, May 10, 1985, box 12, HWF, Series II, RRPL.

Chapter 48: "We Can Do Business Together"

1. Schweizer, *Reagan's War*, 245.
2. Volkogonov, *Autopsy*, 438, 445.
3. Brown, *Human Factor*, 133.
4. Savranskaya and Blanton, *Gorbachev and Reagan*, 6.
5. Miller, *Struggle*, 59–60.
6. Ibid., 60, 147.
7. Gorbachev: Taubman, *Gorbachev* (4, "decent"; 7, "devil"; 201, "business"); Brown, *Human Factor*; Gorbachev, *Memoirs*; Wilson, *Triumph*, 89 ("stop"); Thatcher, *Downing Street*, 459–463.
8. MemCon, RR and Thatcher, Dec. 22, 1985, MTF.
9. McFarlane, *Trust*, 295 ("nurturing"); RR, *Life*, 611 ("dying"); Dobrynin, *In Confidence*, 574 ("stern").
10. RR to Gorbachev, March 11, 1985, FRUS, V.1–2 ("visit me"); Gorbachev to RR, March 24, 1985, FRUS, V.36 ("court"); Dobrynin, *In Confidence*, 572–573 (Geneva).
11. RR, "Exchange with Reporters on Death of Major Nicholson," March 25, 1985, RRPL.

12. JWJ, March 4, 1985 ("soul"); Gates, *Shadows*, 332 ("not reformers"); Lenczowski to McFarlane, March 12, 1986, FRUS, V.3–6 ("quintessential"); Richard Burt to Michael Armacost, April 5, 1985, FRUS, V.50 (Luca Brasi); Buchanan to RR, July 26, 1985, box 13, HWF, Series II, RRPL (NR article).

13. RRD, April 19 and June 24, 1985.

14. Matlock, *Reagan and Gorbachev*, 132–133.

15. RRD, May 20, 1986; RR to Daniel C. Sabatos, Feb. 15, 1988, box 20, HWF, Series II, RRPL; Massie, *Trust but Verify*, 19.

16. Savranskaya and Blanton, *Gorbachev and Reagan*, 42–44.

17. Ibid., 42–44.

18. Kuhn, *In Private*, 172.

19. Dobrynin, *In Confidence*, 585.

20. Wilson, *Improvisation*, 100.

21. Kuhn, *In Private*, 165–168 ("rolling"); Savranskaya and Blanton, *Gorbachev and Reagan*, 44 ("no talk"); Dobrynin, *In Confidence*, 583 ("springboard").

22. Morris, *Dutch*, 558.

23. Savranskaya and Blanton, *Gorbachev and Reagan*, 56–57.

24. Ibid., 57–59.

25. Ibid., 59–60.

26. Ibid., 60–61.

27. Ibid., 65.

28. Ibid., 69.

29. Gorbachev, *Memoirs*, 406.

30. Savranskaya and Blanton, *Gorbachev and Reagan*, 75.

31. Ibid., 77.

32. Korda, *Life*, 471.

33. RRD, Nov. 19, 1985.

34. Savranskaya and Blanton, *Gorbachev and Reagan*, 82.

35. Regan, *Record*, 314 ("dame"); NR, *Turn*, 336–339 ("rough").

36. Savranskaya and Blanton, *Gorbachev and Reagan*, 81.

37. Deaver, *Drummer*, 118.

38. Savranskaya and Blanton, *Gorbachev and Reagan*, 84–85.

39. Gorbachev, *Memoirs*, 406.

40. Savranskaya and Blanton, *Gorbachev and Reagan*, 87–91; Gorbachev, *Memoirs*, 406 ("fend off").

41. Shultz, *Turmoil*, 603; RRD, Nov. 20, 1985.

42. "Joint Soviet-US Statement on Summit Meeting," Nov. 21, 1985, RRPL.

43. Savranskaya and Blanton, *Gorbachev and Reagan*, 109.

44. MemCon, RR and North Atlantic Council, Nov. 21, 1986, MTF.

45. President's Daily Diary, Nov. 1985, RRPL.

46. RRD, Nov. 21, 1985.

47. AI/RD.

48. Savranskaya and Blanton, *Gorbachev and Reagan*, 15.

49. Dobrynin, *In Confidence*, 592; Gorbachev, *Memoirs*, 405.

Chapter 49: Despotism and Terrorism

1. Korda, *Life*, 470.

2. Rogers Commission Report, June 6, 1986, NASA.

3. Kuhn, *In Private*, 176 ("stricken"); Speakes, *Speaking Out*, 93 (emotion); RRD, Jan. 28, 1986 ("horror").

4. *Christian Science Monitor*, Jan. 28, 2011 ("girl"); PNEI, RRPL ("trek").

5. RR, "Address on Explosion of Challenger," Jan. 28, 1986, RRPL.

6. O'Neill, *Man of the House*, 363–363.

7. Gotlieb, *Diaries*, 346.

8. Marcos: Shultz, *Turmoil*, 608–643 (613, "convinced"); Inboden, *Peacemaker*, 397–398; Speakes, *Speaking Out*, 203–217 (213, "disappointed"); AI/PWOLF ("agreement," "brilliant"); AI/EA; AI/GSH; Debate transcript, Oct. 21, 1984, Commission on Presidential Debates ("alternative"); Laxalt, *Memoir*, 276 (support), 279 ("cut"); Phillip D. Brady to RR, June 16, 1988, box 2, KDP, RRPL (indict); Marcos to RR, June 9, 1988, box 2, KDP, RRPL (merciful).

9. *NYT*, Dec. 10, 1988.

10. *American Prospect*, Dec. 19, 2001.

11. Inboden, *Peacemaker*, 407 (two factions); Buchanan to RR, July 9, 1986, box 16, HWF, Series II, RRPL ("retarded"); Buchanan, *Right*, 374 ("America's place").

12. RR to Joan Joyce Sellers, Jan. 28, 1985, in Skinner, *Letters*, 518 ("repugnant"); Lucks, *Reconsidering*, 196 ("tell them"); *American Prospect*, Dec. 19, 2001 ("side").

13. Lucks, *Reconsidering*, 201 ("immoral"); RRD, Dec. 7, 1984 ("unaware").

14. *WP*, Aug. 27, 1985 ("segregation"); RR interview with LAT, June 23, 1986, box 2, PJBP, RRPL ("rid"); *Atlantic*, March 1986 ("minority rights").

15. Davis to RR, June 13, 1986, box 16, HWF, Series II, RRPL.

16. "Back Door to Sanctions," n.d., box 3, PJBP, RRPL.

17. Wirthlin to Regan, July 15, 1986, box 3, PJBP, RRPL.

18. RR, "Remarks to World Affairs Council," July 22, 1986, RRPL.

19. Gotlieb, *Diaries*, 394 ("father"); Buchanan to RR, August 18, 1986, box 16, HWF, Series II, RRPL ("Jo'burg"); Crocker, *High Noon*, 323 ("tilt").

20. AI/CC.

21. TWA: Inboden, *Peacemaker*, 344–347; Crist, *Twilight Wars*, 155; Naftali, *Blind Spot*, 162–165; RRD, June 17, 1985 ("dealing"); NSDD 138, April 3, 1984, RRPL ("hostile").

22. *Achille Lauro*: Inboden, *Peacemaker*, 367–370; Naftali, *Blind Spot*, 171–174; Timberg, *Song*, 346–349; Speakes, *Speaking Out*, 176–179; Crowe, *Line of Fire*, 119–126.

23. El Dorado Canyon: CIA, "Libyan-Soviet Cooperation: The View from Tripoli," August 1986, box 105, ONP, RRPL ("closer"); Poindexter to RR, "Response to Libyan Terrorist Attacks," box 5, HTP, RRPL ("smoking gun"); Stanik, *El Dorado Canyon* (157, "mad dog"); Inboden, *Peacemaker*, 393–397; Naftali, *Blind Spot*, 219–221; Strober and Strober, *Reagan*, 349 (maps); NESA to DDI, June 29, 1985, box 48, ONP, RRPL ("secretly"); North, *Under Fire*, 216 ("tears"); Crowe, *Line of Fire*, 129–145 (135, "meaningfully"); Moore, *Thatcher: Zenith*, 505, 508 ("international law," "cycle"); CIA, "Prospects for West European Assistance in Further US Military Moves Against Libyan Terrorism," box 105, ONP, RRPL ("goad"); "National Security Adviser Talking Points," box 4, HTP, RRPL ("not true").

Chapter 50: The Surprise Summit

1. Baker, *Work Hard*, 217.

2. KDM, SDVRR, May 28, 1985.

3. RR, "Address on Tax Reform," May 28, 1985, RRPL; JWJ, Dec. 30, 1983.

4. AI/JABIII.

5. Birnbaum and Murray, *Gucci Gulch*, 169–174, 284; Baker and Glasser, *The Man*, 262–263; RRD, Dec. 17, 1985.

6. "Federal Tax Code and Income Inequality," April 19, 2012, Center for American Progress; Birnbaum and Murray, *Gucci Gulch*, Appendices A-B.

7. Mulroney, *Memoirs*, 840.

8. Savranskaya and Blanton, *Gorbachev and Reagan*, 143.

9. Coll, *Ghost Wars*, 148–150; Westad, *Global Cold War*, 355–356, 371 ("wound"); Crile, *War*, 419–402, 436–439.

10. Crocker, *High Noon*, 289–303.

11. Matlock, *Reagan and Gorbachev*, 199 ("mad"); RR press conference, Nov. 19, 1986, RRPL (quid pro quo).

12. Savranskaya and Blanton, *Gorbachev and Reagan*, 153.

13. *NYT*, Oct. 12, 1986 ("boots"); NR, *Turn*, 344.

14. Shultz, *Turmoil*, 753.

15. Gorbachev, *Memoirs*, 416.

16. Shultz, *Turmoil*, 758.

17. Savranskaya and Blanton, *Gorbachev and Reagan*, 175–177.

18. Ibid., 178; Fitzwater, *Briefing*, 138 ("sparkle").

19. Wilson, *Triumph*, 124–126; Hoffman, *Dead Hand*, 213–221.

20. Savranskaya and Blanton, *Gorbachev and Reagan*, 232.

21. Ibid., 191.

22. Ibid., 210.

23. Ibid., 212.

24. Ibid., 212; "Operation Frantic," World War II Database (sorties); Shultz, *Turmoil*, 600–601 ("facts").

25. Moore, *Thatcher: Zenith*, 588, 598; Crowe, *Line of Fire*, 267; Poindexter to RR, Oct. 16, 1986, box 3, AKP, RRPL.

26. Matlock, *Reagan and Gorbachev*, 237–238.

27. Savranskaya and Blanton, *Gorbachev and Reagan*, 234–235.

28. RRD, Oct. 12, 1986; Speakes, *Speaking Out*, 142; Kuhn, *In Private*, 192–194; Adelman, *Reykjavik*, 1 ("passions"); Taubman, *Gorbachev*, 304 ("primitive").
29. Dolan to RR, n.d., box 16, HWF, Series II, RRPL; *NYT*, Oct. 13, 1986 ("sad").
30. Savranskaya and Blanton, *Gorbachev and Reagan*, 238.
31. Rosebush, *True*, 96.
32. Mayer and McManus, *Landslide*, 280.
33. Kornbluh and Byrne, *Iran-Contra*, 305.

Chapter 51: "A Dark and Hurtful Time"

1. AI/RM (Kissinger); McFarlane, *Trust*, 21–23 ("responsibility"); Kuhn, *In Private*, 197 ("plight"); RR to Peggy Say, Nov. 26, 1986, box 17, HWF, Series II, RRPL ("ordeal").
2. McFarlane, *Trust*, 23.
3. McFarlane, *Trust*, 26–27; Speakes, *Speaking Out*, 192 ("cancer").
4. AI/RM.
5. McFarlane, *Trust*, 32–34.
6. "North on Lying to Congress," July 8, 1987, Understanding the Iran Contra Affairs, Brown University (admit falsehoods); Timberg, *Song*, 353 ("habitual"); Persico, *Casey*, 389 ("haze"); William Lytton to A. B. Culvahouse, May 6, 1987, box 2, KDP, RRPL (private meetings).
7. Crist, *Twilight War*, 183.
8. McFarlane, *Trust*, 40 ("price"); Kornbluh and Byrne, *Iran-Contra*, 245 (408 TOWs).
9. AI/RM.
10. Byrne, *Iran-Contra*, 105–107; William B. Lytton III to A. B. Culvahouse, "December 7, 1985, Meeting," box 5, HBP, RRPL.
11. Kornbluh and Byrne, *Iran-Contra*, xix, 235.
12. RRD, Nov. 22, 1985.
13. Mayer and McManus, *Landslide*, 190–192.
14. AI/JP.
15. RR, "Remarks at Annual Dinner of CPAC," March 1, 1985, RRPL ("equal"); Kornbluh and Byrne, *Iran-Contra*, 54 ("liars"); McFarlane, *Trust*, 68 ("body and soul").
16. Byrne, *Iran-Contra*, 42; Kornbluh and Byrne, *Iran-Contra*, 6–8.
17. Contra funds: Buchanan to Regan, May 14, 1985, and RR to Bill Simon, May 30, 1985, box 2, PJBP, RRPL ("Canadian"); Byrne, *Iran-Contra*, 222; Kornbluh and Byrne, *Iran-Contra*, 43 ("spark"), 63 (Brunei); Mayer and McManus, *Landslide*, 153; A. B. Culvahouse to RR, Nov. 16, 1986, box 2, KDP, RRPL.
18. Mayer and McManus, *Landslide*, 234.
19. Teicher and Teicher, *Twin Pillars*, 370.
20. RRD, May 28, 1986.
21. Crist, *Twilight War*, 195.
22. Byrne, *Iran-Contra*, 247–248.
23. AI/KO.
24. Kornbluh and Byrne, *Iran-Contra*, xviii, 244.
25. Byrne, *Iran-Contra*, 253–254 (C-123); North, *Under Fire*, 9 ("shut").
26. Abshire, *Saving*, 3 ("pay off"); RRD, Nov. 7, 1986.
27. AI/JP ("leaked"); AI/RM (cried); Byrne, *Iran-Contra*, 256–258 ("drain").
28. RRD, Nov. 12, 1986.
29. RR, "Address on Iran Arms and Contra Aid," Nov. 13, 1986, RRPL.
30. RR press conference, Nov. 19, 1986, RRPL; Timberg, *Song*, 440; Speakes, *Speaking Out*, 292–294.
31. Byrne, *Iran-Contra*, 271–274 ("residual," "shit," shredding); AI/WW ("Roy Cohn").
32. Regan, *Record*, 38.
33. AI/PW.
34. RRD, Nov. 25, 1986.
35. Byrne, *Iran-Contra*, 2.
36. Gotlieb, *Diaries*, 425.
37. AI/FC ("agree," "flattering"); Gotlieb, *Diaries*, 418.
38. AI/CP.
39. AI/CP ("reading," "properly"); AI/FC ("60 percent"); Nicholas Rostow, Memo for File, Aug. 2, 1988, box 3, CPP, RRPL ("cost free").
40. Strober and Strober, *Reagan*, 495 ("focus"); Powell, *Journey*, 323.
41. Woodward, *Veil*, 517.
42. AI/JP.

43. McFarlane, *Trust*, 14.

44. Tower Commission: Abshire, *Saving*, 120 ("piece of paper"), 121 ("slack"); Wallison, *Reagan*, 262 (recollection), 266 ("horrified"); AI/PW.

45. Presidential Job Approval Center, Gallup; Woodward, *Shadow*, 105 (14 percent); Fitzwater, *Briefing*, 118.

46. RRD, Nov. 19, 1986 ("Dreyfus"), Nov. 22, 1986 ("lynched"), Dec. 6, 1986 ("implementing"); Speakes, *Speaking Out*, 112 ("hero").

47. Liman, *Lawyer*, 305.

48. RPR, *My Father*, 214 ("fog"); AI/RPR.

49. NR, *Turn*, 319–320.

50. Kuhn, *In Private*, 203.

51. Tower Commission Report, Internet Archive.

52. AI/PW.

53. AI/RPR.

54. AI/JE; AI/RD.

55. Tumulty, *Triumph*, 484–485 (Wallace); MR, *First Father*, 365 ("pain"); Abshire, *Saving*, 39 ("ass").

56. Meacham, *Destiny*, 308.

57. Regan, *Record*, 96–98, 366–371.

58. AI/FC ("Okay," "volcano"); box 189, DRP, LC (letter); Fitzwater, *Briefing*, 170; Regan, *Record*, 373 ("humiliate").

59. Box 214, DRP, LC ("Revenge"); NR, *Turn*, 52–53.

60. AI/ER.

61. RRD, Feb. 26, 1987.

62. HBOH, UVA.

63. Mayer and McManus, *Landslide*, vii–ix.

64. Wilson, *Triumph*, 127 ("reality"); Persico, *Casey*, 306 ("barely").

65. Mayer and McManus, *Landslide*, x–xi.

66. HBOH, UVA ("boys"); AI/KD ("duck").

67. AI/TG.

68. AI/ABC; AI/FC.

69. AI/SS.

70. RR, "Address on Iran-Contra," March 4, 1987, UVA; Abshire, *Saving*, 148–150.

71. AI/ABC.

72. RR to Alfred Kingon, Aug 5, 1987, box 18, HWF, Series II, RRPL.

73. Crist, *Twilight War*, 250 ("macho"); RR to Charlton Heston, July 9, 1987, box 18, HWF, Series II, RRPL ("heart"); Timberg, *Song*, 474 ("lied").

74. Culvahouse to RR, Nov. 16, 1987, box 2, KDP, RRPL; Report of the Iran-Contra Committee, Internet Archive, 21.

75. Strober and Strober, *Reagan*, 453; Walsh, *Firewall*, 528–529.

76. Iran-Contra Independent Counsel, "Summary of Prosecutions," Federation of American Scientists.

77. Johnson, *Sleepwalking*, 183.

Chapter 52: Culture Wars

1. Bell, *Thirteenth*, 30.

2. AI/AK.

3. *WP*, Jan. 23, 1985.

4. Robinson to Pat Buchanan, Feb. 6, 1985, box 4, PJBP, RRPL.

5. Engel, *Epidemic*, 5–6; Shilts, *Band*; "Global HIV and AIDS Statistics," UN AIDS; *Scientific American*, Dec. 1, 2021.

6. Jim Cicconi to Craig Fuller, May 19, 1983, box 2, JWCP, RRPL ("concerned"); *Vox*, Dec. 1, 2016 (joke); RR, press conference, Sept. 17, 1985, RRPL; RRD, June 24, 1985 (Hudson).

7. Morris, *Dutch*, 458; Speakes, *Speakes Out*, 103 ("slap").

8. AI/RPR.

9. Engel, *Epidemic*, 70–71.

10. Strober and Strober, *Reagan*, 127, 129.

11. Engel, *Epidemic*, 76–77.

12. Farrell, *Ted Kennedy*, 437–449.

13. Karen Tumulty interview with Anthony Fauci (provided to author).

14. Koop, *Koop*, 195, 204.

15. Ibid., 198, 212.

16. Koop, "Surgeon General's Report to the American Public on HIV Infection and AIDS," National Library of Medicine.
17. *NYT*, Oct. 23, 1986 ("explicit"); Koop, *Koop*, 215–217 ("praised"); Bauer to Howard Baker, March 29, 1986, box 2, GBP, RRPL ("details").
18. Koop, *Koop*, 223–224.
19. Shilts, *Band*, 585–586.
20. AI/GB; Koop, *Koop*, 224.
21. RR, "Remarks at AIDS Research Awards Dinner," May 31, 1987, APP; Shilts, *Band*, 588 ("hero"), 594–596; *NYT*, June 1, 1987 ("concurrence").
22. Bauer to RR, June 30, 1987, box 2, GBP, RRPL.
23. Engel, *Epidemic*, 80, 100–101; *NYT*, June 28, 1988 ("muted").
24. Glaser, *Angels*, 145–150; AI/DW.
25. Koop, *Koop*, 236 (fifty thousand); Strober and Strober, *Reagan*, 126 ("dreadful").
26. Shilts, *Band*, 595.
27. Engel, *Epidemic*, 102.
28. "Judgeship Appointments by President," US Courts.
29. AI/ABC.
30. RR to WFB, July 15, 1981, box 2, WFBP, YALE ("next"); AI/ABC.
31. "Bork Nomination," box 3, HBP, RRPL ("qualified"); Bronner, *Battle*, 52 (ugliness), 59 (*Griswold*), 78 (*Roe*), 66 (Cox).
32. Bronner, *Battle*, 84–85.
33. Bork, *Tempting*, 268.
34. Culvahouse to Baker, Sept. 8, 1987, box 3, HBP, RRPL.
35. RR to Charlton Heston, July 9, 1987, box 18, HWF, Series II, RRPL.
36. "Fairness Doctrine," RRPL; RR interview, *Broadcast* magazine, June 25, 1987, box 18, HWF, Series II, RRPL ("fair"); Johnson, *Sleepwalking*, 141 ("toaster").
37. Bork, *Temptation*, 296.
38. Bronner, *Battle*, 193 (civil rights), 202 (literacy tests), 204 (criminal rights), 245 ("feast").
39. RRD, Sept. 19, 1987; AI/TG.
40. AI/ABC.
41. AI/KD.
42. RRD, Oct. 23, 1987 ("regret"); RR to Walter Annenberg, October 29, 1987, box 19, HWF, Series II, RRPL ("shenanigans"); RR, *Life*, 754.
43. Kuhn, *In Private*, 214; NR, *Turn*, 294 (wept).
44. "Stock Market Crash of 1987," Federal Reserve History.
45. NR, *Turn*, 300–301 ("daze"); PD, *Dear Mom*, 201.
46. HBOH, UVA.
47. RR to Murphy, Oct. 29, 1987, box 19, HWF, Series II, RRPL.
48. "Douglas H. Ginsburg: Biographical Information," box 1, KDP, RRPL ("able"); AI/KD ("us").
49. Bronner, *Battle*, 298–305.
50. AI/KD.
51. "Anthony M. Kennedy: Biographical Information," box 1, KDP, RRPL ("enigma"); AI/KD ("boring"); AI/ABC ("Mary").

Chapter 53: Tear Down This Wall

1. Shultz, *Turmoil*, 900.
2. CWOH, UVA; William Webster to RR, Nov. 24, 1987, GWU, NSA ("detect").
3. Wilson, *Triumph*, 128–129 ("fruit"); RR to Nackey Loeb, Dec. 18, 1987, box 19, HWF, Series II, RRPL.
4. RR, "Remarks on East-West Relations," June 12, 1987, RRPL.
5. Ratnesar, *Tear Down*, 155.
6. Brown, *Human Factor*, 209 (harder); Mann, *Rebellion*, 119 ("irrelevant," Shultz).
7. MemCon, RR and Shevardnadze, Sept. 23, 1988, FRUS VI, doc. 177.
8. AI/FC.
9. Wilson, *Triumph*, 134.
10. *NYT*, Nov. 4, 1987.
11. Annis, *Howard Baker*, 200 ("administration"); AI/KD ("shape").
12. AI/FC.
13. AI/CP.

14. RR to Warner L. Atkins, May 23, 1985, box 12, HWF, Series II, RRPL ("systems"); James L. Hooley to Thomas Griscom, Sept. 23, 1987, box 1, CPP, RRPL ("tour").
15. Powell, *Journey*, 349 (astrologer); *WP*, Jan. 9, 1987.
16. Powell, *Journey*, 350.
17. Savranskaya and Blanton, *Gorbachev and Reagan*, 317; Powell, *Journey*, 350–351; RR, *Life*, 715.
18. Nixon, "Memorandum to the File," April 28, 1987, box 51, JMP, HI; Powell, *Journey*, 350–351.
19. Savranskaya and Blanton, *Gorbachev and Reagan*, 345–348.
20. Ibid., 328–329; Brown, *Human Factor*, 165, 187–188; Hoffman, *Dead Hand*, 219.
21. NR, *Turn*, 346–348.
22. *NYT*, Dec. 11, 1987; AI/TG.
23. Savranskaya and Blanton, *Gorbachev and Reagan*, 355.
24. Witcher, *Right*, 122, 129 ("idiot"); Brett Dawson to Howard Baker, April 27, 1987, box 1, HBP, RRPL ("worst thing").
25. AI/KD; Crist, *Twilight War*, 352.
26. Crist, *Twilight War*, 363–371.
27. Matlock, *Reagan and Gorbachev*, 277; Nixon, "Memorandum to the File," April 28, 1987, box 51, JMP, HI.
28. Savranskaya and Blanton, *Gorbachev and Reagan*, 374–376.
29. NR, *Turn*, 301.
30. Matlock, *Reagan and Gorbachev*, 298; NR, *Turn*, 355.
31. AI/TG; Fitzwater, *Briefing*, 159–161.
32. RR to Armand Deutsch, June 7, 1988, box 20, HWF, Series II, RRPL; Matlock, *Reagan and Gorbachev*, 302.
33. Mann, *Rebellion*, 304–305.
34. Page, *Matriarch*, 129.
35. Mulroney, *Memoirs*, 600.
36. *NYT*, Dec. 3, 2018.
37. Gorbachev, "Address to UN General Assembly," Dec. 7, 1988, Wilson Center; Wilson, *Triumph*, 144–145 ("vision").
38. Frank Donatelli to Ken Duberstein, Nov. 7, 1988, box 3, KDP, RRPL.
39. RRD, Dec. 7, 1988.
40. Shultz, *Turmoil*, 1136.

Chapter 54: Fadeout

1. Noonan, *Revolution*, 292–293.
2. Noonan to RR, n.d., WHORM, SP-1314: 589277 (8/8), RRPL.
3. Noonan, *Revolution*, 325–334.
4. Noonan to RR, n.d., WHORM, SP-1314: 589277 (8/8), RRPL.
5. RR, "Farewell Address," Jan. 11, 1989, RRPL.
6. Clancy to RR, Sept. 19, 1989, KOPPP, RRPL.
7. Budget figures: "Historical Tables," Office of Management and Budget, White House.
8. Krugman, *Peddling Prosperity*, 152, 169.
9. Korda, *Life*, 472.
10. Goldwater to RR, Nov. 11, 1988, box 21, HWF, Series II, RRPL.
11. Fitzwater, *Briefing*, 364.
12. RRD, Jan. 20, 1989; RR, *Life*, 721–723.
13. Tumulty, *Triumph*, 510.
14. RR to Nixon, Jan. 31, 1989, box 1, PPC, RMNPL.
15. *NYT*, April 9, 1988 (1987 income); *WP*, Oct. 28, 1989 ($2 million); AI/KO.
16. Lindsey, *Ghost Scribbler*, 164 ($7 million), 154–155 (memory), 160 ("analytical"), 161 ("changed"); RR, *Life*, 263 ("mixed-up").
17. Korda, *Life*, 468 ("genial"), 469 ("critics," "prodding"), 475 ("to read it").
18. Ibid., 467.
19. AI/FR (phones); AI/EMIII ("airs"); AI/KO ("humble").
20. MER, *Lessons*, 137.
21. *WP*, Aug. 4, 1991; *WP*, Aug. 1, 1991.
22. RR to Buckley, Feb. 6, 1989, KOPPP, RRPL; RR to Nixon, April 5, 1990, box 1, PPC, RMNPL.
23. *WP*, March 2, 2018.
24. RR to Lawrence Coughlin, May 31, 1990, KOPPP, RRPL.
25. Korda, *Life*, 471.
26. AI/JB; AI/JN; Mulroney, *Memoirs*, 687.

27. Tumulty, *Triumph*, 542.
28. RPR, *My Father*, 218; AI/DLB.
29. AI/FR.
30. AI/DLB.
31. AI/RPR.
32. AI/RONP.
33. AI/JB; AI/KO.
34. AI/RONP; AI/SS.
35. Noonan, *Revolution*, 268; LNI, JBRPP.
36. Skinner, *Hand*, x.
37. "Mastermind," *Saturday Night Live*, Dec. 6, 1986.
38. Winik, *Brink*, 494, 498.
39. AI/SS.
40. AI/DLB.
41. AI/JB.
42. Kruse and Zelizer, *Myth America*, 296.
43. *BuzzFeed News*, July 10, 2015.
44. Axios, May 7, 2021.
45. Fred Ryan to author, email, June 8, 2021; CNBC, Dec. 12, 2019.
46. Tony Dolan to RR, July 24, 1989, KOPPP, RRPL; C-SPAN, "Presidential Historians Survey 2021"; Mulroney, *Memoirs*, 370.
47. Bunch, *Myth*, xiv.
48. AI/HK.
49. Wilentz, *Reagan*, 2.
50. *WP*, Oct. 28, 1989.

Acknowledgments

1. The Council on Foreign Relations (CFR) is an independent, nonpartisan membership organization, think tank, and publisher dedicated to being a resource for its members, government officials, business executives, journalists, educators and students, civic and religious leaders, and other interested citizens in order to help them better understand the world and the foreign policy choices facing the United States and other countries. The Council on Foreign Relations takes no institutional positions on policy issues and has no affiliation with the U.S. government. All views expressed in its publications and on its website are the sole responsibility of the author or authors.

Bibliography

Abbreviations Used in Notes

AP	*Associated Press*
CT	*Chicago Tribune*
DP	*Daily Pantagraph* (Bloomington, Ill.)
DET	*Dixon Evening Telegraph*
DMR	*Des Moines Register*
DMT	*Des Moines Tribune*
HUAC 1947	US House Un-American Activities Committee, 1947 hearings
HUAC 1951	HUAC, 1951 hearings
JW	Jane Wyman
LADN	*Los Angeles Daily News*
LAECN	*Los Angeles Evening Citizen News*
LAT	*Los Angeles Times*
MEMCON	Memorandum of Conversation
MER	Michael Edward Reagan
MR	Maureen Reagan
NR	Nancy Reagan
NYT	*New York Times*
PD	Patti Davis
RPR	Ronald P. (Ron) Reagan
RR	Ronald Reagan
RRD	Ronald Reagan Diaries
SB	*Sacramento Bee*
SEP	*Saturday Evening Post*
TT	*Tampico Tornado*
WP	*Washington Post*
WSJ	*Wall Street Journal*

Author Interviews (AI)

AA	Annelise Anderson	CFR	Charles Fried
ABC	A. B. Culvahouse	CHP	Charles Powell
AG	Alan Greenspan	CJ	Clark Judge
AK	Alfred Kingon	CP	Colin Powell
AL	Arthur Laffer	DB	Douglas Brinkley
BD	Bob Dole	DC	David Chew
BM	Brian Mulroney	DD	David Dreier
BRI	Bobby Ray Inman	DG	David Gergen
CB	Charles Black	DPG	Donald P. Gregg
CC	Chester Crocker	DLB	Dennis LeBlanc
CD	Carolyn Deaver	DR	Dennis Revell
CF	Craig Fuller	DW	Douglas Wick

EA	Elliott Abrams		LB	Laurence Barrett
EM	Edmund Morris		MF	Martin Feldstein
EMIII	Edwin Meese III		MR	Michael Reagan
ER	Ed Rollins		MT	Margaret Tutwiler
FC	Frank Carlucci		NR	Nancy Reynolds
FR	Fred Ryan		PD	Patti Davis
GAB	Gahl Burt		PH	Peter Hannaford
GB	Gary Bauer		PM	Peter Metzger
GFW	George F. Will		PR	Peter Robinson
GJ	Galen Jackman		PS	Pete Souza
GS	George Skelton		PT	Paula Trivette
GSC	George Schlatter		PV	Paul Volcker
GSH	George Shultz		PW	Peter Wallison
GSI	Gary Sick		PWOLF	Paul Wolfowitz
GST	George Steffes		RD	Richard Davis
HD	Helene von Damm		RG	Richard Gephardt
HK	Henry Kissinger		RM	Robert McFarlane
JABIII	James A. Baker III		RONP	Ron Petersen
JB	Jerry Brown		RP	Richard Perle
JBAR	John Barletta		RPR	Ronald P. (Ron) Reagan
JBELL	Jeff Bell		RQ	Ruth Quigley
JBR	John B. Roberts II		RS	Roger Stone
JD	Jack Danforth		RT	Robert Tuttle
JE	Jane Erkenbeck		RVA	Richard V. Allen
JFL	John F. Lehman		RZ	Robert Zoellick
JK	James Kuhn		SK	Sven Kraemer
JL	James Lake		SS	Stuart K. Spencer
JLIM	John Limbert		TG	Thomas Griscom
JM	Joel McCleary		TL	Trent Lott
JN	John Negroponte		TO	Ted Olson
JP	John Poindexter		TR	Thomas Reed
JR	Junius Rodriguez		WB	Willie Brown
JS	John Sears		WG	William Galston
KD	Kenneth Duberstein		WW	William Weld
KO	Kathleen Osborne			

Archives

APP	American Presidency Project, University of California, Santa Barbara.
BCD	Barber Conable Diary, Division of Rare and Manuscript Collections, Cornell University Library, Ithaca, New York.
BSPP	Bob Spitz private papers, New York, New York.
BJT	Bill and Jean Thompson interview with Anne Edwards, March 2, 1985
CSA	California State Archives, Sacramento, California.
JMUP	Jesse M. Unruh Papers
CSUF	California State University, Fullerton.
KCOH	Kitchen Cabinet Oral History, 1983
RBOH	Robert Beverly Oral History, 1983
DDEPL	Dwight D. Eisenhower Presidential Library, Abilene, Kansas.
PPP	Post Presidential Papers
EC	Melick Library, Eureka College, Eureka, Illinois.
RH	Raymond Holmes, "Ronald Reagan and Segregation in the Midwest," October 1, 2001
RMC	Reagan Memorabilia Collection
FRUS	*Foreign Relations of the United States, 1981–1988*, Department of State, Washington, DC.
GARF	State Archive of the Russian Federation, Moscow, Russia.
VOKS	All-Union Society of Cultural Contacts with Abroad
GF	Gorbachev Foundation, Moscow, Russia.
GFPL	Gerald Ford Presidential Library, Ann Arbor, Michigan.
RNP	Ron Nessen Papers

GHWBL	George H. W. Bush Presidential Library, College Station, Texas.	
	CBGF	C. Boyden Gray Files
GWU/NSA	George Washington University, National Security Archive, Washington, DC.	
HDCR	Hollywood Democratic Committee Records, 1942–1950, Wisconsin Historical Society, Madison, Wisconsin.	
HI	Hoover Institution, Stanford University, Stanford, California.	
	CFRR	Citizens for Reagan Records
	EMP	Edwin Meese Papers
	JMP	Jim Mann Papers
	RRSC	Ronald Reagan Subject Collection
	WJCP	William J. Casey Papers
	WPCP	William P. Clark Papers
JBRPP	John B. Roberts II Personal Papers.	
	LNI	Lyn Nofziger interview
	RDI	Richard Darman interview
JCPL	Jimmy Carter Presidential Library, Atlanta, Georgia.	
JRPP	Junius Rodriguez Personal Papers, Eureka, Illinois.	
JWJ	Jim Wright Journal, Mary Couts Barnett Library, Texas Christian University, Fort Worth, Texas.	
LC	Library of Congress, Washington, DC.	
	AHP	Alexander M. Haig Papers
	CWP	Caspar Weinberger Papers
	DRP	Donald Regan Papers
	RSOH	Ricardo Sanvictores Oral History
	WRP	William Rusher Papers
LCHGS	Lee County Historical and Genealogical Society, Dixon, Illinois.	
MHL	Margaret Herrick Library, Fairbanks Center for Motion Picture Study, Academy of Motion Picture Arts and Sciences, Beverly Hills, California.	
	DS	Don Siegel interview, 1980
MTF	Margaret Thatcher Foundation, London.	
	JRFD	James Rentschler Falklands Diary
PCCA	Palmer College of Chiropractic Archives, Davenport, Iowa.	
RMNPL	Richard M. Nixon Presidential Library, Yorba Linda, California.	
	PPC	Post-Presidential Correspondence with RR
	PPP	Pre-Presidential Papers
	WHCF	White House Central Files
RRFBI	Ronald Reagan FBI Files, FBI Records, The Vault, https://vault.fbi.gov/ronald-wilson-reagan.	
RRPL	Ronald Reagan Presidential Library, Simi Valley, California.	
	1980	1980 Campaign Series I
	AKP	Alton Keel Papers
	CFP	Craig Fuller Papers
	CN	Condolence Notes to NR
	CPP	Colin Powell Papers
	DD	Desk documents
	DGP	David Gergen Papers
	EMP	Edwin Meese Papers
	ES/NSC	Executive Secretariat, NSC
	ESD/NSC	European and Soviet Directorate, NSC
	FMPUOH	First MPU Oral Histories
	GBP	Gary Bauer Papers
	GJKP	George "Jay" Keyworth Papers
	GKP	Geoffrey Kemp Papers
	GP/CO	Governor's Papers, Correspondence
	GP/CS	Governor's Papers, Campaign Speeches
	GP/CU	Governor's Papers, Cabinet Unit
	GP/RF	Governor's Papers, Research Files
	HBP	Howard Baker Papers
	HWF	Handwriting File
	HTP	Howard Teicher Papers

	JBOH	Juanita Brown Oral History
	JMP	Jack Matlock Papers
	JWCP	James W. Cicconi Papers
	KDP	Kenneth Duberstein Papers
	KKP	Kenneth Khachigian Papers
	KOPPP	Kathy Osborne Post-Presidential Papers
	MDP	Michael Deaver Papers
	MSR	Military Service Records
	NRP	Nancy Reagan Papers
	ONP	Oliver North Papers
	P1966	Pre 1966 Speeches
	PJBP	Patrick J. Buchanan Papers
	PBP	Presidential Briefing Papers
	PDD	President's Daily Diary
	PDP	Paula Dobriansky Papers
	PF	Personal file
	PNEI	Peggy Noonan exit interview
	PP	Presidential personal
	PPP	Pre-presidential papers
	RC/NR	Robert Colacello/Nancy Reagan files
	RGDP	Richard G. Darman Papers
	RVAP	Richard V. Allen Papers
	SFP	Sara Fritz Papers
	WCOH	William Cotworthy Oral History
	WCP	William Clark Papers
	WHORM	White House Office of Records Management
RRRC		Ronald Reagan Ranch Collection, Young America's Foundation, Santa Barbara, California.
	LW	Lorraine Wagner Letter Collection
SDVRR		State Department Virtual Reading Room, Washington, DC.
	KDM	Kenneth W. Dam Memos
SHSI		State Historical Society of Iowa, Des Moines, Iowa.
SML		Seeley Mudd Library, Princeton University, Princeton, New Jersey.
	JABIII	James A. Baker III Papers
TMP		Tanya M. Melich Papers, M. E. Grenadier Special Collections and Archives, State University of New York at Albany, New York.
	RNC	Republican National Convention, 1964
UCB		Bancroft Library, University of California, Berkeley.
	EDOH	Earl B. Dunckel Oral History
	FCNOH	Franklyn C. Nofziger Oral History
	GBPOH	Gaylord B. Parkison Oral History
	GCOH	George Christopher Oral History
	NBLOH	Norman B. "Ike" Livermore Jr. Oral History
	EGBP	Edmund G. "Pat" Brown Papers
	RROH	Ronald Reagan Oral History
	WEBOH	William E. Roberts Oral History
	WFSOH	William French Smith Oral History
UCLA		Charles Young Library, Special Collections, University of California, Los Angeles.
	AEP	Anne Edwards Papers
	GDOH	George Dunne Oral History
	HKSM	Herbert Knott Sorrell Memoirs
	JDOH	Jack Dales Oral History
	NROH	Neil Reagan Oral History
	SPOH	Stanley Plog Oral History
UCSB		Special Research Collections, University of California, Santa Barbara.
	LCP	Lou Cannon Papers
UVA		Presidential Oral History Program, Miller Center of Public Affairs, University of Virginia, Charlottesville.
	CWOH	Caspar Weinberger Oral History
	HBOH	Howard Baker Oral History
	KAOH	Kenneth Adelman Oral History

	LNOH	Lyn Nofziger Oral History
	MDOH	Michael Deaver Oral History
	SSOH	Stuart Spencer Oral History
	WCOH	William Clark Oral History
WBA	Warner Brothers Archives, USC School of Cinematic Arts, Los Angeles.	
	JW	Jane Wyman files
	RR	Ronald Reagan files
YALE	Sterling Memorial Library, Yale University, New Haven, Connecticut.	
	JVRP	Joseph Verner Reed Papers
	WFBP	William F. Buckley Jr. Papers

Books and Articles

Abshire, David M. *Saving the Reagan Presidency: Trust Is the Coin of the Realm.* College Station: Texas A&M University Press, 2005.

Adams, Harold. *The History of Eureka College, 1855–1982.* Eureka, IL: Trustees of Eureka College, 1982.

Adelman, Ken. *Reagan at Reykjavik: Forty-Eight Hours That Ended the Cold War.* New York: Broadway Books, 2014.

Aldous, Richard. *Reagan and Thatcher: The Difficult Relationship.* New York: W. W. Norton, 2012.

Allyson, June, with Frances Spatz Leighton. *June Allyson.* New York: G. P. Putnam's Sons, 1982.

Alter, Jonathan. *His Very Best: Jimmy Carter, a Life.* New York: Simon & Schuster, 2020.

Ambinder, Marc. *The Brink: President Reagan and the Nuclear War Scare of 1983.* New York: Simon & Schuster, 2018.

Anderson, Martin. *Revolution.* San Diego: Harcourt Brace Jovanovich, 1988.

Anderson, Sherwood. *Poor White.* New York: New Directions, 1993.

Andrew, Christopher, and Oleg Gordievsky. *Comrade Kryuchkov's Instructions: Top Secret Files on KGB Operations, 1975–1985.* Stanford, CA: Stanford University Press, 1993.

Angelo, Bonnie. *First Mothers: The Women Who Shaped the Presidents.* New York: Harper, 2000.

Annis, J. Lee Jr. *Howard Baker: Conciliator in an Age of Crisis.* Lanham, MD: Madison Books, 1995.

Attali, Jacques. *Verbatim, Part I: 1981–1983.* Paris: Librairie Artheme Fayard, 1993.

Bagley, William T. *California's Golden Years: When Government Worked and Why.* Berkeley, CA: Berkeley Public Policy Press, 2009.

Baker, James A. III. *"Work Hard, Study . . . and Keep Out of Politics!" Adventures and Lessons from an Unexpected Public Life.* New York: G. P. Putnam's Sons, 2006.

Baker, Peter, and Susan Glasser. *The Man Who Ran Washington: The Life and Times of James A. Baker III.* New York: Doubleday, 2020.

Balio, Tino. *Grand Design: Hollywood as a Modern Business Enterprise, 1930–1939.* Vol. 5 of *History of the American Cinema.* Berkeley: University of California Press, 1993.

Barbas, Samantha. *The First Lady of Hollywood: A Biography of Louella Parsons.* Berkeley: University of California Press, 2005.

Barge, William D. *Early Lee County: Being Some Chapters in the History of the Early Days of Lee County, Illinois.* Chicago, 1918.

Barletta, John R., with Rochelle Schweizer. *Riding with Reagan: From the White House to the Ranch.* New York: Citadel, 2005.

Barrett, Laurence I. *Gambling with History: Ronald Reagan in the White House.* New York: Doubleday, 1983.

Bartlett, Bruce. *The New American Economy: The Failure of Reaganomics and a New Way Forward.* New York: Palgrave Macmillan, 2009.

Bartley, Robert L. *The Seven Fat Years: And How to Do It Again.* New York: Free Press, 1992.

Beilenson, Anthony C. *Looking Back: A Memoir—Vol. 2: California Years.* Signature Book Printing, 2012.

Bell, Terrel H. *The Thirteenth Man: A Reagan Cabinet Memoir.* New York: Free Press, 1988.

Bellamann, Henry. *Kings Row.* New York: Simon and Schuster, 1942.

Bent, Charles. *History of Whiteside County, Illinois, From Its First Settlement to the Present Time.* Morrison, IL, 1877.

Bergman, Ronen. *The Secret War with Iran: The 30-Year Clandestine Struggle against the World's Most Dangerous Terrorist Power.* New York: Simon & Schuster, 2008.

Berman, Ari. *Give Us the Ballot: The Modern Struggle for Voting Rights in America.* New York: Picador, 2015.

Betancourt, Mark. "World War II: The Movie." *Air and Space* (March 2012).

Bingen, Steven. *Warner Bros.: Hollywood's Ultimate Backlot.* Lanham, MD: Taylor Trade, 2014.

Bird, Kai. *The Outlier: The Unfinished Presidency of Jimmy Carter.* New York: Crown, 2021.

Birnbaum, Jeffrey H., and Alan S. Murray. *Showdown at Gucci Gulch: Lawmakers, Lobbyists, and the Unlikely Triumph of Tax Reform.* New York: Vintage, 1988.

Bogus, Carl T. *Buckley: William F. Buckley Jr. and the Rise of American Conservatism*. New York: Bloomsbury, 2011.

Boller, Paul F. Jr., and John George. *They Never Said It: A Book of Fake Quotes, Misquotes and Misleading Attributions*. New York: Oxford University Press, 1989.

Bork, Robert H. *The Tempting of America: The Political Seduction of the Law*. New York: Simon & Schuster, 1990.

Bowden, Mark. *Guests of the Ayatollah: The First Battle in America's War with Militant Islam*. New York: Grove, 2006.

Boyarsky, Bill. *Big Daddy Jesse Unruh and the Art of Power Politics*. Berkeley: University of California Press, 2008.

——. *The Rise of Ronald Reagan*. New York: Random House, 1968.

Brady, John. *Bad Boy: The Life and Politics of Lee Atwater*. Reading, MA: Addison Wesley, 1997.

Brands, H. W. *Reagan: The Life*. New York: Doubleday, 2015.

Brilliant, Mark. *The Color of America Has Changed: How Racial Diversity Shaped Civil Rights Reform in California, 1941–1978*. Oxford: Oxford University Press, 2010.

Bronner, Ethan. *Battle for Justice: How the Bork Nomination Shook America*. New York: Union Square Press, 2007.

Brown, Archie. *The Human Factor: Gorbachev, Reagan and Thatcher, and the End of the Cold War*. New York: Oxford University Press, 2020.

Brown, Edmund G. *Reagan and Reality: The Two Californias*. New York: Praeger, 1970.

Bruck, Connie. *When Hollywood Had a King: The Reign of Lew Wasserman, Who Leveraged Talent into Power and Influence*. New York: Random House, 2003.

Buchanan, Patrick J. *Right from the Beginning*. Washington, DC: Regnery, 1990.

Buckley, William F. Jr. *The Reagan I Knew*. New York: Basic, 2008.

Bunch, Will. *Tear Down This Myth: The Right-Wing Distortion of Reagan's Record*. New York: Free Press, 2009.

Burke's Peerage. "Presented to Honorable Ronald Reagan, Fortieth President of the United States by Burke's Peerage." London: Burke's Peerage, 1984.

Butler, Jon, Grant Wacker, and Randall Balmer. *Religion in American Life: A Short History*. New York: Oxford University Press, 2000.

Byrne, Malcolm. *Iran-Contra: Reagan's Scandal and the Unchecked Abuse of Presidential Power*. Lawrence: University Press of Kansas, 2014.

Cannon, Lou. *Governor Reagan: His Rise to Power*. New York: PublicAffairs, 2003.

——. *President Reagan: The Role of a Lifetime*. New York: PublicAffairs, 2000.

——. *Reagan*. New York: G. P. Putnam's Sons, 1982.

——. *Ronnie & Jesse: A Political Odyssey*. Garden City, NY: Doubleday, 1969.

Caro, Robert A. *The Years of Lyndon Johnson—Vol. 4: The Passage of Power*. New York: Vintage, 2013.

Carter, Dan T. *From George Wallace to Newt Gingrich: Race in the Conservative Counterrevolution, 1963–1994*. Baton Rouge: Louisiana State University Press, 1996.

Carter, Jimmy. *Keeping Faith: Memoirs of a President*. Fayetteville: University of Arkansas Press, 1995.

——. *White House Diary*. New York: Farrar Straus Giroux, 2010.

Cavanaugh, Jack. *The Gipper: George Gipp, Knute Rockne, and the Dramatic Rise of Notre Dame Football*. New York: Skyhorse, 2010.

Census Bureau. *Statistical Abstract of the United States*. Washington, DC: US Census Bureau, 1999.

Chait, Jonathan. *The Big Con: Crackpot Economics and the Fleecing of America*. Boston: Houghton Mifflin, 2007.

Clarridge, Duane R., with Digby Diehl. *A Spy for All Seasons: My Life in the CIA*. New York: Scribner, 1997.

Colacello, Bob. *Ronnie & Nancy: Their Path to the White House—1911 to 1980*. New York: Warner Books, 2004.

——. "Ronnie and Nancy, Part II." *Vanity Fair*, May 29, 2009.

Ceplair, Larry, and Steven Englund. *The Inquisition in Hollywood: Politics in the Film Community, 1930–1960*. Garden City, NY: Anchor, 1980.

Clymer, Adam. *Drawing the Line at the Big Ditch: The Panama Canal Treaties and the Rise of the Right*. Lawrence: University Press of Kansas, 2008.

Coffin, Lesley L. *Lew Ayres: Hollywood's Conscientious Objector*. Jackson: University Press of Mississippi, 2012.

Cole, Lester. *Hollywood Red: The Autobiography of Lester Cole*. Palo Alto, CA: Ramparts, 1981.

Cole, Ronald H. *Operation Urgent Fury: The Planning and Execution of Joint Operations in Grenada*. Washington, DC: Joint History Office, Office of the Chairman of the Joint Chiefs of Staff, 1997.

Coll, Steve. *Ghost Wars: The Secret History of the CIA, Afghanistan, and Bin Laden, from the Soviet Invasion to September 10, 2001*. New York: Penguin, 2004.

Collier, Peter. *Political Woman: The Big Little Life of Jeane Kirkpatrick*. New York: Encounter, 2012.

Collins, Robert M. *More: The Politics of Economic Growth in Postwar America*. New York: Oxford University Press, 2000.

Continetti, Matthew. *The Right: The Hundred-Year War for American Conservatism*. New York: Basic, 2022.

Cowie, Jefferson. *Freedom's Dominion: A Saga of White Resistance to Federal Power*. New York: Basic, 2022.

Crafton, William. "The Incremental Revolution: Ronald Reagan and Welfare Reform in the 1970s." *Journal of Policy History* 26, no. 1 (November 2014): 27–47.

Cramer, Richard Ben. *What It Takes: The Way to the White House.* New York: Open Road Media, 2011.

Crespino, Joseph. *In Search of Another Country: Mississippi and the Conservative Counterrevolution.* Princeton, NJ: Princeton University Press, 2007.

Crile, George. *Charlie Wilson's War.* New York: Grove, 2003.

Crist, David. *The Twilight War: The Secret History of America's Thirty-Year Conflict with Iran.* New York: Penguin, 2012.

Crocker, Chester A. *High Noon in Southern Africa: Making Peace in a Rough Neighborhood.* New York: W. W. Norton, 1992.

Cronon, William. *Nature's Metropolis: Chicago and the Great West.* New York: W. W. Norton, 1991.

Crowe, William J. Jr., with David Chanoff. *The Line of Fire: From Washington to the Gulf, the Politics and Battles of the New Military.* New York: Simon & Schuster, 1993.

Cunningham, Douglas. "Imaging/Imagining Air Force Identity: 'Hap' Arnold, Warner Bros., and the Formation of the USAAF First Motion Picture Unit," *Moving Image* 5, no. 1 (Spring 2005): 96–124.

Curtis, Jesse. "'Will the Jungle Take Over?' National Review and the Defense of Western Civilization in the Era of Civil Rights and African Decolonization." *Journal of American Studies* 53 (2019): 997–1023.

Dallek, Matthew. *The Right Moment: Ronald Reagan's First Victory and the Decisive Turning Point in American Politics.* New York: Free Press, 2000.

Dallek, Robert. *Flawed Giant: Lyndon Johnson and His Times, 1961–1975.* New York: Oxford University Press, 1998.

Dalzell, Tom. *The Battle for People's Park, Berkeley 1969.* Berkeley, CA: Heyday, 2019.

Darman, Jonathan. *Landslide: LBJ and Ronald Reagan at the Dawn of a New America.* New York: Random House, 2014.

Darman, Richard. *Who's in Control? Polar Politics and the Sensible Center.* New York: Simon & Schuster, 1996.

Davis, Kathy Randall. *But What's He REALLY Like?* Menlo Park, CA: Pacific Coast Publishers, 1970.

Davis, Loyal. *A Surgeon's Odyssey.* Garden City, NY: Doubleday, 1973.

Davis, Patti. *Dear Mom and Dad: A Letter about Family, Memory, and the American We Once Knew.* New York: Liveright, 2024.

———. *Floating in the Deep End: How Caregivers Can See beyond Alzheimer's.* New York: Liveright, 2021.

———. *The Long Goodbye.* New York: Alfred A. Knopf, 2004. Kindle e-book.

———. *The Way I See It: An Autobiography.* New York: G. P. Putnam's Sons, 1992.

Deaver, Michael K. *A Different Drummer: My Thirty Years with Ronald Reagan.* New York: HarperCollins, 2001.

———, with Mickey Herskowitz. *Behind the Scenes: In Which the Author Talks about Ronald and Nancy Reagan . . . and Himself.* New York: William Morrow, 1987.

DeFrank, Thomas M. *Write It When I'm Gone: Remarkable Off-the-Record Conversations with Gerald R. Ford.* New York: Berkley, 2007.

DeGroot, Gerard. "Ronald Reagan and Student Unrest in California, 1966–1970." *Pacific Historical Review* 65, no. 1 (February 1996): 107–129.

———. *Selling Ronald Reagan: The Emergence of a President.* London: I. B. Tauris, 2015.

D'Haeseleer, Brian. *The Salvadoran Crucible: The Failure of U.S. Counterinsurgency in El Salvador, 1979–1992.* Lawrence: University Press of Kansas, 2017.

Dick, Bernard F. *The President's Ladies: Jane Wyman and Nancy Davis.* Jackson: University Press of Mississippi, 2014.

Dickstein, Morris. *Dancing in the Dark: A Cultural History of the Great Depression.* New York: W. W. Norton, 2009.

Didion, Joan. *The White Album: Essays.* New York: Open Road Media, 1979.

Dmytryk, Edward. *It's a Hell of a Life but Not a Bad Living.* New York: Times Books, 1978.

Dobrynin, Anatoly. *In Confidence: Moscow's Ambassador to America's Six Cold War Presidents.* New York: Times Books, 1995.

Doherty, Brendan J. "Presidential Travel at Home and Abroad, 1977–Sept. 2020." White House Transition Project.

Doherty, Thomas. *Show Trial: Hollywood, HUAC, and the Birth of the Blacklist.* New York: Columbia University Press, 2018.

Drew, Elizabeth. *Portrait of an Election: The 1980 Presidential Campaign.* New York: Simon and Schuster, 1981.

Dubois, Jim. "Dutch Reagan the Lifeguard." *U.S. Life Saving* 3, no. 2 (Summer 1981).

Dunne, George H. *Hollywood Labor Dispute: A Study in Immorality.* Los Angeles: Conference Publishing, 1952.

———. *King's Pawn: The Memoirs of George H. Dunne, S.J.* Chicago: Loyola University Press, 1990.

Edgerton, Gary R. *The Columbia History of American Television.* New York: Columbia University Press, 2007.

Edsall, Thomas, with Mary D. Edsall. *Chain Reaction: The Impact of Race, Rights, and Taxes on American Politics.* New York: W. W. Norton, 1992.

Edwards, Anne. *Early Reagan: The Rise of Power.* Lanham, MD: Taylor Trade, 1987.

Egan, Timothy. *The Worst Hard Time: The Untold Story of Those Who Survived the Great American Dust Bowl.* Boston: Mariner, 2006.

Ehrgott, Roberts. *Mr. Wrigley's Ball Club: Chicago and the Cubs during the Jazz Age.* Lincoln: University of Nebraska Press, 2013.

Eig, Jonathan. *King: A Life.* New York: Farrar, Straus and Giroux, 2023.

Eliot, Marc. *Reagan: The Hollywood Years.* New York: Harmony, 2008.

Engel, Jonathan. *The Epidemic: A Global History of AIDS.* New York: HarperCollins, 2006.

English, John. *Just Watch Me: The Life of Pierre Elliott Trudeau, 1968–2000.* Toronto: Alfred A. Knopf Canada, 2009.

Evans, Thomas W. *The Education of Ronald Reagan: The General Electric Years and the Untold Story of His Conversion to Conservatism.* New York: Columbia University Press, 2006.

Farrell, John A. *Ted Kennedy: A Life.* New York: Penguin, 2022.

———. *Tip O'Neill and the Democratic Century.* Boston: Little, Brown, 2001.

Fehrman, Craig. "Reagan and the Rise of the Blockbuster Political Memoir." *American Literary History* 24, no. 3 (Fall 2012): 468–490.

Feldstein, Mark. *Poisoning the Press: Richard Nixon, Jack Anderson, and the Rise of Washington's Scandal Culture.* New York: Farrar, Straus and Giroux, 2010.

Feldstein, Martin, ed. *American Economic Policy in the 1980s.* Chicago: University of Chicago Press, 1994.

Felzenberg, Alvin S. *A Man and His Presidents: The Political Odyssey of William F. Buckley Jr.* New Haven, CT: Yale University Press, 2017.

Fischer, Ben B. *A Cold War Conundrum: The 1983 Soviet War Scare.* Washington, DC: CIA Center for the Study of Intelligence, 1997.

Fitzgerald, Frances. *Way Out There in the Blue: Reagan, Star Wars, and the End of the Cold War.* New York: Simon and Schuster, 2000.

Fitzwater, Marlin. *Call the Briefing! Reagan and Bush, Sam and Helen: A Decade with Presidents and the Press.* New York: Times Books, 1995.

Flynn, John T. *The Road Ahead: America's Creeping Revolution to Socialism.* New York: Committee for Constitutional Government, 1949.

Ford, Gerald R. *A Time to Heal: The Autobiography.* New York: Harper & Row, 1979.

Friedrich, Otto. *City of Nets: A Portrait of Hollywood in the 1940's.* New York: Harper Perennial, 2014.

Frost, Jennifer. *Hedda Hopper's Hollywood: Celebrity Gossip and American Conservatism.* New York: New York University Press, 2011.

Fuller, Kathryn H. *At the Picture Show: Small-Town Audiences and the Creation of Movie Fan Culture.* Charlottesville: University Press of Virginia, 1996.

Gabler, Neal. *An Empire of Their Own: How the Jews Invented Hollywood.* New York: Anchor, 1989.

Gaddis, John Lewis. *The Cold War.* New York: Penguin, 2005.

Garcia, Gilbert. *Reagan's Comeback: Four Weeks in Texas That Changed American Politics Forever.* San Antonio, TX: Trinity University Press, 2012.

Gardiner, Gordon P. "Nelle Reagan: Mother of Ronald Reagan, President of the United States." *Bread of Life* 30 (May 1981).

Garrison, Winfred Ernest. *An American Religious Movement: A Brief History of the Disciples of Christ.* Loki's Publishing, n.d.

Gates, Robert M. *From the Shadows: The Ultimate Insider's Account of Five Presidents and How They Won the Cold War.* New York: Simon & Schuster, 2006.

Gentry, Curt. *The Last Days of the Late Great State of California.* New York: Ballantine, 1968.

Germond, Jack W. *Fat Man in a Middle Seat: Forty Years of Covering Politics.* New York: Random House, 2002.

——— and Jules Witcover. *Blue Smoke and Mirrors: How Reagan Won and Carter Lost the Election of 1980.* New York: Viking, 1981.

——— and Jules Witcover. *Wake Us When It's Over: Presidential Politics of 1984.* New York: Macmillan, 1985.

Gibler, Bob. *Images of America: Dixon, Illinois.* Charleston, SC: Arcadia, 1998.

Gilbert, Robert E. "Ronald Reagan's Presidency: The Impact of an Alcoholic Parent." *Political Psychology* 29, no. 5 (October 2008): 737–765.

Giorgione, Michael. *Inside Camp David: The Private World of the Presidential Retreat.* New York: Little, Brown, 2017.

Gitlin, Todd. *The Sixties: Years of Hope, Days of Rage.* New York: Bantam, 1993.

Glaser, Elizabeth, with Laura Palmer. *In the Absence of Angels: A Hollywood Family's Courageous Story.* New York: G. P. Putnam's Sons, 1991.

Goldwater, Barry. *Conscience of a Conservative.* LaVergne, TN: Bottom of the Hill, 2010.

———, with Jack Casserly. *Goldwater.* New York: Doubleday, 1988. Kindle e-book.

Gorbachev, Mikhail. *Memoirs.* New York: Doubleday, 1995.

Gordon, Linda. *The Second Coming of the KKK: The Ku Klux Klan of the 1920s and the American Political Tradition.* New York: Liveright, 2017.

Gotlieb, Allan. *The Washington Diaries, 1981–1989.* Toronto: McClelland & Stewart, 2006.

Graff, Garrett M. *Raven Rock: The Story of the U.S. Government's Secret Plan to Save Itself—While the Rest of Us Die.* New York: Simon & Schuster, 2017.

Graham, Katharine. *Personal History.* New York: Vintage, 1998.

Green, Mark, and Gail MacColl. *Reagan's Reign of Error: Expanded and Updated.* New York: Pantheon, 1987.

Greider, William. *The Education of David Stockman and Other Americans.* New York: E. P. Dutton, 1982.

Gritter, Matthew. "The Kerr-Mills Act and the Puzzles of Health-Care Reform." *Social Science Quarterly* 100, no. 6 (August 2019): 2209–2222.

Gronner, Curt J. "The Family of Ronald W. Reagan." Morrison, IL: self-published, 2000.

Haig, Alexander M. Jr. *Caveat: Realism, Reagan, and Foreign Policy.* New York: Macmillan, 1994.

Haines, Gerald K. *Watching the Bear: Essays on CIA's Analysis of the Soviet Union.* Washington, DC: CIA, 2001.

——, and Robert E. Leggett. *CIA's Analysis of the Soviet Union, 1947–1991: A Documentary Collection.* Washington, DC: CIA, 2001.

Hannaford, Peter. *The Reagans: A Political Portrait.* New York: Coward-McCann, 1983.

——. *Ronald Reagan and His Ranch: The Western White House, 1981–1989.* Bennington, VT: Images from the Past, 2002.

Hayek, F. A. *The Road to Serfdom: Text and Documents.* Chicago: University of Chicago Press, 2007.

Hayes, James Todd. "Ronald Reagan as a 'Thoughtful' Speaker—the Sources of Evidence for Selected Assertions from his Campaign Speech of October 27, 1964." MS thesis, Kansas State Teachers College, August 1965.

Heidenry, John. *Theirs Was the Kingdom: Lila and DeWitt Wallace and the Story of the Reader's Digest.* New York: W. W. Norton, 1993.

Hertsgaard, Mark. *On Bended Knee: The Press and the Reagan Presidency.* New York: Farrar Straus Giroux, 1988.

Hess, Stephen, and David S. Broder. *The Republican Establishment: The Present and Future of the G.O.P.* New York: Harper & Row, 1967.

Hinton, Elizabeth. *From the War on Poverty to the War on Crime: The Making of Mass Incarceration in America.* Cambridge, MA: Harvard University Press, 2016.

Hoffman, David E. *The Dead Hand: The Untold Story of the Cold War Arms Race and Its Dangerous Legacy.* New York: Doubleday, 2009.

Horne, Gerald. *Class Struggle in Hollywood, 1930–1950: Moguls, Mobsters, Stars, Reds and Trade Unionists.* Austin: University of Texas Press, 2001.

Inboden, William. *The Peacemaker: Ronald Reagan in the White House and the World.* New York: Dutton, 2022.

Johnson, Haynes. *Sleepwalking through History: America in the Reagan Years.* New York: W. W. Norton, 2003.

Johnson, Thomas R. *United States Cryptologic History, Vol. 4: The NSA Period, 1952–Present.* Washington, DC: National Security Agency, 1999.

Jones, Nate, ed. *Able Archer 83: The Secret History of the NATO Exercise That Almost Triggered Nuclear War.* New York: New Press, 2016.

Jones, Seth G. *A Covert Action: Reagan, the CIA, and the Cold War Struggle in Poland.* New York: W. W. Norton, 2018.

Kabaservice, Geoffrey. *Rule and Ruin: The Downfall of Moderation and the Destruction of the Republican Party, from Eisenhower to the Tea Party.* New York: Oxford University Press, 2012.

Kaplan, Fred. *The Bomb: Presidents, Generals, and the Secret History of Nuclear War.* New York: Simon & Schuster, 2020.

Kelley, Kitty. *Nancy Reagan: The Unauthorized Biography.* New York: Simon & Schuster, 1991.

Kelly, John. *The Graves Are Walking: The Great Famine and the Saga of the Irish People.* New York: Picador, 2012.

Kengor, Paul, and Patricia Clark Doerner. *The Judge: William P. Clark, Ronald Reagan's Top Hand.* San Francisco: Ignatius, 2007.

Kennedy, David M. *Freedom from Fear: The American People in Depression and War, 1929–1945.* New York: Oxford University Press, 1999.

Kennedy, Matthew. *Edmund Goulding's Dark Victory: Hollywood's Genius Bad Boy.* Madison: University of Wisconsin Press, 2004.

Kennedy, Paul. *The Rise and Fall of the Great Powers: Economic Change and Military Conflict from 1500 to 2000.* New York: Vintage, 1989.

Koop, C. Everett. *Koop: The Memoirs of America's Family Doctor.* New York: Random House, 1991.

Korda, Michael. *Another Life: A Memoir of Other People.* New York: Random House, 1999.

Kornbluh, Peter, and Malcolm Byrne, eds. *The Iran-Contra Scandal: The Declassified History.* New York: New Press, 1993.

Krist, Gary. *The Mirage Factory: Illusion, Imagination, and the Invention of Los Angeles*. New York: Crown, 2018.

Krugman, Paul. *Peddling Prosperity: Economic Sense and Nonsense in the Age of Diminished Expectations*. New York: W. W. Norton, 1994.

Kruse, Kevin, and Zelizer, Julian E., eds. *Fault Lines: A History of the United States since 1974*. New York: W. W. Norton, 2019.

——. *Myth America: Historians Take on the Biggest Legends and Lies about Our Past*. New York: Basic, 2022.

Kuhn, Jim. *Ronald Reagan in Private: A Memoir of My Years in the White House*. New York: Sentinel, 2004.

Kukielski, Philip. *The U.S. Invasion of Grenada: Legacy of a Flawed Victory*. Jefferson, NC: McFarland, 2019. Kindle e-book.

Kynaston, David. *Austerity Britain, 1945–51*. London: Bloomsbury, 2007.

Illinois Secretary of State. "Hard Times in Illinois, 1930–1940: A Selection of Documents from the Illinois State Archives."

Lamb, Chris. *Conspiracy of Silence: Sportswriters and the Long Campaign to Desegregate Baseball*. Lincoln: University of Nebraska Press, 2012.

Lamb, George. *Dixon: A Pictorial History*. St. Louis: G. Bradley, 1987.

Laurie, Piper. *Learning to Live Out Loud*. New York: Crown Archetype, 2011.

Laxalt, Paul. *Nevada's Paul Laxalt: A Memoir*. Reno, NV: Jack Bacon, 2000.

Leamer, Laurence. *Make-Believe: The Story of Nancy and Ronald Reagan*. New York: Harper & Row, 1983.

Lehman, John. *Oceans Ventured: Winning the Cold War at Sea*. New York: W. W. Norton, 2018.

LeoGrande, William M. *Our Own Backyard: The United States in Central America, 1977–1992*. Chapel Hill: University of North Carolina Press, 1998.

Lettow, Paul. *Ronald Reagan and His Quest to Abolish Nuclear Weapons*. New York: Random House, 2005.

Leuchtenberg, William E. *In the Shadow of FDR: From Harry Truman to Barack Obama*. 4th ed. Ithaca, NY: Cornell University Press, 2009.

Lev, Peter. *Transforming the Screen, 1950–1959*. Vol. 7 of *History of the American Cinema*. Berkeley: University of California Press, 2003.

Levin, Josh. *The Queen: The Forgotten Life behind an American Myth*. New York: Back Bay, 2019.

Levy, Emanuel. *George Cukor, Master of Elegance*. New York: William Morrow, 1994.

Lewis, Bernard. "In Defense of History." *Proceedings of the American Philosophical Society* 143, no. 4 (December 1999): 573–587.

Lewis, Joseph. *What Makes Reagan Run? A Political Profile*. New York: McGraw-Hill, 1968.

Lewis, Tom. *Empire of the Air: The Men Who Made Radio*. New York: HarperCollins, 1991.

Liman, Arthur L. *Lawyer: A Life of Counsel and Controversy*. New York: PublicAffairs, 1998.

Lindsey, Robert. *Ghost Scribbler: Searching for Reagan, Brando, and the King of Pop*. Lindsey Family Trust, 2014.

Link, William A. *Righteous Warrior: Jesse Helms and the Rise of Modern Conservatism*. New York: St. Martin's, 2008.

Logevall, Fredrik. *JFK: Coming of Age in the American Century, 1917–1956*. New York: Random House, 2020.

Lott, Trent. *Herding Cats: A Life in Politics*. New York: ReganBooks, 2005.

Lowitt, Richard, and Maurine Beasley, eds. *One Third of a Nation: Lorena Hickock Reports on the Great Depression*. Urbana: University of Illinois Press, 1981.

Lucks, Daniel S. *Reconsidering Reagan: Racism, Republicans, and the Road to Trump*. Boston: Beacon, 2020.

Mailer, Norman. *Cannibals and Christians*. New York: Dell, 1966.

Mann, James. *The Rebellion of Ronald Reagan: A History of the End of the Cold War*. New York: Penguin, 2009.

Mann, Robert. *Becoming Ronald Reagan: The Rise of a Conservative Icon*. Lincoln, NE: Potomac, 2019.

Massie, Suzanne. *Trust but Verify: Reagan, Russia, and Me*. Rockland: Maine Authors Publishing, 2013.

Matlock, Jack Jr. *Reagan and Gorbachev: How the Cold War Ended*. New York: Random House, 2004.

Matthews, Chris. *Tip and the Gipper: When Politics Worked*. New York: Simon & Schuster, 2013.

Mayer, Jane, and Doyle McManus. *Landslide: The Unmaking of the President, 1984–1988*. Boston: Houghton Mifflin, 1988.

Mayer, Martin. *The Greatest Ever Bank Robbery: The Collapse of the Savings and Loan Industry*. New York: Charles Scribner's Sons, 1990.

McClelland, Doug. *Hollywood on Ronald Reagan: Friends and Enemies Discuss Our President, the Actor*. Winchester, MA: Faber and Faber, 1983.

McCullough, David. *Truman*. New York: Simon & Schuster, 1992.

McDougal, Dennis. *The Last Mogul: Lew Wasserman, MCA, and the Hidden History of Hollywood*. New York: De Capo, 2001.

McElvaine, Robert S. *The Great Depression: America, 1929–1941*. New York: Three Rivers, 2009. Kindle e-book.

McFarlane, Robert C., and Zofia Smardz. *Special Trust*. New York: Cadell & Davies, 1994.

McGirr, Lisa. *Suburban Warriors: The Origins of the New American Right*. Princeton, NJ: Princeton University Press, 2001.

McMartin, Joseph A. *Collision Course: Ronald Reagan, the Air Traffic Controllers, and the Strike That Changed America*. New York: Oxford University Press, 2011.

McWilliams, Carey. *Southern California: An Island on the Land*. Salt Lake City: Peregrine Smith, 1973.

Meacham, Jon. *Destiny and Power: The American Odyssey of George Herbert Walker Bush*. New York: Random House, 2015.

Meese, Edwin III. *With Reagan: The Inside Story*. Washington, DC: Regnery Gateway, 1992.

Menges, Constantine C. *Inside the National Security Council: The True Story of the Making and Unmaking of Reagan's Foreign Policy*. New York: Simon & Schuster, 1988.

Miles, Simon. "The War Scare That Wasn't: Able Archer 83 and the Myths of the Second Cold War." *Journal of Cold War Studies* 22, no. 3 (Summer 2020): 86–118.

Miller, Chris. *The Struggle to Save the Soviet Economy: Mikhail Gorbachev and the Collapse of the USSR*. Chapel Hill: University of North Carolina Press, 2016.

Miller, Donald L. *City of the Century: The Epic of Chicago and the Making of America*. New York: Simon & Schuster, 1997.

Miller, Edward H. *A Conspiratorial Life: Robert Welch, the John Birch Society, and the Revolution of American Conservatism*. Chicago: University of Chicago Press, 2022.

Miller, John J. *The Big Scrum: How Teddy Roosevelt Saved Football*. New York: HarperCollins, 2011.

Moldea, Dan E. *Dark Victory: Ronald Reagan, MCA, and the Mob*. New York: Open Road Media, 2017.

Mondale, Walter F., with David Hage. *The Good Fight: A Life in Liberal Politics*. New York: Scribner, 2010.

Moore, Charles. *Margaret Thatcher at Her Zenith: In London, Washington and Moscow*. New York: Alfred A. Knopf, 2016.

——. *Margaret Thatcher: The Authorized Biography—From Grantham to the Falklands*. New York: Alfred A. Knopf, 2013.

Morella, Joe, and Edward Z. Epstein. *Jane Wyman: A Biography*. New York: Delacorte, 1985.

Morgan, Michael Cotey. *The Final Act: The Helsinki Accords and the Transformation of the Cold War*. Princeton, NJ: Princeton University Press, 2018.

Morris, Edmund. *Dutch: A Memoir of Ronald Reagan*. New York: Modern Library, 1999.

Morser, Eric J. *Hinterland Dreams: The Political Economy of a Midwestern City*. Philadelphia: University of Pennsylvania Press, 2010.

Mulroney, Brian. *Memoirs, 1939–1993*. Toronto: McClelland & Stewart, 2007.

Naftali, Timothy. *Blind Spot: The Secret History of American Counterterrorism*. New York: Basic, 2005.

Neal, Patricia. *As I Am: An Autobiography*. New York: Simon & Schuster, 1988.

Niskanen, William A. *Reaganomics: An Insider's Account of the Politics and the People*. New York: Oxford University Press, 1988.

Niven, David. *Bring on the Empty Horses: True Tales from the Golden Age of the Silver Screen*. London: Hodder, 1995.

Nofziger, Lyn. *Nofziger*. Washington, DC: Regnery Gateway, 1992.

Noonan, Peggy. *What I Saw at the Revolution: A Political Life in the Reagan Era*. New York: Random House, 1990.

——. *When Character Was King: A Story of Ronald Reagan*. New York: Penguin, 2001.

Norris, Robert S., and Thomas B. Cochran. *US-USSR/Russian Strategic Offensive Nuclear Forces, 1945–1996*. Washington, DC: Natural Resources Defense Council, 1997.

North, Oliver L., with William Novak. *Under Fire: An American Story*. New York: HarperCollins, 1991.

Novak, Robert D. *The Agony of the G.O.P., 1964*. New York: Macmillan, 1965.

——. *The Prince of Darkness: 50 Years of Reporting in Washington*. New York: Crown Forum, 2007.

Obama, Barack. *A Promised Land*. New York: Crown, 2020.

Oberlander, Jonathan. *The Political Life of Medicare*. Chicago: University of Chicago Press, 2003.

O'Brien, Pat. *The Wind at my Back*. New York: Avon, 1967.

O'Neill, Tip, with William Novak. *Man of the House: The Life and Political Memoirs of Speaker Tip O'Neill*. New York: Random House, 1987.

Oreskes, Naomi, and Erik M. Conway. *The Big Myth: How American Business Taught Us to Loathe Government and Love the Free Market*. New York: Bloomsbury, 2023.

Page, Susan. *The Matriarch: Barbara Bush and the Making of an American Dynasty*. New York: Twelve, 2019.

Palmer, David D. *The Palmers: Memoirs of David D. Palmer*. Davenport, IA: Bawden, 1977.

Palmer, John L., and Isabel V. Sawhill, eds. *The Reagan Record: An Assessment of America's Changing Domestic Priorities*. Cambridge, MA: Ballinger, 1984.

Parr, Jerry, with Carolyn Parr. *In the Secret Service: The True Story of the Man Who Saved President Reagan's Life*. Carol Stream, IL: Tyndale House, 2013.

Parry, Robert. *America's Stolen Narrative: From Washington and Madison to Nixon, Reagan and the Bushes to Obama*. Arlington, VA: Media Consortium, 2012.

Patrick, Curtis. *Reagan: What Was He Really Like?* 2 vols. New York: Morgan James, 2011.

Patterson, James T. *The Eve of Destruction: How 1965 Transformed America*. New York: Basic, 2012. Kindle e-book.

———. *Grand Expectations: The United States, 1945–1974*. New York: Oxford University Press, 1996. Kindle e-book.

———. *Restless Giant: The United States from Watergate to Bush v. Gore*. New York: Oxford University Press, 2005.

Paulsen, Duane. *Dixon, Illinois, and the Great War, 1917–1919*. Self-published, 2013.

———. *Dixon Stories*. Self-published, 2016.

Pawel, Miriam. *The Browns of California: The Family Dynasty That Transformed a State and Shaped a Nation*. New York: Bloomsbury, 2018.

Perlstein, Rick. *Before the Storm: Barry Goldwater and the Unmaking of the American Consensus*. New York: Bold Type, 2009.

———. *Invisible Bridge: The Fall of Nixon and the Rise of Reagan*. New York: Simon & Schuster, 2014.

———. *Nixonland: The Rise of a President and the Fracturing of America*. New York: Scribner, 2009.

———. *Reaganland: America's Right Turn, 1976–1980*. New York: Simon and Schuster, 2020.

Persico, Joseph E. *Casey: From the OSS to the CIA*. New York: Viking, 1990.

Philips-Fein, Kim. *Invisible Hands: The Businessman's Crusade against the New Deal*. New York: W. W. Norton, 2009.

Pipes, Richard. *Vixi: Memoirs of a Non-Believer*. New Haven, CT: Yale University Press, 2003.

Podvig, Pavel. "Did Star Wars Help End the Cold War? Soviet Response to the SDI Program." *Science & Global Security* 25, no. 1 (2017): 3–27.

Powdermaker, Hortense. *Hollywood: The Dream Factory: An Anthropologist Looks at the Movies*. Mansfield Center, CT: Martino, 2013.

Powell, Colin, with Joseph Persico. *My American Journey*. New York: Ballantine, 1996.

Priess, David. *The President's Book of Secrets: The Untold Story of Intelligence Briefings to America's Presidents*. New York: PublicAffairs, 2016.

Prindle, David F. *The Politics of Glamour: Ideology and Democracy in the Screen Actors Guild*. Madison: University of Wisconsin Press, 1988.

Quigley, Joan. *"What Does Joan Say?" My Seven Years as White House Astrologer to Nancy and Ronald Reagan*. New York: Birch Lane, 1990.

Quirk, Lawrence J. *Jane Wyman: The Actress and the Woman*. New York: Dembner Books, 1986.

Radosh, Ronald, and Allis Radosh. *Red Star over Hollywood: The Film Colony's Long Romance with the Left*. New York: Encounter, 2006.

Rankin, Jeff. "Dutch's Memorable Year in Monmouth." *Galesburg Register-Mail*, August 2, 2016.

———. "Reagan's 1976 Monmouth Visit Mixed Nostalgia with Politics." *Medium.com*, April 15, 2020.

Raphael, Timothy. *The President Electric: Ronald Reagan and the Politics of Performance*. Ann Arbor: University of Michigan Press, 2009.

Ratnesar, Romesh. *Tear Down This Wall: A City, a President, and the Speech That Ended the Cold War*. New York: Simon & Schuster, 2009.

Reagan, Maureen. *First Father, First Daughter: A Memoir*. Boston: Little, Brown, 1989.

Reagan, Michael, with Jim Denney. *Lessons My Father Taught Me: The Strength, Integrity and Faith of Ronald Reagan*. West Palm Beach, FL: Humanix, 2016.

——— with Joe Hyams. *On the Outside Looking In*. New York: Zebra, 1988.

Nancy Reagan, with Bill Libby. *Nancy*. New York: William Morrow, 1980.

———, with William Novak. *I Love You, Ronnie: The Letters of Ronald Reagan to Nancy Reagan*. New York: Random House, 2000.

———, with William Novak. *My Turn: The Memoirs of Nancy Reagan*. New York: Random House, 1989.

Reagan, Ronald P. *My Father at 100: A Memoir*. New York: Plume, 2011.

Reagan, Ronald W. *An American Life*. New York: Threshold Editions, 1990.

———. *The Reagan Diaries*. Edited by Douglas Brinkley. 2 vols. New York: Harper, 2009.

———. *A Time for Choosing: The Speeches of Ronald Reagan, 1961–1982*. Chicago: Regnery, 1983.

———, with Richard G. Hubler. *Where's the Rest of Me?* New York: Duell, Sloan and Pearce, 1965.

Reagan's Dixon. Dixon, IL: Official Dixon Press, 1980.

Reed, Thomas C. *At the Abyss: An Insider's History of the Cold War*. New York: Ballantine, 2005.

———. *The Reagan Enigma, 1964–1980*. Los Angeles: Figueroa, 2014.

Reeves, Richard. *President Reagan: The Triumph of Imagination*. New York: Simon & Schuster, 2005.

Regan, Donald T. *For the Record: From Wall Street to Washington*. San Diego: Harcourt Brace Jovanovich, 1988.

Revsine, Dave. *The Opening Kickoff: The Tumultuous Birth of a Football Nation*. Guilford, CT: Lyons, 2014.

Ritchie, Donald A. *The Columnist: Leaks, Lies, and Libel in Drew Pearson's Washington*. New York: Oxford University Press, 2021.

Roberts, John B. II. *Reagan's Cowboys: Inside the 1984 Reelection Campaign's Secret Operation against Geraldine Ferraro.* Jefferson, NC: McFarland, 2020.

Rollins, Ed, with Tom DeFrank. *Bare Knuckles and Back Rooms: My Life in American Politics.* New York: Broadway, 1996

Rorabaugh, W. J. *Berkeley at War: The 1960s.* New York: Oxford University Press, 1989.

Rosebush, James. *True Reagan: What Made Ronald Reagan Great and Why It Matters.* New York: Center Street, 2016.

Rosenfeld, Seth. *Subversives: The FBI's War on Student Radicals and Reagan's Rise to Power.* New York: Picador, 2012.

Rossinow, Doug. *The Reagan Era: A History of the 1980s.* New York: Columbia University Press, 2015.

Rothkopf, David. *Running the World: The Inside Story of the National Security Council and the Architects of American Power.* New York: PublicAffairs, 2005.

Rowland, Robert C., and John M. Jones. *Reagan at Westminster: Foreshadowing the End of the Cold War.* College Station: Texas A&M Press, 2010.

Saltoun-Ebin, Jason. *The Reagan Files: Inside the National Security Council.* 2nd ed. Seabec Books, 2014.

Sandburg, Carl. *Prairie-Town Boy.* New York: Harcourt, Brace, 1952.

Savranskaya, Svetlana, and Thomas Blanton, eds. *Gorbachev and Reagan: The Last Superpower Summits: Conversations That Ended the Cold War.* Budapest: Central European University Press, 2020.

Sbardellati, John. *J. Edgar Hoover Goes to the Movies: The FBI and the Origins of Hollywood's Cold War.* Ithaca, NY: Cornell University Press, 2012.

Schatz, Thomas. *Boom and Bust: The American Cinema in the 1940s.* Vol. 6 of *History of the American Cinema.* New York: Charles Scribner's Sons, 1997.

Schickel, Richard. *Ronald Reagan: A Life in Film.* Boston: New Word City, 2012. Kindle e-book.

Schlafly, Phyllis. *A Choice Not an Echo.* Alton, IL: Pere Marquette, 1964.

Schlesinger, Robert. *White House Ghosts: Presidents and Their Speechwriters.* New York: Simon & Schuster, 2008.

Schlozman, Daniel, and Sam Rosenfeld. "The Long New Right and the World It Made." American Political Science Association, Boston, August 31, 2018.

Schmidt, Helmut. *Men and Powers: A Political Retrospective.* New York: Random House, 1989.

Schuknecht, Ludger. *Public Spending and the Role of the State: History, Performance, Risk and Remedies.* Cambridge: Cambridge University Press, 2020.

Schulberg, Budd. *What Makes Sammy Run?* New York: Vintage, 1993.

Schwartz, Nancy Lynn. *The Hollywood Writers' Wars.* Lincoln, NE: iUniverse, 2001.

Schweizer, Peter. *Reagan's War: The Epic Story of His Forty-Year Struggle and Final Triumph over Communism.* New York: Doubleday, 2002.

Schwieder, Dorothy. *Iowa: The Middle Land.* Iowa City: University of Iowa Press, 1996.

Shilts, Randy. *And the Band Played On: Politics, People, and the AIDS Epidemic.* New York: St. Martin's, 2007.

Shirley, Craig. *Last Act: The Final Years and Emerging Legacy of Ronald Reagan.* Nashville, TN: Nelson, 2015.

———. *Reagan's Revolution: The Untold Story of the Campaign That Started It All.* Nashville, TN: Thomas Nelson, 2005.

———. *Rendezvous with Destiny: Ronald Reagan and the Campaign That Changed America.* Wilmington, DE: ISI, 2009.

Shortridge, James R. *The Middle West: Its Meaning in American Culture.* Lawrence: University Press of Kansas, 1989.

Shultz, George P. *Turmoil and Triumph: My Years as Secretary of State.* New York: Charles Scribner's Sons, 1993.

Sick, Gary. *October Surprise: America's Hostages in Iran and the Election of Ronald Reagan.* New York: Times Books, 1991.

Siegel, Don. *A Siegel Film: An Autobiography.* London: Faber and Faber, 1993.

Silber, William L. *Volcker: The Triumph of Persistence.* New York: Bloomsbury, 2012.

Sisson, Richard, Christian Zacher, and Andrew Clayton, eds. *The American Midwest: An Interpretive Encyclopedia.* Bloomington: Indiana University Press, 2007.

Sitton, Tom, and William Deverell, eds. *Metropolis in the Making: Los Angeles in the 1920s.* Berkeley: University of California Press, 2001.

Skinner, Kiron K., Annelise Anderson, and Martin Anderson, eds. *Reagan: A Life in Letters.* New York: Free Press, 2003.

———. *Reagan in His Own Hand: The Writings of Ronald Reagan That Reveal His Revolutionary Vision for America.* New York: Free Press, 2001.

Smith, George H. *Who Is Ronald Reagan?* New York: Pyramid, 1968.

Smith, Hedrick. *The Power Game: How Washington Works.* New York: Ballantine, 1988.

Smith, Jean Edward. *FDR.* New York: Random House, 2007.

Speakes, Larry, with Robert Pack. *Speaking Out: The Reagan Presidency from Inside the White House*. New York: Charles Scribner's Sons, 1988.

Sperling, Cass Warner, and Cork Millner. *The Brothers Warner: The Intimate Story of a Hollywood Studio Family Dynasty*. Rocklin, CA: Prima, 1994.

Spitz, Bob. *Reagan: An American Journey*. New York: Penguin, 2018.

Stanik, Joseph T. *El Dorado Canyon: Reagan's Undeclared War with Qaddafi*. Annapolis, MD: Naval Institute Press, 2003.

Steffgen, Kent H. *Here's the Rest of Him*. Reno, NV: Foresight, 1968.

Steinbeck, John. *The Grapes of Wrath*. New York: Penguin, 2006.

Stevens, Frank E. *History of Lee County, Illinois*. 2 vols. Chicago: S. J. Clarke, 1914.

Stockman, David A. *The Triumph of Politics: Why the Reagan Revolution Failed*. New York: PublicAffairs, 2013.

Stoll, Ira. *JFK, Conservative*. New York: Houghton Mifflin Harcourt, 2013.

Strober, Deborah Hart, and Gerald Strober. *The Reagan Presidency*. London: Thistle, 2015.

Talbot, Margaret. *The Entertainer: Movies, Magic, and My Father's Twentieth Century*. New York: Riverhead, 2012.

Tate, Sheila. *Lady in Red: An Intimate Portrait of Nancy Reagan*. New York: Crown Forum, 2018.

Taubman, Philip. *In the Nation's Service: The Life and Times of George P. Shultz*. Stanford, CA: Stanford University Press, 2023.

Taubman, William. *Gorbachev: His Life and Times*. New York: W. W. Norton, 2017.

Teicher, Howard, and Gayle Radley Teicher. *Twin Pillars to Desert Storm: America's Flawed Vision in the Middle East from Nixon to Bush*. New York: William Morrow, 1993.

Thatcher, Margaret. *The Downing Street Years*. New York: HarperCollins, 1993.

Theoharis, Athan. *Chasing Spies: How the FBI Failed in Counterintelligence but Promoted the Politics of McCarthyism in the Cold War Years*. Chicago: Ivan R. Dee, 2002.

Thomas, Evan. *First: Sandra Day O'Connor*. New York: Random House, 2019.

Thomas, Tony. *The Films of Ronald Reagan*. Secaucus, NJ: Citadel, 1980.

Thomson, David. *Warner Bros: The Making of an American Movie Studio*. New Haven, CT: Yale University Press, 2017.

Timberg, Robert. *The Nightingale's Song*. New York: Simon & Schuster, 1995.

Torrey, E. Fuller. *American Psychosis: How the Federal Government Destroyed the Mental Illness Treatment System*. New York: Oxford University Press, 2014.

Trudeau, Pierre. *Memoirs*. Toronto: McClelland & Stewart, 1993.

Tumulty, Karen. *The Triumph of Nancy Reagan*. New York: Simon & Schuster, 2021.

Tyler, Patrick. *A World of Trouble: The White House and the Middle East—from the Cold War to the War on Terror*. New York: Farrar, Straus, Giroux, 2009.

Untermeyer, Chase. *When Things Went Right: The Dawn of the Reagan-Bush Administration*. College Station: Texas A&M Press, 2013.

US House October Surprise Task Force. "Joint Report of the Task Force to Investigate Certain Allegations Concerning the Holding of American Hostages in Iran in 1980." Washington, DC: US Government Printing Office, 1993.

US House Un-American Activities Committee. "Communist Infiltration of Hollywood Motion Picture Industry—Part I." 82nd Congress, 1st Session, March–April 1951.

——. "Hearings Regarding the Communist Infiltration of the Motion Picture Industry." 80th Congress, 1st Session, October 20–30, 1947.

Vaughn, Stephen. "The Moral Inheritance of a President: Reagan and the Dixon Disciples of Christ." *Presidential Studies Quarterly* 25, no. 1 (Winter 1995): 109–127.

——. *Ronald Reagan in Hollywood: Movies and Politics*. Cambridge: Cambridge University Press, 1994.

Volkogonov, Dmitri. *Autopsy for an Empire: The Seven Leaders Who Built the Soviet Regime*. New York: Free Press, 1998.

Von Damm, Helen. *At Reagan's Side*. New York: Doubleday, 1989.

——. *Sincerely, Ronald Reagan: The Heartwarming Personal Correspondence of Ronald Reagan as Governor of California*. Ottawa, IL: Green Hill, 1976.

Walker, James R. *Crack of the Bat: A History of Baseball on the Radio*. Lincoln: University of Nebraska Press, 2015.

Wallis, Hal, and Charles Higham. *Starmaker: The Autobiography of Hal Wallis*. New York: Macmillan, 1980.

Wallison, Peter J. *Ronald Reagan: The Power of Conviction and the Success of His Presidency*. Cambridge, MA: Westview, 2003.

Walsh, Kenneth T. *Family of Freedom: Presidents and African Americans in the White House*. Boulder, CO: Paradigm, 2011.

Walsh, Lawrence E. *Firewall: The Iran-Contra Conspiracy and Cover-Up*. New York: W. W. Norton, 1997.

Wanniski, Jude. *The Way the World Works*. 4th ed. Washington, DC: Regnery, 1998.

Watts, Trent. "Mississippi's Giant House Party: Being White at the Neshoba County Fair." *Southern Cultures* 8, no. 2 (Summer 2002): 38–55.

Weigel, George. *Witness to Hope: The Biography of Pope John Paul II*. New York: Harper Perennial, 1999.

Weinberg, Mark. *Movie Nights at the Reagans: A Memoir*. New York: Simon & Schuster, 2018.

Weinberger, Caspar. *Fighting for Peace: Seven Critical Years in the Pentagon*. New York: Warner Books, 1991.

Weiner, Tim. *Enemies: A History of the FBI*. New York: Random House, 2012.

Weisberg, Jacob. *Ronald Reagan*. New York: Times Books, 2016.

Westad, Odd Arne. *The Global Cold War*. Cambridge: Cambridge University Press, 2007.

Whipple, Chris. *The Gatekeepers: How the White House Chiefs of Staff Define Every Presidency*. New York: Broadway, 2018.

White, F. Clifton, and William J. Gill. *Why Reagan Won: A Narrative History of the Conservative Movement, 1964–1981*. Chicago: Regnery Gateway, 1981.

White, Theodore H. *America in Search of Itself: The Making of the President, 1956–1980*. New York: Harper & Row, 1982.

———. *The Making of the President 1964*. New York: HarperCollins, 2010.

———. *The Making of the President 1968*. New York: HarperCollins, 2010.

Wilber, Del Quentin. *Rawhide Down: The Near Assassination of Ronald Reagan*. New York: Henry Holt, 2011.

Wilentz, Sean. *The Age of Reagan: A History, 1974–2008*. New York: HarperCollins, 2008.

Wills, Garry. *Reagan's America: Innocents at Home*. New York: Penguin, 1985.

Wilson, James Graham. *The Triumph of Improvisation: Gorbachev's Adaptability, Reagan's Engagement, and the End of the Cold War*. Ithaca, NY: Cornell University Press, 2014.

Wilson, Tom. *Remembering Galesburg*. Charleston, SC: History Press, 2009.

Winik, Jay. *On the Brink: The Dramatic, Behind-the-Scenes Saga of the Reagan Era and the Men and Women Who Won the Cold War*. New York: Simon & Schuster, 1996.

Winkler, Adam. *Gun Fight: The Battle over the Right to Bear Arms in America*. New York: W. W. Norton, 2013.

Wirthlin, Dick, with Wynton C. Hall. *The Greatest Communicator: What Ronald Reagan Taught Me about Politics, Leadership, and Life*. Hoboken, NJ: John Wiley, 2004.

Witcher, Marcus. *Getting Right with Reagan: The Struggle for True Conservatism, 1980–2016*. Lawrence: University Press of Kansas, 2019.

Witcover, Jules. *Marathon: The Pursuit of the Presidency, 1972–1976*. New York: Viking, 1977.

Wood, Grant. *Revolt against the City*. Iowa City, IA: Clio, 1935.

Woodward, Bob. *Shadow: Five Presidents and the Legacy of Watergate*. New York: Simon & Schuster, 1999.

———. *Veil: The Secret Wars of the CIA, 1981–1987*. New York: Simon & Schuster, 1987.

Wright, Harold Bell. *That Printer of Udell's*. Gretna, LA: Pelican, 2011.

Index

Page numbers in *italics* refer to illustrations.

Nicholson, Arthur, 621

Nickles, Don, 478

Niebuhr, Reinhold, 231–32

Night unto Night, 155, 170

9 to 5, 446

1960s counterculture, 257, 273, 302–3, 319, 324, 326, 446

   See also campus unrest

1981–82 recession, 513–14, 518–20, 590

Nir, Amiram, 661

Niven, David, 117, 166

Nixon, Richard M.

   arms control and, 704

   Battaglia scandal and, 309

   Bitburg controversy and, 615

   Robert Bork and, 690

   California politics and, 259

   Cambodia invasion and, 329

   campus unrest and, 328, 329

   China initiative, 334, 347–48

   détente and, xxxvi, 347–48, 362

   economic policies, 470

   environmental policies, 342

   financial deals and, 286–87

   John Birch Society and, 268

   King assassination and, 314

   liberal initiatives, 334, 347

   1968 presidential election and, 311, 317

   racism and, 279, 329

   Reagan administration economic policies and, 464

   Reagan administration initial appointments and, 429

   RR as international envoy for, 349

   on RR's intellectual superficiality, 349

   on RR's late-presidency decline, 702, 706

   RR's opposition to, 163, 194

   RR's racism and, 250, 251

   RR's support for, 237–38, 347–48, 350, 361, 362

   George Shultz and, 550

   television and, 206

   Vietnam War and, 328, 347

   Watergate scandal, 348, 349–50, 434, 664, 674

   Caspar Weinberger and, 306

   welfare reform and, 338–39

   World War II and, 129

Nofziger, Lyn

   conviction of, 678

   Reagan administration initial appointments and, 428

   RR assassination attempt and, 455, 460

   on RR's antipathy to federal government, 428

   RR's California governorship and, 288, 294, 303, 307, 308–9, 310

   RR's California governorship campaign and, 276, 277

   on RR's intellectual superficiality, 725

   RR's 1968 presidential campaign and, 310, 314

   RR's 1976 presidential campaign and, 357, 360, 369

RR's 1980 presidential campaign and, 375, 376, 387, 388, 389, 392, 397, 404

   on RR's personal aloofness, 336

   RR's post-gubernatorial career and, 351

   RR's post-presidential life and, 721

   on White House adviser rivalry, 425

None Dare Call It Conspiracy (Allen), 269

None Dare Call It Treason (Stormer), 233

Noonan, Peggy

   Challenger disaster and, 633, 634

   Normandy speech and, 603

   Reagan administration initial appointments and, 424

   Donald Regan and, 611, 713

   RR's farewell speech and, 713–14, 716, 717

   on RR's intellectual superficiality, 725

North, Oliver L.

   conviction of, 677

   dismissal of, 666

   document destruction and, 665

   Flight 847 crisis and, 642

   Iran arms profit diversion and, 660, 665

   Iran arms sale negotiations and, 658, 659, 661, 662

   Iran-Contra affair congressional hearings and, 675, 692

   Iran-Contra affair plot revelation and, 663

   Libya bombing and, 644

   personality of, 657–58

   RR's responses to Iran-Contra scandal and, 670

North American Free Trade Agreement (NAFTA), 386, 648

Novak, Robert D., 179, 245, 283, 376, 465, 473

nuclear freeze movement, 539

nuclear weapons policy

   Europe missile deployment, 489, 539, 562, 569

   JFK's policies, 230

   RR's 1980 presidential campaign and, 377, 379–80

   See also Reagan administration arms control policy; Reagan administration nuclear weapons policy

Obama, Barack, 434, 450–51, 486, 730

O'Brien, Pat, 105, 121, 122, 133

Obringer, R. J., 120, 130

Occupational Health and Safety Administration (OSHA), 347, 525

O'Connor, John, 687

O'Connor, Sandra Day, xxv, 405, 478–79, 688, 689–90

October Surprise. *See* Iran hostage crisis

October Surprise (Sick), 410

Ogarkov, Nikolai, 491

Olivier, Laurence, 128

O'Neill, Thomas "Tip"

   background of, 13, 471–72

   Challenger disaster and, 634

   Lebanon and, 584

   1984 presidential election and, 604

   Reagan administration economic policies and, 474, 475, 516, 519–20, 521, 523, 525, 647

   on RR's 1980 presidential victory, 415